W9-BFH-877

PSYCHOLOGY
AN INTRODUCTION
SEVENTH EDITION

JOSH GEROW ■ KENNETH BORDENS

INDIANA UNIVERSITY — PURDUE UNIVERSITY AT FORT WAYNE

Alliance Press

Copyright © 2002 by Alliance Press.

All rights reserved. No part of this book may be reproduced in any form whatsoever, by photograph or xerography or by any other means, by broadcast or transmission, by translation into any kind of language, nor by recording electronically or otherwise, without permission in writing from the publisher, except by a reviewer, who may quote brief passages in critical articles and reviews.

Printed in the United States of America.

ISBN: 0-75930352-5

1.800.355.9983
5101 Madison Rd., Cincinnati OH 45227

Address all correspondence and order information to the above address.

Brief Table of Contents

DETAILED TABLE OF CONTENTS

PREFACE

The seventh edition of *Psychology: An Introduction* welcomes back Ken Bordens as coauthor and Jon Hughes Fuller as editor, consultant, advisor. She saw to it that everything got done as it should be done, when it should be done. As with previous editions, Nancy Gerow has read and reviewed every word that follows. Her skills in psychology—as editor and researcher—are reflected throughout the text, and we are grateful. New to the team this year is Thomson Learning Custom Publishing and all their supportive folks in Cincinnati, including Rich Foley, Melissa Acuna, and Dreis Van Landuyt. Joann Piet, our developmental editor, has evolved as the team's quarterback, handling layouts, designing, questioning, suggesting—essentially making words and pictures into a book.

Our primary goal with this edition is much the same as it was for the last: produce a solid, academically sound, yet accessible introduction to psychology at the most reasonable price possible. To keep costs down, we are again publishing the text in a black-and-white format. Our experience with the sixth edition has convinced us that students will gladly (may I say, enthusiastically?) give up flashy, glitzy color photos here and there in order to save cash at the bookstore. Beyond that, our goals are quite the same as they have been for many years now. They include:

- **Sharing the excitement of the <u>science</u> of psychology for beginning students who will take few, if any, additional psychology classes.** We bring to this book the same attitude we bring to our introductory psychology classrooms: "This may be our only chance to share with students the concepts, principles, and challenges of psychology." If nothing else (and one always hopes for more), students who read this book should have a keen appreciation of what psychology is and what it is not. They should be familiar with the vocabulary of the discipline and understand what it is that psychologists do.

- **Using what we know about the psychology of learning and memory to help the student/reader understand psychology.** The study of psychology need not be boring, nor should it be difficult. We do everything we can to make the content of our discipline accessible. Specifics are detailed later in this Preface, in a section called "Aids to Enhance Learning."

- **Demonstrating that psychology has emerged from a historical context.** We believe that students need to appreciate that everything important in psychology did not happen within the last six months—or six years. We have made every effort for the seventh edition of *Psychology: An Introduction* to be as up-to-date as possible, but we also take pains to bring a historical perspective to our discussion.

- **Responding to the diversity of psychology in the 21st century.** No longer a passing fad in social science, attending to matters of culture, ethnicity, gender, and sexual orientation, and the like, has become a mainstream reality in each of psychology's content areas. Our goal here is to reflect our belief that this is a good thing. And our goal is to speak to these issues in the context in which they belong, not as a separate issue or topic.

Highlights of the Seventh Edition

There is little doubt that the most remarkable (certainly the most talked-about) feature of *Psychology: An Introduction* is its low cost to the student. In many cases, the cost of the text <u>AND</u> the Student Study Guide is less than half of what many introductory psychology textbooks cost alone. But, an inexpensive text that was short on content, or missing adequate pedagogy, would be no bargain at all. We are proud of the coverage of psychology presented within these pages. Although it is true that both authors teach the History of Psychology course and value a historical context, the new topics, and the new, updated reference citations make this a text for the twenty-first century.

A feature newly available with this text is customization. We are most excited about the possibilities! We will have "modules" available on such topics as industrial/organizational psychology, prejudice, conflict resolution, environmental psychology, statistics in psychology, and the like. In truth, there is no end to the number and variety of modules that can be written and integrated into the core text, not just "tacked on" at the end. Additionally, instructors will be invited to prepare and provide materials (course notes, lecture notes, syllabi, course outlines, exam schedules) that also can be integrated into the core text. Another exciting aspect of customization is the ability to add material from the vast selection of titles Thomson Learning publishes. In many ways, this process makes textbook production a collaborative effort between us and the classroom instructor, facilitated by the talent and technology that Thomson Learning Custom Publishing can provide. If you are interested in any of the modules or would like to discuss customization options, please contact your local Thomson Learning Representative or call the Custom Publishing group at 1-800-355-9983.

Changes in the Seventh Edition, Chapter-by-Chapter

Chapter 1: The Science of Psychology. Topic 1A reorganized. Clarified the accepting and rejecting of scientific hypotheses. New section on "Contemporary Approaches to Psychology" which introduces biological, evolutionary, psychodynamic, behavioral, cognitive, and cross-cultural approaches. New section on "An emerging new approach: Positive Psychology." Correlational research section rewritten with new examples. New, lengthy example of the experimental method. Section on factorial experiments rewritten.

Chapter 2: The Nervous System and Behavior. The source and nature of myelin made clearer. Added new discussion on salutatory conduction in vertebrates and invertebrates. Clarified the processes by which neurotransmitters are cleared from the synaptic region. Expanded the discussion of serotonin and its role in behavior, and the discussion of the use of fetal brain cells as a treatment for Parkinson's disease. Significantly updated data on split-brain operations and the differences between left- and right-cerebral hemispheres.

Chapter 3: Sensation and Perception. Added the concept of "rock-and-roll" threshold. Expanded the section on taste. Improved photo examples of concepts in the text.

Chapter 4: Varieties of Consciousness. "Contemporary Investigations of the Unconscious" rewritten to include subliminal perception and blindsight. Completely revised section on stages of sleep. Added discussion on the physiology of REM sleep with respect to brain chemistry and electrical activity (PGO waves). Added a new section on dreams and dreaming covering both traditional approaches (e.g., Freudian analysis) and more contemporary approaches (e.g., activation-synthesis models).

Chapter 5: Learning. Included Mary Cover Jones' work on systematic desensitization. Added material on the physiology of both classical and operant conditioning.

Chapter 6: Memory. Updated material on repressed memories and eyewitness testimony. Updated section on the physiological bases of memory.

Chapter 7: Intelligence, Language, and Problem Solving. Expanded the discussion of multiple varieties of intelligence. Added a new section on "emotional intelligence." Added a section on "mainstreaming" exceptional children. Added more examples of ill-defined problems. Expanded the discussion of creative problem solving.

Chapter 8: Human Development. Expanded the coverage of factors that impact on prenatal development—smoking in particular. Added new material to discussion of neonatal brain and sensory development. Extended discussion of information-processing approaches to cognitive development. Enhanced section on developing gender identity. New research included in sections on early and middle adulthood.

Chapter 9: Personality. Recast and expanded the section on the definition of personality. Expanded the treatment of Adlerian psychology. Rewrote the section on Maslow's self-actualizers. Expanded the section on interview techniques.

Chapter 10: Motivation and Emotion. Expanded and updated the discussion of sexual dysfunctions. Expanded and updated the discussion of the physiology of emotion.

Chapter 11: Psychology, Stress, and Physical Health. Recast some of the discussion of healthy and unhealthy reactions to stressors. Updated nearly all of the statistics in this chapter, adding 13 new reference citations from 1999 or later.

Chapter 12: The Psychological Disorders. Updated and expanded the section on Alzheimer's dementia. Added table of new material on Types of Schizophrenia. Expanded the discussion of insanity and the insanity defense. Expanded the section on mental illness and violence. Clarified distinction between somatization disorder and hypochondriasis. Clarified distinctions between major depressive disorder and dysthymia. Added a new section on the diathesis-stress model of mental illness. Added 31 new reference citations.

Chapter 13: Treatment and Therapy. Updated all of the statistics in the chapter. Added to the discussion of the treatment of psychological disorders.

Chapter 14: Social Psychology. Expanded—with new, relevant examples—the section on persuasion and attitude change. Extended discussion of who is likely to conform and factors affecting conformity data.

Aids to Enhance Learning

The seventh edition of *Psychology: An Introduction* retains its focus on making learning an interesting, meaningful experience for students. The effectiveness of these pedagogical features is, perhaps more than anything else, what has given this text the success it has enjoyed over the years. Students actually read the book, and they learn from it. This pleases instructors, as test scores increase, demonstrating the usefulness of these learning aids. Here is a summary of these features.

Opening Vignette. Each chapter begins with a short story illustrating some key issue of the chapter. These vignettes are designed to provide students with an engaging welcome to the issues that follow. We have made a special effort to refer back to the opening vignette throughout the chapter.

Key Questions. The list of questions at the beginning of each Topic encourages the student to become actively involved in looking for the answers throughout the Topic that follows. This technique is consistent with Robinson's SQ3R method, and fosters elaborative rehearsal.

Topical Organization. Dividing the book's 14 chapters into two shorter, coherent Topics encourages distributed practice, long known to be superior to massed practice. A topical approach also fosters flexibility in making reading assignments.

Examples and Applications. We know that the more meaningful the material, the more effective the learning, and the better the retention of that material. Our rule of thumb is to provide examples and applications at every possible opportunity. The more we can demonstrate psychology's relevance to our students' everyday lives, the more effective we will be.

Boldface Key Terms, Marginal Glossary, and Alphabetized Glossary. In large measure, learning about psychology—for the beginning student—is a matter of vocabulary development. Hence, key words and concepts are printed in the text in boldface type and are defined immediately. Then, each term is defined again in a marginal glossary, and all are brought together in alphabetical order at the back of the text.

Before You Go On Questions. This feature has been a staple of the Gerow texts since the first edition. Not only does the notion make sense, but mostly we keep this feature because our students keep telling us that a) They use it! and b) They like it! Among other things, these questions help to foster distributed practice by indicating the location of a reasonable stopping place. Students also find them very helpful when reviewing for an exam.

Topic Reviews. At the end of each Topic is a review. This feature remains expanded, as with the 6th edition. The reviews are organized around the set of Key Questions that begin each Topic.

We have prepared an extensive **Student Study Guide**. This Guide provides students with several useful learning aids for each chapter. The major sections of the Student Study Guide include for each chapter:

- A complete and detailed outline.

- A "how-to-study" tip, or hint, that provides information applicable to the study of psychology—and every other college-level course.

- A discussion of the usefulness of flash cards for mastering the basics of psychology, with examples included for the first five chapters.

- A complete set of "Practice Tests," including multiple-choice and true-false questions. Answers are provided in annotated form with an explanation of why the designated answer is correct and, perhaps more importantly, why alternatives are incorrect.

- "Experiencing Psychology" projects. These are simple, straightforward projects that students can carry out with no supervision required. Again, the intent is to help make psychology real, relevant, and fun.

Supplements for the Instructor

Just as we have tried to make learning as easy as possible for the student, so have we strived to make teaching as effortless as possible for the instructor. Granted that nothing is more helpful to an instructor than a well-written, error-free, easy-to-read text, there are a few supplements available that instructors will find helpful.

The **Instructor's Resource Manual** has been revised yet again to reflect the changes made in the text. This instructor's guide has consistently been one of the most useful in the marketplace, and this edition continues to offer a wealth of information for the beginning teacher and the experienced teacher as well. Features include chapter learning objectives, detailed outlines, suggested lecture topics, discussion ideas, classroom projects and demonstrations, updated timelines, critical thinking exercises, media references, and lists of suggested readings.

A **Test Item File**, written by Josh R. Gerow, includes more than 2,000 multiple-choice items, keyed to the text. The test bank includes many new items, reflecting changes in the text itself and many classroom-tested items.

A **Computerized Test Bank** allows an instructor to *easily* construct tests using the items from the Test Item File. Instructors can *easily* add new items or revise existing ones.

Transparencies, **Powerpoint slides** and an accompanying **website** will also be available.

ABOUT THE AUTHORS

Josh R. Gerow began his college training at Rensselaer Polytechnic Institute, where he majored in chemistry. He earned his B.S. in psychology at the University of Buffalo. At the University of Tennessee–Knoxville, he was awarded a doctorate in experimental psychology. His graduate area of specialization was developmental psycholinguistics. After teaching for two years at the University of Colorado at Denver, he joined the faculty at Indiana University–Purdue University at Fort Wayne (IPFW), an undergraduate institution, where he still teaches. Dr. Gerow has conducted research and published articles in the field of instructional psychology, focusing on factors that affect performance in introductory psychology. His teaching background is extensive. During his more than 30 years as a college professor, he has taught courses on the psychology of learning, memory, the history of psychology, and his favorite course, introduction to psychology. He has also brought college-level introductory psychology to high school students and has made frequent presentations at regional and national conferences on the teaching of psychology.

Kenneth S. Bordens received his Bachelor of Arts degree in Psychology from Fairleigh Dickinson University (Teaneck, New Jersey campus) in 1975. He earned a Master of Arts and Doctor of Philosophy degree in Social Psychology from the University of Toledo in 1979. After receiving his Ph.D., he accepted a position at Indiana University–Purdue University at Fort Wayne (IPFW). Dr. Bordens has taught there for the past 20 years and currently holds the rank of Professor of Psychological Sciences. Dr. Bordens' main research area is in psychology and law. Specifically, he has published several studies on juror and jury decision making. His most recent research is on the impact on jurors of consolidating multiple plaintiffs in complex trials. He has co-authored three textbooks (*Research Design and Methods: A Process Approach*, *Psychology of Law: Integrations and Applications*, and *Social Psychology*) in addition to the sixth and seventh editions of *Psychology: An Introduction*. He is also currently writing a text on statistics. Dr. Bordens teaches courses in social psychology, child development, research methods, the history of psychology, and introductory psychology.

DEDICATION

This edition is dedicated to the memories of our fathers,

J. R. Gerow, Jr., and Walter Bordens

Psychology:
An Introduction

Chapter 1

The Science of Psychology

*A*t 11:21 A.M. mountain standard time on April 20, 1999, five calls were received by the Jefferson County Sheriff's Office. Residents living near Columbine High School in Littleton, Colorado reported hearing loud noises. Two students were seen in the school's southeast parking lot. They were shooting at the school and throwing bombs. One of the shooters was observed unloading duffel bags filled with the bombs and ammunition from his car. The two entered the school cafeteria, shooting as they walked. At least 1,500 students fled the school as soon as the shooting began, while others hid in classrooms for hours. Fourteen students, including the shooters, Dylan Klebold and Eric Harris, and one teacher, died during the attack. About 25 students and teachers were seriously wounded.

Those of us who watched the events on television are not likely to forget the images of students running from the high school building, hands high above their heads, surrounded by police SWAT team members. We were reminded of other, similar, horrific school shootings. On May 21, 1998, a 15-year-old student in Springfield, Oregon entered his school's cafeteria, pulled out a rifle and killed two students, wounding 22 others. Earlier in the day, he had killed his parents before heading off to school. Only two days before, an 18-year-old honor student shot and killed a classmate who was dating his ex-girlfriend. The week before, a science teacher was shot to death in front of students at an eighth-grade graduation dance. A 14-year-old student is charged with the murder. One month earlier, four girls and a teacher were shot to death and 10 people were wounded when two boys, aged 11 and 13, opened fire from the cover of nearby woods during a school fire alarm. And again more recently, on March 5, 2001, we see images of the aftermath of a school shooting. Charles Andrew Williams, a 15-year-old freshman, is accused of killing two students and wounding 13 people. He used a .22-caliber pistol. He talked about doing just such a thing the weekend before. None of his friends took him seriously. He surrendered on his knees in a school restroom, saying, "It's only me."

Topic 1A WHAT IS PSYCHOLOGY?

The shootings at Columbine High School had everyone—psychologists and nonpsychologists—asking, "Why?"

Whenever such grisly events take place, we inevitably search for answers to the question of "Why?" How can we explain such seemingly unexplainable events? Were the youngsters who committed these crimes mentally ill? Were they born violent? Did they learn violence at home from their parents? Or is violence, as some would have us believe, the fault of television, movies, and song lyrics?

How are we to know which of the many possible causes of violent behavior are actually at the root of school violence? Psychology may provide at least partial answers to some of our questions. As a science, psychology attempts to provide descriptions and explanations for the wide variety of human and animal behaviors. Among other things, psychologists ponder and study the forces that shape behaviors in an attempt to isolate the complex causes of behaviors, even school violence (Arman, J.F., 2000).

Key Questions to Answer

In this Topic, we will explore what psychology is, what psychologists do, and how psychology originated as a science. As you read the material in this Topic, you should find the answers to the following questions:

1. What is the definition of psychology?

2. What qualifies psychology as a true science?

3. How does the scientific method work?

4. What are hypotheses, and where do they come from?

5. What are the major goals of psychology?

6. What is the subject matter for psychology?

7. What are operational definitions, and why are they important?

8. What are the philosophical roots of psychology?

9. What contributions did early natural scientists and physiologists make to psychology?

10. Who is credited with being the founder of psychology as a separate science?

11. What were the major themes and methods of the structuralists?

12. What is functionalism, and how did it differ from structuralism?

13. Who was the founder of the school of behaviorism, and what were the major assumptions of this school of psychology?

14. What is psychoanalytic psychology, and who was its founder?

15. What are the major ideas presented in humanistic psychology, and who are some of the important people who developed these ideas?

16. What is gestalt psychology?

17. What are the main thrusts of the biological, evolutionary, psychodynamic, behavioral, cognitive, cross-cultural, and positive approaches to psychology?

WHAT IS PSYCHOLOGY?

Let's get started by considering a definition of psychology. **Psychology** is the science of behavior and mental processes. It will be worth our time to take a few minutes now to dissect this definition to look at its component parts.

> **psychology** the science of behavior and mental processes

First and foremost, the definition tells us that psychology is a *science*, just like biology, physics, and chemistry. As a science, psychology approaches its subject matter from a scientific perspective. This means that psychologists use accepted scientific techniques to build a body of knowledge about behavior and mental processes. Second, the definition tells us that psychologists have an interest in both humans and animals. We'll see many examples of psychological research that uses animals in an effort to help us understand human behaviors and mental processes. On the other hand, some psychologists study the behaviors and mental activity on non-human animals simply because they find them interesting and worthy of study in their own right. Finally, our definition suggests that psychologists study both behavior and mental processes.

We first need to discuss what it means to say that psychology is a science. Then we'll move on to explore psychology's subject matter in a bit more detail.

Psychology: Science and Practice

There are many ways to find out about ourselves and the world in which we live. Some of our beliefs are a matter of faith (for example, there is a God or there isn't). Such faith-based beliefs require no **empirical evidence**—evidence gathered through direct sensory experience or observation. Some beliefs come through tradition, passed on from one generation to the next, accepted simply because "they said it is so." Some beliefs are credited to common sense (for example, beat a dog often enough and sooner or later it will get mean). Some of the insights we have about the human condition are taken from art, literature, poetry, and drama. For example, some of our ideas about romantic love may have roots in literature, such as Shakespeare's *Romeo and Juliet*. Although all of these

> **empirical evidence** evidence gathered through direct sensory experience or observation

ways of learning about ourselves and the world have value in certain contexts, psychologists maintain that there is a better way: by applying the values and methods of science.

When psychologists try to learn about behavior and mental processes, they avoid faith-based and common sense explanations. Instead, they approach problems from a scientific perspective. This involves 1) attempting to isolate the factors that contribute to behavior, and 2) developing theories and laws to account for the behavior of interest.

theory a set of assumptions concerning the causes for behavior, including statements of how the causes for behavior work. Theories are rigorously evaluated and may be retained, modified, or rejected.

A **theory** is a set of testable assumptions concerning the causes for behavior. A theory also includes statements of how the causes for behavior work. Theories are subjected to rigorous evaluation and may be retained, modified, or rejected (Bordens & Abbott, 1999). If enough evidence exists to support a theory, it may be elevated to the status of a *law*. In psychology, our theories or laws about behavior and mental processes are based solely on empirical evidence, and not on faith, tradition, or common sense.

science an organized body of knowledge gained through the application of scientific methods

What qualifies psychology to be a science? Simply put, a **science** is an organized body of knowledge gained through application of scientific methods. So to call itself a science, a discipline has to demonstrate two things: 1) an organized body of knowledge and 2) the use of scientific methods.

Ever since psychology began as a separate science, psychologists have learned a great deal about the behaviors and mental processes of organisms, both human and non-human. Yet it is still the case that we can ask interesting and important questions for which psychologists do not yet have adequate answers. Not having all of the answers can be frustrating, but that is part of the excitement of psychology—there are still so many things to discover. The truth is, however, that psychologists have learned a great deal, and what is known is well organized. This book is but one version of the organized collection of knowledge that is psychology. Another version of the organized body of knowledge can be found in the vast collection of scientific literature found in scientific journals (for example, the *Journal of Experimental Psychology, Child Development*, and the *Journal of Personality and Social Psychology* among scores of others). So in terms of our first requirement, then, psychology qualifies as a science.

scientific method a method of acquiring knowledge which involves observing a phenomenon, formulating hypotheses, further observing and experimenting, and refining and retesting hypotheses

Psychology meets the second requirement of a science because what is known in psychology has been learned mostly through the application of the scientific method. The **scientific method** is a method of acquiring knowledge by observing a phenomenon, formulating hypotheses, further observing and experimenting, and refining and re-testing hypotheses (Bordens & Abbott, 1999). Scientific methods reflect an attitude or an approach to problem solving. It is "a process of inquiry, a particular way of thinking," rather than a special set of procedures that must be followed rigorously (Graziano & Raulin, 1993, p. 2).

There may not be specific rules to follow in doing science, but there are guidelines. The basic process goes like this: The scientist (psychologist) makes observations about his or her subject matter. For example, he or she notices that when there are several bystanders to an emergency, help is <u>less</u> likely to be given than if there is only one bystander. On the basis of such preliminary observations, the scientist develops a hypothesis. A **hypothesis** is a tentative explanation of some phenomenon that can be tested and then either supported or rejected (Bordens & Abbott, 1999); it is an educated guess about one's subject matter. It links together two things: factors believed to control behavior and

hypothesis a tentative explanation of some phenomenon that can be tested and then either supported or rejected

the behavior itself. In our example, the scientist might hypothesize that as the number of bystanders to an emergency increases, the likelihood of the person in need receiving help decreases. In this hypothesis, a causal factor (number of bystanders) is tentatively linked to behavior (helping or lack of helping).

Hypotheses are logically deduced from preliminary observations and from the reading of existing scientific literature. Hypotheses, although they may sound intuitively obvious, are not accepted as the final explanation for behavior. Instead, the scientist proceeds by systematically testing his or her hypothesis with empirical research, making careful observations of behavior (this time under specified and controlled conditions). For example, the psychologist could test the hypothesis linking the number of bystanders and helping behavior by designing a study in which she systematically increases the number of bystanders to a staged emergency and observes the bystanders' behaviors. These new observations would then be analyzed to see if they confirm the previously stated hypothesis.

An interesting reality about the scientific method is that once a hypothesis is confirmed, the research process does not stop. Instead, as is often the case, more questions may be raised by a study than are answered. These new questions, in turn, serve as the basis for new hypotheses and new research. For example, after confirming that increasing the number of bystanders decreases helping, the psychologist might want to explore if the nature of the bystanders makes a difference. Would it make a difference if the bystanders were all friends of the "victim" or all strangers? What if they were all police officers on vacation? New hypotheses could be developed and tested. In this way, the acquisition of knowledge becomes an ongoing process of attempting to refine explanations, theories, and laws of behavior.

There is one important thing to remember about science, the scientific method, and hypotheses. A scientific hypothesis may be rejected or supported, but it cannot be "proven" as true. No matter how much support one finds for a hypothesis, there still may be

Psychology is not just the science of <u>human</u> behaviors and mental processes. Psychologists concern themselves with nonhuman animals as well.

other hypotheses (perhaps, as yet, unthought of) that will do a better job of explaining what has been observed. Thus, psychologists avoid statements or claims that their research "proves" something. Instead, interpretations of results are couched in terms of a hypothesis being supported or rejected.

The goal of many psychologists is to use scientific methods to learn more about their subject matter. But while all psychologists are scientists, most are *scientist-practitioners*. This means that they are not so much involved in discovering new scientific laws about behavior and mental processes as they are in applying what is already known. For example, a clinical psychologist treating a patient with a psychological disorder might use a new therapy technique that research shows is more effective than existing treatments. Of those psychologists who are practitioners, most are clinical or counseling psychologists. Their goal is to apply what is known to help people deal with problems that affect their ability to adjust to the demands of their environments, including other people.

Psychological practitioners can be found in many settings in addition to clinical settings where therapy is conducted. For example, even before classes resumed at Columbine High School, students—and their parents—met not only with teachers and school administrators, but also with teams of counselors and therapists who were there to help students cope with what had happened. Other scientist-practitioners apply psychological principles to situations that arise in the workplace; these are industrial/organizational (or I/O) psychologists. Some use psychology to improve the performance of athletes. For example, at least a part of the phenomenal recent success of the U.S. women's national soccer team has been credited to Colleen Hacker, Ph.D., a sport psychologist who worked to boost confidence, build team unity, and eliminate media distractions. Others advise attorneys on how best to present arguments in the courtroom. Some intervene to reduce ethnic prejudice and to teach others how differing cultural values affect behaviors. Some establish programs to increase the use of automobile safety belts, while others help people train their pets.

BEFORE YOU GO ON

- What is the definition of psychology?
- What makes psychology a science?
- What are the major goals of psychology?

Thus, we say that psychology has two interrelated goals: 1) using scientific methods to better understand the behaviors and mental processes of organisms, and 2) applying that understanding to help solve problems in the real world. The science of psychology and the practice of psychology are not mutually exclusive endeavors. Many psychologists who are practicing industrial/organizational psychology or clinical counseling are also active scientific researchers. And much of the scientific research in psychology gets its initial spark or impetus from problems that arise in real-world applications of psychology (Hoshmand & Polkinghorne, 1992).

The Subject Matter of Psychology

Trying to list everything that psychologists study would not be very instructive; the list would be much too long to be of any use. However, as our definition says, the subject matter of psychology is behavior and mental processes. Let's explore more fully just what that means.

behavior the actions and responses of organisms, which are the focus of psychological research and theory

Psychologists study behavior. **Behavior** is what organisms do—their actions and reactions. The behaviors of organisms are observable and, at least potentially, measurable. If we are concerned with whether a rat will press a lever in some situation, we can observe its behavior directly. If we wonder about Susan's ability to draw a circle, we can ask her to do so and observe her efforts. Observable, measurable behaviors offer an advantage as the subject matter of a science because they are *publicly verifiable*. That is, several observers (public) can agree on (verify) the behavior or the event being studied. We can agree that the rat did or did not press the lever, or that Susan drew a circle rather than a triangle. If you were interested in how violent movies contribute to aggression, you would focus your study on overt, observable, aggressive behaviors, not on how such movies make the viewer feel or think.

Psychologists also study mental processes. As we will soon see, when psychology emerged as a separate discipline in the late nineteenth century, it was *defined* as the science of mental processes, or the science of consciousness. There are two types of mental processes: *cognitions* and *affects*. **Cognitions** are mental events such as perceptions, beliefs, thoughts, ideas, and memories. Cognitive processes, then, include activities such as perceiving, thinking, knowing, understanding, problem solving, and remembering. **Affect** (af'-ekt) refers to mental processes that involve one's feelings, mood, or emotional state. It may be that students who behave very violently toward others have *cognitions* that fellow students are rejecting them and also experience the *affect* of despair and anger.

cognitions mental events such as perceptions, beliefs, thoughts, and memories that comprise part of the subject matter of psychology

affects mental processes that involve one's feelings, mood, or emotional state and that comprise part of the subject matter of psychology

Here we have a scheme we will encounter repeatedly: the ABCs that make up the subject matter of psychology. Psychology is the science of affect, behavior, and cognition. To understand a person at any given time, or to predict what he or she will do next, we must understand what he or she is feeling (A), doing (B), and thinking (C).

Behavior and mental processes have one important difference between them. Behavior is directly observable. We can see if a person behaves aggressively, or cries, or laughs. We can see how many items on a test a person answers correctly. These are overt behaviors that can be directly observed and quantified (publicly verified). On the other hand, the mental processes of affect and cognition are not directly observable. We must infer their existence and effects through the observation of behaviors related to their mental processes. For example, we infer that someone is "sad" (affect) if we see him or her with a long face or crying. Similarly, we infer that jurors used certain pieces of evidence to make a decision (cognition) by what they tell us on a post-trial questionnaire.

Many sports psychologists can be considered "practitioners" of psychology. Using their knowledge of the scientific principles of psychology, they help athletes attain their best performances.

Psychologists find it useful, and occasionally imperative, to define the subject matter of a given study using operational definitions. An **operational definition** defines concepts in terms of the procedures used to measure or create them. Let's look at a few examples.

operational definition defining a concept in terms of the procedures used to measure or create them

Imagine that we wanted to look at the relationship, if any, between exposure to television and violence. Before we got very far, we would have to define what we meant by "exposure to television," and we would have to specify exactly how we would go about measuring "violence." We would have to generate operational definitions for the behaviors we were to study. What if we wanted to compare the behaviors of hungry and non-hungry rats in a maze? What do we mean when we talk about a "hungry rat"? What we can do is offer an operational definition, specifying that—at least for our study—a "hungry" rat is one that has been deprived of food for 24 hours. We could also operationally define a hungry rat as one that has lost 20 percent of its normal body weight, thus defining the concept in terms of the procedures used to create the hunger.

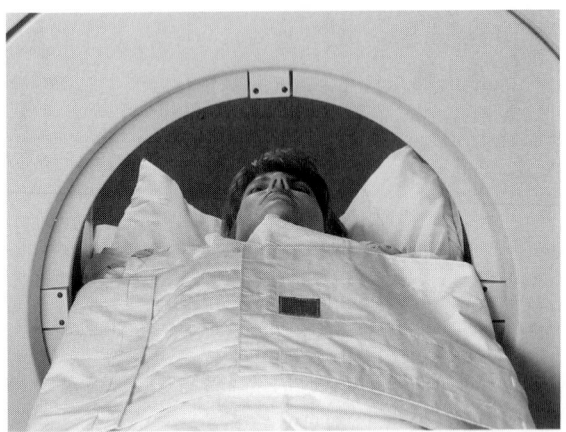

Medical tests often raise one's level of anxiety. In this context, how might we operationally define "anxiety"?

Operational definitions are particularly useful when we are dealing with mental processes. How will we define *anxiety* in a study comparing the exam performance of students who experience either high or low anxiety levels when taking tests? How will we define *intelligence* if we want to compare the intelligence of students who have had access to a preschool program with students who have not? Terms such as *anxiety* and *intelligence* are difficult to define precisely, or to define in ways with which all psychologists agree. Our only recourse is to use operational definitions and specify how we intend to measure these concepts. We might operationally define anxiety in terms of measurable changes in physiological processes such as heart rate, blood pressure, and sweat gland activity. We might operationally define intelligence as the score on a certain psychological test.

Operational definitions have their limitations. They may oversimplify truly complex concepts (surely there is more to intelligence than a test score). On the other hand, they do allow us to specify exactly how to measure the behavior or mental process we are studying, so they help us communicate accurately with others. We will see many examples of operational definitions throughout this text.

BEFORE YOU GO ON

- What are the ABCs of the subject matter of psychology?
- What is an operational definition?

PSYCHOLOGICAL APPROACHES PAST AND PRESENT

No two psychologists approach subject matter exactly the same way. Each brings unique experiences, expertise, values, and prejudices to the study of behavior and mental processes. This is true today and has always been the case. In this section, we add to our definition of psychology by considering some of the major perspectives, or approaches, that have been developed throughout psychology's history.

Psychology's Roots in Philosophy

Psychology did not suddenly appear as the productive scientific enterprise we know today. The roots of psychology are found in philosophy and science.

We credit philosophers for first suggesting that it is reasonable and potentially profitable to seek explanations of human behaviors at a human level. Early explanations tended to be at the level of God—or the gods. If someone suffered from fits of terrible depression, for example, it was believed that person had offended the gods. A few philosophers successfully argued that they might be able to explain why people behave, feel, and think as they do, without constant reference to God's intentions in the matter.

The French philosopher René Descartes (1596–1650) is a good example of such a philosopher. Descartes liked to think about thinking. As he "lay abed of a morning thinking" (which his schoolmaster allowed, because Descartes was so good at it), he pondered how the human body and mind produced the very process he was then engaged in—thinking. Descartes envisioned the human body as a piece of machinery: intricate and complicated, to be sure, but machinery nonetheless. If the body consisted essentially of tubes, gears, valves, and fluids, its operation must be subject to natural physical laws, and those laws could therefore be discovered. This is a philosophical doctrine known as **mechanism**.

Descartes went further. According to the doctrine of **dualism**, humans possess more than just a body: They have minds. It is likely, thought Descartes, that the mind similarly functions through the actions of knowable laws, but getting at these laws would surely be more difficult. Here's where Descartes had a truly important insight. We can learn about the mind because the mind and the body interact with each other. That interaction takes place in the brain. In these matters, Descartes' position is called *interactive dualism*; dualism because the mind and the body are separate entities, and interactive because they influence each other. Thus, we have with René Descartes the real possibility of understanding the human mind and how it works.

René Descartes (1596-1650) Descartes believed we can learn about the mind because the mind and the body interact with each other—a concept called *interactive dualism*.

Nearly a hundred years later, a group of British thinkers brought that part of philosophy concerned with the workings of the human mind very close to what was soon to become psychology. This group got its start from the writings of John Locke (1632–1704). Locke was sitting with friends after dinner one evening discussing philosophical issues when it became clear that no one in the group really understood how the human mind understands anything, much less complex philosophical issues. Locke announced that within a week he could provide the group with a short explanation of the nature of human understanding. What was to have been a simple exercise took Locke many years to finish, but it gave philosophers a new set of ideas to ponder.

One of Locke's major concerns was how we come to represent the world "out there" in the internal world of the mind. Others (including Descartes) had asked this question, and many assumed that we are born with certain basic ideas about the world, ourselves, and, of course, God. Locke thought otherwise. He believed we are born into this world with our minds quite empty, like blank slates (the mind as a blank slate, or *tabula rasa*, was not new with Locke; Aristotle introduced it in the third century B.C.). So how <u>does</u> the mind come to be filled with all its ideas and memories? Locke answered, "In one word, from *experience*." Locke and his followers came to be known as British empiricists, those who credit experience and observation as the source of mental life. Their philosophical doctrine is known as **empiricism**. Generally speaking, the major contribution of the early philosophers to the emergence of psychology as a science was to make psychology empirical.

mechanism the philosophical doctrine suggesting that the human body is a piece of machinery subject to natural physical laws, which can be identified

dualism a philosophical doctrine that states that humans possess both body and mind

empiricism a philosophical doctrine that states that the source of mental life is experience and observation

Few nonpsychologists have influenced the science of behavior and mental processes to the extent that Charles Darwin has. Darwin emphasized the adaptation of species to their environment.

Psychology's Roots in Science

Philosophers had gone nearly to the brink. They had raised intriguing questions about the mind, how it worked, where its contents (ideas) came from, how ideas could be manipulated, and how the mind and body might influence each other. Could the methods of science provide answers to any of the philosophers' questions? A few natural scientists and physiologists believed that they could.

During the nineteenth century, natural science was making progress on every front. Charles Darwin (1809–1882) was a naturalist/biologist. In 1859, just back from a lengthy sea voyage on the *H.M.S. Beagle*, Darwin published his revolutionary *The Origin of Species*, which explained the details of evolution. Few non-psychologists were ever to have as much influence on psychology. Darwin confirmed for psychology that the human species was part of the natural world of animal life. The methods of science could be turned toward understanding this creature of nature called the human being.

Darwin made it clear that all species of this planet are, in a nearly infinite number of ways, related to one another. The impact of this observation, of course, is that what scientists discover about the sloth, the ground squirrel, or the rhesus monkey may enlighten them about the human race. Another concept that Darwin emphasized was adaptation. Species will survive and thrive only to the extent that they can, over the years, adapt to their environments. Psychologists were quick to realize that *adaptation* to one's environment was often a mental as well as a physical process.

A year after the publication of *The Origin of Species*, a German physicist, Gustav Fechner (1801–1887), published a volume that was unique as a physics text. Fechner applied his training in the methods of physics to the psychological process of sensation. How are psychological judgments about events in the environment made? What, Fechner wondered, was the relationship between the physical characteristics of a stimulus and the psychological experience of sensing that stimulus? For example, if the intensity of a light is doubled, will an observer see that light as twice as bright? Fechner found that the answer was no. Using the scientific procedures we would expect from a physicist, Fechner went on to determine the precise relationships between the physical aspects of a stimulus and a person's psychological experience of those stimuli (Link, 1995). Fechner succeeded in applying the methods of science to a psychological question about the mind and experience.

The mid–1800s also found physiologists better understanding how the human body functions. By then it was known that nerves carried electrical messages to and from various parts of the body, that nerves serving vision are different from those serving hearing and the other senses, and are also different from those that activate muscles and glands. Of all the biologists and physiologists of the nineteenth century, the one whose work is most relevant to psychology is Hermann von Helmholtz (1821–1894). In the physiology laboratory, Helmholtz performed experiments and developed theories on how long it takes the nervous system to react to stimuli, how we process information through our senses, and how we experience color. These are psychological issues, but in the mid–1800s there was no recognized science of psychology as we know it today.

Even before psychology became established, scientists had been looking for relationships between structures in the brain and the behavior of organisms. One of the first to have a significant impact in this area of study was Franz Joseph Gall (1758–1828). Gall argued that mental processes have their origins in the brain; to understand mental activity meant that one must understand the brain. Then he went further. Gall claimed that specific areas of the brain house specific psychological characteristics or faculties, such as aggressiveness, honesty, intelligence, and self-esteem. It seemed clear to Gall that there were significant individual differences in the extent to which persons possessed these traits, which he assumed were inborn.

So far, so good. But then Gall suggested that one could measure a person's psychological faculties by examining the size and location of bumps on the skull. Speech, for example, was located at the very front of the brain, where orators seemed to have large protrusions; self-esteem was housed at the top, toward the rear. An associate, Johann Spurzheim, popularized Gall's ideas (to Gall's embarrassment). Spurzheim coined the term **phrenology**, to mean the science of determining personal characteristics by the careful interpretation of bumps on the head! The new "science" became extremely popular, particularly in the United States, but gained little status among the scientific community.

phrenology a discredited science that sought to determine personal characteristics by the careful interpretation of bumps on the head

One reason for the demise of phrenology and Gall's view of the brain was the work of Pierre Flourens (1758–1828). Flourens used the technique of *ablation*, or the systematic removal of small parts of the brain from living animals, to study each part's function. Flourens believed that human brains were not significantly different from those of other animals, so he used mostly dogs and pigeons in his work. He found that some lower brain structures (e.g., the cerebellum) did have rather specific functions, but he was unable to locate any specific functions in the largest structure of the brain, the cerebral cortex. He discovered, for example, that if some behavior were lost following the removal of part of the cerebral cortex, some other area of the brain often could reacquire that behavior.

A different means of studying relationships between the brain and behavior was discovered by Gustav Fritsch (1838–1927) and Eduard Hitzig (1838–1907) in 1870. They found that a mild electric current delivered to one side of a surgically exposed cerebral cortex elicited the movement of muscles in the opposite side of the body. Using dogs, they soon mapped areas on each side of the brain that corresponded to different muscle groups on the opposite side of the dog's body. Soon other scientists were using fine wire electrodes to search for other functions of brain areas. In 1929, Hans Berger, a German psychiatrist who had been experimenting with the technique for 20 years, reported that recording electrodes attached to a person's scalp could pick up and record the general electrical activity of the brain. This was the first reported use of an electroencephalogram (EEG).

The contribution of early physiologists to the emergence of psychology as a separate science was substantial. Whereas early philosophers contributed the idea of empiricism to psychology, the physiologists contributed the idea of approaching issues relating to the mind and behavior experimentally and systematically. "Only when researchers came to rely on carefully controlled observation and experimentation to the study of the human mind did psychology begin to attain an identity separate from its philosophical roots" (Schultz & Schultz, 2000, p.4).

BEFORE YOU GO ON

- How did the philosophies of Descartes and Locke prepare the way for psychology?

- What contributions did early physiologists make to psychology?

By the late nineteenth century, the stage was set for the emergence of a new science. Psychology's time had come. Philosophy had become intrigued with mental processes, the origin of ideas, and the contents of the mind. Physiology and physics had begun to look at the nervous system, at sensation and perception, and were doing so using scientific methods. Biologists were raising questions about relationships between humans and other species. What was needed was someone with a clear vision to unite these interests and methods and to establish a separate discipline. That person was Wilhelm Wundt.

The Early Years: Structuralism and Functionalism

It is often claimed that, as a science, psychology began in 1879, when Wilhelm Wundt (1832–1920) opened his laboratory at the University of Leipzig. Wundt had been trained to practice medicine, had studied physiology, and had served as a laboratory assistant to the great Helmholtz. He also held an academic position in philosophy. Wundt was a scientist-philosopher with an interest in such psychological processes as sensation, perception, attention, word associations, and emotions.

Although others might be credited with founding psychology, Wundt receives credit for getting psychology recognized as a separate science. Wundt wrote in the preface of the first edition of his *Principles of Physiological Psychology* (1874), "The work I here present is an attempt to mark out a new domain of science." Clearly, Wundt's intention was to define the parameters of a new science.

It is no accident that psychology began in Germany. Toward the end of the nineteenth century, the *zeitgeist* (loosely translated as the intellectual "spirit of the times") in Germany favored the emergence of a new science. Experimental physiology was well established in Germany, which was not the case in France or England. Biology and physiology were stressed in Germany, while physics and chemistry were stressed in France and England. In short, the climate was perfect in Germany for the emergence of the new science of psychology.

For Wundt, psychology was the scientific study of the mind. Under carefully controlled laboratory conditions, Wundt and his assistants tested and re-tested his hypotheses. The work performed in Wundt's laboratory focused on the discovery of basic elements of thought. Beyond that, Wundt wanted to see how elements of thought were related to one another and to events in the physical environment—the latter notion picked up from the work of Fechner. Wundt wanted to systematically describe the basic elements of mental life. Because the psychologists in Wundt's laboratory were mostly interested in describing the structure of the mind and its operations, Wundt's approach to psychology is referred to as **structuralism**.

Along with the careful observation and experimentation, an important method used to dissect mental activity into its component parts was introspection. **Introspection** required a great deal of training as individuals were asked to describe in great detail their basic sensations, thoughts and feelings of conscious experience when presented with a particular stimulus. For example, if one of Wundt's assistants were introspecting on an apple, it would not be enough to say, "Oh yes, that's an apple—a red one." Instead, one would have to describe the actual sensations experienced and the feelings elicited by those experiences.

Wilhelm Wundt (1832-1920). For Wundt, psychology was the scientific study of the mind.

structuralism the school of psychology founded by Wundt that studied the mind by attempting to break mental activity into its component parts

introspection the method used by structuralists to study the mind, which involves describing mental responses to conscious experience in great detail

A student of Wundt's, Edward Titchner, attempted to export structuralism to the United States when he took a position at Cornell University. However, structuralism never caught on in America as it had in Germany because the zeitgeist in America was much different than Germany's. America in the nineteenth century was an expanding nation. People were most concerned about adapting to new environments. Quite simply, Americans were not interested in a psychology that focused so much attention on dissecting mental activity into components, or elements.

As Wundt's new laboratory was flourishing in Germany, an American philosopher at Harvard University, William James (1842–1910), was opposed to the type of psychology that was being studied in Leipzig. James agreed that psychology should study consciousness and should use scientific methods to do so. He defined psychology as "the science of mental life," a definition very similar to Wundt's. Still, he thought the German-trained psychologists were off base trying to discover the contents and structure of the human mind. James argued instead that consciousness could not be broken down into elements. He believed consciousness to be dynamic, a stream of events, personal, changing, and continuous. According to James, psychology should therefore be concerned not with the structure of the mind but with its function. The focus of psychology should be on the practical uses of mental life. In this regard, James was responding to Darwin's lead. To survive requires that a species adapt to its environment. How does the mind <u>function</u> to help organisms adapt and survive in the world?

James's practical approach to psychology found favor in North America, and a new type of psychology emerged, largely at the University of Chicago. Psychologists there continued to focus on the mind, but emphasized its adaptive functions. This approach is known as **functionalism**. Functionalists still relied on experimental methods and introduced the study of animals to psychology, again reflecting Darwin's influence. One of the most popular textbooks of this era was *The Animal Mind* (1908) by Margaret Floy Washburn (1871–1939), the first woman to be awarded a Ph.D. in psychology. She addressed questions of animal consciousness and intelligence. One of the characteristics of functionalism was its willingness to be open to a wide range of topics—as long as they related in some way to mental life, adaptation, and practical application. The origins of child, abnormal, educational, social, and industrial psychology can be traced to this approach.

functionalism the school of psychology suggested by James that studied the adaptive functions of the mind and consciousness

In the early days of American psychology, societal pressure was such that earning a graduate-level education, or any academic appointment, was exceedingly difficult for women, no matter how capable (Furumoto & Scarborough, 1986; Scarborough & Furumoto, 1987). Still, one woman, Mary Calkins (1863–1930), so impressed William James that he allowed her into his classes, although Harvard would not allow her to enroll formally (nor would Harvard award her a Ph.D., for which she had met all academic requirements). Mary Calkins went on to do significant experimental work on human learning and memory and, in 1905, was the first woman elected president of the American Psychological Association (Madigan & O'Hara, 1992). Christine Ladd-Franklin (1847–1930) did receive a Ph.D., but not until 40 years after it was earned and Johns Hopkins University lifted its ban on awarding advanced degrees to women. In the interim, she authored an influential theory on how humans perceive color.

BEFORE YOU GO ON

- When and where did psychology originate?
- Who is credited with founding psychology?
- Why did psychology emerge where it did?
- Compare and contrast structuralism and functionalism.

As bright young students were drawn to the science of psychology, new academic departments and laboratories began to prosper throughout the United States and Canada. Scientific psychology was well underway as the scientific study of the mind, its structures, or its functions. This was the case until early in the twentieth century when John Watson turned psychology's attention to the study of behavior.

Behaviorism

While John B. Watson (1878–1958) was a student at Furman University, his mother died, thus relieving one of the pressures he felt to enter the ministry. He enrolled instead as a graduate student in psychology at the University of Chicago. As an undergraduate, he had read about the new science of psychology, and he thought Chicago, where many leading functionalists were, would be the best place to study. However, he was soon disappointed. It turned out he had little sympathy or talent for attempts to study mental processes with scientific methods. He was not very good at giving introspective reports and failed to see how they could be useful. Even so, he stayed on at the university as a psychology major, studying the behavior of animals.

With his new Ph.D. in hand, Watson went to Johns Hopkins University, where, almost single-handedly, he changed both the focus and the definition of psychology. Watson argued that if psychology was to become a mature, productive science, it had to give up the preoccupation with consciousness and mental life that characterized functionalism and concentrate instead on events that can be observed and measured.. He felt psychology should give up the study of the mind and study behavior. The new approach became known as **behaviorism**.

behaviorism the school of psychology founded by Watson that emphasized the study of overt, observable behavior and not the mind

Neither Watson nor the behaviorists who followed him claimed that people do not think or have ideas. What Watson did say was that such processes were not the proper subjects of scientific investigation. After all, no one else can share the thoughts or feelings of the next person. Watson argued that the study of psychology should leave private, mental events to the philosophers and theologians and instead make psychology as rigorously scientific as possible. Watson once referred to behaviorism as "common sense grown articulate. Behaviorism is a study of what people do." (Watson, 1926, p. 724)

No one has epitomized the behaviorist approach to psychology more than B.F. Skinner (1904–1990). Skinner took Watson's ideas and spent a long and productive career in psychology trying to demonstrate that the behaviors of organisms can be predicted and controlled by studying relationships between their observable responses and the circumstances under which those responses occur (Lattal, 1992). What mattered for Skinner is how behaviors are modified by events in the environment. Behaviorists did not address the question of why a rat turns left in a maze by talking about what the rat wanted or what the rat was thinking at the time. Rather, they tried to specify the environmental conditions (the presence of food, perhaps) under which a rat is likely to turn left. For more than 50 years, Skinner consistently held to the argument that psychology should be defined as "the science of behavior." (Skinner, 1987, 1990)

Wundt's structuralism, the functionalism of the early American psychologists, and the behaviorism of Watson were mainstream academic
approaches to psychology. Both structuralism and behaviorism dominated
the way psychologists thought about their discipline. Since the late 1800s,
there have been other approaches to the science of behavior and mental
processes. Some were influential in the past and continue to influence the
way we think about psychology today. We will briefly consider three.

BEFORE YOU GO ON

- What were the major assumptions of behaviorism?

- How did behaviorism deal with the concept of mental processes?

Psychoanalytic Psychology

Early in the twentieth century, Sigmund Freud (1856–1939), a practicing physician in
Vienna, became intrigued with what were then called "nervous disorders." He was struck
by how little was known about these disorders and, as a result, he chose to specialize in
identifying and treating "nervous disorders," a discipline now called *psychiatry*.

Freud was not a laboratory scientist. Most of his insights about the mind came from
his careful observations of his patients and himself. Freud's works were particularly per-
plexing to the behaviorists. Just as they were arguing against a psychology that concerned
itself with consciousness, here came Freud declaring that we are often subject to forces
of which we are not aware. Our feelings, actions, and thoughts (A, B, and C) are often
under the influence of the *unconscious mind*, wrote Freud, and many of our behaviors are
expressions of instinctive strivings. Freud's views were clearly at odds with Watson's. We
call the approach that traces its origin to Sigmund Freud and that emphasizes innate strivings and the unconscious mind **psychoanalytic psychology**. Psychoanalytic psychology
can be viewed as the beginning of modern clinical psychology.

Humanistic Psychology

In many respects, the approach we call humanistic psychology arose as a reaction against
behaviorism and psychoanalysis. The leaders of this approach were Carl Rogers
(1902–1987) and Abraham Maslow (1908–1970). **Humanistic psychology** takes the
position that the individual, or the self, should be the central concern of psychology. If
psychologists concern themselves only with stimuli in the environment and observable
responses to those stimuli, they leave the person out of the middle; that's dehumanizing.
Such matters as caring, intention, concern, will, love, and hate are real phenomena and
worthy of scientific investigation whether they can be directly observed or not. Attempts
to understand people without considering such processes are doomed. To the humanistic
psychologists, the Freudian reliance on instincts was too controlling. Our biology
notwithstanding, we are—or can be—in control of our destinies. Rogers, Maslow, and
their intellectual heirs emphasized the possibility of personal growth and achievement.
This approach led Rogers to develop a system of psychotherapy, and Maslow to develop
a theory of human motivation.

Sigmund Freud brought the psychoanalytic approach to psychology. Among
other things, this approach emphasized the importance of instinctive
strivings and the reality of an unconscious mind.

psychoanalytic psychology the
school of psychology founded by
Freud that emphasized innate
strivings and the unconscious
mind

humanistic psychology an
approach to psychology that proposed that the individual, or the
self, should be the central concern
of psychology

Gestalt Psychology

Gestalt psychology an approach to psychology that focuses on perception and how we select and organize information from the outside world

In the first quarter of the twentieth century, a group of German scientists took an approach to psychology that was decidedly different from that of Wundt, James, Watson, or Maslow. Under the leadership of Max Wertheimer (1880–1943), this approach became known as Gestalt psychology. **Gestalt psychology** focuses on perception, concerned in particular with how we select and organize information from the outside world. "Gestalt" is a German word difficult to translate literally into English. It means roughly "configuration," "whole," or "totality." In general terms, if you can see the big picture—if you can focus on the forest rather than the trees—you have formed a gestalt. Gestalt psychologists argued that to analyze perception or consciousness into discrete, separate entities would destroy the very essence of what was being studied. "The whole is <u>more</u> than the sum of its parts," they said. When we look at a drawing of a cube, we do not see the individual lines, angles, and surfaces, but naturally combine these elements to form a whole, a gestalt, which we experience as a cube.

BEFORE YOU GO ON

- What are the major ideas attributed to psychoanalytic psychology?

- What is humanism?

- Describe the Gestalt school of psychology.

The Gestalt school of psychology was important in that it focused attention away from breaking down consciousness into component parts or studying only observable behavior. It led psychology to view psychological events such as perception in a more holistic way.

Contemporary Approaches to Psychology

Psychology has come a long way since those few students gathered around Wilhelm Wundt in his laboratory at Leipzig back in the late 1800s. There are more than 500,000 psychologists at work in the world today. The Bureau of Labor Statistics reports that nearly 200,000 Americans are employed as psychologists (U.S. Dept. of Labor, 2000). The oldest professional organization of psychologists, the American Psychological Association (APA), claims more than 159,000 members and lists over 50 divisions (areas of specialization) to which its members belong (APA, 2000). The American Psychological Society (APS), formed in 1988, has about 15,000 members dedicated to the advancement of scientific psychology.

A recent survey from the APA listed 236 "psychological specialty areas" in which psychologists are employed. Some areas of specialization are defined in terms of the behaviors studied (e.g., aviation psychology, social psychology, instructional psychology, health psychology, personality psychology, military psychology, cognitive psychology, psychology of religion). Others are defined in terms of the population (individuals) being studied (e.g., animal psychology, industrial psychology, child psychology, cultural psychology). Others include the practitioners of psychology (e.g., clinical psychologists, counseling psychologists, consumer psychologists, and sport psychologists).

Each psychologist approaches the scientific study of behavior and mental processes in a unique way. Each brings his or her own background, personal experiences, training, and set of values to the tasks that are unlike those of any other psychologist. What unites them all, however, is the search to better understand the affects, behaviors, and cognitions of organisms. Moreover, there are a few major approaches, or perspectives, that psychologists may take in their study or practice. Here we review some of the more common perspectives or points of view that guide psychologists in their work. Some have a history dating back to psychology's early days, while some are much more contemporary in origin.

The Biological Approach. Underlying all of our thoughts, feelings, and behaviors is a living biological organism, filled with tissue, fibers, nerves, and chemicals. Psychologists who take a biological perspective seek to explain psychological functioning in terms of genetics and the operation of the nervous system, the brain in particular. Their argument is that, <u>ultimately</u>, every single thing you do, from the simplest blink of an eye to the deepest, most profound thought you've ever had, can be explained by biochemistry. To be sure, experience may modify or alter one's biological structure. Must there not be some changes that take place in our brains as memories are formed? Even most types of cancer are not directly inherited. That is, they do not come from our genes, but from substances to which we are exposed (Lichtenstein et al, 2000; Hoover, 2000). Psychologists who subscribe to a biological point of view might look at violence in schools as a reflection of some inherited predisposition, some hormonal imbalance, or, perhaps, some problem with the activity of a section of the lower brain—a section deep in the center of the brain known to be involved in raw, primitive emotions, such as fear and rage.

The Evolutionary Approach. Yes, psychologists with this point of view are closely allied with those who have a biological perspective. However, they take a broader, long-range view of human and animal behaviors. Although this tradition can trace its roots to Darwin, it is one of the newer perspectives in psychology (Buss, 1999). Here, the argument is that we should explain behaviors and mental processes in terms of how they promote the species' survival and help members of the species adapt to their environments. It is something of an oversimplification, but the point is that we do what we do in order to pass our genes along to those who will survive us. We help others on the chance that they will help us later or that they will assist our offspring if they should need help. An evolutionary approach may suggest that members of the human race are becoming more aggressive (even violent), because *in the long run*, more aggressive behaviors are adaptive.

The Psychodynamic, or Psychoanalytic Approach. As you might have guessed, this approach is one of psychology's oldest, originating with Sigmund Freud and his students. Psychoanalysis as Freud practiced it is not as common today as it was 50 years ago, but many psychologists approach their subject matter with many Freudian notions in mind (Robins, Gosing, & Craik, 1999; Westen, 1998). What are some of the basic premises of this approach today? Much of one's behavior as an adult has its roots or foundation in early childhood experiences. Behaviors and mental processes often reflect an interaction, or downright conflict, among <u>unconscious</u> urges, drives, instincts, and the perceptions of societal pressures. As an adolescent, one's body and hormones provide a message ("having sex is a good thing") while parents and society are telling them something else ("sex is dirty, bad, and sinful"). School violence might be at least partially explained in terms of inadequate nurturing in young childhood and feelings of isolation turned outward.

The Behavioral Approach. John B. Watson first brought behaviorism to psychology and B.F. Skinner championed it. Their approach to psychology no longer dominates (as it did from, roughly, 1920 to 1970), but focusing one's study on observable behavior is still a popular point of view. A basic premise of this perspective is that who we are, what we do, think, and feel is the result of our unique experiences in the world. Yes, we may be born with certain inherited predispositions, but to try to explain what we do in terms of evolution or biology or any sort of inner consciousness is silly. We do not need "theories of personality"; we need only a better understanding of learning. If you want people to stop littering, don't try to make them feel guilty or threaten them, but reinforce their appropriate behaviors (Zelezny, 1999). Behavior-based psychotherapy takes the position that if one can change unfortunate behaviors, unpleasant feelings and disruptive thoughts will change as well. On the other hand, people, even high school students, can learn to react to upsetting events in their lives with aggression, horrific, openly violent, aggression.

The Cognitive Approach. We have seen that cognitions include such mental contents as ideas, beliefs, knowledge, and understanding. Those psychologists who favor a cognitive approach argue that the focus of our attention should be on how an organism processes information about itself and the world in which it lives. Just what do we believe? Where did these beliefs come from? Why are we able to remember some things, yet forget others? How are perceptions turned into memories? How do existing memories affect what we perceive? How do we make decisions? How do we solve problems? Are there better ways to make decisions or to solve problems? How do humans acquire their language, and once acquired, how do we produce language utterances in order to communicate with others? Why do French children acquire their language so easily, while I struggle so to learn it? What is intelligence? Are there different ways to be intelligent? Might people become depressed because they believe things that are not true? Might young high school boys turn to violence if they come to believe that no one likes them and that there is no other way to gain the attention of others? Now that's quite a list of questions, and it only scratches the surface of the sorts of issues that cognitive psychologists pursue. As a subfield of psychology, cognitive is one of the fastest growing (Anderson, 2000; Robins, Gosling & Craik, 1999).

Recognizing that people live in a variety of cultures and ethnic environments, one of the aims of cultural psychology is to examine cultural sources of psychological diversity.

The Cross–Cultural Approach. If psychologists understood all there was to know about the affects, behaviors, and cognitions of young, white, middle-class, American males, they would know a lot—surely a lot more than they know now. However, wouldn't we still have to ask, "But what about females? What about the elderly? What about the poor? What about African-Americans or Cuban-Americans? What about Mexicans or Australians or Germans?" Do we have any reason to believe that what is true of young, middle-class American males is also true of elderly, poor, Jordanian women? Of course not. Such is the thrust of what has lately been referred to as a cross-cultural approach to psychology (Gergen, et al., 1996; Graham, 1992; Hall, 1997; Shweder, 1999). Even very basic psychological issues, such as what an individual finds reinforcing or what motivates an individual to action, vary enormously from culture to culture. How East Asians and Americans perceive and account for cause-and-effect relationships may be significantly different (Norenzayan & Nisbett, 2000). How members of different cultures define mental illness and the treatment/therapy options that are available are significantly different from one culture to another (Lopez, 2000; Triandis, 1996). Please understand: Psychologists have always been aware of cultural differences. It has only been recently, however, that so many others have recognized the value of taking a cross-cultural perspective to the study of psychology.

An Emerging Approach: Positive Psychology. Only recently have two psychologists, Martin Seligman and Mihaly Csikszentmihayi introduced an approach to psychology that is qualitatively quite different from those we've mentioned so far. They, and a growing group of colleagues, call their new perspective "positive psychology" (Buss, 2000, Myers, 2000; Seligman & Csikszentmihalyi, 2000). On the surface, the approach seems simple. For too long, psychologists followed the medical model (or perspective) of looking to "fix" that which is "wrong." Instead of a focus on stress and mental illness, we should focus on mental health. Instead of trying to understand depression, we seek an understanding of happiness. What leads to well-being, to enjoyment, to individuals and communities that thrive? Positive psychology asks about the kinds of families who produce children who flourish, the kinds of work situations that lead to productivity and worker satisfaction. Seligman says that there are three pillars to positive psychology, "First, the study of subjective well-being—life satisfaction and contentment when about the past; happiness, joy, and exuberance when about the present; and optimism, faith and hope when about the future…the second pillar is the study of positive individual traits—intimacy, integrity, leadership, altruism, vocation and wisdom, for example. Third, the study of positive institutions." (Quoted in Volz, 2000.) Those who are comfortable with a positive approach to psychology would not say that we should ignore the causes of violence in public schools. They would only argue that we spend equal effort, time, and money investigating why so many school youngsters are not violent and contribute to their school environments in positive and healthy ways.

This is, no doubt, quite enough for now. You get the point: There are many ways to approach the scientific study of behavior and mental processes. No one way is best. And few psychologists adhere to only one perspective. Most psychologists understand the benefits that each of these approaches can bring to our understanding. You shall encounter these approaches as you continue your study of psychology.

BEFORE YOU GO ON

- Briefly describe the main thrust of the biological, evolutionary, psychodynamic, behavioral, cognitive, cross-cultural, and positive approaches to psychology.

Topic Review 1 A

1. **What is the definition of psychology?**

   Psychology is the science of behavior and mental processes.

2. **What makes psychology a science?**

   Two requirements must be fulfilled before any discipline can be considered a science: having an organized body of knowledge and using scientific methods. Psychology meets both requirements. First, scientific journals and psychology books in a variety of areas house a vast body of literature and knowledge dating back to the latter nineteenth century. Second, psychological research follows the requirements of the scientific method, which is as much a way of thinking as it is a way of discovering new knowledge.

3. **What are the major goals of psychology?**

   Psychology has several goals. One is to investigate how, from a scientific perspective, we perceive ourselves and the world around us. The primary goal of psychology is to discover and better understand the factors that affect behavior and mental processes. Any laws discovered are based on empirical evidence and not on faith, tradition, or common sense. Another goal of psychology is to apply the findings from psychological research to the solution of real-world problems.

4. **What are the ABC's of the subject matter of psychology?**

   The basic subject matter of psychology is the behavior of organisms. Psychologists also study two types of mental processes: cognitions (mental events like perceptions and memories) and affects (feelings, moods, or emotional states). These make up the ABCs of the subject matter of psychology: affect, behavior, and cognitions. Behavior is overt and directly observable, whereas affect and cognition are not directly observable. Psychologists must infer certain affective and cognitive states from overt behavior.

5. **What are operational definitions?**

   Operational definitions are a way to define the subject matter of psychology. Operational definitions define concepts according to the methods used to measure or create them. They are important because they precisely specify just what psychologists mean when defining a behavior or motivational state. They are particularly useful when dealing with mental processes.

6. **How did the philosophies of Descartes and Locke prepare the way for psychology?**

   Psychology owes its early existence to several philosophical doctrines that set the stage for the emergence of psychology as a science. Descartes' doctrines of mechanism (the body is essentially a machine) and dualism (mind and body are separate, but interacting, systems) made important contributions to the emergence of psychology. Over a hundred years after Descartes, the British philosopher John Locke made another important contribution: empiricism. According to this doctrine, all knowledge is acquired through experience.

7. **What contributions did early physiologists make to psychology?**

   Early natural scientists such as Darwin showed that the methods of science could be used to understand human behavior. Darwin's idea that all creatures on earth were in some way related opened the possibility that animal behavior could tell us something about human behavior. Other natural scientists, like Fechner, worked on applying the methods of physics to study sensation. Natural scientists (for example, Helmholtz) were busy working on isolating the physical mechanisms involved in color vision and hearing. The early physiologists suggested that the origins of mental processes were in the brain. Gall, for example, postulated that different parts of the brain were involved in specific psychological functions. Subsequent research provided support for this idea. Overall, the work of natural scientists and physiologists made psychology experimental.

8. **Who is credited with founding psychology?**

   Although several people could be credited for getting psychology rolling, traditionally, Wilhelm Wundt is credited with founding psychology as a separate science. He specifically intended to carve out a new domain of science and in 1879 established the first psychological laboratory in Leipzig, Germany.

9. **Compare and contrast structuralism and functionalism.**

   Structuralism was the school of thought Wundt proposed. Structuralists attempted to discover the basic elements of thought and how they related to one another. An American philosopher, William James, was skeptical about Wundt's brand of psychology. He maintained that psychology should study consciousness from a scientific perspective. He believed that consciousness could not be broken down into component parts and studied in the way Wundt advocated, because consciousness was constantly changing. James's approach asked how consciousness functioned in helping people adapt to the environment. Thus, the school of thought became known as functionalism.

10. What were the major assumptions of behaviorism?

John B. Watson founded the school of behaviorism. Watson was not thrilled with the focus of psychology on mental processes. Instead he focused his attention on studying overt behavior that could be directly measured. He did not deny that mental processes took place; he just believed that they were not the proper subject matter for psychology because they could not be directly observed. Later, B. F. Skinner took up the banner of behaviorism and tried to isolate the external forces that controlled behavior.

11. What are the major ideas attributed to psychoanalytic psychology?

Psychoanalytic psychology was founded by Sigmund Freud. Psychoanalysis was developed based on Freud's experiences with his patients. Contrary to behaviorism, Freud placed emphasis on mental activity that motivated behavior. He believed that most behavior was motivated by the unconscious mind and instinctive forces.

12. What is humanism?

Humanism came about as a reaction to both behaviorism and psychoanalysis. Humanists believe that the self should be psychology's central concern. They suggested that focusing on external stimuli was dehumanizing, and that things like caring, intention, love, and hate should be psychology's focus. To humanists, psychoanalysis proposed a system that was too controlling (deterministic). Humanistic psychologists like Maslow and Rogers stressed free will and personal growth.

13. Describe the Gestalt school of psychology.

Gestalt psychology emerged in Germany, and it stressed laws of perception and how individuals organize and select information from the outside world. The Gestalt psychologists disagreed with Wundt's idea that psychologists could break consciousness down into its component parts and still understand how it worked. For the Gestaltists, the whole was greater than the sum of its parts.

14. Briefly describe the main thrust of the biological, evolutionary, psychodynamic, behavioral, cognitive, cross-cultural, and positive approaches to psychology.

Psychologists who take a *biological approach* to the study of affect, behavior, and cognition, argue that each of these psychological processes has an underlying biological/physiological/genetic basis that needs to be understood. The *evolutionary approach* takes the long-range view that psychological functioning can best be understood in terms of how a species adapts to its environment. The *psychodynamic* view, originated by Freud, seeks to understand the impact of innate, largely unconscious processes and the influence of early childhood. The *behavioral approach* focuses on overt, observable behaviors. What matters is learning and experience. The *cognitive perspective* concentrates on how organisms process information about themselves and the world in which they live, dealing with processes such as perception, learning, memory, decision-making, and problem solving. A *cross-cultural approach* acknowledges that what may be true of persons in one cultural context may not be true of persons in other contexts. Psychologists who take this approach argue that we have for too long focused on the affect, behavior, and congitions of middle-class, white, Americans. *Positive psychology* is the name of a new, emerging focus on what is good, right, and positive about psychological functioning, rather than focusing on problems and issues of mental illness. It focuses on subjective well-being of individuals and institutions.

Topic 1B METHODS OF PSYCHOLOGY

As we discussed in Topic 1A, psychology is a science because it has an organized body of knowledge and because it uses scientific methods to understand behavior. Scientific methods are defined in general terms as systematic procedures of observation, description, control, and replication. It is time to see what this definition means as it applies to the methods psychologists use. To understand psychology, we must understand its research methods. The range of research methods available to psychologists is vast. However, we will focus only on research issues that will help you better understand the material in the following chapters. Our goal is to provide you with the information needed to understand the research methods discussed throughout this book.

correlational research a method of research in which variables are not manipulated. Instead, two or more variables are measured and a relationship between or among them is investigated.

Research methods in psychology can be divided into two categories: correlational or experimental. In **correlational research**, variables are not manipulated. (A variable is something that can take on a wide range of values, as opposed to a constant, which has one value. Manipulating a variable simply means changing its value.) Instead, correlational research depends on observing and measuring behavior and looking for relationships among variables that relate to that behavior. For example, if you were interested in the play patterns of boys and girls in a day care center, you could observe free play times and categorize play behaviors (e.g., being aggressive or helping) and record a child's gender. You could then determine if there is a relationship between the children's gender and their type of play, while making no attempt to influence either variable.

experimental research a method of research in which scientists manipulate one or more variables and then look for a relationship between manipulation and changes in behavior

In **experimental research**, researchers actually manipulate a variable (or perhaps more than one), and then look for a relationship between the manipulation and changes in behavior. For example, if a researcher wants to examine children's willingness to donate candy to needy children, the researcher could have one group of children watch a prosocial television program (such as an episode of "Mr. Rogers' Neighborhood" portraying generosity) and another group of children watch a neutral show. Afterwards, the children can be instructed to play a game where they donate candy to needy children. In this instance, the researcher manipulates the variable of the type of show watched and then determines if exposure to a different television program leads to a change in behavior—in this case generosity (operationally defined as the number of pieces of candy donated).

Key Questions to Answer

While reading this Topic, find the answers to the following key questions:

1. What is the difference between correlational and experimental research?

2. In what situations is correlational research most useful?

3. What is the correlation coefficient?

4. What does the sign of a correlation coefficient tell you?

5. What is a positive correlation?

6. What is a negative correlation?

7. What does the magnitude of a correlation coefficient tell you?

8. Why can't you logically conclude that a causal relationship exists between variables based on correlational research?

9. Can correlational research allow you to predict individual behavior? Why or why not?

10. What type of research allows you to discover causal relationships between variables?

11. What is an independent variable? A dependent variable?

12. What is needed in the most basic experiment?

13. How can a basic experiment be expanded?

14. What advantage does a factorial experiment offer over single independent variable experiments?

15. Why is it important in an experiment to exercise control over extraneous variables?

16. What is a confounding variable? Why is it so important to consider its effect?

17. What techniques can be used to ensure that an experimental group and a control group are equivalent at the beginning of an experiment?

18. What is meant by the generality of research results?

19. What is the relationship between tight control over extraneous variables and generality?

20. What is a field experiment? What are its advantages and disadvantages?

21. What is a meta-analysis? What can it tell you?

22. What are the main ethical guidelines for research using human participants?

23. What are the main ethical guidelines for research using animal subjects?

24. What traps await the consumer of psychological research?

CORRELATIONAL RESEARCH

Correlational research involves measuring two or more variables and looking for a relationship between them. For example, what is the relationship between the amount of alcohol consumed during pregnancy and the rate of birth defects? In this case, you would look for a relationship between two variables: the amount of alcohol consumed and the rate of birth defects.

Correlational research can be useful in several research situations. If it is not possible (or proper) to manipulate a variable of interest, then correlational research is the way to go. In a study of the relationship between birth defects and alcohol consumption, you surely would not want to encourage a pregnant woman to drink alcohol. But you might be able to find women who <u>did</u> drink during their pregnancies and use that information to see if it is related to birth defects. In other words, correlational research is useful when you are looking for relationships between or among variables that occur in the real world. Correlational research is often used in early stages of research to establish relationships

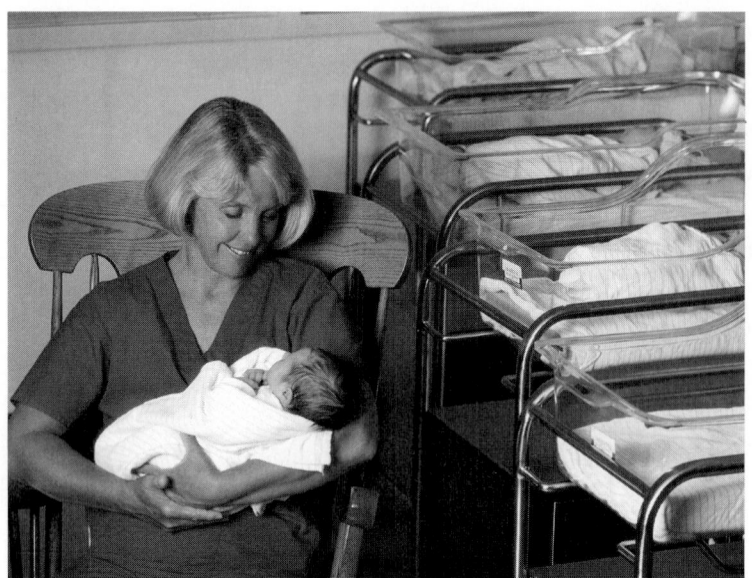

Is alcohol consumption related to birth defects?

between variables that are later explored with experimental research. For example, based on the early correlational findings concerning alcohol consumption and birth defects, subsequent experimental research (using animal subjects) might further explore the link between prenatal alcohol consumption and specific types of birth defects.

Any research involving the age of a person as a variable is correlational; after all, you cannot manipulate a person's age! When discussing factors that relate to intelligence, correlational research is used to establish those relationships. Because of the importance of correlational research approaches, we will explore them in detail.

Let's try a simple example to see how correlational research works. Imagine that we are interested in learning whether a relationship (a correlation) exists between reading ability and performance in introductory psychology. First, we must generate acceptable operational definitions for the responses which interest us. How are reading ability and performance in introductory psychology measured? Performance in introductory psychology is easy: total the number of points and divide by the number of exams to obtain an average earned by a student on classroom exams. Reading ability is a bit more challenging. We could design a test to measure behaviors we think reflect reading ability, but we're in luck. Several tests which measure reading ability are already available, so we decide to use the Nelson Denny Reading Test, the NDRT (Brown, 1973).

Now we're ready to collect some data (make observations). We give a large group of students the reading test (the NDRT). Once the tests are scored, we have one large set of numbers. At the end of the semester, we add up the points each student earned (performance), find the average, and we have a second set of numbers. For each student we have a pair of numbers—one indicating reading ability and one indicating performance in the introductory psychology course. Our goal is to figure out if these numbers are correlated.

The Correlation Coefficient

correlation coefficient a statistic that yields a number between -1 and +1 that shows the strength and nature of the relationship between variables. The sign of the coefficient shows the direction of the relationship between variables and the magnitude shows the strength of the relationship between variables.

From here on, the method is more statistical than psychological. We enter our pairs of numbers into a calculator or a computer. A series of arithmetic procedures is applied, following prescribed formulas. The result is the **correlation coefficient** (denoted with a lower case r), which is a statistic that yields a number between -1.00 and +1.00 that tells us about the nature and the extent of the relationship between the responses we have measured. What does this number mean? How can one number be the basis for a scientific law? It takes experience to be truly comfortable with the interpretation of correlation coefficients, but one general observation we can make is that you get two pieces of information from the correlation coefficient: the sign and the magnitude of the correlation coefficient.

The sign of the correlation coefficient will be positive (+) or negative (-). A positive coefficient tells us that as the value of one variable increases (or decreases) the value of the second also increases (or decreases). The direction of change for each variable is in the same direction. In our example, a **positive correlation** means that a high score on the NDRT is related to a high number of points in the psychology course. It also means that a low score on the NDRT is related to a low number of points. As it happens, there is evidence that such a relationship exists between reading ability and performance in an introductory psychology course (e.g., Gerow & Murphy, 1980). Figure 1.1(A) shows what a graph of the scores in our example might look like and depicts a positive correlation. Here we see a major use of correlations: If we determine that two responses are correlated, we can use our observation of one to make predictions about the other.

positive correlation a correlation indicating that as the value of one variable increases (or decreases), the value of a second increases (or decreases) as well

What if the calculations yield a correlation coefficient that is a negative number? A negative sign indicates a negative, or inverse, relationship between our variables. With a **negative correlation**, as the value of one variable *increases* the value of the second *decreases*. The direction of change for each variable is different. For example, if you were to measure body size to see if it were related to gymnastic ability, it is likely that you would find a negative correlation: large body sizes (high scores) associated with poor gymnastic ability (low scores) and small body sizes associated with good gymnastic ability. Although these two sets of scores are negatively correlated, we can still use body size to predict gymnastic ability. Figure 1.1 (B) shows data depicting a possible relationship between gymnastic ability and body size, a negative correlation.

negative correlation a correlation indicating that as the value of one variable increases, the value of the second decreases

What does the numerical value of the correlation coefficient indicate? Again, it takes a little practice to get used to working with numbers such as -.46, +.55, and +.002. For now, the closer we get to the extreme of +1.00 or -1.00, the stronger the relationship between the responses measured. That is, as our correlation coefficient approaches +1.00 or -1.00 (say, +.84 or -.93), we will have increased confidence in our ability to predict one response knowing the other. The closer it gets to zero (say, -.12 or +.004), the weaker the relationship, or the less useful it is in making predictions. In general, the larger the sample (the more observations made) the greater the confidence we can put in our correlation coefficient, whatever its value.

What if our correlation coefficient turns out to be zero, or nearly so (say, .003)? In this case, we would conclude that the two sets of observations are simply not related to each other in any consistent, useful way. Let's say we worked from the faulty notion that, for normal college students, intelligence is a function of brain size, and that head size indicates brain size. If we measured both the head sizes of many students and their grade point averages, we would find that the correlation coefficient would be very close to zero. As correlations approach zero, predictability decreases. Figure 1.1(C) shows what a graph of data from two sets of unrelated measures would look like.

As you read this text, you will encounter many studies that use a correlational analysis of measured observations. As you do, keep in mind two more important points. First, just because a correlation between two variables exists, changes in the value of one variable do not necessarily *cause* changes in the value of the second. Simply put, it is logically inappropriate to infer a causal relationship exists between variables based on a correlational study. This is true even if two variables are highly correlated with each other. For

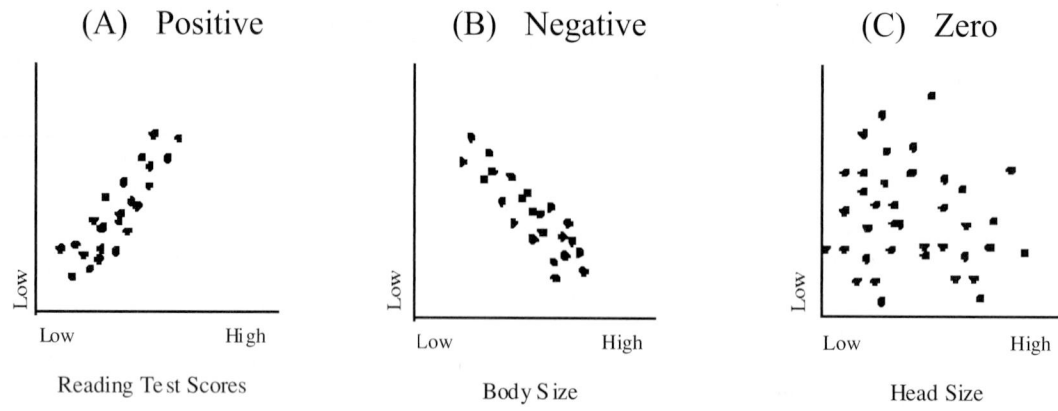

FIGURE 1.1

Graphical representations of positive, negative and zero correlations, using examples cited in the text.

example, even if r = .90, we cannot claim that one causes the other. This can be a difficult point to remember even if sometimes logic overwhelms us. It does make sense that an inability to read will *cause* some students to do poorly in an introductory psychology class where reading is so important. But if all we know is that reading ability and grades are correlated, we can make no statement at all about cause and effect; we can say only that the two responses are related to each other.

There are two reasons you should not draw causal inferences from correlational research. First is the **third-variable problem**, which means that another variable may exist, which we did not measure, that is the true causal variable influencing reading scores. Perhaps, for example, poor reading ability may give rise to high levels of anxiety. The anxiety may turn out to be the true causal variable affecting performance in introductory psychology, and perhaps even reading ability as well. Second is the **directionality problem**, which means that it is sometimes difficult to determine the direction in which the causal arrow runs based on correlational data. For example, in a correlational study of the relationship between preference for violent television programming and violent behavior, you might find a strong positive correlation (greater preference for violent television positively related to overt aggression). It would be tempting to conclude that watching violent television causes a person to be more aggressive. However, based on what is known, you could just as easily argue that the causal arrow runs in the other direction: Violent children prefer watching violent television programs. Results from a correlational study cannot always provide absolute, definitive answers.

The second important thing to keep in mind about correlational data is that even when two responses are highly correlated, we cannot make predictions for individual cases. Reading ability and introductory psychology grades are positively correlated. By and large, students who read well do well in the course, and, by and large, students who do not read well do poorly. So, in general, we can use reading test scores to predict grades, but we have to allow for exceptions. A few poor readers may do very well, and a few excellent readers may still fail the course. Exceptions are to be expected. The farther from +1.00 or -1.00 our correlation coefficient is, the more exceptions we can expect. Like

third-variable problem a reason you should not infer a causal relationship between variables that from correlational research: There may be a third, unmeasured variable that is the actual causal variable

directionality problem a reason you should not infer a causal relationship between variables from correlational research: It is often logically difficult to specify the direction of causality between variables based on correlational data.

most of the scientific laws in psychology, statements of correlation hold true only "by and large," "generally," "in the long run," or "more often than not."

EXPERIMENTAL RESEARCH

A major goal of any science, and psychology is no exception, is to establish clear causal connections among variables of interest. Although it is useful to know that a relationship exists between variables based on correlational research, what we really want to know is whether variables are causally related. For example, as a researcher you want to know if exposure to sec-ondhand cigarette smoke *causes* cancer. You want to know if heavy alcohol consumption during pregnancy *causes* birth defects. You want to know if being reared in an impoverished environment *causes* lower intelligence. Unfortunately, with correlational research, such causal relationships cannot be estab-lished. The only way to establish causal relationships is to conduct well-designed exper-imental research.

Most of what is known today in psychology has been learned by doing experiments. An **experiment** is a series of operations used to investigate relationships between manipulated events and measured events, while other extraneous events are controlled or eliminated. In the abstract that's quite a mouthful, but the actual procedures are not that difficult to understand.

experiment a series of operations used to investigate relationships between manipulated events and measured events, while other events are controlled or eliminated

The Basic Process

When researchers perform an experiment, they are no longer content to discover that two measured observations are simply related; they want to be able to claim that, at least to some degree, one causes the other. To determine if such a claim can be made, researchers *manipulate* one variable to see if that manipulation causes any measurable change in another variable. An **independent variable** is the variable that the experimenter manip-ulates. Its value is determined solely by the experimenter and nothing that the participant in the experiment does affects its value. For example, if you were interested in the effects of different doses of alcohol on the frequency of birth defects, you could give three groups of pregnant mice different amounts of alcohol in their diets (0 ounces/day, .5 ounce/day, or 1 ounce/day). As the experimenter, you determine which mice get which dosage because the amount of alcohol is an independent variable. Conversely, a **dependent variable** (sometimes called a dependent measure) provides the measure of the participant's performance. As such, the value of the dependent variable *is* dependent on what the participant does or what happens to the participant. In our experiment on alcohol consumption and birth defects, the measure of birth defects (for example, the number of limb malformations) would be the dependent variable. One way to keep the concepts of independent and dependent variables straight is to remember that the value of the independent variable is independent of the participants' behavior, whereas the value of the dependent variable *depends* on the participants' behavior or reaction.

independent variable the variable in an experiment that is manipu-lated by the experimenter. Its value is determined by the experi-menter.

dependent variable the variable that provides the measure of a subject's behavior. Its value depends upon what the subject does.

BEFORE YOU GO ON

- How is correlational research conducted?
- When is correlational research most useful?
- What do the sign and magnitude of the correlation coefficient indicate?
- What is the difference between a positive and negative correlation?
- Why shouldn't causality be inferred from correlational research?

experimental group the group in an experiment that receives a nonzero level of the independent variable

control group the group in the experiment that receives a zero level of the independent variable and provides a baseline of behavior to which performance of subjects in the experimental group is compared

placebo something given to research participants that has no identifiable effect on performance

factorial experiment an experiment that includes more than one independent variable

interaction when the effect of one independent variable on the dependent variable differs over levels of a second independent variable

In its simplest form, an experiment has two groups. Participants in the **experimental group** are exposed to some value of the independent variable. For example, in an experiment on the effects of alcohol on simulated driving ability, ten participants in the experimental group could be given an amount of alcohol equivalent to three drinks. If all you had were the experimental group, you would not have a true experiment. What would you conclude if you found that participants in the experimental group had an average of three simulated accidents each? Would you be able to unambiguously say that it was the alcohol that caused the poor performance? If you said no, you are correct. But why not? It might be, for example, that ten of the worst drivers in the world, who would have gotten into accidents even without the alcohol, participated in the experiment. In order to show that alcohol caused the poor performance, you would need a second group of participants, who did not receive alcohol, to perform the same simulated driving task. Participants in this group comprise the **control group**. Thus, the control group involves a zero level of the independent variable. The control group provides a baseline of behavior to which the behavior of the subjects in the experimental group is compared. Hence, in the simplest experiment you *must* have at least two levels of your independent variable.

In practice, experiments get much more complex than the one just described. Even with a control group added, an experimenter may still have trouble saying that it is the psychoactive ingredients in alcohol that cause poor performance. Could it be possible that participants in the experimental group expect to perform poorly because they know that they are not supposed to drive well under the influence? To see if this happens, the experimenter could add an additional control group of subjects who receive a nonalcoholic beverage that tastes exactly like the alcoholic beverage. Such a control group is commonly called a *placebo control group*. A **placebo** is something given to participants that has no identifiable effect on performance. If participants in the placebo control group and those in the experimental group perform equally poorly, the experimenter knows that something beyond the physical effects of alcohol is causing changes in driving behavior.

In addition to adding control groups to one's experiment, experimental groups also can be added to expand the scope of the research. For example, in the study considering the possible relationship between alcohol dosage and simulated driving ability, we might add the variable of the *type of alcoholic beverage consumed* (say, mixed drinks vs. beer). So in this study we would have four groups of participants. One group gets low dosages of alcohol in beer, and a second group gets high dosages in beer, and a third group gets low dosages in mixed drinks, while a fourth group would get high dosages of alcohol in mixed drinks. Everyone then takes the same simulated driving test to see if either alcohol level or beverage type (*or both*) influence errors. This design is called a **factorial experiment** because two (or more) independent variables are included in the same experiment. Figure 1.2 shows two possible outcomes from the study outlined here. In Figure 1.2(A) we see that increased alcohol dosage has exactly the same effect (increases errors equally) as dosage is increased, no matter what the beverage type. When this is the case, we say that there was no *interaction* between the two independent variables. In Figure 1.2(B) we do see an interaction. Here, we see that both independent variables have an effect on what we are measuring (errors). Mixed drinks produce more errors than beer, *and* the difference between the effects of beer and mixed drinks *changes* as dosage increases. An **interaction** occurs if the effect of one independent variable (here, type of beverage) changes as levels of a second independent variable (dosage) change.

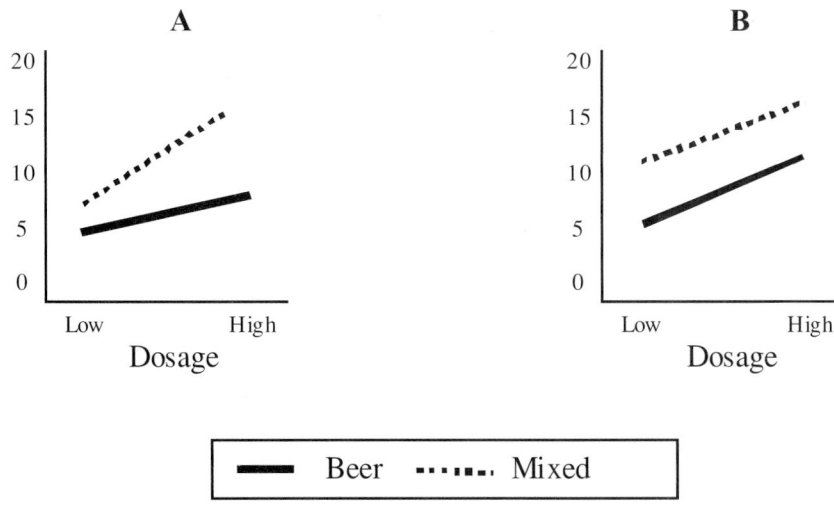

FIGURE 1.2

Hypothetical results from an experiment on the effects of alcohol on driving ability. Panel A shows an interaction between drink type and dosage of alcohol. Panel B shows no interaction.

Let's work through just one more example in an effort to make sure we have all of our variables well in mind. After a few quizzes in your biology class you notice that the student sitting in front of you is consistently scoring higher than you are—not by much, but by enough to be disturbing to you. You ask this student how she does it, and she tells you she has a system she learned in high school. To better remember a series of unrelated concepts, she weaves the terms together to form a story. Remembering the story is fairly easy and can be used to help recall terms for quizzes. This system sounds sensible to you, and you decide to test whether there is a cause-and-effect relation here (a decision that was also made by Gordon Bower and M. C. Clark, who performed such an experiment in 1969).

You get some volunteers from your introductory psychology class and divide them into two groups. One group (A) is asked to memorize a list of ten unrelated nouns. They are left to their own resources to learn the list however they choose. The other group (B) is asked to memorize the very same list of nouns, but they are told about the scheme of tying the words together to form a meaningful story and asked to use this strategy in learning the list.

Now for some terminology. Your hypothesis is that how people go about memorizing has an effect on how much one remembers. You have manipulated this process, so using or not using a strategy in memorizing is your *independent variable*. You believe this variable will have an effect on memory. How will you measure this to see if it is so—that is, what will be your dependent variable? You ask all of the students to return three weeks later. At that time you ask them to "write down as many of the words as you can recall from the list you learned three weeks ago." Thus, you operationally define your *dependent variable* to be the average number of words from the list recalled three weeks later. When you look at your data, you discover that on average, students in group A recall 3.5 words of the original 10, and those in group B (who made up stories) recall 8.2 words correctly. It seems that a story-generating strategy is useful in memorizing words. That strategy seems to cause significantly better recall.

Before we get too carried away, we had better consider the *extraneous variables* that might have been operating in this experiment. These are factors that might have affected the average recall of our two groups of students over and above what was manipulated (memorization strategy). Such factors should have been considered before you actually carried out the experiment, of course. What extraneous variables might be involved in this experiment? For one thing, we need to be certain that the students in each of our groups are of essentially the same academic ability to begin with. We'd have a problem if most of the students in group A were struggling students and those in group B were honor students. Furthermore, both groups of learners need to be presented with identical materials to be learned, and the words need to be presented in the same way to both groups.

When we are done with our experiment and find differences in the dependent variable, we want to be able to claim that these differences are due to our manipulation of the independent variable and to nothing else. This is a very important point. It is the extent to which extraneous variables are anticipated and eliminated that determines the quality of an experiment. Figure 1.3 reviews the steps in our example experiment.

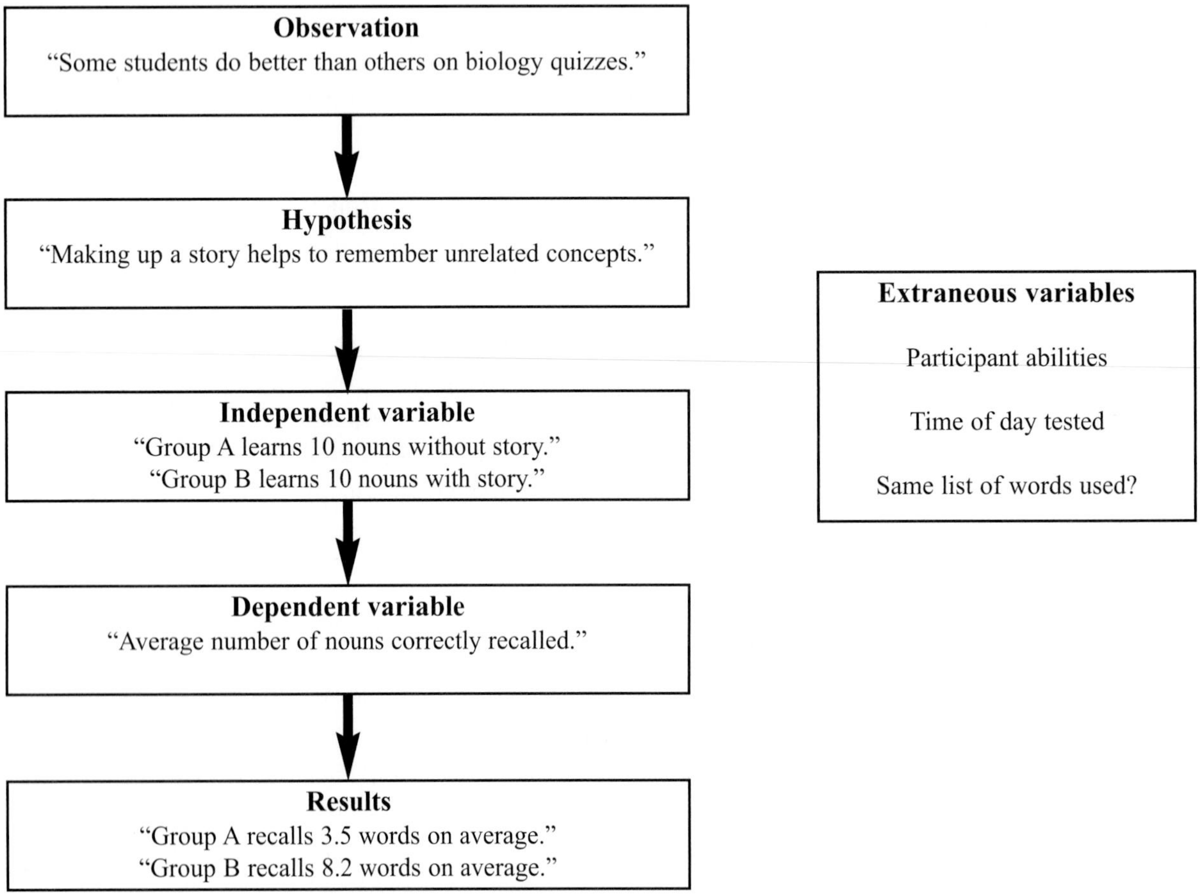

BEFORE YOU GO ON

- How does experimental research differ from correlational research?

- What are independent and dependent variables?

- What comprises a basic experiment?

- How can you expand on the basic experiment?

- What is a factorial experiment, and what are its advantages?

Observation
"Some students do better than others on biology quizzes."

Hypothesis
"Making up a story helps to remember unrelated concepts."

Independent variable
"Group A learns 10 nouns without story."
"Group B learns 10 nouns with story."

Dependent variable
"Average number of nouns correctly recalled."

Results
"Group A recalls 3.5 words on average."
"Group B recalls 8.2 words on average."

Extraneous variables

Participant abilities

Time of day tested

Same list of words used?

FIGURE 1.3

The steps, or stages, involved in doing an experiment. Note how the various types of variables are related to each other.

Exercising Control Over Variables

The essence of an experiment is to look for changes occurring in the value of the dependent variable because of the manipulation of the independent variable.

The hope is that the manipulation of the independent variable will cause predictable changes in the dependent variable—changes predicted by a hypothesis. If the dependent variable changes, the experimenter would like to claim that these changes are due solely to the influence of the manipulated independent variable. To make such a claim, the experimenter must show that all other variables that could have influenced what is being measured have been controlled or eliminated. Factors that need to be eliminated from consideration are **extraneous variables** (extraneous means "not essential"). So to do an experiment, the experimenter manipulates independent variables, measures dependent variables, and eliminates or controls the effects of extraneous variables.

extraneous variable a variable which, if not controlled or eliminated in an experiment, can affect the outcome of that experiment

Think back to our experiment on the effects of alcohol on driving ability. We systematically manipulated the dosage of alcohol and the type of alcohol. We would like to say that it was the alcohol-related variables that changed driving performance. To do this, however, we need to control the potential extraneous variables that could interfere with our ability to make a clear causal connection between our independent variables and dependent variable. For example, we would use the same driving test for all participants, run the experiment in the same room with the same equipment, read the same instructions to all participants in the same way, and maintain a controlled environment. By controlling these variables, we eliminate them as potential alternative explanations for any results we find.

It is particularly important to identify and control a form of extraneous variable called a confounding variable. A **confounding variable** is a type of extraneous variable that varies systematically with the independent variable. If a confounding variable is present, establishing a causal relationship between the independent and dependent variable becomes difficult. For example, in the alcohol experiment, say that on the days when the high alcohol dosage group participates, the laboratory is very warm, whereas on days when the low alcohol dosage group participates, the laboratory is cooler. It may be that participants perform poorly when it is hot rather than when it is cool. In this case, was it the alcohol dosage or the room temperature that caused the change in performance across groups? The obvious way to deal with this is to bring the room temperature under control and keep it constant across conditions of the experiment. Not all confounding variables are this obvious. The time to worry about confounding variables is during the design phase of an experiment.

confounding variable a type of extraneous variable that varies systematically with the independent variable in an experiment and clouds one's ability to clearly establish a causal relationship between the independent and dependent variables

To make sure your control and experimental groups begin the experiment on equal footing, you might try a number of things. For example, try matching the groups on the characteristic of interest. In the experiment on alcohol consumption and driving ability, you could give all participants a driving skills test before the experiment began and then assign them to either group A or B so that the average scores on this test were equal, or nearly so.

random assignment a technique used to equalize groups in an experiment before the experiment is run. Each participant has an equal chance of being assigned to any group in the experiment.

A more common technique is **random assignment**, which means that each participant in the research has an equal chance of being assigned to any one of the experimental groups. If assignment is truly random, good and poor drivers would be equally likely to be in either the experimental or control group. By using random assignment, individual differences will, in the long run, equalize across groups. Decisions to match or randomly assign participants to groups must be made before the experiment begins. Truly matching all participants of an experiment on all relevant characteristics is often very difficult at best—which is why we claim that random assignment is a more common approach.

baseline design an experimental design in which subjects are included in both the control and experimental groups. Behavior observed while the subject is in the experimental phase of the experiment is compared to behavior observed in the control phase.

Another method of controlling differing past experiences of participants is called a **baseline design**. Although there are several such designs, each amounts to arranging conditions so that each participant serves in both experimental and control group situations. Imagine, for example, that you wanted to see if a particular drug caused an increase in the running speed of white rats. Using a baseline design, first you would measure the running speed of rats without giving them the drug (a control, or baseline measure). Then you would check the running speed of the same rats after they were given some of the drug. Changes in their behavior (dependent variable) could then be attributed to the drug (independent variable). You would then check the running speed of the rats again, after the effects of the drug wore off, to see if running behavior returned to its baseline rate.

> ## BEFORE YOU GO ON
>
> - What are extraneous variables, and why is it important to control them?
>
> - What is a confounding variable? Why should it be of concern?
>
> - How can you ensure equivalence between groups before running an experiment?

The Generality of Psychological Research

We have made a strong case for tight control over extraneous variables. This is necessary if research is to produce results that provide an unambiguous test of the research hypotheses and yield data free of confounding variables. However, like life in general, there is a cost adhered to the tight control exercised in many psychological experiments. Experiments that tightly control extraneous variables tend not to be terribly realistic. For example, people drive in all kinds of temperature, weather, and road conditions. These factors could interact with alcohol consumption to raise or lower driving ability. An experiment conducted in a controlled, sterile laboratory is nothing like an actual driving experience. Consequently, the results obtained from research may not apply well to real-world driving. The ability to apply results beyond the restricted conditions of the experiment is known as **generalization**. Usually, the more tightly controlled your experiment, the less generality your data have.

generalization the ability to apply research results beyond the restricted conditions of an experiment

field experiment an experiment run in the real world and not in an artificial laboratory setting

Not all research is conducted under tightly controlled laboratory conditions. Some experiments, known as **field experiments**, are actually conducted in the real world. Instead of bringing participants into the laboratory, the laboratory is essentially brought to the participants. Take a look at an example of an imaginative field experiment conducted by Middlemist, Knowles, and Matter (1976). The experiment examined how people react to invasions of personal space. The experimenters considered personal space to be an invisible bubble which surrounds a person. When an unfamiliar person approached another and came too close, the reaction was negative. For example, if you were approached by someone taking a survey in a mall and she stood six inches from you, undoubtedly, you would feel uncomfortable. Middlemist, et al., wondered if invasions of personal space were *physiologically* arousing as well as psychologically arousing.

They conducted their field experiment in a public men's lavatory (that's lavatory, not laboratory). By closing off one urinal or another, the researchers were able to manipulate how far a participant was from another person while urinating. (That other person, by the way, worked for the researchers. Someone working in an experiment in this capacity is known as a *confederate* of the experimenter.) In the "close" condition, an end urinal was closed off, leaving a center and another end urinal available. The confederate positioned himself at the center urinal before the participant arrived. In the "far" condition, the center urinal was closed off so the confederate and participant used the end urinals. Another confederate positioned in a toilet stall observed the participant's behavior using a periscope. This confederate timed the latency to onset of urination and duration of urination. These are both accepted measures of physiological stress. Under stressful conditions, onset is delayed and duration is shorter. The question was whether there

In order to determine how people might respond in crowded conditions, sometimes it is worthwhile to go into the real world, find a crowd, and observe how people are reacting.

would be a difference in these two measures as a function of the distance between the confederate and participant. Before moving on, can you identify the independent and dependent variable? If you said that distance between the confederate and participant (close or far) was the independent variable, you are correct. If you identified the latency to onset and duration of urination as the dependent variables, you are correct. Middlemist, et al., found that invasions of personal space are, in fact, physiologically arousing. Latency to onset was delayed and duration of urination was shorter in the "close" compared to "far" condition.

As you can see, a field experiment is run in an individual's natural environment. Because of this, the experimenter can have greater assurance that results will generalize beyond the confines of the experiment. However, don't forget the trade-off: Expect some loss of control due to extraneous variables. For example, in the Middlemist, et al., experiment it is not possible to control the amount of commotion in the hallway outside the lavatory or the possibility of interruption by others wanting to use the bathroom. So, the experimenter trades some experimental control over extraneous variables for greater generality.

Which should be of greater concern, tight control or generality? This question has no simple answer other than striking a balance between experimental control and generality. However, one broad rule of thumb applies. If the research is primarily designed to test some theory or model, the experimenter should be more concerned with tight control and less concerned with generality. In such instances, the experimenter may not be interested in applying the results to real-world behavior. On the other hand, if the intent is to apply research results to a real-world problem, then the experimenter should be more concerned with generality than tight control. However, by relaxing tight control too much, the experiment could be fraught with confounding and extraneous variables that will produce results that are of little use.

META-ANALYSIS

There is another popular technique that deserves mention. Some experiments or correlational studies are impossible (or too expensive) to do on a large scale with many participants.

For example, ethics prevent researchers from rearing children in isolation, deprived of environmental stimulation. However, researchers might be able to identify a few adolescents who had relatively isolated, deprived childhoods and compare their learning abilities with those adolescents who had apparently normal childhoods and also with those adolescents who had stimulating childhoods. The findings, based on only a few adolescents and with many variables not under careful control, would be tentative at best, no matter what those findings happened to be. But what if, over the years, many similar studies were conducted by different researchers in different places? Although each study in and of itself would not be convincing, what if there were some way to combine the results of these studies? This is precisely the intent of a procedure called **meta-analysis**, a statistical procedure of combining the results of many studies to more clearly see the relationship, if any, between independent and dependent variables. A meta-analysis minimizes the errors that can plague single, smaller studies (Schmidt, 1992).

Meta-analysis research sometimes uncovers relationships that are not clear in individual studies and sometimes produces results that even contradict some of the studies being included. A meta-analysis by psychologist Janet Hyde and her associates (Hyde et al., 1990) examined gender differences in mathematics performance. These researchers analyzed 100 studies that involved the testing of a combined total of 3,175,188 participants (it is difficult to imagine one research project that could involve over three million people). These researchers found few differences between males and females in mathematical performance on average. Females do have a slight edge in computational skills in elementary and middle school, while males do a little better in mathematical problem solving in high school and college, particularly in tests of advanced mathematics. But any differences found were small, and in most comparisons there were no real differences at all. This is the sort of finding that any one study, no matter how well conceived, is unlikely to provide.

meta-analysis a statistical procedure used to combine the results of many studies to see more clearly if a relationship exists between independent and dependent variables

BEFORE YOU GO ON

- What is meant by the generality of research findings?
- How do tight control over variables and generality relate to one another?
- What are the advantages and disadvantages of a field experiment?
- What is meta-analysis?

ETHICS IN PSYCHOLOGICAL RESEARCH

The goals of science are more often than not, noble: finding a cure for cancer, developing programs to help disadvantaged children in school, or finding a way to effectively treat schizophrenia, for example. However, does having a noble goal justify <u>any</u> research practice? Are there ethical boundaries that should not be crossed in the quest for scientific knowledge and practical applications of that knowledge? As you continue reading, you will find the answer to be a resounding "yes." Researchers in psychology must adhere to a strict code of ethics when conducting research. These ethical codes are designed to protect research subjects from potentially harmful experiments and ensure the well-being of the subjects.

Psychology has something of a unique problem with regard to ethics. To be sure, ethical matters are important in the application of psychological knowledge, be it in diagnosis, therapy, counseling, or training. But in psychology, concerns about ethics are crucial in the *gathering* of information. After all, the objects of psychological research are living organisms. Their physical and psychological welfare must be protected as their behaviors and mental processes are being investigated.

Psychologists have long been concerned with the ethical implications of their work. Since 1953, the American Psychological Association has regularly revised Ethical Principles of Psychologists for practitioners and researchers (APA, 1992, 2001). In fact, concern over how humans are treated in research predates the APA's involvement. Concern over how subjects in experiments are treated can be traced back to the **Nuremberg Code** developed after the Nuremberg war-crime trials that followed World War II. During the war, the Nazis conducted many medical "experiments" on unwilling inmates in concentration and death camps. For example, research was conducted to find the best way to sterilize "inferior races" through surgery done without anesthetic. Josef Mengle conducted a series of sadistic experiments using twin children as subjects. Once the news of these research abuses came to light, the Nuremberg code was put into place. The code of ethics eventually adopted by the APA and other professional organizations closely followed the guidelines set down in the Nuremberg Code.

Nuremberg Code this code mandated that participation in research be voluntary and that the participant be fully informed of the nature and purposes of the research. It also stated that steps should be taken to avoid unnecessary suffering (physical or psychological) of subjects and that subjects have the freedom to withdraw at any time during an experiment.

Ethics and Research With Human Participants

How are the current **APA ethical guidelines** applied to modern-day psychological research? In planning research, psychologists assess the degree to which participants will be put at risk. What are the potential dangers, physical or psychological, that might accompany participation? Even if potential risks are deemed slight, they need to be considered. Researcher Gregory Kimble put it this way: "Is it worth it? Do the potential benefits to science and eventually to animal and human lives justify the costs to be extracted here and now?" (Kimble, 1989, p. 499) Seldom will any one psychologist have to make the ultimate decision about the potential benefits or risks of research. An institutional review board (IRB) typically reviews research proposals to ensure that all research meets the requirements of ethical research practice.

APA ethical guidelines a set of guidelines adopted by the American Psychological Association specifying ethical treatment of human and animal subjects used in psychological research

Here are some other ethical issues related to research in psychology:

1. Participants' confidentiality must be guaranteed. Often names are not used; instead, they are replaced with identification numbers. No matter what participants are asked to do or say, they should be confident that no one will have access to their responses but the researchers.

2. Participation in research should be voluntary. No one should feel coerced or compelled to participate in psychological research. For example, college students cannot be offered extra credit for participating in psychological research unless other options are available for earning the same amount of extra credit. Volunteers should be allowed the option of dropping out of any research project, even after it has begun.

3. Persons should be included in experiments only after they have given their consent. Participants must know the risks of participation, why a project is being done, and what is expected of them. For example, a participant in an experiment on the effects of punishment on learning must be told why the project is being done (to determine if punishment is an effective teaching tool), what they will be doing in the experiment (receiving a mild shock for an incorrect response), and potential risks (pain from the shocks). In some cases, it is not possible to fully disclose the true nature and purpose of a study to participants. Some small amount of deception may be required when doing experiments. In this case, the amount of deception needs to be balanced against the potential benefits of the research and justified to an institutional review board.

4. Particularly if participants have been deceived about the true nature of an experiment, and even if they haven't been, all participants should be debriefed after the experiment has been completed. That means that the project and its basic intent should be fully explained to all those who participated in it. Participants should also be provided with a copy of the results of the project when they are available.

Think back to the Middlemist, Knowles, and Matter (1976) field experiment on the physiological effects of invasions of personal space. What are some ethical questions raised by that experiment? Were the participants informed in advance of their participation? Did the participants have an opportunity for informed consent? Is it ethical to engage in clandestine observation of a private behavior? These and perhaps other questions must be considered when evaluating any research project, especially one done in the field.

Note that there are additional guidelines if children are used as participants in research or if other specialized populations are used (for example, mentally retarded individuals). These guidelines are enforced in addition to the normal APA guidelines.

Ethics and the Use of Animal Subjects in Research

Published ethical guidelines for the use of animals in research are also quite stringent, sometimes more stringent than those published for humans. Current APA ethical guidelines for using animals in research include the following points:

1. Obtaining, caring for, using, and disposing of animals used in research must comply with all federal, state, and local laws, and be consistent with professional standards.

2. A psychologist trained in the care and use of animals must supervise any procedures involving animals and is ultimately responsible for the comfort, health, and humane treatment of the animals.

3. The psychologist must ensure that all assistants are trained in research methods and the care, maintenance, and handling of the animal species being used.

4. Roles assigned to assistants must be consistent with their training.

5. Efforts must be made to minimize any discomfort, infection, illness, or pain of animal subjects.

6. Procedures that subject animals to pain, stress, or privation should only be used when no alternatives are available.

7. When an animal's life is to be terminated, it must be done rapidly with an effort to minimize pain.

8. Proper anesthesia must be used for all surgical procedures.

In addition to these guidelines established by the APA, government regulations must be followed. These government regulations not only specify how animals are to be treated in research, but also dictate minimum standards for housing and caring for animal research subjects.

Just like research using human participants, research using animal subjects must be screened for adherence to ethical guidelines before it can be done. Proposals for research using animal subjects must be reviewed by an institutional animal care and use committee (IACUC). The IACUC normally has the following make-up:

1. A veterinarian who is trained and has experience either with laboratory science or with the species being used.

2. At least one practicing scientist who has experience using animals in research.

3. At least one member of the public to represent the general community's attitudes about the care and use of animals in research. Public members must not be involved in animal research, be affiliated with the institution where the research is to be conducted, or be members of the immediate family of a person affiliated with the institution where the research is being done.

In practice, animal care and use committees exceed the minimum specified. For example, the Purdue University animal care and use committee has more than 30 members and a full-time staff. Every effort is made to avoid research that inflicts undue pain and suffering on animals.

BEFORE YOU GO ON

- What are the major ethical guidelines for research using human participants?

- What are the major ethical guidelines for research using animal subjects?

MAKING SENSE OUT OF PSYCHOLOGICAL RESEARCH

Psychological research can produce results that are fascinating to consider and sometimes difficult to understand. A few traps should be avoided as you read about the research in the remainder of this book. Let's take a look at three such traps.

That Can't Be Right; I Would Never Do That

Imagine you are in class and your professor is lecturing on helping behavior. He tells you about the "bystander effect" that involves less help given to a person in need when many, as opposed to few, bystanders are present. He tells you that when there are many bystanders, individuals tend not to help. You are sitting there thinking to yourself, "That's not right. I remember I helped once when there were loads of bystanders around!" Does your experience mean that the research on the bystander effect is invalid? No. Here's why.

When you read about research, or when your professor talks about it in class, keep in mind that the differences we are talking about are *average differences across groups* and not individual behaviors within a group. For example, let's say you run a bystander-helping experiment with two groups. In Group One, you approach a person walking alone and drop some papers in front of him or her. In Group Two, you approach a person walking near five others and do the same thing. Count the number of people who help you pick up the papers. Let's say in Group One, 80 percent (eight out of ten) stop and help and in Group Two, only 30 percent (three out of ten) stop and help. You conclude that helping is more likely to occur when there is only one bystander than if there are six. Notice, however, that not *all* participants in Group One helped and not *all* participants in Group Two failed to help. So, it is entirely possible that *for you* the bystander effect doesn't apply all the time. But on average, we would still expect more people to help if they were the only bystander as opposed to being with several other bystanders.

The Hindsight Bias

hindsight bias the belief that results from a psychological study are so obvious that no research was needed

Another trap to avoid when considering the results of psychological research is the **hindsight bias** (Slovic & Fischolff, 1977), also known as the "I knew it all along" effect. Sometimes the results from psychological research might seem so obvious that you say to yourself, "Why did they bother doing an experiment on that? I knew that all along." This is a strong tendency, mainly because psychology deals with topics and issues with which we are all familiar. However, keep this fact in mind: If a person is told how a study came out, the results might not seem surprising. However, if the person is told how an experiment was conducted and then asked to predict how it came out, the results can be predicted no better than a guess (Slovic & Fischoff, 1977). You can demonstrate this for yourself using ten friends. Give half of them the following statement:

- "Psychological research has shown that the old adage 'birds of a feather flock together' is true. Do you agree or disagree with this statement?"

Give the other half the following statement:

- "Psychological research has shown that the old adage 'opposites attract' is true. Do you agree or disagree with this statement?"

Most of your friends in each group will probably agree with the statement given, even though they diametrically oppose each other.

Avoiding Circular Explanations

As noted, the goal of the science of psychology is to provide explanations for behavior such as why people fail to help when bystanders are present or why people commit suicide. After years of research in psychology, psychologists have at least partial explanations for these and other psychological events. However, sometimes when an explanation is offered, it is not a true explanation at all. Rather, what is offered is a **circular explanation** (also known as a pseudoexplanation). A circular explanation does nothing more than provide a new label for some observed behavior. For example, Sigmund Freud had some ideas about why a person might commit suicide. Freud proposed that much of behavior is instinctive. He proposed that there are two major instincts: the life instinct (eros) and the death instinct (thanatos). The life instinct impels us toward self-preserving behaviors, such as eating and drinking. On the other hand, the death instincts cause us to engage in self-destructive behaviors like smoking and suicide. So, Freud would say that suicide is caused by an activation of the death instinct.

circular explanation an "explanation" that is not a true explanation. Rather, it does nothing more than give a new label for observed behavior.

Although instincts were a popular "explanatory" concept in the nineteenth and early twentieth centuries, they are not true explanations. Rather, they are circular. Let's see why. The death instinct is used to explain suicide. So far, so good. But something is amiss: When we ask the question of how we know that there is a death instinct, suicide is used to verify the existence of the death instinct. Whenever a situation arises in which the behavior that you are trying to explain is used as evidence for the existence of the underlying explanation, the result is a circular explanation. A similar relationship exists with concepts like explaining hallucinations with a label like schizophrenia. Why do people hallucinate? They are schizophrenic. How do you know the person is schizophrenic? Because they hallucinate. Round and round we go.

To avoid the trap of circular explanations, independent operational definitions for the explanatory concept and the behavior being explained are needed. For example, we could explain hallucinations by postulating that an overabundance of a certain brain chemical triggers hallucinations. We could measure the concentration of this chemical independently from the frequency or seriousness of hallucinations. If we show that increases in the chemical are associated with increased hallucinations, then we have a true explanation for hallucinations that does not merely relabel the behavior we are trying to explain.

BEFORE YOU GO ON

- Explain why exceptions do not invalidate research findings.

- What is the hindsight bias?

- What is a circular explanation, and how do you avoid such an explanation?

Topic Review 1 B

1. **What is the difference between correlational and experimental research?**

   In correlational research, variables are not manipulated (do not change value). Instead, two or more variables are measured and then studied to see if a relationship exists. In experimental research, one or more variables are manipulated and measured for behavior. The relationship between manipulation and changes in behavior is studied.

2. **In which situations is correlational research most useful?**

   Correlational research is useful when it is not possible to manipulate a variable, when relating naturally occurring variables, and during the early stages of research to identify variables that might later be explored with experimental research.

3. **What is the correlation coefficient?**

   The correlation coefficient is a statistic that provides information about the strength and the direction of a relationship between variables measured. It can range from -1 through 0 to $+1$.

4. **What does the sign of a correlation coefficient indicate?**

   The sign of a correlation coefficient indicates the nature of the relationship between variables. It indicates whether you have a positive or negative relationship between variables.

5. **What is a positive correlation?**

   A positive correlation occurs when increases in the value of one variable are associated with increases in the value of a second. That is, a positive correlation exists when changes in both variables are in the same direction (increasing or decreasing).

6. **What is a negative correlation?**

   A negative correlation exists when increases in the value of one variable are related to decreases in the value of the second. That is, a negative correlation exists when the direction of change for the two variables is in an opposite direction.

7. **What does the magnitude of a correlation coefficient indicate?**

   The magnitude of the correlation coefficient indicates the strength of the relationship between variables. The closer the value of the coefficient is to one ($+1$ or -1, it doesn't matter), the stronger the correlation. A correlation coefficient of zero means there is no relationship between variables.

8. **Why can't you logically conclude a causal relationship exists between variables based on correlational research?**

   Although correlational research can be useful in identifying important relationships among variables, it cannot be used to establish causal connections among those variables. There are two reasons why you should not draw causal inferences from correlational research. First is the third-variable problem, which states there may be a third, unmeasured variable that actually is the cause for the behavior of interest. Second is the directionality problem, which says it is difficult to determine in which direction a causal arrow points based solely on correlational research. A correlation coefficient might suggest, for example, that changes in one variable cause changes in a second variable (which may make intuitive sense). However, it might be argued just as strongly that changes in the second variable cause changes in the value of the first variable.

9. **Can correlational research allow prediction of individual behavior? Why or why not?**

   Correlational research does not allow prediction of individual behavior. Since correlation coefficients are rarely, if ever, plus or minus one (indicating a perfect correlation), there will be some error in prediction. So precise predictions about individual behavior is not possible.

10. **What type of research allows discovery of causal relationships among variables?**

    Experimental research, in which certain variables are manipulated and others are controlled, is the research method that allows for discovery of causal relationships among variables.

11. **What is an independent variable and a dependent variable?**

An independent variable is one whose value is set by the experimenter. Nothing the subject in the experiment does can affect the value of the independent variable. The dependent variable is the measure of the subject's behavior. As such, its value depends on what the subject does. In an experiment, look for changes in the value of the dependent variable that occur as a function of changes in the value of the independent variable.

12. What is needed in the most basic experiment?

The most basic experiment must have two levels, or values of the independent variable. In the simplest experiment, one group (experimental group) receives some value of the independent variable. The other group (control group) receives a zero value of the independent variable.

13. How can a basic experiment be expanded?

Expand a basic experiment by adding control groups and experimental groups. Sometimes a placebo control group is included to rule out alternative explanations. For example, in experiments on the effects of drugs on behavior, one group of subjects will receive a nonactive substance. This group helps control the anticipation of expecting a drug to have an effect. Adding experimental groups allows the experimenter to test more refined hypotheses. Additionally, the experimenter can also have more than one independent variable in an experiment, resulting in a factorial experiment.

14. What advantage does a factorial experiment offer over separate, single independent variable experiments?

A factorial experiment allows you to assess separate effects of each independent variable, just like you could do with separate one-variable experiments. In a factorial experiment, you can assess the interaction between independent variables. An interaction is present if the effect of one independent variable changes over levels of a second independent variable.

15. Why is it important in an experiment to control extraneous variables?

Extraneous variables are variables that, if left uncontrolled, can affect your dependent variable. By controlling extraneous variables, you can be sure that variation in the independent variable is the sole cause of changes in the value of the dependent variable.

16. What is a confounding variable and why is it so important to consider its effects?

A confounding variable is an extraneous variable that varies systematically with the independent variable. If a confounding variable is present, it prevents you from unambiguously concluding that a variation in your independent variable caused observed changes in the dependent variable. The time to worry about confounding variables is when an experiment is being designed. If they are detected after an experiment has been conducted, the results of the experiment are worthless.

17. What techniques are used to ensure that experimental and control groups are equivalent at the beginning of an experiment?

Groups must be equivalent at the outset of an experiment; nonequivalence is a source of confounding. Ensure equivalence in three ways. First, measure participants along important dimensions (for example, intelligence or personality characteristics) and match them along those dimensions, assigning one matched participant to the experimental and the other to the control group. By far the most common method to ensure equivalence is random assignment of participants to groups. Each subject has an equal chance of being assigned to either the experimental or control group. In the long run, assume that individual differences will equalize across groups. Finally, use a baseline design in which each subject participates in both the experimental and control group.

18. What is meant by the generality of research results?

Generality refers to the extent to which results can be applied beyond the conditions of an experiment. High generality means that results apply well to situations beyond the experiment. Low generality means the opposite: Results don't apply well beyond the conditions of the experiment.

19. What is the relationship between tight control over extraneous variables and generality?

Overall, the more tightly you control extraneous variables and other conditions of your experiment, the lower the generality of your results. This is because when variables are tightly controlled, your experimental situation becomes less and less like the conditions under which the behavior of interest occurs in the real world. A balance must be struck between tight control and generality. If you are most interested in testing a theory or model, you might be more concerned with tight control over variables and less with generality. On the other hand, if you are doing research and want to apply your results to a real-world problem, you will probably be more concerned with generality than tight control. However, you cannot ignore tight control in these situations.

20. **What is a field experiment? What are its advantages and disadvantages?**

A field experiment is an experiment run in your subjects' natural environment rather than in a laboratory setting. Field experiments have the advantage of producing results that generalize well beyond the conditions of the experiment. However, you give up some ability to tightly control extraneous variables, which is a disadvantage.

21. **What is a meta-analysis, and what can it show?**

Meta-analysis is a research technique that allows you to combine and compare different studies in a field. It can tell you if particular variables are important in affecting the target behavior.

22. **What are the main ethical guidelines for research using human participants?**

The American Psychological Association has established a set of ethical guidelines that must be followed when doing research. These guidelines include participant confidentiality, voluntary participation, freedom to withdraw from the research with no penalty, full disclosure of the purposes and methods of research before participation, and debriefing of participants (especially if deception is used). There are additional guidelines for children and other special populations.

23. **What are the main ethical guidelines for research using animal subjects?**

Researchers who use animals in their research are also bound by a set of ethical guidelines that include the following: Animals should be housed and cared for in ways that comply with federal, state, and local laws; a trained psychologist must supervise any procedures involving animals and ultimately is responsible for their care; the psychologist must ensure that all assistants are properly trained in handling animals; efforts must be made to minimize pain, illness, infection, and discomfort of the animals; if procedures are used that cause pain, they should be used only if no alternatives exist; proper anesthesia must be used for all surgical procedures; and when an animal's life is to be terminated, it must be done rapidly with an effort to minimize pain.

24. **What traps await the consumer of psychological research?**

When reading and considering results from psychological studies, it is easy to fall into three traps. First, the existence of exceptions to findings does not invalidate the findings. Psychologists make statements about average differences between people, not individual differences. Second, some results of psychological research may seem painfully obvious once you hear about them. However, you probably couldn't predict how an experiment would turn out if only given the methods. This is known as the hindsight bias. Finally, watch out for circular explanations that do nothing more than provide a new label of a behavior to be explained. To avoid this trap, there should be independent operational definitions for the explanatory concept and the behavior being explained.

Chapter 2

The Nervous System and Behavior

*A*ll of your behaviors, from simple to complex; every emotion you've ever experienced, from mild to extreme; all your thoughts, from the trivial to the profound—all of these can ultimately be reduced to molecules of chemicals racing in and out of the microscopically tiny cells that comprise your nervous systems. Regardless of the complexity of a stimulus or a behavior, there is a remarkable series of biochemical and physiological reactions that take place in your body. These reactions are the focus of this chapter.

Topic 2A
Nerve Cells and How They Communicate

Topic 2B
The Central Nervous System

Topic 2A NERVE CELLS AND HOW THEY COMMUNICATE

You are sitting in your room studying for an important exam while listening to a CD. When your favorite song comes on, you break from your studies and listen carefully to the music. On your desk a fragrant candle burns. As you pick it up to get a better smell, a drop of hot wax hits your hand, resulting in a small amount of pain. You utter a few colorful metaphors, nearly drop the candle, and abruptly put it down. Soon, you sense your stomach beginning to rumble and grab a bag of chips. With your hunger satisfied, you return to your studies.

Sequences like this occur each day. You are bombarded by sights, sounds, smells, tastes, and tactile stimuli. You enjoy listening to music and smelling the scent of something fragrant, like a candle burning. You sense and satisfy hunger. These are things taken for granted. Have you considered how those notes wafting from your stereo's speakers get to your brain so that you can enjoy them? Or how your brain and nervous system operate to produce an emotional reaction to your favorite music? As you will see in this Topic, the process of getting information to and from the brain (and other parts of your body) involves a complex set of processes that take place on a cellular level.

Key Questions to Answer

In this Topic we will explore how information is transmitted within your nervous system. While reading this Topic, find the answers to the following key questions:

1. What is a neuron?
2. What are the parts of a neuron?
3. What does a dendrite do?
4. What does an axon do?
5. What is myelin, and what functions does it perform?
6. What is the function of an axon terminal?
7. What changes take place in the nervous system after birth?
8. What is a neural impulse?
9. What is the resting potential of a neuron, and how does it occur?
10. What is the action potential, and how does it come about?
11. How does the neuron return to its resting potential after a neural impulse?
12. What is the refractory period of a neuron?
13. What is the all-or-none principle, and why does it hold true?
14. What is the neural threshold?
15. How does your nervous system respond to stimuli of differing intensities?

16. What is a synapse, and how does the neural impulse travel from one neuron to another?

17. What are neurotransmitters, and what functions do they serve?

18. What role does a receptor site play?

19. What do the neurotransmitters acetylcholine, norepinephrine, dopamine, and endorphins do?

20. What are the central and peripheral nervous systems?

21. What are the somatic and autonomic nervous systems?

22. What does the endocrine system do?

23. What is the pituitary gland, and what function does it serve?

24. What does the thyroid gland do?

25. What are the adrenal glands, and what do they do?

26. How does the level of the hormone testosterone affect behavior?

THE NEURON: THE BASIC BUILDING BLOCK OF THE NERVOUS SYSTEM

Our exploration of the nervous system begins at the level of the nerve cell, or **neuron**, the microscopically small cell that transmits information—in the form of *neural impulses*—from one part of the body to another. Neurons were not recognized as separate structures until the turn of the century. To put things in perspective, there are approximately 125 million specialized neurons that line the back of each human eye, and an estimated *100 billion neurons* in the human brain (Hubel, 1979; Kolb, 1989).

neuron a nerve cell that transmits information from one part of the body to another via neural impulses

Even though, much like snowflakes, no two neurons are exactly alike, there are some commonalities among neurons. Figure 2.1 illustrates these common features.

One structure that all neurons have is a **cell body**, the largest concentration of mass in the neuron. The cell body contains the nucleus of each cell. It is in the nucleus of any living cell that we find the genetic information that keeps the cell functioning as it should. Protruding from the cell body are several tentacle-like structures called dendrites, and one particularly long structure called the axon. Typically, **dendrites** reach out to receive messages, or neural impulses, from nearby neurons. These impulses are sent to the cell body and down the **axon** to other neurons, muscles, or glands. Some axons are quite long—as much as two to three feet long in the spinal cord. Within a neuron, impulses travel from dendrite to cell body to axon, and most of the trip is made along the axon.

cell body the largest concentration of mass in a neuron; contains the cell's nucleus

dendrites extensions from a neuron's cell body that receive impulses

axon a long, tail-like extension of a neuron that carries impulses away from the cell body to other cells

The neuron illustrated in Figure 2.1 has a feature not found on all neurons. The axon of this neuron has a cover, or sheath, of myelin. **Myelin** is a white substance composed of fat and protein found on about half the axons in an adult's nervous system. Myelin is produced by special glia cells and is not an outgrowth of the axon itself. Myelin covers an axon in segments, rather than in one continuous coating. Between each segment of myelin is an unmyelinated segment of axon called a **node**. It is the absence or presence of myelin that allows us to distinguish between the gray matter (dendrites, cell bodies, and unmyelinated axons) and white matter (myelinated axons) of nervous system tissue.

myelin a white, fatty covering found on some axons that insulates and protects them and speeds impulses along

node a segment of exposed axon membrane between segments of myelin

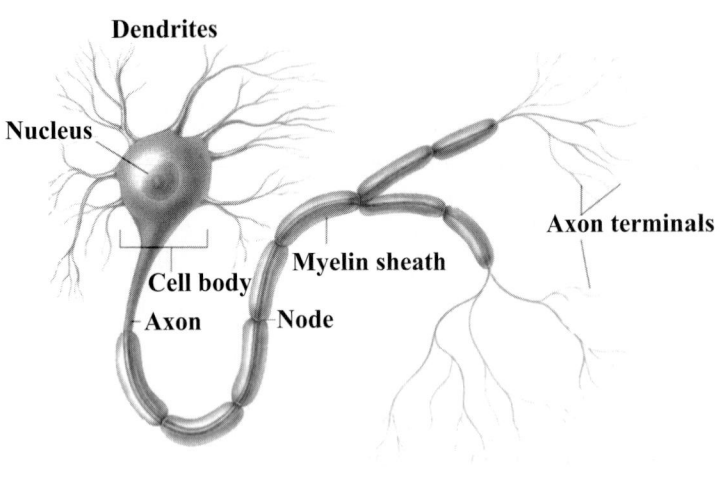

FIGURE 2.1

A typical neuron with its major structures.

saltatory conduction the movement along myelinated axons in which the neural impulse "jumps" from node to node, increasing the rate of neural transmission

axon terminals the set of branching end points of an axon; where neurons begin to communicate with adjacent neurons

We tend to find myelin on axons that carry impulses relatively long distances. Neurons that carry messages up and down the spinal cord, for instance, have myelinated axons, whereas those that carry impulses back and forth across the spinal cord do not.

Myelin serves several functions. It protects the long, delicate axon. It also acts as an insulator, separating the activity of one neuron from those nearby. Myelin speeds impulses along the length of the axon. As we will see later in this chapter, this is because the neural impulse that travels down the axon can "jump" from node to node in a process called **saltatory conduction**. Because of this form of conduction, myelinated neurons carry impulses nearly ten times faster than unmyelinated ones (up to 120 meters per second). Interestingly, myelin can be found only in vertebrate animals. Invertebrates (e.g., worms) have neurons and axons, but no myelin. In order to speed neural impulses, invertebrates have developed some very fat (i.e., large diameter) axons, which are easier to study than the thinner vertebrate axons. Because they don't have myelin, the speed of impulse conduction in invertebrates is quite slow, thereby limiting the size of these organisms. Complex, coordinated behaviors are impossible if invertebrates become too large. Such complex behavior requires more rapid impulse transmission.

Whether myelinated or not, axons end in a branching series of bare end points called **axon terminals**. At the axon terminal, a neuron communicates with other neurons. To review: within a neuron, impulses travel from the dendrites to the cell body, to the axon (which may be myelinated), and then to axon terminals.

Very few new neurons are generated after birth. We are born with more neurons than we will ever have again. In fact, we are born with about twice as many neurons as we'll ever use. What happens to the rest? Those that are not strengthened by experience eventually die off. Bryan Kolb (1989) of the University of Lethbridge in Canada gives us this analogy: In normal development, the brain is "constructed" in a manner rather like that in which a statue is chipped away from a block of granite. Rather than building up the finished product one small piece at a time, more material than one needs is available. What is needed or used is retained, and the rest dies away. For example, a young infant (six to ten months old) has neural circuitry that allows him or her to distinguish between most human speech sounds. Experience with his or her native language environment strengthens those neurons that are important to the native language, whereas those that are not, die off. The result is that an infant that at six to ten months of age could discriminate between speech sounds from his or her non-native language can no longer do so at ten to twelve months of age (Werker & Tees, 1989). In a sense, we are born with a "generic brain" that, much like sculpture, is molded by experience. However, the sculpture analogy goes just so far. While it is true that unnecessary neurons die off, the interconnections between neurons become more numerous and complex as the brain develops.

Here is a related observation: To have billions of neurons in our brains at birth, brain cells must be generated at a rate of about 250,000 per minute while the brain is being formed (Cowan, 1979).

In most cases, dead neurons are not replaced with new ones. We constantly make new blood cells to replace lost ones; if we didn't, we could never donate a pint of blood. Lost skin cells are rapidly replaced by new ones. You rinse away skin cells by the hundreds each time you wash your hands. Most neurons are different; once they're gone, they're gone forever. We're often in luck, however, because the *functions* of lost neurons can be taken over by other surviving neurons. There is also evidence that in the primate brain some new neurons are generated in adulthood through a process called neurogenesis (Gould, Reeves, Graziano, & Gross 1999). These new neurons are found predominately in those areas of the brain that only process incoming sensory information (Gould, et al., 1999a). There is also evidence that new nerve cell growth can be stimulated in rats with exposure to a chemical called "recombined human nerve growth factor," when it is given early in life (Brandner, Vantini, & Schneck, 2000). Rats exposed to the nerve growth factor showed better learning skills than did untreated rats, and this difference persisted into adulthood. Results like these suggest that the brain has the capacity to regenerate lost neurons, but certainly not at the rate that is seen in prenatal and early postnatal development. These new neurons end up in areas associated with higher cognitive functions and may relate to one's ability to continue to learn throughout life or after brain injury. Furthermore, exposure to the growth factor is not the only condition that can produce neurogenesis. Gould et al., (1999b) found that learning stimulated growth of new neurons in specific parts of the hippocampus of rats. There is also evidence that neurogenesis occurs in the adult human brain (Eriksson et al., 1998). Eriksson and his colleagues found clear evidence of new neuron production in the hippocampus, an area of the brain associated with memory. They concluded that neurogenesis occurs in this area of the brain throughout life.

Discussing the structure of the neuron is impossible without reference to the function of the neuron: the transmission of neural impulses. We have seen that impulses are typically received by dendrites, passed on to cell bodies, then to axons, and ultimately to axon terminals. We know that myelin insulates some axons and speeds neural impulses along, but what exactly is a neural impulse? We will explore the neural impulse in the next section.

BEFORE YOU GO ON

- What is a neuron?

- What are the parts of a neuron?

- What is the myelin sheath, and what functions does it serve?

- What are axon terminals, and what do they do?

THE FUNCTION OF NEURONS

The function of a neuron is to transmit neural impulses from one place in the nervous system to another. Let's start with a definition. A **neural impulse** is a rapid, reversible change in the electrical charges within and outside a neuron. This change in electrical charge travels from the dendrites to the axon terminal when the neuron fires. Now let's see what all that means.

Neurons exist in a complex biological environment. As living cells, they are filled with and surrounded by fluids. Only a very thin membrane (like a skin) separates the

neural impulse a rapid and reversible change in the electrical charges inside and outside a neuron. It travels from the dendrite to the axon terminal of a neuron.

chemical ions electrically charged (+ or -) chemical particles inside and outside the axon of a neuron

fluids inside a neuron from those outside. These fluids contain chemical particles called ions. **Chemical ions** are particles that carry a small, measurable electrical charge that is either positive (+) or negative (-). Electrically charged ions float around in all the fluids of the body, but are heavily concentrated in and around the nervous system. If you examine the distribution of ions inside and outside the neuron, you find that the inside of the neuron has a more negative charge than the outside. What does this mean? There are more negative ions than positive ions inside the axon. Conversely, there are more positive ions outside the neuron than negative ions. At rest, the axonal membrane does not allow the negatively and positively charged ions to pass across the membrane. The physiology of the neuron keeps the inside of the axon negatively charged compared to the outside. A tension develops between the electrical charge of ions that have been trapped *inside* the neuron (predominantly negative ions) and the electrical charge of ions that have been trapped *outside* the neuron (predominantly positive ions). Positive and negative ions are attracted to each other; however, they cannot come into contact because the neuron's membrane separates them.

resting potential the electrical tension resulting from the difference in electrical charge of a neuron. The inside is negatively charged, and the outside is positively charged (about -70 mV).

The tension that results from the positive and negative ions' attraction to each other is called a **resting potential**. The resting potential of a neuron is about -70 millivolts (mV), which makes each neuron rather like a small battery. A D-cell battery (the sort used in a flashlight) has two aspects (called poles): one positive and the other negative. The electrical charge possible with one of these batteries—its resting potential—is 1500 mV, much greater than that of a neuron. The resting potential of a neuron is *negative* 70 millivolts (-70 mV) because we measure the inside of a neuron relative to the outside, and the negative ions are concentrated inside. At rest, the neuron is in a *polarized* state.

When a neuron is stimulated to fire, or produce an impulse, the electrical tension of the resting potential is released. Very quickly, the polarity of the nerve cell changes—a process called *depolarization*. This occurs when the axon membrane suddenly allows positively charged sodium ions to flood into the interior of the axon, drastically changing the electrical potential of the axon. Then, the membrane allows positively charged potassium ions to exit the axon. For an instant (about one one-thousandth of a second), the electrical charge within the cell becomes more *positive* than the area outside the cell. This new charge is called the **action potential**, which is about +40 mV. The positive sign indicates that the inside of the neuron is now more positive than the outside (there are more positive ions inside than outside). In a fraction of a second, the neuron returns to its original state with the tension redeveloped, and after a few thousandths of a second it is ready to fire again.

action potential the short-lived electrical burst caused by the sudden reversal of electric charges inside and outside a neuron in which the inside becomes positive (about +40 mV)

Before the neuron returns to its normal resting state, it actually becomes *hyperpolarized*—its negative charge is even <u>more</u> negative than the normal -70mV. This occurs because the neuron's membrane allows too much potassium to leak out of the cell making the inside of the cell too negative. For a few thousandths of a second, there is a *refractory period* during which the neuron cannot fire. Eventually, the membrane returns to normal and the sodium–potassium pump restores the normal distribution of ions across the cell membrane.

To repeat, when a neuron is at rest, there is a difference between the electrical charges inside and outside the neuron (the inside is more negative). When the neuron is stimulated, the difference reverses, so that the inside becomes slightly positive. The tension of

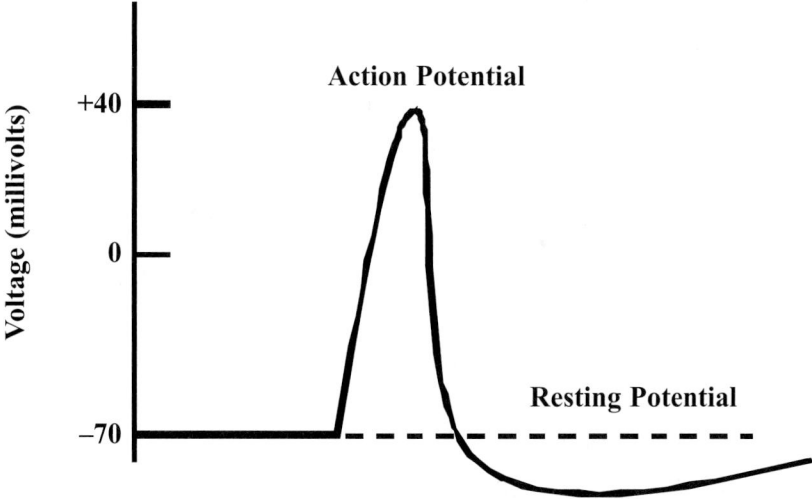

FIGURE 2.2

Changes in electrical potential that occur during the firing of a neuron. Note that the voltage is negative (-70 millivolts) when the neuron is "at rest," and positive (+40 millivolts) during the firing of the impulse. Note, too, that the entire process lasts but a few milliseconds.

the resting potential then returns (see Figure 2.2). Note: When an impulse "travels down a neuron," nothing physically moves from one end of the neuron to the other. The only movement of physical particles is the movement of the electrically charged ions in to and out of the neuron through its membrane.

When a neuron is stimulated by another neuron, it may or may not transmit a neural impulse. It either fires or it doesn't, a fact called the **all-or-none principle**. There is no such thing as a weak or strong neural impulse; the impulse is either there or it isn't. Based on your knowledge of the physiology of the neuron, you can see why this is so. The depolarization of the neuron during the action potential is an all-or-none proposition. When the membrane of the axon is depolarized, it cannot stop. This raises a psychological question: How does the nervous system react to differences in stimulus intensity? How do neurons react to the difference between a bright light and a dim one; a soft sound and a loud one; or a tap on the shoulder and a slap on the back? The electrical charge of the resting potential is either released or it isn't. We cannot say that a neuron fires partially for a dim light, releasing some of the tension of its resting potential, while more ions are exchanged for brighter lights. Part of the answer involves neural thresholds.

all-or-none principle the fact that a neuron will either produce a full impulse, or action potential, or will not fire at all

Neurons do not generate impulses every time they are stimulated. Each neuron has a level of stimulation that must be surpassed to produce an impulse. The minimum level of stimulation required to fire a neuron is the **neural threshold**. This concept, coupled with the all-or-none principle, lends insight into how we process stimulus intensities. High-intensity stimuli (bright lights, loud sounds, etc.) do not cause neurons to fire more vig-

neural threshold the minimum amount of stimulation needed to fire a neuron orously; they stimulate more neurons to fire or to fire more frequently. High-intensity stimuli are above the threshold of a greater number of neurons than are low-intensity stimuli. The difference in your experience of a flashbulb going off in your face and a candle viewed at a distance reflects the *number* of neurons involved and the *rate* at which they fire, not the degree or extent to which they fire.

BEFORE YOU GO ON

- What is a neural impulse?

- What role do chemical ions play?

- What are the resting and action potentials?

- What basic process occurs when a neuron fires?

- What is the all-or-none principle?

Now that we've examined the individual nerve cell in detail, we are ready to learn how neurons communicate with each other—how impulses are transmitted from one cell to another. The story of how impulses travel between neurons is just as remarkable, but quite different from, how impulses travel within neurons.

FROM ONE CELL TO ANOTHER: THE SYNAPSE

synapse where one neuron communicates with other cells

synaptic cleft the space between a neuron and the next cell at a synapse

In your nervous system there are billions of points where neurons interact with one another. The location at which an impulse is relayed from one neuron to another is called the **synapse**. In the cerebral cortex of the human brain alone, there are billions of synaptic interconnections among neurons (Edelman, 1992). At these synapses, neurons do not physically touch one another. Instead, there is a microscopic gap between the axon terminal of one neuron and another neuron. This gap is called the **synaptic cleft**. Here's what happens at the synapse.

Synaptic Transmission

vesicles small containers concentrated in a neuron's axon terminals that hold neurotransmitter molecules

neurotransmitters chemical molecules released at the synapse that, in general, will either excite or inhibit a reaction in the cell on the other side of the synapse

receptor sites places on a neuron where neurotransmitters can be received

As we've noted, at the end of an axon there are many branches called axon terminals (see Fig. 2.1). Throughout any neuron, but concentrated in its axon terminals, are incredibly small membrane sacs called **vesicles**, which hold complex chemicals called neurotransmitters. **Neurotransmitters** are chemical molecules that either excite or inhibit the transmission of a neural impulse in the next neuron after crossing the synapse. When an impulse reaches the axon terminal, the vesicles near the neural membrane burst open and release the neurotransmitter they have been holding. The released neurotransmitter floods out into the synaptic cleft, the tiny space between two neurons. Once in the synaptic cleft, some neurotransmitter molecules move to the membrane of the next neuron where they may fit into **receptor sites**, which are special places on a neuron where neurotransmitters can be received. Think of the neurotransmitter as being a key that fits into a particular lock on the receptor site. Once the key fits into the lock, the neurotransmitter enters the membrane of the next neuron. (See Figure 2.3.)

Then what happens? Actually, any number of things. Let's look at a few. The most reasonable scenario for synaptic activity is that neurotransmitters float across the synaptic cleft, enter into receptor sites in the next neuron in a chain of nerve cells, excite that neuron to release the tension of its resting potential, and fire a new impulse down its axon

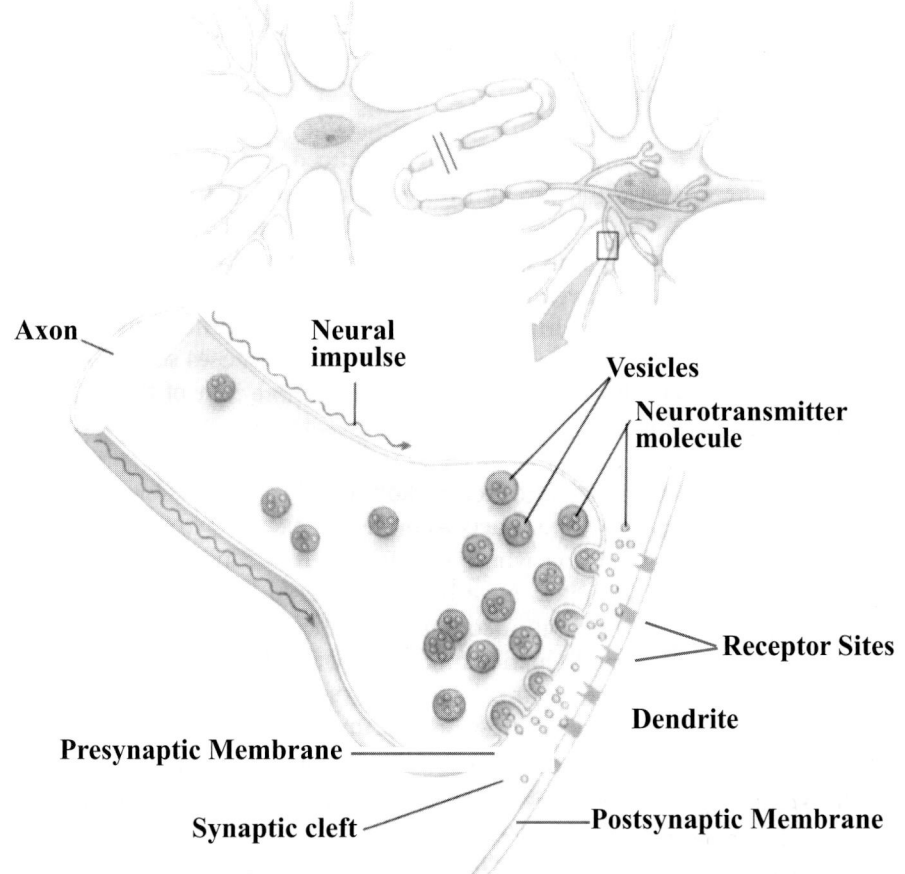

Axon

Neural impulse

Vesicles

Neurotransmitter molecule

Receptor Sites

Dendrite

Presynaptic Membrane

Postsynaptic Membrane

Synaptic cleft

FIGURE 2.3

A synapse, in which transmission is from upper left to lower right. As an impulse enters the axon terminal, vesicles release neurotransmitter chemicals into the synaptic space or cleft. The neurotransmitter then either excites or inhibits an impulse in the next neuron.

terminals. There, new neurotransmitter chemicals are released from vesicles, which cross the synaptic cleft and stimulate the next neuron in the sequence. This is the case when the neurotransmitter excites and stimulates the next neuron to fire in a sequence. These neurotransmitters are referred to as *excitatory*. As it happens, there are many neurons throughout our nervous systems that hold neurotransmitters that have the opposite effect. When they are released, they flood across the synaptic cleft and prevent the next neuron from firing. We refer to these synapses as *inhibitory*.

The final step in the process of synaptic transmission is the elimination of the neurotransmitter from the synaptic cleft. This is done in one of two ways: destruction by an enzyme or reuptake. Some neurotransmitters, such as acetylcholine, are broken down by special enzymes secreted into the synaptic cleft. In the case of acetylcholine the enzyme is acetylcholinesterase. Other neurotransmitters, such as serotonin, are reabsorbed by the presynaptic membrane (the membrane of the neuron from which the neurotransmitters originated) through a process called reuptake. Many psychoactive drugs work by affecting the breakdown or reuptake of neurotranmitters. For example, Prozac (a popular antidepressant drug) operates by inhibiting the reuptake of serotonin. Myasthenia Gravis, a disease relating to the underactivity of acetylcholine is effectively treated with drugs that block acetylcholinesterase. The entire sequence of events is illustrated in Figure 2.4.

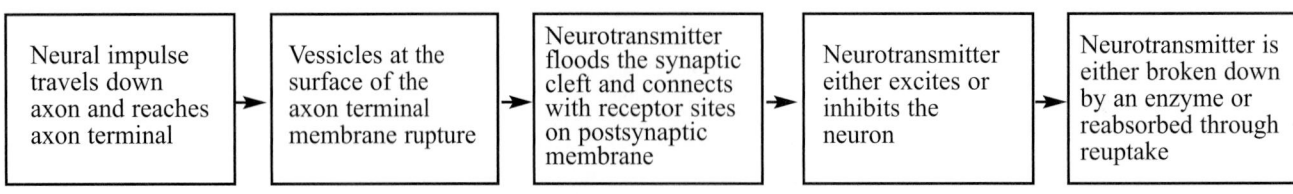

| Neural impulse travels down axon and reaches axon terminal | → | Vessicles at the surface of the axon terminal membrane rupture | → | Neurotransmitter floods the synaptic cleft and connects with receptor sites on postsynaptic membrane | → | Neurotransmitter either excites or inhibits the neuron | → | Neurotransmitter is either broken down by an enzyme or reabsorbed through reuptake |

FIGURE 2.4

Summary of the sequence of events that occur in synaptic transmission

If you recall the last section in which we talked about neural thresholds, you may now appreciate how that concept works. Imagine a neuron's dendrite at rest, with many axon terminals (of many neurons) just across the synaptic cleft. For this neuron to begin a new impulse, it may require a greater amount of excitatory chemical than just one axon terminal can provide, particularly if nearby terminals are releasing inhibitory neurotransmitters at about the same time. The process just described also occurs at the synapse of neurons and nonneural cells. When a neuron forms a synapse with a muscle cell, for instance, the release of neurotransmitter from the neuron's axon terminals may excite that muscle to contract momentarily. Similarly, neurons that form synapses with a gland may cause that gland to secrete a hormone when stimulated by the appropriate neurotransmitter.

Neurotransmitters

To understand how neurotransmitters work, we must examine the two components involved in synaptic transmission: the neurotransmitter and its receptor site. Not long ago, it was believed that neurons produced and released one of two neurotransmitters: those that excite further action and those that inhibit neural impulse transmission. Now we realize that this view is too simplistic. We now know of nearly sixty neurotransmitters, and it is virtually certain that there are many others yet to be discovered. With respect to receptor sites, the once–held view that each neurotransmitter had one type of receptor site is no longer valid. Were you to count the number of receptors for all possible neurotransmitters, you would probably find more than 1,000 (Cooper, Bloom, & Roth, 1996), even though only sixty neurotransmitters have been identified. To complicate matters further, a single neurotransmitter may have more than one type of receptor site. Thus there are *subtypes* of receptor sites for the various brain chemicals. The search for and identification of these receptor sites has become one of the hottest areas of brain research.

The discovery of more neurotransmitters and receptor site subtypes teaches us more about the biochemistry of the brain and how it works. For example, the belief that there was a limited number of neurotransmitters placed a limitation on the nature and complexity of potential synaptic communication. More neurotransmitters, receptor sites, and specialized sites indicates a potential for clearer and more complex communication within the nervous system. Imagine that a part of the brain receives separate signals indicating two different emotions (fear and surprise). Were only one neurotransmitter and receptor site involved, the different emotions could not be recognized. More neurotransmitters and receptor sites allow the independent signals to be separated, sorted, and more clearly recognized (Wilson, 1998, personal communication).

Despite the complexities involved in the biochemistry of the nervous system, we can provide a few details about the activity of some of the neurotransmitters that have been discovered. For now, let's briefly note five of the better–known neurotransmitters.

Acetylcholine (pronounced "uh-see-til-koh-leen"), or ACh, is found throughout the nervous system, where it acts as either an excitatory or inhibitory neurotransmitter, depending on where it is found. It is a common neurotransmitter and the first discovered (in the 1920s). Not only is ACh found in the brain, but it commonly works in synapses between neurons and muscle tissue cells. One form of food poisoning, botulism, blocks the release of acetylcholine at neuron–muscle cell synapses; this can cause paralysis of the respiratory system and may result in death unless an antitoxin is given. The poisonous drug curare works in much the same fashion. Some other poisons (e.g., the venom of the black widow spider) have just the opposite effect, causing excess amounts of ACh to be released, resulting in muscle contractions or spasms so severe as to be deadly. Nicotine is a chemical that in small amounts tends to increase the normal functioning of ACh, but in large doses acts to override the normal action of acetylcholine—a reaction that can lead to muscle paralysis and even death. Smoking or chewing tobacco seldom causes such a dramatic effect because large amounts of nicotine first stimulate a brain center that causes vomiting before too much nicotine has been absorbed into one's system (Palfai & Jankiewicz, 1991, p. 141). Low levels of acetylcholine are associated with loss of cognitive functioning in patients with Alzheimer's disease. Two drugs that act on acetylcholine mechanisms are currently being used to treat Alzheimer's disease. One drug, tacrine, inhibits the action of acetylcholinesterase which breaks down acetylcholine after synaptic transmission. Use of this drug in patients with mild to moderate cases of Alzheimer's disease has led to slight memory enhancement (Delagarze, 1998). Unfortunately, prolonged use of this drug may lead to liver problems, so it is no longer a treatment of choice. The other drug, donepezil, is also an acetylcholinesterase inhibitor and has shown promise as a treatment for memory loss in Alzheimer's patients. It is necessary for the patient to remain on the drug in order for the memory inmprovement to persist. Finally, the link between nicotine and enhanced acetylocholine activity would suggest this drug as another treatment for Alzheimer's disease. Delagarza (1998) reported that nicotine is associated with some memory enhancement in Alzheimer's patients, but it is not now recommended for treatment of the disease.

Norepinephrine is a common and important neurotransmitter that is associated with mood regulation. Norepinephrine is involved in the physiological reactions associated with high levels of emotional arousal, such as increased heart rate, perspiration, and blood pressure (Groves & Rebec, 1992). When there is an abundance of norepinephrine in a person's brain or spinal cord, feelings of arousal, agitation, or anxiety may result. (Cocaine increases the release of norepinephrine leading to a state of agitation and a "high" mood state.) Too little norepinephrine in the brain and spinal cord is associated with feelings of depression.

Dopamine is also a common neurotransmitter associated with mood regulation. It has intrigued psychologists for some time. It is involved in a wide range of reactions. Either too much or too little dopamine within the nervous system seems to produce a number of effects, depending primarily on which system of nerve fibers in the brain is involved. Dopamine has been associated with the thought and mood disturbances of some psychological disorders. It is also associated with the impairment of movement: when there is not enough dopamine, we find difficulty in voluntary movement; too much and we find involuntary tremors.

Serotonin is another important neurotransmitter. Its action in the nervous system is quite complex and not completely understood. We do know, however, that serotonin is related to various behaviors. For example, serotonin is involved in the sleep/waking cycle. An increase in levels of serotonin in parts of the brain associated with sleep are related to sleep onset (Rosenzweig, Leiman, & Breedlove, 1996). Serotonin has also been found to play a role in depression. Depleted levels of serotonin are related to depressive symptoms. Drugs, like Prozac, that increase serotonin levels reduce depressive symptoms. Finally, low levels of serotonin have been implicated in aggressive behavior (Coccaro, Kavoussi, & McNamee, 2000). In one study, for example, monkeys with low levels of serotonin tended to be much more aggressive and prone to risky behavior than monkeys with higher levels of serotonin. In fact, Higley, et al. (1996) found that monkeys with low levels of serotonin—which made them more aggressive—were more likely to be dead four years after the study began, largely due to those monkeys attacking larger monkeys. In contrast, none of the high–level serotonin monkeys were dead.

Endorphins (there are several of them) are natural pain suppressors. The pain threshold—the ability to tolerate different levels of pain—is a function of endorphin production (Watkins & Mayer, 1982). With excess levels of endorphins, we feel little pain; a deficit results in an increased experience of pain. When we are under extreme physical stress, endorphin levels rise. Many long–distance runners, for instance, often report a near–euphoric "high" after they run great distances, as though endorphins have kicked in to protect them against the pain of physical exhaustion.

We could easily continue this list, but for now our focus is on what neurotransmitters do: they are the agents that either excite or inhibit the transmission of neural impulses throughout the nervous system. That excitation or inhibition can have a considerable effect on our thoughts, feelings, and behavior.

So that a simplified description does not leave a false impression, neural impulse transmission is seldom a matter of one neuron stimulating another neuron in a chain reaction. Any neuron can have hundreds or thousands of axon terminals and synapses, and has the potential for exciting or inhibiting (or being excited by or inhibited by) many other neurons.

BEFORE YOU GO ON

- What is a synapse?
- How is the neural impulse transmitted from neuron to neuron?
- Name and briefly describe the actions of four neurotransmitters.

THE HUMAN NERVOUS SYSTEMS: THE BIG PICTURE

Now that we know how neurons work individually and in combination, let's consider the context in which they function. Behaviors and mental activities require large numbers of integrated neurons working together in complex, organized systems. Figure 2.5 depicts these systems. We have also depicted the endocrine system in Figure 2.5. Although it is not composed of neurons, the endocrine system interacts with the nervous systems to control behaviors and mental processes.

Organized Systems of Neurons

The major division of the nervous systems is determined wholly on the basis of anatomy. The **central nervous system (CNS)** includes all neurons and supporting cells found in the spinal cord and brain. This system of nerves is the most complex and intimately involved in the control of behavior and mental processes. The **peripheral nervous system (PNS)** consists of all neurons in our body that are *not* in the CNS—the nerve fibers in our arms, face, fingers, intestines, and so on. Neurons in the peripheral nervous system carry impulses either from the central nervous system to the muscles and glands (on *motor neurons*) or to the CNS from receptor cells (on *sensory neurons*).

The peripheral nervous system is divided into two parts, based largely on the part of the body being served. The **somatic nervous system** includes those neurons that are outside the CNS and serve the skeletal muscles and pick up impulses from our sense receptors, e.g., the eyes and ears. The other component of the PNS is the **autonomic nervous system (ANS)** ("autonomic" means "automatic"). This implies that the activity of the ANS is largely (but not totally) independent of central nervous system control. The nerve fibers of the ANS are involved in activating the smooth muscles, such as those of the stomach and intestines and the glands. The ANS provides feedback to the CNS about this internal activity.

Because the autonomic nervous system is so intimately involved in emotional responses, we'll examine it in that context later. For now, note that the ANS consists of two parts: the sympathetic division and the parasympathetic division which commonly work in opposition to each other. The sympathetic division is active when we are emotionally excited or under stress, like riding up that first huge incline of a roller coaster at an amusement park. The parasympathetic division is active when we are relaxed and quiet as we might be late at night after a long day at that amusement park, half asleep in the back seat on the drive home. Both divisions of the ANS act on the same organs, but do so in opposite ways.

There is good reason to categorize the various organizations of neurons as it makes a very complex system easier to understand, and it reminds us that not all neurons in our body are doing the same thing for the same reason at the same time. Note that the outline of Figure 2.5 is very simplified to this extent: the nerve fibers in each of the systems have profound influences on one another. They are not at all as independent as our diagram might imply.

central nervous system (CNS) neurons and supporting cells in the spinal cord and the brain

peripheral nervous system (PNS) neurons not found in the brain and spinal cord but in the periphery of the body

somatic nervous system (SNS) sensory and motor neurons outside the CNS that serve the sense receptors and the skeletal muscles

autonomic nervous system (ANS) neurons in the peripheral nervous system that activate smooth muscles and glands

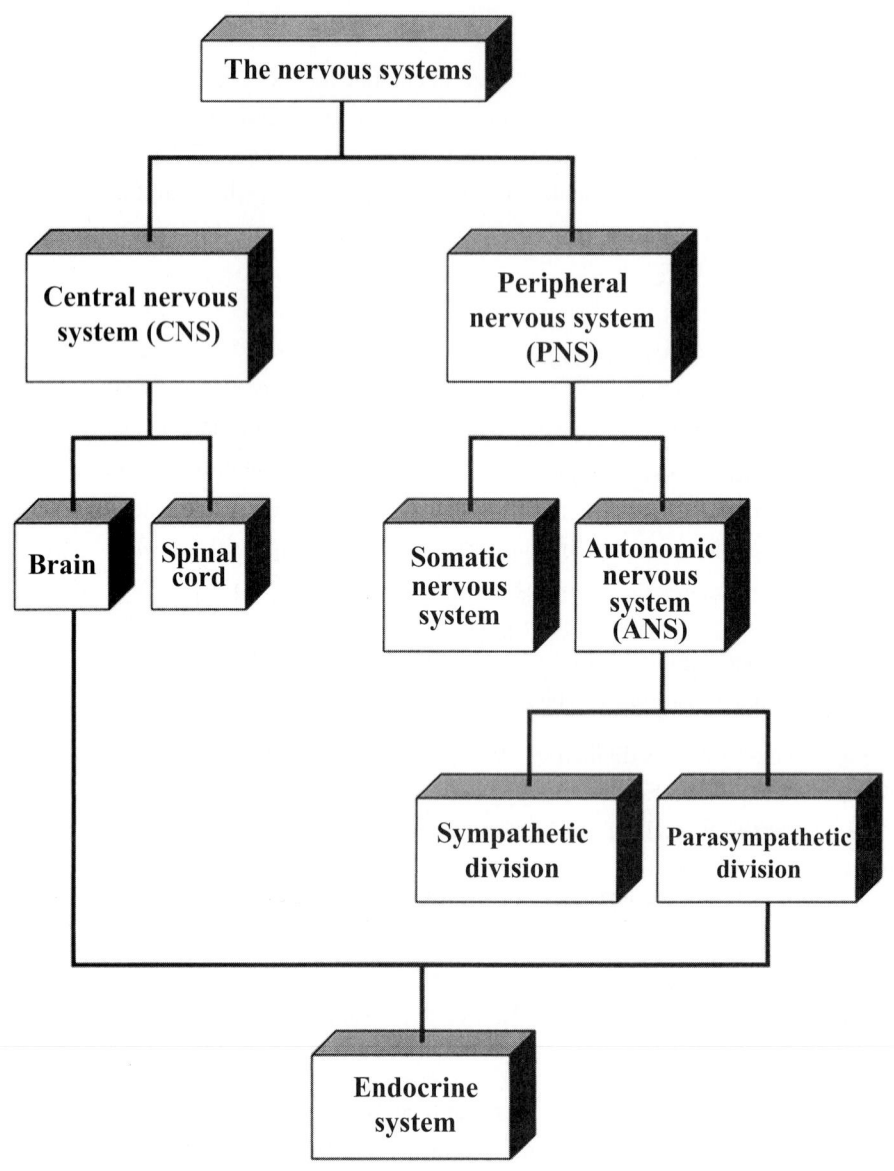

Figure 2.5

The various human nervous systems and how they are interrelated

The Endocrine System

endocrine system a network of
glands that secrete hormones
directly into the bloodstream

As you can see, there is another system depicted in the overview of Figure 2.5: the **endocrine system**, a network of glands that effects behaviors by secreting chemicals called *hormones*. All hormones travel through the bloodstream and impact organs far from where the hormones are produced. The endocrine system is influenced by the central nervous system, which in turn influences nervous system activity, but it is not a system of nerves. Many of the hormones produced by the glands of the endocrine system are chemically similar to neurotransmitters and have similar effects. The endocrine system's glands and hormones are controlled by both the brain of the central nervous system and the autonomic nervous system. We have included the endocrine system in this discussion for two reasons. First, its function is like that of the nervous system: to transmit information from one part of the body to another. Second, hormones exert a direct influence on behavior.

Consider the male hormone *testosterone* secreted by the testes. High testosterone levels are associated with increased aggression (Christiansen & Knussmann, 1987); however, the relationship between testosterone and aggression is quite complex. Testosterone's impact is experienced most before birth (prenatally) and at puberty. During prenatal development, the male genetic code produces high levels of testosterone in the male brain, which causes the male brain to be wired for aggression. This is known as the *organization function* of testosterone. At puberty, testosterone serves an *activation function* (Carlson, 1991) for aggression. Generally, research on animal subjects has confirmed the organization and activation functions of testosterone levels (Conner & Levine, 1969).

Hormones alone don't drive aggressive behavior; however, testosterone levels tend to interact with environmental conditions to increase or decrease aggression. In an experiment (Albert, Petrovic, & Walsh, 1989) male rats were castrated and implanted with a capsule. Half of the rats received empty capsules; however, the other capsules contained testosterone. The rats were housed in a cage with another rat under one of two conditions. In one condition, there was one feeding tube, creating competition for food. In the other condition, there were two feeding tubes, eliminating competition for food. The rats who had the testosterone capsules were tested for aggression. The results showed that only the testosterone–treated males housed in a cage with one feeding tube exhibited an increased level of aggression. So, testosterone levels interacted with the competitive/noncompetitive environment to influence aggression.

Endocrine Glands

There are several endocrine glands throughout our bodies. We'll discuss the pituitary gland, the thyroid gland, and the adrenal gland to examine how this system works. The sex glands are part of this system, but we'll discuss their operation later. (Glands in our bodies that are not part of the endocrine system because their secretions do not enter the bloodstream are called *exocrine* glands. Tear glands and sweat glands are two examples.)

Perhaps the most important endocrine gland is the **pituitary gland**. It is often referred to as the *master gland,* reflecting its direct control over the activity of many other glands in the system. The pituitary is nestled under the brain and secretes many different hormones.

One hormone released by the pituitary is the growth hormone, which regulates the growth of the body during its fastest physical development. Extremes of overproduction or underproduction cause the development of giants or dwarfs. The so–called growth spurt associated with early adolescence is due to the activity of the pituitary gland. It is the pituitary gland that stimulates the release of hormones on the kidneys to regulate the amount of water held within the body. It is the pituitary that directs the mammary glands

pituitary gland the "master gland" of the endocrine system that influences many others and controls such processes as body growth rate, water retention, and the release of milk from the mammary glands

in the breasts to release milk after childbirth. In its role as master over other glands, the pituitary regulates the output of the thyroid and the adrenal glands, as well as the sex glands.

thyroid gland endocrine gland that releases thyroxine, the hormone that regulates the pace of the body's functioning

The **thyroid gland** is located in the neck and produces a hormone called *thyroxine*. Thyroxine regulates the pace of the body's functioning—the rate at which oxygen is used and the rate of body function and growth. When a person is easily excited, edgy, having trouble sleeping, and losing weight, he or she may have too much thyroxine in the system, a condition called *hyperthyroidism*. Too little thyroxine leads to a lack of energy, fatigue, and an inability to do much, a condition called *hypothyroidism*.

adrenal glands endocrine glands that release adrenaline, or epinephrine, into the bloodstream to activate the body in times of stress or danger

The **adrenal glands**, located on the kidneys, secrete a variety of hormones into the bloodstream. The hormone adrenaline (more often referred to as *epinephrine*) is very useful in times of stress, danger, or threat. Adrenaline quickens breathing, causes the heart to beat faster, directs the flow of blood away from the stomach and intestines to the limbs, dilates the pupils of the eyes, and increases perspiration. When our adrenal glands flood epinephrine into our system during a perceived emergency, we usually feel the resulting reactions; but, typical of endocrine system activity, these reactions may be delayed. For example, as you drive down a busy street, a child suddenly darts out in front of you from behind a parked car and races to the other side of the street. You slam on the brakes, twist the steering wheel, and swerve to avoid hitting the child. As the child scampers away, oblivious to the danger just past, you proceed down the street. Then, about half a block later, your hormone–induced reaction strikes. Your heart pounds, a lump forms in your throat, your mouth dries, and your palms sweat. Why now when the incident is past, the child is safely across the street, and you are no longer in danger? The reason is that your reaction is largely hormonal, involving the adrenal glands, and it takes that long for the epinephrine to get from those glands through the bloodstream.

BEFORE YOU GO ON

- What are the central and peripheral nervous systems, and how do they relate to each other?

- What do the somatic and autonomic nervous systems do?

- What is the function of the endocrine system?

- How does testosterone relate to aggression?

- Describe the function of the pituitary gland, thyroid gland, and the adrenal glands.

Topic Review 2 A

1. What is a neuron?

A neuron is the basic cell of the nervous system. The microscopically small neuron transmits information in the form of neural impulses from one part of the body to another.

2. What are the parts of a neuron?

Every neuron in the nervous system has three parts: the cell body, dendrites, and axon. The cell body contains the structures needed to sustain the life of the neuron.

3. What does a dendrite do?

Dendrites extend from the cell body and receive messages from other neurons.

4. What does an axon do?

The axon extends from the cell body and carries the neural message away from the cell body.

5. What is myelin, and what functions does it perform?

Myelin is a white fatty substance that coats the axons of some neurons of the nervous system. The myelin sheath is segmented along the length of the axon leaving nodes of exposed axon membrane between segments. The myelin sheath has several functions. First, it protects the delicate axon from damage. Second, it insulates the axon against signals from other neurons. Third, it speeds the rate of the neural impulse through a process called saltatory conduction where only the exposed segments of the axon undergo a biochemical change.

6. What is the function of an axon terminal?

The axon terminal is found at the end of an axon. It has vesicles that contain chemicals known as neurotransmitters. When stimulated, vesicles rupture and flood the synaptic cleft with a neurotransmitter. Neurotransmitters are responsible for communication between neurons.

7. What changes take place in the nervous system after birth?

We are born with more neurons than we will ever use. Typically, new neurons do not develop after birth (although recent research suggests that under special circumstances they can). What do increase in number (greatly) are dendrites, axon endings, and synapses among neurons. Additionally, myelin develops after birth.

8. What is a neural impulse?

A neural impulse is the electrical signal that travels down the axon after a neuron has been stimulated.

9. What is the resting potential of a neuron, and how does it occur?

The resting potential of a neuron is its electrical charge while it is at rest, which is –70mV. It arises because the inside of the axon is negatively charged relative to the outside. The lining up of negative ions on the inside and positive ions on the outside creates tension along the axon.

10. What is the action potential, and how does it come about?

The action potential is the change in the electrical charge in an axon after the neuron is stimulated, which is +40mV. During the action potential the axon membrane becomes more permeable to positive ions (sodium), which flood into the interior of the axon changing the inside to a positive charge. Then the membrane becomes more permeable to potassium, which is also a positively charged ion. The potassium is forced out of the axon, and for an instant, the inside of the axon becomes even more negatively charged relative to the outside than in its resting state.

11. How does the neuron return to its resting potential after a neural impulse?

The neuron returns to its resting potential when the axonal membrane again becomes less permeable to sodium, thus not allowing any sodium into the axon. The membrane, however, remains permeable to potassium, which flows out of the axon returning the inside of the axon to its negatively charged state. The sodium–potassium pump restores the relative concentrations of sodium and potassium ions inside and outside the cell.

12. What is the refractory period of a neuron?

The refractory period is the brief interval after the action potential when the neuron cannot fire due to hyperpolarization—when the membrane potential overshoots its −70mV resting potential. This happens because while the membrane is receptive to potassium, too much leaks out of the cell making the inside of the cell too negative. Eventually, the membrane returns to normal, and the sodium–potassium pump restores the normal distribution of ions across the cell membrane.

13. What is the all-or-none principle, and why does it hold true?

The all–or–none principle means that if a neuron fires, the neural impulse must travel all the way down the axon. Thus, there is no such thing as a strong or weak neural impulse; it is either present or not. This happens because when the axon undergoes the depolarization process, it cannot stop.

14. What is the neural threshold?

The neural threshold is the minimum level of stimulation required to fire a neuron.

15. How does your nervous system respond to stimuli of differing intensities?

Stimulus intensity is communicated by the nervous system through the number of neurons that fire or the frequency with which they fire. High–intensity stimuli (bright lights, loud sounds, etc.) stimulate more neurons to fire or to fire more frequently than low–intensity stimuli. Perception of different intensities of stimuli depends on the number of neurons that fire and the rate at which they fire, not the degree or extent to which they fire.

16. What is a synapse, and how does the neural impulse travel from one neuron to another?

A synapse is where two neurons come into contact with each other. The neurons do not physically touch one another; there is a small gap called the synaptic cleft separating them. Communication between neurons across the synaptic cleft is accomplished chemically. When the neural impulse reaches the axon terminal a neurotransmitter is released into the synaptic cleft. It is through this chemical that the neural impulse is communicated across the synapse.

17. What are neurotransmitters, and what functions do they serve?

Neurotransmitters are chemicals that flood the synaptic cleft transmitting the neural impulse from one neuron to another. Some neurotransmitters have an excitatory function, which causes the next neuron to fire. Others have an inhibitory function, which makes it more difficult for the next neuron to fire. Approximately 60 neurotransmitters have been identified, and many more are likely to be discovered. The discovery of different receptor sites for neurotransmitters has widened our knowledge of how they work.

18. What role does a receptor site play?

A receptor site is a place on a neuron that is sensitive to a particular neurotransmitter. The receptor site is like a lock into which the neurotransmitter key fits.

19. What do the neurotransmitters acetylcholine, norepinephrine, dopamine, and endorphins do?

Acetylcholine is a neurotransmitter that can have an excitatory or inhibitory function depending on where it is found. Acetylcholine commonly works in synapses between neurons and muscles, and also plays a role in memory. Norepinephrine is a neurotransmitter involved in mood regulation and physiological reactions associated with high levels of arousal. Dopamine is a neurotransmitter that has been associated with thought and mood psychological disorders, as well as voluntary movements. Endorphins are natural pain suppressors.

20. What are the central and peripheral nervous systems?

The central nervous system includes all of the neurons and supporting cells found in the brain and spinal cord. It is a complex system involved in the control of behavior and mental processes. The peripheral nervous system comprises all of the neurons in our body that are *not* in the central nervous system. It includes the nerve fibers in our arms, face, fingers, intestines, etc. Neurons in the peripheral nervous system carry impulses either from the central nervous system to the muscles and glands or to the central nervous system from receptor cells.

21. What are the somatic and autonomic nervous systems?

The somatic and autonomic nervous systems are subdivisions of the peripheral nervous system. The somatic nervous system includes the neurons that serve the skeletal muscles and pick up impulses from our sense receptors. The autonomic nervous system comprises the nerve fibers which activate the smooth muscles, such as those of the stomach, intestines, and glands. The autonomic nervous system has two subsystems. The sympathetic system is activated under conditions of excitement or arousal, and the parasympathetic system is activated when you are relaxed and calm.

22. What does the endocrine system do?

The endocrine system is a network of glands that affect behaviors through the secretion of chemicals called *hormones*. The hormones, which circulate through the blood system, can have an effect on behavior.

23. What is the pituitary gland, and what function does it serve?

The pituitary gland is often called the master gland because it controls many other glands in the endocrine system. It is located under the brain and secretes a variety of hormones. Pituitary hormones impact growth, lactation, regulation of the amount of water held in the body, and the regulation of other glands.

24. What does the thyroid gland do?

The thyroid gland, which is located in the neck, produces a hormone called thyroxine that regulates the body's "pace" (e.g., the rate at which oxygen is used). Hyperthyroidism occurs when too much thyroxine in the blood results in excitability, edginess, insomnia, and weight loss. Too little thyroxin leads to hypothyroidism, which is associated with fatigue and lack of energy.

25. What are the adrenal glands, and what do they do?

The adrenal glands, located on the kidneys, secrete a variety of hormones into the blood. One such hormone, adrenaline, is released during times of danger, which increases respiration, heart and perspiration rates, directs the flow of blood away from the digestive system toward the limbs, and causes pupils to dilate.

26. How does the level of the hormone testosterone affect behavior?

High levels of testosterone are associated with elevated levels of aggression. However, the relationship between testosterone and aggression is complex. Testosterone impacts two points in development: prenatally (organizing function) and at puberty (activation function). Prenatal exposure to testosterone is necessary for testosterone's ability to later increase levels of aggression. Additionally, the presence of testosterone interacts with environmental conditions to affect levels of aggression.

Topic 2B THE CENTRAL NERVOUS SYSTEM

Imagine the following situation: A good friend whom you have known for years is injured in a motorcycle accident in which he suffered brain damage. You visit him in the hospital after he has recovered substantially. When you walk into his room, he looks puzzled and asks who you are. Stunned, you say, "Come on Bill, we've known each other for years." Upon hearing your voice, his face lights up and he says, "Hi Tina, it's really great to see you." You are pleased but totally confused.

How can such a sequence of events be possible? How can your friend fail to recognize a face so familiar to him and yet recognize your voice? The answer, as we will see in this Topic, relates to how your central nervous system, the brain and spinal cord, is organized and how it functions. Physiological structures and functions regularly impact behavior and mental processes. When we examine the functions of the spinal cord, we discover how certain environmental stimuli can produce simple, reflexive responses.

Then there's the brain. What is the human brain like? A vast computer? The seat of understanding? The processor of information? A storehouse of memories? A reservoir of emotion? The source of motivation? It is all of these and more. It is in the brain that our conscious, voluntary actions begin, our emotions are experienced, and our cognitions are manipulated and stored.

We will group the central nervous system into small, manageable structures and discuss them one at a time. Still, when we fragment our discussion of the spinal cord and brain, we can lose sight of the fact that they comprise a unified system in which all parts work together and interact with other complex systems. Some functions are localized in specific areas or structures of the central nervous system; but the adaptability and integration of its many functions often forces us to consider the CNS as an entity that is greater than the sum of its parts.

Key Questions to Answer

While reading this Topic, find the answers to the following key questions:

1. What is the spinal cord, and what does it do?

2. What are the functions of sensory neurons, motor neurons, and interneurons?

3. What are the communication and integration functions of the spinal cord?

4. How does a spinal reflex work?

5. What is meant by the proliferation and migration of neurons?

6. How can environmental factors affect the development of the brain?

7. What is meant by "lower centers" of the brain?

8. What structures comprise the brainstem?

9.   What does the medulla do?

10.   What does cross laterality mean?

11.   What does the pons do?

12.   What is the cerebellum, and what does it do?

13.   What is the function of the reticular formation?

14.   What are the basal ganglia, and what do they do?

15.   What brain structure is most associated with Parkinson's disease and why?

16.   What is the thalamus, and what functions does it have?

17.   What is the limbic system?

18.   What are the functions of the amygdala and septum?

19.   What role does the hippocampus play in behavior?

20.   What is the hypothalamus, and how is it structured?

21.   What is the ventromedial nucleus, and what does it do?

22.   What are the lateral and medial nuclei, and what functions do they serve?

23.   What is the cerebral cortex?

24.   What are the cerebral hemispheres?

25.   What are the lobes of the cerebral cortex, and where are they located?

26.   What are the sensory areas of the cerebral cortex, and what does each do?

27.   What are the motor areas of the cerebral cortex, and what does each do?

28.   What are the association areas of the cerebral cortex?

29.   What are Broca's area and Wernicke's area, and what happens if each is damaged?

30.   What are the main differences between the left and right hemispheres of the brain?

31.   What major structure connects the left and right cerebral hemispheres?

32.   What is the split-brain procedure, and what are its results?

33.   What are the two cerebral hemispheres specialized for?

34.   How do the brains of males and females differ?

THE SPINAL CORD

As we have noted, the central nervous system consists of the brain and the spinal cord. In this section, we'll consider the structure and function of the spinal cord, reserving our discussion of the brain for the next section.

The Structure of the Spinal Cord

The **spinal cord** is a mass of interconnected neurons within the spinal column, which looks rather like a section of rope or thick twine. It is surrounded and protected by the hard bone and cartilage of the vertebrae. A cross–sectional view of the spinal column and

spinal cord a mass of interconnected neurons within the spinal column that transmits impulses to and from the brain and is involved in spinal reflex behaviors

sensory neurons neurons that carry impulses from the sense receptors to the central nervous system

motor neurons neurons that carry impulses away from the central nervous system to muscles and glands

interneurons neurons within the spinal cord or brain

the spinal cord is illustrated in Figure 2.6. A few structural details need to be mentioned. Note that the spinal cord is located in the middle of the spinal column, and extends from your lower back to high in your neck just below your brain. Then note that nerve fibers enter and leave the spinal cord from the side. Neurons or nerve fibers that carry impulses toward the brain or spinal cord are called **sensory neurons** or sensory fibers. Sensory neurons and the impulses they transmit enter the spinal cord on dorsal roots (dorsal means toward the back). Neurons and nerve fibers that carry impulses away from the spinal cord and brain to muscles and glands are called **motor neurons** or motor fibers. Impulses that leave the spinal cord on motor neurons do so on ventral roots (ventral means toward the front). Neurons within the central nervous system are called **interneurons**.

Also notice that the center area of the spinal cord consists of gray matter in the shape of a butterfly, while the outside area is light, white matter. This means that the center portion is filled with cell bodies, dendrites, and unmyelinated axons, while the outer section is filled with myelinated axons. Both of these observations about the structure of the spinal cord are key to understanding its functions.

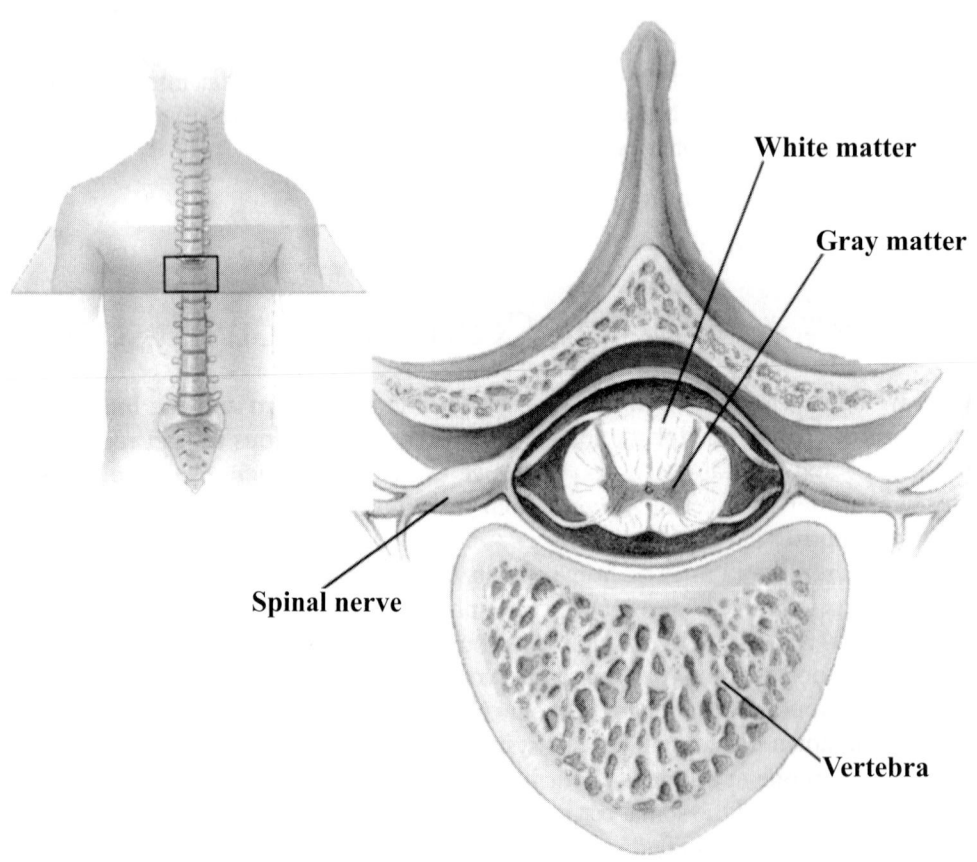

FIGURE 2.6

A cross-sectional view of the spinal column. Only the white matter and gray matter in the center represent actual spinal cord tissue. Note that spinal nerves enter and leave the spinal cord at its sides.

The Functions of the Spinal Cord

The spinal cord has two major functions. The **communication function** of the spinal cord involves transmitting impulses rapidly to and from the brain. When sensory impulses originate in sense receptors below the neck and make their way to the brain, they do so through the spinal cord. When the brain transmits motor impulses to move or activate parts of the body below the neck, those impulses first travel down the spinal cord. For example, if you stub your toe, pain messages travel up the spinal cord and register in the brain. Motor impulses are then sent down your spinal cord causing you to lift your foot, grab it, and hop around.

Impulses to and from various parts of the body leave and enter the spinal cord at different points (impulses to and from the legs, for example, enter and leave at the very base of the spinal cord). If the spinal cord is damaged, the communication function may be disrupted. This is what happened to actor Christopher Reeves, who was thrown from his horse and severed his spine near his neck. The consequences of such an injury are disastrous, resulting in a loss of feeling from the part of the body severed and a loss of voluntary movement (paralysis) of the muscles in the region. The higher in the spinal cord that damage takes place, the greater the resulting losses. In Reeves' case his injury led to *quadraplegia*, or the loss of function of all four limbs, because his injury was so high on the spinal cord. Had his injury been closer to the base of his spine he would have had a condition called *paraplegia*, or loss of function in the legs and lower body.

The second major function of the spinal cord is known as the **integration function**, which has a role in **spinal reflexes**. Spinal reflexes are simple, automatic behaviors that occur without conscious voluntary action of the brain. To understand how these reflexes work, see Figure 2.7. In this drawing of the spinal cord we have added receptor cells in the skin, sensory neurons, motor neurons to muscles in the hand, and have labeled the neurons within the spinal cord as interneurons.

Let's trace your reaction to dripping hot wax on your hand while smelling a fragrant candle. Receptor cells in your hand respond to the hot wax, sending neural impulses racing along sensory neurons, through a dorsal root, and into the spinal cord. Then two things happen at almost the same time. Impulses rush up the ascending pathways of the spinal cord's white matter to your brain. Impulses also travel on interneurons and leave the spinal cord through a ventral root on motor neurons to your arm and hand where muscles are stimulated to contract, and your hand jerks back, causing you to nearly drop the candle.

This is a simple spinal reflex. Impulses travel *in* on sensory neurons, *within* on interneurons, and *out* on motor neurons. We have an environmental stimulus (a flame), activity in the central nervous system (neurons in the spinal cord), and an observable response (withdrawal of the hand).

There are a few observations we must make about the reflex of the type shown in Figure 2.7. First, the fact that impulses enter the spinal cord and immediately race to the brain is not indicated in the drawing. In a situation such as the candle example, you may jerk your hand back "without thinking about it," but very soon thereafter you *are* aware

communication function the function of the spinal cord involving transmission of information to and from the brain

integration function the function of the spinal cord involving the control of the spinal reflexes

spinal reflexes involuntary responses to a stimulus that involve sensory neurons, the spinal cord, and motor neurons

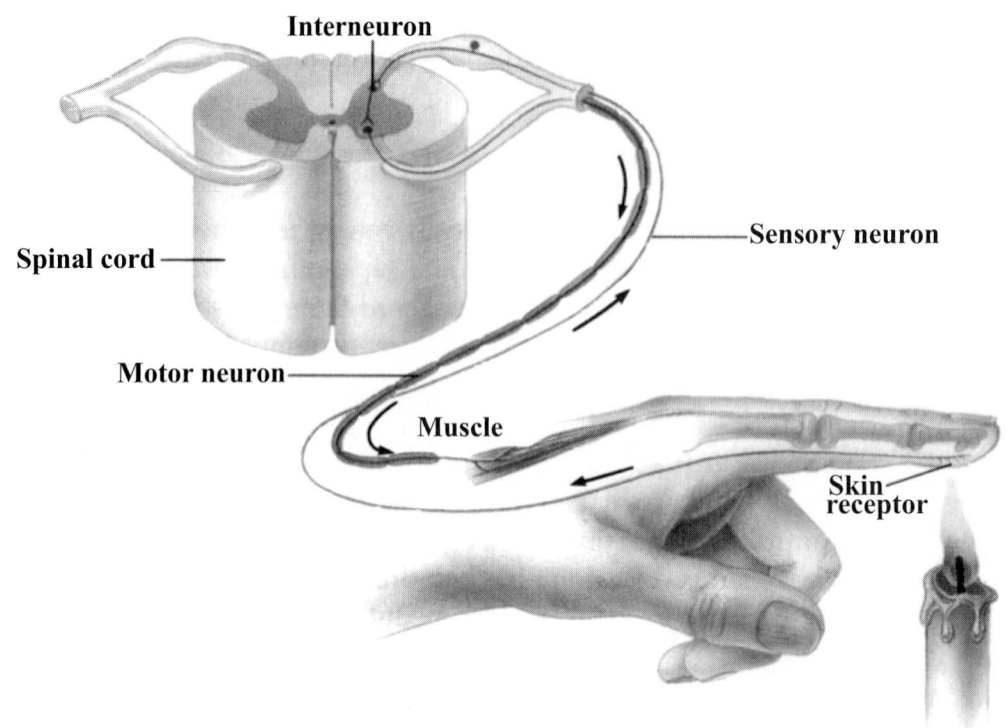

FIGURE 2.7

A spinal reflex. Stimulation of receptor cells in the skin, in turn, stimulated sensory neurons, interneurons, and motor neurons. Although a response is made without the involvement of the brain, impulses also travel up fibers in the spinal cord's white matter to the brain.

BEFORE YOU GO ON

- What is the spinal cord?

- What are sensory neurons, motor neurons, and interneurons?

- What are the communication and integration functions of the spinal cord?

- Describe the major features of a spinal reflex.

of what has happened. Awareness occurs in the brain, not in the spinal cord. It is also true that some reflexes are more simple than the one in Figure 2.7. The reflex shown in Figure 2.7 involves three neurons: a sensory neuron, an interneuron, and a motor neuron. Other reflexes involve only a sensory and a motor neuron which synapse directly. The knee jerk reflex is an example of such a reflex where a sensory and motor neuron synapse directly in the spinal cord with no interneuron.

THE BRAIN

Perched atop your spinal cord, encased in bone, is a wonderful and mysterious organ: your brain. Your brain is a mass of neurons, glia cells and other supporting cells, blood vessels, and ventricles (hollow tubes and spaces containing fluid). Your brain accounts for a small fraction of your body weight, but due to its importance, it receives almost 20 percent of the blood in your body. It contains a storehouse of memories and is the seat of your emotions and your motivation. It regulates your breathing and the beating of your heart.

For convenience, we will divide the brain into two major categories of structures. We will first discuss the role of some of the "lower brain centers," which are involved in several important aspects of behavior. Then we will examine the role of the cerebral cortex, the largest structure in the brain. The cerebral cortex, generally speaking, is the part of the brain that controls higher mental functions. Before we look at how the brain is structured and how it functions, let's look at how the brain develops.

How Does the Brain Develop?

Your adult brain contains billions of neurons and connections, intricately woven together to give you the capabilities you have. The process by which this marvelous organ develops is fascinating and begins with the fertilization of an egg by a sperm. After fertilization, the *zygote* (the first new cell created after fertilization) begins to divide rapidly until it forms a hollow ball of cells that implants itself onto the uterine wall. Development now proceeds very rapidly. During the next phase, the period of the embryo which lasts for about two months, all of the major organ systems of the body are formed.

One of these systems is the central nervous system, which begins as a primitive neural tube that eventually becomes the spinal cord and brain. One end of the neural tube begins to swell. This swelling will eventually become the brain. Brain cells (neurons and glia cells) begin to proliferate. What happens next is nothing short of miraculous. Guided by *radial glia cells*, the proliferating neurons migrate to specific locations where they take up permanent residence (Barinaga, 1996). This process is helped by a protein nicknamed *sonic hedgehog* (after the popular video game), which sends out a signal that helps the migrating neurons find their correct locations. Connections between neurons are formed when the neuron sends out an axon with a *growth cone* at its tip. This growth cone acts like a bloodhound following a chemical scent that helps the axon find its proper synaptic location. Axons that are produced early in development do not have to worry about other axons getting in the way. In contrast, axons that develop later must weave their way around existing axons by following axon tracts that already exist (Tessier-Lavigne & Goodman, 1996). Over the course of several months of prenatal development, axons branch out to their designated locations in waves. The net result of all of this guided migration is the brain's intricate network of neurons and synapses.

Toward the end of prenatal development, the proliferation and migration of neurons slows and eventually stops. Thus we are born with all (or nearly all) of the neurons we will have. Although few, if any, new neurons develop after birth, the brain still undergoes considerable development. Axons need to be myelinated, interconnections between neurons must form, and the various parts of the brain must mature. Take, for example, the visual system, which is underdeveloped at birth. During the first six months of life, the brain cells involved in vision mature and vision improves. Generally, the most rapid period of postnatal brain growth spans the first three years of life, during which time, the brain reaches about 80 percent of its adult size.

Two factors affect brain development. First, a genetic code directs the proliferation and migration of neurons and axonal connections. Second, environmental events also can influence brain development. For example, substances known as *teratogens* (substances that can cause malformations in an unborn child) can have profound effects on the "wiring" of the brain (Cooper, Porter, Young, & Beachy, 1998). One way this happens is by interrupting the normal operation of the sonic hedgehog signaling process (Cooper et al., 1998) sending neurons to the wrong place after migration. For example, alcohol (a powerful teratogen which crosses the placenta very easily) causes neurons to overshoot their destinations in the brain. This results in a jumble of neurons above where the normal surface of the brain should be. This abnormal cell migration is associated with reduced levels of intelligence in children with *fetal alcohol syndrome*. Other teratogens, for example radiation, cause neurons to undershoot their target locations which also results in mental retardation.

The brain that results from normal prenatal and postnatal development is a complex organ capable of many things. In the sections that follow, we will explore the regions of the brain and see what each of them does for you. We'll use a simple organizational scheme and divide the brain into two parts: the cerebral cortex and everything else, which we will refer to as lower brain centers.

The "Lower" Brain Centers

One morning Cheryl Jones woke up with a blinding headache, which went away almost as fast as it started. Her headache was followed by nausea, dizziness, and loss of motor coordination. On her way to the bathroom she stumbled. She woke her husband who rushed her to the hospital. A CT–scan (a sophisticated x–ray procedure that provides a detailed picture of the brain) quickly revealed that Cheryl had an aneurysm (a ballooning of a blood vessel) the size of a grape at the base of her brain. Without surgery, the aneurysm would surely burst, shutting down Cheryl's critical body functions (breathing and heartbeat) and she would die. Opting for surgery that put not only her life, but the life of her unborn baby at risk, Cheryl and the baby survived (Pekkanen, 1998).

What could have been so important in the structures at the very base of Cheryl's brain that caused her to risk her life and the life of her child? As we will see, these "lower centers" of the brain contain vital structures involved in regulating crucial, involuntary functions like respiration and heartbeat. Though we call these structures "lower," they are by no means unimportant to an organism's functioning. Lower brain centers are "lower" in two ways. First, they are physically located beneath the cerebral cortex. Second, these brain structures develop first—both in an evolutionary sense and within the developing human brain. They are the structures we most clearly share with other animals. In no way are these centers less important. As you will soon see, our very survival depends on them. Use Figure 2.8 as a guide to locate the various structures as we discuss them.

The Brain Stem

brain stem the lowest part of the brain, just above the spinal cord, consists of the medulla and the pons

As you look at the spinal cord and brain, you cannot tell where one ends and the other begins. There is no abrupt division of these two aspects of the central nervous system. Just above the spinal cord there is a slight widening of the cord that suggests the transition to brain tissue. Here two important structures form the **brainstem**: the medulla and the pons.

The lowest structure in the brain is the **medulla**. In many ways, the medulla acts like the spinal cord in that its major functions involve involuntary reflexes. There are several small structures called *nuclei* (collections of neural cell bodies) in the medulla that control such functions as coughing, sneezing, tongue movements, and reflexive eye movements. You don't have to think about blinking your eye as something rushes toward it, for example; your medulla produces that eye blink reflexively.

The medulla also contains nuclei that control breathing reflexes and monitor the muscles of the heart to keep it beating rhythmically. We *can* exercise some voluntary control over the nuclei of the medulla, but only within limits. For example, the medulla controls our respiration (breathing), but we can override the medulla and hold our breath. We cannot, however, hold our breath until we die. We can hold our breath until we lose consciousness, which is to say until we give up voluntary control; then the medulla takes over and breathing continues.

At the level of the medulla, most nerve fibers to and from the brain cross from right to left and vice versa. Centers in the left side of the brain receive impulses from and send impulses to the right side of the body, although some are also sent to the left side. Similarly, the left side of the body sends impulses to, and receives messages from, the

medulla the structure in the brain stem where cross laterality begins. It contains centers that monitor reflex functions such as heart rate and respiration.

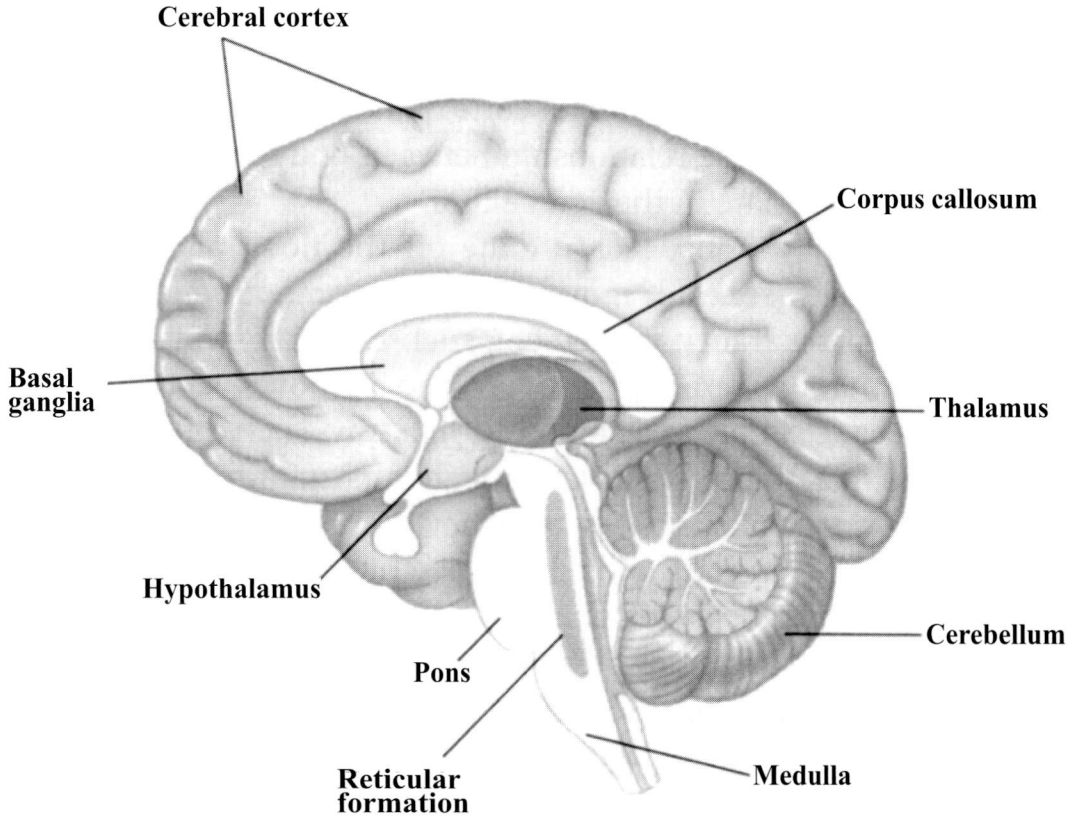

FIGURE 2.8

Some of the major structures of the human brain, of which the cerebral cortex is clearly the largest

cross laterality the arrangement of nerve fibers crossing from the left side of the body to the right side of the brain, and from the right side of the body to the left side of the brain

pons a brain stem structure that forms a bridge that organizes fibers from the spinal cord to the brain and vice versa

cerebellum a spherical structure at the rear base of the brain that coordinates fine and rapid muscular movements

right side of the brain (which explains why electrically stimulating the correct area in the *left* side of the brain produces a movement in the *right* arm). This arrangement of fibers crossing from one side of the body to the opposite side of the brain is called **cross laterality** (also known as *contralateral control*), and it takes place in the brain stem. Note that there is some same–side control. The left side of the brain has some control over the left side of the body, and the right side of the brain has some control over the right side of the body. This control is known as *ipsilateral control*. Ipsilateral control is extremely limited.

Just above the medulla is a structure called the pons. (The pons is one structure; there is no such thing as a "pon.") The **pons** serves as a relay station or bridge (which is what *pons* means), sorting out and relaying sensory messages from the spinal cord and the face up to higher brain centers and reversing the relay for motor impulses coming down from higher centers. The cross laterality that begins in the medulla continues in the pons. Nuclei in the pons are also responsible, at least in part, for the rapid movement of our eyes that occurs when we dream (e.g., Sakai, 1985). Other centers in the pons are involved in determining our cycles of being awake and being asleep (Vertes, 1984).

BEFORE YOU GO ON

- What happens during prenatal and postnatal brain development?

- What do the medulla and pons do?

- Describe what cross laterality and ipsilateral control mean.

The Cerebellum

The **cerebellum** sits behind your pons, tucked up under the base of your skull. Your cerebellum (literally, "small brain") is about the size of your closed fist and is the second largest part of your brain. Its outer region (its cortex) is convoluted—the tissue is folded in upon itself creating many deep crevices and lumps.

The major role of the cerebellum is to smooth and coordinate rapid body movements. Most intentional voluntary movements originate in higher brain centers (usually the motor area of the cerebral cortex) and are coordinated by the cerebellum. Because of the close relationship between body movement and vision, many eye movements originate in the cerebellum.

Our ability to stoop, pick a dime off the floor, and slip it into our pocket involves a complex series of movements made smooth and coordinated by our cerebellum. When athletes train a movement, such as a golf swing or a gymnastic routine, we may say that they are trying to "get into a groove," so that their trained movements can be made simply and smoothly. In a way, the athletes are training their cerebellums. In fact, the cerebellum plays an important role in making movements that are "ballistic," meaning they occur without any sensory feedback. Examples would be catching a fast line drive hit right to you, playing a well–practiced piano piece, or quickly reaching out to save a priceless vase you just knocked off a table with your elbow. The cerebellum *learns* to make such movements, and this process is the focus of research by psychobiologists interested in how learning experiences are represented in the brain (Glickstein & Yeo, 1990; Kornhuber, 1974).

The ability of an athlete, such as this golfer, to perform a complex, coordinated sequence of movements over and over again requires the involvement of the cerebellum.

Few of our behaviors are as well–coordinated or as well–learned as the rapid movements we need to speak. The next time you're talking to someone, focus on how quickly and effortlessly your lips, mouth, and tongue, are moving thanks to the cerebellum. Damage to the cerebellum slurs speech. In fact, damage to the cerebellum disrupts all coordinated movements. One may shake and stagger when walking. Someone with cerebellum damage may appear to be drunk. (On what region of the brain do you suppose alcohol has a direct effect? The cerebellum.)

Damage to the cerebellum can disrupt motor activity in other ways. If the outer region of the cerebellum is damaged, **tremors**, involuntary trembling movements that occur when the person tries to move (called intention tremors) result. Damage to inner, deeper areas of the cerebellum leads to "tremors at rest," and the limbs or head may shake or twitch rhythmically even when the person tries to remain still.

tremors involuntary trembling movements

The Reticular Formation

The **reticular formation** is hardly a brain structure at all. It is a complex network of nerve fibers that begins in the brain stem and works its way up through and around other structures to the top portions of the brain (Carlson, 1991).

What the reticular formation does, and how it does so, remains something of a mystery; however, we do know that it is involved in determining our level of activation or arousal. It influences whether we are awake, asleep, or somewhere in between.

reticular formation a network of nerve fibers extending from the base of the brain to the cerebrum. It controls one's level of activation or arousal.

Electrical stimulation of the reticular formation can produce EEG patterns of brain activity associated with alertness. Classic research has shown that lesions of the reticular formation cause a state of constant sleep in laboratory animals (Lindsley et al., 1949; Moruzzi & Magoun, 1949). In a way, the reticular formation acts like a valve that either allows sensory messages to pass from lower centers up to the cerebral cortex or shuts them off, partially or totally. We don't know what stimulates the reticular formation to produce these effects.

The Basal Ganglia

basal ganglia a collection of structures in front of the limbic system involved in the control of large, slow movements; a source of much of the brain's dopamine

A curious set of tissues is the **basal ganglia**. The basal ganglia are collections of small, loosely connected structures in front of the limbic system. Like the cerebellum, the basal ganglia primarily control motor responses. Unlike the cerebellum, the role of the basal ganglia is involved in the initiation and coordination of large, slow movements. Although the basal ganglia are clearly related to the movements of some of our body's larger muscles, there are no pathways that lead directly from the ganglia down the spinal cord and to those muscles.

Some functions of the basal ganglia have become clearer as we have come to understand Parkinson's disease, a disorder involving the basal ganglia in which the most noticeable symptoms are impairment of movement and involuntary tremors. At first there may be a tightness or stiffness in the fingers or limbs. As the disease progresses, it becomes difficult, if not impossible, to initiate bodily movements. Walking, once begun, involves a set of stiff, shuffling movements. In advanced cases, voluntary movement of the arms is nearly impossible. Parkinson's disease is more common with increasing age, afflicting approximately 1 percent of the population.

The neurotransmitter dopamine is usually found in great quantity in the basal ganglia. Indeed, the basal ganglia are the source of much of the brain's dopamine. In Parkinson's disease, the cells that produce dopamine die off, and levels of the neurotransmitter in the basal ganglia (and elsewhere) decline. As dopamine levels in the basal ganglia become insufficient, behavioral consequences are noted as symptoms of the disease. Treatment, you might think, would be to inject dopamine back into the basal ganglia. Unfortunately, that isn't possible. There's simply no way to get the chemical in there so that it will stay. But another drug, L–dopa (in pill form), has the same effect: L–dopa increases dopamine availability in the basal ganglia, and as a result, the course of the disease is slowed.

One treatment for Parkinson's disease has received considerable attention in the 1990s: the transplantation of brain cells from fetuses directly into the brain of someone suffering from the disease. After many studies demonstrated that cells from the fetuses of rats could grow in the brains of adult rats and increase the amount of dopamine there (e.g., Bjorklund et al., 1980), the procedure was tried with humans. The results so far have been promising. Studies have shown that transplanting fetal brain cells into the brains of individuals with Parkinson's disease can reverse the course of the disease (Fahn, 1992; Lindvall, 1998, Widner, et al., 1992). For example, Lindvall (1998) reported that fetal cells survived for up to six years after implantation and significant regeneration of damaged brain areas occurred. As a consequence, most of the 13 patients studied showed significant long-term improvement. Although fetal cells can form synapses in the adult brain, not all fetal cells survive the transplant and relief from the symptoms of Parkinson's disease is often moderate. Additionally, for the surgery to have a chance at success the cells from six to eight fetuses are needed (Kalat, 2001). The issue of harvesting cells from aborted fetuses is, as you might expect, highly controversial. There are people who strongly oppose abortion to begin with, and the addition of the prospect of fetuses being harvested adds to that opposition. The issue was so controversial that the director of the National Institute of Health (NIH) stopped all research using fetal cells in 1999. The ban was lifted in August 2000 when a strict set of guidelines for using fetal tissue was put into place. The star of movies and television, Michael J. Fox, was recently diagnosed with Parkinson's disease, cutting short his run in a successful TV comedy series. The Michael J. Fox Foundation recently merged with the Parkinson's Action Network (PAN) with the goal of increasing awareness of and research funding for Parkinson's disease.

> ## BEFORE YOU GO ON
>
> - What role does the cerebellum play? What happens if it is damaged?
> - What is the main function of the reticular formation?
> - What do the basal ganglia do, and how are they related to Parkinson's disease?

The Thalamus

The **thalamus** sits just below the cerebral cortex and is involved in its functioning. Like the pons, it is a relay station for impulses traveling to and from the cerebral cortex. Many impulses traveling from the cerebral cortex to lower brain structures, the spinal cord, and the peripheral nervous system pass through the thalamus. Overcoming the normal function of the medulla (e.g., by voluntarily holding your breath) involves messages that pass through the thalamus. The major role of the thalamus, however, involves the processing of information from the senses.

In handling incoming sensory impulses, the thalamus collects, organizes, and then directs sensory messages to the appropriate areas of the cerebral cortex. Sensory messages from the lower body, eyes, and ears, (not the nose) pass through the thalamus. For example, at the thalamus, nerve fibers from an eye are spread out and projected onto the back of the cerebral cortex.

Because of its role in monitoring impulses to and from the cerebral cortex, the thalamus has long been suspected to be involved in the control of our sleep–wake cycle (Moruzzi, 1975). Although the issue is not settled, some evidence (Lugaresi et al., 1986) suggests that nuclei in the thalamus (as well as the pons) do have a role in establishing a person's normal pattern of sleep and wakefulness.

thalamus a structure located just below the cerebral cortex, which is the last sensory relay station. It projects sensory impulses to the appropriate areas of the cerebral cortex.

The Limbic System

The **limbic system** is actually a collection of structures rather than a single unit. It is important in controlling the behaviors of animals which do not have the large, well–developed cerebral cortexes of humans. In humans, the limbic system controls many of the complex behavioral patterns considered instinctive. The limbic system is in

limbic system a collection of structures near the middle of the brain involved in emotionality (amygdala and septum) and long-term memory storage (hippocampus)

the middle of the brain and comprises several structures including the amygdala, septum, hippocampus, hypothalamus, parts of the thalamus (anterior nuclei) and parts of the basal ganglia (Guyton, 1972). Its major parts are shown in Figure 2.9.

Within the human brain, parts of the limbic system are intimately involved in the display of emotional reactions. One structure in the limbic system, the *amygdala,* produces reactions of rage or aggression when stimulated, while another area, the *septum,* has the opposite effect, reducing the intensity of emotional responses when it is stimulated. The influence of the amygdala and the septum on emotional responding is immediate and direct in nonhumans. In humans, it is more subtle, reflecting the influence of other brain centers. The amygdala also plays an important role in deciding whether a stimulus is dangerous or not (Ekman, 1992; LeDoux, 1995).

Another structure in the limbic system, called the *hippocampus,* is less involved in emotion and more involved with the formation of memories for experiences (Vargha–Khadem et al., 1997). People with a damaged hippocampus are often unable to "transfer" experiences (e.g., a birthday party) into permanent memory storage. They may remember events for short periods and may be able to remember events from the distant past, but only if these events occurred before the hippocampus was damaged. Interestingly, hippocampal damage does not interfere significantly with verbal aspects of memory, for example, learning and remembering a list of words (Vargha–Khadem et al., 1997).

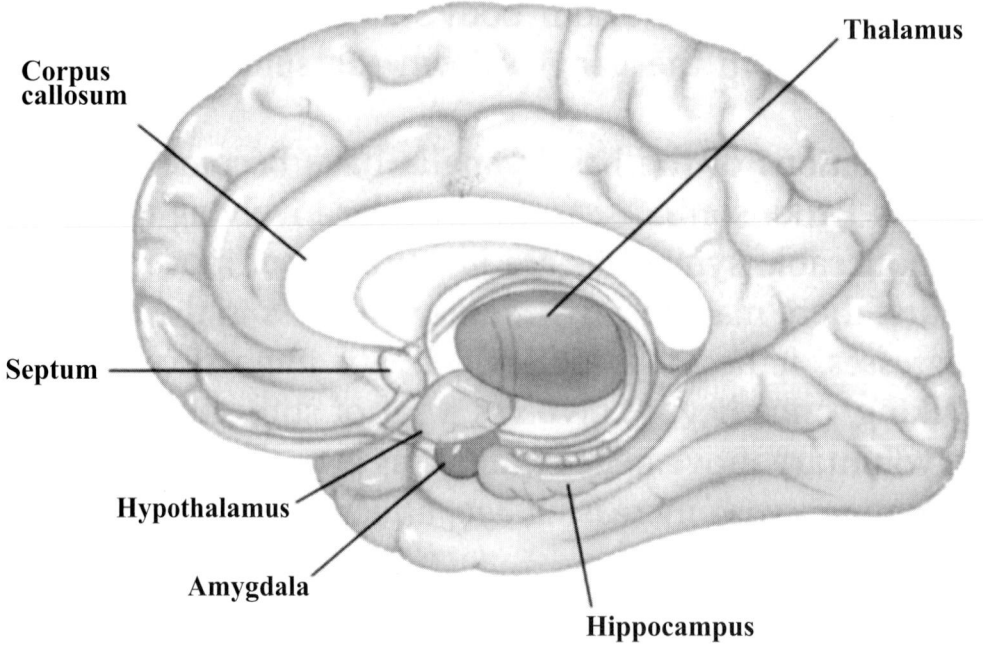

FIGURE 2.9

A view of the brain showing structures deep within it. Among these, the septum, amygdala, and hippocampus constitute the limbic system. Given its proximity, it is easy to see why many scientists include the hypothalamus as part of the limbic system as well.

The **hypothalamus** is a structure that plays a complex role in motivational and emotional reactions. Among other things, it influences many of the functions of the endocrine system, which, as we have seen, is involved in emotional responding. Actually, the hypothalamus is not a unitary structure; instead it is a collection of smaller structures known as *nuclei*. Each nucleus plays a different role in the regulation of motivation and emotion.

The major responsibility of the hypothalamus is to monitor critical internal bodily functions. The *ventromedial nucleus*, for example, mediates feeding behaviors. Destruction of this nucleus in a rat results in a condition called *hyperphagia* which causes the animal to lose its ability to regulate food intake and become obese. Similarly, the anterior hypothalamus involves the detection of thirst and the regulation of fluid intake.

The hypothalamus also plays a role in aggression. Stimulation of the *lateral nucleus* in a cat produces aggression that looks much like predatory behavior. The cat is highly selective in what it attacks and stalks it before pouncing. Stimulation of the *medial nucleus* results in an anger–based aggression. The cat shows the characteristic signs of anger (arched back, ears flattened, hissing and spitting) and will attack anything in its way. Interestingly, the role of the hypothalamus in hunger and aggression is not as simple as it may seem. For example, if you apply mild stimulation to the lateral nucleus, the cat shows signs of hunger (but not aggression). Increase the strength of the stimulation to the same site, and aggression is displayed.

The hypothalamus also acts something like a thermostat, triggering a number of automatic reactions should we become too warm or too cold. This small structure is also involved in sexual behaviors. It acts as a regulator for many hormones. The hypothalamus has been implicated in the development of sexual orientations (LaVay, 1991), an implication we'll discuss when we study needs, motives, and emotions in later chapters.

hypothalamus a small structure in the middle of the brain made up of several nuclei involved in feeding, drinking, temperature regulation, sex, and aggression

BEFORE YOU GO ON

- Describe the function of the thalamus.
- What major structures make up the limbic system?
- Describe some of the functions of the amygdala, septum, and hippocampus.
- What are the major functions of the hypothalamus?
- Describe what happens when various parts of the hypothalamus are stimulated or destroyed.

The Cerebral Cortex

The human brain is a homely organ. There's nothing pretty about it. When we look at a human brain, the first thing we are likely to notice is the large, soft, lumpy, creviced outer covering of the cerebral cortex (cortex means "outer bark," or covering). The **cerebral cortex** (also referred to as the cerebrum) of the human brain is significantly larger than any other brain structure. It is the complex and delicate cerebral cortex that makes us uniquely human by giving us our ability to think, reason, and use language.

cerebral cortex the large convoluted outer covering of the brain that is the seat of voluntary action and cognitive functioning

Lobes and Localization

Figure 2.10 presents two views of the cerebral cortex: a top view and a side view. You can see that the deep folds of tissue provide us with markers for dividing the cerebrum into major areas. The most noticeable division of the cortex can be seen in the top view.

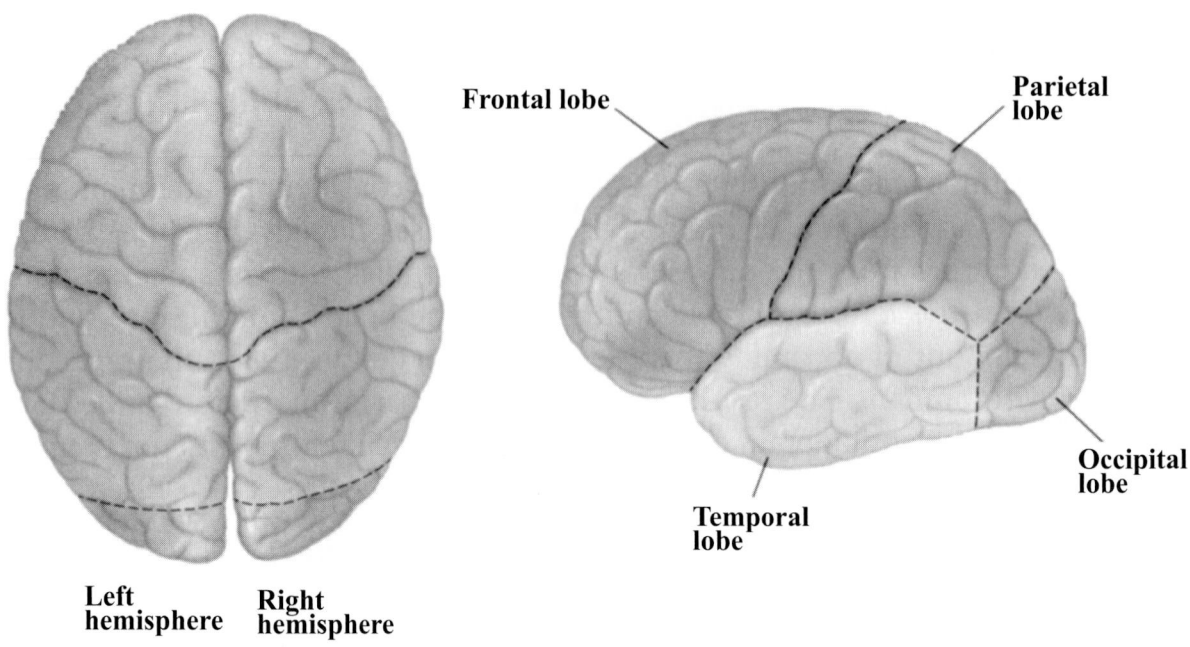

Left   Right
hemisphere   hemisphere

FIGURE 2.10

The human cerebral cortex is divided into left and right hemispheres, which, in turn, are divided into frontal, temporal, occipital, and parietal lobes.

We clearly see the deep crevice that runs down the middle of the cerebral cortex from front to back, dividing it into the left and right *cerebral hemispheres.*

A side view of a hemisphere (Figure 2.10 shows us the left one) allows us to see the four major divisions of each hemisphere, called "lobes." The *frontal lobes* (plural because there is a left and a right) are the largest and are defined by two large crevices called the central fissure and the lateral fissure. The *temporal lobes* are located at the temples below the lateral fissure, with one on each side of the brain. The *occipital lobes,* at the back of the brain, are defined somewhat arbitrarily, with no large fissures setting them off, and the *parietal lobes* are wedged behind the frontal lobes and above the occipital and temporal lobes.

Researchers have learned much about what normally happens in the various regions of the cerebral cortex, but many of the details of cerebral function are yet to be understood. Three major areas have been mapped: *sensory areas,* where impulses from sense receptors are sent; *motor areas,* where most voluntary movements originate; and *association areas,* where sensory and motor functions are integrated, and where higher mental processes are thought to occur. We'll now review each of these in turn, referring to Figure 2.10 as we go along.

Sensory Areas

Let's review for a minute. Receptor cells (specialized neurons) in our sense organs respond to stimulus energy from the environment. These cells then pass neural impulses along sensory nerve fibers, eventually to the cerebral cortex. Senses in our body below our neck first send impulses to the spinal cord. Then, it's up the spinal cord, through the brain stem, where they cross from left to right and from right to left, on up to the thalamus, and beyond to the cerebrum. After impulses from our senses leave the thalamus, they go to a **sensory area**, an area of the cerebral cortex that receives impulses from our senses. The sensory area involved depends on the sense that was activated.

Large areas of the cerebral cortex are involved with vision and hearing. Virtually the entire occipital lobe processes visual information (labeled "visual area" in Figure 2.11). Auditory (hearing) impulses take up large centers ("auditory areas") in the temporal lobes. In addition to being involved in hearing, the undersides of the temporal lobes have a curious function. If certain parts of the underside of the temporal lobes are damaged, a condition called *prosopagnosia* exists. In this curious disorder, a person loses the ability to recognize faces (but not voices). Remember the story about your friend who was in a motorcycle accident, with which we began this chapter? Where do you think he had brain damage?

sensory areas those areas of the cerebral cortex that ultimately receive neural impulses from sense receptors

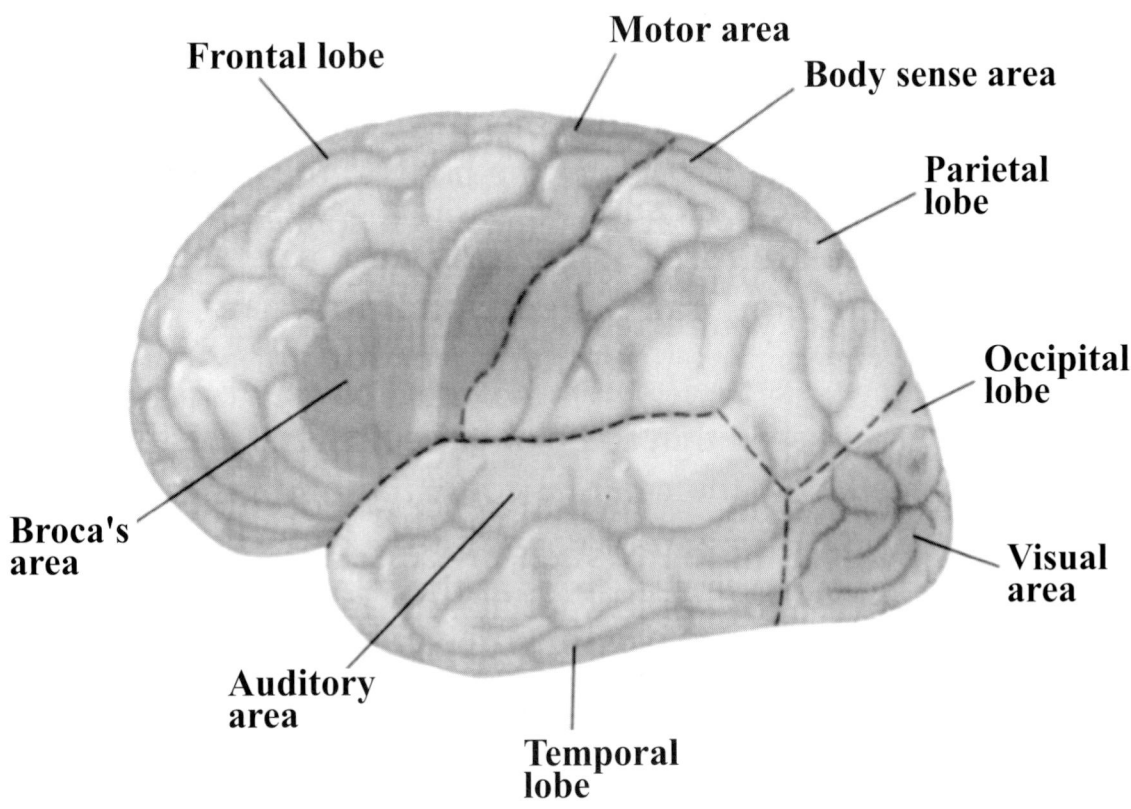

FIGURE 2.11

A side view of the left cerebral hemisphere, showing the four lobes of the cerebral cortex and areas of localization of function.

Our bodily senses (touch, pressure, pain, etc.) send impulses to a strip at the very front of the parietal lobe (labeled "body sense area" in Figure 2.11). In this area of the parietal lobe, we can map out specific regions that correspond to various parts of the body. When we do so, we find that some body parts—the face, lips, and fingertips, for example—are overrepresented in the body sense area of the cerebral cortex, reflecting their high sensitivity. In other words, some parts of the body, even some very small ones, are processed in larger areas of the cortex than are other parts.

Finally, let's remind ourselves of cross laterality, the crossing over of information from senses on the left side of the body to the right side of the brain, and vice versa, that occurs in the brain stem. When someone touches your *right* arm, that information ends up in your *left* parietal lobe. A tickle to your left foot is processed by the right side of your cerebral cortex.

Motor Areas

motor areas those areas at the rear of the frontal lobes that control voluntary muscular movement

We have seen that some of our actions, at least very simple and reflexive ones, originate below the cerebral cortex. Although lower brain centers, such as the basal ganglia, may be involved, most *voluntary* activity originates in the **motor areas** of the cerebral cortex in strips at the very back of our frontal lobes. These areas (remember, there are two of them, left and right) are directly across the central fissure from the body sense areas in the parietal lobe (see Figure 2.11). We need to make the disclaimer that the actual, thoughtful, decision–making process of whether one *should* move probably occurs elsewhere, almost certainly farther forward in the frontal lobes.

Electrical stimulation techniques have allowed us to map locations in the motor areas that correspond to, or control, specific muscles or muscle groups. As is the case for sensory processing, we find that some muscle groups (such as those that control movements of the hands and mouth) are represented by disproportionally larger areas of cerebral cortex.

As you know, we also find cross laterality at work with the motor area. It is your right hemisphere's motor area that controls movements of the left side of your body, and the left hemisphere's motor area that controls the right side. Someone who has suffered a cerebral stroke (a disruption of blood flow in the brain that results in the loss of neural tissue) in the left side of the brain will have impaired movement in the right side of his or her body.

Association Areas

association areas those areas of the frontal, temporal, and parietal lobes in which mental processes (planning, thinking, problem solving, memory) occur and where incoming sensory information is integrated with outgoing motor responses

Once we have located the areas of the cerebral cortex that process sensory information and originate motor responses, we still have a lot of cortex left. The remaining areas of the cerebral cortex are called **association areas**, which are areas of the cerebrum where sensory input is integrated with motor responses, and where cognitive functions such as problem solving, memory, and thinking occur. There are three association areas in each hemisphere: frontal, parietal, and temporal. The occipital lobe is so "filled" with visual processing, there is no room left over for an occipital association area.

There is considerable support for the idea that so–called higher mental processes occur in the association areas. Frontal association areas are involved in many such processes. For instance, more than a century ago, Pierre-Paul Broca (1824–1880) discovered that speech production and some other language behaviors are localized in the left frontal association area. Broca's conclusions were based on observations he made of human brains during autopsy. Persons with similar speech disorders commonly had noticeable damage in the very same region of the left hemisphere of the cerebral cortex. Logic led Broca to suspect that normal speech functions are controlled by this portion of the brain, which we now call *Broca's area* (see Fig. 2.11). Broca's area controls the *production* of speech. That is, it coordinates the actual functions needed to express an idea. A person with damage to Broca's area shows an interesting pattern of speech defects. If asked a question, such as "Where is your car?" a person with Broca's area damage could communicate to you the location of his or her car, but only in broken, forced language. For example, the person might say, "Car...lot...parked by...supermarket."

Another part of the brain involved in language and speech is *Wernicke's area*, which is involved in speech comprehension and organizing ideas. A bundle of nerve fibers connects Wernicke's and Broca's areas so that the language comprehended and organized in Wernicke's area is transmitted to Broca's area, which then coordinates the speech output. If Wernicke's area is damaged (or if the fibers connecting it to Broca's area are damaged), a different speech problem is manifested. If a person with Wernicke's area damage is asked where her car is parked the answer that comes out will be in beautiful, grammatically correct language. The only catch is that it will make no sense whatsoever. For example, the person might say, "Isn't the seashore beautiful this time of year?"

Damage to the very front of the right frontal lobe or to an area where the parietal and temporal lobes come together often interrupts or destroys the ability to plan ahead, to think quickly, or to think things through. Interestingly, these association areas of the brain involved in forethought and planning nearly cease to function when we are feeling particularly happy (e.g., George et al., 1995).

We should not get carried away with cerebral localization of function. Let's not fall into the trap of believing that separate parts of the cerebral cortex operate independently and have the sole responsibility for any one function. This will be particularly important to keep in mind as we look at the division of the cerebral cortex into right and left hemispheres.

BEFORE YOU GO ON

- Describe the location of the four lobes of the cerebral cortex.

- Name and describe the functions of the sensory areas of the cortex.

- Name and describe the functions of the motor areas of the cortex.

- What do the association areas of the cortex do?

The Two Cerebral Hemispheres: Splitting the Brain

The ancient Greeks knew that the cerebral cortex was divided into two major sections, or hemispheres. That the cerebral cortex is divided in half seems quite natural. After all, we have two eyes, arms, legs, lungs, and so forth. Why not two divisions of the brain? In the last thirty years, interest in this division into hemispheres has heightened as scientists have accumulated evidence that suggests that each half of the cerebral cortex may have primary responsibility for its own set of mental functions.

In most humans, the left hemisphere is the larger of the two halves, contains a higher proportion of gray matter, and is considered the dominant hemisphere (active to a greater degree in more tasks). We have already noted that a major language center (Broca's area) is housed in the left cerebral hemisphere. At least this is true for virtually all right–handed people. For some left–handers, language may be processed primarily by the right hemisphere. Because humans are so language oriented, little attention was given to the right hemisphere until a remarkable surgical procedure performed in the 1960s gave us new insights about the cerebral hemispheres (Sperry, 1968, 1982; Springer & Deutsch, 1981).

Normally, the two hemispheres of the cerebral cortex are interconnected by a network of hundreds of thousands of fibers collectively called the **corpus callosum** (see Figures 2.8 and 2.9). Through the corpus callosum, one side of our cortex remains in constant and immediate contact with the other. Separating the functions of the two hemispheres is possible, however, through a surgical technique called a **split–brain procedure**, which is neither as complicated nor as dangerous as it sounds. The procedure destroys the corpus callosum's connections between the two hemispheres and was first performed on a human in 1961 by Joseph Brogan to lessen the severity of the symptoms of epilepsy. As an irreversible treatment of last resort, the split–brain procedure has been very successful.

Most of what we know about the activities of the cerebral hemispheres has been learned from split–brain subjects, both human and animal. One of the things that makes this procedure remarkable is that under normal circumstances split–brain patients behave normally. Only in the laboratory using specially designed tasks can we see the results of independently functioning hemispheres of the cerebral cortex (e.g., Gazzaniga & LeDoux, 1978; Hellige, 1983; Metcalfe et al., 1995).

Experiments with split–brain patients confirm that speech production is a left–hemisphere function in a majority of people. Imagine you have your hands behind your back. I place a house key in your left hand and ask you to tell me what it is. Your left hand feels the key. Impulses travel up your left arm, up your spinal cord, and cross over to your right cerebral hemisphere (remember cross laterality). You tell me that the object in your hand is a key because your brain is intact. Your right hemisphere passes information about the key to your left hemisphere, and your left hemisphere directs you to say, "It's a key."

Now suppose that you are a split–brain subject. You cannot answer my question even though you understand it perfectly. Why not? Your right brain knows that the object in your left hand is a key, but without an intact corpus callosum, it cannot inform the left hemisphere where speech production is located. Under the direction of the right cerebral hemisphere, you *would* be able to point out with your left hand the key from among other objects placed before you. Upon seeing this, your eyes would communicate that information to your left hemisphere.

A major task for the left hemisphere is the production of speech and processing of language. But, we must be cautious about making too much of the specialization of function. When the results of the original split-brain research were published, many drew faulty conclusions. We now know that virtually no behavior, or mental process, is the product of the operation of one hemisphere alone (Hellige, 1990). For example, Gazzaniga (1998) reports that one split-brain patient learned to speak from the right hemisphere 13 years after surgery severing the corpus callosum. This individual can report on information ver-

corpus callosum the network of nerve fibers that connects the two hemispheres of the cerebral cortex

split-brain procedure the surgical lesioning of the corpus callosum, which separates the functions of the left and right hemispheres of the cerebral cortex and is a treatment of last resort for epilepsy

bally, regardless of which hemisphere receives the information. Further, although the left hemisphere is dominant for language, the right hemisphere does do some language processing even if full language functions are not present. For example, the right hemisphere is involved in processing common phrases and clichés, such as "have a nice day" (Kempler & Van Lanker, 1987). Thus, it is more reasonable to say that one hemisphere is *dominant* with respect to a given task, or that one hemisphere may be better than the other at processing certain types of information.

Despite the early overinterpretation of findings from split-brain research, most of the research conducted shows a remarkable amount of hemispheric specialization. Gazzaniga (1998) points out that split-brain research has led to the conclusion that *brain modules* develop in the brain. Each module is designed to carry out a specific function. When the brain is split, modules devoted to specific functions are not affected (Gazzaniga, 1998). So when the brain is split, the left hemisphere retains its superior linguistic ability, presumably because the modules needed for language processing are located in the left hemisphere. The information processing modules in the left hemisphere also function better with information that comes in serially, one piece at a time, although the data in this area are tenuous (Hellige, 1990). Finally, the left hemisphere also has an *interpreter mechanism* that can create explanations for events presented to the right hemisphere in a split-brain patient (Gazzaniga, 1998). Gazzaniga and his colleagues selectively presented information to the right and left hemispheres. When tested, the right hand correctly identified the picture presented to the left hemisphere, and the left hand did the same for the information presented to the right hemisphere. However, when the patient was asked why the left hand was pointing to a given picture, the left hemisphere instantly made up an explanation to fit the situation.

What about the right hemisphere? The clearest evidence is that the right hemisphere dominates the processing of visually presented information (Bradshaw & Nettleton, 1983; Kosslyn, 1987). Putting together a jigsaw puzzle, for instance, uses the right hemisphere more than the left. Skill in the visual arts (e.g., painting, drawing, and sculpting) is associated with the right hemisphere. It is involved in the interpretation of emotional stimuli and in the expression of emotions. While the left hemisphere is analytical and sequential, the right hemisphere is considered better able to grasp the big picture—the overall view of things—and tends to be somewhat creative.

These possibilities are intriguing. While it seems that there are differences in the way the two sides of the cerebral cortex normally process information, these differences are slight and many are controversial. In fact, the more we study hemispheric differences, the more we discover similarities.

BEFORE YOU GO ON

- What is the split-brain procedure, and what have we learned from it?
- What is the left hemisphere specialized for?
- What is the right hemisphere specialized for?

We should be careful about overgeneralizing, but we can say that the left hemisphere of the cerebral cortex is involved in processing language, as when working a crossword puzzle. A major task of the right hemisphere is more involved in interpreting emotional stimuli and in expressing emotions (i.e., painting, drawing, sculpting).

The Two Sexes: Male and Female Brains

The anatomical differences between women and men are obvious. When we discuss the function of the brain, however, we may fairly ask if there are any differences between the brains of men and women. Remember, we are asking about general differences; no two human beings' brains are precisely the same. If there are differences in the anatomy of male and female brains, we must then ask if these differences are significant. Do they have measurable impact on psychological functioning?

It turns out that what appears to be a loaded issue can be resolved easily. Except for those differences in the brains of males and females that are directly related to reproductive function (which are significant), there are very few differences of real consequence (e.g., Unger & Crawford, 1992).

Here's an example of how research in this area has gone. One intriguing possibility is that the hemispheres of the cerebral cortex are more separate and distinct (more *lateralized*) in males than in females. At least one part of the corpus callosum in the brains of females is consistently larger than it is in the brains of males. There is also evidence that women are more likely to recover from strokes than are men, perhaps because functions lost as a result of damage in one hemisphere can be taken over more easily by the other undamaged hemisphere (McGlone, 1977, 1978, 1980). Another implication—usually unspoken—is that intellectual functioning in women is more "balanced" than in men, whereas men are more likely to excel in the functioning of one hemisphere or the other. Further research failed to find any differences in lateralization (Bleier et al., 1987). Nor is there evidence that differences in lateralization are associated with any differences in cognitive abilities between men and women (e.g., Unger & Crawford, 1992). There is a difference in the lateralization of the brains of left–handed persons and right–handed persons (brains of left–handed persons are less lateralized or separate), but there are no significant differences in the cognitive abilities of left– and right–handed persons (Kocel, 1977).

Then, just as some researchers were prepared to give up researching gender–based differences in lateralization, a husband–and–wife team at Yale University, Drs. Sally and Bennett Shaywitz (she's a psychologist, he's a neurologist) published their work (Shaywitz et al., 1995). They watched the functioning intact brains of men and women as they read nonsense words and tried to determine if they rhymed. The Shaywitzes used a new method of brain imaging (functional magnetic resonance imaging) that shows glimpses of areas of the brain that are active during even a very brief task. They found that when men attempted to sound out nonsense words, they used a small portion of their left cerebral cortex near Broca's area. Women used the same area but also involved a similar area on the right side of their brains. Interestingly, the men and women performed the task equally well; the differences were only in *how their brains approached the task.* This was the first research to find a significant difference in brain function, not just brain structure.

BEFORE YOU GO ON

- Are there any significant differences between the male and female brain?

- Do the differences between the male and female brain translate into any significant behavior differences?

Topic Review 2 B

1. **What is the spinal cord, and what does it do?**

   The spinal cord, which is encased in the spinal column, is a mass of interconnected neurons resembling a piece of rope that extends from the lower back to just below the brain. It has nerve fibers that carry messages to and from the brain and to and from the body. The spinal cord has two functions—communication and integration.

2. **What are the functions of sensory neurons, motor neurons, and interneurons?**

   Sensory neurons carry sensory information from the body to the central nervous system. Motor neurons carry information from the central nervous system to the body and control movement. Interneurons are neurons within the central nervous system.

3. **What are the communication and integration functions of the spinal cord?**

   The communication function carries messages to and from the brain and body. The integrative function is behavioral and controls spinal reflexes such as withdrawing your hand from a hot surface.

4. **How does a spinal reflex work?**

   There are two types of spinal reflexes. When a receptor is stimulated (e.g., your hand placed on a hot surface) sensory neurons transmit the information to the spinal cord, and interneurons send motor impulses to the muscles in your arm and hand to withdraw your hand. This behavior is mediated totally at the spinal cord level. However, information is transmitted up the spinal cord, and you consciously experience the pain. Alternatively, some reflexes do not involve interneurons that mediate sensory experience and motor response and, instead, work through direct synaptic connections between sensory and motor neurons.

5. **What is meant by the proliferation and migration of neurons?**

   During prenatal development, neurons are produced at a rapid rate. This is proliferation. Migration of neurons means that once produced, the neurons move to a position in the nervous system determined by your genetic code. The neurons are guided to their appropriate positions by specialized cells and chemicals.

6. **How can environmental factors affect the development of the brain?**

   Environmental factors, such as exposure to alcohol, affect the migration of neurons in the nervous system. In the case of prenatal alcohol exposure, alcohol causes neurons to migrate too far, and they overshoot their appropriate place. The result is a jumble of brain cells above the cortex, which causes the mental retardation associated with fetal alcohol syndrome. Other environmental factors, such as radiation exposure, cause migrating neurons to stop short of their intended target positions, which also results in mental retardation.

7. **What is meant by the term "lower centers" of the brain?**

   The "lower centers" of the brain are structures located at the base of the brain below the cortex. They are the first to develop both in an evolutionary sense and a developmental one. Even though these structures are located at the base of the brain, they perform important functions. Lower brain centers keep vital functions such as heart rate and respiration rate going.

8. **What structures comprise the brainstem?**

   The brainstem includes the medulla, pons, and parts of the reticular formation.

9. **What does the medulla do?**

   Like the spinal cord, the medulla's major functions involve involuntary reflexes. There are several small structures called nuclei (collections of neural cell bodies) in the medulla that control functions such as coughing, sneezing, tongue movements, and reflexive eye movements. The medulla also sends out impulses that keep your heart beating and your respiratory system breathing.

10. **What does cross laterality mean?**

    Cross laterality means that the left side your body is controlled largely by the right side of your brain, and the right side of your body is controlled largely by the left side of your brain. Although most communication is cross lateral, there is some ipsilateral control; that is, the left side of the brain communicates with the left side of your body, and the right side of your brain communicates with the right side of your body.

11. What does the pons do?

The pons serves as a relay station, sorting and relaying sensory messages from the spinal cord and the face to higher brain centers, and reversing the relay for motor impulses coming down from higher centers. The pons is also responsible, at least in part, for the rapid movement of our eyes that occurs when we dream and the sleep/waking cycle.

12. What is the cerebellum, and what does it do?

The cerebellum is the second largest part of the brain and is located under the base of the skull. Its cortex (outer layer) is convoluted. The major function of the cerebellum is to smooth out and coordinate rapid body movements. Most voluntary movements originate in the higher brain centers and are coordinated by the cerebellum. The cerebellum is the point of origin for many eye movements. Damage to the cerebellum can lead to a variety of motor problems including loss of coordination, tremors, and speech problems.

13. What is the function of the reticular formation?

The reticular formation is more a network of nerve fibers than a true brain structure. Most of the functions of the reticular formation remain a mystery. However, we know it is involved in alertness and the sleep/waking cycle.

14. What are the basal ganglia, and what do they do?

The basal ganglia are a collection of small loosely connected structures in front of the limbic system. The basal ganglia primarily control motor response. Unlike the cerebellum, the role of the basal ganglia is related to the initiation and the coordination of large, slow movements.

15. What brain structure is most associated with Parkinson's disease and why?

The basal ganglia are the structures most associated with Parkinson's disease. The neurotransmitter dopamine is found in large quantities in the basal ganglia. In Parkinson's disease the cells that produce dopamine die and the levels of dopamine in the basal ganglia drop, which produces the characteristic motor problems associated with the disease.

16. What is the thalamus, and what functions does it perform?

The thalamus is a lower brain structure located below the cerebral cortex. It relays impulses traveling to and from the cortex. Many of the impulses traveling from the cerebral cortex to lower brain centers, the spinal cord, and the peripheral nervous system pass through the thalamus. The primary function of the thalamus is to relay sensory information to the cerebral cortex.

17. What is the limbic system?

The limbic system is a collection of structures rather than a single one. The limbic system is comprised of the amygdala, hippocampus, hypothalamus, thalamus, septum, and basal ganglia. The limbic system controls many of the behaviors that we consider instinctive.

18. What are the functions of the amygdala and septum?

When stimulated, the amygdala evokes reactions of rage or aggression. It also helps you to decide whether a stimulus is dangerous or not. The septum reduces the intensity of emotional responses when it is stimulated. The influence of the amygdala and the septum on emotional responding is immediate and direct in nonhumans. In humans, it is more subtle, which reflects the influence of other brain centers.

19. What role does the hippocampus play in behavior?

The hippocampus is less involved in mediating emotional responses than other structures in the limbic system. Instead it is involved with the formation of memories. Individuals with damage to the hippocampus have difficulty transferring memories from temporary memory to permanent memory. However, they can still transfer verbal memories from temporary memory to permanent memory.

20. What is the hypothalamus, and how is it structured?

The hypothalamus is a part of the limbic system involved in the mediation of motivation. It is not a unitary structure but rather a collection of smaller structures called nuclei. Each nucleus plays a different role in the regulation of motivation and emotion. The major function of the hypothalamus is to monitor and control internal body functions such as hunger, thirst, and body temperature as well as to regulate many hormones.

21. What is the ventromedial nucleus, and what does it do?

The ventromedial nucleus is part of the hypothalamus and regulates the feeding cycle. If the ventromedial nucleus is damaged, an organism will overeat leading to a condition known as hyperphagia.

22. What are the lateral and medial nuclei, and what function do they have?

The lateral and medial nuclei are involved in aggression. Electrical stimulation of the lateral nucleus produces predatory aggression in which an animal stalks and attacks a carefully selected target. Electrical stimulation of the medial nucleus produces emotional aggression in which an animal shows signs of anger and is not selective in what it will attack.

23. What is the cerebral cortex?

The cerebral cortex, also known as the cerebrum, is the largest part of the human brain. It is associated with all of the mental processes and cognitive functions that make us human by giving us our ability to think, reason, and use language.

24. What are the cerebral hemispheres?

The cerebral cortex is divided down the center, from front to back, into two hemispheres. The left half is called the left hemisphere and the right half the right hemisphere.

25. What are the lobes of the cerebral cortex, and where are they located?

The lobes of the cerebral cortex are divisions of each hemisphere. The cerebral lobes are the frontal lobe, parietal lobe, temporal lobe, and occipital lobe. The frontal lobes are defined by two large crevices called the central and lateral fissures, which are located at the front of the brain. The temporal lobes are located at the temples of the skull below the lateral fissure on each side of the brain. The occipital lobes are located at the very back of the brain and have no large fissures. The parietal lobes are sandwiched between the frontal, occipital, and temporal lobes.

26. What are the sensory areas of the cerebral cortex, and what does each do?

The sensory areas of the brain are portions of the brain specialized for receiving neural impulses from the senses. Almost all of the occipital lobe is dedicated to receiving information from visual stimuli. Impulses relating to hearing go to the temporal lobes. Information from the body senses go to the body sense areas located in the parietal lobe.

27. What are the motor areas of the cerebral cortex, and what does each do?

The motor areas of the cerebral cortex control most vol-untary motor movements. The motor areas of the cortex are located at the back of the frontal lobes.

28. What are the association areas of the cerebral cortex?

The association areas of the cortex are the parts of the cortex not directly involved in the mediation of sensory and motor activities. The association areas make up a large portion of the cortex and are involved in the integration of sensory input, motor responses, and higher cognitive functions (e.g., problem solving and memory).

29. What are Broca's area and Wernicke's area, and what happens if each is damaged?

Broca's area is an area of the cortex involved in producing speech. If it is damaged, a person has difficulty speaking. Wernicke's area plays a role in organizing and comprehending speech. Damage to this area results in a person being able to speak fluently, but not coherently.

30. What are the main differences between the left and right hemispheres of the brain?

In most people, the left hemisphere of the brain is larger and contains more gray matter. The left hemisphere is often referred to as the "dominant hemisphere" because it is active in many tasks and is the seat of language in most people. The right hemisphere appeared to play a minor role until some of its important functions were discovered.

31. What is the major structure connecting the left and right cerebral hemispheres?

A large bundle of fibers called the corpus callosum connects the left and right cerebral hemispheres.

32. What is the split-brain procedure, and what are its results?

The split-brain procedure is a surgical procedure that is performed to relieve the symptoms of severe epilepsy. The procedure involves cutting the corpus callosum. The result is that the two hemispheres become largely disconnected and can be studied independently.

33. What are the two cerebral hemispheres specialized for?

The left hemisphere is specialized for the comprehension and production of speech, although the right hemisphere is involved in processing common phrases and clichés. The left hemisphere is also involved in mathematical abilities and processing information that comes in one piece at a time. The right hemisphere is specialized for visual and spatial information. Artistic skills like painting and sculpting are also associated with the right hemisphere, as is the interpretation of emotional stimuli.

34. How do the brains of males and females differ?

The cerebral hemispheres of the brain are more lateralized in the male brain than in the female brain. In females the corpus callosum is larger, which implies greater cooperation between the hemispheres. When processing speech, male brains show activity on the left side of the brain, whereas women show activity in both hemispheres. Despite these differences, men and women perform equally well on many cognitive tasks though their brains solve the tasks differently.

Chapter 3

Sensation and Perception

*I*n a grand old lecture hall at the University of Tennessee, nearly 600 students settled down to listen to the day's lecture on perception. Suddenly a student burst through the doors at the rear of the hall. Unknown to the class, he was the lecturer's graduate student assistant. He stomped down the center aisle of the lecture hall screaming obscenities at the professor. "Dr. X, you failed me for the last time, you *&@#$ so-and-so! You're going to pay for this!" The class was stunned. No one moved as the student leaped over the lectern to grab the professor. The two struggled briefly, then—in clear view of everyone—a chrome-plated revolver appeared. Down behind the lectern they fell. Bang! The students sat frozen in their seats as the graduate student raced out the side door that their professor entered just minutes earlier. The professor lay sprawled on the floor moaning loudly. Six hundred stunned students just sat there. At the proper dramatic moment, the professor slowly drew himself up to the lectern and in a calm, soft voice said, "Now I want everyone to write down exactly what you just saw."

You can guess what happened. The "irate student" was described as being from 5'4" to 6'3" tall, weighing between 155 and 230 pounds, and wearing either a blue blazer or a gray sweatshirt. But the most remarkable misperception had to do with the gun. When the professor first reached the lectern, he reached into his suit coat pocket, removed the gun, and placed it on top of his notes. When the student crashed into the room, the first thing that the professor did was to reach down, grab the pistol, and point it at the student. In fact, the student never had the gun. It was the professor who fired the shot that startled the class. Fewer than twenty of the 600 students in class reported the events as they actually occurred. The overwhelming majority of witnesses claimed that a crazy student burst into the class with a gun in his hands.

Here we begin our discussion of information processing—how we find out about the world, make judgments about it, learn from it, and remember what we have learned. As the above example demonstrates, our perception of the world often depends on factors that are not immediately apparent. This chapter addresses how we find out about ourselves and the world in which we live. We begin with a look at how our senses work.

Topic 3A SENSORY PROCESSES

This Topic introduces you to sensory processes or sensation. Sensation is the process whereby your sense organs (e.g., your eyes, ears, nose) detect external stimuli. Detection of external stimulation is crucial because only those stimuli that you detect can be transmitted to your brain for further processing and interpretation. As you will see in the sections that follow, sensory processes are more complex than meet the eye (no pun intended). We will explore all of your major senses and show how they respond to and transmit sensory information to your brain.

Key Questions to Answer

While reading this Topic, find the answers to the following key questions:

1.   What is the difference between sensation and perception?

2.   What evidence suggests that sensation and perception are distinct processes?

3.   What is a sensory threshold?

4.   What is psychophysics?

5.   What are absolute and difference thresholds, and how do they differ?

6.   How does signal detection theory conceptualize stimulus detection?

7.   How does signal detection theory apply to lineup identifications?

8.   What is meant by sensory adaptation?

9.   What is dark adaptation, and what accounts for it?

10.   What are the three properties of light, and what sensory experience does each provide?

11.   How do monochromatic and white light differ?

12.   What structures of the eye are involved in focusing light on the back of the eye?

13.   What is the retina, and what structures comprise it?

14.   What are the functions of the rods and cones?

15.   How does the process of dark adaptation demonstrate the existence of two separate visual systems?

16.   How is visual neural energy transmitted from the retina to the brain?

17.   What are the two theories of color vision?

18.   What are the properties of sound, and what sensory experience does each provide?

19.   What are the structures of the ear, and how are they involved in transduction?

20.   How is the stimulus for hearing transduced into an auditory neural impulse?

21.   What are the chemical senses, and how do they work?

22.   How do the senses of smell and taste relate to each other?

23.   What is the vomeronasal organ (VNO), and what does it appear to do?

24.   What are the skin senses, and what do they do?

25.   What are the position senses, and what information do they provide?

26.   What is pain, and how is it detected?

27.   What techniques are used to control pain?

SENSATION AND PERCEPTION

Generally, we divide the initial stages of information processing into two subprocesses—sensation and perception. **Sensation** is the process of detecting external stimuli and changing those stimuli into nervous system activity. Sensation yields our immediate experience of the stimuli in our environment. The psychology of sensation deals with how our various senses do what they do. Sense receptors are the specialized neural cells in sense organs that change physical energy into neural impulses. In other words, each of our sense receptors is a **transducer**—a mechanism that converts energy from one form to another. A light bulb is a transducer. It converts electrical energy into light energy (and a little heat energy). Your eye is a sense organ that contains sense receptors that transduce light energy into neural energy. Your ear is a sense organ that contains sense receptors that transduce the mechanical energy of sound waves into neural energy.

sensation the process of receiving information from the environment and changing it into nervous system activity

transducer a mechanism that converts energy from one form to another—a basic process common to all of our senses

Compared to sensation, perception is a more active, complex, even creative, process. It acts on stimulation received and recorded by the senses. **Perception** is a process that involves the selection, organization, and interpretation of stimuli. Perception is a more cognitive and central process than sensation. We say that our senses *present* us with information about the world in which we live, whereas perception *represents* (re-presents) that information, often flavored by our motivational states, our expectations, and our past experiences. In other words, "...we sense the presence of a stimulus, but we perceive what it is" (Levine & Shefner, 1991, p. 1).

perception the cognitive process of selecting, organizing, and interpreting stimuli

As we have characterized sensation and perception, they appear to be separate but integrated processes. Is there any evidence suggesting that sensation and perception are, in fact, separate processes? The answer to this question is yes. What do you think would happen if we projected a different image to each of your eyes? Each of your eyes senses and responds to the image projected. You should, then, "see" both images simultaneously if there were only sensation. However, that is not what happens. Quite the contrary, your brain perceives the images alternately and spontaneously shifts from one to the other (Lumer, Friston, & Rees, 1998). Moreover, researchers have demonstrated that areas of the frontal and parietal lobes are responsible for this alternation. Interestingly, those areas of the frontal and parietal lobes are not active when only one image is projected. Thus, rather than sensing both images, the perceptual system in your brain makes sense out of the competing images by providing alternating perceptions of each.

BEFORE YOU GO ON

- Define sensation and perception.

- How do sensation and perception differ?

- What evidence exists suggesting that sensation and perception are different processes?

SENSORY PROCESSES

In this Topic, we explore how our senses detect and respond to external stimulation. However, before we get into the story of how each of our sense organs goes about transducing physical energy from the environment into neural energy, we'll consider a few concepts common to all of our senses.

Sensory Thresholds

Think about an electronic device that runs on a solar battery, for example, a calculator. If you use it in the dark, it will not work. In dim light, you might see some signs of life from the calculator. In bright light, the calculator functions fully: the display is bright and easy to read, and all of its features work properly. The calculator's power cell requires a minimum amount of light to power the calculator sufficiently. This is the *threshold* level of stimulation for that device. Light intensities below the threshold will not allow the electronics of the calculator to work. Light intensities at or above threshold allow the calculator to operate properly.

Your sense organs operate in a manner similar to the photoelectric cell in the calculator. A minimum intensity of a stimulus must be present for the sense organ to transduce the external physical stimulus from the environment (for example, light, sound, pressure on your skin) into a neural impulse that your nervous system can interpret. This intensity is known as the **sensory threshold**, or the minimum intensity of a stimulus needed to operate your sense organs.

sensory threshold the minimum intensity of a stimulus that will cause sense organs to function

Physiologists and psychologists have studied sensory thresholds for over a century. This was one of the pioneering areas of research in the early days that led to psychology's emergence as a separate science. **Psychophysics** is the study of relationships between the physical attributes of stimuli and the psychological experiences they produce. It is one of the oldest subfields of psychology. Many methods of psychophysics were developed before Wundt opened his psychology laboratory in Leipzig in 1879.

psychophysics the study of the relationship between the physical attributes of stimuli and the psychological experiences they produce

There are two ways to think about psychophysics. First, at an applied level, we can say that the techniques of psychophysics are designed to assess the sensitivity of our senses providing answers to such questions as, "Just how good *is* your hearing after all these years of playing in a rock band?" Second, at a theoretical level, psychophysics provides a systematic means of relating the physical world to the psychological world. Now we might ask, "How much of a change in the physical intensity of this sound will it take for you to experience a difference in loudness?" Most psychophysical methods are designed to measure *sensory thresholds*, indicators of the sensitivity of our sense receptors. There are two types of sensory thresholds: absolute thresholds and difference thresholds.

Absolute Thresholds

Imagine the following experiment. You are seated in a dimly-lighted room staring at a small box. The side of the box facing you is covered by a sheet of plastic. Behind the plastic is a light bulb. The physical intensity of the light bulb can be decreased to the point where you cannot see it at all. The light's intensity can also be increased so that you can see it very clearly. There are many intensity settings between these extremes. At what point of physical intensity will the light first become visible to you? Common sense suggests that there should be a level of intensity below which you cannot see the light and above which you can. That level is your absolute threshold. In other words, sensory thresholds are inversely related to sensitivity. That is, as threshold values decrease, sensitivity increases. The lower the threshold of a sense receptor, the more sensitive it is.

Let's return to our imaginary experiment. The light's intensity is repeatedly varied, and you are asked to respond, "Yes, I see the light," or "No, I don't see the light." (In this experiment, you won't be allowed the luxury of saying you don't know or aren't sure.)

When this experiment is done, we discover something that seems strange. The intensity of the light *can* be reduced so low that you never report seeing it, and the light *can* be presented at intensities so high that you always say you see them. However, there are light intensities to which you sometimes respond "yes" and sometimes respond "no," even though the physical intensity of the light is constant.

In reality, there isn't much about absolute thresholds that is absolute. They change from moment to moment, reflecting subtle changes in the sensitivity of our senses. They also reflect such factors as momentary shifts in our ability to pay attention to the task at

absolute threshold the physical intensity of a stimulus that one can detect 50 percent of the time

hand—an issue we'll get back to soon. Because there are no absolute measures of sensory sensitivity, psychologists use the following operational definition of **absolute threshold**: the physical intensity of a stimulus that a person reports detecting 50 percent of the time. In other words, intensities below threshold are those detected less than 50 percent of the time, and intensities above threshold are those detected more than 50 percent of the time. This complication occurs for all of our senses, not just vision.

What good is the concept of absolute threshold? Determining absolute thresholds is not just an academic exercise. Absolute threshold levels as a measure of sensitivity are used to determine if one's senses are operating properly and detecting low levels of stimulation (which is what happens when you have your hearing tested, for example). Engineers who design sound systems need to know about absolute thresholds; stereo speakers that do not reproduce sounds above threshold levels aren't of much use. Warning lights must be well above absolute threshold to be useful. How much perfume do you need to use for it to be noticed? How low must you whisper so as not to be overheard in a classroom? Do you really smell natural gas in the

Absolute threshold is not simply an academic exercise. Why put an expensive spice or herb in your cooking if no one can taste it? How much is needed so that it can be detected? These are questions of psychophysics.

Vision	A candle flame seen from a distance of 30 miles on a clear, dark night
Hearing	The ticking of a watch under quiet conditions from a distance of 20 feet
Taste	One teaspoon of sugar dissolved in two gallons of water
Smell	One drop of perfume in a three-room apartment
Touch	The wing of a bee dropped on your cheek from a height of one centimeter

From Galanter, 1962

FIGURE 3.1

Examples of Absolute Threshold Values for Five Senses (i.e., These Stimuli Will Be Detected 50 Percent of the Time)

BEFORE YOU GO ON

- What is psychophysics?
- What is a sensory threshold?
- Describe an absolute threshold.

house, or is it your imagination? Can one basil leaf in the tomato sauce be detected, or will two be required? These are psychophysical questions about absolute thresholds that pertain to everyday experiences outside the laboratory. As it happens, our sense receptors are remarkably sensitive, as the examples in Figure 3.1 attest.

Difference Thresholds

Imagine that one day a friend makes a claim that you just can't believe. She states that she can tell the difference between the tastes of the various colored M&M candies. That is, she claims that she can tell the difference in taste between a red M&M and a brown M&M. Of course, you are skeptical and decide to test her amazing taste abilities. You set up an experiment. You blindfold your friend and feed her pairs of M&Ms, one at a time, giving her a small drink of water between each one. Sometimes you give her pairs of M&Ms that have different colors, and other times you give her pairs of the same color. You keep track of the number of times she correctly discriminates between the pairs of M&Ms. To your amazement, your friend can tell the difference between the differently colored M&Ms!

The truth is, we don't often encounter situations that test our abilities to detect differences between or among very low–intensity stimuli as in our M&M test. However, we *are* often called upon to detect differences between or among stimuli that are above our absolute thresholds. The issue is not whether the stimuli can be detected, but whether they are in some way different from each other. So, a **difference threshold** is the smallest difference between stimulus attributes that can be detected. As you may have anticipated, we encounter the same complication as when we try to measure absolute thresholds. One's difference threshold for any stimulus attribute varies slightly from moment to moment. So, again we say that to be above one's difference threshold, differences between stimuli must be detected more than 50 percent of the time.

difference threshold the differences in a stimulus attribute that can be detected 50 percent of the time

Here's an example. You are presented with two tones. You hear them both (they are above your absolute threshold), and you report that they are equally loud. If I gradually increase the intensity of one of the tones, I will eventually reach a point at which you can just detect a difference in the loudness of the tones. This **just noticeable difference**, or jnd, is the amount of change in a stimulus that makes it just noticeably different from what it was.

The concept of just noticeable difference is relevant in many contexts. A parent tells a teenager to "turn down that stereo!" The teenager reduces the volume, but not by a noticeable difference from the parent's perspective, and trouble may be brewing. Does the color of the shoes match the color of the dress closely enough? Can anyone notice the difference between the expensive ingredients in the stew and the cheaper ones?

Signal Detection

When we are asked to determine if a stimulus has been presented, we are being asked to judge if we can detect a signal against a background of other stimuli and randomly changing neural activity called "noise." When we consider thresholds this way, we are using the basics of signal detection theory. **Signal detection theory** states that stimulus detection is a decision-making process of determining if a signal exists against a background of noise (Green & Swets, 1966).

According to this point of view, one's absolute threshold is influenced by many factors in addition to the actual sensitivity of one's senses. Random nervous system activity has to be accounted for, as do the person's attention, expectations, and biases. For example, in experiments that determine one's absolute threshold, people are more likely to respond positively when asked if they can detect a stimulus. In other words, when in doubt, people simply have a tendency to say "yes" more often than "no" (Block, 1965).

Remember the absolute threshold study with which we began our discussion of psychophysics? The intensity of a light in a box changed and you were asked if you could notice. Your absolute threshold was the intensity of light to which you responded "yes" 50 percent of the time. Signal detection theory considers all of the factors that might have prompted you to say "yes" at any exposure to the light. What might some of these factors be? One might be the overall amount of light in the room. Wouldn't you be more likely to detect the signal of the light in a room that was totally dark as opposed to a room in which all of the lights were on? What if you were offered a $5 reward each time you detected the light? Wouldn't you tend to say "yes" more often, whether you were really sure of yourself or not? By the same token, if we were to fine you $1 for each time you said "yes" when the light was not really on, might you not become more conservative, saying "yes" only when you were very sure of yourself? Might we expect a difference in your pattern of saying "yes" or "no" depending on whether you were tested mid-morning or late in the day?

If you think that signal detection theory only applies to detecting lights in boxes, you are wrong. Think back to the classroom demonstration that opened this chapter. An irate "student" came into a classroom, argued with the professor over a grade, and a shot was fired. Following the event, the professor asked the students to write down everything they had seen. As you may recall, the students' memories were not terribly accurate. Now, let's

just noticeable difference (jnd) the minimal change that can be detected in a stimulus attribute, such as intensity

signal detection theory the view that signal detection is decision-making; separating a signal from background noise

do things a bit differently. Instead of having the students recall what took place, ask them to pick the irate student out of a lineup. Let's say that a short time after the incident, six males are brought to the front of the room, and each student is asked if the irate student is present in the lineup. In this situation, we are asked to determine if the perpetrator (the irate student) is or is not in the lineup, which is a signal detection task.

In the lineup situation there are two possibilities: the perpetrator is present in the lineup (target present lineup) or the perpetrator is not present (target absent lineup). This is analogous to the light being present or absent in our previous example. There are two possible decisions you could make: the perpetrator is present in the lineup or he is not. The matrix shown in Figure 3.2 shows what could happen given this set of parameters. A *hit* results if you said that the perpetrator was present in the lineup when, in fact, he was present. A *miss* occurs if you said the perpetrator was not in the lineup when he was. A *false alarm* is when you pick someone out as the perpetrator when the perpetrator was not present in the lineup. Finally, a *correct rejection* happens when you correctly state that the perpetrator is not present in the lineup.

As is the case with a more traditional signal detection task, we can change the probabilities of making a hit, miss, false alarm, or correct rejection. For example, let's say that the irate student was 6'2" tall with dark hair and a mustache. If we put him in a lineup with four foils (other persons put into the lineup) who are 5'6" tall with blond hair and no facial hair, we would increase the probability of a hit. However, we also increase the probability of a false alarm if we are dealing with a target absent lineup (that is, someone who resembles the irate student is in the lineup). We can virtually eliminate the problem of false alarms by putting the irate student in a lineup with four foils that resemble him almost exactly. The problem is you decrease the rate of hits and increase the rate of misses. This is because the suspect, if present, is not sufficiently different from the foils, making it difficult for the witness to make a selection (increased misses). It also raises the likelihood that a foil will be selected instead of the suspect (decreased hits). To make matters even more complicated, the witness's motivation can affect his or her decision criterion. If you are told that it is crucial you make an identification, you are more likely to pick *someone* out of the lineup, even if the suspect is not present. A well-constructed lineup will maximize the likelihood of a hit while controlling the likelihood of false alarms and misses.

BEFORE YOU GO ON

- What is a difference threshold and a jnd?

- What are the major assumptions of signal detection theory?

- What factors affect a decision concerning whether a signal is present or absent?

- How can signal detection theory be applied to eyewitness identification?

- What is a hit, miss, false alarm, and correct rejection?

		ACTUAL LINEUP COMPOSITION	
		Perpetrator Present	Perpetrator Absent
DECISION	Perpetrator Present	HIT	FALSE ALARM
	Perpetrator Absent	MISS	CORRECT REJECTION

FIGURE 3.2

A decision matrix showing possible outcomes of lineup decisions when the perpetrator is present or absent.

Sensory Adaptation

Sensory adaptation occurs when our sensory experience decreases with continued exposure to a stimulus. There are many examples of sensory adaptation. When we jump into a pool or lake, the water feels very cold. After a few minutes, we adapt and are reassuring our friends to "Come on in; the water's fine." When we walk into a house in which cabbage is cooking, the odor is nearly overwhelming, but soon we adapt and do not notice it. When the compressor motor of the refrigerator turns on, it seems to make a terribly loud noise which we soon do not notice until the motor stops and silence returns to the kitchen.

> **sensory adaptation** the process in which our sensory experience diminishes with continued exposure to a stimulus

There is an important psychological implication in these common examples of sensory adaptation: One's ability to detect the presence of a stimulus depends in large measure on the extent to which our sense receptors are being newly stimulated or have adapted. Our sense receptors respond best to *changes* in stimulation. The constant stimulation of a receptor leads to adaptation and less of a chance that the stimulation will be detected.

There is an exception to this use of the term *adaptation*. What happens when you move from a brightly lit area to a dimly lit one? You enter a darkened movie theater on a sunny afternoon. At first you can barely see, but in a few minutes, you see reasonably well. What happened? We say that your eyes have "adapted to the dark." Here we use the term *adaptation* differently. **Dark adaptation** refers to the process in which the visual receptors become *more* sensitive with time spent in the dark. There is also **light adaptation** which occurs when you move from a darkened area to a lighted one. For example, imagine you need to use the bathroom in the middle of the night. You stumble out of bed and head to the bathroom. Without thinking, you reach for the light switch and are nearly blinded by the light, which, as you know, can even be painful. After a short period of time, you adapt to the light and are no longer bothered by it. This occurs because while you are asleep, your eyes are maximally dark adapted (that is they are very sensitive to light). When you turn on the light, the visual sense receptors in your eyes fire all at once, flooding your brain with visual stimulation. It takes a shorter period of time for your eyes to light adapt than it takes them to dark adapt.

> **dark adaptation** the process by which our eyes become more sensitive to light as we spend time in the dark

> **light adaptation** the process by which our eyes become more sensitive to dark as we spend time in the light

> ## BEFORE YOU GO ON
>
> - What is sensory adaptation?
> - What are dark and light adaptation?

VISION

Which of our senses is "most important" is debatable. Each sense helps us process information about the environment. Many enjoy eating and think highly of the sense of taste. Others enjoy listening to music and think highly of the sense of hearing. Nonetheless, vision is a very important sense for humans. Occasionally we equate our visual experience with truth or reality, as in, "Seeing is believing."

In this section, we will discuss both the stimulus for vision (light) and the receptor for vision (the eye).

The Stimulus for Vision: Light

Light, in the form of electromagnetic energy, is the stimulus for vision. Appreciating the nature of light can help us understand how it is related to our visual experiences. Light is a wave form of energy; that is, light radiates from its source in a manner we represent as waves and call light waves.

Light waves have three important physical characteristics that are related to psychological experience: *wave amplitude, wavelength,* and *wave purity.* Light energy varies in its intensity. Differences in intensity correspond to differences in the wave amplitude of light. Refer to Figure 3.3, and assume that the two waves represent two different light waves. One of the physical differences between light A and light B is the wave amplitude of each. Our psychological experience of wave amplitude, or intensity, is *brightness.* The difference between a bright light and a dim light is due to the difference in wave amplitude. Dimmer switches that control the brightness of light fixtures control the amplitude of light waves.

Wavelength is the distance between any point in a wave and the corresponding point on the next wave, or cycle. In Figure 3.3, another difference between waves A and B is that A has the longer wavelength. It is difficult to imagine distances so small, but we can measure the length of a light wave. The unit of measurement is the *nanometer (nm),* which is equal to one one-billionth of a meter, or one one-millionth of a millimeter.

Wavelength determines the *hue* or color of light we perceive. The human eye responds only to radiant energy that has a wavelength between roughly 380 nm and 760 nm. This is the range of energy waves that constitutes the *visible spectrum.* As light waves increase from the short 380 nm wavelengths to the long 760 nm lengths, we experience these changes as violet, blue, green, yellow-green, yellow, orange, and red—the color spectrum. Wave forms of energy with wavelengths shorter than 380 nm (e.g., X-rays and ultraviolet rays) are too short to stimulate the receptors in our eyes and go unnoticed. Wave forms of energy with wavelengths longer than 760 nm (e.g., microwaves and radar) do not stimulate the receptor cells in our eyes either.

Here's an apparently easy problem: We have two lights, one red (700 nm) and the other yellow-green (550 nm). We adjust the physical intensities of these lights so that they are equal. Will the lights appear equally bright with equal amplitudes? Actually, they won't. The yellow-green light is much brighter than the red one. It also appears brighter than a blue light of the same amplitude. Wavelength and wave amplitude interact to produce apparent brightness. Wavelengths in the middle of the spectrum (such as yellow-green) appear brighter than do wavelengths of light from either extreme if their amplitudes are equal. We *can* get a red light to appear as bright as a yellow-green one, but to do so we'll have to increase its amplitude, which requires more energy and is thus more expensive. Here is a fairly good argument that the lights on emergency vehicles should be yellow-green—not red. With everything else being equal, yellow-green lights appear brighter than red ones.

Now we need to consider a third characteristic of light waves: their *saturation*—which is the degree of purity of the light. Imagine a light of medium amplitude with all of its wavelengths exactly 700 nm long. Because the wavelengths are all 700 nm, it would

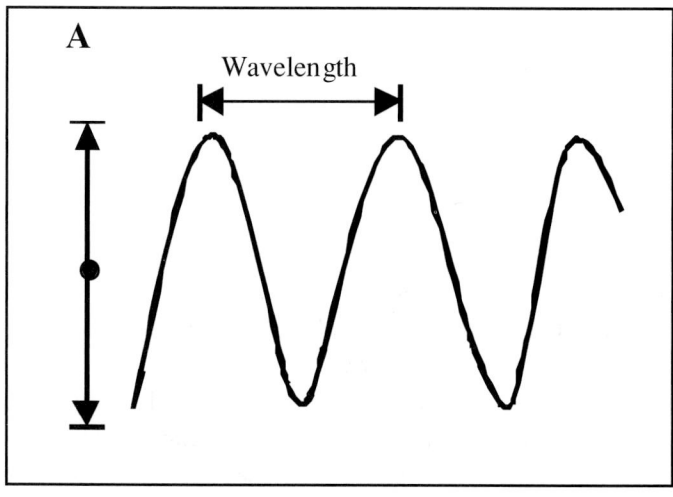

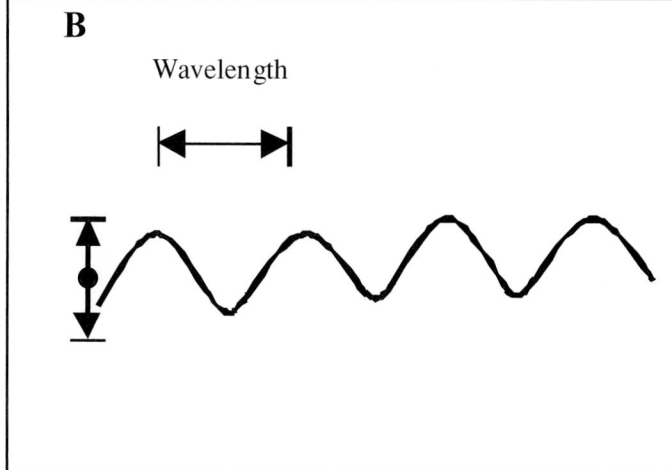

FIGURE 3.3

Representations of lightwaves differing in wavelength and wave amplitude. Wavelength gives rise to our experience of hue (or color) and wave amplitude determines our experience of brightness.

appear red. Moreover, it would appear as a pure, rich red. We call such a light *monochromatic* because it consists of light waves of one (mono) length or hue (chroma), that is, monochromatic light is highly saturated. We seldom see such lights outside the laboratory because producing a pure monochromatic light is expensive. The reddest of lights we see in our everyday experience have other wavelengths of light mixed with the predominant 700 nm red. (If the 700 nm wave did not predominate, the light wouldn't look red.) Even the red light on top of a police car has some violet, green, and yellow light in it.

As different wavelengths are mixed into a light, it lowers in saturation and looks pale and washed out. Light of the lowest possible saturation, a light consisting of a random mixture of wavelengths, is *white light*. It is something of a curiosity that white light is in fact as *impure* a light as possible. A pure light has one wavelength; a white light contains many wavelengths. True white light is as difficult to produce as is a pure monochromatic light. Fluorescent bulbs produce a reasonable approximation, but their light contains too

BEFORE YOU GO ON

- What are the three physical characteristics of light?

- What psychological experience does each characteristic of light yield?

- What is the difference between monochromatic and white light?

many wavelengths from the short or blue- violet end of the spectrum to be truly white. Light from incandescent bulbs contains too many light waves from the orange and red end of the spectrum, even if we paint the inside of the bulb with white paint. A prism can break a beam of white light into its various parts and produces a rainbow of hues. Where did all those hues come from? They were there all along, mixed together to form the white light.

We have seen that three physical characteristics of light influence our visual experience. These relationships are summarized in Figure 3.4.

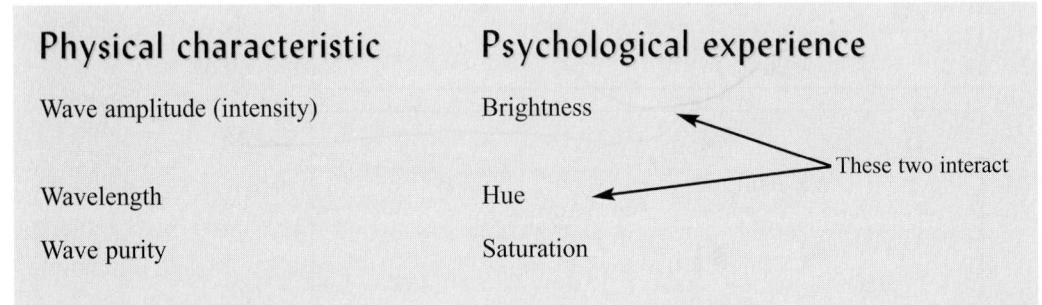

FIGURE 3.4

Relationships Between Physical Characteristics of Light and Our Psychological Experience of That Light

The Receptor for Vision: The Eye

pupil the opening of the iris, which changes size in relation to the amount of light available and in relation to emotional factors

iris the colored structure of the eye that reflexively opens or closes the pupil

lens the structure behind the iris that changes shape to focus visual images in the eye

ciliary muscles small muscles attached to the lens that control its shape and focusing capability

accommodation the vision process in which the shape of the lens is changed by the ciliary muscles to focus an image on the retina

Vision involves changing, or transducing, light wave energy into the neural energy of the nervous system, i.e., causing neurons to transmit impulses to the brain. The sense receptor for vision is the eye. The eye is a complex organ comprising several structures, most of which are involved in focusing light on the back of the eye where transduction of light energy into neural energy takes place.

Figure 3.5 illustrates the structure of the human eye. The *cornea* is the tough, round, virtually transparent outer shell of the eye. The cornea has two functions. It protects the delicate structures at the front of the eye. Also important, it is the first point where light rays are bent. In fact, about three-fourths of the bending of light waves is done by the cornea.

The **pupil** is an opening through which light enters the eye. The **iris** (the colored part of your eye) operates like the aperture of a camera lens. It can expand or contract depending on the intensity of light hitting the eye. In bright light situations, the iris closes down and lets small amounts of light into the eye. Conversely, in dim light situations the iris expands and allows more light to enter. The **lens** is a flexible structure whose shape is controlled by powerful **ciliary muscles** which expand or contract to reflexively change the shape of the lens that brings an image into focus. The lens becomes flatter when we try to focus on an object at a distance and rounder when we try to view something up close. The changing of the shape of the lens is called **accommodation**. Often an image

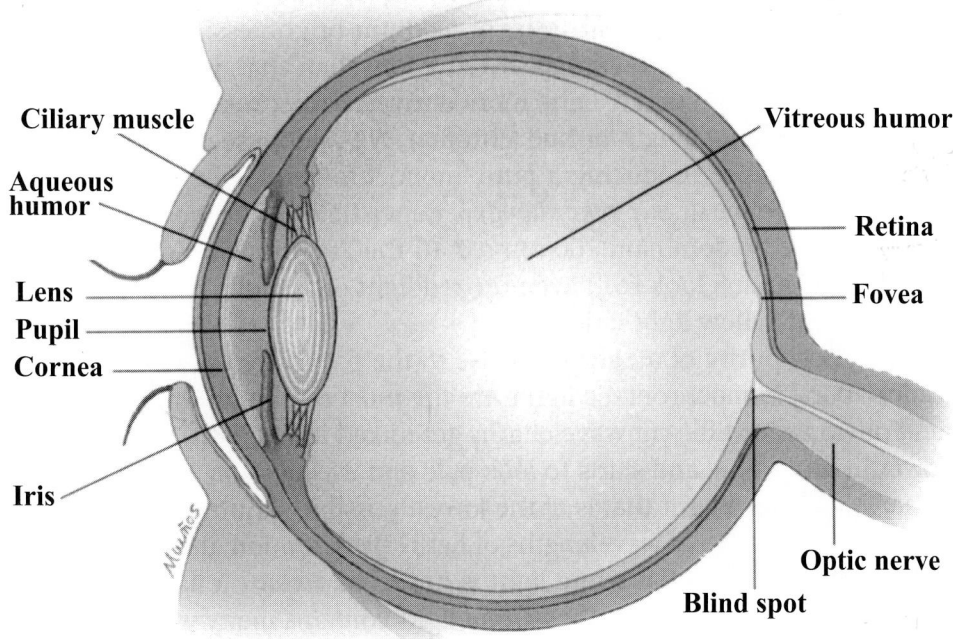

FIGURE 3.5

The major structures of the human eye

does not focus as it should because of the shape of the lens or a failure of accommodation. Sometimes even a healthy lens and functioning ciliary muscles can't focus on an image because of the shape of the eyeball. The result is either nearsightedness or farsightedness. With age, lenses harden and ciliary muscles weaken which makes it difficult to focus.

As you can see in Figure 3.5, the eye is filled with two fluids. The **aqueous humor** (humor means fluid) provides nourishment to the cornea and the other structures at the front of the eye. The aqueous humor is constantly produced and supplied to the space behind the cornea filtering out blood to keep the fluid clear. If the fluid cannot easily pass out of this space, pressure builds within the eye, causing distortions in vision or, in extreme cases, blindness. This disorder is known as *glaucoma*. The interior of the eye (behind the lens) is filled with a thicker fluid called **vitreous humor**. Its major function is to keep the eyeball spherical.

At the back of the eye is the **retina** where vision begins to take place. Light energy is transduced into neural energy here. The retina is really a series of layers of specialized nerve cells at the back surface of the eye. The location of the retina and its major landmarks are shown in Figure 3.5. Figure 3.6 shows the retina in more detail.

To describe the retina, let's move from the back of the retina toward the front. The layer of cells at the very back of the retina are the receptor cells for vision, the transducers or photoreceptors, of the eye. It is here that light wave energy is changed into neural energy. There are two types of photoreceptor cells: **rods** and **cones.** They are aptly named

aqueous humor watery fluid found in the space between the cornea and the lens that nourishes the front of the eye

vitreous humor the thick fluid behind the lens of the eye that keeps the eyeball spherical

retina layers of cells at the back of the eye that contain the photosensitive rod and cone cells

rods photosensitive cells of the retina that are most active in low levels of illumination and do not respond differentially to various wavelengths of light

cones photosensitive cells of the retina that operate best at high levels of illumination and that are responsible for color vision

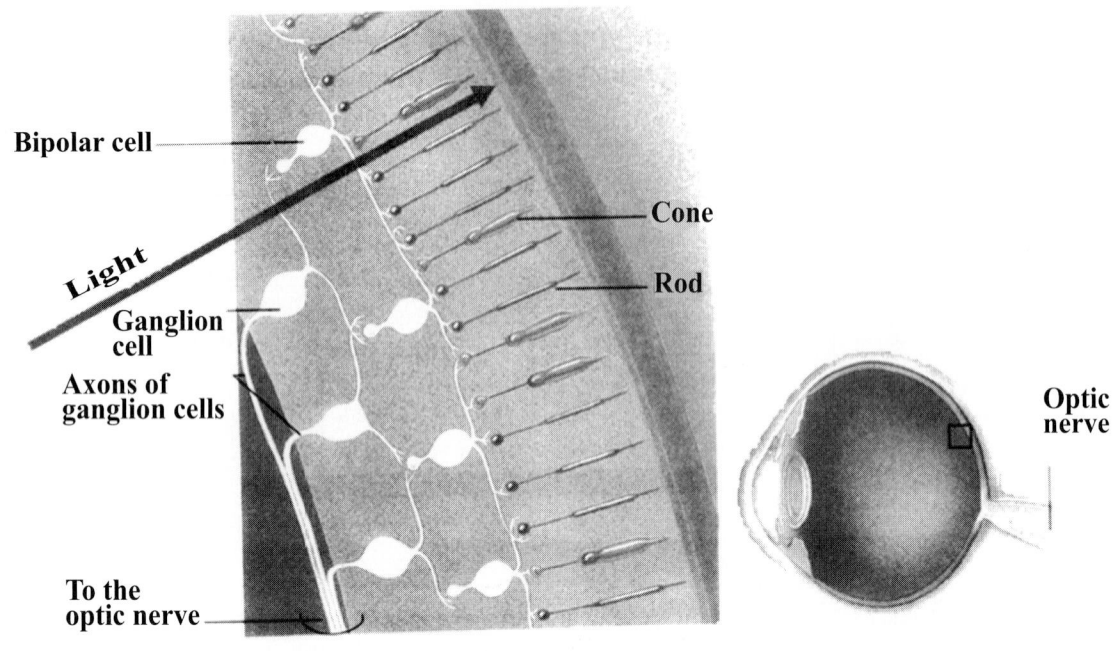

FIGURE 3.6

The major features of the human retina.

optic nerve the fiber consisting of many neurons that leaves the eye and carries impulses to the occipital lobe of the brain

fovea the region at the center of the retina consisting solely of cones where acuity is best in daylight

blind spot the small region of the retina containing no photoreceptors where the optic nerve leaves the eye

because they look like tiny rods and cones. Their tips respond to light wave energy and begin a neural impulse. The impulses travel down the rods and cones and pass on to (form a synapse with) other cells arranged in layers. Within these layers there is considerable combination and integration of neural impulses. No rod or cone has a single direct pathway to the cerebral cortex of the brain. Impulses from many rods and cones are combined within the eye by *bipolar cells* and *ganglion cells* among others. Fibers from ganglion cells form the **optic nerve**, the collection of neurons that leaves the eye and starts back toward other parts of the brain.

Two main features of the retina depicted in Figure 3.5 are the fovea and the blind spot. The **fovea** is a small area of the retina where there are few layers of cells between the entering light and the cone cells that fill the area. There are no rods in the fovea, only cones, which are tightly packed together. At the fovea our *visual acuity*, or ability to discern detail, is best, at least in daylight or in reasonably high levels of illumination. When you thread a needle, you focus the image of the needle and thread on the fovea.

The **blind spot** is where the nerve impulses from the rods and cones, having passed through many layers of cells, exit the eye. There are no rods or cones at the blind spot—nothing is there except the optic nerve threading its way back into the brain. Because there are no rods or cones, there is no vision here, which is why this area is called the blind spot. Figure 3.7 shows you how to locate your own blind spot.

BEFORE YOU GO ON

- What structures of the eye are involved in focusing light rays onto the back of the eye?
- What is the function of the retina?
- What cells comprise the retina?
- What is the fovea, and why is it important in vision?
- How does a neural impulse leave the eye?

A

B

FIGURE 3.7

This figure provides two ways to locate your blind spot. (A) Close your right eye and stare at the cross (+). Hold the page about a foot from your left eye and slowly move the page around until the star falls on your blind spot and disappears. (B) Close your right eye and stare at the cross (+). Hold the page about a foot from your left eye and slowly move the page around until the break in the line falls on your blind spot. The line will then appear to be unbroken.

More on Rods and Cones and What They Do

Let's continue our discussion about rods and cones—the two types of receptor cells in our retinas. Although they are both nerve cells, rods and cones do not look alike and have many other differences. The fact that the retina of the eye contained two different types of cells was first observed by one Max Schultze in 1865 (Goldstein, 1999). In each eye, there are about 120 million rods but only 6 million cones. They are not distributed evenly throughout the retina. Cones are concentrated in the center of the retina in the fovea, and rods are concentrated on the periphery in a band or ring around the fovea. These observations led scientists to wonder if rods and cones have different functions.

In fact, cones function best in medium to high levels of illumination (e.g., daylight) and are primarily responsible for our experience of color. On the other hand, rods operate best under conditions of reduced illumination (e.g., twilight). They are more sensitive to low-intensity light. Rods do not discriminate among wavelengths of light, which means that rods do not contribute to our appreciation of color.

Some of the evidence for these claims can be verified by our own experiences. Do you find it difficult to distinguish among colors at night or in the dark? The next time you are at the movies eating pieces of different colored candy, see if you can tell them apart without holding them up to the light of the projector. You probably won't be able to tell a green piece from a red one because they all appear black. You can't discriminate colors very well in a dark movie theater because you are seeing them primarily with your rods, which are very good at seeing in the reduced illumination of the theater but don't differentiate among wavelengths of light.

If you are looking for something small outside at night, you probably won't see it if you look directly at it. Imagine you are changing a tire at night, and you can't find one of the lug nuts you know is somewhere in the gravel. If you look directly at it, the image of the lug nut falls on your fovea. Remember, your fovea consists almost entirely of cones. Cones do not operate well in relative darkness, so you won't see the nut. To increase your chance of finding it, you have to get the image of the nut to fall on the periphery of your eye, where rods are concentrated.

Animals that see well at night have a preponderance of rods in their retinas.

One of the reasons nocturnal animals (e.g., many varieties of owls) function so well at night is because their retinas are packed with rods, which enable them to see well in the dark. Such animals usually have little or no fovea, or at least fewer cones, and are color-blind.

Let's consider another piece of evidence that supports the idea that our rods and cones provide us with two distinct types of visual experience. Dark adaptation is the process of our becoming more sensitive (our thresholds lowering) as we spend time in the dark. Figure 3.8 is a graphic representation of the dark adaptation process. It illustrates that time spent in the dark increases our sensitivity or decreases our threshold. At first, we can see only very bright lights (e.g., the light reflected from a movie screen). Later we can see dimmer lights (reflected from people in the theater), and soon still dimmer ones (reflected from pieces of candy) are detected as our threshold drops. The entire process takes about thirty minutes.

BEFORE YOU GO ON

- What are the functions of the cones?
- What are the functions of the rods?
- Describe the dark adaptation curve.
- What does the dark adaptation curve suggest about the nature of the human visual system?

But there is something strange going on. The dark adaptation curve is not smooth and regular (see Figure 3.8). After eight to ten minutes, there is a change in the shape of the curve. This break in the smoothness of the curve is called the *rod-cone break*. For seven or eight minutes, the cones increase their sensitivity (represented by the first part of the curve). But cones are basically daylight receptors. They're not designed for seeing in the dark, and after a few minutes, they become as sensitive as they can get. They "drop out" of the curve. At about the same time, the rods lower their threshold and become even more sensitive (represented by the part of the curve after the "break"). This explanation of rods and cones acting differently has remain unchallenged for over 60 years (Hecht, 1934).

We've reviewed the nature of light and the basic structures of the eye. Now let's examine how neural impulses that leave our retinas travel to the occipital lobes of the cerebral cortex.

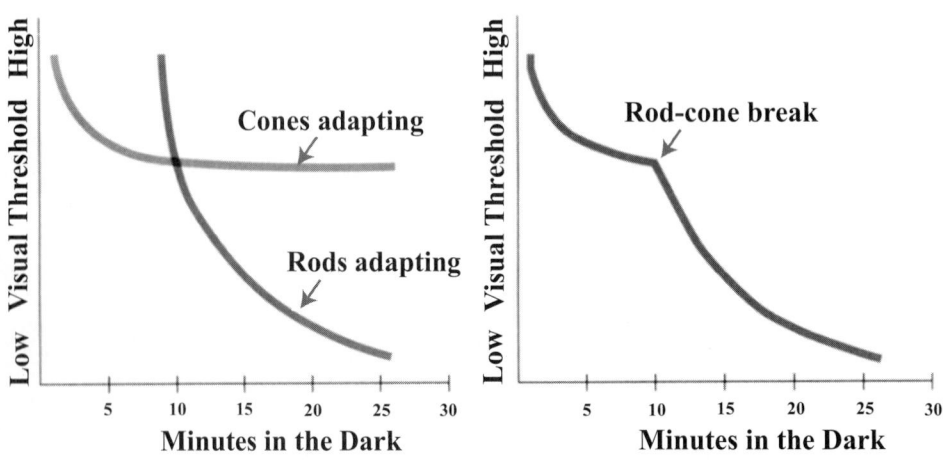

FIGURE 3.8

The dark adaptation curve. In the graph on the left we see that the cones begin adapting immediately, but then begin "dropping out" at about the 10-minute mark. Rods then begin adapting and continue until about 30 minutes have been spent in the dark. When these two curves are combined to give us a view of what happens in general with time spent in the dark, we have the curve at the right which shows the "rod-cone break."

The Visual Pathway After the Retina

Considerable visual processing takes place within the layers of the retina; there are, after all, many more rods and cones in the retina than there are ganglion cell fibers leaving it. Visual information continues to change as it races back to the visual area of the occipital lobe of the cerebral cortex.

To trace the pathway of nerve fibers between the eyes and the cortex, we need to introduce the concept of left and right visual fields. When you view the world, everything to your left is in your left visual field, whereas everything to your right is in your right visual field. In Figure 3.9 the left visual field is white and the right visual field is gray. Stimuli in our left visual field end up represented in our right occipital lobe, and stimuli in our right visual field end up represented in our left occipital lobe.

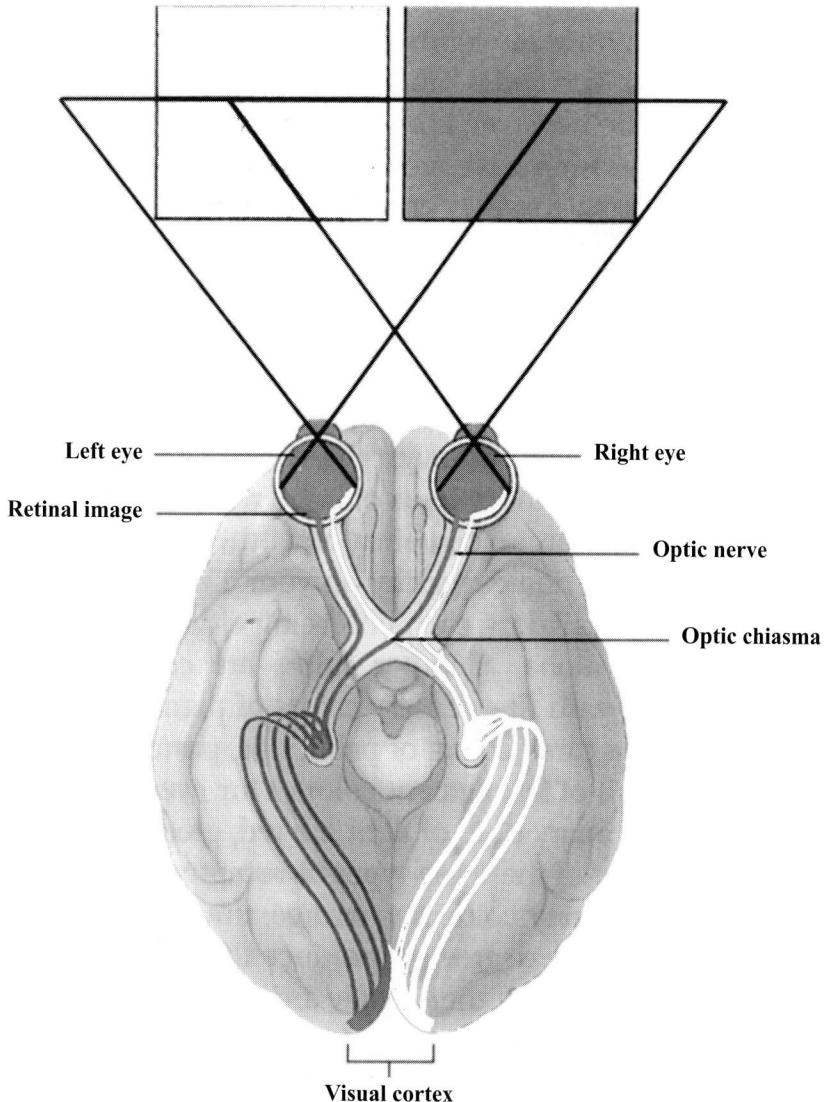

FIGURE 3.9

In keeping with the principle of cross laterality, stimuli from the left visual field are sent to the right occipital lobe for further processing, whereas stimuli from the right visual field are sent to the left occipital lobe.

optic chiasma the location in the brain where impulses from light in the left visual field cross to the right side of the brain, and impulses from light in the right visual field cross to the left side of the brain

Where and how fibers in the optic nerve get directed occurs largely in the **optic chiasma.** Notice in Figure 3.9 that, in fact, each eye receives light energy from both visual fields. Light that enters our left eye from the left initiates neural impulses that cross to the right side of the brain at the optic chiasma, whereas light that enters our left eye from the right visual field initiates neural impulses that go straight back to the left hemisphere. Now see if you can describe what happens to light that enters the right eye.

From the optic chiasma, nerve fibers pass through other centers in the brain including the lateral geniculate nucleus. Nerve fibers also pass through a cluster of cells on each side of the brain called the *superior colliculus* that controls the movement of our eyes over a patterned stimulus, perhaps fixing our gaze on some aspect of the pattern. Curiously, people who are totally blind because of damage to the occipital lobes of their cerebral cortex can often locate visual stimuli in space. That is, they can point to a light they cannot "see"—probably an example of the superior colliculus at work (e.g., Weiskrantz et al., 1974). Beyond the superior colliculus, nerve cells form synapses with neurons in the thalamus, which project neural impulses to the layers of cells in the visual cortex of the occipital lobe.

BEFORE YOU GO ON

- Trace the course of the visual neural impulse after it leaves the retina.

- What does the superior colliculus do?

- What are the right and left visual fields and where does information from each end up in the brain?

- Where is the final representation of a visual stimulus located in the brain?

It is important to note that vision doesn't really happen in our eyes. The eye is the structure that contains the transducers that convert light energy into neural impulses, but the experience of "seeing" a stimulus occurs in our brain. Our brain reassembles a myriad of neural impulses into one image in our awareness—one complete visual field, not one divided into left and right The detection and interpretation of patterns of light, shade, color, and motion are functions of the cerebral cortex.

Color Vision and Color Blindness

Explaining how the eye responds to various intensities of light is simple. High-intensity lights cause more rapid firings of neural impulses than do low-intensity lights, and high-intensity lights stimulate more cells to fire than do lights of low intensity. How the eye responds to differing wavelengths of light to produce differing experiences of color, however, is another story. Here things are not simple at all. Two theories of color vision, proposed many years ago, have received research support. As is often the case with competing theories that explain the same phenomenon, both are probably partially correct.

trichromatic theory a theory of color vision postulating the existence of three types of color photoreceptors in the eye (red, green, and blue)

The older of the two theories of color vision is the **trichromatic theory**. It was first proposed by Thomas Young early in the nineteenth century and was revised by Hermann von Helmholtz, a noted physiologist, about 50 years later. As its name suggests, the trichromatic theory proposes that the eye contains *three* distinct receptors for color. Although there is some overlap, each receptor responds best to one of three *primary hues* of light: red, green, or blue. These hues are primary because the careful combination of the three produces all other colors. This happens every day on your TV screen because the picture consists of a pattern of very small red, green, or blue dots. From these three wavelengths, all other colors are constructed or integrated. (Don't confuse the three primary hues with the primary colors of pigment, which are red, blue, and yellow. The primary colors of paint, dye, pastel, etc., can be mixed together to form all other pigment colors. Our eyes respond to light, not pigment, and the three primary hues of light are red, green, and blue.)

Because the sensitivity of the three types of receptors overlaps, when our eyes are stimulated by a nonprimary color, for example, orange, the orange-hued light stimulates each receptor to varying degrees to produce the experience of orange. What gives this theory credibility is that there are such receptor cells in the human retina: cones, which are responsible for color vision. The relative sensitivity of these three cone systems is shown in Figure 3.10.

Ewald Hering thought the Young-Helmholtz theory left a bit to be desired, and in 1870 he proposed the **opponent-process theory.** Hering believed there are three pairs of visual mechanisms that respond to different wavelengths of light: a blue-yellow processor, a red-green processor, and a black-white processor.

Each mechanism is capable of responding to either of the two hues that give it its name, but not both. That is, the blue-yellow processor can respond to blue or to yellow, but cannot handle both simultaneously. The second mechanism responds to red or to green, but not both. The third mechanism codes brightness. Thus, the members of each pair work in opposition, hence the theory's name. If blue is excited, yellow is inhibited. If red is excited, green is inhibited. A light may appear to be a mixture of red and yellow,

opponent-process theory a theory of color vision suggesting that there are three pairs of visual mechanisms that respond to different wavelengths of light (blue-yellow, red-green, and black-white)

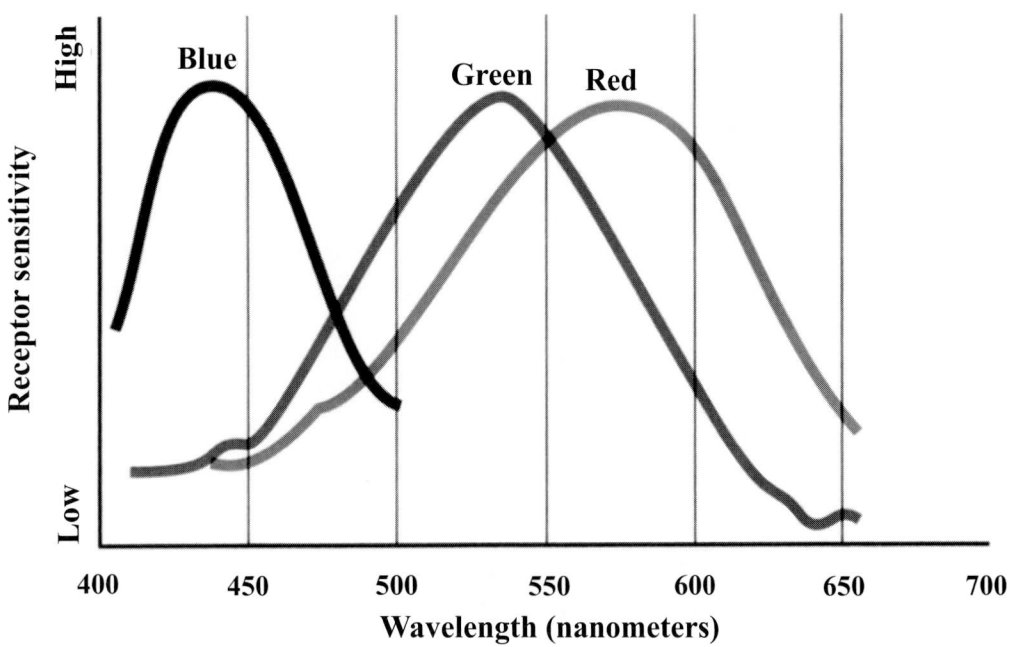

FIGURE 3.10

The relative sensitivities of three types of cones to lights of differing wavelengths. Although there is considerable overlap, each type is maximally sensitive to wavelengths corresponding to the primary hues of light: blue, green, and red.

but it cannot be seen as a mixture of red and green because red and green cannot be excited at the same time. (It *is* difficult to imagine what "reddish green" or "bluish yellow" would look like. Can you picture a light that is bright and dim at the same time?)

Although the opponent-process theory may seem complicated, there are some strong signs that Hering was on the right track. Excitatory-inhibitory mechanisms such as he proposed for red-green, blue-yellow, and black-white have been found. They are not at the level of rods and cones in the retina as Hering thought, but at the layer of the ganglion cells (see Figure 3.6) and in a small area of the thalamus.

Support for Hering's theory also comes from our experiences with *negative afterimages*. If you stare at a bright green figure for a few minutes and then shift your gaze to a white surface, you notice an image of a red figure. Where did that come from? While you stared at the green figure, the green component of the red-green process fatigued because of the stimulation it received. When you stared at the white surface, the red and green components were equally stimulated; but because the green component was fatigued, the red predominated and produced the image of a red figure.

Evidence supporting both theories of normal color vision comes from studies of persons with color vision defects. Defective color vision of some sort occurs in about 8 percent of males and slightly less than 0.5 percent of females. Most cases are genetic. It makes sense that if cones are our receptor cells for the discrimination of color, people with some deficiency in color perception would have a problem with their cones. This is consistent with the Young-Helmholtz theory. In fact, there *is* a noticeable lack of one particular type of cone in the most common of the color vision deficiencies (dichromatism); which type depends on the color that is "lost." Those people who are red-green color-blind, for instance, have trouble distinguishing between red and green. People with this type of color blindness also have trouble distinguishing yellow from either red or green. The deficiency is not in actually seeing reds or greens. It is in distinguishing reds and greens from other colors. Put another way, someone who is red-green color-blind can clearly see a bright red apple; it just looks no different than a bright green apple.

Some color vision defects can be traced to cones in the retina, but damage to cells higher in the visual pathway is implicated in some rare cases of color vision problems. When such problems do occur, there are losses for both red and green or both yellow and blue as predicted by the opponent-process theory (e.g., Schiffman, 1990).

Because cone cells that respond differently to red, blue, and green light have been found in the retina, we cannot dismiss the trichromatic theory. However, there are cells that operate the way the opponent-process theory predicts, so we cannot dismiss that theory either. Which one is right? Probably both. Our experience of color likely depends on the interaction of cone cells and opponent-process cells within our visual pathway—a marvelous system indeed.

BEFORE YOU GO ON

- How does the trichromatic theory of color vision account for color vision?

- How does the opponent-process theory account for color vision?

- What evidence exists to support the theories of color vision?

- What is color blindness, and how does what we know about color blindness inform us about the mechanisms underlying normal color vision?

AUDITION: THE SENSE OF HEARING

Vision is an important sense. Try this experiment on your own. Attempt to bypass your reliance on vision and spend the better part of a day doing without it. Try to go about your normal everyday activities blindfolded. One thing you will realize almost immediately is just how heavily you rely on vision. Consider for a moment the quantity and quality of information you receive from your other senses. You may gain a new appreciation of how well they inform you of the wonder of your environment: the aroma and taste of a well-prepared barbecue; the sounds of birds and music; the touch and feel of textures and surfaces; the sense of where your body is and what it's doing; the feedback from your muscles as you move.

The Stimulus for Hearing: Sound

The stimulus for vision is light; the stimulus for hearing is sound. Sound is a series of air pressures (or some other medium, such as water) beating against our ear. These pressures are sound waves. As a source of sound vibrates, it pushes air against our ears in waves. Like light waves, sound waves have three major physical characteristics: amplitude, frequency (the inverse of wavelength), and purity. Each is related to a different psychological experience. We'll briefly consider each.

The *amplitude* of a sound wave depicts its intensity—the force with which air strikes the ear. The intensity of a sound determines the psychological experience of *loudness*; the higher its amplitude, the louder the sound. Quiet, soft sounds have low amplitudes.

The physical intensity of sound is measured in units of force per unit area (or pressure). Loudness is a psychological characteristic, measured by people's experiences, not by instruments. The *decibel scale* of sound intensity measures perceived loudness. Its zero point is the absolute threshold, or the lowest intensity of sound that can be detected.

Our ears are very sensitive receptors and respond to very low levels of sound intensity. In fact, if our ears were any more sensitive then they are, we would hear molecules of air bouncing against our eardrums. Hudspeth (1997) gives us this analogy: Individual receptor cells for sound, deep in our inner ears, need only to be displaced by a distance as small as the diameter of a hydrogen atom (!) to produce the experience of sound.

If sound intensities are high enough, we literally can "feel" sound. Sounds in the 90-120 decibel range (such as those produced by jet aircraft engines or fast-moving subway trains) are often "felt" as much as heard. Because sounds in this range of loudness are commonly encountered in dance clubs and at concerts, this shift from hearing a sound to feeling a sound has been named "the rock and roll threshold" (Dibble, 1995; McAngus-Todd & Cody, 2000). Any kind of prolonged exposure to very loud, high intensity sounds can cause deafness. When then-President Bill Clinton turned 51, he was fitted with hearing aids. His hearing loss attributed—at least in part—to his playing a saxophone in a jazz band. Hearing loss among rock musicians is a real and serious concern. There is even a webpage (www.hearnet.com) posting advice and treatment options under the title page "Hearing Education and Awareness for Rockers." On the other hand, the San (or "Bushmen") of the Kalahari desert in Africa have significantly better hearing at older ages than do natives of the United States. There may be several reasons for this, but the relative quiet of the desert environment seems to be a significant factor (Berry et al., 1992).

The second physical characteristic of sound is *wave frequency* or the number of times a wave repeats itself within a given period. For sound, frequency is measured in terms of how many waves of pressure are exerted every second. The unit of sound frequency is the *hertz*, which is abbreviated Hz. If a sound wave repeats itself fifty times in one second, it is a 50- Hz sound; 500 repetitions is a 500-Hz sound.

The psychological experience produced by sound wave frequency is pitch. *Pitch* is our experience of how high or low a tone is. The musical scale represents differences in pitch. Low frequencies correspond to bass tones, such as those made by foghorns or tubas. High frequencies correspond to high-pitched sounds, such as the musical tones produced by flutes or the squeals of smoke detectors.

Just as the human eye cannot respond to all possible wavelengths of radiant energy, the human ear cannot respond to all possible sound wave frequencies. A healthy human ear responds to sound wave frequencies between 20 Hz and 20,000 Hz. If air strikes our ears at a rate less than twenty times per second, we do not hear a sound. Sound vibrations faster than 20,000 Hz cannot be heard, at least not by the human ear. Many animals *can* hear sounds with frequencies above 20,000 Hz, such as those produced by dog whistles.

A third characteristic of sound waves is *wave purity,* or *wave complexity*. You'll recall that we seldom experience monochromatic lights. Pure sounds are also uncommon in our everyday experience. A pure sound would be one in which all waves from the sound source vibrate at exactly the same frequency. Such sounds can be produced electronically, and tuning forks produce approximations, but most of the sounds we hear every day are complex sounds consisting of many different sound wave frequencies.

A tone of middle C on the piano is a tone of 256 Hz. (The source of the sound, here a piano wire, is vibrating 256 times per second.) A pure 256-Hz tone consists of sound waves (vibrations) of only that frequency. As it happens, the middle C of the piano has many other wave frequencies mixed in with the predominant 256-Hz wave frequency. (If the 256-Hz wave did not predominate, the tone wouldn't sound like middle C.)

The psychological quality or character of a sound that reflects its degree of purity is called *timbre*. For example, each musical instrument produces a unique variety or mixture of overtones, so each type of musical instrument sounds a little different from others. If a trumpet, a violin, and a piano play the same note, we can tell the instruments apart because of our experience of timbre. In fact, any instrument can display different timbres depending on how it is constructed and played.

We learned that the opposite of a pure light was white light—a light consisting of all wavelengths of the visible spectrum. Again we see the parallel between vision and audition. If a sound source produces all the possible sound wave frequencies, it sounds like a buzzing noise. The best example is what one hears when a radio is tuned to a position between stations (FM works better than AM). This soft, buzzing sound, containing a range of many audible sound frequencies, is useful in masking or covering other unwanted sounds. We call a random mixture of sound frequencies *white noise*, just as we called a random mixture of wavelengths of light, white light. If you tune your radio between stations you will get a good example of white noise.

The analogy between light and sound and vision and hearing is striking. Both types of stimulus energy can be represented as waves. In both cases, each of the physical characteristics of the waves (amplitude, length or frequency, and purity or complexity) is correlated with a psychological experience. All of these relationships are summarized in Figure 3.11.

> **BEFORE YOU GO ON**
>
> - What are the three physical characteristics of sound?
>
> - What psychological experiences are related to the three characteristics of sound?

Physical characteristic	Psychological experience for vision	Psychological experience for hearing
Wave amplitude	Brightness	Loudness
Wavelength or frequency	Hue	Pitch
Wave purity or mixture	Saturation	Timbre

FIGURE 3.11

A Summary of the Ways in Which the Physical Characteristics of Light and Sound Waves Affect Our Psychological Experiences of Vision and Hearing

The Receptor for Hearing: The Ear

The energy of sound wave pressures is transduced into neural impulses deep inside the ear. As with the eye, most of the structures of the ear simply transfer energy from without to within. Figure 3.12 is a drawing of the major structures of the ear. We'll use it to follow the path of sound waves from the environment to the receptor cells.

The outer ear is called the *pinna*. Its function is to collect sound waves from the air around it and funnel them through the *auditory canal* toward the eardrum. Air waves push against the **eardrum** (technically called the *tympanic membrane*) setting it in motion so that it vibrates at the same rate as the sound source. The eardrum then transmits vibrations to three very small bones (collectively called *ossicles*) in the middle ear. In order from the eardrum inward, they are the **malleus**, **incus**, and **stapes** (pronounced *stape-eez*). These bones pass vibrations, while amplifying them, to the *oval window* membrane, which is like the eardrum but smaller. As the ossicles pass sound vibrations to the oval window they amplify them which increases their force.

When sound waves pass beyond the oval window, the vibrations are in the *inner ear*. The major structure of the inner ear is the snail-like **cochlea**, which contains the actual receptor cells, the transducers, for hearing. As the stapes vibrates against the oval

eardrum the outermost membrane of the ear which is set in motion by the vibrations of a sound and transmits vibrations to the ossicles

malleus, incus, and **stapes** three small bones collectively known as the ossicles that intensify sound vibrations and transmit them from the eardrum to the oval window

cochlea the snail-like part of the inner ear where sound waves become neural impulses

basilar membrane a structure within the cochlea that vibrates and thus stimulates the hair cells of the inner ear

hair cells the receptor cells for hearing located in the cochlea and stimulated by the vibrating basilar membrane; they send neural impulses to the temporal lobe of the brain

window, fluid inside the cochlea is set in motion at the same rate. When the fluid within the cochlea moves, the **basilar membrane** is bent up and down. The basilar membrane is a small structure that runs about the full length of the cochlea. Hearing takes place when very tiny mechanical receptors called **hair cells** are stimulated by the vibrations of the basilar membrane. Through a process not fully understood, the mechanical pressure of the basilar membrane causes the hair cells to bend. The neural impulses leave the ear traveling on the auditory nerve toward the temporal lobe. Thus, most of the structures of the ear are responsible for amplifying and directing waves of pressure to the hair cells in the cochlea where the neural impulse begins.

BEFORE YOU GO ON

- Through what structures does sound pressure enter the ear?

- What are the principal functions of the ossicles?

- What happens to sound once it reaches the oval window?

- What is the function of the basilar membrane and hair cells?

- To what part of the brain does the auditory nerve transmit its neural impulse?

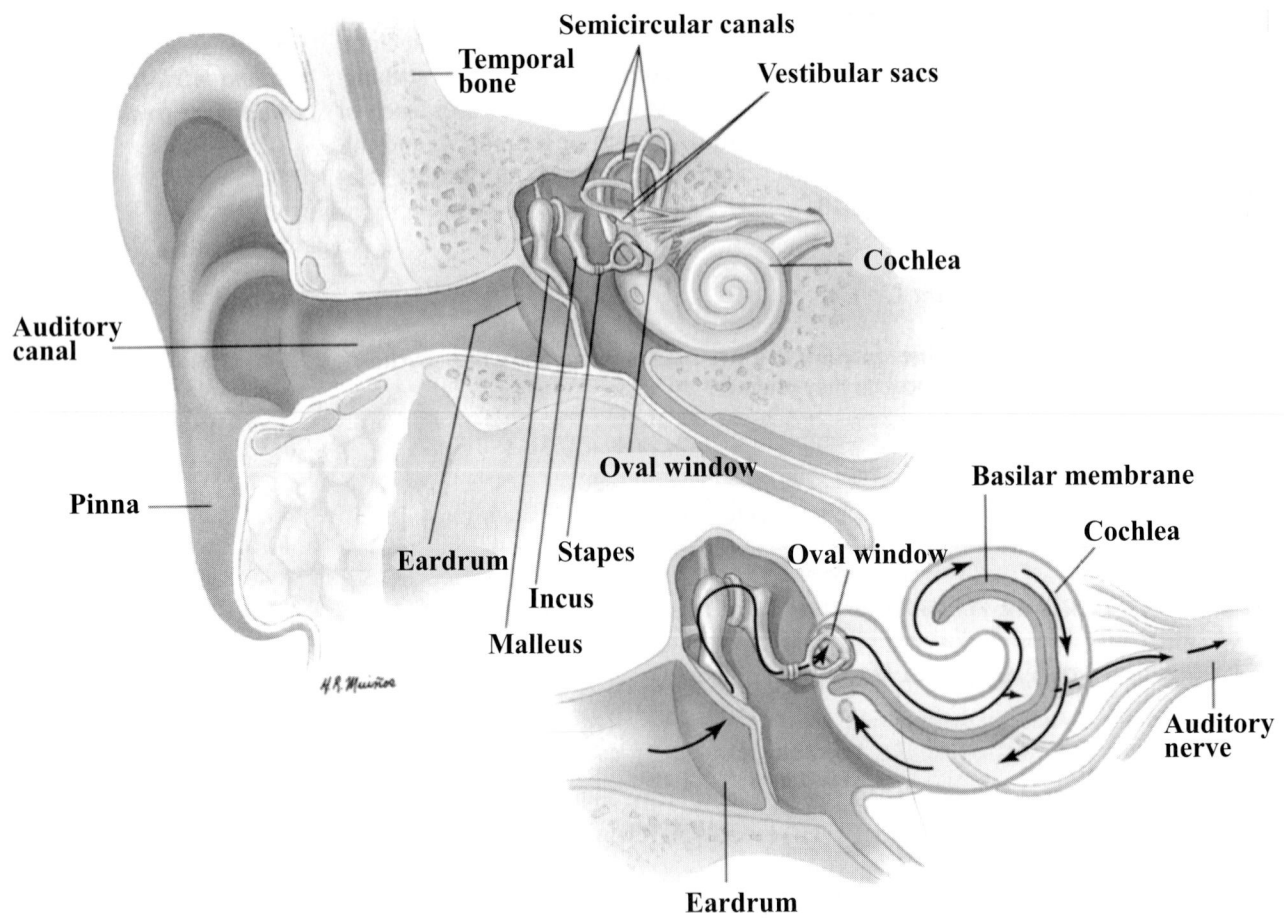

FIGURE 3.12

The major structures of the human ear

THE CHEMICAL SENSES

Taste and smell are referred to as chemical senses because the stimuli for both are molecules of chemical compounds. For taste, the chemicals are dissolved in liquid (usually the saliva in our mouths). For smell, they are dissolved in the air that reaches the smell receptors high inside our noses. The technical term for taste is *gustation*; for smell, it is *olfaction.*

If you have ever eaten while suffering from a head cold, you appreciate the extent to which our experiences of taste and smell are interrelated. Most foods seem to lose their taste when we cannot smell them. This is why we differentiate between the *flavor* of foods (which includes such qualities as odor and texture) and the *taste* of foods. A simple test demonstrates this point. While blindfolded, eat a small piece of peeled apple and a small piece of peeled potato. See if you can tell the difference between the two. You shouldn't have any trouble with this discrimination. Now hold your nose very tightly and try again. Without your sense of smell to help you, discrimination on the basis of taste alone is very difficult.

Taste (Gustation)

Our experience of the flavors of foods depends so heavily on our sense of smell, texture, and temperature that we sometimes have to wonder if there is truly a sense of taste. Well, there is. Even with odor and texture held constant, tastes can vary. Taste has four basic psychological qualities (and many combinations of these four): sweet, salt, sour, and bitter. Most foods derive their special taste from a unique combination of these four basic taste sensations. You can generate a list of foods that produce each of these sensations. Notice that it is more difficult to think of examples of sour- and bitter-tasting foods than of sweet or salty ones. This reflects the fact that we usually don't like bitter and sour tastes and have learned to avoid them. Beyond that, specific taste preferences are culturally conditioned—a reality you may have experienced the first time you visited a restaurant that serves food from another culture (e.g., Berry et al., 1992 p. 135). Even newborn infants can discriminate among the four basic taste qualities of sour, sweet, salty, and bitter. A newborn will, for example, make a face, wrinkle his nose and turn away when a sour liquid such as grapefruit juice is placed in his mouth. As we develop through childhood, adolescence, and adulthood, our preferences for foods (and tastes) may change, but changes have more to do with learning and experience than with our gustatory receptors. With old age, however, as taste buds begin to fail, persons often find themselves using more sugar, more salt, more pepper, etc., than they did when they were younger.

The receptor cells for taste are located in the tongue and are called **taste buds.** We have about 10,000 taste buds, and each one consists of several parts (Figure 3.13). When parts of taste buds die (or are killed by foods that are too hot, for example), new segments

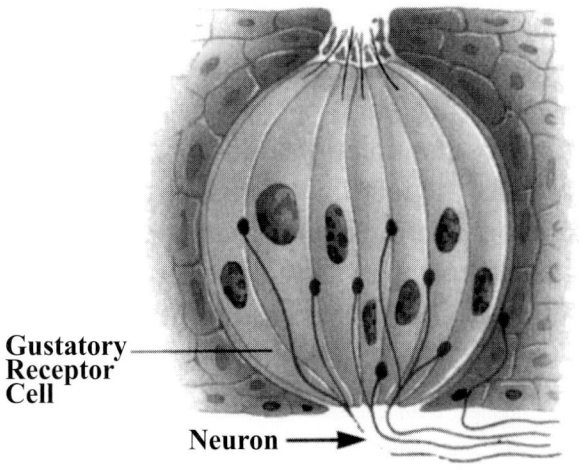

Gustatory Receptor Cell

Neuron

FIGURE 3.13

Enlarged view of a taste bud, the receptor for gustation.

taste buds receptors for taste that are located on the tongue

are regenerated. Fortunately, we always grow new taste receptor cells. This makes taste a unique sense: its receptor cells, the taste buds, are nerve cells, and we've already noted that nerve cells are usually not replaced when they die.

Taste buds respond primarily to chemicals that produce one of the four basic taste qualities. However, some receptor cells respond best to salts, whereas others respond primarily to sweet-producing chemicals, such as sugars. These receptors are not evenly distributed on the surface of the tongue; receptors for sweet tastes are concentrated at the tip of the tongue, for example. Nonetheless, all four qualities of taste can be detected at all locations of the tongue. Recent research (Cruz & Green, 2000) provides evidence that in addition to responding to the various chemicals that we put in our mouths, our taste buds also respond to different temperatures. In fact, as many as half of the neurons in mammalian taste pathways—from the taste buds to the brain—respond to temperature. For example, warming the very tip of the tongue from a cold temperature gives rise to the experience of sweetness.

Smell (Olfaction)

Smell is a poorly understood sense. It often gives us great pleasure; think of the aroma of bacon frying over a wood fire or of freshly picked flowers. Smell can also produce considerable displeasure; consider the smell of a skunk, old garbage, or rotten eggs.

The sense of smell originates in hair cells located high in the nasal cavity, very close to the brain itself. We know that the pathway from these receptors to the brain is the most direct and shortest of all the senses (see Figure 3.14). What we don't understand is how molecules suspended in air and gases stimulate the small hair cells of the olfactory receptors to fire neural impulses.

pheromones chemicals that produce an odor used as a method of communication between organisms

The sense of smell is very important for many nonhumans. Many animals, including humans, emit chemicals called **pheromones** that produce distinctive odors. Sometimes pheromones are released by cells in the skin, sometimes in the urine, and occasionally from special glands (in some deer, this gland is located near the rear hoof). One purpose of pheromones is to mark territory. If you take a dog for a walk and discover that he wants to stop and deposit small amounts of urine on almost every signpost, he is leaving a pheromone message that says, "I have been here; this is my odor; this is my turf."

vomeronasal organ (VNO) organs located along the nasal septum believed to be involved in the detection of pheromones

Pheromones are detected by a mechanism different from the receptors involved in the detection of common odors. The primary organ involved in the detection of pheromones is the **vomeronasal organ (VNO).** It has long been acknowledged that animals have the VNO. However, for a time it was believed that the human VNO disappeared during prenatal development. We now know that the VNO can also be found in humans. The human VNO comprises two small sacs (about 2mm deep) located on each side of the nasal septum (Taylor, 1994).

The VNO in most animals and humans appears to be involved in detecting pheromones that regulate behaviors like mating, territoriality, and aggressiveness (Hines, 1997, Taylor, 1994). The possibility has been raised that the human VNO is involved in sexual attraction. In fact, there are companies that make perfumes for men and women that sup-

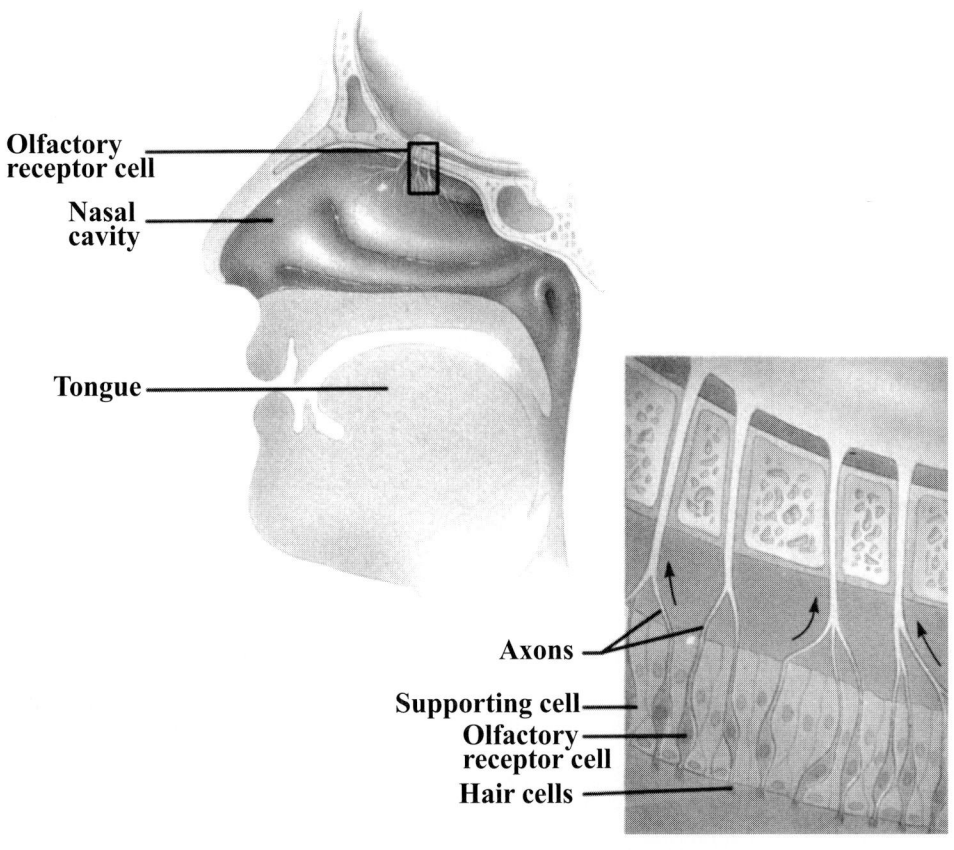

FIGURE 3.14

The olfactory system, showing its proximity to the brain and the transducers for smell— the hair cells.

posedly stimulate the VNO. Even though it makes sense that the VNO would be involved in human sexuality (as it is in animal sexuality), we must keep in mind that humans respond to many more sexual signals than pheromones. Taylor (1994) points out that humans rely on a host of sexual signals including visual (attractiveness), auditory and tactile cues. That notwithstanding, it is possible that the VNO plays a role in the mediation of sexuality in humans. Not enough research is available to date to say what, if any, role the VNO plays in this area (Cutler, Friedmann, & McCoy, 1998).

There is some evidence that human pheromone production is related to the sex hormones. For example, women who live in close quarters and share the same air supply (and the same pheromones, it is presumed) for a long time, soon synchronize their menstrual cycles. The same thing occurs in rats when the only contact between them is the same air supply and the same odors (McClintock, 1971, 1979).

BEFORE YOU GO ON

- What are the four basic psychological qualities of taste?
- Where are the receptors for taste located, and what are they called?
- Where are the receptors for the sense of smell located?
- What is the vomeronasal organ, and what does it do?
- What are pheromones, and what is their function?
- How do the senses of smell and taste interact?
- What is the vomeronasal organ, and what is it believed to do?

THE SKIN, OR CUTANEOUS, SENSES

Most of us take our skin for granted; we seldom think about it very much. We frequently abuse our skin by overexposing it to the sun's rays in summer and to excess cold in winter. We scratch it, cut it, scrape it, and wash away millions of its cells every time we shower or bathe.

Figure 3.15 is a diagram of some of the structures found in an area of skin from a hairy part of the human body. Each square inch of the layers of our skin contains nearly 20 million cells including many special sense receptors. Some skin receptor cells have *free nerve endings*, whereas others have some sort of covering. We call these latter cells *encapsulated nerve endings*, of which there are many types. Our skin somehow gives rise to our psychological experience of touch or pressure, and of warmth and cold. It would be convenient if each of the various receptor cells within our skin gave rise to a different type of psychological sensation, but this does not seem to be the case.

One of the problems in studying the cutaneous senses is trying to determine which cells in the skin give rise to different sensations of pressure and temperature. We can discriminate clearly between a light touch and a strong jab in the arm and between vibrations, tickles, and itches. A simple proposal is that there are different receptors in the skin responsible for each sensation, but this is not supported by facts. Although some types of receptor cells are more sensitive to some types of stimuli, current thinking is that our ability to discriminate among types of cutaneous sensation is due to the unique combination of responses the many receptor cells have to various types of stimulation.

As good as our cutaneous senses are, those of the common cockroach are—in some ways—even more remarkable. Cockroaches are incredibly good at avoiding a swat from a newspaper or the heel of a shoe because they have tiny hairs on their posterior that

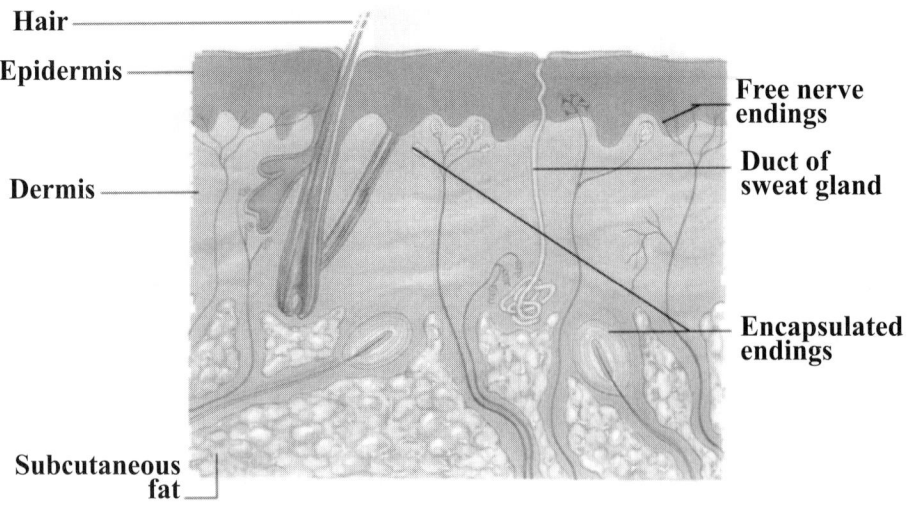

FIGURE 3.15

A patch of hairy skin, showing the layers of skin and several nerve cells

detect even the most minute changes in air flow around them. This sense (which few other organisms have) allows a cockroach to "surmise the direction of an attack and scurry away to avoid being eaten" (or squished) (Rinberg & Davidowitz, 2000, p. 756).

By carefully stimulating very small areas of the skin, we can locate areas that are sensitive to temperature. We are convinced that warm and cold temperatures each stimulate specific locations on the skin. Even so, there is no consistent pattern of receptor cells found at these locations, called temperature spots. That is, we have not yet located specific receptor cells for cold or hot. Our experience of hot seems to come from the simultaneous stimulation of both warm and cold spots. A rather ingenious demonstration shows how this works. Cold water is run through one metal tube, and warm water is run through another. The tubes are coiled together (Figure 3.16). If you grasp the coiled tubes, you would experience heat; the tubes would feel hot even if you knew they weren't.

Warm water　　**Cold water**

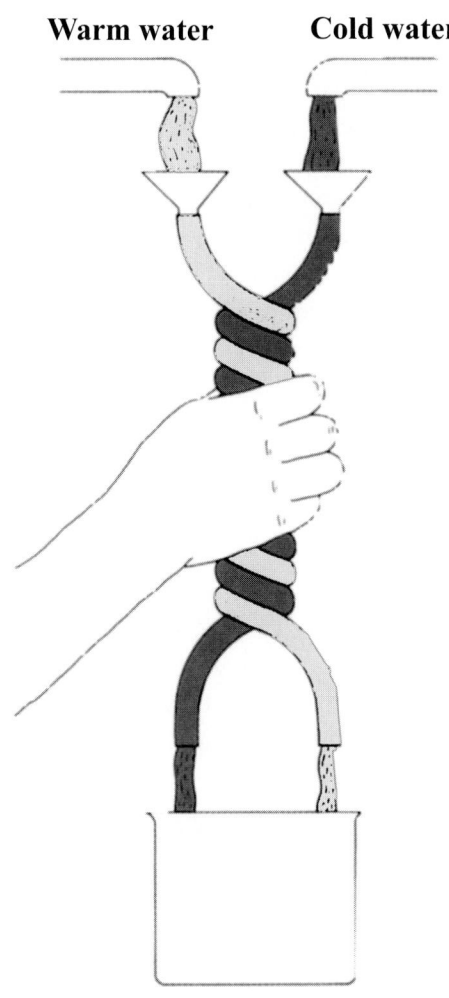

FIGURE 3.16

A demonstration that our sense of what is hot can be constructed from sensations of what is warm and cold. Even if you know that the coiled tubes contain only warm and cold water, when you grasp the tubes they will feel very hot.

THE POSITION SENSES

Another sensory capacity we often take for granted is our ability to know how and where our bodies are positioned in space. Although we seldom worry about it, we can quickly become aware of how our bodies are positioned in regard to the pull of gravity. We also get sensory information about where various parts of our body are in relation to one another. We can tell if we are moving or standing still. And, unless we are on a roller coaster or racing across a field, we usually adapt to these sensory messages quickly and pay little attention to them.

Most of the information about where we are in space comes from our sense of vision. If we want to know how we are oriented in space, we simply look around. But we can do the same sort of thing with our eyes closed. We have two systems of position sense over and above what vision can provide. One, the **vestibular sense**, tells us about balance, about where we are in relation to gravity, and about acceleration or deceleration. The other, the kinesthetic sense, tells us about the movement or position of our muscles and joints.

vestibular sense the position sense that conveys balance, where we are in relation to gravity, and acceleration or deceleration

The receptors for the vestibular sense are located on either side of the head near the inner ears. Five chambers are located there: three semicircular canals and two vestibular sacs. Their orientation is shown in Figure 3.12. Each of these chambers is filled with fluid. When our head moves in any direction, fluid in the semicircular canals moves, drawn by gravity or the force of our head accelerating in space. The vestibular sacs contain very small solid particles that float in the fluid within the sacs. When we move, these particles are forced against one side of a sac, and they stimulate hair cells that start neural impulses. Overstimulation of the receptor cells in the vestibular sacs or semicircular canals can lead to feelings of dizziness or nausea, reasonably enough called *motion sickness*.

kinesthetic sense the position sense that tells us the position of various parts of our bodies and what our muscles and joints are doing

Receptors for our **kinesthetic sense** are located primarily in our joints, but some information also comes from muscles and tendons. These receptors sense the position and movements of parts of the body—again, information to which we seldom attend. Impulses from these receptors travel to the brain through pathways in the spinal cord. They provide excellent examples of reflex actions. As muscles in the front of your upper arm (your biceps) contract, the corresponding muscles in the back of your arm (triceps) relax so you can bend your arm at the elbow. How fortunate it is that our kinesthetic receptors, operating reflexively through the spinal cord, take care of these details without our having to consciously manipulate all of the appropriate muscular activity. In fact, about the only time we realize that our kinesthetic system is functioning is when it stops working well, such as when our leg "falls asleep" and we have trouble walking.

BEFORE YOU GO ON

- What are the cutaneous senses, and what are the transducers for each?

- What are the two major position senses, and what do they detect?

- Where are the receptors for the position senses located?

- How does the experience of motion sickness relate to the position senses?

An example of a person with very keen vestibular and kinesthetic senses.

PAIN: A SPECIAL SENSE

The sense of pain is a curious and troublesome one for psychologists interested in sensory processes. Pain, or the fear of it, can be a strong motivator; we'll do much to avoid it. Pain is surely unpleasant, but it is also very useful. Pain alerts us when a problem occurs somewhere in our bodies and warns us that steps might need to be taken to remove the source of pain. It is the experience of pain that prompts more than 80 percent of all visits to the doctor's office (Turk, 1994). Feelings of pain are private sensations and are difficult to share or describe (Verillo, 1975).

What *is* pain? What causes the experience of pain? What are its receptors? We have only partial answers to these questions. Many stimuli cause pain. Intense stimulation of any sense receptor produces pain. Too much light, strong pressures on the skin, excessive temperatures, very loud sounds, and even very "hot" spices cause pain. In the right circumstances, even a light pinprick is painful. Our skin has many receptors for pain, but pain receptors can also be found deep inside our bodies; consider stomachaches, lower back pain, and headaches. Pain is experienced in our brain, and the thalamus seems to play an important role, but pain is the only "sense" for which we cannot find one specific center in the cerebral cortex (Groves & Rebec, 1992, p. 265; Rainville et al., 1997).

One theory claims that pain is experienced within the central nervous system rather than in the periphery, and that a *gate control mechanism* (high in the spinal cord) opens to let pain messages race to the brain, or acts to block pain messages by "closing the gate" so that messages never get to the brain for processing (Melzack, 1973; Melzack & Wall, 1965). A *cognitive-behavioral theory* of pain also suggests that central mechanisms are important, noting that pain is influenced by a person's attitudes, expectations, and behaviors (Turk, 1994).

Even without a full understanding of how pain is sensed, there are techniques that can be used to reduce, or manage, the experience of pain. If pain is really experienced in the brain, what sorts of things can we do to keep pain messages from reaching those brain centers?

Drug therapy is one choice for pain management. Opiates such as morphine, when administered systematically, are believed to inhibit pain messages at the level of the spinal cord, as well as at the specific site of the pain (Bausbaum & Levine, 1991; Clinton, 1992; Randall, 1993; Richmond et al., 1993).

Hypnosis and cognitive self-control (trying very hard to convince yourself that the pain you're experiencing is not all that bad and will go away soon) can also be effective in lessening the experience of pain (Litt, 1988; Melzack, 1973).

placebo an inactive substance that produces an effect because a person believes it to be effective

That psychological processes can inhibit pain is reinforced by data on *placebo effects*. A **placebo** is a substance (perhaps a pill) a person believes will be useful in treating some symptom, such as pain. When a person takes a placebo that he or she believes will alleviate pain, endorphins are released in the brain and effectively keep pain-carrying impulses from reaching the brain (Levine et al., 1979). This placebo effect is particularly strong when the health care provider is prestigious, empathic, and shows a positive attitude about the placebo (Turner et al., 1994).

Another process that eases the feeling of pain, particularly pain from or near the surface of the skin, is called *counterirritation*. The idea is to forcefully (but not painfully, of course) stimulate an area of the body *near* the location of the pain. Dentists have learned that rubbing the patient's gum near the spot of a Novocain injection significantly reduces the pain of the needle.

The ancient Chinese practice of *acupuncture* is also effective in the treatment of pain. We don't yet know why acupuncture works as well as it does. There are cases where it doesn't work at all, but these usually involve patients who are skeptics, which suggests that at least one of the benefits of acupuncture is its placebo effect. As many as 12 million acupuncture therapies for pain management are performed in the United States each year (George, 1992; Parson, 1993), although more recent evidence suggests that acupuncture is less effective than pain-killing drugs (Taub, 1998).

Individual responses to pain are unique and are influenced by many factors, such as prior experience, memory of those experiences, and how one feels about pain. It is clear that gender and cultural differences can be involved in the expression or display of pain. In Japan, for instance, individuals are socialized not to show pain or any intense feeling. In Western culture, men are often socialized not to show pain and to "take it like a man." Among other things, these socialization issues often create difficulties in the diagnosis and treatment of an illness or disease where pain is an informative symptom. Finally, we should also explode the widely-held misconception that newborns cannot feel pain because of immature pain receptors. Research on the newborn's sensitivity to pain clearly shows that newborns do experience pain.

BEFORE YOU GO ON

- What stimuli can cause an experience of pain?

- Explain how the "gate control mechanism" relates to the experience of pain.

- What does the "cognitive-behavioral theory" of pain say about the experience of pain?

- Name and describe the ways that pain can be controlled or managed.

Topic Review 3 A

1. What are sensation and perception and how do they differ?

Sensation is the process of receiving information from the environment and changing it into nervous system activity. The process of transforming external stimuli into a form that the nervous system can interpret is known as transduction. Perception is the process that involves selection, organization and interpretation of stimuli. Sensation and perception differ in that perception is a more active, cognitive and central process than sensation.

2. What evidence exists to suggest that sensation and perception are distinct processes?

If different images are projected to each of your eyes, your brain perceives the images alternately, spontaneously shifting from one image to the other. The frontal and parietal lobes of the brain are responsible for this spontaneous alteration between images. Rather than sensing both images at the same time, the perceptual system lodged in your brain makes sense of the competing images by alternating between them.

3. What is a sensory threshold?

A sensory threshold is the minimum intensity of a stimulus that causes your sense organs to begin the process of transduction.

4. What is psychophysics?

Psychophysics is the study of the relationships between the physical attributes of a stimulus and the psychological reactions that those attributes produce. It is one of the oldest fields of study in psychology. Psychophysics helps you understand the sensitivity of your senses. It also helps you understand how you represent those stimuli psychologically.

5. What are absolute and difference thresholds, and how do they differ?

Essentially, an absolute threshold is the minimum amount of stimulus necessary to trigger a reaction from a sense organ. However, because there are no set absolute measures of sensory sensitivity, an absolute threshold is defined as the physical intensity of a stimulus that a person reports detecting 50 percent of the time. Thus, an absolute threshold deals with your ability to detect a particular stimulus. On the other hand, a difference threshold refers to the minimum difference between stimuli that can be detected 50 percent of the time. A just noticeable difference (or jnd) is the amount of change in a stimulus that makes it just noticeably different from another stimulus.

6. How does signal detection theory conceptualize stimulus detection?

According to signal detection theory, stimulus detection is a decision-making process. The decision is whether a stimulus is present against a background of noise. A decision about the presence or absence of a stimulus depends on many factors, such as the sensitivity of one's sense organs, attention, one's expectations, motivations and biases. In signal detection theory a "hit" is saying a signal is present when it is present. A "miss" occurs when a signal is undetected. A "false alarm" occurs when you say a signal is present when it is not. Finally, a "correct rejection" occurs when you say no signal is present, when in fact it is not present.

7. How does signal detection theory apply to lineup identifications?

A lineup facing an eyewitness is essentially a signal detection task. The suspect (the signal) is presented against a background of noise (foils). The eyewitness is required to make a decision concerning whether the suspect is in the lineup. If the eyewitness correctly says that the suspect is in the lineup, a "hit" occurs. If the witness fails to identify the suspect in a suspect present lineup, a "miss" has occurred. If the eyewitness says the suspect is present in a suspect absent lineup (that is, identifies a foil), a "false alarm" has occurred. Finally, if the eyewitness fails to identify the suspect in a suspect absent lineup, a "correct rejection" has occurred. The same rules apply to lineup identifications that apply to more general signal detection tasks. For example, putting a suspect in a lineup with foils that do not resemble the suspect raises hit rates, but may also result in false identification of a suspect (who is not the perpetrator).

8. What is meant by sensory adaptation?

Sensory adaptation occurs when our sensory experience decreases as a result of continued exposure to a stimulus.

For example, when you enter a dark room, you cannot see very well. After a few minutes your eyes adapt to (or get used to) the dark, and you can begin to make out objects in the room. In an adaptation situation your sense organs are subjected to the same stimulus continuously and are not newly stimulated. Because your sense organs are geared to detect changes in stimulation, you do not detect the continuous stimulation.

9. What is dark adaptation, and what accounts for it?

Dark adaptation occurs when your visual receptors become increasingly sensitive to light with more time spent in the dark. Your cones, adapted for daylight vision, reach their maximum sensitivity very quickly. On the other hand, your rods, responsible for low light vision, adapt more slowly. The rods eventually become more sensitive to light than the cones, allowing you to see in low light situations. Light adaptation also occurs when you move from a dark room to a lighted room, and it is a faster process than dark adaptation.

10. What are the three properties of light, and what sensory experience does each provide?

Light is a form of radiant energy that emanates from its source in waves. Light has three properties: wave amplitude (the height of the wave), wavelength (the distance between peaks of the wave, measured in nanometers), and wave purity (the number of different types of waves making up the stimulus). Differences in wave amplitude determine the brightness of light; the higher the wave, the brighter the light. Wavelength determines the hue or color of the light. The range of the visual spectrum for the human eye is 380 nanometers to 760 nanometers. Finally, wave purity refers to its saturation. The more saturated a light wave the more pure its hue.

11. How do monochromatic and white light differ?

Monochromatic light comprises a single wavelength. For example, light with all of its wavelengths at 700 nanometers (highly saturated) will appear as a deep rich red. White light, conversely, is a mixture of wavelengths and is the least saturated light possible.

12. What are the structures of the eye involved in focusing light on the back of the eye?

Several structures of the eye are involved in bending or focusing light onto the back of the eye. The cornea is the first structure that bends light. This tough, virtually transparent structure does about 75 percent of the bending of light waves. The pupil (the opening through which light passes) and the iris (the colored part of your eye) work like the aperture of a camera. The pupil can expand or contract letting in more or less light respectively. In dim light the pupil will be larger, and in bright light it will be smaller. The lens is a flexible structure whose shape is controlled by the ciliary muscles. The ciliary muscles change the shape of the lens to focus light as it enters the eye. The lens becomes flatter when we try to focus on a distant object and more round when we try to focus on a nearby object. This changing of the shape of the lens is called accommodation.

13. What is the retina, and what structures comprise it?

The retina is the photosensitive structure located at the back of the eye. It is actually a series of layers of specialized cells that is considered a part of the brain. The layer of cells at the very back of the retina are the photoreceptors, which actually transduce light energy into a neural impulse. There are two types of photoreceptors: rods and cones. Rods are responsible for achromatic, low light vision. Cones are responsible for color, daylight vision. Signals from the rods and cones are then processed through the bipolar cells and ganglion cells. Fibers from the ganglion cells form the optic nerve.

Cones are concentrated in an area of the retina called the fovea where there are only a few layers of cells between the light entering the eye and the cones. In the fovea the cones are densely packed and there are no rods. The rods are found outside the fovea. Visual acuity is highest at the fovea. The point where the optic nerve connects to the eye is called the blind spot. There are no rods or cones at this spot, consequently, there is no vision there.

14. What are the functions of the rods and cones?

In the eye there are about 120 million rods, but only 6 million cones. The cones are concentrated in the fovea, whereas the rods are distributed in a ring around the fovea. Not only do rods and cones differ in location and number, they also differ in function. The cones function most efficiently in medium to high levels of illumination and are responsible for color vision. Conversely, the rods function most effectively under low light conditions. As a consequence, they are responsible for twilight and night vision. Rods are not capable of discriminating between different wavelengths of light. As a consequence, the rods are not involved in color vision.

15. How does the process of dark adaptation demonstrate the existence of two separate visual systems?

After a period of time in darkness, the cones reach their maximum sensitivity to light. At the same time that the cones are adapting to light by becoming more sensitive, so are the rods. However, after the sensitivity of the cones levels off, the sensitivity of the rods continues to increase markedly. The point where the sensitivity curves for the cones and rods cross is called the rod-cone break. After the rod-cone break, the rods are primarily responsible for low light vision. Because the cones are not able to respond well to low levels of light intensity, color vision is limited under low light conditions.

16. How is visual neural energy transmitted from the retina to the brain?

Once nerve fibers leave the eye at the blind spot, they travel to the optic chiasma, where some are sent straight back and others cross to the opposite side of the brain. Images from the left visual field are processed in the right side of the brain, and images from the right visual field are processed in the left side of the brain. From the optic chiasma, impulses travel through the superior colliculi, the thalamus, and to the occipital lobes of the cerebral cortex where visual experiences are processed.

17. What are the two theories of color vision?

The two theories of color vision are the Young-Helmholtz trichromatic theory and Hering's opponent-process theory. These theories explain how the visual system codes wavelengths of light to give us the experience of color. The trichromatic theory claims that there are three types of cones, each maximally sensitive to one of the three primary hues: red, green, and blue. Hering's opponent-process theory claims that there are three pairs of mechanisms involved in our experience of color: a blue-yellow processor, a red-green processor, and a black-white processor. Processors respond to either of the characteristics that give it its name, but not to both at the same time. There is evidence that supports both theories, some of which comes from our understanding of why some people have defects in color vision.

18. What are the properties of sound, and what sensory experience does each provide?

Like light, sound may be represented as a wave form of energy with three major physical characteristics: wave amplitude, frequency, and purity. Wave amplitude provides our experience of the loudness of a sound. Frequency determines pitch, and purity determines timbre.

19. What are the structures of the ear, and how are they involved in transduction?

Most of the structures of the ear (pinna, auditory canal, eardrum, malleus, incus, stapes, and oval window) intensify and transmit the pressure of sound waves to the fluid in the cochlea, which then vibrates the basilar membrane.

The basilar membrane stimulates tiny hair cells to transmit neural impulses along the auditory nerve to the temporal lobes of the cerebral cortex.

20. How is the stimulus for hearing transduced into an auditory neural impulse?

The three small bones of the middle ear (the malleus, incus, and stapes) amplify and pass vibrations to the oval window, a membrane like the eardrum. The sound waves then enter a structure in the inner ear called the cochlea, which is a snail-like structure. The cochlea contains the actual receptor cells, the transducers, for hearing. As the stapes vibrates against the oval window, fluid inside the cochlea moves at the same rate. When the fluid within the cochlea moves, the basilar membrane, a small structure that runs about the full length of the cochlea, is bent up and down. Hearing occurs when very tiny hair cells are stimulated by the vibrations of the basilar membrane. The mechanical pressure of the basilar membrane on the hair cells starts neural impulses that leave the ear, traveling on the auditory nerve toward the temporal lobe.

21. What are the chemical senses, and how do they work?

The chemical senses are gustation (taste) and olfaction (smell). The receptors for taste are cells in the taste buds located on the tongue. Taste appears to have four primary qualities: sweet, salt, sour, and bitter. For smell, the sense receptors are hair cells that line the upper regions of the nasal cavity.

22. How do the senses of smell and taste relate to each other?

The senses of gustation (taste) and olfaction (smell) are interrelated and are referred to as chemical senses because both respond to chemical molecules. Much of what we call taste actually relies on the sense of smell.

This is why when you have a stuffy nose you have difficulty tasting foods.

23. What is the vomeronasal organ (VNO), and what does it appear to do?

The vomeronasal organ (or VNO) is the primary organ involved in the detection of pheromones. The VNO has long been acknowledged in animals, but it was once believed that the VNO in humans was absorbed during prenatal development. We now know that humans also possess a VNO which are two small sacs located on each side of the nasal septum. The VNO is involved in detecting pheromones involved in mating, aggression, and territoriality. The VNO might be involved in human sexual attraction.

24. What are the skin senses, and what do they do?

The skin senses comprise the senses of touch, pressure, warmth, and cold. Specific receptor cells for each of the skin senses have not yet been identified, although they no doubt include free nerve endings and encapsulated nerve endings, which most likely work together.

25. What are the position senses, and what information do they provide?

One of our position senses is the vestibular sense, which responds to the movement of small particles suspended in a fluid within our vestibular sacs and semicircular canals and informs us about orientation with regard to gravity or accelerated motion. The other position sense is kinesthesis, which uses receptors in our tendons, muscles, and joints to inform us about the orientation of various parts of our bodies.

26. What is pain and how is it detected?

A wide variety of stimuli can give rise to our experience of pain, from high levels of stimulus intensity to light pinpricks, and to internal stimuli of the sort that produce headaches. The central nervous system is involved in the experience of pain, perhaps as a gate-control mechanism in the spinal cord that either blocks or sends impulses carrying information about pain to the brain.

27. What techniques are used to help control pain?

Anything that can effectively block the passage of pain impulses can control our experience of pain. This is directly accomplished by the action of endorphins and counter-irritation. The experience of pain can be controlled by hypnosis, placebo effects, self-persuasion, and acupuncture.

Topic 3B PERCEIVING THE WORLD AROUND US

A deep space probe orbiting Saturn sends back radio signals that are detected by sophisticated, highly sensitive antennae. The radio signals eventually show up on your television screen as sharp images of Saturn's rings and moons. However, before you see the beautifully detailed photos, the radio signals must be decoded and the images enhanced by computers. The end product of this "computer enhancement" is what you see on your television screen.

Your sensory and perceptual systems work in a similar fashion. Like the antennae that detect the radio signals from space and the receivers that convert those radio signals into an interpretable format, your senses receive information in the form of energy, and convert that energy into neural impulses that are sent to your brain. Your brain, like the computer working on the signal from space, cleans up the image transmitted by your senses. Consider, for example, visual perception. If you were to look at the image falling on your retina you would find that it is blurry (light has to pass through the fluids of the eye), inverted, two- dimensional, and mosaic-like. Yet, your final experience of a visual stimulus is clear, in its proper orientation, three-dimensional and continuous (smooth). The visual information processing systems in your brain take the original "signal" and enhance it much like those beautiful photographs of Saturn's rings.

By and large, our senses can detect very low levels of stimulus intensity. Our senses, then, are constantly bombarding us with bits and pieces of information. It is the process of perception that first selects incoming stimulus information to attend to and then organizes, interprets, and tries to make meaningful the data that sensation provides us.

Key Questions to Answer

In this Topic, we will examine some of what we know about the cognitive process called perception.

While reading this Topic, find the answers to the following key questions:

1.   What is the difference between a salient detail and a peripheral detail?

2.   What are the stimulus factors that control perceptual selectivity?

3.   What are the personal factors that control perceptual selectivity?

4.   What factors can influence how we organize stimuli in perception?

5.   What is the figure-ground relationship?

6.   What is meant by bottom-up processing?

7.   What is a subjective contour?

8. What is top-down processing?

9. What cues relating to the visual system help us discriminate depth and distance?

10. What are the cues from the environment that help us discriminate depth and distance?

11. What role does culture play in depth perception?

12. What, generally, are the perceptual constancies?

13. What are the specific perceptual constancies?

14. What is an illusion?

PAYING ATTENTION: A PROCESS OF SELECTION

Let's return to the classroom exercise that opened this chapter. You sit in class listening to your professor lecture, and from time to time, your mind wanders (we hope not too frequently). You think that wearing your new shoes was not a good idea as your feet hurt. To your left, a student rips open a bag of chips. You turn your head and feel annoyed. You smell someone's perfume and think what a pleasant fragrance it is. Your senses are being bombarded simultaneously by all sorts of information: sights, sounds, tastes, smells, even pain. Suddenly, someone enters the room and begins arguing with your professor. A scuffle breaks out, and eventually you see a gun and hear a shot. Your heart is pounding, you are breathing heavily, and you don't know what to do next.

salient detail a detail that captures our attention

What determines which stimuli attract our attention and which get ignored? One thing is for sure: you cannot attend to every stimulus at once. Typically, we select a few details to which we attend. A detail that captures our attention is called a **salient detail**. These details not only catch our attention, they are also remembered more often than *peripheral details*. Peripheral details make up our perceptual background, so we tend to pay less attention to them.

In this section, we'll discuss some of the important variables that influence what we attend to. These variables are of two general types: stimulus factors and personal factors. By *stimulus factors* we mean those characteristics that make some stimuli more compelling than others no matter who the perceiver is. By *personal factors* we mean those characteristics of the perceiver that influence which stimuli get attended to or perceived. Personal factors may be transient, such as the emotional arousal that accompanies witnessing an automobile accident. Or, personal factors can be more permanent, such as poor vision or personal prejudices. First, we will take a look at some stimulus factors that affect our perceptual processes.

Stimulus Factors in Perceptual Selectivity

contrast the extent to which a stimulus is in some physical way different from surrounding stimuli

The most important stimulus factor in perceptual selection is **contrast**, the extent to which a stimulus is physically different from the other stimuli around it. One stimulus can contrast with other stimuli in a variety of ways. We are more likely to attend to a stimulus if its intensity is different from the intensities of other stimuli. Generally, the more intense a stimulus, the more likely we are to select it for further processing. Thus, we are more likely to attend to an irate student in a classroom if he is shouting rather than whispering. In other contexts, a bright light is more attention-grabbing than a dim one; an extreme temperature is more likely to be noticed than a moderate one. This isn't always the case, however, as context can make a difference. A shout is more compelling than a whisper, unless everyone is shouting; then it may be the soft, quiet, reasoned tone that gets our attention. If we are faced with a barrage of bright lights, a dim one by contrast may be the one we process more fully.

The same argument holds true for the stimulus characteristic of physical *size*. In most cases, the bigger the stimulus, the more likely we are to attend to it. There is little point in building a small billboard to advertise your motel or restaurant. You want to construct the biggest billboard you can in hopes of attracting attention. Still, faced with many large stimuli, contrast effects often cause us to attend to the one that is smaller. The easiest player to spot on a football field is often the placekicker, who tends to be smaller and not wearing as much protective padding as the other players.

A third dimension for which contrast is relevant is *motion*. Motion is a powerful factor in determining visual attention. Walking through the woods, you may nearly step on a chipmunk before you notice it, as long as it stays still—an adaptive camouflage that chipmunks do well. If it moves to escape, you easily notice it scurrying across the leaves. Again, the *contrast* created by movement is important.

Although intensity, size, and motion are three characteristics of stimuli that readily come to mind, there are others. Indeed, any way in which two stimuli are different (i.e., contrast) can provide a dimension that determines which stimulus we attend to. (Even a small grease spot can easily grab one's attention if it's located in the middle of a solid yellow tie.) Because contrast guides attention, important terms are printed in **boldface type** throughout this book—so you'll notice them, attend to them, and recognize them as important stimuli.

There is another stimulus characteristic that determines attention, but for which contrast is not relevant; that is *repetition*. The more often a stimulus is presented, the more likely it will be attended to—with all else being equal. Note that we have to say "all else being equal" or we develop contradictions. If stimuli are repeated too often, we adapt to them as they are no longer novel. Even so, there are many examples that convince us of the value of repetition in getting someone's attention. Instructors who want to make an important point seldom mention it just once, but repeat it. This is why we repeat the definitions of important terms in the text, in the margin, and again in the glossary. The people who schedule commercials on television want you to attend to their messages, and obviously repetition is one of their main techniques.

There are many ways in which stimuli differ. The greater the contrast between any stimulus and the others around it, the greater the likelihood that that stimulus captures our attention. All else being equal, the more often a stimulus is presented, the greater the likelihood that it is perceived and selected for further processing.

Personal Factors in Perceptual Selectivity

Sometimes attention is determined less by the physical characteristics of the stimuli present than by personal characteristics of the perceiver. For example, imagine two students watching a football game on television. Both are presented with identical stimulation from the same TV screen. One asks, "Wow, did you see that tackle?" The other responds, "No, I was watching the cheerleaders." The difference in perception here is hardly attributable to the nature of the stimuli because both students received the same sensory information from the same TV. The difference is due to characteristics of the perceivers, or personal factors, which we categorize as motivation, expectation, or past experience.

We often perceive what we want to perceive, and we often perceive what we *expect* to perceive. We may not notice stimuli when they are present simply because we did not "know" they were coming—we didn't expect them. When we are psychologically predisposed to perceive something, we form a **mental set.**

mental set a predisposed (set) way to perceive or respond to something; an expectation

Take a second and quickly glance at the message in Figure 3.17. What does the message say? (If you have seen this before, you'll have to try it with someone who hasn't.) Many people say the message is "Paris in the spring." In fact, there are two *thes* in the triangle: "Paris in the the spring." Most people familiar with the English language (and with this phrase) do not expect to see two *thes* next to each other. Following their mental set, they report seeing only one. Others may develop a different mental set. Their reasoning may go something like this: "This is a psychology text, so there's probably a trick here, and I'm going to find it." In this instance, such skepticism is rewarded. There *is* a trick, and if their mental set is to find one, they do. Our inability to change a set way of perceiving a problem may interfere with finding a solution to that problem. What we call "creative" problem solving is often a matter of perceiving aspects of a problem in new or unexpected ways. Thus, even as complex a cognitive process as problem solving often hinges on basic perceptual processes.

FIGURE 3.17

How we perceive the world is determined at least in part by our mental set or our expectations about the world. How many THEs did you see when you first glanced at this figure? Why?

When we say that what we attend to is due to motivation and expectation we are claiming that what we perceive is often influenced by our *past experiences*. Much of our motivation and many of our expectations develop from past experiences. We are likely to perceive, or be set to perceive, what we have perceived in the past. Perhaps a personal example will make this clear. One of us (Gerow) took a course in comparative psychology that examined the behaviors of nonhuman organisms. One of the teachers of the course was an ornithologist (a scientist who studies birds). Participation in early morning bird-watching was a requirement of the course. The memory is still vivid: cold, tired, clutching the thermos of coffee, slopping through the marshland looking for birds as the sun was just rising. After twenty minutes of this unpleasantness, the instructor identified ten or eleven different birds. Gerow wasn't certain, but he thought he saw a duck. "I didn't know what sort of duck it was, but I thought I saw a duck. The differences in perception between my instructor and me that cold, wet morning can be explained in terms of motivation (he *did* care more than I); but I suspect his ability to spot birds so quickly also reflected his past experience. He knew where to look and what to look for."

Our perception of stimuli is usually accomplished without conscious effort, and the process is influenced by several factors, some of which depend on the stimuli themselves. What we perceive is determined to some extent by the bits and pieces of information we receive directly from our senses. We may attend to a particular stimulus because it is significantly larger, smaller, more colorful, louder, or slower than the other stimuli around it. We then try to organize, identify, and store that stimulus in our memory. This is called *bottom-up processing*. On the other hand, whether or how stimuli are perceived can also be influenced by the perceiver. In this case, selection of stimuli is a matter of applying concepts and information already processed. Examples include the use of motivation, mental set, and past experience to influence perceptual selectivity. When what one selects and perceives depends on what the perceiver already knows, this is *top-down processing*.

BEFORE YOU GO ON

- What is the difference between a salient and peripheral detail?
- List and define the stimulus factors that affect perceptual selectivity.
- What is a mental set, and how does it affect perceptual selectivity?
- List and define the personal factors that affect perceptual selectivity.

ORGANIZING OUR PERCEPTUAL WORLD

One of our basic perceptual reactions to the environment is to select certain stimuli from among all those that strike our receptors so they may be processed further. A related perceptual process is to organize and interpret the bits and pieces of experience into meaningful, organized wholes. We do not hear individual sounds of speech; we perceive words, phrases, and sentences (Feng & Ratnam, 2000). Our visual experience is not one of bits of color and light and dark but of identifiable objects and events. We don't perceive a warm pat on the back as responses from hundreds of individual receptors in our skin.

Perceptual organization was of considerable interest to the Gestalt psychologists. Perhaps you recall that **gestalt** is a German word that means "configuration" or "whole." You form a gestalt when you see the "big picture." When you perceive the whole as being more than the sum of its parts, you've formed a gestalt.

gestalt term meaning whole, totality, configuration; a gestalt is more than the sum of its parts

A basic principle of Gestalt psychology is the **figure-ground relationship**. Those stimuli you attend to and group together are *figures*, whereas all the rest are the *ground*. As you focus your attention on the words on this page, they form figures against the ground (or background, if you'd prefer) provided by the rest of the page. When you hear your instructor's voice during a lecture, it is the figure against the ground of all other sounds in the room. The irate student who barged into the classroom to confront a professor became a figure quite quickly. Do you see the relationship between these classic, Gestalt psychology terms (figure and ground) and the more modern, technical terminology (salient and peripheral details) we introduced at the very beginning of this Topic? What the Gestalt psychologists called a *figure*, we also can call a *salient detail* of our sensory world. Those stimuli which make up our perceptual *ground* are the *peripheral details*. Figure 3.18 provides a couple of visual examples of the figure-ground relationship.

figure-ground relationship the Gestalt psychology principle that stimuli are selected and perceived as figures against a ground (background)

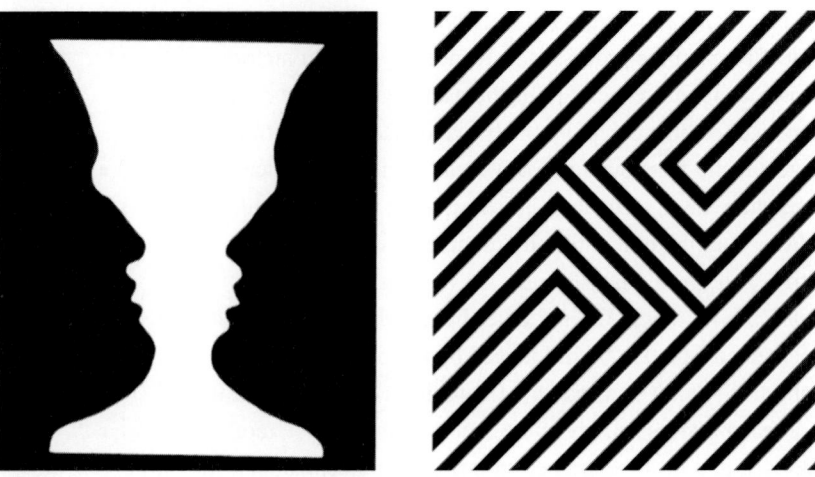

FIGURE 3.18

(A) A classic reversible figure-ground pattern. What do you see here? A white vase or two black profiles facing each other? Can you see both figures clearly at the same time? (B) After a few moments' inspection, a small square should emerge as a figure against a ground of diagonal lines.

Gestalt psychologists were intrigued by how we group and organize perceptual stimuli to form meaningful gestalts. As with perceptual selection, many factors influence how we organize our perceptual world. Again, it will be useful to consider both stimulus factors, or bottom-up processing, and personal factors, or top-down processing.

Grouping Stimuli with Bottom-Up Processing

Bottom-up processing occurs when we select stimuli as they enter our senses and process them "higher" into our cognitive systems by organizing them, interpreting them, making them meaningful, and storing them in our memories. When we talk about bottom-up processing in this context, we're talking about forming gestalts, putting stimuli together based solely on the characteristics of the stimuli themselves. We call these "stimulus factors." We'll consider five of the most influential: proximity, similarity, continuity, common fate, and closure.

proximity the Gestalt principle of organization claiming that stimuli will be perceived as belonging together if they occur together in space or time

1. **Proximity**. Glance quickly at Figure 3.19(A). Without giving it much thought, what did you see? A bunch of Xs yes; but more than that, there were two identifiable groups of Xs, weren't there? The group of Xs on the left seems separate from the group on the right, whereas the Xs within each group seem to go together. This illustrates what the Gestalt psychologists called proximity, or contiguity—events occurring close together in space or time are perceived as belonging together and part of the same figure.

    Proximity operates on more than just visual stimuli. Sounds that occur together (are contiguous) in speech are perceived together to form words or phrases. In written language there are physical spaces between words on the printed page. Thunder and lightning usually occur together, thunder following shortly after the lightning. As a result, it's difficult to think about one without also thinking about the other.

2. **Similarity**. Now glance at Figure 3.19(B) and describe what you see there. A collection of Xs and Os are clearly organized into a simple pattern—as two columns of Xs and two of Os. Perceiving rows of alternating Xs and Os is difficult, which demonstrates the Gestalt principle of similarity. Stimuli that are alike or share properties tend to group together in our perception—a "birds of a feather are perceived together" sort of thing. Most of us perceive Australian koalas as bears because they look so much like bears, when, in fact, they are related to kangaroos and wallabies.

> **similarity** the Gestalt principle of organization claiming that stimuli will be perceived together if they share some common characteristics

3. **Continuity**. The Gestalt principle of continuity (or good continuation) is operating when we see things as ending up consistent with the way they started off. Figure 3.19(C) illustrates this point with a simple line drawing. The clearest, easiest way to organize this drawing is as two separate but intersecting lines—one straight, the other curved. It's difficult to imagine seeing this figure any other way.

> **continuity** the Gestalt principle of organization claiming that a stimulus or a movement will be perceived as continuing in the same smooth direction as first established

Continuity may account for how we organize some of our perceptions of people. Aren't we surprised when a hardworking, award-winning honor high school student suddenly does poorly in college and flunks out? That's not the way we like to view the world. We would not be as surprised to find that a student who barely made it through high school fails to pass at college. We want things to continue as they began, as in "as the twig is bent, so grows the tree."

4. **Common fate**. Common fate is our tendency to group together in the same figure those elements of a scene that appear to move together in the same direction and at the same speed. Common fate is like continuity, but it applies to moving stimuli. Remember our example of a chipmunk sitting motionless on the leaves in the woods? As long as both the chipmunk and the leaves remain still, the chipmunk isn't noticed. When it moves, all of the parts of the chipmunk move together, sharing a common fate, and we see it scurrying away.

> **common fate** the Gestalt principle of organization claiming that we group together, within the same figure, elements of a scene that move together in the same direction and at the same speed

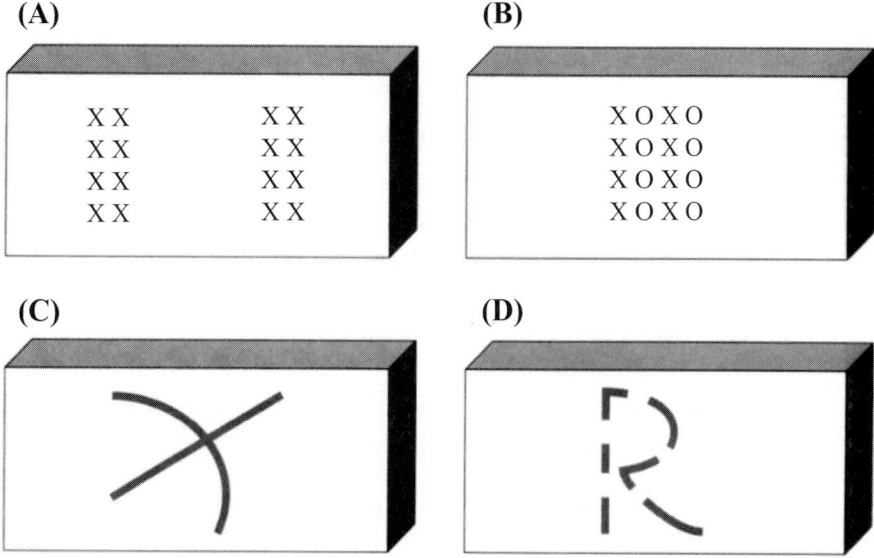

(A) **(B)** **(C)** **(D)**

FIGURE 3.19

Four Gestalt psychology examples of grouping. (A) These Xs are organized as two groups, not as four rows or four columns, because of proximity. (B) Here we see two columns of Os and two columns of Xs because of similarity. (C) We tend to see this figure as two intersecting lines—one curved, the other straight—because of continuity. (D) This figure is perceived as the letter R, not because it is a well-drawn representation, but because of closure.

closure the Gestalt principle of organization claiming that we tend to perceive incomplete figures as whole

5.   **Closure**. One of the most commonly encountered Gestalt principles of organization, or grouping, is closure. We tend to fill in gaps in our perceptual world. Closure provides an excellent example of perception as an active process. It underscores the notion that we constantly seek to make sense out of our environment, whether that environment presents us with sensible stimuli or not. This concept is illustrated by Figure 3.19(D). At a glance, we see this figure as the letter R, but, of course, it is not. That's not the way you make an R, however, it is the way we perceive an R because of closure.

As an example of closure, make an audio tape of a casual conversation with a friend, and write down exactly what you both say. A truly faithful transcription will reveal that many words and sounds were left out. Although they were not actually there as stimuli, they were not missed by the listener, because he or she filled in the gaps (closure) and understood what was being said.

A phenomenon that many psychologists believe is a special case of closure is the perception of **subjective contours**, in which arrangements of lines and patterns enable us to see figures that are not actually there. If that sounds a bit strange, look at Figure 3.20, in which we have an example of subjective contour. In this figure, you can "see" a solid triangle that is so clear it nearly jumps off the page. There is no accepted explanation for subjective contours (Bradley & Dumais, 1975; Coren, 1972; Kanizsa, 1976; Rock, 1986), but it seems to be another example of our perceptual processes filling in gaps in our perceptual world in order to provide us with sensible information.

subjective contours the perception of a contour (a line or plane) that is not there, but is suggested by other aspects of a scene

FIGURE 3.20
An example of subjective contour.

Grouping Stimuli with Top-Down Processing

Remember that when we refer to top-down processing, the implication is that we take advantage of motivations, expectations, and previously stored memories in order to deal with incoming stimuli. In terms of perceptual organization, this means that we often perceive stimuli as going together, as part of the same gestalt or figure, because we want to, because we expect to, or because we perceived them together in the past.

We can think of no better example in our experience than the one used to open this chapter. Six hundred students claimed to see something that did not happen. The problem was not one of perceptual selection; everybody saw the gun. The problem was one of organization—with whom did they associate the gun? No one was *mentally set* for the professor to bring a gun to class. No one *wanted* to see the professor with a gun. And no one had *experienced* a professor with a gun in class before. (Seeing crazed students with guns is not a common experience either, but with television and movies and recent school killings, it is certainly a more probable one.)

BEFORE YOU GO ON

- How does the term "Gestalt" apply to organizing your perceptual world?

- What is a figure-ground relationship? Give an example.

- What is bottom-up processing?

- List and describe the characteristics of a stimulus that affect bottom- up processing.

- What is top-down processing?

Perceiving Depth and Distance

Perception requires that we select and organize stimulus information. One of the ways in which we organize visual stimuli is to note where they happen to be in the world. We perceive the world as three-dimensional. As long as we pay attention (surely a required perceptual process), we won't fall off cliffs or run into buildings. We know with considerable accuracy just how far we are from objects in our environment. What is remarkable about this ability is that light reflected from objects and events in our environment falls on two-dimensional retinas. The depth and distance in our world is not something we directly *sense;* it is something we *perceive.*

The ability to judge depth and distance accurately is an adaptive skill that plays an important role in determining many of our actions. Our ability to make such judgments reflects the fact that we are simultaneously responding to a large number of cues to depth and distance. Some cues are built into our visual systems and are referred to as *ocular cues. Physical,* or *pictorial cues,* have to do with our appreciation of the physical environment. We'll also see that our culture plays a role in the perception of depth and distance.

Ocular Cues

Some of the cues we get about distance and depth reflect the way our eyes work. Cues that involve both eyes are called *binocular cues* (*bi* means "two"). When we look at a nearby three-dimensional object, each eye gets a somewhat different view of it. Hold a pen with a clip on it a few feet in front of your eyes. Rotate the pen until the clip can be viewed by the left eye, but not the right. (You check that by first closing one eye, then the other, as you rotate the pen.) Now each eye (retina) gets a different (disparate) view of the same object. This phenomenon is called **retinal disparity**. It is a cue that what we are looking at must be solid or three-dimensional. Otherwise, each eye would see the same image, not two disparate ones (Figure 3.21).

Another binocular cue to depth and distance is **convergence**—our eyes turning toward each other when we view something up close. As we gaze off into the distance, our eyes aim outward in almost parallel fashion. As we focus on objects close to us, our eyes come together, or converge, and we interpret that convergence as an indication that what we are looking at is close to us. Convergence is illustrated in Figure 3.21.

The rest of the cues we'll consider are *monocular,* implying that they require only one eye to have their influence. (Even the physical cues that follow are monocular cues because they can be appreciated by persons who can see with one eye.) A unique monocular cue, at least for relatively short distances, is accommodation. This process is the changing of the shape of the lens by the ciliary muscles to focus images on the retina. When we focus on distant objects, accommodation flattens our lens, and when we focus on nearby objects, our lens gets rounder or fatter. Although the process is reflexive and occurs automatically, our brains react to the activity of our ciliary muscles in terms of the distance of an object from our eyes. Accommodation does not function well as a cue for distances beyond arm's length because the changes in the activity of the ciliary muscles

retinal disparity the phenomenon in which each retina receives a different (disparate) view of the same three-dimensional object

convergence the tendency of the eyes to move toward each other as we focus on objects close up

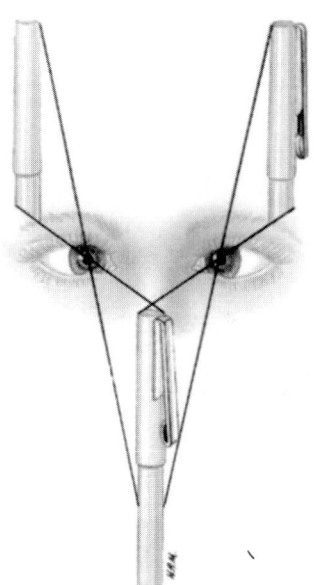

FIGURE 3.21

When looking at a three-dimen-sional object, such as a pen, the right eye sees a slightly different image than does the left eye—a phenome-non called retinal disparity. This disparity gives us a cue that the object we are viewing is three-dimensional. Here we also note convergence—our eyes turn toward each other when we view an object that is close to us.

are too slight to be noticed. But it is within arm's length that decisions about distance are often critical.

Physical Cues

The physical cues to distance and depth are those we get from the structure of our environment. These are sometimes called *pictorial cues* because they are used by artists to create the impression of three-dimensionality on a two-dimensional canvas or paper. Here are some of the most important.

1. **Linear perspective** (see Figure 3.22): As you stand in the middle of a road, looking off into the distance, the sides of the road, which you know to be parallel, seem to come together in the distance. Using this pictorial cue in drawing takes some time and experience to develop.

2. **Interposition** (see Figure 3.23): This cue to distance reflects our appreciation that objects in the foreground tend to cover, or partially hide from view, objects in the background, and not vice versa. One of the reasons a professor knows that people sitting in the back of a classroom are farther away than people sitting in the front row is the information that he or she gets from interposition. People (and other objects) in the front partially block the view of the people sitting behind them.

3. **Relative size** (see Figure 3.24): This is a commonly used clue to our judgment of distance. Very few stimuli in this world change their size, but a lot of things get nearer to or farther away from us. Objects that are near to you cast a larger image on your retina than objects that are farther away. So, all else being equal, we tend to judge the object that produces the larger retinal image as being closer to us.

FIGURE 3.22

Although we know that the sides of a road are parallel, they appear to come together in the distance–an example of linear perspective.

FIGURE 3.23

Interposition occurs when objects in the foreground partially block or obscure objects that are farther away.

FIGURE 3.24

All of these hot air balloons are about the same size. Those in the distance project much smaller images in our retinas, however, demonstrating the importance of relative size as a cue to distance.

4. **Texture gradient**: Standing on a gravel road, looking down at your feet, you can clearly make out the details of the texture of the roadway. You can see individual pieces of gravel. As you look on down the road, the texture gradually changes, and details give way to a smooth blend of a textureless surface. We interpret this gradual change (gradient) in texture as a change in distance.

5. **Patterns of shading** (see Figure 3.25): Drawings that do not use shading look flat and two-dimensional. Children eventually learn that if they want their pictures to look lifelike, they should shade in tree trunks and apples and show them casting shadows. Two-dimensional objects do not cast shadows, and how objects create patterns of light and shade tell us a great deal about their shape and solidity.

6. **Motion parallax**: This rather technical label names something with which we are all familiar. The clearest example may occur when we are in a car, looking out a side window. Even if the car is going at a modest speed, nearby utility poles and fence posts seem to race by. Objects farther away from the car seem to be moving more slowly, and mountains or trees way off in the distance seem not to be moving at all. This difference in apparent motion is known as motion parallax. Observations of this phenomenon during a train ride in 1910 are what first got Max Wertheimer interested in what eventually evolved into Gestalt psychology.

Figure 3.25

We see depth and distance in this image of sand dunes largely because patterns of light and shadow provide us with information about the three-dimensionality of objects in our environment.

The Role of Culture

Even something as "natural" as perceiving depth and distance is susceptible to cultural constraints. Here are two classic examples. Turnbull (1961) reported that the Bambuti people of the African Congo live much of their lives in the dense Ituri Forest where they seldom see much farther than 100 feet. When Turnbull first took his Bambuti guide out of the forest onto the open plains, the guide, Kenge, was disoriented with regard to cues for distance. Kenge thought that buffalo grazing a few miles away were, in fact, tiny insects, responding more to retinal size than relative size as a cue to distance. Interestingly, with just a little training in how the real, physical world can be represented most cultural differences in the perception of depth disappear (Mshelia & Lapidus, 1990).

> ### BEFORE YOU GO ON
>
> - What do the binocular cues for depth include?
> - Name and describe the monocular cues for depth.
> - List and describe the physical cues for depth.
> - How does culture play a role in depth perception?

The Constancy of Visual Perception

Perceptual constancies help us organize and interpret the stimulus input we get from our senses. Because of the constancy of perception, we recognize a familiar object as being the same regardless of how far away it is, the angle from which we view it, or the color or intensity of the light reflected from it. You can recognize your textbook whether you view it from a distance or close up, straight on or from an angle, in a dimly or brightly lighted room, or in blue, red, or white light; it is still your textbook, and you will perceive it as such regardless of how your senses detect it. Were it not for perceptual constancy, each sensation might be perceived as a new experience and little would appear familiar to you.

perceptual constancies perceptual mechanisms that allow you to perceive various aspects of your world as constant

size constancy the perceptual constancy that allows you to perceive the size of an object viewed at different distances as constant despite changes in the size of the retinal image

Size constancy is the tendency to see objects as constant in size regardless of the size of the retinal image. A friend standing close to you may fill your visual field. At a distance, the image of the same person may take up only a fraction of your visual field. The size of the image on your retina may be significantly different, but you know very well that your friend has not shrunk but has simply moved farther away. Our ability to discern that objects remain the same size depends on several factors, most importantly the quality of the depth perception cues available to us and our familiarity with the stimulus object.

shape constancy the perceptual constancy that allows you to perceive the shape of an object as constant despite different viewing angles and changes in the retinal image

Shape constancy refers to our perception that objects maintain their shape even though the retinal image they cast may change. Shape constancy may be demonstrated with any familiar object, such as the nearest door in your field of view. As you look at that door from various angles, the shape of the image of the door on your retina changes radically. Straight on it appears to be a rectangle; partially open, the image is that of a trapezoid; from the edge, fully open, the retinal image is of a straight line. But despite the retinal image, you still see that object as a door because of shape constancy (see Figure 3.26)

brightness constancy the perceptual constancy that allows you to perceive the apparent brightness of a familiar object as constant despite changes in the actual amount or type of light under which it is viewed

Brightness constancy causes the apparent brightness of familiar objects to be perceived as the same regardless of the actual amount or type of light under which they are viewed. The white shirt you put on this morning may be *sensed* as light gray when you pass through a shadow, or as even a darker gray when night falls, but it is still *perceived* as a white shirt and in no way darker than it was in the morning. The same is true for color perception. **Color constancy** allows you to perceive the color of a familiar object as constant, despite changing lighting conditions. For example, if you know you put on a white shirt this morning, you would still perceive it as white even if we were to illuminate it with a red light. Most of the light waves reflected by the shirt would be associated with the experience of red (about 700 nm), and someone else, who didn't know any better, might perceive the shirt as red, but you'd perceive it as white because of color constancy.

color constancy the perceptual constancy that allows you to perceive a familiar object as having a constant color despite changes in the hue of the light illuminating the object

FIGURE 3.26

At the level of the retina, we experience different images, yet we know we are looking at the same door because of shape constancy.

When Constancy Fails:
Geometric Illusions and Impossible Figures

By now you appreciate that the relationship between the "real world" and your perceptual world is not as straightforward as you might think. What we perceive is often flavored by factors above and beyond any physical reality that impinges on our sense receptors. The interaction between physical reality and our psychological experience can be appreciated when we consider illusions and impossible figures. **Illusions** are experiences in which our perceptions are at odds with what we know as physical reality. In most cases, illusions occur when our reliance on perceptual constancies is challenged.

illusion a perception that is at odds with (different from) what we consider physical reality

Several simple and compelling geometrical illusions are presented in Figure 3.27. Figure 3.27 (A) depicts the vertical-horizontal illusion. Figure 3.27 (B) is the same illusion in slightly more meaningful terms. Are the lines in Figure 3.27 (A) the same length? Yes, you know they are. But do they *appear* to be the same length? No, they do not. The vertical line seems much longer than the horizontal one. The hat in Figure 3.27 (B) seems to be considerably taller than it is wide. Notice that the vertical-horizontal illusion works even after you measure the two lines to confirm that they are the same length. They *still* don't look equal. This is one of three fundamental facts about illusions: they do not depend on our ignorance of the situation.

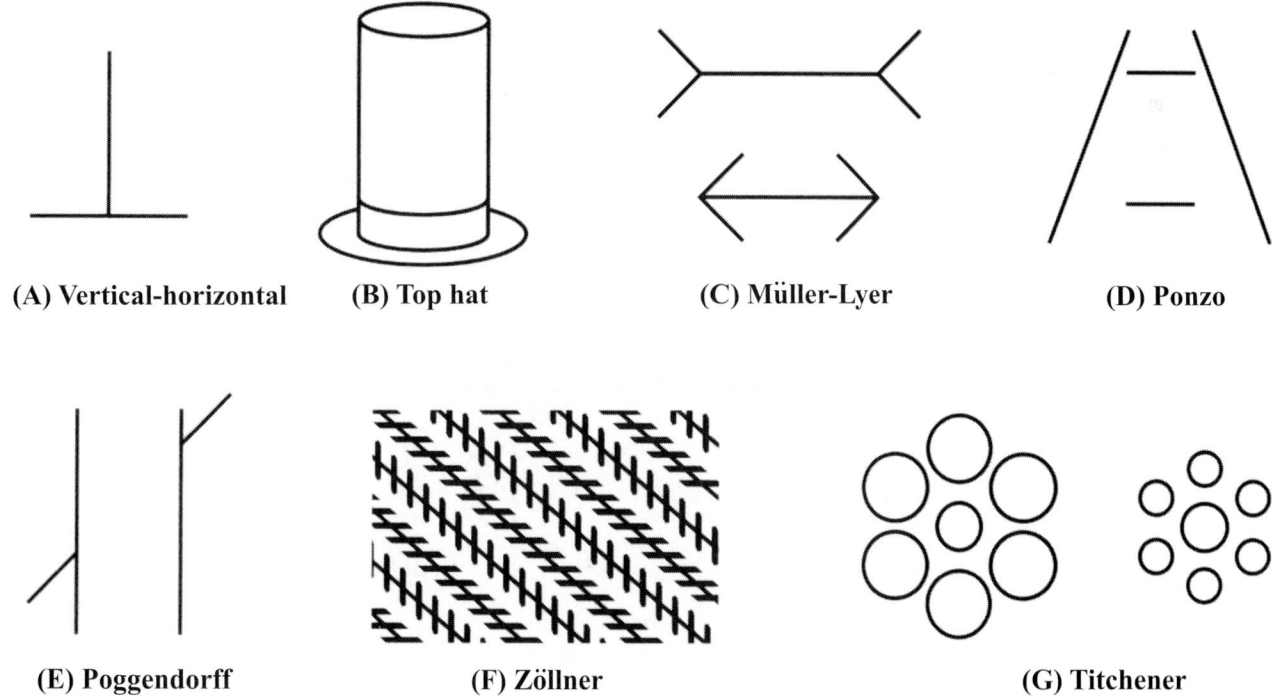

| (A) Vertical-horizontal | (B) Top hat | (C) Müller-Lyer | (D) Ponzo |

| (E) Poggendorff | (F) Zöllner | (G) Titchener |

FIGURE 3.27

A few classic geometrical illusions. In each case, you know the answer, but the relevant questions are: (A) Are the vertical and horizontal lines the same length? (B) Is the brim of the hat as wide as the hat is tall? (C) Are the two horizontal lines the same length? (D) Are the two horizontal lines the same length? (E) Are the two diagonals part of the same line? (F) Are the long diagonal lines parallel? (G) Are the two center circles the same size?

A second fact about illusions is that they do not occur at the retina. Figure 3.27 (C) is the well-known Müller-Lyer illusion named for the man who first drew it. The top line would continue to appear longer than the bottom one even if the two (equal) lines were presented to one eye, and the arrowlike vanes were presented to the other. A third fact about illusions is that their effects do not depend on eye movements. Illusions appear vividly even when they are flashed before the eyes so quickly that there is no opportunity to scan the presented image (Gillam, 1980).

Illusions of the sort presented in Figure 3.27 are not new. Scientists have been searching for reasonable explanations for illusions for well over a hundred years. How *do* geometrical illusions give rise to visual experiences that are at odds with the physical reality detected by the eyes? Frankly, we can't say. Several factors seem to work together to create illusions. A reasonable observation about illusions is that they provide evidence of our perceptual constancies being overapplied. Illusions largely depend on how we perceive and interpret clues to the size of objects in a three-dimensional world, and on inferences we make about the world, given our experience with it (Coren & Girgus, 1978; Gillam, 1980; Gregory, 1977; Hoffman, 1983).

Here's just one example. A reasonable-sounding explanation of the Müller-Lyer illusion is that the vanes of the arrows are taken to represent corners, as in a room. Refer to Figure 3.28 (A). When corners are near to us or far away, we are presented with perspective cues to their distance. Hence, we see the arrows of the illusion as representing corners and edges. This view is known as the "carpentered world hypothesis" (e.g., Davidoff, 1975; Gregory, 1977). In fact, in those cultures such as the Zulu in Africa, who through most of their history have lived in circular houses with round doors and domed roofs, the effects of the Müller-Lyer illusion are difficult to find (Segal et al., 1966). The carpentered world hypothesis sounds pretty good, doesn't it? Why, then, in Figure 3.28 (B), do we see the distance between circles *A* and *B* as greater than the distance between circles *B* and *C* when they are, in fact, equal?

The main instructional point of illusions is that they remind us that perception is a higher-level process than simple sensation; perception involves the organization and interpretation of the information we get from our senses, and things are not always as they seem. This point is made even more dramatically with what are known as impossible figures (see Figure 3.29).

BEFORE YOU GO ON

- What is meant by the term "perceptual constancies"?
- List and describe the specific perceptual constancies.
- What are illusions, and what best explains them?

(A)

(B)

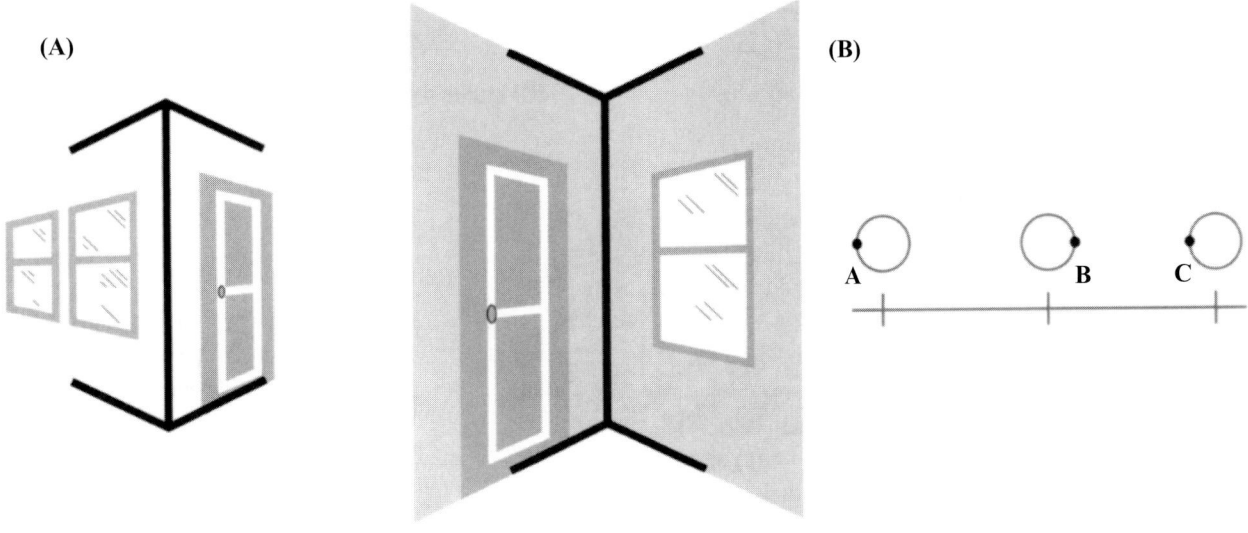

FIGURE 3.28

(A) One attempt to "explain" the Müller-Lyer illusion as the representation of edges and corners. (B) A variant of the Müller-Lyer illusion. The distance between the circles A and B is equal to the distance between the circles B and C. An explanation in terms of edges and corners no longer seems reasonable.

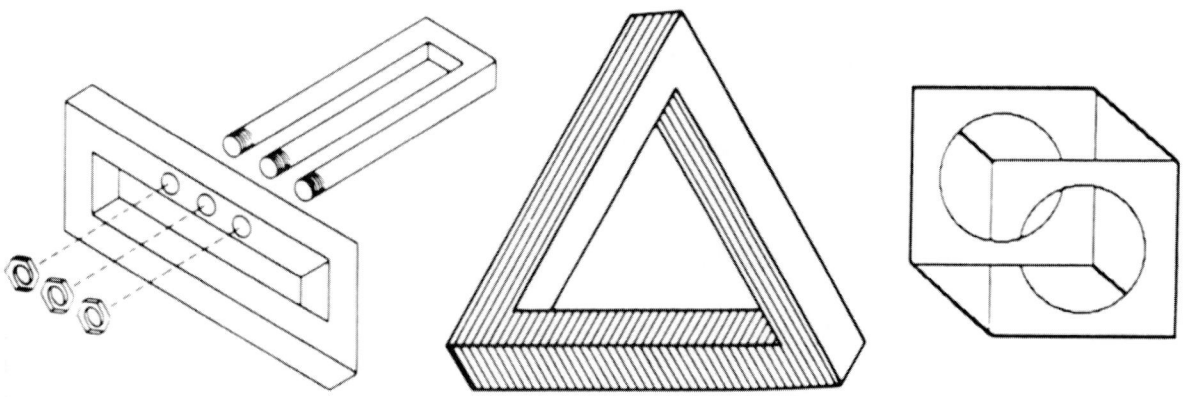

FIGURE 3.29

Impossible figures—examples of conflicting visual information.

Topic Review 3 B

1. **What is the difference between a salient detail and a peripheral detail?**

   A salient detail is one that is important enough to capture our attention. Salient details are remembered best. Peripheral details are part of the background and are less important than salient details. As a consequence, they are not remembered as well as salient details.

2. **What two major classes of factors control perceptual selectivity?**

   The two major classes of factors controlling perceptual selectivity are stimulus and personal factors. Stimulus factors refer to aspects of the stimulus perceived that affect perception. Personal factors refer to things about the perceiver that can influence what details in a scene are attended to.

3. **What are the stimulus factors that control perceptual selectivity?**

   Only a small portion of the information that stimulates our receptors is attended to, or selected, for further processing. Characteristics of the stimuli themselves may determine which stimuli will be attended to. We are more likely to attend to a stimulus if it contrasts with others around it in terms of intensity, size, motion, novelty, or any other physical characteristic. The repetition of a stimulus also increases the likelihood that we will attend to it.

4. **What are the personal factors that control perceptual selectivity?**

   The selection of stimuli is partly based on characteristics of the perceiver. Such factors as motivation, expectation (or mental set), and past experience often determine which stimuli are attended to. When characteristics of the perceiver are influential, we say that information is processed from the top down, rather than from the bottom up.

5. **What factors can influence how we organize stimuli in perception?**

   The organization of stimuli depends in part on the characteristics of the available stimuli, such as proximity, similarity, continuity, common fate, and closure. When these factors influence organization, we have bottom-up processing again. The personal factors that affect perceptual organization are the same as those that influence attention: motivation, mental set, and past experience.

6. **What is the figure-ground relationship?**

   The figure-ground relationship is a basic principle of Gestalt psychology. *Figures* are the stimuli in your environment that you attend to and group together, whereas all the rest are the *ground*. Figure is what we pay the most attention to and remember best. Elements of the background are not attended to as carefully, so we cannot remember things about ground well. For example, when you look at a painting, that painting is the figure, and the wall on which it is hanging, is the ground.

7. **What is meant by bottom-up processing?**

   Bottom-up processing involves grouping stimuli together based solely on the characteristics of the stimuli or stimulus factors. Five influential bottom-up processing factors are: proximity (grouping objects that are close together physically), similarity (grouping similar items together), continuity (seeing things as ending up consistent with the way they started off), common fate (grouping elements of a scene that appear to move together in the same direction and at the same speed), and closure (completing incomplete objects).

8. **What is a subjective contour?**

   Subjective contour is a phenomenon that is a special type of closure. With subjective contours, arrangements of lines and patterns cause us to see figures that are not actually there. There is no accepted explanation for subjective contours, but is considered another example of our perceptual processes filling in gaps in our perceptual world in order to provide us with sensible information.

9. **What is top-down processing?**

   Top-down processing involves the role of personal factors such as one's motivations, expectations, and information already stored in memory when processing incoming information. This means that we often perceive stimuli as related, as part of the same gestalt or figure, because we want to, because we expect to, or because we have perceived them together in the past.

10. What cues relating to the visual system help us discriminate depth and distance?

We are able to perceive three-dimensionality and distance even though we sense the environment on two-dimensional retinas because of the many cues with which we are provided. Some have to do with the visual system and are called ocular cues. Three such cues are retinal disparity, convergence, and accommodation. Retinal disparity involves each eye getting a slightly different view of three-dimensional objects. Convergence occurs when we look at something near our eyes and they move in toward each other. Retinal disparity and convergence are called binocular cues because they require both eyes. Accommodation, a monocular cue requiring only one eye, occurs when our lenses change shape to focus images as objects move toward or away from us.

11. What are the cues from the environment that help us discriminate depth and distance?

Cues for depth and distance also come from the environment, including many physical cues such as linear perspective (parallel lines seem to come together in the distance), relative size (everything else being equal, the smaller the stimulus, the farther away we judge it to be), interposition (near objects partially obscure our view of more distant objects), texture gradients (details of texture that we can see clearly up close are difficult to determine at a distance), patterns of shading, and motion parallax (as we move toward stationary objects, those close to us seem to move past us more rapidly than do objects in the distance).

12. What role does culture play in depth perception?

Depth and distance perception have been found to be susceptible to cultural influences. For example, the Bambuti people of the African Congo live so much of their lives in the dense Ituri Forest that they seldom can see much farther than 100 feet. If a Bambuti is taken out of the forest onto the open plains he or she will become disoriented with regard to cues for distance.

13. What, generally, are the perceptual constancies?

Perceptual constancies are mechanisms that help us organize and interpret the stimulus input we receive from our senses. The perceptual constancies allow us to recognize a familiar object as being the same regardless of how far away it is, the angle from which we view it, or the color or intensity of the light reflected from it.

14. What are the specific perceptual constancies?

Perceptual constancies comprise size, shape, brightness, and color constancy. Size constancy is the tendency to see objects as being of constant size regardless of the size of the retinal image. Shape constancy refers to our perception that objects maintain their shape even though the retinal image they cast may change. Brightness constancy means that the apparent brightness of familiar objects is perceived as being the same regardless of the actual amount or type of light under which they are viewed. Finally, color constancy allows us to see the color of objects as stable despite illumination with different colored lights.

15. What is an illusion?

An illusion is an example of when our perceptual constancies break down. Illusions are experiences in which our perceptions are at odds with what we know about physical reality. Illusions occur because of the way our brains process visual information, although no one explanation exists for why illusions occur.

Chapter 4

Varieties of Consciousness

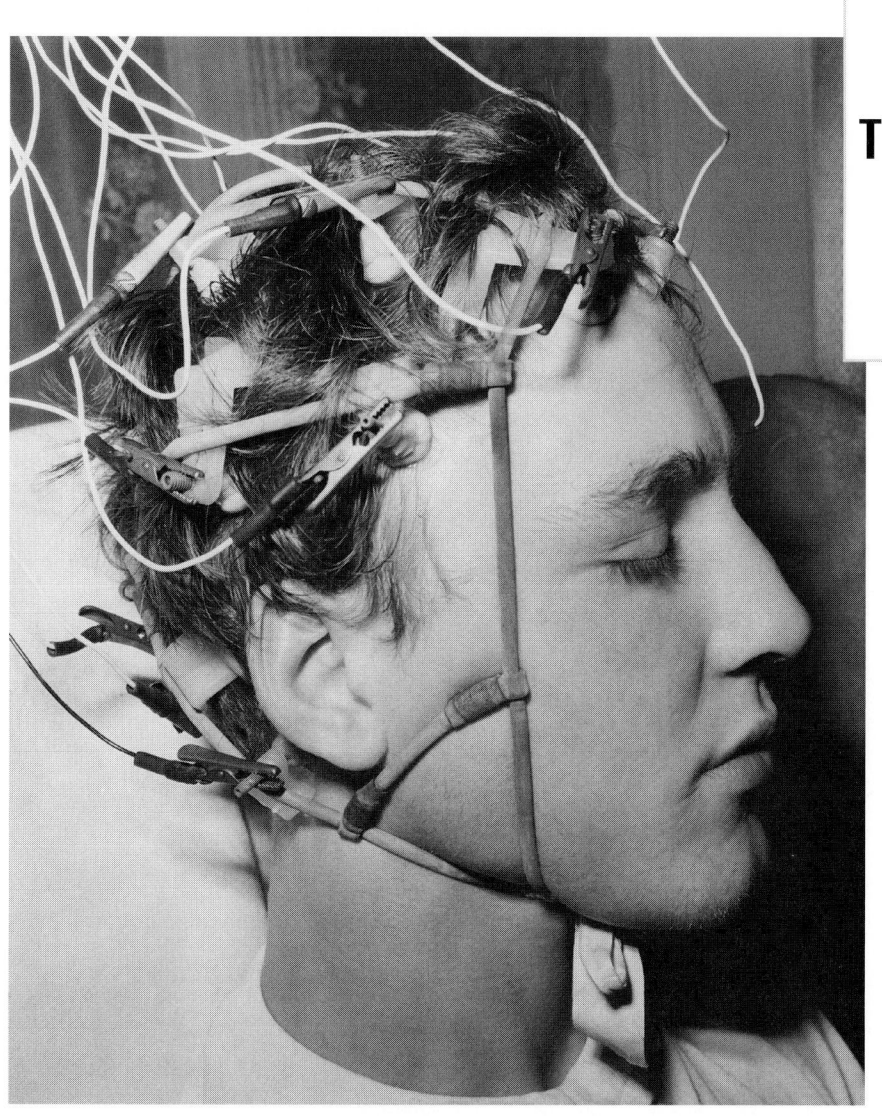

Topic 4A
Consciousness: Awake and Asleep

Topic 4B
Voluntary Alterations of Consciousness

Topic 4A CONSCIOUSNESS: AWAKE AND ASLEEP

Consciousness is such an integral part of our lives, we might argue that to be alive is to be conscious. Remember that the earliest psychologists (e.g., Wilhelm Wundt and William James) *defined* psychology as the science of consciousness or mental activity. Dealing with consciousness scientifically proved to be a very tricky business. After years of struggling with a science of consciousness, psychologists abandoned consciousness completely and turned their attention to observable behavior, as John B. Watson (and behaviorism) argued they should. But consciousness would not go away, and within the past 25 years, the scientific study of consciousness has reemerged, resuming its place in mainstream psychology.

consciousness the awareness of the environment and of one's own mental processes

Consciousness is the awareness of the environment and of one's own mental processes. Normal, waking consciousness is the awareness of those thoughts, feelings, and perceptions that are active in our minds. With this as a working definition, we might ask how to best characterize consciousness.

Humans, as well as other animals, experience a wide range of states of consciousness. Some of these are involuntary, representing the natural changes in alertness throughout the day. You feel refreshed after a good night's sleep. Later in the day, you may find yourself becoming drowsy during a late afternoon class. Later that evening, you go to bed and fall asleep and your brain experiences several alterations in consciousness. Other alterations in consciousness we bring upon ourselves: we meditate, undergo hypnosis, and perhaps even take drugs or drink alcohol. In this chapter we will explore these varieties of consciousness.

Key Questions to Answer

While reading this Topic, find the answers to the following key questions:

1. What are the four factors in normal waking consciousness?

2. What is meant by "levels of consciousness"?

3. What is Freud's classic approach to levels of consciousness?

4. What are the modern approaches to unconscious processing of information?

5. What are the stages of sleep and what kind of brain activity do you see in each?

6. What is meant by the terms REM and NREM sleep?

7. When do periods of REM sleep occur and how long do they last?

8. How are the stages of sleep distributed over the course of a night's sleep?

9. Does everyone experience the dreaming associated with REM sleep?

10.   What happens when we are deprived of sleep?

11.   What else, besides dreaming, happens during REM sleep?

12.   What happens if a person does not get enough REM sleep?

13.   What are the explanations for dreaming?

14.   What are the major sleep disorders?

15.   What is insomnia?

16.   Are drugs effective in combating insomnia?

17.   What effects does melatonin have on sleep onset and the sleep cycle?

18.   Is alcohol an effective sleep-inducing drug?

19.   What are the cognitive and behavioral underpinnings of insomnia?

20.   What are some of the things one can do to break bad sleep habits and negative thoughts?

21.   What is narcolepsy?

22.   What is sleep apnea?

NORMAL WAKING CONSCIOUSNESS

We probably have no better description of consciousness than that provided by William James a hundred years ago (1890, 1892, 1904). According to James, there are four basic aspects of what we call our normal, waking consciousness. Keep these four factors in mind—in your own consciousness—as we work through this chapter.

1.   *Consciousness is always changing*. Consciousness doesn't hold still. It cannot be held before the mind for study. "No state once gone can recur and be identical with what was before," James wrote (1892, p. 152).

2.   *Consciousness is a very personal experience*. Consciousness does not exist without an individual to have it. My consciousness and yours are separate and different. The only consciousness I can experience with certainty is mine. You may try to tell me about yours, but I will never be able to fully appreciate the state of mind that is your consciousness.

3.   *Consciousness is continuous*. Our awareness of our environment and of our own mental processes cannot be broken into pieces. There are no gaps in our awareness. We can't tell where one thought begins and another leaves off. James wrote, "Consciousness, then, does not appear to itself chopped up in bits. Such words as 'chain' or 'train' do not describe it fitly as it presents itself in the first instance. It is nothing jointed; it flows. A 'river' or 'stream' is most naturally described. In talking of it hereafter, let us call it the stream of thought, of consciousness…" (1890, p. 243).

4.   *Consciousness is selective*. Awareness is often a matter of making choices, of selectively attending to some aspect of experience while ignoring others. "We find it [consciousness] always doing one thing, choosing one out of several of the materials so presented to its notice, emphasizing and accentuating that and suppressing as far as possible all the rest" (James, 1890, p. 139).

BEFORE YOU GO ON

- What is meant by the term "consciousness"?

- What are the four major factors of consciousness?

You can appreciate that studying human consciousness scientifically, or experimentally, has been a challenge to psychologists over the years. An even more slippery notion is that consciousness is not an either-or proposition; it functions to different degrees, or levels, of awareness. Let's now consider levels of consciousness and the possibility of subconscious mental processes.

LEVELS OF CONSCIOUSNESS

The observation that levels or degrees of consciousness vary throughout the day seems intuitively obvious. At times we are wide awake, paying full attention to nearly everything around us. At other times our "minds wander" and we're "unfocused"—not paying attention to or processing much information of any sort from anywhere. And, of course, when we are asleep there are long periods when we are virtually unconscious, seemingly unaware of what is happening either in the environment or in our own minds.

It also seems intuitively obvious that the higher the level of our consciousness, the better able we are to process (i.e., interpret, understand, recall, or react to) information. Is it not more likely that you will remember something said in class if your consciousness is focused; if you are attentive, wide awake, and straining your attention to understand what is being said? Are you not more likely to trip over something on the sidewalk if you are daydreaming about this weekend's plans rather than remaining fully conscious of the environment around you?

Now we come to an interesting question: Is it possible to process information without being aware of it? Is it possible to process information *unconsciously*? The idea of an unconscious aspect of mind has a long history in philosophy and psychology (Epstein, 1994; Greenwald, 1992; Hilgard, 1992; Kihlstrom, 1987; Whyte, 1960). In this section, we'll focus first on a classic view of the unconscious as proposed by Sigmund Freud and then briefly consider some contemporary research.

The Freudian View of Levels of Consciousness

Sigmund Freud was trained in medicine and can rightfully be called the Father of Psychiatry, where psychiatry refers to that subfield of medicine that studies, diagnoses, and treats mental disorders. Early in his career, Freud became intrigued by what were then called "nervous disorders." He was struck by how little was known about disorders wherein one's psychological experiences and mental life seemed to produce pain and suffering for which there was no medical explanation. Freud proposed an elaborate theory of personality and put his ideas about human nature into practice by developing a new technique for treating mental disorders. For now, we focus on Freud's view of consciousness, a central aspect of both his theory and of his therapy.

Freud's vision of consciousness is often depicted as an iceberg nearly totally submerged in the sea (Figure 4.1). This iceberg analogy is one that Freud used himself. What does it imply?

Freud wrote that only a small portion of one's mental life was readily available to one's awareness at any given time. Ideas, memories, feelings, or motives of which we are actively aware are said to be *conscious*. It is hoped you are conscious of the words you are reading, what they mean, and how you can relate them to your own experience. Aspects of our experience that are not conscious at any moment, but that can easily be brought to awareness, are stored at a *preconscious* level. Right now you may not be thinking about what you had for dinner last night or what you might have for dinner tonight, but with just a little effort these matters—now in your preconscious—can be brought into your conscious awareness.

Cognitions, feelings, or motives that are not available at the conscious or the preconscious level are said to be in the *unconscious*. At this level are ideas, desires, and memories of which we are not aware and cannot easily become aware. This is a strange notion: there are thoughts and feelings stored in our minds of which we are completely unaware. Freud theorized that the unconscious level of mind can and does influence us. Much of the content of our unconscious mind is there because if we were to think about or dwell on these issues we would experience anxiety and distress. A husband, for instance, who constantly forgets his wedding anniversary and occasionally cannot even remember his wife's name when he tries to introduce her may be having some unconscious conflict or doubts about being married in the first place. (There are, of course, other explanations.) Unconscious mental content passing through the preconscious can show itself in dreams, humor, and slips of the tongue. It might be significant that following a lively discussion of some issue, Nathan says to Heather, "Let's rape more about this some time," when he *meant* to say, "Let's rap more about this some time." As we'll see, many Freudian techniques of psychotherapy are aimed at helping the patient learn about the contents of his or her unconscious mind.

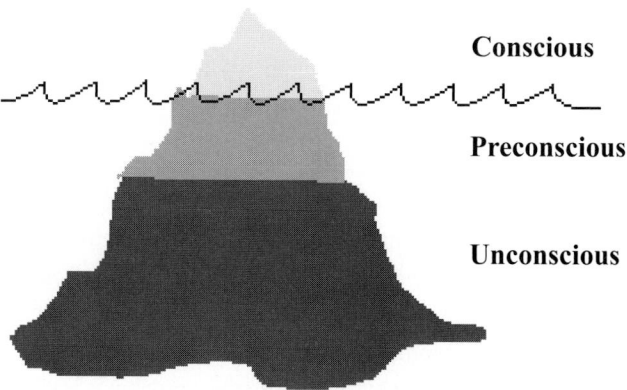

Conscious

Preconscious

Unconscious

FIGURE 4.1

In the theories of Sigmund Freud, the mind is likened to an iceberg where only a small portion of one's mental life is available in normal waking consciousness; more is available, with some effort of retrieval, at a preconscious level; and most is stored away at an unconscious level from which intentional retrieval occurs only with great effort.

Demonstrating the reality of levels of consciousness as Freud proposed them has proven difficult in controlled laboratory research. Nonetheless, Freud's basic ideas about levels of consciousness have gained wide acceptance in psychology, particularly among practicing clinical psychologists (Epstein, 1994; Greenwald, 1992).

Contemporary Investigations of the Unconscious

Interest in the unconscious is not limited to Freud and other psychoanalysts. Currently, researchers are investigating if (and how) the unconscious mind can process information and influence behavior. There are two major ways in which psychologists have approached the study of the unconscious. These are: subliminal perception, and blindsight. **Subliminal perception** is the process of perceiving and responding to stimuli presented at levels of intensity that are below our absolute threshold of conscious processing. **Blindsight** is a phenomenon that occurs in individuals with damage to the primary visual areas of the brain. Despite the fact that these individuals are blind in the area of the visual field associated with the damage, some can still "see" simple stimuli.

subliminal perception the process of perceiving and responding to stimuli presented at levels of intensity that are below our absolute threshold—below our level of conscious processing

blindsight a phenomenon that occurs in individuals with damage to the primary visual areas of the brain but can still see simple stimuli

Subliminal Perception

Can a subliminal message implanted in an advertisement induce you to buy a product? Can you improve your memory by listening to tapes with subliminal messages embedded within the material? The answer to these questions, based on available research is clearly no. For example, in one experiment, motivated participants listened to audio tapes that were supposed to either improve memory or enhance self-esteem through subliminal suggestion (Greenwald, et al., 1991). The participants were not aware that the labels of some of the tapes had been switched so that some participants who believed they were using the memory tape were actually using the self-esteem tape (and vice versa). The results showed little evidence for the power of subliminal messages. Although there was some improvement in memory or self-esteem for everyone, neither effect could be attributed to the subliminal tapes (Greenwald, et al., 1991). Interestingly, more than one-third of the participants had the illusion of improvement. The bottom line seems to be that if a person genuinely believes that self-help tapes will work, and invests money and time in them, he or she can become convinced that the tapes work and may show improvement (Balay & Shevrin, 1988; Dixon, 1971; Duncan, 1985; Vokey & Read, 1985).

Does the failure of subliminal tapes mean that it is not possible to process *any* information subliminally? The answer here is also no. Subliminal messages that are complex and meaningful (e.g., subliminal tapes) cannot be processed unconsciously. However, more simple stimuli can. In one experiment, for example, a person sits in front of a small screen. A word is flashed on the screen so dimly and so quickly that the person does not report seeing the word. Let's say the word is *stars*. Now two words that the subject can see clearly are flashed on the screen. The task is to choose the word that is related in some way to the word that was not seen. Let's say the words used in this example are *stripes* and *pencil*. Even when subjects claim they are only guessing, they choose *stripes* significantly more frequently than chance would predict. If the "unconscious prompt" were *eraser*, not *stars*, they would more likely choose *pencil*. It is as if the initially presented word influenced their choice (Cheesman & Merikle, 1984; Dixon, 1971, 1981; Fowler et al., 1981; Tulving & Schacter, 1990). For that matter, simply reading a list of words at one point in time increases the ability of subjects to read those words later when they are flashed very briefly on a computer screen, even if the subjects did not recognize that the words had been read previously (Jacoby & Dallas, 1981).

Blindsight

In normal vision, visual pathways extend from the retina through the lateral geniculate body and then on to the primary visual cortex. If something happens to damage this normal pathway, a person will be rendered blind in that part of the visual field served by the damaged area. However, as noted above, the damage does not totally eliminate vision in those parts of the visual field. The phenomenon of blindsight was first discovered by Lawrence Weisenkrantz. In the course of research with patients having damage to the visual cortex, he noted that a person could not "see" a stimulus presented in the damaged area of the visual field. However, when the individual was encouraged to guess whether something was presented, the individual correctly identified the presence of a stimulus above chance levels, indicating that there was detection of the stimulus on some level (Scharli & Harman, 1999; Wessinger & Fendrich, 1997; Kentridge & Heywood, 1997).

Some persons who are totally blind can—in certain circumstances—still respond to visually-presented stimuli, a phenomenon that some argue demonstrates "blindsight."

This phenomenon has been demonstrated in other aspects of vision. In one case, a patient with brain damage could not identify even the simplest of shapes. However, when she was asked to place a letter in a mail slot, she successfully adjusted the position of the envelope to fit the slot (Zeman, 1998). Thus, "the loss of certain kinds of activity in certain crucial areas of the visual cortex impairs or extinguishes visual awareness, without necessarily abolishing visually guided behavior" (Zeman, 1998, p. 1696). An analogous phenomenon can be found with hearing (called "deaf hearing"). In one experiment, a deaf patient was found to react reflexively to sounds and later identified auditory stimuli above chance levels when asked to guess whether a stimulus was presented (Garde & Cowey, 2000).

Why does blindsight occur? The answer to this question is not yet totally clear. It may be that subcortical visual pathways that remain intact after a lesion or surgery are responsible for blindsight (Kentridge & Heywood, 1999). However, there is evidence that fibers and tissue that were spared damage in the primary visual pathways may account for blindsight (Scharli & Harman, 1999; Scharli, Harman, & Hogben, 1999). At this point, there is no one good explanation for all cases of blindsight. However, it does raise some fascinating questions about the nature of the mind.

Is There an Unconscious Mind?

So, is there an unconscious mind, and if so, what is it like? There is little doubt that individuals can process information below the level of awareness, or unconsciously. The evidence we have just reviewed suggests, however, that unconscious processing is relatively primitive. Only simple, subliminal messages can be received, and only very basic visual information can be processed with blindsight. It may be that what we call the unconscious mind comprises primitive pathways in the brain that can handle only limited information.

Most of the research available clearly points to the existence of unconscious processes. Although there is no agreement about just how sophisticated unconscious processes are, there is absolute agreement that there are exciting times ahead for research on the unconscious mind (Loftus & Klinger, 1992).

BEFORE YOU GO ON

- What is meant by the idea of "levels of consciousness"?

- What are the three levels of consciousness proposed by Freud and what role does each play?

- What are the contemporary approaches to consciousness?

- What are subliminal perception and blindsight, and what do they say about the unconscious mind?

SLEEP

Sleep reduces our alertness, awareness, and perception of events occurring around us. Sleep is a normal process, yet it is one we do not understand well. We are seldom aware or conscious of our own sleeping, even though we may spend more than 200,000 hours of our lifetime asleep. Just as the level or degree of our awareness varies during the day, so does our sleep vary in its level or quality throughout the night and from night to night. The study of sleep and dreams has intrigued psychologists for many years. Here, we will examine some of what we know about the altered state of consciousness we call sleep.

The Stages of a "Good Night's Sleep"

How do we know when someone is asleep? Self-reports of sleeping are notoriously unreliable. A person who claims that he or she "didn't sleep a wink last night" may have slept soundly for many hours (Dement, 1974). Our best indicators of sleep are measurements of brain activity and muscle tone. The electroencephalograph (EEG) is an instrument that measures and records the electrical activity of the brain. It does so by means of small electrodes pasted onto the scalp. Each of those electrodes is measuring the summation of the action potentials of hundreds of the neurons that lie below it. The process is slightly messy, but it is in no way painful. The electromyogram (EMG) similarly produces a record of a muscle's activity, tone, or state of relaxation.

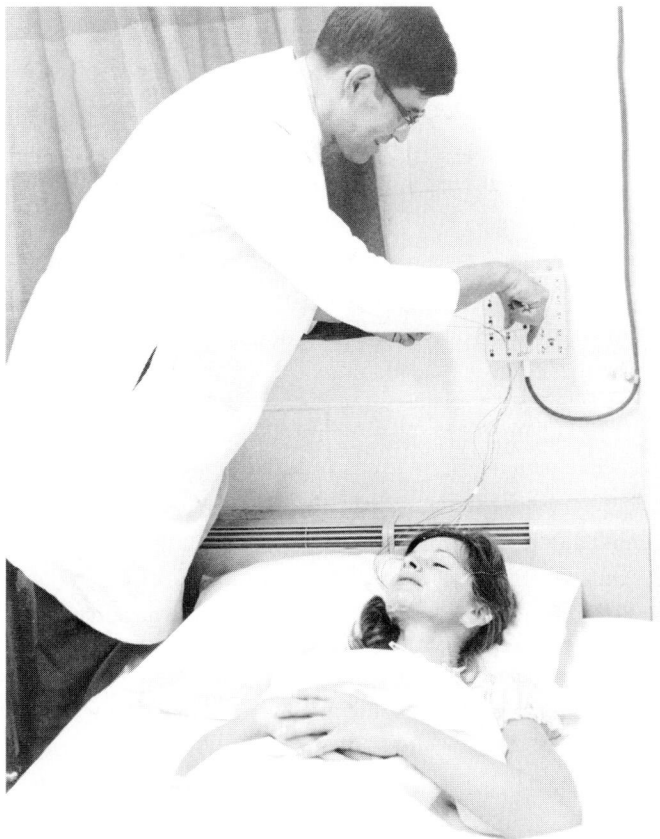

Our understanding of the stages of sleep comes, in large measure, from the studies of persons who report problems sleeping, and have their sleep habits monitored in a clinical setting.

When you are awake and alert, your EEG pattern shows fast, small, irregular patterns called gamma waves and beta waves. Gamma waves occur more than 30 times per second, while beta waves occur between 12 and 30 times per second. You have fast eye movements as you look around at things in your environment, and your breathing may be fast and shallow or slow and deep, depending on your level of physical activity.

When you are in a calm, relaxed state with your eyes closed but not yet asleep, your EEG pattern shows a rhythmic cycle of brain wave activity called *alpha waves*. In this presleep stage, we find smooth EEG waves cycling eight to twelve times per second. If, as you lie still, you start worrying about an event of the day or try to solve a problem, the alpha waves become disrupted and are replaced by an apparently random pattern of heightened electrical activity typical of that found in wakefulness.

As you enter sleep, your brain waves change as alpha waves give way to the brain waves that occur during the stages of sleep. The transition between the waking state and the sleep state is not sudden or abrupt. The onset of sleep is more like someone gradually turning down the brightness of a light than shutting off a switch. Once asleep, EEG tracings of the electrical activity of the brains of sleeping subjects reveal that sleep can be divided into five stages (Foulkes, 1966). As we review these stages, you can refer to Figure 4.2, which shows the EEGs of a person in each stage of sleep.

Stage 1: This is a very light sleep developing from the waking state. Sometimes this stage 1 sleep is referred to as *descending stage 1 sleep* because it represents a descent from wakefulness to sleep. The smooth cyclical alpha pattern disappears, and is replaced by the slower theta waves (4-7 cycles per second). The amplitude, or magnitude, of the electrical activity is becoming more regular. Your breathing is becoming more regular, your heart rate is slowing, and your blood pressure is decreasing. Some slow, rolling eye movements may occur or the eyes may be still. If aroused from sleep, individuals report being in a light sleep or just "drifting off" to sleep. This stage does not last long—generally less than ten minutes. Then, you start to slide into stage 2 sleep.

Stage 2: In this stage, the EEG pattern is similar to descending stage 1—low amplitude, with no noticeable wavelike pattern. The difference is that we now see *sleep spindles* in the EEG record. These are brief bursts of electrical activity (12-14 cycles per second) that occur with regularity (about every fifteen seconds). In addition to sleep spindles, we also see *K–complexes* in the EEG record. A *K–complex* is indicated by a large, sharp waveform made up of a single positive wave followed by a single negative wave.

Stage 3: You're getting into deep sleep now. There is a reduction in the brain's electrical activity. We can clearly make out *delta wave* activity in your EEG. Delta waves are high, slow waves (from 0.5 to 4 cycles per second). In this stage, delta waves constitute between 20 percent and 50 percent of your EEG pattern. Your internal functions (temperature, heart rate, breathing) are lowering and slowing. It's going to be difficult to wake you now.

Stage 4: Now, you're in deep sleep. Your EEG record is virtually filled with slow, recurring delta waves (as opposed to stage 3 sleep, where delta waves made up only a portion of your brain wave activity). Readings from an electromyogram indicate that your muscles have become almost totally relaxed. About 15 percent of your night's sleep will be spent in this stage.

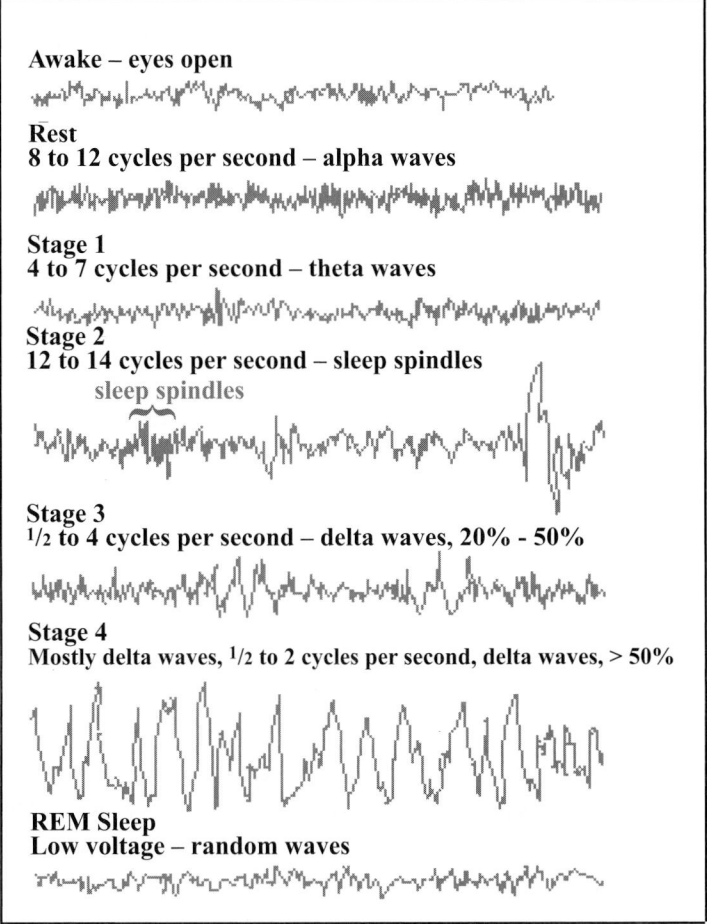

Awake – eyes open

Rest
8 to 12 cycles per second – alpha waves

Stage 1
4 to 7 cycles per second – theta waves

Stage 2
12 to 14 cycles per second – sleep spindles
sleep spindles

Stage 3
$^1/_2$ to 4 cycles per second – delta waves, 20% - 50%

Stage 4
Mostly delta waves, $^1/_2$ to 2 cycles per second, delta waves, > 50%

REM Sleep
Low voltage – random waves

FIGURE 4.2

EEG records showing the general electrical activity of the brain for a person at various stages of sleep and wakefulness.

In the early 1950's, Nathaniel Kleitman and Eugene Aserinsky discovered that during the course of a night's sleep, there were times when you would see the sleeping person's eye darting around rapidly. These eye movements are called rapid eye movements that occur during the **REM** stage of sleep. They also noted that there were other times during the night when these rapid eye movements were absent (Aserinsky & Kleitman, 1953; Kleitman, 1963b). Sleep stages two, three, and four are referred to as **NREM sleep** because of the lack of rapid eye movements. If you were to awaken a person during a period of NREM sleep they would not report a vivid dream, rather they would report fragmented thoughts (Kleitman, 1963a; NCSDR, 1993).

Stage 5, REM sleep: Following stage 4 sleep, we enter the stage of REM sleep, or rapid eye movement, sleep. This type of sleep is sometimes referred to as *ascending stage 1* sleep because there is ascent from the brain wave activity characteristic of deep sleep to brain wave activity that looks more like the waking state. During this stage, slow theta waves are evident, as is the case in stage 1. During REM sleep, there is a periodic return

REM sleep a period of sleep during which the eyes move rapidly and is associated with vivid, story-like dreams

NREM (nonREM) sleep a period of sleep during which there are no rapid eye movements and is associated with fewer, more fragmented dreams

to alpha wave activity (around 8 cycles per second in contrast to the 10 cycles per second for the waking brain) (Foulkes, 1966), making the brain appear to be in a waking state. If you refer to Figure 4.2, you will find an EEG tracing typical of the sort found during REM sleep. Note that it looks much like the tracing indicating wakefulness. Your muscles are completely relaxed. The sleeping individual displays a reduced sensitivity to external stimuli, is immobile, and is difficult to arouse. If awakened, the person will report being in a deep sleep.

If a person is awakened during REM sleep, he or she would most likely (about 85 percent of the time) report a vivid, story-like dream. At first, it was believed that the rapid eye movements during REM sleep were being made as the dreamer literally viewed, or scanned, images produced by the dream. This also led to the myth that dreams lasted only a few seconds. We now know that this is not the case. A dreamer's eye movements are unrelated to the content of the dream.

If REMs are not a result of watching one's dream, what are they? The best evidence we have suggests that rapid eye movements are a byproduct of the activation of the visual system that occurs during REM sleep. According to J. Allan Hobson (1994), a complex sequence of neurophysiological events trigger REM sleep and rapid eye movements. A simplified representation of these events is shown in Figure 4.3. According to Hobson, cells in the pons (a structure located in the brainstem) are responsible for the transition into REM sleep and the rapid eye movements characteristic of that type of sleep. During NREM sleep, cells in the pons which produce the neurotransmitters norepinephrine and serotonin are at first active, but gradually become less active as NREM sleep continues. As norepinephrine and serotonin levels fall, other cells in the pons create a flood of another neurotransmitter (acetylcholine), which triggers REM sleep. With the surge of acetylcholine, the brain begins to produce what are called *"PGO waves."* These are brain waves that originate in the pons (P), go up through the geniculate bodies (G), midbrain structures involved in vision, and end in the occipital lobe (O) of the cortex, where visual representation normally takes place.

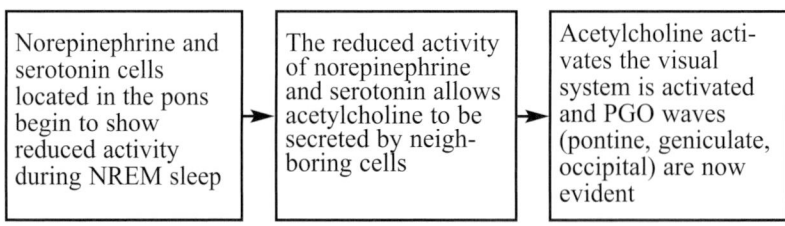

FIGURE 4.3

A simplified representation of the physiological mechanisms involved in rapid eye movements.

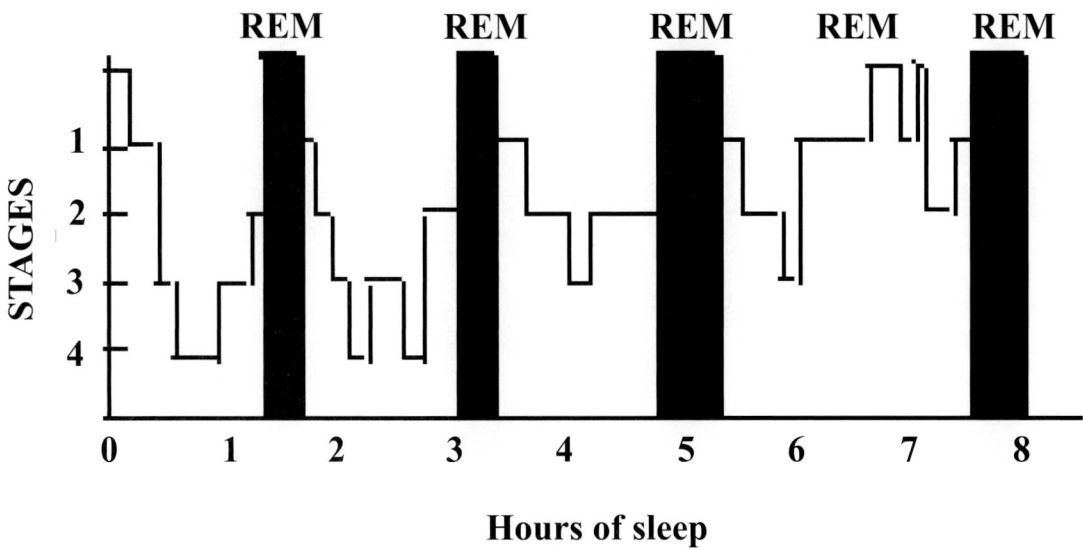

FIGURE 4.4

A typical sequence of sleep stages during a night's sleep for a young adult. Notice the recurring REM sleep throughout the night, and note that one does not need to enter each stage of sleep in the same order or sequence.

Periods of REM sleep occur throughout the night and normally last from a few minutes to half an hour and occupy about 20 percent to 25 percent of the sleep of adult humans. About 90 to 120 minutes each night are spent in REM sleep. As one goes through a night's sleep, REM episodes tend to become longer and dreams more vivid (NCSDR, 1993). The normal pattern of REM episodes is presented in Figure 4.4.

During the course of a night's sleep, there is a recurring pattern of stages of sleep. However, one does not necessarily pass through all stages of sleep in an orderly fashion. Occasionally stage 3 may be passed over completely; later in the evening, stage 4 may be absent. Indeed, toward the end of our sleeping, we tend not to return to the deep sleep of stage 4 between REM episodes.

Dreaming isn't all that happens during REM sleep. From the outside, someone in REM sleep seems quiet and calm, except for those barely noticeable eye movements and irregular breathing. On the inside, however, is quite a different story. One change is a muscular immobility, called *atonia*, caused by the total relaxation of the muscles (Chase & Morales, 1990). It does seem adaptive to have the body lie still so that the dreamer does not react to the action of his or her dreams. This state of immobilization is occasionally interrupted by slight muscle "twitches." Some people do not demonstrate normal atonia but thrash about wildly during REM sleep, a condition reasonably called *REM sleep disorder* (Mahowald & Schenck, 1989).

In many ways, the REM sleeper is very active even though not conscious of most external stimulation. During REM sleep there is often an excitement of the sex organs, males having a penile erection, females having a discharge of vaginal fluids (although

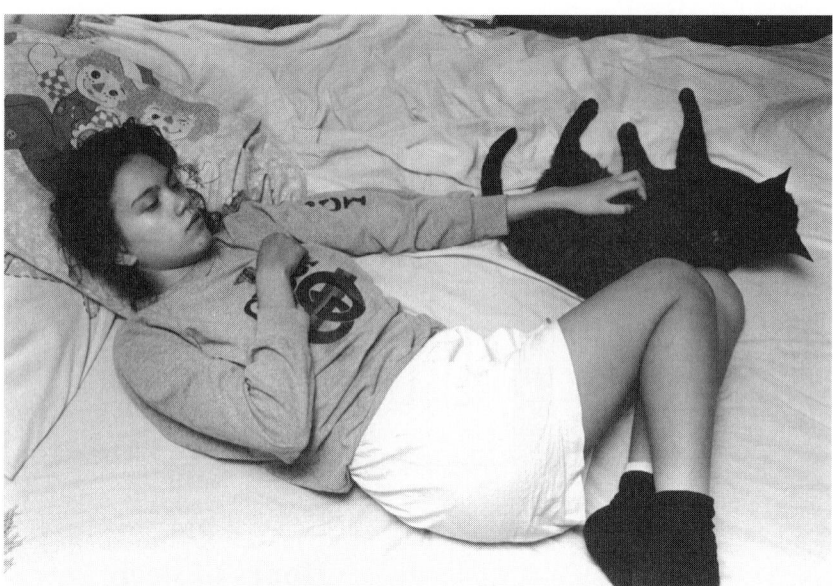

Freud believed that dreams allow the unconscious mind the freedom to express itself without burdening the conscious mind with fears and anxieties.

BEFORE YOU GO ON

- Describe the five stages of sleep and the brain activity associated with each.

- How do Stage 1 and REM sleep differ?

- What is the difference between REM and NREM sleep?

- What causes REMs to occur?

- What physiological changes occur during REM sleep?

---

this latter finding is not as common). Breathing usually becomes shallow and rapid. Blood pressure levels may sky-rocket and heart rates increase, all while the person lies "peace-fully" asleep. This marked increase in physiological activity during REM sleep has long been suspected to be related to heart attacks, strokes, and other cardiovascular problems that can develop "even though the patient was asleep" (King et al., 1973; Kirby & Verrier, 1989; Somers et al., 1993).

Sleep Deprivation

"Each year, the lives of millions of American men, women, and children are disturbed, disrupted, or destroyed by sleep deprivation, sleep disorders, or sleep disturbances." So begins the report of the National Commission on Sleep Disorders Research (NCSDR, 1993, p. 15). In this section, we'll consider some of the issues that have concerned this commission.

We are a nation in need of a good night's sleep. On average, Americans get about 1.5 hours less sleep each night than they need. This reflects an average reduction in nightly sleep of nearly 20 percent over the last century—due to a myriad of factors, including demands of the workplace, school, home, and family. Interstate truck drivers, for instance, regularly get less than five hours of sleep a night (NCSDR, 1993; Mitler et al., 1997). In fact, Mitler, et al., concluded that long-haul truckers get less sleep than is required for optimal alertness for their jobs and are at particular risk for falling asleep at the wheel late at night and early in the morning. Each of us requires a specific amount of sleep in a twenty-four-hour period to maintain optimal waking activity. "A good night's sleep" is the amount of sleep that will allow a person to awaken without the use of some device or environmental influence, such as an alarm clock. If a person does not get an adequate amount of sleep (yes, there are individual differences in terms of how much sleep is adequate), he or she will be less alert and less able to function well in the short run (the next day). What is particularly troubling is that sleep loss accumulates from one night to the next as a "sleep debt." The more sleep lost each day, the greater the debt and the more severe the consequences.

Most sleep deprivation studies, in which humans are awakened so as to disrupt their sleep, show remarkably few long-term adverse side effects (Horne, 1988; Martin, 1986; Webb & Cartwright, 1978). Even if sleep is disrupted over several nights, there are few lasting changes in a person's reactions, particularly if the person is in good physical and psychological health to begin with. In fact, Thomas Edison, one of the 20th century's greatest inventors, rarely got more than a couple of hours of sleep per night. If, after deprivation, a task is interesting enough and if it is not lengthy or time-consuming, there is little impairment of intellectual functioning (Dement, 1974; Webb, 1975). At least up to a point, we can adapt to deprivation, perhaps by taking little catnaps while we're awake. Very short episodes of sleep, called microsleeps, can be found in the EEG records of waking subjects, both animal and human. Thomas Edison took many such catnaps during the day. These microsleep episodes increase in number when normal sleep is disrupted.

That's not to say that there aren't any effects of being deprived of sleep. Some people show marked signs of depression and irritability when their sleep is interrupted (Moorecroft, 1987, 1989). People deprived of REM sleep for a few nights and then left alone will spend long periods REMing, as if to catch up on lost REMs. This REM rebound effect is generally found only for the first night after deprivation, then patterns return to normal. There is some evidence that NREM sleep (particularly stage 4 deep sleep) also rebounds (Agnew et al., 1964). There is now evidence that sleep loss may affect crucial endocrine functions related to some chronic diseases (Spiegel, Leproult, & Van Cauter, 1999). Diabetes, coronary heart disease and impairment of the immune system may be affected by sleep deprivation.

BEFORE YOU GO ON

- What is the definition of a "good night's" sleep?
- What happens when a person is selectively deprived of REM sleep?
- What is the REM "rebound effect"?
- What are the consequences of sleep deprivation?

Dreaming

In the previous section we explored the physiological mechanisms that trigger the stage of sleep in which "dreams" take place. Consequently, you now know how dreams are switched on. However, there is more to dreaming than simply switching on a physical mechanism. Dreams have meaning. When you wake up in the morning and recall a particularly strange dream, you probably try to figure out what the dream was all about. Was it related to what happened to you the day before? Or was it related to something that you were planning to do the next day? Or, yet again, was it related to something that happened to you years ago?

The question of what the content of a dream means has been a topic of interest for humans ranging (at least) back to the ancient Greek philosophers. For example, Aristotle believed that dreams were simply the contents of sensory experiences that manifested themselves during sleep. Aristotle did not attach much significance to the imagery one experienced during sleep because those images were assumed to be directly related to the sensations and perceptions that occurred during the day.

The most influential view of the nature of dreams was provided by Freud (1900a) in his book *Interpretation of Dreams*. Recall that Freud placed a great deal of emphasis on the role of the unconscious in our everyday lives. Unfortunately, we are not privy to what goes on in the unconscious. Freud saw dreams as a way of finding out what mischief was going on in the unconscious. In fact, Freud in his third lecture presented at Clark University in 1910, stated that the "interpretation of dreams is in fact the via regia [royal road] to the interpretation of the unconscious."

Freud's theory of dreams underscores the importance of the meaning of dreams. He suggested that many dreams serve a wish-fulfillment purpose. That is, the content of a dream is related to something you need or want. So, if you are thirsty when you go to bed and you dream of drinking water, your wish for water has been fulfilled in the dream. Further, Freud suggested that all dreams are related to events that occurred on the day before the dream or on events that occurred in the few days preceding the dream (Freud, 1990b/1952).

manifest content the content that the dreamer is consciously aware of

In his theory of dreams, Freud made a distinction between two types of dream content. The **manifest content** was the content of which the dreamer was aware. So, when you awake in the morning and remember being chased by a bear in a clown suit riding a motorcycle, that is the manifest content. Of course, the manifest content was important in the analysis and interpretation of dreams. However, the manifest content was only important in that it gave Freud a pathway to the latent content of the dream. The **latent content** is the true, underlying meaning of the dream that resides in a person's unconscious mind. Through a process called *dream work*, latent content shows itself in a highly disguised form. Freud said that dream work comprised several processes. The *condensation* process took elements of the latent content and fused them together into a composite that would show up in the manifest content. So, for example, that bear that was chasing you could be a composite of your father, your boss, and your pet dog. Another process was *dramatization* which operated to translate thoughts into actions. So the bear riding the motorcycle could be a dramatization of some unconscious thought (e.g., a desire to get away from your parents). A third, and crucial, process was *dream displacement* which allowed for elements of the latent content to affect the importance or vividness of the manifest content. The catch is, however, that something that is vivid in the manifest content may relate to something insignificant in the latent content and vice versa. That is, maybe a bear and a motorcycle chase are relatively unimportant matters. Maybe it is the clown suit that is important, signaling an inner embarrassment you feel about the way your mother dresses in public.

latent content the true, underlying meaning of the dream that resides in a person's unconscious mind

Although Freud's theory on dreams was well articulated and comprehensive, not everyone agreed with it. For example, Carl Jung (a fellow psychoanalytic theorist) believed that dreams were more transparent than did Freud. Jung did not emphasize the disguised nature of dream content. Instead he suggested that the symbolism inherent in dreams was related to universal human concerns (Hobson, 1988). Despite these differences, the psychoanalytic theory of dreams dominated most of the thinking on dreams in the 20th century.

A wholly different theory of dreams was proposed by Hobson and McCarley in 1977. This theory is known as the **activation-synthesis theory** of dreaming. According to this theory, dreams are activated via physiological mechanisms in the brainstem (see our previous discussion of REM sleep and PGO waves). This activation produces the images that form the content of our dreams. Synthesis takes place in the cerebral cortex and subcortical areas associated with processing memories. This involvement of memory provides the "plot" or "story" for the dream and is responsible for the meaningfulness of the content. Hobson (1988) maintains that dreams are "neither obscure nor bowdlerized, but rather transparent and unedited" (p.214). This position is in sharp contrast to Freud's view of dreams as being highly disguised and distorted.

activation-synthesis theory theory that dreams are activated via physiological mechanisms in the brainstem

Which position is "correct?" This is still open to debate. Many psychologists and psychiatrists adhere—to one degree or another—to Freud's characterization of dreams. However, like almost all of Freud's theoretical concepts, there is little empirical support for his theory of dreams. Conversely, the activation-synthesis theory is based on years of research on both animals and humans and has a more firm scientific foundation than psychoanalytic theory. What is most important, however, is that both approaches say that our dreams have meaning and the content of our dreams is important to us. The major difference lies in the characterization of a dream as being highly distorted (psychoanalysis) or transparent (activation-synthesis).

Sleep Disorders

A good night's sleep is a wonderful and apparently necessary thing. Some people have no difficulty sleeping. Others experience problems, either in getting to sleep in the first place, or during sleep itself. Still others fall asleep at unwanted times. As is the case for so many psychological processes, we often take sleep for granted until we experience problems with it.

The Association of Sleep Disorders Centers (ASDC) has classified sleep disorders into four groups: disorders of initiating or maintaining sleep (insomnias), disorders of excessive sleep, disorders of the sleep-waking cycle (disorders of the circadian rhythm), and disorders of sleep stages or partial arousals (parasomnias) (Rothenberg, 1997). The *Diagnostic and Statistical Manual (4th edition) of the American Psychiatric Association* (DSM-IV) classifies sleep disorders into three main groups: primary sleep disorders (including insomnias and parasomnias), disorders of sleep relating to other disorders, and "other" sleep disorders (sleep disturbances related to medical conditions or substance abuse) (Rothenberg, 1997). In the sections that follow we will explore some of the major sleep disorders.

Insomnia

insomnia the inability to fall asleep or stay asleep

At some time or another, each of us has suffered from a bout of **insomnia**—the inability to fall asleep or stay asleep when we want to. Insomnia may occur in brief episodes lasting a few days or episodes lasting weeks or months. Bouts of insomnia can be brought on by many things, such as excitement over upcoming events, life stress, psychological disorders, and a host of illnesses (Rothenberg, 1997). Also, insomnia may occur if we overstimulate our autonomic nervous systems with drugs such as caffeine. Chronic, debilitating insomnia affects nearly 30 million Americans, women more commonly than men, and the elderly about one and one-half times as often as younger adults (Fredrickson, 1987; NCSDR, 1993). Because there are many possible causes for insomnia, it is often difficult to pinpoint a single factor causing a person's insomnia (Rothenberg, 1997). In fact, most people who chronically suffer from insomnia haven't the slightest idea why they are unable to get a good night's sleep.

An interesting finding from the sleep laboratory is that many people who believe they are not getting enough sleep are, in fact, sleeping much more than they think. The phenomenon is called *pseudoinsomnia*, and one hypothesis is that such people spend several dream episodes each night dreaming that they are awake and trying to get to sleep. Then, in the morning, they remember their dreams and come to believe that they haven't slept at all (e.g., Dement, 1974). Pseudoinsomnia can usually be cured simply by demonstrating to patients that they really are getting a good night's sleep, as indicated by their EEG records. Regardless of whether insomnia is real or imagined, individuals suffering from insomnia often take steps to combat the disorder.

Drugs Used to Induce Sleep

In the quest for that elusive good night's sleep, many insomniacs resort to medications to help them fall or stay asleep. Prescribing sleeping pills (common in nursing homes) and using over-the-counter medications to treat insomnia may cause more problems than it solves. The medication (usually sedatives or depressants) may have a positive effect for a while, but eventually dosages have to be increased as tolerance builds. When the medications are discontinued, a rebound effect occurs that makes it more difficult to get to sleep than it had been before (Kales et al., 1979; Kripke & Gillin, 1985; Palfai & Jankiewicz, 1991). Also, certain sedatives suppress stages 3 and 4 sleep. For these reasons, sleep experts recommend that drugs be used only for transient, short-term insomnia, limited to four weeks or less (Roehrs & Roth, 1997).

One controversial substance that has been implicated in the sleep cycle is *melatonin*. Melatonin is a hormone that is produced by the pineal gland during the night and appears to play a role in the sleep-waking cycle (Garfinkel & Laudon, 1995). Research shows that taking melatonin at bedtime can decrease the time to sleep onset in normal young adults (Zhdanova & Wurtman, 1997; Zhdanova, Wurtman, Morabito, Piotrovska, & Lynch, 1996). It has also been found to decrease sleep onset time in elderly individuals who may show lowered levels of naturally-occurring melatonin (Dawson, et al., 1998; Garfinkel & Laudon, 1995). Research on the effects of melatonin on sleep onset latency for insomniacs is mixed (Mendelson, 1996). For example, one experiment showed that individuals who have trouble falling asleep and waking spontaneously at a desired time in the morning were helped by a 5-mg dose of melatonin, compared to a placebo control group. On the other hand, Ellis, Lemmens and Parks (1996) reported no benefits of melatonin for insomniacs. A review of the literature on melatonin confirms the limited effectiveness of melatonin for insomniacs (Mendelson, 1997).

BEFORE YOU GO ON

- How are sleep disorders classified?
- What is insomnia?
- What is pseudoinsomnia?
- What are some of the benefits and drawbacks of using sleep medications to fight insomnia?
- Is melatonin an effective drug for inducing sleep in insomniacs?
- What effects does alcohol have on the sleep cycle?

The Cognitive and Behavioral Roots of Insomnia

Many cases of insomnia have roots in learning and perpetuating poor sleep habits. For example, after a poor night's sleep or two one might begin to dwell on not being able to sleep, leading to anxiety at bedtime. Individuals learn to associate the bedroom and bed with negative feelings, which are incompatible with the relaxation that is needed to fall asleep. Eventually, the negative thoughts and feelings associated with insomnia give rise to maladaptive sleep habits. In an interesting study (Libman et al., 1997) comparing the behaviors of good and poor sleepers, it was found that good and poor sleepers differ on a number of behavioral dimensions. When good sleepers do wake up in the middle of the night, they are able to fall back to sleep quickly. On the other hand, poor sleepers tend to engage in counterproductive activities such as tossing and turning, or worrying about personal problems.

According to the National Commission on Sleep Disorder Research (NCSDR), we are a nation badly in need of sleep. The commission reports that interstate truck drivers regularly get fewer than five hours of sleep a night.

Because so many cases of insomnia relate to cognitive, affective, and behavioral problems, a person suffering from insomnia may find success with techniques that target unproductive sleep-related thoughts and behaviors. There are several such behavioral techniques that one can use to fall asleep (Pawlicki & Heitkemper, 1985). These are summarized in Figure 4.5.

BEFORE YOU GO ON

- What are the cognitive and behavioral underpinnings of insomnia?

- How do good and poor sleepers differ in terms of their sleep habits?

- What are the behavioral techniques used to fight insomnia?

- How effective are the behavioral techniques in reducing insomnia?

Behavioral techniques can be helpful in treating insomnia. In one study, for example, several behavioral techniques were assessed including stimulus control instructions (use one's bedroom only for sleep, get up and leave bed if one doesn't fall asleep in a reasonable amount of time, wake at a regular time, no napping), relaxation training, biofeedback, and cognitive therapy (Bootzin & Rider, 1997). The results showed that the stimulus control technique had the strongest effect in treating insomnia. Additionally, stimulus control techniques have been found to be effective in helping medicated insomniacs fall asleep after withdrawal from medication as well as nonmedicated insomniacs (Riedel et al., 1998).

Narcolepsy

narcolepsy going to sleep, even during the day, without any intention to do so

Narcolepsy involves going to sleep, even during the day, without any intention to do so. Periods of narcoleptic sleep overcome a person, regardless of the number of hours of sleep obtained the night before (Rothenberg, 1997). Narcolepsy has a genetic component and appears to be transmitted by the expression of a dominant gene (Rothenberg, 1997). There are several other symptoms which can accompany narcolepsy. These include a

1.   Avoid caffeine within four to six hours of bedtime.

2.   Avoid the use of nicotine close to bedtime or during the night.

3.   Do not drink alcoholic beverages within four to six hours of bedtime.

4.   While a light snack before bedtime can help promote sound sleep, avoid large meals.

5.   Avoid strenuous exercise within 6 hours of bedtime.

6.   Minimize light, noise, and extremes in temperature in the bedroom.

7.   Try to sleep when you are drowsy.

8.   If you are unable to fall asleep or stay asleep, leave your bedroom and engage in a quiet activity elsewhere. Do not permit yourself to fall asleep outside the bedroom. Return to bed when—and only when—you are sleepy. Repeat this process as often as necessary throughout the night.

FIGURE 4.5

Techniques recommended by the American Academy of Sleep Medicine for getting a good night's sleep. Downloaded from the World Wide Web, January 31, 2001. http://www.asda.org/ Reprinted with permission.

sudden decrease in muscle tone even while awake (called "cataplexy"), a paralysis upon falling asleep, and dream-like images that occur as soon as one goes to sleep or wakes up. Recent research has shown that narcolepsy is associated with a loss of specific types of neurons in the hypothalamus (Thannickal et al., 2000). For years, the only treatment for narcolepsy was the prescription of stimulants to help people stay awake during the day, but this approach had many side effects. Recently a drug called modafinil has been approved to treat narcolepsy, with promising results. Although only around 50,000 cases have been diagnosed, estimates are that nearly 350,000 Americans suffer from narcolepsy (NCSDR, 1993). The big problem with narcolepsy (in addition to the embarrassment it may cause) is the total relaxation of muscle tone that happens when the person is wide awake. This relaxation of muscle tone can occur without warning but it is usually triggered by an emotional event, either happy or sad. A person with narcolepsy can have an attack of muscle weakness before giving a speech or after hearing a funny joke. The danger in suddenly going to sleep or losing muscle control during one's daily activities (such as driving a car) is obvious.

Sleep Apnea

Apnea means a sudden stoppage in breathing, literally "without breath." If we were to stop breathing when awake and conscious, we could do something about it. We can exercise conscious, voluntary control over our breathing. We cannot do so, however, when we are asleep. **Sleep apnea** involves patterns of sleep during which breathing stops entirely. There are three types of sleep apnea: obstructive sleep apnea, central sleep apnea, and mixed sleep apnea. In *obstructive sleep apnea*, which is the most common type, the soft tissues at the back of the throat close off air passages blocking the flow of air. *Central sleep apnea* occurs when the brain does not send signals to muscles involved in breathing. *Mixed sleep apnea* involves a combination of obstructive and central sleep apnea (American Sleep Apnea Association, 2001). Sleep apnea is a widespread problem with as many as 12 million sufferers in America. Although it can occur at any age or to men or women, it is most common among men over age 40 who are overweight (American Sleep Apnea Association, 2001). Episodes of sleep apnea are usually short. When apnea episodes are longer—say, a minute or two—carbon dioxide in the lungs builds to such a level that the sleeper is awakened, draws a few gasps of air, and returns to sleep, probably oblivious to what just happened. Potential consequences of sleep apnea include hypertension, coronary heart disease, stroke, psychiatric problems, impotence, and memory loss. The Commission on Sleep Disorders Research estimates that 38,000 cardiovascular deaths due to sleep apnea occur each year (1993, p. 33).

sleep apnea patterns of sleep, usually short, during which breathing stops entirely

Sleep apnea is also a prime suspect in the search for a cause of Sudden Infant Death Syndrome, or SIDS. In this syndrome, young infants, apparently without any major illness, but sometimes with a slight cold or infection, suddenly die in their sleep. Such sudden death occurs at a rate of about two infants per thousand.

BEFORE YOU GO ON

- What is narcolepsy?
- What are the characteristics associated with narcolepsy?
- What is sleep apnea?
- Why might sleep apnea be dangerous?

Topic Review 4 A

1. What are the four factors in normal waking consciousness?

According to William James, the four factors in normal waking consciousness are: Consciousness is always changing (thus it cannot be held in mind to be studied), consciousness is a personal experience (each person's consciousness is different), consciousness is continuous (it cannot be broken down into separate pieces), and consciousness is selective (allowing one to selectively attend to some things while ignoring others).

2. What is meant by "levels of consciousness"?

Levels of consciousness refer to the notion that throughout the day we experience many different degrees of consciousness (for example, wide awake and attentive, mind wandering, sleepy). We perform at optimal levels when we are at the highest level of consciousness. Another level of consciousness is the unconscious where it may be possible to process information without being aware of it.

3. What is Freud's classic approach to levels of consciousness?

Freud believed that consciousness existed on three levels: the conscious, preconscious, and unconscious. Freud also believed that consciousness was much like an iceberg, with only a small portion of the iceberg jutting from the surface of the water. Likewise, Freud believed that the part of consciousness that existed above the water was the conscious mind, which represents the ideas, memories, feelings and motives of which we are actively aware. Just below the waterline is the preconscious. In the preconscious are things you are not immediately aware of, but can access quite easily (for example, what you did yesterday). Deep under the water is the unconscious which has ideas, desires, and memories of which we are not aware, and cannot easily become aware. Freud believed that impulses from the unconscious were important in motivating behavior.

4. What are the modern approaches to unconscious processing of information?

There are two approaches to the problem of unconscious processing of information: processing information while not attending to it and subliminal perception. Research evidence suggests that some unconscious processing of information is possible. In subliminal perception a message is flashed at a rate below your threshold of detection, so you are not consciously aware of it. The existence of blindsight also provides evidence for the unconscious processing. In blindsight even though, as the result of brain damage, a blind individual can still detect simple visual stimuli. Generally, research shows that subliminal processing of complex messages is not likely to occur. However, we are sensitive to some stimuli presented below the level of awareness. Generally, the unconscious is unsophisticated and primitive with respect to the type or amount of information it can handle.

5. What are the stages of sleep and what kind of brain activity do you see in each?

In the period immediately preceding sleep, while you are relaxed, your brain produces alpha waves (8 to 12 cycles per second). Once asleep, the electrical activity of the brain shows that sleep is divided into five stages: descending stage 1, stages 2, 3, and 4, and REM sleep. In stage 1 sleep, alpha waves are replaced by theta waves (3-7 cycles per second), heart rate slows, breathing becomes more regular, and blood pressure decreases. The eyes are either still or showing slow movement. If awakened during this stage a person reports being in a light sleep or drifting off to sleep. During stage 2 sleep, the sleep spindles appear. Sleep spindles are brief, high amplitude bursts of electrical activity (12-14 cycles per second) that appear regularly around every 15 seconds. During stage 2 you enter deeper sleep, but you can still be easily awakened. During stage 3 sleep, delta waves are high and slow (.5 to 3 cycles per second) and comprise between 20 and 50 percent of the EEG pattern. Normal bodily functions slow during stage 3, and it is difficult to wake a person up from stage 3 sleep. In stage 4, sleep delta waves make up almost all of the brain's electrical activity, and your muscles are relaxed. Stage 4 sleep accounts for about 15 percent of the total night's sleep. REM sleep develops from the sleep state after a reversal of stages from 4 to 3 to 2, unlike stage 1 sleep which develops from a waking state. During REM sleep, there are periods of alpha wave activity accompanied by rapid eye movements. Although the brain looks like it is awake, it is difficult to arouse a person from this type of sleep. If awakened the person reports being in a deep sleep.

6. What is meant by the terms REM and NREM sleep?

REM sleep refers to periods of sleep during which the sleeping person's eyes can be seen moving rapidly under his or her eyelids, thus the term rapid eye movement (or REM). It is during periods of REM sleep that people usually report having vivid, story-like dreams. Rapid eye movements are not associated with a person "watching" a dream. Instead, they are a by-product of brain activation. NREM sleep (or nonREM sleep) are periods of sleep where rapid eye movements are absent. Persons awakened during NREM sleep report fewer and much more fragmented dreams.

7. When do periods of REM sleep occur, and how long do they last?

Periods of REM sleep occur throughout the night during ascending stage 1 sleep, usually lasting between a few minutes and half an hour. The length of REM periods and the vividness of dreams increase as a night's sleep progresses. REM sleep accounts for about 20 to 25 percent of the sleep of adults. Overall, around 90 to 120 minutes are spent in REM sleep per night.

8. How are the stages of sleep distributed over the course of a night's sleep?

During a typical night's sleep, there is a recurring pattern of sleep stages. However, one doesn't necessarily pass through all stages of sleep in a fixed sequence. At times, stage 3 may be missed. Late in the sleep cycle stage 4 may be totally absent.

9. Does everyone experience the dreaming associated with REM sleep?

Yes. Everyone experiences REM sleep and dreams. Some people have difficulty remembering their dreams in the morning. But, during the course of a normal night's sleep each of us has several dreams. Unless we make a conscious effort to remember a dream, it will be forgotten.

10. What else, besides dreaming, happens during REM sleep?

Although the sleeper may look peaceful during REM sleep, his or her body physiology suggests anything but peacefulness. During REM sleep muscles are totally relaxed, a condition called atonia, which is probably a mechanism to prevent the sleeper from thrashing around.

During REM sleep sex organs are aroused, blood pressure increases markedly, breathing becomes shallow and irregular. Generally, the person in REM sleep is experiencing arousal of many body functions.

11. What happens when we are deprived of sleep?

It is generally true that most people get less sleep than they need. Sleep loss tends to accumulate from night to night resulting in a "sleep debt." Surprisingly, however, sleep deprivation studies show few long-term adverse effects of sleep deprivation. Sleep deprivation may lead to a person taking short catnaps called microsleeps, which become more frequent when normal sleep is disrupted. Even though there are no serious long-term effects of sleep deprivation, a person who does not get a good night's sleep may show signs of depression and irritability.

12. What happens if a person does not get enough REM sleep?

If a person is selectively deprived of REM sleep for a few nights, when allowed undisturbed sleep the person will show REM rebound. That is, the person spends more time than normal in REM sleep. A similar rebound effect of NREM sleep has also been observed.

13. What are the explanations for dreaming?

Aristotle characterized dreams as being residuals of sensations and perceptions that were encountered during the day. Freud developed the most elaborate system for understanding dreams. According to Freud's view, dreams originate in the unconscious and are related to issues of the unconscious. The manifest content of a dream is what the dreamer is aware of and can recall. The manifest content is tied to an underlying latent content. The latent content transforms into the manifest content through a process called dream work. According to Freud, dreams have meaning and can tell a therapist about an individual's unconscious impulses. The activation-synthesis theory is a recent theory which suggests that the vivid images experienced during dreaming are caused by activation of the visual system in the brain. Once activation takes place, synthesis occurs when higher parts of the brain provide meaning for the images. In this approach no special, unconscious significance is attached to dreams.

14. What are the major sleep disorders?

The Association of Sleep Disorders Centers (ASDC) classifies sleep disorders as insomnias (disorders of initiating or maintaining sleep), disorders of excessive sleep, disorders of the sleep-waking cycle, and parasomnias (disorders of sleep stages).

15. What is insomnia?

Insomnia is the inability to fall asleep or stay asleep. It may occur in brief episodes or become chronic, lasting weeks or months. Insomnia may be brought on by anticipation of an important event, life stress, illness, and drug use. Chronic insomnia affects about thirty million Americans with women reporting more insomnia than men. Insomnia is more common among older adults than younger adults. Interestingly, many people who report insomnia actually get more sleep than they think, a condition called pseudoinsomnia.

16. Are drugs effective in combating insomnia?

Although many people try a variety of drugs to help them fall asleep, using drugs as hypnotics may cause more problems than it solves. One problem with using drugs is that they may be effective initially, but gradually lose their effectiveness as tolerance builds. When medications are stopped, a rebound effect occurs, making it more difficult to get to sleep. Some drugs may also lead to less stage 3 and 4 sleep. Sleep experts recommend using drugs on a short-term basis only.

17. What effects does melatonin have on sleep onset and the sleep cycle?

Melatonin is a hormone produced naturally by the pineal gland during the night that appears to play a role in the sleep-waking cycle. Melatonin is available as an over-the-counter product. Many people have tried melatonin as a sleep-inducing drug. Melatonin is effective in reducing sleep onset time in normal, healthy young adults and older adults who may show lower levels of naturally-produced melatonin. However, the effectiveness of melatonin in treating insomnia has not been firmly established. Melatonin is most effective when treating insomnia relating to a disruption of the normal circadian rhythm (for example, people who change shifts at their jobs frequently), but less effective for psychologically-based insomnia. Because little is known about the dosages and side effects of melatonin, it should be used with caution and under the direction of a physician.

18. Is alcohol an effective sleep inducing drug?

In the short run it may be. However, in the long run using alcohol to induce sleep may cause more harm than good. Alcohol consumption (as little as three drinks) sup-presses REM sleep during the first part of the night. After the alcohol wears off, REM rebound occurs and a person is likely to experience periods of wakefulness. Generally, alcohol disrupts the normal distribution of stages of sleep leading to low-quality sleep.

19. What are the cognitive and behavioral underpinnings of insomnia?

Many cases of insomnia boil down to learning and perpetuating poor sleep habits. After a couple of poor nights' sleep a person may begin to worry about sleep. Eventually, negative sleep thoughts, emotions, and behaviors develop. In fact, good and poor sleepers differ on many sleep-related thoughts and behaviors (for example, poor sleepers are more likely to toss and turn than good sleepers). Individuals experiencing this form of insomnia may benefit from cognitive and behavioral treatments.

20. What are some of the things one can do to break bad sleep habits and negative thoughts?

Behavioral techniques have been developed to help a person correct poor sleep habits. Such techniques include keeping a sleep diary, withdrawal from sleep medications, eliminating napping, not staying in bed for more than ten minutes, getting up and going to another room to do something relaxing until tired, only going to bed when tired, counting backwards, getting up the same time every day, exercising, and monitoring the intake of bedtime stimulants. These techniques have been found to be effective in managing and treating insomnia.

21. What is narcolepsy?

Narcolepsy involves falling asleep, even during the day, without the intention to do so. The symptoms of narcolepsy are excessive sleepiness, muscle weakness or paralysis, paralysis upon falling asleep, dreamlike hallucinations upon falling asleep or upon waking up. Narcolepsy may affect up to 350,000 Americans, although only 50,000 cases have been diagnosed.

22. What is sleep apnea?

Sleep apnea involves periods of sleep during which breathing stops entirely. It appears mostly in obese, middle-aged males and may be a cause of sudden infant death syndrome. Short episodes of sleep apnea are not dangerous. However, long episodes may be life-threatening.

Topic 4B VOLUNTARY ALTERATIONS OF CONSCIOUSNESS

We have reviewed some of the evidence and theories that focus on how consciousness normally changes throughout the day when we are awake, and how it varies throughout the night as we sleep. The changes in consciousness that we've addressed so far are quite automatic and involuntary. We don't really decide when we'll go to sleep, when we'll REM and dream, or when we'll spontaneously awaken. These alterations in consciousness just "happen." Now we direct our attention to those altered states of consciousness that normally require some effort to attain. We'll consider three processes that alter consciousness: hypnosis, meditation, and the use of psychoactive drugs.

Key Questions to Answer

While reading this Topic, find the answers to the following key questions:

1. What is hypnosis?

2. Can everyone be hypnotized?

3. Will a person be made to do things under hypnosis that they wouldn't ordinarily do?

4. Does hypnosis represent a state of consciousness distinctly different from normal waking or sleeping consciousness?

5. Can hypnosis relieve physical pain?

6. Can one remember things under hypnosis that could not be remembered otherwise?

7. What is meditation?

8. What are the benefits of meditation?

9. What are stimulant drugs, and what are their effects?

10. What are depressant drugs, and what are their effects?

11. What are the effects of alcohol?

12. Is alcohol consumption related to aggression?

13. What are the hallucinogenic drugs, and what are their effects?

14. What is the active ingredient in marijuana, and what are its effects?

15. What are the effects of ecstasy?

HYPNOSIS

hypnosis   a state of consciousness characterized by (1) a marked increase in suggestibility, (2) a focusing of attention, (3) an exaggerated use of imagination, (4) an unwillingness or inability to act on one's own, and (5) an unquestioning acceptance of distortions of reality

Hypnosis is a state of consciousness that typically requires the voluntary cooperation of the person being hypnotized. Hypnosis is characterized by (1) a marked increase in suggestibility, (2) a focusing of attention, (3) an exaggerated use of imagination, (4) an unwillingness or inability to act on one's own, and (5) an unquestioning acceptance of distortions of reality (Hilgard & Hilgard, 1975). There is little truth to the belief that being hypnotized is like going to sleep. Few of the characteristics of sleep are to be found in the hypnotized subject. EEG patterns, for example, are significantly different.

Hypnosis has been used, with varying degrees of success, for several purposes. As you know, it is used as entertainment, as a show business routine where members of an audience are hypnotized—usually to do silly things in public. Hypnosis has long been seen as a method for gaining access to memories of events not in immediate awareness. It has been touted as a treatment for a wide range of psychological and physical disorders. In this section, we'll consider some common issues concerning hypnosis.

Can everyone be hypnotized? No, probably not. The susceptibility to hypnosis varies from person to person. Some people resist and cannot be hypnotized. Contrary to popular belief, you cannot be hypnotized against your will, which is one reason why we say that one enters a hypnotic state voluntarily (some hypnotists claim that they can hypnotize anyone under the right conditions, which is why we hedged and said "probably" not) (e.g., Lynn et al., 1990).

Although not everyone can be easily hypnotized, some people are excellent subjects, can readily be put into deep hypnotic states, and can easily learn to hypnotize themselves (Hilgard, 1975, 1978). A number of traits are correlated with one's ability to be hypnotized. The most important factor seems to be the ability to engage easily in daydreaming and fantasy, to be able to "set ordinary reality aside for awhile" (Lynn & Rhue, 1986; Wilkes, 1986, p. 25). Other factors include suggestibility and a degree of passivity or willingness to cooperate, at least during the hypnotic session. An intriguing notion is that persons who were often punished in childhood, or are avid readers, runners, or actors, are good subjects for hypnosis. The logic is that these people have a history of self-induced trance-like states (to escape punishment, to focus and become absorbed in a task at hand, and so on), which makes them more likely to be hypnotizable (Hilgard, 1970).

Can I be made to do things under hypnosis that I would not ordinarily do? Next to being unknowingly hypnotized, the greatest fear associated with hypnosis is doing things that one would not ordinarily. That is, can a hypnotist make you do something dangerous or embarrassing? Actually, this question leads us to a distinction between clinical/forensic and stage hypnosis. Hypnosis used in clinical settings is used as a therapeutic tool. In the forensic area, hypnosis is sometimes used to help witnesses remember details of a crime. Stage hypnosis, with which most people are familiar, involves using hypnosis for entertainment. Typically, the hypnotist calls several people to the stage for a hypnosis demonstration. Bear in mind that these "volunteers" are carefully selected and undergo an on-stage series of tests for their susceptibility to suggestion (Barber, Spanos, & Chaves, 1974).

When hypnosis is used in a "show business" setting, ordinary people may do some very silly things, but they are not likely to do anything that they would not do otherwise.

The bottom line on stage hypnosis is this: Under the influence of a skilled hypnotist, you may do some pretty silly things and do them publicly. Under the right circumstances, you might do those same things without being hypnotized. It is unlikely you would do under hypnosis anything you would not do otherwise. However, under certain (unusual) circumstances, people can do outrageous—and dangerous—things, which is why hypnosis should be used with caution.

Does hypnosis really represent an altered state of consciousness? The issue of whether hypnosis represents a unique state of consciousness, different from the normal waking state or sleep, is in dispute. Some believe that hypnosis is really no more than a heightened level of suggestibility (Barber, 1972; Spanos & Barber, 1974), whereas others believe it to be a special state, separate from the compliance of a willing subject. When hypnotized subjects are left alone, they usually maintain the condition induced by their hypnosis. Subjects not hypnotized, but simply complying as best they can with an experimenter, revert quickly to normal behaviors when left alone (Hilgard, 1975; Orne, 1969). However, EEG recordings of brains of hypnotized individuals reveal few, if any, alterations from normal consciousness (Barber, Spanos, & Chaves, 1974).

A person in a hypnotic state is aware of what he or she is doing, but in a strange way. Within the hypnotized subject is what Hilgard calls a "hidden observer" who may be aware of what is going on. In one study (Hilgard & Hilgard, 1975), a person was hypnotized and told that he would feel no pain as his hand was held in a container of ice water (usually very painful). When asked, the person reported feeling little pain, just as expected. The hypnotic suggestion was working. The Hilgards then asked the person if "some part of him" was feeling any pain and to indicate the presence of such pain by using his free hand to press a lever (or to write out a description of what he was feeling). Although the person continued to verbally report no feeling of pain, the free hand (on behalf of the "hidden observer") indicated that it "knew" there was pain in the immersed hand.

Can hypnosis be used to alleviate physical pain? Yes. It won't (can't) cure the under-lying cause, but it can be used to control the feeling of pain. Hypnosis can be used to create hallucinations in the hypnotized subject. *Hallucinations* are perceptual experiences that occur without sensory input. Some hallucinations are said to be *positive* when a person perceives something that is not there. Pain reduction uses *negative* hallucinations: a failure to perceive something (e.g., pain) that is there. If a person is a good candidate for hypnosis, there is a significant chance that at least a portion of perceived pain can be blocked from conscious awareness (Hilgard & Hilgard, 1975; Long, 1986).

Is it true that one can remember things under hypnosis that could not otherwise be remembered? Probably not, although there is no more hotly contested issue related to hypnosis. In the sense of "Can you hypnotize me to remember psychology material better for the test next Friday?" the answer is an apologetic, "Almost certainly not." Someone might be able to convince you under hypnosis that you'd better remember your psychology and lead you to want to remember your psychology, but there is no evidence that hypnotic suggestion can directly improve your ability to learn and remember new mate-rial. In the more restrictive sense of "I don't remember all the details of the accident and the trauma that followed. Can hypnosis help me recall those events more clearly?" the answer is less sure. Distortions of memory can easily occur in normal states. In hypnotic states, the subject is suggestible and susceptible to distortions in recall furnished by the hypnotist (even assuming that the hypnotist has no reason to cause distortions). To the extent that hypnosis can reduce feelings of anxiety and tension, it may help in the recol-lection of anxiety-producing memories. The evidence is neither clear nor convincing on this issue in either direction (Dywan & Bowers, 1983; Kihlstrom, 1985). What of the related questions, "Can hypnosis make me go back in time (regress) and remember what it was like when I was only three or four years old?" or "Can hypnosis help me recall past life experiences?" Here, we do have a clear-cut answer, and the answer is no. So-called age-regression hypnotic sessions have simply not proved valid (e.g., Nash, 1987; Spanos et al., 1991). Often there is no way to verify the validity of memories "recovered" during age or past life regression.

One area in which this issue has been important is the use of hypnosis to "refresh" the memories of witnesses to crimes. The most famous example of this took place in California when a school bus full of children was hijacked. The children were being held hostage. The driver of the bus managed to escape and gave police a partial description of the perpetrators and the vehicle they had used. Under hypnosis the driver was able to recall more details, including a partial license plate number for the truck used by the kid-nappers. The driver's information led to the children being found unhurt and the kidnap-pers being arrested.

Despite this, and other anecdotal evidence that hypnosis can help witnesses recall things they couldn't recall under standard interrogation, there is little research support for the memory-enhancing powers of hypnosis. In a meta-analysis of 24 experiments on the hypnosis-memory link, Steblay and Bothwell (1994) found that there is no significant difference between the memory capabilities of hypnotized and nonhypnotized witnesses. However, hypnosis does appear to produce more accurate memory after a 24-hour delay between viewing an event and recall. Unfortunately, this small difference can be disrupted if leading questions are asked during the delay period and if the delay period extends to a week. The bottom line is that any benefit of using hypnosis to refresh witness's memories can be compromised by several factors.

One area of particular concern in the use of hypnosis to refresh witness's memories is the potential for hypnosis to lead to the creation of *pseudomemories*, or false memories. Under hypnosis the witness is in a highly suggestible state. It may be easy to implant in a witness's memory, through suggestive questions, facts or events that never occurred. The research in this area is mixed. Some studies show that hypnosis does not lead to inordinately high levels of pseudomemories (Sheehan & Statham, 1989; Weekes, Lynn, Green, & Brentar, 1992), whereas other studies show an increase in pseudomemories among hypnotized witnesses, especially those highly susceptible to hypnosis (Sheehan, Statham, & Jamison, 1991, Sheehan, Green, & Truesdale, 1992). Pseudomemories are not unique to hypnosis. Human memory is malleable, or open to suggestion, with or without hypnosis. Under some conditions hypnosis may enhance this effect.

> ## BEFORE YOU GO ON
>
> - What is hypnosis?
> - Does hypnosis represent a unique state of consciousness?
> - Can everyone be hypnotized?
> - What are the effects of hypnosis on behavior?
> - Can hypnosis improve one's memory?
> - How does hypnosis relate to pseudomemories?

MEDITATION

Meditation is a self-induced state of altered consciousness characterized by a focusing of attention and relaxation. Meditation is usually associated with ancient, particularly Eastern, cultures and has been practiced for centuries. We tend to think of meditation in a religious context. Meditation became popular in North America in the 1960s. It was then that psychologists began to study the process seriously. In this section we'll first review the process of meditation and then look at some of the claims that have been made about its potential benefits.

meditation self-induced state of altered consciousness characterized by a focusing of attention and relaxation

There are several types of meditation, but the most popular are those that require mental focusing or concentration. *Transcendental meditation (TM)* is a type of meditation of this sort (Maharishi, 1963). In TM, one begins meditating by assuming a comfortable position and becoming calm and relaxed. The meditator then directs his or her attention to one particular stimulus. This could be some simple bodily function, such as one's own breathing. Attention could be focused on some softly spoken or chanted word or phrase, or mantra, such as "oom," "one," or "calm." As attention is focused, other stimuli, either external (events in the environment) or internal (thoughts, feelings, or bodily processes), can be blocked from consciousness. The challenge is to stay relaxed, to remain peaceful

Mediation may not enable the mind to "transcend" the real world and open one to a "cosmic wholeness," but it *is* a very effective means of relaxation and reducing somatic arousal.

and calm. A state of meditation cannot be forced. Its practitioners claim that reaching an altered state of awareness through meditation is not difficult (Benson, 1975).

Once a person is in a meditative state, measurable physiological changes do take place that allow us to claim meditation to be an altered state of consciousness. The most noticeable is a predominance of alpha waves in the EEG record. Such waves characterize a relaxed state of the sort experienced just before one enters into sleep. Breathing slows and becomes deeper. Oxygen intake is reduced, and the heart rate may decrease.

There is no doubt that people enter meditative states of consciousness. Doubts that have arisen concerning meditation center on the claims of its benefits. One of the major claims for meditation is that it is a reasonably simple, very effective, even superior way to enter into a state of relaxation. The reduction of somatic (bodily) arousal is taken to be one of the main advantages of meditation. The claim is that by meditating, one can slow bodily processes and enter into a state of physical as well as psychological calm. Researcher David Holmes (1984, 1985, 1987) has reviewed the evidence for somatic relaxation through meditation. On several measures of arousal and relaxation, including heart rate, respiration rate, muscle tension, and oxygen use, Holmes concluded that there were no differences between meditating persons and people who were "simply" resting or relaxing.

Another claim made for meditation is that those who practice it are better able to cope with stress, pressure, or threatening situations than are those who do not practice meditation. Once again, Holmes (1984, 1985) reports that he could find no evidence to support this claim. In fact, in four of the studies he reviewed, Holmes found that under mild threat, meditating subjects showed greater arousal than did nonmeditating subjects. We must add two important notes here: (1) Some psychologists have taken issue with Holmes's methods and conclusions, and argue that meditation does offer advantages over simply resting, suggesting also that "resting" is a difficult concept to define (e.g., Shapiro, 1985; Suler, 1985; West, 1985). (2) Holmes does not argue that meditation is useless. He simply says that with regard to somatic arousal there is no evidence that it is any better than resting.

BEFORE YOU GO ON

- What is the definition of meditation?

What is involved in practicing transcendental meditation?

What physiological changes take place when a person is in a meditative state?

Are people who meditate better able to cope with anxiety and stress?

Can one be raised to new heights of awareness through meditation?

Some of the claims made for meditation techniques go well beyond relaxation and somatic arousal reduction. Claims that meditation can raise one's consciousness to transcendental heights of new awareness and thus make one a better person are viewed with considerable skepticism in psychology. Some people claim that they have an incredible "openness" to ideas and feelings, that they have hallucinatory experiences, and that they can divorce themselves from their bodies and minds when they meditate. Such experiences might, in some instances, be true. The idea that a meditating person can exist apart from present experience and view life "as if from without" isn't far removed from Hilgard's concept of a "hidden observer" in hypnosis. Nonetheless, the majority of psychologists who have investigated meditation continue to question any claims for a heightened state of well-being that is achieved through such little effort and that relies more on testimonials of personal experience than on scientific evidence (Webb, 1981).

ALTERING CONSCIOUSNESS WITH DRUGS

In this final section, we will discuss some of the chemicals that alter consciousness by inducing changes in perception, mood, or behavior. Because of their ability to alter psychological processes, these chemicals are referred to as psychoactive drugs.

Drugs have been used for centuries to alter consciousness. Psychoactive drugs are taken, at least initially, to achieve a state of consciousness the user considers to be positive, pleasant, even euphoric. No reasonable person would take a drug because he or she expected to have a negative, unpleasant experience. However, the use of drugs that alter our mood, perception, and behaviors often has seriously negative outcomes. In this regard, there are a few terms that will be relevant for our discussion. Although there is not total agreement on how these terms are used, for our purposes, we'll use the following definitions:

1. *Dependence*: a state in which (a) the use of a drug is required to maintain bodily functioning (called physical dependence), or (b) continued use of a drug is believed to be necessary to maintain psychological functioning at some level (called psychological dependence). "I just can't face the day without my three cups of coffee in the morning."

2. *Tolerance*: a condition in which the use of a drug leads to a state in which more and more of it is needed to produce the same effect. "I used to get high with just one of these; now I need three."

3. *Withdrawal*: a strongly negative response, either physical or psychological (including reactions such as headaches, vomiting, and cramps), that results when one stops taking a drug. "When I take these, I don't feel real good, but it sure does hurt when I stop."

4. *Addiction*: an extreme dependency, physical or psychological, in which signs of tolerance and painful withdrawal are usually found (Schuckit, 1989). Addiction also implies seeking a short-term gain (say, a pleasurable feeling) at the expense of long-term negative consequences (Miller, 1992). "No way I'm gonna give it up; no matter what. It feels too good. And who cares if I lose my job?"

Another important distinction we should make is between drug use and drug abuse. We are dealing with abuse when we find (1) a lack of control, as evidenced by daily intoxication and continued use, even knowing that one's condition will deteriorate; (2) a disruption of interpersonal relationships or difficulties at work that can be traced to drug usage; and (3) indications that maladaptive drug use has continued for at least one month (American Psychiatric Association, 1987). Hidden in this distinction is the reality that although drug use may not have negative consequences, drug abuse will. There is no clear dividing line between drug use and drug abuse. For that matter, there are no clear dividing lines between drug use, dependency on drugs, and drug addiction. There is, instead, a continuum from total abstinence through heavy social use to addiction (Doweiko, 1993; Peele et al., 1991).

There are many psychoactive drugs that can alter consciousness. We'll focus on four types, or categories: stimulants, depressants, hallucinogens, and (as a separate category) marijuana.

BEFORE YOU GO ON

- How do drugs (chemicals) alter consciousness?

- What is meant by the terms dependence, tolerance, withdrawal, and addiction?

- How does drug use differ from drug abuse?

- What are the four categories of consciousness-altering drugs?

Stimulants

stimulants chemicals that activate an organism, producing a heightened sense of arousal and an elevation of mood

Chemical **stimulants** do just that—they stimulate or activate an organism, producing a heightened sense of arousal and an elevation of mood. Most of the time, these drugs also activate neural reactions, but at this level we have to be careful. For example, one stimulant administered directly to the reticular formation can awaken and arouse a sleeping cat, but if that same drug is administered to a different area of the reticular formation, the cat will go to sleep.

Caffeine is one of the most widely used stimulants. It is found in common foods and drinks (coffee, tea, and chocolate), as well as in several varieties of painkillers. It is an ingredient in many soft drinks, notably colas. In moderate amounts, it seems to have no life-threatening effects on the user. At some point, a mild dependence may develop. Caffeine temporarily increases cellular metabolism (the general process of converting food into energy), which then results in a burst of newfound energy. It also blocks the effects of some inhibitory neurotransmitters in the brain (Julien, 1985). Caffeine disrupts sleep, making it more difficult to get to sleep in the first place and more difficult to stay asleep.

We seldom think of coffee and tea as containing a psychoactive drug, but they do—caffeine, which may create a mild dependence.

After long or excessive use, giving up sources of caffeine may result in the pain of withdrawal. If you tend to drink a lot of coffee and cola during the week, but take a break from them during the weekend, you may experience headaches of caffeine withdrawal. You may drink coffee to help stay awake during an all-night study session, but a few hours after you stop drinking the caffeine, you may experience a streak of extreme mental and physical fatigue—perhaps right at exam time!

Nicotine is another popular stimulant, usually taken by smoking and absorption by the lungs. It is carried to the brain very quickly—in a matter of seconds. Nicotine *is* a stimulant of central nervous system activity, but it does relax muscle tone slightly, which may explain the rationalization of smokers who claim that they can relax by having a cup of coffee and a cigarette. Nicotine produces its effects by activating excitatory synapses in both the central and peripheral nervous systems (McKim, 1986).

Many individuals (but not all) develop a tolerance to nicotine requiring more and more to reach a desired state of stimulation (Food and Drug Administration, 1995; Hughes, et al., 1987). Nicotine is now known to be an addictive drug, despite earlier claims that it was not. For example, the Food and Drug Association (1995) clearly states nicotine's addictive qualities, and the Royal College of Physicians of London, England has also determined that nicotine is addictive (Maxhom, 2000).

Smokeless tobacco has recently become more popular and is being used by many as an alternative to smoking. In fact, 20.4 percent of male children between the ages of 9 and 12 use smokeless tobacco (Center for Disease Control, 1993), and 7.8 percent of students in the 9th to 12th grade reported using smokeless tobacco (Centers for Disease Control, 1999).

Unfortunately, the news is not good. The nicotine in smokeless tobacco is absorbed into the blood and gets to the brain almost as quickly as nicotine from tobacco smoke and is just as addictive (Food and Drug Administration, 1995).

The unfortunate consequences of addiction to cigarettes are serious health hazards such as cardiovascular disease, stroke, and lung cancer. According to the Centers for Disease Control (1996), cigarette smoking results in more than 400,000 deaths in the United States and is the single most preventable cause of death.

Cocaine is a stimulant derived from leaves of the coca shrub (native to the Andes Mountains in South America). The allure of cocaine and its derivative "crack" is the rush of pleasure and energy it produces when it first enters the bloodstream, either through the mucous membranes when inhaled as smoke ("free basing"), inhaled through the nose as a powder ("snorting"), or injected directly as a liquid. A cocaine "high" doesn't last very long; 15 to 20 minutes is average.

There are many physiological reactions that result from cocaine use. It elevates blood pressure and heart rate. Cocaine also blocks the reuptake of two important neurotransmitters (Julien, 1988). This means that once these neurotransmitters have entered a synapse, cocaine will prohibit their being taken back up into the neuron from which they have been released. The result is that, for a time at least, excessive amounts of the neurotransmitters are available in the nervous system. The two neurotransmitters in question are norepinephrine, which acts in both the central and peripheral nervous systems to provide arousal and the sense of extra energy, and dopamine, which acts in the brain to produce feelings of pleasure and euphoria.

Some of the effects of cocaine use are long-lasting, if not permanent, even though the psychological effects last but a few minutes. Not only is the rush of the psychological reaction to cocaine or "crack" short-lived, but it is followed by a letdown approaching depression. As users know, one way to combat letdown and depression is to take more of the drug—a vicious cycle that invariably leads to dependency and addiction. Cocaine is such a powerfully addictive drug that many individuals can become psychologically and physically dependent on its use after just one or two episodes. Determining the number of cocaine users or addicts is difficult (after all, the drug is illegal), however, according to the National Institute on Drug Abuse (1999a), an estimated 1.7 million people in the United States over the age of 12 are current cocaine users. Cocaine addiction tends to run in families to such an extent that current research is exploring the hypothesis that there is a genetic basis for cocaine addiction. Cocaine is a drug that no one can handle safely.

Amphetamines are synthetically manufactured stimulants that usually come in the form of capsules or pills, and are known by many "street names," such as bennies, wake-ups, uppers, dexies, or jellie babies. In addition to blocking reuptake, amphetamines cause the release of excess dopamine and norepinephrine. However, their action is considerably slower and less widespread than that of cocaine. Once an amphetamine takes effect, users feel alert, awake, aroused, filled with energy, and ready to go. These results are short-lived. The drug does not create alertness so much as it masks fatigue, which will ultimately overcome the user when the drug wears off. These are not the only effects of amphetamine use; it has a direct effect on the heart and circulatory system, causing, for example, irregular heartbeat and increased blood pressure (McKim, 1986).

Depressants

depressants chemicals that reduce one's awareness of external stimuli, slow bodily functioning, and decrease levels of overt behavior

In terms of their effects on consciousness, **depressants** are the opposite of stimulants. They reduce one's awareness of external stimuli, slow bodily functioning, and decrease levels of overt behavior. Predictably, one's reaction to depressant drugs depends largely on how much is taken. In small doses, they may produce relaxation, a sense of freedom from anxiety, and a loss of stifling inhibitions. In greater amounts, they may produce sedation, sleep, coma, or death.

Alcohol is the most commonly used of all depressants. It has been in use for thousands of years—perhaps since as long ago as 8000 B.C. (Ray & Ksir, 1987). Alcohol is a dangerous drug because of its popularity and widespread use, if for no other reason. It can be a deadly drug. Over 100,000 deaths a year in the United States are attributed to alcohol use. The devastating effects of alcohol consumption by pregnant women are also well-documented. Alcohol use has been associated with a myriad of problems with newborn babies.

Perhaps the first thing to remember about alcohol is that it is a depressant. Some folks may feel that they are entertaining and stimulating when drinking alcohol, but their nervous system activity is actually being slowed. Alcohol increases urination, leading to an overall loss of fluids. It raises visual thresholds, making it more difficult to detect dim lights. Alcohol affects mood, leading to friendly elation as levels rise, and to depression, anger, and fatigue as alcohol levels drop (Babor et al., 1983).

The specific effects of alcohol on the drinker reflect several interacting factors. Primary among them (again) is amount. What matters most is the amount of alcohol that gets into a person's bloodstream. Blood alcohol level (BAL) is affected by how much one drinks and by how fast the alcohol can get into the bloodstream, which in turn is affected by what else is in the stomach and is related to gender (females absorb alcohol faster than males). Drinking on an empty stomach is more dangerous than drinking while or soon after eating, because the alcohol will be more quickly absorbed. One-tenth of 1 percent alcohol in the bloodstream is enough to declare someone legally drunk in most states. At this level, brain activity is so depressed that decision making is distorted and motor coordination is impaired (and both are skills required to drive safely). Drinking more than one mixed drink or one can of beer or glass of wine per hour will raise blood alcohol levels (Maguire, 1990).

Alcohol use and abuse are related to *sociocultural* factors, including ethnic background, religion, and socioeconomic level. For example, Europeans constitute about one-eighth of the world's population, but they consume nearly half of all the alcohol produced. Think about the impact of the social pressures derived from religious beliefs and attitudes toward alcohol. The use of alcohol is virtually nonexistent among Muslims and Mormons, and used sparingly—usually in religious settings—by the Chinese and Orthodox Jews. Alcoholism rates are very low among these groups. In the United States, Irish Americans are six times more likely to suffer alcoholism than are Greek Americans—*in general*. Remember, there *are* Irish Americans who do not use alcohol at all (Valliant, 1983). Adolescent Native Americans, especially those living on reservations, have much higher rates of alcohol use and abuse than any other American ethnic-racial population (Moncher et al., 1990; Swaim et al., 1993). Peer pressure, a major determining factor in drug and alcohol use for Anglo youths, is much less important in the culture of adolescent Native Americans (Oetting & Beauvais, 1987). Economics are also relevant. Research clearly demonstrates a relationship between alcohol use and economic indicators such as poverty, unemployment, and lack of opportunity (Gefou-Madianou, 1992; Ley, 1985).

BEFORE YOU GO ON

- What effects do stimulants (for example, caffeine, nicotine, cocaine) have on consciousness?

- What effects do depressants have on consciousness?

- How does alcohol affect consciousness and behavior?

Opiates, Heroine, and Barbiturates

Opiates, such as morphine and codeine, are called analgesics because they can be used to reduce or eliminate sensations of pain. They were first used for this purpose. In small doses, they create feelings of well-being and ease, relaxation, and a trance-like state. Unlike alcohol, they seem to have little effect on motor behavior. The catch, again, is that they produce dependence and addiction. Their removal results in extreme pain and depression.

Heroin is an opiate, originally (in the 1890s) derived from morphine but considered less addictive—a notion soon proven wrong. Strong dependency and addiction occur rapidly. Estimates suggest that more than 500,000 persons in the United States are addicted to heroin—and nearly half of them live in New York City. As with other drugs, we find that the addictive nature of heroin may be related to its rapid entry into the brain. Methadone, used in some treatment programs for long-term heroin users, is a drug with many of the chemical properties of heroin and many of the same effects. A difference is that methadone is slow to reach the brain and thus tends not to produce heroin's pre-dictable "rush," which makes methadone somewhat less addictive.

The psychological effects of heroin (above whatever painkilling use it may have) are mostly related to one's emotional state and mood. Unlike alcohol or the opiates, there seldom are hallucinations or thought disturbances associated with heroin use. But as increased amounts of heroin become needed to produce the desired emotional states of pleasant euphoria, tolerance builds, and increased dosages of heroin can cause breathing to stop, often for long enough periods that death results.

Barbiturates are synthetically produced sedatives of which there are many varieties. Well over 2,500 barbiturate chemicals have been isolated in laboratories (Doweiko, 1993). All barbiturates slow nervous system activity—in small amounts producing a sense of calm and tranquillity, in higher doses producing sleep or coma. They have this effect either by blocking receptor sites of excitatory synapses or by enhancing the effects of inhibitory neurotransmitters. Barbiturates also depress the cells and organs outside the central nervous system, slowing muscular responses and reducing respiration and heart rates. Some barbiturates are addictive, producing strong withdrawal symptoms when dis-continued. All produce dependency if used with regularity. As is generally the case, once addiction develops, getting off these drugs is very difficult.

Hallucinogens

hallucinogens chemicals that lead to the formation of hallucinations, usually visual

The chemicals called **hallucinogens** have unpredictable effects on consciousness. One of the reactions to these drugs is the formation of hallucinations, usually visual. That is, users often report seeing things when there is nothing there to see, or they see things in ways that others do not. Hallucinations of hearing, smell, taste, and touch are possible but much less common.

There are nearly a hundred different types of hallucinogenic substances around the world, and many have been in use for centuries. In many cultures, the drugs are used in religious practices to induce trance-like states that may help the user communicate with the supernatural; in such settings, the drug may be given to young people by their elders. In these cases, "unauthorized" use of the drug, or abuse of the drug, is nearly unheard of (e.g., Chagnon, 1983; Grob & Dobkin de Rois, 1992).

LSD (lysergic acid diethylamide), a potent and popular hallucinogen in most Western cultures, was introduced in the United States in the 1940s. LSD raises levels of emotionality that can produce profound changes in perception, usually vivid, visual hallucinations. One of the first steps in discovering how LSD works was finding that levels of the neurotransmitter serotonin increased when LSD was given to animals (Jacobs, 1987; Jacobs & Trulson, 1979). In itself this was not surprising, because LSD and similar hallucinogens (such as mescaline) have a chemical composition much like that of serotonin. Serotonin has its effects, both excitatory and inhibitory, on many areas of the brain (Jacobs, 1987). Now we know that serotonin levels increase because LSD acts on serotonin receptor sites, much like a neurotransmitter. Small doses (measured in millionths of a gram) can produce major behavioral effects.

The changes in mood that take place with LSD are usually exaggerations of one's present mood. From the start, this has been viewed as one of the dangers of the drug. Some people may be drawn to drugs such as LSD because things are not going well for them. Perhaps they are depressed and feeling hopeless. They think LSD might help cheer them up. In fact, it may worsen their mood, resulting in a "bad trip" by exaggerating their unpleasant feelings.

Hallucinations under the influence of LSD usually involve exaggerations of some actual perception. Colors seem more vivid, dimly lit stimuli take on a glow, stationary objects move, and otherwise unnoticed details become apparent. On some occasions, LSD gives rise to an experience of synesthesia, in which a stimulus of one modality is perceived in a different modality. For example, the individual may "hear" colored lights, "see" sounds, "feel" odors, and so forth.

BEFORE YOU GO ON

- What effects do opiates and heroin have on consciousness?

- How do barbiturates affect consciousness?

- What are hallucinogens?

- What effects do hallucinogens have on consciousness?

- How does LSD influence consciousness and behavior?

Other Popular Drugs

Some drugs do not fit easily into the categories of stimulants, depressants or hallucinogens. These may produce some of the effects associated with other classes of drugs, but they are really in a different class. In this section we shall discuss two such drugs: marijuana and ecstasy.

Marijuana

Marijuana can act as a depressant. In small doses its effects are similar to those of alcohol: decreased nervous system activity and depression of thought and action. In greater doses, marijuana acts as a hallucinogen, producing hallucinations and alterations in mood.

Marijuana is produced from the cannabis, or hemp plant—the source of most of the rope manufactured for sailing ships in the eighteenth century. It was an important crop in the American colonies, grown by George Washington among other notables. The plants were farmed in great numbers throughout the Midwest during World War II. The cannabis plant is hardy, and many of the remnants of those farms of the early 1940s are still found in Illinois and Indiana, where every summer, adventurers come in search of a profitable— albeit illegal—harvest. More marijuana is grown in the United States than anywhere else in the world. Use of the drug is widespread. In 1998, 72 million Americans over the age of 12 indicated that they had tried marijuana at least once during their lifetime. Additionally, nearly 18.7 million Americans reported using marijuana in the past year (National Institute on Drug Abuse, 1999b).

The active ingredient in marijuana is the chemical tetrahydrocannabinol, or THC. THC is also the active ingredient in hashish, a similar but more potent drug, also made from the cannabis plant. Although marijuana, in large doses, has been found to increase overall levels of some neurotransmitters, it is not known just how it produces this effect.

Marijuana is a difficult drug for society to deal with. In the United States, it is illegal to sell, possess, or use marijuana. There is evidence that marijuana tolerance may develop rapidly, but little evidence that it is addictive. Is marijuana dangerous? Certainly, if for no other reason than that it is usually smoked, and smoking is a danger to one's health. But smoking marijuana is more dangerous than cigarette smoking in terms of causing cancers, lung disease, and respiratory problems. It is also dangerous in the sense that alcohol is dangerous. Excessive use leads to impaired judgment, impaired reflexes, unrealistic moods, poor physical coordination, and hallucinations (Bennett, 1982). Excessive use is also related to deficits in tasks requiring sustained attention and cognitive flexibility. Heavy users of marijuana also show lower verbal intelligence quotients than light users (Pope & Yurgelun-Todd, 1996).

The most debatable aspect of marijuana use involves the results of moderate to heavy long-term use. The use of marijuana may have genetic implications (producing chromosomal abnormalities in nonhumans). It can adversely affect the body's immune system and white blood cells. It is partially responsible for lowering the sperm count of male users. It can impair memory function, affecting memories of recent events in particular. It has predictably negative effects when taken during pregnancy, resulting in smaller babies, increased numbers of miscarriages, and so on (Bloodworth, 1987; Doweiko, 1993; Grinspoon, 1977; Julien, 1985; McKim, 1986). One issue of genuine concern is the considerable variability in the potency and quality, or purity, of marijuana available on the street today.

Ecstasy

ecstasy a drug that is classified as a psychedelic amphetamine

Ecstasy (the street name for MDMA) is a drug that is classified as a psychedelic amphetamine. Because of its euphoric effects, ecstasy has become a very popular drug over the past 20 years, especially among young people. In one survey conducted in Boston, it was found that 14 percent of boys and 7 percent of girls in high school were using ecstasy. The drug most often comes in tablet form, but in some cases it can be found in capsule or powder form (Erowid, 2001). Ecstasy produces feelings of emotional openness, reduced critical thoughts, a decrease in inhibitions, and euphoria (Erowid, 2001). It has also been associated with an increase in trust and a lowering of barriers between people (National Institute on Drug Abuse, 1999c). Because of these effects, ecstasy is popular with young adults and adolescents while attending concerts or raves (all night, intense dance parties). The effects of ecstasy can be felt by a person in as little as 30 minutes and the euphoria can last for as long as 3 to 4 hours (Erowid, 2001). Regular users of ecstasy may develop a tolerance for the drug, requiring higher and higher doses to obtain the desired effect.

As is the case with most drugs, there is a downside to ecstasy use. On the physical side, ecstasy has been associated with symptoms such as teeth clenching, nausea, blurred vision, rapid eye movement, faintness, and chills or sweating (National Institute on Drug Abuse, 1999c). On the psychological side, ecstasy can produce confusion, sleep problems, depression, severe anxiety, and paranoia. These adverse psychological reactions may be felt immediately or be experienced weeks after the drug has been taken. There is also emerging evidence that claims ecstasy may lead to some brain damage in those parts of the brain associated with thought and memory—probably from damage to the serotonin systems in the brain (National Institute on Drug Abuse, 1999c). The seriousness of side effects is tied to the dose taken. As tolerance develops and higher doses are taken, negative side effects become more pronounced (Erowid, 2001). Finally, ecstasy can interact with other drugs a person may be taking. For example, ecstasy interacts negatively with some antidepressant medications.

BEFORE YOU GO ON

- What effects does marijuana have on the nervous system and consciousness?

- What is the active ingredient in marijuana?

- What are the negative effects of heavy, long-term use of marijuana?

- What are the effects of ecstasy?

- What are the negative physical and psychological effects of ecstasy?

Type of Drug	Examples	Likely Effects
Stimulants	Caffeine	increases CNS activity and metabolism; disrupts sleep; rebound possible
	Nicotine	activates excitatory synapses; leads to tolerance or addiction
	Cocaine	produces 15-20 minute high; raises blood pressure and heart rate; blocks reuptake; powerfully addictive
	Amphetamines	release excess norepinephrine and dopamine; slower acting than cocaine; mask fatigue; lead to dependence
Depressants	Alcohol	decreases nervous system activity; releases inhibitions; impairs decision making; causes birth defects; dependency and addiction
	Opiates	reduce pain; produce feelings of calm and ease; cause dependency and addiction
	Heroin	produces "rush" of euphoria; reduces pain; is very addictive
	Barbiturates	slow nervous system activity; from calm to sleep to coma; slow muscle responses; reduce heart rate; cause addiction
Hallucinogens	LSD	produces hallucinations, increases serotonin levels; raises levels of emotionality
Others	Marijuana	produces slight depressant effects and hallucinations in high doses; alters mood; causes lung disease, chromosomal abnormalities and impairs memory
	Ecstasy	produces a euphoria and decreased inhibitions; has hallucinogenic properties and has negative physical and psychological side effects

FIGURE 4.6

Psychoactive Drugs—A Few Examples

Topic Review 4 B

1. What is hypnosis?

Hypnosis is a state of consciousness that is characterized by a marked increase in suggestibility, focusing of attention, exaggerated use of imagination, unwillingness or inability to act on one's own, and acceptance of distortions of reality. It is a state of consciousness that must be entered into voluntarily. Hypnosis has been used in entertainment (stage hypnosis), to enhance memory, and as a way to treat a variety of psychological and physical disorders.

2. Can everyone be hypnotized?

Susceptibility to hypnosis varies from person to person, and some people can successfully resist hypnosis. A person who can easily engage in daydreaming and fantasy is most hypnotizable. Other factors relating to susceptibility to hypnosis are passivity, a willingness to cooperate, having been punished as a child, being an avid reader, and being a runner or an actor.

3. Will a person be made to do things under hypnosis that they wouldn't ordinarily do?

Stage hypnotists often make people behave in silly and embarrassing ways. However, a person under hypnosis may comply with such suggestions because he or she has been selected for readiness to respond to suggestion. Also, if the subject believes that the hypnotist has a strong reputation, he or she will be more willing to perform outlandish acts. The stage hypnotist carefully observes his subjects and picks those who are most willing to comply. Finally, the hypnotized subject does not want to disappoint the audience. Despite all of this, you probably would not do something under hypnosis that was dangerous to yourself or others.

4. Does hypnosis represent a state of consciousness distinctly different from normal waking or sleeping consciousness?

There is some debate here. Some evidence suggests that hypnosis does represent a unique state of consciousness. However, EEG recordings of hypnotized subjects show little alteration from normal consciousness. A hypnotized person is aware of what he or she is doing, but in a vague way.

5. Can hypnosis relieve physical pain?

Hypnosis has been used as a successful tool in helping people manage pain. Although hypnosis cannot cure the underlying cause for the pain, it can be used to control the conscious experience of pain.

6. Can one remember things under hypnosis that could not be remembered otherwise?

Probably not. Hypnosis can't improve your memory for information learned (for example, for a test). Hypnosis can't make you recall long-forgotten childhood memories or memories of past lives. Hypnosis has been used successfully in refreshing the memories of eyewitnesses in some cases. However, research shows that there is little support for the idea that hypnosis can markedly improve a witness's memory. There is also a danger that a hypnotized witness will report pseudomemories, or things that never happened.

7. What is meditation?

Meditation is a self-induced state of consciousness characterized by an extreme focusing of attention and relaxation. There are several types of meditation. Transcendental meditation is a type of meditation that involves mental focusing or concentration. Practicing transcendental meditation involves assuming a comfortable position, relaxing, and directing attention to a particular stimulus (for example, breathing) or a softly spoken word called a mantra. Once in a meditative state, breathing slows and the brain produces alpha waves, indicating a relaxed state.

8. What are the benefits of meditation?

Proponents of meditation claim that it is an easy way to enter a relaxed state. Other claims are that meditation can help a person better cope with stress, pressure, and threatening situations than one who does not practice meditation. Although it is true that meditation is an efficient way to enter a relaxed state, other claims have not been supported by research.

9. What are stimulant drugs, and what are their effects?

Stimulants are psychoactive drugs such as caffeine, nicotine, cocaine, and the amphetamines. Their basic effect is to increase levels of arousal and elevate mood, often by affecting the neural synapse, or by increasing effective levels of norepinephrine and dopamine. With heavy or continued use, tolerance to stimulants may develop, as may dependence and addiction.

10. What are depressant drugs, and what are their effects?

The depressants include such drugs as alcohol, the opiates (e.g., morphine, codeine, and heroin), and a variety of synthetically produced barbiturates. All depressants slow nervous system activity, reduce one's awareness of outside stimulation, and, in small doses, may alleviate feelings of nervousness and anxiety. In large doses, however, they produce sedation, sleep, coma, or death. Tolerance, dependence, and addiction may result from the use of these drugs. The use of these drugs (and virtually all others) is influenced to some degree by sociocultural factors.

11. What are the effects of alcohol?

Alcohol is the most commonly used depressant. Although individuals under the influence of alcohol feel stimulated, alcohol actually depresses nervous system activity. Alcohol leads to alterations in mood, with mood becoming positive as alcohol levels rise and anger and depression as they fall.

12. What are the hallucinogenic drugs, and what are their effects?

Hallucinogens (such as LSD) are drugs that alter mood or perceptions. They get their name from their ability to induce hallucinations, where a user may have experiences that are unrelated to what is going on in the user's environment. Hallucinogens may intensify already unpleasant moods. Synesthesia, a hallucinatory experience that crosses sense modalities ("hearing" lights, for example), may occur under the influence of LSD.

13. What is the active ingredient in marijuana, and what are its effects?

The active ingredient in marijuana is the chemical compound THC. The use of marijuana through smoking is more dangerous to lungs and the respiratory system than is the smoking of regular cigarettes. Negative effects have been associated with long-term use: impaired judgment, unrealistic mood, impaired coordination, and hallucinations. Also, marijuana may have an adverse effect on the body's immune system and has been implicated in producing a range of negative consequences when taken before or during pregnancy.

14. What are the effects of ecstasy?

Ecstasy is a drug with the qualities of amphetamines and hallucinogens that produces feelings of emotional openness, reduced critical thoughts, a decrease in inhibitions, euphoria, and an increase in trust and a lowering of barriers between people. The drug has negative physical side effects (e.g., nausea, blurred vision, rapid eye movement, faintness, and chills or sweating) and negative psychological side effects (e.g., confusion, sleep problems, depression, and severe anxiety).

Chapter 5

Learning

*W*hen David was 12 years old, he developed a fear of loud noises, most notably thunder. Eventually, David also began to show a fear of rain, because it was associated with thunder. His father decided to try to help David overcome his fear of thunder and rain before it got too far out of hand. First, David's father taught him to relax his body progressively, starting with his feet and working up to his head. Next, he had David imagine a noise that didn't scare him too badly, and relax while he was thinking of that noise. They continued this process in steps, until David could think of thunder and stay relaxed. Finally, David was taught to relax when it was actually thundering! David had been "cured" of his fear of loud noises. Follow-ups with David showed that his lack of fear of loud noises did not come back (based on a case reported by Tasto, 1969).

What happened in David's case? The answer is rooted in classical conditioning. David began to fear thunder, which is understandable; children often are afraid of thunder. However, the fear was subsequently attached to rain. David was associating a previously neutral stimulus (the rain) with a stimulus that did produce fear (thunder). David's father helped him by teaching him to associate a new emotion (relaxation) with the feared stimuli. As we'll see, David's case is an example of the application of classical conditioning techniques, discovered in the laboratory of a Russian physiologist well over 100 years ago.

Topic 5A CLASSICAL CONDITIONING

In this Topic, we begin by considering definitions of learning and conditioning. We'll focus on classical conditioning in this Topic, first by reviewing Pavlov's work with salivating dogs. Then we'll see why classical conditioning is so important to all of us and how it can be applied in our daily lives. We'll also examine how contemporary psychology views the process, discovering that some of Pavlov's assumptions may not have been correct.

Key Questions to Answer

While reading this Topic, find the answers to the following key questions:

1. How do we define learning?

2. What is the difference between learning and performance?

3. What are the basic procedures of classical conditioning?

4. What is the unconditioned stimulus (UCS) and unconditioned response (UCR) in classical conditioning?

5. What is the conditioned stimulus (CS) and conditioned response (CR) in classical conditioning?

6. In classical conditioning, what is acquisition?

7. In classical conditioning, what is extinction?

8. What is spontaneous recovery?

9. In classical conditioning, what are generalization and the generalization gradient?

10. In classical conditioning, what is discrimination?

11. What sorts of responses are most readily formed by classical conditioning?

12. What was the "Little Albert" demonstration?

13. What is systematic desensitization?

14. Can any two stimuli be associated with equal ease?

15. What is the modern view of classical conditioning?

16. Can any stimulus serve as a CS?

17. Must the interval between a CS and UCS always be brief in order for classical conditioning to occur?

WHAT IS LEARNING?

Directly or indirectly, learning has an impact on every aspect of our being. The human organism is poorly suited to survive without learning. If we are to survive, much less prosper, we must profit from our experiences. **Learning** is demonstrated by a relatively permanent change in behavior that occurs as the result of practice or experience. This is a rather standard definition, and it raises some important points that we should explore.

First, when we say that learning is *demonstrated* by a change in behavior, we mean that learning (like many other psychological processes) cannot be observed directly. In a literal sense, there is no way that anyone can directly observe, or measure, what you have learned. Thus, we have to make a distinction between "learning," which is an internal process that is not directly observable and "performance," which is overt, observable behavior. All we can measure directly is your performance, or your behavior. To determine if you have learned something, we ask you to perform and then make inferences about your learning on the basis of your performance. Unfortunately, there are times when performance may not adequately reflect underlying learning. For example, you may learn a great deal while studying for a test. However, you may perform poorly because you are anxious, or ill.

A second aspect of our definition that takes a bit of explaining is that learned changes in behavior are *relatively permanent*. This means that they are not fleeting, short-lived, or cyclical changes, such as those due to fatigue or brief shifts in motivation. Consider, for example, the change in typing behavior that occurs—even for a skilled typist—between 8 a.m. and 10 a.m. each morning. There is likely to be a significant improvement in typing behavior that we ought not attribute to learning, but to *warm-up*. That same typist might not function as well at the end of the day—a change in behavior better attributed

learning the demonstration of a relatively permanent change in behavior that occurs as the result of practice or experience

Who we are in this world, and who we shall become, reflects our inheritance and our ability to profit from our experiences, i.e., our learning.

to fatigue than to forgetting. These are important changes in behavior, but they are not due to learning. Learned changes are relatively permanent.

Another term in our definition reminds us that there are other changes in behavior that do not result from learning. By definition, learned changes in behavior result from *practice* or *experience*. Some behavioral changes may be due to maturation. The fact that birds fly, that salamanders swim, or that humans walk probably has more to do with genes and physical development than with learning and experience. For another thing, some changes in our behaviors are due to automatic physiological reactions, such as sensory adaptation, and are not learned. When we enter a darkened theater, we don't "learn" to see in the dark. Our vision improves and our behaviors change as our eyes adapt to the change in lighting.

One final point about learning: We often fall into the habit of thinking that learning is a good thing. Clearly, that isn't always true. We can learn maladaptive, ineffective habits just as readily as we learn good, adaptive ones. No one we know honestly claims to have enjoyed the first cigarette that he or she smoked. Yet many people have learned the habit, which is hardly an adaptive one. Learning is simply reflected in a change in behavior, be it for better or worse.

When we put these ideas together, we have our definition: Learning is demonstrated by (or inferred from) a relatively permanent change in behavior that occurs as the result of practice or experience.

BEFORE YOU GO ON

- What is the definition of learning?
- What is the difference between learning and performance?

We now begin our discussion of learning by considering *classical conditioning*. Although *conditioning* and *learning* are not technically synonymous terms, they can be used interchangeably. For the sake of simplicity, we follow common usage here and agree to call the most basic and fundamental types of learning "conditioning."

PAVLOV AND CLASSICAL CONDITIONING

When we think about learning, we typically think about such activities as memorizing the Bill of Rights, studying for an exam, or learning to do things, such as ice skate. But our study of learning begins over a hundred years ago in the laboratory of a Russian physiologist who taught dogs to salivate in response to tones. How salivating dogs could be relevant to college students may be difficult to imagine at first, but the relevance will become apparent soon.

Late in the nineteenth century, Ivan Pavlov was studying the basic processes of digestion—work for which he was awarded a Nobel Prize in 1904. Pavlov focused on the salivation reflex in dogs. He knew that he could get his dogs to salivate by forcing food powder into their mouths. He measured the number of drops of saliva that were produced

Russian physiologist Ivan Pavlov (center) observes a dog in one of his laboratory's testing chambers.

when food was introduced. Salivation is a *reflex*—an unlearned, automatic response that occurs in the presence of a specific stimulus. Every time Pavlov presented the food powder, his dogs salivated.

Pavlov made an interesting observation that led him to one of the most important discoveries in psychology. He noticed that his dogs sometimes began salivating *before* food was put in their mouths. They would salivate at the sight of the food or even at the sight of the laboratory assistant who usually delivered the food. With this observation, Pavlov went off on a tangent that he pursued for the rest of his life (Pavlov, 1927, 1928). The phenomenon he studied is now called **classical conditioning**, a learning process in which a neutral stimulus is paired with a stimulus that elicits an unconditioned response. After conditioning, the neutral stimulus alone elicits a conditioned response. In the abstract that may not make much sense, but as we go through the process step by step, you will realize that the process *is* simple and straightforward.

To demonstrate classical conditioning, we first need a stimulus that reliably, or consistently, produces a predictable response. The relationship between this stimulus and the response it elicits is usually an unlearned, reflexive one. Given this stimulus, the same response always follows. Here is where the food powder comes in. If we present the food powder to a dog, the salivation response reliably follows. We call the stimulus an **unconditioned stimulus (UCS)** and the response an **unconditioned response (UCR)**. A UCS (food powder) produces a UCR (salivation) with no prior learning. That is, a dog does not need to learn to salivate at food. It happens naturally. Thus, anytime you see the term "unconditioned" you will know that there is no learning involved.

Now we need a *neutral stimulus* that, when presented, produces a minimal response, or a response of no particular interest. For this neutral stimulus, Pavlov chose a tone. At first, when a tone is sounded, a dog *will* respond. It will, among other things, perk up its

classical conditioning a learning process in which a neutral stimulus is paired with a stimulus that elicits an unconditioned response. After conditioning, the conditioned stimulus alone elicits a conditioned response

unconditioned stimulus (UCS) in classical conditioning, a stimulus (e.g., food powder) that reflexively and reliably elicits a response

unconditioned response (UCR) in classical conditioning, a response (e.g., salivation in response to food) reliably and reflexively elicited by a stimulus

orienting reflex the simple, unlearned response of orienting toward, or attending to, a new or unusual stimulus

habituation in classical conditioning, a simple form of learning in which an organism comes to ignore a stimulus of little or no consequence

ears and try to orient toward the source of the sound. We call this response an **orienting reflex**—a simple, unlearned response of attending to a new or unusual stimulus. After a while, however, the dog will get used to the tone and will ignore it. This process is called **habituation**, a form of learning in which an organism comes to ignore a stimulus of little or no consequence. Essentially, the dog learns not to orient toward the tone. We're ready to go. We have two stimuli: a tone that produces a minimal response and food powder (UCS) that reliably produces salivation (UCR).

Neutral Stimulus (NS)   **No Response**
(a tone)   (no salivation)

UCS ⟶ **UCR**
(food powder)   (salivation)

Once we get our stimuli and responses straight, the rest is easy. The two stimuli are paired. That is, they are presented at about the same time—the tone first, then the food powder. The salivation then occurs automatically in response to the food powder. We have a neutral stimulus, then a UCS, followed by the UCR (or tone-food-salivation).

Neutral Stimulus (NS)   +   **UCS** ⟶ **UCR**
(a tone)   (food powder)   (salivation)

conditioned stimulus (CS) in classical conditioning, an originally neutral stimulus (such as a tone) that, when paired with a UCS, comes to evoke a new response

conditioned response (CR) in classical conditioning, the learned response (such as salivation in response to a tone) evoked by the CS after conditioning

Each pairing of the two stimuli may be considered a conditioning *trial*. If we repeat this procedure several times—for several trials—conditioning, or learning, takes place. We find a relatively permanent change in behavior as a result of this experience. After a number of trials, when we present the tone by itself, the dog salivates, something it did not do before in response to the tone. Now the dog salivates not just in response to the food powder, but to the tone as well. The tone is no longer "neutral." Now it produces a response, so we call the tone a **conditioned stimulus (CS)**. To keep the salivation response that it elicits separate from the salivation in response to the food powder, we call it a **conditioned response (CR)**, indicating that it has been conditioned, or learned. Thus, anytime you see the term "conditioned," you will know that you are dealing with the *learned* component of classical conditioning.

CS ⟶ **CR**
(a tone)   (salivation)

Let's review: (1) We start with two stimuli: the neutral stimulus (the CS), which elicits no UCR and the UCS, which elicits the UCR. (2) We repeatedly present the CS and UCS together. (3) As a result, we find that when we present the CS alone, it now elicits a CR.

The same type of stimulus—a tone, for example—can be either a neutral stimulus (before learning occurs) or a conditioned stimulus (when it elicits a learned response). Similarly, the same type of response—say, salivation—can be either an unconditioned response (if it is elicited without learning) or a conditioned response (if it is elicited as the result of learning).

If you have a pet, you have seen this process in action. If you keep your pet's food in the same cabinet all the time, you may note a range of excited, anticipatory behaviors every time your pet hears you open that cabinet door. The open door (CS) has been paired with the food within it (UCS), which produces the same sort of reaction (CR) that was originally reserved for the food (UCR).

Shortly, we'll look at how classical conditioning influences human behaviors, but let us make it clear that classical conditioning is not something that occurs only in dogs and cats. You demonstrate a classically conditioned salivation response when you see pictures or smell the aromas of your favorite foods (particularly if you're hungry). If you respond with anxiety at the sight of your instructor entering the classroom with exam papers, you're displaying a classically conditioned response.

There are two technical points we need to make. The CR and UCR are *not* identical. The CR is usually weaker than the UCR, regardless of the number of times the CS and the UCS are paired. For example, in salivation conditioning, we never get as much saliva in response to the tone (as a CR) as we originally got in response to the food powder alone (as a UCR). Second, *how* the conditioned stimulus and the unconditioned stimulus are paired does matter. If you think about it, you'll realize that there are many ways in which two stimuli can be presented at about the same time (e.g., simultaneously, or UCS then CS, or CS then UCS, with varying time intervals in between). Of all the alternatives, one method consistently works best: the CS comes first, followed shortly (within a second or so) by the UCS, or, again, tone-food-salivation. (Think of it this way: Pavlovian conditioning is basically a matter of "ding-food-slobber.")

> ## BEFORE YOU GO ON
>
> - What is classical conditioning?
> - What is the unconditioned stimulus (UCS) and unconditioned response (UCR)?
> - What is the conditioned stimulus (CS) and conditioned response (CR)?
> - How do the UCR and CR relate to one another?
> - How is classical conditioning accomplished?

CLASSICAL CONDITIONING PHENOMENA

Now that we have the basics of classical conditioning in mind, we can examine some of the procedures developed in Pavlov's laboratory. We'll first see how a classical conditioning experiment actually proceeds.

Acquisition

The stage of classical conditioning during which the CS and UCS are paired and the strength of the CR increases (for example, a dog acquires the response of salivating to a tone) is called **acquisition**. When conditioning begins, the conditioned stimulus (CS) does not produce a conditioned response (CR), which is why we refer to it as a neutral stimulus at this point. After a few pairings of the CS and UCS (conditioning trials), we can demonstrate the presence of a CR. To do that, of course, we'll have to present the conditioned stimulus (CS) by itself. We now discover that there is some saliva produced in response to the tone presented alone. The more trials of the CS and UCS together, the

acquisition the process in classical conditioning in which the repeated pairing of a CS and a UCS increases the strength of a CR

more the dog salivates in response to the tone when it is presented alone. Over repeated trials, the increase in CR strength (the amount of saliva in response to the tone) is rapid at first, but it soon slows and eventually levels off. The first part of Figure 5.1 illustrates the acquisition phase of classical conditioning.

Extinction and Spontaneous Recovery

Assume we have a well-conditioned dog producing a strong CR. Continuing to present the CS-UCS pair adds little to the amount of saliva we get when we present the CS alone. Now we go through a series of trials during which the CS (the tone) is presented but is *not* paired with the UCS (food powder). The result is that the CR will weaken. As we continue to present the tone alone the CR becomes progressively weaker; the dog provides less and less saliva. If we keep it up, the dog eventually will stop salivating to the tone. This is called **extinction**—the process in which the strength of a CR decreases with repeated presentations of the CS alone (that is, the tone without the food powder).

extinction the process in classical conditioning in which the strength of the CR decreases with repeated presentations of the CS alone (without the UCS)

It would appear that we're right back where we started. Because the CR has been extinguished, our dog no longer salivates when we present the tone. Let's return our dog to the kennel for a rest. When the dog comes back to the laboratory and the tone is sounded, the dog salivates again! Not a lot, perhaps, but the salivation does return, or recover. It recovers automatically, or spontaneously, so we call this phenomenon **spontaneous recovery**. Extinction and spontaneous recovery are also illustrated in Figure 5.1.

spontaneous recovery the phenomenon in classical conditioning in which a previously extinguished CR returns following extinction and a rest interval

Spontaneous recovery occurs after extinction and following a rest interval, which indicates two things. First, one series of extinction trials may not be sufficient to eliminate a conditioned response. Because of the possibility of spontaneous recovery, we may have to run more than one series of extinction trials to get our dog to stop salivating altogether. Second, what is happening during extinction is not "forgetting"—at least not in

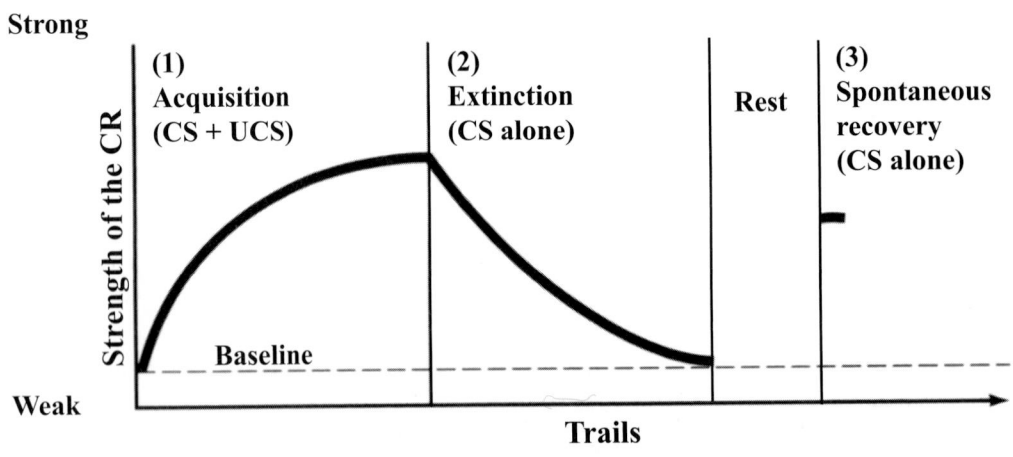

FIGURE 5.1

The stages of conditioning. (1) Acquisition is produced by the repeated pairing of a CS and a UCS. The strength of the CR increases rapidly at first, then slows, and eventually levels off. (2) Extinction is produced by presenting the CS without pairing it with the UCS. The strength of the CR then decreases. (3) After a rest interval (and following extinction), spontaneous recovery is demonstrated by a partial return of the CR.

the usual sense. The response is not forgotten; it is suppressed. That is, the learned salivation response is still there, but it is not showing up in performance during extinction, which is why it can (and does) return later in spontaneous recovery.

At this point we can differentially affect the strength of the CR, depending on what we do. If we again pair the CS with the UCS, the strength of the CR increases. This is called *relearning*. On the contrary, if we again present the CS alone (without the UCS) the strength of the CR diminishes as it did during extinction.

Generalization and Discrimination

During the course of conditioning, assume we consistently use a tone of a given pitch as the conditioned stimulus. After repeated pairings of this tone with food powder, a dog salivates when the tone is presented alone. What will happen if we now present a different tone, one the dog has not heard before? Typically, the dog will salivate in response to it also. This response may not be as strong as the original CR (there may not be as much saliva). How strong it is depends on how similar the new tone is to the original CS. The more similar the new tone is to the original, the more saliva will be produced. This is **generalization**—a process by which a conditioned response is elicited by stimuli different from but similar to the original CS.

generalization the phenomenon in classical conditioning in which a CR is elicited by stimuli different from, but similar to, the CS

This is a powerful process. It means that an unconditioned stimulus need not be paired with all possible conditioned stimuli. If you choose a mid-range tone (CS), a conditioned response automatically generalizes to other, similar tones. Conditioning does not have to be applied over and over for separate tones. A graph of this process is presented in Figure 5.2. If a dog is conditioned to salivate to a tone of middle pitch, it will also salivate to slightly higher and lower tones through generalization. Notice that the strength of the CR

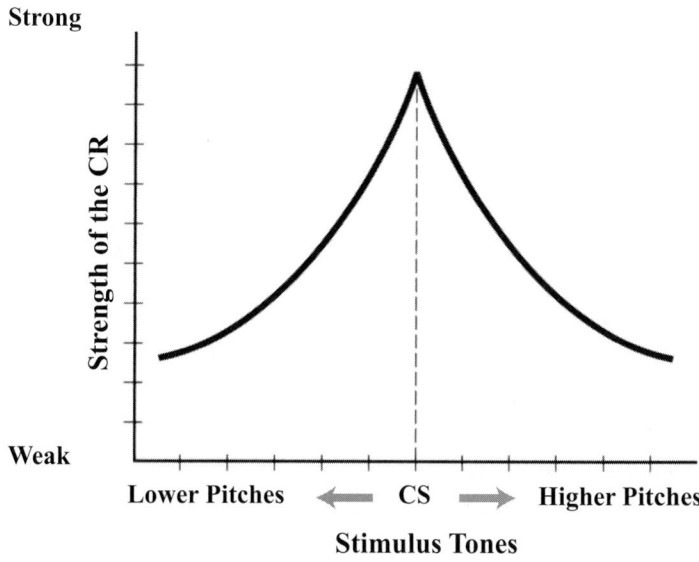

FIGURE 5.2

Generalization gradient. Presenting stimuli other than the CS may produce a CR. How much conditioned response is produced depends on the similarity between the new stimulus and the original CS.

gets weaker and weaker as the new CS becomes more and more different from the original CS. This phenomenon is called the *generalization gradient*.

Look at the outer "tails" of the graph depicted in Figure 5.2. The strength of the CR is very weak at those points. The dog is no longer salivating at the sound of the very different (relative to the initial CS) tone. This points out another important learning phenomenon called **discrimination learning**. Discrimination learning means that the dog has learned to discriminate between different stimuli, emitting the CR in the presence of some stimuli and withholding it in the presence of others. In a sense, discrimination is the opposite of generalization. To demonstrate discrimination learning, we would present a dog with many tones, but would pair the UCS food powder with only one of them—the CS we want the dog to salivate to. We might, for example, pair food powder with a tone of middle C. A lower tone, say A, would also be presented to the dog but *would not* be followed by food powder. At first there would be some saliva in response to the lower A tone (generalization), but eventually our subject would learn to discriminate and would no longer salivate to it.

discrimination learning the phenomenon in classical conditioning in which an organism learns to make a response to only one CS, but not to other CSs

BEFORE YOU GO ON

- What is meant by acquisition?
- How does extinction occur?
- What is spontaneous recovery?
- What is the process of generalization?
- What is a generalization gradient?
- What is discrimination?

THE SIGNIFICANCE OF CLASSICAL CONDITIONING FOR PEOPLE

It is time to leave our discussion of dogs, tones, salivation, and Pavlov's laboratory and turn our attention to the practical application of classical conditioning. We can find examples of classically conditioned human behaviors everywhere.

One of the significant aspects of classical conditioning is its role in the development of emotional responses to stimuli in our environment. There are few stimuli that naturally, or instinctively, produce an emotional response. Yet think of all those things that *do* directly influence how we feel.

For example, very young children seldom seem afraid of spiders, plane rides, or snakes. (Some children actually seem to enjoy them.) How many people do you know who *are* afraid of these things? There are many stimuli in our environments that cause us to be afraid. There are stimuli that produce feelings of pleasure, calm, and relaxation. What scares you? What makes you feel relaxed? Why? Might you feel upset in a certain store because you once had an unpleasant experience there? Might you fondly look forward to a vacation at the beach because of a very enjoyable vacation you had there as a child? Do you shudder at the sight of a police car or smile at the thought of a payroll envelope? In each case, we are talking about classical conditioning. (Not all our learned emotional reactions are acquired through classical conditioning alone. As we will see, there are other possibilities.)

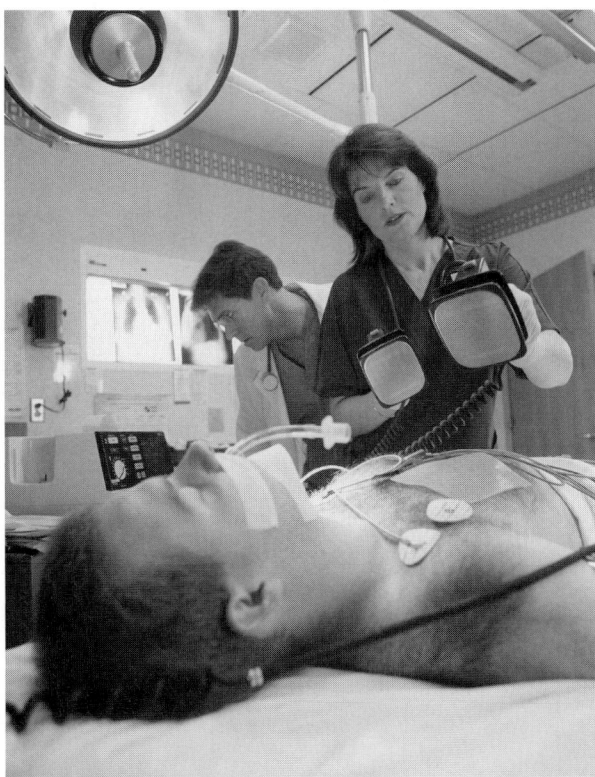

Someone who has had a traumatic experience in a hospital setting may feel "uneasy" about all hospitals for a long time thereafter. This would reflect both classical conditioning and generalization.

Consider the following example experienced by one of the authors (Gerow). When he was a senior in high school, he agreed to have surgery on his nose. (As an uncoordinated basketball player, he had broken it a number of times.) The surgery was done under local anesthetic and was painful, messy, and altogether unpleasant. For nearly 20 years after that surgery, whenever he visited a hospital, his nose ached! He knew that the pain was just "in his head," but his nose hurt nonetheless. This is an example of some relatively permanent classical conditioning, isn't it? The CS of hospital sights, sounds, and odors was paired with the UCS of an operative procedure that caused a UCR of pain and discomfort. This pairing, which lasted for a few days, led to the establishment of a CR of discomfort associated with the CS of the hospital. His CR obviously generalized to many other hospitals, not just the one in which the surgery was performed. And the CR took a very long time to extinguish.

An Example: The Case of "Little Albert"

In 1920, John B. Watson (the founder of behaviorism) and his student assistant, Rosalie Rayner, published a summary article about a series of experiments they had performed with "Little Albert." Albert's experiences have become well-known. Although Watson and Rayner's summary of their own work tended to oversimplify matters (Samuelson, 1980), the story of Little Albert provides a good model for the classical conditioning of emotional responses, in this case, fear.

Eleven-month-old Albert was given many toys to play with. Among other things, he was allowed to play with a live white rat. Albert showed no sign of fearing it. At this point, the rat was a neutral stimulus (NS) with respect to fear. Then conditioning began. One day as Albert reached for the rat, one of the experimenters (Rayner) made a sudden loud noise by striking a metal bar with a hammer. The loud noise frightened Albert. Two months earlier, Watson and Rayner had established that a sudden loud noise frightened Albert—at least he behaved in a way that Watson and Rayner felt indicated fear.

After repeated pairings of the rat and the loud noise, Albert's reaction to the rat underwent a relatively permanent change. Albert would at first start to reach toward the rat, but then would recoil and cry, often trying to bury his head in his blanket. He was making emotional responses to a previously neutral stimulus (NS) that did not elicit those responses before it was paired with a sudden loud noise. This sounds like classical conditioning: the rat is the CS, and the sudden loud noise is the UCS that elicits the UCR of an emotional fear response. After repeated pairings of the rat and the noise (CS and UCS), the rat elicits the same sort of fear response (or CR). Figure 5.3 presents a diagram of the procedures used to condition Little Albert to be afraid of a white rat.

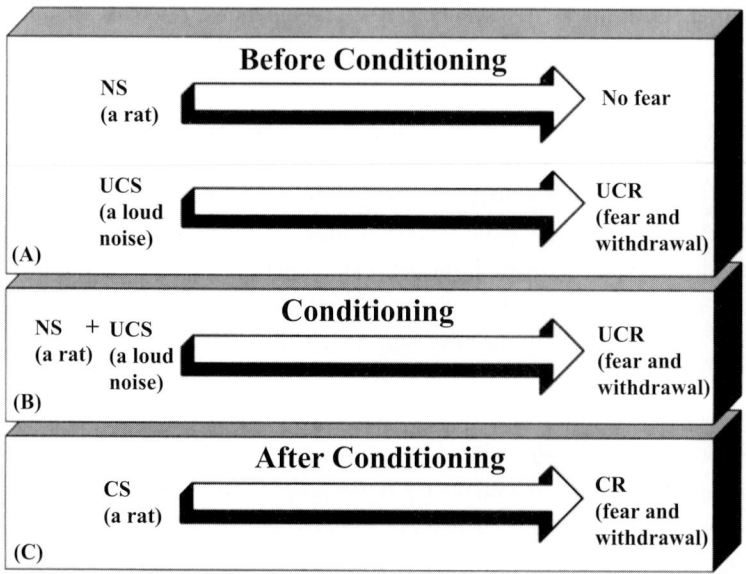

FIGURE 5.3

Conditioning Albert to fear a neutral stimulus (NS) by pairing it with a fear producing stimulus (UCS). The NS becomes a CS when it has been associated with the UCS and will come to elicit a learned fear response (CR).

Watson and Rayner then demonstrated that Albert's fear of the white rat generalized to all sorts of stimuli: a dog, a ball of cotton, even a Santa Claus mask with a white beard and mustache. In some cases, however, Watson and Rayner did not test for generalization as they should have. They occasionally paired the loud noise (UCS) with new stimuli before testing to see what the reaction might be (Harris, 1979).

Several issues have been raised concerning Watson and Rayner's demonstration of learned fear—not the least of which is the unethical treatment of Albert. It is unlikely that anyone would even attempt such a project today. Watson had previously argued (1919) that emotional experiences of early childhood can affect an individual for a lifetime, yet he purposely frightened a young child (and without the advised consent of the boy's mother). Albert's mother removed him from the hospital before Watson and Rayner had a chance to undo the conditioning. They were convinced that they could reverse Little Albert's fear, but as fate would have it, they never got the chance. A number of researchers who tried to replicate Watson and Rayner's experiment, despite ethical considerations, were not totally successful (Harris, 1979).

Even with these disclaimers, it is easy to see how the Little Albert demonstration can be used as a model for describing how fear or any other emotional response can develop. When the project began, Albert didn't respond fearfully to a rat, a cotton ball, or a Santa Claus mask. After a few trials of pairing a neutral stimulus (the rat) with an emotion-producing stimulus (the loud noise), Albert appeared to be afraid of all sorts of white, fuzzy objects.

> ## BEFORE YOU GO ON
>
> - What classical conditioning principles can explain Little Albert's acquisition of a fear?
> - What process explains why Little Albert came to fear other stimuli?
> - Was Watson and Rayner's treatment of Little Albert ethical?

An Application: Treating Fear with Classical Conditioning

There are many things in this world that are life-threatening and downright frightening. Being afraid of some stimuli is often a wise, rational, and adaptive reaction. Occasionally, however, some people experience distressing fears of stimuli that are not threatening in any real or rational sense.

Some people are intensely afraid of heights, spiders, the dark, riding on elevators, or flying. Psychologists say that these people are suffering from a *phobic disorder*—an intense, irrational fear of an object or event that leads a person to avoid contact with it. There are many explanations for how phobic disorders, or phobias, occur, but one clear possibility is classical conditioning. The classical conditioning explanation for phobias suggests that a previously neutral stimulus (a spider, for example), is associated with a fear inducing event (perhaps a painful spider bite). Through a process of association the previously neutral stimulus (the CS) comes to elicit a fear response.

Sadly, phobic disorders are far from rare. Estimates place prevalence between 7 percent and 20 percent of the population, and that's tens of millions of people (Kessler, 1994). Phobic reactions seldom extinguish on their own. Why? There are many reasons, but one is that someone with a phobia is usually successful at avoiding the conditioned stimulus that elicits the fear. Someone with a fear of flying may simply get where he or she wants to go by driving or taking a bus or train.

An effective way to treat fears and phobias is to make use of the principles of classical conditioning. Mary Cover Jones (1924) made one of the earliest attempts to apply classical conditioning to the elimination of a fear. Jones worked with a young boy who had a fear of rabbits. Jones began pairing a pleasing food with the rabbit. The food, by itself (the CS) does not elicit fear, but rather feelings of pleasure. By pairing the food with the fear-producing stimulus (the UCS, the rabbit) Jones was able to condition the boy to substitute the feelings of pleasure with the feelings of fear that had been associated with the rabbit. Over 30 years later the application of classical conditioning to the treatment of fears was elaborated by Joseph Wolpe (1958, 1969, 1981). Wolpe pioneered a technique called *systematic desensitization* which gradually teaches a patient to associate positive feelings with a feared stimulus.

In its standard form, there are three stages of systematic desensitization. First, the therapist instructs or trains the client to relax. There are several ways to do this. Some therapists use hypnosis, but most simply have the client relax one foot, then both feet, one leg, then both, and so on, until the entire body is relaxed. Whatever method is used, this stage generally doesn't take very long. After a few hours of training, the subject knows how to enter a relaxed state quickly.

The second stage is to construct an "anxiety hierarchy"—a list of stimuli that gradually decrease in their ability to elicit anxiety. The most feared stimulus is placed at the top of the list (for example, giving a formal speech to a large group, being called on in class, talking to a small group of strangers, being introduced to two or more people, talking with friends, etc.).

Now treatment begins. The client relaxes completely and thinks about the stimulus lowest on the anxiety hierarchy. The client is then instructed to think about the next highest stimulus, and the next, and so on, all the while remaining as relaxed as possible. As he moves up the list toward the anxiety-producing stimulus at the top, the therapist constantly monitors the client's level of tension or relaxation. When anxiety seems to be overcoming relaxation, the client is told to stop thinking about that item on the hierarchy and to think about an item lower on the list.

counterconditioning in systematic desensitization, when a new response (relaxation) is being acquired to "replace" an old one (fear)

BEFORE YOU GO ON

- How can classical conditioning be used to explain the development of phobias?

- What is systematic desensitization?

- How is systematic desensitization used to treat phobic disorders?

- What is meant by counterconditioning?

Systematic desensitization is more than the simple extinction of a previously conditioned fear response. A new response (relaxation) is being acquired to "replace" an old one (fear). This process is called **counterconditioning**. The logic is that a person cannot be relaxed and anxious at the same time. These are incompatible responses. If one pairs a stimulus (CS) with the feeling of being relaxed (UCS), classical conditioning will produce a reaction of calm (a CR) not the incompatible response of tension and anxiety (the old CR). For many people, this technique can be effective (e.g., Wilson, 1982). It works best for fears or anxieties associated with specific, easily identifiable stimuli; it works least well for a diffuse, generalized fear, for which hierarchies are difficult to generate.

RETHINKING WHAT HAPPENS IN CLASSICAL CONDITIONING

Pavlovian conditioning continues to be an active area of research. Psychologists continue to be interested in understanding precisely what happens in classical conditioning and what factors influence the effectiveness of the procedure (Adler & Cohen, 1993; Domjan, 1987; Lavond et al., 1993; Rescorla, 1987, 1988; Spear et al., 1990).

Pavlov believed, as did generations of psychologists who followed him, that any stimulus paired with an unconditioned stimulus could effectively serve as a conditioned stimulus. It's easy to see how psychologists came to this conclusion. A wide variety of stimuli *can* be paired with food powder and as a result come to elicit salivation.

Psychologists now see classical conditioning in a broader light: as a process of learning about relationships among events in the world; as a search for information that one stimulus provides about another. Previously, it was believed that the time interval between the CS and the UCS had to be brief. We now recognize that there are biological constraints on which sorts of conditioning are likely to occur easily.

Can Any Stimulus Serve as a CS?

Research suggests that one cannot pair just any stimulus with an unconditioned stimulus and expect conditioning to result. For example, a rat can be conditioned to fear the sound of a tone by presenting that tone and consistently following it with an electric shock. It doesn't take many pairings of the tone and the shock for the conditioned response (fear of tone) to develop a straightforward example of classical conditioning. Assume that we also present a different rat with a tone and occasionally follow it with a mild shock. For this rat, we also present the shock from time to time, but *without the preceding tone*. This rat will end up with several shocks without a preceding tone, but it will have as many tone-shock pairings as our first rat. Will this rat demonstrate a conditioned response to the tone when it is presented alone? No, it won't. Although this rat experienced the same number of tone-shock pairings, there will be no conditioning (Rescorla, 1968, 1987).

In this case (and in others, e.g., Miller & Spear, 1985; Pearce & Hall, 1980; Rescorla & Wagner, 1972), what matters most in determining whether a stimulus will act as a CS is the extent to which that stimulus provides information or predicts the occurrence of another stimulus. In the original Pavlovian demonstration, the tone was highly informative. Every time the tone was presented, food powder followed, so the tone was an effective CS. In Rescorla's experiments, we see that if the tone does not reliably predict the presence of a shock (as when some shocks occur without the previous tone), that tone will not be an effective CS no matter how many times it is paired with the UCS.

Let's recast this issue in human terms. If we can talk about rats representing their environments by learning which stimuli predict other stimuli, isn't it reasonable to think about classical conditioning in humans along a similar vein? We may experience a pleasant feeling when we see a picture of a mountain stream because it is associated with one of our best vacations. The fact that we happened to have left for that vacation on a

Tuesday is not. Mountain streams predict fun and good times; Tuesdays do not. We have not been conditioned to associate a fireplace with the pain of being burned, even though we may have first been burned when we placed our hand into a fire. Little Albert's fear of a rat generalized to many stimuli, but he developed no particular fear of blankets, even though he was sitting on a blanket every time Rayner created the loud noise that Albert came to associate with the rat.

BEFORE YOU GO ON

- Can any stimulus serve as a CS for any response?

Now, let's consider an additional complication that has arisen in the search to understand the basic process of classical conditioning: the fact that the CS and the UCS do not have to be paired close together in time.

Must the Time Interval Between the CS and UCS Always Be Brief?

Pavlov thought that the time interval between the CS and the UCS was a critical variable in classical conditioning. For nearly 50 years it was assumed that the most appropriate interval between the CS and UCS was a brief one—a few seconds at most (Beecroft, 1966; Gormezano, 1972). Previously, the claim in most textbooks on learning was that the shorter the interval between the CS and UCS, the faster conditioning would be. It now appears that there is at least one excellent example of classical conditioning in which the CS-UCS interval may be much longer than a few seconds—even hours long. This example also reinforces the point that some stimuli make more effective conditioned stimuli than others. The example is found in the research on the formation of aversions (very strong dislikes) to certain tastes.

Many experiments have confirmed that rats and people (and many other animals) can be classically conditioned to avoid particular foods (Garcia et al., 1966; Gemberling & Domjan, 1982; Revulsky & Garcia, 1970). For example, rats eat or drink a food that has been given a distinctive taste. Then they are given a poison, or treated with X rays, so that they will develop nausea. However, the feelings of nausea do not occur until hours after the food has been eaten. (In a few days, the rats are perfectly normal and healthy again.) Even though there has been a long delay between the flavored food (CS) and the feelings of nausea (UCS), the rats learn to avoid the food, often in just one trial. Patients being treated for cancer may experience nausea as an unpleasant side effect of chemotherapy. Such patients will often show a strong taste aversion for whatever they ate hours before their treatment—even if what they ate was something pleasant, such as ice cream (Bernstein, 1978).

The time delay between the CS and UCS here is clearly at odds with the standard belief that to be effective the CS and UCS need to be presented together in time. A related question is why the *taste* of previously eaten food should so commonly serve as the CS for nausea that occurs hours later. That is, why is the nausea associated with the taste of food instead of some other stimulus event that could be paired with the nausea? Imagine

To keep coyotes from their sheep, ranchers treat a sheep carcass with a substance that makes the coyotes very sick. They develop a taste aversion and avoid the sheep—classical conditioning in action.

this experience happening to you. At a restaurant, you order a piece of pumpkin pie. Hours later, you suffer severe stomach cramps and nausea. Recalling our previous example, why might you associate your illness with the food and not the chair you sat on or the music that was playing during dinner? We may have a biological predisposition, or bias, for making some associations easily (for example, taste and illness), and others with difficulty or not at all (for example, music and illness), particularly if they have a functional basis (Mackintosh, 1975, 1983; Revulsky, 1985). Food followed by nausea is an example of just such a predisposed association. It is biologically adaptive for an organism (a human or a rat) to learn, based on one encounter, not to eat things that make it ill. The second time could be fatal. However, it is still true that shorter CS-UCS intervals lead to stronger associations than longer ones.

BEFORE YOU GO ON

- What was the major assumption for 50 years concerning the timing of the CS and UCS?

- Under what conditions can an association between stimuli be learned, even after a long delay between the CS and UCS?

Topic Review 5 A

1. How do we define learning?

Learning is demonstrated by a relatively permanent change in behavior that occurs as the result of practice or experience. We can use the same definition for "conditioning" in that it is a simple, basic, form of learning.

2. What is the difference between learning and performance?

Learning refers to an internal process that cannot be observed directly and is demonstrated by a change in behavior or performance. It may also occur without being demonstrated through performance.

3. What are the basic procedures of classical conditioning?

In classical, or Pavlovian, conditioning, a neutral stimulus that originally does not elicit a response of interest is paired with another stimulus that reliably elicits a given response. As a result, the once-neutral stimulus acquires the ability to elicit a response that is similar to the original reflexive response.

4. What are the unconditioned stimulus (UCS) and unconditioned response (UCR) in classical conditioning?

The UCS is the stimulus that reliably elicits a reflexive response. The UCR is the reflexive response elicited by the UCS. In classical conditioning, the relationship between the UCS and UCR is unlearned.

5. What are the conditioned stimulus (CS) and conditioned response (CR) in classical conditioning?

The CS is the previously neutral stimulus, which after being paired with the UCS comes to elicit a learned response that resembles the UCR. The learned response is the CR, and it is not identical to the UCR. Typically, it is weaker than the UCR.

6. In classical conditioning, what is acquisition?

In classical conditioning, acquisition refers to the process of learning an association between the CS and the UCS. Acquisition is represented by an increase in the strength of the CR as the CS and the UCS continue to be presented together.

7. In classical conditioning, what is extinction?

If the CS is repeatedly presented without the UCS, the strength of the CR decreases. This is the process of extinction.

8. What is spontaneous recovery?

Spontaneous recovery occurs if an organism is given a rest period following extinction of a CR. After the rest period and presentation of the CS, the CR is once again observed. If the CS and UCS are paired again, reacquisition of the CR occurs. If the CS is again presented alone, the CR again extinguishes.

9. In classical conditioning, what are generalization and the generalization gradient?

In generalization, a response (CR) conditioned to a specific stimulus (CS) will also be elicited by other, similar stimuli. The generalization gradient refers to the fact that the more similar the new stimuli are to the original CS, the greater the resultant CR. As the new stimulus becomes more and more dissimilar to the original CS, the CR becomes progressively weaker.

10. In classical conditioning, what is discrimination?

In many ways, discrimination is the opposite of generalization. It is learning to make a CR in response to a specific CS (paired with the UCS) while learning not to make the CR in response to other stimuli, which are not paired with the UCS.

11. What sorts of responses are most readily formed by classical conditioning?

Classical conditioning has its most noticeable effect on emotion or mood. Most of the stimuli to which we respond emotionally have probably been classically conditioned to elicit those responses, called conditioned emotional responses.

12. What was the "Little Albert" demonstration?

In the Watson and Rayner 1920 "Little Albert" demonstration, a sudden loud noise (the UCS) was paired with the presentation of the neutral stimulus, a white rat. As a result of such pairings, eleven-month-old Albert came to display a learned fear response (a CR) to the originally neutral rat (now the CS). The conditioned fear generalized to other, similar stimuli. The demonstration has been used to explain learned emotional reactions to events in our environments.

13. What is systematic desensitization?

Systematic desensitization involves counterconditioning—training a person to relax and stay relaxed while thinking about a hierarchy of stimuli that are more and more likely to elicit anxiety or fear. If relaxation can be conditioned to thoughts of anxiety-producing stimuli, the sense of calm and relaxation will come to replace the competing response of anxiety. The procedure is often used to treat phobic disorders.

14. Can all stimuli be associated with one another with equal ease?

Although it was assumed for a long time that any stimulus paired with a UCS could serve as a conditioned stimulus, this assumption is no longer accepted because research demonstrated that some stimuli are not readily associated in classical conditioning.

15. What is the modern view of classical conditioning?

The modern view of classical conditioning is that it is a process of learning about relationships among events in the world. It is now known that there are biological limitations on the forms of conditioning that are likely to occur easily. The organism is now conceptualized as an information seeker using relations among events and preconceptions to form representations of its world.

16. Can any stimulus serve as a CS?

The short answer is no. The key factor in determining whether a stimulus will become an effective CS is whether it reliably predicts the occurrence of another stimulus. A stimulus will not be an effective CS if it does not predict another stimulus, regardless of the number of times the stimuli are paired.

17. Must the interval between a CS and UCS always be brief in order for classical conditioning to occur?

In the early days of classical conditioning this was considered true. However, we now know that some stimuli can be associated even after a long delay between the presentation of the CS and the UCS. One example is learned taste aversions. A taste can be associated with feelings of illness even after a delay of several hours between experiencing the taste and first feeling ill. There may be a biological predisposition to associate certain stimuli that predict dangerous conditions even after long delays.

Topic 5B OPERANT CONDITIONING AND COGNITIVE APPROACHES

Imagine yourself in a large child psychology class. The instructor in that class has a terribly boring style—he simply sits at his desk and reads from his notes for the entire period. Imagine further that you and several other students just left a psychology of learning lecture, where the professor suggested you try a "little experiment" to see if you could modify someone's behavior.

You decide to reward the child psychology instructor for doing what you want him to do by smiling, looking attentive, and taking notes. Whenever he does what you don't want him to do, you appear bored, gaze around the room, and stop taking notes. The experiment begins on a Wednesday, but little is accomplished because the experiment isn't well organized. Agreement is needed on exactly which behaviors to reward and which to ignore. By the end of class on Friday, progress is being made. The instructor looks up from his notes more frequently, and he starts squirming in his chair.

Monday's class brings a breakthrough: the instructor rises from his chair! From time to time he sits down (only to be ignored), however, he does not give up physical contact with his notes. He is still reading, but occasionally he stands to do so.

On the following Friday, about halfway through the class period, the instructor is standing in the corner of the room. Notes still on the desk, he is simply talking to the class about child psychology.

Think about that. In just five class days a small group of students lifts their instructor out of his chair and stands him in the corner. No doubt that in another 10 minutes they could move him from one corner to the other. And all this is done by rewarding some behaviors with attention and by ignoring other behaviors. The class is impressed, but the students find themselves thinking about the ethical implications of their experiment.

The premise of operant conditioning is that behaviors are shaped by the consequences they have produced in the past. In this example, the class was able to modify the instructor's behavior by providing different consequences (attention or inattention) for different behaviors.

Key Questions to Answer

While reading this Topic, find the answers to the following key questions:

1. What is operant conditioning?

2. What is the "Law of Effect"?

3. How did B. F. Skinner demonstrate operant conditioning?

4.   In operant conditioning, what is acquisition?

5.   What is shaping through successive approximations?

6.   In operant conditioning, what is extinction?

7.   In operant conditioning, what is spontaneous recovery?

8.   What is meant by the term "reinforcement"?

9.   How does "reinforcement" differ from a "reinforcer"?

10.   How does a "reinforcer" differ from a "reward"?

11.   What is a positive reinforcer?

12.   What is a negative reinforcer?

13.   What is a primary reinforcer?

14.   What is a secondary reinforcer?

15.   What are contingency contracting and token economies?

16.   What are continuous and partial reinforcement schedules?

17.   What is the partial reinforcement effect?

18.   What are fixed-ratio, fixed-interval, variable-ratio, and variable-interval schedules of reinforcement?

19.   What is punishment?

20.   How does punishment differ from negative reinforcement?

21.   What forms does punishment take?

22.   How can punishment be used effectively?

23.   What are the drawbacks to using punishment to modify a child's behavior?

24.   In operant conditioning, what are generalization and discrimination?

25.   What is latent learning?

26.   What is a cognitive map?

27.   What are the basic concepts of social learning theory?

28.   What are the possible outcomes of social learning?

29.   What are vicarious reinforcement and vicarious punishment?

30.   What is an aggressive script?

THE BASICS OF OPERANT CONDITIONING

Most of the early research on operant conditioning was done by B. F. Skinner. Although we correctly associate operant conditioning with Skinner, he did not discover it. The techniques of operant conditioning had been in use for hundreds of years before Skinner was born. What Skinner did was bring that earlier work—most of it casual, some of it scientific—into the laboratory. There he studied the process of operant conditioning with a unique vigor that helped the rest of us realize the significance of the process.

Defining Operant Conditioning

operant conditioning a procedure that changes the rate of a response on the basis of the consequences that result from that response

Skinner used the term *operant* to refer to a behavior or group of behaviors an organism uses to operate on its environment. Operants are controlled by their consequences: they will maintain or increase their rate if they are reinforced; they will decrease their rate if they are not reinforced or if they are punished. Thus, **operant conditioning** changes the rate, or probability, of responses on the basis of the consequences that result from those responses. We are not claiming here that the future governs what happens in the present, but that past experiences influence present ones. Skinner put it this way: "…behavior is shaped by its consequences, but only by consequences that lie in the past. We do what we do because of what *has* happened, not what *will* happen" (Skinner, 1989).

Actually, the first clear statement of operant conditioning came not from Skinner but from E. L. Thorndike, a psychologist at Columbia University in the early twentieth century, who worked to discover the "laws of learning." In one experiment, he placed a cat inside a wooden box. The door of the box was latched with a wooden peg. If manipulated correctly, the peg could be moved, the latch opened, and the cat could go outside the box to eat a small piece of fish that Thorndike had placed there (Figure 5.4). When it was first placed in the box, the cat engaged in a wide range of behaviors: clawing, licking, biting, scratching, hissing, and stretching. But eventually—and, at first, by chance—the door was unlatched and the cat got to the food. The next time the cat was in Thorndike's "puzzle box," it exhibited many of the same behaviors, but it did unlatch the door and escape a bit sooner. Over a series of trials, Thorndike noted that his cat reduced its irrelevant behaviors and directly moved to open the door more and more quickly. After some experience, a cat placed in the box would go immediately to the latch, move the peg, open the door, and eat the fish provided by its trainer. Thorndike had discovered a law of learning—the *law of effect*.

FIGURE 5.4

After noting that cats became more and more proficient at escaping from his "puzzle box," E.L. Thorndike came to believe that they were demonstrating lawful behaviors. Those behaviors could be explained, Thorndike argued, in terms of his law of effect.

The **law of effect** embodies the basics of operant conditioning, claiming that responses are learned ("stamped in," Thorndike said) when followed by a "satisfying state of affairs" (Thorndike, 1911). On the other hand, if a response is not followed by a satisfying state of affairs, or if a response leads to "discomfort," an organism will tend not to make that response again. Thorndike seemed to be saying, "We tend to do, and continue to do, whatever makes us feel good." This seemingly simple observation is also a profound one because it is true. Behaviors are shaped by their consequences.

> **law of effect** Thorndike's law stating that responses that lead to a "satisfying state of affairs" tend to be repeated; responses that do not lead to a satisfying state of affairs tend not to be repeated

Examples of operant conditioning are all around us. You don't need any special apparatus to observe the principle. Imagine a father rushing through a supermarket with his toddler seated in a shopping cart. The youngster is screaming at the top of his lungs for a candy bar, "I wanna candy bar! I wanna candy bar!" Father is doing a good (and an appropriate) job of ignoring this monstrous behavior until he spies a neighbor coming down the next aisle. The neighbor has her three children with her, all of whom are acting like perfect angels. What's a parent to do? He races by the checkout lanes, grabs a chocolate bar, and gives it to his child. He has *reinforced* the child's tantrum by giving the child the candy (a *reinforcer*). Does one have to be an expert in child psychology (or operant conditioning) to predict what will happen on the next visit to the store? Screaming "worked" this time, so it will be tried again. Reinforced behaviors tend to recur.

Demonstrating Operant Conditioning

To demonstrate operant conditioning in the laboratory, Skinner built a special apparatus, which he called an operant chamber. Although Skinner never used the term, and said he didn't like it (Skinner, 1984), some psychologists call this device a "Skinner box." Figure 5.5 shows a standard operant chamber. The chamber pictured here is designed for rats. The box is empty except for a small lever that protrudes from one wall and a small cup that holds a piece of rat food. Food pellets are automatically dispensed through a tube into the food cup. They are released one at a time when the lever is pressed all the way down.

Now that we have our chamber, we need a learner. If we put a hungry rat into the chamber and do nothing else, the rat will occasionally press the lever. There's little else for it to do in there. Rats naturally explore their environments and tend to manipulate objects in it. The rate at which the rat freely presses the lever is called its *base rate* of responding. Typically, a rat will press the lever eight to ten times an hour.

After a period of observation, we activate the food dispenser so that a food pellet is delivered every time the lever is pressed. As predicted by Thorndike's law of effect, the rate of the lever-pressing response increases. The rat may reach the point of pressing the lever as many as 500 to 600 times an hour. Learning has taken place. There has been a relatively permanent change in behavior as a result of experience.

Here is a little subtlety: has the rat learned to press the lever? In any sense can we say that we have taught the rat a lever-pressing response? No. The rat "knew" how to press the lever and did so long before we introduced the food pellets as a reward for its behavior. The change in behavior that took place was a change in *the rate* of the response, not in *the nature* of the response.

BEFORE YOU GO ON

- What is operant conditioning?
- What is the law of effect?
- How did Skinner demonstrate operant conditioning?

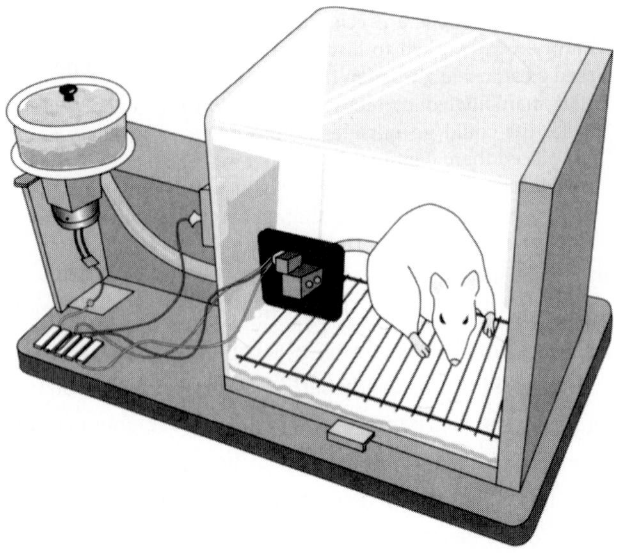

FIGURE 5.5

A drawing of a typical operant chamber.

The Course of Conditioning

Now that we have the basic principles of operant conditioning in mind, let's briefly review how to use the procedure. A reality of operant conditioning is that before you can reinforce a response, you have to get that response to occur in the first place. If your rat never presses the lever, it will never get a pellet. What if you place your rat in an operant chamber and discover that after grooming itself, it stops, stares off into space, and settles down, facing away from the lever and the food cup? Your operant chamber is prepared to deliver a food pellet as soon as your rat presses the lever, but you may have a long wait.

shaping a procedure of reinforcing successive approximations of the response you ultimately want to condition

In such circumstances, you could use a procedure called **shaping**, reinforcing *successive approximations* of the response you ultimately want to condition. You have a button that delivers a pellet to the food cup of the operant chamber even though the lever is not pressed. When your rat turns to face the lever, you deliver a pellet, reinforcing that behavior. This isn't exactly the response you want, but at least the rat is facing in the correct direction. You don't give your rat another pellet until it moves toward the lever. It gets another pellet for moving even closer to the lever. The next pellet doesn't come until the rat touches the lever. Eventually the rat will press the lever to deliver a pellet by itself. Shaping is over, and the rat is on its own.

Once an organism emits the responses you wish to reinforce, the procedures of operant conditioning are simple. Immediately following the response, a reinforcer is provided. As responses produce reinforcers, those responses become more and more likely to occur. The increase in response rate that follows reinforcement will generally be slow at first, become more rapid, and eventually level off. This stage in which response rates increase is **acquisition**. Figure 5.6 is a curve showing the stages of operant conditioning. Note that the vertical axis is a measure of *rate of response*, not response strength—that is, what increases in acquisition for operant conditioning is the rate of a response.

acquisition the process in operant conditioning in which the rate of a reinforced response increases

Once an organism is responding at a high rate of response, what will happen if reinforcers are withheld? Let's say that because we have reinforced its lever pressing, a rat is pressing a lever at a rate of 550 presses an hour. From now on, however, it will receive no more pellets of food for its efforts—no more reinforcers. Although we would expect the rat to stop pressing the lever, which will happen eventually, quite the opposite happens for the first few nonreinforced behaviors. In fact, the rate of responding actually *increases* for a while. Not only does the rate of responding initially increase, but the force exerted on the lever by the rat also increases. That is, the rat will hit the lever harder than before. Eventually, however, the rate of lever-pressing response decreases gradually until it returns to the low base rate. That is, eventually the lever pressing returns to base rate (not to zero, because it didn't start at zero), and **extinction** has taken place. In operant conditioning, extinction is the decrease in the rate of a response as reinforcers are withheld.

Now assume that extinction has occurred, and that the rat has been removed from the operant chamber and returned to its cage for a few days. When we again deprive it of food and return it to the chamber, what will it do? It will go to the lever and begin to press it again. Although the lever pressing has undergone extinction (the last time this rat was in the operant chamber, it was not pressing the lever), it will resume once the rat is given a rest interval. This return of an extinguished response following a rest interval is called **spontaneous recovery**. Figure 5.6 also shows extinction and spontaneous recovery for operant conditioning.

What happens to the spontaneously recovered response depends on what you do next. If you continue to withhold reinforcement, the behavior once again undergoes extinction. That is, the rate of responding falls off. If, on the other hand, you again begin to reinforce the operant response, *reacquisition* occurs. The operant response again gains its heightened rate.

extinction the process in operant conditioning in which the rate of a response decreases as reinforcers are withheld

spontaneous recovery the phenomenon in operant conditioning in which the rate of an extinguished response returns above base rate, following a rest period

---

BEFORE YOU GO ON

- To what does the term shaping refer?

- Describe acquisition of an operant response.

- What is extinction?

- What is spontaneous recovery?

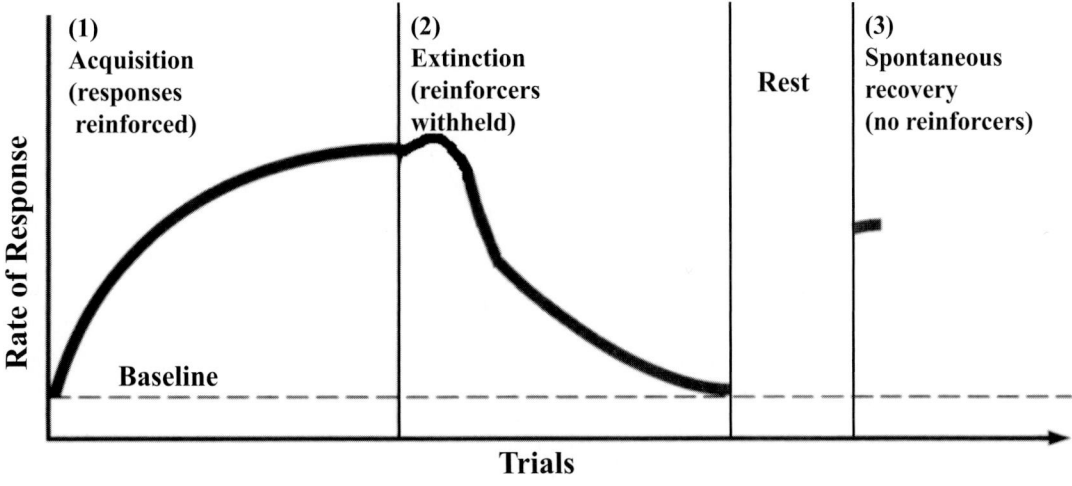

FIGURE 5.6

The stages of operant conditioning. (1) During acquisition, response rates increase as responses are reinforced. (2) In extinction, reinforcers are withheld and response rates return to their original baseline rates. In spontaneous recovery, an increase in response rate is noted following a rest interval after extinction. Note that the vertical axis indicates a measure of the rate of a response, not its strength.

REINFORCEMENT

reinforcement a process that increases the rate, or probability, of the response it follows

reinforcer a stimulus that increases or maintains the rate, or probability, of a response it follows

From what we've said so far, it is obvious that reinforcement is a crucial concept in operant conditioning. At this point, it is useful to make a distinction between two related, but different concepts: reinforcement and reinforcer. **Reinforcement** refers to the *process* of strengthening a response. Anytime you see the term "reinforcement" you should know that the intention is to strengthen or increase the probability of a behavior. A **reinforcer** refers to the actual *stimulus* used in the process of reinforcement that increases the probability or strength of a response. It is important to keep the related concepts of reinforcement and reinforcer separate. A stimulus is classified as a reinforcer based on its effect on behavior. If the stimulus increases the rate of responding, or at least maintains its level, it is a reinforcer. It is important that you divorce the term reinforcer from reward. The term reward implies that a stimulus that increases behavior is something positive (for example, a piece of food to a hungry rat, or a piece of candy to a child). Although many reinforcers are positive and desired by an organism, some are not. For example, if a child shows an increase in aggressive behavior following spankings, the spankings are acting as a reinforcer. Thus, the inherent nature of a stimulus has little to do with whether it is a reinforcer. The only criterion for establishing something as a reinforcer is its effect on behavior.

Positive and Negative Reinforcers

What qualifies as an effective reinforcer? What creates that satisfying state of affairs that Thorndike claimed is necessary to increase response rate? For hungry rats in operant chambers, the answer seems simple. Here we can ensure that a rat is hungry and can confidently predict that receiving food will be reinforcing. For people, or for rats who are no longer hungry, the answer may not be as obvious.

Skinner and his students have long argued that we should define reinforcers only in terms of their effect on behavior. Reinforcers are stimuli. If a stimulus presented after a response increases the strength of that response, then that stimulus is a reinforcer regardless of its nature. For example, imagine the following scenario: A parent spanks his four-year-old child each time the child pulls the cat's tail. The parent notices that instead of pulling the tail less, the child is actually pulling the tail more often. If the operant behavior we are trying to influence is pulling of the cat's tail, then the spanking is serving as a reinforcer because the frequency of the operant behavior has gone up. This is despite the fact that the parent sees the spanking as something negative. Perhaps the child is being reinforced by the attention from the parent attached to the spanking! In short, identifying which stimuli will act as reinforcers may be difficult to do ahead of time. We need to observe the effect of a stimulus on the operant, base, level of a behavior before we can really know if that stimulus is a reinforcer.

Cultural influences impact what will or will not be reinforced. In many cultures (mostly Eastern and African), the group is valued above the individual. In such cultures, reinforcing an individual's achievements will have less effect than in those cultures (mostly Western) in which individual effort and achievement are valued (e.g., Arnett,

1995; Brislin, 1993; Triandis, 1990). In traditional Hawaiian culture, the sense of family is strong, and personal independence is not a sought-after goal. Thus, "the Hawaiian child may not be motivated by individual rewards (gold stars, grades) to the extent that his or her Caucasian counterpart may be" (Cushner, 1990). The point is that we cannot tell whether a stimulus will be reinforcing until we try it. It is reinforcing only if it increases the rate or the likelihood of the response it follows.

Now that we have a general idea of what a reinforcer is and have distinguished it from the process of reinforcement, we can get more specific. A **positive reinforcer** is a stimulus given to an organism after a response is made that increases (or maintains) the rate of a response it follows. This sounds familiar and even redundant: if something is positive, it ought to be reinforced. Examples include such stimuli as food for hungry organisms, water for thirsty ones, high-letter grades for well-motivated students, and money, praise, and attention for most of us. Remember, the intention of the person doing the reinforcing does not matter at all. This explains how an aversive stimulus (for example, a spanking) can actually be a positive reinforcer. If a child shows increased aggression after spankings, the aggression is being positively reinforced by the spanking. The attention, although "negative," from the parent in the form of the spanking, is actually reinforcing the aggression. Remember, reinforcers are defined solely on the basis of their effect on behavior.

A **negative reinforcer** is a stimulus that increases (or maintains) the rate of a response that precedes its removal. In order to increase the rate of a response with a negative reinforcer, one presents an aversive stimulus *before* the behavior to be learned is emitted. For example, you could administer a weak electric shock to a rat in an operant chamber. Any behavior that immediately precedes the *removal* of the negative reinforcer will increase in strength. So, if we want the rat to learn to press a lever, we make termination of the negative reinforcer contingent upon the lever press. When the animal presses the lever, the shock is terminated. It is the *removal* of an aversive event that is reinforcing.

Negative reinforcer is a strange term. If something is negative, how can it be a reinforcer? Remember that the key word here is *reinforcer*, and reinforcers increase the rate of responses. In terms of the law of effect, negative reinforcement must produce some sort of satisfying state of affairs. It does. The reinforcement comes not from the delivery or presentation of negative reinforcers, but from their removal. (Another secret is to remember that reinforcement is a process. You may think of negative reinforcers as unpleasant stimuli, whereas negative reinforcement is a pleasant process or outcome.)

So negative reinforcers are stimuli that increase the probability of a response when they are removed. They may include such stimuli as shocks, enforced isolation, or ridicule—exactly the sorts of things a person would work to avoid or escape. Although it may not sound like it, negative reinforcement is desirable. If one is offered negative reinforcement, "one should accept the offer. It is always good to have bad things terminated or removed" (Michael, 1985). Figure 5.7 illustrates how positive and negative reinforcers work.

positive reinforcer a stimulus that increases the rate of a response it follows. Positive reinforcers are presented after a response has been made.

negative reinforcer a stimulus that increases the rate of a response when that stimulus is removed after the response is made. Negative reinforcers are presented before a response is made.

Positive Reinforcement

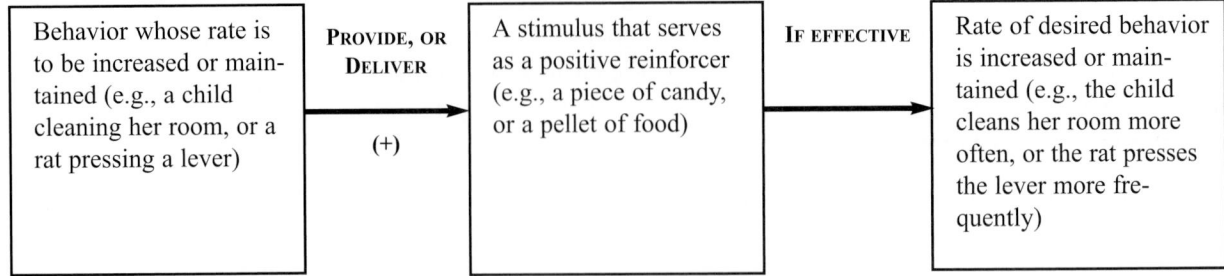

Negative Reinforcement

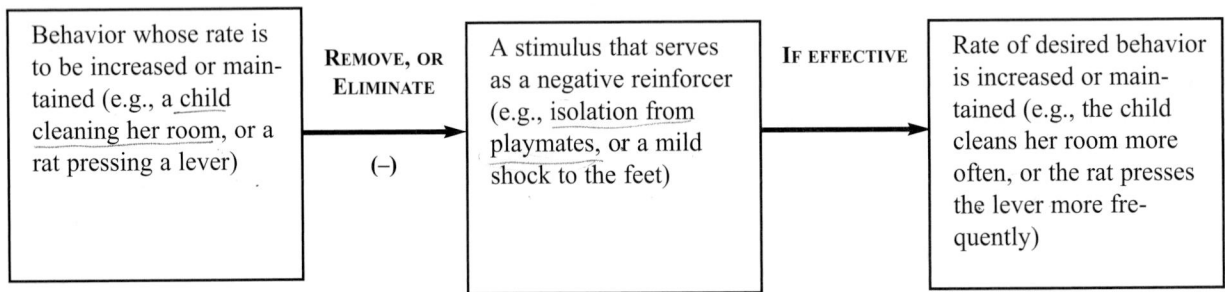

FIGURE 5.7

The major differences between Positive and Negative Reinforcement

Consider a few examples. A rat in an operant chamber is given a constant shock (through the metal floor of the chamber). As soon as the rat presses a lever, the shock is turned off. The lever press has been reinforced. Because an unpleasant, painful stimulus was terminated, negative reinforcement occurred. The negative reinforcer was the shock. You take an aspirin when you have a headache and are reinforced: the pain stops. You will be likely to try aspirin the next time you have a headache. When Wayne says "uncle" to get Ken to stop twisting his arm, Ken does stop, thereby reinforcing Wayne's saying "uncle." If this negative reinforcement is effective, Wayne will be more likely to say "uncle" in the future when Ken asks him to. (Note that Ken could have used a positive reinforcer to get Wayne to say "uncle," perhaps by offering him five dollars to do so.) When a prisoner is released from prison early "for good behavior," the good behavior is being reinforced. The process is negative reinforcement.

Here's one more hint for you. Don't think of positive and negative reinforcement in terms of good and bad, but in terms of plus (+) and minus (−). When using positive reinforcement, one adds (+) a stimulus, and in negative reinforcement one takes away, or subtracts (−), a stimulus. Remember, any time you see the term reinforcement or reinforcer, you should know that the intention is to *increase the rate of a* behavior.

BEFORE YOU GO ON

- What is reinforcement?
- What is a reinforcer?
- Distinguish between reinforcement and reinforcer.
- What is a positive and a negative reinforcer? How do they differ?

Primary and Secondary Reinforcers

We've seen that reinforcers are defined in terms of their effects on behavior, and that both positive and negative reinforcers increase response rate. When we distinguish between primary and secondary reinforcers, the issue is the extent to which reinforcers are natural and unlearned or acquire their reinforcing capability through learning or experience.

Primary reinforcers do not require previous experience to be effective. They are related to the organism's survival in some way and are usually physiological or biological in nature. Food for a hungry organism or water for a thirsty one are common examples. Providing a warm place by the fire to a cold, wet, stray dog involves primary reinforcement. A **secondary reinforcer** may be referred to as a *conditioned, acquired,* or *learned reinforcer.* There is nothing about a secondary reinforcer that implies that they are inherently reinforcing in any biological sense, yet they strengthen responses. Most of the reinforcers we all work for are of this sort. Money, praise, high-letter grades, and promotions are good examples. Money, in itself, is not worth much. But previous experiences have convinced most of us of the reinforcing nature of money because it can be traded for something we need (such as food). Thus, money can serve to increase the rate of a variety of responses.

primary reinforcer a stimulus (usually biologically or physiologically based) that increases the rate of a response with no previous experience or learning required

secondary reinforcer a stimulus that increases the rate of a response because of an association with other reinforcers; also called conditioned, or learned, reinforcers

Weeding a flowerbed may not be very pleasant, but if one has learned the value of money, being paid to do so can be reinforcing.

The use of secondary reinforcers and operant conditioning can be illustrated by a type of psychotherapy called *contingency contracting.* Contingency contracting is achieved by setting up a system called a token economy that provides secondary reinforcers for appropriate behaviors. For example, a child earns a checkmark on the calendar for each day he or she makes the bed (or takes out the trash, or walks the dog, or clears the table). The "economy" hinges on the extent to which the checkmarks serve as tokens, or as secondary reinforcers. The child must first learn that a certain number of checkmarks can be exchanged for something that already reinforces his or her behaviors (for example, an extra dessert, an hour of playing a video game, or a new toy). Techniques such as this, when applied consistently, can be very effective in modifying behaviors.

Perhaps because of their effectiveness, examples such as this one often disturb students and parents. "Why, this isn't psychology," they argue. "You're just bribing the child to behave." There are at least two reasons why we need not be overly concerned. First, bribery involves contracting to reward someone to do something that both parties view as

BEFORE YOU GO ON

- What is a primary reinforcer?
- What is a secondary reinforcer?
- What is contingency contracting and when is it used?

inappropriate. People are bribed to steal, cheat, lie, change votes, or otherwise engage in behaviors they know they should not. Token economies reinforce behaviors judged in the first place to be appropriate. Second, as Skinner argued for many years, the long-term hope is that the child (in our example) will come to appreciate that having trash removed, or walking the dog, or having a clean room is a valued end in itself and can be its own reward. The hope is that the use of reinforcers will no longer be needed as appropriate behaviors become reinforced by more subtle, intrinsic factors.

Schedules of Reinforcement

In all of our discussions and examples so far, we have implied that operant conditioning requires that a reinforcer be provided after every desired response. In fact, particularly at the start, it may be best to reinforce each response as it occurs. But as response rates begin to increase, there is good reason for reinforcing responses intermittently.

continuous reinforcement (CRF) schedule a reinforcement schedule in which every response is followed by a reinforcer

The procedure of reinforcing each and every response after it occurs is called a **continuous reinforcement (CRF) schedule**. One problem with CRF schedules is that earning a reinforcer after each response may reduce the effectiveness of that reinforcer. For example, once a rat has eaten its fill, food pellets will no longer serve to reinforce its behavior, and the rat will have to be removed from the operant chamber until it becomes hungry again (Skinner, 1956). Another problem is that responses acquired under a CRF schedule tend to extinguish (go through extinction process) very quickly. Once reinforcement is withheld, response rates decrease drastically.

partial reinforcement schedules a schedule in which responses are not reinforced every time they occur

Alternatives to reinforcing every response are **partial reinforcement schedules**. Simply put, these are strategies for reinforcing a response less frequently than every time it occurs. There are several ways in which one might reinforce responses according to a partial schedule. We will review four: the fixed-ratio, fixed-interval, variable-ratio, and variable-interval schedules.

fixed-ratio schedule the partial reinforcement schedule calls for delivering one reinforcer after a set number of responses (e.g., one reinforcer after every five responses)

With a **fixed-ratio schedule** (FR), one establishes (fixes) a ratio of reinforcers to responses. In an FR 1:5 schedule, for example, a reinforcer is delivered after every five responses. A 1:10 fixed-ratio schedule for a rat in an operant chamber means that the rat receives a pellet only after it presses the lever ten times. Piecework is an example of a fixed-ratio schedule, "I'll pay you twenty-five cents for every twelve gizmos you assemble," or "You'll earn ten points of credit for every three book reports you hand in." Understandably, there is a high and steady rate of responding under a fixed-ratio schedule. After all, the more one responds, the more reinforcement there will be. For most organisms, there is a brief pause, known as a *postreinforcement pause*, just after a reinforcement occurs. Responses acquired under an FR schedule are more resistant to extinction than those acquired under a CRF schedule.

With a **fixed-interval schedule** (FI), time is divided into set (fixed) intervals. After each fixed interval, a reinforcer is delivered when the next response occurs. An FI thirty-second schedule calls for the delivery of a food pellet for the first lever press a rat makes after each thirty-second interval passes. With such a schedule, you know from the start that you won't be dispensing more than two pellets every minute. Note that the rat doesn't get a pellet just because thirty seconds has elapsed; it gets a pellet for the first response it makes after the fixed interval. A commonly cited example is employees paid on a regular interval of, say, every Friday or once a month. Under an FI schedule, response rates decrease immediately after a reinforcer, then increase as the time for the next reinforcer approaches. FI schedules also produce responses that are resistant to extinction.

There are two variable schedules of reinforcement: a **variable-ratio schedule** (VR) and a **variable-interval schedule** (VI). From the learner's point of view, these schedules are very much alike. They differ from the perspective of the dispenser of reinforcers. With a VR schedule, one varies the ratio of reinforcers to responses. With a VR 1:5 schedule, the experimenter provides one reinforcer for every five responses *on the average*, but always in a different ratio. The first reinforcer may come after five responses, the next after six, the next after nine, the next after one, and so on. On the average, the ratio of reinforcers to responses is 1:5, but the patterning of actual ratios is variable. From the learner's point of view, this is a random schedule. The most commonly cited examples of VR reinforcement schedules are gambling devices, such as slot machines. They pay off (reinforce) on a variable-ratio schedule where the ratios are usually quite large. The variable-ratio schedule produces a high rate of responding with no post-reinforcement pauses. Behavior maintained on a VR schedule is very resistant to extinction.

fixed-interval schedule the partial reinforcement schedule calling for a reinforcer at the first response following a specified, or fixed, interval

variable-ratio schedule the partial reinforcement schedule that randomly changes the ratio of reinforcers to responses but maintains a given ratio as an average

variable-interval schedule the partial reinforcement schedule calling for a reinforcer at the first response after a time interval whose length is randomly varied

Because gambling devices "reinforce" on variable schedules, gambling behaviors are difficult to extinguish.

Variable-interval (VI) schedules follow the same logic as variable-ratio schedules. The difference is that for VI schedules, time intervals are established randomly. For a rat on a VI thirty-second schedule, a food pellet comes following the first lever press response after a thirty-second interval; the next follows the first response after a fifty-second interval; then after a ten-second interval, and so on. For a VI thirty-second schedule, the varied intervals *average* thirty seconds in length. An instructor who wants to keep a class studying regularly and attending class consistently may schedule quizzes on a variable-interval schedule. The students will learn that the quizzes are coming, but they never know when. What we find when VI schedules are used is a slower but very steady pattern of performance. If you know when your exams are coming, you may hold off studying until just before they occur. If they are scheduled to occur randomly throughout the semester, you'll keep your studying rate up just in case there's a test the next class period.

The terminology we have used is standard, but it is somewhat technical. The main point to remember is that operant conditioning does not require that each response be reinforced. The scheduling of reinforcers influences the pattern of the learned responses. Maintaining behavior on a partial schedule of reinforcement also affects a behavior's resistance to extinction. The **partial reinforcement effect** refers to the phenomenon that a behavior maintained on a partial schedule of reinforcement is more resistant to extinction than one maintained on CRF (see Figure 5.8). This is because on a partial schedule an organism "gets used to" not being reinforced for every response. When an extinction period begins, responses persist because extinction looks a lot like what the organism had gotten used to. In contrast, on CRF the organism is used to receiving reinforcement for every response. During periods of extinction, the lack of reinforcement is more evident and the organism gives up responding more quickly.

Another point should be made regarding the scheduling of reinforcers. No matter whether one is using a continuous or a partial schedule, reinforcers should come immediately after the desired response is made. Delayed reinforcement is likely to be ineffective.

We are not saying that delaying reinforcement destroys the possibility of learning, but in most cases, the more immediate the reinforcer, the better the learning. In one study, for example, rats were reinforced for entering a black box instead of a white one. The task was learned readily when reinforcers were delivered immediately. If the delivery of reinforcers was delayed only a second or two, very little learning took place; with a ten-second delay, there was no learning at all (Grice, 1948). Several experiments have demonstrated the same phenomenon with human subjects (Hall, 1976). This point has many practical applications. What if parents buy tickets to the circus to reinforce their son's behavior with the babysitter? The circus is not until Saturday. When the family goes to the circus Saturday afternoon, what is reinforced may not be the child's "good behaviors" of last Tuesday night but inappropriate behaviors of Wednesday, Thursday, Friday, and Saturday morning.

partial reinforcement effect
the phenomenon that behavior maintained on a partial reinforcement schedule is more resistant to extinction than behavior maintained on CRF

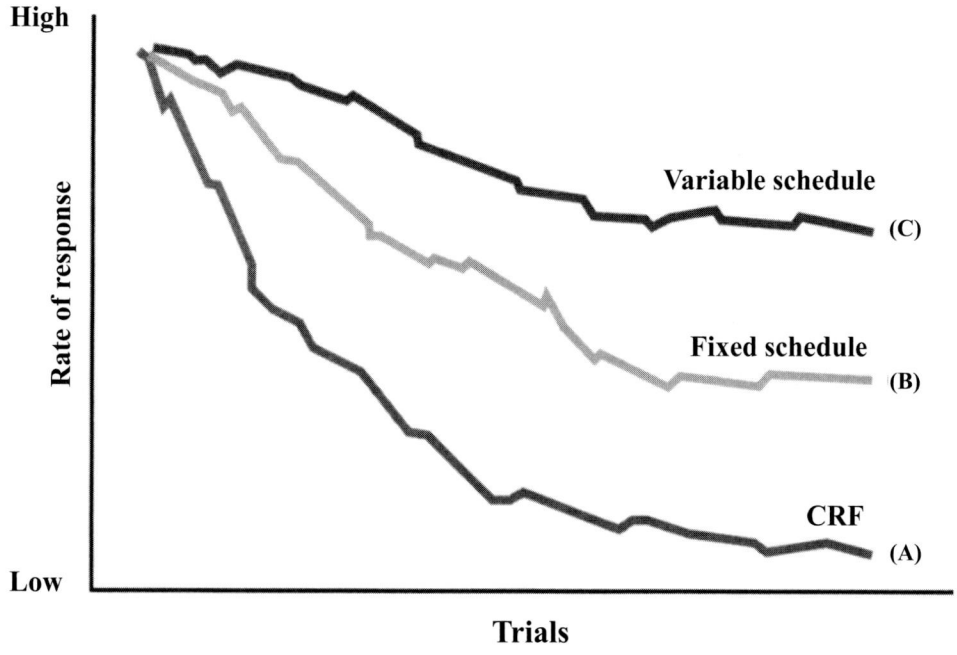

FIGURE 5.8

The effects of a schedule of reinforcement on extinction. These are three hypothetical extinction curves following operant conditioning on (A) continuous reinforcement (CRF), (B), a fixed schedule (FR or FI), and (C), a variable schedule VR or VI).

PUNISHMENT

We've talked about reinforcers—positive and negative, primary and secondary—and how they can be scheduled. Let's now consider punishment. **Punishment** occurs when a stimulus delivered to an organism *decreases* the rate, or probability, of the response that preceded it. In common usage, punishment is usually in some way hurtful or painful, either physically (a spanking) or psychologically (ridicule). It is a painful, unpleasant stimulus presented to an organism after some response is made. It may have occurred to you that if punishers are removed, the result will be reinforcing; in fact, we would have an example of negative reinforcement.

Determining ahead of time what stimulus will be punishing is as difficult to do as determining what stimulus will serve as a reinforcer. Once again, one's intentions are irrelevant. We'll know for sure that something is a punisher only after observing its effect on behavior. We may think we are punishing Jon by sending him to his room because he has begun to throw a temper tantrum. It may be that "in his room" is exactly where Jon would like to be. We may have reinforced Jon's temper tantrum behaviors simply by attending to them. The only way to know for certain is to note the effect on behavior. If Jon's tantrum-throwing behaviors become less frequent, sending him to his room may indeed have been a punishing thing to do.

We can think of punishers as being positive and negative in the same way that we explain positive and negative reinforcers. Positive punishment means delivering or giving (adding, +) a painful, unpleasant stimulus (e.g., a slap on the hand) following an inappropriate response. Negative punishment means removing (subtracting, -) a valued, pleasant stimulus (e.g., "No more TV for a week!") following an inappropriate response.

punishment the administration of a punisher, which is a stimulus that decreases the rate, or probability, of a response that precedes it

Is punishment an effective way of controlling behavior? Does punishment work? Yes, it does—sometimes. Punishment *can* be an impressive modifier of behavior. A rat has learned to press a lever to get food. Now you decide that you no longer want the rat to press the lever. You pass an electric current through the lever so that each time the rat touches the lever it receives a strong shock. What will happen? Actually, several things may happen, but—if your shock is strong enough—there's one thing of which we can be sure: the rat will stop pressing the lever. If punishment is effective, why do psychologists argue against its use, particularly the punishment of children for the misbehavior?

There are many potential problems, or side-effects, of the use of punishment, even when it is used correctly. And often it is used incorrectly. Let's review some of what we know about the use of punishment (e.g., Axelrod & Apsche, 1983; Azrin & Holz, 1966; Walters & Grusec, 1977).

1.   To be effective, punishment should be delivered immediately after the response. The logic here is the same as for the immediacy of reinforcement. Priscilla is caught in mid-afternoon throwing flour all over the kitchen. Father counts to ten in an attempt to control his temper (good), then says, "Just wait 'til your mother gets home" (not good). For the next three hours, Priscilla's behavior is angelic. When mother does get home, what is punished, Priscilla's flour tossing or the appropriate behaviors that followed?

2.   For punishment to be effective, it needs to be administered consistently. If one chooses to punish a certain behavior, it should be punished whenever it occurs—and often that is difficult to do.

3.   Punishment may decrease (suppress) overall behavior levels. Although an effectively punished response may end, so may other responses. That rat who has been shocked for pressing the bar not only will stop pressing the bar, but also cower in the corner, doing very little of anything.

4.   When responses are punished, alternatives should be introduced. Think about your rat for a minute. The poor thing knows what to do when it is hungry: press the lever. Now it gets shocked for doing that very thing. With no alternative response to make in order to get food, the rat is in a conflict that has no solution. There is no way out. The result may be fear, anxiety, and even aggressiveness. One way to make this point is to say that punishment does not convey any information about what to do; it only communicates what not to do. Rubbing your puppy's nose in a "mess" it just made on the living room carpet doesn't give the dog much of a sense of what it is supposed to do when it feels a need to relive itself; taking it outside will.

5.   Among other things, spanking or hitting—physical approaches to punishment—provide a model for aggressive behavior. It conveys the message that when one is frustrated, to hit and to strike out is acceptable behavior—and it conveys the message that it's okay for "big" people to hit smaller people. As we will soon see, such a message, provided by important models, can easily be taken as a model for the behavior of youngsters.

BEFORE YOU GO ON

- What are punishers, and how can they be used effectively?

GENERALIZATION AND DISCRIMINATION

In classical conditioning, we saw that a response conditioned to one stimulus could be elicited by other, similar stimuli. We have a comparable process in operant conditioning, and again we call it **generalization**—a process in which responses conditioned in the presence of a specific stimulus appear in the presence of other, similar stimuli. For example, little Leslie receives a reinforcer for saying "doggie" as a neighbor's poodle wanders across the front yard. "Yes, Leslie, good girl. That's a doggie." Having learned that calling the poodle "doggie" earns her parental approval, the response is tried again, this time with a German shepherd. Leslie's operantly conditioned response of saying "doggie" in the presence of a poodle has generalized to the German shepherd. When it does, it will no doubt be reinforced again. The problem is, of course, that Leslie may overgeneralize "doggie" to virtually any furry, four-legged animal and start calling cats and raccoons "doggie" also. When a child turns to a total stranger and utters "Dada," generalization can (usually) be blamed for the embarrassing mislabeling.

generalization the phenomenon in operant conditioning in which a response that was reinforced in the presence of one stimulus appears in response to other, similar stimuli

The process of generalization can be countered with **discrimination** training. Discrimination training is basically a matter of *differential reinforcement*. In other words, responses made to appropriate stimuli will be reinforced, while responses made to inappropriate stimuli will be ignored or extinguished (by withholding reinforcers, not by punishing the response). To demonstrate how discrimination training works, consider a strange question. Are pigeons color-blind? Disregarding why anyone would care, how might you go about testing the color vision of a pigeon? The standard tests we use for people certainly wouldn't work.

discrimination the process of differential reinforcement wherein one stimulus is reinforced while another stimulus is not

A pigeon can be readily trained to peck at a single lighted disk in order to earn a food reward. A pigeon in an operant chamber pecks at a lighted disk, and a few grains of food are delivered. Soon the pigeon pecks the disk at a high rate. Now let's present the pigeon with two lighted disks, one red, the other green. Otherwise, they are identical: the same shape, brightness, and size. Can the pigeon tell the difference between red and green? We make the green disk the discriminative (positive) stimulus since pecking at it earns a reinforcer. Pecks at the red disk are not reinforced. The position of the colored disks is randomly altered, of course. We don't want to demonstrate that the pigeon can tell left from right.

The results of this sort of manipulation are depicted in Figure 5.9. At first, the red and green lighted disks are responded to at an approximately equal rate. But in short order, the pigeon is ignoring the red disk and pecking only at the green one, for which it receives its reinforcer. In order to maintain such behavior, the pigeon must be able to discriminate between the two colored disks. We still don't know what red and green look like to a pigeon, but we may conclude that pigeons can tell the difference between the two. This is sensible because the eyes of pigeons contain cones in their retinas, and as you'll recall, cones are the receptors for color vision. Some varieties of owls are virtually without cone receptor cells and thus are color-blind. They cannot discriminate between red and green and appear frustrated in a discrimination learning task based on color.

When a pigeon in an operant chamber is presented with both a red disk and a green disk, it will soon learn to discriminate between the two, pecking only at the disk for which pecking is reinforced.

Please don't think that generalization and discrimination learning are processes relevant only to young children, rats, and pigeons. A great deal of our own learning has

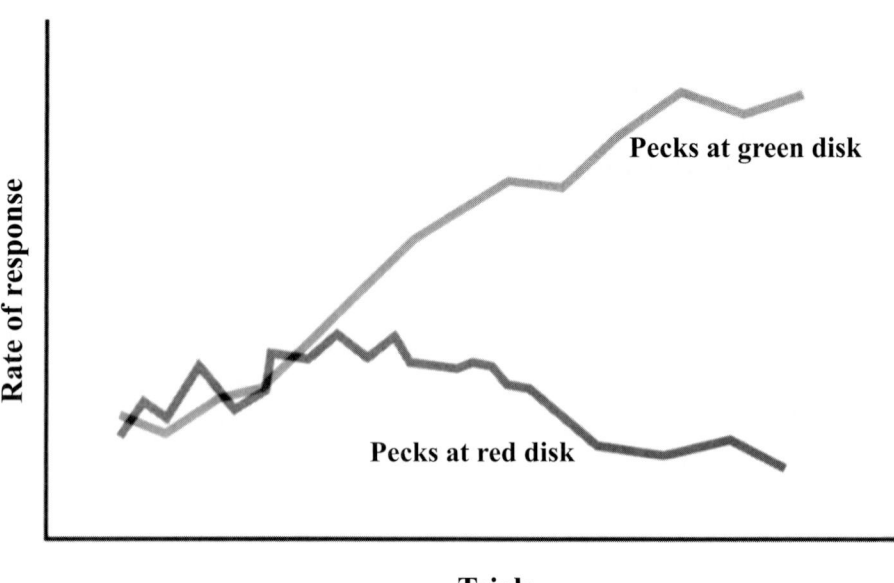

FIGURE 5.9

Discrimination training. Response rates for a pigeon presented with a green disk and a red disk. Pecks at the green disk are reinforced; those at the red disk are not.

involved learning to discriminate when behaviors are appropriate and are likely to be reinforced, and when they are inappropriate and likely to be ignored or punished. You have learned that many of the behaviors that may be reinforced at a party are inappropriate responses to make in the classroom. You may have learned that it's okay to put your feet up on the coffee table at home but not when you're at your boss's house or at Grandma's. Learning to interact with people from different cultures is also a matter of discrimination learning. In Saudi Arabia, for example, if two people approach a door at the same time, the person on the right always enters first. Being courteous by holding the door open for someone to the left of you and insisting that they enter is a generalized response that is simply not proper in all situations.

BEFORE YOU GO ON

- In operant conditioning, what are generalization and discrimination?

COGNITIVE APPROACHES TO LEARNING

Cognitive approaches to learning accent changes that occur in an organism's system of cognitions—its mental representations of itself and its world. *Cognitive learning* involves the acquisition of knowledge or understanding, and need not be reflected in behavior. We first alerted you to this issue when we discussed the definition of learning. We said that learning is demonstrated by, or inferred from, changes in behavior. The implication is that there may be less than a perfect correspondence between what one has learned and what one does. We anticipated this issue with our coverage of the work of Rescorla and Kamin in the previous Topic. There, we noted that a stimulus acted as an effective conditional stimulus only when it informed the organism about something happening in its world as in, "When this tone sounds, food will follow." Extracting useful information from one's experience in the world is largely a cognitive one (Bolles, 1975). In this section, we'll review the work of two theorists who stressed cognitive approaches to learning from the outset: Edward Tolman and Albert Bandura.

Latent Learning and Cognitive Maps

Do rats have brains? Of course they do. While their brains aren't very large, and their cerebral cortex is small indeed, they do have brains. A more intriguing question is whether rats form and manipulate cognitions. Can they figure things out? Can they understand? They can form simple associations. They can learn to associate a light with a shock and a lever-press response with a reinforcer, and they can modify their behaviors on the basis of these associations. Can they do more?

Consider a now-classic experiment performed over 70 years ago by Tolman and Honzik (1930). Even then, it was well-established that a rat could learn to run through a complicated maze of alleyways and dead ends to get to a goal box, where it would find a food reward. Tolman and Honzik wanted to understand just what the rats were learning when they negotiated such a maze. They used three groups of rats with the same maze.

One group of hungry rats was given a series of exposures (trials) to the maze. Each time the rats ran from the starting point to the goal box, they were given a food reward for their efforts. Over the course of 16 days, the rats in this group demonstrated a steady improvement in maze running. Their rate of errors dropped from approximately nine per trial to just two. Getting quickly and errorlessly from the start box to the goal box was what earned them their reinforcers.

A second group of rats was also given an opportunity to explore the maze for 16 days. However, they were not given a food reward for making it to the end of the maze. When they got to the goal box, they were simply removed from the maze. The average number of errors made by the rats in this group also dropped over the course of the experiment (from about nine errors per trial to about six). That the rats in this group did improve their maze-running skills suggests that simply being removed from the maze provided some measure of reinforcement. Even so, after 16 days, this group was having much more difficulty in their maze running than was the group receiving a food reinforcer.

Now for the critical group. A third group of rats was allowed to explore the maze on their own for ten days. The rats were not given a food reward upon reaching the goal box. But, beginning on day 11, a food reinforcer was introduced when they reached the goal box. The food was provided as a reinforcer on days 11 through 16. Introducing the food reward had a very significant effect on the rats' behaviors. Throughout the first ten days in the maze—without food—the group's performance showed only a slight improvement. Soon after the food was introduced, however, the rats' maze running improved markedly. In fact, on days 13 through 16, they made fewer errors than did the rats who received food all along! Figure 5.10 shows the relative performance of these three groups.

What do you make of this experiment? Why did that third group of rats do so much better after the food reward was introduced? Did they learn something about the pattern of

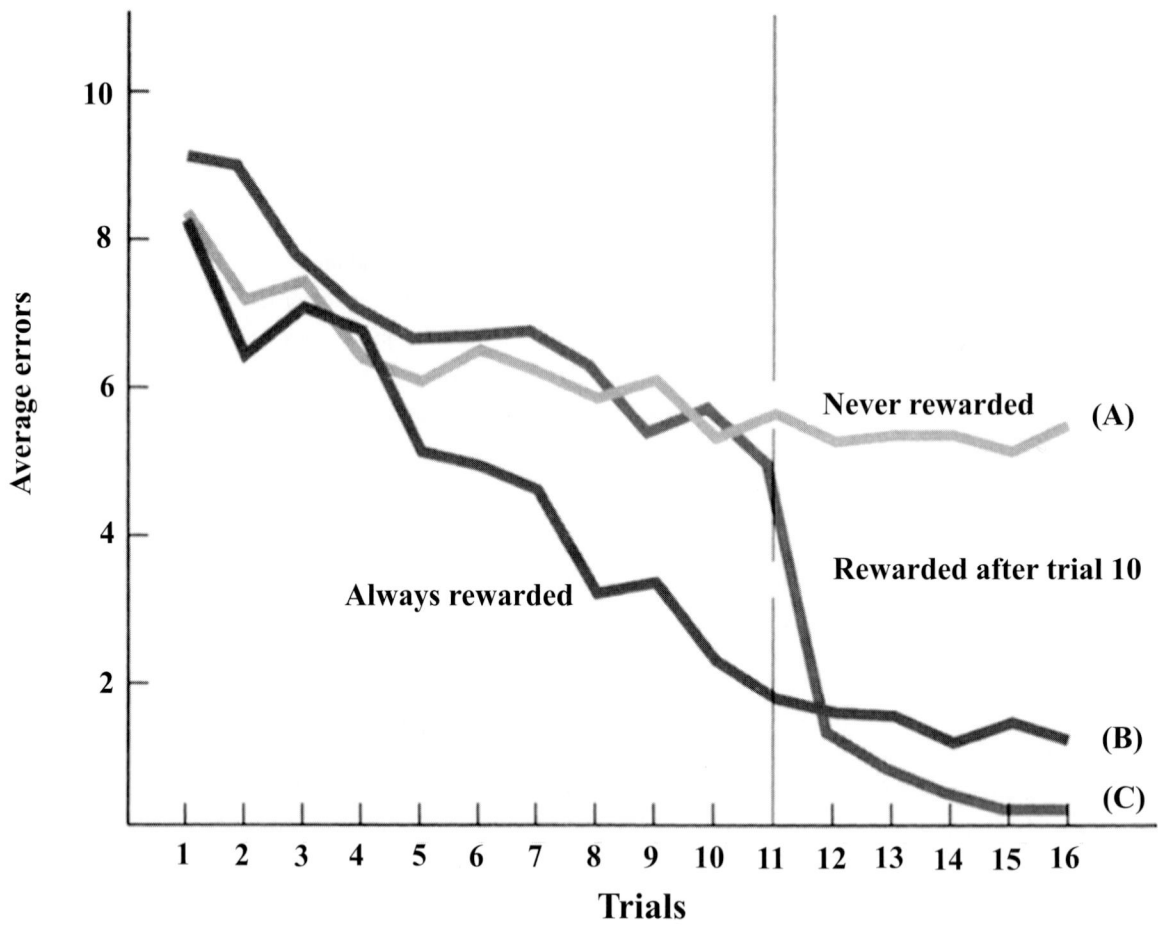

FIGURE 5.10

The performance of rats in a complicated maze were (A) never rewarded for reaching the end of the maze, (B) rewarded every time they reached the end of the maze, and (C) rewarded for reaching the end of the maze only on days 11-16 (Tolman & Honzik, 1930).

the maze before they received reinforcement for getting to the goal box? Did they "figure out" the maze early on but fail to rush to the goal box until there was a good reason to do so?

Tolman thought they did. He argued that the food rewarded a change in the rats' performance, but that the actual learning took place earlier. This sort of learning is called **latent learning** because it is, in a sense, hidden and not shown in behavior until it is reinforced.

During those first ten days in the maze, the rats developed what Tolman called a **cognitive map** of the maze; they formed a mental picture, or representation, of their physical environment, noting significant landmarks when possible. The rats knew about the maze, but until food was provided at the goal box, there was no reason, or purpose, for getting there in a hurry. This logic led Tolman to refer to his approach as "purposive behaviorism" (Tolman, 1932). Introducing a distinction between performance and

latent learning hidden learning that is not demonstrated in performance until that performance is reinforced

cognitive map a mental representation of the learning situation or physical environment

learning focused attention on what happened to the learner during learning, which was one of Tolman's goals. If you stop and think for a minute about what Tolman's rats did, you have to be impressed. But cognitive maps learned by small birds that live in the Alps are even more impressive. These small birds spend most of the summer and early fall hiding seeds in the ground (about four or five at a time). During the winter, they find their hidden supplies of seeds with remarkable accuracy. Have they formed cognitive maps of their seed placements? Apparently so. Making their judgments on the basis of nearby landmarks, these small birds, Clark's nutcrackers, can remember the location of at least 2,500 hiding places (Vander Wall, 1982).

You can find examples from your own experiences that approximate latent learning and the formation of cognitive maps. You may take the same route home from campus every day. If one day an accident blocks your path, won't you be able to use your knowledge of other routes (a cognitive map) to get where you are going? When you park your car in a large parking lot, what do you do as you walk away from your car? Do you look around, trying to develop a mental image, a cognitive representation, of the parking lot and some of its features? You are to meet a friend in a new classroom building on campus. You arrive early, so you stroll around the building for a few minutes. Isn't it likely that this unreinforced, apparently aimless behavior will be useful if you have to locate a room in that building for class the next semester?

Another setting in which we find Tolman's behaviorism at work is athletics. Before the big game, the coaching staff devises a perfect game plan—a set of ideas or cognitions dealing with what the team should do. The team members may learn the coaches' strategy and all of the new plays they are to use. They know what they are supposed to do to win (latent learning), but what will decide the contest is not their understanding but their performance. In sports, this is called execution. Knowing what to do and actually doing it are often different things.

> ## BEFORE YOU GO ON
>
> - What is cognitive learning?
> - What is latent learning?
> - What is a cognitive map?

Social Learning and Modeling

Albert Bandura's approach to learning is also cognitive, but it adds a decidedly social flavor and, for that reason, is referred to as **social learning theory** (Bandura, 1974, 1982, 2001a, 2001b). The central idea is that learning often takes place through the observation and imitation of models. What makes social learning theory *social* is the idea that we often learn from others. What makes it *cognitive* is that what is learned through observation or modeling are changes in one's cognitions that may never be expressed as behavior nor be directly reinforced.

social learning theory the theory that learning takes place through observation and imitation of models

According to social learning theory, there are three possible outcomes associated with learning from the behavior of others. First, a person can learn a new behavior, one that the person did not have in his or her repertoire of behaviors prior to exposure to a model. Second, a person can inhibit a behavior that is in his or her repertoire if the model is seen punished for that behavior. Finally, a person can *disinhibit* a behavior after watching a model. Disinhibition means removing any inhibitions against performing a behavior already in one's repertoire. Once the inhibitions are removed, the behavior can be displayed. This occurs if the individual sees a model reinforced for a particular behavior.

The classic study of observational learning was reported in 1963 by Bandura, Ross, and Ross. For this demonstration, 96 preschoolers were randomly assigned to one of four experimental conditions. One group of children observed an adult model act aggressively toward an inflated plastic "Bobo" doll. The adult model vigorously attacked the doll. Children in the second group watched the same aggressive behaviors directed toward the "Bobo" doll, but in a movie. The third group watched a cartoon version of the same aggressive behaviors, this time performed by a cat. Children in the fourth group constituted the control group and did not watch anyone or anything interact with "Bobo" dolls, neither live nor on film.

Then each child, tested individually, was given new and interesting toys to play with for a brief time. The child was soon led to another room containing fewer, older, and less interesting toys, including a small version of the inflated "Bobo" doll. Each child was left alone in the room while researchers, hidden from view, watched the child's behavior.

The children who had seen the aggressive behaviors of the model, live, on film, or in a cartoon, were much more aggressive in their play than were the children who did not have the observational experience. Children in the first three experimental conditions attacked the "Bobo" doll the same way the model had.

According to social learning theory, the children had learned simply by observing. As with latent learning, the learning was separated from performance. The children had no opportunity to imitate (to perform) what they had learned until they had a "Bobo" doll of their own. The learning that took place during observation was cognitive. As Bandura puts it, "Observational learning is primarily concerned with processes whereby observers organize response elements into new patterns of behavior at a symbolic level on the basis of information conveyed by modeling stimuli" (Bandura, 1976).

Later studies have shown that reinforcement and punishment play a major role in observational learning. For example, a twist was added to an experiment that replicated the one just described. The difference was that after attacking the "Bobo" doll, the adult models were either rewarded or punished for their behavior. Children who observed the model being punished for attacking the doll engaged in very little aggressive behavior toward their own "Bobo" dolls. Those who saw the model receive reinforcement for attacking the doll acted aggressively, imitating the model's behaviors in considerable detail (Bandura, 1965).

Learning about the consequences of one's own behavior by observing what happens to someone else is **vicarious reinforcement** or **vicarious punishment**. Vicarious reinforcement leads to acquisition of new behaviors or disinhibition of behavior, whereas vicarious punishment leads to inhibition of behavior.

The application of this sort of data is very straightforward. For example, Bandura's research suggests that children can learn many potential behaviors by watching TV. Subsequent research confirms the idea that children can learn aggressive behavior from watching violent television programs (citations). There is a small, but rather consistent relationship between the amount of violent television a child watches and the level of aggressive behavior displayed. Our real concern should be reserved for occasions in which inappropriate behaviors are left unpunished. This logic suggests that it would be

There is little doubt that the behaviors and mannerisms of children are in large measure a reflection of their attempts to imitate adult models.

vicarious reinforcement (or punishment) increasing the rate (with reinforcement) or decreasing the rate (with punishment) of responses due to observing the consequences of someone else's behaviors

unfortunate for one of a child's TV heroes to get away with murder, much less be rewarded for doing so. As it happens, reinforced behaviors of valued models are more likely to be imitated than punished behaviors of less valued models (Bandura, 1965).

How does exposure to violent television contribute to elevated levels of aggression? One cognitive approach to answering this question was proposed by Huesmann (Huesmann, 1986; Huesmann & Malamuth, 1986). According to Huesmann, when a child is exposed to high levels of violent television programming, they form an **aggressive script** which is an internalized representation of an event that leads to increased aggression and a tendency to see the world as an aggressive, hostile place. The latter effect of aggressive scripts increases the likelihood that a child will interpret an unintentional, accidental behavior as aggression directed at him or her. So, an innocent bump in the hallway at school escalates into a full-blown fight because it is interpreted by the child with the aggressive script as an act of aggression.

aggressive script an internalized representation of an event that leads to increased aggression and a tendency to see the world as an aggressive, hostile place

Another medium that has the potential for transmitting aggression via observational learning involves violent video games. Much of the early research on this issue did not show any significant relationship between playing violent video games and aggression. More recent research does show a relationship. For example, Anderson and Dill (2000) found a correlation between self-reported violent video game play and aggressive delinquent behavior among college students. Participants who played video games often were most likely to show delinquent aggressive behavior. However, the relationship was not as simple as it first appears. Anderson and Dill found that individuals with an aggressive personality (versus individuals without aggressive personalities) were most likely to show high levels of aggression after a high degree of exposure to video game violence. Additionally, this relationship was stronger for males than females. In a follow-up laboratory experiment, participants played either a violent or nonviolent video game, and then played a competitive game against what the participant believed was an opponent (actually, the "opponent's" responses were controlled by a computer). The participant was told that whomever pressed a button first after seeing a stimulus could punish the other with a burst of noise. Anderson and Dill found that playing a violent video game led to higher levels of aggression than playing a nonviolent video game. Other research shows that when individuals (male or female) play a video game competitively, they display a more aggressive style of play while playing the game than individuals playing cooperatively (Anderson & Morrow, 1995).

Learning through observation and imitation is a common form of human learning. Your television on any Saturday provides many examples, particularly if you watch a PBS station. All day long there are people (role models) trying to teach us how to paint landscapes, build solar energy devices, do aerobic exercises, improve our golf game, remodel the basement, replace a carburetor, or prepare a low-calorie meal. The basic message is, "Watch me; see how I do it. Then, try it yourself."

BEFORE YOU GO ON

- What are the main ideas behind social learning theory?
- What is a model?
- What are vicarious reinforcement and vicarious punishment?
- What is an aggressive script?

Topic Review 5 B

I. What is operant conditioning?

Operant conditioning occurs when the probability, or rate, of a response is changed as a result of the consequences that follow that response. Reinforced responses increase in rate, while nonreinforced responses decrease in rate.

2. What is the "Law of Effect"?

E.L. Thorndike provided the first clear demonstration of what we now call operant conditioning. Thorndike placed a cat in "puzzle box" and noticed that, at first, the cat's behaviors were random. Eventually the cat hit upon a wooden peg that opened the box, giving the cat access to food. On successive trials the cat's behavior became more efficient until it eventually went to the peg right away. Thorndike developed the law of effect, which stated that learning occurs when a response is followed by a "satisfying state of affairs."

3. How did B.F. Skinner demonstrate operant conditioning?

Skinner constructed a special apparatus he called an operant chamber (later it came to be known as the "Skinner Box"). The chamber allowed Skinner to tightly control an organism's environment during a learning experiment. A typical chamber would have a bar or lever (or some other device for the subject to use to make a response) and a food cup to deliver reinforcement. A hungry animal was placed in the chamber and taught an operant response.

4. In operant conditioning, what is acquisition?

Acquisition is the process whereby an organism learns to associate a behavior with its consequence. In operant conditioning, acquisition is produced by reinforcing a desired response so that its rate increases.

5. What is shaping through successive approximations?

Shaping is used to establish a response, that is, to get an organism to make a desired response. We shape a response by reinforcing successive approximations to the desired one. This means that we first reinforce a distant approximation of the desired behavior until that behavior is firmly established (for example, a rat turns its head toward the wall of an operant chamber where a lever is located) and then reinforce closer and closer approximations of the behavior (for example, reinforce when the rat approaches the lever, then when the rat touches the lever, etc.). At each stage of the shaping process, approximations of the desired behavior are reinforced until an approximation is reliably made.

6. In operant conditioning, what is extinction?

Extinction occurs when you withhold reinforcement from a previously reinforced behavior. Initially, you observed an increase in the rate of responding over the first few trials into extinction as well as an increase in the force exerted on the lever. Eventually, extinction decreases the rate of a response to its original baseline rate.

7. In operant conditioning, what is spontaneous recovery?

After a rest interval, a previously extinguished response will return at a rate above baseline; that is, in the same situation, it will spontaneously recover. If the reinforcer is withheld from the spontaneously recovered response, it will once again be extinguished. If the spontaneously recovered response is again followed by a reinforcer, reacquisition occurs.

8. What is meant by the term reinforcement?

Reinforcement refers to the process of strengthening a response. Whenever you see the term reinforcement, remember the intent is to increase the strength of a response.

9. How does reinforcement differ from a reinforcer?

As we have just noted, reinforcement refers to the process of strengthening an operant response. A reinforcer is the actual stimulus used in the process of reinforcement. It is important to keep the concepts of reinforcement and reinforcer distinct. A reinforcer is any stimulus that increases or maintains the rate of a response, regardless of the nature of the stimulus.

10. How does a reinforcer differ from a reward?

The term reward is avoided in operant conditioning because it implies that a reinforcer must always be something an organism wants to acquire. The term reinforcer is a more general term relating to the idea that any stimulus that increases or maintains behavior is a reinforcer, even if it is something the organism doesn't like.

11. What is a positive reinforcer?

A positive reinforcer is a stimulus given to an organism after a response that increases or maintains the rate of the response it follows. A positive reinforcer causes positive reinforcement of that behavior. Food for a hungry animal, water for a thirsty animal, and high-letter grades for students are examples of positive reinforcers.

12. What is a negative reinforcer?

This is a tricky one for most students of psychology because most think of something positive when they see the term reinforcer. However, there is a class of reinforcers that work differently from positive reinforcers. A negative reinforcer is an aversive stimulus presented before an operant behavior occurs. When the behavior is emitted, the aversive stimulus is removed. Any behavior that comes immediately before the removal of the negative reinforcer will be strengthened or maintained. Thus, it is the removal of an aversive stimulus that is negatively reinforcing. Negative reinforcers bring about the process of negative reinforcement.

13. What is a primary reinforcer?

A primary reinforcer is a stimulus that is in some way biologically important or related to an organism's survival, such as food for a hungry organism or warm shelter for a cold one. No learning is required for a primary reinforcer to strengthen or maintain behavior.

14. What is a secondary reinforcer?

A secondary reinforcer strengthens or maintains response rates through a process of learning. Secondary reinforcers, unlike primary reinforcers, have no direct biological significance for an organism. Instead, they take on reinforcing qualities by being associated with something else. That is, secondary reinforcers, such as praise, money, and letter grades have reinforcing qualities because they are associated with something else (for example, money can be exchanged for food).

15. What are contingency contracting and token economies?

Contingency contracting is an application of secondary reinforcement to psychotherapy. It involves setting up a token economy in which secondary reinforcers are used to reinforce appropriate behavior. For example, a poker chip could be earned if a depressed person gets out of bed, two chips could be earned if the person socializes with others. The secondary reinforcers can be saved and traded for things the patient desires (for example, candy, a weekend at home, etc.).

16. What are continuous and partial reinforcement schedules?

On a continuous reinforcement schedule, an organism is reinforced for each and every response made. Unfortunately, on this type of schedule an organism becomes full very quickly and will no longer respond. Also, behaviors maintained on a continuous schedule extinguish quickly. On a partial reinforcement schedule an organism is not reinforced for every response made. There are four main partial schedules: fixed-ratio, fixed-interval, variable-ratio, and variable-interval.

17. What is the partial reinforcement effect?

The partial reinforcement effect refers to the fact that behaviors maintained on a partial schedule of reinforcement are more resistant to extinction than behaviors maintained on a continuous schedule of reinforcement.

18. What are fixed-ratio, fixed-interval, variable-ratio, and variable-interval schedules of reinforcement?

The FR (fixed-ratio) schedule calls for delivering one reinforcer after a set number of responses (e.g., one reinforcer after every five responses). The FI (fixed-interval) schedule calls for a reinforcer at the first response following a specified, or fixed, interval. A VR (variable-ratio) schedule randomly changes the ratio of reinforcers to responses, but maintains a given ratio as an average. A VI (variable-interval) schedule calls for a reinforcer for the first response after a time interval whose length is randomly varied. In general, responses reinforced with fixed schedules are more resistant to extinction than are responses that have been reinforced each time they occur (a CRF, or continuous reinforcement schedule). Responses acquired under variable schedules are even more resistant to extinction than are those acquired by fixed schedules.

19. What is punishment?

Punishment is the process of decreasing the strength of a behavior by delivering a stimulus that an organism is motivated to avoid after a behavior has occurred.

20. How does punishment differ from negative reinforcement?

Unlike negative reinforcement, which is intended to increase or maintain behavior, punishment is intended to reduce or eliminate a behavior. Also, the two processes differ when the stimulus is presented. In negative reinforcement, the negative reinforcer is presented before the behavior occurs. In punishment, the punisher is delivered after the behavior occurs. The same stimulus could serve as a negative reinforcer or punisher depending on when it is delivered. Whether a stimulus is classified as a negative reinforcer or a punisher depends on its effect on behavior.

21. What forms does punishment take?

Punishment can either involve administering a punisher after an undesired behavior has occurred, or it can involve withdrawing a stimulus that an organism desires. For example, a child can be spanked for aggressive behavior in the former case, or have television privileges suspended in the latter case.

22. How can punishment be used effectively?

Punishment can be effective in suppressing a response when it is strong enough and is delivered immediately after the response to be punished. Punishment must also be used consistently. Inconsistent use of punishment reduces the effectiveness of punishment for the immediate behavior and desensitizes the organism to the effects of future punishment. Punishing one response should be paired with the reinforcement of another, more appropriate one.

23. What are the drawbacks to using punishment to modify a child's behavior?

There are several drawbacks to using punishment with children including: punishment alone only leads to a temporary suppression of behavior; physical punishment provides children with aggressive role models and a lesson that the way to deal with frustration and anger is through aggression.

24. In operant conditioning, what are generalization and discrimination?

Generalization has occurred when a response reinforced in the presence of one stimulus also occurs in the presence of other, similar stimuli. Discrimination involves differential reinforcement—reinforcing responses to some stimuli while extinguishing responses to other (inappropriate) stimuli.

25. What is latent learning?

According to Tolman, latent learning is the acquisition of information (an internal, mental, cognitive process) that may not be demonstrated in performance until later, if at all. The phenomenon of latent learning demonstrates the distinction between learning and performance.

26. What is a cognitive map?

A cognitive map is a mental picture, or representation, of one's physical environment, noting significant landmarks when possible. The formation of a cognitive map can be viewed as a type of latent learning. When one acquires a cognitive map, one develops a cognitive representation (or picture) of one's surroundings—an appreciation of general location and location of key objects.

27. What are the basic concepts of social learning theory?

Bandura's social learning theory emphasizes the role of the observation of others (models) and imitation in the acquisition of cognitions and behaviors. We often learn by imitating models.

28. What are the possible outcomes of social learning?

An individual can acquire a totally new response that was not in the person's behavioral repertoire. An individual can learn to inhibit a behavior that he or she was performing. Or, a person can learn to disinhibit (remove the inhibitions from) a behavior that is currently in one's repertoire.

29. What are vicarious reinforcement and vicarious punishment?

Vicarious reinforcement occurs when a person sees a model reinforced for behavior. This increases the likelihood that the same behavior will be imitated. Vicarious reinforcement leads to the acquisition of new behavior or disinhibition of behavior. Vicarious punishment occurs when a person sees a model punished for performing a behavior. This makes it less likely that the behavior will be imitated. Vicarious punishment, then, leads to response inhibition.

30. What is an aggressive script?

An aggressive script is an internalized representation of an event that leads to increased aggression and a tendency to see the world as a hostile place.

Chapter 6

Memory

A few years ago, I (Gerow) was asked to return to my hometown to give a short speech. The occasion was my mother's retirement from her job as secretary to the principal at the village elementary school. She had begun working at the school when I was in the fifth grade, and had served at least four principals. It was widely known that if you needed anything at the school, Mrs. Gerow was the person to contact. She was, perhaps, the *only* person who knew where everything was. A big retirement party was scheduled at the local Holiday Inn.

I was honored and pleased. But, I was also very anxious about "making a speech" there, in front of old family friends—and many of my old teachers as well. Here I was a college professor, experienced at all sorts of "public speaking." Nonetheless, I was worried. I wanted to look good, and I did not want to use any notes. Then I remembered a "trick"—a mnemonic device—that was supposed to help one remember such things as short speeches. The trick is called "the method of loci." The word *loci* means "locations."

Here's what I did. I visualized several locations in the small house of my childhood. At the front door, I "placed" my greetings to those assembled. I pictured myself moving into the living room, talking about all that Mother was able to do for my brother and me while we were in school. On to the dining room, where I had "placed" a bit about how. Mother had gotten to know so many families in town because of her association with their children. Then, as I mentally strolled into the kitchen, I could move to the part of the speech in which I spoke about her helping so many teachers over the years. My thank-you and closing I "located" at the back door. A smile. A wave. Sit down; it's over.

Nearly to my amazement, the technique actually worked! I visualized moving through the house, and as I did so, the various parts of my little talk that I had "stored" in each location, readily came to mind. It can be very refreshing to discover that advice given to others works as you have claimed.

In this chapter, we will describe the nature of human memory. Then we will discuss how we might improve its workings.

Topic 6A HOW CAN WE DESCRIBE HUMAN MEMORY?

You awaken in the morning to the sound of your alarm clock. Stumbling out of bed, you make your way to the bathroom, turn on the light and begin your daily routine: brushing your teeth, taking a shower, drying your hair, getting dressed. You go down to the kitchen and fix yourself a quick breakfast before leaving for class. After breakfast you walk out the front door of your apartment building, look around the parking lot for your car, and then walk to it. You start the engine and take your usual route to school. In your first class you are having an exam, so you get there early and find a seat. After taking the exam, you go through the rest of your day, returning home at 6 p.m. Upon entering your apartment, you put down your books and make yourself dinner. Then it's off to the couch for an evening of your favorite TV shows.

Imagine what life would be like without memory. You would not be able to accomplish even the most routine tasks. For example, you wouldn't remember where your bathroom was or where you keep your toothbrush or hair dryer. You would not remember to make yourself breakfast, nor would you be able to find your car in the parking lot. You would have no recollection of how to get to school. And anything you studied for your exam would be nonexistent. In fact, the sentences in your text would make no sense. Without your memory, you would have no idea what a textbook is or why you had it open in front of you. The patterns of print you now recognize as words would appear as no more than random marks. We care about memory in an academic, study-learn-test sense, but the importance of memory goes well beyond classroom exams. All of those things that define us as individuals, our feelings, beliefs, attitudes, and experiences, are stored in our memories.

In this Topic, we'll formulate a working definition of memory. We will consider how information gets into memory and how it is stored there. We will explore the possibility that there are several types of memory and see what these varieties of memory might be. We'll also take a moment to see what scientists can tell us about the physiological changes that occur when new memories are formed.

Key Questions to Answer

While reading this Topic, find the answers to the following key questions:

1. What is memory?

2. What are the interrelated processes of encoding, storage, and retrieval?

3. What are reconstructive and constructive memory?

4. What reconstruction processes could account for inaccurate reports of memories?

5. What is the tip-of-the-tongue effect?

6. What is the multistore model of memory?

7. What is the levels-of-processing model of memory?

8. What is sensory memory?

9. What is short-term memory?

10. How much information can be stored in short-term memory (STM)?

11. How is information represented in STM?

12. What is long-term memory (LTM)?

13. What are repressed memories, and what do they tell us about LTM?

14. What are compromise memory and the misinformation effect?

15. What are elaborative rehearsal and maintenance rehearsal?

16. What is declarative and nondeclarative memory?

17. What is semantic memory, and how is it organized?

18. What is episodic memory?

19. What is procedural memory?

20. At the level of the neuron, what changes take place when memories are formed?

21. What do recent brain imaging studies suggest about the physiology of memory?

MEMORY AS INFORMATION PROCESSING

One way to think about human memory is to consider it as a final step in a series of psychological activities that process information. The processing of information begins when sensory receptors are stimulated above threshold levels. The process of perception then selects and organizes the information provided by the senses. With memory, a record of that information is formed.

Although we often give a single label to what we commonly refer to as memory, it is not a single structure or process. Instead, **memory** is a set of systems involved in the acquisition, storage, and retrieval of information (Baddeley, 1998; Ashcraft, 1994). Memory comprises systems that can hold information for periods of time ranging from fractions of a second to a lifetime, and have storage capacities that range from the very limited (e.g., just a few simple sounds) to the very vast (e.g., a complex event, such as a high school graduation ceremony) (Baddeley, 1998).

Using memory is a cognitive activity that involves three interrelated processes. The first is **encoding**, a process of putting information into memory, which is a matter of forming cognitive representations of information. Encoding is an active process involving a decision (usually unconscious) as to which details to place into memory. Once the representations are in memory, they must be kept there. This process is called **storage**. In order to use stored information, it must be gotten out again. This process is called **retrieval** (Murdock, 1974).

memory the cognitive capacity to encode, store, and retrieve information

encoding the active process of representing or putting information into memory

storage the process of holding encoded information in memory

retrieval the process of locating, removing, and using information stored in memory

The Constructive Nature of Memory

One popular misconception is that memory works much like a camcorder. That is, when placing something into memory, the record button is pressed (encoding), and that information is recorded exactly on tape (storage). Information is gotten out of storage by pressing the rewind button, immediately followed by the play button (retrieval). Although this common view of memory is elegant in its simplicity, it is not how memory works. In reality we tend to store *features* of what is experienced, and then, through a process called **reconstructive memory**, those features are retrieved and a report of what was encoded and stored in memory is reconstructed (Bartlett, 1932).

reconstructive memory an approach to memory suggesting that we retrieve features stored about an event and reconstruct a report of what was encoded and stored in memory

Recent research and theory on the psychology of memory supports the general idea that memory involves an active construction process and that memories based on such processes may be inaccurate because information may be left out or added (Schacter, Norman, & Koutstaal, 1998). The view emerging from research in this area is that the construction process, known as the **construction memory framework (CMF)**, involves, as Frederick Bartlett suggested nearly 70 years ago, storing patterns of features in which each feature represents a different aspect of what is experienced. Furthermore, the features stored are widely scattered over different parts of the brain. Consequently, no single part of the brain houses a complete memory. Retrieval of information within the CMF framework is much like putting together a jigsaw puzzle. Features stored in various parts of the brain are reactivated, which, in turn, reactivate other features. This reactivation process continues until a memory is reconstructed (Schacter et al., 1998).

construction memory framework (CMF) an emerging view of memory stating that we store patterns of features of experience scattered over different parts of the brain with each feature representing a different aspect of what is experienced. Retrieval involves successively reactivating features.

As Bartlett first noted in 1932, sometimes the reconstruction process results in inaccurate reports of what is in memory. According to the construction view of memory, there are several reasons why the recall of information from memory may not be accurate. At the time of encoding, inadequate separation of episodes from other similar episodes may cause a person not to remember a feature or features as specific to a given episode. Inadequate connections among the features associated with an event stored in memory can lead to inaccurate reconstruction, and consequently, to inaccurate memories. Finally, retrieval cues may match more than one set of features representing more than one episode. So, a person may not be able to get the episode he or she wants out of memory. Another similar, but incorrect, set of features is activated, resulting in inaccurate reporting (Schacter et al., 1998).

Evidence for construction-based memory comes from something we have all experienced. Has anything like this ever happened to you? One of the authors (Bordens) was trying to remember the name of an amusement ride on the Boardwalk in Seaside Heights, New Jersey, that he had ridden a few years ago. No matter how hard he tried, he could not remember the name of the ride. In fact, the harder he tried to remember, the worse it got. He could remember where it was located on the Boardwalk and that there were paintings of the Beatles on the sides of the ride. He could even remember the shape of the cars on the ride. Everything came to him, except, of course, the name. He felt at any minute, he would remember the name. Then one night, out of the blue, he woke up at 2 A.M., sat up and said, "The Matterhorn."

This phenomenon is known as the *tip-of-the-tongue effect* (Brown & McNeill, 1966), and it tells us something about how memory works. When we are trying to remember something, we go into our memory stores and begin fishing out details (where the ride is located, how the ride is decorated, etc.). When enough details are retrieved, the memory usually comes back. Sometimes this process is fraught with errors. For example, when Bordens tried recalling the ride's name, he came up with other similar names, but not the correct name. (This is called the *ugly sister effect* [Reason & Lucas, 1984].) The tip-of-the-tongue effect tells us that memories may not be stored as they are on videotape. Rather, memories are stored in a fragmented, but organized, way. And, as Bartlett suggested, we retrieve as many fragments as possible and reconstruct memories.

Modern theories view memory as being complex and multidimensional. That is, not all of the information that gets into memory necessarily gets encoded or stored in the same way or even in the same place. As it happens, there is considerable disagreement over just how we should conceptualize human memory. Theories are plentiful, and often at odds with each other (Baddeley, 1992; Cowan, 1994; Loftus, 1991; Roediger, 1990; Schacter, 1992; Squire et al., 1993; Watkins, 1990).

Theories on How Memory is Structured

Some psychologists argue that there are various memory storehouses, each with its own characteristics and mechanisms for processing information. Psychologists who talk about separate, distinct memories, or stores of information, support what are called *multistore models of memory* (Atkinson & Shiffrin, 1968; Cowan, 1993; Tulving, 1985; Waugh & Norman, 1965). The most widely known multistore model of memory is Atkinson and Shiffrin's (1968) **modal model** of memory. According to this model, information is processed through three distinct memory storage systems: sensory memory, short-term memory (STM), and long-term memory (LTM). We will explore these in more detail later.

modal model the model of memory stating that information is processed through three distinct memory storage systems: sensory memory, short-term memory (STM), and long-term memory (LTM)

The modal model of memory was, and still is, a popular theory of memory which appeared to rest on a firm foundation of research support (Baddeley, 1998). However, like any model or theory, there were some cracks in the foundation. For example, a key assumption of the modal model was that the likelihood that information would be transferred into LTM related to the amount of rehearsal devoted to it. However, research on this issue has produced mixed results. Some research, for example, shows little effect of the amount of rehearsal on whether something is transferred from STM to LTM (Baddeley, 1998). We can all think of times when we have put information into LTM with little or no rehearsal. For example, you might encode the telephone number of your new love interest directly into LTM because it is important to you. And there are times when several presentations of information do not lead to long-term recollection of the information.

The problems associated with the modal model of memory led researchers and theorists to an alternative view of memory. This model suggests that there is only one type of human memory, or storehouse of information, but that within that memory are various levels or depths to which information can be processed (Cermak & Craik, 1979; Craik, 1970; Craik & Lockhart, 1972; Crowder, 1993). Their claim is that information can get more (deep) or less (shallow) processing within the same memory.

Depth of processing is seen as a function of work or effort and is related to the likelihood of retrieval. This position gives rise to what is called a *levels-of-processing model of memory*. According to this model, the more deeply we process information, the better we can later recall that information. For example, if you look up a number in the telephone book that you anticipate using only once, you will not process it deeply. Consequently, you probably won't remember that number the next day. If, on the other hand, the number is important (the number of your doctor or a possible dating partner you just met) you will process that number more deeply and will probably remember it the next day. Although it has wide support, it is but one theory that views memory as a single, unitary process.

So, which model will we use? We can construct our own conceptualization of memory by combining major aspects of both of these dominant positions. Our model will include three stores, or levels, of memory: *sensory memory, short-term memory (STM),* and *long-term memory (LTM).* Sometimes we'll refer to sensory, short-term, and long-term memories as if they were memory stores, or structures—something you put information in. Sometimes we will refer to memory in terms of levels of processing, as if the levels referred to activities—what you do with information in order to remember it. This mix of viewpoints is intentional because, at the moment, no one can claim with any certainty which model of memory provides the "best" way to think about human memory.

In any event, we'll have questions about each memory structure or level. What is its *capacity:* how much information can it deal with? What is its *duration:* how long will the information be held there without further processing? How does information get into this memory: how does it get *encoded?* In what form is it stored?

BEFORE YOU GO ON

- What is the definition of memory?

- What are encoding, storage, and retrieval?

- What is the construction view of memory and what accounts for inaccurate memories?

- What is the tip-of-the-tongue effect, and what does it tell us about how memory works?

- What are the multistore and levels-of-processing models of memory?

SENSORY MEMORY

sensory memory a type of memory that stores large amounts of information for very brief periods (a few seconds or less)

iconic memory the sensory memory system associated with the sense of vision

echoic memory the sensory memory system associated with the sense of hearing

Sensory memory stores large amounts of information for very short periods (only a few seconds or less). There are sensory memory systems for each of your senses. However, we usually consider only two of them. Visual sensory memory or **iconic memory** is the sensory store associated with vision. Think of information in iconic memory as being similar to a photocopy that lasts for only about a half second (Sperling, 1960, 1963). The sensory storage system associated with the sense of hearing is known as **echoic memory**, which, as its name implies, is something like a brief echo which can last five to ten seconds.

The concept of such very brief memory systems is a strange one (we usually don't think about remembering something for only a few seconds), but it has a place in information-processing models. All of the information that gets stored in our memories must first have entered through our senses. Simply, to be able to recall what a lecturer says, you must first hear the lecture. To remember a drawing from this book, the image of the drawing must first stimulate your visual system. You can't remember the aroma of fried onions if you've never smelled them.

The basic idea of a sensory memory is that information does not pass immediately and directly through our sensory systems; instead, it is held in sensory memory for a brief time. Even after a stimulus has left our environment and is no longer physically present, it has left its imprint, having formed a sensory memory.

The capacity of sensory memory seems, at least in theory, to be very large. At one time it was believed that we are able to keep as much in our sensory memory as our sense receptors can respond to at any one time. Everything above our sensory thresholds—everything to which our senses react—gets stored in our sensory memory. Such claims may give sensory memory more credit than it is due. Sensory memory can hold much more information than we can attend to, but there are limits on its capacity.

Sensory memory is typically viewed as being a rather mechanical or physical type of storage. Information is not encoded in sensory memory; you have to take it pretty much as your receptors deliver it. It's as if stimuli from the environment make an impression on our sensory systems, reverberate momentarily, and then rapidly fade or are replaced by new stimuli.

Here are two demonstrations of sensory memory. In a reasonably dark area, stand about 20 feet from a friend who is pointing a flashlight at you. Have your friend swing the flashlight around in a small circle, making about one revolution per second. What do you see? Your *experience* is that of a circle of light. At any one instant, you are seeing where the light is, and you are experiencing—from your sensory memory—where the light has just been. If your friend moves the light slowly, you may see a "tail" of light following it, but you will no longer see a full circle because the image of the light's position will have decayed from sensory memory. (A similar situation occurs when we experience a streak of lightning during a thunderstorm. In fact, the lightning is only present in the sky for two-tenths of a second or less. It's the impression of lightning in sensory memory that we experience.)

Has this ever happened to you? Someone asks you a simple question, to which your reply is something like "Huh? What'd you say?" Then, before the person even gets a chance to repeat the question, you answer it (which may, in turn, provoke a response such as, "Why didn't you answer me in the first place?"). Perhaps you did not hear all of the question you were asked, but while it was still reverberating, or echoing, in your sensory memory, you listened to it again and formed your answer.

As we said, the idea of a sensory memory as a very brief storage space for large amounts of minimally processed information is a strange one. There is evidence that some kind of sensory memory is a real phenomenon, at least for vision and audition. Perhaps that extra fraction of a second or two of storage in sensory memory gives us the time we need to attend to information so that we can then move it further along in our memory.

BEFORE YOU GO ON

- What is sensory memory?

- What are iconic and echoic memory?

- What is the capacity and duration of iconic and echoic memory?

SHORT-TERM MEMORY (STM)

short-term memory (STM) a type of memory with limited capacity and limited duration; also called working memory

Information can get into sensory memory with relative ease. Once it gets there, where does it go next? Most of it fades rapidly or is quickly replaced with new stimuli. But with a little effort, we can process material from our sensory memories more fully by moving it to short-term memory. **Short-term memory (STM)** is a level, or store, in human memory with a limited capacity and, without the benefit of rehearsal, a brief duration.

What we are calling short-term memory is often referred to as *working memory* (Baddeley, 1982, 1992, 1998). It is viewed as something like a workbench or desktop on which we pull together, use, and manipulate the information to which we pay attention.

Figure 6.1 presents a schematic diagram of the model of memory we are building. At the top are stimuli from the environment affecting our senses and moving directly to sensory memory. In the middle is short-term memory. We see that information from sensory memory *or* from long-term memory can be moved into STM. To get material into short-term memory requires that we attend to it.

Stimuli in the Environment

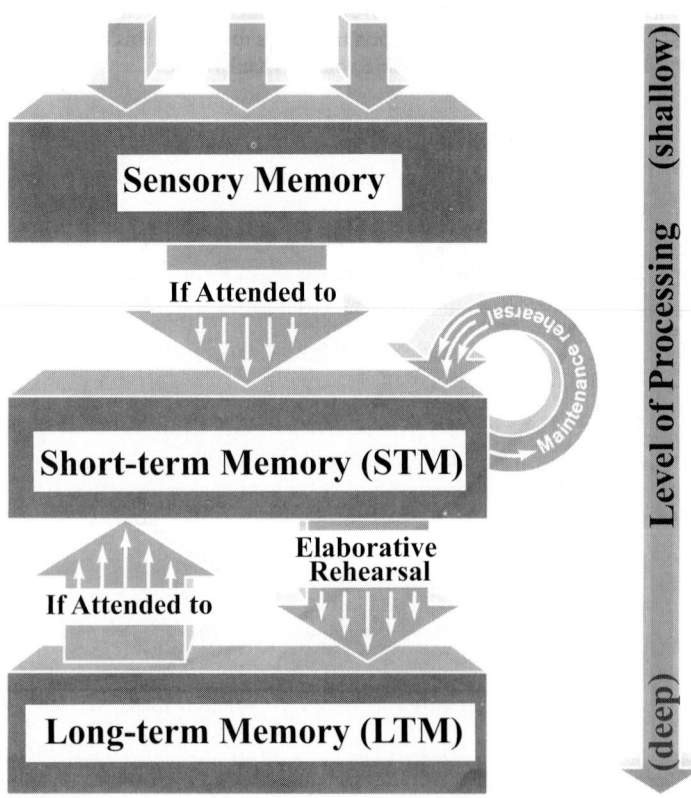

FIGURE 6.1

A simplified model of human memory.

The Duration of STM

Interest in short-term memory can be traced to two experiments reported independently in the late 1950s (Brown, 1958; Peterson & Peterson, 1959). In one experiment, a student is shown three consonants, such as KRW, for three seconds. Presenting the letters for a full three seconds ensures that they are attended to and encoded into STM. The student is then asked to recall the three letters after retention intervals ranging from zero to 18 seconds. This doesn't sound like a difficult task, and it isn't. Anyone can remember a few letters for 18 seconds. In this study, however, students are kept from rehearsing the letters during the retention interval. They are given a "distractor" task to perform right after they see the letters. They are to count backward, by threes, from a three-digit number.

If you were a participant in this sort of experiment, you would be shown a letter sequence—say, KRW—and then asked to immediately start counting backward from, say, 397 by threes, or "397, 394, 391, 388," and so on. You would be instructed to count out loud as rapidly as possible. The idea is that the counting keeps you from rehearsing the three letters you were just shown.

Under these conditions, your correct recall of the letters will depend on the length of the retention interval. If you are asked to recall the letters after just a few seconds of counting, you'll do pretty well. If you have to count for as long as 15 to 20 seconds, your recall of the letters will drop to almost zero (see Figure 6.2). Distracted by the counting task, you cannot rehearse the letters, and they are soon unavailable to you.

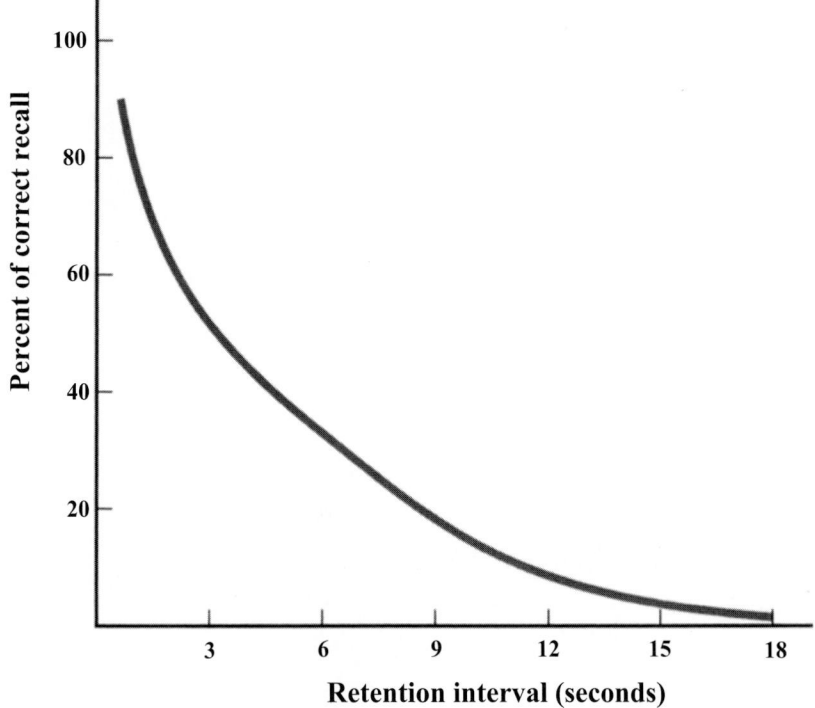

FIGURE 6.2

The recall of a stimulus of three letters as a function of retention interval when maintenance rehearsal is minimized (Peterson & Peterson, 1959).

This laboratory example isn't as abstract as it may appear. Consider this scenario. Having studied psychology for hours, you decide to reward yourself with a pizza. Never having called Pizza City before, you turn to the yellow pages to find the number: 555-5897. You repeat the number to yourself: 555-5897. You close the phone book and dial the number without error. Buzzz-buzzz-buzzz-buzzz. Darn, the line's busy! Well, you'll call back in a minute.

Just as you hang up, the doorbell rings. It's the paper carrier. You owe $11.60 for the past two weeks' deliveries. Discovering that you don't have enough cash on hand to pay for the paper and a pizza, you write a personal check. Your thought processes go something like this, "Let's see, what is today's date? 09-01-02. How much did you say I owed you? Oh yes, $11.60, and a dollar and a half for a tip, comes to $13.10. This is check number 1079; I'd better write that down. There you go. Thanks a lot."

The paper carrier leaves, and you return to your studying. Then you recall that you were going to order a pizza. Only five or six minutes have passed since you got a busy signal from Pizza City. As you go to dial, you cannot remember the phone number. Back to the yellow pages. A number once attended to was active in your short-term memory. When you were kept from rehearsing it, and when other numbers entered as interfering information, that original telephone number was soon inaccessible.

maintenance rehearsal a process of rote repetition (reattending) to keep information in short-term memory

We can increase the duration of short-term memory by rehearsing the information stored there. The rehearsal we use to keep material active in our short-term memory is **maintenance rehearsal**, or rote rehearsal, and amounts to little more than the simple repetition of the information already in our STM. To get material into STM (encoding), we have to attend to it. By repeating that material (as we might if we wanted to remember a telephone number until we could dial it), we are reattending to it with each repetition.

If we are not interrupted or distracted, we can easily hold a seven-digit telephone number in STM long enough to dial it.

The duration of STM *is* long enough for us to use it in many everyday activities. Usually all we want to do with a telephone number is remember it long enough to dial it. Few people feel the need to make a permanent record of every telephone number they dial. Using STM in mathematical computations is a good example, particularly when we do computations "in our heads." Multiply 28 by 6 without paper and pencil, "Let's see. Six times 8 is 48. Now I have to keep the 8 and carry the 4." Stop right there. Where do you "keep the 8" and where do you store the 4 until they are needed? Right, in STM. For that matter, where did the notion that 6 x 8 = 48 come from in the first place? Where did the idea of what "multiply" means come from? Right again. This is an example of information entering STM, not "from the outside," through our senses and sensory memory, but from long-term storage (see Figure 6.1).

Another example of STM in action is in the processing of language. As you read one of our longer sentences, such as this one, it is useful to have a short-term storage place to keep the beginning of the sentence in mind until you finally get to the end of the sentence, so that you can figure out the basic idea of the sentence before deciding whether anything in the sentence is worth remembering.

Having discussed the duration of short-term memory, let's now deal with its capacity. Just how much information can we hold in STM for that fifteen to twenty seconds?

The Capacity of STM

In 1956, George Miller wrote a paper about "the magical number seven, plus or minus two." In it, he argued that the capacity of short-term memory is very small—limited to just 5 to 9 (or 7 ± 2) bits, or "chunks," of information.

In the context of short-term memory, the concept of a *chunk* is actually a technical, and at the same time, imprecise term (Anderson, 1980). A **chunk** may be defined as the representation in memory of a meaningful unit of information. Thus, the claim is that we can store 7 ± 2 meaningful pieces of information in STM.

chunk an imprecise concept referring to a meaningful unit of information represented in short-term memory

We can easily attend to, encode, and store five or six letters in STM. Holding the letters YRDWIAADEFDNSYE in short-term memory, however, would be a challenge. Fifteen randomly presented letters exceed the capacity of STM for most of us. What if you were asked to remember the words *Friday* and *Wednesday*? Keeping these two simple words in STM is easy—even though they contain (the same) fifteen letters. Here you are storing just two chunks of meaningful information, not fifteen. In fact, you can easily store 50 letters in short-term memory if you recode them into the one meaningful chunk: "days of the week."

We can readily store a telephone number in short-term memory. Adding an area code makes the task somewhat more difficult because the ten digits now come fairly close to the upper limit of our STM capacity. Notice, though, how we tend to cluster the digits of a telephone number into a pattern. The digit series 2195553661 is more difficult to deal with as a simple string than when it is seen and encoded as a telephone number: (219) 555-3661 (Bower & Springston, 1970). Grouping the digits into chunks lets us see them in a new, more meaningful way.

Many mathematical calculations require that we briefly hold information in STM until we are ready to use it.

At best, short-term memory works something like a leaky bucket. From the vast storehouse of information available in sensory memory, we scoop up some (not much, at that) by paying attention to it and holding it for a while until we either use it, hang onto it with maintenance rehearsal, move it along to long-term storage, or lose it.

How Information Is Represented in STM

The material or information stored in sensory memory is kept there in virtually the same form in which it was presented. Visually presented stimuli are held as visual images, auditory stimuli form auditory memories, and so on. Getting information into STM is not an automatic process. We have to attend to the material to encode it into STM. How is that material stored, or represented, there?

Conrad (1963, 1964) was one of the first to argue that information is stored in STM with an acoustic code. This means that material is processed in terms of how it sounds. Conrad's conclusion was based on his interpretation of the errors people make in short-term memory experiments. In one experiment, he presented a series of letters visually, one at a time, and asked participants to recall the letters they had just seen. Many errors were made over the course of the experiment. What was surprising was that when people responded incorrectly, it was often with a letter that *sounded like* the correct one. For example, if participants were to recall the letter E and failed to do so, they would recall V, G, or T, letters that sound like the E they were supposed to recall. They rarely responded with F, which certainly looks more like the E they had just seen than do V, G, and T. (This was true whether recall was given orally or in writing.)

It seems that using STM is largely a matter of talking to ourselves. Regardless of how it is presented, we tend to encode information acoustically, the way it sounds. At least that's what the early evidence suggested. Psychologists still believe that acoustic coding is the most important means of representing information in STM, but some may be encoded in other ways, for example, visually or spatially (Martindale, 1981; Shulman, 1971, 1972; Squire et al., 1993). Perhaps the most we can say is that there is a tendency to rely heavily on the acoustic coding of information in STM, but that other codes may also be used.

BEFORE YOU GO ON

- What is short-term memory?
- What is maintenance rehearsal?
- What is the capacity of short-term memory?
- How is information represented in short-term memory?

LONG-TERM MEMORY (LTM)

Long-term memory (LTM) is memory as we all usually think of it: memory for large amounts of information that is held for long periods. Our own experience tells us that the capacity of long-term memory is huge—virtually limitless. At times we even impress ourselves with the amount of material we have stashed away in LTM (for instance, when we play Trivial Pursuit or TV game shows). How much can be stored in human memory may never be measured, but we can rest assured there is no way we will ever learn so much that there won't be room for more. (Getting that information out again when we want it is another matter, which we'll get to later.)

long-term memory (LTM)
a type of memory with virtually unlimited capacity and very long, if not limitless, duration

How Long Do Long-Term Memories Last?

On an experiential basis, we can again impress ourselves with the duration of some of our own memories. Assuming you remain free from disease or injury, you're likely never to forget some information, such as your own name or the words to "Happy Birthday."

At the moment, it is difficult to imagine an experiment that could tell us with any certainty how long information or experiences remain stored in LTM. One thing we know for a fact is that we often cannot remember things we once knew. We do tend to forget. The issue is *why*. Do we forget because the information is no longer available to us in our long-term memories—it just isn't there anymore? Or do we forget because we are unable to get the information out of LTM, which implies that it is still available but somehow not accessible? In other words, "How can we ever be sure that a memory failure is due to the relevant information being unavailable and hence inaccessible under all conceivable conditions rather than just merely being inaccessible under the prevailing conditions?" (Watkins, 1990, p. 330).

An article by Elizabeth and Geoffry Loftus (1980) focused on the issue of the duration of long-term memories. They concluded, "The evidence in no way confirms the view that all memories are permanent and thus potentially recoverable" (p. 409). They claim that the bulk of such evidence is neither scientific nor reliable and that when we think we recall specific events of the long-distant past, we may be reconstructing a reasonable facsimile of that information from bits and pieces of our past. In other words, when we do remember something that happened to us a long time ago, we don't recall the events as they actually happened. Instead, we recall a few specific details and then actively reconstruct a reasonable story. But even if we do reconstruct recollections of our past experiences, that would not necessarily mean that our original memory was no longer available. It might only suggest that we can maintain several versions of the same event in long-term memory (e.g., McCloskey & Zaragoza, 1985).

How Does Information Get into Long-Term Memory?

Simple repetition (maintenance rehearsal) can be used to keep material active in short-term memory. This type of rehearsal is also one way to move information from STM to LTM. Within limits, the more one repeats a bit of information, the more likely it will be remembered beyond the limits of short-term memory. However, the simple repetition of information is seldom sufficient to process it into long-term storage. Simply attending to information—the essence of repetition—is an inefficient means of encoding information in long-term memory.

elaborative rehearsal a means of processing information into LTM that involves thinking about information, organizing it, and making it meaningful

To get information into long-term memory we need to think about it, organize it, form images of it, make it meaningful, or relate it to something already in our long-term memories. In other words, to get information into LTM we need to use **elaborative rehearsal**, a term proposed by Craik and Lockhart (1972). Elaborative rehearsal is not an either/or process. Information can be elaborated to greater or lesser degrees.

Do you see how the distinction between maintenance rehearsal and elaborative rehearsal fits the levels-of-processing model of memory we discussed earlier? When we do no more than attend to an item, as in maintenance rehearsal, our processing is fairly minimal, or shallow, and that item is likely to remain in memory for a relatively short time. The more we rehearse an item elaboratively, the deeper into memory it is processed. And, as the model claims, the more we elaborate on it, the easier it will be to remember.

Consider a hypothetical experiment in which students are asked to respond to a list of words in different ways. In one instance, they are asked to count the number of letters in each word on the list. In another, they are asked to generate a word that rhymes with each one they read. In a third, they are asked to use each word in a sentence. The logic is that in each case, the words are processed at an increasingly "deeper" level as students focus on (1) the simple, physical structure of the words, (2) the sounds of the words as they are said aloud, and (3) the meaning of the words and their role in sentence structure. In such an experiment, as processing increases, so does recall of the words being processed (Cermak & Craik, 1979; Craik & Tulving, 1975).

Are There Different Types of Long-Term Memories?

Our own experiences tell us that what we have stored in LTM can be retrieved in various forms. We can remember the definitions of words. We can visualize people and events from the past. We can recall the melodies of songs. We can recall how our bodies moved when we first tried to roller-skate or ski.

Are there different LTM storage systems that encode and store information differently? Apparently, there are. LTM can be divided into two subsystems: declarative memory and nondeclarative memory (Gabrieli, 1998; Squire, 1992). **Declarative memory** includes memory systems from which information can be intentionally recalled (Gabrieli, 1998). Declarative memory includes subsystems for verbally-oriented, factual information (semantic memory) and memory for events (episodic memory). **Nondeclarative memory** (also known as procedural memory) involves the acquisition, retention, and retrieval of performance skills such as a tennis stroke, a golf swing, or riding a bicycle (Gabrieli, 1998).

Declarative Memory

As we just noted, declarative memory is divided into two subsystems: semantic memory and episodic memory (Tulving, 1972, 1983, 1985, 1986). In **semantic memory** we store all our vocabulary, simple concepts, and rules (including the rules that govern our use of language). Here we have stored our concepts and knowledge of the world in which we live. Our semantic memories are crammed with facts, both important and trivial. Can you answer the following questions?

> *Who opened the first psychology laboratory in Leipzig in 1879?*
> *How many stripes are there on the American flag?*
> *Is "Colorless green ideas sleep furiously" a well-formed, grammatically correct sentence?*
> *What do dogs eat?*

If you can, you found the answers in your long-term semantic memory.

Information in semantic memory is stored there in an organized fashion. We're not yet sure how to characterize the complex structure of semantic memory, but several ideas have been put forth. At the very least, concepts seem to be related in terms of their ability to elicit each other as associates. If we asked you to say the first thing that comes to mind when you hear the word "hot," aren't you likely to say "cold" in response? When people are asked to recall a list of randomly presented words from various categories (e.g., pieces of furniture, fruits, sports, and colors), they do so by category, recalling first furniture pieces, then names, then fruits, and so on (e.g., Bousfield, 1953). This is a process called **clustering**.

Interestingly, even if there is no inherent, obvious basis on which to cluster words, we organize them anyway. The phenomenon of *subjective organization* refers to the fact that given a list of unrelated words to recall, individuals will impose their own personal (subjective) organization on the list (Tulving, 1966).

Over the past 20 years, several *hierarchical network models* have been proposed to describe the structure of semantic LTM. Each theory is somewhat different, but they all propose that the concepts (animal, bird, canary, yellow) or propositions (birds are animals, birds can fly, canaries are birds, canaries are yellow) stored in semantic memory are interrelated in highly structured, predictable ways (Anderson, 1976, 1983a, 1983b; Collins & Loftus, 1975).

declarative memory a memory system that includes memory systems from which factual information and memories of events can be intentionally recalled

nondeclarative memory a long-term memory system (also known as procedural memory) that involves the acquisition, retention, and retrieval of performance skills

semantic memory a subsystem of LTM and a type of declarative memory in which vocabulary, facts, simple concepts, and rules are stored

clustering the process of recalling related items of information together on the basis of shared associations

Basic activities or procedures, such as those acquired when one learns how to ride a bicycle, are stored in procedural memory. Words, facts, meanings, and rules are stored in *semantic memory*. Life experiences, both mundane and dramatic, are stored in *episodic memory*.

Semantic long-term memory is also abstract. For example, although we may know how many stripes are on the American flag, and although we have a general idea of what dogs eat, we have difficulty remembering how, why, or when we acquired that information. The information in semantic memory is not tied in any real way to our memories of our own life experiences, which sets it apart from the next variety of LTM.

episodic memory a subsystem of LTM, and a type of declarative memory in which personal experiences are stored

In **episodic memory** we store the memories of our life events and experiences. It is a time-related memory, and the experiences stored there are laid down in chronological order. Episodic memory registers, or catalogues, all of our life's events. In other words, episodic memories are memories of specific events, not abstract events. Eye witness memory for a crime is an example of episodic memory. Other examples are:

> *What did you have for lunch yesterday?*
> *Did you have a good night's sleep last night?*
> *How did you spend last summer's vacation?*
> *What did your dog eat yesterday?*
> *What was your fifth birthday like?*

The answers to these sorts of questions are stored in episodic memories.

Some researchers claim that there is a separate category of episodic memory called *autobiographical memory* (e.g., Baddeley, 1990; Berscheid, 1994). Episodic memory contains things that have happened to us, but the events in autobiographical memory are particularly significant. What you had for lunch last Monday may be in your episodic memory, but your experience of your first day in college is probably in your autobiographical memory, as well. One's autobiographical memory does not seem to develop until about the age of 3 to 3 $\frac{1}{2}$ years, or until we are old enough to talk to ourselves and to others about the events of our lives (Nelson, 1993; Pillemer & White, 1989).

Nondeclarative Memory

Another, different type of long-term memory is nondeclarative or *procedural memory*. In this memory, we have stored recollections of learned responses, or chains of responses. Stored here are the patterned responses we have learned well, such as how to ride a bicycle, type, shave, or apply makeup. Simply stated, procedural memory stores the basic procedures of our lives. What we have stored here is retrieved and put into use with little or no effort. At one time in your life, handwriting was difficult, as you strained to form letters and words correctly. But by now, your writing skills, or procedures, are so ingrained that you can retrieve the processes involved almost without thinking. John Anderson (1986, 1987) calls the information in this subsystem *procedural knowledge,* or "knowing how." The other types of LTM hold what Anderson calls *declarative knowledge,* or "knowing that."

How Accurate Are Long-Term Memories?

When we try to remember a fact we learned in school many years ago, it is often easy to determine the accuracy of our recall. As on many classroom tests, we are either right or wrong. Note that if we learned something many years ago that was wrong and recalled that incorrect information now, it might still be wrong, even though our memory would be accurate.

Determining the accuracy of our memories for real past experiences is difficult at best and sometimes simply impossible. Do we *really* remember all the details of that vacation we took with our family when we were six years old, or are we recalling bits and pieces of what actually happened, bits and pieces of what we have been told happened, and adding in other details to reconstruct a likely story? Most of the time, the accuracy of our recollection of experiences from the distant past is of little or no consequence. In some situations, the accuracy of long-term memory can be of critical importance. In the following sections, we will consider two such situations: repressed memory and eyewitness memory.

BEFORE YOU GO ON

- What is long-term memory?
- How long do long-term memories last?
- How does information get into long-term memory?
- What are the different types of long-term memories?
- What is declarative memory, and what memory systems comprise it?
- What is nondeclarative memory?
- How accurate are long-term memories?

Repressed Memories

One example of the importance of accuracy in the retrieval of information from long-term storage involves what is called **repressed memory**. Repression is said to have occurred when extremely unpleasant or traumatic events are pushed deep into the unconscious cor-

repressed memory
traumatic memories pushed into an individual's unconscious that are very difficult to retrieve

ners of memory, from which retrieval is, at best, very difficult. A repressed memory is one that is so disturbing to a person that it is pushed deep into that person's unconscious and is no longer readily available for retrieval.

The idea that repression, or "motivated forgetting," can help us forget unpleasant past events has gained wide acceptance in psychology (Baddeley, 1990; Byrd, 1994; Erdelyi, 1985; Erdelyi & Goldberg, 1979; Gold et al., 1994; Loftus, 1993a, 1994). However, in recent years, the idea of repressed memory has created quite a stir. Repressed memories have been linked to several psychological symptoms, including eating disorders, anxiety, and depression. The prevailing theory is that a repressed memory of childhood sexual abuse is at the root of these and other disorders, and the only way to deal with an individual's symptoms is to recover the repressed memory (or memories) and deal with it.

The central controversy over repressed memory is whether memories recovered in therapy are actual or false memories, perhaps resulting from the suggestions made during the course of therapy. In recent years, thousands of individuals have come forth with accusations that they were sexually abused as children, usually by a close relative. Based on memories recovered during therapy, individuals have been tried and convicted. Some were guilty, whereas others were not. For example, in May 1994 a jury in Napa, California awarded Gary Ramona $500,000 from a therapist who "uncovered" repressed memories of childhood sexual abuse from his daughter, Holly. Holly had entered therapy for an eating disorder and was convinced that her disorder related to childhood sexual abuse. The jury agreed that the therapist had planted the ideas of abuse in her memory and awarded damages accordingly.

Sigmund Freud recognized the inherent problems in reports of childhood sexual abuse he heard from some of his female patients. Freud (1943) wrote:

> Sexual experiences in childhood reconstructed and recollected in analysis are on some occasions undeniably false, while others are just as certainly quite true, and that in most cases truth and falsehood are mixed up (p. 321).

In Freud's assessment, then, it may be difficult to determine which memories recovered in therapy are true, false, or a blend of the two.

Without questioning the enormity of the problem of child abuse or challenging reports of its prevalence, Elizabeth Loftus (1993a, 1993b) has challenged the authenticity of the repressed memories of some adults who "remember" events that may never have happened in the first place. Loftus has never argued that child abuse is not a real phenomenon. It may be, however, that *some* people genuinely come to believe that they were abused as children in order to help make sense of the difficulties they are now encountering as adults (Frankel, 1993; Gardner, 1993; Powell & Boer, 1994). It is possible that repressed memories recovered during therapy may be implanted by a therapist who uses suggestive therapy techniques. Imagine a patient who is told that the therapist has "seen hundreds of cases" like the patient's, and that in most cases, symptoms relate to repressed memories of childhood sexual abuse. The therapist encourages the patient to uncover and elaborate on the repressed memory. To make matters worse, the therapist may encourage the patient to let his or her imagination run wild. Some therapists even have patients imagine that they were sexually abused (Loftus, 1997). Research by Elizabeth Loftus has shown that such imagination techniques can lead to the formation of false memories. She terms this effect *imagination inflation*, which may occur because the imagined event becomes familiar to the individual.

What is the bottom line on repressed and recovered memories? There is research showing that memories can be implanted. However, this does not mean that *all* recovered memories are false memories. The problem lies in the ability to distinguish between those recovered memories that are actual memories and those that are false memories resulting from suggestive therapy techniques. The problem of repressed memory recovery not only presents a challenge to psychology, but also to the legal system which must deal with cases relying on recovered memories.

Eyewitness Testimony

Another area in which the accuracy of long-term memory is of critical importance is eyewitness testimony. If, in fact, memories are not permanent, and can be distorted or replaced by events processed later, we may have to reconsider the weight given to eyewitness testimony (Clifford & Lloyd-Bostock, 1983; Loftus, 1984; McLeod & Ellis, 1986; Ross et al., 1993; Wells et al., 1994). Most wrongful convictions can be traced to inaccurate eyewitness identifications and testimony (Rattner, 1988).

The challenges posed to eyewitnesses occur at each phase of the memory process: encoding, storage, and retrieval. Remember from our previous discussion that when you encode information, you select information to be placed into memory. Also, not all details of an event are equally attended to and encoded into memory. Only details that are salient to the individual are encoded. For example, if you saw a person with a gun holding up a bank, you might encode information about the gun, the robber's clothing, height, weight, etc. Other information (e. g., the color of the robber's shoes) may not be encoded.

Once information is encoded, it must be stored for later use. As much eyewitness memory research points out, human memory is a dynamic process. Information placed into storage can be influenced by information already in memory and information coming in after a memory is stored (Loftus, 1979a,b).

The effects of information encountered after an event is witnessed are quite varied. Imagine that you were a witness to a bank robbery. You originally believed that the getaway car was green. However, the next day you read in the newspaper that another witness described the same car as blue. Through a process of **compromise memory** (Loftus, 1979a) you may blend the green with the blue and come to believe that the car was a bluish-green color. Loftus (1979a,b) and others (McCloskey & Zaragoza, 1985; Tversky & Tuchin, 1989; Lindsay & Johnson, 1989; Dodson & Reisberg, 1991) have found in a variety of studies that *postevent information* in a variety of forms can influence what eyewitnesses have in memory and their reports of crimes. This effect of biasing postevent information is known as the **misinformation effect** (Loftus, Schooler, & Wagenaar, 1985).

compromise memory the blending of conflicting information in memory so that an "averaged" version of information will be recalled

misinformation effect the biasing effect of postevent information on the recall of an event

There are several reasons why some people are more reliable eyewitnesses than others. Just because someone says that he or she can clearly recall what happened does not mean that his or her retrieval is accurate. Two people can see the same woman, but when asked to describe her, their descriptions can be completely different.

Although the misinformation effect has been demonstrated quite frequently, some controversy exists over *why* it occurs. In fact, some research suggests that two memory traces are superimposed on one another, forming a single blended entity (Metcalfe, 1990).

BEFORE YOU GO ON

- What is a repressed memory?

- In recent years why has repressed memory become important?

- What are the major criticisms of repressed memory?

- What is compromise memory?

- What is the misinformation effect?

- What explanations have been proposed for the misinformation effect?

- How can the wording of a question affect an eyewitness's report of an event?

There are a variety of factors that can influence how information is retrieved by an eyewitness. To illustrate how question wording can affect retrieval of information, let's review a classic study in this area (Loftus & Zanni, 1975). Students view a short film showing the collision of two cars. Later, the viewers are asked about what they had seen and to estimate the speed of the cars at the time of the collision. Actually, some were asked about the cars "colliding," some were asked about the cars "hitting", and others were asked about cars "contacting," "bumping," or "smashing." Estimates of the speeds of the cars varied according to the verb used in the question. The cars were reported as going nearly 41 mph when they "smashed" together, but only about 31 mph when they "contacted" each other.

WHERE AND HOW ARE MEMORIES FORMED IN THE BRAIN?

We may safely assume that memories of our experiences are stored in our brains. Logic suggests that as information is encoded, stored, and retrieved, reliable changes occur in the central nervous system. Trying to discover where and how memories are formed in the nervous system is not a new line of research, but over the last decade, it has become one of the most exciting and most promising.

Where Are Memories Formed?

A rabbit can be conditioned to close the nictitating membrane of its eyes when a tone is sounded. That response, once learned, is at least partially stored in the rabbit's cerebellum.

Karl Lashley (1890–1958), a student of John B. Watson, spent over 30 years trying to find the particular part of the brain that stored memories. Lashley taught rats, cats, and monkeys to negotiate all sorts of complex mazes. Then he systematically removed or lesioned (cut) portions of the subject's cerebral cortex. Once he destroyed a part of the brain, Lashley tested his subject's memory for the previously learned task. What Lashley found was quite unexpected (Lashley, 1950). He discovered that specific memories do not have a specific location in the brain. When he went looking for a memory in the brain to lesion, he could not find one. What he did find was that, in general, the more brain tissue he destroyed, the more impaired the organism's performance, but *it seemed to matter very little where the damage occurred.*

We now recognize a few of the limitations of Lashley's studies. For one thing, he studied mostly maze learning, a rather complex set of procedures that involves the interaction of many senses and many muscle groups. Lashley may have been correct about memories for mazes; they are probably not stored in one location. But some types of memories do seem to be found in certain predictable locations. Individual experiences of sight, sound, or touch may very well be stored in—or near—the relevant sensory area of the cerebral cortex, and memories for the images of faces and for images of animals may have storage places of their own (e.g., Squire, 1986, 1987, 1992).

Another limitation of Lashley's work is that it focused only on the cerebral cortex. Some evidence suggests that many lower brain centers are intimately involved in encoding and storing information (Gluck & Myers, 1995; McCormick et al., 1982; Mishkin & Appenzeller, 1987; Thompson, 1969, 1981, 1986). For example, we know that rabbits can be classically conditioned to close the protective tissue (nictitating membrane) that covers their eyes, in response to the sound of a tone. Once this response has been learned, the only way to destroy the association is to make small lesions in areas of the cerebellum. For rabbits, then, we know that there is at least one conditioned response stored in the cerebellum (Thompson, 1990).

Scientists assume that most human memories are stored in the cerebral cortex, but they also argue that other, lower structures are involved. It is the *hippocampus* that seems most necessary for memory formation. Much of what we know about the role of the hippocampus we have learned from observations of a few unfortunate individuals for whom at least one aspect of memory had been stolen away by illness or disease (Baddeley, 1990; Corkin, 1984; Milner, 1959, 1965; Milner et al., 1968; Squire, 1992).

A patient known to us only as "H.M." suffered from epilepsy. For nearly 11 years he experienced an average of one major convulsive attack and several partial seizures every day. Finally, it was decided that drastic treatment was needed. Parts of the temporal lobe were severed and the hippocampus removed from both sides of H.M.'s brain. The surgery was successful. Epileptic seizures became rare. Sensory, perceptual, and most intellectual functioning were left intact.

However, there were disastrous effects on H.M.'s memory. He could not form new long-term memories. Failure to recall events before his surgery would have meant a diagnosis of **retrograde** (backward-acting) **amnesia**—the loss of memory of events that occurred before the onset of the amnesia. However, this was not the problem. H.M. could remember all that had happened to him *before* his surgery, but he could not form memories of events that happened after the surgery. H.M. had **anterograde** (forward-acting) **amnesia**. If asked what year it was, H.M. would say, "1953"—the year the surgery was performed. If you were to interact with H.M. and then leave for a few minutes, he would have no idea who you were when you returned.

Consider the fate of Clive Wearing, a bright musician who contracted encephalitis, which ultimately damaged his brain. He, too, was left after treatment with an inability to form new, lasting memories. "If his wife left the room for a few minutes, when she returned he would greet her with great joy, declaring that he had not seen her for months and asking how long he had been unconscious. Experienced once, such an event could be intriguing and touching, but when it happens repeatedly day in, day out, it rapidly loses its charm" (Baddeley, 1990, p. 5). Unlike H.M.'s experience, Mr. Wearing also had signs of retrograde amnesia. His recollections of events that preceded his illness were spotty and seldom included detail. One marvelous exception is that throughout all of his memory problems, his memory for making beautiful music remained.

From other similar cases, we find that if damage is localized to the hippocampus and the rest of the brain is unscathed, the degree of amnesia (retrograde or anterograde) is considerably less than that of either H.M. or Mr. Wearing, each of whom had damage to the temporal lobes, as well (Squire, 1992).

How Are Memories Formed?

When human memories are formed, changes occur in the cerebral cortex that are, at least in part, influenced by the action of the hippocampus. That sounds simple enough, but what sorts of changes take place as memories are stored? Exactly what is changed, and in what ways? Answers to these questions are not yet available, and what hints we do have tell us that the processes involved are incredibly complex. If the nervous system is in some way altered as memories are formed, that alteration must be at the level of the neuron or the synapse.

By the late 1970s, there was evidence that memory formation could be found by examining changes at the synapse (Bartus et al., 1982; Kandel & Schwartz, 1982; Lavond et al., 1993; Matthies, 1989; McNaughton & Morris, 1987). One change that occurs at the synapse is that with experience, the synapse becomes more efficient. More specifically,

retrograde amnesia the loss of the memory of events stored before the onset of the amnesia

anterograde amnesia the inability to form or retrieve new memories

when a synapse stimulates another neuron several times, future synaptic transmission at that site becomes easier (Kalat, 2001). Another important synaptic mechanism involved in learning and memory involves the neurotransmitter glutamate, the most abundant neurotransmitter in the brain. Repeated stimulation at a glutamate receptor site causes a change in the ion balance on the postsynaptic membrane. This allows glutamate to more easily stimulate a neuron at the synapse.

If memories are formed because repetition, experience, or practice allows some neurotransmitters to work more effectively at the synaptic level, what would happen if something disrupted or blocked the action of those neurotransmitters? You would predict that memories formed at synapses that used those neurotransmitters would be disrupted as well. Studies show that this is essentially what happens. The neurotransmitters most often involved in studies such as these are acetylcholine (ACh) and serotonin.

A slightly different line of research claims that experience does not increase (or alter in any way) the neurotransmitter released at synapses. What matters are changes in the postsynaptic membrane. The most common changes are thought to be increases in the number of effective or useful receptor sites (Lynch & Baudry, 1984). As synapses are used repeatedly, the number of receptor sites increases, and this is what makes for more efficient use of the synapse.

In brief, the formation of memories involves making some synaptic transmissions easier than they once were. What remains to be seen is whether changes at the synapse involve the amount of neurotransmitters present or produce physical changes in the neuronal membranes to allow existing neurotransmitters to function more effectively.

More recent research has moved the search for the physiology of memory from the cellular level to larger parts of the brain that are involved in storing memories. The advent of new brain imaging technologies, like *functional magnetic resonance imaging* (fMRI), has given neuroscientists new insights into how information is encoded and stored in memory. For example, research investigating nondeclarative memory using fMRI has found that about six hours after initial training on a motor task, different parts of the brain are active than were active during the training period (Shadmehr & Holcomb, 1997). Specifically, during initial training, association areas in the prefrontal cortex were active. After six hours, brain activity associated with the learned motor behavior shifted to other areas of the brain, including the left posterior parietal cortex and the right anterior cerebellum.

There is also evidence that the temporal lobes are important in the declarative memory functions of remembering new events and facts (Gabrieli, Brewer, Desmond, & Glover, 1998). Gabrieli, et al., found that during the encoding of visual information, areas of the temporal cortex on both sides of the brain were activated. During retrieval of the same information, there was an increase in activity in a different area of the temporal lobes on both sides of the brain. Thus, different parts of the temporal lobes are activated during encoding and retrieval of information. Encoding verbal experiences is related to activation in the left prefrontal and temporal areas of the brain (Wagner et al., 1998).

Interestingly, the amount of activation of the brain is related to how well something is recalled later (Brewer et al., 1998). Brewer, et al., showed participants 24 color photographs of indoor or outdoor scenes. Thirty minutes later, participants were given an unexpected memory test for the pictures. They were shown a group of pictures that included those that were seen previously along with new ones. Participants indicated whether they had seen a photograph before. If participants reported seeing a photograph previously, they were asked to state whether their judgment was based on a distinct recollection of a picture or a feeling of familiarity with a picture. Brewer, et al., found that several parts of the brain were involved in the memory of the pictures. Activation in these areas predicted which pictures were remembered and which were forgotten. They also found that activation in these areas of the brain was greater for photographs that were distinctly recalled than for those which participants had a feeling they had seen before. Thus, activation of specific parts of the brain were not only associated with whether or not a photograph was remembered, but also with the degree to which a photograph was remembered.

BEFORE YOU GO ON

- Where are memories stored in the brain?

- What are retrograde and anterograde amnesia?

- How are neurons and neurotransmitters involved in storing memories?

- What is the role of synaptic transmission in the formation of memories?

- What does research using functional magnetic resonance imaging suggest about how memories are formed?

- What changes in brain activity are noticed during the encoding and storage of information?

Topic Review 6 A

1. What is memory?

Memory is a set of systems involved in the acquisition, storage, and retrieval of information. Memory comprises systems that can hold information for periods of time ranging from fractions of a second to a lifetime and systems that have very limited storage capacities to those with vast storage capacities.

2. What are the interrelated processes of encoding, storage, and retrieval?

Encoding refers to the active process of deciding what should be placed into memory and forming cognitive representations for encoded information. Storage refers to the process of keeping information in memory after cognitive representations have been formed. Retrieval is the process of getting information out of memory.

3. What is reconstructive memory?

Unlike the common view of memory working like a camcorder, recording information exactly for later playback, memory is a constructive process. Features of information are stored, and recall involves a reconstruction of those features. Modern views of memory refer to the feature construction process as the construction memory framework (CMF). According to this view, stored features are scattered in different areas of the brain. When we want to remember something, a feature is activated which sets off a chain reaction in other related features.

4. What reconstruction processes could account for inaccurate reports of memories?

Within the construction-based explanation for memory there are a number of causes for inaccurate memories. Weak connections among features associated with an episode can cause inaccurate memory. At the time of encoding, inadequate separation of similar episodes and features can also cause faulty memory. Finally, retrieval cues may activate more than one set of features causing a person to recall an episode other than the one desired.

5. What is the tip-of-the-tongue effect?

The tip-of-the-tongue effect is a demonstration of how constructive memory processes work. When you are try-

ing to recall something, there are times where you can recall many features associated with the to-be-recalled information. When enough features have been retrieved, the desired information may be recalled. In some cases, something similar is recalled, an effect known as the "ugly sister effect."

6. What is the multistore model of memory?

The multistore model of memory holds that there are a number of separate memory storage systems, each with its own ways of processing information. The most widely accepted multistore model is the Atkinson and Shiffrin modal model which divides memory into sensory memory, short-term memory, and long-term memory.

7. What is the levels-of-processing model of memory?

The levels-of-processing model of memory suggests that there is a single process representing memory, not multiple, separate processes. According to this model, the amount of processing that information receives determines how well information can be remembered. Information processed to a shallow level cannot be remembered for a long period of time. Conversely, information processed to a deep level becomes long-lasting.

8. What is sensory memory?

Sensory memory is a memory storage system that stores large amounts of information for very short periods of time. Iconic memory is the sensory storage system associated with the sense of vision and can hold information for about a half second. Echoic memory is the sensory store associated with the sense of hearing, which can hold auditory information for up to five to ten seconds.

9. What is short-term memory?

Short-term memory is a storage system in which information can be held for several seconds (occasionally up to one minute) before it fades or is replaced. Encoding information into this memory requires that we attend to it. Information may enter short-term storage from sensory memory or be retrieved from long-term memory. We keep material in STM by reattending to it, a process called maintenance rehearsal.

10. How much information can be stored in short-term memory?

The capacity of short-term memory is approximately 7 ± 2 "chunks of information," where a chunk is an imprecise measure of a unit of meaningful material. Organizing information into meaningful clusters or units can expand the apparent capacity of STM.

11. How is information represented in STM?

Information in our short-term memories may be encoded in several forms, but acoustic coding seems to be the most common.

12. What is long-term memory?

Long-term memory is a storage system that houses large amounts of information for long, virtually limitless, periods of time. Barring illness or injury, memories of a lifetime are stored in long-term memory. Determining the accuracy of long-term memories is difficult. In most instances, complete accuracy is not crucial.

13. What are elaborative rehearsal and maintenance rehearsal?

Maintenance rehearsal (rote repetition) is used to hold information in STM. Although maintenance rehearsal may sometimes be sufficient to move information from STM to LTM, the best way is elaborative rehearsal. Elaborative rehearsal involves thinking about the material, organizing the material, and forming associations with or images of the material and relating it to something already stored in LTM. The more one elaborates, or the "deeper" the elaboration, the better retrieval will be.

14. What is declarative and nondeclarative memory?

Declarative memory is a storage system with subsystems for verbally-oriented, factual information and memory for events. Nondeclarative memory (also known as procedural memory) is involved in memory for the acquisition, retention, and retrieval of performance skills.

15. What is semantic memory and how is it organized?

Semantic memory is one subsystem of declarative memory where we store all of our vocabulary, simple concepts, and rules for vocabulary and language use. Information is stored in semantic memory in an organized fashion. During recall from semantic memory, words are organized according to category membership through a process called clustering. Even in the absence of any inherent organization of a list of words a person has to learn, the individual will find a way to organize.

This is known as subjective organization. Most likely, information in semantic memory is organized in a hierarchical network.

16. What is episodic memory?

Episodic memory is another subsystem of declarative memory. Episodic memories record life events and experiences. They are tied to specific times and places. There is a separate category of episodic memory known as autobiographical memory in which we store important events from our own lives (for example, your high school graduation or the day you got your driver's license).

17. What is procedural memory?

Procedural memory is part of the nondeclarative memory system. In this storage system we keep recollections of learned responses or chains of responses. Procedural memories involve knowing how to perform a skill (for example, riding a bike or hitting a golf ball).

18. What are repressed memories, and what do they tell us about LTM?

Repressed memories are events presumed to be in one's long-term memory but that cannot be retrieved because to do so would be anxiety-producing. Some psychologists have challenged the reality of some repressed memories, as when adults remember incidents of abuse when they were children. Some critics of repressed memories maintain that influential suggestions from therapists may cause a person to believe that his or her psychological problems stem from repressed memories of events that may, in fact, never have taken place. It may be that our recall of events long past has been influenced by events that have occurred since.

19. What are compromise memory and the misinformation effect?

Eyewitness testimony is another example of how one's recollection of events can be influenced by factors other than the events themselves. Compromise memory occurs when an eyewitness blends conflicting sources of information into an "average" memory. According to the misinformation effect, postevent information can influence what an eyewitness remembers about an event. The exact cause for the misinformation effect is not known exactly. However, it appears that the original memory (based on viewing the event) and the new memory (based on postevent information) coexist and may both be used when recalling an event. Eyewitness memory can also be affected at the time of questioning if questions are worded in a biased way. Overall, the research on eyewitness memory suggests that information held in long-term memory is not carved in stone. Rather, it is susceptible to many outside influences.

20. At the level of the neuron, what changes take place when memories are formed?

In ways yet unknown, human memories are probably stored throughout the cerebral cortex. The hippocampus is surely involved in the consolidation of long-term memories, as studies of patients with amnesia have shown. At the neural level, synaptic pathways that are used repeatedly become more and more efficient in their ability to transmit neural impulses.

21. What do recent brain imaging studies suggest about the physiology of memory?

Research using functional magnetic resonance imaging techniques finds that different areas of the brain are involved in encoding and storing information. For example, research shows the encoding of nondeclarative, procedural memories activates one part of the brain. But, six hours later, the information activated a different part of the brain. Similar processes are involved in encoding and storing declarative memories. The amount of brain activity during encoding is related to how well information can be recalled later.

Topic 6B FACTORS AFFECTING FORGETTING

In this Topic, we turn to the practical matter of accounting for why we forget things. In the terminology we've been developing, forgetting is a matter of retrieval failure. Our focus, then, will be on factors that affect the retrieval of information from memory. Whether we are talking about a simple, well-learned habit stored in procedural memory, a precise definition stored in semantic memory, a personal experience stored in episodic memory, or a telephone number temporarily stored in short-term memory, if retrieval fails at a critical time, that information will be of no use to us.

What factors influence whether information can be retrieved on demand? What can be done to increase the likelihood that retrieval will succeed? In truth, the list is *not* a very long one. We have organized this discussion around four different but related factors: (1) how memory is measured, (2) how encoding strategies influence later retrieval, (3) how encoding is scheduled, and (4) how interference can affect retrieval. Throughout this Topic, we will assume that the to-be-remembered information is actually stored in memory. That is, we will focus on problems of retrieval, not retention. Occasionally, we may feel that we have "forgotten" something when it was never really stored in memory in the first place.

Key Questions to Answer

While reading this Topic, find the answers to the following key questions:

1. What is meant by a direct or explicit measure of memory?

2. What is recall?

3. What is recognition?

4. Is recall or recognition a more sensitive measure of memory?

5. Are there any similarities between recognition and recall?

6. What are implicit measures of memory?

7. What is relearning?

8. How does the context in which one encodes information affect the retrieval of that information?

9. What is the encoding specificity principle?

10. What is state-dependent memory?

11. What are flashbulb memories?

12. How is meaningfulness related to retrieval?

13. What is a mnemonic device?

14   How do narrative chaining, mental imagery, and the method of loci help memory?

15.   What is a schema?

16.   What are the different types of schemas?

17.   How do schemas affect retrieval?

18.   How does overlearning affect retrieval?

19.   How does distributing one's practice affect retrieval?

20.   What are retroactive interference and proactive interference?

HOW WE MEASURE RETRIEVAL

There are a variety of ways in which we can retrieve information from memory. In some cases, we may be directly asked to recall or recognize something. For example, when you are taking an exam, you are consciously and actively trying to retrieve information from memory. In other instances, retrieval of information is not as direct or conscious. For example, you may have learned to play golf many years ago. When you try the game now, you find your skills have diminished. However, it does not take long to sharpen your skills and get close to where you were before. Obviously, you retained some of your previous learning. Relearning the task was not all that difficult.

Direct, Explicit Measures of Memory

Measures of retrieval are called *direct,* or *explicit,* when someone must consciously or purposively retrieve specified information from his or her memory (as on a classroom exam).

One direct measure of memory is recall. **Recall** occurs when someone produces information to which he or she has been previously exposed. There are different types of recall tasks. In *free recall* an individual is allowed to recall information in any order. For example, if I presented you with a list of 15 words to learn and then asked you to write down as many words as possible, in any order, you would be using free recall. In free recall, we provide the fewest *retrieval cues* to aid the retrieval process. We merely specify the information wanted and say, "Go into your long-term memory, locate that information, get it out, and write it down." Another type of recall is *serial recall* in which a person is required to recall information in the order presented. For example, when a child is being taught the months of the year, she will be required to recall them in the order learned. In another form of recall, called *cued recall*, we provide retrieval cues. For example, if we asked you to learn a list of word pairs (cat-dog or car-boat), we could use the first word from each pair as a stimulus word, or cue. You would be required to produce the correct second word from each pair after receiving the cue word.

recall a direct measure of retrieval in which one is given the fewest possible cues to aid retrieval and must produce information to which he or she has been previously exposed

Another explicit measure of memory is recognition. For **recognition,** we ask someone to identify material previously experienced. A good example of a recognition task is when an eyewitness must try to pick a suspect out of a lineup. The witness was exposed to the perpetrator at the scene of the crime. An image of the perpetrator's face was

recognition a direct measure of retrieval in which an individual is required to identify material previously learned

encoded into memory. During a lineup, the witness is asked if he or she recognizes any one in the lineup. Recognition memory is a two-step process. First, the individual must retrieve information stored in memory (the memory of the perpetrator's face, for example). Second, the individual must match that memory with the material to be recognized and make a decision concerning whether the material (or person) was seen before.

When recall and recognition memory are directly compared, recognition memory turns out to be a more sensitive measure of memory than recall. That is, we can often recognize things we cannot recall. For example, have you ever seen someone you know walking toward you and you recognize the person (perhaps an acquaintance from high school), but you cannot recall the person's name? In virtually every case, retrieval by recognition is superior to retrieval by recall (Bahrick, 1984; Brown, 1976; Schacter, 1987). Figure 6.3 provides some clear-cut (and classic) data of this point. Over a two-day period, tests of retrieval by recognition are superior to tests of retrieval by recall. Most students would rather take a multiple-choice exam, in which they only have to recognize the correct response from among a few alternatives, than a fill-in-the-blank test (or an essay test), which requires recall.

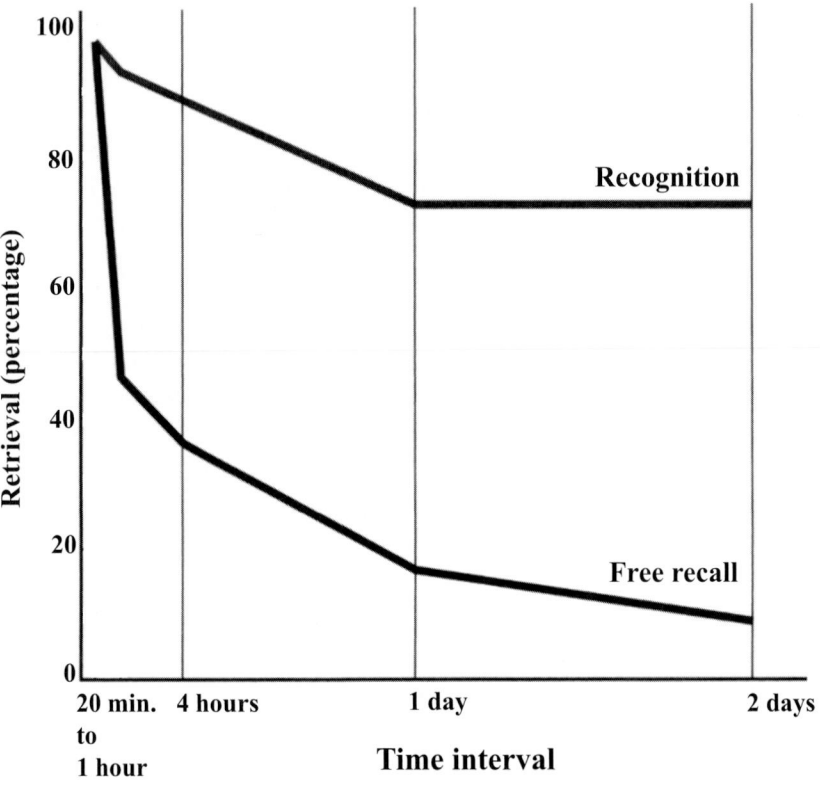

FIGURE 6.3

Differences in retrieval scores for the memory of nonsense syllables over a two-day period. In one case retrieval is measured with a test for recall, whereas in the other case, retrieval is measured with a test for recognition (Luh, 1922).

Despite the differences between recall and recognition, the two forms of retrieval have common elements. Both involve the retrieval of material stored in semantic memory or episodic memory (Hayman & Tulving, 1989; Tulving, 1983). Also, both seem to involve the same physiological underpinnings in the brain (Haist et al., 1992; Squire et al., 1993).

Indirect, Implicit Measures of Memory

Measures of memory classified as *indirect* or *implicit* are more subtle than either recall or recognition. With indirect measures, someone demonstrates that information is stored in memory when he or she can take advantage of previous experiences without consciously trying to do so.

For example, suppose a person in a memory experiment came back to the laboratory two weeks after memorizing a list of words and could neither recall nor recognize any of the items. We'd be a bit surprised, but, we might be wrong to assume that nothing was retained from the learning experience two weeks earlier. What if we ask this student to relearn the list of 15 words? Two weeks ago it took ten presentations of the list, or trials, before the words were learned. Now, relearning the same list takes only seven trials. This is a common finding in memory research.

Relearning is the change in performance that occurs when a person is required to learn material for a second time and almost always requires fewer trials, or less time, than did original learning. The difference is attributed to the benefit provided by a person's memory of the original learning. Because relearning does not require the direct, conscious retrieval of information from memory, it qualifies as an indirect, or implicit, test of memory retention (Graf & Schacter, 1985; Schacter, 1987, 1992).

relearning the change in performance that occurs when one is required to learn material for a second time

Implicit tests of memory have become an active area of research in cognitive psychology (Richardson-Klavehn & Bjork, 1988; Roediger, 1990). Among other things, this research supports the hypothesis that information is stored in various types of long-term memory. Although we may think of the relearning of verbal materials, such as words or nonsense syllables, as a typical example of an indirect measure of memory, many implicit tests of retention focus on *procedural memories,* or procedural knowledge. You'll recall from our last Topic that procedural memories include the storage of "knowing how to go about doing things," such as tying a shoelace, typing, speaking, or riding a bicycle. Remembering how to do such things is virtually automatic or unconscious. When we specifically try to recall how to do them—when we really pause and think about what we're doing—our performance often deteriorates. "In some sense, these performances reflect prior learning, but seem to resist conscious remembering" (Roediger, 1990, p. 1043).

Implicit memory tests also help us better understand the processes underlying amnesia. Some people with amnesia are unable to transfer information from STM to LTM. What is learned today is forgotten by tomorrow. Research suggests that individuals with and without amnesia differ with respect to how they respond to tests of memory (Warrington & Weiskrantz, 1968). When tested with explicit memory techniques (e.g., recall), individuals without amnesia performed better than those with amnesia. However,

BEFORE YOU GO ON

- What is a direct measure of memory?

- What is the difference between recall and recognition?

- What is an indirect measure of memory?

- What is relearning?

- What do indirect measures of memory tell us about long-term memory?

on an implicit test of memory (i.e., identify a word learned earlier that begins with a certain string of letters), individuals with and without amnesia do not differ (Bowers & Schacter, 1990; Graf & Mandler, 1984; Simamura, 1986; Warrington & Weiskrantz, 1968). These findings suggest that even in the worst cases of amnesia, some memory processing may be saved. At least some long-term memories, especially those in procedural memory, are maintained. Sometimes a person with amnesia cannot remember various long-term memories, but they can still remember how to talk (how to tell us they do not remember something), how to eat and how to get dressed, all procedural memories.

HOW WE ENCODE INFORMATION

Encoding, storage, and retrieval are interrelated memory processes. The issue is simple: if you do not encode information properly, you will have difficulty retrieving it. You cannot recall a stranger's name simply because you never knew it in the first place. You have had countless encounters with pennies. Can you draw a picture of a penny, locating all of its features? Can you recognize an accurate drawing of a penny (Figure 6.4)? In fact, few of us can, and even fewer can recall all of its essential features. Nearly 90 percent forget that the word *Liberty* appears right behind Lincoln's shoulder (Nickerson & Adams, 1979; Rubin & Kontis, 1983). These retrieval failures do not result from a lack of experience but from a lack of proper encoding. Few of us have ever sat down to study (encode) exactly what a penny looks like. We'll cover four encoding issues: context effects, meaningfulness, mnemonic devices, and schemas.

The Power of Context

encoding specificity principle
the hypothesis that we can retrieve only what we have stored and that retrieval is enhanced to the extent that retrieval cues match encoding cues

Retrieval is best when the situation, or context, in which retrieval takes place matches the context that was present at encoding. When cues present at encoding are also present at retrieval, retrieval is enhanced. This observation reflects the main point of the **encoding specificity principle**, which asserts that how we retrieve information depends on how it was encoded in the first place (Flexser & Tulving, 1982; Newby, 1987; Tulving & Thompson, 1973). Not only do we encode and store particular items of information, we also note and store the context in which those items occur. The encoding specificity principle is as valid for animals as it is for humans. "Ease of retrieval…is quite strongly influenced by the context in which the animal is asked to retrieve it. The closer the test context is to training conditions and the more unique the context is for specific memories, the better the retrieval" (Spear et al., 1990, pp. 190–191).

Here's a hypothetical experiment that demonstrates encoding specificity (based on Tulving & Thompson, 1973). Students are asked to learn a list of 24 common words. Half the students are given cue words to help them remember each item on the list. For the stimulus word *wood,* the cue word is *tree;* for *cheese,* the cue is *green,* and so on for each

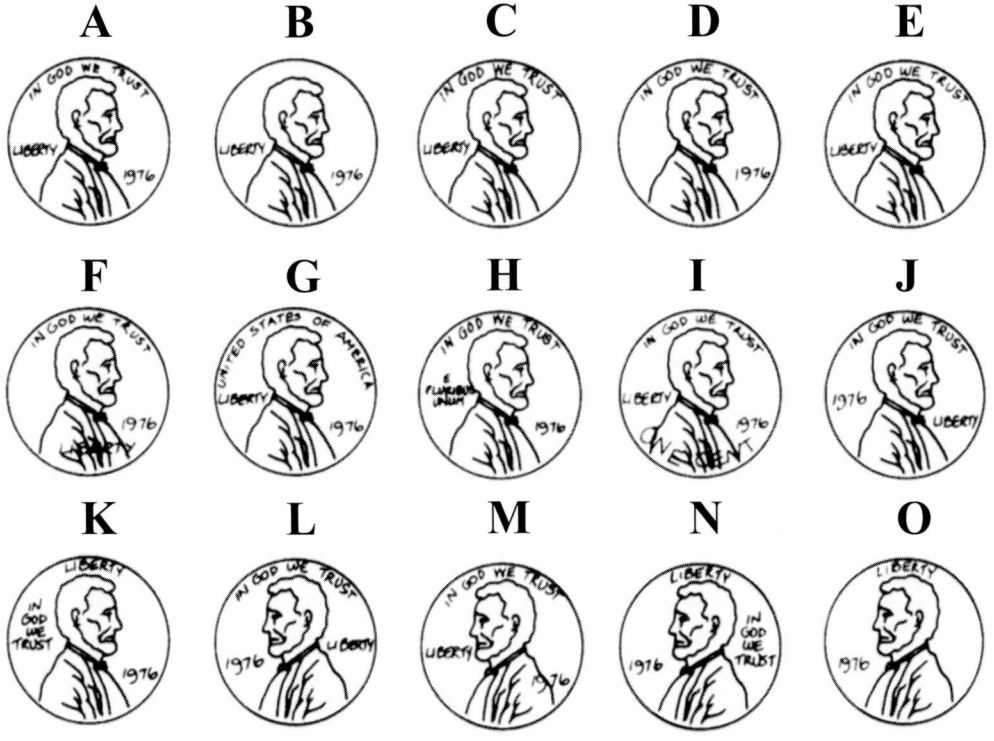

FIGURE 6.4

Fifteen drawings of the head of a penny. The fact that we cannot easily identify the correct rendition emphasizes that simple exposure to a stimulus does not guarantee it will be adequately encoded in long-term memory (Nickerson & Adams, 1979).

of the 24 words. The other students receive no such cue during their memorization (i.e., while encoding). Later, students are asked to recall as many words from the list as they can. What we discover is that presenting the cue at recall helps those students who had seen it during learning but *decreases* the recall for those who had not seen it during learning. If learning takes place without a cue, recall will be better without it.

How-to-study-in-college books often recommend that you choose one place for studying. Your kitchen table is not likely to be a good choice because it is associated with eating experiences (and many others). In other words, the context of a kitchen is not a good one for encoding information unless you expect to be tested for retrieval in that same context—which seems highly unlikely. This advice was reaffirmed by a series of experiments by Steven Smith (1979). He had students learn some material in one room and then tested their recall for that material in either the same room or a different one. When a new room—a different context with different cues—was used, retrieval scores dropped substantially. Simply instructing students to try to remember and think about the room in which learning took place helped recall considerably.

These context effects may be related to what has been called **state-dependent memory**. The idea here is that, to a degree, retrieval depends on the extent to which a person's

state-dependent memory
the hypothesis that retrieval can be enhanced by the extent to which one's state of mind at retrieval matches one's state of mind at encoding

state of mind at retrieval matches the person's state of mind at encoding (Leahy & Harris, 1989, p. 146). If learning takes place while a person is under the influence of a drug, for example, being under the influence of that drug at retrieval often has beneficial effects (Eich et al., 1975; Goodwin et al., 1969; Parker et al., 1976). Intriguing research by Gordon Bower (Bower, 1981; Bower et al., 1978; Bower & Mayer, 1989) suggests that mood may also predict retrieval. Using moods (sad or happy) induced by posthypnotic suggestion, Bower found that retrieval was best when mood at retrieval matched mood at learning. This effect is more pronounced for females than for males (Clark & Teasdale, 1985). Unfortunately, this "mood-dependent memory" effect has proven to be somewhat unreliable. Neither the circumstances under which it occurs nor the mechanisms that produce it are well understood (Eich, 1995; Eich et al., 1994). There is also considerable evidence that a given mood or frame of mind tends to evoke memories that are consistent with that mood (e.g., Blaney, 1986). Simply put: when you are in a good mood, you tend to remember pleasant things, and when you are in a bad or depressed mood, you tend to remember unpleasant, depressing things.

flashbulb memory a particularly clear and vivid (although not necessarily accurate) recollection from one's past

Furthermore, our memories for emotionally arousing experiences are easier to recall than memories of emotionally neutral events (Thompson, 1982). This may be because emotional arousal increases the levels of certain hormones that, in turn, help form vivid memories associated with the emotional arousal (Gold, 1987; McGaugh, 1983). Emotional arousal may help to form particularly vivid memories and may help us understand what Brown and Kulik (1977) call **flashbulb memories**—memories that are unusually clear and vivid. You probably have flashbulb memories of several events: your high school graduation, the funeral of a close friend, or how you learned about some significant news event. Although flashbulb memories *are* particularly clear and vivid, there is little reason to believe that they are necessarily any more complete or accurate than any other memories. Although we seem to recall these events in vivid detail, much of that detail may be totally wrong or may never have happened (McCloskey et al., 1988; Neisser, 1982, 1991).

BEFORE YOU GO ON

- What is the encoding specificity principle?
- What is state-dependent learning?
- What are flashbulb memories?
- How does the context in which information is encoded affect how it is retrieved?

The Usefulness of Meaningfulness

We have a hypothesis. We believe we can determine the learning ability of students by noting where they sit in a classroom. The best, brightest students choose seats farthest from the door. Poorer students sit by the door, apparently interested in getting easily into and out of the room. (There may be some truth to this, but we are not serious.) To make our point, we do an experiment. Students seated away from the door are asked to learn a list of words. They can read the list aloud only once. We need a second list of words for the students seated by the door because they've already heard the first list. The list our "smart students" hear contains words such as *university, registrar, automobile, environmental,* and *psychology.* As predicted, they have little problem recalling this list after just one presentation. The students huddled by the door get the second list: *insidious, tachistoscope, sophistry, flotsam,* and *episcotister.* Needless to say, our hypothesis will be confirmed.

This obviously is not a fair experiment. Those students sitting by the door will yell foul. The second list of words is clearly more difficult to learn and recall than the first. The words on the first list *are* more familiar, and they are easier to pronounce. However, the major difference between these lists is the **meaningfulness** of the items—the extent to which they elicit existing associations in memory. The *university, registrar, automobile* list is easy to remember because each word in it is meaningful. Each word makes us think of many other things or produces many associations. These items are easy to elaborate. Words like *episcotister* are more difficult because they evoke few, if any, associations.

Meaningfulness is not a characteristic or feature built into materials to be learned. Meaningfulness resides in the learner. *Episcotister* may be a meaningless collection of letters for many, but for others it is a word rich in meaning, a word with which they can readily form many associations. What is or is not meaningful is a function of individual experiences. (An episcotister, by the way, is a type of apparatus used in psychology. To make this word meaningful for you, you might want to do some research on episcotisters.)

It follows, then, that one of your tasks as a learner is to do whatever you can to make the material you are learning as meaningful as possible. You need to seek out and form associations between what you are learning and what you already know. You need to elaboratively rehearse what you are encoding so that you can retrieve it later. You need to ask about what you are studying. What does this mean? What does it make me think of? Does this remind me of something I already know? How can I make this more meaningful? Perhaps you now see the reason for including "Before You Go On" questions within each chapter.

The Value of Mnemonic Devices

Retrieval is enhanced when we elaborate on the material we are learning—when we organize it and make it meaningful during the encoding process. Now we'll look at a few specific encoding techniques, or **mnemonic devices**, that can aid our retrieval by helping us to organize and add meaningfulness to new material.

Research by Bower and Clark (1969) shows us that we can improve the retrieval of otherwise unorganized material if we weave that material into a meaningful story—a technique called *narrative chaining*. A group of college students learned a list of ten simple nouns in a specific order. This is not a difficult task, and students had little trouble with it. Then they were given another list of ten nouns to learn, and then another, until they had a total of 12 lists. These students were given no instructions other than to remember each list of words in order.

A second group of students learned the same 12 lists. They were asked to make up stories that used each of the words on the list in order. After each list was presented, both groups were asked to recall the list of words they had just heard. At this point, there was no difference in the recall scores for the two groups. Then came a surprise. After all 12 lists had been recalled, the students were tested again on their recall for each of the lists. Students were given a word from one of the twelve lists and were asked to recall the other

meaningfulness the extent to which new information evokes associations with information already in LTM

mnemonic device a strategy for improving retrieval that takes advantage of existing memories in order to make new material more meaningful

nine words from that list. Now the difference in recall between the two groups of students was striking (see Figure 6.5). Those who used a narrative-chaining technique recalled 93 percent of the words (on average), whereas those who did not organize the words recalled only 13 percent. The message is clear and consistent with what we've learned so far: organizing unrelated words into sensible stories helps us remember them.

imagery a memory strategy that involves forming mental images to improve memory

Forming *mental images* can also improve memory. Using **imagery** at encoding to improve retrieval has proven to be very helpful in many different circumstances (Begg & Paivio, 1969; Marschark et al., 1987; Paivio, 1971, 1986). It is Paivio's contention that visual images provide a unique way of encoding meaningful information; that is, we are at an advantage when we can encode not only what a stimulus means, but also what it looks like. Imagery helps us retrieve words such as *horse, rainbow,* and *typewriter* more readily than words such as *treason, session,* and *effort*—even when the frequency and meaningfulness of the words are equated.

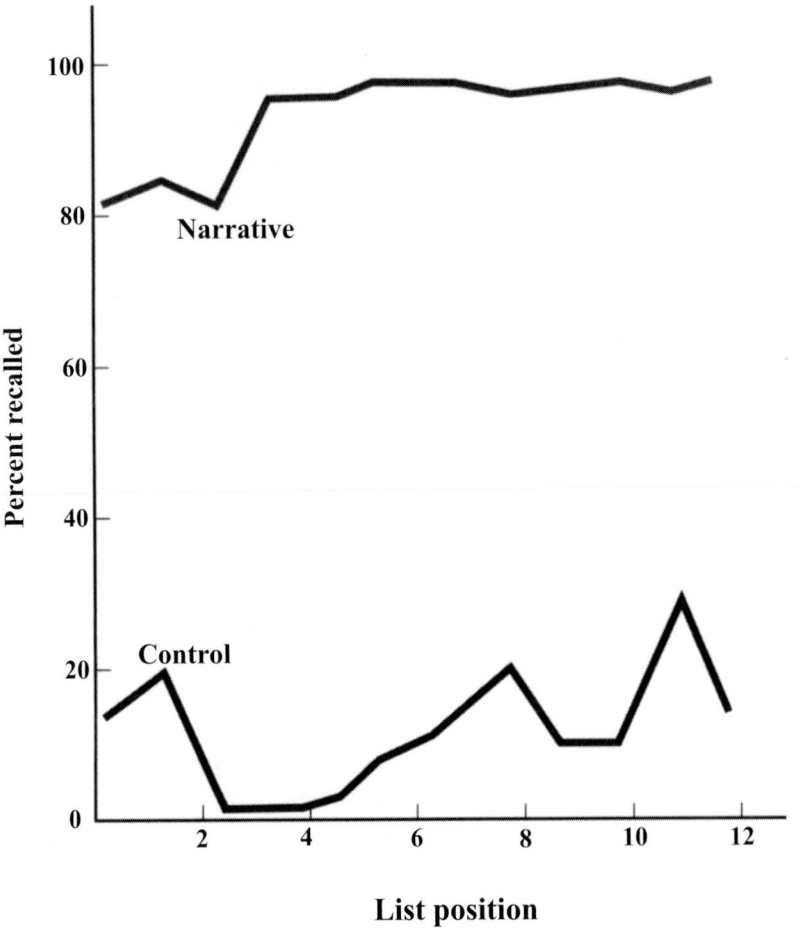

List position

FIGURE 6.5

Percent correct recall for words from twelve lists learned under two study, or encoding, conditions. In the narrative condition, students made up short stories to relate the words meaningfully, whereas in the control condition, simple memorization without any specific mnemonic device was used (Bower & Clark, 1969).

Assume that you have to learn the meanings of a large number of Spanish words. You could use simple rote repetition, but this technique is tedious and not very efficient. Atkinson (1975) suggested that to improve memory for foreign language vocabulary, it is useful to imagine some connection visually tying the two words together. He calls this the *key word method* of study. The Spanish word for "horse," for example, is *caballo,* which is pronounced *cab-eye-yo.* To remember this association, you might choose *eye* as the key word and picture a horse actually kicking someone in the eye. Or, if you are not prepared to be that gruesome, you might imagine a horse with a very large eye. The Spanish word for "duck" is *pato.* Here your key word might be *pot,* and you'd picture a duck wearing a pot on its head (Figure 6.6) or sitting in a large pot on the stove. This may sound strange, but research suggests that it works very well (Pressley et al., 1982).

The same basic technique works whenever you need to remember any paired items. Gordon Bower (1972), for example, asked students to learn lists of pairs of English words. Some students were instructed to form mental images that showed an interaction between the two words. One pair, for instance, was *piano-cigar.* Recall for word pairs was much better for those students who formed mental images than for those who did not.

Given the power of mental imagery, is it true that the more strange and bizarre the image, the better you will be able to recall it? Although some research suggests that common, interactive images are more useful than strange and bizarre ones (Bower, 1970; Wollen et al., 1972), recent research shows that bizarre images work better than common ones (Worthen, 1997, Worthen & Marshall, 1996). For example, Worthen (1997) found that recall was better when a bizarre image was used (for example a cat with a bowl hovering over its tail) than when a more common image (a cat drinking from a bowl) was used. This was true regardless of whether subjects generated their own mental images or had them provided for them. So, to remember the *piano-cigar* pair, it is probably more useful to picture a piano smoking a cigar than a cigar placed on a piano. It may sound silly, but it works.

The last imagery-related mnemonic device may be the oldest. It is attributed to the Greek poet Simonides and is called the *method of loci* (Yates, 1966). The idea here is to get in your mind a well-known location (loci are locations); say, the floor plan of your house or apartment. Visually place the material you are trying to recall in various places throughout your house in a sensible order. When the time comes for you to retrieve the material, mentally walk through your chosen locations, recalling the information you have stored at each place. (This is the technique referred to at the very beginning of this chapter.)

Mnemonic devices don't have to be formal techniques with special names. You used a mnemonic trick to learn which months of the year had 30 days and which had 31 when you learned the ditty "Thirty days hath September, April, June, and November. All the rest have…." Some students originally learned the colors of the rainbow (we called it the visible spectrum) in order by remembering the name "ROY G. BIV," which we grant you isn't terribly meaningful, but it does help us remember "red, orange, yellow, green, blue, indigo, and violet." Our guess is that you can think of several mnemonic devices you have used to organize and make meaningful material to be learned. In each case, the message is that when we can organize otherwise unrelated material in a meaningful way,

FIGURE 6.6

An illustration of how the key word method can be used to help foreign language retrieval. The Spanish word for "duck" is *pato,* pronounced "pot-oh" (Atkinson, 1975).

retrieval will be enhanced. However, the benefit of such devices may be temporary. For example, while one of the authors (Bordens) was in college, he learned the names of the cranial nerves for a biology class. Each nerve's name was attached to the first letter of the following ditty: "On old Olympus' towering tops, a fat American German viewed some hops." To this day, he can recall the ditty. Unfortunately, the names of most of the cranial nerves are gone.

The Role of Schemas

The encoding specificity principle tells us that how we retrieve information is affected by how we encoded it. One of the processes that influences how we encode and retrieve information is our use of schemas. A **schema** is an internal, organized, general knowledge system stored in long-term memory (Mayer, 1983). Schemas come in a variety of forms. A *person schema* helps us organize information about the characteristics of people (for example, attractiveness or weight) and store them in memory. A *role schema* includes information and expectations about how individuals in certain roles should behave. For example, when a person is in the role of "professor," that person is expected to come to class and present material, give and grade exams, and assign final grades. *Event schemas* (or *scripts*) house our ideas about how events occur. For example, you have an idea of what should happen at a basketball game or ballet performance.

schema an organized mental representation of the world that is adaptive and formed by experience

Generally, schemas help us organize information about various aspects of our world. They help us remember things by allowing us to organize related information together and activate that information when needed. Generally, information for which we have a schema is remembered better than information for which we have no schema. Additionally, schemas direct our search for new information (Neisser, 1976). We pay more attention to information that is consistent with an existing schema than information that is not.

Sir Frederic Bartlett, who first used the term in the context of memory, saw schemas as an organized part of our memories that held what we knew about some aspect of the world and guided our expectations about it (Bartlett, 1932). Schemas give us a general framework to understand new information and to remember or retrieve that information later (Alba & Hasher, 1983; Lord, 1980).

You may never have learned to play chess. However, you undoubtedly know what a chessboard looks like and you could probably name most of the pieces. You know that there are restrictions on how pieces can be moved in a chess game, but you don't know what those restrictions are. In other words, you have a very sketchy schema for chess. If we were to show you a chessboard with the pieces positioned as if in the midst of a game and then later asked you to reconstruct what you had seen, you would probably do very poorly. When chess experts are shown the board and are later asked to reconstruct the positions of the pieces from memory, they do very well (DeGroot, 1965, 1966). Part of the explanation for their success is that they have a complete, detailed schema for chess games, which helps them encode and later retrieve the positions of the pieces on the board. When chess pieces are positioned *randomly* on a chessboard (not consistent with the rules of the game), the memory of chess experts for the location of the pieces is no

Having a complex, complete schema for chess makes it easier to recall the position of pieces on a chess board—so long as the position of the pieces reflects a true game situation. If pieces are placed randomly on a board, the chess-playing schema will be of little value.

better than yours or that of other novices (Chase & Simon, 1973). This is because the randomly positioned pieces don't fit the experts' schemas for chess, taking away their advantage. A detailed schema is not necessarily going to help one's retrieval unless the retrieval task takes advantage of the information stored in that schema (Brewer & Nakamura, 1984). This result has been found for expertise in several areas, including computer programming (Adelson, 1984) and medicine (Norman et al., 1989).

Think in terms of your memory. If I ask you to tell me all of the details of your last trip to the dentist, won't you rely heavily on your knowledge of what it is like to go to the dentist in general— your schema? You'll supplement the recall of your last specific visit by adding whatever details you can.

BEFORE YOU GO ON

- How does the meaningfulness of information affect memory?

- What is a mnemonic device?

- How do narrative chaining, imagery, and the method of loci help improve memory?

- How do schemas affect retrieval?

HOW WE SCHEDULE PRACTICE

As we've seen repeatedly, retrieval, no matter how it is measured, depends on how one goes about encoding, rehearsing, or practicing information in the first place. Retrieval is a function of the *amount* of practice and how that practice is spaced or *distributed*. One of the reasons some students do not do as well on classroom exams as they would like is that they simply do not have (or make) enough time to study or practice the material covered on exams. Another reason is that some students do not schedule wisely what time they do have.

Overlearning

overlearning the practice, or rehearsal, of material over and above what is needed to learn it

Once we decide to learn something we read, practice, and study the material until we know it. We study until we are satisfied that we have encoded and stored the information in our memories, and then we quit. In other words, we often fail to engage in **overlearning**, the process of practicing or rehearsing material over and above what is needed to learn it. Consider this example, and see if you can extend this evidence to your own study habits.

A student comes to the laboratory to learn a list of syllables such as *dax, wuj, pib,* and *zuw.* There are 15 items on the list, and the material has to be presented repeatedly before our student can recall all of the items correctly. Having correctly recalled the items once, our student is dismissed with instructions to return two weeks later for a test of his recall of the syllables. Not surprisingly, he does not fare very well on the retrieval task.

What do you think would have happened if we had continued to present the list of syllables at the time of learning, well beyond the point at which it was first learned? Let's say the list was learned in 12 trials. We have the student practice the list for six additional presentations (50 percent overlearning—practice that is 50 percent over and above that required for learning). What if we required an additional 12 trials of practice (100 percent overlearning), or an additional 48 trials of practice (400 percent overlearning)?

The effects of overlearning are well documented and very predictable. The recall data for this imaginary experiment might look like those in Figure 6.7. Note three things about these data: (1) If we measure retrieval at various times after learning, forgetting is rather impressive and quite sudden, (This is one of the results of research on memory reported by Ebbinghaus in 1885.) (2) Overlearning improves retrieval and has its greatest effects with longer retention intervals, and (3) There is a "diminishing returns" phenomenon present; that is, 50 percent overlearning is much more useful than no overlearning; 100 percent overlearning is somewhat better than 50 percent; and 400 percent overlearning is better than 100 percent, but not by very much. For any learning task, or individual, there is probably an optimum amount of overlearning. How a person *schedules* practice or learning time is also an important factor in determining the likelihood of retrieval, and it is to this issue we turn next.

Scheduling, or Spacing, Practice

Some of the oldest data in psychology tell us that retrieval will be improved if practice (encoding) is spread out over time with rest intervals spaced in between. The data in Figure 6.8 are fairly standard. In fact, this experiment, first performed in 1946, provides such reliable results that it is commonly used as a student project in psychology classes. The

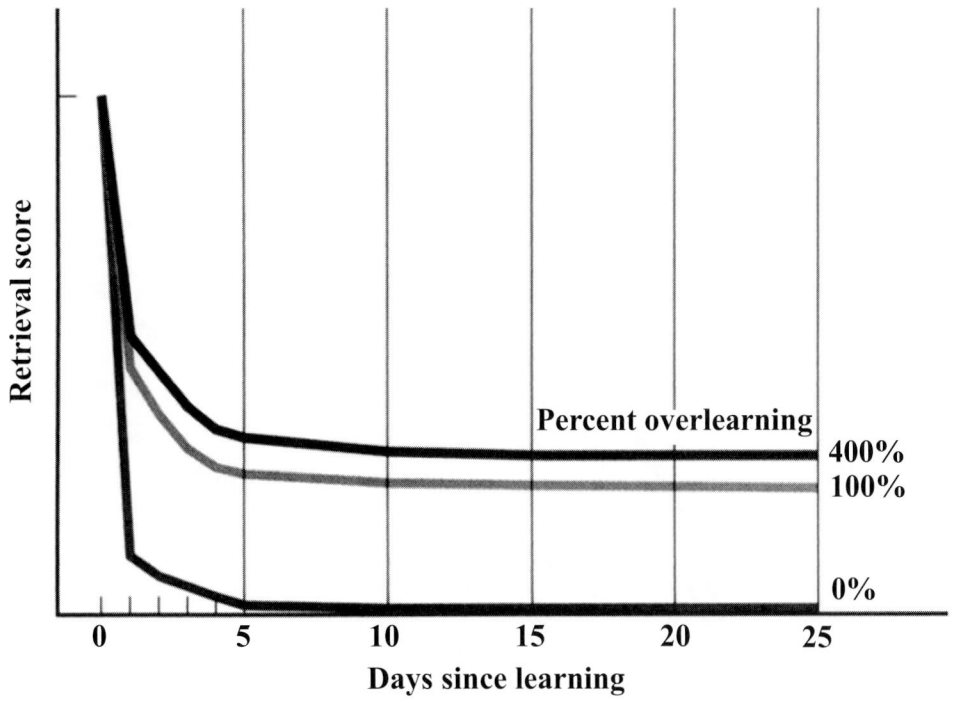

FIGURE 6.7

Idealized data showing the short-term and long-term advantages of overlearning. Note the "diminished returns" with additional overlearning (Krueger, 1929).

task is to write the letters of the alphabet, upside down and from right to left. (If you think that sounds easy, give it a try.)

Subjects are given the opportunity to practice the task under four conditions. The *massed-practice* group works with no break between trials. The three *distributed-practice* groups receive the same amount of practice, but get rest intervals interspersed between each one-minute trial. One group gets a three-to five-second rest between trials, a second group receives a 30-second rest, and a third group gets a 45-second rest between trials.

As we can see in Figure 6.8, subjects in all four groups begin at about the same (poor) level of performance. After 20 minutes of practice, the performance of all groups shows improvement, but by far, the massed practice (no rest) group does the poorest, and the 45-second rest group does the best.

The conclusion from years of research is that, almost without exception, distributed practice is superior to massed practice. There are exceptions, however. Some tasks may suffer from having rest intervals inserted in practice time. In general, whenever you must keep track of many things at the same time, you should mass your practice until you have finished what you are working on. If, for example, you are working on a complex math

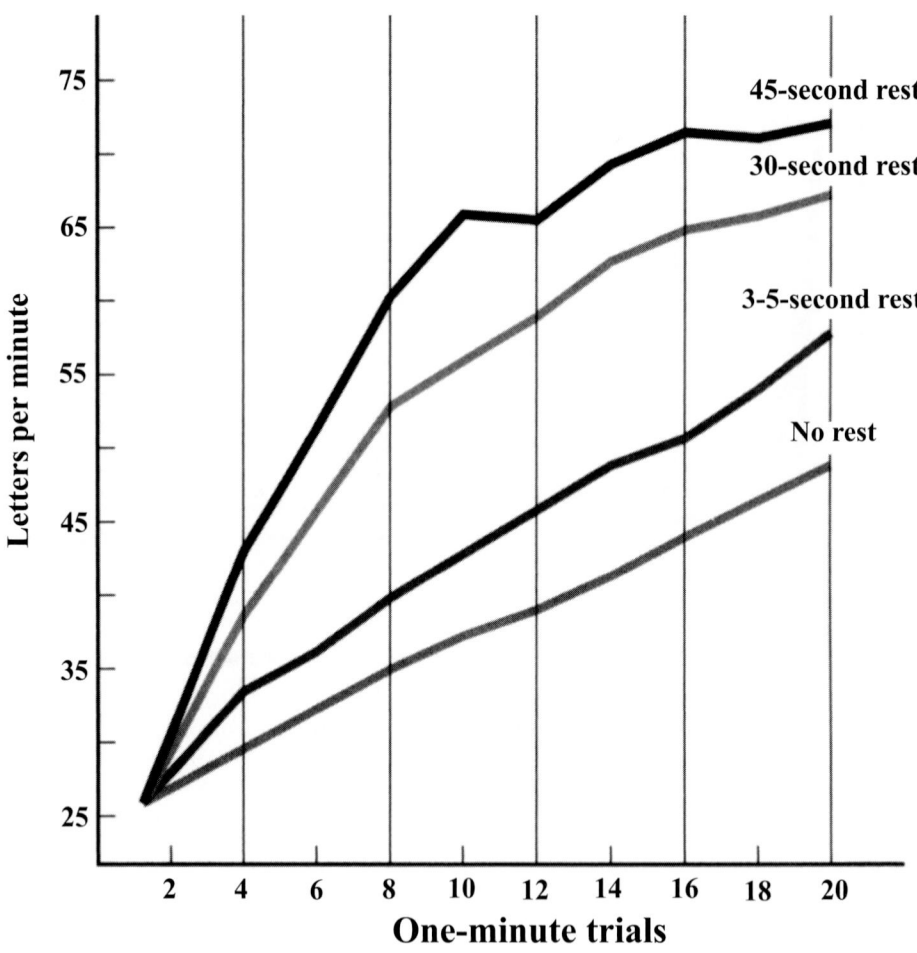

FIGURE 6.8

Improvement in performance as a function of the distribution of practice time. The task involved was printing the letters of the alphabet upside-down and backward with 20 one-minute trials separated by rest intervals of various lengths (Kientzle, 1946).

problem, you should work it through until you find a solution, whether it's time for a break or not. And, of course, you should not break up your practice in such a way as to disrupt the meaningfulness of the material you are studying.

BEFORE YOU GO ON

- What is overlearning, and how does it affect retrieval?

- What are massed and distributed practice?

- How does spacing practice affect learning and memory?

What we're talking about here is the scheduling of study time. The message is always the same: short (and meaningful) study periods with rest periods interspersed are more efficient than study periods massed together. There may be times when cramming is better than not studying at all, but as a general strategy, cramming is inefficient.

HOW WE OVERCOME INTERFERENCE

Think back to when you were in third grade. Can you remember the name of the student who sat behind you at school? Most of us can't. You can guess who it might have been, but there seems to be no way you can directly access and retrieve that piece of information from long-term memory with certainty. One possibility is that information is simply no longer there. It may, in some literal sense, be lost forever. Perhaps you never encoded that name in a way that would allow you to retrieve it effectively. Another possibility is that the name of that student *is* available in memory, but inaccessible at the moment because you have been in so many classes since third grade. So much has happened and entered your memory since third grade that the material you are looking for is "covered up" and being interfered with by information that entered later.

How about your most recent class? Can you recall who sat behind you in your last class? That may be a little easier, but remembering that name with confidence is still not easy. Again, our basic retrieval problem may be one of interference. Assuming that what we are searching for is still there, we may not be able to retrieve it because so many previous experiences are getting in the way, interfering with retrieval.

Retroactive Interference

The idea that interference can account for retrieval failure is an old one in psychology. Some early experiments, for example, demonstrated that subjects who were active for a period after learning remembered what they had learned less well than did subjects who used the intervening period for sleep (Jenkins & Dallenbach, 1924). The graphs in Figure 6.9 show reasonably comparable data from two experiments, one with college students

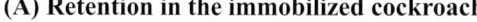
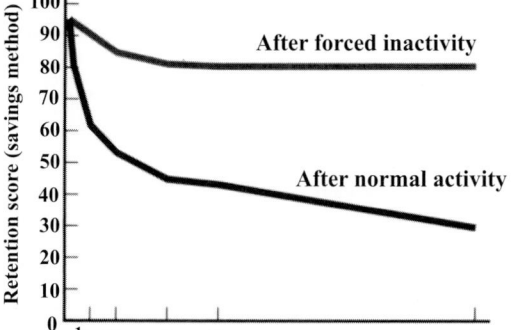
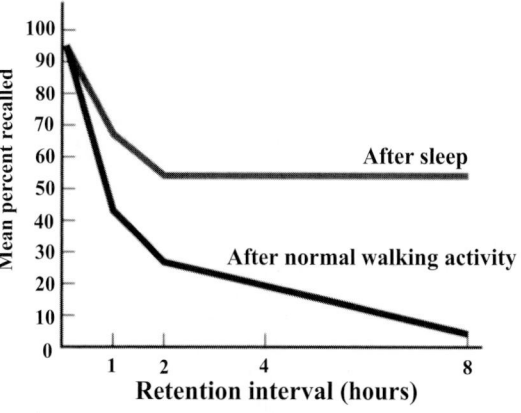

FIGURE 6.9

These graphs illustrate how activity following learning can interface with the retrieval of the learned behavior or materials. In both cases, normal waking activity caused more interference than did forced inactivity (for cockroaches) or sleeping (for college students) (Minami & Dallenbach, 1946).

who had learned a list of nonsense syllables, and the other with cockroaches that had learned to avoid an area of their cage. In both cases, subjects who engaged in normal waking activity did more poorly on tests of retrieval over all retention intervals.

When interfering activities come *after* the learning that is to be remembered or retrieved, we have **retroactive interference**. Let's go back into the laboratory. (You can follow along with the summary diagram in Figure 6.10). Students are randomly assigned to either a control group or an experimental group. Students in both groups are required to learn something (almost anything will do; we'll assume it's a list of nonsense syllables). Having learned their lists, the groups are treated differently. Students in the experimental group are now required to learn something else, perhaps a new list of nonsense syllables. At the same time, control group subjects are asked to do nothing (which is impossible, of course, in a literal sense). They might be asked to rest quietly or to play some simple game.

Now for the test. Both groups are asked to remember whatever was presented in the first learning task. Students in the control group will show a higher retrieval score than students in the experimental group. For the experimental group, the second set of learned material interferes with the retrieval of the material learned first. Figure 6.10 (A) summarizes this research design.

Most of us are familiar with retroactive interference from our own experiences. A student who studied French in high school takes a few Spanish courses in college and now can't remember very much French. The Spanish keeps getting in the way. Two students are scheduled to take a psychology test tomorrow morning at 9 A.M. Both are equally able and equally well motivated. One is taking only one class—the psychology class. She studies psychology for two hours, watches TV for two hours, and goes to bed.

retroactive interference the inhibition of retrieval of previously learned material caused by material learned later

(A) Retroactive interference

	Learn	Learn	Test
Experimental group	Task A	Task B	Retrieval of Task A
Control group	Task A	Nothing	Retrieval of Task A

(B) Proactive interference

	Learn	Learn	Test
Experimental group	Task A	Task B	Retrieval of Task B
Control group	Nothing	Task B	Retrieval of Task B

Note: If interference is operating, the control group will demonstrate better retrieval than will the experimental group.

FIGURE 6.10

Designs of Experiments to Demonstrate Retroactive Interference and Proactive Interference

She comes in the next morning to take the test. The second student also studies psychology for two hours, but then reads a chapter and a half from her sociology text, just in case she is called on in class. After reading sociology, she goes to bed, comes to class, and takes the test. Everything else being equal, this student will be at a disadvantage. The sociology she studied will retroactively interfere with her retrieval of the psychology she learned previously. What is this student to do? She has to study psychology, and she knows that she had better read her sociology, too. About all she can do is to set herself up for proactive interference.

Proactive Interference

Proactive interference occurs when *previously* learned material interferes with the retrieval of material learned later. First follow along in Figure 6.10 (B), then we'll get back to our student and her studying problem. We have two groups of students, experimental and control. The experimental group again starts by learning something—that same list of syllables, perhaps. This time the control group students begin by resting quietly while the experimental group goes through the learning task. Both groups then learn a new list of syllables. We test for retrieval, but this time we test for the retrieval of the more recently learned material. Again, the control group students have an advantage. They have none of that first list in their memories to interfere with retrieval. However, the advantage is not as great as it was in the case of retroactive interference. Proactive interference is not as detrimental as retroactive interference, which is why we would advise our student to study what she thinks is her most important assignment last.

proactive interference the inhibition of retrieval of recently learned material caused by material learned previously

Americans learn to drive on the right side of the road. If they find themselves in a country where one must drive on the left side of the road, interference effects from previous learning can be very powerful.

Although both retroactive and proactive interference are well documented, there are many factors that influence the extent of such interference (Underwood, 1957). For example, meaningful, well-organized material is less susceptible to interference than is less meaningful material, such as nonsense syllables. As a rule, the more similar the interfering material is to the material being retrieved, the greater will be the interference (McGeoch & McDonald, 1931). The student who had to study for a psychology test and read a sociology text will experience more interference (retroactive or proactive) than will a student who has to study for the psychology test and work calculus problems. In this context, we might suggest that working on calculus is rather like "doing nothing." We would make such a suggestion only in the sense that there is little about calculus to get in the way, or interfere, with the psychology lesson.

BEFORE YOU GO ON

- What is retroactive interference, and how does it affect retrieval?

- What is proactive interference, and how does it affect retrieval?

Topic Review 6 B

1. **What is meant by a direct or explicit measure of memory?**

   An explicit, or direct, measure of memory involves a person consciously or purposively retrieving information from memory. Recall and recognition both qualify as explicit measures of memory.

2. **What is recall?**

   Recall involves asking a person to produce information to which he or she had been previously exposed. On a free recall task, an individual is asked to get as much information out of memory as possible in any order (for example, answering the question "What did you have for breakfast yesterday?"). Serial recall requires an individual to recall information in the same order in which it was learned (for example, recalling the months of the year). Cued recall involves providing a person with a retrieval cue (for example, the first word from a word pair) for what is to be recalled (the second word from a word pair). Recall is a one-step process involving going into memory and pulling out as much information as possible.

3. **What is recognition?**

   Recognition is a direct measure of memory in which we actually provide the information to be retrieved and ask that it be identified as familiar. Recognition is a two-step process involving retrieving information and then comparing it to what is to be recognized. A decision must be made as to whether the information has been seen before.

4. **Is recall or recognition a more sensitive measure of memory?**

   Retrieval measured by recognition is generally superior to retrieval measured by recall. We can often recognize things that we cannot recall.

5. **Are there any similarities between recognition and recall?**

   Despite the differences between recall and recognition, there are some points of overlap. First, both involve retrieval of information from semantic or episodic memory. Second, similar brain processes are involved in recall and recognition.

6. **What are implicit measures of memory?**

   Implicit tests of memory assess the extent to which previously experienced material is helpful in subsequent tasks. Implicit tests of memory do not require conscious efforts to recall information. For example, relearning shows us that even when information can be neither recalled nor recognized, it will be easier to relearn than it was to learn in the first place.

7. **What is relearning?**

   Relearning is the change in performance when a person is required to learn material for a second time. Relearning almost always requires fewer trials than the original learning because some of the previously learned material is still in memory. Relearning is an indirect measure of memory because no conscious effort to recall the original material is required.

8. **How does the context in which one encodes information affect the retrieval of that information?**

   The greater the extent to which the cues or context available at retrieval match the cues or context available at encoding, the better retrieval will be. Even matching a person's state of mind at encoding and retrieval may improve retrieval. Heightened emotionality at encoding may also produce memories that seem more vivid than others, even if they are not more accurate.

9. **What is the encoding specificity principle?**

   The encoding specificity principle suggests that we not only encode what we are trying to learn, but also encode aspects about the place where the learning took place. Recall for information should be easier if memory is tested in the place where learning took place rather than another, unfamiliar place.

10. **What is state-dependent memory?**

    State-dependent memory means that the ability to retrieve information depends on a person's state of mind when the information was encoded. For example, if you lose your keys while drunk, it would be easier to find them if you were again drunk. Mood has also been found to be a state that affects memory. If one's mood at the time of retrieval matches one's mood at the time of encoding, memory is better than if there is a mismatch, especially for females.

11. What are flashbulb memories?

Flashbulb memories are unusually clear and vivid memories for events that are of great importance. For example, many people can remember quite vividly where they were when they heard about the bombing in Oklahoma City. Although these memories are clear and vivid, there is no reason to assume that they are any more complete or accurate than any other memories.

12. How is "meaningfulness" related to retrieval?

Meaningfulness reflects the extent to which material is associated with, or related to, information already stored in memory. In general, the more meaningful the material, the easier it will be to retrieve. Meaningfulness resides in the individual and not in the material to be learned.

13. What is a mnemonic device?

Mnemonics are specific encoding techniques that can help us retrieve information. They help us organize and add meaningfulness to new information by taking advantage of existing memories.

14. How do narrative chaining, mental imagery, and the method of loci help memory?

In general, mnemonic devices are strategies used at encoding to organize and increase the meaningfulness of material to be retrieved. Narrative chaining involves making up a story that meaningfully weaves together otherwise unorganized words or information. Forming mental images, or "pictures in one's mind," of to-be-remembered information is also helpful. Sensible, interactive images seem to work best. The method of loci is an imagery method in which one "places" pieces of information at various locations (loci) in a familiar setting and then retrieves those pieces of information while mentally traveling through the setting.

15. What is a schema?

A schema is an internal, organized, general knowledge system stored in long-term memory. Schemas influence how we encode and retrieve information.

16. What are the different types of schemas?

Schemas come in a variety of forms. A person's schema helps organize information about the characteristics of people (for example, attractiveness or weight) and store them in memory. A role schema includes information and expectations about how individuals in certain roles should behave. An event schema (or script) houses ideas about how events occur.

17. How do schemas affect retrieval?

Schemas are organized, general knowledge systems stored in LTM. Based on past experiences, schemas summarize the essential features of common events or situations. They are used to guide the organization of and give meaning to new information. The more relevant one's available schemas for to-be-remembered information, the better encoding and retrieval will be.

18. How does overlearning affect retrieval? How does distributing one's practice affect retrieval?

Overlearning is the rehearsal or practice of material above and beyond that necessary for immediate recall. Within limits, the more one overlearns, the greater the likelihood of accurate retrieval. In massed practice, study or rehearsal continues without intervening rest intervals. Distributed practice uses shorter segments of rehearsal interspersed with rest intervals. In almost all cases, distributed practice is superior to massed practice.

19. What are retroactive interference and proactive interference?

Retroactive interference occurs when material or information cannot be retrieved because it is inhibited or blocked by material or information learned later. Proactive interference occurs when information cannot be retrieved because it is inhibited or blocked by material or information learned earlier. Retroactive interference is typically more detrimental to retrieval than is proactive interference.

Chapter 7
Intelligence, Language, and Problem Solving

$\mathcal{H}$e was a most intelligent person. His colleagues in the psychology department called him "Ted," but because his initials were E.E., he was also called "E^2." No disrespect was intended; it somehow seemed fitting. His teaching specialty was "multivariate statistical analysis," an advanced course in correlational methods. There was no text for this class. Every day, E^2 wrote out the text in class on the blackboards he had installed to encircle the room. In truth, few students followed all of his reasoning, as he derived formulas from one blackboard to another. From time to time his eyes would sparkle, and he seemed to no longer notice where he was. He sometimes muttered something to himself, "No, that shouldn't be r, it should be capital R. No, no. It should be R ! Yes, that's it, R !" And off he'd go writing his equations on the board faster than anyone could copy, much less comprehend.

Over his sixty-year career, he authored scores of scientific articles and wrote several books. None of his students will ever forget his brilliance. Nor will anyone tire of telling "E^2 stories," such as the time he and his wife (also a well-respected psychologist) traveled to a psychology convention two states away. When the meetings were over, E^2 got in his car and drove home, leaving his wife behind, apparently forgetting that she had accompanied him. On several other occasions he would "get lost" in his equations, toss a lighted cigarette into the trash, start a fire in the wastebasket, and continue without pause, as someone carried the flaming receptacle out of the room. One dreary morning, he left his car lights on and had locked the car doors. When someone told him about it, he said thanks, put on his topcoat, and left the office. About 45 minutes later, his phone rang and it was E^2, calling from home. He could not remember why he had gone home. You see, when E^2 put on his coat, left his office, and got in his car, he went home. Now he was confused because it was only 9:00 in the morning.

We cannot think of a better example of an "absentminded professor." Memories of E^2 and the stories about him also reinforce the point that intelligence is a multifaceted concept. One can be "intelligent" in one area (multivariate statistics) yet seemingly less than intelligent in others.

Topic 7A INTELLIGENCE

In this Topic, we focus on the most complex of all cognitive processes: intelligence. We will find that even defining the concept of intelligence is difficult. We'll look at how intelligence is measured, and we'll end the Topic by examining group and individual differences in measured intelligence.

Key Questions to Answer

While reading this Topic, find the answers to the following key questions:

1.   How is intelligence defined?

2.   How did Spearman, Thurstone, Guilford, and Vernon define intelligence?

3.   How did Sternberg and Gardner define intelligence?

4.   What is emotional intelligence?

5.   How do Western and non-Western concepts of intelligence differ?

6.   What is the definition of a psychological test?

7.   What determines the quality of psychological tests?

8.   What is the Stanford-Binet intelligence test?

9.   What are crystallized and fluid-analytic abilities?

10.   What is the intelligence quotient?

11.   What are the major features of the Wechsler intelligence scales?

12.   What is the difference between a paper-and-pencil intelligence test and an aptitude test?

13.   Are there gender differences in IQ?

14.   Does intelligence increase, decrease, or remain the same with increasing age?

15.   What are fluid and crystallized intelligence?

16.   Are there racial differences in IQ scores?

17.   What is a stereotype threat and how does it relate to racial differences in IQ?

18.   What defines the mentally gifted?

19.   How do we define mental retardation?

20.   What are the causes of mental retardation?

JUST WHAT *IS* INTELLIGENCE?

Intelligence is a troublesome concept in psychology. We all know what we mean when we use the word, but we have a terrible time trying to define intelligence concisely. We wonder if John's failure in school is due to his lack of intelligence or to some other factor. You may argue that locking my keys in the car was not very intelligent. We may claim that a student with any intelligence can see the difference between positive and negative reinforcement. In this section, we'll develop a working definition of intelligence, and then we'll review some of the ways in which psychologists have described the concept.

To guide our study through this Topic, we will accept two definitions of **intelligence**, one academic and theoretical, the other operational and practical. For our theoretical definition of intelligence, we will use the one offered by David Wechsler: "The capacity of an individual to understand the world about him [or her] and his [or her] resourcefulness to cope with its challenges" (1975, p. 139). This definition, and others like it, sounds sensible at first, but it does present some ambiguities. What does "capacity" mean in this context? What is meant by "understand the world"? What if the world never really challenges one's "resourcefulness"? Would such people be considered less intelligent?

intelligence One of the most difficult concepts in psychology to define. A theoretical definition is that intelligence is the capacity to understand one's world and one's resourcefulness to cope with it. Another definition is that intelligence is what intelligence tests measure.

We have suggested that defining concepts operationally can help us deal with conceptually abstract concepts. We have to be careful here, but, as E.G. Boring put it in 1923, "Intelligence is what the intelligence tests measure" (Hunt, 1995, p. 356). Before we get to a discussion of intelligence tests, it will be helpful to spend a bit of time reviewing some of the ways in which psychologists have described intelligence. Although there are some difficulties with Wechsler's definition, most psychologists today take a similar approach to intelligence, emphasizing adaptation, problem solving, and finding ways to meet one's goals (Das, 1973; Matthews, 1997; Sternberg, 1988).

Classic Models of Intelligence

Theoretical models of intelligence are attempts to categorize and organize cognitive or intellectual abilities into groupings that make sense. In a way, they are sophisticated attempts to provide a definition for "intelligence." British psychologist Charles Spearman was one of the pioneers of mental testing and the inventor of many statistical procedures used to analyze test scores. Spearman's characterization of intelligence came from his inspection of scores earned by people on a wide range of psychological tests designed to measure cognitive skills. What impressed Spearman was that no matter what cognitive ability a specific test was designed to measure, some people always seemed to do better than others. People who scored high on some tests tended to score high on all the tests. It seemed as if there was an intellectual power that facilitated performance in general, whereas variations in performance reflected strengths and weaknesses for specific tasks.

g-factor (g) general intelligence; a global measure of intellectual abilities

Spearman (1904) concluded that intelligence consists of two things: a general intelligence, called a **g-factor**, and a collection of specific cognitive skills, or **s-factors**. Spearman believed that "g" was independent of knowledge, of content—it went beyond knowing facts. It involved the ability to understand and apply relationships in all content

s-factors specific cognitive or intellectual skills; in Spearman's theory, part of intelligence in addition to "g"

areas. In this view, everyone has some degree of general intelligence (which Spearman thought was inherited), and everyone has specific skills that are useful in some tasks but not in others. A controversy remains over the extent to which "g" is an all-important, sometimes-important, or never-important factor in intelligence (Barrett & Depinet, 1991; Helms, 1992; Hunt, 1995; Ree & Earles, 1992; Sternberg & Wagner, 1993; McClelland, 1973, 1993). Still, looking at intelligence in terms of what a variety of tests measure and how such measures are interrelated became a popular way to think about intelligence.

When L.L. Thurstone examined correlations among various tests of cognitive abilities he administered, he found something different from what Spearman had found. Thurstone (1938) saw little or no evidence to support the notion of a general g-factor of intellectual ability. Instead, he claimed that abilities fall into seven categories, which he called the seven **primary mental abilities** (Figure 7.1). Thurstone argued that each factor in his model is independent, and to know one's intelligence requires that you know how one fares on all seven factors.

With the model of J.P. Guilford (1967), matters get more complicated than with either Spearman's or Thurstone's theory. Guilford claimed that intelligence can be ana-

primary mental abilities in Thurstone's model, the seven distinct abilities that constitute intelligence

Verbal comprehension (V) —	the ability to understand ideas, concepts, and words, as in a vocabulary test
Number (N) —	the ability to use numbers to solve problems quickly and accurately
Spatial relations (S) —	the ability to visualize and manipulate patterns and forms in space, as in the ability to recognize an object viewed from a different perspective
Perceptual speed (P) —	the ability to determine quickly and accurately whether or not two complex stimuli are identical or in some way different
Word fluency (W) —	the ability to use words quickly and fluently, as in the ability to solve anagrams and produce rhymes
Memory (M) —	the ability to remember lists of materials, such as digits, letters, or words presented previously
Inductive reasoning —	the ability to discover a general rule from presented information, to discover relationships, as in, "What number comes next? 2, 4, 6, 8, –"

Thurstone, 1938.

FIGURE 7.1

Thurstone's Seven Primary Mental Abilities

lyzed as three intersecting dimensions. Guilford said that any intellectual task can be described in terms of the mental *operations* used in the task, the *content* of the material involved, and the *product* or outcome of the task. Each of these three dimensions has a number of possible values. There are five operations, four contents, and six possible products. The three dimensions of this model, and their values, are found in Figure 7.2.

If you study Figure 7.2, you will see that there are 120 possible combinations of content, operations, and products in Guilford's model. (In 1988, Guilford increased the possible number of combinations to 150 by coming up with two memory operations. His basic logic remained the same.) Just to give you an idea of how this system works, let's choose one of the "cells" depicted in Figure 7.2—where cognition, figural, and units intersect (the little "block" in the uppermost left corner). What would this intellectual skill be like? Guilford says it's a matter of recognizing (cognitive) diagrams or pictures (figural) of simple, well-defined elements (units). To test this ability, one might be shown an incomplete drawing of a simple object and be asked to identify it as quickly as possible.

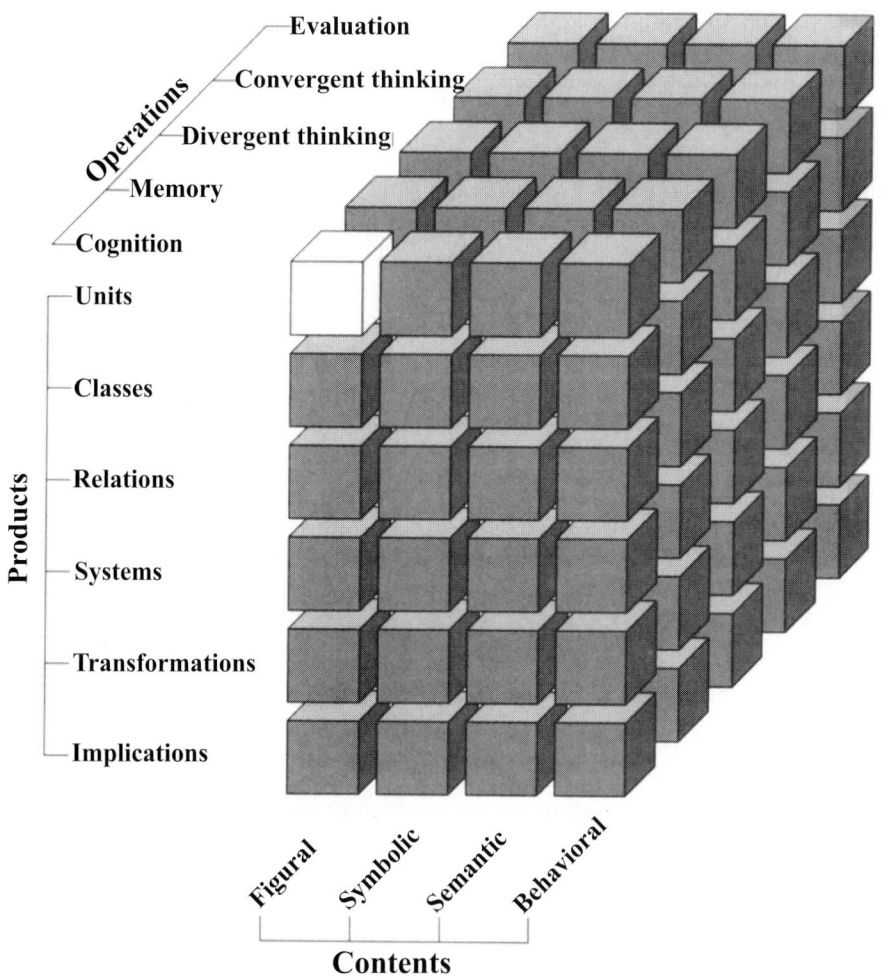

FIGURE 7.2

Guilford's model of intelligence. In this model, there are three major divisions (contents, products, and operations), each with its own subdivisions. Each subdivision may interact with all others, yielding 120 specific intellectual skills or abilities (Guilford, 1967).

Philip Vernon (1960, 1979) suggests we think of intelligence as a collection of skills and abilities arranged in a hierarchy (Figure 7.3). At the top is a general cognitive ability similar to Spearman's "g." Under it are two factors; one is a verbal, academic sort of intelligence, whereas the other is a mechanical, practical sort. Either of these, in turn, is thought of as consisting of yet more specific intellectual skills. The verbal-academic skill, for example, consists of numerical and verbal abilities, among others. Each of these can be broken down further (verbal skills include word usage and vocabulary, for instance); and then further still because vocabulary includes knowing synonyms and antonyms. Seeing intelligence as including a general factor and a structured set of specific factors gives us a model that combines some of the thinking of Spearman, Thurstone, and Guilford.

BEFORE YOU GO ON

- How is intelligence defined?
- Briefly describe the classic models of intelligence.

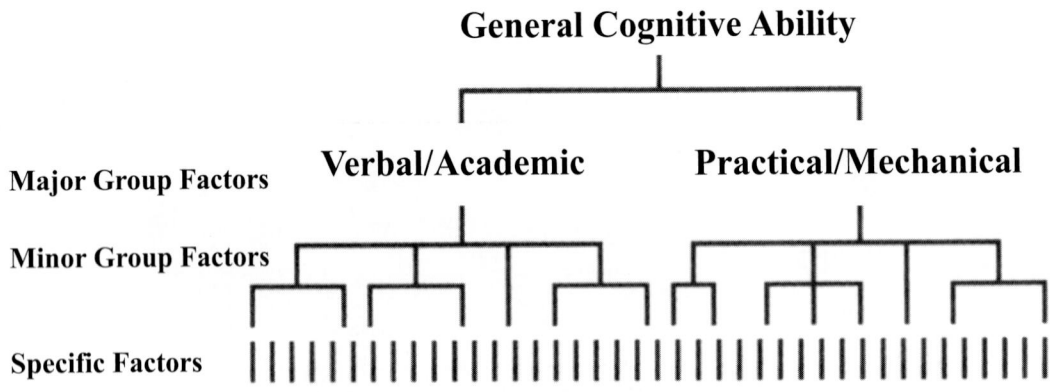

FIGURE 7.3

According to Philip Vernon, intellectual abilities may be represented in a hierarchy from very general intellectual skills at the top to very specific abilities at the bottom (Vernon, 1960).

Contemporary Models of Intelligence

During the past 20 years, theories about intelligence have taken a different approach than those we've reviewed so far. First, they assume that intelligence is a multidimensional concept. Second, they view intelligence as an active processing of information rather than a "thing" that one either has or doesn't have to some degree.

Robert Sternberg (1979, 1988, 1990) is a cognitive psychologist who views intelligence as multifaceted. He focuses on how one *uses* one's intellectual abilities rather than trying to describe a particular set of skills or talents. Sternberg sees one sort of intelligent behavior as a reflection of three different processes, or components . He calls this *componential intelligence,* which includes: (1) skills we bring to bear when we set about to solve a problem. "Just what is the problem here?" "How shall I get started?" "What will I need to see this through?" "How will I know when I've succeeded?"; (2) the skills we actually use in our attempt to solve problems—for example, when we work on a math

plied—this component of our cogni-
ues or strategies for collecting and
onstrating that one can profit from

dds two others. *Experiential intel-*
king. It is a measure of the extent
nd useful ways and is reflected in
ts, writers, actors, and scientists
ce is commonly referred to as
very good at getting along with
ions. It is a practical, nitty-gritty
of the extent to which one can
clearly, how one demonstrates
ure—and from one situation to
nce are not the sorts of things

A
t
h
d
"s
otl
set
ma
con
the
that

How.
peopl
of the
made
adds (
intellig

igence has been proposed by
1989). Gardner suggests that
nt ways (or in a combination
lastic, academic intelligence,
guistic abilities. To these he
ect or designer; (4) *musical*

intellig ... produce, but also to appreciate pitch, rhythm, tone, and
the subtleties of music; (5) *body/kinesthetic* intelligence—reflected in the ability to
control one's body and to handle objects, as one finds in skilled athletes and dancers; (6)
interpersonal intelligence—the ability to get along with others, and to "read other
people" (Rosnow et al., 1995); and (7) *intrapersonal* intelligence—required to understand one's own self, to realize one's strengths and weaknesses. Obviously, a person can
find success in life with any one (or more) of these multiple intelligences, but which are
valued the most depends on the demands of one's culture. Highly technological societies,
such as ours, value the first two types of intelligence. In cultures where one must climb
tall trees or hunt wild game for food, body/kinesthetic skills are valued—as they are in
the American subculture we identify as "professional athletics." Interpersonal skills are
valuable in cultures that emphasize family and group activities.

In the 1990s, John Mayer of the University of New Hampshire and Peter Salovey of
Yale University introduced the term "emotional intelligence" into psychology's vocabulary (Mayer & Salovey, 1994, 1995, 1997; Mayer & Geher, 1996). The concept was an
immediate hit with the general public. It was discussed on television talk shows and in
the popular news magazines. Daniel Goleman's 1995 book on the topic, *Emotional
Intelligence*, became a non-fiction best seller. **Emotional intelligence** is characterized by
the ability to accurately perceive emotions, to generate emotion so as to assist thought, to
understand emotions, and to regulate emotions so as to promote better emotion and
thought.

emotional intelligence the
ability to perceive, generate,
and regulate emotions in
order to promote better emotional reactions and thoughts

Some people are successful in life, particularly in social situations, not because they are so "smart" in a cognitive, academic sense, but because they are good at controlling their own feelings and are sensitive to understanding the feelings of others. As you drive down a four-lane highway, you notice a sign warning of construction ahead and indicating that the left lane is closed. You move to the right lane. Whizzing by you and other drivers who have responded to the warning sign, a red car zips down the left lane until the very last minute; jogging back to the right just before hitting the barricades. Is this driver rude, aggressive, obnoxious and worthy of scorn and rage or did he or she simply not attend to the warning signs? Perhaps the driver was responding to an emergency. Being able to weigh such alternatives and monitor one's own response accordingly is a sign of emotional intelligence. A manager needs to discipline an employee. Doing so in a constructive way, without causing embarrassment, resentment, or anger would demonstrate emotional intelligence. There is little doubt that the concept of emotional intelligence (or EQ, as opposed to IQ) makes common sense. Can EQ be measured? Is it a scientifically useful term for assessing and predicting behavior? These questions are now under active research review (Ciarrochi, Chan, & Caputi, 2000; Davies, Stankov, & Roberts, 1998; Schutte, Malouff, et. Al., 1998).

Intelligence Across Cultures

The definitions and theories of intelligence we just reviewed have a decidedly *Western* flavor. The very concept of intelligence and intelligence testing is a Western invention, originating in Europe and the United States. However, Western ideas about intelligence are not always shared by non-Western cultures (Sternberg & Kaufman, 1998). For

Contemporary theories of intelligence (such as that proposed by Gardner) suggest that there are several ways in which intelligence can be manifested, including interpersonal intelligence (the ability to get along with others [A]), intrapersonal intelligence (the ability to introspect and understand one's self [B]), and kinesthetic intelligence (the ability to control one's body [C]).

example, the Western emphasis on speed of processing as an index of intelligence flies contrary to cultures that do not value such speed, and even value the opposite.

To illustrate how Western and non-Western cultures differ in how intelligence is conceptualized, consider how intelligence is defined and viewed in China. Yang and Sternberg (1997) found five factors underlying the Chinese concept of intelligence. These are (as listed by Sternberg & Kaufman, 1998):

- a general cognitive factor similar to Spearman's g-factor
- interpersonal intelligence
- intrapersonal intelligence
- intellectual self-assertion
- intellectual self-effacement

These five dimensions underlying the Chinese concept of intelligence are different from the Western concept of intelligence that emphasizes verbal ability, the ability to solve practical problems, and social competence (Sternberg & Kaufman, 1998). Sternberg and Kaufman also point out that cultural differences are not limited to American and Chinese cultures. African concepts of intelligence, centering on abilities that foster intragroup harmony and cooperation, differ from more technologically-based concepts of intelligence in the United States. These differences most likely reflect differences in what is valued within a culture.

What we have reviewed here is only a sampling of the theoretical approaches to intelligence that have been proposed over the years. None of these models has been tested fully enough to evaluate the extent to which it characterizes human intelligence. As is often the case when we are faced with multiple descriptions or explanations—it is important to keep an open mind and to select from each approach aspects that are best supported by the evidence.

Now that we have an idea of the sorts of theoretical issues psychologists have struggled with, we can turn our attention to tests of intelligence.

> ## BEFORE YOU GO ON
>
> - Briefly describe the contemporary models of intelligence.
> - How do Western and non-Western concepts of intelligence differ?
> - How is "emotional intelligence" different from "cognitive" or "academic" intelligence?

PSYCHOLOGICAL TESTS OF INTELLIGENCE

Just as there are several ways to define intelligence, so are there several ways to measure it. Most involve psychological tests. Although the focus of our discussion here is intelligence, we must recognize that psychological tests have been devised to measure the full range of human traits and abilities. For that reason, we start with a few words about tests in general.

Testing the Tests

A **psychological test** is an objective, standardized measure of a sample of behavior (Anastasi, 1988; Dahlstrom, 1993). Tests are used as an aid in the understanding and pre-

psychological test an objective, standardized measure of behavior

diction of behavior (Kaplan & Saccuzzo, 2001). A psychological test measures *behavior* because that is all we can measure. We cannot directly measure feelings, aptitudes, abilities, or intelligence. We can and do make inferences about such things on the basis of our measure of behavior, but we cannot measure them directly. Psychological tests can only measure a *sample* of one's behaviors. If we want to know about your tendency to be aggressive, we cannot very well ask you everything that relates to aggression in your life. We can sample (identify a portion of) the behaviors of interest. Then we assume that your responses to a sample of items predict, or are similar to, responses to unasked questions. Even a classroom final exam only asks you about a sample of the material you have learned.

A psychological test should also be *objective.* The objectivity of tests refers to the evaluation of the behaviors being measured. Several examiners (at least those with the same level of expertise) should give the same interpretation and evaluation to a test response. If the same responses to a psychological test lead one psychologist to say that a person is perfectly normal, a second to consider the person a mass of inner conflict, and a third to wonder why this person is not in a psychiatric institution, we have a problem, and it is probably with the objectivity of the test.

As a consumer and as a student of psychology, you should be able to assess the value or *quality* of a psychological test. The quality of a psychological test depends on the extent to which it has three characteristics: reliability, validity, and adequate norms.

reliability in psychological testing, the extent to which a test measures whatever it measures consistently

A test's **reliability** refers to its ability to produce the same or highly similar results across similar testing situations. Suppose someone gives you a test and on the basis of your responses claims that you have an IQ slightly below average—94, let's say. Three weeks later, you retake the same test and are told that your IQ is now 127, nearly in the top 3 percent of the population. We haven't yet discussed IQ scores, but we recognize that one's IQ as a measure of intelligence does not change by 33 points in a matter of three weeks.

validity in psychological testing, the extent to which a test measures what it claims to be measuring

When people worry about the usefulness of a test, their concern is usually with **validity**. Measures of validity tell us the extent to which a test actually measures what it claims to be measuring. It is the extent to which there is agreement between a test score and the quality or trait that the test is believed to measure (Kaplan & Saccuzzo, 2001). There are different forms of validity. *Face validity* is the lowest level of validity. One inspects the items on a test, and if the items cover a wide range of topics related to the behavior being evaluated, the test is said to have face validity. *Predictive validity* occurs when the results of a test predict a behavior known to be related to the construct being tested. For example, intelligence test scores should reliably predict (correlate with) school performance. With *concurrent validity*, validity is established by demonstrating that a test produces scores that correlate well with another established test in the area. Finally, *construct validity* involves the results of a test relating to a construct predicted by a theory. For example, if a theory of intelligence predicts that "intelligent" people are successful in life, then test scores must correlate highly with success. Although it may be acceptable to demonstrate validity in one way, the more dimensions along which a test is valid the better.

There is one more issue that we need to address: the adequacy of test norms. Suppose you have filled out a long paper-and-pencil questionnaire designed to measure the extent to which you are outgoing. You know that the test is a reliable and valid instrument. You are told that you scored a 50 on the test. So what? What does *that* mean? It does not mean that you answered 50 percent of the items correctly—on this test there are no correct or incorrect answers. The point is that if you don't have a basis of comparison, one test score by itself is meaningless. You need to compare your score with the scores of other people like yourself who have also taken the test. Results of a test taken by a large group of people whose scores are used to make comparisons are called **norms**. You may discover by checking the norms that a score of 50 is average, or it might indicate a very high or a very low level of extroversion.

norms in psychological testing, scores on a test taken by a large number of persons that can be used for making comparisons

As we review some of the psychological tests used to measure intelligence, keep in mind the many ways in which psychologists have described intelligence. Given the difficulty that psychologists have coming to any agreement on the nature of intelligence, you won't be surprised to learn that not all psychologists are pleased with the intelligence tests that are currently available.

BEFORE YOU GO ON

- What is a "psychological test"?
- What is the reliability of a psychological test?
- What is the validity of a psychological test?
- What is a norm?

The Stanford-Binet Intelligence Scale

Alfred Binet (1857–1911) was the leading psychologist in France early in the twentieth century. Of great concern in those days were children in the Paris school system who seemed unable to profit from the educational experiences they were being given. Binet and his collaborator, Théodore Simon, wanted to identify students who should be placed in special (remedial) classes, where their education could proceed more efficiently than it had in the standard classroom. As we will see later, this original use of the intelligence test sowed the seeds of controversies that would emerge throughout the twentieth century.

Binet's first test appeared in 1905 and was an immediate success. It caught the attention of Lewis M. Terman at Stanford University, who supervised a translation and revision of the test in 1916. Since then, the test has been called the *Stanford-Binet test* and has undergone subsequent revisions, the most recent of which was published in 1986. This edition, the fourth, made several significant changes in the test and in its scoring. So, what is this test like?

The test follows what its authors call a three-level, hierarchical model of cognitive ability (Thorndike et al., 1986). As did Binet's original test, the current edition yields an overall test score that reflects "g," or general intellectual ability, which the authors describe as "what an individual uses when faced with a problem that he or she has not been taught to solve" (Thorndike et al., 1986, p. 3). Underlying "g" are three second-level factors (Figure 7.4): crystallized abilities, fluid-analytic abilities, and short-term memory. *Crystallized abilities* represent those skills needed for acquiring and using information about verbal and quantitative concepts. These abilities are influenced by schooling and

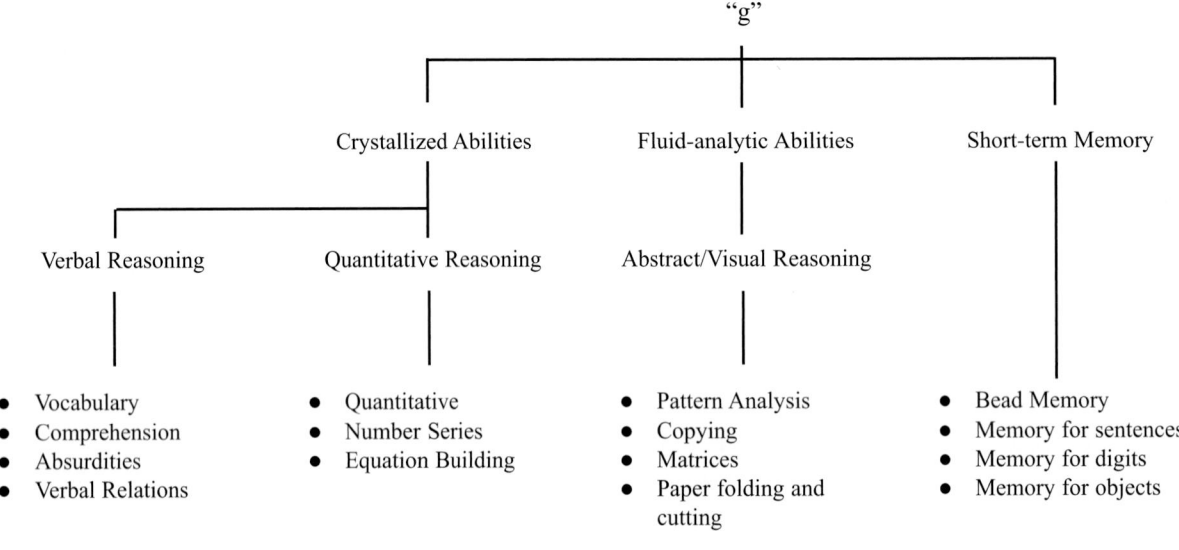

FIGURE 7.4

The factors tested by the Stanford-Binet Intelligence Scale, Fourth Edition, arranged in three levels below "g," or general intellectual ability. Each subtest is noted at the lowest level (Thorndike et al., 1986).

can be called an academic ability factor. *Fluid-analytic abilities* are those needed to solve problems that involve figural or nonverbal types of information. They involve the ability to see things in new and different ways, and are less tied to formal schooling. The third factor at this level of the model is *short-term memory.* Items that test one's ability to hold information in memory for short periods can be found on Binet's original test.

The next level of abilities provides more specific, content-oriented definitions of the factors from level two. As you can see from Figure 7.4, at this level, crystallized abilities are divided into verbal and quantitative reasoning, fluid-analytic abilities are seen as abstract/visual reasoning, and there is no ability at this level under short-term memory. At the base of the hierarchy are the 15 subtests that constitute the actual Stanford-Binet test.

What all of this means is that the authors of the 1986 revision of the Stanford-Binet test acknowledge that a person's measured intelligence should be reflected in more than just one test score. Not only can we determine an overall "g" score (the only score available from earlier editions), but we can also calculate scores for each factor at each level. There are also scores for the 15 subtests by themselves. Figure 7.5 shows the way "g" scores on the Stanford-Binet are distributed for the general population.

Before we go on, let's take a minute to discuss what has happened to the concept of IQ. **IQ** is an abbreviation for the term *intelligence quotient.* As you know, a quotient is the result you get when you divide one number by another. In dividing 8 by 6, the quotient is 1.33. For the early versions of the Stanford-Binet, the examiner's job was to determine a person's mental age (or *MA*), the age level at which the person functioned in terms of intellectual abilities. A person with the intellectual abilities of an average eight-year-old would have an MA of 8. IQ was determined by dividing the person's mental age by

IQ (Intelligence Quotient) a measure of general intelligence that results from dividing one's mental age by one's chronological age and multiplying the result by 100

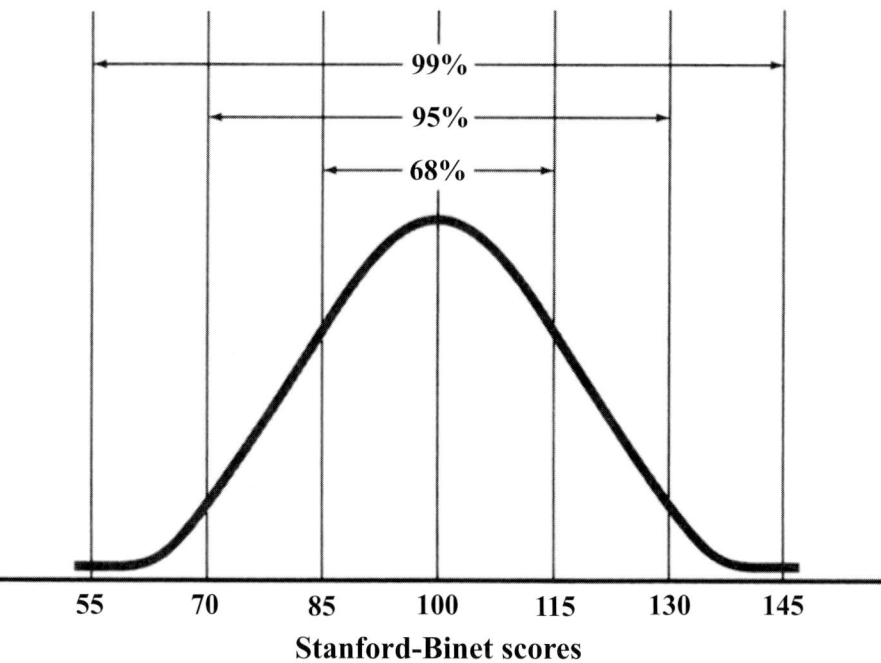

FIGURE 7.5

An idealized curve that shows the distribution of scores on the Stanford-Binet Intelligence Scale taken by a very large sample of the general population. The numbers at the top of the curve indicate the percentages of the population expected to score within the range of scores indicated; that is 68 percent earn scores between 85 and 115, 95 percent score between 70 and 130, and 99 percent earn scores between 55 and 145.

his or her actual age (called chronological age, or CA). This quotient was then multiplied by 100 to determine IQ:

If an eight-year-old girl had a mental age of eight, she would be average, and her IQ

$$IQ = \frac{MA}{CA} \times 100$$

would equal 100 (or 8/8 x 100 = 1 x 100). If the eight-year-old were above average, with the intellectual abilities of an average ten-year-old, her IQ would be 125 (10/8 x 100, or 1.25 x 100). If she were below average, say with the mental abilities of an average six-year-old, her computed IQ would be 75.

It didn't take long for psychometrists to criticize the traditional IQ. For example, Thurstone argued that mental age was an ambiguous measure of mental ability (Cohen, Montague, Nathanson, & Swerdlik, 1988). As it happens, two individuals with identical MAs may not have equivalent levels of intelligence. For example, a 20-year-old with a MA of 10 has an IQ of 50. However, a nine-year-old with the same MA has an IQ of 111. Additionally, two individuals with the same IQ, could have different levels of intelligence. For example, a six-year-old with an MA of seven has an IQ of 116.7. A 12-year-old with an MA of 14 has the same IQ despite the fact that the 12-year-old is two mental

BEFORE YOU GO ON

- What is the Stanford-Binet test, and what was it originally designed to do?

- What is a person's "mental age"?

- What is IQ, and how is it calculated?

- Why was the original IQ test abandoned, and what took its place?

years above his chronological age and the six-year-old is only one year above (Cohen et al., 1988). In its place, the *deviation IQ* is now used. The deviation IQ uses established group norms and allows for comparing intelligence scores across age groups. However, because it is a term ingrained in our vocabulary, we will continue to use the term "IQ" for a measure of general intelligence even though we now use established norm groups, and no longer calculate MAs or compute quotients.

The Wechsler Tests of Intelligence

David Wechsler published his first intelligence test in 1939. Unlike the Stanford-Binet test that existed at the time, it was designed for use with adult populations and to reduce the heavy reliance on verbal skills that characterized Binet's tests. With a major revision in 1955, the test became known as the *Wechsler Adult Intelligence Scale (WAIS)*. The test was revised in 1981 (*WAIS-R*), and again in 1997 (*WAIS-III*). The WAIS-III is appropriate for persons between 16 and 74 years of age and is reported to be the most commonly used of all psychological tests (Lubin et al., 1984).

A natural extension was the *Wechsler Intelligence Scale for Children (WISC)*, originally published 11 years after the WAIS. With updated norms and several new items (among other things, designed to minimize bias against any ethnic group or gender), the *WISC-III* appeared in 1991. It is appropriate for children ages six to 16 (there is some overlap with the WAIS-III). A third test in the series is for younger children, between the ages of four and six. It is called the *Wechsler Preschool and Primary Scale of Intelligence,* or *WPPSI.* It was published in 1967, was revised in 1989, and is now the *WPPSI-R.* There are some subtle differences among the three Wechsler tests, but each is based on the same logic. Therefore, we will consider only one, the WAIS-III, in detail.

The WAIS-III consists of 14 subtests organized in two categories. Seven subtests define the *verbal scale,* and seven subtests constitute a *performance scale.* Figure 7.6 lists the subtests of the WAIS-III and describes some of the types of items found on each.

Each item on each subtest is scored. (Some of the performance items have time limits that affect scoring.) As is now the case with the Stanford-Binet, each subtest score is compared to a score provided by the test's norms. How a person's earned score compares to the scores earned by persons in the norm group (others of the same sex and age who have already taken the test) determines the person's standard score for each Wechsler subtest. In addition to one overall score, the Wechsler tests provide verbal and performance scores, which can tell us something about a person's particular strengths and weaknesses.

There has been controversy for many years about individually administered intelligence tests such as the Wechsler tests and the Stanford-Binet. The extent to which the tests are culturally biased, thus favoring one group of subjects over another, whether they truly measure intelligence and not just academic success, and whether test results can be used for political purposes, perhaps as a basis for racial discrimination, are just some of the concerns that keep surfacing. Although experts allow that the tests may be somewhat biased on racial and socioeconomic grounds, they "believe that such tests adequately measure more important elements of intelligence" (Snyderman & Rothman, 1987, p.143).

VERBAL SUBTESTS

Vocabulary	person must provide an acceptable definition for a series of words
Similarities	person must indicate the way(s) in which two things are alike; for example, "In what way are a horse and a cow alike?"
Arithmetic	simple math problems that must be answered without paper and pencil; for example, "How far will a bird travel in 90 minutes at the rate of 10 miles per hour?"
Digit span	person is to repeat a series of digits, given at the rate of one per second, both forward and backward
Information	person must answer questions about a variety of topics dealing with one's culture; for example, "Who wrote Huckleberry Finn?" or "How many members are there in the U.S. Congress?"
Comprehension	test of judgement, common sense, and practical knowledge; for example, "Why do we bury the dead?" or "Why do we have prisons?"
Letter-number sequencing	letters and numbers in scrambled order, person is to re-order them correctly; for example, "Given Z, 3, B, 1, 2, A," the correct response would be, "1, 2, 3, A, B, Z."

PERFORMANCE SUBTESTS

Picture completion	person must identify or name the missing part or object in a drawing; for example, a truck with only three wheels
Digit symbol coding	each nine digit "key" is paired with a simple symbol. Given a random series of digits, the person must provide the paired symbol within a time limit.
Block design	using blocks whose sides are all red, all white, or diagonally red and white, person must copy a pattern provided on a card
Matrix reasoning	person is presented with nonverbal, figural stimuli and is to describe a pattern or relationship between the stimuli
Picture arrangement	series of cartoon-like pictures must be arranged in order to tell a story
Object assembly	free-form jigsaw puzzles must be put together to form familiar objects
Symbol search	person is given a geometric figure and must locate that figure from among five figures in a search group of figures as quickly as possible

FIGURE 7.6

The Subtests of the Wechsler Adult Intelligence Scale, Third Edition WAIS-III

Group Tests of Intelligence

There are advantages of individually administered tests such as the Wechsler tests and the Stanford-Binet. Both have demonstrated considerable reliability and validity, at least with respect to predicting academic or scholastic achievement (Tulsky, Zhu, & Ledbetter, 1997; Thorndike, 1986). One of the most important advantages is that the examiner has the opportunity to interact with the person taking the test. The examiner can develop opinions about the examinee and observe how he or she goes about responding to test items. A disadvantage of the individually administered tests is that they are time-consuming and expensive. There are alternatives. Group IQ tests are generally paper-and-pencil tests that can be administered to many individuals at one time.

By the beginning of World War I, Binet's test had gained wide approval, and the basic notion of using psychological methods to measure intellectual abilities had been generally accepted. There was good reason to know the intellectual capabilities of the recruits who were entering the armed services, but obviously not all could be individually tested. A committee of psychologists was charged with the task of creating a group test of intelligence. The result, published in 1917, was the *Army Alpha Test,* a paper-and-pencil test that made rough discriminations among examinees on the basis of intelligence. In the same year, the committee published the *Army Beta Test,* designed for illiterates who could not read the Army Alpha. It was a performance test, the instructions of which were given orally or acted out.

The military continues to be a major publisher and consumer of group intelligence tests. The U.S. Army now uses the *Armed Forces Qualification Test (AFQT),* and anyone who goes through military induction will have firsthand experience with this test.

When psychological tests of cognitive ability are used to predict future behaviors, we call them **aptitude tests**. Many of the aptitude tests used in the context of education are tests of general intellectual ability. The difference is in the use to which the score is put: predicting future academic success. The two most commonly used college entrance tests are the *ACT (American College Testing Program)* and the *SAT (Scholastic Aptitude Test),* which yield verbal and mathematics scores as well as an overall score. In 1994, a major revision of the test, the SAT-I was published. The SAT-I includes math items that are not in the usual multiple-choice format, and the verbal section places more emphasis on reading comprehension. A new, optional SAT-II is also available. The SAT-II includes a written essay section, language proficiency tests for native speakers of Japanese and Chinese, and tests for non-native English speakers.

aptitude tests psychological tests of cognitive abilities used to predict future behaviors

Aptitude tests have long been used outside the realm of education and academics. Employers often rely on specific aptitude tests to help them decide which candidate might be best suited for a particular job. You may have had some experience with such tests. There are specific aptitude tests for just about every skill or ability you can imagine; mechanical aptitude, aptitude for sales, for leadership, for dexterity, and for artistic expression. In fact, a long-standing debate in psychology centers on the usefulness of specific predictors of performance when compared to tests of general intelligence. The latter tests often provide better results than do specific aptitude tests (Hogan, Hogan, & Roberts, 1996; Hunt, 1995; Sternberg & Wagner, 1993).

BEFORE YOU GO ON

- What are the Wechsler intelligence tests?
- Briefly describe how the Wechsler tests are organized.
- What are group tests?
- What is an aptitude test?

GROUP DIFFERENCES IN MEASURED INTELLIGENCE

For the remainder of this topic, we'll be focusing on IQ scores. Please keep in mind that IQ is simply a convenient abbreviation for intelligence as it is measured by psychological tests. *We should not take IQ to equal one's intelligence.* IQ scores reflect only a particular measure of intelligence.

Recognizing that there are individual differences in intelligence, can we make any statements about differences in IQ in general? Who are smarter, women or men? Do we become less intelligent with age? Are there differences in intelligence among ethnic groups? As you are aware, simple answers to such questions are often misleading and, if interpreted incorrectly, can be harmful to some groups of people.

Reported average differences in IQ test scores are often misleading. Let's imagine that two large groups of people are tested: 1,000 Alphas and 1,000 Thetas. On the average, the IQ score for Alphas is 95, and for Thetas, it is 110. An appropriate statistical analysis tells us that the difference of 15 points is too large to have been expected by chance. Are Thetas smarter than Alphas? Yes, on the average they are—that is exactly what has been discovered.

Now look at Figure 7.7. Here are two curves that represent the IQ scores from the study. We can see the difference in the averages (means) of the two groups. However, there *are* Thetas whose IQs are below the average IQs of Alphas. And there *are* Alphas with IQs above that of the average Thetas. We may draw conclusions about average IQs, but making definitive statements about individual Thetas and Alphas is not possible.

Being able to demonstrate a significant difference between the average IQs of two groups in itself tells us nothing about *why* those differences exist. Are Thetas genetically superior to Alphas? Maybe, maybe not. Have Alphas had equal access to the sorts of experiences that IQ tests ask about? Maybe, maybe not. Are the tests biased to provide Thetas with an advantage? Maybe, maybe not. Learning that two groups of persons have different average IQ scores usually raises more questions than it answers.

Gender Differences in IQ

Here's a question to which we have a reasonably definitive answer: Is there a difference between the IQs of males and females? The answer is no. At least there are very few studies that report any differences between men and women on any test of general intelligence of the sort represented by an IQ score. What small differences have been found seem to be getting smaller (Aiken, 1984; Halpern, 1986; Hyde et al., 1990; Maccoby & Jacklin, 1974). Note that there may be no measured differences between the IQs of men and women because IQ tests are constructed to minimize or eliminate any such differences. Usually, if an item on an intelligence test discriminates between women and men, it is dropped from consideration.

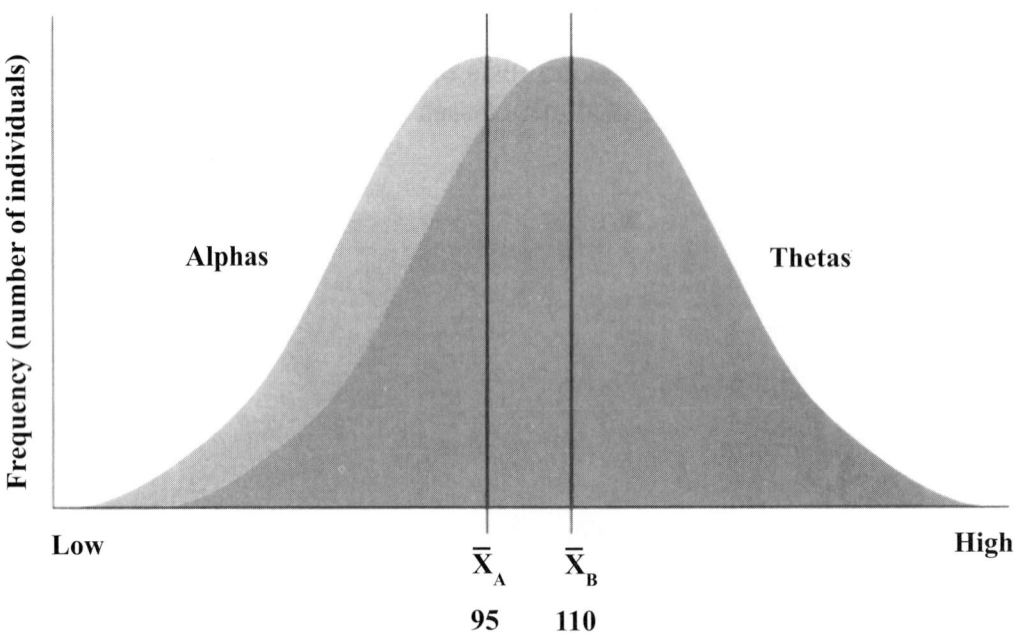

FIGURE 7.7

Hypothetical distributions of IQ scores for two groups (ALPHAs and THETAs). The average IQ for THETAs is higher than that for ALPHAs, but there is considerable overlap between the two distributions. That is, some ALPHAs have IQs higher than the average for THETAs (110), and some THETAs have IQs lower than the average for ALPHAs (95).

When we look beyond global measures of IQ, however, there are signs of gender differences on specific intellectual skills (which offset each other on general IQ tests). For example, males score significantly higher than females on tests of spatial relations—particularly on tests that require one to visualize what a three-dimensional object would look like when rotated in space (Eagly, 1995; Masters & Sanders, 1993). What is curious about this rather specialized ability is that males perform better than females on such tasks from an early age, widening the gap through the school years, even though this particular ability is only marginally related to academic course work (Linn & Peterson, 1985; McGee, 1979). This suggests that these sex differences cannot be easily attributed to differences in educational opportunity.

On the other hand, educational experiences may be related to some differences in mathematical ability. Scores on tests of mathematics skills are well correlated with the number and type of math classes taken while a student is in high school (Kimball, 1989). For many reasons, males enroll in more advanced math courses than females. It is not surprising, then, that by the time they leave high school, there are differences between men and women on tests of mathematical ability (particularly for those that assess mathematical reasoning and problem solving). There is evidence that average differences between males and females on tests of mathematical abilities have been declining steadily over the past 25 years (Hyde, 1994; Hyde et al., 1990; Jacklin, 1989). Other researchers argue that although average differences may be small and shrinking, significant differences remain in the respective proportions of males and females who score at the very top or the very bottom of ability tests (Feingold, 1993, 1994, 1995). Still other researchers, noting the higher scores males have earned on the math portion of the SAT over the past 17 years, suspect genetic factors are at work.

An analysis by Larry V. Hedges and Amy Nowell of the University of Chicago examined the performances of male and female teenagers on tests of mental ability over the past 30 years (Hedges & Newell, 1995). In every case, *average differences* were small. However, on some tests there were disproportionally larger numbers of boys at the top or the bottom of the distributions of scores. For example, seven times as many boys as girls scored in the top 5 percent on science tests, and twice as many boys as girls scored in the top 5 percent on math tests. On the other hand, boys were much more likely than girls to score near the bottom of the distribution on tests of perceptual speed and reading comprehension. Boys also showed an "alarming" disadvantage on tests of writing skills. A significant aspect of this study was that differences in the scores of males and females showed remarkably little change between 1960 and 1992, the dates of testing sessions used in the research. Although their research in no way addressed the cause of any observed differences, Dr. Hedges felt compelled to state that he believes that "the sex differences in abilities are caused by social constraints rather than biology."

Some psychologists argue that males generally outperform females in tests of mathematics and spatial relations because of the courses they are encouraged to take in school. As more females are drawn to classes in math and science, differences in test scores most likely will continue to decline.

Age Differences in IQ

You know a great deal more now than you did when you were 12. You knew more when you were 12 than you did when you were ten. Many 12-year-olds think they know more than their parents do. *What* we know changes with age, even *how much* we know changes with age, but neither provides a measure of intelligence. IQ scores are computed so that, by definition, they remain consistent with age. The IQ of the average 12-year-old is 100, the same as the IQ of the average 30-year-old and the average 60-year-old, regardless of which test is used. But what about the IQ of any one individual? If Kim's IQ is 112 at age four, will it still be 112 at age 14, or age 40?

Infant and preschool IQ tests are poor predictors of IQ at older ages (Baumeister, 1987; Bayley & Schaefer, 1964). IQ test scores of children younger than seven simply do not correlate well with IQs measured later. This does not mean that testing young children is without purpose. Having even a rough idea of the intellectual abilities of young children is often useful, particularly if there is concern about retardation or some thought that the child may be exceptional. The resulting scores may not predict adult intelligence well, but they may help in assessing the development of the child compared to other children.

What about intellectual changes throughout the life span? Does IQ decrease with old age? You may have guessed the answer: yes, no, and it depends. Most of the data on age differences in IQ scores have been gathered using a *cross-sectional method,* in which tests are given at about the same time to many people of varied ages. When this is done, the results indicate that overall IQ peaks in the early twenties, remains stable for about 20 years, and then declines sharply (e.g., Schaie, 1983; Wechsler, 1958, 1981). A different approach is to test the same individuals repeatedly, over a period of time. This is the *longitudinal method.* With this method, things don't look quite the same, showing IQ scores rising until the mid-fifties and then very gradually declining (Schaie, 1974; Schaie & Strother, 1968).

So far we have qualified "yes" and "no" answers to our question about age and IQ. Probably the best answer is "it depends." Studies of cognitive abilities demonstrate that we should ask about specific intellectual skills because they do not all decline at the same rate, and some do not decline at all. For example, tests of vocabulary often show no drop in scores with increasing age (Blum et al., 1970), whereas tests of verbal fluency often show steep declines beginning at age 30 (Schaie & Strother, 1968). A longitudinal study of more than 300 bright, well-educated adults showed a slight *increase* in general intellectual performance throughout adulthood (ages 18 to 54) on the Wechsler Adult Intelligence Scale (Sands et al., 1989). A closer look at scores on the Wechsler subtests for people between the ages of 40 and 61 showed improvement on the Information, Comprehension, and Vocabulary subtests, but a decline in scores on Digit Symbol and Block Design (see Figure 7.6).

fluid intelligence abilities related to speed, adaptation, flexibility, and abstract reasoning

Another "it depends" answer surfaces when we consider what are called fluid and crystallized intelligence (Cattell, 1963; Horn, 1982, 1985; Horn & Cattell, 1966). **Fluid intelligence**—abilities related to speed, adaptation, flexibility, and abstract reasoning—includes the skills that show the greatest decline with age. Fluid intelligence is not dependent on specific learning. As an example of an item that taps into fluid intelligence, try to complete this analogy: *Here:Now::There:_____* (the correct answer is "then."). This item requires abstract reasoning and a minimal knowledge of the English language. **Crystallized intelligence**—abilities depending on acquired knowledge, accumulated experiences, and general information—remains constant or even increases throughout one's lifetime (Horn, 1976, 1985; Vernon, 1979). Try the following analogy: *Oberon:Puck::Prospero::_____*. The abstract reasoning necessary is identical to the previous analogy. However, to solve this analogy correctly, you must know something of the plays of William Shakespeare. The relationship asked for in the "Oberon" analogy is between "master" and "servant." In *Midsummer Night's Dream*, Oberon is the King of the Fairies and Puck is his servant. In *The Tempest*, Prospero is the master and Ariel is his servant. If the concepts of fluid and crystallized intelligence sound familiar, you may be reminded of two of the dimensions the Stanford-Binet Intelligence Scale measures. As you may have guessed, high levels of crystallized intelligence are very helpful for working crossword puzzles.

crystallized intelligence abilities related to acquired knowledge, accumulated experiences, and general information

BEFORE YOU GO ON

- On a general level, describe what the research on gender differences in global intelligence finds.

- In what specific areas do men and women differ?

- How can we account for gender differences in specific abilities?

- What are fluid and crystallized intelligence?

- In what areas is there a decline in intelligence with age, and in what areas is there little decline or even an increase?

With age, the ability to acquire new information or to solve new and different types of problems may decline, but there is no reason to expect a decline in those intellectual abilities already acquired (Salthouse, 1989, pp. 19–20). Research supporting this idea comes from the National Institute on Aging (Grady et al., 1995). Older volunteers (average age 69) had greater difficulty than younger volunteers (average age 25) recognizing pictures of faces they had been shown 15 minutes earlier. Using PET scan imaging techniques, which show the brain centers that are active during a given task, the researchers noted that fewer areas of the brain were active when the older subjects tried memorizing the faces. They could not remember the faces because they had not encoded them effectively.

Racial and Ethnic Differences in IQ

That there are significant differences between the IQ test scores of African Americans and Caucasian Americans is not a new discovery. It was one of the conclusions drawn from the testing of army recruits during World War I. Since then, many studies have reconfirmed the fact that—on average—Caucasians score about 15 points higher on general intelligence (IQ) tests than do African Americans. African Americans earn lower scores on performance tests and on tests designed to minimize the influence of one's cultural background (so-called culture-fair tests) (Helms, 1992; Jensen, 1980; Rushton, 1988). At the same time, Japanese children between the ages of six and 16 score higher on IQ tests—about 11 points on the average—than do Caucasian American children of the same age (e.g., Lynn, 1982, 1987). The superiority of Japanese children on mathematics tests is even greater (Stevenson et al., 1986). Curiously, there are no real differences in math abilities or in general intelligence between Asian and Caucasian American children at ages four or five—*before* formal schooling begins (Geary, 1995). Asian American students score higher on the math portion of the SAT than other students in math (e.g., average math scores on the SAT of 525 compared to 476) (Caplan, 1989; College Board, 1989; Hsia, 1988; Lynn, 1991; Sue & Okasaki, 1990). The nagging question, of course, is why? Why do these differences appear?

The proposed answers have been controversial and point to several possibilities: (1) The *tests are biased* and unfair. Current IQ tests may reflect mainstream life and the experiences of Caucasian Americans to a greater extent than they reflect the experiences of most African Americans or Hispanics, (2) Differences in IQ scores can be attributed to *environmental factors,* such as available economic or educational opportunities, or the extent to which one is exposed to a wide range of stimuli, (3) There are *genetic factors* that place some groups at a disadvantage. (4) There are *cultural differences in motivation* and attitudes about performance on standardized tests. In most Western cultures, poor performance on an academic test is typically attributed to factors other than one's effort, "The test was bad; my teachers were lousy, and I had the flu." In some cultures, including most Asian cultures, failure is more likely to be attributed to lack of effort, "I didn't work hard enough to prepare and will try harder next time."

Test bias may account for some of the differences in IQ scores, but assume for the moment that available techniques for assessing general intelligence are as valid as they can be. First, let's remind ourselves that even the best and fairest of tests only measure one or a few of the various possible dimensions of intelligence. What then? Some (e.g., Suzuki & Valencia, 1997) find intelligence tests to be racially biased and favoring middle class and upper class test takers. Others (e.g., Gregory, 1999) argue that current intelligence tests do a very good job of establishing standards of intellectual competence and potential.

In the 1950s and 1960s, social scientists were confident that most, if not all, of the difference between the average IQ scores of Caucasians and African Americans could be accounted for in terms of environmental, sociocultural, and motivational factors. There may not have been a lot of research to support this position, but the logic was compelling and was consistent with prevailing attitudes. African Americans were at a disadvantage on standard IQ tests because they were often denied access to enriching educational opportunities. Their generally lower socioeconomic status deprived African Americans of many of the sorts of experiences that could raise their IQ scores.

In 1969, Arthur Jensen shocked the scientific community with an article published in the *Harvard Educational Review.* Jensen argued that there was insufficient evidence to justify the conclusion that the environment alone produced such large differences in IQ scores. The alternative was obvious to Jensen: differences were attributable to genetic factors. Many readers took Jensen's claim to mean that African Americans are genetically inferior to Caucasians. Jensen says that his argument was meant only as a reasonable hypothesis, intended to provoke scientific efforts to explore such a possibility (Jensen, 1981).

Perhaps you can imagine the furor created by Jensen's article. Researchers took up the challenge to find convincing evidence to demonstrate that the environment is the cause of lower African American IQ scores. After reviewing the body of evidence that accumulated from these efforts, one scientist, Brian Mackenzie, asserted that "what is finally clear from such research is that environmental factors have not been identified that are sufficient to account for all or even most of the 15-point mean difference in IQ between African Americans and Caucasians in the United States. Jensen's conclusion that one-half to two-thirds of the gap remains unaccounted for by any proposed combination of environmental influences is still unrefuted" (Mackenzie, 1984, p. 1217). Now what does *that* mean? Does it mean that racial differences in IQ *are* caused by genetic factors? *Are* African Americans genetically less able than Caucasians? *Of course not.* There is not sufficient evidence to support such a conclusion (Mackintosh, 1986).

Just as many were coming to believe that the debate over racial differences in IQ was settling down, the controversy was reignited late in 1994 with the publication of a book titled, *The Bell Curve.* (The "bell curve" refers to the symmetrical curve of IQ scores we saw in Figure 7.5.) The book, by psychologist Richard Herrnstein and political analyst Charles Murray, raises several points about intelligence and IQ testing. Relevant to our discussion are their assertions that intelligence (1) is largely inherited (up to 60 percent inherited, they claim), (2) is virtually unchangeable from very early childhood on, (3) accounts for the "winners and losers" in today's society, and (4) is possessed in varying degrees by members of different races. Murray and Herrnstein predict the emergence of one class of "cognitive elite" and an impoverished low-IQ class, the former being Caucasian, the latter mostly African American. Objections to nearly every aspect of *The Bell Curve* were loud and immediate (Bower, 1995; Jacoby & Glauberman, 1995; Kamin, 1995).

To understand why the issue of the inheritance of IQ has not yet been resolved requires that we understand three points: (1) Any evidence that genetic factors may affect differences in intelligence *within* races does not imply that genetic factors influence differences in intelligence *between* races, (2) A failure to identify specific environmental causes of racial differences in IQ is insufficient reason to drop the environmental factors argument, and (3) Just because we have not identified the specific environmental factors that can cause racial differences in IQ does not mean we must accept genetic explanations.

One intriguing hypothesis about why African Americans might not score as well on standard tests of IQ comes from an experiment conducted by Steele and Aronson (1995). According to Steele and Aronson, when a person is asked to perform a task for which there is a negative stereotype attached to their group, that person will perform poorly because the task is threatening. They call this idea a *stereotype threat*. To test the hypothesis that members of a group will perform more poorly on tasks that relate to prevailing negative stereotypes, Steele and Aronson conducted the following experiment. African American and Caucasian participants took a test comprised of items from the verbal section of the Graduate Record Exam (GRE). One-third of the participants were told that the test was diagnostic of their intellectual ability (diagnostic condition). One-third were told that the test was a laboratory tool for studying problem solving (nondiagnostic condition). The final one-third were told that the test was of problem solving and would present a challenge to the participants (nondiagnostic/challenge condition). Steele and Aronson then determined the average number of items answered correctly within each group.

The results of this experiment showed that when the test was said to be diagnostic of one's intellectual abilities, African American and Caucasian participants differed significantly, with African American participants performing more poorly than Caucasian participants. However, when the *same* test was presented as nondiagnostic, African American and Caucasian participants did equally well. There was no significant difference between African Americans and Caucasians in the nondiagnostic/challenge condition. Overall, across the three conditions, African Americans performed most poorly in the diagnostic condition. In a second experiment, Aronson and Steele produced results that were even more pronounced than in their first. They also found that African American participants in the diagnostic condition finished fewer items and worked more slowly than African American participants in the nondiagnostic condition. Steele and Aronson point out that this is a pattern consistent with impairments caused by test anxiety, evaluation apprehension, and competitive pressure.

In a final experiment, Steele and Aronson had participants perform word completion tasks (e.g., _ _ c e; L a _ _; _ _ ack; _ _ or) that could be completed in a racially stereotyped way (e.g., Race; Lazy; Black; Poor) or a nonstereotyped way (e.g., Pace; Lace; Stack; Door). This was done to see if stereotypes are activated when participants were told that a test was either diagnostic or nondiagnostic. Steele and Aronson found that there was greater stereotype activation among African Americans in the diagnostic condition compared to the nondiagnostic condition. They also found that in the diagnostic condition African Americans were more likely than Caucasians to engage in self-handicapping strategies (that is, developing behavior patterns that actually interfere with performance, such as losing sleep the night before a test). African Americans and Caucasians did not differ on self-handicapping behaviors in the nondiagnostic condition.

What does this tell us about the performance of African Americans and Caucasians on intelligence tests? Intelligence tests, by their very nature and purpose are diagnostic of one's intellectual abilities. According to Steele and Aronson's (1995) analysis, when an African American is faced with the prospect of taking a test that is diagnostic of intellectual ability, it activates a stereotype threat because a common stereotype of African Americans is that they are not supposed to perform well on tests of intellectual ability.

According to Steele and Aronson, the stereotype threat impairs performance by generating evaluative pressures. Recall that participants who were under stereotype threat in the diagnostic condition spent more time doing fewer items. As they became more frustrated, performance was impaired. It may also impair future performance because more self-handicapping strategies are used by African Americans facing diagnostic tests. In short, the stereotype threat creates an impairment in the ability to cognitively process information adequately which, in turn, inhibits performance. So, lower scores on IQ tests by African Americans may relate more to the activation of the stereotype threat than any genetic differences between African Americans and Caucasians.

So where do we stand on the issue of racial-ethnic differences in IQ? We stand in a position of considerable uncertainty. For one thing, even the very concept of race is being challenged as a meaningful descriptor of persons. As we have seen, there are data that underscore the contributions of both genetic and environmental influences on intelligence. We would do well to keep in mind the following: "whether intelligence is largely genetically or largely environmentally determined is actually irrelevant in the context of group differences. The real issue is whether intelligence can be changed, an issue that does not go hand in hand with the issue of heritability" (Angoff, 1988, p. 713). And, the whole argument over the causes for race differences may someday become moot. Between 1973 and 1988 the gap between African Americans and Caucasians on intelligence tests has been closing (Williams & Ceci, 1997). In the areas of reading ability and mathematical ability, the gap has narrowed between 1973 and 1994 (Williams & Ceci, 1997). The narrowing of the gap, according to Williams and Ceci is more related to gains by African Americans rather than declines by Caucasians.

BEFORE YOU GO ON

- Describe the racial differences in intelligence test scores.

- What factors contribute to racial differences in IQ?

- What is a stereotype threat, and how could it affect performance on an IQ test?

- Describe why within-group measures on inheritance do not inform us about between-group differences in IQ.

- What is the current status of the gaps between racial and ethnic groups on IQ scores?

EXTREMES OF INTELLIGENCE

When we look at the IQ scores earned by large random samples of people, we find that they are distributed in a predictable pattern. The most frequently occurring score is the average score, 100. Most other earned scores are close to this average. In fact, about 95 percent of all IQ scores fall between 70 and 130 (see Figure 7.5). We'll end this Topic by considering those people who score at the extremes.

The Mentally Gifted

There are several ways in which a person can be gifted. The United States Office of Education (1972) defines giftedness as a demonstrated achievement or aptitude for excellence in any one of six areas. These categories are similar to those proposed by Gardner's model of intelligence.

1. Psychomotor ability: An overlooked area in which some people clearly excel. We are dealing with people of outstanding abilities in behaviors or skills that require agility, strength, speed, quickness, coordination, and so forth.

2. Visual and performing arts: Some people, even as children, demonstrate an unusual talent for art, music, drama, or writing.

3. Leadership ability: Leadership skills are valued in most societies, and there are individuals who are particularly gifted in this area, even as very young children. Youngsters with good leadership skills tend to be bright, but they are not necessarily the smartest of the group.

4. Creative or productive thinking: Here we are talking about individuals who may be intellectually or academically above average, but not necessarily. Scores on measures of creativity are typically unrelated to measures of general intelligence (e.g., Kershner & Ledger, 1985). Among other things, people with this type of giftedness are able to generate unique and different, but useful, solutions to problems. Persons with exceptional creative talents in one area (art, math, or language, for instance) usually show no special creativity in other areas (Amabile, 1985; Weisberg, 1986).

5. Specific academic aptitude: In this case we are talking about people who have a special ability in a particular subject or two. Someone who is a whiz in math, history, or computer science without necessarily being outstanding in other academic areas would fit this category.

6. Intellectually gifted: Inclusion in this group is based on scores earned on a general intelligence test. It is likely that when people use the term mentally gifted, they are referring to individuals who fit this category—people of exceptionally high IQ. (IQ scores of 130 or above usually qualify for this category. Some reserve the label for those with IQs above 135. In either case, we are dealing with a very small portion of the population: fewer than 3 percent.)

Consistent with the notion that there may be many kinds of "intelligence," there may be many ways in which one can demonstrate giftedness, including musical ability.

How can we describe intellectually gifted individuals? Actually, there have been few large-scale attempts to understand mental giftedness or the cognitive processing of people at the upper end of the IQ distribution (Horowitz & O'Brien, 1985; Reis, 1989; Winner, 2000). A lot of what we do know about the mentally gifted comes from a classic study begun by Lewis M. Terman in the early 1920s (the Lewis Terman who revised Binet's IQ test in 1916). Terman supervised the testing of more than 250,000 children throughout California. His research group at Stanford University focused on those children who earned the highest scores, 1,528 in all, each with an IQ above 135.

Lewis Terman died in 1956, but the study of those mentally gifted individuals who were between the ages of eight and 12 in 1922 continues. Ever since their inclusion in the study, and at regular intervals, they continue to be retested, surveyed, interviewed, and polled by psychologists and others (Friedman et al., 1995; Goleman, 1980; Oden, 1968; Sears & Barbee, 1977).

The Terman study has its drawbacks. Choosing a narrow definition of gifted in terms of IQ alone is one. Failing to account for the educational or socioeconomic level of each child's parents is another. The researchers may also have excluded from the sample any children who showed signs of psychological disorders or problems, whether their IQ scores were high enough or not. Nonetheless, the study is an impressive one for having continued for more than 80 years. What can this longitudinal analysis tell us about people with very high IQs?

Most of Terman's results fly in the face of the classic stereotype of the bright child as skinny, anxious, clumsy, sickly, and a wearer of thick glasses (Sears & Barbee, 1977). In fact, if there is any overall conclusion to be drawn from the Terman-Stanford study it is that, in general, gifted children experience advantages in virtually everything. They are taller, faster, better coordinated, have better eyesight, fewer emotional problems, and tend to stay married longer than average. These findings have been confirmed by others with different samples of subjects (Holden, 1980; Winner, 1996; 2000). Many obvious things are also true: the mentally gifted received more education; found better, higher-paying jobs; and had brighter children than did people of average intelligence. By now, we know better than to overgeneralize. Not all of Terman's children (sometimes referred to as "Termites") grew up to be rich and famous or live happily ever after. Many did, but not all.

Mental Retardation

Our understanding of mental retardation has changed markedly over the past 25 years. We've seen changes in treatment and care and great strides in prevention. There have also been significant changes in how psychology defines mental retardation.

Intelligence, as measured by IQ tests, is often used to confirm suspected cases of mental retardation. As is true for the mentally gifted, however, there is more to retardation than IQ alone. The American Association of Mental Deficiency (AAMD) cites three factors in its definition of **mental retardation**: "subaverage general intellectual functioning which originated during the developmental period and is associated with impairment in adaptive behavior" (Grossman, 1973). Let's look at each of these three points.

mental retardation a condition indicated by an IQ score below 70 that begins during development and is associated with an impairment in adaptive functioning

The IQ cutoff for mental retardation is usually taken to be 70, with IQs between 70 and 85 considered "borderline" or "slow" (Zigler & Hodapp, 1991). Standard IQ cutoff scores for the four major degrees of retardation are:

- IQ 50–69: mildly mentally retarded (approximately 80 percent of all cases of retardation)

- IQ 35–49: moderately mentally retarded (approximately 12 percent of all cases of retardation)

- IQ 20–34: severely mentally retarded (approximately 8 percent of all cases of retardation)

- IQ less than 19: profoundly mentally retarded (less than 1 percent of all cases of retardation)

(American Psychiatric Association, 1994)

As you review this list, keep two things in mind. First, these scores are suggested limits. Given what we know about IQ tests, it is ridiculous to claim after one administration of a test that a person with an IQ of 69 is mentally retarded, while someone else with an IQ of 71 is not. Second, a diagnosis of mental retardation is not (should not be) made on the basis of IQ score alone. Of late, there has been much controversy over where to place the upper limit of mental retardation, with some (e.g., the American Association of Mental Retardation) arguing that it should be at 75 rather than 70.

To fit the AAMD definition of mental retardation, the cause or the symptoms of the below-average intellectual functioning must show up during the period of intellectual development (up to age eight). In many circles, the term *developmentally delayed* is beginning to replace the narrower term *mentally retarded*. Diagnosis may come only after the administration of an IQ test, but initial suspicions generally come from perceived delays in developmental or adjustive patterns of behavior. Even more common these days is the reference to persons—children in particular—as "exceptional." The term is meant to offset some of the negative stereotyping associated with such terms as "retarded" or "handicapped."

By making "impairment in adaptive behavior" a part of their definition of mental retardation, the AAMD is acknowledging that there is more to getting along in this world than the intellectual and academic sorts of skills IQ tests emphasize. Being mentally retarded does not mean being helpless, particularly for those at borderline or mild levels of retardation. Of major consideration is the ability to adapt to one's environment. In this regard, such skills as the abilities to dress oneself, follow directions, make change, or find one's way home from a distance become relevant (Coulter & Morrow, 1978).

Even without a simple definition of retardation based solely on IQ, the population of mentally retarded or developmentally delayed citizens is large. Estimates indicate that approximately 3 percent of the population at any one time falls within the IQ range for retardation. Two other relevant estimates are that nearly 900,000 children and young adults with mental retardation between the ages of three and 21 years are being served in the public schools (Schroeder et al., 1987) and that nearly 200,000 mentally retarded persons are found in community residential facilities: state and county mental hospitals and nursing homes (Landesman & Butterfield, 1987). Let's now turn to a brief discussion of the causes, treatment, and prevention of mental retardation.

The Causes of Mental Retardation

Approximately one-fourth of all cases of mental retardation reflect a problem that developed before, during, or just after birth. Between 15 and 20 percent of those persons referred to as mentally retarded were born prematurely—at least three weeks before the due date or at a weight below 5 pounds, 8 ounces.

We appreciate that the health of the mother during pregnancy and the health of the father at conception can affect the health of the child. Many prenatal conditions can cause developmental delays, including hypertension, exposure to X rays, low oxygen intake, rubella, maternal syphilis, and the mother's use of drugs, from powerful narcotics to the frequent use of aspirin, alcohol, or nicotine. To greater and lesser degrees, all of these can be linked to mental retardation. In addition, some cases stem from difficulties or injuries during the birth process itself.

Down syndrome a condition of several symptoms, including mental retardation, caused by an extra (47th) chromosome

As we've seen, the extent to which normal levels of intelligence are inherited is open to debate. Some types of mental retardation, however, are clearly genetic in origin. One of the clearest examples is the intellectual retardation accompanying **Down syndrome**, first noted in 1866. We don't know exactly why it happens, but occasionally a fetus develops with 47 chromosomes instead of the usual 46, or 23 pairs. We do know that Down syndrome is more likely to occur as the age of *either* parent increases. The physical signs are well-known: small, round skull; flattened face; large tongue; short, broad nose; broad hands; and short, stubby fingers. During childhood, behavioral development is delayed. A Down syndrome child may fall into any level of retardation. Many are educable and lead lives of considerable independence; although, even as adults many will require supervision at least some of the time.

Fragile X syndrome is a variety of mental retardation with a genetic basis that was discovered more recently—in the late 1960s (Bregman et al., 1987). Although it can occur in females, it is found primarily in males. Males with Fragile X syndrome usually have long faces, big ears, and, as adults, large testes (Zigler & Hodapp, 1991). Individuals with this form of retardation have difficulty processing sequences of events or events in a series, which means that they have problems with language skills. One curiosity is that whereas males with Down syndrome show a gradual but steady decrease in IQ scores with age, males with Fragile X syndrome show their most noticeable declines during puberty.

Most cases of mental retardation do not have obvious causes. About one-half to three-quarters of cases of mental retardation do not have known biological or genetic causes (Zigler & Hodapp, 1991).

Dealing effectively with mental retardation has been difficult. Special education programs have helped, but not all have been successful (Zigler & Hodapp, 1991). Preparing teachers and mental health professionals to be sensitive to the wide range of behaviors and feelings of which mentally retarded persons are capable has also helped. Impressive changes *can* be made in raising the IQs of some mildly retarded and a few moderately retarded children (Landesman & Ramey, 1989). As strange—and as frustrating—as it may be, there are still many more basic questions about how best to accommodate exceptional children with intellectual deficits than there are answers. For example, *main-streaming*, placing mildly retarded and borderline children in regular classroom settings, has been a common practice for several years. Is it a beneficial practice? Is it any better than segregating exceptional children in special schools or special classrooms? As yet, there is simply no clear-cut evidence one way or the other (Cole et al., 1991; Detterman & Thompson, 1997). For severely and profoundly retarded persons, the outlook is not bright—at least in terms of raising IQ points (Spitz, 1986). But we always need to remind ourselves that quality of life is not necessarily a function of IQ. The emphasis in recent years has been less on overall intellectual growth and more on those specific skills and abilities that can be improved.

There is greater hope in the area of prevention. As we continue to appreciate the influences of the prenatal environment on the development of cognitive abilities, we can educate mothers and fathers about how their behaviors can affect their child even before it is born. An excellent example of how mental retardation can be prevented concerns a disorder called *phenylketonuria,* or *PKU.* This disorder is genetic in origin, and over 50 years ago it was found to be a cause of mental retardation. PKU results when a child inherits genes that fail to produce an enzyme that normally breaks down chemicals found in many foods. Although a newborn with PKU usually appears normal, a simple blood test can detect the disorder soon after birth. Once PKU has been detected, a prescribed diet (which must be maintained for about four years) can reduce or eliminate any of the retardation effects of the disorder.

BEFORE YOU GO ON

- How is giftedness defined?

- Briefly describe the six categories used to define giftedness.

- How is mental retardation defined?

- Describe the different categories of mental retardation.

- Describe the biological/genetic causes for retardation.

- Describe the environmental causes for retardation.

Topic Review 7 A

1. **How is intelligence defined?**

   Intelligence can be defined in an academic/theoretical sense and in an operational/practical sense. The academic/theoretical definition of intelligence is that intelligence is the capacity of an individual to understand the world and use resourcefulness to cope with its challenges. On the operational/practical level, intelligence can be defined as that which intelligence tests measure.

2. **How did Spearman, Thurstone, Guilford, and Vernon define intelligence?**

   Spearman viewed intelligence as consisting of one general factor ("g") and a number of specific abilities ("s"). Thurstone saw intelligence as a combination of seven unique and primary mental abilities. Guilford argued that there are as many as 150 cognitive skills that constitute one's intelligence. Vernon suggested that intellectual skills or cognitive abilities can be arranged in a hierarchy from general at the top to specific at the bottom.

3. **How did Sternberg and Gardner define intelligence?**

   Sternberg argued that intelligence should be conceptualized as an organized set of three cognitive processes: (1) a componential, "academic" type of intelligence, (2) an experiential, "creative" type of intelligence, and (3) a contextual, "practical" type of intelligence. Gardner also proposed multiple intelligences: mathematical, verbal, spatial, musical, bodily, interpersonal, and intrapersonal.

4. **What is emotional intelligence?**

   Emotional intelligence (or EQ), as introduced by Mayer and Salovey and popularized by Goleman in the mid-1990s, is characterized by the ability to perceive emotions accurately, to appreciate the emotional states of others, and to generate and manage one's emotions to promote more effective thinking. It is thought to be independent of cognitive, or academic intelligence.

5. **How do Western and non-Western concepts of intelligence differ?**

   Western cultures place a great deal of emphasis on the speed of processing information as an index of intelligence, whereas non-Western cultures do not. Chinese culture acknowledges a general intelligence (like Spearman's g-factor) but emphasizes other aspects of intelligence not recognized by Western cultures. These are interpersonal intelligence, intrapersonal intelligence, intellectual self-assertion, and intellectual self-effacement. Western concepts of intelligence emphasize verbal ability, the ability to solve practical problems, and social competence. The African concept of intelligence stresses skills and abilities that foster intragroup harmony and cooperation, whereas Western culture stresses technologically-based concepts.

6. **How is "emotional intelligence" different from "cognitive" or "academic" intelligence?**

   Although both may be helpful in real-life problem solving, emotional intelligence is more involved in how one feels and how accurately one can assess one's own emotional states and those of others. Academic or cognitive intelligence, on the other hand, deals more with what one "knows," the accumulation of knowledge, facts, and ideas.

7. **What is the definition of a psychological test?**

   A psychological test is an objective, standardized measure of a sample of behavior. Psychological tests are used as an aid in the understanding and prediction of behavior.

8. **What determines the quality of psychological tests?**

   Psychological tests are objective, standardized measures of samples of behaviors. To be a "good" quality test, an instrument must demonstrate: (1) reliability—that it measures something consistently, (2) validity—that it measures what it says it's measuring, and (3) adequate norms that can be used to assign meaning to an individual score.

9. **What is the Stanford-Binet intelligence test?**

   The Stanford-Binet is the oldest of general intelligence tests (commonly called IQ tests). Its most recent (1986) revision yields an overall score ("g"), as well as subscores for a number of abilities assumed to underlie general intelligence. The test consists of 15 subtests, each assessing a specific cognitive task. Scores on the test compare the performance of an individual to that of others of the same age level.

10. What are crystallized and fluid-analytic abilities?

Crystallized abilities are skills needed to acquire and use information about verbal and quantitative concepts that are influenced by schooling. Fluid-analytic abilities are those needed to solve problems that involve figural or nonverbal information. Fluid-analytical abilities are less influenced by formal schooling.

11. What is the intelligence quotient?

The intelligence quotient (IQ) is a number that is computed to represent a person's intelligence. The IQ score used to be computed as MA/CA x 100. The traditional IQ score is no longer used. IQ scores are now tied to established group norms and statistics.

12. What are the major features of the Wechsler intelligence scales?

The three Wechsler scales are individually administered tests of general intelligence, each appropriate for a specific age group. Each scale consists of verbal or performance subtests of varied content. Hence, three scores can be determined: an overall score, a score on the verbal subtests, and a score on the performance subtests. Scores on the Wechsler tests are standard scores that compare one's abilities to those of others of the same age.

13. What is the difference between a paper-and-pencil intelligence test and an aptitude test?

Most educational aptitude tests (such as the SAT or ACT) are essentially paper-and-pencil tests of general intellectual abilities that are used to make predictions about future academic performance. That is, the difference between the two types lies in how the scores are used, assessment or prediction.

14. Are there gender differences in IQ?

No and yes. There are no significant differences between men and women on virtually any test that yields a general IQ score. There are some specific skills and abilities that demonstrate gender differences, but the differences are "on the average" and quite slight. Exceptions are spatial relations skills and advanced math (males score higher) skills and verbal fluency and writing skills (females score higher).

15. Does intelligence increase, decrease, or remain the same with increasing age?

Overall intelligence does tend to decline slightly as one approaches the age of fifty or sixty. Various skills and abilities are differentially affected by age. Fluid intelligence declines with age, whereas crystallized intelligence remains constant or even increases slightly with age. Although with advanced age one may have a more difficult time encoding new information, there is little reason to believe that other intellectual skills will diminish.

16. What are Fluid and Crystallized intelligence?

Fluid intelligence is intelligence manifesting itself in abilities related to speed, adaptation, flexibility, and abstract reasoning which are the skills that show the greatest decline with age. Fluid intelligence is not dependent on specific learning. Crystallized intelligence comprises abilities depending on acquired knowledge, accumulated experiences, and general information and remain constant or even increase throughout one's lifetime.

17. Are there racial differences in IQ scores?

There are reliable differences between the IQs of African Americans and Caucasians, with most studies putting the average difference at about 15 points in favor of Caucasians, whereas Asian-American students, on average, perform better on tests of academic achievement, mathematics in particular. The data on group differences tell us nothing, however, about their source. Arguments have been made favoring genetic and environmental causes, including different emphases put on testing in different cultures. Group differences tell us nothing, again, about their source.

18. What is a stereotype threat, and how does it relate to racial differences in IQ?

A stereotype threat is activated whenever a person is required to do a task for which a negative group stereotype exists. Performance on such a task will be generally poor because of evaluative pressure, self-handicapping, and frustration.

19. What defines the mentally gifted?

Giftedness can mean several things in addition to overall intellectual ability as measured by IQ tests (usually an IQ over 130). Other abilities in which individuals may be gifted include psychomotor skills, the visual and performing arts, leadership, creativity, and abilities in specific academic areas. The Terman-Stanford research tells us that persons who are mentally gifted experience other physical, educational, social, and economic advantages.

20. How do we define mental retardation?

Mental retardation is indicated by below-average intellectual functioning (IQ scores less than 70), originating during the developmental period (within eighteen years) and associated with impairment in adaptive behavior (as well as academic behaviors).

21. What are the causes of mental retardation?

In addition to genetic causes (as in Down syndrome and Fragile X syndrome), most known causes of mental retardation involve the health of the parents at conception and the care of the mother and fetus during pregnancy and delivery. Drugs, lack of oxygen, and poor nutrition have been implicated in mental retardation. In other words, many causes of mental retardation appear to be preventable.

Topic 7B LANGUAGE AND PROBLEM SOLVING

In Topic 7B we consider two examples of human intelligence in action: the use of language as a means of communication and as a means of problem solving.

Key Questions to Answer

While reading this Topic, find the answers to the following key questions:

1. What are the defining characteristics of language?

2. What is the difference between communication and language?

3. What are arbitrary symbolic reference, productivity, semanticity, and displacement?

4. How are rules and structure reflected in the use of phonemes, morphemes, and syntax?

5. What is the study of "pragmatics," and what does it tell us about language use?

6. What is babbling?

7. What are the characteristics of a child's first word?

8. What is telegraphic speech?

9. What happens after the two-word stage of language development?

10. What is the learning theory of language acquisition?

11. What is the nativist theory of language acquisition?

12. What is overregularization, and what does it tell us about language development?

13. What is the interactionist theory of language acquisition?

14. What are well-defined and ill-defined problems?

15. In the context of problem solving, what is meant by problem representation?

16. How are algorithmic and heuristic strategies used to solve problems?

17. How might mental sets or functional fixedness hinder problem solving?

18. Which heuristics hinder problem solving?

19. What is involved in creative problem solving?

LANGUAGE

Language is a social process, a means of communication, which reflects a marvelously complex cognitive activity. The philosopher Suzanne Langer put it this way:

> Language is, without a doubt, the most momentous and at the same time the most mysterious product of the human mind. Between the most clear animal call of love or warning or anger, and a man's least, trivial word, there lies a whole day of Creation or in modern phrase, a whole chapter of evolution. (1951, p. 94)

Let's Talk: What Is Language?

How will we characterize this mysterious product of the human mind called language? **Language** is a large collection of arbitrary symbols that have a shared significance for a language-using community and that follow certain rules of combination (Morris, 1946). We need to make a clear distinction between *communication* and *language.* Communication is the act of transferring information from one point to another. Language, on the other hand, is a specific means of communication. You may find yourself arguing with someone who insists that animals (e. g., chimpanzees, dolphins, bees) use language. They don't. They do have elaborate communication systems. For example, chimpanzees use vocalizations and gestures to communicate messages. However, this and other animal communication systems do not qualify as a language. As we explore the definition of language and examine its properties, you will see why animal communication systems don't qualify as true languages.

language a large collection of arbitrary symbols that have a shared significance for a language-using community and that follow certain rules of combination

Language consists of a large number of *symbols* that can be combined in an infinite number of ways to produce an infinite number of utterances. The symbols that constitute language are commonly referred to as words—labels we have assigned to concepts, or our mental representations. When we use the word *chair* as a symbol, we don't use it to label just one specific instance of a chair. We use the word as a symbol to represent our concept of chairs. As symbols, words need not stand for real things in the real world. We have words to describe objects or events that cannot be perceived, such as *ghost* or, for that matter, *mind.* With language we can communicate about owls and pussycats in teacups and a four-dimensional, time-warped hyperspace. Words stand for cognitions, or concepts, and we have a great number of them.

Language use is a social process, a means of communicating our understanding of events to others.

One property of all true languages is **arbitrary symbolic reference** (Glucksburg & Danks, 1975), which means that there need be no resemblance between a word and its referent. In other words, there is no requirement for using the particular symbol for a given object. You call what you are reading a book (or a textbook, to use a more specific symbol). We have all agreed (in English) that *book* is the appropriate symbol for what you are reading. But we don't have to. We could agree to call it a *relm*. Or a *poge*. The symbols of a language are arbitrary, but once established by common use or tradition, they become part of one's language and must be learned and applied consistently by each new language user. Notice also that the arbitrary reference for symbols in one's language can change over time. Think how the symbols, "gay," or "cool," or "the web" have changed in terms of what they reference today compared to just 50 years ago. Consider what the year 2000 presidential election (particularly in Florida) did for the symbol "chad" or "hanging chad" much less "pregnant chad."

arbitrary symbolic reference the property of human language that there does not have to be any relationship between a word and its referent

To be part of a language, at least in a practical sense, language symbols need to have shared *significance for a language-using community.* That is, people have to agree on both the symbols used in a language and what those symbols mean. This refers to the property of language known as **semanticity** which refers to the meaning that words take on in language. Because language has semanticity it can be used as a social enterprise. You and I might decide to call what you are now reading a *relm*, but then you and I would be in a terribly small language-using community.

semanticity the property of human language that gives language its meaning

The final part of our definition tells us that the symbols of a language must follow certain *rules of combination.* What this means is that language is structured or rule-governed. It is used to communicate ideas and to share our thoughts and feelings with others. Of course, there are ways of communicating that do not involve language. What makes language use a special form of communication is the fact that it is governed by rules of combination. For one thing, there are rules about how we can and cannot string symbols together in language. In English we say, "The small boy slept late." We do not say, "Slept boy late small the." Well, we could say it, but no one will know for sure exactly what we mean by it. The utterance violates the rules of combination in English. When the rules of language are violated, utterances lose their meaning, and the value of language as a means of communication is lost.

Although "The small boy slept late." is sensible in English, "Slept boy late small the." is not, demonstrating that word order matters in language utterances.

Even with this complex definition of language, a few points are left out. For one, using language is a remarkably *creative, generative process.* This refers to the property of language known as **productivity**. Productivity means that with a limited number of language symbols, we can express an infinite number of ideas. Nearly everything we say is something we've never said before. It's unlikely, for example, that you have ever

productivity the property of human language that it is possible to produce an unlimited number of utterances with a limited number of speech sounds

Your dog may be able to communicate to you all sorts of feelings, needs, or desires. But because your dog lacks language, it cannot communicate with you about what it did last week or what it would like to do next weekend. Lacking *displacement*, your dog can only communicate about the here and now.

displacement the property of language that allows us to refer to the past and future, and not just the present

before read a sentence just like this one. Almost every time we use language, we use it in a new and creative way, which emphasizes the importance of the underlying rules, or structure, of language. Another property of language is **displacement**, the ability to communicate about the "not here and the not now." We can use language to talk about yesterday's lunch and tomorrow's class schedule. We can talk about things that are not here, never were, and never will be. Language is the only form of communication that allows us to do so.

Finally, language and speech are not synonymous terms. Speech is one way in which language is expressed as behavior. There are others, including writing, coding (as in Morse code), or signing (as in American Sign Language).

The properties of language give it unique qualities, and set it apart from animal communication systems. No animal communications system known has the properties of language we just described. For example, chimpanzee vocalizations and gestures have specific meaning (not arbitrary symbolic reference). They also cannot be combined to express an infinite number of ideas (they lack productivity), and they refer only to the here and now (there is no capacity for displacement). Thus, although animals communicate with one another, they do not have true language.

Describing the Structure in Language

Psycholinguistics is a hybrid discipline consisting of scientists trained in psychology *and* linguistics. When psycholinguists analyze a language, they usually do so at three levels. The first level involves the sounds that are used when we express language as speech. The second level deals with the meaning of words and sentences, and the third involves the rules used for combining words and phrases to generate sentences. At each of these three levels we can see structure and rules at work (Best, 1999).

Individual speech sounds of a language are called **phonemes**. They are the sounds we make when we talk to each other. Phonemes by themselves have no meaning, but when put together in the proper order they result in a meaningful utterance. For example, the word *cat* consists of three phonemes: an initial consonant sound (a "k" sound here), the vowel sound of "a," and a consonant sound, "t." How phonemes are combined to form words and phrases is governed by *phonological rules*. If we were to interchange the consonant sounds in *cat* we would have an altogether different utterance, *tack,* with an altogether different meaning. To use a language requires knowing which speech sounds are part of that language and how they may be combined to form larger language units. There are approximately 45 phonemes in English. (Because those 45 sounds are represented by only 26 letters in our alphabet, it is little wonder many of us have problems spelling.) As we noted above, because language is productive, we can express an infinite number of ideas with this limited set of speech sounds.

> **phoneme** the smallest distinguishable unit of sound in the spoken form of a language

Describing a language's phonemes, noting which sounds are relevant and which combinations are possible, is only a small part of a complete description of a language. Another level of analysis involves *meaning* in the language. The study of meaning is called **semantics**. Researchers interested in semantics take the morpheme as their unit of analysis. A **morpheme** is the smallest unit of *meaning* in a spoken language. A morpheme is a collection of phonemes that means something. In many cases, a *morpheme* is a *word*. For example, *write* is a morpheme and a word; it has meaning, and it is not possible to subdivide it into smaller, meaningful units. This type of morpheme is called a *free morpheme* because it can stand alone. Other morphemes, known as *bound morphemes* are not words and cannot stand alone. Prefixes (for example, re-and un-) and suffixes (for example, -ing and -ed) are bound morphemes because they must be attached to another morpheme to be used properly. *Rewrite* is a word and has meaning, but it consists of two morphemes, *write* (a free morpheme) and *re* (a bound morpheme), which in this context means roughly, "do it again." *Tablecloth* is another word composed of two morphemes, *table* and *cloth* (this time two free morphemes).

> **semantics** the study of the meaning of words and sentences
>
> **morpheme** the smallest unit of meaning in a language

The use of morphemes is governed by *morphological rules*. For example, we cannot go around making nouns plural in any old way. The plural of ox is oxen, not oxes. The plural of mouse is mice, not mouses, mousen, or meese. If you want to write something over again, you have to rewrite it, not write-re it. Note how morphemes are verbal labels for concepts (mental representations). Asking you to rewrite something would make no sense if we did not share the concepts of "writing" and of "doing things over again."

The aspect of our language that most obviously uses rules is the generation of sentences—stringing words (or morphemes) together to create meaningful utterances (Hörmann, 1986). The rules that govern how sentences are formed (or structured) in a language are referred to as the **syntax** of a language. The formal expression of the syntax of a language is its *grammar.*

> **syntax** the rules that govern how the morphemes of a language are combined in order to form meaningful utterances

To know the syntax, or syntactic rules, of one's language involves a peculiar sort of knowledge or cognitive ability. We all know the rules of English in the sense that we can and do use them, but few of us know what those rules are in the sense that we can tell anyone else what they are. We say that people have a *competence,* a cognitive skill that governs language use. That skill allows us to judge the extent to which an utterance is a meaningful, well-formed sentence (Howard, 1983; Slobin, 1979). We know that "The dog looks terrifying" fits the rules of English and that "The dog looks barking" does not, and somehow we recognize that "The dog looks watermelon" is downright absurd. At the same time, we recognize that "Colorless green ideas sleep furiously" *does* fit the rules of English, even though it doesn't make sense (Chomsky, 1957). It may be a silly thing to say, but we realize that it is a grammatically correct thing to say.

We also know that these two utterances communicate the same message, even though they look (and sound) quite different:

The student read the textbook.

The textbook was read by the student.

In either case, we know who is doing what. Another linguistic intuition that demonstrates our competence with the rules of our language is in our ability to detect ambiguity. Look at these two sentences:

They are cooking apples.

They are cooking apples.

There is no doubt that the sentences appear to be identical, but upon reflection we can see that they may be communicating different (ambiguous) ideas. In one case, we may be talking about what some people are cooking (apples as opposed to spaghetti). In another, we may be identifying a variety of apple (those best suited for cooking as opposed to those best suited for eating). In yet another case, we may be describing what is being done to the apples (cooking them as opposed to eating them). You may be able to think of other ways in which this simple sentence can be interpreted. This is not an isolated example of ambiguity in language. There are many: "The shooting of the policemen was terrible," or "Flying airplanes can be dangerous."

Language Use as a Social Process

The main purpose of language is communication. Language helps us share our thoughts, feelings, intentions, and experiences with others. Language use is social behavior. **Pragmatics** is the study of how language is related to the social context in which it occurs. Our understanding of sarcasm (as in "Well, it certainly is a beautiful day!" when in fact it is rainy, cold, and miserable), or simile (as in "Life is like a sewer…"), or metaphor (as in "His slam dunk to start the second half was the knockout blow"), or cliché (as in "It rained cats and dogs") depends on many things, including an appreciation of the context of the utterance and the intention of the speaker. The rules of conversation (turn taking) are also part of the pragmatics of speech. We have learned that it is most efficient to listen while others speak and to speak when they listen. We all know what it is like to have a "conversation" with someone who violates this rule.

pragmatics the study of how social contexts affect the meaning of linguistic events

In their classic comedy movies, Laurel and Hardy often found themselves in significant—and silly—predicaments, usually because of the actions of Stan Laurel. Oliver Hardy would then declare, "This is a fine kettle of fish you've gotten us into!" Because of the pragmatics of the situation, no one in the audience would take the words literally, looking for actual fish in an actual kettle.

Pragmatics involve decisions based on the perception of the social situation at the moment. Think how you modify your language use when you talk to your best friend, a preschool child, a professor in her office, or a driver who cuts you off at an intersection. Contemporary concerns about "political correctness" seem relevant here, don't they? In most contexts, words such as *pig, Uncle Tom, boy,* and *girl* are reasonable and proper; in other contexts they can evoke angry responses. In some American Indian cultures, periods of silence—even lengthy periods of silence—during conversation are common and acceptable. Someone not familiar with this pragmatic reality could become anxious and upset about long pauses in the midst of a conversation (e.g., Basso, 1970; Brislin, 1993, pp. 217–221). As you can imagine, translations from one language to another can cause huge changes in meaning as cultural contexts change. Two of my favorites (from Berkowitz, 1994) are the translation of the slogan "Finger Lickin' Good" into Chinese, yielding, "Eat Your Fingers Off," and in Taiwan, the slogan "Come alive with the Pepsi Generation" becomes "Pepsi will bring your ancestors back from the dead."

BEFORE YOU GO ON

- What is language, and how does it differ from communication?

- Briefly describe the properties of all human languages.

- What are phonemes and morphemes?

- What is the syntax of a language?

- What are the pragmatics of a language?

LANGUAGE ACQUISITION

One of the most significant achievements of childhood is the acquisition of language. Few, if any, cognitive skills can compare to language use in complexity and utility. Language acquisition is nothing short of miraculous. Think about it for a moment: When you were a newborn you had no capacity for language production. The only way you could communicate was through crying. Over the course of the first year you began to modify your crying pattern to communicate different messages (hunger, anger, pain). You eventually began making speech sounds (cooing) and began stringing them together (babbling). By the time you were one year old, you used your first word. By 18 months you were stringing two words together into simple (although grammatically correct) sentences. By the time you were five years old, you had mastered most of the complexities of language and were a proficient language user. In five short years, you acquired language.

It is important to understand that you did not specifically set out to "learn language," as you would in your college Spanish or French class. Instead, you set out to learn how to communicate with other members of your species. The way humans communicate is through a structured, rule-governed language. In order to fit in with other humans and adapt to your world you had to learn to communicate. Along the way, you learned language.

Children acquire language behaviors with an ease and facility that is a marvel to behold.

What Happens in Language Acquisition

babbling speech phonemes produced in rhythmic, repetitive patterns

Infants create speech sounds spontaneously. They come into the world with a cry and make noise with regularity forever after. At about the age of six months, random cries and noises are replaced by the more regular sounds of babbling. **Babbling** is the production of strings of phonemes which begins somewhere between four and six months of age (Shaffer, 1999). Babbling occurs in repetitive, rhythmic patterns, such as "ma-ma-ma" or "lu-lu-nah-nah." All babies babble in the same way for the first six months of the babbling period (Shaffer, 1999, Nakazima, 1962; Oller, 1981). An adult cannot distinguish the babbling of a Chinese infant from that of a Greek or an American infant. This shows that the *onset* of babbling is related to the maturation of the infant's brain. However, the *course* of babbling is related to the language environment to which the infant is exposed. Eventually, phonemes that are not part of the native language are dropped, and babbling of babies from different language environments begins to sound different.

Another piece of evidence that the onset of babbling is maturational comes from the fact that congenitally deaf infants begin to babble at the same time as hearing infants and that their early babbling is indistinguishable from hearing infants (Oller & Eilers, 1988, Lenneberg et al., 1965). However, the babbling of the deaf infant begins to fall off just as the babbling of the hearing infant reaches its peak. Deaf babies also "babble" with their fingers and hands. These motions are meaningless, but are the basis for what will later become (for many of them) their native (sign) language.

Does the frequency and nature of babbling relate to later language acquisition? Strictly speaking, there is virtually no relationship between how frequently and what an infant babbles and the later acquisition of the verbal aspects of language. However, during the babbling period infants learn about important nonverbal aspects of language such as control of attention, turn taking, and beginning and ending a conversation. Parents often engage their infants in face-to-face "interactions" during which the parent says something to the infant and waits for a response from the infant. The infant responds with babbling, and the parent waits while the infant babbles. The parent will then respond to the infant. It is through these early face-to-face language sessions that the infant begins to learn about the nonverbal aspects of language.

The acquisition of vocabulary follows soon after babbling begins. In all cases, comprehension, or understanding, comes before production. Children understand and respond appropriately to the meaning of utterances long before they are able to produce those utterances themselves. A child's first word or two usually appears at about the age of one (parents often argue that the onset of speech is earlier, but independent observers often fail to confirm what may be parental wishful thinking). Once begun, word acquisition is remarkable. A one-year-old may produce only two or three words. By the age of two, word production is up to about 50. In terms of comprehension, by age two, a child understands 200 to 300 words; by age three, over 1,000; and by age six, between 8,000 and 14,000 words (Benedict, 1979; Brown, 1973; Carey, 1978).

Describing the development of syntactic rules in children has proven difficult. As linguists began to understand the rules of adult language, it seemed reasonable to look for these same rules in the language of children. What soon became apparent was that the syntax of adult forms of language do not emerge until long after children have begun stringing words and morphemes together in utterances. Even though we do not find adult structure or rules in the language use of young children, they still use language in a rule-governed way. In other words, children do not speak adult language badly; instead, their language follows its own rules (e.g., Radford, 1990).

The first use of vocalization as language is called **holophrastic speech**—the use of just one word to communicate a range of intentions and meanings dependent on gestures, intonation, and so on. Before this stage a child may produce words, but only as a naming exercise. Words are used as labels for concepts and nothing else. With holophrastic speech, individual words are used to communicate a range of possibilities. Imagine it yourself. Picture a young child sitting in a high chair. Can't you just see how the utterance *milk* could be used to communicate such things as "I want my milk!" or "Uh-oh, I dropped my milk," or "Oh yea! here's my milk," or "Yuck, not milk again."

holophrastic speech the use of one word to communicate several meanings

Around 18 months, the child begins to produce simple sentences comprising two words. When carefully analyzed, these utterances are very regular, as if they were being put together according to strict rules. Given an understanding of the words *big* and *little* and many nouns, a child may say, "big ball," "big plane," "big doggie," "little stick," or "little cup." What is interesting is that the child will never reverse this word order. He or she will not say "ball big" or "cup little" (Braine, 1976).

telegraphic speech utterances characterized by the use of nouns, verbs, and adjectives, and few function words

During and immediately after the two-word stage a child's language is known as **telegraphic speech**, which is spoken language consisting of short sentences resembling a telegram. In telegraphic speech the child uses *content words* that convey meaning. Content words include nouns, verbs, and adjectives. The child drops *function words* from his or her telegraphic sentences. Function words include articles, prepositions, and conjunctions. We hear children say such things as "want milk" or "throw ball" rather than *"I* want milk" or "throw *the* ball." The simple sentence "want milk" conveys meaning to the listener efficiently. Imagine a parent's confusion if the child said, "I want."

BEFORE YOU GO ON

- What is babbling, and what contributes to its onset and course?

- What is the relationship between babbling and later language acquisition?

- What is holophrastic speech?

- What is telegraphic speech?

- Describe the course of language acquisition after the two-word stage.

At roughly $2^{1}/_{2}$ years of age, language use expands at an explosive rate. There really is no noticeable three-word or four-word stage of development. Phrases are lengthened, noun phrases first, so that "Billy's ball" becomes "Billy's red ball," which soon becomes "Billy's red ball that Mommy got at the store." When children are ready to begin grade school, at age five or six, they demonstrate both the understanding and the production of virtually every acceptable type of sentence structure in their language.

Theories of Language Acquisition

How is language acquired? If you studied a foreign language in high school or are studying one now, did it occur to you that there were children somewhere in the world who were easily acquiring the same language you were struggling with? Acquiring one's language is a cognitive feat at which all humans (without physical or developmental problems) succeed.

Language acquisition may have a biological foundation, but it requires the interaction of language users and language learners to progress normally.

There are three major theories of how language develops: Learning, Nativist, and Interactionist (Shaffer, 1999).

The Learning Theory of Language Development

The **learning theory of language development** maintains that language, like any other behavior, is learned. Originally, the theory stressed the role of *selective reinforcement* in the acquisition of language (Skinner, 1957). According to Skinner's view, children learn language because they are selectively reinforced for certain language constructions. For example, during babbling, parents (according to learning theory) selectively reinforce those speech sounds that are part of the infant's native language and do not reinforce those that are not. Later, parents selectively reinforce grammatically correct sentences. So, through a process of *shaping*, the child learns language.

A later addition to learning theory came from the work of Albert Bandura (1971) on how children learn through imitation. According to Bandura, much of what a child learns about the vocabulary, semantics, syntax, phonology, and pragmatics of language comes from imitating the speech of others (Shaffer, 1999).

We can be most comfortable with learning approaches when we try to account for the acquisition of phonemes and morphemes. Acquiring the phonemes of one's language seems to be a straightforward process, albeit slightly backward. The infant spontaneously produces phonemes from all languages but learns through imitation and reinforcement which sounds need to be "saved" for use in his or her language. Sounds not appropriate for the child's language are simply not used and disappear from the child's repertoire (deVillers & deVillers, 1978).

learning theory of language development a theory of language development that postulates that language, like any other behavior, is learned

One significant difficulty for language-acquisition theories is that children acquire the grammatical rules of their language without anyone teaching them those rules.

There are several varieties of learning involved in word acquisition. Some of the meaning of words comes from classical conditioning. The use of some morphemes or words is reinforced and the use of others is not, as operant conditioning predicts. Some growth in vocabulary results from observational learning—using words that others use. Some word meanings develop through direct instruction. Yes, learning seems to handle morpheme acquisition rather nicely, but there are a few problems.

For one thing, as children acquire morphemes that change the meaning of a word (called bound morphemes), they do so with a disturbing regularity. For no good reason that learning theory can account for, children learn to add *-ing* to words before they learn to form possessives (by adding *-'s*), which they learn before they learn to form the past tense of verbs (by adding *-ed*). When asked what he is doing, a child may be expected first to respond, "I draw." Later will come "I drawing." Only later may we expect "That Billy's picture." Still later we'll hear something like "I drawed it yesterday." In short, there is a predictable sequence in which many morphemes are acquired. This sequencing may reflect limits set by the child's genetic constitution or by the child's cognitive growth (i.e., he or she may not understand the basic concept of past tense until the concept of possessive is acquired), but in either case, simple learning theory is strained.

Another point often raised against the learning approach is that when it comes to the rules of syntax, most adults cannot begin to tell us what the rules of their language *are.* How, then, can you teach something to someone else if you don't have any idea what it is you're teaching? The argument is sensible. Yet as adults, we do have certain linguistic intuitions. We can tell when an utterance is correctly formed, even if we can't specify why. Perhaps we use these intuitions to reinforce proper use and to correct improper use. The problem is that when we carefully watch adults interacting with young children, we find that they are much more likely to correct the *content* of what the child says than the *form* in which it is said. If a child says, "Me no like cereal," a parent is likely to respond with a statement such as, "Sure you do; you eat it all the time" (Brown, 1973; Brown et al., 1969). "Explicit language teaching from adults is not necessary. In fact, if adults try to structure and direct a child's language learning, the outcome may be interference…" (Rice, 1989, p. 153).

overregularization the over-application of an acquired language rule (e.g., for forming plurals) in a situation in which it is not appropriate

Another problem of learning theory is called **overregularization**—the continued application of an acquired language rule (e.g., forming plurals or past tense) in a situation for which it is not appropriate. A child might say, "I have two foots," "I saw four mans," or "I goed to the store," even after using the words *feet, men,* and *went* appropriately in similar contexts. This is a grammatical construction unique to children. Children do not hear adults making overregularization errors. Nor do adults selectively reinforce such errors. Quite the contrary, parents endlessly correct these errors, albeit with very little success.

The Nativist Theory of Language Development

nativist theory of language development a theory of language development that postulates that there is a significant biological component to language development. One idea of this theory is that humans are born with a "language acquisition device."

The **nativist theory of language development** (Chomsky, 1965, 1975, 1986; Lenneberg, 1967; McNeil, 1970, Pinker, 1995; Seidenberg, 1997) states that language development has a significant biological component. According to this theory, there is an innate, "prewired" biological mechanism that compels the child to seek out and apply rules during acquisition (thus the term "nativist"). This mechanism, often called a *language acquisition device,* or *LAD,* becomes active when we are about one year old, and usually turns off by the time we are five or six years old. Further, the theory states that only humans possess the LAD, so only humans are capable of developing language.

It is important to understand that the nativists are not saying that language itself is innate. That is, the child is not born with an innate knowledge of all languages. Rather, the *capacity and mechanisms* required for language development are innate. According to the nativist perspective, a child is born with a concept of what language is. Nativists do not discount the role of the language environment. The LAD receives input from the language environment and processes that input, figuring out the syntax, semantics, and pragmatics of language. The language environment is of tremendous importance because it provides the raw materials for the LAD. The child then acts like a scientist, forming hypotheses about what language is like and testing those hypotheses against the language environment. Some hypotheses are retained; some are discarded and some modified.

This approach accounts for overregularization "errors" with this theoretical process. Early in language development, a child may use a correctly pluralized word (for example, teeth). However, eventually the child learns a rule for pluralization: "add -s or -es to form plurals." The child begins to apply this rule to regular words (for example, hats) *and* irregular words (for example, tooth becomes tooths). This is a creative error in that the child is now applying a rule for pluralization and tests it against language reality. Eventually, the hypothesis is modified based on input from the language environment, and the child stops making the overregularization errors.

Reliance on some sort of innate LAD is even more sensible when we consider the acquisition of rules reflected in the generation of sentences. The argument for an innate predisposition for the acquisition of language rules comes once again from the orderliness of language development. The ages are not always the same, but with uncanny regularity, children everywhere go about acquiring their different languages in virtually the same pattern. Holophrastic speech, the stability of the two-word utterance, the expansion of noun phrases, and the ordered acquisition of bound morphemes have been noted over and over as a consistent pattern—a pattern much more consistent than we could ever expect of the learning histories of the children being observed (Slobin, 1979).

Although the nativist theory represented a step forward in our understanding of language development, it too has some drawbacks. First, it casts the child in a relatively passive role in the language development process. One gets the image of the child waiting around for input from the language environment. With the LAD the child should be able to learn language by passively listening to language. In reality, the child plays a more active role in the language development process, actively communicating with those around him or her. Second, there is not much evidence for the existence of the LAD, let alone how the LAD works (Shaffer, 1999).

The Interactionist Theory of Language Development

interactionist theory of language development a theory of language development that acknowledges the roles of learning and biological mechanisms

Because of the shortcomings of the learning and nativist theories, a third theory was developed to account for language development. This is the **interactionist theory of language development**. The interactionist theory acknowledges the roles of reinforcement, imitation, and innate language structures in the language acquisition process. However, the theory suggests that the essence of language development lies in the child's need to interact or communicate with other members of the species. Interactionists suggest that *conversation* (not just passive receipt of language) is necessary for the child to become a skillful language user (Shaffer, 1999). Further, the theory stresses the role of general cognitive development over innate mechanisms like the LAD, and stresses the importance of social interactions between a child and older, more accomplished language users. In short, the interactionist perspective blends the best of the learning and nativist theories into a unified theory that takes into account other aspects of development (cognitive and social) that we know are important to development.

BEFORE YOU GO ON

- Briefly describe the learning theory of language acquisition and its drawbacks.

- Briefly describe the nativist theory of language acquisition and its drawbacks.

- What is an overregularization error, and what does it say about language acquisition?

- Briefly describe the interactionist theory of language acquisition.

PROBLEM SOLVING

Our daily lives are filled with problems of various sorts. Some are simple, straightforward, even trivial; others are complex and very important to us. Here we'll focus on cognitive, or intellectual, problems, those that require the manipulation of cognitions for their solution. The first thing to do is define what a problem is, and then we can consider how to go about solving one.

Just What *Is* a Problem?

Sometimes our goals are obvious, our present situation is clear, and the way to get from where we are to where we want to be is also obvious. In such cases, we don't have a problem, do we? Say you want to have a nice breakfast. You have eggs, bacon, bread, and butter available. You also have the implements needed to prepare these foods, and you know how to use them. You know that, for you, a nice breakfast would be two eggs over easy, three strips of fried bacon, and a piece of buttered toast. With little hesitation, you engage in the appropriate behaviors and reach your goal.

problem a discrepancy between one's present state and one's goal state with no apparent way to get from one to the other

A **problem** exists when there is a discrepancy between one's present state and one's perceived goal state and no readily apparent way to get from one to the other. In situations in which the path to goal attainment is not clear a problem exists, and you need to engage in problem solving behaviors—as might be the case if halfway through the preparation of breakfast you discover you have no butter or margarine.

A problem has three major components: (1) an *initial state*—the situation as it is, or is perceived to exist, at the moment; (2) a *goal state*—the situation as the problem solver would like it to be, or the end product; and (3) possible *routes or strategies* for getting from the initial state to the goal state.

Psychologists also distinguish between well-defined and ill-defined problems. *Well-defined problems* are those in which both the initial state and the goal state are clearly defined. We know what the current situation is, what the goal is, and we may even know some of the possible ways to go about getting from one to the other. "What English word can be made from the letters *teralbay*?" We see that this question presents a problem. We understand what the question is asking, have some ideas about how we might go about answering it, and will surely know when we have succeeded. "How do you get home from campus if you discover that your car, which is in the campus parking lot, won't start?" Again, we know our initial state (on campus with a car that won't start), and we'll know when we have reached our goal (we're at home), but we have to find a different way to get there.

Most of the problems we face every day are *ill-defined*. In such cases, we do not have a clear idea of what we are starting with, nor are we able to clearly identify or define any ideal solution. "What should my college major be?" Many high school seniors (and some college seniors) don't even know what their options are. They have few ideas about how to find out about college majors. And once they have selected a major, they are not at all sure that their choice was the best one—which may explain why so many college students change their majors so often. Ill-defined problems usually involve many variables that are difficult to define (much less control), so psychologists usually study problems that are at least reasonably well defined.

Problem Representation

Once we realize we're facing a problem, the first thing we should do is put it in some form that allows us to think about it in familiar terms. We need to *represent* the problem in our own minds, interpreting the problem so that the initial state and the goal state are clear to us. We also need to note if there are any restrictions on how we can go about seeking solutions. In short, we need to understand the nature of the problem and should try to make it meaningful by relating it to information we have available in our memories.

By examining a few problems of the sort that have been used in the psychology laboratory, we can see that how we represent a problem can be critical. Consider the following classic example (from Duncker, 1945):

> One morning, exactly at sunrise, a Buddhist monk began to climb a tall mountain. A narrow path, only a foot or two wide, spiraled around the mountain to a glittering temple at the summit. The monk ascended at varying rates of speed, stopping many times along the way to rest and eat dried fruit which he carried with him. He reached the temple shortly before sunset. After days of fasting and meditation, he began his journey back down along the same path, starting at sunrise again and walking at variable speeds, with many pauses along the way. His

average speed going down was, of course, greater than his average climbing speed. Show that there is a spot along the path that the monk occupied on both trips at precisely the same time of day.

Thinking about this problem as it is presented—in words—can be maddening. As is often the case with real-life problems, this statement contains a lot of irrelevant information. Useful problem representation often involves sorting out what matters and what doesn't. The fact that we're dealing with a monk is not relevant, nor is the temple, the dried fruit, the fact that the path is narrow, or that the trip was made on two different days.

You might represent this problem in terms of just one climber making the trip in one day. Or, better still, imagine that there are two climbers: one starting from the top of the mountain, the other starting from the bottom. Because they both take the same path, surely they will meet somewhere on that mountain trail sometime during the day. When you represent the problem this way, the solution is readily apparent. So it might help to represent the mountain-climbing problem visually, drawing out the ascending and descending pathways on a sheet of paper.

Representing the following problem visually would not be wise:

> Imagine that you have a very large sheet of paper, 1/100 of an inch thick. Imagine folding it over on itself so that now you have two layers of paper. Fold it again so that there are four layers. It is impossible to actually fold a sheet of paper 50 times, but imagine that you could. About how thick would the paper be if it were folded over on itself 50 times? (From Adams, 1974)

On the one hand, it sounds so simple: imagine what it would be like to fold a piece of paper over and over. Unfortunately, picturing just what a piece of paper folded 50 times really would look like is very difficult. Some people guess a few inches. Some say that the folded paper would be a few feet thick. Many have no idea at all. Representing this problem in visual terms is of little help. If one recognizes this as a mathematics problem, involving exponents, a correct solution is more likely. Actually, 50 folds would increase the paper's thickness by a factor of 250. That comes to 1,100,000,000,000,000 inches, and the resulting paper would be so thick it would nearly reach from the earth to the sun!

Problem representation often provides *the* stumbling block to problem solution. Once you realize you're faced with a problem, your first step should be to represent it in a variety of ways. Eliminate nonessential information. Try to relate the problem to other problems you have solved before. Having done so, if the solution is still not obvious you may have to develop some strategy to move from your representation of the problem to its solution. We now turn to how one might go about generating possible problem solutions.

Problem-Solving Strategies

Once you have represented the initial state of a problem and have a clear idea of what an acceptable goal state might be, you still have to figure out how to get to that goal. You might spend a few minutes guessing wildly at a solution, but soon you'll have to settle on some strategy. In this context, a **strategy** is a systematic plan for generating possible solutions that can be tested to see if they are correct. The main advantage of cognitive strategies is that they permit the problem solver to exercise some degree of control over the task at hand. They allow solvers to choose the skills and knowledge they will bring to bear on any particular problem at any time (Gagné, 1984). There are several strategies one might choose to try. We'll consider two types of strategies: algorithms and heuristics.

An **algorithm** is a strategy that guarantees that eventually you will arrive at a solution if the strategy is correctly applied. Algorithms systematically explore and evaluate all possible solutions until the correct one is found. It is sometimes referred to as a *generate-test strategy,* in which one generates hypotheses about solutions and then tests each one in turn. Given their speed of computation, most computer programs designed to solve problems use algorithmic strategies.

Simple anagram problems (letters of a word shown in a scrambled fashion) can be solved using an algorithmic strategy. "What English word has been scrambled to make *uleb*?" With sufficient patience, you can systematically rearrange these four letters until you hit on a correct solution: *leub, lueb, elub, uleb, buel, beul, blue.* There it is, *blue.* With only four letters to deal with, finding a solution generally doesn't take very long; there are only 24 possible arrangements of four letters ($4 \times 3 \times 2 \times 1 = 24$).

On the other hand, consider the eight-letter anagram *teralbay.* In fact, there are 40,320 possible combinations of these eight letters: $8 \times 7 \times 6 \times 5 \times 4 \times 3 \times 2 \times 1 = 40,320$ (Reynolds & Flagg, 1983). Unless your system for moving letters around just happens to start in a good place, you could spend a lot of time trying to come up with a combination that produces an English word. If we were dealing with a ten-letter word, there would be 3,628,800 possible combinations to check!

Imagine that you go to the supermarket to buy a jar of horseradish. You're quite sure the store has horseradish, but you have no idea where to find it. One plan would be to go up and down every aisle of the store, checking first the top shelf, then the second, then the third, until you spied the horseradish. This (algorithm) strategy would work if the store carried horseradish and if you searched carefully enough. There must be a better way to solve such problems. Here's where heuristic strategies come in.

A **heuristic** is an informal, rule-of-thumb strategy of generating and testing problem solutions. Heuristics are more economical for solving problems than are algorithms, but when one uses a heuristic, there is no guarantee of success. On the other hand, heuristics are usually much less time-consuming than algorithm strategies and lead searches for goals in a logical, sensible way.

A heuristic strategy for finding horseradish in a supermarket might take you to various sections in the store in the order you believed to be most reasonable. You might start with spices, but you would be disappointed. Next, you might look among the fresh

strategy in problem solving, a systematic plan for generating possible solutions that can be tested to see if they are correct

algorithm a problem-solving strategy in which all possible solutions are generated and tested until an acceptable solution appears

heuristic an informal, economical, yet reasonable, method of testing problem solutions without the guarantee of success

vegetables. Then, upon recalling that horseradish needs to be refrigerated, you go next to the dairy case, and there you'll find the horseradish. You would not have wasted time searching the cereal aisle or the frozen food section—real possibilities if you tried an algorithmic strategy. Another, more reasonable, heuristic would be to ask an employee where the horseradish is kept.

If you tried the *teralbay* anagram problem, it is likely you used a heuristic strategy. To do so, you rely on your experience with the English language. You seriously consider only those letter combinations you know occur frequently. You generate and test the most common combinations first. You just don't worry much about the possibility that the solution may contain a combination such as *brty*. Nor do you search for a word with an *aae* string in it. You explore words that end in *able* because you know these to be fairly common. But that doesn't work. What about *br* words? No, that doesn't work. How about words with *tray* in them? *Traybeal*? No. *Baletray*? No. "Oh! Now I see it: *betrayal*." This heuristic strategy is a *means-ends analysis,* a strategy in which one always keeps the final goal in mind, but first works toward reaching subgoals (Newell & Simon, 1972). In the *teralbay* example, subgoals are letter combinations that make sense or are commonly found. Once subgoals are reached, they are manipulated in an attempt to reach the final goal. The example of the search for horseradish also involved a means-ends analysis: first find the right section of the store, then search for the specific product.

BEFORE YOU GO ON

- What is the definition of a problem?

- How does the manner in which a problem is represented affect problem solving?

- Describe algorithms and heuristics.

Barriers to Effective Problem Solving

It is difficult, often impossible, to solve problems without relying heavily on one's memory. If you couldn't remember the recipe for something you wanted for dinner, you'd have a hard time buying the correct ingredients when you went to the store. Regardless of the type of problem or the strategy employed to solve it, solving problems effectively requires that we use our memories. There are times, however, when previous experiences (and memories of them) create difficulties in problem solving. We'll look at three such cases.

Mental Set and Functional Fixedness

Perceptions can be influenced by expectations, or mental set. We often perceive what we are set to perceive. The concept of mental set is also very relevant in problem solving. A **mental set** is a tendency to perceive or respond to something in a given, or set, way. It is, in essence, a cognitive predisposition. We may have or develop expectations that interfere with effective problem solving.

mental set a predisposed (set) way to perceive or respond to something; an expectation

Figure 7.8 provides an example of how an inappropriate mental set can interfere with problem solving. When first presented with this problem, most people make an assumption (form a mental set). They assume the nine dots form a square and that their lines somehow must stay within that square. Only when this mental set is "broken" can the problem be solved. Figure 7.11 at the end of this topic provides one solution to the nine-dot problem.

Mental sets do not necessarily interfere with problem solving. The appropriate mental set can be facilitating. For example, if we told you to look beyond the confines of any imagined square when attempting the nine-dot problem, that mental set—which seems strange and out of context—could have made the problem easier to solve.

Also, mental sets may lead to less than efficient problem-solving strategies. Consider the following incident. Two friends were helping a third move from his apartment to a new one (let's call them Moe, Larry, and Curley). Moe rented a truck which, at the time, had doors that swung open and rested against the sides of the truck. After a full day of moving things into the truck it came time to close the truck and move on. When Moe, Larry and Curley tried to swing the doors shut, they found that there was a car in the way, preventing them from closing one of the doors. What to do? With their mental set squarely fixed on the car being in the way of the door, and failing to locate the owner of the car, they struck upon what to them was the *only* logical solution: pick the car up and move it. Moe, Larry and Curley picked up the front of the car, bouncing it along, and moved it sufficiently so they could close the door. It was only after they were in the truck, driving out of the parking lot that it dawned upon them, in a great epiphany, that all they had to do was move the truck forward a few feet to close the door!

Functional fixedness is a type of mental set defined by Duncker (1945) as the inability to discover an appropriate new use for an object because of experience using the object in some other function. The problem solver fails to see a solution to a problem because he or she has "fixed" some "function" to an object that makes it difficult to see how it could help with the problem at hand.

A standard example is one used by Maier (1931). Two strings are hung from the ceiling. The problem is that they are so far apart a subject cannot reach both of them at the same time. The goal is to do just that: to hold on to both strings at once. If there were nothing else in the room, this problem might never get solved. However, there are other objects in the room that the subject can use, including a pair of pliers. One solution to this problem is to tie the pliers to one string and start the pliers swinging like a pendulum. As the person holds the other string, the string with the pliers attached can be grasped as it swings over to the person. Because many people fail to see pliers as useful (functioning) for anything but turning nuts and bolts, they fail to see the pliers as a potential pendulum weight and thus may fail to solve the problem. They have "fixed" the "function" of the pliers in their mind.

Another famous example that demonstrates functional fixedness was reported by Duncker (1945). Here, someone is provided with a box of tacks, a candle, and some matches. The task is to use these materials to mount the candle on the wall and light it. Obviously one cannot just tack a candle to the wall. The solution to this problem requires

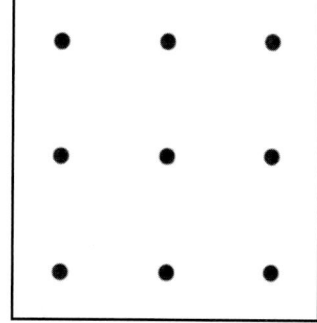

FIGURE 7.8

Without lifting your pen or pencil from the page, connect these nine dots with four straight lines.

functional fixedness a type of mental set that interferes with problem solving, involving the inability to discover a new use for an object because of prior experience with the object

breaking the mental set of functional fixedness for the box containing the tacks, seeing it as a potential candleholder, tacking it to the wall, and mounting the candle on it (Figure 7.9).

A number of experiments (e.g., Glucksberg & Danks, 1968) have shown that some subtle changes in the way in which the materials are presented have an effect on solving this problem. When the box of tacks is labeled *tacks,* the problem is much more difficult to solve. Using an empty box and having the tacks scattered about increases the likelihood that subjects will overcome the functional fixedness of seeing the box as something that holds things.

Biased Heuristics and Decision Making

For some of the problems we encounter in real life, we are provided with possibilities from which we must choose a correct or "best" alternative. Looked at this way, we see that some decision-making tasks are much like the problems we have been considering in this Topic. We've seen that problem solving requires us to use our past experience to devise strategies for reaching goal states. Occasionally our heuristic strategies—those rules of thumb used to guide problem solving—are biased because of perceptions of past experience. Such biases create a barrier to effective problem solving.

Some strategies we use to make decisions require us to estimate the probability of events, and many of these strategies are notoriously poor (Hastie & Park, 1986; Payne et al., 1992). Most of the research on judging probabilities and frequencies has been reported by Daniel Kahneman and Amos Tversky (1973, 1979, 1984; Tversky & Kahneman, 1974).

availability heuristic the assumption that whatever comes to mind readily must be more common or probable than what does not easily come to mind

The **availability heuristic** is the assumption that things that readily come to mind are more common, or frequently occurring, than things that less readily come to mind. For example, I show you a list that includes the names of 19 famous women and 20 less

FIGURE 7.9

The materials provided in the candle problem—and one solution (Duncker, 1945).

famous men. Later, you will almost certainly overestimate the number of women on the list, because those famous names were more available to you. The media (newspapers, TV, radio) often draw our attention to events (make them available) in such a way that we tend to overestimate their frequency of occurrence. When reports of terrorist bombings at foreign airports make the news, many Americans cancel their plans for European vacations, overestimating the risk of flying to Europe. Even without terrorists, most people will overestimate the number of airplane crashes that occur each year compared to the number of automobile crashes that occur, simply because we tend to hear more about the airplane accidents; they are more available in our memories.

The **representativeness heuristic** is the assumption that any judgments made about the most prototypic member of a category will hold for all members of the category. For example, you know that a particular group of men consists of 70 percent lawyers and 30 percent engineers. You are told that one of the men, chosen at random, has hobbies that include carpentry, sailing, and mathematical puzzles. Is this man an engineer or a lawyer? Because you believe these hobbies to be representative of engineers, not lawyers, you may say that the man is an engineer, even though the likelihood that he is a lawyer is more than twice (seven to three) the chance that he is an engineer.

representativeness heuristic the assumption that judgments made about a very typical member of some category will hold for all members of that category

Which group includes more tobacco chewers, professional baseball players or college students? The answer is college students (because there are so many of them, even though a smaller percentage of them uses chewing tobacco). If you flip a coin and it turns up heads five times in a row, what is the chance of getting tails on the next flip? The probability is no better than it's been all along, 50/50 (the fact that heads have appeared the previous five times is of absolutely no consequence to the coin).

There are other heuristics that can bias our decision making and interfere with problem solving. A multiple-choice test item is the sort of problem that requires you to decide which of a number of alternatives best answers a question. A problem-solving heuristic that may cause trouble is called the **positive test strategy**—the strategy that claims that if something works, don't drop it to try something else (Klayman & Ha, 1987). This is the heuristic that suggests "If it isn't broken, don't fix it." This approach is often a sensible one, but there are instances when even better solutions—more useful decisions—could be found if only one continued to look. Have you fallen into the "trap" of saying that alternative A was the correct answer to a multiple-choice item simply because it was correct, only to discover later that alternatives B and C were also correct, thus making alternative D, "all of the above," the best answer to the question?

positive test strategy the heuristic of sticking with an acceptable decision or solution, even if better ones may exist

Successful problem solving requires that we break out of the restraints imposed by improper mental sets, functional fixedness, and some heuristic strategies. To be able to overcome these barriers reflects an ability to solve problems creatively, and it is to this subject that we turn next.

BEFORE YOU GO ON

- What is a mental set, and how can it interfere with problem solving?

- What is functional fixedness, and how can it interfere with problem solving?

- How can the availability and representativeness heuristics interfere with problem solving?

- What is the positive test strategy?

Overcoming Barriers with Creative Problem Solving

Creative solutions to problems are new, innovative, and useful. In the context of problem solving, "creative" means more than unusual, rare, or different. Someone may generate a very original plan to solve a given problem, but unless that plan works, we shouldn't view it as creative (Newell et al., 1962; Vinacke, 1974). Creative solutions should be put to the same test as more ordinary solutions: do they solve the problem at hand?

Creative solutions generally involve a reorganization of problem elements. As mentioned earlier, it is often at the stage of problem representation that creativity is most noticeable. Seeing a problem in a new light, or combining elements of a problem in a new and different way, can lead to creative solutions.

There is virtually no correlation between creative problem solving and intelligence (Barron & Harrington, 1981; Horn, 1976; Kershner & Ledger, 1985). At least there are virtually no significant correlations between tests for creativity and tests for intelligence.

divergent thinking the creation of many ideas or possible solutions from one idea

convergent thinking the reduction or focusing of many ideas or solutions into one, or a few

We say that creative problem solving often involves **divergent thinking**, that is, starting with one idea and generating from it a number of alternative possibilities and new ideas (Dirkes, 1978; Guilford, 1959b). When we engage in **convergent thinking**, we take many ideas, or bits of information, and try to reduce them to just one possible solution (Figure 7.10). Obviously, convergent thinking has its place in problem solving. But for creative problem solving, divergent thinking is generally more useful because many possibilities are explored. Remember, however, that all these new possibilities for a problem's solution ultimately need to be judged in terms of whether or not they really solve the problem.

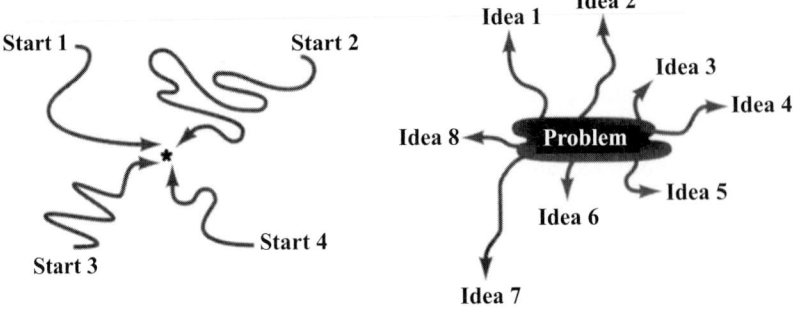

Convergent thinking: where many different starting points all come together (converge) on the same one solution to a problem

Divergent thinking: where one problem generates a number of different (divergent) ideas that take the solver in different directions

FIGURE 7.10

A schematic representation of convergent and divergent thinking in the context of problem solving.

For obvious reasons, businesses and industries are constantly on the lookout for "creative problem solvers"—people who will come up with the next generation of cordless communication device or application of Internet technology (Fontenot, 1993). Advertisements beckon employees who can "think outside the box." The data suggest that most creative discoveries are not that different from ordinary problem solving (Boden, 1990; Weisberg, 1993). Creative problem solvers are usually experts in their fields and are motivated to find unique and practical solutions (Sternberg & Lubart, 1996). Businesses which actively encourage and reward creative problem solving have found their efforts to be very reinforcing (Amabile, 1988; Simonton, 1997; Van Gundy, 1995). Encouraging creativity in the workplace involves such things as allowing time for reflective thought, collaboration among workers from different parts of the business, brainstorming sessions in which negative assessments of new ideas are forbidden, and permitting more opportunities for child-like periods of play and exploration. In business and industry, perhaps even more than elsewhere, the criterion of utility (does it work?) is every bit as valuable as the criterion of uniqueness (is it different?).

Creative problem solving can be divided into four interrelated stages. This view of the problem-solving process is an old one in psychology, but it has held up over the years (Wallas, 1926).

1. Preparation: This is not unlike problem representation. The basic elements of the problem are considered. Past experience is relevant but should not become restrictive. At this stage of problem solving, it is important to overcome the negative effects of mental set and functional fixedness. Various ways of expressing the problem are considered, but a solution is not found.

2. Incubation: In this stage, the problem is "put away" and not thought about. Perhaps fatigue that developed during failed efforts can then dissipate. Perhaps inappropriate strategies can be forgotten. Perhaps unconscious processes can be brought to bear on the problem. Why setting aside a problem may lead to its creative solution we cannot say for sure. We do know, however, that it is often very useful (Koestler, 1964; Yaniv & Meyer, 1987).

3. Illumination: This is the most mysterious stage of the process. Like insight, a potential solution to a problem seems to materialize as if from nowhere. A critical analogy becomes apparent, as does a new path to the problem's solution (Glass et al., 1979; Metcalfe & Wiebe, 1987).

4. Verification: Now the proposed solution must be tested, or verified, to see if it does in fact provide an answer to the question posed by the problem.

You have probably noted that there is really nothing extraordinary about Wallas's description of the creative problem-solving process. It sounds very much like the sort of thing anyone should do when faced with a problem. The truth is, however, that we often fail to go through these stages in any systematic fashion. To do so consciously often helps problem solving. Good problem solvers show more conscious awareness of what they are doing during the course of problem solving than do poor problem solvers (Glaser, 1984).

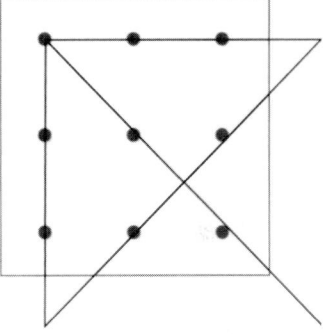

FIGURE 7.11

A possible solution to the nine-dot problem. Note that one has to break the "mental set" that the four lines must remain inside the rectangle defined by the dots.

BEFORE YOU GO ON

- Describe how creative solutions can help problem solving.

- What are divergent and convergent thinking?

- Describe the four stages of creative problem solving.

Topic Review 7 B

1. What are the defining characteristics of language?

Language is a complex and creative cognitive skill used for communication. A language consists of a large number of arbitrary symbols, usually words, that stand for, or label, our conceptualization of objects and events that have meaning for users of that language and that are combined in accordance with certain rules. The use of language is a generative process that, among other things, allows us to communicate about the "not here and the not now."

2. What is the difference between communication and language?

Communication is the general process of transferring information from one point to another. Language is a specific means of communication. Members of many species communicate with one another, but no true animal language has been identified.

3. What are arbitrary symbolic reference, productivity, semanticity, and displacement?

Arbitrary symbolic reference means that the sound of a word need not resemble its referent. Productivity refers to the fact that with a limited number of language units (e. g., speech sounds) one can express an infinite number of ideas. Semanticity refers to the meaningfulness of language. Displacement means that language is not restricted to referring to the present. Language can be used to talk about past and future events. Together, these four are defining properties of all human languages.

4. How are rules and structure reflected in the use of phonemes, morphemes, and syntax?

A phoneme is the smallest unit of sound in the spoken form of a language (i.e., a speech sound). How phonemes can be combined in a language follows strict rules. Morphemes are the smallest units of meaning in a language, including words, prefixes, and suffixes. How morphemes are ordered, or structured, in language affects their meaning. Syntax refers to the rules that govern the way morphemes are ordered, or structured, to produce sentences. Language speakers are competent in

the use of these rules even though they may not be able to state them explicitly. We can determine intuitively (without being able to explain why) when utterances are syntactically correct and when they are not. We can tell when two sentences that take different forms are communicating the same idea or message. We can identify ambiguous sentences and can often remove that ambiguity, but only when we are aware of a larger context in which the utterance occurred.

5. What is the study of "pragmatics," and what does it tell us about language use?

Pragmatics is the study of how the social situation, or context, in which language is used influences the meaning of what is being said. An appreciation of that context allows us to recognize the use of sarcasm, simile, metaphor, and the like.

6. What is babbling?

Babbling is the production of strings of phonemes that begins between four and six months of age. The onset of babbling is most closely related to physical maturation of the brain. This is supported by the facts that babies from all language environments babble in the same way early in the babbling stage and that congenitally deaf infants begin to babble at the same time as hearing infants. The course of babbling is determined by the language environment. Although there is no relationship between babbling and the acquisition of the verbal aspects of language, many nonverbal aspects of language are learned during the babbling period.

7. What are the characteristics of a child's first word?

Sometime around the end of a child's first year of life he or she will utter his or her first word. The child's first linguistic utterances are found in holophrastic speech, which occurs when one word is used to communicate a range of feelings, intentions, and meanings.

8. What is telegraphic speech?

A child begins to string words together in simple sentences. The two-word utterances show structure in word ordering. Language in this stage is called telegraphic speech because the child economizes on speech by eliminating words that convey little or no meaning (function words) while retaining words that convey meaning.

9. What happens after the two-word stage of language development?

From the two-word utterance on, language development is extremely rapid. By the time a child is five years old, he or she will know thousands of words (will understand more than she or he will produce) and be able to combine those words in virtually every acceptable sentence structure in the language.

10. What is the learning theory of language acquisition?

The learning theory of language acquisition states that language is acquired through selective reinforcement of language sounds and sentences. Imitation is another learning mechanism involved in the learning of language.

11. What is overregularization, and what does it tell us about language development?

Overregularization is when a child overapplies a rule of language. For example, saying "runned" instead of "ran." The fact that children make overregularization errors shows that selective reinforcement and imitation cannot account adequately for language development. Overregularized words are seldom used by adults.

12. What is the nativist theory of language acquisition?

The nativist theory of language acquisition states that humans have an innate concept of language. According to this theory humans have a language acquisition device (LAD) that accepts language input and figures out language. A child learning language acts as a scientist, developing and testing hypotheses about language.

13. What is the interactionist theory of language acquisition?

The interactionist theory of language acquisition combines elements of the learning and nativist theories. The theory states that there is a biological component to language acquisition and that social interaction through conversation is necessary for language acquisition.

14. What are well-defined and ill-defined problems?

A problem has three components: (1) an initial state—the situation as it exists, (2) a goal state—the situation as the problem solver would like it to be, and (3) routes or strategies for getting from the initial state to the goal state. Whether a problem is well-defined or ill-defined is a matter of the extent to which the elements of the initial state and goal state are well delineated and clearly understood by the problem solver. An example of a well-defined problem might be that which you face when a familiar route home from campus is blocked. An example of an ill-defined problem might be that which you face when you have to write a term paper on the topic of your choice.

15. In the context of problem solving, what is meant by problem representation?

Problem representation involves the mental activity of thinking about a problem and putting it into familiar terms.

16. How are algorithmic and heuristic strategies used to solve problems?

Algorithms and heuristics are types of strategies, or systematic plans, used to solve problems. Algorithms involve a systematic search of all possible solutions until the goal is reached; with algorithms, a solution is guaranteed. A heuristic strategy—of which there are many—is a more informal, rule-of-thumb approach that involves generating and testing hypotheses that may lead to a problem solution in a sensible, organized way.

17. How might mental sets or functional fixedness hinder problem solving?

A mental set is a predisposition to perceive or respond in a particular way. Mental sets develop from past experience and involve the continued use of strategies that have been successful in the past. Because those ways of perceiving or solving a problem that have worked in the past may no longer be appropriate for the problem at hand, mental sets can hinder effective problem solving. Functional fixedness is a type of mental set in which an object is seen as serving only a few fixed functions.

18. Which heuristics hinder problem solving?

We tend to judge as more likely or more probable those events readily available to us in memory—the "availability heuristic." We also tend to overgeneralize about events that are prototypic representatives of a category or concept—the "representativeness heuristic." Additionally, "positive test strategy" may have us accept a successful solution that is still not the best solution to a problem.

19. What is involved in creative problem solving?

Divergent thinking, in which a large number of alternative possibilities are generated to be tested, is seen as a useful technique in problem solving. Convergent thinking involves taking a large number of ideas or possibilities and reducing them to one or a few. Problem solving in general, and creative problem solving in particular, has four interrelated stages: (1) preparation (the problem is represented mentally), (2) incubation (the problem is put aside for a while), (3) illumination (a potential solution becomes known), and (4) verification (the potential solution is tested to see if it does solve the problem at hand).

Chapter 8

Human Development

W hen Kenny was born, it was obvious that something was not right. He didn't look normal. His eyes were too close together; he had an extra fold of skin on his eyelids; his nose was flat; and his head was smaller than normal. He also seemed less responsive to his surroundings. As Kenny grew, the early suspicions that something was wrong were reinforced. He lagged behind his peers in almost every area of development. At two years old, Kenny was functioning physically and mentally at the level of a nine-month old. His language skills were limited and he was showing signs of mental retardation.

As Kenny grew into an adolescent, his situation worsened. He was hyperactive and had difficulty focusing his attention. He suffered seizures and was photophobic (had an aversion to light). His vision was very poor. And, despite being in an enriched environment, he still lagged behind children of his own age in intelligence and motor coordination.

What could possibly have gone wrong? Was there some genetic defect that led to Kenny's problems? Or, was it something about Kenny's environment that was responsible? For most people, development proceeds normally, with few serious impediments. In Kenny's case, however, he encountered an impediment before he was born. His mother was an alcoholic and drank heavily throughout her pregnancy. The result was that Kenny's development was permanently altered.

In this chapter, we will explore the forces that influence human development. We will look at the major stages of development: childhood, adolescence, young adulthood, middle adulthood, and late adulthood. We will also explore the special challenges of the elderly and the death and dying process.

**Topic 8A
The Development of Children**

**Topic 8B
Development in Adolescence and Adulthood**

Topic 8A THE DEVELOPMENT OF CHILDREN

From conception to death, human beings share certain developmental events that unite us as one species. However, it is also true that each of us is unique. Developmental psychologists are interested in both the common patterns of our growth and development and the ways in which we differ as we grow and develop throughout our lives. We tend to think that a person's development begins at birth. In fact, growth and development begin earlier, at conception and with the first division of one cell into two, so that is where we will start.

Throughout this discussion, we will use *growth* and *development* to mean different things. Growth refers to simple enlargement—getting bigger. Development refers to a differentiation of structure or function. Something develops when it appears for the first time and remains. Thus, we say that the nervous system *develops* between week two and week eight after conception.

Key Questions to Answer

While reading this Topic, find the answers to the following key questions:

1. What is the prenatal period of development, and why do psychologists study it?

2. What happens during fertilization?

3. What happens during the germinal stage?

4. What changes take place during the embryo stage?

5. What happens during the fetal stage?

6. What effect does maternal nutrition have on prenatal development?

7. What effects do smoking, alcohol, and drugs have on prenatal development?

8. What role does the father play in problems of prenatal development?

9. What general observations can we make about physical growth and motor control in childhood?

10. What is the course of brain development in childhood?

11. What are the sensory capacities of the neonate?

12. What do we know about infant face perception?

13. What is cognitive development, and what are the two approaches to studying it?

14. What are the main elements of Piaget's theory of cognitive development?

15. What characterizes each of the four stages of cognitive development proposed by Piaget?

16.   What are the two main criticisms of Piaget's theory?

17.   What age-related changes are there in learning?

18.   What age-related changes occur in memory?

19.   What are the main points of Kohlberg's theory of moral development?

20.   What are the first four stages (crises) of development according to Erikson?

21.   What conclusions may we draw about the development of gender identity in children?

22.   In child development, what is "attachment," and what are the consequences of developing secure attachments?

PRENATAL DEVELOPMENT

Human development begins at conception, when the father's sperm cell unites with the mother's ovum. At that time, all of the genes on the 23 chromosomes from each parent pair off within a single cell. We have in that one action the transmission of all inherited characteristics. Within the next 30 hours, the one-celled zygote will divide and become two. In three days, there may be about ten to 15 cells; after five days, there will be slightly more than 100. No one knows how many cells the human organism has at birth, and few are willing to even hazard a guess; "more than a trillion" is a conservative estimate (Moore, 1982). The time from conception to birth is the **prenatal period**. Many events that can have lifelong consequences occur during this very sensitive period.

prenatal period the period of development from conception to birth

The journey of human development begins when a single sperm produced by the father fertilizes the egg provided by the mother. After ejaculation, the sperm make their way to the *fallopian tubes*. In the fallopian tubes their numbers divide, some going up one fallopian tube, the remainder going up the second. Once the sperm reaches the egg, the fertilization process begins. When the head of one sperm penetrates the outer membrane of the egg, the membrane instantly changes so that no other sperm can penetrate the egg. Thus, in all normal pregnancies, a single sperm fertilizes the egg. This is true even for identical twins who develop from a single egg. The production of identical (or monozygotic, meaning one egg) twins occurs after fertilization. The production of fraternal (or dizygotic, meaning two eggs) twins develop when two separate sperm fertilize two separate eggs.

Fertilization continues as the head of the sperm burrows into the egg. Once inside, the head of the sperm ruptures, spilling the genetic material from the father (23 chromosomes) into the egg. There it joins up with the genetic material from the egg (23 chromosomes), resulting in 46 chromosomes arranged in twenty-three pairs. Two chromosomes (one pair) are the *sex chromosomes* and carry the genetic instructions that will lead the child to be male or female. The normal chromosomal configuration is "XY" for the male, and "XX" for the female. The genetic sex of the child is determined by the father. The father produces two types of sperm: 22+X (22 chromosomes plus an X sex chromosome) and 22+Y (22 chromosomes plus a Y sex chromosome). The egg contains only an X chromosome. The genetic sex of the child depends on which of the two types of sperm fertilizes the egg.

Prenatal development is divided into three stages: the *germinal stage*, the *embryonic stage*, and the *fetal stage*. Each stage is characterized by its own landmarks of growth and development.

The Germinal Stage

zygote the one-cell product of the union of sperm and ovum at conception

germinal stage the first stage of prenatal development, lasting from conception to implantation into the uterine wall, around two weeks after conception

Once the sperm fertilizes the egg, the first new cell of the unborn child, called the **zygote**, is formed. During the **germinal stage** of prenatal development the zygote begins to move down the fallopian tube toward the uterus. As it travels to the uterus, it undergoes rapid cell growth, eventually forming into a hollow ball called the *blastocyst*. The germinal stage lasts from the time of fertilization until the blastocyst implants itself into the wall of the uterus—about two weeks.

The blastocyst is an interesting entity. The outer layer of cells is genetically programmed to develop into the placenta (this forms the interface between the blood systems of the mother and unborn child. The two blood systems do not intermix directly), the amniotic sac (the sac in which the fetus will grow), and the umbilical cord (which connects the fetus to the placenta). The inner layer of cells is programmed to become the fetus itself. The blastocyst includes hundreds of cells, and for the first time it is clear that not all of the cells are exact replicas of each other. That is, there is now some differentiation among the cells in the zygote.

The Embryonic Stage

embryonic stage the second prenatal developmental period from two to eight weeks during which all the organ systems of the body are put into place

The **embryonic stage** lasts about six weeks. During this period, the embryo develops at a rapid rate and all of the organ systems of the body are laid in place. At the beginning of this stage, we can identify only three types of cells: (1) those that will become the nervous system, the sense organs, and the skin; (2) those that will become the internal organs; and (3) those that will become the muscles, skeleton, and blood vessels. By the end of the embryonic stage, we can identify the face, eyes, ears, fingers, and toes.

During this stage, within the first three months of prenatal development, the unborn child is most sensitive to external or environmental influences. If prenatal problems (for example, birth defects) occur, they are most likely to develop during this stage. For example, if the heart, eyes, and hands do not differentiate and develop during this embryonic period, there will be no way to compensate later. The central nervous system is at risk throughout the prenatal period, particularly in weeks three through six. The reason for this heightened sensitivity is simple: when organs are growing at a very rapid rate, they are in their *vulnerable period*. The greatest potential for prenatal problems is during these vulnerable periods.

Two months after conception, the embryonic stage draws to a close. The one-inch-long embryo now has enough of a primitive nervous system to respond to a light touch, exhibiting a simple reflex movement.

The Fetal Stage

The final stage of prenatal development is the longest, the **fetal stage**. It includes months three through nine. Not only do the organs of the body continue to increase in complexity and size, but they also begin to function. The arms and legs move spontaneously by the end of the third month. In two more months, these movements will be substantial enough for the mother to feel them. At the end of the fifth month, the fetus can be ten inches long. Internal organs have developed, but not to the point of sustaining life outside the uterus. The brain has developed, but neurons within it have not formed many synapses.

fetal stage the third stage of prenatal development from week eight until birth during which the organs that developed in the embryonic stage develop further

Development and growth continue through the last few months of pregnancy. The most noticeable change, at least to the mother, is the significant increase in weight and overall movement of the fetus. Sometime during the seventh month, most fetuses have reached the point of *viability*—the point at which the fetus could survive if he or she were born. During its last few weeks in the uterus, the fetus grows more slowly. Its movements may be more powerful, but overall activity is slowed because of the cramped quarters in which the fetus finds itself. After nearly 270 days, the fetus is ready to enter the world as a newborn.

> ## BEFORE YOU GO ON
>
> - Why do developmental psychologists study prenatal development?
> - Describe the fertilization process.
> - What happens during the germinal period?
> - What happens during the embryonic stage?
> - What happens during the fetal stage?

Environmental Influences on Prenatal Development

In a vast majority of cases, the growth and development of the human organism from zygote to fetus progresses according to the blueprint laid down in the genes, but in the prenatal stage, the human organism is not immune to influences from the environment. Most external influences on prenatal development have negative consequences.

Nourishment

Never meant to be taken literally, the old expression, "You are what you eat" does have some truth to it. By the same token, before we are born, we are what our mothers eat. Maternal malnutrition often leads to an increase in miscarriages, stillbirths, and premature births. At best, we can expect the newborn child of a malnourished mother to be similarly malnourished.

Deficiencies in specific vitamins and minerals affect the prenatal organism. For example, a mother's calcium deficiencies affect the development of bones and teeth in the fetus. As is the case for many nutrients, it may very well be the mother who suffers more. If there are inadequate supplies of calcium in the mother's system, "the fetal need for calcium will be met at the expense of the mother" (Hughes & Noppe, 1985, p. 140). Taking vitamins *can* be overdone. Overdosing some vitamins (vitamins A and D, in particular) can be toxic, with negative effects for both mother and unborn child. What works best is a balanced, sensible diet.

Smoking, Drinking, and Drugs

There is ample evidence that cigarette smoking has harmful effects on the smoker. Smoking during pregnancy is associated with low birth weight and premature birth, especially for mothers pregnant with twins (Pollack, Lantz, & Frohna, 2000). Smoking has also been associated with retarded prenatal growth (Golbus, 1980), increased risk of hearing defects with greater risks attached to heavier smoking (Fried, 1993). There is also evidence that children whose mothers smoked at least a pack of cigarettes a day during pregnancy have *a 75 percent increase* in the risk for mental retardation, even when other risk factors (e.g., maternal age, education, and alcohol use) were controlled (Drews & Murphy, 1996). Older children of mothers who smoked during pregnancy have also been found to have higher rates of behavioral problems such as aggression and hyperactivity (Orlebeke, Knol, & Verhulst, 1999) and poorer performance on visual perceptual tasks (Fried & Watkinson, 2000), compared to children of nonsmokers.

Smoking during (and after) pregnancy is also associated with an increased risk of sudden infant death syndrome (Blair & Fleming, 1996). Although the exact mechanism involved with this association is not yet known, there are at least two possible answers. First, prenatal exposure to nicotine from maternal smoking reduces the effectiveness of the oxygen monitoring systems of the lungs (Cutz & Perrin, 1996). Second, infants born to smokers require higher levels of stimulation to arouse from sleep (Franco et al., 1999). It is well known that one factor contributing to sudden infant death syndrome is that some of these infants don't arouse to reactivate respiration during periods of sleep apnea.

So, the bad news is that smoking during pregnancy relates to a wide range of physical and behavioral problems. There is some good news, however. There is evidence that if the mother stops smoking early in pregnancy at least some of the negative effects of smoking can be avoided (Lindley, Becker, Gray & Herman, 2000). For example, Lindley et al., found that if a pregnant mother stopped smoking between her first visit to the doctor and the 32nd week of pregnancy, there was reduced risk of low birth weight, small head circumference and abnormal brain to body weight ratio.

Alcohol is a drug that can be extremely injurious to unborn children. Alcohol is quickly and directly passed through the placenta from the mother to the fetus. Alcohol then collects in organs with a high water content, most ominously in the gray matter of the brain. To make matters worse, the fetus eliminates alcohol at half the rate of the mother. The bottom line is that alcohol gets into the fetus easily and stays in for a long time.

Heavy drinking (three drinks or more per day) or binge drinking during vulnerable periods of organ development significantly increases the chance of having smaller babies with retarded physical growth, poor coordination, poor muscle tone, intellectual retardation, and other problems, collectively referred to as **fetal alcohol syndrome (FAS)** (Jones et al., 1973; Mattson et al., 1988). Lower doses of alcohol consumption during critical periods of pregnancy can produce a condition that is less severe than full-blown fetal alcohol syndrome known as *fetal alcohol effects*. Alcohol also can have subtle effects on development at low to moderate doses. For example, light alcohol consumption (as little as one drink per day) during early or mid-pregnancy is related to deficits in fine motor

fetal alcohol syndrome (FAS) a cluster of symptoms (for example, low birth weight, poor muscle tone, and intellectual retardation) associated with a child born to a mother who was a heavy drinker of alcohol during pregnancy

skills (Barr, Streissguth, Darby, & Sampson, 1990). The more alcohol the mother drinks, the greater the impairment in fine motor skills. The case of "Kenny" we used to open this chapter is a perfect example of a child born with FAS.

In the United States, fetal alcohol syndrome is the leading preventable cause of birth defects that produce mental retardation (Streissguth et al., 1991). The Centers for Disease Control and Prevention estimate that 8,000 babies with FAS are born in the United States every year. In the summer of 1995, the CDC released a report that the rate of babies born with fetal alcohol syndrome increased *sixfold* from 1979 to 1993. Back in the 1970s, it was believed that an occasional drink or two had no lasting effect on prenatal development. We now know better; alcohol is a powerful drug that can have profound effects on an unborn child. Because no absolute safe level of alcohol has been established, experts agree that the best advice is total abstinence.

There are racial and ethnic differences in the rates of alcohol-related birth complications. According to a 1996 CDC study, African American mothers who drink have a far higher rate of alcohol-related fetal deaths than Caucasian mothers who drink. The highest rate of fetal alcohol syndrome is among the Native American population of the Southwest, with a rate three times that of Caucasians (Shelton & Cook, 1993).

Mothers who use or abuse psychoactive drugs such as heroine, cocaine, or crack-cocaine during pregnancy may cause considerable complications for their unborn children. For example, 70 percent of newborns of mothers who used heroine during pregnancy showed symptoms of drug withdrawal (e.g., tremulousness, irritability, hyperactivity and respiratory problems) after birth (Weitraub et al., 1998). These newborns are also more likely than normal newborns to have a low birth weight and retarded fetal growth.

Even common aspirin has become suspect as a cause of prenatal complications (Briggs et al., 1986; Govoni & Hayes, 1988; Sibai et al., 1993). Researchers have also looked at the relationship between caffeine consumption and birth problems. The results tend to show that the effects of caffeine can be complex. One study found that caffeine was associated with low birth weights, but only among women who also smoked during pregnancy (Cook, et al., 1996). Another study found no association between caffeine consumption and pre-term delivery (Peacock & Bland, 1995). However, there is an association between caffeine consumption and the risk of miscarriage. Women who consume an amount of caffeine equivalent to five or more cups of coffee per day nearly doubled the rate of miscarriage (Klebanoff, 1999). Lower doses of caffeine, for example the caffeine equivalent of one to two cups of coffee per day, did not significantly increase the risk of miscarriage.

Having said all of this, we need to caution against overreactions. Yes, ingesting a potentially harmful substance such as alcohol raises the likelihood of birth defects and mental retardation. But, there are a few things to bear in mind about the impact of these substances on prenatal development (Hetherington & Parke, 1981): First, the genetic make-up of the mother and fetus relate to the impact of harmful substances. Some mothers and fetuses are more resilient than others. Second, the physical health of the mother is important. Harmful substances are less harmful when the mother is healthy than when she is unhealthy. Third, exposure to multiple harmful substances is more damaging than exposure to one. In short, just because a mother is exposed to a harmful substance does not *guarantee* that birth defects or mental retardation will result. For example, among alcoholic mothers, 40 percent of infants show effects of prenatal alcohol exposure (Shelton & Cook, 1993). Among moderate drinkers, the rate of alcohol exposure effects is 11 percent. This, however, does not mean that a woman should ignore the potential impact of harmful substances. Our best advice is to avoid as many of these substances as possible, get good prenatal care, eat a healthy diet, and follow your doctor's advice.

What About Dad?

As you read through the last sections on nourishment and drugs, did it sound at all sexist to you? All of what we've covered puts the focus on mothers—what mothers should and should not do. Eat a balanced diet. Don't drink. Don't do drugs. Don't smoke. There has been little concern expressed about the father's role in the process. A review of the literature on factors that influence the pathological development of children and adolescents found that only 1 percent of the 577 studies cited focused on the role of fathers (Phares & Compas, 1993).

This situation is changing. Researchers are now looking at the role of the father in determining the quality of life of the prenatal child. The main issue revolves around factors affecting the quality of the father's sperm at the moment of conception. As one example, consider the known causes of Down syndrome, a collection of birth defects associated with mental retardation. Down syndrome is the result of a child being born with 47 chromosomes per cell instead of the standard 23 pairs. It was assumed that a problem with the mother's ovum caused this syndrome since the likelihood of having a child with Down syndrome increases as the mother's age increases (much beyond the age of 35 to 40).

We now recognize that the age of *the father* is related to some cases of Down syndrome. As many as one-third of all Down syndrome cases reflect difficulties with the father's sperm and that the syndrome is more likely in children whose fathers have jobs that subject them to toxic chemicals. Alcohol use by fathers has also been implicated as a probable cause of prenatal and birth abnormalities, but nearly all of this research has been on rats and mice (Hood, 1990). Obviously, some difficulties of pregnancy, birth, and development are due to the condition of the father at or near the time of conception (Brown, 1985; Soyka & Joffee, 1980).

BEFORE YOU GO ON

- How can malnutrition affect prenatal development?

- What are Fetal Alcohol Syndrome and Fetal Alcohol Effects?

- What dosages of alcohol are necessary before effects are shown on the unborn child?

- How do smoking and drugs affect prenatal development?

- What role does the father play in the transmission of birth defects?

MOTOR AND PERCEPTUAL DEVELOPMENT

Now we turn our attention to development in *childhood*, that period between birth and adolescence. We'll begin by considering the orderly sequence of the development of the motor responses of children—their ability to do things with their bodies.

The Neonate

When a baby is first born, it looks like it can't do much of anything. Mostly it just sleeps. In fact, newborns *do* sleep a lot, about 15 to 17 hours a day. But as parents are quick to find out, that sleep occurs in short naps, seldom lasting more than a few hours at a time. A careful examination of the **neonate**, a newborn through the first two weeks of life, reveals a capability for a wide range of behaviors.

neonate the newborn from birth through the first two weeks

Most of the behaviors of the neonate are *reflexive*—simple, unlearned, involuntary reactions to specific stimuli. The neonatal reflexes fall into two categories: *survival reflexes* and *primitive reflexes* (Shaffer, 1996). The survival reflexes help the infant survive and adapt to its environment, and include the rooting reflex (a reflex that helps the neonate locate a nipple), the sucking reflex (which allows the neonate to take in milk) and the swallowing reflex. The primitive reflexes do not have direct survival value. These include the stepping reflex (if you support a newborn and have its feet touch a hard surface it makes a stepping response) and the Moro reflex (a sudden noise or change in

Whether a child begins to walk at ten months or 13 months, he or she will still follow the age-old patterns of sitting, crawling, and then walking. Although walking may not be learned in the usual sense, it is an accomplishment that often brings pleasure to parents.

body position causes the neonate to throw its arms out, arch its back, and bring the arms together). Regardless of whether a reflex is classified as a survival or primitive reflex, neonatal reflexes serve another important function: they give doctors a window into the health of the neonate's nervous system. A reflex that is absent, weak, persists beyond when it should disappear, or one that reappears indicates possible damage to the central nervous system.

The Motor Development of Children

Parents who try to keep their young children in properly fitting clothes know how quickly children grow. During the first three years, a child's height and weight normally increase at a rate never again equaled. Although changes in size and motor skills are rapid, they do tend to be orderly and well sequenced. Additionally, no two children can be expected to grow at the same rate or to develop control over their bodies at the same time. Joan may walk at the age of ten months. Bill may not venture forth until he's 13 months. The rate of motor development in early childhood is largely unrelated to adult characteristics, such as intelligence or physical coordination.

Regardless of the *rate* of motor development, there are regularities in the *sequence* of motor development. No matter when Joan walks, she will first sit, then crawl. Figure 8.1 summarizes the development of common motor skills. There are two important things for you to notice about this figure: first, the sequence of events is regular, and second, *when* each stage develops includes a wide range of ages that should be considered normal. It is also true that the sequence and timing of the events listed in this figure hold equally true for boys and girls. That is, in the development of these basic motor skills there are no significant sex differences.

The regularity of physical growth and development is guided by two "principles." (1) *Cephalocaudal sequencing* refers to the fact that a child's growth and bodily control proceed from top to bottom, or from head to upper torso to lower body. Children's heads and upper torsos develop before their trunks and lower bodies; hands and arms can be manipulated before feet and legs. (2) *Proximodistal sequencing* refers to the fact that a child's growth and bodily control proceed from the center core to the extremities, from the internal organs to the arms and legs, then to the hands and feet, then to the fingers and toes.

The Development of the Brain

During the first two to three years of a child's life, the brain undergoes its most rapid development. After age three the rate of brain growth slows but continues throughout childhood. A neonate is born with all (or nearly all) of the neurons that he or she will have. There are, however, other areas of brain development that occur after birth. Connections between neurons (synapses) are formed, and many of the myelinated axons of the brain develop their myelin sheath, speeding up the rate of transmission of neural impulses.

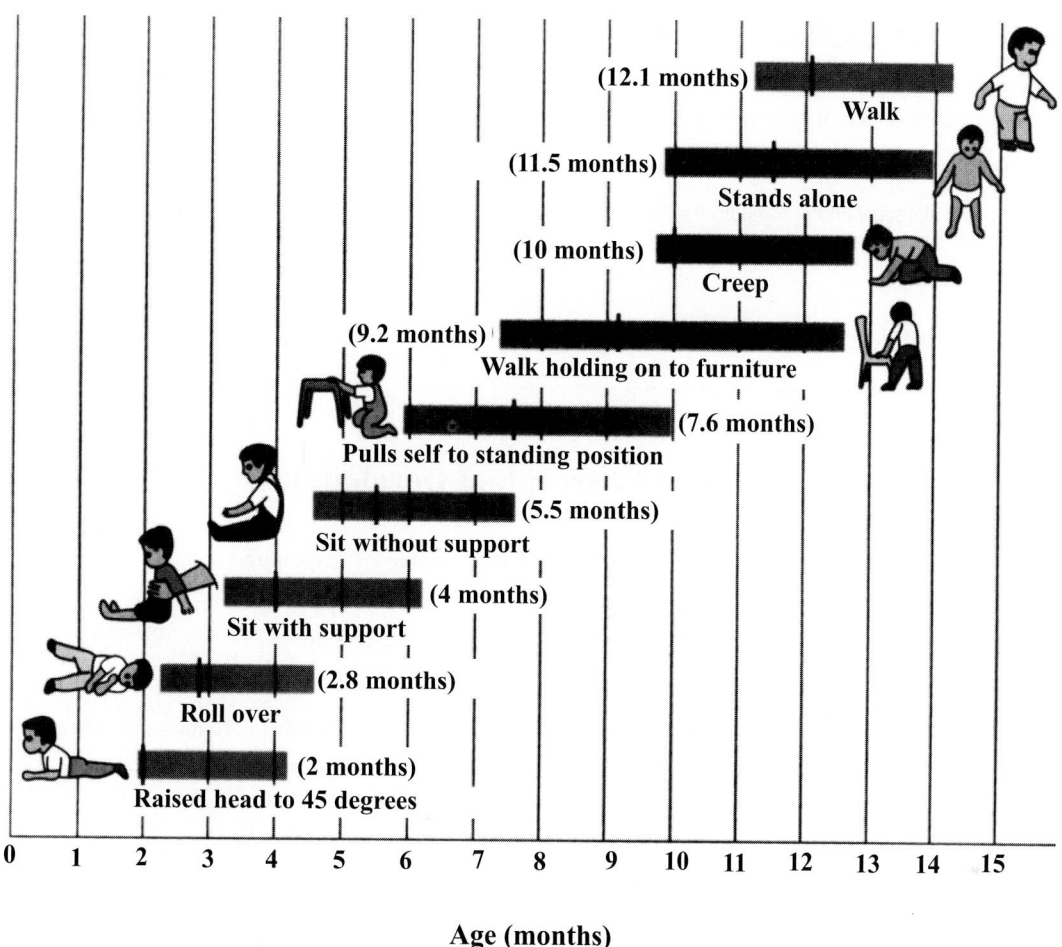

FIGURE 8.1

The sequence of human motor development. Each bar represents the ages at which between 25 percent of children (left end) and 90 percent (right end) engage in a given behavior. The short vertical line through the bar indicates the age at which 50 percent of children exhibit that behavior.

Different parts of the brain develop at different rates. The most highly developed parts of the brain at birth are the brain stem and midbrain (involved in arousal and involuntary body functions, such as respiration). Most of the cerebral cortex thickens during the first three months of life. At this time the primary motor areas (that control limb and other body movements) are developing most rapidly. By six months, the primary sensory and motor areas are highly developed (Shaffer, 1996). The parts of the brain involved in higher functioning and integrating information, called the *association areas* (which make up around three-fourths of the capacity of the cortex), develop more slowly. Between six and 15 months, growth in the primary motor areas slows and the visual association areas are more advanced than the auditory areas. By two years of age, the primary sensory and motor areas are well developed, and rapid development in the association areas is taking place.

BEFORE YOU GO ON

- Describe the capabilities of the neonate.

- What are the survival and primitive reflexes, and what do they tell us?

- What are cephalocaudal and proximodistal growth and development?

- What general observations can you make about physical growth in childhood?

- Describe the major changes in brain development during childhood.

Eventually, the brain will reach its adult proportions. The advances made during the first three years of life are considerable. As the primary motor areas develop, the child gets better at motor skills like reaching and grasping. Continued development of the association areas allows the child to better integrate sensory experience and motor behavior and allows for the emergence of more complex behaviors.

Sensory and Perceptual Development

A newborn comes into the world capable of responding to a wide range of stimuli. At birth, the newborn's senses are not fully developed. However, some senses (for example, smell and taste) are more advanced than others (for example, vision) (Shaffer, 1999). In this section, we will explore sensory and perceptual development.

The neonate's ability to sense even subtle changes is remarkable. However, there are limitations. The ability of the eyes to focus on an object, for example, does not fully develop until the child is about four months old. The neonate can focus well on objects held one to two feet away, but everything nearer or farther appears out of focus. This means that even newborns can focus on the facial features of the persons cradling or feeding them. Visual acuity—the ability to discern detail—shows a threefold to fourfold improvement in the first year (Aslin & Smith, 1988). Newborns can detect differences in brightness, and soon develop the ability to detect surfaces, edges, borders, and the differences among colors (Cohen et al., 1978; Termine et al., 1987).

The other senses are more highly developed at birth. Neonates can hear nearly as well as adults. Even three-day-old newborns are able to discriminate the sound of their mother's voice from other sounds (DeCasper & Fifer, 1980; Kolata, 1987; Martin & Clark, 1982).

Newborns also respond to differences in taste and smell. They can discriminate among the four basic taste qualities of salt, sweet, bitter, and sour. Neonates show pleasure to and prefer sweet tastes, and show displeasure to bitter and sour tastes (Shaffer, 1996). Although they are unable to use it then, the sense of smell is established before birth. Immediately after birth, neonates respond predictably, drawing away and wrinkling their noses to a variety of strong odors (e.g., Bartoshuk & Beauchamp, 1994). A one-to two-week-old infant can distinguish its own mother's smell from the smell of an unfamiliar woman (Cernoch & Porter, 1985). Neonates are also capable of detecting touch and temperature stimulation and can most definitely feel pain (Shaffer, 1996).

Form and pattern perception also develop rapidly during the first year of life. Infants prefer patterned over unpatterned stimuli (Fantz, 1961) and moving over stationary stimuli (Slater et al., 1985). When given a choice of looking at a face-like stimulus and another patterned stimulus, infants prefer to look at the face-like stimulus. Newborns just a few hours old can recognize a picture of their own mother's face and prefer to look at it over any other face paired with it (Bushnell et al., 1989; Walton et al., 1992; Walton & Bower, 1993). Young infants can also discriminate among facial expressions of emotions and spend more time looking at facial expressions of joy than of anger (Malatesta & Izard, 1984).

In summary, a wide range of sensory and perceptual capabilities appears to be available to the newborn child. The neonate may require some time to learn what to do with the sensory information it acquires from its environment, but many of its senses are operational. What the newborn makes of the sensations it receives will depend on the development of its mental, or cognitive, abilities. This is the subject we turn to now.

BEFORE YOU GO ON

- Describe the sensory capabilities of neonates.

- What do we know about infant face perception?

COGNITIVE DEVELOPMENT

Cognitive development refers to the age-related changes in learning, memory, perception, attention, thinking and problem solving. Starting from the moment you are born, there are a number of changes in the basic psychological processes underlying cognition. Developmental psychologists look at cognitive development from two perspectives. First, there is the **structural-functional approach** developed by Jean Piaget. According to this approach, there are age-related changes in the structures involved in cognition, whereas the functions remain fixed. In Piaget's theory, at each stage of development a child uses a *qualitatively different* form of intelligence. Second, there is the **information processing approach**, which is not a unified theory like Piaget's. Instead, those advocating the information processing approach focus on *quantitative* changes in basic information processing systems like memory, attention, and learning. From the information processing approach, cognitive development means that a child becomes a faster, more efficient processor of information. The information processing systems we are born with grow and develop; they are not replaced by qualitatively different systems as suggested by Piaget.

Piaget's Structural-Functional Approach

Jean Piaget proposed a comprehensive theory of cognitive development that describes the course of cognitive development from birth through adolescence. Like Freud, Piaget was *not* trained as a psychologist. Instead, his education was in the natural sciences. From an early age, Piaget was a keen observer of the world around him. In 1919, Piaget went to France to work with Alfred Binet to help develop the first IQ test. While there, Piaget became fascinated with the incorrect answers children gave to items on the test. He noticed that children of about the same age gave very similar *incorrect* answers. His observations eventually led Piaget to conclude that cognitive development was represented by qualitative changes in the way children think. He decided to dedicate the rest of his life to studying the development of children.

cognitive development age-related changes in a child's learning, memory, perception, attention, problem solving, and thinking

structural-functional approach the approach Piaget took to explain cognitive development that says that structures (schemas) change with development, while functions remain fixed. Cognitive development is seen as a series of qualitative changes in intelligence.

information processing approach an approach to explaining cognitive development that proposes that cognitive development is represented by quantitative changes in basic information processing systems, such as attention and memory

Jean Piaget's observations about the cognitive development of children are the most comprehensive and influential. Nonetheless, some of Piaget's ideas have been challenged.

schema an organized mental representation of the world that is adaptive and formed by experience

organization one of the functions in Piaget's theory involving a predisposition to integrate individual schemas into organized units

adaptation a function in Piaget's theory involving a child adapting cognitive abilities to the demands of the environment

assimilation in Piaget's theory, the process of adding and "fitting in," new material or information to an existing schema

accommodation in Piaget's theory, the process of changing or revising an existing schema as a result of new experiences

equilibration in Piaget's theory, the idea that a child attempts to maintain a balance between cognitive abilities and demands of the environment. Once a child reaches a balance, the environment places more demands on the child, requiring cognitive change.

Piaget's roots in the natural sciences show up in his theory of cognitive development. Piaget used observational methods along with informal testing of children while developing his theory. In fact, much of his theory of cognitive development is based on his careful observations of his own children.

According to Piaget, "intelligence" had two components: structures and functions. Piaget suggested that a cognitive knowledge structure is involved in processing information. Such a structure is called a **schema** and is integrated within the nervous system (Piaget, 1952). Functions are the mechanisms that help a child adapt to his or her environment. Unlike the structures which change with age, functions remain invariant throughout development. According to Piaget, schemas (knowledge structures) help to accomplish functions.

The two basic functions for Piaget are **organization** and **adaptation**, which are two complementary processes. Organization refers to the interrelatedness of cognitive schemas. For example, when an infant is born it has some basic, reflexive schemas (rooting or finding a food source, head turning, and sucking, for example). Initially, these schemas operate independently. However, with development they are organized into an integrated behavior: rooting for food, turning the head to find a nipple, and sucking.

Adaptation comprises two complementary processes: **assimilation** and **accommodation**. Assimilation occurs when a child incorporates new information into an existing scheme. For example, the first thing that infants do with an object is to put it in their mouth and suck the object. In Piaget's terminology, the child has assimilated the object (a rattle, for example) into the sucking. If assimilation were the only process available, cognitive development would be hindered. What happens when an infant comes across an object that cannot be sucked (for example, a large ball). According to Piaget, through the process of accommodation the infant will modify its schemas to account for the new object. So, after several aborted attempts at sucking the ball, the infant may roll it on the floor.

One final process is important in Piaget's theory. **Equilibration** is the main mechanism of change in Piaget's theory. According to Piaget, a child strives to maintain a state of equilibrium (balance) between cognitive abilities and the demands of the environment. However, when the child brings his or her level of cognitive functioning up to the level demanded by the environment, the environment (via the parents, for example) ups the ante, requiring more complex cognition and behavior. Thus, the child adapts mentally to a changing psychological environment.

BEFORE YOU GO ON

- Describe in general terms Piaget's structural-functional approach.

- What are schemas, and what role do they play in cognitive development?

- What are organization and adaptation?

- What are assimilation and accommodation?

- What is equilibration?

Stages of Development

Piaget's theory is a *stage theory*. The theory maintains that a child passes through four qualitatively different stages of cognitive development. These are the sensorimotor stage (birth to two years), the preoperational stage (two to seven years), the concrete operations stage (seven to 11 years) and the formal operations stage (12 years and up). Piaget stated that movement through these stages was unidirectional (progressing from lower forms of intelligence to higher ones) and universal across cultures.

In the **sensorimotor stage**, children discover by sensing (sensori-) and by doing (motor). A child may come to appreciate, for example, that a quick pull on a dog's tail (a motor activity) reliably produces a loud yelp (a sensory experience), perhaps followed, in turn, by parental attention.

sensorimotor stage the first stage of development in Piaget's theory, from birth to two years, when a child learns by sensing and doing

One of the most useful schemas to develop in the sensorimotor stage is that of *causality*. Infants gradually come to realize that events may have knowable causes and that some behaviors cause predictable reactions. Pushing a bowl of oatmeal off the high chair causes a mess and gets mommy's attention: if A, then B—a very practical insight. Another important discovery that occurs during this developmental stage is that objects may exist even when they are not immediately in view. Early in this stage, an object that is out of sight is more than out of mind. The object ceases to exist for the child. By the end of the sensorimotor period, children have learned that objects can and do still exist even if they are not physically present and that their reappearance can be anticipated. This awareness is called **object permanence**.

object permanence the appreciation that an object no longer in view can still exist and reappear later

Another useful skill that characterizes the sensorimotor period is imitation. As long as it is within its range of abilities, a baby will imitate almost any behavior it sees. A cognitive strategy has developed, one that will be used for a lifetime: trying to imitate the behaviors of a model.

Throughout most of the **preoperational stage** a child's thinking is self-centered, or *egocentric*. According to Piaget, the child has difficulty understanding life from someone else's perspective. In this stage, the world is very much *me-*, *mine-*, and *I*-oriented.

preoperational stage the second stage of development in Piaget's theory, from ages two to six years, characterized by egocentrism and the beginning of symbol development

In the preoperational stage, children begin to develop symbols, usually in the form of words, to represent concepts. At this stage, children do not know how to manipulate symbols in a consistent, rule-governed way. It's not until the end of this period that they can play word games or understand why riddles about rabbits throwing clocks out of windows in order to "see time fly" are funny. It is similarly true that children at this stage have great difficulty with many "abstract" concepts, such as those involved with religious beliefs.

Children in the **concrete operations stage** begin to develop many concepts *and* show that they can manipulate those concepts. For example, they can organize objects into categories of things: balls over here, blocks over there, plastic soldiers in a pile by the door, and so on. Each of these items is recognized as a toy, ultimately to be put away in the toy box and not in the closet, which is where clothes are supposed to go. It is in this period that rule-governed behavior begins. The concrete, observable objects of the child's world can be classified, ranked, ordered, or separated into more than one category, according to rules.

concrete operations stage the third stage of development in Piaget's theory, from ages seven to 12 years, when concepts can be manipulated, but not in an abstract fashion

conservation in Piaget's theory, an appreciation that changing the physical properties of an object does not necessarily change its essence

A sign of the beginning of the concrete operations stage is the ability to solve *conservation problems*. **Conservation** involves the awareness that changing the form or the appearance of something does not change what it really is. Many observations convinced Piaget that conservation marked the end of the preoperational stage. We can show size conservation by giving two equal-size balls of clay to a four-year-old. One ball is then rolled into a long cigar shape, and the child will now assert that it has more clay in it than the ball does. A seven-year-old will seldom hesitate to tell you that each form contains the same amount of clay. The seven-year-old has moved on to the next stage of cognitive development.

As its name suggests, in the concrete operations stage children begin to use and manipulate (operate on) concepts and ideas. Their manipulations are still very concrete, however-tied to real objects in the here and now. An eight-year-old can be expected to find her way to and from school, even if she throws in a side trip along the way. What she will have a difficult time doing is telling you with any precision just how she gets from one place to another. Drawing a sensible map is difficult for her. If she stands on the corner of Maple Street and Oak Avenue, she knows where to go next to get home. Dealing with the concrete reality, here and now, is easy. Dealing with such knowledge in abstract terms is tough.

formal operations stage the fourth stage in Piaget's theory; ages older than twelve years, when one can generate and test abstract hypotheses and manipulate symbolic concepts

The logical manipulation of abstract, symbolic concepts appears in the last of Piaget's stages: **formal operations**. The key to this stage, usually begun in adolescence, is abstract, symbolic reasoning. By the age of twelve, most children can develop and mentally test hypotheses—they can work through problems in their mind.

In the stage of formal operations, youngsters can reason through hypothetical problems: "What if you were the only person in the world who liked rock music?" "If nobody had to go to school, what would happen?" Similarly, children are now able to deal with questions that are literally contrary to fact: "What if John F. Kennedy or Ronald Reagan were still president of the United States?" The stages of Piaget's theory and the cognitive milestones associated with each are summarized in Figure 8.2.

BEFORE YOU GO ON

- Describe the four stages of Piaget's theory of cognitive development.

- What is object permanence?

- What is conservation?

Reactions to Piaget

There can be no doubt of the significance of Piaget's influence. His observations and insights about intellectual development spanned decades. Considerable research has supported many of these insights. Finding evidence of Piagetian stages is one of the success stories of cross-cultural research. That evidence tells us that the stages we have just reviewed can be identified in children around the world (Brislin, 1993; Dasen & Heron, 1981; Dasen & de Ribaupierre, 1987; Segall et al., 1990). There will be some individual differences, of course. Remember the example of conservation that involved estimating the amount of clay when it is rolled into varied shapes? Sons and daughters of potters understand the conservation of sizes of clay with great ease (Price-Williams et al., 1969). In other words, experience does matter.

1. **Sensorimotor stage (ages birth to two years)**

   - "Knows" through active interaction with environment

   - Becomes aware of cause-effect relationships

   - Learns that objects exist even when not in view

   - Crudely imitates the actions of others

2. **Preoperational stage (ages two to six years)**

   - Begins by being very egocentric

   - Language and mental representations develop

   - Objects are classified on just one characteristic at a time

3. **Concrete operations stage (ages seven to 12 years)**

   - Develops conservation of volume, length, mass, etc.

   - Organizes objects into ordered categories

   - Understands relational terms (e.g., bigger than, above)

   - Begins using simple logic

4. **Formal operations stage (ages over 12)**

   - Thinking becomes abstract and symbolic

   - Reasoning skills develop

   - A sense of hypothetical concepts develops

FIGURE 8.2

Piaget's Stages of Cognitive Development

The two major criticisms of Piaget's theory are that (1) the borderlines between his proposed stages are much less clear-cut than his theory suggests, and (2) Piaget underestimated the cognitive talents of preschool children (Flavell, 1982, 1985; Gelman, 1978; Wellman & Gelman, 1992).

For example, the egocentrism said to characterize the preoperational child may not be as flagrant as Piaget believed. In one study (Lempers et al., 1977), children were shown a picture pasted inside a box. They were asked to show the picture to someone else. In showing the picture, they turned it so that it would be right side up to the viewer. Every child over two years old indicated such an appreciation of someone else's point of view. More than that, recent research makes it clear that young children (18 months old) readily ascribe goals and intentions to the action of others. That is, preschoolers *can* observe someone else doing something and appreciate what it is they are trying to do (Meltzoff, 1995).

Similarly, object permanence may be neither universal nor consistently found in any one child; it depends on how you test for it (Harris, 1983). For example, psychologist Renée Baillargeon (1993, 1995) reports that even "infants aged 2 ½ to 3 ½ *months* are aware that objects continue to exist when masked by other objects, that objects cannot remain stable without support, that objects move along spatially continuous paths, and that objects cannot move through the space occupied by other objects" (p. 133, emphasis added). Piaget's theory suggests that these sorts of abilities do not appear until a child is about two years old.

Piaget's notion of conservation may not be such an obvious indicator of cognitive development either. When experimenters pour liquid from a short beaker into a tall one, a five-year-old will probably say that the taller beaker now holds more liquid-evidence of preoperational stage thinking. If the child does the pouring from one beaker to the other, as opposed to just watching, five-year-olds show conservation and recognize that the amount of liquid is the same in both containers (Rose & Blank, 1974).

A further criticism is that Piaget's theory, focusing on a stage approach, gives little attention to the impact of language development. Nor did Piaget have much to say about the smooth and gradual increase in the capacity of a child's memory.

BEFORE YOU GO ON

- Which areas of Piaget's theory have been supported?
- What are the two main criticisms of Piaget's theory?
- What does research suggest about object permanence and conservation?

Some of Piaget's observations and assumptions have come under attack. This is to be expected in science. However, Piaget made some important contributions. For example, Piaget focused attention on the social and emotional development of children and had considerable influence on the American educational system (Shaffer, 1999). He also showed that children are not passive during the development process but rather active participants in their own cognitive development. One of the most important contributions of Jean Piaget is that he developed a theory of cognitive development in children that was so detailed, so thought-provoking, that it will continue to challenge researchers for years to come.

The Information Processing Approach

Piaget's theory served as a catalyst for developmental psychologists to explore cognitive development. The information processing approach grew out of the research that developmental psychologists were conducting on infant learning, memory, and attention. In the sections that follow, we will briefly review research in these areas.

The Development of Learning

Newborns are able to perform simple learning tasks. A neonate (only two hours old) is stroked on the forehead and seems not to respond. This stimulus is then paired with a sugar solution delivered to the infant's lips. The unconditioned stimulus of the sugar solution elicits the unconditioned response of turning the head and making sucking movements. After several trials of pairing the stroking of the forehead and the sugar solution, the baby makes sucking and head movements simply when its forehead is touched (Blass et al., 1984). This is an example of classical conditioning. Headturning and sucking movements of neonates can also be brought under the control of operant conditioning. The rates of these responses increase when they are followed by reinforcers such as sugar solutions, the sound of the mother's voice, or the recorded sound of the mother's heartbeat (DeCasper & Sigafoos, 1983; Moon & Fifer, 1990).

Imitation is the ability to reproduce a behavior that is observed. There is evidence that infants as young as one week old are capable of imitating simple facial expressions (Meltzoff & Moore, 1983). However, these early imitations are not very stable (Shaffer, 1996) and disappear between 20 to 21 weeks of age (Abravanel & Sigafoos, 1984). True imitation of complex behaviors is not reliably evident until the child is eight to 12 months old (Piaget, 1951). Once developed, imitation plays an important role in the transmission of a wide range of behaviors, including prosocial behaviors (for example, helping) and antisocial behaviors (for example, aggression).

The Development of Memory

To benefit from learning, one must be able to store and retrieve information. *Memory* is the cognitive system that performs these tasks. Memory can be demonstrated in very young infants. For example, Friedman (1972) reported a demonstration of memory in neonates only one to four days old. Babies were shown a picture of a simple figure—say, a checkerboard pattern—for 60 seconds. Experimenters recorded how long the baby looked at the stimulus. After the same pattern was shown repeatedly, the baby appeared to be bored and gave it less attention. When a new stimulus pattern was presented, the baby stared at it for the full 60 seconds of its exposure. So what does this have to do with memory? The argument is that for the neonate to stare at the new stimulus, it must have formed some memory of the old one. How else would it recognize the new pattern as being new or different? In fact, if the new stimulus pattern was very similar to the old one, the baby would not give it as much attention as it would if it were totally different.

By the time the infant is two to three months old, it can remember an interesting event for several days (Shaffer, 1996). In an experiment, Rovee-Collier (1984) tied one end of a string to the foot of an infant and the other end to a mobile. Each time the infant kicked its foot, the mobile moved. When tested days later, two to three month old infants remembered the relationship and they got upset if they kicked their foot and the mobile did not move. Memory for the event was also evident after three weeks if the experimenters provided the infant with a retrieval cue (moved the mobile). Generally, over the course of infancy, recall memory shows steady improvement (Shaffer, 1996).

By the time the child is two to three years of age, their memories have improved markedly. Children as young as three can understand the temporal nature of events and form coherent representations (scripts) of those events in memory (Nelson, 1986). By far, however, the most impressive gains in childhood memory take place between three and 12 years of age (Shaffer, 1996). There are strides in both short-term and long-term memory. For example, short-term memory capacity increases with age, most likely because the child becomes a more efficient processor of information.

Children's memory also improves because they become more proficient at using *memory strategies* such as rehearsal, organization, retrieval cues, and elaboration. The use of spontaneous verbal rehearsal to learn material gets progressively better with age. Flavell (1977) found that only 10 percent of kindergartners used verbal rehearsal spontaneously (without being told to do so), whereas 60 percent of second graders and 85 percent of fifth graders used rehearsal spontaneously. Interestingly, younger children have the *ability* to rehearse (which helps memory) if they are told to do so. Additionally, with age, children use more efficient rehearsal strategies. Young children (five to eight years old) rehearse one item at a time, whereas older children (12 years old) rehearse items in related clusters (Ornstein, Naus, & Liberty, 1975).

Semantic memory of adults is organized hierarchically. Organization is a powerful strategy that aids memory during encoding, storage, and retrieval. As you might expect, younger children do not organize information in memory as efficiently as do older children. It is not until a child is around nine or ten years old that they can benefit from semantic organization, or organizing information by category (Shaffer, 1996). With respect to retrieval cues, young children (preschool age) don't use retrieval cues effectively. Compared to 11-year-olds and adults, seven-year-olds have difficulty using retrieval cues effectively (Kee & Bell, 1981). However, seven-year-olds can use retrieval cues more effectively if they are provided for them during encoding and retrieving information. Furthermore, 11-year-olds and adults can generate their own retrieval cues to help memory. Elaboration is a sophisticated memory strategy that involves forming mental images of material to be learned. Generally, elaboration is a memory strategy that is "discovered" late in childhood and is rarely used before adolescence (Shaffer, 1996). Unlike rehearsal, a younger child's memory will not be improved much if they are told to use elaboration.

Much of the research on the development of memory has focused on the development of semantic memory. The research in this area leads to the conclusion that a child's memory is not very efficient at younger ages. When we consider episodic memory, however, a different picture emerges. Nelson (1986) points out that children as young as three can be accurate when reporting events that are familiar. Young children are capable of forming coherent event representations, which can be used to help memory for an experienced event. Research looking at the memory capabilities of children in eyewitness situations shows that a child's memory for an event is much better than previously believed. Ornstein, Gordon, and Baker-Ward (1992) evaluated children's memories (three-year-olds and six-year-olds) for a familiar event: a trip to the doctor. They found that older children had better memory for what took place during a routine visit to the doctor than younger children, and that difference was accentuated after an extended retention interval. However, the performance of the three-year-olds was still quite good (66.9 percent of recalled events were correct after three weeks). Additionally, children tended to provide very little false information when asked about things that were not part of the doctor's examination. Other research confirms that younger children (three-year-olds) have the greatest memory problems and that six-year-olds and adults perform at equivalent levels (Goodman & Reed, 1986). Overall, a child's memory for an event is much better than previously believed.

BEFORE YOU GO ON

- Can newborns be classically and operantly conditioned?

- When does the capacity to imitate behaviors develop?

- Describe what is known about infant memory.

- Describe the changes in the use of memory strategies that occur with age.

- Describe a child's episodic memory capabilities.

MORAL DEVELOPMENT

How children learn to reason and make judgments about what is right and wrong is an aspect of cognitive development that has received considerable attention (Darley & Schultz, 1990; Vitz, 1990). Piaget included the study of moral development in his theory, arguing that morality is related to cognitive awareness and that children are unable to make moral judgments until they are at least three or four years old (Piaget, 1932/1948).

Lawrence Kohlberg (1963, 1969, 1981, 1985) has offered a theory that focuses on moral development. Like Piaget's approach, Kohlberg's is a theory of stages—of moving from one stage to another in an orderly fashion. Kohlberg's data came from young boys who responded to questions about stories that involve a moral dilemma. A commonly cited example concerns whether a man should steal a drug in order to save his wife's life after the pharmacist who invented the drug refuses to sell it to him. Should the man steal the drug? Why or why not?

On the basis of responses to such dilemmas, Kohlberg proposed three levels of moral development, with two stages (or "orientations") at each level. The result is the six stages of moral development summarized in Figure 8.3. For example, a child at the level of **preconventional morality** would reason that the man should not steal the drug because "he'll get caught and be put in jail," or that he should steal the drug because "the drug didn't cost all that much." The major concern of a person in the first level of moral reasoning are the rewards and punishments that come from breaking a rule. A child who says the man should steal the drug because "it will make his wife happy, and most people would do it anyway," or that he shouldn't steal the drug because "you always have to follow rules, even if the situation is serious" is reflecting a type of reasoning at the second level, **conventional morality**. At this level the judgment is based on an accepted social convention. Social approval and disapproval matter as much as or more than anything else. The argument that he should steal the drug because "human life is more important than a law," or that "he shouldn't steal the drug for a basically selfish reason, which in the long run would promote more stealing in the society in general" is an example of moral reasoning at the third level, or **postconventional morality**. Moral reasoning at this highest level reflects complex, internalized standards. Notice that what matters is not the choice the child makes but the reasoning behind that choice.

Research tells us that the basic thrust of Kohlberg's theory has merit (Rest, 1983). It also has cross-cultural application. To varying degrees, Kohlberg's descriptions are valid for several cultures, including Isreal, Turkey, India, and Nigeria (Nisan & Kohlberg, 1982; Snarey, 1987; Snarey et al., 1985).

Problems with the theory also exist. For one thing, few people (including adults) operate at the higher stages of moral reasoning described by the theory (Colby & Kohlberg, 1984). This is particularly true in cultures that emphasize communal or group membership, such as the Israeli kibbutz or tribal groups in New Guinea, more than individuality (Snarey, 1987).

preconventional morality the first level of moral reasoning in Kohlberg's theory in which the prime interest of the child is simply with the punishment that comes from breaking a rule

conventional morality the second level of moral reasoning in Kohlberg's theory in which a judgment is based on an accepted social convention. During this stage social approval matters as much as or more than anything else.

postconventional morality the highest level of moral reasoning in Kohlberg's theory in which moral reasoning reflects complex, internalized standards

Level 1	**Preconventional morality**
1. Obedience and punishment orientation	Rules are obeyed simply to avoid punishment: "If I take the cookies, I'll get spanked."
2. Naive egotism and instrumental orientation	Rules are obeyed simply to earn rewards: "If I wash my hands, will you let me have two desserts?"
Level 2	**Conventional (conforming) morality**
3. Good boy/girl orientation	Rules are conformed to in order to avoid disapproval and gain approval: "I'm a good boy 'cause I cleaned my room, aren't I?"
4. Authority-maintaining orientation	Social conventions blindly accepted to avoid criticism from those in authority: "You shouldn't steal because it's against the law, and you'll go to jail if the police catch you."
Level 3	**Postconventional morality**
5. Contractual-legalistic orientation	Morality is based on agreement with others to serve the common good and protect the rights of individuals: "I don't like stopping at stop signs, but if we didn't all obey traffic signals, it would be difficult to get anywhere."
6. Universal ethical principle orientation	Morality is a reflection of internalized standards: "I don't care what anybody says, what's right is right."

FIGURE 8.3

Kohlberg's Stages of Moral Development

This observation brings us to a key concept in cross-cultural psychology: the dimension of individualism-collectivism (Bhawuk & Brislin, 1992; Erez & Early, 1993; Triandis, 1990, 1993; Triandis et al., 1988). People in some cultures are socialized from early childhood to take others (the family, the tribe, the neighborhood, the society) into account when setting goals or making decisions. Such a tendency toward *collectivism* is found more commonly in Asia and South America. People in many other cultures are socialized to think mostly about themselves and their own individual behaviors, a sort of "pull yourself up by your own boot straps; make it on your own; you'll get what you deserve" sort of mentality. This tendency toward *individualism* is common in North America and Western Europe. We are talking about a dimension of comparison here; even within the same culture, individualism and collectivism exist to varying degrees. This discussion relates to Kohlberg's theory because most measures of moral reasoning put a high value on the sort of thinking found in individualistic (largely Western) cultures and devalue the sorts of thinking typical of collective cultures. This does not mean that Kohlberg was wrong, of course. It just means that what is true for one culture may not be for another, and neither is necessarily any "better" or more moral.

Judgments concerning what constitutes moral reasoning need to take into account gender and cultural differences. Members of some cultures in Japan, for instance, or other Asian or South American countries, place a strong emphasis on collectivism, on adherence to the values and goals of the group, the family, the tribe, or the society.

A similar argument has been raised about Kohlberg's theory as it applies to females (Ford & Lowery, 1986; Gilligan, 1982). All of Kohlberg's original data came from the responses of young boys, remember. Later, when girls were tested, some studies seemed to suggest that the girls showed less advanced moral development when compared to boys. Carol Gilligan's argument is that comparing the moral reasoning of females and males is problematic because the moral reasoning of females is simply *different* from the moral reasoning of males. Males (at least in Western cultures) are concerned with rules, justice, and an individual's rights. As a result, they approach moral dilemmas differently than females, who are characteristically more concerned with caring, personal responsibility, and interpersonal relationships (Gilligan, 1982). The issue is not a judgmental one in the sense of determining if men are more or less moral in their thinking than women. The question is whether women and men develop different styles of moral reasoning. So far, most studies have shown that any differences between men and women in resolving moral conflicts are insignificant (Darley & Schultz, 1990; Donneberg & Hoffman, 1988; Mednick, 1989; Walker, 1989) and that males and females both consider justice and concern for others when reasoning about moral issues (Smetana, Kilen, & Turiel, 1991).

ERIKSON'S PSYCHOSOCIAL THEORY OF DEVELOPMENT

Erik Erikson (1902–1994) Erikson developed the psychosocial theory of development, which focuses on the social environment and its effects.

Erik Erikson (1902-1994) was a psychologist who, like Piaget, proposed a stage theory of human development (Erikson, 1963, 1965, 1968). Unlike Piaget, his theory focuses on more than cognitive development; although, this aspect is included. Erikson's theory is based on his observations of a wide range of peoples of various ages. As we will see, his theory extends from childhood through adolescence into adulthood and has a cross-cultural basis. Erikson was born in Germany, studied with Anna Freud (Sigmund Freud's daughter) in Vienna, and then came to the United States to do his research. Erikson's views were influenced more by Freud than by Piaget. Unlike Freud, Erikson focused on the social environment, which is why his theory is called *psychosocial*.

Erikson lists eight stages of development through which a person passes. These stages are not so much time periods as they are a series of conflicts, or crises, that need to be resolved. Each of the eight stages is referenced by a pair of terms that indicates the nature of the conflict that needs to be resolved in this period of development. As a stage theory, Erikson implies that we naturally go through the resolution of each conflict in order and that facing any one type of crisis usually occurs at about the same age for all of us. Figure 8.4 is a summary of each of Erikson's eight stages of development.

As you can see, only the first four stages are relevant for children. In fact, a major strength of Erikson's view of development is that it covers the entire life span. For now, we'll describe Erikson's first four crises, but we will return to his theory in Topic 8B.

According to Erikson, during the first year of life, one's greatest struggle centers around the establishment of a sense of *trust* or *mistrust*. There's not much a newborn can accomplish on its own. If its needs are met in a reasonable fashion, the child will develop a basic sense of safety and security, optimistic that the world is a predictable place. If a child's needs aren't adequately met, what develops is a sense of mistrust—feelings of frustration and insecurity.

During the period of *autonomy versus self-doubt*, from ages one and one-half to three years, what emerges most is a sense of self-esteem. The child begins to act independently; to dress and feed himself, for example. Physically more able, the child strikes off on his own, exploring ways of assuming personal responsibility. Frustration at this level of development leads to feelings of inadequacy and doubts of self-worth.

Erikson calls the period from ages three to six *initiative versus guilt*. Now the challenge is to develop as a contributing member of social groups, particularly the family. If the child is encouraged to do so, he or she should develop a strong sense of initiative—a

Approximate Age	Crisis	Adequate resolution	Inadequate resolution
0-1½	Trust vs. mistrust	Basic sense of safety	Insecurity, anxiety
1½-3	Autonomy vs. self-doubt	Perception of self as agent capable of controlling own body and making things happen	Feelings of inadequacy to control events
3-6	Initiative vs. guilt	Confidence in oneself as initiator, creator	Feeling of lack of self-worth
6-puberty	Competence vs. inferiority	Adequacy in basic social and intellectual skills	Lack of self-confidence, feelings of failure
Adolescent	Identity vs. role confusion	Comfortable sense of self as a person	Sense of self as fragmented; shifting, unclear sense of self
Early adult	Intimacy vs. isolation	Capacity for closeness and commitment to another	Feeling of aloneness, separation; denial of need for closeness
Middle adult	Generativity vs. stagnation	Focus on concern beyond oneself to family, society, future generations	Self-indulgent concerns; lack of future orientation
Later adult	Ego-integrity vs. despair	Sense of wholeness, basic satisfaction with life	Feelings of futility, disappointment

FIGURE 8.4

Erikson's Eight Stages of Development

certain joy of trying new things. How reinforcing it is to a five-year-old to be asked for an opinion on what the family should do this evening. Without such encouragement, a child is likely to feel guilty and resentful.

The final childhood period, *competence versus inferiority*, lasts from about age six to puberty. During this period of choices, the child is challenged to move beyond the safety and comfort of the family unit. The main focus of development is "out there" in the neighborhood and the school. Children have to begin to acquire those skills that will enable them to become fully functioning adults in society. If the child's efforts of industry are constantly belittled or ignored, the child may develop a sense of inadequacy and inferiority and thus remain dependent on others even into adulthood.

BEFORE YOU GO ON

- List and define Kohlberg's three levels of moral reasoning.

- What are the weaknesses of Kohlberg's theory?

- What are the main differences between Freud and Erikson's theories of personality?

- List and define Erikson's stages of development that apply to childhood.

DEVELOPING GENDER IDENTITY

The theories of Piaget, Kohlberg, and Erikson deal with how (and when) children develop concepts or cognitions about themselves and the world in which they live. In this section we'll focus on the concept of **gender**—one's maleness or femaleness, as opposed to one's sex, which is a biological term. Gender has been defined as "the socially ascribed characteristics of females and males, their roles and appropriate behaviors" (Amaro, 1995, p. 437), and "the meanings that societies and individuals ascribe to female and male categories" (Eagly, 1995, p. 145).

gender one's maleness or femaleness; socially ascribed characteristics of males and females, as opposed to their biological characteristics

One of the first proclamations made upon the birth of a baby is "It's a girl!" or "It's a boy!" Parents wrap little girls in pink, boys in blue, and dress an infant or small child in clothes that clearly label the child as a boy or a girl.

One question we might ask is what differences do we find between boys and girls in childhood? Let's discuss the general answer first and then go into specifics. Differences between male and female infants and children are few and subtle. They are more likely to be in the eye of the beholder than in the behaviors of children.

As infants, boys develop a bit more slowly than girls, have a little more muscle tissue than girls, and are somewhat more active, but even these differences are slight (e.g., Eaton & Enns, 1986). During the first year of life there are virtually no differences in temperament or "difficulty" between boys and girls (Thomas & Chess, 1977). Adults often believe that there ought to be differences between the sexes (Paludi & Gullo, 1986) and choose toys, clothing, and playmates based on what they believe is acceptable (Schau et al., 1980). However, when averaged over many studies, there are few areas in which parents consistently treat their sons and daughters differently (Lytton & Romney, 1991).

The only area in which North American parents show significant differentiation is in the encouragement of different sex-typed activities for girls and boys. For example, in one study (Snow et al., 1983), fathers were more likely to give dolls to one-year-old girls than to boys. However, even at this age, children themselves already have their own toy preferences; when offered dolls, boys are less likely to play with them. In the first few years of elementary school, girls have a different view of areas of their own competence and activities of value than boys do. Girls tend to value (and see themselves as competent in) reading and instrumental music, for example, whereas boys value math and sports activities (Eccles et al., 1993.)

Children's peer groups provide significant experiences for both girls and boys (Maccoby, 1988, 1990; Maccoby & Jacklin, 1987). By the age of three or four, girls and boys gravitate toward playmates of the same sex, a pattern that is shown cross-culturally. Boys tend to dominate in mixed-sex interactions (Jacklin & Maccoby, 1978). Boys develop the tendency to use direct commands to influence others, whereas girls tend to use polite suggestions, which are effective with other girls but not with boys (Serbin et al., 1984). Girls develop more intensive friendships than boys and are more distressed when those friendships end. Maccoby (1990) has suggested that the interactive styles that develop in same sex groups in childhood lay the foundation for differences in social relationships of adult men and women, with more supportive, intimate relationships among women and more direct, hierarchical relationships among men.

Here's a different but related question: At what age do boys and girls begin to see each other as "different"? When do children develop gender identity, the basic sense or self-awareness of maleness or femaleness? Even five-month-old infants are able to distinguish gender in faces shown to them in pictures (Fagan & Singer, 1979). Most of us develop a sense of gender identity by the time we are two or three years old (Money, 1972; Paludi & Gullo, 1986). By the age of four, most children demonstrate gender stereotypes, showing that they believe that certain occupations, activities, or toys go better with males and some go better with females. By the time they are ready to start school, most children have a notion of associating various personality traits with men and women. This pattern has been found in several cultures (Williams & Best, 1990). Once gender identity is established, it remains quite invulnerable to change (Bem, 1981; Spence, 1985).

Cognitive psychologists believe that once children can discriminate between the sexes, they develop schemas for gender-related information (Martin, 1991). You'll recall that a schema is an organized system of general information, stored in memory that guides the processing of new information. For example, children remember toys better if they are gender consistent than if they are gender inconsistent. That is, male children remember male-oriented toys better than female-oriented toys, and female children remember female-oriented toys better than male-oriented toys (Cherney & Ryalls, 1999; Brandbard & Endsley, 1983). This effect extends to when children are asked to remember situations depicting gender-consistent versus gender-inconsistent information (Signorella, Bigler, & Liben, 1997). In one experiment, male and female children (Kindergarten to 3rd grade) were asked to recall a series of pictures depicting men and women in either traditional or nontraditional roles. The results showed that male children remembered more pictures showing a male in a traditional male role (e.g., firefighter) than a male in a nontraditional role (e.g., schoolteacher). Female children better remembered a female in a traditional role than in a nontraditional role (Liben & Signorella, 1993). According to Liben and Signorella, this gender difference is most likely due to distorting or forgetting material in memory that is inconsistent with one's gender schemas. These memory distortions help perpetuate a child's gender schema because information that does not fit with the schema is changed so that it fits with the schema (Martin, 1991).

> ## BEFORE YOU GO ON
>
> - What is meant by the term "gender"?
>
> - What reliable gender differences exist in behavior?
>
> - What role does the peer group play in the development of gender roles?
>
> - When do boys and girls see each other as different?

DEVELOPING SOCIAL ATTACHMENTS

To a large degree, we adapt and thrive in this world to the extent that we can profit from interpersonal relationships (Hartup, 1989). The roots of social development can be found in early infancy—in the formation of attachment. **Attachment** is a strong emotional relationship between a child and mother or primary caregiver (Bowlby, 1982). Attachment has survival value, "increasing the chances of an infant being protected by those to whom

attachment a strong emotional relationship between a child and parent or primary caregiver that develops over the first year of life

Social attachments between parents and children are a two-way street in which signs of mutual interest and affection are exchanged. Studies tell us that early father-child attachments are beneficial later in life.

he or she keeps proximity" (Ainsworth, 1989). A well-formed attachment provides a child with freedom to explore the environment, curiosity, adaptive problem solving, and competence when interacting with peers (Collins & Gunnar, 1990).

Forming an attachment between infant and mother, for example, involves regular interaction and active give-and-take between the two. Strong attachments are most likely to be formed if the parent is optimally sensitive and responsive to the needs of the child. Sensitivity refers to the parent's ability to correctly read the signals coming from an infant (for example, correctly identifying when the infant is hungry by the nature of the infant's crying pattern). Responsiveness refers to how the parent responds to the child's signals, for example picking up the infant when he or she cries, changing the diaper as soon as it is soiled, feeding on a regular basis, and so on. Interestingly, there is an optimal level of sensitivity and responsiveness that relates to positive, secure attachments. Too much or too little can result in negative, insecure attachment (Belsky, Rovine, & Taylor, 1984).

Simply spending time with an infant is seldom enough to produce successful attachment. Attachment is promoted by spontaneous hugging, smiling, eye contact, and vocalizing (Lamb et al., 1982). It is fostered by qualities such as warmth and gentleness. When the process is successful, we say that the child is "securely attached." Forming an attachment is a two-way street. Attachment will be most secure when the baby reciprocates by smiling, cooing, and clinging to mother when attended to (Ainsworth, 1979; Pederson et al., 1990). About 65 percent of American children become securely attached by the age of one year—a percentage close to that found in seven other countries (van Ijzendoorn & Kroonenberg, 1988).

Are there long-term benefits of becoming securely attached? Yes. Secure attachment is related to: (1) sociability (less fear of strangers, better relationships with peers, more popularity, and more friends), (2) higher self-esteem, (3) better relationships with siblings, (4) fewer tantrums or less aggressive behaviors, (5) less concern by teachers over controlling behaviors in the classroom, (6) more empathy and concern for the feelings of others, (7) fewer behavioral problems at later ages, and (8) better attention spans (from Bee, 1992). Securely attached children also show greater persistence at problem solving and are less likely to seek help from adults when injured or disappointed (Goldsmith & Harman, 1994).

We need to make it clear that infants can and do form attachments with persons other than their mothers. Father-child attachments are quite common and are beneficial for the long-term development of the child (Lamb, 1977, 1979; Lynn, 1974). One researcher found that she could predict the extent to which a child showed signs of attachment to its father simply by knowing how often Dad changed the baby's diaper (Ross et al., 1975). There is no evidence that fathers are less sensitive to the needs of their children than are mothers (Parke, 1981); although, they may be a little more physical and a little less verbal in their interactions (Parke & Tinsley, 1987).

Finally, we need to consider attachment formation for those children who spend time—sometimes a lot of time—in day care facilities. In the United States, more than half the mothers of children younger than three are employed, and the care of those children is at least, in part, taken over by others. There is evidence that children who are placed in high quality day care benefit cognitively and socially (Shaffer, 1999). How do these children fare with respect to attachment? It depends to a large extent on the quality of the care the children are given—no matter where they get it. Children who receive warm, supportive, attentive care, adequate stimulation, and opportunities for exploration demonstrate secure attachment (Howes, 1990; Phillips et al., 1987). The impact of day care depends on the likelihood that the child would have received good, warm, supportive, loving care at home (Scarr & Eisenberg, 1993). Additionally, the quality of day care and quality of maternal care combine to affect attachment security. Children who experience both low quality day care and insensitive/unresponsive parenting show the poorest attachment security (NICHD Early Child Care Research Network, 1997).

The benefits or harm of nonparental child care may also depend on the age of the child. "There is little dispute about the conclusion that children who enter day care at 18 months, two years, or later show no consistent loss of security of attachment to their parents" (Bee, 1992, p. 510). The debate centers on children less than one year old, and there is some evidence that secure attachment is less likely among those children who are not cared for at home during their first year (Belsky, 1990; Belsky & Rovine, 1988; Hennessy & Melhuish, 1991; Lamb & Sternberg, 1990). Two other studies suggest that early infant day care has little effect on a child's later social and emotional development. In one study conducted in France, there was no difference in the amount of aggression and other behavior problems between three to four-year-old children who had attended day care during the first three years of life and those who had not (Balleyguier & Melhuish, 1996). Early day care has also been found *not* to affect mother-infant interactions or cognitive outcomes for the child (Caruso, 1996). Thus, it appears that there is no consistent relationship between early infant day care and later social and emotional development.

It may tentatively be concluded that forming secure attachments is important for the later development of the child. There are long-term benefits (ranging from improved emotional stability to improved problem-solving skills) to be derived from the development of strong attachments formed early in childhood (Ainsworth, 1989; Bowlby, 1982; Etaugh, 1980; Schwartz, 1983). Further, attachments formed with the father or other caregivers seem as useful for long-term development as do attachments to the mother.

BEFORE YOU GO ON

- What is attachment?

- How do sensitivity and responsiveness contribute to attachment?

- Describe the course of attachment formation.

- What are the benefits of developing a secure attachment?

- How does day care affect attachment?

Topic Review 8 A

1. **What is the prenatal period of development, and why do psychologists study it?**

The prenatal period of development is the period of development that takes place before birth. It begins at conception when the egg is fertilized by a sperm and ends with birth. The prenatal period is a period of extreme rapid development. Developmental psychologists are interested in studying prenatal development because there is great potential for genetic and/or environmental factors to influence development which will impact postnatal development.

2. **What happens during fertilization?**

Fertilization involves a single sperm transferring its genetic material from the father to the mother's egg. Fertilization takes place in a fallopian tube. During fertilization the head of the sperm penetrates the outer membrane of the egg, which then cannot be penetrated by another sperm. The head of the sperm burrows into the egg and ruptures, releasing the father's genetic material into the egg where it links up with the mother's genetic material housed in the egg. The genetic sex of the child is determined by one of the two types of sperm which fertilizes the egg.

3. **What happens during the germinal stage?**

The first new cell created after fertilization is the zygote. The zygote begins to divide as it moves down the fallopian tube toward the uterus. A hollow ball of cells called the blastocyst forms. The outer layer of the blastocyst will become the amniotic sac, the placenta, and the umbilical cord. The inner layers of cells will become the fetus. The germinal period lasts for about two weeks and ends when the blastocyst implants itself in the uterine wall.

4. **What changes take place during the embryonic stage?**

During the embryonic stage, which lasts about six weeks, all of the organ systems of the body are put into place. During the embryonic stage, the embryo is most susceptible to prenatal problems that could lead to defects. This is because organs are growing at such a fast rate and are in their vulnerable periods. By the end of the embryonic stage, the embryo is one-inch long but has a functioning nervous system and is capable of simple reflexive movements.

5. **What happens during the fetal stage?**

The fetal stage is the longest stage of prenatal development, spanning the last six months of pregnancy. The organs laid down during the embryonic stage increase in complexity and size and begin to function. The arms and legs develop, the brain is developing rapidly, and at the end of the fifth month the fetus can be ten inches long. The age of viability, or the age at which the fetus could survive if born prematurely, is reached in the seventh month.

6. **What effect does nutrition have on prenatal development?**

A mother's diet and use of drugs can have profound effects on prenatal development. Malnutrition in the mother or deficiencies of specific vitamins or minerals are usually shared by the embryo or the fetus.

7. **What effects do smoking, alcohol, and drugs have on prenatal development?**

Although the exact mechanisms are not known, cigarette smoking can cause retarded prenatal growth, increased risk of hearing defects, miscarriages, stillbirths, and neonatal death. Alcohol is a powerful drug that reaches the fetus easily. It stays in the fetus longer than it stays in the mother and collects in organs with a high water content (like the gray matter of the brain). Exposure to high levels of alcohol throughout pregnancy or binge drinking during a vulnerable period of organ development can lead to fetal alcohol syndrome. Fetal alcohol syndrome includes retarded physical growth, poor coordination, poor muscle tone, intellectual retardation, and other problems. Lower doses are associated with a less severe condition known as fetal alcohol effects. Even light alcohol consumption can lead to deficits in motor skills. There is no safe level of alcohol that can be consumed during pregnancy. Mothers who abuse psychoactive drugs put their infants at risk for low birth weights, difficulty regulating the sleep-waking cycle, and drug addiction, as well as a host of other problems.

8. **What role does the father play in problems of prenatal development?**

Although the father cannot directly influence the unborn child during prenatal development, as the mother can, there is still the potential for the father to cause prenatal problems. If the father's age or behavior (for example, drinking or doing drugs) causes defective sperm to be produced, the potential for birth defects exists if one of the defective sperm fertilizes the egg.

9. **What general observations can we make about physical growth and motor control in childhood?**

The neonate is born with several reflexes that have survival value. Other reflexes seem to serve no particular function for the neonate but can be used to confirm normal physical development. The age at which motor skills develop varies from child to child, but the sequence is predictable. Growth and development follow two patterns: (1) cephalocaudal, from head to torso to feet, and (2) proximodistal, from center to extremities.

10. **What are the sensory capacities of the neonate?**

The neonate's senses function reasonably well from birth. The eyes can focus at arm's length; although they will require a few months to focus over a range of object distances. Hearing and auditory discrimination are quite good, as are the senses of taste, smell, and touch.

11. **What do we know about infant face perception?**

Although neonates can make distinctions between faces and facial expressions, there is no evidence that there is an innate preference for the human face. Young infants prefer complex stimuli over simple ones.

12. **What is cognitive development and what are the two approaches to studying it?**

Cognitive development refers to the age-related changes in learning, memory, perception, attention, thinking, and problem solving. The structural-functional approach says that there are qualitative, age-related changes in the structures and functions that underlie intelligence. The information processing approach proposes that there are quantitative changes in basic information processing systems that relate to age.

13. **What are the main elements of Piaget's theory of cognitive development?**

Piaget proposed that there were cognitive structures called schemas that helped a person deal with information. During development these structures undergo significant change. The functions involved in cognitive development do not change with age. The functions are organization and adaptation. Organization is the predisposition to integrate schemas into more complex units. Adaptation comprises two subprocesses: assimilation (incorporating new information into existing schemas) and accommodation (adjusting existing schemas to account for new information). Another important concept is equilibration, which is the predisposition to maintaining a balance between one's cognitive abilities and the demands of the environment.

14. **What characterizes each of the four stages of cognitive development proposed by Piaget?**

During the sensorimotor stage a baby develops schemas (assimilating new information and accommodating old concepts) through an interaction with the environment—by sensing and doing. The baby begins to appreciate cause-and-effect relationships, imitates the actions of others, and by the end of the period, develops a sense of object permanence. Egocentrism is found in the preoperational stage of development. The child becomes me-and I-oriented, unable to appreciate the world from anyone else's perspective. In addition, children begin to develop and use symbols in the form of words to represent concepts.

In the concrete operations stage, a child organizes concepts into categories, begins to use simple logic and to understand relational terms. Conservation involves coming to understand that changing something's form does not change its nature or quantity. The essence of the formal operations stage is the ability to think, reason, and solve problems symbolically or in an abstract rather than a concrete, tangible form.

15. **What are the two main criticisms of Piaget's theory?**

Piaget's theory of cognitive development has been very influential and has received support from cross-cultural studies, but it has not escaped criticism. Two criticisms of the theory are that (1) there is little evidence that cognitive abilities develop in a series of well-defined stages (that is, the borders between stages are poorly defined), and (2) preschool children seem to have more cognitive abilities than Piaget suggested.

16. **What age-related changes are there in learning?**

Newborns just a few hours old give evidence of learning through classical and operant conditioning. They also show the ability to imitate simple facial expressions; although, early imitation is unstable. Imitation of complex behaviors is not reliably shown until the child is between eight and twelve months old. Imitation becomes an important channel of learning as the child gets older, contributing to the development of prosocial and antisocial behaviors.

17. What age-related changes in memory occur?

Neonates (in one study, only one to four days old) demonstrate memory. They will attend to a new visual pattern after ignoring a familiar one, showing an appreciation of the difference between familiar and new. By the time the infant is two to three months of age, they can remember an interesting event for up to three weeks. Children as young as three years can form coherent representations of events; but the most impressive changes in memory occur between three and twelve. As the child gets older they are better able to use the memory strategies of rehearsal, organization, using retrieval cues, and elaboration (which is discovered later than the other strategies). Research on a child's episodic memory shows that children's memory is better than previously believed. Only very young children show memory problems. Six-year-olds perform at adult levels.

18. What are the main points of Kohlberg's theory of moral development?

Kohlberg claims that moral reasoning develops through three levels of two stages each. First, one decides between right and wrong on the basis of avoiding punishment and gaining rewards (preconventional morality), then on the basis of conforming to authority or accepting social convention (conventional morality), and finally on the basis of one's understanding of the common good, individual rights, and internalized standards (postconventional morality). Although much of the theory has been supported, there is little evidence that many individuals reach the higher levels of moral reasoning. Also, there may be serious deficiencies in applying the theory equally to both genders or to all cultures, wherein what is "moral" or "right" may vary.

19. What are the first four stages (crises) of development according to Erikson?

Of Erikson's eight stages of development, four occur during childhood. These stages are described in terms of crises that need resolution and include: (1) trust versus mistrust (whether the child develops a sense of security or anxiety), (2) autonomy versus self-doubt (whether the child develops a sense of competence or doubt), (3) initiative versus guilt (whether the child gains confidence in his or her own ability or becomes guilty and resentful), and (4) competence versus inferiority (whether the child develops confidence in intellectual and social skills or develops a sense of failure and lack of confidence.)

20. What conclusions may we draw about the development of gender identity in children?

Gender identity is the sense or self-awareness of one's maleness or femaleness and the roles that males and females traditionally play in one's culture. Most children have a sense of their own gender by the age of 2 to three years, with gender identity most strongly reinforced by peer groups and play activities. A child's cognitive sense of gender stereotypes may flavor how new information is accommodated.

21. In child development, what is "attachment," and what are the consequences of developing secure attachments?

Attachment is a strong emotional relationship formed early in childhood between the child and primary caregiver(s). It has survival value in an evolutionary sense, keeping the child in proximity to those who can best care for him or her. Secure attachment in childhood has been associated with improved self-esteem later in life. A secure attachment is most likely to occur if the parents are optimally sensitive and responsive to the infant and develop a reciprocal pattern of behavior with the infant. Fathers, as well as mothers, demonstrate appropriate attachment-related behaviors, and to date, most evidence is that day care for children (at least those older than two years) need not have negative consequences (depending mostly on the quality of care).

Topic 8B DEVELOPMENT IN ADOLESCENCE AND ADULTHOOD

If you were to look at a timeline representing the development of an individual, you would find that the most rapid development and most dramatic changes occur between conception and around 11 years of age. So much happens during this time span, such as the development of language, memory, and social relationships, that it is easy to lose sight of the fact that development, as suggested by Erikson, is a lifelong proposition. Although the changes we see in development after childhood are not as rapid or dramatic as those seen during childhood, development progresses until the day we die.

Key Questions to Answer

In this Topic, we will explore development in adolescence and adulthood. While reading this Topic, find the answers to the following key questions:

1. How is adolescence defined?

2. How has adolescence been characterized?

3. What is the challenge of puberty in adolescence?

4. What is the challenge of identity formation in adolescence?

5. How did Erikson describe an adolescent's search for identity?

6. What are Marcia's four ways that identity issues can be resolved?

7. What is the relationship between age and identity status?

8. What is the challenge of drug use in adolescence?

9. What is the challenge of adolescent sexuality and teenage pregnancy?

10. What developments characterize early adulthood?

11. What are the issues surrounding interpersonal relationships in young adulthood?

12. What considerations are there in the choice of a career?

13. What challenges does the birth of a first child pose in adulthood?

14. What are some of the tasks typically faced during the middle years of adulthood?

15. What do we know about the elderly?

16. What are the stages of dying outlined by Kubler-Ross?

17. How general are the stages of dying?

18. How do elderly people feel about death?

ADOLESCENT DEVELOPMENT

adolescence the developmental period between childhood and adulthood, often begun at puberty and ending with full physical growth, generally between the ages of 12 and 20

puberty the stage of physical development at which one becomes capable of sexual reproduction

Adolescence is a period of transition from the dependence of childhood to the independence of adulthood. It is the period of development that begins at puberty (sexual maturity) and lasts through the teen years—essentially the second decade of life.

Adolescence can be viewed from a number of different perspectives. As we have noted in our definition of adolescence, in biological terms, adolescence begins with **puberty**—sexual maturity and an ability to reproduce—and concludes with the end of physical growth, which is usually late in the teen years. A more psychological perspective emphasizes the development of the cognitions, feelings, and behaviors that characterize adolescence. Such approaches emphasize the development of problem-solving skills and an increased reliance on the use of symbols, logic, and abstract thinking. Such perspectives stress the importance of identity formation and the appreciation of self and self-worth. A social perspective looks at the role of adolescents in their societies, and defines adolescence in terms of being "in between," not yet an adult, but no longer a child. In this context, adolescence usually lasts from the early teen years through the highest educational level, when a person is thought to enter the adult world.

Actually, whether we accept a biological, psychological, or social perspective, we are usually talking about people who, in our culture, are between the ages of 12 and 20. An intriguing issue in the psychology of adolescence today is how to characterize this stage of development in a general way. Is it a time of personal growth, independence, and positive change? Or is adolescence a period of rebellion, turmoil, and negativism?

The view that adolescence can be described in terms of turmoil, storm, and stress is actually the older of the two, attributed to G. Stanley Hall (who wrote the first textbook on adolescence in 1904) and to Anna Freud (who applied psychoanalytic theory to adolescents). This position claims that normal adolescence involves many difficulties of adjustment. "To be normal during the adolescent period is by itself abnormal" (Freud, 1958, p. 275). In this view, "Adolescents may be expected to be extremely moody and depressed one day and excitedly 'high' the next. Explosive conflict with family, friends, and authorities is thought of as commonplace" (Powers et al., 1989, p. 200).

As we'll see, the teen years often present conflicts and pressures that require difficult choices, and some teenagers react to the pressures of their adolescence in maladaptive ways (Larson & Ham, 1993; Quadrel et al., 1993; Takanishi, 1993). s 1,855,022 individuals in the United States under the age of 18 were arrested. This represents a 23.98 percent increase over the 1,298,436 recorded in 1989 (Bureau of Justice Statistics, 1999). Also, between 1989 and 1998 the number of arrests for violent crimes increased by 14.1 percent. Additionally, although the physical health and general well being of the North American population has consistently improved over recent decades, it has declined for adolescents. For example, according to the American Diabetes Association (2001), type II diabetes (where your body doesn't make enough insulin or use insulin effectively), which usually has a late onset, is rapidly becoming more prevalent among adolescents. The risk of developing diabetes is increased in overweight adolescents (80 percent of newly diagnosed type II diabetics are overweight at time of diagnosis). Risks also increase if there is a family history of type II diabetes, and if a child is over age ten or in middle to late puberty (but cases are being observed in children as young as four years). The risk of developing diabetes is closely associated with obesity. According to the Youth Behavior Risk Survey from the Centers for Disease Control (1999), there has been a 6 percent increase in the number of overweight adolescents over the past few years. As the number of overweight adolescents increases, we can expect an increase in the number of adolescents diagnosed with type II diabetes.

Yes, adolescence requires changes and adjustments, *but* those adjustments and changes are usually made in psychologically healthy ways (Feldman & Elliott, 1990; Jessor, 1993; Manning, 1983; Millstein et al., 1993; Peterson & Ebata, 1987; Rutter et al., 1976). As adolescents struggle for independence and for means of self-expression, some engage in behaviors that may be considered reckless. Such behaviors are often a reflection of the socialization process of the teenagers' culture (Arnett, 1995; Compas et al., 1995). "While many adolescents face occasional periods of uncertainty and self-doubt, loneliness and sadness, and anxiety and concern for the future, they are also likely to experience joy, excitement, curiosity, a sense of adventure, and a feeling of competence as they master new challenges" (Conger, 1991, p. 24). Here we have a theme we've seen before: There is a "wide variability that characterizes psychological development during the second decade of life" (Compas et al, 1995, p. 271).

Adolescence presents the individual with a series of challenges. In the sections that follow, we will examine a few of the challenges faced by an adolescent: puberty, identity formation, drug use, and adolescent sexuality.

The Challenge of Puberty

The onset of adolescence is marked by two biological changes. First, there is a marked increase in height and weight, known as a *growth spurt*, and second, there is sexual maturation. The growth spurt of adolescence usually occurs in girls at an earlier age than it does in boys. Girls begin their growth spurt as early as age nine or ten and then slow down at about age 15. Boys generally show increased rates of growth between the ages of 12 and 17. Males usually don't reach adult height until their early twenties; females generally attain maximum height by their late teens (Roche & Davila, 1972; Tanner, 1981).

At least some of the challenge of early adolescence is a direct result of the growth spurt. It is common to find increases in weight and height occurring so rapidly that they are accompanied by real, physical growing pains, particularly in the arms and legs. The spurt of adolescent growth seldom affects all parts of the body uniformly, especially in boys. Boys around the ages of 13 and 14 often appear incredibly clumsy and awkward as they try to coordinate their large hands and feet with the rest of their body. One of the most noticeable areas of growth in boys is that of the larynx and vocal cords. As the vocal cords lengthen, the pitch of the voice lowers. This transition is seldom a smooth one, and a teenage boy may suffer through weeks of a squeaking, cracking change of pitch in his voice (Adams, 1977; Adams & Gullotta, 1983).

Puberty occurs when one becomes physically capable of sexual reproduction. With the onset of puberty, there is a marked increase in levels of the sex hormones, androgens in males and estrogens in females. (All of us have androgens and estrogens in our bodies. Males simply have more androgens; females have more estrogens.) Boys seldom know when their own puberty begins. For some time they have experienced penile erections and nocturnal emissions of seminal fluid. Puberty in males begins with the appearance of live sperm in the semen, and most males have no idea when that happens; such determinations require a laboratory test. In females, the onset of puberty is recognizable. It is indicated by the first menstrual period, called **menarche**.

menarche a female's first menstrual period, a sure sign of the beginning of adolescence

With puberty, adolescents are biologically ready to reproduce. Dealing with that readiness and making the adjustments that we associate with psychological maturity, however, do not come automatically with sexual maturity. Some boys and girls reach puberty before or after most of their peers, and are referred to as *early* or *late bloomers.* Reaching puberty well before or after others of the same age may have some psychological effects, although few are long-lasting. Let's first get an idea of what early and late puberty means. The age range during which the major developments associated with puberty may be expected to occur are between ten and 15 years of age for girls and between 11 and 16 years of age for boys. In some cases, the age range is quite large. Many of the ages in this figure are subject to change. For example, in the United States 150 years ago, the average age of menarche was 16; now it's close to 12 (Hamburg & Takanishi, 1989). However, this trend has leveled off recently (Shaffer, 1999).

What are the advantages and disadvantages of early maturation? A girl who enters puberty early will probably be taller, stronger, faster, and more athletic than other girls (and many boys) in her class at school. She is more likely to be approached for dates, have earlier sexual encounters, and marry at a younger age than her peers. She may have self-image problems, particularly if she puts on weight and shows marked breast development (Conger & Peterson, 1984; Crockett & Peterson, 1987).

Because of the premium put on physical activity in boys, the early-maturing boy is at a greater advantage than the early-maturing girl. He will have more dating and sexual experiences than his peers, which will raise his status among his peers. He'll have a better body image and higher self-esteem (Peterson, 1988). Also, physically mature adolescents are expected to show higher levels of social and emotional maturity by parents, teachers, and friends (Jaffe, 1998). This presents the physically mature adolescent with quite a challenge because physical development usually progresses faster than social and emotional development.

BEFORE YOU GO ON

- What is adolescence, and from what perspectives can it be viewed?

- What adjustments are required during adolescence?

- What is the challenge of puberty?

- What are the advantages and disadvantages of early maturation?

For teens of both sexes, being a late bloomer is more negative in its impact (at the time) than is being an early bloomer (Gross & Duke, 1980). Late-maturing boys may carry a sense of inadequacy and poor self-esteem into adulthood (Jones, 1957). Late maturity for girls has virtually no long-term negative consequences. Some feel, at least in retrospect, that being a late bloomer was an advantage because it allowed them to develop other, broadening interests, rather than becoming "boy-crazy" like so many of their peers in early adolescence (Tobin-Richards et al., 1984).

The Challenge of Identity Formation

Adolescents around the world give the impression of being great experimenters. They experiment with hairstyles, music, religions, drugs, sexual outlets, fad diets, part-time jobs, part-time relationships, and part-time philosophies of life. It often appears that most of a teenager's commitments are made on a part-time basis. Teens are busy trying things out, doing things their own way, off on a grand search for Truth.

This perception of adolescents as experimenters is not without foundation. It is consistent with the view that one of the major tasks of adolescence is the resolution of an **identity crisis**—the struggle to define and integrate the sense of who one is, what one is to do in life, and what one's attitudes, beliefs, and values should be. The concept of identity formation is associated with Erik Erikson (1963), where the search for identity is the fifth stage of psychosocial development and occurs during the adolescent years. During adolescence we come to grips with questions like: "Who am I?" "What am I going to do with my life?" "What is the point of it all?" Needless to say, these are not trivial questions.

> **identity crisis** the effort to define and integrate one's sense of self and what one's attitudes, beliefs, and values should be

For many young people, resolving their identity crisis is a relatively simple and straightforward process. In such cases, the adolescent years bring very little confusion or conflict in terms of attitudes, beliefs, or values. Many teenagers are able and willing to accept the values and sense of self they began to develop in childhood. For many teenagers, however, the conflict of identity formation is quite real. They have a sense of giving up the values of parents and teachers in favor of new ones—their own. Physical growth, physiological changes, increased sexuality, and the perception of societal pressures to decide what they want to be when they "grow up" may lead to what Erikson calls role confusion, in which wanting to be independent, to be one's own self, does not fit in with the values of the past, of childhood. As a result, the teenager experiments with various possibilities in an attempt to see what works best, often to the dissatisfaction of bewildered parents.

Another perspective on identity formation comes from the work of James Marcia (1980). According to Marcia, identity development begins in infancy but becomes a dominant theme in adolescence when the child has reached a point where he or she can sort out and synthesize childhood identity. At this point the child develops a plan for movement into adulthood. Marcia has identified four ways that identity issues can be resolved during adolescence: *identity achievement, foreclosure, identity diffusion,* and *moratorium.* Identity achievers have experienced a decision-making period during which they have settled on a career and ideological path that they have chosen for themselves. A person in identity foreclosure is also set on a career and ideological path. However, that path was chosen by someone else, most likely the parents. Identity diffusers are individuals who have not yet set a career or ideological path, even if they have gone through a decision-making process. Finally, those in moratorium are in a state of struggle over their futures. These individuals can be characterized as being in "crisis."

One of the challenges of adolescence is identity formation. Who am I? What kind of a person am I to be? What shall be my values? What will I do with my life as I give up my dependence on my parents?

BEFORE YOU GO ON

- What is an "identity crisis," and how is it resolved?

- List and define Marcia's dimensions of identity formation.

- What ages are associated with Marcia's dimensions of identity formation?

Alan Waterman (1985) looked at identity status across eight cross-cultural studies for individuals of varying ages. Waterman found that identity achievement is most frequently found for college juniors and seniors. Foreclosure and identity diffusion are most common for younger children (sixth to tenth grade). Moratorium was less common for most age groups, except for individuals in their first two years of college where around 30 percent were in moratorium. Finally, once an identity has been formed it may not be stable. Individuals typically fluctuate among identity statuses (for example, between moratorium and identity achievement) (Lerner, 1988).

The Challenge of Drug Use

There is no doubt that many adolescents experiment with drugs. Many use drugs on a regular basis while others abuse drugs. Smoking (79 percent) and alcohol use (81 percent) lead the list of drug-related activities teenagers have tried at least once by the ninth grade (Centers for Disease Control, 1999b). With respect to smoking, the Centers for Disease Control (2000) estimate that 1.22 million individuals under the age of 18 began smoking in 1996 (66.2 percent of all individuals who started smoking that year). Overall, a minimum of 4.5 million adolescents (age 12-17) smoke cigarettes, 70 percent of whom wish they had never started. Despite this wish, a majority of adolescent smokers remain smokers into adulthood, increasing their risk of developing lung cancer versus individuals who start smoking in adulthood (Centers for Disease Control, 2000). In 1998, the tobacco industry spent almost 7 billion dollars to advertise and promote their products (Centers for Disease Control, 1999c). At least some of this advertising reached adolescents and may have been a factor in their decision to start smoking.

Drug use among teens rose steadily during the 1970s, dropped slowly during the 1980s, and increased again in the 1990s. A survey by the University of Michigan Institute for Social Research showed a significant rise in drug use by secondary school students between 1993 and 1994, reporting that over 45 percent of twelfth graders (and over 25 percent of eighth graders) admitted to using illegal drugs, most often marijuana. In September 1995, the Substance Abuse and Mental Health Services Administration released the results of their survey of 22,181 teens between the ages of 12 and 17. In this group, marijuana use had doubled since 1992. On the basis of this survey, we may estimate that nearly 1.3 million teenagers use marijuana on a monthly basis. There are no racial differences in drug use among adolescents (Oetting & Beauvais, 1990). Perceptions to the contrary, there are no differences in the rates of drug use between adolescents and adults (Warner et al., 1995). The Center for Disease Control (1999) reports that 47.2 percent of teens used marijuana at some point in their lives. Males (51.0 percent) were more likely than females (43.4 percent) to be lifetime marijuana users.

The most widely tried drug, by far, is alcohol. In the CDC risk survey, 81 percent of high school students reported having one or more drinks at some point in their life.

Heavy, episodic alcohol use was reported by 31.5 percent of students, with males (34.9 percent) being more likely than females (28.1 percent) to report heavy episodic alcohol use. Alcohol use tends to increase as a child gets older. For both males and females, alcohol use was more pervasive in grades 10-12 than in grade 9. Alcohol, as you know, impairs one's ability to drive. In the CDC risk survey, 13.1 percent of high school students reported drinking before driving. Males were more likely to drink and drive than females, a difference that cut across racial and ethnic lines. More chillingly, 33.1 percent of the students reported being a passenger in a car with a teen driver who had been drinking. Couple inexperience behind the wheel and alcohol consumption and the results are often deadly. In 1997, alcohol was involved in 20 percent (or a total of 7,719) of fatal car crashes involving drivers between the ages of 16 and 20 (National Institute of Health, 2000). And, it is the teen driver who is most likely to be killed (35.7 percent), followed by being a passenger in a drinker's car (31.1 percent). The good news is that number is down from the rates for the 1980s, when most of the rates were above 30 percent. Additionally, teens who drink are more likely than nondrinkers to have behavioral problems, skip school, engage in violence, use illegal drugs, and get involved in criminal activity (Substance Abuse and Mental Health Services Administration, 2000).

Researchers have looked at the relationship between adolescent drug use and psychological health (Shedler & Block, 1990). Participants in this investigation were 18 year olds who had been under study since they were three years old. Based on their level of drug use, they were divided into one of three groups: (1) *abstainers* (N = 29), who had never tried any drug; (2) *experimenters* (N = 36), who had used marijuana "once or twice, or a few times," and who tried no more than one other drug; and (3) *frequent users* (N = 20), who used marijuana frequently and tried at least one other drug. There were no socioeconomic or IQ differences among the groups.

The researchers found that *frequent users* were generally maladjusted, alienated, deficient in impulse control, and "manifestly" distressed. The *abstainers* were overly anxious, "emotionally constricted," and lacking in social skills. These same results were apparent when the researchers examined records from when the same subjects were seven and 11 years old. Generally, the *experimenters* were better adjusted and psychologically "healthier" than either of the other two groups. The authors of this study are concerned that their data will be misinterpreted—that their data might be taken to indicate "that drug use might somehow improve an adolescent's psychological health" (p. 628). Clearly this interpretation would be in error. You may recognize these as correlational data from which no conclusion regarding cause and effect is justified.

While drug use among adolescents is a matter of great concern, there is evidence that one need not get hysterical about infrequent drug use among teenagers. In a review of substance use among teenagers, Newcomb and Bentler (1989, p. 247) put it this way:

> Not all drug use is bad and will fry one's brain (as the commercials imply). Such claims as reflected in the national hysteria and depicted in media advertisements for treatment programs repeat the failed scare tactics of the past. All drug abuse is destructive and can have devastating consequences for individuals, their families, and society. The difference or distinction lies in the use versus abuse of drugs.

The Challenge of Sexuality

For the adolescent, puberty is an intensely personal, private, and potentially confusing process. Under the direction of the hypothalamus and the pituitary gland, large doses of sex hormones enter the bloodstream, stimulating the development of secondary sex characteristics. In males, the neck and shoulders expand, hips narrow, facial and body hair begins to sprout, and the voice crackles and then lowers in pitch. In females, the breasts begin to develop, hips broaden and become more rounded, and the shoulders narrow. All of this takes time, but then, puberty is more of a process than a single event. It is during this process that sex hormones give rise to sex drives, which are expressed in sexual behaviors. With puberty, sexual behaviors can lead to pregnancy.

As you might imagine, collecting data on the sexual behaviors of adolescents isn't easy. Many surveys are biased because samples are small or not representative of the general population due to the difficulty of obtaining consent of schools and parents. Truthfulness can be a problem with survey data, even if anonymity is ensured. This is particularly true when asking young people about an issue as sensitive as their own sexual behaviors. Some respondents stretch reality with tales of numerous sexual exploits, whereas others, perhaps somewhat anxious or guilt-ridden, tend to minimize reports of their sexual activities. Still, quality data can be found, and they tell us that adolescents are a sexually active group.

According to the Youth Risk Behavior Surveillance report from the CDC (1999), 49.9 percent of high school teenagers had engaged in sexual behavior. When we look at sexual behavior and gender, 47.7 percent of females and 52.2 percent of males had engaged in sexual behavior. blacks tended to engage in sexual behavior at higher rates than whites or Hispanics (71 percent, 45.1 percent, and 54.1 percent respectively). Males were slightly more likely to have four or more sexual partners (19.3 percent) than females (13.1 percent). Blacks had a higher rate of multiple partners (34.4 percent) than whites (12.4 percent). In terms of one's first sexual experience, 8.3 percent of teens had their first sexual experience before age 13, with more males (12.2 percent) than females (4.4 percent) reporting early sexual experience. A vast majority of teenage women (93 percent) indicated that their first sexual experience was voluntary. However, 25 percent of these women stated that the sex was unwanted (Guttmacher Institute, 1999). Generally, the frequency of sexual intercourse increases progressively between the ages of 15 and 19 among both males and females (Guttmacher Institute, 1999).

Most teens do not "plan" to be sexually active; it "just happens" (Chilman, 1983). The implication is that there is little consideration of short-and long-term consequences when behaviors "just happen." There are gender differences in how sexual activity is evaluated. One study (Coles & Stokes, 1985) tells us that about 60 percent of the males, but only 23 percent of the females, "felt glad" about their first intercourse (34 percent of the males and 61 percent of the females reported feeling "ambivalent"). A similar study reports that 67.4 percent of the males were "psychologically satisfied after their first sexual experience," whereas only 28.3 percent of the females shared in that satisfaction (Darling & Davidson, 1986).

With the relatively high rates of sexual behavior among teens, it should not be too surprising that teen pregnancy has become a serious social concern. Teen pregnancy rates in the United States are nearly twice as high as other industrialized countries such as England, Canada and Wales, and it is nine times higher than the rates in the Netherlands and Japan (Guttmacher Institute, 1999). According to the CDC (1999), 6.3 percent of high school students reported becoming pregnant or getting someone pregnant. Alcohol or drug use was a factor in 24.8 percent of the sexual activities of teenagers, with a higher percentage of males (31.2 percent) than females (18.5 percent) reporting use of alcohol or drugs prior to their last sexual intercourse. This gender difference was true for all racial and ethnic groups studied. Overall, the rate of teen pregnancy has declined by 17 percent between 1990 and 1996 (Guttmacher Institute, 1999). Unfortunately, the drop in teen pregnancy rates was true for persons between the ages of 18 and 19. Pregnancy rates for teens 15 and younger actually increased (CDC, 1998). The drop in teen pregnancy rates can be attributed to the fact that 20 percent of the decline is due to reduced sexual activity and 80 percent to using more effective contraceptive techniques (Guttmacher Institute, 1999). While the frequency of use of oral contraceptives declined from 1988 to 1995, the use of condoms and other methods increased (CDC, 1998).

What are the outcomes for teen pregnancies? Having the baby is most likely (56 percent). However, about 30 percent of teenage pregnancies are ended through abortion. The three most likely reasons given for teen abortion are concerns over finances, not feeling mature enough to have a baby, and how a baby would change one's life (Guttmacher Institute, 1999).

For those who elect to have and keep their baby, the physical, psychological and financial costs can be high. A large majority of births to teen mothers occur outside of marriage (78 percent). Teen births account for 31 percent of all births outside of marriage, which is down from 50 percent in the 1970s (Guttmacher Institute, 1999). One-quarter of teen mothers will have a second child within two years of having their first child (Guttmacher Institute, 1999). According to statistics compiled by the Guttmacher Institute, 70 percent of teen mothers complete high school, but are not as likely as women who do not have children as teens to go to college. Most teen mothers come from economically deprived backgrounds and remain in that situation after giving birth.

Teenage mothers face innumerable hurdles: they are much more likely to drop out of school, to be on welfare, to have inadequate access to health care, and to suffer economic hardships (Hayes, 1987; Hofferth & Hayes, 1987). But, remember, most adolescents do not plan to become pregnant. Teenage pregnancy may reflect a poor understanding of sexuality. For example, a significant number of adolescents do not believe they can become pregnant the first time they have intercourse, and teenagers generally hold negative attitudes about the use of contraceptives (Morrison, 1985). More and better education is needed at a younger age to prevent these statistics from climbing.

What can we conclude about adolescents on the basis of the statistics we have reviewed here? Millions of adolescents are sexually active, and many are ignorant of the consequences of their own sexual behaviors. Those for whom sexual activity results in pregnancy may exceed a million each year. But let's not lose sight of the fact that most

BEFORE YOU GO ON

- What is the challenge of drug use?

- What have been the trends in teenage drug use over the past decades?

- What is the relationship between drug use and psychological health?

- What is the challenge of sexuality?

- What do we know about the frequency and causes for teenage sexual activity?

- What are the physical, psychological, and financial costs of teenage pregnancy?

teenagers are not involved with unwanted pregnancies. Many adolescents know a great deal about sex. Dealing with sexuality effectively may not be easy, but it is just one of the challenges that must be addressed as a person passes through adolescence. Adolescence is a developmental stage of challenge, and for some it is a stage of risk and danger. On the other hand, adolescence is a stage of growth, newfound freedom, responsibility, and independence.

DEVELOPMENT DURING EARLY ADULTHOOD

The changes that occur during our adult years may not seem as striking or dramatic as those that typify our childhood and adolescence, but they are no less real. Many of the adjustments we make as adults go unnoticed as we accommodate physical changes and psychological pressures. As an adult, health may become a concern for the first time. Psychological adjustments need to be made to marriage, parenthood, career, the death of friends and family, retirement, and, ultimately, one's own death.

Following the lead of Erikson (1968) and Levinson (1978, 1986), we will consider adulthood in terms of three overlapping periods, or seasons: *early adulthood* (roughly ages 18 to 45), *middle adulthood* (ages 45 to 65), and *late adulthood* (over age 65). Presenting adult development in this way can be misleading, so we'll have to be careful. Although there is support for developmental stages in adulthood, these stages may be better defined by the individual adult than by the developmental psychologist (Datan et al., 1987). Some psychologists find little evidence of orderly transitions in adulthood (Costa & McCrae, 1980; McCrae & Costa, 1984), while others find that there are sex differences in what determines the stage of adult life (Reinke et al., 1985).

If anything marks the transition from adolescence to adulthood it is choice and commitments made independently. The sense of identity fashioned in adolescence now needs to be put into action. In fact, the achievement of a sense of self by early adulthood is a good predictor of the success of intimate relationships later in adulthood (Kahn et al., 1985). With adult status, there are new and often difficult choices to be made. Advice may be sought from elders, parents, teachers, or friends, but as adults, individuals make their own choices. Should I get married? Which job should I pursue? Do I need more education? What sort? Where? Should we have children? How many? Many of these issues are first addressed in adolescence, during identity formation. But for the adult, these questions are no longer abstract. They are real questions that demand a response.

Levinson calls early adulthood the "era of greatest energy and abundance and of greatest contradiction and stress" (1986, p. 5). In terms of our physical development, we are at something of a peak during our twenties and thirties, and we are apparently willing to work hard to maintain that physical condition (McCann & Holmes, 1984). On the one hand, young adulthood is a season for finding our niche, for working through aspirations of our youth, for raising a family. On the other hand, it is a period of stress, finding the "right" job, taking on parenthood, and maintaining a balance among self, family, job, and society at large. Let's take a look at two important decision-making processes of young adulthood: the choice of mate and family, and the choice of job or career.

Marriage and Family

Erikson (1963) claims that early adulthood revolves around the choice of *intimacy* or *isolation*. Failure to establish close, loving, intimate relationships may result in loneliness and long periods of social isolation. Marriage is not the only source of interpersonal intimacy, but it is the first choice of most Americans. More young adults than ever before are postponing marriage plans, but 95 percent of us marry (at least once).

Young adults may value marriage, but the choice of whom to marry is of no small consequence. We've learned over the past 30 years that mate selection is a complex process. At least three factors influence the choice of a marriage partner (Newman & Newman, 1984). The first deals with *availability*. Before we can develop an intimate relationship with someone, we need the opportunity to develop the relationship in the first place. Availability is one thing, *eligibility* is a second. Here, matters of age, religion, race, politics, and background come into play. Available and eligible, a third factor enters the picture: *attractiveness*. Attractiveness in this context means physical attractiveness, but as

One of the markers of early adulthood is independence from one's parents. At the same time, early adulthood is marked by interdependence–often in the form of marriage and the beginning of a new family.

we all know, judgments of physical beauty depend on who's doing the judging. Attractiveness also involves psychological characteristics, such as understanding, emotional supportiveness, and similarity in values and goals.

Psychologist David Buss reviewed the evidence on mate selection with a focus on the question of whether opposites attract. He concluded that, in marriage, they do not. He found that "we are likely to marry someone who is similar to us in almost every variable" (Buss, 1985, p. 47). Most important (in order) are age, education, race, religion, and ethnic background, followed by attitudes and opinions, mental abilities, socioeconomic status, height, weight, and even eye color. Buss and his colleagues found that men and women are in nearly total agreement on the characteristics they seek in a mate (Buss, 1985; Buss & Barnes, 1986). Figure 8.5 presents 13 such characteristics ranked by men and women. There is a significant difference in ranking for only two: good earning potential and physical attractiveness.

Let's pause here and remind ourselves of two points that have come up before. First, the conclusions of the studies cited above are true only in general, on the average. There may be happy couples that have few of the traits listed in Figure 8.5 in common. Second, these conclusions only hold in Western, largely Anglo, North American cultures. Buss and many others are studying preferences in selecting mates around the world. In one report of their efforts (Buss et al., 1990), people from 33 countries on six continents were studied. There were some similarities among all of the cultures studied, but cultures tended to show significantly different rankings of preferences for mates. The trait that varied most across cultures was *chastity*.

> Samples from China, India, Indonesia, Iran, Taiwan, and Arab Palestine placed great importance on chastity in a potential mate. Samples from Ireland and Japan placed moderate importance on chastity. In contrast, samples from Sweden, Finland, Norway, the Netherlands, and West Germany generally judged chastity to be irrelevant or unimportant. (Buss et al., 1990, p. 16).

You'll note that chastity is nowhere to be found on the list of preferred characteristics presented in Figure 8.5.

Rank (most important)	Male choices	Female choices
1	Kindness and understanding	Kindness and understanding
2	Intelligence	Intelligence
3	Physical attractiveness	Exciting personality
4	Exciting personality	Good health
5	Good health	Adaptability
6	Adaptability	Physical attractiveness
7	Creativity	Creativity
8	Desire for children	Good earning capacity
9	College graduate	College graduate
10	Good heredity	Desire for children
11	Good earning capacity	Good heredity
12	Good housekeeper	Good housekeeper

FIGURE 8.5

Characteristics Sought in Mates

Choosing a marriage partner is not always a matter of making sound, rational decisions, regardless of one's culture. Several factors, including romantic love and the realities of economic hardship, sometimes affect such choices. As sound and sensible as choices at the time of marriage may seem, approximately 50 percent of all first marriages end in divorce (75 percent of second marriages suffer the same fate) (Gottman, 1994). In the United States, 9.4 years is the average life span of a first marriage (U.S. Bureau of the Census, 1991). In 1993, there were 10.9 million single parents rearing children in the United States, and over 4.7 million children lived with their grandparents and not with either parent (U. S. Bureau of the Census, 1994).

Just as men and women tend to agree on what matters in choosing a mate, so do they agree on what matters in maintaining a marriage, listing such things as liking one's spouse as a friend, agreeing on goals, and a mutual concern for making the marriage work (Lauer & Lauer, 1985). Typically, men are more satisfied with their marriage than are women (Rhyne, 1981). One of the best predictors of a successful marriage is the extent to which marriage partners were able to maintain close relationships (such as with parents) *before* marriage (Wamboldt & Reiss, 1989).

BEFORE YOU GO ON

- How can we characterize the changes that occur during early adulthood?

- What challenges define the transition to adulthood from adolescence?

- What are some of the recent trends in the decision to get married?

- What factors contribute to choosing a mate?

- How do marital choices differ across cultures?

The Transition to Parenthood

Beyond establishing an intimate relationship, becoming a parent is often taken as a sure sign of adulthood. For many couples, parenthood is more a matter of choice than ever before because of more available means of contraception and new treatments for infertility. Having a family fosters the process of *generativity*, which Erikson associates with middle adulthood. **Generativity** reflects a concern for family and for a person's impact on future generations. Although such concerns may not become central until a person is over age 40, parenthood usually begins much sooner.

generativity a concern in adulthood for one's family and for one's impact on future generations

There is no doubt that having a baby around the house significantly changes established routines. Few couples have a realistic vision of what having children will do to their lives. The freedom for spontaneous trips, intimate outings, and privacy is in large measure given up in trade for the joys of parenthood. As parents, men and women take on the responsibilities of new social roles—of father and mother. These new adult roles add to the already established roles of being male or female, son or daughter, or husband or wife. It seems that choosing to have children (or at least choosing to have a large number of children) is becoming less popular. Although many people see the decision not to have children as selfish, irresponsible, and immoral (Skolnick, 1979), there is no evidence that such a decision leads to a decline in well-being or satisfaction later in life (Beckman & Houser, 1982; Keith, 1983).

What changes occur in a relationship when a child is born? There is overwhelming evidence that marital satisfaction tends to drop during the child rearing years of a marriage (Glenn, 1990; Rollins & Feldman, 1970). The good news is that marital satisfaction increases again once the children leave the nest (Glenn, 1990; Rollins & Feldman, 1970). In fact, Glenn (1990), after reviewing the literature in this area concluded that the u-shaped curve representing marital satisfaction before, during, and after the child rearing years is one of the most reliable in the social sciences. Other research confirms that indicators of marital satisfaction tend to go down, although not tremendously, in the months immediately following the birth of a first child (Belsky, Lang, & Rovine, 1985).

Why does dissatisfaction increase after the birth of a child? The most likely explanation is that *role conflict* (a person having to play more than one role at a time, such as wife and mother) and *role strain* (when the demands of a role are higher than a person's abilities) both increase (Bee, 1996). The competing demands of multiple roles and constantly changing demands on role as parent contributes to high levels of stress and dissatisfaction.

Career Choice

By the time a person has become a young adult, it is generally assumed that he or she has chosen a vocation or life's work. However, in today's marketplace, one's initial career choice need not be a life-long decision, as multiple career changes are commonplace. Choice of occupation and satisfaction with that choice go a long way toward determining self-esteem and identity. For women in early adulthood, being employed outside the home is a major determinant of self-worth (Stein et al., 1990). These days, "dual-career" families, in which both the woman and the man are pursuing lifelong careers, are becoming quite common (Gilbert, 1994; Wisensale, 1992). Women now constitute about 46.5 percent of the professional labor force in this country.

Selection of a career is driven by many factors; family influence and the potential for earning money are just two (Rhodes, 1983; Shertzer, 1985). Choosing a career path involves several stages (Turner & Helms, 1987).

1. *Exploration*: There is a general concern that something needs to be done; a choice needs to be made, but alternatives are poorly defined, and plans for making a choice are not yet developed.

2. *Crystallization*: Some real alternatives are being weighed: pluses and minuses are associated with each possibility, and although some are eliminated, a choice is not yet made.

3. *Choice*: For better or worse, a decision is made. There is a sense of relief that at least a person knows what he or she wants, and an optimistic feeling develops that everything will work out.

4. *Career* clarification: The person's self-image and career choice become intertwined. Adjustments and accommodations are made. This is a matter of fine-tuning the initial choice: "I know I want to be a teacher; but what do I want to teach, and to whom?"

5. *Induction*: The career decision is implemented, presenting a series of potentially frightening challenges to a person's own values and goals. "Is this really what I want to do?"

6. *Reformation*: A person discovers that changes need to be made if he or she is to fit in with fellow workers and do the job as expected. "This isn't going to be as simple as I thought it would be. I'd better take a few more classes."

7. *Integration*: The job and the work become part of a person's self, and a person gives up part of himself or herself to the job. This is a period of considerable satisfaction.

Occasionally a person makes a poor career decision. This is most likely to occur, of course, in the third stage of choosing a career path but probably won't be recognized until the fourth or fifth stage. In such cases, there is little to do but begin again and work through the process, seeking the self-satisfaction that comes at the final stage.

BEFORE YOU GO ON

- What challenges does the transition to parenthood pose?

- Why does having a child relate to marital dissatisfaction?

- List and describe the seven stages of choosing a career path.

Development During Middle Adulthood

As the middle years of adulthood approach, many aspects of life have become settled. By the time most people reach the age of 40, their place in the framework of society is fairly set. They have chosen their lifestyle and have grown accustomed to it. They have a family (or have decided not to). They have chosen their life work. "Most of us during our forties and fifties become 'senior members' in our own particular worlds, however grand or modest they may be" (Levinson, 1986, p. 6). In reality, the notion of a *mid-life crisis* is mostly a myth (Costa & McCrae, 1980; Farrell & Rosenberg, 1981; Hunter & Sundel, 1989).

There are several tasks that a person must face in the middle years. For starters, adjusting to the physiological changes of middle age. Middle-aged persons can surely engage in many physical activities, but they may have to be selective or modify the vigor with which they attack such activities. Heading out to the backyard for pickup basketball with the neighborhood teenagers is something a 45-year-old may have to think twice about.

While career choices have been made, in middle age one comes to expect satisfaction with work. If career satisfaction is not attained, a mid-career job change is possible. Of course, there are also situations in which changing jobs in middle age is more a matter of necessity than choice. In either case, the potential for crisis and conflict or for growth and development exists.

A major set of challenges that middle-aged persons face is dealing with family members. At this stage in life, parents are often in the throes of helping their teenagers adjust to adolescence and prepare to "leave the nest," while at the same time caring for their own parents. Adults in this situation have been referred to as "the sandwich generation" (Brody, 1981; Neugarten & Neugarten, 1989). Individual responsibility and concern for the care of the elderly has not deteriorated in recent years. In fact, 80 percent of all day-to-day health care for the elderly is provided by family members.

By middle adulthood, most people have chosen their career paths and have devel-oped lifestyles that allow for more leisure time. At least this is presented as part of the American dream.

One task of middle adulthood is similar to Erikson's crisis of generativity versus stagnation. People shift from thinking about all they have done with their life to thinking about what they will do with what time is left for them and how they can leave a mark on future generations.

BEFORE YOU GO ON

- Briefly describe middle adulthood.

- What are the main tasks faced during middle adulthood?

Although all of the "tasks" we've noted so far are interdependent, this is particularly true of these last two: relating to a spouse as a person and developing leisure-time activities. As children leave home and financial concerns diminish, there may be more time for a person's spouse and for leisure. In the eyes of adults, these tasks can amount to enjoying each other, enjoying status, enjoying retirement, vacations, and travel. In truth, taking advantage of these opportunities in meaningful ways provides a challenge for some adults whose lives have previously been devoted to children and career.

DEVELOPMENT DURING LATE ADULTHOOD

The transition to *late adulthood* generally occurs in our early to mid-sixties. Perhaps the first thing to acknowledge is that persons over the age of 65 constitute a sizable and growing proportion of the population. By the year 2020, Americans over 65 will constitute nearly 20 percent of the population (Cavenaugh & Park, 1993). Because of the coming of age of the "baby boom" generation, by the year 2030, there will be about 66 million older persons in the United States. According to a Census Bureau report, by the year 2050, the number of persons of age 65-plus years will be *78.9 million*—with an average life span of 82.1 years (AARP, 1993). The data also tell us that "aging is disproportionally a women's issue." The vast majority of those over age 80 are women, and the number of older ethnic minority adults is increasing more rapidly than for the population in general (Cavenaugh & Park, 1993).

What It Means to Be Old

Ageism is the name given to discrimination and prejudice against a group on the basis of age. Ageism is particularly acute in our attitudes about the elderly. One misconception about the aged is that they live in misery. We cannot ignore some of the difficulties that come with aging, but matters may not be as bad as many believe they are. Sensory capacities, for example, are not what they used to be. But as Skinner (1983) suggested, "If you cannot read, listen to book recordings. If you do not hear well, turn up the volume of your phonograph (and wear headphones to protect your neighbors)." Some cognitive abilities decline with age, but others develop to compensate for most losses (Salthouse, 1989). Some apparent memory loss may reflect more of a choice of what one wants to remember than an actual loss. Mental speed is reduced, but the accumulated experience of living often outweighs any advantages of speed.

ageism discrimination or prejudice against someone formed solely on the basis of age

Children have long since left the nest, but they're still in touch, and now there are grandchildren with whom to interact. Further, the children of the elderly have reached adulthood themselves, and are more able and likely to provide support for aging parents. Most older adults live in family settings. In fact, only about 5 percent of Americans over the age of 65 live in nursing homes (Papilia, Camp, & Feldman, 1996). However, the number of elderly living in nursing homes increases with age, reaching a high of 15 percent for individuals aged 85 and older. In 1995, a majority of individuals over the age of 65 lived with their families (67 percent) and another 30 percent lived alone (American Association of Retired Persons, 1997).

Some individuals dread retirement, but most welcome it as a chance to do things they have planned on for years (Haynes et al., 1978). Many people over the age of 65 become *more* physically active after retiring, perhaps from a job in which they sat at a desk all day long.

We often assume that old age necessarily brings with it the curse of poor heath. However, in 1994 only 28 percent of elderly individuals reported their health to be fair or poor. That compares to a 10 percent rate for non-elderly individuals. Finally, only 5 percent of individuals between the ages of 65 and 69 reported needing assistance for important daily activities (American Association of Retired Persons, 1997).

One scheme developmental psychologists are finding useful is to divide those over age 65 into two groups: *the young-old* and *the old-old*. This distinction is not made on the basis of actual age, but on the basis of psychological, social, and health characteristics (Committee on an Aging Society, 1986; Neugarten & Neugarten, 1986). This distinction reinforces the notion that aging is not some sort of disease. The young-old group is the large majority of those over 65 years of age (80 percent to 85 percent). They are "vigorous and competent men and women who have reduced their time investments in work or homemaking, are relatively comfortable financially and relatively well-educated, and are well-integrated members of their families and communities" (Neugarten & Neugarten, 1989).

The concept of *successful aging* is one that, until recently, seldom got much attention. Most research on the elderly has focused on *average* age-related losses. John Rowe and Robert Kahn (1987) argue "that the role of aging per se in these losses has often been overstated and that a major component of many age-associated declines can be explained in terms of lifestyle, habits, diet, and an array of psychosocial factors extrinsic to the aging process" (p. 143). The argument is that the declines, deficits, and losses of the elderly are not the result of advanced age but of factors over which we all can exercise some degree of control (Schaie, 1993). The major contributors to decline in old age include such things as poor nutrition, smoking, alcohol use, inadequate calcium intake, failure to maintain a sense of autonomy or control over life circumstances, and lack of social support (as long as the support does not erode self-control). Attention to these factors may not lengthen the life span but should extend what Rowe and Kahn call the "health span, the maintenance of full function as nearly as possible to the end of life" (1987, p.149). Research suggests, for example, that close family relationships and involvement in effective exercise programs predict successful aging (Clarkson-Smith & Hartley, 1989; Valliant & Valliant, 1990). If it comes from the initiative of the individual, a growing dependency on others can be a positive, adaptive strategy for successful aging (Baltes, 1995; Baltes & Baltes, 1990).

Death and Dying

Of the two sure things in life, death and taxes, the former is the surer. There are no loopholes. Dealing with the reality of our own death is the last major crisis we face in life. Many people never have to deal with their own death in psychological terms. These are the people who die young or suddenly. Many individuals *do* have time to contemplate their own death, and this usually takes place in late adulthood.

Much attention was focused on the confrontation with death in the popular book, *On Death and Dying* by Elisabeth Kübler-Ross (1969, 1981). Her description of the stages one goes through when facing death was based on hundreds of interviews with terminally ill patients who were aware that they were dying. Kübler-Ross suggests that the process takes place in five stages: (1) denial—a firm, simple avoidance of the evidence; a sort of "No, this can't be happening to me" reaction, (2) anger—often accompanied by resentment and envy of others, along with a realization of what is truly happening; a sort of "Why me? Why not someone else?" reaction, (3) bargaining—a matter of dealing, or bartering, usually with God; a search for more time; a sort of "If you'll just grant me a few more weeks, or months, I'll go to church every week; no, every day" reaction, (4) depression—a sense of hopelessness that bargaining won't work, that a great loss is imminent; a period of grief and sorrow over both past mistakes and what will be missed in the future, and (5) acceptance—a rather quiet facing of the reality of death, with no great joy or sadness, simply a realization that the time has come.

Kübler-Ross's description may be idealized. Many dying patients do not fit this pattern at all (Butler & Lewis, 1981; Kastenbaum & Costa, 1977). Some may show behaviors consistent with one or two of the stages, but seldom all five (Schultz & Alderman, 1974). There is some concern that this pattern of approaching death may be viewed as the "best" or the "right" way to go about it. The concern is that caretakers may try to force dying people into and through these stages, instead of letting each face the inevitability of death in his or her own way (Kalish, 1976, 1985).

Although elderly people have to deal with dying and death, they are less morbid about it than are adolescents (Lanetto, 1980). In one study (Kalish, 1976), adults over age 60 did more frequently think about and talk about death than did the younger adults surveyed. However, of all of the adults in the study, the oldest group expressed the least fear of death, some even saying they were eager for it.

BEFORE YOU GO ON

- When does the transition to late adulthood take place?

- What are the main challenges faced during late adulthood?

- What is meant by "successful aging"?

- List and define the five stages of the dying process.

Topic Review 8 B

1. **How is adolescence defined?**

   Physically, adolescence begins with puberty (attainment of sexual maturity) and lasts until the end of one's physical growth. Psychologically, it is defined in terms of cognitions and feelings that characterize the period, searching for identity, and abstract thinking. Socially, it is a period of transition, coming between childhood and adulthood, reflecting how the adolescent is viewed by others.

2. **How has adolescence been characterized?**

   Historically, the period has been seen as one of stress, distress, and abnormality. More contemporary views see adolescence as a period of challenges, but a period that most survive with no lasting negative consequences.

3. **What is the challenge of puberty in adolescence?**

   Two significant physical developments mark adolescence: a spurt of growth, seen at an earlier age in girls than in boys, and the beginning of sexual maturity, a period called puberty. As adolescents, individuals are for the first time physically prepared for sexual reproduction and begin to develop secondary sex characteristics. The consequences of reaching puberty early are a bit more positive for males than females; although, the long-term consequences for both are few and slight.

4. **What is the challenge of identity formation in adolescence?**

   The challenge of identity formation is to establish a personal identity that is separate from the parents. Thus, one major task of adolescence is the resolution of an identity crisis, which is the struggle to define and integrate the sense of who one is, what one is to do in life, and what one's attitudes, beliefs, and values should be.

5. **How did Erikson describe an adolescent's search for identity?**

   The search for one's identity—a sense of who one is and what one is to do with one's life—is, for Erikson, the major crisis of adolescence. Most develop such a sense of identity, but some enter adulthood in a state of what Erikson calls role confusion.

6. **What are Marcia's four ways that identity issues can be resolved?**

   Marcia's four dimensions of identity formation are identity achievement, foreclosure, identity diffusion, and moratorium. Resolution through identity achievement means that a person has gone through a period of decision making and has settled on a self-chosen career and ideological path. An individual in foreclosure has had an ideological and career path chosen by someone else, most likely the parents. Individuals who have not yet chosen an ideological or career path, but may have gone through a decision-making phase are said to be identity diffusers. Those in moratorium are in "crisis" and are in a state of struggle over the future.

7. **What is the relationship between age and identity status?**

   Identity achievement is most common among college juniors and seniors. Foreclosure and identity diffusion are most often seen in younger children in sixth to tenth grades. Moratorium is most commonly seen in students in their first two years of college.

8. **What is the challenge of drug use in adolescence?**

   Most teenagers have experimented with drugs, and many use drugs frequently. One study showed that among frequent users, experimenters and abstainers, adolescents classified as experimenters evidenced the fewest psychological problems. Drug use among teenagers is no worse (but no better) than among the adult population.

9. **What is the challenge of adolescent sexuality and teenage pregnancy?**

   About half of all adolescent females and males report being sexually active. Teens' first sexual encounters most often just "happen," which may help to explain why so many become pregnant each year. Slightly over half of all teenage pregnancies result in live births.

10. **What developments characterize early adulthood?**

    Early adulthood (ages eighteen to forty-five) is characterized by choices and commitments made independently. One assumes new responsibilities and is faced with decisions about career, marriage, and family. For

Erikson, the period is marked by the conflict between intimacy and social relationships on the one hand and social isolation on the other.

11. What are the issues surrounding interpersonal relationships in young adulthood?

Mate selection and marriage are two issues that young adults face. Individuals tend to "match" on a variety of characteristics (for example, age, education, or race). Some people postpone marriage, whereas others marry in young adulthood. Many marriages do fail, but most young adults list a good marriage as a major source of happiness in their lives. Many factors determine the selection of a mate. There is little support for the notion that opposites attract. Characteristics of desired mates vary among cultures.

12. What considerations are there in the choice of a career?

Choosing a career or occupation is a decision of early adulthood. Choosing the right career contributes in positive ways to self-esteem and identity. It is a process that goes through several stages: exploration, crystallization, choice, career clarification, induction, reformation, and integration. Occasionally, a person makes a poor career choice and may have to begin the process of career selection over.

13. What challenges does the birth of a first child pose in adulthood?

There is a u-shaped function relating family status and marital satisfaction. Before the birth of the first child, marital satisfaction is high. During the child rearing years, marital satisfaction declines but recovers again after the children leave the home. The birth of a child adds stress to a marriage through role conflict and role strain.

14. What are some of the tasks typically faced during the middle years of adulthood?

Middle adulthood (ages forty-five to sixty-five) may be troublesome for some, but most find middle age a period of great satisfaction and opportunity. The individual comes to accept his or her own mortality in several ways. Tasks of middle age involve adapting to one's changing physiology, occupation, aging parents and growing children, social and civic responsibilities, and the use of leisure time.

15. What do we know about the elderly?

There are more than thirty million Americans over age sixty-five, and the number of elderly is growing rapidly. Although there may be sensory, physical, and cognitive limits forced by old age, only 31 percent of elderly people rate health problems as a major concern. Although some elderly are isolated and lonely, fewer than 5 percent live in nursing homes. Older people may be concerned about death, but they are neither consumed by it nor morbid about it. With good nutrition and diet, the development of a healthy lifestyle, proper social support, and the maintenance of some degree of autonomy and control over one's life, "successful aging" can become even more common than it is today. This is another way of saying that we can increase the already large percentage (80 percent to 85 percent) of those over the age of sixty-five who have been characterized as young-old, as opposed to old-old.

16. What are the stages of dying outlined by Kübler-Ross?

Kübler-Ross described five stages of the dying process. The first stage is denial involving avoidance of evidence of impending death. The second stage is anger which is often accompanied by resentment and envy of others who are not dying. Bargaining is the third stage in which the dying person tries to make a deal with God for more time. The fourth stage is depression, or a sense of hopelessness that bargaining won't work, sorrow over past mistakes, and what will be missed in the future. The final stage is acceptance where the dying person finally accepts the reality of death with no great joy or sadness.

17. How general are the stages of dying?

Not all dying patients progress through the five stages of death outlined by Kübler-Ross. Some patients may show behavior consistent with one or two stages, but not all. There is also the danger that caretakers might force people to go through the stages.

18. How do elderly people feel about death?

Elderly people have to deal with death (their own and that of others) more than individuals of other ages. They tend to be less morbid about it than adolescents, and they think about it more than younger adults. However, elderly people express less fear of death than younger individuals. Some even express eagerness for death.

Chapter 9

Personality

$\mathcal{P}$ersonality...it is a term that we use regularly, without giving much thought to exactly what we mean when we say it. Personality is not only something that we can have in large or small amounts, but personality is also something that can be evaluated as great or awful with many ratings in between. Each of us likes to think that we are reasonably accurate in our assessments of the personalities of others—the truth is, we are. Consider the statements listed below. To what extent do you believe that each applies to you?

- You have a rather strong need for other people to like you and for them to admire you, at least a little.

- You have a tendency to be critical of yourself.

- You feel somewhat uncomfortable when called upon in class, even if you know the answer to the question.

- While you have some personality weaknesses, you are generally able to compensate for them.

- Disciplined and controlled on the outside, you tend to be a bit insecure on the inside.

- You prefer a certain amount of variety and become dissatisfied when hemmed in by restrictions.

- You have found it unwise to be too open in revealing yourself to others you do not know well.

- Sometimes you are extroverted, and easy-going. Other times you are introverted, and reserved.

- Some of your aspirations tend to be pretty unrealistic.

- Your sexual adjustments have presented some problems for you.

- At times, you doubt if you made the right decision or did the right thing.

How do you feel about those assessments? Fit you well? Describe your personality with reasonable accuracy? The truth is that almost everyone thinks that these statements provide an accurate appraisal. Some students are shocked at how insightful these statements are. And that, of course, is the very problem with them. We really do not know you at all, yet here we have generated a list of statements that seems to describe your personality with precision.

**Topic 9A
Theories of
Personality**

**Topic 9B
Issues
Related to
Personality**

Topic 9A THEORIES OF PERSONALITY

The major task of this Topic is to describe some of the theories of personality. We'll organize this discussion of specific personality theories into four basic approaches. Before we do, let's see what we mean by *theory* and *personality* in this context.

A theory is a series of assumptions; in our particular case, these assumptions are about people and their personalities. The ideas or assumptions that constitute a theory are based on observations and are reasonably and logically related to each other. The ideas of a theory should lead, through reason, to specific, testable hypotheses. In short, a *theory* is an organized collection of testable ideas used to explain a particular subject matter.

What then is personality? Few terms have been as difficult to define. Actually, each of the theoretical approaches we will study in this Topic generates its own definition of personality. We'll say that **personality** includes the affects, behaviors, and cognitions of people that characterize them in a number of situations over time. (Here again is our *ABC* mnemonic.) Personality also includes those dimensions we can use to judge people to be different from one another. With personality theories we are looking for ways that allow us to describe how people remain the same over time and circumstances, and to describe differences that we know exist among people (R. F. Baumeister, 1987). Note that personality is something a person brings to his or her interactions with the environment. Somehow, personality originates within the individual (Burger, 2000).

personality the affects, behaviors, and cognitions that characterize a person in a variety of situations

Key Questions to Answer

While reading this Topic, find the answers to the following key questions:

1. What is the definition of personality?

2. What are the main characteristics of Freud's theory of personality?

3. What are the three levels of consciousness proposed by Freud?

4. What role do instincts play in Freud's theory?

5. What are the three structures of personality as Freud saw them?

6. What are defense mechanisms?

7. What were the contributions of Adler, Jung, and Horney to the psychoanalytic approach to personality?

8. What are the strengths and weaknesses of the psychoanalytic approach to personality?

9. What were the contributions to the concept of personality made by Watson, Skinner, Dollard and Miller, and Bandura?

10. What criticisms have been made against the behavioral-learning approach?

11. What is the cognitive approach to personality?

12. What are the assumptions of Mischel's approach to personality?

13. What is social intelligence and how does it relate to personality?

14. What is the humanistic-phenomenological approach to personality as epitomized by Rogers and Maslow?

15. How has the phenomenological-humanistic approach been evaluated?

16. What are the major personality traits according to Allport and Cattell?

17. What are the Big Five personality dimensions?

18. How can we evaluate the trait approach?

THE PSYCHOANALYTIC APPROACH

We begin our discussion of personality with the **psychoanalytic approach** associated with Sigmund Freud and his students. We begin with Freud because he was the first to present a unified theory of personality.

psychoanalytic approach
the approach to personality associated with Freud and his followers that relies on instincts and the unconscious as explanatory concepts

Freud's theory of personality has been one of the most influential and, at the same time, most controversial in all of science. There are many facets to Freud's theory, but two basic premises characterize the approach: (1) a reliance on innate drives as explanatory concepts for human behavior, and (2) an acceptance of the power of unconscious forces to mold and shape behavior.

Freud's Theory

Freud's ideas about personality arose from his reading of the works of philosophers, his observations of his patients, and intense self-examination. His private practice provided Freud with experiences from which he proposed a general theory of personality and a technique of therapy. Here we review some of Freud's basic ideas about the structure and dynamics of human personality.

Levels of Consciousness

Central to Freudian personality theory is the notion that information, feelings, wants, drives, desires, and the like can be found at various levels of awareness or consciousness. Mental events of which we are actively aware at the moment are *conscious* or "in consciousness." Aspects of our mental life of which we are not conscious at any moment but that can be easily brought to awareness are stored at a *preconscious* level. When you shift your awareness to think about something you may do this evening, those plans were probably already there, in your preconscious mind.

The first grand theory of personality was authored by Sigmund Freud, a physician practicing in Vienna.

Cognitions, feelings, and motives that are not available at the conscious or preconscious level are said to be in the *unconscious*. Here we keep ideas, memories, and desires of which we are not aware and cannot easily become aware. Remember the significance of the unconscious level of the mind: even though thoughts and feelings are stored there so that we are completely unaware of them, the contents of the unconscious mind still influence us. Unconscious content, passing through the preconscious, may show itself in slips of the tongue, humor, neurotic symptoms, and dreams. Freud believed that unconscious forces could explain behaviors that otherwise seemed irrational and beyond description. He also maintained that most of our mental life took place on the unconscious level.

Basic Instincts

According to Freudian theory, our behaviors, thoughts, and feelings are largely governed by innate biological drives, referred to as *instincts* in this context. These are inborn impulses or forces that rule our personalities. There may be many separate drives or instincts, but they can be grouped into two categories.

life instincts (eros) inborn impulses, proposed by Freud, that compel one toward survival; they include hunger, thirst, and sex

On the one hand are **life instincts (eros)**, or impulses for survival, including those that motivate sex, hunger, and thirst. Each instinct has its own energy that compels us into action (drives us). Freud called the psychic energy through which the sexual instincts operate **libido**. Opposed to life instincts are **death instincts (thanatos)**. These are largely impulses of destruction. Directed inward, they give rise to feelings of depression or suicide; directed outward, they result in aggression. In large measure, life (according to Freud) is an attempt to resolve conflicts between these two natural but opposed sets of instincts.

The Structure of Personality

Freud believed that the mind operates on three interacting levels of awareness: conscious, preconscious, and unconscious. Freud proposed that personality also consists of three separate, though interacting, structures or subsystems: the id, ego, and superego. Each of these structures or subsystems has its own job to do and its own principles to follow.

The **id** is the totally inborn portion of personality. It resides in the unconscious level of the mind, and it is through the id that basic instincts are expressed. The driving force of the id is *libido*, or sexual energy; although, it may be more fair to say "sensual" rather than "sexual" so as not to imply that Freud was always talking about adult sexual intercourse. The id operates on the **pleasure principle**, indicating that the major function of the id is to find satisfaction for basic pleasurable impulses. Although the other divisions of personality develop later, our id remains with us always and is the basic energy source in our lives.

The **ego** is the part of the personality that develops through one's experience with reality. In many ways, it is our "self," at least the self of which we are consciously aware at any time. It is the rational, reasoning part of our personality. The ego operates on the **reality principle**. One of the ego's main jobs is to try to find satisfaction for the id, but it does so in ways that are reasonable and rational. The ego may delay gratification of some libidinal impulse or may need to find an acceptable outlet for some need. Freud said that "the ego stands for reason and good sense while the id stands for untamed passions" (Freud, 1933).

The last of the three structures to develop is the **superego**, which we can liken to one's sense of morality or conscience. It reflects our internalization of society's rules. The superego operates on the **idealistic principle**. One problem we have with our superegos is that they, like our ids, have no contact with reality and, therefore, often place unrealistic demands on the individual. For example, a person's superego may have that person believe that he or she should *always* be kind and generous and *never* harbor unpleasant or negative thoughts about someone else, no matter what. The superego demands that we do what *it* deems right and proper, no matter what the circumstances. Failure to do so may lead to guilt and shame. Again, it falls to the ego to try to maintain a realistic balance between the conscience of the superego and the libido of the id.

Although the dynamic processes underlying personality may appear complicated, the concepts underlying these processes are not as complicated as they sound. Suppose a bank teller discovers an extra $20 in his cash drawer at the end of the day. He certainly

libido in Freud's theory, the energy that activates the sexual instincts

death instincts (thanatos) the inborn impulses, proposed by Freud, that compel one toward destruction; they include feelings of depression and aggression

id in Freud's theory, the instinctive aspect of personality that seeks immediate gratification of impulses; it operates on the pleasure principle

pleasure principle the impulse of the id to seek immediate gratification to reduce tensions

ego in Freud's theory, the aspect of personality that encompasses the sense of "self"; it is in contact with the real world and operates on the reality principle

reality principle the force that governs the ego, arbitrating between the demands of the id and the realities of the world

superego in Freud's theory, the aspect of personality that refers to ethical or moral considerations; it operates on the idealistic principle

idealistic principle the force that governs the superego; opposed to the id, it seeks adherence to standards of ethics and morality

Life often presents us with situations in which the aspects of our personality—id, ego, and superego—may be in conflict.

could use an extra $20. "Go ahead. Nobody will miss it. The bank can afford a few dollars here and there. Think of the fun you can have with an extra $20," is the basic message from the id. "The odds are that you'll get caught if you take this money. If you are caught, you may lose your job; then you'll have to find another one," reasons the ego. "You shouldn't even think about taking that money. Shame on you! It's not yours. It belongs to someone else and should be returned," the superego protests. Clearly, the interaction of the three components of one's personality isn't always this simple and straightforward, but this example illustrates the general idea.

The Defense Mechanisms

defense mechanisms unconsciously applied techniques that protect the self (ego) from feelings of anxiety

If the ego cannot find acceptable ways to satisfy the drives of the id, or if it cannot deal with the demands of the superego, conflict and anxiety result. Then ways must be found to combat the resulting anxiety. Freud observed that we use **defense mechanisms**, unconsciously applied techniques that protect the conscious self (the ego) against strong feelings of anxiety. What follows is a list of some of the more common ego defense mechanisms with an example of each.

repression a defense mechanism referring to motivated forgetting of an anxiety-producing event or desire

Repression is the most basic defense mechanism. It is sometimes referred to as *motivated forgetting*, which gives you a good idea of what is involved. Repression is a matter of forgetting about some anxiety-producing event or desire. For example, Paul had a teacher with whom he did not get along. After spending an entire semester trying to do his best, Paul failed the course. The following summer, while Paul was walking with his girlfriend, the teacher approached Paul, and Paul could not remember the instructor's name. He had repressed it. Forgetting about everything and everyone who ever caused you anxiety is not an adaptive response, but pushing some anxiety-producing memories into the depths of the unconscious can protect us from dwelling on unpleasantness.

Sublimation is a defense mechanism involving the repression of unacceptable sexual or aggressive impulses and allowing them to surface in socially acceptable behaviors that are neither sexual nor aggressive in nature (Hall, 1954). For example, if a person has sexual urges for his sister, these urges can be repressed and channeled into an acceptable behavior. The person may channel the sexual energy into his artistic abilities and become an accomplished artist. For individuals with more ordinary talents such sexual energy might be channeled into a hobby or excelling at one's job.

> **sublimation** a defense mechanism involving the repression of unacceptable sexual or aggressive impulses and channeling them into socially acceptable behaviors

Denial is a defense mechanism in which a person refuses to acknowledge the realities of an anxiety-producing situation. When a physician first tells a patient that he or she has a terminal illness, a common reaction is denial; the patient refuses to believe or accept that the diagnosis is accurate.

> **denial** a defense mechanism wherein one refuses to believe the realities of an anxiety-producing situation

Rationalization amounts to making up excuses for one's behaviors rather than facing the (anxiety-producing) real reasons for them. For example, the real reason Kevin failed his psychology midterm is that he didn't study for it and had missed several classes. Kevin hates to admit, even to himself, that he could have been so stupid as to flunk this exam because of his own actions or inactions. So he rationalizes, "It really wasn't my fault. I had a terrible instructor. The test was grossly unfair. We used a lousy textbook. And I've been fighting the flu all semester."

> **rationalization** a defense mechanism that excuses one's behaviors rather than facing the anxiety-producing reasons for them

Fantasy provides an escape from anxiety through imagination or daydreaming. It is a defense mechanism commonly used by college students. After a week of exams and term paper deadlines, isn't it pleasant to sit back in a comfortable chair and fantasize about graduating from college with honors? To engage in fantasy from time to time is a normal and acceptable reaction to stress and anxiety. On the other hand, there are potential dangers. One needs to be able to keep separate those activities that are real and those that occur in fantasies. Fantasy by itself will not solve the problems or resolve the conflicts that caused the anxiety in the first place. Daydreaming about academic success may help one feel better for a while, but it is not likely to make anyone a better student.

> **fantasy** a defense mechanism that involves the imagination or daydreaming as a reaction to stress and anxiety

Projection is a matter of seeing one's own unacceptable, anxiety-producing thoughts, motives, or traits in others. For example, under enormous pressure to do well on an exam, Kirsten decides to cheat. But at exam time, her conscience (superego) won't let her. Because of projection, Kirsten may think that she sees cheating going on all around her. Projection is a defense mechanism often used in conjunction with aggression or hostility. When people feel uncomfortable with their own hostility, they often project their aggressiveness onto others, coming to believe that others are "out to get me."

> **projection** a defense mechanism that involves seeing one's own unacceptable, anxiety-producing characteristics in others

Regression is a return to earlier, more primitive, even childish levels of behavior that were once effective. We often see regression occurring in children. Imagine a four-year-old who until recently was an only child; mommy has just returned from the hospital with a new baby sister. The four-year-old is no longer the "center of attention." He reverts to earlier behaviors and starts wetting the bed, screaming for a bottle of his own, and crawling on all fours.

> **regression** a defense mechanism that involves returning to earlier, more primitive levels of behavior that were once effective

Fantasy is a common anxiety defense mechanism often used by college students. You are frustrated with traffic and parking problems on campus. Couldn't you just fantasize about a pleasant vacation on the beach to escape your hectic daily schedule?

displacement a defense mechanism in which one's behaviors or motives (usually aggressive) are directed at a substitute rather than the real object of those behaviors or motives

The defense mechanism of **displacement** is usually discussed in the context of aggression. It's a matter of directing one's motives or behaviors at a substitute person or object rather than expressing them directly, which would be anxiety-producing. For example, Dorothy expects to get promoted at work, but someone else gets the new job she wanted. She's upset and angry at her boss but feels, perhaps correctly, that blowing her top at her boss will do more harm than good, so she displaces her hostility toward her husband, the children, or the family cat.

This list of defense mechanisms is not an exhaustive one. These are among the more common, however, and should give you an idea of what Freud had in mind. There are two points that deserve special mention. (1) Using defense mechanisms is a natural reaction. You shouldn't be alarmed if you find that some of these mechanisms sound like reactions you have used. In moderation they help us to cope with the anxieties and conflicts of everyday life. (2) Although they are normal, these mechanisms *can* become maladaptive. As long as defense mechanisms are successful in easing the unpleasant feelings of anxiety, we may no longer feel a need to search for the true sources of anxiety and, thus, will be less likely to resolve the conflicts that produced the anxiety in the first place. After all, if these mechanisms do nothing else, they distort reality, at least to some degree. We'll have more to say about this point when we discuss effective and ineffective strategies for dealing with stress and anxiety.

BEFORE YOU GO ON

- What is the definition of personality?

- Describe Freud's ideas about the role of instincts and levels of consciousness in behavior.

- What are the id, ego, and superego and what principles does each operate under?

- Describe each of the defense mechanisms listed above.

The Psychoanalytic Approach After Freud

Sigmund Freud was a persuasive communicator. His ideas were challenging, and they attracted many students. Freud founded a psychoanalytic society in Vienna. There was an inner circle of colleagues and friends who shared his ideas, but some did not entirely agree with all aspects of his theory. Among other things, they were bothered by the very strong emphasis on biological instincts and libido and what they perceived as a lack of concern for social influences. Some of these analysts proposed theories of their own. They became known as **neo-Freudians**. Because they had their own ideas, they had to part from Freud; he would not tolerate disagreement with his theory. One had to accept all of Freudian theory, or one had to leave Freud's inner circle.

neo-Freudians theorists (including Adler, Jung, and Horney) who supported the basics of psychoanalytic theory but differed from Freud

The theories proposed by the neo-Freudians are complex and comprehensive. Each consists of logically interrelated, assumptions. We realize that it is not possible to do justice to someone's theory of personality in a short paragraph or two. We can, however, sketch the basic idea(s) behind the theories of a few neo-Freudians.

Alfred Adler (1870–1937). As the psychoanalytic movement was beginning to take shape, Adler was one of Freud's closest friends. However, Adler left Freud's inner circle and, in 1911, founded his own version of a psychoanalytic approach to personality. Two things seemed most to offend Adler: the negativity of Freud's views (for example, the death instinct) and the idea of sexual libido as the prime impulse in life.

Adler argued that we are a product of the social influences on our personality. We are motivated not so much by drives and instincts as we are by goals and incentives. The future and one's hope for what it holds are often more important than one's past. For Adler, the goal in life is the achievement of success or superiority. This goal is fashioned in childhood when, because we are then weak and vulnerable, we develop an **inferiority complex**—the feeling that we are less able than others to solve life's problems and get along in the world. Although we may seem inferior as children, with the help of social support and our own creativity, we can overcome and succeed. Simply striving for superiority—to be the best—was viewed by Adler as a healthy reaction to early feelings of inferiority, only if it were balanced with a sort of "social interest," or "community feeling," or a genuine desire to be helpful and of service to others.

inferiority complex the feeling that we are less able than others to solve life's problems and get along in the world

Carl Jung (1875–1961). Carl Jung left Freud's inner circle in 1913. Jung was chosen by Freud to be his successor, but several disagreements developed, mostly about the role of sexuality and the nature of the unconscious, two central themes in psychoanalysis. Jung was more mystical in his approach to personality and, like Adler, was more positive about an individual's ability to control his or her own destiny. He believed the major goal in life is to unify all of the aspects of our personality, conscious and unconscious, introverted (inwardly directed) and extroverted (outwardly directed). Libido was energy for Jung, but not sexual energy; it was energy for personal growth and development.

Jung accepted the idea of an unconscious mind and expanded on it, claiming that there are two types of unconscious: the *personal unconscious*, which is very much like Freud's view of the unconscious, and the *collective unconscious*, which contains very basic ideas that go beyond an individual's own personal experiences. Jung believed that the concepts

Karen Horney

contained in the collective unconscious are common to all of humanity and are inherited from all past generations. The contents of our collective unconscious include what Jung called *archetypes*—universal forms and patterns of thought. These are basic "ideas" that transcend generations and all of history. They include certain themes that repeatedly show up in myths: motherhood, opposites, good, evil, masculinity, femininity, and the circle as a symbol representing travel from a beginning back to where one started, or the complete, whole self.

Karen Horney (1885-1952). Trained as a psychoanalyst in Germany, Karen Horney (pronounced "horn-eye") came to the United States in 1934. She held onto a few Freudian concepts but changed most of them significantly. Horney believed that the idea of levels of consciousness made sense, as did anxiety and repression, but she theorized that the prime impulses that motivate behavior are not biological and inborn or sexual and aggressive. A major concept for Horney was *basic anxiety*, which grows out of childhood when the child feels alone and isolated in a hostile environment. If proper parental nurturance is forthcoming, basic anxiety can be overcome. If parents are overly punishing, inconsistent, or indifferent, however, children may develop *basic hostility* and may feel very hostile and aggressive toward their parents. However, young children cannot express hostility toward their parents openly, so the hostility gets repressed (into the unconscious), building even more anxiety.

Horney did emphasize early childhood experiences, but from a perspective of social interaction and personal growth. Horney claimed that there are three distinct ways in which people interact with each other. In some cases, people *move away from others*, seeking self-sufficiency and independence. The idea here is, "If I am on my own and uninvolved, you won't be able to hurt me." On the other hand, some move toward others, and are compliant and dependent. This style of interaction shields against anxiety in the sense of "If I always do what you want me to do, you won't be upset with me." Horney's third interpersonal style involves *moving against others*, where the effort is to be in control, to gain power and dominate, "If I am in control, you'll have to do what I want you to." The ideal, of course, is to maintain a balance among these three styles, but Horney argued that many people have just one style that predominates their dealings with others.

Horney also disagreed with Freud's position regarding the biological basis of differences between men and women. Freud's theories have been taken to task several times for their male bias (Fisher & Greenberg, 1977; Jordan et al., 1991). Karen Horney was one of the first to do so.

Evaluating the Psychoanalytic Approach

Given that we have reviewed only a few major ideas from a very complex approach to personality, can we make any value judgments about its contribution? We suspect that you can anticipate our answer. There are critics and supporters of each of the theoretical approaches summarized in this Topic. Each can tell us something about ourselves and about human personality in general.

The psychoanalytic approach, particularly as modified by the neo-Freudians, is the most comprehensive and complex of the theories we'll review. Psychologists have debated the relative merits of Freud's works for decades, and the debate continues. On the positive side, Freud and other psychoanalytically-oriented theorists must be credited for focusing our attention on the importance of the childhood years and for suggesting that some (even biologically determined) impulses may affect our behaviors even though they are beyond our immediate awareness. Although Freud may have overstated the matter, drawing our attention to the impact of sexuality and sexual impulses as influences on personality and human behavior is also a significant contribution. Freud's concept of defense mechanisms has generated considerable research and has found general acceptance (Feshbach et al., 1996), as has the basic notion that the unconscious may influence our pattern at responding to the world (Westen, 1998).

On the other hand, many psychologists have been critical of several aspects of psychoanalytic theory. We've seen how the neo-Freudians tended to downplay innate biological drives and take a more social approach to personality development than did Freud. One of the major criticisms of the psychoanalytic approach is that so many of its insights appear to be untestable. Freud thought of himself as a scientist, but he tested none of his ideas about human nature experimentally. Some seem beyond testing. Just what *is* libidinal energy? How can it be measured? How would we recognize it if we saw it? Concepts such as id, ego, and superego may sound sensible, but how can we prove or (more importantly) disprove their existence? Such a heavy reliance on instincts, especially with sexual and aggressive overtones, as explanatory concepts goes beyond where most psychologists are willing to venture.

BEFORE YOU GO ON

- How did neo-Freudian theories differ from Freud's theory?

- What is the inferiority complex?

- What are Jung's personal unconscious and collective unconsciousness?

- What is basic anxiety?

- Describe the strengths and weaknesses of the psychoanalytic approach to personality.

THE BEHAVIORAL-LEARNING APPROACH

Many American psychologists in the early twentieth century did not think much of the psychoanalytic approach, regardless of its form or who happened to propose it. From its beginnings, American psychology was oriented toward the laboratory and theories of learning. Explaining personality in terms of learning and observable behaviors seemed a reasonable course of action. In this section we'll briefly review some of the behavioral approaches to personality.

Learning theorists see no particular need for a separate theory of personality. Who we are is determined by our learning experiences, and early childhood experiences count heavily. Bandura, for example, argued that much of who we are is learned by imitating others.

Learning Theorists

John B. Watson (1878-1958) and his followers in behaviorism argued that psychology should turn away from the study of consciousness and the mind because the contents of mental life were unverifiable and ultimately unscientific. They argued that psychologists should study observable behavior. Yet here were Freud and the psychoanalysts arguing that *un*conscious and *pre*conscious forces are determiners of behavior. "Nonsense," the behaviorist would say. "We don't even know what we mean by consciousness, and you want to talk about levels of unconscious influence!"

Watson emphasized the role of the environment in shaping one's behaviors. Behaviorists could not accept the Freudian notion of inborn traits or impulses, whether called id or libido or anything else. What mattered was *learning*. A personality theory was not needed. A theory of learning would include all of the details about personality that one would ever need.

Who we are is determined by our learning experiences, and early experiences count heavily; on this point Watson and Freud would have agreed. Even our fears are conditioned (remember Watson's "Little Albert" study?). So convinced was Watson that instincts and innate impulses had little to do with the development of behavior that he could write, albeit somewhat tongue in cheek, "Give me a dozen healthy infants, well-formed, and my own specified world to bring them up in, and I'll guarantee to take any one at random and train him to become any type of specialist I might select—doctor, lawyer, artist, merchant, chief, and yes, even beggarman and thief, regardless of his talents, penchants, tendencies, abilities, vocations, and race of his ancestors" (Watson, 1925).

B.F. Skinner (1904-1990) refused to refer to any internal variables to explain behavior, which is the essence of what we normally think of as personality. Skinner believed that psychology should focus on observable stimuli, observable responses, and the relationships between them. Skinner argued that one should not go meddling about in the mind of the organism. Behavior is shaped by its consequences. Some behaviors result in reinforcement and, thus, are repeated. Other behaviors are not reinforced and, thus, tend *not* to be repeated. Consistency in behavior simply reflects the consistency of one's reinforcement history. The important question—from a Skinnerian point of view—is how will external conditions be manipulated to produce the sorts of consequences that we want?

John Dollard (1900-1980) and *Neal Miller* (b. 1909) tried to see if they could use the principles of learning theory to explain personality and how it developed. What matters for one's personality, they argued, was the system of habits one developed in response to cues in the environment. Behavior was motivated by biological *primary drives* (upon whose satisfaction survival depended) and *learned drives*, which developed through experience. Motivated by drives, habits that get reinforced tend to be repeated and, thus, become part of the stable collection of habits that constitute personality. For example, repression into the unconscious is simply a matter of learned forgetfulness; forgetting about some anxiety-producing experience is reinforcing and, consequently, tends to be repeated. It was Miller (1944) who proposed that conflict can be explained in terms of tendencies (habits) to approach or avoid goals and has little to do with the id, ego, and superego or with unconscious impulses of any sort.

Albert Bandura (b. 1925) is one learning theorist more than willing to consider the internal cognitive processes of the learner. He claims that many aspects of personality are learned, but often through observation and social influence. For Bandura, learning is more than forming connections between stimuli and responses or between responses and resulting reinforcers; it involves a cognitive rearrangement and representation of the world. In simpler terms, this approach argues that you may learn to behave honestly, for example, through the observation of others. If you observe your parents as being honest and see their behaviors being reinforced, you may acquire similar responses.

Evaluating the Behavioral-Learning Approach

Many critics of the behavioral-learning approach to personality argue that Watson, Skinner, and others dehumanize personality and that even the social learning theory of Bandura is too deterministic. The impression is that virtually everything a person does, thinks, or feels is in some way determined by his or her environment or learning history. This leaves nothing for the person, for personality, to contribute. Behavioral-learning approaches to personality often are not theories at all, at least not very comprehensive theories. To their credit, learning theorists demand that theoretical terms be carefully defined and that hypotheses be verified experimentally. It is also the case that many of the ideas reflected in approach to personality theory have been successfully applied in behavior therapy.

BEFORE YOU GO ON

- What were the behaviorists' views of personality?

- Describe Bandura's ideas about personality.

- What are some of the strengths and weaknesses of the learning approach to personality?

THE COGNITIVE APPROACH

According to the cognitive approach, many of the basic cognitive processes humans use (for example, memory and accessing information) intersect with patterns of thought and perception normally thought to be involved in personality (Funder, 1997).

An early cognitive theory of personality was proposed by George Kelly (1955). According to Kelly, each person has a set of *personal constructs* that direct a person's thoughts and perceptions. One idea is that these personal constructs are part of one's long-term memory and exert a directive influence over how information is stored and processed in other memory stores. Unfortunately, Kelly's work was being done just as the "cognitive revolution" in psychology was beginning, and Kelly never really made a connection between his notion of personal constructs and the then developing ideas about human cognitive functioning (Funder, 1997).

Walter Mischel, who was a student of Kelly, provided the links between personal constructs and human cognition. Mischel (1973) proposed a cognitive model of personality that included the following four "person variables":

1. *Cognitive and behavioral construction competencies*: Included in this set of competencies are personal abilities such as intelligence, social skills, and creativity. These competencies would be part of one's procedural memory, or memory involving how to do things.

2. *Encoding strategies and personal constructs*: Included here are one's conceptual categories used to make sense out of the world. They include categories for beliefs about oneself (for example, "I am a friendly person") and make up part of one's declarative memory.

3. *Subjective stimulus values*: Here a person houses his or her expectations about achieving goals, as well as the weight placed on possible outcomes for goal achievement (for example, rewards).

4. *Self-regulatory systems and plans*: This dimension comprises strategies for self-reinforcement and how those strategies control one's cognitions. This would also be part of one's procedural memory.

social intelligence in the cognitive theory of personality, all the skills, abilities, and knowledge that a person brings to all social situations

Another cognitive approach, proposed by Cantor and Kihlstrom (1987), focuses on an individual's **social intelligence**, which includes all the skills, abilities, and knowledge that a person brings to all social situations (McAdams, 1990). Individuals use their social intelligence to solve immediately pressing *life tasks*. A life task, for example, could be attending college or deciding on a career. According to this view, individuals face a wide range of life tasks that change over time. An individual must bring to bear his or her social intelligence and problem-solving strategies to deal with these tasks. Individuals facing life tasks must make use of information that they have stored in declarative and procedural memory (McAdams, 1990).

Cantor and Langston (1989) report results from a study that tracked student strategies for dealing with relevant life events. They identified two major "life task-strategy packages." One such package is *defensive pessimism*, which involves approaching life tasks with a "worst case scenario" in mind. These individuals tend to set low expectations for themselves and feel anxious about facing life tasks. The second package identified comprised *optimists* who approach life tasks with a set of more positive expectations, experience less anxiety, and generally have more positive attitudes toward academic tasks. Despite these differences, pessimists and optimists did not differ in their first semester college performance Although optimists may have performed no better than defensive pessimists during their first semester in college, there is ample evidence that persons with an optimistic outlook on life reap other benefits,including better physical health (Myers, 2000; Scheier & Carver, 1992).

Evaluating the Cognitive Approach

The cognitive approach to personality fits in well with what is known about human cognition. Kelly's and Mischel's approach to personality has withstood the test of time. In fact, over 20 years since Mischel first proposed his theory it has undergone only one change: the addition of a fifth, affective, factor. Other cognitive systems have also been proposed which incorporate the time-honored cognitive concepts of schemes and scripts. There has been a "blending" of trait and cognitive theories of personality that has provided a rich new area for research into personality (Funder, 1997).

> **BEFORE YOU GO ON**
>
> - What is the major premise of the cognitive approach to personality?
>
> - What is a personal construct?
>
> - Describe Mischel's dimensions of personality.
>
> - What is social intelligence and how is it involved in solving life tasks?

THE HUMANISTIC-PHENOMENOLOGICAL APPROACH

To some degree, the humanistic-phenomenological approach to personality contrasts with both the psychoanalytic and behavioral approaches. It claims that people have the ability to shape their own destiny and to chart and follow their own course of action, and that biological, instinctive, or environmental influences can be overcome or minimized. The humanistic view may be thought of as more optimistic than either the Freudian approach (with its death instincts and innate impulses) or the learning approach (with its emphasis on control exerted by forces of the environment). It tends to focus more on the "here and now" than on early childhood experiences as important molders of personality. The humanistic-phenomenological point of view emphasizes the wholeness or completeness of personality, rather than focusing on its structural parts. What matters most is how people view themselves and others, which is essentially what *phenomenological* means.

Humanistic Theorists

Carl Rogers' (1902-1986) approach to personality is referred to as a *person-centered* or self theory. Like Freud, Rogers developed his views of human nature through the observation of clients in a clinical setting. (Rogers preferred the term *client* to *patient* and preferred the term *person-centered* to *client-centered* to describe his approach.) Rogers believed that the most powerful of human drives is the one to become fully functioning.

To be *fully functioning* implies that the person is striving to become all that he or she can be. To be fully functioning is to experience "optimal psychological adjustment, optimal psychological maturity, complete congruence, complete openness to experience…" (Rogers, 1959, p. 235). People who realize this drive can be described as living in the present, getting the most from each experience, not moping around over opportunities lost or anticipating events to come. As long as we act only to please others, we are not fully functioning. To be fully functioning involves an openness to one's own feelings and desires, an awareness of one's inner self, and a positive self-regard.

Helping children become fully functioning requires that we offer what Rogers calls *unconditional positive regard*. As children, some of the things we do bring reward, but other things do not. How we behave often influences how we are regarded by those we care about. If we behave in a positive manner, others regard us positively. Conversely, if we behave in a negative manner, others regard us negatively. Thus, we tend to receive only conditional positive regard. *If* we do what is expected or desired, *then* we get rewarded. As a result, we try to act in ways that bring rewards and avoid punishment; we try to act in ways that please others. Feelings of self and self-worth are thus dependent on the actions of others who either reward us, don't reward us, or punish us. Rogers also argued that we should separate the child's behaviors from the child's self. That means that we may punish a child for doing a bad thing, but never for being a bad child (for example, "I love you very much, but what you have done is inappropriate and, therefore, will be punished"). Helping people achieve positive self-regard is one of the major goals of Carl Rogers' person-centered therapy.

Note that what matters here is not so much what *is*, but what is *felt* or *perceived*. One's true self (whatever it may be) is less important than one's *image* of oneself. How the world is experienced is what matters, clearly a phenomenological point of view. You may be an excellent piano player (better, perhaps, than 98 percent of the population), but if you feel you are a poor piano player, that perception or self-regard is what matters most.

Abraham Maslow's (1908-1970) basic criticism of the psychology he had studied was that it was altogether too pessimistic and negative. The person was seen as being battered about by either a hostile environment or by depraved instincts, many of which propelled the person on a course of self-destruction.

There must be more to living than this, thought Maslow. He preferred to attend to the positive side of human nature. Maslow felt that people's needs are not low and negative, but are positive, or, at worst, neutral (Maslow, 1954). Our major goal in life is to realize and put into practice those needs, or to *self-actualize*.

Let's look, Maslow argued, at the very best among us. Let's focus our attention on the characteristics of those who have realized their fullest positive potential and have become self-actualized (see Figure 9.1). Compare this point of view with Freud's who drew many of his ideas about personality from interactions with his patients, people who hardly could be categorized as self-actualizers. In his search for such individuals, Maslow could not find many. Most were historical figures, such as Thomas Jefferson and Eleanor Roosevelt.

1. They tend to be realistic in their orientation.
2. They accept themselves, others, and the world for what they are, not for what they should be.
3. They have a great deal of spontaneity.
4. They tend to be problem-centered rather than self-centered.
5. They have a need for privacy and a sense of detachment.
6. They are autonomous, independent, and self-sufficient.
7. Their appreciation of others (and of things of the world) is fresh, free, and not stereotyped.
8. Many have spiritual or mystical (although not necessarily religious) experiences.
9. They can identify with mankind as a whole and share a concern for humanity.
10. They have a number of interpersonal relationships, some of them very deep and profound.
11. They tend to have democratic views in the sense that all are created equal and should be treated equally.
12. They have a sense of humor that tends more to the philosophical than the hostile.
13. They tend to be creative in their approaches.
14. They are hard working.
15. They resist pressures to conform to society.

After Maslow, 1954.

FIGURE 9.1

Some of the Characteristics or Attributes of Self-Actualizers

Evaluating the Humanistic-Phenomenological Approach

Like the others, the humanistic-phenomenological approach has a number of strengths. For one, it reminds us of the *wholeness* of personality and of the danger in analyzing something as complex as personality in artificial segments. Additionally, the humanistic approach is more positive and optimistic, stressing personal growth and development. This view contrasts with Freud's darker, more pessimistic approach. As we will see in our discussion of psychotherapy, the humanistic-phenomenological approach has had a significant impact on many therapists and counselors.

Humanistic theories also have some drawbacks. A major problem with this approach is much like the basic problem with Freud's theory: it seems to make sense, but how does one go about *testing* any of the observations and statements made by proponents of the approach? Many of the key terms are defined in general, fuzzy ways. What is self-image? How do we really know when someone is "growing"? How can one document the advantages of unconditional positive regard? In many ways, what we have here is a blueprint for living, a vision for the nature of personality, not a scientific theory. There are also critics who claim that the notions of striving to become fully functioning or self-actualized are both naive and far from universal.

BEFORE YOU GO ON

- Describe the basic ideas behind the humanistic-phenomenological approach to personality.

- What is Carl Rogers' view of personality?

- Describe Maslow's approach to personality.

- What are some of the strengths and weaknesses of the humanistic-phenomenological approach?

THE TRAIT APPROACH

Trait theories of personality have a markedly different flavor from any of the approaches we have looked at thus far. Trait theories have two important aspects. First, the trait approach is an empirical one, relying on research using carefully constructed tests. Second, the trait approach focuses on individual differences in personality and not on measuring which traits are dominant in a given individual (Funder, 1997). Arnold Buss put it this way: "Trait psychologists typically seek to reveal the psychological dimensions along which people differ and ways in which traits cluster within individuals" (1989, p. 1379). We may define a **trait** as "any distinguishable, relatively enduring way in which one individual differs from others" (Guilford, 1959a, p. 5).

trait a distinguishable, relatively enduring way in which individuals may be described and in which they may differ

Traits are descriptive *dimensions*. In other words, any trait (for example, friendliness) is not a simple either/or proposition. Friendliness falls on a continuum, ranging from extremely unfriendly to extremely friendly, with many possibilities in between. To be useful, traits need to be measurable so we can assess the extent to which people may differ on those traits (Hogan & Nicholson, 1988; Ozer & Reise, 1994; Wiggins & Pincus, 1992). We'll briefly summarize two classic trait theories and then look at a contemporary trait theory.

Two Classic Examples

For *Gordon Allport* (1897-1967), personality traits exist within a person and can help to explain the consistency in that person's behavior. In various situations, a personality trait of friendliness might produce a range of specific responses, but those responses would be, in their essence, very much alike.

Allport proposed that there are two types of personality traits: *common traits* and *personal traits* (personal dispositions) (Allport, 1961). By common traits Allport means those dimensions of personality shared by almost everyone, to greater or lesser degrees perhaps, but shared in common with nearly everyone. Aggressiveness is an example of a common trait, as is intelligence. These are traits we can use to make comparisons among people. Personal dispositions, on the other hand, are traits unique to just some persons. How one displays a sense of humor (sharp wit, cutting sarcasm, philosophical puns, dirty jokes, and so on) is usually thought of as being a unique disposition.

Allport went on to claim that personal traits are of three subtypes: cardinal, central, and secondary. A *cardinal trait* is so overwhelming that it influences virtually everything a person does. The personalities of few of us are ruled by cardinal traits. Allport could imagine only a few examples (Don Quixote, the Marquis de Sade, Mohandas Gandhi, and Don Juan among them). No, what influences your behaviors and mine are not likely to be cardinal traits, but *central traits*, or dispositions. These can usually be described in just one word. They are the five to ten traits that best characterize someone (for example, honesty, friendliness, neatness, outgoingness, fairness, and kindness). Finally, each of us is occasionally influenced by *secondary traits*. These traits (dispositions) seldom govern many of our reactions but may be found in specific circumstances. For example, people who are basically very calm and easygoing, even when threatened (reflecting their central traits), may be very aggressive and excited when threatened in their own homes (by intruders, let's say).

Another classic approach is that of *Raymond Cattell* (b. 1905-1998). Cattell's is an empirical approach, relying on psychological tests, questionnaires, and surveys. Talking about personality traits without talking about how they are measured made little sense to Cattell. Cattell used a technique called *factor analysis*, a correlational procedure that identifies groups of highly related variables that may be assumed to measure the same underlying factor (here, a personality trait). The logic is that if you know that some people are outgoing, you don't need to test them to see if they are sociable or extroverted; such information would be redundant.

Cattell argues that there are two major types of personality traits (1973, 1979). *Surface traits* are clusters of behaviors that go together, like those that make up curiosity, trustworthiness, or kindliness. These traits are easily observed and can be found in many settings. More important than surface traits are the fewer number of underlying traits from which surface traits develop. These are called *source traits*. One's pattern of source traits determines which surface traits get expressed in behavior. Source traits are not as easily measured as surface traits because they are not directly observable. Cattell's source traits are listed in Figure 9.2.

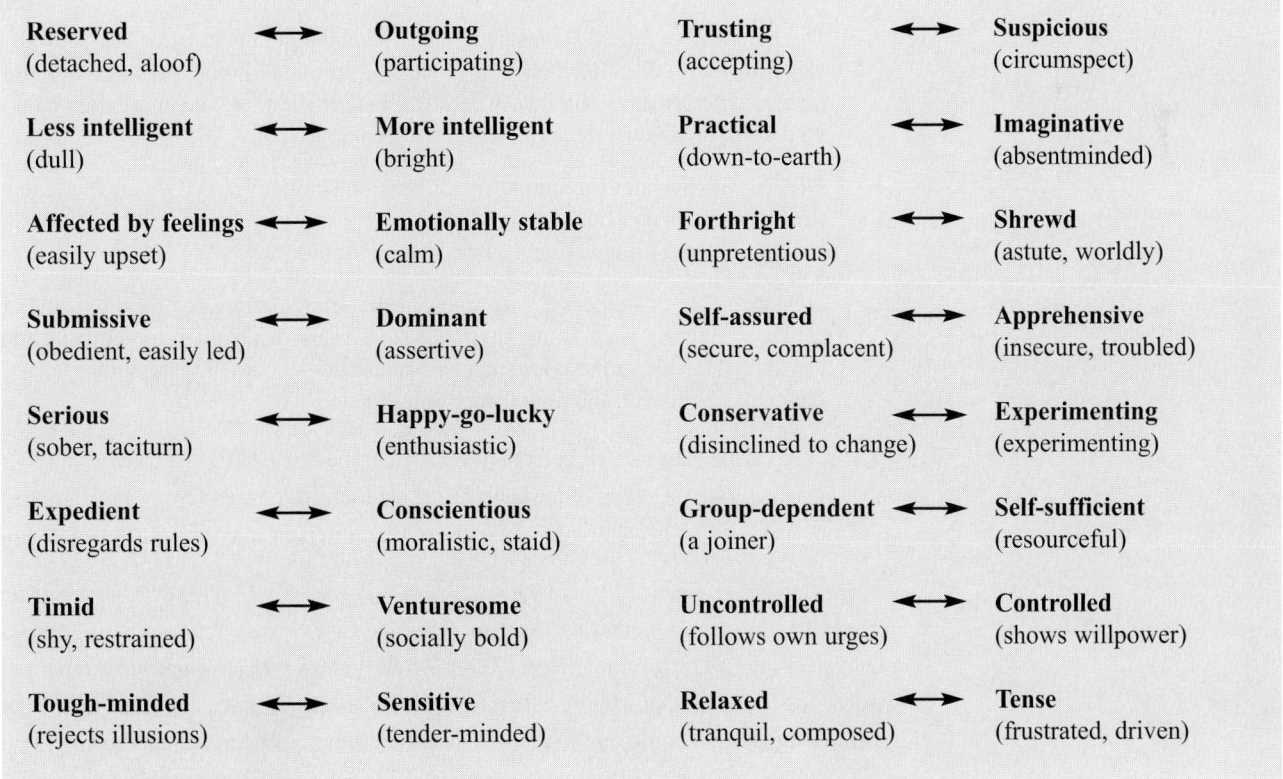

Reserved (detached, aloof)	⟷	Outgoing (participating)	Trusting (accepting)	⟷	Suspicious (circumspect)
Less intelligent (dull)	⟷	More intelligent (bright)	Practical (down-to-earth)	⟷	Imaginative (absentminded)
Affected by feelings (easily upset)	⟷	Emotionally stable (calm)	Forthright (unpretentious)	⟷	Shrewd (astute, worldly)
Submissive (obedient, easily led)	⟷	Dominant (assertive)	Self-assured (secure, complacent)	⟷	Apprehensive (insecure, troubled)
Serious (sober, taciturn)	⟷	Happy-go-lucky (enthusiastic)	Conservative (disinclined to change)	⟷	Experimenting (experimenting)
Expedient (disregards rules)	⟷	Conscientious (moralistic, staid)	Group-dependent (a joiner)	⟷	Self-sufficient (resourceful)
Timid (shy, restrained)	⟷	Venturesome (socially bold)	Uncontrolled (follows own urges)	⟷	Controlled (shows willpower)
Tough-minded (rejects illusions)	⟷	Sensitive (tender-minded)	Relaxed (tranquil, composed)	⟷	Tense (frustrated, driven)

FIGURE 9.2

Sixteen Source Traits as Identified by Cattell (Each trait is a dimension)

A Contemporary Perspective: The Big Five

We've taken a brief look at just two theories that have tried to identify relatively enduring personality traits, and we've generated quite a list. Allport focused on common traits and personal dispositions, and Cattell found many surface traits and a smaller number of source traits. Which scheme is right? Which set is most reasonable? Is there even a set of personality traits that is acceptable?

It may surprise you to learn that personality theorists are coming to a consensus concerning which traits have the most research support to best qualify as descriptors of personality. This model is referred to as the *Five-Factor Model* (Digman, 1990; McCrae & Costa, 1986, 1987, 1997; DeRaad, 1998; McCrae & John, 1992; Ozer & Reise, 1994). What are the dimensions of personality that are now being referred to as the "Big Five"?

Although there may be some consensus that five major dimensions will suffice to characterize human personality, there is disagreement on exactly how to describe these five. The following dimensions are from Digman (1990) and Goldberg (1993):

1. *Dimension I*, called "Extroversion/Introversion," embodies such things as assurance, talkativeness, openness, self-confidence, and assertiveness, on the one hand, and silence and passivity on the other.

2. *Dimension II* is "Agreeableness" or "Friendliness," with altruism, caring, and emotional support at one end and hostility, indifference, selfishness, and distrust on the other.

3. *Dimension III* is called "Conscientiousness" and amounts to a "will to achieve" (or simply a "will"). It includes self-control, dependability, planning, thoroughness, and persistence paired with carelessness, negligence, and unreliability. It is well correlated with educational achievement.

4. *Dimension IV* is an "Emotionality" dimension. In many ways, this is the extent to which one is emotionally stable or in some way psychologically disordered. It includes such things as nervousness and moodiness.

5. *Dimension V* is "Openness to Experience and Culture." (In this context, "culture" refers to aspects of experience such as art, dance, literature, music, and the like.) This factor includes such characteristics as curiosity, imagination, and creativity. Some call the dimension "Intelligence."

The recurrent finding that all personality traits can be reduced to just five, with these names (or names like these), is remarkable. Each of these five traits represents a dimension of possible habits and individual responses that a person may bring to bear in any given situation.

These five traits have emerged from nearly 50 years of research in many cultures (Paunonen et al., 1992; Stumpf, 1993; Wiggins & Pincus, 1992). They have emerged regardless of the individuals being assessed, and "the Big Five have appeared now in at least five languages, leading one to suspect that something quite fundamental is involved here" (Digman, 1990, p. 433). On the other hand, Revelle (1987) notes that "the agreement among these descriptive dimensions is impressive, [but] there is a lack of theoretical explanation for the how and the why of these dimensions" (p. 437).

Evaluating the Trait Approach

As we've already mentioned, trait approaches to personality are different from the others, even in their basic intent. Trait theories have a few obvious advantages. They provide us not only with descriptive terms, but also with the means of measuring the important dimensions of personality. They give us an idea of how measured traits are related to one another. On the other hand, there continues to be debate concerning the number of traits that are important in personality and predicting behavior. Even with the so-called Big Five traits, which is the most widely accepted trait theory, there continues to be disagreement concerning whether the five traits are completely independent and whether personality can be reduced down to five traits.

The basic relevance or value of personality traits also varies from one culture to another (Segall, Lonner, & Berry, 1998). The notion of individual personality traits seems to be relevant and sensible to people in individualistic societies, such as ours and most other Western cultures. In these cultures, people are viewed as individuals, and knowing about the characteristics of those individuals is viewed as helpful. If people are viewed in terms of their membership in a group or a collective (as in collectivistic cultures, such as are found in Asia and South America), then their individual traits will be of less interest than their roles, duties, group loyalties, and responsibilities, for example (Kitayama, et. al., 1997; Shwedler & Sullivan, 1993).

So, as we might have predicted, when we try to evaluate various approaches to or theories of personality, there are no real winners or losers. Each approach has its shortcomings, but each adds something to our appreciation of the complex concept of human personality.

BEFORE YOU GO ON

- What is the trait approach to personality, and what is a trait?

- Describe Allport's trait approach to personality.

- What is Cattell's approach to personality?

- Describe the "Big Five" personality traits.

- What are the strengths and weaknesses of the trait approach?

Topic Review 9 A

1. **What is the definition of personality?**

   Personality includes the affects, behaviors, and cognitions of people that characterize them in a number of situations over time. Personality also includes the dimensions that we can use to judge people to be different from one another. Personality resides within an individual and comprises characteristics that he or she brings to interactions with the environment.

2. **What are the main characteristics of Freud's theory of personality?**

   Freud's theory of personality has been one of the most influential and controversial theories of personality. There are two basic premises to Freud's theory: a reliance on innate drives to explain human behavior and an acceptance of the powerful role of the unconscious in motivating behavior.

3. **What are the three levels of consciousness proposed by Freud?**

   Freud proposed that at any given time we are only aware, or *conscious*, of a few things. With a little effort, some ideas or memories can be accessed from our *preconscious*, whereas others—those in our unconscious mind—may be accessed only with great difficulty. Freud believed that unconscious motives could explain behaviors that seem irrational and that most of our mental lives took place on the level of the unconscious.

4. **What role do instincts play in Freud's theory?**

   Freud believed that human behavior was guided by innate biological drives called instincts. He divided instincts into two broad categories. The life instincts, or eros, are instincts related to survival and include motives for hunger, thirst, and sex. The death instincts, or thanatos, are instincts related to destruction, such as depression and aggression. The libido is the psychic energy through which the instincts operate.

5. **What are the three structures of personality as Freud saw them?**

   The three structures of personality according to Freud are the instinctive *id*, operating on the *pleasure principle* and seeking immediate gratification; the *ego*, or sense of self, which operates on the *reality principle*, mediating needs in the context of the real world; and the superego, or sense of morality or conscience, which operates on the *idealistic principle*, attempting to direct one to do what is right and proper.

6. **What are defense mechanisms?**

   Defense mechanisms are unconscious devices employed to defend the ego against feelings of anxiety. They include *repression*, or motivated forgetting, in which anxiety-producing ideas or experiences are forced into the unconscious; *denial*, in which one refuses to acknowledge the reality of anxiety-producing situations; *rationalization*, in which one generates excuses for anxiety-producing behaviors rather than facing the real reasons for those behaviors; *fantasy*, in which a person uses daydreaming to escape the anxieties of daily living; *projection*, in which one sees in others those traits or desires that make one anxious when seen in oneself; *regression*, in which one retreats to earlier, primitive levels of behavior that were once effective as a means of dealing with anxiety; and *displacement*, in which one's anxiety-producing motives or behaviors are directed at some "safe" object or person rather than the person for whom they are intended.

7. **What were the contributions of Adler, Jung, and Horney to the psychoanalytic approach to personality?**

   Adler, Jung, and Horney each parted with Freud on theoretical grounds, while remaining basically psychoanalytic in their respective approaches to personality. For Adler, social influences and *inferiority complexes* mattered much more than did innate drives. Jung was less biological, more positive, and expanded on Freud's view of the unconscious mind, adding the notion of the *collective unconscious*. Horney rejected the notion of instinctual impulses and discussed instead the concept of *basic anxiety* and how one reacts to it as the sculptor of one's personality.

8. **What are the strengths and weaknesses of the psychoanalytic approach to personality?**

The strengths of the psychoanalytic approach include the fact that Freud and other psychoanalytic theorists focused attention on the importance of the childhood years. Other strengths are that the approach highlighted the role of the unconscious in motivating behavior and the introduction of defense mechanisms as important psychological concepts. The greatest weakness of the approach is that many of its central concepts cannot be empirically tested.

9. What were the contributions to the concept of personality made by Watson, Skinner, Dollard and Miller, and Bandura?

Many psychologists have argued that personality can be explained using learning principles and observable behavior. Watson emphasized behavior and argued that psychology should abandon mental concepts. Skinner emphasized the notion of operant conditioning and the consequences of one's behavior. Dollard and Miller tried to explain personality development in terms of learning and habit formation. Bandura stressed the role of observation and social learning in the formation of personality.

10. What criticisms have been made against the behavioral-learning approach?

The behavioral-learning approach has been criticized for dehumanizing personality and being too deterministic. Also, the various learning approaches to personality are not comprehensive theories. However, on the positive side, the approach demands that terms be carefully defined and verified experimentally.

11. What is the cognitive approach to personality?

According to the cognitive approach, basic information processing strategies such as memory and attention, intersect with patterns of thought and perception normally thought to be involved in personality. An early cognitive theory proposed by Kelly suggested that personal constructs, which are a part of long-term memory, direct an individual's thoughts and perceptions.

12. What are the assumptions of Mischel's approach to personality?

Mischel's cognitive approach to personality more clearly linked personality constructs with cognitive psychology. According to this approach there are four "person variables" that make up personality. These are: cognitive and behavioral competencies, encoding strategies and personal constructs, subjective stimulus values, and self-regulatory systems and plans.

13. What is social intelligence and how does it relate to personality?

Cantor and Kihlstrom (1987) proposed that social intelligence is at the heart of personality. Social intelligence includes all the skills, abilities, and knowledge that a person brings to all social situations. Social intelligence is used to deal with a wide range of life tasks. Two major life task "packages" are optimism and pessimism, which are characteristic ways that a person deals with life tasks. Although the two approaches are very different, they appear equally successful in dealing with some life tasks.

14. What is the humanistic-phenomenological approach to personality as epitomized by Rogers and Maslow?

The theories of Rogers and Maslow are alike in many ways, emphasizing the integrity of the self and the power of personal development. Both theorists challenge the negativity and biological bias of psychoanalytic theory, as well as the environmental determinism of behaviorism.

15. How has the phenomenological-humanistic approach been evaluated?

On the positive side, this approach reminds us of the wholeness of personality and the inherent dangers in trying to break down a complex concept like personality into artificial segments. Another strength of the approach is its focus on personal growth and striving. Additionally, the approach has had a positive impact on therapy techniques. On the negative side, the central concepts of the approach are difficult to test.

16. What are the major personality traits according to Allport and Cattell?

A personality trait is a characteristic and distinctive way in which an individual may differ from others. According to Allport, there are two varieties of traits: *common traits* and *personal dispositions*. The former is found in virtually everyone, and the latter is unique to some individuals. Cattell also feels that there are two varieties of traits: *surface traits*, which are readily observable, and source traits, from which surface traits develop.

17. What are the Big Five personality dimensions?

Recent research in personality trait theory suggests that from all of those traits that have been proposed, five emerge most regularly; although, there is as yet no agreement on what to call these dimensions. One version calls them (1) Extroversion-Introversion, (2) Agreeableness or Friendliness, (3) Will or Conscientiousness, (4) Stability-Instability, and (5) Intelligence.

18. How can we evaluate the trait approach?

The trait approach has provided a powerful way of describing and measuring personality dimensions. Modern trait theories have made great strides in showing how traits predict behavior. On the other hand, there is still debate over the number of traits that are involved in personality and whether the so-called "Big Five" traits are independent of one another and can adequately represent personality.

Topic 9B ISSUES RELATED TO PERSONALITY

Not all psychologists who claim "personality" as one of their areas of interest are actively involved in trying to devise a grand theory to describe or explain human nature. Many are involved in research that focuses on one or a few aspects of the complex concept we call personality. In this section we'll look at three areas: the extent to which personality is a useful concept when trying to explain behavior, gender differences in personality, and personality assessment or measurement.

Key Questions to Answer

While reading this Topic, find answers to the following key questions:

1. What are the assumptions of the temperament theory of personality development?

2. What are the main assumptions of the learning theory of personality development?

3. What are the key assumptions of the psychoanalytic approach to personality development?

4. What are Freud's psychosexual stages of development?

5. What are the gender differences in personality traits?

6. What are the goals of personality assessment? How are behavioral observations used to assess personality?

7. What is behavioral observation?

8. Name one advantage and one disadvantage of the interview as a technique for personality assessment.

9. How was the MMPI-2 constructed?

10. What is a projective technique?

11. What is the Rorschach inkblot test?

12. What is the Thematic Apperception Test (TAT)?

IS THERE A PERSONALITY?

Each approach to personality has its own perspective. There is one theme, however, that they have in common: all address the *consistency* of personality. Someone with an "overdeveloped superego" should be consistently conscientious and feel guilty whenever established standards are not met. Someone who has learned to behave aggressively should behave aggressively in a range of settings. Someone trying to "grow personally and to self-actualize" should be consistently open to a wide variety of new opinions and ideas. Someone with a trait of extraversion should appear outgoing and extroverted most of the time.

About 30 years ago, this very basic assumption about personality was challenged by Walter Mischel (1968). One problem with arguing for the consistency of personality is that personality just may not be consistent at all (Council, 1993; Epstein, 1979; Mischel, 1968, 1979; Mischel & Peake, 1982). Think carefully about your own behavior and your own personality. Assume for the moment you think of yourself as easygoing. Are you *always* easygoing, easy to get along with? Are there some situations in which you would be easygoing, but others in which you might fight to have your way? Are there some situations in which you tend to be social and outgoing, yet different situations in which your preference is to be alone and not mix in? Such was the thrust of Mischel's challenge: personality characteristics appear to be consistent only when they are viewed in similar or consistent situations.

We may observe consistency in the personality of others for two reasons: (1) It is convenient. We like to think that we can quickly and accurately categorize people. If we see someone do something dishonest—pick up change left as a tip for a waiter—we find it convenient to label that person as basically dishonest. It's easy to assume that the mean, aggressive football player will probably be mean and aggressive off the field as well. Such assumptions may not be true, but they make it easy to form judgments about others. (2) We tend to see others only in a restricted range of situations, where their behaviors and attitudes may very well *be* consistent. The real test would be to see those people in varied situations on many occasions (Epstein, 1979; Kendrick & Funder, 1991).

As you might suspect, arguments challenging the very definition of personality created quite a stir. Since Mischel raised the challenge, there has been an exciting barrage of research and debate on this issue. We now see that things may not be as unstable and situation-bound as Mischel suggested. One analysis, using methodology borrowed from the field of behavior genetics, argues that most of the variability we see in behaviors does reflect individual differences, even more than the pressures of the situation (Rowe, 1987; see also Digman, 1990; McCrae & Costa, 1994; Wiggins & Pincus, 1993).

In fact, most personality theorists today are ready and willing to declare the debate of "personality traits versus the situation as determinants of behavior" resolved (Carson, 1989; Digman, 1990; Kendrick & Funder, 1988, 1991). Depending on how you look at it, neither side or both sides won. By and large, research supports the position that, indeed, there are some person-related characteristics that show remarkable stability over a wide range of time and situations. The research also supports the notion that it is folly not to take into account the situation in which behaviors occur.

One outcome of the debate triggered by Mischel is a view of personality and situational variables known as *interactionism*, or the *transactional* approach (Bandura, 1978; Magnusson, 1990; Magnusson & Edler, 1977; Mischel, 1981). This approach says that how one behaves is a function of an interaction of stable personality characteristics *and* the individual's perception of the situation. Neither personality characteristics (inside the person) nor the situation (external environment) can be fully relied on to explain an individual's reaction.

Let's say that Robin agrees to a friendly racquetball game, just for the exercise. At first all goes well, and Robin, a superior player, takes it easy on her opponent. After all, they are just playing for the exercise. In the second game, Robin's opponent makes a few good shots and moves ahead in the score. Robin now notices that a small group of spectators is watching them play. As the situation changes, so does Robin's perception of it. "This is no longer fun and games," she thinks to herself, as she starts smashing low line drives off the front wall. Within just a few minutes, Robin's behavior is considerably different. The situation has been altered, and now her behavior is aggressive and forceful. As the situation changed, it brought about a change in Robin's behavior: a perceived challenge to her ability brought out competitive reactions. Robin's personality also brought about a change in the situation; to some degree, her competitiveness turned a friendly game into an athletic contest. With interactionism we have an approach that acknowledges the impact of the environment but also allows for the influence of stable, internal personality traits.

BEFORE YOU GO ON

- Describe Mischel's challenge to traditional personality approaches.

- What is interactionism?

THE ORIGINS OF PERSONALITY

One of the most interesting and sometimes controversial topics in personality is the origins of personality. Ideas and debate over the origins of personality rekindle age-old questions about the development of human behavior, most notably the nature-nurture question. That is, is personality more related to inherited biological factors (nature) or environmental factors (nurture)? In this section we will explore the major theories concerning the origins of personality.

Theories of personality development fall into three broad categories (Bee, 1995): biological theory, learning theory, and psychoanalytic theory. We will begin by looking at the biological theory.

The Biological Theory of Personality Development

The main proposition of the biological approach to personality development is that there are inborn behavioral predispositions. The most popular biological approach to personality is **temperament theory**, which suggests that one's temperamental qualities (such as activity level, sociability, and emotionality) are inborn and influence behavior. Temperament theory has four basic propositions (Bee, 1995, pp. 261-262):

1. *Individuals are born with a characteristic way of responding to the environment and to people.* There is evidence that at least some portion of one's temperament is related to genetic factors. For example, Buss & Plomin (1984) report that the correlations between temperamental qualities of identical twins are higher than those of fraternal twins. However, other research suggests that infant temperament is also influenced by the environment (Scarr & Kidd, 1983).

temperament theory a theory of the origins of personality which suggests that one's temperamental qualities (such as activity level, sociability, and emotionality) are inborn and influence behavior

2. *These characteristic ways of responding are rooted in the way a person's brain, nervous system, and endocrine system operate.* There is evidence that temperament and physiological functioning are related. Kagan, Reznick and Snideman (1990) found strong correlations between a child's shyness and various physiological measures (for example, heart rate, muscle tension, and hormone levels).

3. *There is consistency between one's temperament in infancy and childhood and one's adult temperament.* Although mixed, research evidence suggests that there is consistency of temperament over time, with the greatest consistency being temperament in toddlerhood and later temperament (Bee, 1995).

4. *Temperamental characteristics interact with the environment to affect behavior.* There is some evidence that temperamental characteristics interact with the environment (for example, parental behavior) to affect behavior. However, in general, temperamental characteristics of a child are less important than parental behaviors in the development of behavior. For example, attachments are driven more by the sensitivity and responsiveness of the parents and less by infant temperament. In short, parents find ways to effectively deal with temperamentally difficult children (Bee, 1995).

The Learning Theory of Personality Development

The basic idea behind the learning theory approach is that personality, like anything else, is acquired via the traditional mechanisms of learning (reinforcement, punishment, and observational learning). There are four basic propositions to this theory (Bee, 1995):

1. Reinforcement strengthens behavior. There is a massive amount of research showing that this is true. The basic laws of learning discovered in animal laboratories generalize well to human behavior.

2. Behaviors maintained on a partial schedule of reinforcement are more resistant to extinction than those maintained on a continuous schedule. Once again, there is ample evidence that this basic law of learning applies to the development of human behavior.

3. Children learn many behaviors from watching models. One of the most important channels of behavior development is observational learning. Through observational learning, children can learn new behaviors, learn to inhibit behaviors, or learn to remove inhibitions from behaviors. There is ample psychological evidence (for example, Bandura, 1977) of the power of modeling.

4. In addition to learning behaviors through reinforcement and modeling, children also learn attitudes, self-concept, and internal standards for behavior through these mechanisms. Once again, there is ample evidence that children learn a wide range of characteristics via learning channels.

The learning theory is one of the most widely accepted models of behavior and personality development. Additionally, recent updates to classical learning theory have been proposed that include cognitive elements as well. These new approaches suggest that based on reinforcement and modeling, children develop internalized schemes and scripts that guide thinking and behavior. For example, a child who is exposed to a great deal of violence will develop an aggressive script that causes the child to view the world as an aggressive place and respond to social situations aggressively (Huesmann, 1986). In

January, 2001, a 13-year-old boy, tried as an adult, was convicted of murdering a 6-year-old girl and sentenced to life imprisonment. The thrust of his defense was that he was only "acting out" moves and "throws" that he had seen on television. You see, he was an avid fan of televised professional wrestling.

The Psychoanalytic Theory of Personality Development

Psychoanalytic theories of personality development have been around for many years. Theories proposed by Freud and Erikson are two premier psychoanalytic theories of personality. Psychoanalytic theories have the following propositions:

1. Behavior is guided by both conscious and unconscious forces.

2. The basic structure of personality develops over time.

3. Personality develops across a series of stages.

4. An individual's personality develops according to how well an individual moves through the stages of development.

Freud put a lot of stock in the biological bases of personality, relying on concepts such as drive and instinct. This same orientation flavored his view of personality development. According to Freud, personality develops naturally in a biologically-based series of overlapping stages. The events that occur in early stages have the potential to produce profound effects on later development. At each stage of development, except for the latency period, there is a "crisis" that must be resolved. If the crisis is not resolved, there will be an overinvestment of psychic energy at that stage, and a person is said to have a **fixation** in that stage. Be clear on this point, a fixation does not mean that a person is stuck in a particular stage, not going on to the next stage. A fixation means that the failure to resolve a crisis will leave an indelible mark on the personality that will show up as part of that person's adult personality. For example, the crisis in the first stage of development (the oral stage) is weaning. If weaning is accompanied by stress and anxiety, the crisis may not be successfully resolved. As adults this may show up as an excessive need for oral stimulation and gratification. A person who smokes a large number of cigarettes per day could be said to have an oral fixation. But then again, maybe not. Apparently, Freud (an avid cigar-smoker himself) once really did say that, "Sometimes a cigar is just a cigar."

fixation in Freud's theory, an overinvestment of psychic energy resulting from a failure to adequately deal with a crisis leading to characteristics of a particular stage showing up in adult personality

One of Freud's most controversial assumptions about human behavior was that even infants and young children were under the influence of the sexual strivings of the id and its libidinal energy. The outlet for the sexual impulses (again, "sensual" may be a better term in today's usage) of young children is not the reproductive sex act. But Freud thought that much of the pleasure derived by children *is* essentially sexual; hence, we refer to Freud's stages of development as *psychosexual*. Freud claimed that there are four such stages and one "period" during which no significant developmental challenges arise.

1. *Oral Stage (Birth to one year)*. Pleasure and satisfaction come from oral activities: feeding, sucking, and making noises. If a fixation occurs in the oral stage, the mouth will continue to be a source of pleasure for many people long into adulthood, as demonstrated by overeating, fingernail biting, smoking, or talkativeness.

According to Freud, at puberty we enter a genital stage, with renewed interest in sexual matters and a reawakening of desires.

2. *Anal Stage (Age one to three years).* Sometime in their second year, children develop the ability to control their bladder and bowel habits. At this time, the anus becomes the focus of pleasure. Satisfaction is gained through bowel control. Aggression (the id again) can be displayed (particularly against parents) by either having bowel movements at inappropriate times or by refusing "to go" when placed on the potty chair. Here we can clearly see the thoughtful, reasoning ego emerging and exercising some control. After all, the parents can't make the child do what they want him or her to do. The child is in control, and that can lead to great satisfaction. Hence, the crisis that must be dealt with in the anal stage is toilet training. Toilet training accompanied by high levels of stress and anxiety can lead to an anal fixation. Adult manifestations of such a fixation are people who are overly neat and orderly (known as an anal-retentive personality) or extremely disorganized and messy (an anal-expulsive personality).

3. *Phallic Stage (Age three to five years).* Here there is an awareness of one's sexuality. The genitals become more important than the mouth and the anus as the source of pleasure, and masturbation or fondling of the genitals may become a common practice. Freud admitted that he did not understand women or the psychology of women very well (Fadiman & Frager, 1994, p. 18). He often offended the feminists of his day. (Yes, there were feminists at that time, and Freud was well aware of their criticisms.) One of the things that got him in trouble was suggesting that in the phallic stage, girls come to realize that they do not have a penis and feel inferior, "lacking," and jealous as a result (Freud, 1933, p. 126). Freud said that such "penis envy" led mature women to desire children—a male child in particular, who will bring the "longed-for penis" with him. During this stage of development children tend to form close (sexually

based) attachments to the parent of the opposite sex, and feelings of jealousy or fear of the same-sex parent may arise. This pattern of reaction is called the *Oedipus complex* in boys and the *Electra complex* in girls. It is in the phallic stage that the superego begins to develop. Resolution of the Oedipus/Electra complex is the central crisis of the phallic stage. The resolution of the Oedipus/Electra complex results in the formation of gender-role identity, sexual orientation, and emotions relating to intimacy.

4. *Latency Period (Age six years until puberty).* At this stage, sexual development gets put on hold. The latency stage is not a stage in its truest sense because there is no crisis that must be resolved. However, the ego is developing very rapidly. There is much to be learned about the world and how it operates. Sexual development can wait. Sexuality is repressed. Friends tend to be of the same sex. You have no doubt heard the protestations of a nine-year-old boy, "Oh, yuck; kiss a girl? No way! Yuck!" And you counsel, "Just wait; soon girls won't seem so 'yucky.'"

5. *Genital Stage (After puberty).* With puberty, there is a renewal of sexual impulses, a reawakening of desire, and an interest in matters sexual and sensual. During this stage the individual must deal with new relationships with members of the opposite sex, which presents one of the greatest challenges of this stage. Issues and defense mechanisms related to unresolved conflicts originating in earlier stages come to the forefront at this time. Unless the individual has learned to identify his or her unconscious impulses and conflicts on a conscious and rational level, there will be some degree of difficulty dealing with these challenges (Hill, 1998, personal communication).

> ## BEFORE YOU GO ON
>
> - What are the assumptions of the biological approach to personality development?
>
> - Describe the learning theory of personality development.
>
> - Describe Freud's psychosexual stages of personality development.

GENDER AND PERSONALITY

Personality traits give us reasonable ways to describe people and to express differences we observe among them. We can note Kathy's assertiveness and Juan's sociability. We can say that Chuck is friendlier than Steve or that Melissa is more impulsive than Jesse. An issue that intrigues personality psychologists is the extent to which personality traits can be used to characterize groups of people and determine if there are consistent differences, in general, among groups. The two groups that have been studied most closely in this regard are men and women.

What do you think about the following statements? Boys have higher self-esteem than girls. Girls are more social than boys. Men are more analytical than women. Men are better at rote learning, whereas women are more creative. Women are more open to suggestion and influence than are men.

These assertions might sound sensible, but there is no research evidence to support any of them. According to Eleanor Maccoby and Carol Jacklin, there are no gender differences in self-esteem, sociability, analytic skills, rote learning, creativity, or suggestiveness. These were the findings of the first large-scale exploration of gender differences, reported by Maccoby and Jacklin in 1974. Maccoby and Jacklin's work was not the first to ask whether there are differences between males and females (theirs was a re-analysis of data that existed at the time). It did, however, stimulate others to join in the search for ways in which gender could be used to predict how one might behave in a range of situations. That search has turned up little. The research tells us that gender differences tend to be insignificant and inconsistent (Huston, 1985; Hyde, 1984, 1986; Maccoby, 1990). "There appear to be relatively few basic psychological differences between the sexes, although members of the two sexes are socialized to behave in different ways" (Feshbach et al., 1996).

There is one glaring exception, and that is overt, physical aggression, which has consistently been found more commonly in males than in females (Eagly, 1987; Eagly & Steffen, 1986; Hyde, 1986; Maccoby, 1990). The difference in aggression found between males and females seems to be there (to varying degrees) at all ages and in all cultural settings (Ashmore, 1990; Maccoby & Jacklin, 1980; Rushton et al., 1986; Whiting & Edwards, 1973). Although we may claim that males are more physically aggressive than females, there are two necessary cautions: (1) This is a generality made "on the average" for groups of persons. Any one female might be significantly more aggressive in all regards than any one male, and (2) We have no certain evidence that this difference is necessarily genetic or biologically based.

On the assumption that you will not overinterpret them, we can list instances, other than aggression, in which small gender differences have occasionally been found.

1. *Communication style.* Men seem to be more talkative in a variety of settings and are more likely to interrupt others (Key, 1975), but in some situations, females are more likely to "self-disclose" and share their inner ideas and feelings (Cozby, 1973). Girls may also be somewhat more compliant to the demands of parents, teachers, and other (older) authority figures (Cowan & Avants, 1988; Maccoby, 1988).

As adults, there are few significant differences in the personalities of men and women. There are several observable differences in the behaviors and preferences of young boys and girls, however.

2. *Body language*. Women may be better at decoding or interpreting the body language of others (Eagly, 1987; Hall, 1978), but there are no differences in the display of postures or gestures associated with dominance in nonverbal social situations (Halberstadt & Saitta, 1987).

3. *Altruism*. Women report that they are more willing to engage in self-sacrifice for the good of others, but whether their behaviors are actually more altruistic than that of men is not clear (Rushton et al., 1986; Sennecker & Hendrick, 1983).

4. *Empathy*. As with altruism, when we rely on self-reports, women appear to be more empathic than men, more able to appreciate and understand another's feelings. But when we look at laboratory or real-life evidence, differences disappear (Eisenberg & Lennon, 1983).

5. *Self-confidence*. Particularly when they are asked to do something usually associated with a male role (for example, take a test on sports figures), women tend to be less self-confident in their performance than men—even when performances are equivalent (Beyer, 1990). This difference occurs only in social situations, in which females may be acting in accord with their perception of what is expected (Daubman et al., 1992).

Well, then, where are we on the issue of personality differences as a function of one's gender? There are gender differences in physical aggression, and there may be gender differences on a few other traits, but even these differences are not found with consistency. On most personality traits, there simply are no differences between females and males.

> **BEFORE YOU GO ON**
>
> - Describe what we know about gender differences in personality.

PERSONALITY MEASUREMENT OR ASSESSMENT

As we know, personality is a difficult concept to define. Common to most definitions is the idea that there are characteristics of an individual that remain fairly consistent over time and over many (if not all) situations. It would be very useful, then, to *reliably* and validly measure personal characteristics.

Why do psychologists engage in personality assessment in the first place? There are three goals that lie behind the measurement of personality. One is related to mental illness and psychological disorders. One question that a psychologist may ask in a clinical setting is, "What is wrong with this person?" In fact, the first question is often, "Is there anything wrong with this person?" (Burisch, 1984). Thus, adequate and proper diagnosis is one aim of personality measurement.

A second use for personality assessment is theory building, where there are a number of interrelated questions (Ozer & Reise, 1994): Which personality traits can be measured? How can traits be organized within the person? Which traits are the most important for describing someone's personality? For trait theorists, this is obviously the major purpose for constructing personality measurement devices.

The third goal involves the extent to which knowledge of personality traits can be used to predict some target behavior or behaviors. This concern is a practical one, particularly in vocational placement. For example, if we know that Joe is dominant and extroverted, what does that knowledge tell us about his leadership potential? Or the likelihood that he will succeed as a sales manager? For that matter, what personality traits best describe a successful astronaut, police officer, or secretary?

In brief, personality assessment has three goals: diagnosis, theory building, and behavioral prediction. These goals often interact. A clinical diagnosis made in the context of some theoretical approach is often used to predict possible outcomes, such as which therapy is most appropriate for a given patient.

Now let's consider a few of the assessment techniques that are used to discover the nature of someone's personality.

Behavioral Observations

behavioral observation the assessment technique of drawing conclusions about one's personality based on observations of that person's behaviors

As we develop our impressions of the personalities of friends and acquaintances, we usually do so by relying on **behavioral observation**, which, as its name suggests, involves drawing conclusions about someone's personality on the basis of observations of his or her behaviors. We judge Dan to be bright because he was the only one who knew the answer to a question in class. We feel that Maria is submissive because she always seems to do whatever her husband demands.

As helpful as our observations may be, there may be problems with the casual, unstructured observations you and I normally make. Because we have observed only a small range of behaviors in a limited range of settings, we may be overgeneralizing when we assume that those same behaviors will show up in new or different situations. Dan may never again know the answer to a question in class. Maria may give in to her husband only because we are there. That is, the behaviors that we observe may not be typical at all.

Nonetheless, behavioral observation can be an excellent source of information, particularly when the observations being made are purposeful, careful, and structured, and when steps are taken to make the observations reliable and valid and to ensure our sample is representative. Among other things, the accuracy of one's observations are related to the degree of acquaintance between the observer and the person being observed (Paulus & Bruce, 1992). Behavioral observations are commonly a part of a clinical assessment. The clinical psychologist may note several behaviors of a client as potentially significant—the style of dress, manner of speaking, gestures, postures, and so on.

Consider an example. A child is reportedly having trouble at school, behaving aggressively and generally being disruptive. One thing a psychologist may do is visit the school and observe the child's behaviors in the natural setting of the classroom. It may be that the child does behave aggressively and engage in fighting behavior, but only when the teacher is in the room. Otherwise, the child is pleasant and passive. It may be that the child's aggressive behaviors reflect a ploy to get the teacher's attention.

In an attempt to add to his or her observations, a psychologist may use *role playing* as a means to collect information. Role playing is a matter of acting out a given life situation. "Let's say that I'm a student, and that you're the teacher, and that it's recess time," the psychologist says to a child. "Let's pretend that somebody takes a toy away from me,

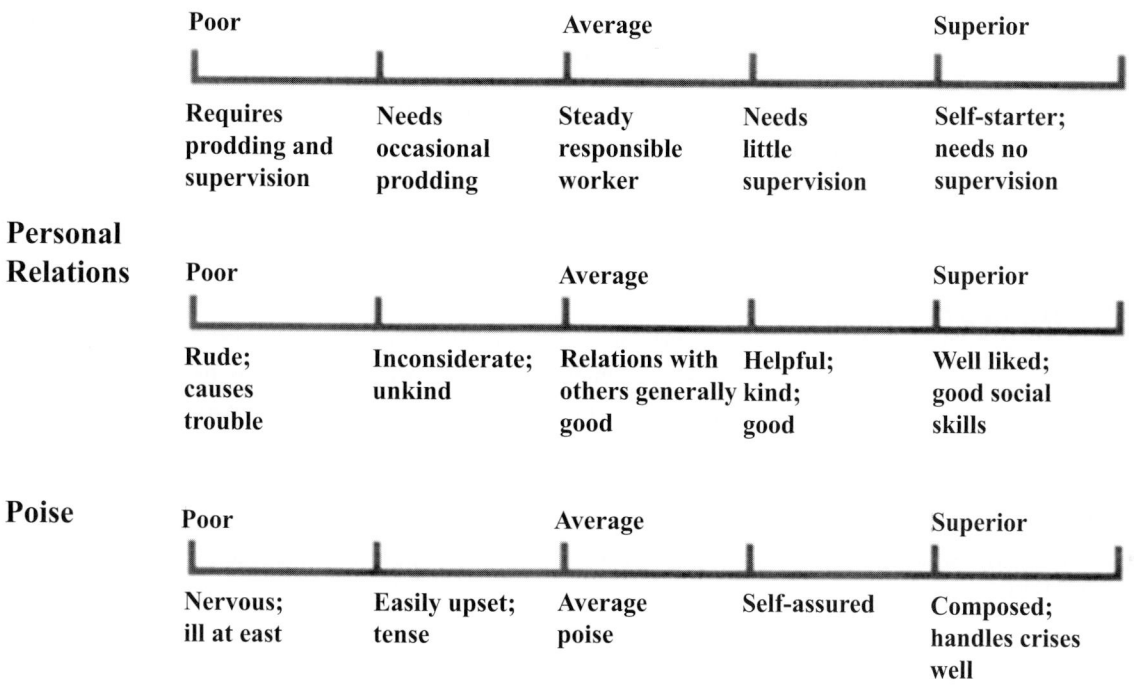

Dependability

Poor · · · **Average** · · · **Superior**

| Requires prodding and supervision | Needs occasional prodding | Steady responsible worker | Needs little supervision | Self-starter; needs no supervision |

Personal Relations

Poor · · · **Average** · · · **Superior**

| Rude; causes trouble | Inconsiderate; unkind | Relations with others generally good | Helpful; kind; good | Well liked; good social skills |

Poise

Poor · · · **Average** · · · **Superior**

| Nervous; ill at east | Easily upset; tense | Average poise | Self-assured | Composed; handles crises well |

FIGURE 9.3

A graphic rating scale such as this might be used by an employer evaluating current or potential employees.

and I hit him on the arm. What will you do?" What is of interest here is the child's response in a role-reversal situation. Can the child mentally "step back" from such a situation and make a realistic observation about what the teacher should do now?

Observational techniques can be supplemented with a rating scale (Figure 9.3). Rating scales provide many advantages over casual observation. For one thing, they focus the attention of the observer on a set of specified behaviors to be observed. Rating scales also yield a more objective measure of behavior. With rating scales, one can have behaviors observed by several raters. If several raters are involved in the observation of the same behaviors (say, children at play in a nursery school), you can check on the reliability of the observations. If all five of your observers agree that Timothy engaged in hitting behavior on the average of six times per hour, the consistency of that assessment adds to its usefulness.

Interviews

We can learn some things about people just by watching them. We can also gain insight about some aspects of their personality by simply asking them about themselves. In fact, the interview is "one of the oldest and most widely used, although not always the most accurate, of the methods of personality assessment" (Aiken, 1984, p. 296). Its popularity is largely due to its basic simplicity and flexibility.

interview the assessment technique involving a conversational interchange between an interviewer and another in order to gain information about the latter's personality

The data of the **interview** are what people say about themselves, rather than what they do. Interview results are usually impressionistic and not easily quantifiable (although some interview techniques are clearly more structured and objective than others). The interview is a technique of discovering more generalities than specifics.

A major advantage of the interview is its flexibility. The interviewer may decide to drop a certain line of questioning if it is producing no useful information to pursue some other area of interest (Whetzel & McDaniel, 1997). Studies conducted nearly 20 years ago demonstrated very clearly that interviews had very little reliability and even less validity (Tenopyr, 1981). The technique was nearly abandoned as a means of adequately assessing personality. It turned out, however, that the low marks that interviewing received only held for free-formed, often rambling, *unstructured* interviews. *Structured* interviews, on the other hand, amount to a specific set of questions to be asked in a prescribed order. This structured interview, then, becomes more like a psychological test to the extent that it is objective and standardized and asks about a particular sample of behavior. Analyses of structured interviews show that their reliability and validity can be very high (Campion, Palmer, & Campion, 1997, 1998; Landy et al., 1994).

BEFORE YOU GO ON

- Describe the goals and uses of personality assessment.

- How are behavioral observations used to assess personality?

- Describe how interviews are used to assess personality.

Paper-and-Pencil Tests

Minnesota Multiphasic Personality Inventory (MMPI) a paper-and-pencil personality test designed to assess several dimensions of personality and to indicate the presence of a psychological disorder

Observational and interview techniques barely qualify as psychological tests. In this section, we'll focus on one of the most often-used paper-and-pencil personality tests, the **Minnesota Multiphasic Personality Inventory**, or **MMPI** for short. The test is called *multiphasic* because it measures several personality dimensions with the same set of items.

The MMPI was designed to aid in the diagnosis of persons with mental disorders and, hence, is not a personality test in the sense of identifying personality traits. The test is the most researched test in psychology and remains one of the most commonly used (Lubin et al., 1984). In 1989, a revision of the MMPI (the MMPI-2) became available. The revision made two major changes and several lesser ones. Antiquated and offensive items (having to do with religion or sexual practices) were replaced. The norm group for the MMPI-2 was much larger (2,600 people) than for the MMPI (about 700 people) and is supposed to reflect a more representative sample of the population in regard to cultural background, ethnicity, and the like (Ben-Porath & Butcher, 1989). The intent of the authors of the MMPI-2 was to update and improve but *not change* the basic design or meaning of test scores.

The MMPI-2 consists of 567 true/false questions that ask about feelings, attitudes, physical symptoms, and past experiences. It is a *criterion-referenced test*, which means that items on the test are referenced to one of the criterion groups—either normal persons or patients with a diagnosis of a particular mental disorder. Some of the items appear sensible. "I feel like people are plotting against me" seems like the sort of item someone with paranoia would call "true," whereas normals would tend to respond "false." Many items, however, are not as obvious. "I like to visit zoos," is not an MMPI-2 item, but it might have been if subjects of one diagnostic group responded to the item differently from other subjects. What the item *appears* to be measuring is irrelevant. What matters is whether subjects of different groups respond differently to the item. We need also mention that no one will make even a tentative diagnosis of a psychological disorder on the basis of a person's response to just a few items. What matters is not just the simple scores or even the pattern of scores on any set of items, but the *interpretation* of those scores by a trained, experienced psychologist.

The MMPI-2's *validity scales* consist of items from among the 567 that assess the extent to which the subject is attending to the task at hand or is trying to present herself or himself in a favorable light instead of responding truthfully to the items. For example, responding "true" to several statements such as "I always smile at everyone I meet" would lead an examiner to doubt the validity of the subject's responses.

Although the MMPI-2 is commonly used, it is not the only paper-and-pencil test of personality. The *California Personality Inventory*, or CPI, was written using only normal people, not those who were diagnosed as having a psychological problem or disorder. It assesses 18 personality traits, including self-acceptance, dominance, responsibility, and sociability. Because it is designed to measure several traits, it can also be referred to as a multiphasic test.

Some multiphasic tests were designed in conjunction with a particular personality theory. For example, Cattell's trait theory approach investigated a number of potential personality traits. These traits are what are measured with *Cattell's 16 PF Questionnaire* (in which PF stands for personality factors). Analysis of responses on this test results in a personality profile that can be compared to one gathered from a large norm group.

Finally, many personality questionnaires or inventories are designed to measure just one trait and, thus, are not multiphasic. One example is the *Taylor Manifest Anxiety Scale*. Taylor began with a large pool of items, many of them from the MMPI, and then asked psychologists to choose those items they thought would best measure anxiety. The 50 items most commonly chosen as indicators of anxiety constitute this test, which has gained wide acceptance. A more recent test, the *Endler Multidimensional Anxiety Scale*, not only assesses anxiety levels, but also claims to distinguish between anxiety and depression (Endler et al., 1992).

BEFORE YOU GO ON

- What is the MMPI-2?
- What is the California Personality Inventory?
- Describe the Taylor and Endler anxiety scales.

Projective Techniques

projective technique a personality assessment technique requiring a person to respond to ambiguous stimuli in the hopes that the person will reveal aspects of his or her personality

A **projective technique** asks a person to respond to ambiguous stimuli. The stimuli can be any number of things, and there are no clearly right or wrong answers. Projective procedures are unstructured and open-ended. The idea is that because there is, in fact, so little content in the stimulus being presented, the person will project some of his or her own self into the response. In many ways, projective techniques are more like aids to interviewing than they are psychological tests (Korchin & Scheldberg, 1981).

Some projective techniques are very simple. The *word association technique*, introduced by Galton in 1879, is a projective procedure. "I will say a word, and I want you to say the first thing that pops into your head. Do not think about your response; just say the first thing that comes to mind." There are no right answers. The hope is that the psychologist can gain some insight, perhaps into the problems of a patient, by using this technique.

A similar technique is the unfinished sentences, or sentence completion test. For example, a sentence is begun, "My greatest fear is…" "The subject is asked to complete the sentence. Although there are published tests available (e.g., the *Rotter Incomplete Sentences Blank*), many psychologists prefer to make up their own forms. Again, there are no right or wrong responses, and interpreting responses is subjective, but a skilled examiner can use these procedures to gain new insights about a subject's personality.

Rorschach inkblot test a projective technique in which a person is asked to say what he or she sees in a series of inkblots

Of the projective techniques, none is as well known as the **Rorschach inkblot test**. This technique was introduced in 1921 by Hermann Rorschach, (see Figure 9.4). There are ten cards in the Rorschach test: five are black on white, two are red and gray, and three are multicolored. People are asked to tell what they see in the cards or what the inkblot represents.

Scoring Rorschach test responses has become controversial. Standard scoring procedures require attending to many factors: what the person says (content), where the person focuses attention (location), mention of detail versus global features, reacting to color or open spaces, and how many distinct responses there are. Many psychologists have questioned the efficiency of the Rorschach as a diagnostic instrument. Much of what it can tell an examiner may be gained directly. For example, Rorschach responses that include many references to death, sadness, and dying are indicative of a depressed person. One wonders if inkblots are really needed to discover such depression. As a psychological test, the Rorschach seems neither reliable nor valid, yet it is still popular. It is used primarily as an aid to assessment.

thematic apperception test (TAT) a projective technique in which a person is asked to tell a series of short stories about a set of ambiguous pictures

The **Thematic Apperception Test**, or **TAT**, was devised by Henry Murray in 1938. This test is a series of ambiguous pictures about which a person is asked to tell a story. The person is asked to describe what is going on, what led up to the situation, and what the outcome is likely to be. The test is designed to provide a mechanism to discover a person's hidden needs, desires, and emotions, which will be projected into his or her stories. The test is a thematic test because scoring depends largely on the interpretation of the themes of the stories told. Although scoring schemes are available, scoring and interpretation are usually subjective and impressionistic. It's likely the TAT is popular for the same reason that the Rorschach is: psychologists are used to it, comfortable with the insights it provides, and willing to accept any source of additional information they can use to make a reasonable assessment or diagnosis.

BEFORE YOU GO ON

- What is a projective technique?

- Describe the Rorschach inkblot test.

- What is the Thematic Apperception Test?

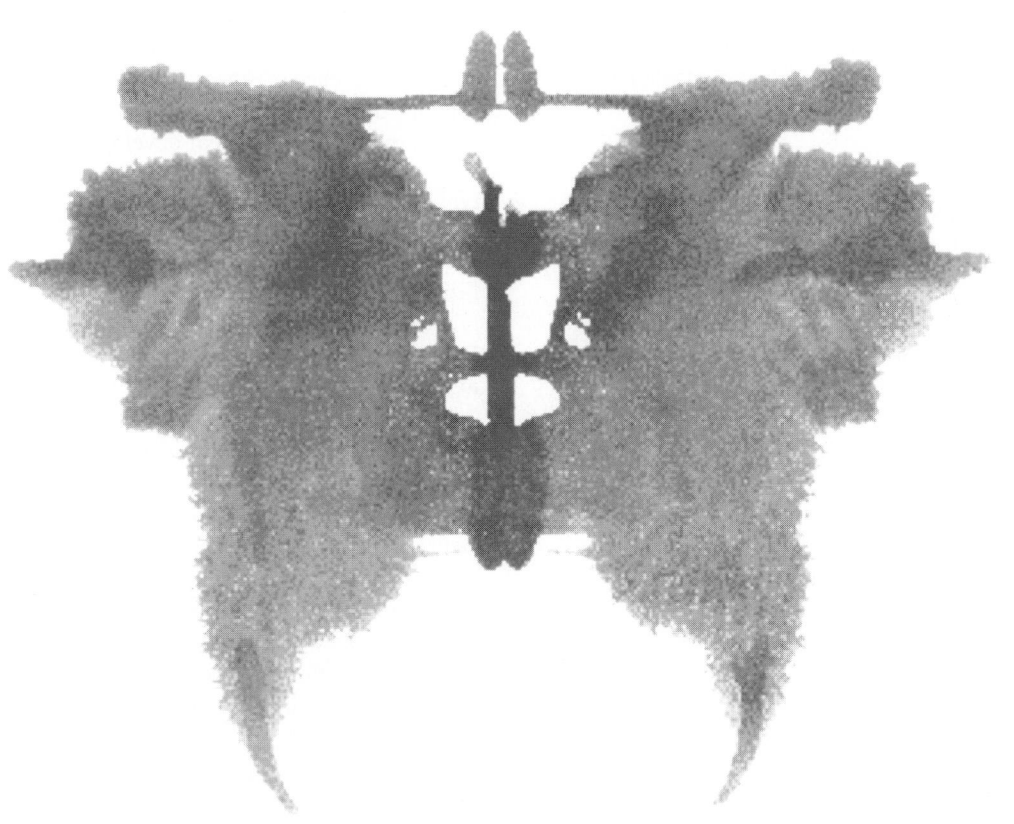

FIGURE 9.4

A sample Rorschach-like inkblot. The subject is asked what the inkblot represents and what she or he sees in it.

Topic Review 9 B

1. **What are the key points in the debate concerning personality versus situational influences on behavior?**

An issue of interest among psychologists who study personality is the extent to which we can claim that there are internal, individual traits that are consistent over time and over situations. One's personal characteristics should be discernible at least within a range of situations. The debate over the stability or consistency of personality variables begun in the late 1960s is essentially over. A point of view called interactionism has emerged that says that predicting how a person will respond in a certain situation is determined by the interaction of stable personality characteristics and that person's perception of the situation.

2. **What are the assumptions of the temperament theory of personality development?**

According to temperament theory, one's temperamental qualities, such as activity level, sociability, and emotionality, are inborn and influence behavior. Temperament theory has four basic assumptions: (1) Individuals are born with a characteristic way of responding to the environment and others; (2) the characteristic ways of responding are rooted in the way a person's brain, nervous system, and endocrine system operate; (3) there is consistency between temperament in infancy, childhood, and adulthood; and (4) temperament interacts with the environment to influence behavior.

3. **What are the main assumptions of the learning theory of personality development?**

The learning theory of personality development proposes that personality development can be explained with the basic learning concepts of reinforcement, punishment, and observational learning. There are four assumptions underlying this approach to personality development: (1) Reinforcement strengthens behavior; (2) behaviors maintained on a partial schedule of reinforcement are more resistant to extinction than those maintained on a continuous schedule; (3) children learn many behaviors from watching others; and (4) children learn attitudes, self-concept, and internal standards for behavior. The

learning theory is the most widely accepted approach to personality development and now includes modern concepts from cognitive psychology (for example, schemes and scripts).

4. **What are the key assumptions of the psychoanalytic approach to personality development?**

Psychoanalytic theories of personality include theories by Freud and Erikson. There are four assumptions of this approach: (1) Behavior is influenced by both conscious and unconscious forces; (2) the basic structure of personality develops over time; (3) personality develops across a sequence of stages; and (4) an individual's personality develops according to how well an individual moves through the stages of development.

5. **What are Freud's psychosexual stages of development?**

Freud believed that personality developed in stages, each related to some expression of sexuality, or sensuality. Freud believed that at each stage there was a "crisis" that must be resolved. If there were an overinvestment of psychic energy at a stage, a fixation could take place. The first stage of development is the *oral stage*, in which pleasure and satisfaction derive from oral activities such as sucking, feeding, and noise making. The second stage is the *anal stage*, in which the control of bladder and bowel movements become a source of satisfaction and pleasure. The third stage is the *phallic stage*, in which one becomes aware of one's sexuality and forms a close attachment with the opposite sex parent. During the *latency period*, which is not a true stage because there is no "crisis," sexuality is "put on hold." The final stage is the *genital stage*, which follows puberty and wherein there is a reawakening of sexual, sensual desires.

6. **What are the gender differences in personality traits?**

As much as our stereotypes would like to convince us that there are differences in the personalities of men and women, research continues to remind us that actual differences are few and slight at best. The one personality trait that does seem to be more common in males than in females is aggression, at least as expressed in overt physical acts. On other personality traits the data are mixed, but some possibilities include differences in communication style, body language, altruism, empathy, and self-confidence.

7. What are the goals of personality assessment? How are behavioral observations used to assess personality?

We would like to be able to reliably and validly measure or assess an individual's personality so that we may (1) make a proper diagnosis of any psychological disorder, (2) construct reasonable theories of personality, or (3) use measurements or assessments to predict future behaviors for that person. Conclusions about personality can be inferred from the observation of that person's behaviors. Behaviors should be observed in a large number of settings. Observations should be as objective as possible and may involve the use of behavioral rating scales to check reliability.

8. What is behavioral observation?

Behavioral observation involves drawing inferences about an individual's personality based on observations of his or her behavior. Behavioral observation can be an important tool for assessing personality, particularly when the observations are made in a purposeful, careful, and structured way, if steps are taken to ensure reliability and validity of observations, and if the sample of individuals observed is representative.

9. What is one advantage and one disadvantage of the interview as a technique of personality assessment?

The major advantage of the interview is its ease and flexibility of administration, as it allows the interviewer to pursue certain avenues of interest and abandon lines of questioning that are not informative. Unfortunately, unstructured interviews lack demonstrated validity. On the other hand, structured interviews show as much reliability and validity as any psychological test.

10. How was the MMPI-2 constructed?

Multiphasic instruments attempt to measure several characteristics or traits with the same set of items. The MMPI was designed (in the early 1940s and revised, as the MMPI-2, in 1989) as an aid to diagnosis. The test includes items that discriminate between persons of differing diagnostic categories (including "normal") and that assess the extent to which the subject is doing a thorough and honest job of answering the 567 true/false questions. Paper-and-pencil tests can serve as screening devices to indicate which traits or patterns of traits are likely to be found within a given individual.

11. What is a projective technique?

With a projective technique, the assumption is that in responding to an ambiguous stimulus, a person will project aspects of him-or herself into his or her responses. Projective techniques include word association tests, sentence completion tests, the Rorschach test, and the TAT.

12. What is the Rorschach inkblot test?

The Rorschach inkblot test is a projective technique that was introduced in 1921 by Hermann Rorschach. The test comprises cards showing inkblot patterns. An individual is asked what he or she sees on the card or what the inkblot represents. Scoring the test involves attending to what the person says, where the person focuses attention, mentions of detail, and how many direct responses are made.

13. What is the Thematic Apperception Test (TAT)?

The TAT is a projective technique introduced by Henry Murray in 1938. The test consists of a series of ambiguous pictures. The individual taking the test is required to tell a story to go with each picture. The subject is asked to describe what is going on in the picture and the likely outcome. Scoring centers on the themes of the stories told by the subject.

Chapter 10

Motivation and Emotion

You had a great time. You and your friends spent the day backpacking in the mountains. The signs of Spring were everywhere, and you enjoyed every minute. After a full day in the fresh mountain air, no one was terribly choosy about what to have for dinner. Large, heaping piles of beef stew and baked beans from the can were enjoyed by everyone. You even found room for dessert: toasted marshmallows and a piece of chocolate squeezed between two graham crackers.

As your friends settle around the campfire, darkness just beginning to overtake the campsite, you excuse yourself. You need to "walk off" some of that dinner, so you head off to stroll down a narrow trail that leads away from the campsite. As you meander down the trail, you feel totally relaxed, at peace with the world. When you are about 200 yards from the campsite you think you hear a strange noise in the woods off to your left. Looking back down the trail, you notice that you can barely see the campfire's glow through the trees and underbrush, even though their leaves are not yet fully formed. Well, maybe you'd better not venture too much farther, perhaps just over that ridge, and then... suddenly, from behind a dense thicket, a large growling black bear appears. It takes one look at you, bares its teeth, and lets out a mighty roar. *What will you do now?*

In this situation, and in many similar, but less dramatic ones, we can be sure of one thing: your reaction will involve motivational and emotional states. You will certainly become emotional. Encountering a bear in the woods is not something that one does with reason and intellect alone. You will be motivated to do something; getting away from that bear seems reasonable. We will return to this meeting-a-bear-in-the-woods story several times throughout this chapter as we explore what psychologists know about motivation and emotion.

Topic 10A MOTIVATION

In this Topic, we'll address some important practical issues. For the first time, our focus is on questions that begin with *why*. "Why did she *do* that (as opposed to doing nothing)?" "Why did she do *that* (as opposed to doing something else)?" "Why does she *keep* doing that (as opposed to stopping)?" As you can see, the study of motivation gets us involved with attempts to explain the causes of certain behaviors.

Motivation involves two subprocesses. First, motivation involves arousal—one's level of activation or excitement. Here we are using "motivation" to describe a force that initiates behaviors, that gets an organism going, energized to do something and to keep doing it. The second subprocess provides *direction*, or focus, to one's behaviors. More than being simply aroused and active, a motivated organism's behavior is in some way goal-directed or purposeful. Thus, **motivation** is the process that arouses, directs, and maintains behavior.

motivation the process that arouses, directs, and maintains behavior

Key Questions to Answer

While reading this Topic, find the answers to the following key questions:

1. How have the concepts of instincts, needs, drives, and incentives been used to explain motivated behaviors?

2. How has the concept of balance, or equilibrium, been used to explain motivated behaviors?

3. How is temperature regulation a physiological drive?

4. What are some of the internal and external cues that motivate eating behaviors?

5. Describe anorexia nervosa and bulimia nervosa.

6. In what ways is the sex drive a unique physiologically based drive?

7. What is homosexuality, and why is sexual preference a difficult concept to define?

8. How can homosexuality and heterosexuality be characterized?

9. What factors relate to one displaying a homosexual orientation?

10. What are the male sexual disorders, and what are their causes?

11. What are the female sexual disorders, and what are their causes?

12. What is achievement motivation, and how is it measured?

13. What are the needs for power, affiliation, and intimacy?

14. What is loneliness?

CHARACTERISTICS OF MOTIVATION

From its earliest days, psychology has tried to find some systematic theory to summarize and organize what various motivational states have in common. Psychologists have struggled to find one general pattern or scheme that could be used to account for why organisms tend to do what they do. In this section, we will review some of these theories in a somewhat chronological order. As you might predict, no one approach to motivation will satisfactorily answer all of our questions.

Instincts

During the 1880s, psychologists often explained behaviors in terms of an **instinct**—an unlearned, complex pattern of behavior that occurs in the presence of certain stimuli. Why do birds build nests? A nest-building instinct. When conditions are right, birds build nests. Why do salmon swim upstream to mate? Instinct. Swimming upstream at mating season is part of what it means to be a salmon. Yes, these behaviors can be modified by the organisms' experiences, but the force behind them is unlearned or instinctive.

instinct an unlearned, complex pattern of behavior that occurs in the presence of certain stimuli

Instinct may explain some of the behaviors of birds and salmon, but what about people? William James (1890) reasoned that because they are more complex, humans had to have more instincts than do "lower" animals. William McDougall championed the instinctual explanation of human behaviors (McDougall, 1908). He said that human behaviors were motivated by 11 basic instincts: repulsion, curiosity, flight, reproduction, gregariousness, acquisitiveness, parenting, construction, self-assertion, self-abasement, and pugnacity. Soon McDougall had to extend his list to include 18 instincts. As different behaviors required explanation, new instincts were devised to explain them.

As lists of human instincts got longer and longer, the problem with this approach became obvious. Particularly for humans, "explaining" behavior patterns by alluding to

Why do bears hibernate in the winter? Why do geese fly south for the winter? We may "explain" these behaviors by referring to instincts, but the concept of instinct has not been useful for explaining human behaviors.

instinct only relabeled them and didn't explain anything. Even so, the psychologists who argued for instincts did introduce and draw attention to an idea very much with us today: We may engage in some behaviors for reasons that are basically physiological and more inherited than learned.

Needs and Drives

An approach that provided an alternative to explaining behavior in terms of instincts was one that attempted to explain the whys of behavior in terms of needs and drives. We will look at two theories that incorporate these concepts.

Clark Hull

need a lack or shortage of some biological essential resulting from deprivation

drive a state of tension resulting from an unlearned need that arouses and directs an organism's behavior

Clark Hull's ideas about motivation were dominant in the 1940s and 1950s (Hull, 1943). In Hull's system, a **need** is a lack or shortage of some biological essential required for survival. A need arises from deprivation. When an organism is kept from food, it develops a need for food. Needs give rise to drives. A **drive** is a state of tension, arousal, or activation. If an organism is in a drive state, it is aroused and directed to engage in some behavior to reduce the drive by satisfying the underlying need. Needs produce tensions (drives) that the organism seeks to reduce; hence, this approach is referred to in terms of *drive reduction.*

Why do we visit aquariums and zoos? Because they are there. Psychologists have argued that we all have needs to explore our environments, needs that are particularly strong in childhood.

Whereas instincts are tied to specific patterns of behavior, needs and drives are not. They are concepts that can be used to explain why we do what we do and still allow for the influence of experience and the environment. Going without food may give rise to a need, which in turn gives rise to a drive, but *how* that drive is expressed in behavior is influenced by one's experiences and learning history.

One problem with a drive reduction approach centers on the biological nature of needs. To claim that needs result only from biological deprivations seems restrictive. It may be that not all of the drives that activate a person's behavior are based on biological needs. Humans often engage in behaviors to satisfy *learned drives.* Drives derived from one's learning experience are called **secondary drives**, as opposed to *primary drives,* which are based on unlearned, physiological needs. Most of the drives that arouse and direct our behavior have little to do with physiology. You may feel you "need" a new car this year. Your brother may convince himself that he "needs" a new set of golf clubs, and you'll both work very hard to save the money to buy what you "need." You may say you are "driven" to work for money, but it's difficult to imagine how your car or your brother's golf clubs could be satisfying a biological need. A lot of advertising is directed at trying to convince people that products and services are needed that will, in fact, have very little impact on survival.

secondary drive a state of tension resulting from a learned or acquired need that motivates an organism's behavior

A related complication is that organisms often continue to behave even after their biological needs are met. Drives are states of arousal or tension. This position claims that we behave as we do in order to reduce tension or arousal. Yet we know that sky divers jump out of airplanes, mountain climbers risk life and limb to scale sheer cliffs of stone, monkeys play with mechanical puzzles even when solving those puzzles leads to no other reward, and children explore the pots and pans in kitchen cabinets even when repeatedly told not to. These actions do not appear to be reducing tension, do they? We might suggest, as some psychologists have, that these organisms are trying to satisfy an exploration drive, a manipulation drive, or a curiosity drive. But then we run the risk of trying to explain why people behave as they do by generating longer and longer lists of drives— the same problem we have when we try to explain behavior in terms of instinct.

So what do these complications mean? It seems that people often behave in ways that reduce drives and thereby satisfy needs. How drives are satisfied, or reduced, may reflect each organism's learning history. The concept of drive reduction is a useful one and is still very much with us in psychology, but it cannot be accepted as a complete explanation for motivated behaviors.

BEFORE YOU GO ON

- What is the definition of motivation?
- What is an instinct, and what are some of the problems with this concept?
- What is a need?
- What is a drive?
- What is a secondary drive?

Maslow's Hierarchy of Needs

Abraham Maslow is one of the persons we associate with the humanistic movement in psychology. *Humanistic psychologists* emphasize the person and his or her psychological growth. Maslow combined his concern for the person with Hull's drive reduction theory and proposed that human behavior does, in fact, respond to needs. Not all of those needs are physiological. Maslow believed that the needs that motivate human action are few and are arranged hierarchically (Maslow, 1943, 1970). Figure 10.1 summarizes this hierarchy of needs.

Maslow's belief is basically a stage theory. It proposes that what motivates us first are *physiological needs.* These include the basic needs related to survival—food, water, and shelter. Until these needs are met, there is no reason to suspect that an individual will be concerned with anything else. Once one's physiological needs are under control, a person is still motivated, now by *safety needs:* the need to feel secure, protected from dangers that might arise in the future. We are now motivated to see to it that the cupboard has food for later, we won't freeze this winter, and there's enough money saved to protect against sudden calamity. The hierarchical nature of this theory is already clear. We are not going to worry about what we'll be eating tomorrow if there's not enough to eat today, but if today's needs are taken care of, we can then focus on the future.

Once safety needs are met, concern shifts to *love and belongingness,* a need for someone else to care about us, to love us. If these needs are satisfied, our concern shifts to *esteem.* Our aim is to be recognized for our achievements and efforts. These needs are not physiological, but social. Now our behaviors are motivated by our awareness of others and a concern for their approval. One moves higher in the hierarchy, on to higher stages, only if needs at lower stages are met. Ultimately, we may reach the highest stage in Maslow's hierarchy: *self-actualization* needs. We self-actualize when we become the best we can be, taking the fullest advantage of our potential as human beings. We are self-actualizing when we strive to be as creative or productive as possible. Pervin (2001) pro-

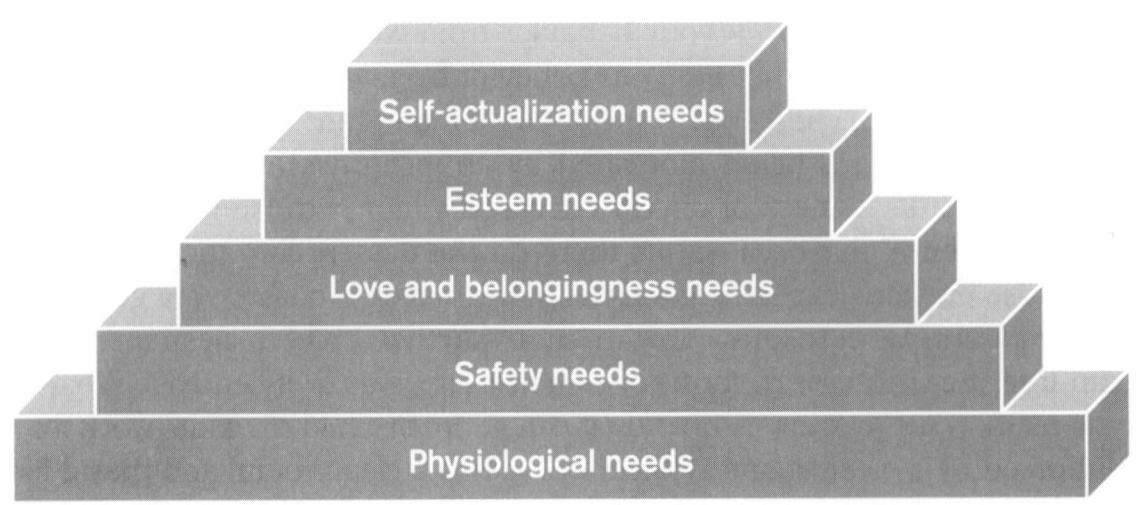

FIGURE 10.1

Maslow's hierarchy of needs.

vides an excellent characterization of what self-actualization means. According to Pervin, self-actualization is "the tendency of an organism to grow from a simple entity to a complex one, to move from dependence toward independence, from fixity and rigidity to a process of change and freedom of expression (p.177)." For example, an individual who early in life toils in a boring job may begin to express himself or herself artistically later in life.

In many ways, Maslow's arrangement of needs in a hierarchical fashion reflects the values of Western culture, particularly those that reflect the notion of the individual working hard to overcome obstacles and achieve. We can hardly expect people to be motivated to grow and to achieve "success" when they are concerned about their very survival on a day-to-day basis. When people's needs for safety, belonging, and esteem are reasonably fulfilled, they don't just die, unmotivated to do anything else. It should be clear to you, as it was to Maslow, that many people never make it to the self-actualization stage in the hierarchy of needs. There are millions of people in this world who have great difficulty dealing with the very lowest stages and who never have the time, energy, or opportunity to be concerned with such issues as self-esteem or belongingness, much less self-actualization.

As a comprehensive theory of human motivation, Maslow's hierarchy has some difficulties. Perhaps the biggest stumbling block is the idea that one can assign ranks to needs and put them in a neat order, regardless of what that order may be. Some persons are motivated in ways that violate the stage approach of this theory. Individuals will, for example, freely give up satisfying basic survival needs for the sake of "higher" principles (as in hunger strikes). For the sake of love, people may abandon their own needs for safety and security. The truth of the matter is that there is little empirical research support for Maslow's approach to ranking needs in a hierarchy. It remains, however, that because of its intuitive appeal, Maslow's theory of human motivation has found favor both in and outside psychology.

Incentives

One alternative to a drive reduction approach to motivation focuses on the *end state,* or goal, of behavior, not needs or drives within the organism. In this view, external stimuli serve as motivating agents, or **incentives**, for behavior. Incentives are external events that act to *pull* our behavior from without, as opposed to drives, which are internal events that *push* our behavior from within.

incentives external stimuli an organism may be motivated to approach or avoid

When a mountain climber says she climbs a mountain "because it is there," she is indicating that she is being motivated by an incentive. After enjoying a large meal, we may order a piece of cherry cheesecake, not because we need it in any physiological sense, but because it's there on the dessert cart and looks so good (and because previous experience tells us that it is likely to taste good as well).

Some parents want to know how to "motivate their child to clean up his room." We can interpret this case in terms of establishing goals or incentives. What those parents

Motivating children to take a bath and brush their teeth can be viewed as an attempt to get the children to share some of the practices that are valued by their parents.

really want to know is how they can get their child to value, work for, and be reinforced by a clean room. What they want is a clean room, and they'd like to have the child clean it. If they want the child to be motivated to clean his or her room, the child needs to learn the value or incentive of having a clean room. How to teach a child that a clean room is a thing to be valued is another story, involving other incentives the child does value. For now, let's just acknowledge that establishing a clean room as a valued goal is the major task at hand, and having a clean room is not an innate, inborn need.

If you think this all sounds like our discussion of operant conditioning, you're right. Remember, the basic tenet of operant conditioning is that behaviors are controlled by their consequences. We tend to do (are motivated to do) what leads to reinforcement (positive incentives), and we tend not to do what leads to punishment or failure of reinforcement (negative incentives).

Balance or Equilibrium

A concept that has proven useful in understanding motivation is *balance* or *equilibrium.* The idea is that we are motivated to maintain a state of balance. What are we motivated to balance? Sometimes balance involves physiological processes that need to be kept at some level, or a restricted range, of activity. Sometimes equilibrium is required among our thoughts or cognitions. We'll review three approaches to motivation that emphasize maintaining a state of balance, equilibrium, or optimum level of functioning.

Homeostasis

One of the first references to a need for equilibrium is found in the work of Walter Cannon (1932). Cannon was concerned with our internal physiological reactions, and the term he used to describe a state of balance within those reactions was **homeostasis**. The idea is that each of our physiological processes has a balanced set point of operation. One's *set point* is a level of activity that is "normal" or "most suitable." When anything upsets this balance, we become motivated, driven to do whatever we can to return to our set point, our optimum, homeostatic level. If we drift only slightly from our set point, our physiological mechanisms return us to homeostasis without our intention or awareness. If these automatic processes are not successful, we may have to take action, motivated by the drive to maintain homeostasis.

homeostasis a state of balance, or equilibrium, among internal, physiological conditions

Everyone has normal set levels for body temperature, blood pressure, heart rate, basal metabolism (the rate at which energy is used by bodily functions), and so on. If any of these processes deviate from their set point, or homeostatic level, we become motivated to do something that will return us to our state of balance. Cannon's concept of homeostasis was devised to explain physiological processes, but the ideas of balance and optimum level of operation have been applied to psychological processes as well.

Arousal

Arousal is defined in terms of overall level of activation or excitement. A person's level of arousal may change from day to day and within the same day. After a good night's sleep and a brisk morning shower, your arousal level may be high. (It also may be high as your instructor moves through class handing out exams.) Late at night, after a busy day at school, your level of arousal may be quite low. Your arousal level is at its lowest when you are in the deepest stages of sleep.

arousal one's level of activation or excitement

Arousal theories of motivation (Berlyne, 1960, 1971; Duffy, 1962; Hebb, 1955) claim that there is an optimal level of arousal (an "arousal set point") that organisms are motivated to maintain. Drive reduction theories, remember, argue that we are motivated to *reduce* tension or arousal by satisfying the needs that give rise to drives. Arousal theories argue that sometimes we seek out ways to *increase* arousal in order to maintain our optimal arousal level. If we find ourselves bored and in a rut, the idea of going to an action-adventure movie may seem like a good one. On the other hand, if we've had a very busy, hectic day, just staying at home doing nothing may sound appealing.

This approach is like Cannon's idea of homeostasis but in more general terms than specific physiological processes. It suggests that for any situation there is a "best," or most efficient, level of arousal. To do well on an exam, for example, requires that a student have a certain level of overall arousal. If a student is tired, bored, or just doesn't care, we can expect a poor performance. If, on the other hand, a student is so worried and anxious that she or he can barely function, we can also expect a poor exam score. The relationship between arousal and the efficiency of performance is depicted in Figure 10.2.

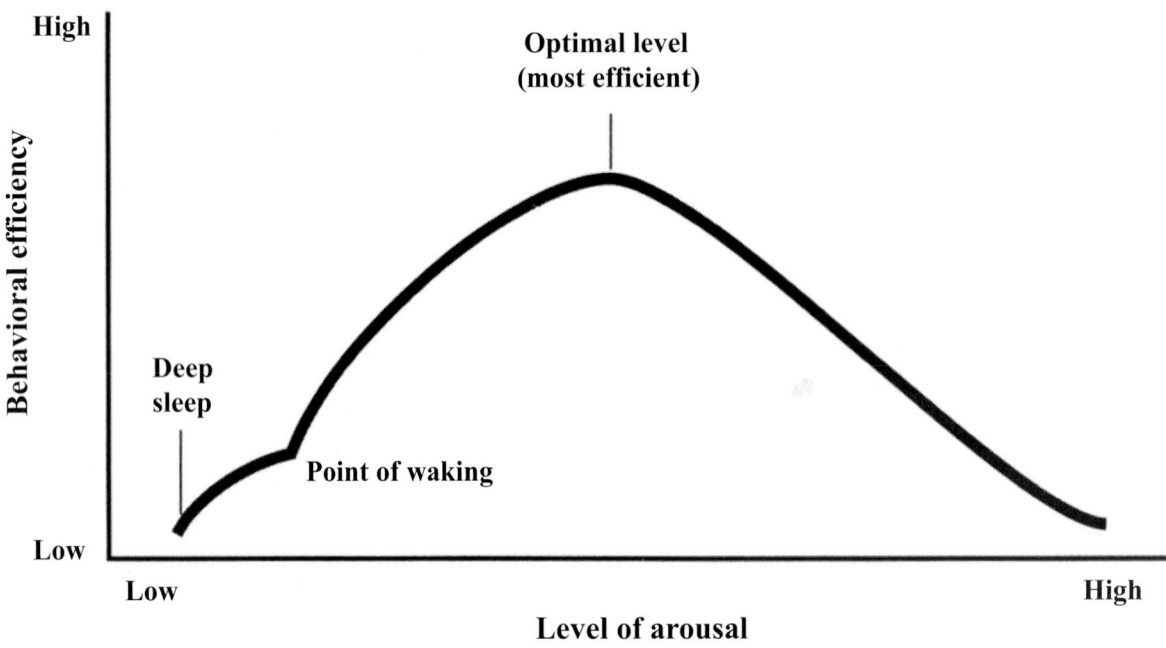

FIGURE 10.2

For each task we attempt, there is an optimal level of arousal. What that level is depends on several factors, including the difficulty of the task. In other words, it is possible to be too aroused (motivated), just as it is possible to be underaroused (Hebb, 1955).

Arousal theory also takes into account the difficulty or complexity of the activity in which a person is engaged. For simple tasks, a high level of arousal may be optimal, whereas that same high level of arousal would be disastrous for difficult, complex tasks (Brehm & Self, 1989). For example, students who were judged to be poorly, moderately, or highly motivated tried a series of difficult anagram problems (identifying a word whose letters have been scrambled). The most highly motivated subjects did significantly worse than did the moderately motivated subjects (Ford et al., 1985). The notion that optimum levels of arousal vary with the difficulty of a task can be traced to an article published in 1908 by Yerkes and Dodson, even though the concept of "arousal" did not appear in psychology until many decades later (Winton, 1987).

An interesting twist on the theory of arousal is that, for some reason, optimum levels of arousal vary widely from individual to individual. Some people seem to need and seek particularly high levels of arousal and excitement in their lives. Marvin Zuckerman calls such people "sensation seekers" (Zuckerman et al., 1978, 1980). They enjoy skydiving or mountain climbing and look forward to the challenge of driving in heavy city traffic. Some recent evidence suggests that there may be a genetic basis for individual differences in sensation-seeking, or risk-taking (Ebstein et al., 1996).

Cognitive Dissonance

There is also a point of view that we are motivated to maintain a state of balance among our ideas or beliefs (our cognitions), as well as among our physiological processes and levels of arousal. That is, we are motivated to maintain what Leon Festinger (1957) calls a *state of consonance* among our cognitions.

You believe yourself to be a good student. You study hard for an exam in biology and think you're prepared. You judge the exam to be a fairly easy one. But when you get your exam paper back, you discover you failed the test! Now that's hard to accept. You believe you studied adequately and that the test wasn't difficult. But you also know you failed the test. Here are cognitions that do not fit together. They are not consonant; they are not balanced. You are experiencing **cognitive dissonance**, a state of tension or discomfort that exists when we hold and are aware of inconsistent cognitions. When this occurs, Festinger argues, we are motivated to bring about a change in our system of cognitions. You may come to believe you're not such a good student after all. Or you may come to believe your paper was unfairly graded. Or you may come to believe you are a poor judge of an exam's difficulty. This theory doesn't predict *what* will happen, but it does predict that cognitive dissonance produces motivation to return to a balanced state of cognitive consonance.

cognitive dissonance a motivating discomfort or tension caused by a lack of balance or consonance among one's cognitions

These days, almost all smokers experience cognitive dissonance. They know that smoking is a very dangerous habit, yet they continue to smoke. Some reduce their dissonance by convincing themselves that although smoking is bad for one's health in general, it really isn't bad for them in particular, at least not when compared to perceived "benefits."

For many of us, jumping off into space with only a parachute to break the fall would be overly arousing, to say the least. For "sensation seekers," however, skydiving may provide a near optimum level of arousal.

Summing Up: Applying Motivational Concepts

Let's go back now to the story about meeting a bear in the woods, which opened this chapter. Granted the example is somewhat far-fetched and we'll have to oversimplify a bit, but let's apply the theoretical approaches we've been discussing to explain your behavior. Let's say that upon seeing the bear you throw your arms straight up in the air, scream at the top of your lungs, and race back to camp as fast as you can. Your friends, still sitting around the campfire, can see and hear you coming. How might they explain your behaviors? (1) "Clearly, it's a matter of instinct. Humans have a powerful and useful instinct for avoiding large animals in the wild. In this instance, running away is just an unlearned, natural, instinctive reaction." (2) "No, I think that the fear that arose upon seeing the bear created a tension—a drive—that needed to be relieved. There were several options available, but in your need to reduce your fear, you chose to run away." (3) "Why do you folks keep relying on all this internal instinct-need-drive nonsense? Previous learning experience, even if it was secondhand, or vicarious, taught you that bears in the wild are incentives to be avoided. They are negative goals. You ran back here simply to reach the goal of safety with us, your friends." (4) "I see your reaction as an attempt to maintain a state of equilibrium or balance. Seeing that bear was an emotional experience that increased many physiological functions. Your running away was just one way to try to return those physiological functions to their normal, homeostatic levels." (5) "Why get so complicated with physiological functions? Why not just say that your overall arousal level was much higher than normal—higher than you wanted it to be—so you ran away from the bear simply to lower your level of arousal?" (6) "The same argument can be made for your cognitions—and cognitive dissonance reduction. You know that you like being safe and free of pain. You believe that bears in the woods can be very hurtful, and there's one in front of you. These two ideas are in conflict. You will do something. In this case, you chose to run away. If you believed that a bear in the woods would be afraid of you and of no potential harm, then there wouldn't have been any dissonance, and you wouldn't have run away."

BEFORE YOU GO ON

- Describe Maslow's need hierarchy.
- What are incentives, and how do they affect behavior?
- How is homeostasis involved in motivation?
- What is arousal, and how is it involved in motivation?
- What is cognitive dissonance?

MOTIVATION AND EVERYDAY BEHAVIOR

Now that we've reviewed a few theoretical approaches to motivation, we can turn to a few specific examples. As we go through this discussion, we will follow convention and use the term *drive* when talking about activators of behavior that have a known biological or physiological basis (for example, a hunger drive) and the term *motive* for those that do not (for example, a power motive).

Temperature Regulation

Most of us seldom give our body temperature much thought beyond the fuzzy notion that 98.6 degrees Fahrenheit is "normal." That body temperature has anything to do with motivation is sensible in the context of homeostasis. Whenever anything happens to raise or lower our body temperature above or below its homeostatic set point range, we become motivated. We become driven to return our body temperature to its normal, balanced 98.6 degrees. (In passing, research confirms the observation that body temperature normally fluctuates throughout the day and suggests that 98.2 degrees is a better estimate of "normal," average body temperature than is 98.6 degrees [Mackowiak et al., 1992].)

Let's say you are outside on a bitterly cold day and are improperly dressed for the low temperature and high wind. Your body temperature starts to drop. Automatically your body responds to elevate your temperature back to its normal level: blood vessels in the hands and feet constrict, forcing blood back to the center of the body to conserve heat (as a result, your lips turn blue); you shiver (those involuntary muscle movements create small amounts of heat energy); and you get "goose bumps" as the skin thickens to insulate against the cold. These are just the sorts of automatic physiological reactions Cannon had in mind when he wrote about homeostasis.

Imagine that you are fully dressed and walking across a desert at noon on a hot day in August. Your temperature rises. Automatically, blood is diverted to the surface of your body, and your face becomes flushed. You perspire, and as moisture on the surface of the skin evaporates, the skin is cooled, as is the blood now near the surface—all in an attempt to return your body's temperature to its homeostatic level.

There are two processes in your brain that act as a thermostat and initiate attempts at temperature regulation. Both are located in the **hypothalamus**, a mid-brain structure near the limbic system that is involved in several physiological drives (see Figure 10.3). One center is particularly sensitive to elevated body temperatures, the other to lowered

hypothalamus a small structure near the limbic system in the center of the brain, associated with temperature regulation, feeding, drinking, and sex

We are driven to maintain our body temperatures within rather strict limits. When our autonomic nervous systems cannot deal adequately with temperature extremes, we may be driven to do something that will lower or raise our body temperatures.

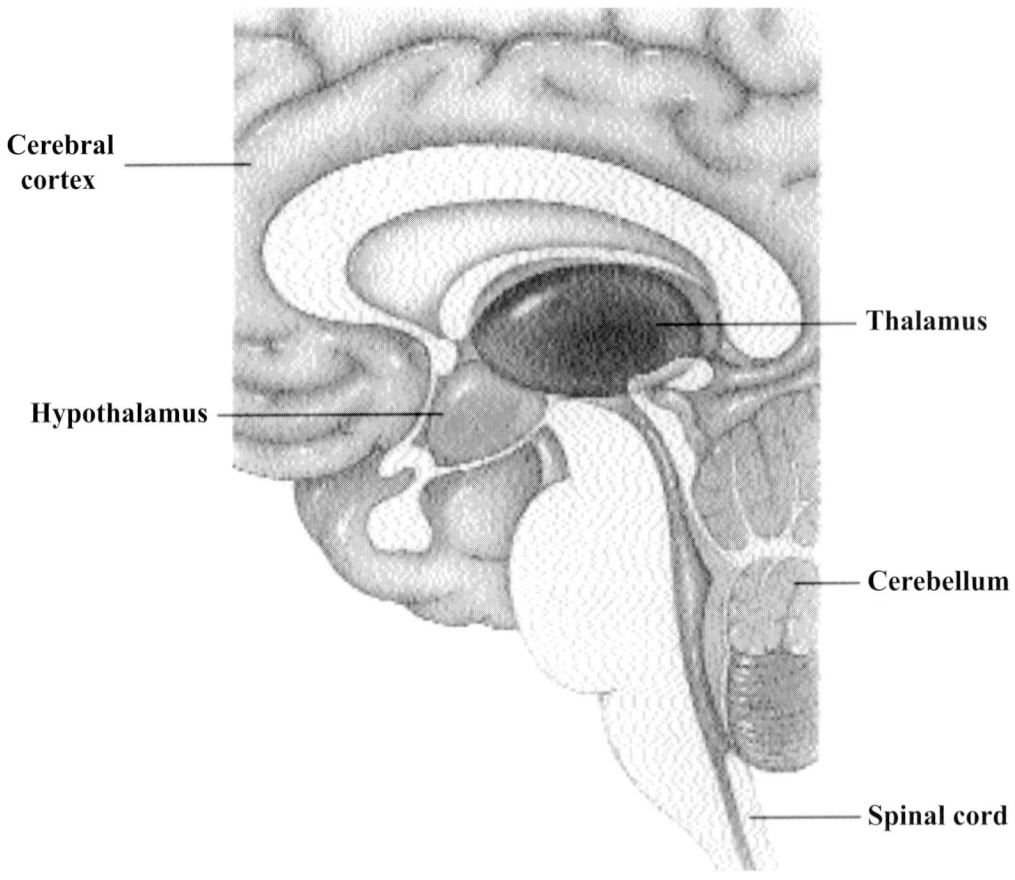

Cerebral cortex

Thalamus

Hypothalamus

Cerebellum

Spinal cord

FIGURE 10.3

A section of the human brain, showing the location of the hypothalamus.

temperatures. Together they act to mobilize the internal environment when normal balance is upset. If these automatic reactions are not successful, you may be driven to take some voluntary action. You may have to get inside, out of the cold or heat. You may need to turn on the furnace or the air conditioner. Over and above what your brain and body do automatically, you may have to engage in learned behaviors in order to maintain homeostasis.

The Thirst Drive and Drinking Behaviors

We need water for survival. If we don't drink, we die. As the need for water increases, it gives rise to a thirst drive. The intriguing issue is not so much that we need to drink, but how we *know* we're thirsty. What actually causes us to seek liquid and drink it?

Internal Physiological Cues

For a long time, psychologists thought that we drank to relieve the discomfort caused by the dryness of our mouths and throats. No doubt, the unpleasantness of a dry mouth and throat *can* cause one to drink, but there must be more to drinking behavior than this. Animals with no salivary glands, whose mouths and throats are constantly dry, drink no more than normal animals (they drink more frequently, but not more in terms of quantity). Normal bodily processes (such as urination, exhaling, and perspiration) cause us to lose about two liters of water a day (Levinthal, 1983). That water needs to be replaced, but what motivates us to do so?

About two-thirds of the fluid in our bodies is contained *within* our body's cells (intracellular); the remaining one-third is held in the spaces *between* cells (extracellular). There seem to be two mechanisms sensitive to losses of fluid. Intracellular fluid loss is monitored by the hypothalamus. One small center acts to "turn on" the thirst drive when fluid levels are low, and another center "turns off" the thirst drive when fluid levels are adequate.

Thirst that stems from extracellular loss is also monitored in the brain through a complex chain of events, involving the kidneys, which stimulate the production of a hormone that leads to a thirst drive.

External Psychological Cues

Drinking behavior may be motivated by a physiological drive arising from a physiological need for water. Sometimes, however, our drinking behavior is influenced by external factors, or incentives. For example, the aroma of freshly brewed coffee may stimulate us to order a second (unneeded) cup. A frosty glass of iced tea may look too good to refuse. We may drink a cold beer or a soda simply because it tastes good, whether we *need* the fluid it contains or not.

Notice also that once we are motivated in terms of being aroused, *what* we drink will be influenced by our previous learning experiences. Choices for what we drink are also shaped by availability. Even with such an obvious physiological drive as thirst and such an obvious physiological need as ours for water, psychological factors can be very relevant.

The Hunger Drive and Eating Behaviors

Our need for food is as obvious as our need for water. If we don't eat, we die. Again, the interesting question is, what gives rise to the hunger drive? As it happens, many factors motivate a person to eat. Some are physiological. Some are psychological and reflect learning experiences. Some involve social pressures.

Internal Physiological and Genetic Cues for Hunger and Eating

People and animals with no stomachs eat the same amounts of food as do people and animals with intact stomachs. Cues from our stomachs, then, don't seem to be very important in producing a hunger drive. The two structures that seem most involved in the hunger drive are the hypothalamus (again) and the liver, which is involved in the production and breakdown of fat.

Theories of hunger that focus on the role of the hypothalamus are referred to as *dual-center theories* because there are two regions in the hypothalamus that regulate food intake. One (the ventromedial hypothalamus) is a "no–eat" center that gives rise to feelings of hunger, while the other (the lateral hypothalamus) is an "eat" center that lets us know when we've had enough. Removing or lesioning the eat center (and leaving the no-eat center intact) in rats, leads to starvation, whereas lesioning the no-eat center (and leaving the eat center intact) leads to extreme overeating. Electrically stimulating the no-eat center will cause even a food-deprived rat to stop eating (Friedman & Stricker, 1976).

Although the hypothalamus is involved in hunger, normal eating patterns are not under the influence of electrical stimulation and brain lesioning procedures. What, then, activates the brain's hunger-regulating centers in a normal organism? Here we are at the level of hypothesis and conjecture, and there are several hypotheses to consider. One proposal is that the body responds to levels of blood sugar, or glucose, that can be metabolized, or converted into energy, for the body's use. When levels of glucose are low, which they are when we haven't eaten for a while, we are stimulated to eat. When glucose levels are adequate, we will stop eating. It may be that our liver most closely monitors such blood chemistry for us.

Another view holds that we respond, through a complex chain of events, to levels of fat stored in our bodies. When fat stores are adequately filled, we feel no hunger. If fat supplies are depleted, a hunger drive arises. Once again, it is the liver that is involved in the cycle of storing and depleting fat supplies.

Another hypothesis that emphasizes the role of internal, physiological cues also relies heavily on the concept of set point, or homeostasis. This position claims that a person's *overall body weight,* like blood pressure or body temperature, is regulated (Nisbett, 1972). "Being so regulated, weight normally is maintained at a particular level or set-point, not only by the control of food intake, as is often assumed, but also by complementary adjustments in energy utilization and expenditure" (Keesey & Powley, 1986). An implication is that if body weight decreases significantly through dieting, exercising, or both, the organism will be driven to return to the set point level. The result may be to abandon the diet, cut down on exercise, or both. Conversely, if one eats too much—more than is necessary to keep a homeostatic level of energy consumption and storage—one will be motivated to expend energy to return to set point levels. Still to be determined are the mechanisms involved in establishing one's set point body weight and energy utilization levels to begin with. There is evidence that these body weight set points are influenced by both genetic factors and feeding behaviors during infancy.

We are learning that there are powerful genetic forces at work that may determine one's body size and the distribution of fat within the body (Stunkard, 1988; Stunkard et al., 1986). One experiment (Bouchard et al., 1990) looked at the effects of overeating on 12 pairs of adult (ages 19 to 27) male identical twins. After eating normally for two weeks, the men were required to consume 1,000 excess calories of food each day for six days a week over a 100-day period. Weight gains *between* twin pairs varied considerably by the end of the study. Significantly, there were virtually no differences in weight gain *within* each pair of twins. In addition, *where* the excess weight was stored (for example, the waist or hips) also varied between pairs, but not within twin pairs. The researchers concluded that "the most likely explanation for the intrapair similarity… is that genetic factors are involved" (p. 1477). A related correlational study looked at the body weights of twins reared together or apart and found that regardless of where or how the twins were reared, there was a significant relationship between genetic similarity and body mass (Stunkard et al., 1990). Even early childhood environments had little or no effect. Such data tell us that genetic factors are important in both the ultimate determination of body weight and size and the distribution of fat within the body. But they do not tell us that the only factors involved in determining body size are genetic (Brownell & Rodin, 1994; Sobal & Stunkard, 1989).

There is one other series of studies to consider before we leave this discussion. In 1994, a group of researchers at the Howard Hughes Medical Institute of Rockefeller University led by Dr. Jeffrey Friedman announced that they had isolated a specific gene related to eating and obesity. They called it the *obese gene,* or the *ob gene* (Baringa, 1995). This gene controls the amount of a hormone the researchers named *leptin* (after the Greek word for *thin*) in the bloodstream. This hormone is a protein called *ob protein* that directly or indirectly tells the brain how much fat is stored in the body. When something goes wrong with the gene, insufficient amounts of *ob protein* are available, and the organism continues to eat, "unaware" that it already has adequate (or more than adequate) fat stored away. The obvious result is an overweight organism. In the summer of 1995 Friedman and his colleagues reported on three independent studies in which *ob protein* was injected into mice that were either obese or of normal weight (Campfield et al., 1995; Halaas et al., 1995; Pelleymounter, 1995). The results were astounding. In just two weeks, the mice ate less and burned energy faster. Obese mice lost about 30 percent of their body weight and had about 9 grams of body fat, compared to 38 grams of body fat in control mice who were not given the protein. Normal mice given *ob protein* injections lost almost all of their body fat—about 12 percent of their weight.

Lest those of us who would like to lose weight the easy way get too excited, we must note that although there appears to be an obese gene in humans (Couce, Burguera, Parisi, Jensen, & Lloyd, 1997), most of the research in this area has been done on animals. To date, there is no "drug" available for humans that can produce the same effects just discussed. Also, the present results with animals show a short-term effect of *ob protein* on obesity. It remains to be seen what the long-term effects will be. Finally, there may be unwanted side effects of the *ob protein* treatment. For example, in one experiment, free-feeding rats that were given an injection of *leptin* (another term for *ob protein*) showed reduced amounts of REM sleep and increased amounts of slow wave sleep. Food deprived rats did not show disruption of the quantity of REM sleep (Sinton, Fitch, & Gershenfeld, 1999).

External Psychological Cues for Hunger and Eating

As we know, eating behaviors are influenced by factors beyond our physiology. We often respond to external cues. Sometimes, the stimulus properties of foods—aroma, taste, or appearance—are enough to get us to eat. You may not want any dessert after a large meal until the waitress shows you a piece of chocolate cake. Eating that cake has nothing to do with your internal physiological conditions (reminding us of the "incentive approach" to motivation described earlier).

Sometimes people eat more from habit than from need. "It's 12 o'clock. It's lunch time; so let's eat." We may fall into habits of eating at certain times, tied more to the clock than to internal cues from our bodies. Some people seem unable to watch television without poking food into their mouths, a behavioral pattern motivated more by learning than by physiology.

Occasionally we eat simply because others around us are eating. Such "socially facilitated" eating has been noted in several species (Harlow, 1932; Tolman, 1969). If a caged chicken is allowed to eat its fill of grain, it eventually stops eating. When other hungry chickens are placed in the cage and begin to eat, the "full" chicken starts right in eating again. Its behaviors are not noticeably different from those of the chickens just added to the cage.

Overweight people may be less sensitive to internal hunger cues and more sensitive to external eating cues from the environment (Schachter, 1971); although, there is evidence that this logical analysis is not always true (Rodin, 1981). We know that many people who are overweight tend to underestimate the amount of food (calories) they eat each day, even when they are in a controlled weight-loss program. They fail to lose weight because they really aren't dieting, even though they believe they are. They also overestimate their level of exercise and physical activity (Lightman et al., 1992).

For those people who are overweight, it would be nice if there were some simple, foolproof way to lose weight. Indeed, 32 percent of men and 35 percent of women over the age of 20 are overweight (National Center for Health Statistics, 1995). Among African American women, 48 percent are overweight, and among Mexican American women, 47 percent are overweight. For adolescents between the ages of 12 and 19, 21 percent are overweight, up from 15 percent in 1987 (National Center for Health Statistics, 1995). We find considerable disagreement among experts over whether dieting can ever be effective (Brownell, 1993; Brownell & Rodin, 1994; Lee et al., 1993). "Fully 95 percent of those starting a weight-loss program will return to their original weight within five years" (Martin et al., 1991, p. 528). Our society's preoccupation with weight and body size may help to explain the increasing rates of eating disorders that have occurred in the last decade (for example, Fairburn & Wilson, 1993). It is to this issue that we turn next.

Many patients with eating disorders see themselves as being overweight—even obese—when in fact their body weights are below normal.

Eating Disorders

Eating well is something few of us do all the time. Some of us simply eat too much—too many saturated fats in particular—sometimes resulting in obesity. There are those, however, whose problems with eating go beyond not eating the right foods or eating too much. Some people eat too little. When a person refuses to maintain a normal weight, he or she is probably suffering from an eating disorder. Two eating disorders are anorexia nervosa and bulimia nervosa. These disorders are fairly common, affecting around 7 million women and 1 million men each year (National Association of Anorexia Nervosa and Associated Eating Disorders, 2001). Although anorexia nervosa and bulimia nervosa are separate disorders, there are cases in which a person shows the symptoms of both at once.

Anorexia nervosa is characterized by an inability (or refusal) to maintain one's body weight. It is essentially a condition of self-starvation, accompanied by a fear of becoming fat and a feeling of being overweight in spite of the fact that the person is considerably underweight (more than 15 percent below normal) (APA, 1987; Yates, 1989). The person

anorexia nervosa an eating disorder characterized by the reduction of body weight through self-starvation and/or increased activity

with anorexia nervosa maintains a reduced body weight by severely reducing food intake, by increasing levels of physical activity, or both. The disorder is surprisingly common, particularly among females. Between .5 percent and 1 percent of young females suffer from the disorder (Eating Disorders Resource Center, 2001). Stated another way, around 1 in 100 females between the ages of 10 and 20 suffer from the disorder. Between 5 percent and 10 percent of patients with anorexia nervosa are male. The costs of treating anorexia can be staggering, reaching as high as $30,000 per month for inpatient care (National Association of Anorexia Nervosa and Associated Eating Disorders, 2001).

bulimia nervosa an eating disorder characterized by recurrent episodes of binge eating and then purging to remove the just-eaten food

Bulimia nervosa is characterized by episodes of binge eating followed by purging—usually self-induced vomiting or the use of laxatives to rapidly rid the body of just-eaten food (APA, 1987; Yates, 1989). The binge eating episodes are often well planned, anticipated with a great deal of pleasure, and involve rapidly eating large amounts of high-calorie, sweet-tasting food. Like the anorexic patient, the person with bulimia is very likely to be female, from an upper socioeconomic class, and usually shows concern about weight. Unlike a person with anorexia nervosa, a bulimic patient need not be well below normal body weight. Another difference involves denial: "The anorexic denies to others and herself that any problem or abnormal eating behavior exists, whereas the bulimic usually denies the existence of a problem to others, but clearly recognizes that her eating is abnormal" (Sherman & Thompson, 1990, p. 4).

What causes eating disorders, and what can be done to treat them effectively? Eating disorders have a number of interacting causes. The value that Western cultures place on thinness is certainly one. We are constantly being bombarded with messages that communicate the same theme: "To be thin is good; to be fat is bad." Role models for many young girls include super-thin fashion models, dancers, and entertainers. More than 75 percent of adolescent girls desire to weigh less than they do (Brownell & Rodin, 1994; Yates, 1989). The cultural emphasis on feminine thinness likely contributes to the greater dissatisfaction among women than men with their weight and body shape (Rolls et al., 1991). One study found that women eat less in the presence of a desirable male partner than when they are with a less desirable partner (Mori & Pliner, 1987).

When we look for specific behavioral or personality traits that might predict the development of an eating disorder, we find little. There is a tendency for adolescent girls with eating disorders to have rather strong needs for achievement and approval. Patients with eating disorders often show relatively high rates of depression, but such depression may be a response to an eating disorder rather than a cause (Garner et al., 1990). Some psychologists have examined parenting and family style as contributors. Anorexia nervosa patients *do* tend to come from very rigid, rule-governed, overprotecting families. And bulimic patients often experienced inordinate blame and rejection in childhood (Bruch, 1980; Yates, 1990). You know by now not to overinterpret findings like these; there are many exceptions.

Obviously, researchers have considered physiological processes as causes of eating disorders. One significant line of scientific detective work stems from the often-confirmed observation that bulimic patients do not "feel full" after they eat, even after they binge (Pyle et al., 1981; Walsh et al., 1989). This may be due to the fact that the hormone *cholecystokinin* (CCK) is found in very low levels in bulimic patients. This is significant because CCK, which is normally produced in the small intestine, signals that one is full and need eat no more. When drug treatment elevates CCK levels in bulimic patients, they often show fewer symptoms of the disorder.

The *prognosis*, or prediction of the course of a disorder, for anorexia nervosa is particularly poor. Nearly 50 percent of those who are released from treatment relapse within one year (Yates, 1990). About 10 percent of patients with anorexia nervosa die from the disorder (Eating Disorders Association, 1999). At first, treatment will be medical, in response to nourishment needs. Hospitalization may be required. Virtually all forms of psychotherapy have been tried, but with little consistent success, and no one form of therapy is significantly more effective than any other. The best predictor of the success of psychotherapy is the extent to which the family gets involved. If all members of the family participate in therapeutic interventions, prognosis is much better than if the patient is left on her (or his) own.

The outlook for bulimia nervosa is usually much better. If nothing else, bulimic patients are seldom malnourished and, for that reason, do not require hospitalization. For persons with bulimia, the prognosis is better with family-oriented therapy than with individual therapy (Fairburn et al., 1993). With bulimic patients there has been some short-lived success with antidepressant medications (Geracioti & Liddle, 1988; Pope et al., 1985; Pope & Hudson, 1986), but when one looks at long-term success, the data are not as encouraging (Pyle et al., 1990; Walsh et al., 1991). A study by Fairburn et al., (1995) looked at the long-term condition (three to 11 years after diagnosis) of 89 persons who had been diagnosed with bulimia. Nearly one in five was still bulimic at the time of the follow-up, and about one-quarter had a different eating disorder. These researchers found that having a father who was overweight was a significant predictor of a negative outcome. They also found that prognosis was best for those patients who had been treated with a form of cognitive therapy.

> ## BEFORE YOU GO ON
>
> - Describe the mechanisms involved in temperature regulation.
> - What are the internal physiological cues for hunger and thirst?
> - What are the external psychological cues for hunger and thirst?
> - Describe eating disorders.

Sexual Motivation and Human Sexual Behaviors

Sex can be an important motivator for humans and nonhumans alike. Sexual motivation varies considerably, not only among individuals, but also among species. Sexuality involves a complex interplay between physiological, cognitive, and affective processes. We begin with a discussion of the physiological basis for sexual motivation. We will then explore the cognitive and affective aspects of sexual motivation and then go on to consider other aspects of human sexuality.

The Physiological Basis for the Sex Motive

On the physiological level, the sex motive is unique in many ways. First, the survival of the individual does not depend on satisfying the sex motive. If we do not drink, we die; if we do not regulate our body temperatures, we die; if we do not eat, we die. If we do not have sex—well, we don't die. The survival of a species requires an adequate number of its members to respond successfully to a sex motive, but an individual member can get along without doing so. Second, most physiologically based motives, including thirst and hunger, provide mechanisms that ultimately replenish or maintain the body's energy. When it is satisfied, the sex motive depletes bodily energy. A third point about the sex motive that makes it different from other drives is that it is not present—in the usual sense—at birth, but requires maturation (puberty) before it is apparent. The other motives are present and most critical early in life. A fourth unique quality of the sex drive is the extent to which internal and external forces have differing degrees of impact on sexual behaviors, depending on the species involved. Internal, physiological states are much more important in "lower" species than they are in humans. For example, matters of sex for rats are simple and straightforward. If adequate testosterone (the male sex hormone)

In so-called lower animals, engaging in sexual behaviors is biologically driven. There is little evidence of any concern over the "quality" of one's "performance."

is present, and if the opportunity presents itself, a male rat will respond to its hormone-induced sex drive and will engage in sexual behaviors. If adequate levels of estrogen (a female sex hormone) are present, and if the opportunity arises, the female rat will engage in sexual behaviors. For rats, learning or experience has little to do with sexual behaviors—they are tied closely to physiology, to hormone level. There is little difference between the mating behaviors of sexually experienced rats—those that have mated once or twice—and virgin rats.

Although there is an important physiological component to human sexual motivation, it cannot adequately account for complex sexual behaviors by itself. Hormones may provide humans with an arousing force toward sexual behavior. However, they may not be necessary or sufficient to account for sexual behaviors. Women, for example, who have hysterectomies often report greater sexual interest and pleasure after their surgery than before. It is obvious that physiological mechanisms cannot account for *what* we do when we are sexually aroused. Sexual behaviors tied to the sexual motivation are shaped by society, religion, family, and personal experience. As we will see, there is a complex system of cognitive activity and affect that contribute to human sexual motivation.

Sexual Orientation

The complexities of human sexuality are no more apparent than when we consider **homosexuality**, which involves sexual attraction and arousal to members of the same sex. **Heterosexuality** involves attraction and sexual arousal to members of the opposite sex. Psychologists argue that homosexuality should be referred to as an orientation, not as a sexual preference. It is certainly not a sexual disorder as defined in the Diagnostic and Statistical Manual–IV published by the American Psychiatric Association (1994). Like handedness or language, sexual orientation is not chosen voluntarily (Committee on Lesbian and Gay Concerns, 1991; Money, 1987). Some even recommend that the term homosexuality not be used to refer to same-sex orientation because of the negative stereotypes associated with the term. The term homosexuality focuses only on the sexual nature of a relationship, while ignoring the *affective preferences* (Kelly, 1995) and identity issues. According to Kelly one can have an affectional orientation toward members of the same sex, yet never express them in sexual behavior because of social pressures. The terms **gay**, which is most often used to refer to males with a same-sex orientation, and **lesbian**, the term for women with a same-sex orientation, are preferred terms of reference (Kelly, 1995). For the sake of simplicity, in the following discussion we will use the terms homosexuality and heterosexuality, recognizing that the terms do not reflect the complexity of human sexual orientations.

Homosexuality and heterosexuality are not mutually exclusive categories, but are endpoints of a dimension of sexual orientations. Alfred Kinsey and his colleagues (1948, 1953) first brought the prevalence of homosexuality to the attention of the general public. Kinsey devised a seven-point scale of sexual orientation, with those who are exclusively heterosexual at one end and persons who are exclusively homosexual at the other (see Figure 10.4). Kinsey found that about half the males who responded to his surveys fell somewhere between the two endpoints. Even though homosexuality is now more openly

homosexuality a sexual orientation involving being sexually attracted to and aroused by members of one's own sex

heterosexuality a sexual orientation involving being sexually attracted to and aroused by members of the opposite sex

gay the preferred term of reference for males with a homosexual orientation

lesbian the preferred term of reference for females with a homosexual orientation

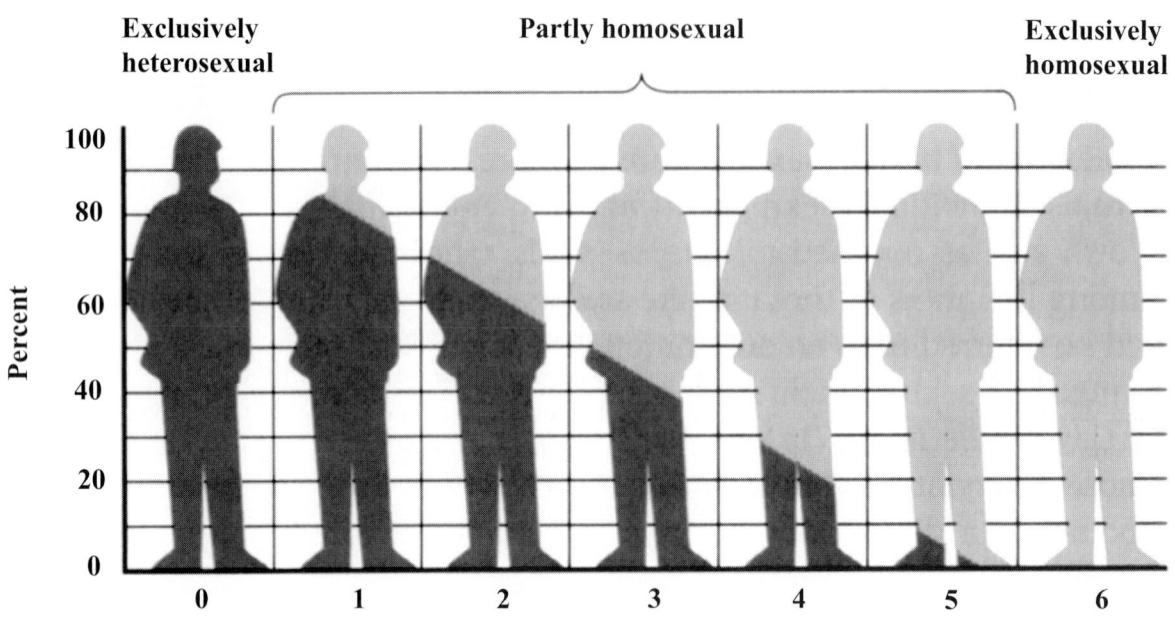

FIGURE 10.4

Kinsey's scale of sexual orientation.

discussed than it was in the 1940s and 1950s, it is still difficult to get accurate estimates of the number of persons who are exclusively or predominantly homosexual. Estimates suggest that about 2 percent of North American males are exclusively homosexual and that 8 percent to 10 percent have had more than an occasional homosexual encounter (Billy et al., 1993). A survey from researchers at the University of Chicago tells us that when asked if they are sexually attracted to persons of the same gender, 6.2 percent of the men and 4.4 percent of the women responded affirmatively. When asked about having an actual sexual encounter with someone of the same gender *within the past year,* 2.7 percent of the men and 1.3 percent of the women responded "yes." When this question was rephrased to read *since puberty,* comparable figures were 7.1 percent and 3.8 percent, respectively (Laumann et al., 1994).

There is little difference between persons with homosexual and heterosexual orientations in the pattern of their sexual responsiveness. Most homosexuals have experienced heterosexual sex. They simply find same-sex relationships more satisfying. In fact, compared to married heterosexual partners, lesbian couples report more intimacy, more autonomy, and more equality in their relationships (Kurdek, 1998). Generally, homosexual couples are more at ease and comfortable with their sexual relationship than most heterosexual couples (Masters & Johnson, 1979).

We have no generally accepted theory of the factors relating to why a person displays a particular sexual orientation. However, a homosexual orientation is probably related to an interaction between genetic, hormonal, and environmental factors (Money, 1987). There is now ample evidence that homosexuality tends to "run in families" (Bailey & Pillard, 1991; Diamond & Karlen, 1980; Pool, 1993; Whitam et al., 1993). A team of researchers has claimed they have located a segment of the X chromosome that seems certain to be the site for genes that influence the development of homosexual orientation in males (Hamer et al., 1993). This is only the first step. These results have not yet been confirmed, and there is much to learn about which genes are found there and how such genes have their effects.

There are no differences in sex hormone levels of adult heterosexuals and adult homosexuals (Gladue, 1994). Providing gay males and lesbians with extra amounts of sex hormones may increase overall sex drive, but it has virtually no effect on sexual orientation. One hypothesis with research support suggests that prenatal hormonal imbalances may affect one's sexual orientation in adulthood (Money, 1987). This hypothesis claims that embryos (genetically male or female) exposed to above-average concentrations of female hormones will develop into adults attracted to persons having masculine characteristics (Ellis & Ames, 1987; Gladue et al., 1984).

In 1991, Simon LeVay of the Salk Institute in San Diego published an article on his research that became headline news (LeVay, 1991). LeVay performed a postmortem examination of the brains of 19 gay males, 16 males with heterosexual orientation, and six women with heterosexual orientation. He found an area in the hypothalamus that was significantly smaller in the gay men. In gay men, this area was precisely the same size as that found in the hypothalamus of women. Note that LeVay has not claimed he located the cause of homosexual orientation. His observations lead us only to an association from which a cause-and-effect conclusion is unwarranted. But as one brain scientist, Dennis Landis of Case Western Reserve University, said of LeVay's work, "It would begin to suggest why male homosexuality is present in most human populations, despite cultural constraints. It suggests it's a biological phenomenon" (Barinaga, 1991).

As the biological evidence accumulates, psychologists remain unwilling to totally abandon hypotheses that emphasize environmental influences. One thing, however, is clear: sexual orientation cannot be attributed to any one early childhood experience. We cannot yet discount them, but environmental, experiential causes of sexual orientation are mostly of theoretical interest, with little research evidence to support them. "With a larger data base... we may be able to construct a biosocial model in which different events—genetic, hormonal, and environmental—occurring at critical times are weighted for their impact on the development of sexual orientation. Associated with this model would be the idea that not all men and women arrive at their sexual orientation following the same path" (Gladue, 1994).

BEFORE YOU GO ON

- Describe the physiological basis for the human sex motive.

- Describe the different sexual orientations, and point out some of the difficulties involved in defining them.

- What, if any, are the differences between people with different sexual orientations?

- What factors relate to displaying a homosexual orientation?

Sexual Dysfunctions

sexual dysfunction any one of a
number of chronic difficulties or
problems with sexual functioning

Sexual drives and behaviors, which seem so natural and virtually automatic in lower species, are often the source of considerable distress for humans. **Sexual dysfunction** is the
name given to any chronic (long-term) problem, disturbance, or inadequacy of sexual
functioning. It is difficult to determine the percentage of persons who experience sexual
dysfunctions. Part of the problem is the commonly held belief that everyone else's sex
life is perfect and that other couples constantly engage in sexual activities. People don't
like to talk about their sex life if they think they are having problems. Physicians and therapists who ask their patients about sexual problems report many more cases than do those
who wait for patients to volunteer such information.

Results from a survey by Laumann, Paik, & Rosen (1999) showed that 43 percent of
women and 31 percent of men reported experiencing sexual dysfunction (including lack
of interest in sex, failure to achieve an orgasm, and performance anxiety). When men and
women (ages 18 to 59) are compared directly, some gender differences emerge. Lack of
interest, inability to achieve an orgasm, and reporting that sex is not pleasurable is more
prevalent among women than men. Men were slightly more likely to report experiencing
performance anxiety. Laumann, et al. point out that sexual dysfunction is more prevalent
among men and women who are in poor health, with men experiencing a greater risk.
However, alcohol consumption, having a sexually transmitted disease, or being circum-
cised did not increase risk for sexual dysfunction. Many individuals who experience
sexual dysfunction do not seek help. Only 10 percent of men and 20 percent of women
were found to seek medical help for their sexual dysfunction. Under the general category
of "sexual dysfunction" there are several male and female sexual disorders defined by the
American Psychiatric Association (1994). We shall explore a few of these next.

Male Sexual Disorders

Male erectile disorder is the inability to attain or maintain an erection long enough to
experience intercourse. It is the preferred term for what many still refer to as "impotence." Impotence literally means "without power," and power is not what sex or sexual
dysfunctions are all about. Male erectile disorder is the most commonly reported dysfunction among men seeking treatment. It can be found in men of any age. In most cases
there has been success at achieving an erection in the past (APA, 1994). Psychological
reactions to erectile disorder can be severe. Self-esteem is often involved.
Embarrassment, depression, fear of future failures, and guilt often accompany erectile
disorder. The causes of male erectile disorder are complex. However, around two-thirds
of the cases involve some biological factor, usually combined with psychological factors
(Davison & Neale, 1998).

There are many causes of erectile disorder. Failure to attain or maintain an erection
may be associated with short-term physical problems such as fatigue, drinking too much
alcohol, being in a strange situation, or stress, but an occasional episode or two does not
constitute a dysfunction. There *are* physical causes of erectile disorder, including under-

lying disorders or diseases, such as heart disease or diabetes, injury to the spinal cord, infection in the testes or prostate, and some prescribed medications (Richardson, 1991). On the other hand, at least half of the cases of erectile disorder seen by therapists have psychological causes, usually involving such factors as fear of failure, anxiety about the quality of one's "performance," guilt about having sex, or a lack of adequate communication with one's partner (Gendel & Bonner, 1988).

Two disorders of male sexual responsiveness involve the timing of ejaculation during vaginal intercourse (or coitus). *Premature ejaculation* is difficult to define. The implication is that the male ejaculates too soon, but what determines what is too soon? The most generally accepted definition has to do with the male's voluntary control over ejaculation, rather than with time per se (Kaplan, 1974). Premature ejaculation is usually self-defined by the person (or his partner) as a condition in which ejaculation chronically occurs too early to provide satisfaction. A less common problem is *retarded ejaculation,* in which the male has difficulty ejaculating at all during coitus; although, he may have little difficulty doing so while masturbating or when he is with a new sex partner. When this disorder occurs, we tend to find frustration on the part of the male and a sense of rejection in his partner. As with all the sexual disorders, retarded ejaculation occurs to varying degrees, with partial failure to ejaculate more common than total failure.

Female Sexual Disorders

Female sexual arousal disorder used to be known as "frigidity" (Kaplan, 1974, 1975). In severe forms of female sexual arousal disorder, a fear or loathing of sexual activities may develop. This disorder is usually self-diagnosed because what may be "acceptably responsive," or pleasurable, varies from person to person. What matters is the extent to which a woman and her partner feel satisfied with the woman's ability to be sexually aroused. The causes of female sexual unresponsiveness are almost always psychological, involving feelings of shame and guilt, accompanied by a belief that sex is somehow "dirty." The disorder can lead to related problems, such as a lack of self-esteem and depression.

Female orgasmic disorder is the inability to experience an orgasm. In many cases there may have been an occasional orgasm, perhaps not as forceful or timely as desired. This sexual disorder is the one most often mentioned by women seeking therapy for sexual problems (Wincze & Carey, 1992). Part of the problem may be the mystique that has been associated with orgasm through coitus. Many women who experience orgasm through masturbation, for example, and seldom experience orgasm through intercourse, come to believe that they are sexually inadequate or a disappointment to their partners. Sex partners may experience guilt if orgasm is not reached. Although most women (nearly 90 percent) can and do experience orgasm, fewer than half do so with only the stimulation from vaginal intercourse (Kaplan, 1974; Wilcox & Hager, 1980).

Female orgasmic disorder may have a biological basis. Orgasmic problems may be related to illness, alcohol consumption, or extreme fatigue. Most cases, however, can be traced to many of the same psychological factors that disrupt sexual functioning in males:

anxiety, fear of failure, becoming a "spectator," and, most commonly, poor communication with one's partner. Sex therapists have noted that women are even more reluctant than men to share with their partners the behaviors, touches, and actions that would bring them pleasure, or orgasm, during sexual intercourse.

Vaginismus is the powerful, spasmodic, and occasionally painful contraction of the muscles surrounding the opening to the vagina. In some cases, the contractions are severe enough to prohibit the penis from entering the vagina. This is a relatively rare disorder, accounting for fewer than 10 percent of women treated for sexual problems (Masters et al., 1992). Hypotheses about why women develop vaginismus usually refer to a reflex-like reaction of the woman against pain, either the anticipated pain of coitus not yet achieved or pain experienced in the past.

There are other difficulties associated with sexual behaviors, to be sure. We've only covered those most commonly encountered by sex therapists. Many adults will suffer the distress caused by one or more of these dysfunctions during their sexually active years. Most sexual disorders are amenable to treatment and therapy.

BEFORE YOU GO ON

- Describe the male sexual disorders and their causes.

- Describe the female sexual disorders and their causes.

PSYCHOLOGICALLY-BASED MOTIVES

From time to time, you may be able to analyze your behaviors in terms of physiologically based needs and drives. That you had breakfast this morning soon after you got up may have reflected your response to a hunger drive. That you got dressed may have been your attempt to do what you could to control your body temperature, which also may have influenced your choice of clothes. Some sexual motivation may also have affected what you chose to wear today.

On the other hand, many of our behaviors are aroused and directed (motivated) by forces that are not clearly biological in origin. In this section we'll review a few of the motivators that reflect learned or social influences on our behaviors; achievement, power, and affiliation and intimacy motivation.

Achievement Motivation

need to achieve (nAch) the learned need to meet or exceed some standard of excellence in one's behaviors

The hypothesis that people are motivated to varying degrees by a need to achieve was introduced to psychology in 1938 by Henry Murray. The **need to achieve (nAch)** is the acquired need to meet or exceed some standard of excellence in one's behaviors. Measuring nAch and determining its implications have been the major work of David McClelland and his associates (McClelland, 1985; McClelland et al., 1953; Smith, 1992).

Although there are short paper-and-pencil tests for the purpose, nAch is usually assessed by means of the **Thematic Apperception Test (TAT)**. This is a projective test in which people are asked to tell short stories about a series of rather ambiguous pictures depicting people in various settings. Stories are interpreted and scored according to a series of objective criteria that note references to attempting difficult tasks, succeeding, being rewarded for one's efforts, setting short-and long-term goals, and so on. There are no right or wrong responses. Judgments are made about the references to achievement a person "projects" into the pictures.

One of the first things McClelland and his colleagues found was that there *were* consistent differences in measured levels of nAch. A reliable finding about people with high needs for achievement is that when given a choice, they attempt tasks in which success is not guaranteed (otherwise, there is no challenge) but in which there still is a reasonable chance of success. Both young children (McClelland, 1958) and college students (Atkinson & Litwin, 1960) who were high in nAch were observed playing a ring-toss game in which the object was to score points by tossing a small ring over a peg from a distance. The farther away from the peg one stood, the more points one could earn successfully. High nAch subjects in both studies stood at a moderate distance from the peg. They didn't stand so close as to guarantee success, but they didn't choose to stand so far away that they would almost certainly fail. People with low nAch scores tended to go to either extreme—very close, earning few points for their successes or so far away they rarely succeeded.

People with high achievement needs are not always interested just in their own success or in personal achievement at the expense of others. Particularly in collectivist societies, people may work very hard to achieve goals that are available only to the group of which they are a part (Brislin, 1993).

McClelland would argue that you are reading this text at this moment because you are motivated by a need to achieve. You want to do well on your next exam. You want to get a good grade in this course, and you have decided that to do so you need to study the assigned text material. Some students, however, may read assignments not because they are motivated by a need to achieve, but because they are motivated by a *fear of failure* (Atkinson & Feather, 1966). In such a case, the incentive is negative (avoid an F) rather than positive (earn an A). Individuals motivated by a fear of failure tend to take few risks. They either choose tasks they are bound to do well or tasks that are virtually impossible (if the task is impossible they don't have to blame themselves for failures).

It seems that the need to achieve is learned, usually in childhood. Children who show high levels of achievement motivation are those who have been encouraged in a positive way to excel ("Leslie, that grade of B is very good. You must feel proud!" versus "What! Only a B?"). High-nAch children are generally encouraged to work things out for themselves, perhaps with parental support and encouragement ("Here, Leslie, see if you can do this" as opposed to "Here, dummy, let me do it; you'll never get it right!"). Also, McClelland is convinced that achievement motivation can be acquired by almost anyone of any age, and he has developed training programs to increase achievement motivation levels (McClelland & Winter, 1969).

thematic apperception test (TAT) a projective personality test requiring a subject to tell a series of short stories about a set of ambiguous pictures

Power Motivation

need for power the learned need to be in control of events or persons

Some people are motivated not only to excel, but also to be in control, to be in charge of both the situation and others. In such cases, we speak of a **need for power** (McClelland, 1982; Winter & Stewart, 1978). Power needs are also measured by the interpretation of stories generated with the Thematic Apperception Test. Note that a high need for power is, in itself, neither good nor bad. What matters is the end to which one uses one's power.

People with high power needs like to be admired. They prefer situations in which they can control the fate of others, usually by manipulating access to information. They present an attitude of "If you want to get this job done, you'll have to come to me to find out how to do it." People with low power needs tend to avoid situations in which others would have to depend on them and tend to be somewhat submissive in interpersonal relationships. Even though the situation is changing slowly in Western cultures, men are more commonly found in positions of power than are women (Darley & Fazio, 1980; Falbo & Peplau, 1980; Mulac et al., 1985). At the same time, there are no reliable differences between men and women in measured *needs* for power (Winter, 1988).

The Need for Affiliation and Intimacy

need for affiliation the need to be with others and to form relationships

Another psychologically based motivator is the **need for affiliation**—a need to be with others, to work with others toward some end, and to form friendships and associations. Individuals with a high need for affiliation express a stronger desire to be with friends than those with a low need for affiliation. For example, college men with a high need for affiliation tend to pick living arrangements that enhance the likelihood of meeting others. As a result, men with a high need for affiliation had more housemates and were more willing to share a room than those with a low need for affiliation (Switzer & Taylor, 1983). Additionally, there are some gender differences in the need for affiliation. Teenage girls, for example, express a greater desire to spend time with girlfriends than teenage boys (Wong and Csikzentmihalyi, 1991).

One interesting implication of having a high need for affiliation is that it is often at odds with a need for power. Logic suggests that if you are simultaneously motivated to be in control and to be with others in a truly supportive way, conflicts may arise. It is more difficult to exercise power over people whose friendship you value than it is to exercise power and control over people whose friendship is of little concern to you. It remains the case, however, that there are circumstances in which we find people who are high on both power and affiliation needs. These are often politicians who enjoy the exercise of power but who also value being public figures and being surrounded by aides and advisors (for example, Winter, 1987). Affiliation and achievement motives are also somewhat independent. Success can be earned either with others (high affiliation) or on one's own (low affiliation).

Although we might be quite confident that achievement and power motives are learned and culturally determined, we are less confident about the sources of affiliation motivation. There is a reasonable argument that the need to affiliate and be with others is at least partly biologically based. We are social animals for whom social isolation is diffi-

Many politicians would rate high on both a need for power and a need for affiliation.

cult, particularly when we are young. On the other hand, some of the degree to which we value affiliation relationships can be attributed to our learning experiences.

Merely affiliating with others does not always satisfy our social needs. Individuals also have a **need for intimacy**, or a need to form and maintain close affectionate relationships (McAdams, 1982). Intimacy in a relationship involves sharing and disclosing personal information, also known as *self-disclosure*. Individuals with a high need for intimacy tend to be warm, affectionate, and express concern for others. There is evidence that women are more likely to show a higher need for intimacy than men (McAdams, 1989).

What happens when our needs for affiliation and intimacy are not met? In this situation a psychological state called **loneliness** results. Note that loneliness is a subjective, psychological state that arises when there is a discrepancy between the types of social relationships we would like to have and those we actually have (Peplau & Perlman, 1982). Being alone does not constitute loneliness. There are people who prefer to be alone and are probably low on the needs for affiliation and intimacy. For some lonely people, loneliness is temporary. For others, loneliness is a chronic way of life with a person having few, if any, close relationships. In many cases, these individuals lack the social skills necessary to form such relationships. A lonely person also tends to have negative expectations for social interactions. That is, they enter social settings (for example, a party) apprehensive and expecting failure. They then act in ways that fulfill this expectation.

need for intimacy the need to form and maintain close, affectionate relationships with others

loneliness a psychological state arising when our actual social relationships are discrepant from the relationships we would like to have

BEFORE YOU GO ON

- Describe the achievement motivation.
- What is the power motivation?
- What is the need for affiliation and the need for intimacy?
- What is loneliness?

Topic Review 10A

1. **How have the concepts of instincts, needs, drives, and incentives been used to explain motivated behaviors?**

   Instincts are complex patterns of unlearned behavior that occur in the presence of certain stimuli. Instinct approaches to explaining why humans do what they do have not proven to be satisfactory. Needs are shortages of some biological necessity. Deprivation leads to a need, which gives rise to a drive, which arouses and directs an organism's behavior. Many drives are more learned than biologically based. Maslow said that needs can be placed in a hierarchy, from survival needs to a need to self-actualize. Focusing on incentives explains behaviors in terms of goals and outcomes rather than internal driving forces. These approaches are not mutually exclusive.

2. **How has the concept of balance, or equilibrium, been used to explain motivated behaviors?**

   The basic idea is that organisms are motivated to reach and maintain a state of balance—a set point level of activity. Homeostasis is a drive to maintain a state of equilibrium among internal physiological conditions, such as blood pressure, metabolism, and heart rate. Others argue for a general drive to maintain a balanced state of arousal, with an optimal level of arousal being best suited for any given task or situation. Festinger claims that we are motivated to maintain consonance, or balance, among cognitive states, thereby reducing cognitive dissonance.

3. **How is temperature regulation a physiological drive?**

   Temperature regulation can be viewed as a physiological drive because we have a need (are driven) to maintain our body temperatures within certain strict (homeostatic) levels. Doing so involves voluntary as well as involuntary, autonomic, responses.

4. **What are some of the internal and external factors that influence drinking behavior?**

   We are motivated to drink for several reasons, including a need to relieve dryness in our mouths and throats and to maintain a homeostatic level of fluid within our bodies (which is monitored by the hypothalamus). We also engage in drinking behavior in response to external cues (incentives), such as taste, aroma, or appearance, and by our previous learning experiences.

5. **What are some of the internal and external cues that motivate eating behaviors?**

   Several factors affect eating behaviors. Internal factors include cues mediated by the hypothalamus, which may be responding to stored fat levels, blood sugar levels, or other indicators that our normal homeostatic balance has been disrupted. Associated with this view is the position that body weight is maintained at a set point by both food intake and exercise levels. Awareness of being full may be stimulated by a hormone (ob protein) produced under the control of an obese gene. There is evidence that body size may be significantly determined by genetic factors. The stimulus properties of foods may motivate eating, as may habit patterns and social pressures.

6. **What are anorexia nervosa and bulimia nervosa?**

   Anorexia nervosa and bulimia nervosa are eating disorders most commonly found in females. The anorexic patient is essentially engaged in self-starvation, significantly reducing body weight. Bulimia involves recurrent episodes of binging and purging of large amounts of sweet, high-calorie foods. We do not know what causes eating disorders, but cultural, family, and hormonal influences have been implicated. All sorts of psychotherapy have been tried as treatments for eating disorders. The prognosis for anorexia is poor. Family-oriented therapy and cognitive therapies seem most effective for bulimia. Antidepressant medication is occasionally effective in the treatment of bulimia, at least for the short term, particularly when paired with psychotherapy.

7. **In what ways is the sex drive a unique physiologically based drive?**

   The sex drive is an unusual physiological drive because: (1) individual survival does not depend on its satisfaction; (2) unlike thirst and hunger, that replenish the body's energy, the sex drive depletes the bodily energy when satisfied; (3) it is not fully present at birth, but matures later; and (4) the extent to which it is influenced by learned or external influences varies among species.

8. **What is homosexuality, and why is sexual preference a difficult concept to define?**

sHomosexuality involves attraction and sexual arousal to members of the same sex. In contrast, heterosexuality involves attraction and arousal to members of the opposite sex. Because of the negative stereotypes attached to the term homosexuality and the fact that it typically refers to a sexual act, some have advocated not using this term. One can have an affectional orientation towards a member of the same sex and not express it because of social pressures. The preferred terms are "gay" for homosexual men and "lesbian" for homosexual women.

9. **How can homosexuality and heterosexuality be characterized?**

There is a continuum that extends from exclusively homosexual on the one extreme to exclusively heterosexual on the other. Kinsey found that about half his sample of males fell somewhere between these two endpoints. Recent surveys indicate that about 2 percent of North American males are exclusively homosexual. There is little difference between individuals with homosexual and heterosexual orientations in terms of sexual responsiveness.

10. **What factors relate to one displaying a homosexual orientation?**

We do not know what "causes" homosexual orientation but strongly suspect a genetic basis, the influence of prenatal hormone levels, and the involvement of the hypothalamus.

11. **What are the male sexual dysfunctions and what are their causes.**

Sexual dysfunctions are chronic problems in sexual functioning. The most commonly reported by males is male erectile disorder, an inability to attain or maintain an erection long enough to experience intercourse. Premature ejaculation and delayed ejaculation are self-diagnosed, and have to do with the timing of ejaculation during intercourse, the former being more common than the latter.

12. **What are the female sexual disorders and what are their causes?**

Female sexual arousal disorder is said to occur when a woman gains little or no satisfaction or pleasure from sexual activities. Female orgasmic disorder is the inability to experience an orgasm to one's satisfaction. It is the dysfunction most commonly reported by women. Vaginismus refers to the powerful, spasmodic contraction of the muscles surrounding the opening to the vagina. These sexual dysfunctions in men and women may, in turn, create additional problems, such as loss of self-esteem, guilt, anxiety, or depression. There may be a physiological cause (illness, fatigue, alcohol use, medication, injury) for sexual dysfunctions, but most often they are caused by psychological factors.

13. **What is achievement motivation and how is it measured?**

Achievement motivation, based on the need to achieve (nAch), is a need to attempt and succeed at tasks so as to meet or exceed a standard of excellence. Achievement needs are usually assessed through the interpretation of short stories generated in response to the Thematic Apperception Test, or TAT, in which one looks for themes of striving and achievement.

14. **What are the needs for power, affiliation, and intimacy?**

The need for power is the need to be in charge, to be in control of a situation. Affiliation needs involve being motivated to be with others, to form friendships and interpersonal relationships. The need for intimacy is the need for close affectionate relationships. Individuals with a high need for intimacy tend to be warm, affectionate, and express concern for others.

15. **What is loneliness?**

Loneliness is a psychological state that results when there is a discrepancy between the types of social relationships a person has and those he or she would like to have. Loneliness does not mean being alone physically. There are those who choose not to affiliate with others who are not lonely.

Topic 10B THE PSYCHOLOGY OF EMOTION

Since its emergence in the late 1800s, psychology has included emotion as part of its subject matter. Psychologists have learned a great deal about emotional reactions, but answers to some critical questions have remained elusive. We wish that psychologists could tell us just what emotions are and where they come from. We want to know how to increase the pleasant emotions and decrease our experience of the unpleasant ones. Some emotional reactions seem quite unpleasant: fear, shame, jealousy, and rage. Just the same, we would not want to give up our ability to experience emotions. To do so would be to surrender the likes of love, joy, satisfaction, and ecstasy. We'll begin this Topic as we have begun many others—trying to generate an acceptable working definition of "emotion." You ought to give that a try yourself before you go on. How would you define *emotion?*

Key Questions to Answer

While reading this Topic, find the answers to the following key questions:

1.   What are the four components of an emotion?

2.   How did Wundt conceptualize emotions?

3.   How did Izard conceptualize emotions?

4.   What are Plutchik's ideas about emotion?

5.   What role does emotionality play in motivation?

6.   What is the bottom line on how emotions are classified?

7.   What components are there to a typical emotional reaction?

8.   What role does the autonomic nervous system play in emotional arousal?

9.   What physiological mechanisms are involved in the sympathetic reaction to an emotional stimulus?

10. What role does the brain play in an emotional reaction?

11. What role do the hypothalamus and limbic system play in emotional reactions?

12. How is the cerebral cortex involved in emotional reactions?

13. How are facial expressions involved in the communication of emotion?

14. What universal facial expressions did Ekman and his colleagues identify?

15. What effect does making a particular face have on emotional responding?

16. What is the frustration-aggression hypothesis?

17. What factors contribute to the amount of frustration experienced?

DEFINING AND CLASSIFYING EMOTIONS

In this section, we'll consider two interrelated issues: defining emotion and classifying primary emotions. The goal for this section is simple: to describe human emotions as best we can.

Defining Emotion

Try to recall the last time you experienced an emotion of some significance—perhaps the fear of going to the dentist, the joy of receiving an "A" on a classroom exam, the sadness at the death of a friend, or the anger at being unable to register for a class you wanted to take. You may be able to identify four components to your emotional reaction: (1) You experience a *subjective feeling,* or *affect,* which you may label fear, joy, sadness, anger, or the like, (2) You have a *cognitive reaction;* you recognize, or "know," what happened, (3) You have an internal, *physiological reaction,* involving glands, hormones, and internal organs, and (4) You engage in an overt *behavioral reaction.* You tremble as you approach the dentist's office. You run down the hallway, a broad smile on your face, waving your exam over your head. You cry at the news of your friend's death. You shake your fist and yell at the registrar when you find you can't enroll in the class of your choice.

Note that when we add an overt behavioral component to emotions, we can see how emotions and motivation are related. Emotions are motivators (Greenberg & Safran, 1989; Lang, 1985; Lazarus, 1991a, 1991b, 1993). To be motivated is to be aroused to action. Emotional experiences also arouse behaviors. Theorist Richard Lazarus put it this way: "Without some version of a motivational principle, emotion makes little sense, inasmuch as what is important or unimportant to us determines what we define as harmful or beneficial, hence emotional" (1991a, p. 352).

There has been considerable debate in psychology concerning how best to define emotion. As one researcher puts it, "Despite the obvious importance of emotion to human

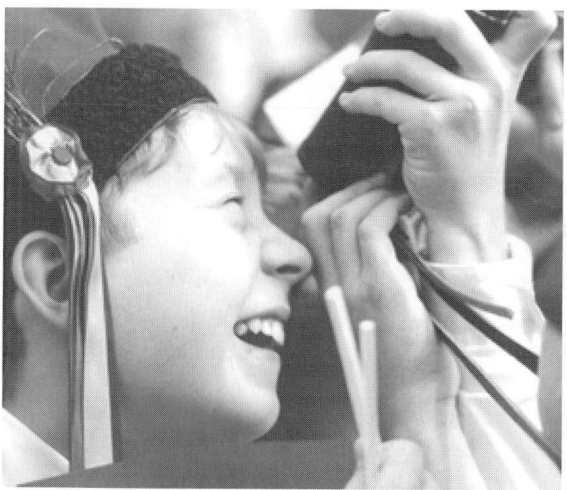

Emotions give flavor and coloring to our lives. If nothings else, emotions can be classified as pleasant or unpleasant. Here, we see joy and sadness.

emotion an experience that includes a subjective feeling, a cognitive interpretation, a physical reaction, and a behavioral expression

existence, scientists concerned with human nature have not been able to reach a consensus about what emotion is and what place emotion should have in a theory of mind and behavior" (LeDoux, 1995, p. 209). For now, however, we need a working definition, and we'll say that an **emotion** is an experience that includes a subjective feeling, a cognitive interpretation, a physiological reaction, and a behavioral expression. With this definition in mind, we turn to the related issue of how to classify emotions.

Classifying Emotions

Although cognitions, physiology, and overt behavior are involved in an emotion, there is little doubt that a very important aspect is the "subjective feeling" component. Perhaps it would help if we had a scheme or plan that described and classified various emotional reactions or feelings in a systematic way.

In fact, there are several ways to classify emotional responses. Wilhelm Wundt, in that first psychology laboratory in Leipzig, was concerned with emotional reactions. He believed that emotions could be described in terms of three intersecting dimensions: pleasantness-unpleasantness, relaxation-tension, and calm-excitement. Let's look at a few more recent attempts to classify emotions.

Carroll Izard (1972, 1977, 1993) has proposed a classification scheme calling for nine primary emotions. From these he claims all others can be constructed. Izard's nine primary emotions are fear, anger, shame, contempt, disgust, distress, interest, surprise, and joy. Izard calls these nine emotions primary because he believes that they cannot be dissected into simpler, more basic emotions and because each is thought to have its own underlying physiological basis. Other emotions are some combination of any two or more of these nine.

Robert Plutchik (1980a,b) argues for eight basic emotions. What makes these emotions primary, Plutchik claims, is that each is directly tied to some adaptive pattern of behavior; they are emotions related to survival. Plutchik's eight primary emotions, and their adaptive significance, are listed in Figure 10.5. Plutchik believes that emotions in

Emotion or feeling	Common stimulus	Typical behavior
1. Anger	Blocking of goal-directed behavior	Destruction of obstacle
2. Fear	A threat or danger	Protection
3. Sadness	Loss of something valued	Search for help and comfort
4. Disgust	Something gruesome or loathsome	Rejection; pushing away
5. Surprise	A sudden, novel stimulus	Orientation; turning toward
6. Curiosity	A new place or environment	Explore and search
7. Acceptance	A member of own group; something of value	Sharing; taking in; incorporating
8. Joy	Potential mate	Reproduction; courting; mating

FIGURE 10.5

Plutchik's Eight Primary Emotions and How They Relate to Adaptive Behavior

addition to these eight are variants of the primary emotions. While rage, for example, may be an extreme emotion, it is viewed as being essentially the same as anger. Anger in a weaker form is annoyance (Plutchik, 1980b).

Richard Lazarus (1991a,b; 1993) proposes a theory of emotion that stresses the motivational role of emotionality. He claims that emotion is the result of specific relationships or interactions between people and their environments. Some relations are perceived as (potentially) harmful to one's well-being and yield negative emotions, such as anger, anxiety, fear, shame, or guilt. These are emotions we are motivated to avoid. Some relations are (potentially) beneficial, give rise to positive emotions, such as joy, pride, gratitude, and love, and are emotions we are motivated to seek or approach. Lazarus's list of basic emotions and their relational themes is presented in Figure 10.6.

You won't be surprised to learn that none of the approaches to classifying emotions listed so far has proven completely satisfactory. Psychologists continue to propose theories to account for the nature of an emotional reaction (Berkowitz, 1990; Buck, 1985; Ekman, 1993; Frijda, 1988; Greenberg & Safron, 1989; Mathews & MacLeod, 1994; Oatley & Jenkins, 1992; Ortony et al., 1988; Ortony & Turner, 1990).

Whether there are eight or nine primary emotions (or more or fewer) and how they might be combined to form other emotions depends on one's theoretical perspective. A review by Ortony and Turner (1990) listed more than a dozen theoretical versions of basic, or primary, emotions. A similar review by Plutchik (1994) lists 16, and *none is in complete agreement with any other.* The only issue on which there appears to be a consensus is that emotions represent a **valenced state**, meaning that emotions can be classified as being either positive (relief or happiness, and the like) or negative (fear, anger, or shame, and the like). Unfortunately, there isn't even complete agreement on how to distinguish between positive and negative emotions. Fear, for example, seems like a reasonable candidate for a list of negative emotions. Yet it is clear that fear can be useful and can serve to guide one's behavior in positive or adaptive ways.

valenced state the idea that emotions can be classified as either positive or negative

So where does this leave us? As sensible as it may sound to try to construct a system of basic, primary emotions, particularly if such a system had a physiological or evolutionary foundation, such an attempt will prove difficult at best. One problem is that there is less than total agreement on just what *basic* or *primary* means when we are talking about emotions. "Thus, the question 'Which are the basic emotions?' is not only one that probably cannot be answered, it is a misdirected question, as though we asked, 'Which are the basic people?' and hoped to get a reply that would explain human diversity" (Ortony & Turner, 1990, p. 329).

If there is one conclusion regarding emotion with which all theorists agree, it is that part of being emotional is a physiological, visceral response. To put it plainly, being emotional is a gut-level reaction. To be emotional involves more than our thinking, reasoning cerebral cortex. We turn next to discuss the physiological aspects of emotion.

BEFORE YOU GO ON

- What are the four components of emotion?

- Describe how emotions are classified.

- What is meant by a valenced state?

Emotion	Relational theme
Anger	A demeaning offense against me and mine
Anxiety	Facing an uncertain, existential threat
Fright	An immediate, concrete, and overwhelming physical danger
Guilt	Having transgressed a moral imperative
Shame	Failing to live up to an ego ideal
Sadness	Having experienced an irrevocable loss
Envy	Wanting what someone else has
Jealousy	Resenting a third party for the loss of, or a threat to, another's affection or favor
Disgust	Taking in or being too close to an indigestible (metaphorically speaking) object or idea
Happiness	Making reasonable progress toward the realization of a goal
Pride	Enhancement of one's ego-identity by taking credit for a valued object or achievement, either one's own or that of some group with which one identifies
Relief	A distressing goal-incongruent condition that has changed for the better or gone away
Hope	Fearing the worst but wanting better
Love	Desiring or participating in affection, usually but not necessarily reciprocated
Compassion	Being moved by another's suffering and wanting to help

From Lazarus, 1993. Reproduced, with permission, from the Annual Review of Psychology, Volume 44, ©1993 by Annual Reviews, Inc.

FIGURE 10.6

Basic Emotions and Their Relational Themes

PHYSIOLOGICAL ASPECTS OF EMOTION

Let's return once again to our opening story about meeting a bear while walking in the woods. One question we asked was, "What will you do now?" We agreed that, if nothing else, your reaction would be an emotional one. You will experience *affect* (call it fear, if not panic). You will have a *cognitive reaction* (realizing you've just encountered a bear and that you'd rather you hadn't). You will engage in some *overt behavior* (either freezing in your tracks or racing back to the campfire). A significant part of your reaction in this situation (or one like it) will be internal, *physiological,* and "gut-level." Responding to a bear in the wild is not something people would do in a purely intellectual sort of way. When we are emotional, we respond with our insides, our viscera.

Our biological reaction to emotional situations takes place at several levels. Of primary interest is the autonomic nervous system, or ANS. The brain has a role to play in emotion, but first we'll consider the autonomic response.

The Role of the Autonomic Nervous System

The *autonomic nervous system (ANS)* consists of two parts that serve the same organs but have nearly the opposite effect on those organs. The *parasympathetic division* is actively involved in maintaining a relaxed, calm, and unemotional state. As you strolled down the path into the woods, the parasympathetic division of your ANS actively directed your digestive processes to do the best they could with the meal you'd just eaten. Blood was diverted from the extremities to the stomach and intestines. Saliva flowed freely. With your stomach full, and with blood diverted to it, you felt somewhat sleepy as your brain responded to the lower levels of blood supply. Your breathing was slow, deep, and steady, as was your heart rate. Again, all of these activities were under the control of the parasympathetic division of your autonomic nervous system.

Suddenly, there's that bear! Now the **sympathetic division** of your ANS takes over. Automatically, many physiological changes take place—changes that are usually quite adaptive.

sympathetic division (of the ANS) the division of the autonomic nervous system that takes over under conditions of emotional arousal and causes dilation of your eyes and increased respiration, blood pressure, and heart rate, among other reactions

1. The pupils of your eyes dilate, letting in as much of what light is available, increasing your visual sensitivity.

2. Your heart rate and blood pressure are elevated (energy needs to be mobilized as fast as possible).

3. Blood is diverted away from the digestive tract toward the limbs and brain, and digestion stops; you've got a bear to deal with; dinner can wait until later. Let's get the blood supply out there to the arms and legs where it can do some good (with what is called the fight-or-flight response).

4. Respiration increases, becoming deeper and more rapid; you'll need all the oxygen you can get.

5. Moisture is brought to the surface of the skin in the form of perspiration; as it evaporates, the body is cooled, thus conserving energy.

6. Blood sugar levels increase, making more energy readily available.

7. Blood will clot more readily than usual—for obvious but, it is hoped, unnecessary reasons.

The sympathetic system makes some of these changes directly (for example, stopping salivation and stimulating the cardiac muscle). Others are made indirectly through the release of hormones into the bloodstream, mostly epinephrine and norepinephrine from the adrenal glands. Because part of the physiological aspect of emotion is hormonal, it takes a few seconds for the effect to be experienced. If you were, in fact, confronted by a bear in the woods, you would probably not have the presence of mind to notice, but the reactions of sweaty palms, gasping breaths, and "butterflies in your stomach" take a few seconds to develop.

Is the autonomic and endocrine system reaction the same for every emotion that we experience? That's a very difficult question. There may be slight differences. There appears to be a small difference in the hormones produced during rage and fear reactions. There may be differences in the biological bases of emotions that prepare us for defense or for retreat—fight or flight (Blanchard & Blanchard, 1988). Consistent differences in physiological reactions for the various emotional states are, at best, very slight indeed. This issue has been controversial in psychology for many years and is likely to remain so (Blanchard & Blanchard, 1988; Plutchik, 1994; Selye, 1976).

The Role of the Brain

When we become emotional, our sympathetic nervous system does not just spring into action on its own. Autonomic nervous system activity is related to, and coordinated by, central nervous system activity.

The two brain structures most intimately involved in emotionality are the *limbic system* and the *hypothalamus,* that small structure in the middle of the brain centrally involved with physiological drives. The limbic system is a "lower" center in the brain, consisting of a number of small structures (the amygdala may be the most important for emotionality). These centers are "lower" in the sense of being well below the cerebral cortex and in the sense of being present (and important) in the brains of "lower" animals, such as rats and cats.

The limbic system is most involved in emotional responses that call for defensive or attacking responses—those emotions stimulated by threat. Electrical stimulation or destruction of portions of the limbic system reliably produces a variety of changes in emotional reaction.

It is to be expected that the hypothalamus would play a role in emotionality. It is involved in many motivational states. Hypothalamic stimulation can produce strong emotional reactions, including those that lead to attacking and killing any nearby prey (Flynn et al., 1970). Precisely how the limbic system and hypothalamus are coordinated in the normal experience and expression of emotion is not yet fully understood.

The role of the *cerebral cortex* in emotionality is also poorly understood. It seems to be largely inhibitory. That is, the limbic system and hypothalamus seem to act as the sources for extreme and rather poorly directed emotional reactions. The cortex *interprets* impulses from these lower centers and other information available to it and then modifies and directs the emotional reaction accordingly.

The clearest involvement of the cerebral cortex in emotionality is in the cognitive aspect of an emotion. It is the cerebral cortex that is involved in the interpretation and memory of emotional events. When you get back to camp, having just been frightened by a bear, you will use your cortex to tell the emotional details of your story. Emotional reactions tend to be processed in the right hemisphere of the brain; the left hemisphere is usually unemotional (Boraod, 1992; LeDoux, 1995; Sperry, 1982; Tucker, 1981).

To review, along with the autonomic nervous system, the limbic system and the hypothalamus are centers of emotion. These centers are coordinated by higher centers in the cerebral cortex, which, among other things, provides the cognitive interpretation of emotional responses.

BEFORE YOU GO ON

- Describe the role of the autonomic nervous system in emotion.

- What role does the brain play in emotion?

OUTWARD EXPRESSIONS OF EMOTION

An aspect of emotion that has long intrigued psychologists is how inner emotional states are communicated to others. Charles Darwin was one of the first to popularize the idea that facial expressions provide indicators of an organism's emotional state. More than a hundred years later, psychologists are discovering new evidence that suggests that Darwin was correct.

It is very useful for one organism to let another know how it is feeling. As one wild animal approaches a second, the second better have a good idea about the emotional state of the first. Is it angry? Does it come in peace? Is it just curious, or is it looking for dinner? Is it sad, looking for comfort, or is it sexually aroused, looking for a mate? An inability to make such determinations quickly can be disastrous. Animals need to know the emotional state of other animals if they are to survive for long.

Nonhuman animals have many instinctive and ritualistic patterns of behavior to communicate aggressiveness, interest in courtship, submission, and other emotional states. Humans also express their emotional states in a variety of ways, including verbal communication. Surely if you are happy, sad, angry, or jealous, you can try to tell us how you feel. In fact, the ability to communicate with language often puts humans at an advantage. Research now tells us that emotional states are reflected in *how* we speak, even if our message is not related to emotion at all (Bachorowski & Owren, 1995; Scherer, 1986). Even without verbal language, there is a school of thought that suggests that the human animal, like the nonhuman, uses *body language* to communicate its emotional condition (Birdwhistell, 1952; Fast, 1970). Someone sitting quietly, slumped slightly forward with head down, may be viewed as feeling sad, even from a distance. We similarly interpret

Because they cannot verbalize how they feel, it is particularly important for animals to be able to convey their emotions through posture and facial expressions.

postural cues and gestures as being associated with fear, anger, happiness, and so on. Such expressions often result from learning and may be modified by cultural influences.

Darwin recognized facial expression as a common cue to emotion in animals, especially mammals. Might facial expression provide the key to underlying emotions in humans, too? Are there facial expressions of emotional states that are universal among the human species, just as there appear to be among nonhumans? A growing body of evidence supports the hypothesis that facial expressions of emotional states are innate responses, only slightly sensitive to cultural influence (Adelmann & Zajonc, 1989; Andrews, 1963; Buck, 1980; Gellhorn, 1964; Oatley & Jenkins, 1992; Tomkins, 1962).

Paul Ekman and his colleagues have conducted several studies trying to find a reliable relationship between emotional state and facial expression across cultures (Ekman, 1972, 1992, 1993; Ekman et al., 1987). In one large study (Ekman, 1973) college students were shown six pictures of people's faces. In each picture, a different emotion was displayed: happiness, disgust, surprise, sadness, anger, or fear. When students from the United States, Argentina, Japan, Brazil, and Chile were asked to identify the emotion experienced by the people in the photographs, their agreement was remarkable. One problem with this study is that all of the subjects did have many shared experiences, even though they were from basically different cultures. They were, after all, college students and had many experiences in common (perhaps they had seen the same movies or watched the same TV shows). Even though Ekman's subjects came from different countries, their agreement could be explained in terms of the similarities of their experiences rather than some innate tendency to express emotions through facial expression.

An argument against this line of reasoning is found in another project by Ekman (Ekman, 1972; Ekman & Friesen, 1971). Here, natives of a remote New Guinea tribe were asked to make faces showing various emotional reactions (for example, "A friend has come and you are happy"). No one in any other culture would have much difficulty identifying the emotion the subjects were trying to display. The New Guinea tribesmen had little contact with persons outside New Guinea, and virtually no contact with magazines, television, or movies that could have introduced them to the facial expressions of people from other cultures. Distinctive, universal facial expressions have been identified for anger, fear, disgust, sadness, and happiness (Ekman, 1993).

Another study of facial expression (Ekman et al., 1983) has shown that simply moving one's facial muscles into the positions associated with emotional expression can cause distinctive physiological changes associated with an emotional state (see also Adelmann & Zajonc, 1989; Laird, 1984; Matsumoto, 1987; Schiff & Lamon, 1989). As bizarre as it sounds, the idea is that if you raise your eyebrows, open your eyes widely, and raise the corners of your mouth, you will produce an internal physiological change not unlike that which occurs when you are happy, and you will smile as a result.

BEHAVIORAL MANIFESTATIONS OF EMOTION

Differing facial expressions are not the only way that emotions are expressed. Often, as we know from experience, emotions directly influence behavior. For example, imagine that you are driving home from school one day and you accidentally cut off another motorist. You think nothing of it because it was an accident. The next thing you know you see this other driver in your rearview mirror inches from your rear bumper. He pulls up next to you, and you notice that his face is all red and he is shouting and making obscene gestures at you. Next, to your shock, he tries to run you off the road. You decide to pull over and let this "maniac" pass you.

aggression any behavior that is intended to inflict physical and/or psychological harm on another organism or the symbol of that organism

In this example, the other motorist was obviously experiencing an emotional episode that was translated into a particular behavior: aggression. Social psychologists define **aggression** as any behavior that is intended to inflict physical and/or psychological harm on another organism (for example, you) or the symbol of that organism (for example, your car). One of the more popular theories of why aggression occurs in situations like the one just described is the **frustration-aggression hypothesis**. In its original form the frustration-aggression hypothesis stated that "aggression is always a consequence of frustration… the occurrence of aggressive behavior always presupposes the existence of frustration and, contrariwise,… the existence of frustration leads to some form of aggression" (Dollard, Doob, Miller, Mowrer, & Sears, 1939, p. 1). In other words, according to the frustration-aggression hypothesis, when we are frustrated, we behave aggressively.

frustration-aggression hypothesis the hypothesis that states that frustration gives rise to aggression and that aggression arises from frustration

Factors Affecting Frustration

An assumption of the frustration-aggression hypothesis is that emotion is aroused when goal-directed behavior is blocked. Frustration is aroused under two conditions. First, we expect to perform certain behaviors, and second, those behaviors are blocked (Dollard et al., 1939).

Frustration can vary in strength, depending on three factors (Dollard et al., 1939). The first is the strength of the original drive. If you are very thirsty, for example, and are deprived of water, your frustration will be greater than if you are only slightly thirsty. The second factor is the degree to which the goal-directed behavior is thwarted. If a water fountain dribbled just enough water for you to drink a little bit, you would be less frustrated than if it didn't work at all. Another factor influencing the amount of frustration experienced is the number of frustrated responses. If your thwarted attempt to get water from a fountain followed another frustrating event, you would experience more frustration than if it had not followed another frustrating event. Thus, frustrating experiences are cumulative. The motorist you cut off may have reacted aggressively because he may have experienced several frustrating events. For example, perhaps he didn't get the raise he expected, he hit a great deal of traffic on his way home, and then you cut him off.

Although the original frustration-aggression hypothesis stated categorically that frustration always leads to aggression, acts of frustration-based aggression can be inhibited (Dollard et al., 1939). If there is a strong possibility that your aggressive behavior will be punished, you may not react aggressively to frustration. If a police officer were behind the frustrated driver, he probably would not have acted aggressively out of fear of being arrested.

The Role of Anger in the Frustration-Aggression Link

The frustration-aggression hypothesis stirred controversy from the moment it was proposed. Some theorists questioned whether frustration inevitably led to aggression (Miller, 1941). Others suggested that frustration only leads to aggression under specific circumstances, such as when the blocked response is important to the individual (Blanchard & Blanchard, 1984).

As criticisms of the original theory mounted, modifications were made. For example, Berkowitz (1989) proposed that frustration is connected to aggression by negative affect, such as anger. If the frustration of goal-directed behavior leads to anger, then aggression will occur. If no anger is aroused, no aggression will result.

What factors lead to the arousal of anger? One factor is how we judge the *intent* of a person who frustrates us. In fact, when acting aggressively we take into account a person's intent, more so than his or her actual behavior (Ohbuchi & Kambara, 1985). So, if we infer that someone intended to frustrate or hurt us, we will experience more anger than if we infer that the harm was not intended.

Another factor that can contribute to anger, and ultimately to aggression, is the perception that we have been treated unjustly. For example, we frequently read about fans at sporting events who riot over a "bad call" or fans at a football game who pelt officials with snowballs or beer cans following a call against a home team. In each case the fans are reacting to what they perceive to be an injustice done to the home team.

Aggression is often seen as a way of restoring justice and equity in a situation. The person you cut off on the highway was using aggressive driving to "even the score" with you. The perceived inequity and injustice in a frustrating situation is more likely to arouse anger and aggression than the frustration itself (Sulthana, 1987).

Of course, not all perceived injustice leads to aggression. There may be more of a tendency to use aggression to restore equity when the recipient of the inequity feels particularly powerless (Richardson, Vandenberg, & Humphries, 1986). In one study, subjects with lower status than their opponents chose higher shock levels than did subjects with equal or higher status than their opponents. We can begin to understand from these findings why groups who believe themselves to be unjustly treated, who have low status, and who feel powerless resort to aggressive tactics, especially when frustrated, to remedy their situation. Riots and terrorism are often the weapons of choice among those with little power.

Think back to the scenario that opened this section. You cut off another driver accidentally, and this person took it as an intentional act and decided to act aggressively. Who might such a person be? There is no set profile of the aggressive driver, but most are relatively young, poorly educated males with a history of violence and drug or alcohol problems (American Automobile Association, 1997).

BEFORE YOU GO ON

- How can emotions be communicated without verbal language?

- How do facial expressions relate to the expression of emotion?

- What is the frustration-aggression hypothesis, and what factors affect frustration?

Topic Review 10B

1. **What are the four components of an emotion?**

   There are four possible components of an emotional reaction: (1) the experience of a subjective feeling, or affective component; (2) a cognitive appraisal or interpretation; (3) an internal, visceral, physiological reaction; and (4) an overt behavioral response.

2. **How did Wundt conceptualize emotions?**

   There have been several attempts to categorize emotional reactions, dating back to Wundt in the late 1800s. Wundt believed that emotions had three intersecting dimensions: pleasantness-unpleasantness, relaxation-tension, and calm-excitement.

3. **How did Izard conceptualize emotions?**

   Izard has a theory that calls for nine primary emotions: fear, anger, shame, contempt, disgust, distress, interest, surprise, and joy. Each of the primary emotions is believed to have its own underlying physiological basis. All other emotions would be combinations of the nine primary emotions.

4. **What are Plutchik's ideas about emotion?**

   Plutchik argues that there are eight basic emotions and many combinations and degrees of them. Other theorists have proposed as few as two or as many as dozens of primary emotions.

5. **What role does emotionality play in motivation?**

   Richard Lazarus proposed a theory of emotion that highlights the motivational aspects of emotion. According to this view, through experience we learn that there are certain emotions that we are motivated to avoid (fear, anger, guilt, for example), whereas others we are motivated to seek out (joy, pride, and love, for example).

6. **What is the bottom line on how emotions are classified?**

   The inconsistency among theories leads some psychologists to wonder if the attempt to classify basic emotions is misguided. It is difficult to determine how many primary or basic emotions exist. One conclusion that can be drawn is that emotions involve a visceral, physiological response that goes beyond the cognitive response to emotional stimuli.

7. **What role does the autonomic nervous system play in emotional arousal?**

   Among the changes that take place when we become emotional are those produced by the sympathetic division of the autonomic nervous system. Occurring to varying degrees and depending on the situation, these reactions include dilation of the pupils, increased heart rate and blood pressure, cessation of digestive processes, deeper and more rapid breathing, increased perspiration, and elevated blood sugar levels.

8. **What physiological mechanisms are involved in the sympathetic reaction to an emotional stimulus?**

   The sympathetic division of the autonomic nervous system influences some responses directly, such as stopping salivation and stimulating the heart. Other reactions are indirectly caused by the release of epinephrine and norepinephrine into the blood. These reactions take a few seconds to take effect.

9. **What role do the hypothalamus and limbic system play in emotional reactions?**

   The two brain structures closely involved in emotional reactions are the hypothalamus and the limbic system. The limbic system is most involved in defensive or attacking responses. The hypothalamus produces strong emotional reactions. Stimulating certain parts of the hypothalamus leads to a predatory response.

10. **How is the cerebral cortex involved in emotional reactions?**

    The role of the cortex in emotional responding is not well understood. However, the cerebral cortex appears to play mainly an inhibitory role in emotionality. The cortex interprets impulses from the hypothalamus and limbic system and then modifies and directs the emotional reaction. The most prominent role of the cortex in emotional responding is cognitive in nature, giving meaning to emotional experiences.

11. **How are facial expressions involved in the communication of emotion?**

From the time of Charles Darwin, who theorized that facial expressions provide information about internal states, a great deal of attention has focused on the role of facial expressions in communicating emotions. Expressing emotions via facial expressions has adaptive value. It allows one to communicate a wide range of emotions that can be interpreted by others.

12. **What universal facial expressions did Ekman and his colleagues identify?**

Ekman and his colleagues identified six facial expressions that appear to be universal. They include: happiness, disgust, surprise, sadness, anger, and fear. Subjects from five countries were able to identify the emotion that went with each face with remarkable accuracy.

13. **What is the frustration-aggression hypothesis?**

Social psychologists define aggression as any behavior that is intended to inflict physical and/or psychological harm on another organism or the symbol of that organism. The frustration-aggression hypothesis is one popular theory of why aggression occurs. In its original form the frustration-aggression hypothesis stated that aggression is always the result of frustration and that frustration always leads to aggression.

14. **What factors contribute to the amount of frustration experienced?**

Frustration, which occurs when a goal-directed behavior is blocked, is affected by three factors. The stronger the original drive to perform a behavior, the more frustration is experienced if that behavior is blocked. A second factor affecting frustration is the degree to which a goal-directed behavior is blocked. More frustration is experienced when a behavior is totally blocked, compared to when a behavior is partially blocked. The third factor affecting frustration is the number of frustrating experiences. The greater the number of frustrating experiences, the more frustration you will experience.

15. **What is the updated version of the frustration-aggression hypothesis?**

Because frustration sometimes does not lead to aggression, an updated version of the hypothesis was proposed. According to the updated version, frustration will lead to aggression only if it arouses a negative emotion such as anger. If no anger is aroused, frustration does not lead to aggression. Anger can be aroused if we perceive that a person intends to harm us or if we feel we have been treated unjustly.

Chapter 11

Psychology, Stress, and Physical Health

- It's Friday, and you have a chance to get away for the weekend. Unfortunately, you have two big exams scheduled for Monday and need the weekend to study.

- Lindsay is almost done typing a term paper on her computer when suddenly the power goes out. Having failed to save her work as she went along, she'll have to redo it all.

- Cindy and Jerry have known each other since grade school. They dated throughout high school and college. Next week, family and friends will join in the celebration of their marriage.

- Doug wants to make the basketball team, but the coach informs him that despite his best efforts, he is too short to make the team.

- Marian is excited about going to Germany in a student-exchange program, but she's also very nervous about getting along in a new country.

- After 11 years on the road as a salesman, Wayne is being promoted to district sales manager—an office job with a substantial raise in pay.

- Jake cut back his smoking to one pack a day and was considering starting an exercise program. Now he is in a coronary intensive care unit, having just suffered a heart attack.

- Three-year-old Trudy keeps asking her mother for a cookie. Mother steadfastly refuses because it's almost dinner time. Trudy returns to her room and promptly pulls an arm off her favorite doll.

- You are late for class, driving down a two-lane road, when someone pulls out in front of you and drives ten miles per hour below the speed limit.

- Shirley wants to be a concert pianist, but her music teacher tells her she does not have the talent or discipline to reach that goal.

Life is filled with stress, frustration, and conflict. This list provides a very small sample of the types of stressful events people encounter every day. We'll return to each of these examples, and provide others throughout this chapter, where our focus is the role of psychological factors as they affect one's physical health and well-being. Here we encounter a familiar theme: biological and psychological processes interact; body and mind are interrelated.

Topic 11A
Stress, Stressors, and How to Cope

Topic 11B
Health Psychology

Topic 11A STRESS, STRESSORS, AND HOW TO COPE

Our study of stress is divided into two main sections. First we'll see, at least in general terms, where stress comes from. What are the common stressors in our lives? Second, we'll examine the complex patterns of responses we make when we experience stress. We begin by trying to understand the causes of stress.

Key Questions to Answer

While reading this Topic, find answers to the following key questions:

1. What is the definition for stress?

2. Under what conditions is stress aroused?

3. What is meant by frustration-induced stress?

4. What are the four common types of motivational conflict?

5. In what ways might life events produce stress?

6. How does socioeconomic status contribute to stress?

7. How do everyday life hassles contribute to stress?

8. What does it mean to say that there are individual differences in reactions to stressors?

9. What is Selye's General Adaptation Syndrome (GAS)?

10. What happens during the alarm stage of the GAS?

11. What happens during the resistance stage of the GAS?

12. What occurs in the exhaustion stage of the GAS?

13. What are some adaptive ways of dealing with stress?

14. What are some maladaptive reactions to stress?

STRESSORS: THE CAUSES OF STRESS

stress a complex set of reactions to real or perceived threats to one's well-being that motivates adaptation

Although each of us is familiar with stress and how it feels, psychologists have struggled with how to characterize stress for nearly 60 years (Hobfoll, 1989; Rice, 1999). We define **stress** as a complex set of reactions made by an individual under pressure to adapt. In other words, stress is a *response* one makes to real or perceived threats to one's sense of well-being. Stress is something that happens inside people. There are physiological reactions and unpleasant feelings (for example, distress and anxiety) associated with stress.

There are many circumstances or events that can produce stress. The *sources* of stress are called **stressors**. We'll consider three types of stressors: frustration, conflict, and life events. As we go along, we'll provide examples as a reminder that stress is not necessarily a reaction to some big, overwhelming, catastrophic event, such as the death of a loved one or a natural disaster. Once we see where stress comes from, we'll consider techniques people use to cope with it.

stressors the sources or stimuli for stress, which include frustration, conflict, and life events

Frustration-Induced Stress

Motivated behaviors can be characterized as *goal-directed*. Whether by internal processes (drives) or external stimuli (incentives), we are pushed or pulled toward positive goals and away from negative goals. Now let us introduce an assumption: Organisms do not always reach all of their goals. Have you always gotten everything you've ever wanted? Have you always been able to avoid unpleasantness, pain, or sorrow? Do you know anyone who has?

Sometimes we are totally prohibited from ever reaching a particular goal. At other times our progress may be slower or more difficult than we would like. In either case, we are frustrated. **Frustration** is the blocking or thwarting of goal-directed behavior— blocking that may be total and permanent or partial and temporary (see Figure 11.1).

frustration a stressor; the blocking or thwarting of goal-directed behavior

Stress that results from frustration is a normal, commonplace reaction. Frustration is a stressor, and the stress it produces is part of life. In no way does it imply weakness, pathology, or illness. What matters is how individuals react to the stressors in their lives.

To someone who is frustrated, the actual source of stress may be of little consequence. However, in order to respond adaptively to frustration-induced stress, it may be helpful to recognize the source of the blocking—the particular stressor—keeping us from our goals. There are two basic types of frustration: environmental and personal.

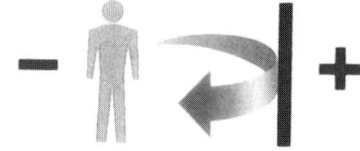

FIGURE 11.1
A depiction of frustration, the blocking or thwarting of goal-directed behavior.

Environmental frustration implies that the blocking or thwarting of one's goal-directed behavior is caused by something or somebody in the environment. (Note that we talk about the *source* of frustration, not *fault* or *blame*, which are evaluative terms.) Remember Lindsay who lost her term paper when the power went out? This is an example of environmental frustration. Lindsay wanted to get her paper typed. Her goal-directed behavior led her to use her computer. Something in her environment—a momentary power outage—kept her from reaching her goal. And remember Trudy? She wanted a cookie, but her mother said, "No, it's almost dinner time." Trudy is also being frustrated by her environment, but in a slightly different way. She wants a cookie, and her mother is blocking that motivated behavior. This type of environmental frustration, in which the source of the blocking is another person, is sometimes called *social frustration*.

Occasionally we are frustrated not because something in our environment blocks our progress, but because of an internal or personal reason. This is *personal frustration*. Doug fails to make the basketball team simply because he is too short. Shirley, who wants to be a concert pianist, may be frustrated in her attempt to do so simply because she doesn't have sufficient talent. Shirley's frustration and resulting stress are not her *fault* (fault and

BEFORE YOU GO ON

- What is the definition of stress?
- When is stress aroused?
- What is meant by frustration-induced stress?

blame are just not relevant, remember), but if she persists in this goal-directed behavior, she will be frustrated. Some of us are learning that simply getting older can be stressful. When someone now has difficulty doing things that at one time were easy to do, the result may be stress. That stress is frustration-induced, and this type of frustration is personal.

Conflict-Induced Stress

conflict a stressor in which some goals can be satisfied only at the expense of others

Sometimes we are unable to satisfy a particular drive or motive because it is in **conflict** with other motives that are influencing us at the same time. Stress may result from conflicts within our own motivational system.

With motivational conflicts, there is the implication of a decision or choice to be made. Sometimes the choice is relatively easy, and the resulting stress will be slight; sometimes decision making is difficult, and the resulting stress will be greater. When discussing conflicts, we talk about positive goals or incentives that one wishes to approach and negative goals or incentives one wishes to avoid. There are four major types of stress-inducing motivational conflicts.

Approach-Approach Conflicts

Conflicts are necessarily unpleasant, stress-producing situations, even when the goals involved are positive. In an approach-approach conflict, an organism is caught between two (or more) alternatives, and each of them is positive, or potentially reinforcing (Figure 11.2). If alternative A is chosen, a desired goal will be reached. If B is chosen, a different desirable goal will be attained. This is a conflict in that both goals and alternatives are not available at the same time. It has to be one or the other.

FIGURE 11.2

A diagram of an approach-approach conflict. In such a conflict, a person is faced with two (or more) attractive, positive goals, and must choose between or among them.

Once an approach-approach conflict is resolved, the person does end up with something positive no matter which alternative is chosen. If Carla enters an ice cream shop with only enough money to buy one scoop of ice cream, she may experience a conflict when faced with all of the flavors from which she can choose. Typical of conflict, we'll probably see some swaying back and forth among alternatives. We can assume that this conflict will be resolved with a choice, and Carla will at least walk out of the store with an ice cream cone of some flavor she likes. Her life might have been easier (less stressful) if the store had just one flavor and she didn't have to make a choice.

Sometimes the choices we have to make are much more serious than those involving ice cream flavors. What will be your college major? On the one hand, you'd like to go to medical school and be a surgeon (that's a positive incentive or goal). On the other hand, you'd like to study composition and conducting at a school of music (also a clear positive goal). At the moment, you can't do both. The courses you would take as a premed

Even if the choices that one has to make are positive (which dessert should I take?), the very process of making those choices can put one in a conflict and produce stress.

student are different from those you'd take if you were to follow music as a career path. Both are constructive, desirable alternatives, but at registration, you have to make a choice, one that may have long-lasting repercussions. The consequences of such a conflict qualify it as a stressor.

Avoidance-Avoidance Conflicts

Perhaps the most stress-inducing of all motivational conflicts are the avoidance-avoidance conflicts (Figure 11.3). In this type of conflict, a person is faced with several alternatives, and each of them is negative or in some way punishing. To be in an avoidance-avoidance conflict is, in a way, to be boxed in so that no matter what you do, the result will be punishing or unpleasant.

This sort of conflict is not at all unusual in the workplace. Imagine that you are a supervisor in charge of a reasonably large department. Your department has been doing

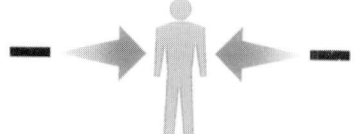

FIGURE 11.3

A diagram of an avoidance-avoidance conflict. In such a conflict, a person is faced with two (or more) unattractive, negative goals, and must choose between or among them. This is sometimes referred to as a "no-win" situation.

well, making a profit, but management directs you to cut your operating budget by 20 percent by next month. There are ways you can reduce expenses—limit travel, cut down on supplies, reduce pay, eliminate expense accounts—but each involves an action you'd rather not take. If you do nothing at all, you may lose your job. The result may be stress, and the stressor is an avoidance-avoidance conflict.

Approach-Avoidance Conflicts

FIGURE 11.4

A diagram of an approach-avoidance conflict. Here, a person is faced with only one goal. What makes this a conflict is that the goal has both positive and negative aspects or features.

With approach-avoidance conflicts, a person is in the position of considering only one goal (Figure 11.4). What makes this situation a conflict is that the person would very much like to reach that goal, but at the same time would very much like not to. It's a matter of "Yes, I'd love to… Well, I'd rather not… Maybe I would… No, I wouldn't… yes… no." Consider the possibility of entering into a relationship with someone you think of as special. On the one hand, such a relationship might turn out to be wonderful and rewarding. On the other hand, such a relationship might put you in the position of being rejected.

Typical of conflict, we'll find vacillation between alternatives—motivated to approach and, at the same time, motivated to avoid. Like Marian in our opening examples, you might find yourself in an approach-avoidance conflict if you want to interact with people who are culturally different, perhaps to show that you are open-minded. At the same time, you may be reluctant to initiate such an interaction for fear that your behaviors will be inappropriate or misinterpreted.

Multiple Approach-Avoidance Conflicts

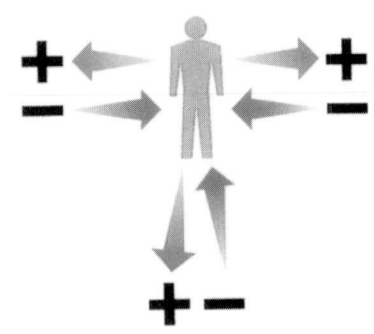

FIGURE 11.5

A diagram of multiple approach-avoidance conflict. In such a conflict, a person is faced with two (or more) alternatives, each of which has both positive and negative aspects or features, and a choice must be made between or among the alternatives.

Multiple approach-avoidance conflicts may be the most common of the conflicts experienced by adults (see Figure 11.5). This type of conflict arises when an individual is faced with a number of alternatives, each one of which is in some way both positive and negative.

Perhaps you and some friends are out shopping on a Saturday morning. You realize that it's getting late, and you're all hungry. Where will you go to lunch? You may have a multiple approach-avoidance conflict here. "We could go to Bob's Diner, where the food is cheap and the service is fast, but the food is terrible. We could go to Cafe Olé, where the food is better, but service is a little slower, and the food is more expensive. Or we could go to The Grill, where the service is elegant and the food is superb, but the price is very high." Granted this is not an earth-shaking dilemma, but in each case, there is a plus and a minus to be considered in making the choice. The more difficult the choice, the greater the induced stress.

Think of your own decision-making processes when you decided to go to college. First, there was the multiple approach-avoidance conflict of whether to go at all. "I could forget about it, just stay here; get a good job; lay back and be happy, BUT all my friends are going. College graduates make more than high school graduates." The conflicts do not go away when one considers all of the pluses and minuses of *where* to go to college.

The choices, both strong and weak points, can be maddening. Stay at home and go to school nearby? Stay in state for lower tuition, but move away from home? Get away from it all to some place you have always wanted to live?

Life is filled with such conflicts, and some of them can cause extreme stress. They may encompass questions of the "What will I do with the rest of my life?" sort. "Should I stay at home with the children (+ and -), or should I have a career (+ and -)?" "Should I get married or stay single, or is there another way (+ and - in each case)?" "Should I work for company A (+ and -), or should I work for company B (+ and -)?" Clearly, such lists could go on and on. Reflect back on the conflicts you have faced during the past few weeks. You should be able to categorize each of them into one of the four types listed here.

> ## BEFORE YOU GO ON
>
> - How can conflict bring about stress?
> - What are the four common types of motivational conflict?

Life-Induced Stress

Frustration and conflict are potent sources of stress and often are simply unavoidable consequences of being a motivated organism. Psychologists have also considered sources of stress that do not fit neatly into our descriptions of either conflict or frustration. One useful approach is to look at events and changes that occur in one's life as potential sources of stress.

Sometimes life events that are evaluated as being positive, such as planning a wedding, can be stressors.

In 1967, Thomas Holmes and Richard Rahe published the first version of their *Social Readjustment Rating Scale,* or *SRRS* (Holmes & Holmes, 1970). The basic idea behind this scale is that stress results whenever life situations change. The scale provides a list of life events that might be potentially stressful. The original list of such events was drawn from the reports of patients suffering from moderate to high levels of stress in their lives. Marriage was arbitrarily assigned a value of 50 stress points, or *life-change units*. With "marriage = 50" as their guide, the patients rated a number of other life changes in terms of the amount of stress they might provide. The death of a spouse got the highest rating (100 units), followed by divorce (73 units). Pregnancy (40 units), trouble with the boss (23 units), changing to a new school (20 units), and minor violations of the law (11 units) are some other stress-inducing life-change events on the scale. In a rather direct way, the SRRS gives us a way to measure the stress in our lives.

There is a positive correlation between scores on the SRRS and the incidence of physical illness and disease (Rahe & Arthur, 1978). People with SRRS scores between 200 and 299 have a 50-50 chance of developing symptoms of physical illness within the next two years, whereas 80 percent of those with scores above 300 develop symptoms within the same time period. Several studies that have looked at correlations between SRRS scores and health problems have found the correlations to be positive (Adler et al., 1994; Brett et al., 1990; and McCrae, 1984).The logic is that stress predisposes one to physical illness. But correlations do not tell us about cause and effect. Some of the SRRS items are worded to include mention of a physical illness or are health related. It is not much of a surprise, then, to find that scores on this scale are related to levels of physical illness.

socioeconomic status (SES) a measure that reflects one's income, education, and occupation

Socioeconomic status, or **SES**, is a measure that reflects income, educational level, and occupation. Sensibly, there is a negative correlation between socioeconomic level and experienced stress. SES is related to stress in at least two ways: (1) Persons of higher socioeconomic status are less likely than are persons of low SES to encounter negative life events, such as unemployment, poor housing, and less access to quality health care (McLeod & Kessler, 1990), and (2) Persons of low SES necessarily have fewer resources to deal with stressful life events when they do occur (Adler et al., 1994).

It doesn't take a lot of imagination to think of other life situations that are likely to be stress-inducing. For example, being a working mother is a stressor, and to a much greater extent than being a working father (Light, 1997; Luecken et al., 1997; Matthews et al., 1997). Isn't it logical that being a single parent, or being a college student with children can be stressful? Certainly, being diagnosed with a serious, life-threatening disease is a stress-producing life event (Anderson, 1997).

Richard Lazarus (1981, 1991c, 1993, 2000) argues that psychologists ought to focus more attention on those causes of stress that are less dramatic than major life changes, such as the death of a family member or marriage. What often matters most are life's little hassles—the traffic that goes too slowly, the toothpaste tube that splits, ants at a picnic, the cost of a pizza compared to what it was just a few years ago. This argument is that big crises or major life-change events are too large to have an impact on us directly. What causes us to feel stressed are the ways in which big events produce little, irritating changes in our lives (hassles). Being retired may mean a lack of access to friendly conversation at coffee-break time. A spouse who returns to work may make life more difficult; the other spouse may have to cook dinner for the first time. Thus, stress is not so much a reaction to an event itself but to the hassles it creates.

Lazarus and his colleagues created a scale to assess the extent to which hassles enter peoples' lives (Kanner, Coyne, Schaefer, & Lazarus, 1981). Respondents to the *Hassles Scale*, as it is called, indicate which hassles have happened to them and rate the severity of the experienced stress. The ten most commonly cited daily hassles for college students and for middle-aged adults are listed in Figure 11.6. *The Hassles Scale* turns out to be a better predictor of problems with physical health and a better predictor of symptoms such as anxiety and depression than is the *Social Readjustment Rating Scale* (DeLongis et al., 1988).

Other scales have been designed to assess the stressors people encounter. One, the *Comprehensive Scale of Stress Assessment* (Sheridan & Smith, 1987), has been revised for use with teenagers (Sheridan & Perkins, 1992). Significant stressors for teens include such things as "having thoughts of losing your parents or someone else dear to you," "being bombarded by questions and requests," "experiencing high-level noise at school or home," "being around angry people," and "having someone call something you have said or done 'stupid.'"

One final note about life-induced stressors: the events in our lives we talk about as stressors do not have to be negative or unpleasant events. Many events that we look forward to and consider changes for the better can bring with them the hassles associated with stress (Folkman & Moskowitz, 2000; Somerfield & McCrae, 2000). For example, everybody is happy about Cindy and Jerry getting married, no doubt a pleasant, positive

For Middle-aged Adults:	For College Students:
1. Concerns about weight	1. Troubling thoughts about the future
2. Health of a family member	2. Not getting enough sleep
3. Rising prices of common goods	3. Wasting time
4. Home maintenance (interior)	4. Inconsiderate smokers
5. Too many things to do	5. Physical appearance
6. Misplacing or losing things	6. Too many things to do
7. Yard work or outside home maintenance	7. Misplacing or losing things
8. Property, investments, or taxes	8. Not enough time to do the things you need to do
9. Crime	9. Concerns about meeting high standards
10. Physical appearance	10. Being lonely

From Kanner, Coyne, Schaefer, & Lazaarus, 1981.

FIGURE 11.6

Ten Common Stressors in the Lives of Middle-aged Adults and College Students

BEFORE YOU GO ON

- In what ways might life events produce stress?

- How does socioeconomic status relate to stress?

- What role do everyday hassles play in the arousal of stress?

life event. At the same time—as anyone who has ever gone through the process will attest—weddings, and preparing for them, are stressors. They may produce new conflicts. If Aunt Sarah is invited, does that mean that Aunt Louise must be invited as well? Cindy and Jerry are planning an outdoor reception. What if it rains? And there's Wayne the experienced salesman, now a sales manager. Wayne may have gotten used to being on the road and setting his own hours. Now that he has a promotion ("good news") his daily routine may be drastically altered by his being confined to an office, which may produce new stress.

REACTING TO THE STRESSORS IN OUR LIVES

So far we have defined stress and reviewed a number of potential stressors. Now we need to consider what someone might do when he or she experiences stress. We often hear about people trying to "cope with the stress in their lives." Consistent with the terminology we've been using, it would be more correct to speak of "coping with, or dealing with, the stressors in one's life." Stress is a reaction to stressors (frustration, conflict, or life events). Stress may motivate us, but it motivates us to do something about the perceived threats to our well-being which we call stressors.

Individual Differences in Responding to Stressors

As with so many other things, there are large individual differences in how one responds to stressors. What constitutes a stressor and what someone may do when he or she experiences stress can vary considerably from person to person. Some people fall apart at weddings; others find them only mildly stressful. For some people, simple choices are difficult to make; for others, choices are not enough, and they seek challenges. The variability in stress we see among different people can usually be found within any one person at different times. For example, on one day, being caught in slow-moving traffic might drive you up the wall. In the very same situation a few days later, you find you couldn't care less. So we need to remember that reactions to stressors vary from time to time and from person to person. The amount of stress one experiences and the means of coping with stress do not appear to be different for men and women (Baum & Grunberg, 1991; Lazarus, 1993).

Some people seem so generally resistant to the negative aspects of stress that they have been labeled as having *hardy personalities* (Kobasa, 1979, 1982, 1987; Maddi & Kobasa, 1984; Neubauer, 1992). Hardiness in this context is related to three things: (1) *challenge* (being able to see difficulties as opportunity for change and growth, not a threat to status); (2) *control* (being in charge of what is happening and believing that a person is the master of his or her fate); and (3) *commitment* (being engaged and involved with life and its circumstances, not just watching life go by from the sidelines).

Here's another observation about how we deal with stress: some responses are more effective or adaptive than others. Stress often follows as a natural consequence of being alive, motivated in the real world. What is unfortunate is that we occasionally develop ineffective or maladaptive strategies for dealing with stress, meaning that one's reaction will not, in the long run, be successful in reducing stress. Before we consider strategies for dealing with stress, let's look more closely at the reaction to stressors that we call stress.

BEFORE YOU GO ON

- What does it mean to say that there are individual differences in reactions to stressors?

Stress as a Physiological Reaction: Selye's General Adaptation Syndrome

No matter how we ultimately cope with stress, stressors produce a series of physiological reactions within us. In this way, stress is much like other reactions to emotion-producing stimuli in our environments. When we experience stress, demands are made on the physiological systems of our bodies. Hans Selye's **general adaptation syndrome**, or **GAS**, describes the most widely accepted description of the physiological reactions one makes to stressors. According to Selye (1956, 1974), the reaction to stressors occurs in three stages: alarm, resistance, and exhaustion.

general adaptation syndrome (GAS) Selye's description of physiological reactions made to stressors, which include three stages: alarm, resistance, and exhaustion

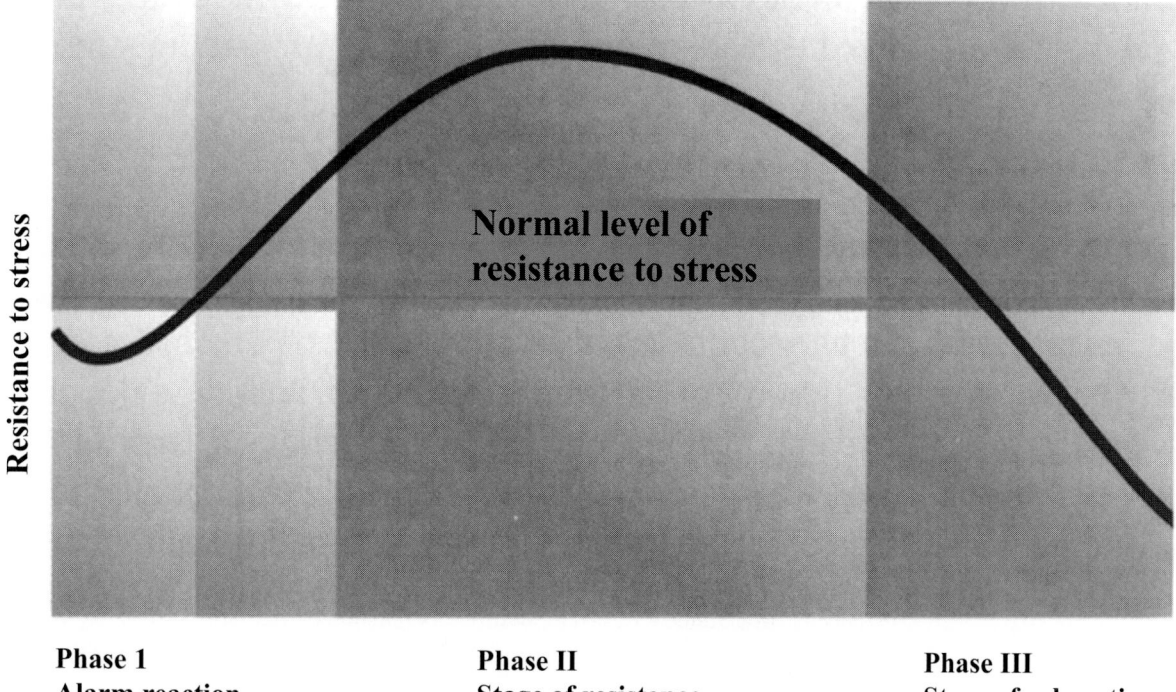

Resistance to stress

Normal level of resistance to stress

Phase 1
Alarm reaction

Phase II
Stage of resistance

Phase III
Stage of exhaustion

FIGURE 11.7

Selye's General Adaptation Syndrome calls for three levels of largely physiological reactions to stressors. In the alarm reaction, resources are quickly mobilized as the sympathetic division of the ANS springs into action. If the stressor remains, the organism enters a defensive resistance stage. Following prolonged exposure to a stressor, the energy necessary for a adaptive resistance may become depleted in a stage of exhaustion.

The first response to the perception of a stressor is *alarm*. Any perceived threat produces rapid and noticeable changes in the sympathetic division of the autonomic nervous system. There will be an increase in blood pressure and heart rate, pupillary dilation, a cessation of digestion, and a rerouting of the blood supply to the extremities of the body. The adrenal glands enlarge and secrete norepinephrine into the bloodstream, mobilizing the body's resources and providing increased levels of blood sugar. These reactions are similar to those we experience in any emotional situation. This strong, dramatic reaction cannot last very long. We usually maintain high levels of sympathetic activity for no more than several minutes, a few hours at the most.

Consider this example. Imagine Pam, a college student in the midst of an important semester. Pam is strongly motivated to do well in her courses. It is just past midterm, and she gets word from home that her father has had a massive heart attack. She leaves school and drives straight home, a sixteen-hour drive, and rushes to the hospital. Her father has never been seriously ill before; now he's in coronary intensive care. The shock and disbelief are nearly overwhelming during Pam's initial alarm-stage reaction.

In *resistance*, the second stage of the general adaptation syndrome, the cause of one's stress remains present, and Pam's body continues to fight off the challenge of the stressor. Pam's father begins to show some signs of recovery, but he will be in intensive care for another three days and will be hospitalized well beyond that. There's little Pam can do to help her father, but she feels she can't leave and go back to school right now. Every day she stays at home, she gets further behind in her classes.

Pam's bodily resources were mobilized in the alarm stage of the GAS. Now she has discovered that there is no means of escaping or lessening the source of her stress. The drain on her body's resources continues as she maintains a high level of arousal. If new stressors appear, Pam will be less able to deal with them effectively. More than that, she will be more sensitive to new stressors that she otherwise might have ignored. She will become vulnerable to physical illness and infection to a greater degree than she would without the constant stress she is experiencing. High blood pressure, ulcers, skin rashes, or respiratory difficulties may develop. Pam may appear to be in control, but the reality of her father's condition and the approach of her final exams continue to eat away at her, intruding into her awareness.

If Pam cannot find some useful way to deal with the stress she is experiencing, her physical reaction to the still-present stressors may be *exhaustion*. In this stage, her bodily resources become nearly depleted. She is running out of energy and out of time. Pam may break down—psychologically, physically, or both. Depression is a real possibility. Although the resistance stage may last for several months, eventually resources become expended. In extreme cases (e.g., if stressors remain or even worsen over the course of several months), the exhaustion stage of the general adaptation syndrome may result in death.

For Selye, stress is a three-stage mobilization of the body's resources to combat real or perceived threats to our well-being. In that sense the process is "adaptive"—at least through the stage of resistance. Unfortunately, we have a limited supply of adaptive resources. Repeated exposure to stressors has a cumulative effect. Dire consequences can result when someone is faced with several stressful situations at about the same time. Selye's model focuses on the physiological aspects of responding to stressors. It does not take into account just how a person can respond to stressors in more cognitive and behavioral ways. Let's first consider effective strategies for dealing with stress and stressors, and then look at some common ineffective strategies.

> **BEFORE YOU GO ON**
>
> - What is Selye's General Adaptation Syndrome?
>
> - What happens in each of the three stages of the General Adaptation Syndrome?

Effective Strategies for Coping with Stressors

In the long run, the most effective way to deal with stress is to make relatively permanent changes in our behaviors as a result of the experience of stress. Learning is defined as a relatively permanent change in behavior that occurs as the result of practice or experience. To respond to a stressor with learning makes particularly good sense for frustration-induced stress. In a frustrating situation, the pathway to our goal is being blocked. An adaptive way to handle such a stressor is to find a new way to reach our goal or to learn to modify our goal (see Figure 11.8).

In fact, much of our everyday learning is motivated by frustration-induced stress. You've had to learn many new responses as a means of coping with frustration. Having been frustrated once (or twice) by locking yourself out of your house or car, you learn to hide another set of keys in a location where you can easily find them. Having been caught at home in a blizzard with no cookies in the house, you have learned to bake them yourself. You may have learned as a child to get what you wanted from your parents by smiling sweetly and asking politely. In each of these cases, what prompted, or motivated, the learning of new responses or the establishment of new goals was the stress resulting from frustration.

Learning that is motivated by stress may also teach the value of escape and avoidance. You now know how to avoid getting into many motivational conflicts. You may have learned that a sensible thing to do once you are in a conflict is to escape or to make major changes in what is motivating you. This is one way in which stress can be seen as a positive force in our lives. If we were never challenged, if we never set difficult goals, if we never faced stressful situations, we would miss out on many opportunities for personal growth and learning. The stress we experience is unpleasant at the time, but it may produce positive consequences (Carver & Scheier, 1999; Cramer, 2000; Folkman & Moskowitz, 2000; Tedeschi, Park & Calhoun, 1998).

To say that we should respond to stressful situations by learning new, effective behaviors is sensible enough, but are there any specific measures we can take to help alleviate the unpleasantness of stress in our lives? Indeed, there are many specific steps we can take. Here we'll review eight such strategies.

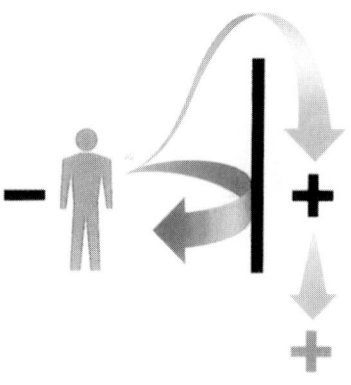

FIGURE 11.8

Reacting to frustration with learning is the most effective long-term reaction to stressors. That is, when one's goal-directed behaviors are continually blocked or thwarted, one should consider bringing about a relatively permanent change in those behaviors, or consider changing one's goals altogether.

Identify the Stressor

Remember that stress is a reaction to any one of several types of stressors. If you are experiencing stress in your life, the first thing you should ask is, "Where is it coming from?" Are you having difficulty resolving a motivational conflict? What positive or negative goals are involved? Is your goal-directed behavior being blocked? If so, what is the source of your frustration? What recent changes or events in your life are particularly upsetting or problematic? Any successful strategy for coping with stress will require change and effort on your part. The first thing to do is to make sure your efforts are well-directed.

Efforts for dealing with stress can be categorized as being either *emotion-focused* or *problem-focused* (Lazarus & Folkman, 1984). The difference is self-evident. Strategies that are emotion-focused deal with how you feel and with finding ways to feel differently. This is often the first reaction to stressors. "I feel miserable and stressed out; how can I feel better?" Real progress usually requires that you look beyond how you feel at the moment to discover the underlying situation causing your present feelings—a problem-focused strategy. "Where did this stress come from, and how can I make it go away?"

Remove or Negate the Stressor

Once a stressor has been identified, the next logical question is, "Can anything be done about it?" Do I have to stay in this situation, or can I bring about a change? If a particular interpersonal relationship has become a constant, nagging source of stress, might this be the time to think about breaking off the relationship? If the stress you experience at work has become overwhelming, might this be a good time to consider a different job? The issue is one of taking control, of trying to turn a challenge into an opportunity. Granted, all of this sounds very cut-and-dry, even easy. What makes the process difficult is that there usually is affect involved, often very strong emotional reactions. What we are describing here is largely a cognitive, "problem-solving" approach. If it is going to be at all successful, negative emotions are going to have to be set aside—at least for the time being. Perhaps you recall that a tendency to take control of potentially stressful situations is one of the characteristics of people with the so-called "hardy personality" who usually manage to avoid many of the negative consequences of stress. Even people with a terminal illness fare much better if they take control, find out everything there is to know about their illness, seek second and third opinions, and make the most of what time they have left (Folkman, 1984).

Reappraise the Situation

We should assess whether the stressors in our lives are real or (even partially) imagined threats to our well-being. Making this determination is part of what is called a cognitive reappraisal of one's situation (Schultz & Decker, 1985). In the context of stress management, cognitive reappraisal means rethinking a situation to put it in the best possible light.

Is that coworker really trying to do you out of a promotion? Do you really care if you are invited to the party? Must you earn an "A" on the next test in order to pass the course? Are things really as bad as they seem? Lazarus (1993, p. 9) sees this as realizing that "people should try to change the noxious things that can be changed, accept those that cannot, and have the wisdom to know the difference"—a paraphrase of an ancient Hebrew prayer.

Meichenbaum (1977) argues that we can deal with a lot of stress simply by talking to ourselves, replacing negative statements (such as, "Oh boy, I'm really in trouble now. I'm sure to be called on, and I'll embarrass myself in front of the whole class") with coping statements (such as, "I'll just do the best I can. I'm as prepared as anybody in here, and in a little while, this will all be over"). This cognitive approach does take a bit of practice, but it can be very effective.

Inoculate Against Future Stressors

Among other things, this strategy involves accepting and internalizing much of what we have been saying about the universality of stress and stressors. It's a matter of convincing yourself that stress has occurred before, will occur again, and that this, too, will pass. It's a matter of anticipation and preparation—truly coming to accept the reality that "worrying about this won't make it any better," or "no matter how bad things look, I'll be able to figure out some plan to deal with it." We know that surgery patients recover faster and with fewer postsurgical complications if they are fully informed before their surgery of what they can expect, how they are likely to feel, and what they can do to aid in their own recovery (MacDonald & Kuiper, 1983).

Inoculating yourself against future stressors amounts to trying to develop a sense of optimism in the belief that good things, as opposed to bad things, will generally happen to you. People with this sort of optimistic outlook "routinely maintain higher levels of subjective well-being during times of stress than do people who are less optimistic" (Scheier & Carver, 1993, p. 27). Optimism also predicts such things as better adjustment in one's first year away at college, less depression among mothers following childbirth, and rate of recovery from heart surgery (Aspinwall & Taylor, 1992; Carver & Gaines, 1987; Scheier & Carver, 1992, 1993; Scheier et al., 1989).

Take Your Time with Important Decisions

Stress often accompanies the process of making tough decisions. You're frustrated. A goal-directed behavior is being blocked. You have to decide if you will pursue a different course of action. Which course of action? Would it be wiser to change your goal? Do you want to do this (+ and -) or do you want to do that (+ and -)? We make matters worse by rushing a decision "just to have it over with." Occasionally we are faced with deadlines by which final decisions must be made. We often add to an already stressful situation by racing to conclusions before we have all of the facts, before we have explored all of the costs and benefits associated with the alternatives we are contemplating (Hogan, 1989).

For example, if you can't make up your mind about a new car you're thinking about buying, why not rent one for a few days to see if you'd be happy with it in the long run?

The strategies listed above make suggestions for dealing with the stressor that has caused stress in one's life. As noted above, being problem-focused, as these strategies are, is the only effective, long-term way to deal with stressors. In the short-term, there *are* some things you can do to combat the unpleasant feelings or effects that accompany stress (that is, emotion-focused strategies). We'll look at three.

Learn Techniques of Relaxation

Learning effective ways to relax may not be as easy as it sounds, but the logic is simple: feeling stressed and being relaxed are not compatible responses. If you can become relaxed, the experience (feelings) of stress will be diminished (Lehrer & Woolfolk, 1984). Hypnosis may help. Meditation may help. So may relaxation training.

A variety of operant conditioning called biofeedback can provide relief from the tension associated with stress (Kamiya et al., 1977; Shirley et al., 1992; Yates, 1980). Biofeedback is "the process of providing information to an individual about his [or her] bodily processes in some form which he [or she] might be able to use to modify those processes" (Hill, 1985, p. 201). One's heart rate, let us say, is constantly monitored, and the rate is fed back to the person, perhaps in the form of an audible tone. As heart rate increases, the pitch of the tone becomes higher. As heart rate decreases, the tone gets lower. Once the learner knows (through the feedback) what his or her heart rate (or blood pressure, or muscle tension, and so on) is doing, a certain degree of control over that response is possible. The reinforcement involved here is simply the newly gained knowledge that a desired change is being made. As a result of being reinforced, the stress-fighting responses increase in their frequency (Kaplan, 1991; Kimmel, 1974; Miller, 1978; Thackwray-Emerson, 1989).

Many believe that a good, physical exercise routine will help reduce the stress we experience each day.

Engage in Physical Exercise

There is a good deal of evidence that physical exercise is a useful agent in the battle against stress (Anshel, 1996; Brown, 1991; Crews & Landers, 1987; McCann & Holmes, 1984; Wheeler & Frank, 1988). Physical exercise is helpful once stress is experienced, but it is difficult to say if exercise combats stress directly or does so indirectly by improving physical health, stamina, self-esteem, and self-confidence. In that regard, exercise can be part of a program to inoculate against stress in the first place. And of course, one must be careful. Deciding that tomorrow you'll start running five miles a day, rain or shine, may be a decision that in itself will create more stress than it will reduce. Exercise should be enjoyable, not overly strenuous, and help you feel better about yourself.

Seek Social Support

Finally, there is the advantage of social support for persons who are experiencing stress. Stress is a common phenomenon. Perhaps no one else knows precisely how you feel, or has experienced exactly the same situation in which you find yourself, but all of us have known stress, and we are all aware of the types of situations that give rise to it. Social support from friends and relatives or from others, such as physicians, clergy, therapists, or counselors, can be very helpful (Adler & Matthews, 1994; Coyne & Downey, 1991; Gottlieb, 1981; Hobfall, 1986; Rook, 1987). If at all possible, one should not face stress alone.

Now that we've reviewed some of the steps one can take to help alleviate the unpleasantness of stress, let's consider some reactions stress can produce that are not as adaptive.

> ## BEFORE YOU GO ON
>
> - What are some adaptive ways of dealing with stress?

Ineffective Strategies for Coping with Stressors

Coping effectively with stress is a matter of bringing about change. If you do not change, you *fixate* and accept the same stress from the same stressor. Fixation is seldom an adequate reaction to stress. The adage, "If at first you don't succeed, try, try again" is sound advice. But, again, and again, and again? At some point, we must give up a particular course of action to try something else.

In a way, procrastination is a form of fixation, isn't it? Your term paper is due in two weeks and you can't seem to start, deciding to "put if off until this weekend." This weekend brings no progress either, and the stress of dealing with the paper is momentarily postponed. The catch is that you are going to pay a price. Eventually you have to do the paper. Then, with very little time before the deadline, you will probably experience stress more than ever before. One long-term study of procrastination in college students found that procrastinators experienced less stress and less illness early in the semester but as the semester progressed, they reported greater stress, more illness, and more serious illnesses. Moreover, procrastinators earned significantly lower grades. As the authors of this study put it, "Procrastination thus appears to be a self-defeating behavior pattern marked by short-term benefits and long-term costs" (Tice & Baumeister, 1997). In addition to not changing one's behavior or one's goals or simply not doing anything at all, there are two other reactions to stressors that are clearly maladaptive: aggression and anxiety.

There are many causes of aggression, and one source of aggressive behaviors is stress; in particular, the stress that results from frustration. A student, expecting a grade of "A" on a paper, receives a grade of "C-", returns to her room and throws her hairbrush at the mirror, shattering it. A driver in a hurry to get to campus rams the rear bumper of the car ahead, judging it to be going far too slowly. Remember Trudy, who was frustrated because she couldn't have a cookie and then tore the arm off her doll? At one time, it was proposed that frustration was the only cause of aggression, the so-called **frustration-aggression hypothesis** (Dollard et al., 1939). This point of view claimed that frustration

frustration-aggression hypothesis the view (now discredited) that all aggression stems from frustration

Aggression, even verbal aggression, often follows from frustration. It does nothing to remove the stressor, however, and is therefore an ineffective reaction to stress.

could produce a number of reactions, including aggression, but that aggression was always caused by frustration. We now recognize that there are other sources of aggression (some view it as innate or instinctive, whereas others see it as a response learned through reinforcement or modeling that need not be stimulated by frustration). It is true, however, that frustration remains a prime candidate as the cause of aggression. Although it usually doesn't do much good in the long run, a flash of aggressive behavior often follows stress (Berkowitz, 1978, 1982, 1989, 1990).

You are in the parking lot trying to get home from class, and your car won't start. Over and over you crank the ignition. Continuing to turn the key without success is a good example of fixation—it's not doing you any good, but you keep at it, perhaps until you run down the battery. Still frustrated, you swing open the door, get out, kick the front left fender, throw up the hood, and glower at the engine. You're mad! Having released a bit of tension, you might feel better for a few seconds, but being angry and kicking at the car, or yelling at someone who offers to assist, won't help you solve your problem.

anxiety a general feeling of tension, apprehension, and dread that involves predictable physiological changes

Another negative consequence of stress is **anxiety**—a general feeling of tension, apprehension, and dread that involves predictable physiological changes. Anxiety is a very difficult concept to define precisely, but everyone "knows" what you're talking about when you refer to anxiety. It is a reaction we have all experienced. Often, it is a reaction that accompanies stress. We can think of anxiety as an unpleasant emotional component of the stress response. As much as anything else, we want to rid ourselves of stress in order to minimize our anxiety.

Sometimes the amount of stress and anxiety in one's life becomes more than one can cope with effectively. Feelings of anxiety start to interfere with normal adaptations to the environment and to other people. Such feelings may become the focus of one's attention. More anxiety follows, and then more distress, and more discomfort, and more pain. For many people—tens of millions of people in the United States and Canada—the anxiety that results from stress is so discomforting and so maladaptive that we say they are suffering from a psychological disorder.

BEFORE YOU GO ON

- What are some maladaptive reactions to stressors?

Topic Review 11 A

1. What is the definition of stress?

Stress is defined as a complex set of reactions made by a person under pressure to adapt. Stress is a response that an individual makes to real or perceived threats to his or her well-being which give rise to physiological reactions and unpleasant feelings like distress and anxiety.

2. Under what conditions is stress aroused?

Feelings of stress are aroused when an individual is exposed to a stressor. There are three types of stressors: frustration, conflict, and life events. Although in some cases stress is aroused because of some major event (for example, the death of a loved one), it need not be. In some cases consistent but relatively minor events can arouse stress.

3. What is meant by frustration-induced stress?

Frustration, a stressor, is the blocking or thwarting of goal-directed behaviors. If someone or something in one's environment blocks goal-directed behaviors, environmental frustration is the result. There are many examples: your car won't start; your pen runs out of ink during an exam; your dog eats your term paper. If the source of the frustration is a personal characteristic we have personal frustration. Examples include someone not succeeding in a physics class due to an inadequate math background, or someone who agrees to go mountain climbing even though they are inexperienced and out of shape.

4. What are the four common types of motivational conflict?

Motivational conflicts are stressors. They are situations in which we find ourselves faced with difficult choices to make with regard to our motivated behaviors. In an approach-approach conflict, one is faced with two or more attractive (positive) goals and must choose between them. In an avoidance-avoidance conflict, a choice must be made between unpleasant (negative) alternatives. In an approach-avoidance conflict, there is one goal under consideration; in some ways that goal is positive, in others it is negative (it attracts and repels at the same time). In a multiple approach-avoidance conflict, one faces a number of alternatives, each of which has its strengths and its weaknesses, and a choice must be made between or among them.

5. In what ways might life events produce stress?

Many psychologists argue that life events, particularly changes in one's life situation, can act as stressors. The Social Readjustment Rating Scale (SRRS) is one example of an instrument that measures the amount of stress by having a person indicate recent life-change events. High scores on such scales are associated with an above-average incidence of physical illness. Some psychologists claim that the little hassles of life can be more stressful than large-scale life events. Life-change events do not have to be negative or unpleasant events to act as stressors.

6. How does socioeconomic status contribute to stress?

Socioeconomic status (SES) relates to stress in at least two ways. First, individuals in higher SES brackets are less likely than lower SES individuals to encounter negative life events that can arouse stress. Second, low SES individuals have fewer resources to deal with life events that arouse stress. Research indicates that being a working mother is more stressful than being a working father.

7. How do everyday life hassles contribute to stress?

Some psychologists suggest that rather than focusing on major life events that arouse stress, scientists should focus on everyday hassles (for example, traffic or dealing with a cranky child or spouse) as sources of stress. Measures of everyday hassles are better predictors of conditions such as depression than are measures of major life events.

8. What does it mean to say that there are individual differences in reactions to stressors?

People may respond differently to the same stressor. What some find merely challenging, others may find overwhelmingly stressful. Reaction to stressors varies over time: events that do not seem stressful today may be very stressful tomorrow. Some people are particularly resistant to stressors and have been called "hardy personalities." Such people tend to see difficulties as opportunities, have a sense of being in control of their lives, and are fully engaged in and committed to life.

9. What is Selye's General Adaptation Syndrome (GAS)?

According to Hans Selye, a prolonged stress reaction progresses through three stages, collectively referred to as the general adaptation syndrome. The three stages are: alarm, resistance, and exhaustion.

10. What happens during the alarm stage of the GAS?

During the alarm stage of the GAS there are rapid changes in the operation of the sympathetic nervous system which leads to increases in blood pressure, heart rate, and to pupillary dilation, cessation of digestion, and rerouting of blood to body extremities. Adrenaline is dumped into the blood stream, which gets the body ready for action. This stage does not last long, usually for a few hours at the most.

11. What happens during the resistance stage of the GAS?

If a stressor is persistent, the body enters the resistance stage of the GAS. The body continues to fight off the challenges of the stressors. Maintaining high levels of arousal drains the body's resources. If other stressors are encountered, a person is less able to deal with them. Some things that might ordinarily not bother a person become important sources of stress. This further depletes the body's resources.

12. What occurs in the exhaustion stage of the GAS?

If stress is not reduced in the resistance stage, exhaustion may occur. Bodily resources become nearly depleted and a person runs out of energy to cope with stressors. There may be a psychological and/or physical breakdown. Depression is a real possibility. In extreme cases, exhaustion can lead to death.

13. What are some adaptive ways of dealing with stress?

The most effective means of dealing with stress is to deal with the stressors that caused it by learning new behaviors that help one cope with those stressors. There are two approaches to dealing with stress. One is problem-focused and includes such things as identifying the specific stressor causing stress, removing or minimizing the stressor, reappraising the situation, inoculating against future stressors, and taking time in making difficult decisions. Battling the feelings associated with stress, called emotion-focused approaches, includes learning relaxation techniques, engaging in physical exercise, and seeking social support.

14. What are some maladaptive reactions to stressors?

Maladaptive reactions to stressors are those that interfere with attempts to change behaviors as a result of experiencing stress. Fixation describes a pattern of behaviors in which a person tries repeatedly to deal with stressors, is unsuccessful, but does not try anything new or different. Aggression often results from stress, particularly frustration. Although aggression may yield a momentary release of tension, it usually does not remove the original stressor. Anxiety is yet another maladaptive response to stress. This general feeling of apprehension and dread is often the aspect of experienced stress that motivates us to do something about it.

Topic 11B HEALTH PSYCHOLOGY

health psychology the field of applied psychology that studies psychological factors affecting physical health and illness

Health psychology became a division of the American Psychological Association in 1978 (Division 38), and now has more than 3,000 members—an increase of 200 percent over 1980 membership. **Health psychology** is the study of psychological or behavioral factors affecting physical health and illness. As applied psychologists, or practitioners, health psychologists help people cope with physical diseases and illnesses and are involved in efforts to try to prevent health problems from occurring in the first place. As researchers, health psychologists seek to better understand the relationships between psychological functioning and physical health.

The involvement of psychologists in the medical realm of physical health and well-being is based on four assumptions:

1.   Certain behaviors increase the risk of certain chronic diseases.

2.   Changes in behaviors can reduce the risk of certain diseases.

3.   Changing behaviors is often easier and safer than treating many diseases.

4.   Behavioral interventions are comparatively cost-effective (Kaplan, 1984).

In this Topic, we'll examine two major thrusts of health psychology. We'll look at the relationships between psychological variables and physical health. Then, we'll consider how psychologists are joining the fight against illness and disease.

Key Questions to Answer

While reading this Topic, find the answers to the following key questions:

1.   What physical diseases have been found to have a significant psychological component?

2.   What are the Type A and B behavior patterns?

3.   What is the relationship, if any, between the Type A behavior pattern and physical illness?

4.   What are the reasons people die?

5.   Why are psychologists so concerned about smoking behaviors?

6.   What are the defining characteristics of sexually transmitted diseases (STDs)?

7.   What are some of the most common STDs, and what are their causes?

8.   What is the scope of the AIDS problem?

9.   What are the causes of AIDS?

10.   What are the symptoms and the course of AIDS?

11.   What role can psychologists play in the fight against AIDS?

PSYCHOLOGICAL FACTORS THAT INFLUENCE PHYSICAL HEALTH

Is there a relationship between aspects of one's personality and one's state of physical health? Can psychological evaluations of an individual predict physical disease as well as psychological disorders? Is there such a thing as a disease-prone personality? "Why do some people get sick and some stay well?" (Adler & Matthews, 1994, p. 229). Our response is tentative, but we can say, "Yes, there is a positive correlation between some personality variables and physical health."

One meta-analysis of 101 published research articles looked for relationships between personality measures and disease (including coronary heart disease, asthma, ulcers, arthritis, and headaches). The strongest associations were those that predicted coronary heart disease (CHD), although depression, anxiety, and anger or hostility were each associated with all of the physical disorders studied (Friedman & Booth-Kewley, 1987). These researchers argued that there are sufficient data linking some personality variables to some physical diseases to "argue for a key role for psychological research on the prevention and treatment of disease" (p. 539). There are now adequate data to claim that psychological stress makes us more susceptible to the common cold, influenza, and other infectious diseases (Cohen, 1996; Cohen, Doyle et al., 1995; Cohen & Williamson, 1991). Recognizing that psychologists can help in the battle to prevent disease and to promote good health, the Centers for Disease Control and the American Psychological Association have begun discussions on how to best work together on these issues (Cavaliere, 1995; Roberts et al., 1997).

When we talk about relating personality to physical diseases, what often comes to mind is the **Type A behavior pattern (TABP)** and coronary heart disease. As it was *originally defined*, the Type A individual is a competitive, achievement-oriented, impatient person who typically works at many tasks at the same time, is easily aroused, and often hostile or angry (Friedman & Rosenman, 1959; Rosenman et al., 1964). Coronary heart disease is a label given to several physical symptoms, including chest pains and heart attacks, caused by a buildup of substances (for example, cholesterol) that block the supply of blood to the heart. People who show none of the characteristics of the TABP and who are relaxed and easygoing are said to have a *Type B behavior pattern.*

Type A behavior pattern (TABP) a collection of behaviors (in which one is competitive, achievement-oriented, impatient, easily aroused, and often hostile or angry) commonly associated with coronary heart disease

For nearly 20 years, from the early 1960s to the early 1980s, many studies found a clear, positive relationship between CHD and behaviors typical of the Type A personality (Jenkins, 1976; Rosenman et al., 1975; Wood, 1986). The National Institutes of Health declared the Type A behavior pattern to be an independent risk factor for heart disease (National Institutes of Health, 1981). The Type A personality pattern profile was implicated in *hypertension* (chronic high blood pressure) even when no other signs of coronary heart disease were present (Irvine et al., 1991). It all seemed clear. Find people with a Type A behavior pattern, intervene to change their behaviors, and watch coronary heart disease rates decline. By now you know that complex problems seldom have simple solutions.

Logan Wright (1988) claims that one important aspect, or "active ingredient," of the Type A behavior pattern is multiphasia—having several things going on all at the same time.

Data began to surface that failed to show a clear relation between TABP and CHD (Fishman, 1987; Hollis et al., 1990; Krantz & Glass, 1984; Matthews, 1982, 1988; Wright, 1988). Perhaps Type A people were no more at risk for heart disease than anyone else. Perhaps studies that failed to find a relation between TABP and CHD were flawed. Both of these hypotheses seem valid. For one thing, the Type A behavioral pattern is complex and difficult to assess. It is likely that simple paper-and-pencil inventories, which have been used in many studies, fail to identify a large number of people with the TABP.

It also may be that the TABP—as originally defined—is too global a pattern of behaviors (Adler & Matthews, 1994; Dembroski & Costa, 1987). Perhaps there is a set of behaviors within the general definition of Type A behaviors that *does* predict coronary heart disease. The best bet right now is that the "active ingredients" of TABP related to CHD are anger and hostility. Of particular interest is "cynical hostility," characterized as being suspicious, moody, distrusting, and quick to get upset and criticize others (Friedman et al., 1994; Houston & Vavak, 1991; Miller et al., 1996; Smith, 1992).

Much more work needs to be done. We need research on adequately diagnosing Type A behavior patterns and on the mechanisms that underlie whatever relationships there may be between TABP and CHD. We also need research on how to bring about psychological changes in Type A persons that would reduce the likelihood of their contracting physical disease (Winett, 1995). The ingredients of TABP appear to be precisely the characteristics many people in our society learn to value and to imitate in their quest to "get ahead." How can psychologists intervene to help people change those behaviors that directly and indirectly impact on their state of health? It is to matters of intervention that we now turn.

BEFORE YOU GO ON

- What diseases have been found to have a psychological component?

- What are the Type A and B behavior patterns?

- What is the relationship, if any, between the Type A behavior pattern and physical illness?

PROMOTING HEALTHY BEHAVIORS

At the very least, it is possible that some personality characteristics have an impact on physical health. The specific traits involved and the nature of that impact are the subject of debate and ongoing research. There is no debate, however, that certain behaviors put people at risk for physical disease and death. One role of the health psychologist is to help change potentially dangerous behaviors (Kirscht, 1983; Levine et al., 1993; Matarazzo, 1980; Miller, 1983).

Why Do People Die?

Obviously, people die for an almost infinite number of reasons. Ultimately, death is unavoidable. On the other hand, many deaths are premature and preventable.

Let's review a few gruesome statistics. The leading causes of death in this country are cardiovascular disorders and cancers, diseases caused by and maintained by the interaction of several factors—genetic, biological, social, environmental, and behavioral. Among the latter, such variables as cigarette smoking, nutrition, obesity, and stress have been identified as important risk factors. This means that millions of people engage in what may be referred to as a deadly lifestyle. Here are more numbers from a review article in the Journal of the American Medical Association.

In 1998, there were 2,337,256 deaths in the United States (Murphy, 2000). Of these, nearly half a million deaths could be traced to tobacco use; diet and activity patterns accounted for 300,000 deaths, firearms 30,000 deaths, sexual behaviors 30,000 deaths, motor vehicles 43,000 deaths, and illegal drug use 17,000 deaths.

In many of these cases, there was probably little or nothing that could have been done to prevent or delay death. However, in other cases, bringing about changes in behavior in a timely fashion might have reduced these numbers.

Notice that a deadly lifestyle may involve behaviors that directly lead to death; for instance, failing to wear safety belts or knowingly engaging in other unsafe behaviors at work or play. Nearly 50,000 children and teenagers were killed by firearms between 1979 and 1991—a number nearly equal to the American casualties in the Vietnam War. By early 1995, the leading cause of death among Americans ages 25 to 44 was AIDS.

Interventions designed to prevent health problems from arising in the first place have been applied to a wide range of behaviors and situations, including smoking and the misuse of alcohol. Programs have tried to change nutrition, physical fitness and exercise, controlling stress and high blood pressure, immunization, and unsafe sexual behaviors (Jeffery, 1989; Matthews, 1997; McGinnis, 1985; Rodin & Salovey, 1989; Winett et al., 1993). Psychologists also use behavioral techniques in attempts to promote healthy and safe behaviors, such as wearing car safety belts (Geller et al., 1987; Geller et al., 1990). Many psychologists argue that we should be doing all we can to help promote healthy environments (smoke-free spaces, safe work places, opportunities for exercise at work, the installation of air bags in cars) while working to change individual behaviors (Aldwin & Stokals, 1988; Fielding & Phenow, 1988; Geller et al., 1982; Stokals, 1992; Winett, 1995).

For the remainder of this topic, we will examine two areas in which psychologists have been particularly active: helping people to stop smoking, and helping people deal with or prevent sexually transmitted diseases.

Helping People to Stop Smoking

Although efforts to bring about behavioral change have moved forward on many fronts, few have received as much attention as those discouraging young people from smoking. One reason for the special efforts in this area is that smoking is so deadly, accounting for about one-third of all cancer deaths and nearly 430,000 of all deaths each year in the

There is now considerable evidence that many deaths in the United States could be postponed if people were to change their behaviors—that is, give up their "unhealthy lifestyles."

United States (Jeffery, 1989; American Heart Association, 2000) and about three million deaths worldwide (Peto et al., 1992). According to a 2000 estimate of the World Health Organization, smoking is the leading cause of premature death in the industrialized world, *killing 11,000 people every day*! Cigarettes are viewed as one of the most addictive substances and among the most deadly (Fiore et al., 1989; Schelling, 1992; American Cancer Society, 2000). Concern now includes the impact of "secondhand smoke," as we see evidence that the children of parents who smoke are at risk for lung cancer even if they, as adults, have never smoked. Secondhand smoke causes enough heart disease in nonsmokers to kill 62,000 Americans and bring on 200,000 nonfatal heart attacks (American Heart Association, 2000).

Of particular concern is the fact that an estimated 2.2 million American children ages 12 to 17 smoke cigarettes, and nine million children under age five live with smokers, according to American Heart Association. Each day an estimated 3,000 children begin smoking. In the summer of 1995, the Journal of the American Medical Association (July 19, 1995) published an editorial supported unanimously by its editorial board. In part the editorial said, "The evidence is unequivocal—the U.S. public has been duped by the tobacco industry. No right-thinking individual can ignore the evidence. We should all be outraged, and we should force the removal of this scourge from our nation."

Yet another reason for concern among health psychologists is that success rates of programs to persuade smokers to quit have not been encouraging. "Habitual heavy users of heroin and cocaine say it is easier to give up these drugs than to stop smoking" (Grinspoon, 1997). Only 5 percent of smokers manage to quit on their first try, and nearly 80 percent relapse within a year (Bartecchi, MacKenzie, & Schrier, 1995; Cohen et al., 1989; Glasgow & Lichtenstein, 1987; Orleans & Slade, 1993). A person who finally does give up smoking permanently has quit, on the average, five times before. Quitters who can cope with other stressors in their lives are significantly more likely to stay off cigarettes than are those who experience additional stress (Cohen & Lichtenstein, 1990). A good predictor of whether an attempt to stop smoking will be successful is the absence of negative affect—unpleasant feelings, including anxiety and depression (Brandon, 1994). Most smokers who quit permanently do so without any special program of intervention. And, in fact, the total number of adult smokers in the United States and Canada *is* decreasing, albeit at a rather slow rate. There is evidence that using a "nicotine patch" in conjunction with therapy can be effective (Cinciripini et al., 1996), and combining psychotherapeutic interventions with a prescription for antidepressant medications also seems promising.

Psychologists have had some success in designing programs aimed at getting people, teenagers in particular, to refrain from smoking in the first place. As more and more facilities declare themselves "smoke-free environments," the more difficult it is for people to begin or continue smoking. The use of role models and peers to teach specific skills to resist smoking has been successful when the focus is on short-term benefits derived from not smoking, such as freedom from coughing and bad breath and positive factors such as improved appearance. Increasing the taxes on, and hence the price of, a pack of cigarettes also provides a negative incentive. There may be promise in a campaign designed to convince youngsters that adults (i.e., the tobacco industry) are trying to trick young people

Antismoking ads, such as this one which provides information on how smoking is harmful to the fetus, are focusing on trying to keep pregnant women from smoking.

into smoking. The logic of this effort (created with input from teenagers) is that if young people come to believe that some adults actually *want* them to smoke, they won't!

BEFORE YOU GO ON

- What are some of the important causes of death?

- Why are psychologists so concerned about smoking behaviors?

Some hope came late in 1995 when researchers at the Columbia-Presbyterian Medical Center in New York reported that they found an area of the limbic system in the mid-brain that responds directly to nicotine (McGehee et al., 1995). It seems that nicotine speeds up and intensifies the flow of *glutamate*, a neurotransmitter in the brain. This, in turn, increases the rate of neural firing in the limbic area, which is experienced as an increase in pleasant mood and alertness. If a drug can be found to block this effect, much of the addictive nature of smoking might be negated.

Sexually Transmitted Diseases (STDs)

Sexually transmitted diseases (STDs) are contagious diseases usually passed on through sexual contact. Sexually transmitted diseases affect millions of individuals each year, and for every person we know of with an STD, there may be two to five others with the disease in an undiagnosed nonsymptomatic stage. We will begin with a description of the more common STDs and then consider psychological interventions aimed at controlling the spread of AIDS, the deadliest of the STDs.

sexually transmitted diseases (STDs) contagious diseases that are usually transmitted through sexual contact

Chlamydia is one of the most common STDs in North America. Chlamydia is caused by a bacterial infection. It is usually diagnosed in sexually active persons younger than 35. Its incidence is soaring; The Centers for Disease Control and Prevention states there are an estimated 3 million new cases of chlamydia every year. Symptoms include burning urination in both men and women. Men may experience a penile discharge; women may experience a disruption in their menstrual cycle. Left untreated in women, chlamydia can lead to pelvic inflammatory disease (PID), which can cause infertility (in about 100,000 women a year). When diagnosed, treatment with an antibiotic, usually erythromycin, is generally effective within one week.

chlamydia a common STD caused by a bacterial infection that can lead to PID and infertility in women if untreated

Gonorrhea is a disease of the young and sexually active. Of the nearly two million cases that will be diagnosed this year, most will be men between the ages of 20 and 24. It is a bacterial infection that affects the moist tissue areas around the genitals. The bacteria that produce the symptoms of gonorrhea can live for only a few seconds outside the human body, so there is little likelihood of contracting the disease from toilet seats, utensils, towels, or drinking fountains. One may be infected with the gonorrhea bacteria and not even know it. This is particularly true for women, most of whom remain relatively free of symptoms. When symptoms do develop, they are like those experienced with chlamydia: frequent, painful urination, vaginal discharges, and a reddening of the genital area. In men, there is a milky discharge from the penis and painful, frequent urination. Treatment for this STD—*penicillin* or *tetracycline*—is usually successful, although drug-resistant strains have been noted.

gonorrhea a STD caused by a bacterial infection of moist tissues in the genital area

Syphilis is caused by the bacterium *spirochete*. If left untreated, the disease may run its course through four known stages, from relatively simple and painless sores all the way to the infection of other, nonsexual organs, and it can lead to death. Not long ago it was believed that syphilis had become a disease of the past. Then, in the fall of 1990, the Centers for Disease Control (CDC) released figures indicating that since 1985, the number of syphilis cases had skyrocketed. Rates were up 60 percent (132 percent among the African American population) to levels not seen since 1949. Nearly 85,000 new cases can be expected this year. Treatment for syphilis is simple once a diagnosis has been confirmed. Penicillin (or tetracycline) is used, and the prognosis is related to length of infection. The sooner treatment begins, the better the prognosis.

syphilis a STD caused by a bacterial infection; the disease may pass through four stages, ultimately resulting in death

Genital herpes (herpes type II) is a skin disease that affects the genital area, producing small sores and blisters. It is not caused by bacteria, but by a virus that was virtually unknown until the mid-1960s. Now, genital herpes is one of the most common STDs. Some estimates place incidence rates as high as 40 million Americans, with 1 million new

genital herpes (herpes type II) the most common STD; a skin infection in the form of a rash or blisters in the genital area

cases each year. At the moment, herpes has no cure, although medication can reduce the occasionally painful symptoms. A person with genital herpes is most infectious when the sores and blisters are active and erupting. There may be periods during which the infected person remains symptom-free, only to have the reddening and sores recur. Levels of stress are related to the onset of herpes symptoms (VanderPlate et al., 1988). There are no life-threatening complications of the disease in males, but genital herpes in females increases the risk of contracting cervical cancer. Another complication arises when pregnant women contract genital herpes. The herpes virus can be passed along during childbirth, which can cause considerable damage, even death, to the newborn.

acquired immune deficiency syndrome (AIDS) a deadly disease caused by a virus (HIV) that destroys the body's natural immune system; can be transmitted by an interchange of blood or semen

No other STD has attracted as much public attention as **acquired immune deficiency syndrome,** or **AIDS**. AIDS was virtually unknown in the United States before 1981. Just 12 years later, over 250,000 cases and more than 160,000 deaths had been reported. AIDS has become the fifth most common killer of women. The United Nations HIV/AIDS office estimates that by mid-2000, AIDS has killed 19 million people worldwide and 34 million more are infected (U.N. AIDS, 2000).

AIDS is caused by the *human immunodeficiency virus*, or *HIV*. HIV almost always enters the body through sexual contact or by the use of contaminated needles in intravenous (IV) drug use. About one infant in three born to an HIV–positive mother will also be infected. Each year, about 2,000 babies are born HIV–positive. In infected persons, concentrations of the virus are highest in the blood, semen, and vaginal fluids. An infected person may experience few symptoms other than those usually associated with the common cold. Then, the person enters a carrier state. He or she may pass the virus on to others, yet remain symptom-free. What is not clear is just how many persons infected with HIV will develop AIDS, or how long the process takes. Of those with a diagnosis of AIDS (not just HIV–positive), virtually all will die within four years.

HIV directly attacks the body's immune system, which normally fights off infections. With a weakened or nonfunctioning immune system, someone with AIDS does not have the resources to defend against other infections that otherwise would not be life-threatening. In other words, patients do not die of AIDS directly, but from other diseases or opportunistic infections (for example, pneumonia or cancer) against which the body cannot defend.

Whereas other sexually transmitted diseases cause discomfort and pain, AIDS is fatal. There is no vaccine to prevent it. At the moment, there is no cure for AIDS, but researchers are beginning to be a bit more optimistic about the future. Some drugs (notably AZT combined with 3TC) seem able to at least increase the life span and the quality of life for many diagnosed with the HIV infection. The only reasonable way to avoid AIDS is through education, understanding the repercussion of sexual behavior, practicing safe sex, and encouraging abstinence. Practicing abstinence is the only way to fully avoid AIDS. We now turn to psychological interventions aimed at preventing the spread of AIDS.

Interventions to Decrease the Incidence of AIDS

"Behavior change remains the only means for primary prevention of HIV disease. Psychology should take a leading role in efforts to curtail the epidemic, but has not contributed to HIV prevention at a level proportionate to the urgency of the crisis" (Kelly et al., 1993, p. 1023). Attempts to prevent AIDS, or at the very least, to reduce its spread, have met with mixed results (Mann, Tarantola, & Netter, 1992). Successful interventions are multifaceted, involving education, the changing of attitudes, increasing motivation to engage in safe (or safer) sexual practices, and providing people with the negotiating skills to avoid high-risk situations (Brigham, 1991, p. 617). Successful interventions are those that attend to larger issues, such as the environment in which targeted behaviors occur, the culture in which the audience resides, and marketing strategies (Fisher & Fisher, 1992; Sheeran, Abraham, & Orbell, 1999; Winett, 1995).

By and large, most Americans are aware of AIDS, have a reasonable idea of what causes the disease, and are aware of what can be done to avoid it (Levine et al., 1993; Sheridan et al., 1990). We are now learning that the logic that claims, "Give people the facts about AIDS and they'll change their risky behaviors" may be flawed. "Unfortunately, the evidence that sex education leads to changes in behaviors intended to prevent AIDS or pregnancy is disappointing" (Helweg-Larsen & Collins, 1997). In one study, IV drug users were either given AIDS education, AIDS education with HIV testing, or were placed in a control group. Four months later, researchers could not detect any differences among the groups in either their knowledge about AIDS (very good in all cases) or the frequency of their risky behaviors (Calsyn, et al., 1992).

On the assumption that many adolescents and adults will not abstain from sex, many experts counsel "safe sex," but there is disagreement on just what safe sex is. In general, the advice seems reasonable. The fewer sexual contacts one has, the less the probability of encountering someone infected with HIV. The more selective one is in choosing a partner, the less risk. The use of condoms reduces (but does not eliminate) the likelihood of infection. Engaging in sexual behaviors in which there is no exchange of bodily fluids (such as mutual masturbation) also contributes to lower-risk sex (Masters et al., 1987). Consistent to our point above, even with considerable knowledge about AIDS, few people, teenagers in particular, seem willing to change their sexual practices (Helweg-Larsen & Collins, 1997; Klepinger et al., 1993). Many teenagers believe that they simply will not get AIDS, and most do not use condoms (Hansen et al., 1990).

Some programs that go beyond providing information and actively seek to change behaviors have been effective—particularly those aimed at small groups identified as members of "high-risk" populations, such as gay men and IV drug users (DeJarlais & Friedman, 1988; Kelly et al., 1993; Stall et al., 1988). What works best are long-term, small-group sessions that present information and provide social support for changing high-risk behaviors (Kelly et al., 1989; Sorensen et al., 1991). Although short-term gains (in changing attitudes and behaviors) have been noted, maintaining those gains for the long term has proven more difficult (Kelly et al., 1991). The "enormous challenge posed by HIV infection suggests that multiple approaches will be necessary to have the largest and most lasting effects" (Levine et al., 1993, p. 549).

AIDS is a physical disease, but it is a disease with unprecedented psychological complications. Patients diagnosed with HIV but who have not yet developed AIDS tend to be more depressed and disturbed than those who have developed the full-blown and fatal symptoms of the disease (Chuang et al., 1989). As you might expect, people with a diagnosis of AIDS experience significant levels of stress, depression, anger, anxiety, and denial (Herek & Glunt, 1988; Kelly & St. Lawrence, 1988; Namir et al., 1987). Males with AIDS are almost 7.5 times more likely to commit suicide than are men in the general population (Coté et al., 1992). Because AIDS can be such a devastating disease, AIDS patients are often shunned by loved ones and even by health care professionals. In 1987, the American Medical Association issued a statement that it is unethical for a physician to refuse treatment to an AIDS patient. In 1994, the U.S. Public Health Service published a 196-page "clinical practice guideline" on how to diagnose and manage patients in the early stages of HIV infection. The Health Service's concern was that too many primary care, general practice physicians were unnecessarily referring suspected HIV patients to "specialists." The fear, alienation, and stress experienced by AIDS patients (and their friends and families) are in many ways as painful as the disease itself and often require psychological treatment (Knapp & VandeCreek, 1989).

BEFORE YOU GO ON

- What is the definition of an STD?

- What are some of the most common STDs?

- What are the causes, symptoms, and course of AIDS?

- What role can psychologists play in the fight against AIDS?

Topic Review 11 B

1. What physical diseases have been found to have a significant psychological component?

Although many diseases may include a psychological component (for example, asthma, ulcers), coronary heart disease has the strongest association with psychological factors. Psychological stress also makes one more susceptible to the common cold, flu, and other infectious diseases.

2. What is the relationship, if any, between the Type A behavior pattern and physical illness?

There is a relationship between some personality variables and physical health; that is, some psychological traits put a person at risk for disease. Beginning in the 1950s, evidence accumulated showing a strong positive relationship between a Type A behavior pattern, or TABP (a person who is competitive, achievement-oriented, impatient, easily aroused, often angry or hostile, and who tends to have many projects going at once) and coronary heart disease (blockage of major arteries). The picture, it now seems, is a little less clear as psychologists seek to identify the "active ingredients" of the TABP. Some claim that time urgency, chronic activation, and multiphasia are the main culprits, whereas others have focused on the influence of anger and hostility as best correlated with physical health.

3. What are the reasons people die?

Some causes of death are unavoidable. However, others are avoidable. The leading causes of death in the United States are cardiovascular disease and cancers, which are related to the interaction of genetic, biological, social, environmental, and behavioral factors (for example, cigarette smoking, nutrition, obesity, and stress). Tobacco and alcohol use account for a high number of deaths. Other factors relating to death are exposure to bacteria and viruses, toxic agents, firearms, sexual behavior, illegal drugs, and motor vehicles. By 1995, the leading cause of death among twenty-five to forty-four year-olds was AIDS.

4. Why are psychologists so concerned about smoking behaviors?

Of the leading causes of death in this country, most could be reduced by behavioral change. Smoking is a central part of what has been called a "deadly lifestyle." Smoking accounts for more than 400,000 deaths each year in the United States. Health psychologists continue to look for effective means of helping people to stop smoking. By and large, efforts have not met with much success. Most smokers who do quit on a permanent basis do so on their own. But overall, the number of adult smokers is decreasing. Current efforts focus on attempts to get children and teens to avoid smoking in the first place.

5. What are the defining characteristics of sexually transmitted diseases (STDs)?

A sexually transmitted disease is passed from one person to another through sexual contact. STDs affect millions of people each year. For every one case that is known, there are perhaps two to five others that are not known.

6. What are some of the most common STDs?

Sexually transmitted diseases (STDs) are common. Among them are: (1) Chlamydia, a bacterial infection of the genitals that results in painful urination and fluid discharge. Left untreated in women, it may lead to pelvic inflammatory disease (PID) and infertility. (2) Gonorrhea, a bacterial infection of the moist tissues around the genitals, is passed on only by sexual contact. If left untreated, its symptoms increase in severity. Penicillin is an effective treatment. (3) Syphilis, a bacterial infection, may progress through four stages as symptoms increase in severity. Left untreated, it may result in death. Again, penicillin is an effective treatment. (4) Genital herpes, a viral infection that affects tissue around the genitals, is a very common STD and has no known cure. (5) Acquired immune deficiency syndrome (AIDS) is a viral (HIV) infection transmitted through the exchange of bodily fluids, usually semen or blood. Once infected, a person may stay symptom-free (but capable of infecting others) in a "carrier state" until full-blown AIDS appears. Virtually all persons with AIDS die within four years.

7. **What are the causes of AIDS?**

    AIDS is caused by the HIV (human immunodeficiency virus) which almost always enters the body through sexual contact or through the use of contaminated needles. About one in three infants born to an HIV-positive mother will contract the disease, resulting in about 2,000 HIV-infected babies every year. Concentrations of HIV are highest in the blood, semen, and vaginal fluid.

8. **What are the symptoms and the course of AIDS?**

    A person infected with HIV may experience few symptoms beyond those of the common cold. At this point the person is a carrier of the virus and can pass the virus to others while remaining symptom-free. Eventually, HIV attacks the body's immune system making the body susceptible to a wide range of diseases. Ordinary diseases become life-threatening. Whereas other STDs may cause pain and discomfort, AIDS is fatal. There is no cure or vaccine at the present time. There are drugs, however, that can control the symptoms of AIDS and prolong life.

9. **What role can psychologists play in the fight against AIDS?**

    There is no vaccine or treatment for AIDS. For this very reason, health psychologists have been involved in helping people change their risky sexual behaviors or their IV drug use. Awareness of AIDS and understanding of the disease have increased markedly, but many people at risk—largely sexually active, heterosexual adolescents—have made few changes in their sexual practices. Some groups at risk—largely gay men and IV drug users—have made changes. Psychologists are also involved in helping AIDS sufferers (and their friends and families) deal with the emotionally charged nature of the disease.

Chapter 12

The Psychological Disorders

M any people in our society could profit from an "attitude adjustment" regarding psychological disorders. "Mental illness" is something that most folks simply do not want to talk about. Many would rather not even think about the commonality of psychological disorders. Few of us like hearing that in a given year about 30 percent of the adult population will experience a diagnosable mental illness (Howard et al., 1996). We do not like to hear, as the surgeon general reported in January of 2001, that one in ten children suffers from mental illness severe enough to impair development.

People who will share the gory details of their abdominal surgery at the dinner table may hesitate to mention their concern that the stress in their lives is growing to unbearable levels. Few of us who saw it will ever forget the image of then President Lyndon Johnson at his Texas ranch hoisting his pajama top to show the television audience the lengthy scar he had earned from his gall bladder surgery. Yet when it became public knowledge that Thomas Eagleton had been in counseling for depression and that perhaps he had an electroconvulsive shock treatment, his candidacy for the vice presidency was doomed.

Psychological disorders *are* common. Some are very dramatic; a few may be devastating. But most are not beyond the experience of any of us. And most can be treated successfully, even cured, if we talk openly about our psychological problems and seek help for them. This chapter provides an overview, a sketch of the basic psychological disorders. As students of psychology, perhaps you can join us in helping to change attitudes about mental illness. The first step is to understand what psychological disorders are.

**Topic 12A
Anxiety,
Somatoform,
Dissociative,
and
Personality
Disorders**

**Topic 12B
Alzheimer's
Dementia,
Mood
Disorders, and
Schizophrenia**

Topic 12A ANXIETY, SOMATOFORM, DISSOCIATIVE, AND PERSONALITY DISORDERS

In this Topic, we will introduce you to some of the "less severe" psychological disorders. We characterize these as less severe because they rarely require hospitalization or involve symptoms typical of more serious psychotic disorders such as schizophrenia.

Key Questions to Answer

While reading this Topic, find the answers to the following key questions:

1. How do we define abnormality in psychology?

2. What is the *DSM-IV-TR*?

3. What are some of the advantages and disadvantages of classifying psychological disorders?

4. What is the difference between psychological disorders, insanity, and competence?

5. Describe the symptoms of generalized anxiety disorder.

6. What are the major symptoms of panic disorder?

7. What characterizes a phobic disorder?

8. Name two main categories of phobias and give examples.

9. What are obsessions and compulsions?

10. What characterizes the obsessive-compulsive disorder?

11. What are the symptoms of posttraumatic stress disorder?

12. What, generally, is a somatoform disorder?

13. What are the symptoms of hypochondriasis?

14. What are the symptoms of conversion disorder?

15. What are the defining symptoms of dissociative disorders?

16. What are the defining characteristics of personality disorders?

17. What are the three clusters of personality disorders?

WHAT IS "ABNORMAL"?

abnormal referring to maladaptive cognitions, affects, and/or behaviors that are at odds with social expectations and result in distress and discomfort

We all have a basic idea of what is meant by such terms as *abnormal*, *mental illness*, or *psychological disorder*. The more we think about abnormality, however, the more difficult it becomes to define. The concept of abnormal as it is used in psychology is not a simple one. We'll use this definition: **Abnormal** refers to maladaptive cognitions, affects, and/or behaviors that are at odds with social expectations and result in distress or discomfort. That is lengthy, but to be complete, our definition must include each of these aspects.

Literally, abnormal means "not of the norm" or "not average." Therefore, those behaviors or mental processes that are rare could be considered abnormal; in a literal sense, of course, they are. The problem with this statistical approach is that it would categorize the behaviors of Michael Jordan, Steven Spielberg, Dave Letterman, and Maya Angelou as abnormal. Statistically, they *are* abnormal. There are very few others who do what these people do, but, as far as we know, none of them has a psychological disorder. Psychological disorders are not determined by statistical averages alone.

The reactions of people with psychological disorders are *maladaptive*. This is a critical part of our definition. Thoughts, feelings, and behaviors are such that the person does not function as well as he or she could without the disorder. To be different, or to be strange, does not in itself mean that someone has a psychological disorder. There must be some impairment, some self-defeating interference with one's growth and functioning (Durand & Barlow, 2000, p.3).

Another observation reflected in our definition is that abnormality may show itself in a number of ways. A person with a psychological disorder may experience abnormal *affect*, engage in abnormal *behaviors*, have abnormal *cognitions*, or any combination of these. Recall our ABCs mnemonic.

Any definition of psychological abnormality should acknowledge social and/or cultural expectations. What may be clearly abnormal and disordered in one culture may be viewed as quite normal or commonplace in another. In some cultures, loud crying and wailing at the funeral of a total stranger is considered strange or deviant; in others, it is common and expected. In some cultures, to claim you have been communicating with dead ancestors would be taken as a sign of mental disturbance; in others, it would be treated as a great gift. "Mexican Americans in the Los Angeles area tend to view people

What is considered abnormal or deviant in one culture may be viewed as quite normal and acceptable in another. One simple example is how people of various cultures dress.

with symptoms of schizophrenia as vulnerable and ill, but they explain those symptoms as resulting from 'nerves' and from being 'sensitive' and assume that recovery is possible. In contrast, Anglo Americans in the same area are more likely to categorize the same people as 'crazy,' with little or no hope of recovery" (NAMHC, 1996). Even in your own culture, behaviors that are appropriate, or at least tolerated, in one situation, say a party, may be judged as inappropriate in another context, say, a religious service.

One additional issue needs to be addressed: psychological disorders involve distress or discomfort. People we consider abnormal are suffering or are the source of suffering in others. Psychological disorders cause emotional distress, and individuals with such disorders are often the source of distress and discomfort to others—friends and family who care and worry about them. Complex as it is, we hope you can see that there is a reason for each point in our definition of abnormal: behaviors or mental processes that are maladaptive, at odds with social expectations, and resulting in distress or discomfort.

BEFORE YOU GO ON

- How do we define abnormality in psychology?

- What are the ways in which abnormality can be expressed?

- What roles do social and cultural factors play in defining abnormality?

Classifying Abnormal Reactions—The DSM

diagnosis the act of recognizing a disorder on the basis of a specified set of symptoms

One way of dealing with the broad concept of psychological abnormality is to consider each psychological disorder separately in terms of how that disorder is diagnosed. **Diagnosis** is the act of recognizing a disorder on the basis of specified symptoms. Once individual disorders are identified, it is helpful to organize them in a systematic way.

Systems of classification are common in science and are not new to psychology. In 1883, Emil Kraepelin published the first classification scheme for what he called "mental disturbances." His system was based on the idea that each disorder had its own collection of symptoms (a syndrome) and its own biological cause.

In 1952, the American Psychiatric Association published its system for classifying psychological disorders, the *Diagnostic and Statistical Manual of Mental Disorders*, which became known as the *DSM*. Reflecting significant changes with each edition, the fourth edition, the *DSM-IV* was published in 1994, and was revised once again, with the *DSM-IV-TR* (where TR stands for "text revision") published in the summer of 2000 (American Psychiatric Association, 2000). For simplicity sake, we will continue to use the abbreviation *DSM-IV* to refer to this most recent classification system.

The *DSM-IV* is the system of classification most widely used in all mental health fields. We've used the *DSM-IV* as a major source of information for this chapter. The *DSM-IV* lists 297 different diagnostic categories, compared to 265 in the *DSM-III*, 182 in the *DSM-II*, and only 106 in the original *Diagnostic and Statistical Manual* (Clark et al., 1995).

etiology referring to the source or cause of a disorder

The *DSM-IV* is more than just an organized list of disorders in terms of symptoms. Except for cases for which there are known biological factors, the manual attempts to avoid any reference to the **etiology**, or causes, of disorders. It is meant to be objective, based on research evidence, described as completely as possible, and theorized as little as possible. Bringing that research evidence up-to-date was the major reason behind the *DSM-IV-TR*. The *DSM-IV* also contains more material and reference to ethnic and cultural issues than did its predecessors, thanks largely to a three-year effort of the "Group on Culture and Diagnosis," sponsored by the National Institute of Mental Health (DeAngelis, 1994).

There are several advantages of having a classification system for psychological disorders. The major advantage, of course, is communication. People cannot hold a reasonable conversation about a patient's problem if they disagree on the basic definition of the diagnoses appropriate for that patient. If everyone agrees on the *DSM-IV's* definition, then at least they are using the same terminology in the same way. At the same time, however, classification can cause difficulties.

Problems with Classification and Labeling

Assigning labels to people may be useful for purposes of communication, but it can also be dehumanizing. It may be difficult to remember that Sally is a complex and complicated human being with a range of feelings, thoughts, and behaviors, not just a "paranoid schizophrenic." In response to this concern, the *DSM-IV* refers only to disordered behaviors and to patterns of behaviors, not to disordered people. That is, it refers to paranoid reactions, not to individuals who are paranoid; to persons with anxiety, not anxious persons.

A second problem inherent in classification and labeling is falling into the habit of believing that labels *explain* behavior. Diagnosing and labeling a pattern of behaviors does not explain those behaviors. It does not tell us why such a pattern of behaviors developed or what we can or should do about them now. Labels can create unfortunate and lasting stigmas of negative attitudes about people. Learning that someone is "psychologically disordered" or is "mentally ill" may cause a wide range of negative reactions, and the label often sticks long after the disorder has been treated and the symptoms are gone.

Another potential problem is **comorbidity**—the occurrence of two or more disorders in the same individual (Clark et al., 1995). Comorbidity has been described as "the premier challenge facing mental health professionals in the 1990s" (Kendall & Clarkin, 1992, p. 833). The 1994 National Comorbidity Survey found that psychological disorders were much more common than previously believed. This study suggested that of the people who experience a disorder in their lifetime, most (79 percent) will have two or more disorders (Kessler et al., 1994). The problem is particularly acute in high-risk samples. A study of incest victims showed an average of nearly two different diagnoses per person (Pribor & Dinwiddie, 1992). A study of combat veterans found an average of 3.1 disorders per person in their sample (Mellman et al., 1992), and an average of four disorders per person was found in a study of suicidal patients (Rudd et al., 1993).

comorbidity the occurrence of two or more disorders within the same individual

A Word On "Insanity"

In common practice, the terms *psychological disorder*, *mental disorder*, and *behavior disorder* are often used interchangeably. There is one term, however, with which we need to exercise particular care, and that is *insanity*. Insanity is not a psychological term. It is a legal term. It relates to problems with psychological functioning, but in a restricted sense. Definitions of **insanity** vary from state to state, but to be judged insane usually requires evidence that a person did not know or fully understand the consequences of his or her actions at a given time, could not discern the difference between right and wrong, and was unable to exercise control over his or her actions at the time a crime was committed. Curiously, the American public has long over estimated the use of an insanity defense in courts of law. The public's perception is that some sort of "insanity plea" is "used too much"—in about 37 percent of all felony cases. In fact, it is used in fewer than 1 percent of all felony cases, and is used successfully in only 26 percent of those cases (Pasework & Seidenzahl, 1979; Silver, Cirincione, & Steadman, 1994; Hans, 1986).

insanity a legal term related to whether one can understand the consequences of his or her actions

A related issue, known as *competence*, has to do with a person's mental state at the time of trial. The central issues are whether a person is in enough control of his or her mental and intellectual functions to understand courtroom procedures and aid in his or her own defense. If not, a person may be ruled "not competent" to stand trial for his or her actions, whatever those actions may have been. Most likely, a person who is judged incompetent will be placed into a mental institution until he or she becomes competent to stand trial.

A Few Cautions

For the remainder of this chapter, we will consider a variety of psychological disorders. As we do so, there are several important points you need to keep in mind.

1. *"Abnormal" and "normal" are not two distinct categories.* They may be thought of as end points on some dimension we can use to describe people, but there is a large gray area between the two in which distinctions get fuzzy. In actual practice, many psychologists/therapists would agree that making an accurate diagnosis is occasionally as much a matter of "art" as "science" (Liebert, 2000).

2. *Abnormal does not mean dangerous.* True, some people diagnosed as having mental disorders may cause harm to themselves or to others, but most people with psychological disorders are not dangerous at all. Even among persons who have been in jail for violent crimes, those with psychological disorders have no more subsequent arrests than do persons without disorders (Teplin et al., 1994). One large-scale, well-controlled study looked at the violent behaviors of approximately 1,700 patients with psychological disorders one year after they were released from treatment (Steadman, et al., 1998). Only two groups of former patients were more likely to engage in violent behaviors than were non-patients: those with personality disorders and those who had a drug-related problem in addition to their psychological disorder. Interestingly, when former patients *were* violent, more than 90 percent of the time their aggression was directed toward friends or family members. All other former patients (the majority) were not more likely to be violent. As David Holmes (2001, p. 546) puts it, "...we do

not see headlines such as 'PERSON WITH NO HISTORY OF MENTAL ILLNESS COMMITS MURDER,' although, in fact, that situation is more prevalent."

3. *Abnormal does not mean bad.* People diagnosed with psychological disorders are not "bad" people, or weak people, in any evaluative sense. They may have done bad things, and bad things may have happened to them, but it is certainly not in the tradition of psychology to make moral judgments about good and bad.

4. Most of our depictions of psychological disorders will be made in terms of extreme and obvious cases. Psychological disorders, like physical disorders, may occur in mild or moderate forms. We know that no two people are exactly alike and that there are individual differences in psychological functioning. Therefore, no two people, even with the same diagnosis of a psychological disorder, will be exactly alike in all regards.

BEFORE YOU GO ON

- What is the *DSM-IV?*

- What are some of the advantages and disadvantages of classifying psychological disorders?

- What is the difference between psychological disorders, insanity, and competence?

ANXIETY DISORDERS

We define **anxiety** as a feeling of general apprehension or dread accompanied by predictable physiological changes: increased muscle tension; shallow, rapid breathing; cessation of digestion; increased perspiration; and drying of the mouth. Thus, anxiety involves two levels of reaction: subjective feelings (e.g., fear or dread) and physiological responses (e.g., rapid breathing). The major symptom of *anxiety disorders* is felt anxiety, often coupled with "avoidance behavior," or attempts to resist or avoid any situation that seems to produce anxiety.

anxiety a feeling of general apprehension or dread often accompanied by physiological changes

Anxiety disorders are the most common of all the psychological disorders. The National Comorbidity Survey claims that 17 percent of the people in its study had some sort of anxiety disorder in the year before the survey was taken, and 25 percent had an anxiety disorder at some point in their lives. Anxiety disorders are two to three times more likely to be diagnosed in women than in men (Kessler et al., 1994; Roth & Argyle, 1988). Percentages of this sort do not convey the enormity of the problem. We're talking about millions of real people here—people like you and me. In this section, we will consider five anxiety disorders: generalized anxiety disorder, panic disorder, phobic disorder, obsessive-compulsive disorder, and posttraumatic stress disorder.

Generalized Anxiety Disorder (GAD)

The major symptom of **generalized anxiety disorder (GAD)** is distressing, felt anxiety. With this disorder we find unrealistic, excessive, persistent worry. People with generalized anxiety disorder report that the anxiety they experience causes substantial interference with their lives and that they need a significant dosage of medications to control their symptoms (Wittchen et al., 1994). The *DSM-IV* adds the criterion that people with this disorder find it difficult to control worry or anxiety.

generalized anxiety disorder (GAD) an anxiety disorder characterized by high levels of chronic anxiety with unrealistic, persistent worry

The experienced anxiety of this disorder may be very intense, but it is also diffuse, meaning that it is not brought on by anything specific in the person's environment; it just seems to come and go (or come and stay) without reason or warning. People with GAD are usually in a state of uneasiness and seldom have any clear insight or ideas about what is causing their anxiety. The self-reports of persons with GAD show that their major concerns are an inability to relax, tenseness, difficulty concentrating, feeling frightened, and being afraid of losing control (Beck & Emery, 1985). Clearly, this is a distressing and disruptive disorder that brings with it considerable pain. Although people with this disorder can often continue to function in social situations and on the job, they may be particularly prone to drug and alcohol abuse—the comorbidity problem alluded to earlier (Brown & Barlow, 1992; Wittchen et al., 1994).

Panic Disorder

panic disorder an anxiety disorder characterized by acute, recurrent, unpredictable attacks of anxiety

In the generalized anxiety disorder, the experience of felt anxiety may be characterized as *chronic*, implying that the anxiety is always present, albeit sometimes more so than at other times. For a person suffering from **panic disorder**, the major symptom is more *acute*—a recurrent, unpredictable, unprovoked onset of sudden, intense anxiety, or a "panic attack." These attacks may last for a few seconds or for hours. Attacks are associated with all sorts of physical symptoms—a pounding heart, labored breathing, sweating, trembling, chest pains, nausea, dizziness, numbness and trembling in the hands and feet. There is no one particular stimulus to bring it on. The panic attack is unexpected. It just happens. The *DSM-IV* points out that panic attacks do occur in conjunction with other disorders—not just panic disorder. With panic disorder, however, there is a recurrent pattern of attacks and a building worry about future attacks.

At some time in their lives, between 1.5 and 3.5 percent of the population will experience panic disorder. (That doesn't sound very significant until we realize that that's four to nine million people!) Interestingly, a study of panic disorder in ten countries around the world found that all had about the same rate of occurrence (in the U.S., Canada, Puerto Rico, France, Germany, Italy, Lebanon, Korea, and New Zealand) except for Taiwan which, for some unknown reason, had a rate of occurrence significantly less than half that of the other countries (Weissman et al., 1997).

BEFORE YOU GO ON

- Describe the symptoms of generalized anxiety disorder.

- What are the major symptoms of panic disorder?

The age of onset for panic disorder is usually between adolescence and the mid-20s (Hayward et al., 1992). Initial panic attacks are often associated with stress, particularly from the loss of an important relationship (Ballenger, 1989). A complication of panic disorder is that it can be accompanied by feelings of depression—another example of comorbidity (Kessler et al., 1998). This may be why the rate of suicide and suicide attempts is so high for persons with a diagnosis of panic disorder (20 percent), which is higher than that for persons diagnosed with depression alone (15 percent) (Johnson et al., 1990; Weissman et al., 1989).

Phobic Disorders

The essential feature of **phobic disorders** (or phobias) is a persistent and excessive fear of some object, activity, or situation that consistently leads a person to avoid that object, activity, or situation. Implied in this definition is the notion that the fear is intense enough to be disruptive. Also implied is the fact that there is no real or significant threat involved in the stimulus that gives rise to a phobia; that is, the fear is unreasonable, exaggerated, or inappropriate.

Many things are life-threatening or downright frightening. For example, if you drive your car down a steep hill and suddenly realize the brakes are not working, you feel an intense reaction of fear. Such a reaction is not phobic, because it is not *irrational*. Similarly, few of us enjoy the company of bees. That we don't like bees and would prefer they not be around does not mean we have a phobic disorder. Key to a diagnosis is intensity of response. People who have a phobic reaction to bees (called *mellissaphobia*) may refuse to leave the house in the summer for fear of encountering a bee and may become genuinely anxious at the buzzing sound of any insect, fearing it to be a bee. They may become uncomfortable reading a paragraph, such as this one, about bees.

There are many phobias. The two main categories of phobic disorder are *specific phobias* and *social phobias*. **Specific phobias** involve the fear of (a) animals; (b) the physical environment (storms, heights, water, etc.); (c) blood, injection, or injury; or (d) a specific situation (tunnels, elevators, airplanes, etc.). **Social phobias** are significant and persistent fears of social or performance situations in which embarrassment may occur. Fears of public speaking or of being in large crowds qualify as social phobias. In one study, 10 percent of the respondents reported that public speaking anxiety had markedly interfered with their work, social life, or education, or had caused them marked distress (Stein, Walker, & Forde, 1996).

Within any one year, as many as 30 percent of the population experiences some type of phobic disorder (Magee et al., 1996). In some cases, a person with a phobia can avoid the source of fear and, as a result, not seek treatment. The **prognosis** (the prediction of the future course of a disorder) is good for phobic disorders. That is, therapy for persons with a phobia is likely to be successful, however, only a small minority of those with phobic fears ever seek professional help (Magee et al., 1996).

A commonly treated phobic disorder is **agoraphobia**, which literally means "fear of open places." It is an exaggerated fear of venturing forth into the world alone. People with this disorder avoid crowds, streets, and stores. They establish a safe base for themselves and may, in extreme cases, refuse to leave. Agoraphobia is often an associated complication of panic disorder (comorbidity again). This is not unreasonable, is it? For example, a person with agoraphobia experiences several panic attacks, brought on by no particular stimulus, and then finds it more and more difficult to venture out in the world for fear of having yet another panic attack.

phobic disorders anxiety disorders characterized by persistent, excessive fear of some object, activity, or situation that leads to avoidance

specific phobias phobias concerning specific objects or events, such as animals, heights, blood, or airplanes

social phobias phobias concerning social or performance situations, such as being in large crowds or speaking in public

prognosis the prediction of the future course of a disease or disorder

agoraphobia an exaggerated fear of venturing into the world alone

BEFORE YOU GO ON

- What is a phobia?
- What characterizes a phobic disorder?
- What are the two categories of phobias?

Riding a ferris wheel would be out of the question for someone suffering from acrophobia, the fear of high places.

Obsessive-Compulsive Disorder (OCD)

obsessive-compulsive disorder (OCD) an anxiety disorder characterized by a pattern of recurrent obsessions and compulsions

obsessions ideas or thoughts that constantly intrude into awareness

compulsions constantly intruding, repetitive, unwanted behaviors

The **obsessive-compulsive disorder (OCD)** is an anxiety disorder characterized by a pattern of recurrent obsessions and compulsions. **Obsessions** are ideas or thoughts that involuntarily and constantly intrude into awareness. Generally speaking, obsessions are pointless, or groundless thoughts, most commonly about cleanliness or violence, disease, danger, or doubt (Grinspoon, 1995). Many of us have experienced mild, obsessive-like thoughts, for example, worrying if you really did turn off the stove during the first few days of a vacation. To qualify as part of OCD, obsessions must be disruptive; they must interfere with normal functioning. They are also time-consuming and are the source of anxiety and distress.

Compulsions are constantly intruding, repetitive behaviors. The most commonly reported compulsions are hand washing, grooming, and counting or checking behaviors, such as checking repeatedly that the door is really locked (Leckman et al., 1997; Swedo et al., 1989a). Have you ever checked an answer sheet to see that you've really answered all of the questions and then checked it again, and again, and again? To do so is compulsive. It serves no real purpose, and it provides no real sense of satisfaction, although it is done very conscientiously in an attempt to reduce anxiety or stress. People with OCD recognize that their behaviors serve no useful purpose; they know that they are unreasonable but cannot stop them. It is as if such a person engages in these compulsive behaviors to prevent some other (even more anxiety-producing) behaviors from taking place.

In many cases, an obsession or compulsion can exert an enormous influence on a person's life. For example, consider the case of a happily married accountant, the father of three. For reasons he cannot explain, he becomes obsessed with the fear of contracting AIDS. There is no reason for him to be concerned; his sexual activities are entirely monogamous; he has never used drugs; he has never had a blood transfusion. Still, he is overwhelmed with the idea that he will contract this deadly disease. Ritualized, compulsive behaviors are associated with his obsessive thoughts: he washes his hands vigorously at every opportunity and becomes anxious if he cannot change his clothes at least three times a day (all in an effort to avoid contact with the dreaded AIDS virus).

Notice that we are using *compulsive* in an altogether different way when we refer to someone being a compulsive gambler, a compulsive eater, or a compulsive practical joker. What's different about the use of the term in such cases is that although the person engages in habitual patterns of behavior, he or she gains pleasure from doing so. The compulsive gambler enjoys gambling; the compulsive eater loves to eat. Such people may not enjoy the long-term consequences of their actions, but they feel little discomfort about the behaviors themselves.

Obsessive-compulsive disorder is much more common than once believed. It afflicts nearly one of every 200 teenagers (OCD is commonly diagnosed in childhood or adolescence), and as many as five million Americans (Rapoport, 1991). It is a disorder with a high rate of comorbidity, often found in conjunction with another disorder (Galbaud du Fort et al., 1993).

It seems that obsessive-compulsive disorder has a biological basis. The most likely candidate for the source of the problem is the pathway that communicates between the frontal lobes and the basal ganglia. The neurotransmitter *serotonin* is also directly implicated (Hollander et al., 1992; Wynchank & Berk, 1998). Support for the biological basis of OCD comes from the observation that drug treatment (using antidepressant medications) is often successful in eliminating many of the symptoms of OCD. Unfortunately, the prognosis for OCD is generally not very good. One study found that even after as many as seven years of treatment, only 6 percent of patients with obsessive-compulsive disorder could be considered totally symptom-free, and 43 percent still met the diagnostic criteria for the disorder (Leonard et al., 1993).

Posttraumatic Stress Disorder (PTSD)

An anxiety disorder that has been the subject of much public discussion over the past decade is **posttraumatic stress disorder (PTSD).** This disorder involves distressing symptoms that arise some time after the experience of a highly traumatic event, where trauma is defined by the *DSM-IV* as an event that meets two criteria: (1) the person has experienced, witnessed, or been confronted with an event that involves actual or threatened death or serious injury, and (2) the person's response involves intense fear, helplessness, or horror.

There are three clusters of symptoms that further define PTSD: (1) re-experiencing the traumatic event (e.g., flashbacks or nightmares), (2) avoidance of any possible

posttraumatic stress disorder (PTSD) an anxiety disorder involving distressing symptoms that arise some time after the experience of a traumatic event

Posttraumatic stress disorder (PTSD) can be expected in some survivors of trauma or catastrophe.

reminders of the event (including people who were there), and (3) increased arousal or "hyperalertness" (e.g., irritability, insomnia, difficulty concentrating).

The traumatic events that trigger this disorder are many, ranging from natural disasters (e.g., floods or hurricanes), to life-threatening situations (e.g., kidnapping, rape, assault, or combat), to the loss of property (e.g., the house burns down; the car is stolen). Nearly 1.7 million veterans—nearly half of all who served in Southeast Asia—have suffered from PTSD at some time since discharge from military service (True et al., 1993).

Posttraumatic stress disorder was not recognized as a distinct diagnostic category of anxiety disorder until 1980. Estimates of the lifetime prevalence of PTSD range from about 2 percent of the population (Robb-Nicholson, 1995) to about 8 percent (Kessler et al., 1995). Nearly 20 percent of women exposed to trauma will experience the symptoms of posttraumatic stress disorder, compared to 8 percent of men (Kessler et al.). Within two weeks, 94 percent of rape victims and 76 percent of female victims of physical assault evidence the symptoms of PTSD (Foa & Riggs, 1995).

We often find comorbidity with PTSD. It is commonly associated with alcohol and substance abuse or depression. In fact, the prognosis for posttraumatic stress disorder is related to the extent to which there *are* comorbid disorders (e.g., alcoholism) attending it, the extent to which the patient experienced psychological problems before the traumatic event, and the extent to which social support is available. There are also data to suggest that higher levels of cognitive ability "protect" against the disorder. This study found that intelligence (measured by a simple IQ test) is a good predictor of which veterans with combat experience are likely to experience PTSD (McNally & Shin, 1995).

BEFORE YOU GO ON

- What characterizes the obsessive-compulsive disorder?

- What are obsessions and compulsions?

- What characterizes the posttraumatic stress disorder?

- What are the symptoms of posttraumatic stress disorder?

SOMATOFORM DISORDERS

Soma means "body." Hence, the **somatoform disorders** in some way involve physical, bodily symptoms or complaints. They are *psychological* disorders in that there is no known medical or biological cause for the symptoms. We'll consider three: two common, *hypochondriasis* and *somatization disorder*; the other rare but very dramatic, *conversion disorder*.

somatoform disorders disorders that involve some physical, bodily complaint

Hypochondriasis and Somatization Disorder

Hypochondriasis is the diagnosis for someone preoccupied with the fear of a serious disease. Persons with this disorder are unusually aware of every ache and pain. They often read popular magazines devoted to health issues, and feel free to diagnose their own ailments. In reality, they have no medical disorder or disease. Even so, they constantly seek medical attention and are not convinced of their good health despite the best medical opinions. A man with occasional chest pains, for example, diagnoses his condition as lung cancer. Even after many physicians reassure him that his lungs are perfectly fine and that he has no signs of lung cancer, the man's fears are not put to rest. "They are just trying to make me feel better by not telling me, but they know, as I do, that I have lung cancer and am going to die soon."

hypochondriasis a somatoform disorder in which one is preoccupied with a fear of a serious disease

It's not difficult to imagine why someone develops hypochondriasis. If a person believes he or she (hypochondriasis is found equally in men and women) has contracted some serious disease, three problems might be solved. (1) The person now has a way to explain otherwise unexplainable anxiety: "Well, my goodness, if you had lung cancer, you'd be anxious, too." (2) The illness may be used to excuse the individual from activities that he or she finds anxiety-producing: "As sick as I am, you don't expect me to go to work, do you?" (3) The illness may be used to gain attention or sympathy: "Don't you feel sorry for me knowing that I have such a terrible disease?"

It is often difficult for mental health professionals to distinguish hypochondriasis from **somatization disorder**, which is indicated by several, recurring, and long-lasting complaints about bodily symptoms for which no physical cause can be found. The subtle difference is that persons with somatization disorder focus primarily on their nonexistent "symptoms," while persons with hypochondriasis focus on some nonexistent "disease"

somatization disorder a somatoform disorder characterized by several, recurrent, long-lasting complaints about physical symptoms for which there is no physical cause.

indicated by their symptoms. Unfortunately, the prognosis for somatization disorder is poor. It is most often a lifelong disorder that truly burdens the health care system (Bell, 1994).

Conversion Disorder

conversion disorder a somatoform disorder involving a loss or altering of physical functioning with no underlying medical cause

Conversion disorder is rare (accounting for fewer than 5 percent of all anxiety disorders). The *DSM-IV* tells us that it is more common in rural areas or in underdeveloped countries. Indeed, in some cultures, some of the symptoms of the disorder are considered quite normal. The symptoms of **conversion disorder** are striking. There is a loss or altering of physical function that suggests a physical disorder. The symptoms are not intentionally produced and cannot be explained by any physical disorder. The "loss of functioning" is typically of great significance; paralysis, blindness, and deafness are classic examples. As difficult as it may be to believe, the symptoms are real in the sense that the person cannot feel, see, or hear.

Again, there is no medical explanation for the symptoms. In some cases, medical explanations run contrary to the symptoms. One type of conversion disorder is *glove anesthesia*, a condition in which the hands lose feeling and become paralyzed from the wrist down. As it happens, it is physically impossible to have such a paralysis and loss of feeling in the hands alone. There would have to be some paralysis in the forearm, upper arm, and shoulder because paralysis must follow neural pathways.

One remarkable symptom of this disorder (which occurs only in some patients) is known as *la belle indifference*—a seemingly inappropriate lack of concern over one's condition. Some persons with this disorder seem to feel comfortable with and accepting of their infirmity. They are blind, deaf, or paralyzed and show very little concern over their condition.

BEFORE YOU GO ON

- What, generally, is a somatoform disorder?
- What are the symptoms of hypochondriasis and somatization disorder?
- Describe the symptoms of conversion disorder.

Conversion disorder holds an important position in psychology's history. This disorder most intrigued Sigmund Freud and ultimately led him to develop a new method of therapy. The disorder was known to the Greeks who named it hysteria, a label still occasionally used, as in "hysterical blindness." They believed the disorder was found only in women and was a disorder of the uterus, or *hysterium*, hence the name *hysteria*. The ancient logic was that the disease would leave the uterus, float through the body, and settle in the eyes, hands, or whatever part of the body was affected. Of course, this idea is no longer considered valid, although the potential sexual basis for the disorder was one of the aspects that caught Freud's attention.

DISSOCIATIVE DISORDERS

dissociative disorders disorders in which a person seeks to escape from some aspect of life or personality that is seen as a source of stress

To *dissociate* means to become separate from or to escape. The underlying theme of the **dissociative disorders** is that a person seeks to escape from some aspect of life or personality seen as the source of stress, discomfort, or anxiety. These disorders can be dramatic and are often the subject of novels, movies, and television shows.

Dissociative Amnesia

Dissociative amnesia is the inability to recall important personal information—an inability too extensive to be explained by ordinary forgetfulness. Before the *DSM-IV*, this disorder was called psychogenic amnesia, where psychogenic means "psychological in origin," and amnesia refers to a loss of memory. What is forgotten is usually some traumatic incident and some or all of the experiences that led up to or followed the incident. As you may suspect, there is no medical explanation for the loss of memory. The extent of forgetting associated with dissociative amnesia varies greatly. In some cases, a person may "lose" entire days and weeks at a time; in other cases, only specific details cannot be recalled. Not surprisingly, cases of this disorder tend to be more common in wartime, when traumatic experiences occur.

dissociative amnesia the inability to recall important personal information for no apparent reason

Dissociative Fugue

Occasionally, amnesic forgetfulness is accompanied by a change of location—seemingly pointless travel. For example, a person finds himself in a strange and different place with no reasonable explanation for how he got there. This is a disorder known as **dissociative fugue**. A typical example is that of Carol who was found wandering around the business district of a large eastern city, inappropriately dressed for the cold winds and low temperatures. Her behaviors seemed aimless, and she was stopped by a police officer who asked if he could be of assistance. It became apparent that Carol did not know where she was, so the officer took her to a nearby hospital. It was discovered that she had no memory of where she had been or what she had been doing for the last two weeks. She had no idea how she had gotten to the city, which was 350 miles from home.

dissociative fugue amnesic forgetfulness accompanied by a change in location

Both dissociative amnesia and fugue disorder are, in their own ways, like the somatoform disorders in that they involve escape from stressful situations. In conversion disorders, for example, a person may escape from stress by taking on the symptoms of a major physical disorder. With amnesia and fugue, escape is more literal. People escape by forgetting, or they avoid stress by psychologically or physically running away.

Dissociative Identity Disorder

This disorder is still commonly known as *multiple personality disorder*, as it was called until the publication of the *DSM-IV*. It is important to note that it is a dissociative disorder and not schizophrenia. We say that because the media quite consistently give the impression that these are one and the same. They are not. Schizophrenia is a different disorder, which we'll discuss shortly.

The major symptom of **dissociative identity disorder** is the existence within the same person of two or more distinct personalities or personality traits. The disorder has been very rare, although for unknown reasons its incidence is increasing markedly. From the 1920s to 1970, only a handful of cases were reported worldwide; since the 1970s, the number of cases reported has "increased astronomically" with thousands reported each year (Carson & Butcher, 1992; Ross, 1997; Spanos, 1994).

dissociative identity disorder the existence within the same person of two or more distinct personalities or personality traits

Dissociative identity disorder used to be called "multiple personality." It is a disorder characterized by evidence of two or more distinct personalities within the same person.

The very idea of two or more personalities inhabiting the same person is difficult to imagine. Perhaps it would help to contrast this disorder with a pattern of behavior typical of all of us. We all change our behaviors, and in a small way, our personalities change every day, depending on the situation. We do not act, think, or feel exactly the same way at school as we do at work, at a party, or at a house of worship. We modify our behaviors to fit the circumstances. But these changes do not qualify as an identity disorder. What's the difference?

The differences are significant. Someone with a dissociative identity disorder has changes in personality that are dramatic and extreme. They do not slightly alter their behavior; they have two or more distinct personalities, implying a change in underlying consciousness, not just a change in behaviors. Another difference is that when we change our behaviors, we do so in response to situational cues. This is not the case for a person with dissociative identity disorder whose changes in personality can take place without warning or provocation. The third major difference involves control. When we change our behaviors, we do so intentionally. Persons with a multiple personality disorder can seldom control or predict which of their personalities are dominant at any one time. Persons diagnosed with dissociative identity disorder have often been the victim of child abuse or sexual abuse (Putnam et al., 1986; Ross, 1997). The significantly higher incidence of multiple personality disorder in women than in men is partially understood when we consider that girls and women are much more likely to be sexually or physically abused than are boys and men (Ross, 1997). Females also tend to have a greater number of separate identities, averaging 15 or more, to the male average of eight identities. One intriguing finding, however, should make us pause: The marked increase in reported cases of dissociative identity disorder that we noted above has been largely restricted to North America. It is a diagnosis hardly ever made in France, and it is very rare in Great Britain, Russia, and India. One study in 1990 failed to find even one case of the disorder in Japan (Spanos, 1994; Takahashi, 1990).

BEFORE YOU GO ON

- What are the defining symptoms of the dissociative disorders?

- What is dissociative amnesia?

- What is dissociative fugue?

- What is dissociative identity disorder?

PERSONALITY DISORDERS

The psychological disorders we have reviewed so far are those that seem to afflict people who at one time were normal and undisturbed. In most cases, the person did not always exhibit the symptoms of the disorder. This is not the case with the personality disorders. **Personality disorders** are long-lasting patterns of perceiving, relating to, and thinking about the environment and oneself that are maladaptive and inflexible and cause either impaired functioning or distress. As we have seen, individual personality is defined by attitudes, behaviors, and traits that persist in many situations over long periods of time. With a personality disorder the traits and habits that constitute one's personality are inflexible and damaging (Grinspoon, 1996). The problems associated with personality disorders are usually identifiable by the time an individual is an adolescent, but a diagnosis of a personality disorder is not appropriate for anyone younger than 18.

personality disorders long-lasting patterns of perceiving, relating to, and thinking about the environment and oneself that are maladaptive and inflexible

The *DSM-IV* lists 11 personality disorders (PDs), grouped together in three clusters. Cluster 1 includes disorders in which the person can be characterized as odd or eccentric. People with disorders from this cluster are often difficult to get along with. Cluster 2 includes disorders in which the person seems overly dramatic, emotional, or erratic, and where behaviors are impulsive. Cluster 3 includes disorders that add anxiety or fearfulness to the standard criteria for personality disorder. Note that it is only for those personality disorders in Cluster 3 that we find any reports of fear, anxiety, or depression.

Rather than deal with all of the personality disorders in detail, we'll simply describe some of the major characteristics of disorders within each of the three main clusters. Then, we'll look at one PD—antisocial personality disorder—in a bit more detail. Keep in mind as we do so that to be a personality disorder, the symptoms must be relatively long-standing, generally beginning in childhood or adolescence.

Cluster I: Disorders of Odd or Eccentric Reactions

Paranoid personality disorder: an extreme sensitivity, suspiciousness, envy, and mistrust of others; the actions of other people are interpreted as deliberately demeaning or threatening. The attitude of suspicion is not justified. A person with this disorder shows a restricted range of emotional reactivity, is humorless, and rarely seeks help. Example: A person who continuously, and without justification, accuses a spouse of infidelity and believes that every wrong number was really a call from the spouse's lover.

Schizoid personality disorder: an inability to form, and an indifference to, interpersonal relationships. A person with schizoid personality disorder seems "cold and aloof," and often engages in excessive daydreaming. Example: A person who lives, as she has for years, in a one-room flat in a poor part of town, venturing out only to pick up a social security check and a few necessities at the corner store.

Cluster II: Disorders of Dramatic, Emotional, or Erratic Reactions

Histrionic personality disorder: overly dramatic, reactive, and intensely expressed behaviors. A person with this disorder is emotionally lively, draws attention to himself or herself, and overreacts to matters of little consequence. Example: A woman who spends an inordinate amount of time on her appearance, calls everyone "Darling!," constantly asks for feedback about her looks, describes most of her experiences as "wonderful!" and "vastly outstanding!" even when such an experience is no more than finding a detergent on sale at the grocery store.

Narcissistic personality disorder: a grandiose exaggeration of self-importance, a need for attention or admiration, and a tendency to set unrealistic goals. Someone with this personality disorder maintains few lasting relationships and in many ways engages in a "childish" level of behavior. Example: A person who always wants to be the topic of conversation and shows a lack of interest in saying anything positive about anyone else. Someone who believes that no one else has ever taken a vacation as stupendous as his or hers, or understood an issue as clearly as he or she, and who will do whatever it takes to be complimented.

Cluster III: Disorders Involving Anxiety and Fearfulness

Avoidant personality disorder: an over-sensitivity to the possibility of being rejected by others and an unwillingness to enter into relationships for fear of being rejected. A person with this disorder is devastated by disapproval, but holds out a desire for social relationships. Example: A man with few close friends who almost never dates, and only talks to women who are older and less attractive than he. He has worked for years at the same job, never seeking a job change or promotion, rarely speaks in public, and may attend meetings and public gatherings but without actively participating.

Dependent personality disorder: allowing and seeking others to dominate and assume responsibility for one's actions; a poor self-image and lack of confidence. A person with this disorder sees himself or herself as stupid and helpless, thus deferring to others. Example: A woman whose husband commonly abuses her. Although she has from time to time reported the abuse, she refuses to take an active role in finding help or treatment, saying it is "her place" to do as he says, and that if she does not please him, it is her fault.

Because personality disorders are difficult to diagnose accurately, estimates of their prevalence tend to be inexact. Most cases of personality disorder first come to the attention of mental health professionals on referral from the courts (or family members), or because of related problems such as child abuse or alcoholism. What we do find is that "while the overall rate of PD may be between 10 percent and 20 percent, the rates of specific disorders are very low" (Weissman, 1993; Zimmerman & Coryell, 1989). About one-fourth of those with symptoms of a personality disorder fit more than one diagnostic category—another example of comorbidity (Zimmerman & Coryell, 1989). Several studies reveal that "relatively few people meet the criteria for a given personality disorder without also meeting criteria for one or more other *DSM* diagnoses" (Clark et al., 1995).

The prognosis for the personality disorders is poor. The maladaptive patterns of behavior that characterize personality disorders have usually taken a lifetime to develop. Changing them is very difficult (Kazdin & Mazurick, 1994).

As we have noted before and will see again, no one of these hypotheses adequately explains why a particular individual will develop a personality disorder. The key, no doubt, is the interaction of two or more of these factors in the life of the individual.

An Example: The Antisocial Personality Disorder

The **antisocial personality disorder** is characterized by an exceptional lack of regard for the rights and property of others. Someone with this disorder often engages in impulsive behaviors with little or no regard for the consequences of those behaviors. One of the things that makes this diagnosis difficult is that, by definition, the symptoms of the disorder include deceit and the manipulation of others. "Lacking in conscience and in feelings for others, they cold-bloodedly take what they want and do as they please, violating social norms and expectations without the slightest guilt or regret" (Hare, 1995, p. 4). Many still refer to people with antisocial PD with the outdated terms "psychopath" or "sociopath." The disorder is included, with the histrionic and the narcissistic personality disorders, in Cluster II in *DSM-IV*.

antisocial personality disorder an exceptional lack of regard for the rights and property of others accompanied by impulsive, often criminal, behaviors

Remember, as is the case for all PDs, the antisocial personality disorder is not an appropriate diagnosis for anyone younger than 18 years old. Still, there is usually a history of "getting into trouble" long before the diagnosis is made. Persons with antisocial personality disorder are impulsive. They change jobs, residences, and relationships frequently. At best, they are irresponsible. At worst, their behaviors are criminal. A person who has committed a crime does not necessarily have antisocial personality disorder. Many criminals, in fact, show genuine sadness and remorse over the crime they have committed. If nothing else, they show remorse for the fact that they were caught and punished. Persons with antisocial personality disorder are likely to be indifferent about their actions, their victims, or even their apprehension. "Well, that's the way it goes." "He shouldn't have been carrying that much money with him." "A few more months in jail won't bother me much." Fifteen to 20 percent of the American prison population is composed of persons with antisocial PD.

The antisocial personality disorder is much more likely to be found among those who are of low socioeconomic status, live in an urban setting, and have a history of antisocial behaviors beginning before age 10. It is also much more likely to be diagnosed in males than in females. Estimates put the disorder at about 3 percent of the population for males and about 1 percent of the population for females. Like many of the other personality disorders, antisocial personality disorder is resistant to treatment. The main problem is that most psychotherapy is designed for people who recognize they have a problem and want to change. Persons with antisocial personality disorder usually enter treatment programs because they have been court-ordered to do so (Hare, 1995). Court-ordered therapy programs are ineffective for the 25 to 35 percent of spouse abusers who are diagnosed with antisocial PD. Interestingly, persons with antisocial personality disorder do not benefit from punishment; it seems to have no effect (Holmes, 2001, p. 352).

Unlike the other personality disorders, there is evidence of a "burnout factor" for antisocial personality disorder (Weiss, 1973). That is, some persons with the disorder have a spontaneous remission of symptoms in their early 40s. In one study, for example, prisoners with antisocial personality disorder were most likely to be in prison when they were between the ages of 31 and 35 (90 percent of the sample), and much less likely to be in prison when they were between the ages of 41 and 45 (less than 60 percent of the sample) (Hare et al., 1988).

BEFORE YOU GO ON

- What are the defining characteristics of the personality disorders?

- What are the three categories or clusters of personality disorders?

- Describe the antisocial personality disorder.

Topic Review 12A

1. **How do we define psychological abnormality in psychology?**

   Within the context of psychological disorders, "abnormal" refers to maladaptive behaviors, cognitions, and/or affect that are at odds with social expectations and that result in distress or discomfort.

2. **What is the *DSM-IV*?**

   The *DSM-IV* is the fourth edition of the *Diagnostic and Statistical Manual of the American Psychological Association*. It is the most widely used classification system for psychological disorders. In addition to classifying disorders, the *DSM-IV* spells out criteria for diagnosing disorders and suggests possible causes.

3. **What are some of the advantages and disadvantages of classifying psychological disorders?**

   The major advantage of classifying psychological disorders is that it provides one standard label and cluster of symptoms for each disorder that all mental health practitioners can use; as such, it is a basis for improved communication. It does have its limitations, however. Many persons have more than one disorder at a time, a phenomenon called comorbidity. Schemes of classification can confuse description with explanation; classifying and labeling persons as having psychological disorders may overlook the larger group or society of which that individual is a part.

4. **What is the difference between psychological disorders, insanity, and competence?**

   Psychological disorder, mental disorder, and behavior disorder are all psychological concepts used to label abnormal mental and behavioral conditions. Insanity is a legal term. It relates to psychological problems but refers to a defendant's state of mind at the time of a crime. The question of insanity centers on whether a person knew or fully understood the consequences of his or her actions, knew the difference between right and wrong, and could exercise control over his or her actions at the time of a crime. Competence refers to a defendant's ability at the time of trial to understand legal proceedings and assist in his or her defense.

5. **What are the symptoms of generalized anxiety disorder?**

   The defining characteristic of generalized anxiety disorder is a high level of anxiety that cannot be attributed to any particular source. The anxiety is chronic, persistent, and diffuse.

6. **What are the major symptoms of panic disorder?**

   The defining symptom of a panic disorder is a sudden, often unpredictable, attack of intense anxiety, called a panic attack, which may last for seconds or for hours. There is no particular stimulus that prompts the attack. It has a high rate of comorbidity and is often coupled with depression.

7. **What characterizes a phobic disorder?**

   By definition, a phobic disorder is typified by an intense, persistent fear of some object, activity, or situation that is in no real sense a threat to the individual's well-being; in brief, an intense, irrational fear. Phobias imply attempts to avoid the phobic object. Most phobias have a reasonably good prognosis.

8. **What are the two main categories of phobias? (Give examples.)**

   The two categories of phobias are specific phobias and social phobias. Examples of specific phobias are phobias of animals, the physical environment (storms, height), blood, injection or injury, or specific situations (tunnels, elevators). Social phobias include fear of social performance, public speaking, and being in large crowds.

9. **What are obsessions and compulsions?**

   Obsessions are thoughts or ideas that involuntarily and constantly intrude into awareness. They tend to be pointless or groundless thoughts commonly about cleanliness, violence, disease, danger or doubt. Compulsions are constantly intruding repetitive behaviors. The most common compulsions are hand washing, grooming, and counting or checking behavior.

10. **What characterizes the obsessive-compulsive disorder?**

Obsessions and compulsions are the main symptoms in the obsessive-compulsive disorder, or OCD. OCD is a relatively common disorder with a biological basis.

11. **What are the symptoms of posttraumatic stress disorder?**

Posttraumatic stress disorder, or PTSD, is an anxiety disorder in which the symptoms of high levels of anxiety, recurrent and disruptive dreams, and recollections of a highly traumatic event (e.g., rape, combat, or natural disaster) occur well after the danger of the event has passed. We often find that persons with PTSD also have alcohol or drug abuse problems or suffer from depression.

12. **What, generally, is a somatoform disorder?**

A somatoform disorder involves some physical, bodily symptom or complaint for which there is no known medical or biological cause.

13. **What are the symptoms of hypochondriasis?**

In hypochondriasis, a person lives in fear and dread of contracting a serious illness or disease when there is no medical evidence for such fears.

14. **What are the symptoms of conversion disorder?**

In conversion disorder, there is an actual loss or alteration in physical functioning— often dramatic, such as blindness or deafness—not under voluntary control, suggesting a physical disorder but without medical basis.

15. **What are the defining symptoms of the dissociative disorders?**

Dissociative disorders are marked by a retreat or escape from (dissociation with) some aspect of one's personality. It may be an inability to recall some life event (amnesia), sometimes accompanied by unexplained travel to a different location (fugue state). In rare cases, aspects of one's personality become so separated that the person suffers from dissociative identity disorder, where two or more personalities are found in the same individual.

16. **What are the defining characteristics of the personality disorders?**

Personality disorders (PDs) are enduring patterns of perceiving, relating to, and thinking about the environment and oneself that are inflexible and maladaptive. They are lifelong patterns of maladjustment and may be classified as belonging to one of three groups, or clusters.

17. **What are the three clusters of personality disorder?**

Cluster 1 includes those PDs involving odd or eccentric reactions, such as the paranoid and schizoid personality disorders. Cluster 2 includes disorders of dramatic, emotional, or erratic reactions, such as the narcissistic and histrionic personality disorders. Cluster 3 includes disorders involving fear and anxiety, such as the avoidant and dependent personality disorders.

Topic 12B ALZHEIMER'S DEMENTIA, MOOD DISORDERS, AND SCHIZOPHRENIA

In this Topic, we continue our discussion of individual psychological disorders. It may be inappropriate, even unfair, to classify some disorders as being more severe or debilitating than others. To the person who is experiencing a disorder, and to those who care about that person, any disorder can seem severe and debilitating. It is nonetheless the case that the disorders in this Topic tend to be more disruptive and discomforting than those we've covered so far. Most of the disorders we'll look at now cause great difficulties in meeting the demands of everyday life and a loss of contact with the real world as the rest of us know it. As a result, persons with these diagnoses frequently require hospitalization.

Key Questions to Answer

While reading this Topic, find the answers to the following key questions:

1. What is Alzheimer's dementia?

2. What are the four signs of Alzheimer's dementia?

3. What are the possible causes for Alzheimer's dementia?

4. What are the mood disorders?

5. What are the symptoms of major depression?

6. What is dysthymia?

7. What is bipolar disorder?

8. What are the biological factors that contribute to the mood disorders?

9. What psychological factors play a role in mood disorders?

10. Why are the mood disorders more prevalent in women than men?

11. What is schizophrenia?

12. How prevalent is schizophrenia, and what is the prognosis?

13. What are the three dimensions of symptoms associated with schizophrenia?

14. What characteristics distinguish the positive and negative symptoms of schizophrenia?

15. What are some of the possible causes of schizophrenia?

ALZHEIMER'S DEMENTIA

dementia a condition characterized by the marked loss of intellectual abilities

By definition, **dementia** is a condition characterized by the marked loss of intellectual abilities. One's attention may be intact, but use of memory is poor and deteriorates. Judgment and impulse control may be adversely affected.

A slow deterioration of one's intellectual functioning is the most common symptom associated with **Alzheimer's disease** (Katzman, 1987). Problems of recent memory mark the early stages of the disease, "Did I take my pills this morning?" Mild personality changes—apathy, less spontaneity, withdrawal—soon follow, perhaps in an attempt to hide one's symptoms from others. Figure 12.1 is from a summary table prepared by the Alzheimer's Association.

Alzheimer's disease a form of dementia associated with personality changes, diagnosed at autopsy

This type of dementia was first described in 1907 by Alois Alzheimer and was thought to be an inevitable process of aging (often incorrectly referred to as *senile psychosis*). The symptoms associated with dementia of the Alzheimer's type are <u>not</u> normal, natural, or a necessary part of growing old, but a general acceptance of this reality did not occur until the early 1970s. Alzheimer's disease has been diagnosed in persons younger than age 65. In such cases, we have what is called an *early onset form* of the disease, but researchers are beginning to conclude that age of onset, by itself, does not define different forms of the disease (Bondareff et al., 1993).

	Normal	**Possible Alzheimer's**
1.	Temporarily forgetting a colleague's name	Not being able to remember the name later
2.	Forgetting the carrots on the stove until the meal is over	Forgetting that a meal was ever prepared
3.	Unable to find the right word, but using a fit substitute	Uttering incomprehensible sentences
4.	Forgetting for a moment where you're going	Getting lost on your own street
5.	Talking on the phone, temporarily forgetting to watch a child	Forgetting a child is present
6.	Having trouble balancing a checkbook	Not knowing what the numbers mean
7.	Misplacing a wristwatch until steps are retraced	Putting a wristwatch in the sugarbowl
8.	Having a bad day	Having rapid mood shifts
9.	Gradual changes in personality with age	Drastic changes in personality
10.	Tiring of housework, but getting back to it	Not knowing or caring that housework needs to be done

From *Is It Alzheimer's? Warning Signs You Should Know*; a pamphlet by the Alzheimer's Association, 919 North Michigan Avenue, Suite 1000, Chicago IL 60611-1676

FIGURE 12.1

Ten Warning Signs of Alzheimer's Disease

Alzheimer's disease is a global problem. Currently, more than 7 million people in North America and Europe have been diagnosed, but an even larger number—perhaps 11 million—suffer from the disorder in the developing nations of the world (Farlow, 2000). Each year nearly 11,000 Americans die of the disease (Fackelman, 1992). The prevalence of Alzheimer's dementia is at only 1 percent of the population of 65 year olds, but it becomes progressively more common, increasing to between 20 percent and 30 percent by age 85 (Evans, et al., 1989; Farlow, 2000).

Although the symptoms of Alzheimer's disease are psychological, it *is* a physical disease caused by abnormal changes in brain tissue. Reliable diagnostic tests may be on the horizon, but as of today, Alzheimer's dementia is diagnosed with certainty only after an autopsy of the brain. There are four signs of Alzheimer's disease: (1) a mass of *tangles*, a "spaghetti-like jumble of abnormal protein fibers" (Butler & Emr, 1982); (2) the presence of *plaques*—waste material, degenerated nerve fibers that wrap around a core of protein; (3) the presence of small cavities filled with fluid and debris; (4) *atrophy*—some structures in the brain are reduced in size (Larner, 1995; Yen et al., 1995). Two problems with these observations are that these signs can sometimes be found in a normal brain (seldom more than one at a time, however), and we don't know what yet causes these signs.

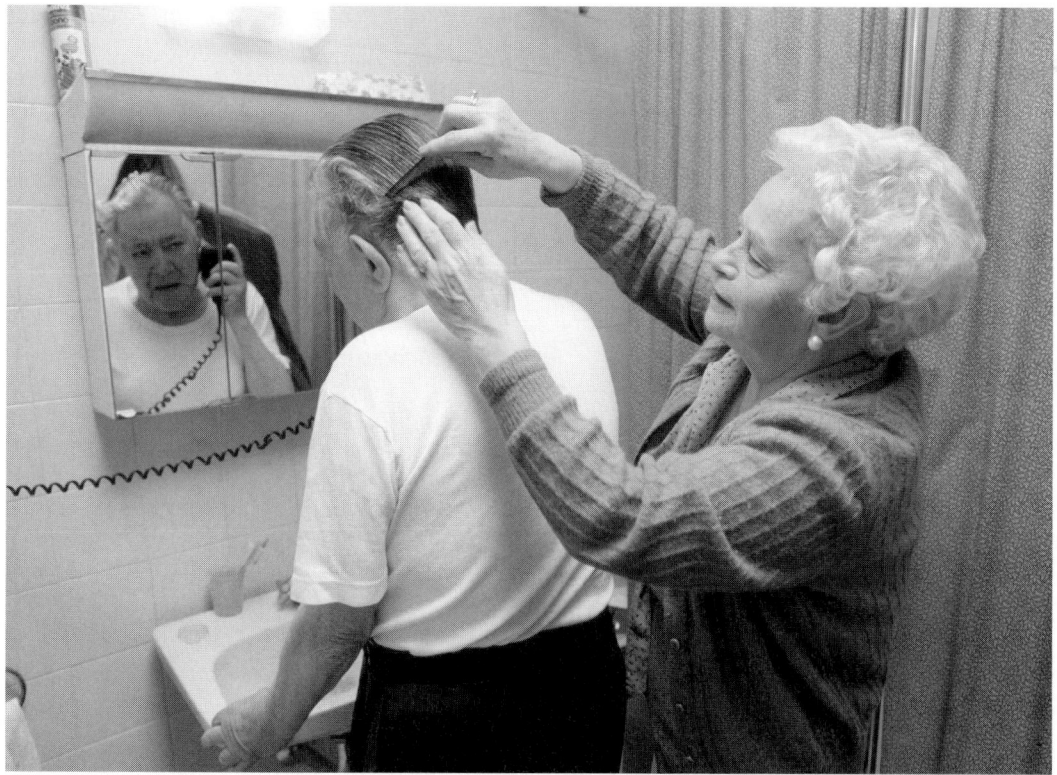

Alzheimer's dementia involves the premature death of brain cells. Early symptoms include mild disorientation and memory loss.

Scientists are beginning to understand the etiology, or causes, of Alzheimer's. We are still at the level of discussing hypotheses, although some do seem more promising than others. The basic issue is that nerve cells in the brains of Alzheimer's patients start to die off sooner than they should, resulting in the tangles, plaques, and other signs we see at autopsy. The crucial question is, how and why do these brain cells die?

As is so often the case with psychological functioning, there is a genetic basis for Alzheimer's disease. There is no doubt that the disease runs in families. This is particularly true for cases in which the age of onset is younger than 60 (Marx, 1990). A breakthrough occurred in 1993, when a team of researchers at Duke University isolated a gene that might be part of the cause of Alzheimer's. By the summer of 1995, two other genes associated with Alzheimer's were discovered. How these genes are involved is another story, yet to be understood.

Another hypothesis about the cause of Alzheimer's dementia is related to the role of a particular protein molecule. This protein is a major component of the plaques found in the brains of Alzheimer's patients. Scientists now know the specific type and structure of the protein involved (Marx, 1990; Mayeux & Sand, 1999; Sinha et al., 1999). Another model involves levels of the neurotransmitter acetylcholine; patients with Alzheimer's dementia often have low levels of acetylcholine (Bodnick et al., 1997; Davis et al., 1998). We've already noted that acetylcholine is involved in memory, so a belief that it is involved in memory deficit is quite reasonable. There is the possibility that Alzheimer's is the result of a poison, or toxin (aluminum salts have been shown to produce similar symptoms). One recent study (Plassman, 2000) demonstrated that head injury in early adulthood is a predictor of the later development of Alzheimer's dementia. The study was conducted with veterans of World War II. Those who had sustained even moderate head injury were more than twice as likely to have Alzheimer's disease 30 years later. Those who had severe head injuries were 4.5 times more likely to have the disorder than age-mates without injury. At present, there seems to be at least a shred of truth in each of these hypotheses.

BEFORE YOU GO ON

- What is Alzheimer's dementia?

- What are the four signs of Alzheimer's dementia found in the brain?

- What are the hypothesized causes for Alzheimer's dementia?

MOOD DISORDERS

mood disorders disorders where a disturbance of affect/mood is the defining symptom

The **mood disorders** (called *affective disorders* until the publication of the *DSM-III-R*) clearly demonstrate a disturbance in emotional reactions or feelings. We have to be careful here. Almost all psychological disorders have an impact on mood or affect. With mood disorders, however, the intensity or extreme nature of a person's mood is the major symptom.

Types of Mood Disorder

Listed under the classification *mood disorder* are several specific disorders differentiated in terms of such criteria as length of episode and severity.

Making a diagnosis of **major depressive disorder** is quite a challenge. For one thing, a person must have experienced two or more depressive episodes, where such an episode is defined as a period of at least two weeks during which the person experienced *five or more* of the following symptoms nearly every day: a) depressed or sad mood, b) loss of pleasure or interest in normal activities, c) weight loss or dramatic change in appetite, d) either significantly more or less sleep than normal, e) either physical slowness or agitation, f) unusual fatigue or loss of energy, and g) recurrent thoughts of death or suicide.

major depressive disorder feeling sad, low, helpless, with a loss of pleasure or interest in most normal activities

This mood disorder is diagnosed about two times more often in women than in men; during any six-month period, approximately 6.6 percent of women and 3.5 percent of men will have an episode of major depression. This ratio holds across nationalities and ethnic groups (Cross-National Collaborative Group, 1992; Papolos & Papolos, 1997). Worldwide, major depression is on the increase, with current rates at more than 100 million persons (Gotlib, 1992; Weissman & Klerman, 1992). Unfortunately, relapse and recurrence are common for those who have had a depressive episode (Coyne, Pepper, & Flynn, 1999). Major depression seldom occurs as just one episode of illness, but rather is a fairly chronic condition, with as many as 10 percent of depressed patients being continuously ill for 15 years or more (Eaton et al., 1997; NDMDA, 1996).

Dysthymia [diss-thigh'-me-a'] is essentially a mild case of major depression. The disorder is also chronic, with recurrent pessimism, low energy level, and low self-esteem. Whereas major depression tends to occur in a series of extremely debilitating episodes, dysthymia is a more continuous sense of being depressed and sad. By definition, the depressed mood must last at least two years—and may last for 20 to 30 years (Akiskal & Cassano, 1997).

dysthymia a mild (but distressing) chronic form of depression

For both major depression and dysthymia, there need not be any identifiable event or situation that precipitates the person's depressed mood. That is, to feel overwhelmingly depressed upon hearing of the death of a close friend is not, in itself, enough to be diagnosed with a disorder of any sort. We all may feel periods of mild depression from time to time. With major depressive disorder, however, the depression is significant and is associated with a myriad of additional symptoms. With dysthymia, the depression is particularly long-lasting (4 to 5 years on average).

In **bipolar disorder**, episodes of depression are occasionally interspersed with episodes of mania. This disorder is still often referred to as "manic depression." **Mania** is characterized as an elevated mood with feelings of euphoria or irritability. In a manic state, one shows an increase in activity, is more talkative than usual, and seems to get by with less sleep than usual. Mania is a condition of mood that cannot be maintained for long. It is too tiring to stay manic for an extended time. As is true for depression, mania seldom occurs as an isolated episode. Follow-up studies show that recurrences of manic reactions are common. Relapse is found in approximately 40 percent of those who have been diagnosed as having a manic episode (Harrow et al., 1990; Tohen et al., 1990). People are rarely manic without also showing interspersed periods of depression. Approximately two million Americans presently suffer from bipolar disorder.

bipolar disorder a mood disorder characterized by swings of mood between extreme depression and (shorter segments of) mania

mania a state of elevated mood, euphoria, or irritability with increased levels of activity

Major depression is a mood disorder characterized by inexplicable feelings of sadness and hopelessness accompanied by a loss of pleasure in common activities.

Observations on the Causes of Depression

The answers to the question "What causes depression?" depend largely on how and where we look. It seems most likely that depression is caused by several different but potentially interrelated causes—both biological and psychological.

Biological Factors

Bipolar mood disorder isn't very common. An individual chosen at random has less than a one-half of one percent chance of developing the symptoms of the disorder. The chances of developing the symptoms rise to 15 percent if a brother, a sister, or either parent had the disorder. This 15 percent figure holds for fraternal twins. If, however, one member of a pair of identical twins has bipolar mood disorder, the chances that the other twin will be diagnosed as having the disorder jump to more than 70 percent (Allen, 1976; Grinspoon, 1997). What this means, of course, is that there is excellent evidence for a genetic, or inherited, predisposition to the bipolar mood disorder. The data are not quite as striking for the *unipolar mood disorder* (depression only). We suspect, however, that there is some sort of genetic basis for major depression as well (Hammen et al., 1990; Kendler et al., 1993). A study of twins confirmed the influence of heredity in major depression and ruled out early childhood experiences as a causative factor. The study found no evidence that growing up at the same time, in the same home with the same parents, in the same neighborhood, or in the same school was related to the development of the symptoms of depression (Kendler et al., 1994).

We may talk about a genetic basis for depression, but clearly, people do not inherit depression—they inherit genes. What the **diathesis-stress model** proposes is that individuals inherit multiple genes, which may give rise to the tendency or *predisposition* to express certain behaviors, and that these behaviors are expressed only if activated by stress or trauma. "Diathesis" is a term that literally means "a condition that makes someone susceptible to developing a disorder." In our current discussion, then, the proposal would be that some people inherit predispositions to develop a depressive disorder when they encounter stress in their lives. Faced with the same—or similar—stress, someone else may have a diathesis to develop coronary heart disease or gastrointestinal problems, while someone else might respond to that stress with no disease or disorder at all.

Even if we knew the site of a specific gene that provided the basis for a disorder, researchers would still be challenged to specify the mechanisms that produce the symptoms of that disorder. For the mood disorders, attention has been focused on neurotransmitters that appear to influence mood directly. Collectively they are referred to as biogenic amines and include such neurotransmitters as serotonin, dopamine, and norepinephrine. A major breakthrough in this research came when it was discovered that reserpine, a drug used to treat high blood pressure, reduced dopamine levels and also produced symptoms of depression. It was then discovered that reserpine lowered the brain's level of norepinephrine, and the search for neurotransmitter involvement in affective disorders began (Delgado, et al., 1994; George, et al., 1995).

Recent studies of the brains of persons with mood disorders have found abnormally large ventricles (openings in the brain that contain cerebrospinal fluid) (Elkis et al., 1995; Damasio, 1997). Patients with bipolar mood disorder have abnormally high levels of white matter in the brain, and tend to have larger thalamuses than control subjects, while patients with major depression have smaller thalamuses than normal (Dupont et al., 1995).

diathesis-stress model the position that the expression of disordered behaviors (particularly depression) results from the interaction of an inherited predisposition and the experience of stress or trauma.

Psychological Factors

Learning theorists have attributed depression to experiential phenomena, including a lack of effective reinforcers. Someone with a history of making responses without earning reinforcement may just stop responding altogether and become quiet, withdrawn, passive, and depressed (Seligman, 1975). Some people, lacking the ability to earn reinforcers, simply respond less often to environmental cues. They enter into a long, generalized period of extinction, ultimately leading to depression. On the other hand, research suggests that the ineffectiveness of reinforcers in some people's lives is more a result of depression than a cause of it. Because they are depressed, they may find less reinforcement for their responses to the world about them (Carson & Carson, 1984).

Other theorists, most notably psychiatrist Aaron Beck (1967, 1976), argue that although depression is a disorder of affect, its causes are largely cognitive. Some people, the argument goes, tend to think of themselves in a poor light; they believe that they are, in many ways, ineffective people. They tend to blame themselves for many of their failures, whether deservedly so or not. Facing life every day with these negative attitudes about oneself tends to foster even more failures and self-doubt, and such cycles then lead to feelings of depression (Gotlib & Krasnoperoua, 1998).

There are other views about the causes of depression, including the psychoanalytic view that depression is a reflection of early childhood experiences that lead to anger that is directed inward. In brief, we can conclude that depression probably stems from a combination of genetic predispositions, biochemical influences, learning experiences, situational stress, and cognitive factors. Which of these is more, or most, important remains to be seen.

Before we go on, let's briefly consider the data on mood disorders that suggests they are twice as likely to be diagnosed in women than in men. Why should this be so? Several hypotheses have been proposed. (1) Perhaps the genetic basis of depression is located on X chromo-somes (males carry an XY pair of chromosomes, whereas women have XX pairs). There are little data to support this hypothesis. (2) Perhaps women, given their roles in our cul-ture, feel more free and open to discuss their feelings—their negative feelings in particu-lar—than do men. More open to sharing their sad, unhappy moods, women may be diagnosed more often as being depressed. In contrast, men are more likely to abuse alcohol: it's a male response to feelings of sadness and depression. In Amish, Jewish, and other groups with a low rate of alcoholism, major depression is equally common in both sexes—possible evidence that men disguise their depression (even from themselves) by trying to treat it with alcohol (Grinspoon, 1998). (3) Perhaps women are more exposed to the types of stressors (less edu-cation, poorer employment, lower pay, responsibilities of child-rearing, etc.) that would lead one to become depressed. This may be a valid observation, but when such factors are controlled for (when men and women are matched for such stressors), the sex difference in diag-nosis remains. Even when factors such as self-esteem are controlled for, the sex difference remains. As you might guess, there are several other hypotheses, including the notion that mental health professionals (males in particular) are simply following a cultural expectation and diagnosing the disorder more commonly in women. Once again, a common theme emerges: sex differences in depression reflect a complex interaction of genetic, biological, psychological, and cultural factors (McGrath et al., 1990; Strickland, 1992).

BEFORE YOU GO ON

- What are the mood disorders?

- What is major depression?

- What is dysthymia and how does it differ from major depression?

- What is bipolar disorder?

- What are the biological and psychological causes for mood disorders?

- What factors have been suggested to account for gender differences in mood disorders?

SCHIZOPHRENIA

schizophrenia a family of serious disorders involving a distortion of reality, a retreat from others, distur-bances in affect; often showing hal-lucinations and delusions

Schizophrenia is a diagnosis for what may be several different disorders, which have in common a distortion of reality and a retreat from other people accompanied by distur-bances in affect, behavior, and cognition (our ABCs again). Schizophrenia can impair every aspect of living. The range of symptoms is so great that it is nearly impossible to specify which are fundamental and which are secondary.

Incidence and Types of Schizophrenia

Schizophrenia can be found around the world at the same rate: about 1 percent of the population (Adler & Gielen, 1994; Bloom et al., 1985; Buckley et al., 1996). People in developing countries tend to have a more acute (intense, but short-lived) course—and a better outcome—of the disorder than do people in industrialized nations. In the United States, schizophrenia accounts for 75 percent of all mental health expenditures (Carpenter & Buchanan, 1994). Schizophrenia occurs at the same rate for both sexes, but symptoms are likely to show up earlier in males, and males are more likely to be disabled by the disorder and have a higher relapse rate (Grinspoon, 1995; Szymanski et al., 1995).

No matter how we state the statistics, we are talking about very large numbers of people. The prognosis for schizophrenia is not very encouraging. About 25 percent recover fully from their first episode of the disorder and have no recurrences; in about 50 percent of the cases, there is a recurrent illness with periods of remission in between, and in the other 25 percent of the cases there are no signs of recovery and a long-term deterioration in functioning. In one study, only 10 to 17 percent of patients with schizophrenia showed complete remission of symptoms in a follow-up five years after initial diagnosis (Carone et al., 1991), and another study reported that overall, fewer than half of the patients diagnosed with schizophrenia showed substantial improvement after follow-up averaging six years (Hegarty et al., 1994). Prognosis is related to when intervention begins. If treatment begins immediately after an initial episode, the prognosis is fairly good, with as many as 83 percent recovering (Lieberman et al., 1993). We see this with many physical ailments: the sooner treatment begins, the better the likelihood of recovery.

Some of the defining symptoms of schizophrenia are disordered or disorganized perceptions and hallucinations. These are some of the key symptoms experienced by those who were tried and convicted of witchcraft in Salem, Massachusetts, late in the 17th century.

Schizophrenia is a label that applies to several disorders. In this way, the term *schizophrenia* is not unlike the term *cancer*. To say that one has cancer communicates only a general diagnosis. We want to know what sort of cancer. Classifying varieties of schizophrenia has been motivated by an attempt to better understand what causes the disorder, which might then lead to more effective treatment. There have been several attempts at "typing" schizophrenia. Only recently has a consensus developed for a system for classifying the disorder into types on the basis of *positive and negative symptoms*.

In 1919, Emil Kraepelin claimed there were two types of schizophrenia depending on the symptoms found at diagnosis. Recent research indicates that schizophrenia has three dimensions of symptoms (Andreasen et al., 1990; Andreasen et al., 1995; Arndt et al., 1995; Brown & White, 1992; Buckley et al., 1996; Eaton et al., 1995; Kay & Singh, 1989). One dimension of schizophrenia is typified by **negative symptoms**—emotional and social withdrawal, reduced energy and motivation, apathy, and poor attention.

The other two dimensions of schizophrenia are typified by *positive symptoms*—positive psychotic and positive disorganized. The **positive psychotic symptoms** include hallucinations and delusions. *Hallucinations* are false perceptions; perceiving that which is not there or failing to perceive that which is. Schizophrenic hallucinations are often auditory, taking the form of "hearing voices inside one's head." **Delusions** are false beliefs; ideas that are firmly held regardless of evidence to the contrary. Delusions of someone with schizophrenia are inconsistent and unorganized. **Positive disorganized symptoms** of schizophrenia include disorders of thinking and speech, bizarre behaviors, and inappropriate affect. A person displaying positive disorganized symptoms may say something like, "When you swallow in your throat like a key it comes out, but not a scissors, a robin too, it means spring" (Marengo & Harrow, 1987, p. 654), or the person may giggle and laugh or sob and cry for no apparent reason, or may stand perfectly still for hours at a time. (See Figure 12.2.)

The usefulness of this negative-positive distinction is that there *may* be differences in both the causes and the most effective treatment plans for the three types. In brief, we find the correlates of negative symptoms to include enlarged ventricles in the brain, a clearer genetic basis, more severe complications at birth, a lower educational level, poorer adjustment patterns before onset, and a poorer prognosis given the relative ineffective-

negative symptoms of schizophrenia emotional and social withdrawal, reduced energy and motivation, apathy and poor attention

positive psychotic symptoms of schizophrenia hallucinations and delusions

delusions false beliefs; ideas firmly held regardless of evidence to the contrary

positive disorganized symptoms of schizophrenia disorders of thinking and speech, bizarre behaviors, and inappropriate affect

---

Schizophrenia with negative symptoms

Characterized by: emotional and social withdrawal, and/or reduced energy and motivation, and/or apathy, and/or poor attention

Schizophrenia with positive psychotic symptoms

Characterized by: hallucinations, or false perceptions, and/or delusions, or false beliefs

Schizophrenia with positive disorganized symptoms

Characterized by: disordered thinking or speech, and/or bizarre behaviors, and/or inappropriate affect

FIGURE 12.2

One Classification Scheme for Schizophrenia

ness of medications. Correlated with both types of positive symptoms are excesses of the neurotransmitter dopamine, relatively normal brain configuration, severe disruptions in early family life, overactivity and aggressiveness in adolescence, and a relatively good response to treatment (Andreasen et al., 1990; Breier et al., 1991; Brown & White, 1992; Cannon et al., 1990; Eaton et al., 1995; Lenzenweger et al., 1989; McGlashan & Fenton, 1992).

As is always the case in such matters, we need to be cautious. Not all of the data on typing schizophrenia have been supportive (Kay, 1990; Pogue-Geile & Zubin, 1988). The distinctions described here are quite new; only time and further research will tell us how useful they will be in the long run.

The *DSM-IV* and its most recent revision characterize schizophrenic subtypes differently. In the *DSM-IV*, schizophrenia is described as being of one of several types—paranoid, disorganized, catatonic, and undifferentiated. These types are summarized in Figure 12.3.

We need to make two things clear. First, as unsettling as these symptoms may be, the average patient with schizophrenia does not present the picture of the crazed, wild lunatic that is often depicted in movies and on television. Day in and day out, the average schizophrenic patient is quite colorless, socially withdrawn, and of very little danger. Although there are exceptions to this rule of thumb, it is particularly true when the patient with schizophrenia is medicated or in treatment. Their "differentness" may be frightening, but people with schizophrenia are seldom more dangerous than anyone else. Second, when literally translated, *schizophrenia* means "splitting of the mind." This term was first used by a Swiss psychia-trist, Eugen Bleuler, in 1911. The split Bleuler was addressing was a split of the mind of the patient from the real world and social relationships as the rest of us experience them. The term has never been used to describe multiple or split personalities of the Jekyll and Hyde variety. Such disorders do occur, but as we have seen, they are classified as dissociative identity disorders.

BEFORE YOU GO ON

- What is schizophrenia?

- How common is schizophrenia and what is the prognosis?

- What are the three dimensions of symptoms that characterize different forms of schizophrenia?

- What distinguishes between the positive and negative symptoms of schizophrenia?

What Causes Schizophrenia?

Schizophrenia is a complex family of disorders, and as you may suspect, any bottom line conclusion on the causes of schizophrenia will be tentative and multidimensional. We may not know what causes the disorder, but we do have several interesting hypotheses.

Schizophrenia has a genetic basis (Buckley et al., 1996; Gottesman & Bertelsen, 1989; Kessler, 1980). The data are not as striking as they are for the mood disorders, but a person is at a higher risk of being diagnosed as having schizophrenia if there is a family history of the disorder. A child of two parents with schizophrenia has about a 40 percent chance of developing the disorder. Schizophrenia occurs at a 30 to 50 percent rate among the identical twins of schizophrenics, but at only a 10 to 15 percent rate in fraternal twins

Paranoid Schizophrenia
- absurd, illogical, and changeable delusions, usually of persecution or grandeur frequently accompanied by vivid hallucinations
- impairment of critical judgment
- erratic and occasionally dangerous behaviors
- usually appears after age 40 and accounts for about 40 percent of all patients with schizophrenia

Disorganized Schizophrenia
- disorganized speech patterns
- peculiar mannerisms and bizarre, often obscene behavior
- emotional distortions with inappropriate silliness and laughter
- often found in younger patients and with high prevalence among homeless persons

Catatonic Schizophrenia
- alternating extreme withdrawal and extreme excitement
- tendency to remain motionless for hours—even days
- agitated states involve rapid talking and shouting, uninhibited, frenzied behaviors
- fewer than 10 percent of schizophrenic cases get this diagnosis

Undifferentiated Schizophrenia
- a rapidly changing mixture of all or most of the primary symptoms of schizophrenia, both positive and negative
- perplexity, confusion, emotional turmoil, depression, fear
- essentially a "catch-all" category for those who do not qualify for one of the types above

FIGURE 12.3

Types of Schizophrenia described in the *DSM-IV-TR*

(Grinspoon, 1995; Kety et al., 1994; Kendler et al., 1994). It is reasonable to say that one may inherit a predisposition to develop schizophrenia, but lest we get too committed to a genetic hypothesis on the causes of schizophrenia, we must consider that 89 percent of persons diagnosed with schizophrenia have no known relative with the disorder (Cromwell, 1993; Plomin, 1988).

There is no doubt that schizophrenia is a disease of the brain, and for some time, the focus has been on the neurotransmitter dopamine. The role of dopamine has come to light from several lines of research. We know that the abuse of amphetamines can lead to many of the symptoms also found in schizophrenia. We know that amphetamines are chemically very similar to dopamine and actually cause an increase in dopamine levels in the brain. Logic leads researchers to wonder if schizophrenic symptoms (in particular those we have recognized as positive symptoms) are caused by excess amounts of dopamine. Although dopamine is found in all human brains, it is present at high levels in late adolescence, which is when schizophrenia usually first appears (Grinspoon, 1995).

Support for the dopamine hypothesis comes from examining the action of drugs that reduce schizophrenic symptoms. Some of the drugs that ease schizophrenic symptoms commonly block receptor sites for dopamine in the brain (Snyder, 1980). If reducing the effectiveness of dopamine by blocking its activity at the synapse can control schizophrenic symptoms, might these symptoms have been caused by dopamine in the first place (Schooler & Keith, 1993; Tandon & Greden, 1989)?

Many patients with schizophrenia, mostly those with negative symptoms, have abnormally large ventricles in their brains (cavities or openings that contain cerebrospinal fluid) (Andreasen et al., 1982, 1990b), and evidence suggests a lack of balance between the two hemispheres of the brain (Gur et al., 1987; Reveley et al., 1987). There are other differences between the brains of persons with schizophrenia and persons without the disorder, although they tend to be less dramatic. Persons with the disorder tend to have a loss of tissue in and around the limbic system (related to the regulation of emotion), larger crevices in the surface of the cerebral cortex, and a smaller thalamus (the structure that relays information between the cerebral cortex and the rest of the brain). Even if these differences in the brain are confirmed, we still don't know if they are causes or effects.

An interesting and potentially helpful point of view concerning the causes of schizophrenia is the "neurodevelopmental hypothesis" (Wyatt, 1996). This hypothesis—with supporting evidence accumulating rapidly—is that schizophrenia first diagnosed in early adulthood may have its roots in very early development. The basic notion is that some physically traumatic event happening either in utero or during delivery disrupts the normal development of the central nervous system. One of the prime suspects for that "physically traumatic event" is influenza contracted in the second trimester of pregnancy (Goldman-Rakic, 1995; Torrey et al., 1994; Wright et al., 1995).

In some people, the symptoms of schizophrenia remain dormant, or unexpressed, until the individual is subjected to environmental stressors (Gottesman & Bertelsen, 1989; Johnson, 1989; Ventura et al., 1989). The theory is that some people are genetically prone to develop the symptoms of schizophrenia when they are exposed to stressors. Other people faced with the same type or amount of stress might develop ulcers, might become excessively anxious, or might show no particular symptoms at all. So, it is possible that some life experiences bring on the symptoms of schizophrenia or tend to make those symptoms worse than they would otherwise be. Here we have the diathesis-stress model once again. The consensus, however, is that we are dealing with a complex disease of the brain, not a "disorder of living" (Johnson, 1989). "How the environment interacts with genetic risk to trigger the development of schizophrenia remains unknown" (Iacono & Grove, 1993).

BEFORE YOU GO ON

- What are some of the possible causes of schizophrenia?

Topic Review 12B

1. **What is Alzheimer's dementia?**

   Alzheimer's dementia is a form of degenerative dementia associated with abnormalities in the brain—among other things, the formation of tangles and plaques. There is a strong likelihood of a genetic basis for the disease. Currently, research is focusing on the formation of certain brain proteins and the neurotransmitter acetylcholine.

2. **What are the four signs of Alzheimer's disease?**

   The four signs of Alzheimer's relate to brain pathology discovered after death. They are (1) a mass of tangles of abnormal protein fibers in the brain, (2) the development of plaques (waste material), (3) the presence of small cavities filled with fluid and debris, and (4) atrophy of parts of the brain.

3. **What are the possible causes for Alzheimer's dementia?**

   Although the exact causes for Alzheimer's dementia are not known, there are several hypotheses concerning why things go wrong in the brain. First, there may be a genetic link (Alzheimer's runs in families), especially if onset occurs before age sixty. Second, a particular protein found in the plaques may play a causal role. Third, Alzheimer's may relate to low levels of the neurotransmitter acetylcholine in the brain.

4. **What are the mood disorders?**

   In the mood disorders, a disturbance in affect or feeling is the prime, and perhaps only, symptom. Most commonly the disorder involves depression; less commonly we find mania and depression occurring in cycles (bipolar mood disorder). Whether the major symptom is depression or mania, there is no reason for the observed mood. Major depression affects about twice as many women as men.

5. **What are the symptoms of major depression?**

   Major depression, or major depressive disorder, comprises a constellation of symptoms including feeling sad, low, and hopeless, coupled with a loss of pleasure or interest in most normal activities. Poor appetite, loss of energy, insomnia, decreased sexual activity, and feelings of worthlessness are also symptoms associated with major depression.

6. **What is dysthymia?**

   Dysthymia is similar to major depression except that the symptoms are milder. It is a chronic disorder characterized by pessimism, low energy level, and low self-esteem. Dysthymia is also characterized by a more continuous sense of depression, whereas major depression is punctuated with a series of extremely debilitating episodes.

7. **What is bipolar disorder?**

   Bipolar disorder is characterized by episodes of depression that may be interspersed with episodes of mania, which is characterized by elevated mood, feelings of euphoria or irritability. The disorder is still referred to as "manic depression."

8. **What are the biological factors that contribute to the mood disorders?**

   Because mood disorders tend to run in families, there is most likely a genetic component. However, no specific genes have been identified as causal factors. Attention has also been focused on the role of neurotransmitters that appear to affect mood, such as serotonin, dopamine, and norepinephrine. One theory suggests that low levels of one or more of these chemicals is the cause for depression. There may also be structural brain abnormalities involved. Persons with depressed moods tend to have abnormally large ventricles and abnormally high levels of white matter in the brain. Additionally, individuals with bipolar disorder tend to have enlarged thalamuses, whereas those suffering from major depression have abnormally small thalamuses.

9. **What psychological factors play a role in mood disorders?**

   Learning theorists suggest that lack of effective reinforcers is associated with depression. Ineffective reinforcers may cause a person to stop responding and become quiet, withdrawn, passive and depressed. Other theorists argue that depression is related to the way people think about themselves. According to this view, depressed individuals think of themselves in a poor way, see themselves as failures, and believe that they are ineffective people. Psychoanalytic theorists point to early childhood experiences. Most likely depression is caused by a combination of genetic factors, biochemical influences, as well as learning experiences, situational stress, and cognitive factors.

10. Why are the mood disorders more prevalent in women than men?

There are several possible reasons for the gender differences in mood disorders. First, it is possible that the gene for depression is carried on the X chromosome. However, there is little support for this hypothesis. Second, women may feel freer than men to express and discuss feelings openly, leading to a higher diagnosis rate for women than men. Third, women may be exposed to more stressors associated with depression (for example, poorer employment, lower pay, child-rearing responsibilities). Most likely, the gender differences relate to an interaction between biological and social factors.

11. What is schizophrenia?

Schizophrenia is a label applied to disorders that involve varying degrees of impairment. It occurs in about 1 percent of the population worldwide. Many believe that there are three distinct types of schizophrenia, depending on the cluster of symptoms found.

12. How prevalent is schizophrenia and what is the prognosis?

About 1 percent of the world's population is afflicted with schizophrenia. Schizophrenia is seen equally in both sexes, although men tend to show symptoms earlier, are more likely to be disabled, and have a higher relapse rate than women. Generally, the prognosis for recovery is not very good. Only 25 percent recover fully from their first episode and have no recurrences. In 50 percent of cases, symptoms are recurrent with periods of remission. In 25 percent of cases, there is no recovery accompanied by long-term deterioration of functioning.

13. What are the three dimensions of symptoms associated with schizophrenia?

Symptoms known as negative symptoms involve emotional and social withdrawal, reduced energy and motivation, apathy, and poor attention. A second dimension of symptoms include the positive symptoms characterized by hallucinations (false perceptions) and delusions (false beliefs). The third dimension is made up of the positive disorganized symptoms including disordered thinking, bizarre behavior, and inappropriate affect.

14. What characteristics distinguish the positive and negative symptoms of schizophrenia?

The negative symptoms of schizophrenia relate to enlarged ventricles in the brain. The negative symptoms also have a clearer genetic basis, more severe complications at birth, poorer adjustment patterns before onset of symptoms, and a poor prognosis. Positive symptoms are related to excesses of the neurotransmitter dopamine (but normal brain configuration), and disruptions in family life. Positive symptoms are more responsive to treatment, especially with medication.

15. What are some of the possible causes of schizophrenia?

Although we do not know the causes of schizophrenia, three lines of investigation have produced hopeful leads: (1) There is a genetic predisposition for the disorder. Schizophrenia is not inherited, but it does run in families. (2) Research on biochemical correlates have localized the neurotransmitter dopamine as being involved in the production of schizophrenia-like symptoms, although dopamine's role in the disorder is now being questioned. (3) Some psychological experiences, or stressful events, may bring on symptoms or make them worse. A reasonable position is that for some individuals, environmental events, such as extreme stress, trigger biochemical and structural changes in the brain that result in the symptoms of schizophrenia.

Chapter 13

Treatment and Therapy

Consumer Reports is a very popular magazine. Each month—with no advertising—it publishes its evaluation of a wide range of products and services, acting as an independent judge of the sorts of things for which we, as consumers, spend our hard-earned money. It rates refrigerators, VCRs, and baby carriages—among other things. It comments on the value of various types of life insurance and home security systems. In 1995, Consumer Reports published a lengthy article on the effectiveness of various types of psychotherapy. The magazine had never before ventured into such an arena. Many readers—and many psychologists—responded with surprise, even indignation. "How dare this popular magazine presume to evaluate such a complex, intricate process as psychotherapy?"

Although it is true that the *Consumer Reports* study is not without its critics, it has stood up to careful scrutiny very well indeed. It was not the standard, carefully controlled, matched-group experimental design. Instead, its approach was the essence of simplicity: It asked people who had "at any time over the past three years" experienced stress or other emotional problems for which they sought help to respond to a survey to describe their experience. Twenty-two thousand readers responded. Of those, nearly 3,000 had seen a mental health professional (as opposed to friends, clergy, or family doctors).

The conclusion: Patients benefited substantially from psychotherapy. Long-term treatment did considerably better than short-term treatment, and psychotherapy alone did not differ in effectiveness from medication plus psychotherapy. Additionally, no particular type or "brand" of psychotherapy did any better than any other, and no particular type of therapist (e.g., psychologist, psychiatrist, or social worker) was any more effective than any other (*Consumer Reports*, 1995; Jacobson & Christensen, 1996; Seligman, 1995; 1996; Strupp, 1996; VandenBos, 1996).

Topic 13A HISTORY AND BIOMEDICAL TREATMENTS

Mental illness is not a new phenomenon. Among the earliest written records from the Babylonians, Egyptians, and ancient Hebrews are descriptions of what we now know as psychological disorders (Murray, 1983). How individuals with disorders were treated was consistent with the prevailing view of what caused the disorder.

Key Questions to Answer

While reading this Topic, find the answers to the following key questions:

1.   How did the ancient Greeks and Romans conceptualize mental illness?

2.   How can treatment of the mentally ill during the Middle Ages be characterized?

3.   What contributions did Philippe Pinel make to the treatment of the mentally ill?

4.   What contributions did Benjamin Rush, Dorothea Dix, and Clifford Beers make to the treatment of the mentally ill?

5.   What is psychosurgery?

6.   What is involved in the procedure known as a lobotomy?

7.   What is ECT, and why is it still being used?

8.   What are the three major types of psychoactive medications used to treat psychological disorders?

9.   What are the antipsychotic drugs, and what are their effects?

10. What are the three classes of antidepressant drugs?

11. What is lithium, and what is it used to treat?

12. What are the antianxiety drugs?

13. What are the advantages and disadvantages of using psychoactive drugs to treat psychological disorders?

A HISTORICAL PERSPECTIVE

Although there were a few bright spots along the way, the history of treating psychological disorders in the Western world is not a pleasant one. By today's standards, *therapy*, in the sense of active, humane intervention to improve the condition of persons in psychological distress, doesn't even seem to be the right term to describe how most disordered persons were dealt with in the past.

The ancient Greeks and Romans believed that individuals who were depressed, manic, irrational, or intellectually retarded, or who had hallucinations or delusions, had in some way offended the gods. In some cases, these individuals were viewed as temporarily out of favor with the gods, and it followed that their condition could improve through prayer and religious ritual. More severely disturbed patients were seen as physically possessed by evil spirits. These cases were more difficult, often impossible, to cure. The goal of treatment was to exorcise the evil spirits and demons inhabiting the minds and souls of the mentally deranged. Many unfortunates died as a result of their treatment or were killed outright when treatment failed. Treatment was left to the priests, who were, after all, thought to be skilled in the ways and means of spirit manipulation.

There *were* those in ancient times who had a more enlightened, or reasonable, view of psychological disorders. Among them was *Hippocrates* (460-377 B.C.), who believed that mental disorders had physical causes, not spiritual ones. He saw epilepsy as being a disorder of the brain, for example. Some of his views were wrong (e.g., that hysteria is a disorder of the uterus), but at least he tried (albeit without success) to demystify psychological disorders.

During the Middle Ages (1000-1500), the oppression and persecution of the disordered were at their peak. During this period, the prevailing view continued to be that psychologically disordered people were "bad people," under the spell of devils and evil spirits. They had brought on their own grief, and there was no hope for them, except that they save their immortal souls and confess their evil ways.

For hundreds of years, well into the eighteenth century, the prevailing attitude toward the mentally ill continued to be that they were in league with the devil or that God was punishing them for sinful thoughts and deeds. They were witches who could not be cured except by confession. When such confessions were not forthcoming, the prescribed treatment was torture. If torture failed to evoke a confession, death was the only recourse, often by being burned at the stake. Between the fourteenth and mid-seventeenth centuries, nearly 200,000 to 500,000 "witches" were put to death (Ben-Yehuda, 1980).

When the disordered (or those who were severely intellectually retarded) were not tortured or immediately put to death, they were usually placed in asylums for the insane. The first insane asylum, opened in 1547, was St. Mary of Bethlehem Hospital in London, to house "fools" and "lunatics." The institution became known as Bedlam (a cockney pronunciation of Bethlehem). It was a terrible place. Inmates were tortured, poorly fed, or starved to death. To remove the "bad blood" from their systems, thought to be a cause of their melancholy or delirium, patients were regularly led to bleeding chambers, where a small incision was made in a vein in the calf of their legs so that their blood would ooze into leather buckets. There was no real professional staff at Bedlam. The "keepers," as they were called, could make extra money by putting their charges on view for the public; viewing the lunatics of Bedlam became entertainment for the nobility. Inmates who were able were sent into the streets to beg, wearing a sign that identified them as "fools of Bedlam." Even today we use the word *bedlam* to describe a condition of uproar and confusion.

Please understand that the horrific treatment of the mentally ill and retarded was not simply the action of mean-spirited, violent, nasty people. No, persons with psychological disorders were simply being treated in accord with the prevailing wisdom (or lack thereof) of the times. It is quite possible that 50 years from now psychologists and their students will look back at *our* treatment of disordered persons and find it equally barbaric.

It would be comforting to think that Bedlam was an exception, an aberration. It was not. In the eighteenth and nineteenth centuries, similar institutions were commonplace. Against this backdrop of misery and despair, the names of a few enlightened individuals deserve mention. One is Philippe Pinel (1745-1826), a French physician who, in the midst of the French Revolution (on April 25, 1793), was named director of an asylum for the insane in Paris. We know of Pinel today largely because of his act of compassion and courage. The law of the day required that asylum inmates be chained and confined. On September 2, 1793, Pinel ordered the chains and shackles removed from about 50 of the inmates of his "hospital." He allowed them to move freely about the institution and its grounds. This humane gesture produced surprising effects: The symptoms of the patients, in many cases, improved markedly. A few patients were even released from the asylum. Unfortunately, Pinel's "humane therapy," as he called it, did not spread to other asylums. Yet Pinel's unchaining of the insane and his belief in moral treatment for the mentally ill can be seen as the beginning of a gradual enlightenment concerning mental illness, even if Pinel's success did not lead to broad, sweeping reforms.

A few other pioneers' efforts also deserve mention here. *Benjamin Rush* (1745-1813) was the founder of American psychiatry. He published the first text on mental disorders in the United States. Although some of the treatments Rush recommended seem crude by today's standards (he believed in bleeding, for example), his general attitudes were very humane. He argued vehemently and successfully, for example, that the mentally ill should not be put on display to satisfy the curiosity of onlookers.

Dorothea Dix (1802-1887) was an American nurse. In 1841 she took a position in a women's prison and was appalled at what she saw there. Among the prisoners were hundreds of women who clearly were mentally retarded or psychologically disordered. Despite her slight stature and her own ill health, she entered upon a crusade of singular vigor. She traveled from state to state, campaigning for reform in prisons, mental hospitals, and asylums.

Clifford Beers, a graduate of Yale University, had been institutionalized in a series of hospitals and asylums. It seems likely that he was suffering from what we now call a bipolar mood disorder. Probably in spite of his treatment rather than because of it, Beers recovered and was released, in itself an unusual occurrence. In 1908, he wrote a book about his experience, *A Mind That Found Itself.* The book became a best seller; William James and Theodore Roosevelt were said to be very impressed with Beers and his story. Clifford Beers's book was read by people in power, and is often cited as one of the main stimuli for the beginning of what we now call the "mental health movement."

Since the early 1900s, progress in providing help for the mentally ill has been both slow and unsteady. World War I and the Great Depression reduced the monies available to support state institutions for mental patients. Within the past 50 years, conditions have improved immeasurably, but there's still a long way to go. There is still a significant stigma attached to persons suffering from psychological disorders.

BEFORE YOU GO ON

- How did the Greeks and Romans view mental illness?

- What were the consequences of assuming that a mentally ill person was in league with the devil?

- What contributions did Pinel make to the treatment of the mentally ill?

- What contributions did Benjamin Rush, Dorothea Dix, and Clifford Beers make to the treatment of the mentally ill?

BIOMEDICAL TREATMENTS OF PSYCHOLOGICAL DISORDERS

Biological and medical approaches to mental illness can be traced to ancient times. As it happens, however, psychologists today cannot use medical treatments—performing surgery, administering shock treatments, and prescribing medications require a medical degree. Psychologists can be involved in biomedical treatments, however, and they may recommend a medical treatment or refer a client to the care of a physician or psychiatrist (a person with a medical degree who specializes in mental disorders). The approaches psychologists use, the *psychotherapies*, will be the subject of our next Topic.

Here we'll review three types of biomedical intervention: psychosurgery, which was common just 50 years ago, but is now rare; electroconvulsive therapy, which is far from uncommon; and drug therapy, one of the most promising developments in the treatment of mental illness.

Psychosurgery

Psychosurgery is the name given to surgical procedures, usually directed at the brain, used to affect psychological reactions. Psychosurgical techniques today are largely experimental, and are aimed at making rather minimal lesions in the brain.

psychosurgery surgical procedure designed to affect one's psychological or behavioral reactions

The surgical destruction of the corpus callosum (in the so-called "split-brain" procedure) can alleviate symptoms in extreme cases of epilepsy. Small surgical lesions in the limbic system have been effective in reducing or eliminating violent behaviors. A surgical technique, a *cingulectomy,* has been used successfully to reduce extreme anxiety and the symptoms of obsessive-compulsive disorders. This is a treatment of last resort that involves cutting a bundle of nerve fibers connecting the very front of the frontal lobe with parts of the limbic system (Baer et al., 1995; Sachdev et al., 1992). Surgical techniques are also being used to treat some cases of Parkinson's disease.

lobotomy psychosurgical technique in which the prefrontal lobes of the cerebral cortex are severed from lower brain centers

Of all of the types of psychosurgery, none has ever been used as commonly as a procedure called a prefrontal lobotomy or, simply, **lobotomy** (Valenstein, 1980, 1986). This surgery severs the major neural connections between the prefrontal lobes (the area at the very front of the cerebral cortex) and lower brain centers.

A lobotomy was first performed in 1935 by a Portuguese psychiatrist, Egas Moniz. For developing the procedure, Moniz was awarded the Nobel Prize in 1949. (The next year, in an ironic twist of fate, Moniz was shot by one of his lobotomized patients. He was rendered paraplegic and was confined to a wheelchair for the rest of his life.) The logic behind a lobotomy was that the prefrontal lobes influence the more basic emotional centers, low in the brain (e.g., in the limbic system). Severely disturbed patients were thought to have difficulty exercising cerebral cortex control over those lower parts of the brain. The reasoning was that if these areas of the brain were separated surgically, the more depressed, agitated, or violent patients could be brought under control.

The operation often appeared to be successful. Always used as a measure of last resort, stories of the changes it produced in chronic mental patients circulated widely. For example, in its November 30, 1942, issue, *Time* magazine called the surgical procedure "revolutionary," claiming that at that time, "some 300 people in the United States have had their psychoses surgically removed." *Life* magazine, in a graphic photo essay titled "Psychosurgery: Operation to Cure Sick Minds Turns Surgeon's Blade into an Instrument of Mental Therapy," called the results of lobotomy procedures "spectacular," claiming that "about 30 percent of the lobotomized patients were able to return to everyday productive lives" (*Life,* March 3, 1947, p. 93).

In the 1940s and 1950s, prefrontal lobotomies were performed regularly. *Time* reported (September 15, 1952) that neurologist Walter Freeman was performing about a hundred lobotomies a week. It is difficult to estimate how many lobotomies were performed in these two decades, but certainly they numbered in the tens of thousands.

Treating severely disturbed patients had always been difficult, so perhaps we should not be surprised that this relatively simple surgical technique was accepted so widely at first. The procedure was done under local anesthetic in a physician's office and took only ten minutes. An instrument that looks very much like an ice pick was inserted through the eye socket, on the nasal side, and pushed up into the brain. A few movements of the instrument and the job was done—the lobes were cut loose from the lower brain centers. Within a couple of hours, patients would be ready to return to their room.

Psychosurgery has always been acknowledged as an irreversible procedure. What took longer to realize was that it often brought terrible side effects. Between 1 and 4 percent of patients receiving prefrontal lobotomies died. Many who survived suffered seizures, memory loss, an inability to plan ahead, and a general listlessness and loss of affect. Many acted childishly and were difficult to manage within institutions. By the late 1950s, lobotomies had become rare. Contrary to common belief, a prefrontal lobotomy is not an illegal procedure, although the conditions under which it might even be considered are very restrictive. Prefrontal lobotomies are not done today for the very simple reason that they are no longer needed. Psychoactive drugs, which have fewer side effects, produce similar results more safely and reliably.

BEFORE YOU GO ON

- What is psychosurgery?
- What is involved in a lobotomy?
- Why are lobotomies rarely performed today?

Electroconvulsive Therapy

As gruesome as the procedures of psychosurgery can be, many people find the very notion of **electroconvulsive therapy (ECT)**, or shock treatments, even more difficult to appreciate. This technique, introduced in 1937, involves passing an electric current of between 70 and 150 volts across a patient's head for a fraction of a second. Patients receive fast-acting general anesthetic and are thus unconscious when the shock is delivered. As soon as the anesthetic is administered, patients receive a muscle relaxant to minimize muscular contractions, which were quite common (and potentially dangerous) in the early days of ECT. The electric shock induces a reaction in the brain not unlike an epileptic seizure; the entire procedure takes about five minutes. One of the side effects of ECT is a loss of memory for events just preceding the administration of the shock and for the shock itself.

At first, the treatment was used to help calm agitated schizophrenics, but it soon became clear that ECT's most beneficial results were for those patients suffering from major depression. It often alleviates the symptoms of depression and, in some cases, has beneficial effects on other symptoms. In fact, the group of patients best suited to the ECT procedure are those for whom depression is a major symptom, but for whom other symptoms (such as hallucinations or delusions) are also present (Joyce & Paykel, 1989). It is also effective for patients demonstrating manic symptoms (Fink, 1997).

Virtually all patients (97 percent) give their consent to the procedure, and negative side effects are rare. The most commonly reported side effects are memory loss and a general mental confusion. In nearly all cases, these effects disappear in a few days or weeks. Once they have experienced the procedure, most ECT patients are far from terrorized by the notion of having an electrical shock sent through their brain. Most report that they feel the procedure helped them, and most would have it done again (Bernstein et al., 1998). In one study, 82 percent of 166 patients surveyed rated ECT as no more upsetting than a visit to the dentist (Sackeim, 1985). After only 10 to 12 treatments, many patients remain free of symptoms for months. In the United States, more than 10,000 patients receive ECT *each day*.

Although ECT is effective, it has a poor reputation among the general population, and among some psychologists and psychiatrists as well. This poor reputation did not develop without foundation. If the procedure is abused, there are negative side effects. At first, the seizures of the shock treatment were induced by drugs, not electricity, and it is largely from these drug-induced treatments that we have stories of convulsions so massive as to result in broken bones. Drug-induced shock/seizure procedures are no longer used. Now, no more than a dozen treatments are given and they are administered over an extended period. Some patients in the past received hundreds of ECT treatments; in such cases, there were reports of brain damage and permanent memory loss.

Administering a shock to just one side of the brain, called a *unilateral ECT,* may be a safer yet equally effective procedure with fewer side effects. More success has been found by creating seizures in the right hemisphere of the cerebral cortex (which is more associated with emotional reactions) than in the left hemisphere (Sackeim et al., 1996; Squire & Slater, 1978).

electroconvulsive therapy (ECT) treatment, usually for severe depression, in which an electric current is passed across a patient's head and causes a seizure

BEFORE YOU GO ON

- What is ECT, and why is it still being used?

- What are some of the problems with ECT?

Just why ECT produces the benefits it does is not fully understood. Although it is a treatment that must be used with extreme care, ECT is very much in practice today. The National Institute of Mental Health estimates that 110,000 American patients receive shock treatments each year. And while the introduction of antidepressant medications has reduced the need for ECT, drug treatment is not always successful; even when it is, drugs often take six to eight weeks to produce their results. Researchers have found that in many cases ECT is a more effective treatment than antidepressant medications (Small et al., 1988) and that adding ECT to antidepressant medication is significantly more effective in the long term than is drug treatment alone (Gagné et al., 2000).

Drug Therapy

Chemicals that alter a person's affect, behavior, or cognitions are referred to as *psychoactive* drugs. As we've seen, there are many drugs, and most are used to produce an altered state of consciousness or awareness. Using chemicals to improve the condition of the mentally disordered is a much more recent development and has been hailed as one of the most significant scientific achievements of the latter half of the twentieth century (Snyder, 1984). In this section we examine the three major types of medication used as therapy: the antipsychotic drugs, antidepressant drugs, and antianxiety drugs.

Antipsychotic Drugs

antipsychotic drugs chemicals, such as chlorpromazine, effective in reducing psychotic symptoms

As their name implies, the **antipsychotic drugs** alleviate or eliminate psychotic symptoms. *Psychotic symptoms* signal loss of contact with reality, such as delusions and hallucinations, and a gross impairment of functioning. Inappropriate affect, or total loss of affect, is also a psychotic symptom. Antipsychotic medications are primarily designed to treat schizophrenia, although they are also used with other disorders, including cases of substance abuse disorders.

The breakthrough in the use of antipsychotic drugs came with the introduction of *chlorpromazine* in the early 1950s. A French neurosurgeon, Henri Laborit, was looking for a drug that would calm his patients before surgery. Laborit wanted to help them relax because he knew that if they did, his patients' postsurgical recovery would be improved. A drug company gave Laborit chlorpromazine. It worked even better than anyone had expected, producing relaxation and calm in the patients. Laborit convinced some of his colleagues to try the drug on their more agitated patients, some of whom were suffering from psychological disorders. The experiments met with great success, and by the late 1950s the drug was widely used in both North America and Europe. Not only did "Laborit's tranquilizer" produce a calm and relaxed state in his patients, it also significantly reduced psychotic symptoms in other patients.

The drug revolution had begun. With the success of chlorpromazine, the search for other chemicals that could improve the plight of the mentally ill began in earnest. By 1956, more than half a dozen antipsychotic medications were available.

Chlorpromazine is one of many drugs currently being used with success to treat psychotic symptoms. Although there are many types of antipsychotic drugs, most work in essentially the same way—by blocking receptor sites for the neurotransmitter dopamine. Antipsychotic drugs are most effective in treating the positive symptoms of schizophrenia: delusions, hallucinations, and bizarre behaviors. Clozapine (trade name *Clozaril*) seems to be an exception, because it is effective in reducing negative symptoms, such as social withdrawal, as well as positive ones. Unfortunately, clozapine carries with it the risk of serious side effects, some of which can be fatal. As a result, use of this drug is very carefully monitored.

The effects of the antipsychotic drugs are remarkable and impressive. They have revolutionized the care of psychotic patients, but they are not the ultimate solution for disorders such as schizophrenia. With high dosages or prolonged use, side effects emerge that are unpleasant at best: dry mouth and throat, sore muscles and joints, sedation, sexual impotence, and muscle tremors. About 30 percent of patients with schizophrenia do not respond to antipsychotic medication (Kane, 1989; American Psychiatric Association, 1997). Like most drugs, antipsychotic medications are most effective when they are used early on, with patients who have recently been diagnosed with schizophrenia, as opposed to those who have exhibited symptoms of the disease for some time (Carpenter & Buchanan, 1994; Lieberman et al., 1993).

Although antipsychotic drugs can suppress symptoms, the question remains: Are they in any sense curing the disorder? In the usual sense of the word *cure,* they are not. Symptom-free patients, who are often released from institutional care to the outside world, soon stop using their medication, only to find that their psychotic symptoms return. A review of 66 studies of 4,365 patients found that relapse was highly associated with sudden withdrawal from antipsychotic medication. Recognizing the unpleasantness and even the danger of the prolonged use of such medications, the authors of this review recommended a slow tapering off of the drugs being used (Gilbert et al., 1995). Other studies (e.g., Viguera et al., 1997) confirm the idea that if antipsychotic drugs are to be discontinued, the withdrawal of the treatment should be gradual.

Antidepressant Drugs

Antidepressant drugs elevate the mood of persons who are depressed. Some antidepressant medications may be useful in treating disorders other than depression, e.g., panic disorder and generalized anxiety disorder (Rickels et al., 1993). An antidepressant drug that has little or no effect on one person may cause severe, unpleasant side effects in another, and yet have markedly beneficial effects for a third person. Antidepressant drugs can elevate the mood of many depressed individuals, but they have no effect on people who are not depressed; that is, they do not produce a euphoric high in people who are already in a good mood.

antidepressant drugs
chemicals that reduce the symptoms of depression

There are three classes of antidepressant drugs: MAO (monoamine oxidase) inhibitors, tricyclics, and the newer class of antidepressants that act on neurotransmitter receptor sites (serotonin and norepinephrine). Some of these drugs inhibit the re-uptake of serotonin (together, these drugs are known as SSRIs [selective serotonin reuptake inhibitors]). Other newer drugs operate on norepinephrine as well as serotonin.

MAO inhibitors are the oldest of the antidepressant medications. These drugs, including Parnate, Marplan, and Nardil, inhibit the enzyme monoamine oxidase, which normally breaks down levels of serotonin, norepinephrine, and dopamine in the brain. The net result is an increase in these neurotransmitters and elevated mood (Julien, 1995). A major drawback to MAO inhibitors is that they can be toxic and can be difficult to use. Among other things, they interact badly with foods containing tyramine, such as aged cheeses, red wine, and chicken livers (Julien, 1995). The tricyclics, including imipramine, desipramine, and trimipramine, are generally safer and more effective than the older MAO inhibitors. Tricyclics affect the operation of the neurotransmitter serotonin.

Drugs in the SSRI class of antidepressants are usually no more effective than tricyclics. However they do act faster to relieve symptoms and have fewer side effects (Julien, 1985). *Prozac* was introduced in 1987. Chemically, *Prozac* is unrelated to most of the other antidepressants, although it, too, affects a brain neurotransmitter (serotonin). Prozac works by inhibiting the re-uptake (or breaking down) of serotonin causing higher levels of serotonin in the brain. This increased serotonin level elevates mood. Often an effective medication, its main advantage is that it produces fewer negative side effects than some of the older antidepressants. Three other SSRI antidepressants are *Zoloft*, *Luvox*, and *Paxil.*

Three other antidepressant drugs, which are not technically SSRIs, are Effexor, Serzone, and Remeron. Of particular note is *Effexor,* which was approved for use in 1993 and has proven to be effective with few side effects. Like *Prozac,* it targets levels of the neurotransmitter serotonin in the brain, but does so more quickly and with slightly more precision. It also inhibits the re-uptake of norepinephrine increasing the levels of this neurotransmitter in the brain (Feighner, 1997). Increased norepinephrine is associated with mood elevation. There are two classes of drugs currently being investigated for possible use with bipolar disorder, the newer antipsychotics (some promise with these, but more for the manic stage than the depression stage) and anti-epileptic or anti-seizure medications. For reasons not yet clear, these drugs do show promise with bipolar disorder and produce significantly fewer side effects (Keck, 2001).

You might be wondering why there are so many "new generation" drugs that appear to do the same thing. Although the net effect of each may be similar to the others in this class, each produces its effect differently. Different individuals respond differently to the various antidepressant medications. What works for one person may not work for another. For example, one person may respond very well to Prozac, while another may not. That second person may respond better to Effexor. The bottom line on antidepressant medications is that the *exact* manner in which they act to relieve symptoms of depression is not well known. Having many drugs available makes it more likely that a physician or psychiatrist can find a medication that will be maximally effective for a given patient.

Another important point about antidepressant medications is that they typically take two to four weeks to show any effect. Their full effect may take six weeks, and they need to be taken long-term to prevent recurrence of the depression (Maxman, 1991). As with the antipsychotics, most antidepressant medications produce unfortunate side effects in some patients, including intellectual confusion, increased perspiration, and weight gain.

Some have been implicated as a cause of heart disease. Another major problem with some antidepressant drugs is that they require adherence to a strict diet and carefully monitored dosages to be most effective.

This is an appropriate context in which to mention *lithium,* or lithium salts, such as lithium carbonate. Lithium salts are referred to as "mood stabilizers" (Maxman, 1991). They have been used with success in treating major depression, but are most useful in controlling the manic stage of bipolar disorders. A major benefit of lithium treatments is that they are often effective in preventing or reducing the occurrence of future episodes of mood disorder (NIMH, 1981, 1989; Kahn, 1995). There are those for whom the drug has no beneficial effects. Furthermore, it was once believed that the prolonged use of lithium treatments caused convulsions, kidney failure, and other serious reactions, but there is little data to support such a belief (Schou, 1997).

Unlike antipsychotic medications, when antidepressant drugs are effective, they may actually bring about long-term cures rather than just symptom suppression. In other words, the changes in mood caused by the drugs may outlast use of the drug itself. The plan, in fact, is to gradually reduce the dosage of the drug over time. For persons with mood disorders who do not respond to drugs presently available, other types are being tested, and for such patients, electroconvulsive therapy may be indicated.

Antianxiety Drugs

The **antianxiety drugs** (tranquilizers) help reduce the felt aspect of anxiety. Some anti-anxiety drugs, e.g., *Miltown* or *Equanil,* are muscle relaxants. When muscular tension is reduced, the patient often reports feeling calm and at ease. The other major variety of antianxiety drugs is the group of chemicals called *benzodiazepines* (e.g., *Librium, Valium,* and *Xanax*). These are among the most commonly prescribed of all drugs. They act directly on the central nervous system, and their impact is significant. They help anxious people feel less anxious. Initially, the only negative side effects appear to be a slight drowsiness, blurred vision, and a slight impairment of coordination.

antianxiety drugs chemicals that alleviate the symptoms of anxiety; also known as tranquilizers

Unfortunately, the tranquilizing effect of the drugs is not long-lasting. Patients can fall into a pattern of relying on the drugs to alleviate even the slightest fears and worries. A dependency and addiction can develop from which withdrawal can be difficult. In fact, a danger of the antianxiety medications is the very fact that they are so effective. As long as one can avoid the unpleasant feelings of anxiety simply by taking a pill, there is little to motivate one to seek out and deal with the actual cause of one's anxiety.

A curiosity is that these drugs are much more likely to be prescribed for women, especially women over age 45, than they are for men (Travis, 1988). This may very well be the result of a tendency on the part of physicians to see women as more likely to be anxious in the first place (Unger & Crawford, 1992).

Figure 13.1 is a summary table of some of the major psychoactive medications listed by their trade name.

BEFORE YOU GO ON

- What are the three major types of psychoactive medications used to treat psychological disorders?

- What are the antipsychotic drugs?

- What are the three types of antidepressant drugs?

- What are the antianxiety drugs?

- What are the advantages and disadvantages of using psychoactive drugs to treat psychological disorders?

Disorder	Medication*	Intended Result
Schizophrenia	Haldol, Navane, Prolixin, Risperdal, Thorazine, Trilifon	Suppresses symptoms
	Clorazil	Used for those resistant to other drugs
Major Depression	Elavil, Effexor, Nardil, Parnate Paxil, Prozac, Tofranil, Zoloft	Decreases depression
Bipolar Disorder	Depakote, Lithium, Tegretol	Reduces both highs and lows
Anxiety Disorder	Ativan, Librium, Valium, Xanax	Reduces feelings of apprehension and dread
Panic Disorder	Paxil, Klonopin, Tofranil, Xanax	Reduces frequency of attacks
OCD	Anafranil, Luvox, Prozac Zoloft	Minimizes compulsive behaviors

*This is only a partial list of some of the more common drugs now in use.

From: Gorman, J.M. (1996). *The Essential Guide to Psychiatric Drugs.* New York: St. Martin Press.

FIGURE 13.1

Trade Names of Psychoactive Drugs Used to Treat Psychological Disorders

Topic Review 13A

1. **How did the ancient Greeks and Romans conceptualize mental illness?**

   Early beliefs about mental illness centered on a person being out of favor with the gods. If a person were temporarily out of favor, treatment took the form of prayer and religious rituals. More severely afflicted individuals were believed to be possessed by an evil spirit. Treatment involved exorcising the evil spirit. More enlightened scholars of the time believed that there was an underlying physical cause for mental illness.

2. **How can treatment of the mentally ill during the Middle Ages be characterized?**

   The Middle Ages saw a return to the belief that the mentally ill were possessed or under the spell of evil spirits. For hundreds of years the prevailing belief was that the mentally ill were in league with the devil. These individuals were tortured until they confessed their sins. If torture did not yield a confession the mentally ill person was killed, often by being burned at the stake. Another "treatment for the mentally ill" was to place them into asylums where conditions and treatment were poor.

3. **What contributions did Philippe Pinel make to the treatment of the mentally ill?**

   Pinel was a French physician who was named director of an asylum in Paris. Pinel ordered that fifty patients be unchained and allowed to move freely about the hospital. This more humane treatment of the mentally ill led some patients to get better, a few even being released from the asylum. Unfortunately, Pinel's humane treatment did not spread to other asylums and did not lead to a widespread reform of treatment for the mentally ill.

4. **What contributions did Benjamin Rush, Dorothea Dix, and Clifford Beers make to the treatment of the mentally ill?**

   Benjamin Rush published the first text on mental disorders in the United States. He supported humane treatment for the mentally ill. He was successful in curbing the practice of putting the mentally ill on display. Dix was a nurse who began a crusade which she took from state to state for reform in prisons, mental hospitals,

and asylums. Clifford Beers was a formal mental patient who wrote a book about his experiences, pointing out that he recovered in spite of his treatment (and not because of it). His book was read by influential people and stimulated the modern "mental health movement."

5. **What is psychosurgery?**

   Psychosurgery is any surgical technique, usually directed at the brain, designed to bring about a change in a patient's affects, behaviors, or cognitions. Because of its inherent danger, and because safer, reversible treatments such as drug therapy are available today, it is no longer used. There are, however, psychosurgical techniques that are used, including the split-brain procedure as a treatment for epilepsy and the cingulectomy as a treatment for anxiety and obsessive-compulsive disorder.

6. **What is involved in the procedure known as a lobotomy?**

   Lobotomy was a commonly used psychosurgical technique. It involved a surgeon severing the major connections between the prefrontal cortex and lower brain centers. It was first performed in 1935 and became popular thereafter. The theory behind the surgery was that the prefrontal lobes influenced the more basic emotional centers in the lower brain. Often, the surgery was successful in reducing a patient's violent emotions. It was used as a measure of last resort because of the potential for serious side effects.

7. **What is ECT, and why is it still being used?**

   ECT stands for electroconvulsive, or shock, therapy. In this treatment, a brain seizure is produced with an electric current. Upon regaining consciousness, the patient has no memory of the procedure. Although there may be negative side effects, particularly with prolonged or repeated use, the technique is demonstrably useful for many patients as a means of reducing or even eliminating severe depression and other symptoms usually associated with schizophrenia.

8. **What are the three major types of psychoactive medications used to treat psychological disorders?**

   Antipsychotic drugs are used to reduce or control psychotic symptoms characterized by a loss of contact with reality and a gross impairment of functioning. When they are effective, antidepressant drugs reduce episodes of depression. And, as their name suggests, antianxiety medications alleviate, or suppress, feelings of anxiety.

9. What are the antipsychotic drugs and what are their effects?

Antipsychotic drugs are used primarily to treat schizophrenia. The first antipsychotic drug was chlorpromazine, introduced in the 1950s. It was first used as a drug to calm patients before surgery. However, it was found to be effective in treating some patients with mental disorders. By 1956 there were a half dozen antipsychotic drugs available. The use of these drugs has steadily increased over the ensuing years. Most of these drugs act to block dopamine and relieve positive psychotic symptoms of schizophrenia. One drug, clozapine, reduces the negative psychotic symptoms of schizophrenia. Although these medications are effective, they can have unpleasant side effects.

10. What are the three classes of antidepressant drugs?

The three classes of antidepressant drugs are MAO inhibitors, tricyclics, and the new generation of SSRI drugs. The MAO inhibitors are the oldest of the antidepressant drugs. They inhibit monoamine oxidase from metabolizing serotonin, norepinephrine, and dopamine in the brain, leading to elevated mood. These drugs have some potentially serious side effects. Tricyclics were the next drugs introduced which were safer than the MAO inhibitors. The new generation drugs include Prozac, Effexor, Serzone, and Remeron. These drugs inhibit the re-uptake of serotonin and in some cases, norepinephrine, resulting in elevated mood. Although the SSRI medications are not more effective than the tricyclics, they have fewer side effects and take effect faster. Most antidepressant drugs take from ten to fourteen days to take effect and longer to reach therapeutic levels in the blood.

11. What is Lithium and what is it used to treat?

Lithium (or lithium salts) is classified as a mood stabilizer. Lithium has been used successfully in treating major depression, but is most widely used to control the manic episodes of individuals with bipolar disorder. In addition to controlling symptoms, Lithium also reduces the occurrence of future mood disorders. There is little support for the old idea that Lithium has serious side effects.

12. What are the antianxiety drugs?

The antianxiety drugs include muscle relaxants (Miltown, for example) and benzodiazepines (Librium, Valium, and Xanax, for example). These drugs act on the central nervous system and relieve anxiety. Short-term side effects include drowsiness, blurred vision, and slight impairment of coordination. The antianxiety drugs tend not to have a long-term effect.

13. What are the advantages and disadvantages of using psychoactive drugs to treat psychological disorders?

Long-term use of psychoactive drugs may produce a number of potentially harmful or unpleasant side effects. The most common antianxiety drugs, or tranquilizers, are the benzodiazepines, including Valium and Librium, which are among the most commonly prescribed drugs in the world. These drugs are effective in reducing felt levels of anxiety. There is evidence that some patients who use antianxiety drugs develop addictions to them. Like antipsychotic drugs, they suppress symptoms; they do not cure the underlying anxiety, and even small overdoses can lead to dependency and addiction.

Topic 13B THE PSYCHOTHERAPIES

The major goal of the various psychotherapy techniques is to help a person to think, feel, or act more effectively. Additionally, different types of therapy have different specific subgoals. In this Topic, we focus on five types of psychotherapy and see that each approaches therapeutic interaction a bit differently. Before we get to our discussion of specific techniques, let's see what sorts of professionals provide treatment or therapy for persons with psychological disorders.

Key Questions to Answer

While reading this Topic, find the answers to the following key questions:

1. Who may offer psychotherapy?

2. What are the major features of Freudian psychoanalysis?

3. How is psychoanalysis different today from when it was practiced by Freud?

4. What are the basic ideas behind humanistic therapy techniques?

5. What are the characteristics of client-centered therapy?

6. What are the characteristics of Gestalt therapy?

7. What are the underlying assumptions of behavior therapy?

8. What are systematic desensitization and exposure and response prevention?

9. What is aversion therapy?

10. What are contingency management and contingency contracting?

11. What is modeling, and how is it used as a therapy technique?

12. What is the basic idea behind cognitive therapy techniques?

13. What is the basic logic behind rational-emotive therapy and cognitive restructuring therapy?

14. What is group therapy?

15. What are some of the advantages of group therapy?

16. What are two assumptions underlying family therapy?

17. Is there any evidence that psychotherapy is effective?

WHO PROVIDES PSYCHOTHERAPY?

Just 30 years ago, only 13 percent of the population sought psychotherapy at any time in their lives. Today, 30 percent will have some experience in psychotherapy in their lifetime. People seek help from mental health professionals twice as often as they visit internists.

What follows is a list of generalities; these descriptions will not hold true for everyone in a given category. Remember also that because of their experience and training, some mental health professionals develop specialties within their fields. That is, some therapists specialize in working with children or adolescents; some work primarily with adults; some prefer to work with families; and some devote their efforts to people with substance and alcohol abuse problems. With these cautions in mind, the following may be considered psychotherapists:

1. *Clinical psychologists* usually have earned a Ph.D. in psychology from a program that provides practical, applied experience in therapeutic techniques, as well as an emphasis on research. Ph.D. clinicians complete a one-year internship, usually at a mental health center or psychiatric hospital, and have extensive training in psychological testing (in general, psychodiagnostics). Some clinical psychologists have a Psy.D. (pronounced "sigh-dee"), which is a Doctor of Psychology, rather than the Doctor of Philosophy degree. Psy.D. programs take as long to complete as Ph.D. programs, but tend to emphasize more practical, clinical work.

2. *Psychiatry* is a specialty area in medicine. In addition to course work required for an M.D., the psychiatrist does a psychiatric internship (usually one year) and a psychiatric residency (usually three years) in a hospital where psychological disorders are treated. During the internship and residency, the psychiatrist specializes in the care of the psychologically disturbed. At the moment, the psychiatrist is the only type of psychotherapist permitted to use the biomedical treatments; a campaign is underway to get some medical privileges for Ph.D. psychologists (Gutierrez & Silk, 1998).

3. *Counseling psychologists* usually have a Ph.D. in psychology. The focus of study (and the required one-year internship) is generally with patients with less-severe psychological problems. For instance, rather than spending an internship in a psychiatric hospital, a counseling psychologist would more likely spend time at a university counseling center.

4. *Licensed professional counselors* have a degree in counselor education (at the master's level) and have met state requirements for a license to practice psychotherapy. Counselors are found in schools and private practice, but also work in mental health settings, specializing in family counseling, marriage counseling, and drug abuse.

5. *Psychoanalyst* is a special label given to a clinical psychologist or a psychiatrist who has also received intensive training (and certification) in the methods of Freudian psychoanalysis.

6. *Clinical social workers* generally acquire a master's degree, although Ph.D.s in social work are becoming more common. Social workers engage in a variety of psychotherapies, but their traditional role has been involvement in family and group therapy.

Some people with a master's degree in psychology provide psychotherapy, but because of certification laws in many states, they cannot advertise themselves as "psychologists." *Occupational therapists* usually have a master's degree (less frequently, a bachelor's degree) in occupational therapy, which includes many psychology classes and internship training in aiding the psychologically and physically handicapped. *Psychiatric nurses* often work in mental hospitals and clinics. In addition to their R.N. degree, psychiatric nurses have training in the care of mentally ill patients. *Pastoral counseling* is a specialty of those with a religious background and a master's degree in psychology or educational counseling. *Mental health technicians* usually have an associate degree in mental health technology (MHT). MHT graduates seldom provide unsupervised therapy, but they may be involved in the delivery of many mental health services.

Some therapists have special training in dealing with clients from various cultures or ethnic groups (Sue, 1998; Sue & Sue, 1990). This can be useful because individuals from different cultures may approach the therapy process very differently. For example, in the United States, "most mental health workers come from middle-class backgrounds and expect their clients to be open, verbal, and psychologically minded. They tend to value verbal, emotional, and behavioral expressiveness" (Koslow & Salett, 1989, p. 3). Clients from non-Western cultures may not be as open and forthcoming with therapists. A therapist who is trained in cross-cultural issues will be in a strong position to adapt to cultural communication differences.

Adler and Gielen (1994) tell the story of an African American woman of Bahamian descent who was complaining of depression. It seems the woman believed that another girlfriend of her lover had placed a "hex" on her. The depressed woman sought treatment from a Haitian spiritual healer who, among other things, took the woman to a cemetery at midnight, placed her in an open grave, and sprinkled some dirt on her before retrieving her. Shortly after this "treatment," the woman was free of her depression, received a raise at her job, and had sent her lover packing. Most American therapists probably would judge this treatment plan to be as bizarre and troubling as the symptoms that prompted it. But in this woman's cultural framework, the ritualistic, symbolic burial allowed her to bury her evil spirits at the cemetery, their source, and come away cleansed. This may be an extreme example, but it is true that members of other cultures and ethnic minorities state a strong preference for "ethnically similar" therapists (e.g., Coleman et al., 1995).

Now that we have an idea of who may offer psychotherapy services, let's consider the types of techniques or approaches they may employ.

How Do I Choose the Right Therapist?

Realizing that so many different professionals offer psychotherapy, how does one go about choosing a psychotherapist? Many people and agencies can serve as a good resource at this point. Do you have any family or friends who have been in therapy or counseling? What (or whom) do they recommend? If you get no useful information from friends or family, there are many other people you could ask (assuming that your symptoms are not acute and that time is not critical). You might check with your psychology instructor. He or she may not be a psychotherapist, but will probably be familiar with the mental health resources of the community. You might also see if your college or university maintains a clinic or counseling center service for students (if nothing else, this is often an inexpensive route to take). Check with your family physician. Among other things, a complete physical examination may turn up some leads about the nature of your problem. You might talk with your rabbi, priest, or minister. Clergy persons commonly deal with people in distress and, again, are usually familiar with community resources. If there is one in your community, call the local mental health center or mental health association. If you think that you may have a problem, the most important thing is not to give up. Find help. And the sooner the better.

Now let's assume that a psychotherapist has been recommended to you. You have scheduled an appointment. How will you know if you've made a wise choice? To be sure, only you can be the judge of that. Two cautions are appropriate here: (1) Give the therapy and the therapist a chance. By now, surely you recognize that psychological problems are seldom simple and easily solved. (In fact, a therapist who suggests that your problem can be easily solved is probably a therapist to be leery of.) It may take three or four sessions before your therapist has learned (from you) what the exact and real nature of your problem *is*. Most psychological problems have developed over a long period of time. An hour or two per week for a week or two cannot be expected automatically to make everything right again, as if by magic. You should expect progress, and you might expect some sessions to be more helpful than others. To expect a miracle cure is to be unreasonable. (2) On the other hand, you may feel that you have given your therapy every opportunity to succeed. If you have been truly open and honest with your therapist and feel that you are in no way profiting from your sessions, say so. Express your displeasure and disappointment. After careful consideration, be prepared to change therapists. Starting over again with someone new may involve costs in time and effort, but occasionally it is the only reasonable option.

BEFORE YOU GO ON

- Who may offer psychotherapy?
- List and briefly define each of the professions that offer psychotherapy. How do they differ?

PSYCHOANALYTIC TECHNIQUES

Psychoanalysis began with Sigmund Freud near the end of the nineteenth century. It did not really evolve from Freudian personality theory; if anything, the reverse is true, for Freud was a therapist first, a personality theorist second. But his techniques of therapy and theory of personality sprang forth from the same mind, and are thus related.

psychoanalysis the form of psychotherapy associated with Freud; aimed at helping the patient gain insight into unconscious conflicts

Psychoanalysis is based on several assumptions, most of them having to do with conflict and the unconscious mind. For Freud, one's life is often a struggle to resolve conflicts between naturally opposing forces. The biological, sexual, aggressive strivings of the *id* are often in conflict with the *superego*, associated with being overly cautious and experiencing guilt. The strivings of the id also can be in conflict with the rational, reality-based *ego*, which may be called upon to mediate between the id and the superego. Anxiety-producing conflicts that go unresolved are *repressed*; that is they are forced out of awareness into the unconscious mind. Conflicts and anxiety-producing traumas of childhood can be expected to produce symptoms of psychological disturbance later in life.

According to Freud, the way to rid oneself of anxiety is to enter the unconscious, identify the details of the repressed, anxiety-producing conflict, bring it out into the open, and then resolve it as well as possible. The first step is to gain insight into the true nature of one's problems; only then can problem solving begin. Thus the goals of Freudian psychoanalysis are insight and resolution of repressed conflict. This process is very slow and gradual, because old, repressed experiences tend to be well-integrated in one's current life situation (Kaplan & Sadock, 1991).

Sigmund Freud died in 1939, but his approach to psychotherapy did not die with him. It has been modified (as Freud himself modified it over the years), but it remains true to the basic thrust of Freudian psychoanalysis.

Freudian Psychoanalysis

In 1881, Freud graduated from the University of Vienna Medical School. From the start, he was interested in what were then called *nervous disorders*. He went to France to study the technique of hypnosis, which many were claiming to be a worthwhile treatment for psychological disorders. Freud was not totally convinced, but when he returned to Vienna, he and a colleague, Josef Breuer, tried hypnosis to treat nervous disorders—conversion reaction (hysteria) in particular. Both became convinced that hypnosis itself was of little benefit because its effects were temporary (Freud, 1943). Hypnosis, according to Freud, did not allow for an in-depth exploration of the underlying causes for nervous disorder. In fact, Freud characterized the difference between hypnosis and psychoanalysis in the following way:

> The hypnotic therapy endeavors to cover up and as it were to whitewash something going on in the mind, the analytic to lay bare and to remove something. The first works cosmetically, the second surgically. (Freud, 1943, p. 392).

What mattered, Freud believed, was to have the patients talk about anything and everything to get at the underlying conflicts that were causing the patient's symptoms. Freud and Breuer's method became known as the "talking cure," better known as psychoanalysis.

Psychoanalysis with Sigmund Freud was a time-consuming (up to five days per week for as many as ten years), often tedious process of aided self-examination. The major task for the patient was to talk openly and honestly about all aspects of his or her life, from early childhood memories to the dreams of the present. The main task of the therapist/analyst, was to interpret what was being expressed by the patient, always on the lookout for clues to possible repressed conflict. Once identified, the patient and the analyst could try together to resolve any conflicts underlying the symptoms that brought the patient to analysis in the first place. Several procedures and processes were used in the search for repressed conflicts.

Free Association

free association the procedure in psychoanalysis in which the patient is to express whatever comes to mind without editing responses

The technique of **free association** was a standard procedure in psychoanalysis. Patients were to say out loud whatever came into their minds. Sometimes the analyst would provide a stimulus word to get a chain of freely flowing associations going. To free associate the way Freud would have wanted is not an easy task. It often required many sessions for patients to learn the technique. Patients were not to edit their associations. They were to be completely honest and say whatever they thought. Many people are uncomfortable, at least initially, sharing their private, innermost thoughts and desires with anyone, much less a stranger; here is where the Freudian couch came in. To help his patients relax, Freud would have them lie down, be comfortable, and avoid eye contact with him. The job of the analyst through all this was to try to interpret the apparently free-flowing verbal responses, always looking for expressions of unconscious desires and conflicts.

Resistance

resistance in psychoanalysis, the inability or unwillingness to discuss freely some aspect of one's life

During the course of psychoanalysis, the analyst listens very carefully to what the patient says. The analyst also carefully listens for what the patient does not say. Freud believed **resistance**—the unwillingness or inability to discuss freely some aspect of one's life—was a significant process in analysis. Resistance can show itself in many ways, from simply avoiding the mention of some topic, to joking about matters as being inconsequential, to disrupting a session when a particular topic comes up for discussion, to missing appointments altogether.

Say, for example, that over the last six months in psychoanalysis a patient has talked freely about a wide variety of subjects, including early childhood memories and all family members—all, that is, except her older brother. She has talked about all sorts of private experiences, some of them sexual, some of them pleasant, some unpleasant. But after six months of talking, she has not said anything about her older brother. Her analyst, noting this possible resistance, suggests that during the next visit, he would like to hear about this older brother. Then, for the first time since analysis began, the patient misses her next appointment. She comes to the following appointment, but ten minutes late. The analyst may now suspect that there is a problem with the relationship between the patient and her older brother, a problem that may have begun in childhood and that has been repressed ever since. Of course, *there may be no problem at all*, but for psychoanalysis to be successful, potential resistance needs to be broken down and investigated.

Dream Interpretation

Analyzing patient dreams is an important aspect of psychoanalysis. Freud referred to dreams as the "royal road" to the unconscious level of the mind. Freud often trained his patients to recall and record their dreams in great detail. He analyzed dreams at two levels: *manifest content*, the dream as recalled and reported, and *latent content*, the dream as a symbolic representation of the contents of the unconscious. Latent content was usually analyzed to identify some sort of unconscious wish fulfillment. Symbolism hidden in the latent content of dreams has been one of the most controversial aspects of Freud's theories. The idea was that true feelings, motives, and desires might be camouflaged in a dream. For example, someone who reports a dream about suffocating under a huge pile of pillows might be expressing feelings about parental overprotectiveness. Someone who dreams about driving into an endless tunnel and becoming lost there might be expressing fears or concerns of a sexual nature. The job for the analyst, Freud argued, was to interpret dreams in terms of whatever insights they could provide about the true nature of the patient's unconscious mind.

Transference

Another controversial aspect of Freudian psychoanalysis is his concept of transference. **Transference** occurs when the patient unconsciously comes to view and feel about the analyst in much the same way he or she feels about another important person in his or her life, usually a parent. As therapy progresses over a long period, the relationship between analyst and patient often does become a complex and emotional one. If feelings once directed toward someone else of significance become directed toward the analyst, they are more accessible, more easily observed, and more readily dealt with. Therapists have to guard against letting their own feelings and experiences interfere with their objective interactions with their patients. Failure to do so is called *countertransference*.

transference in psychoanalysis occurs when the patient comes to feel about the analyst in the same way he or she once felt about some other important person

Post-Freudian Psychoanalysis

Early in this century, Freudian psychoanalysis was the only form of psychotherapy, and through the 1940s and 1950s, it still was the therapy of choice. "Psychoanalytic theory was the dominant force in psychiatry in the postwar period and was embraced by a large number of clinical psychologists. To a certain extent, and for all practical purposes, there was no rival orientation" (Garfield, 1981, p. 176). In recent years though, psychoanalysis has become less common, and strict Freudian psychoanalysis has become rare.

How has the Freudian system of therapy changed? First, note what hasn't changed: to qualify as a psychoanalytic approach, the basic aim of therapy must be the uncovering of deep-seated, unconscious conflict, perhaps caused by childhood experiences, and the removal of defenses so that such conflicts can be resolved (Luborsky et al., 1993; Sandler, Dare, & Holder, 1992).

Probably the most significant change since Freud's practice is the concern for shortening the length of analysis (Bloom, 1997; Strupp & Binder, 1984). Now we talk about time-limited and short-form psychoanalytic therapy (Binder, 1993; Koss & Butcher, 1986). Today's analysts take a more active role than did Freud, using interviews and discussions, and they rely less on free association. The couch as a requirement is gone; the comfort of the patient is what matters, and some patients feel more comfortable pacing or sitting than they do lying on a couch. Modern psychoanalysts, although not insensitive to the impact of childhood experiences, tend to spend more time exploring the

BEFORE YOU GO ON

- What are the major features of Freudian psychoanalysis?

- List and define the various techniques used in Freudian psychoanalysis.

- How is psychoanalysis different today from when it was practiced by Freud?

present. For example, a patient may come for analysis complaining about feelings of depression and anger to the point that the analyst believes there is a real and present danger that the patient might harm himself or herself, or even commit suicide. The thrust of therapy is in the here and now, dealing with the patient's current anger and depression until the analyst is convinced the patient is no longer in danger of harming himself or herself.

HUMANISTIC TECHNIQUES

There are many different types of humanistic psychotherapy and their allied cousins, the *existential therapies*. What they all have in common is a concern for self-examination, personal growth, and development. The goal of these therapies is not to uncover deep seated conflicts, but to foster psychological growth and help a person take full advantage of life's opportunities. Based on the premise that people can take charge of themselves and their futures, and can grow and change, therapy is directed at assisting with these processes.

client-centered therapy the humanistic psychotherapy associated with Rogers; aimed at helping a person grow and self-actualize

Client-centered therapy, also called Rogerian therapy after its founder, Carl Rogers, best typifies the humanistic approach. As its name suggests, the client is the center of the therapeutic interaction. Given his medical training, Freud called the people he dealt with *patients*. Rogers never used the term *patient*, and before his death in 1987 began using the term *person-centered* rather than *client-centered* to describe his approach to therapy.

For Rogers, therapy provides a special opportunity for a person to engage in self-discovery. Another way to express this is to say that a goal of client-centered therapy is to help the individual self-actualize—to grow and develop to the best of one's potential.

What are the characteristics of client-centered therapy? Again, there are variants, but the following ideas characterize a client-centered approach. The focus is on the present, not the past or childhood. The focus is on one's *feelings* or affect, not beliefs or cognitions; that is, you are more likely to hear, "How do you feel about that?" than "What do you think about that?" The therapist will attempt to *reflect*, or mirror, not interpret, how a client is feeling (using statements such as, "You seem angry," or "Does that make you feel sad?"). Assessing and reflecting the true nature of a client's feelings is not necessarily easy to do. To do so requires that the therapist be an active listener and be **empathic**, or be able to understand and share the essence of another's feelings.

empathic able to understand and share the essence of another's feelings, or to view from another's perspective

Throughout each session, the therapist tries to express *unconditional positive regard*. This is the expression of being accepting and noncritical. "I will not be critical. If that is the way you feel, that is the way you feel. Anything you say in here is okay."

Gestalt therapy is associated with Fritz Perls (1893–1970) and shares many of the same goals as Roger's person-centered approach (Perls, 1967, 1971; Perls et al., 1951). Gestalt means (roughly) "whole" or "totality." Thus, the goal of Gestalt therapy is to assist a person to integrate his or her thoughts, feelings, and actions—to assist in increasing the person's self-awareness, self-acceptance, and growth. The therapy is aimed at helping the person become aware of his or her whole self—including conflicts and problems—and to begin finding ways to deal with conflicts and problems.

What we have here is "getting in touch with one's feelings," acknowledging them as valid, and moving to get on with one's life. Although the focus of Gestalt therapy is the individual, sessions are often convened in small group settings. Clients may be given role playing exercises in which they have to play several parts. They may be asked to act out how they feel in a certain situation and then act out how they wish they could respond.

BEFORE YOU GO ON

- What are the main features of humanistic therapy techniques?

- What are the characteristics of client-centered therapy?

- What are the characteristics of Gestalt therapy?

BEHAVIORAL TECHNIQUES

There is no one **behavior therapy**; it is a collection of several techniques. What unites these techniques is that they are "methods of psychotherapeutic change founded on principles of learning established in the psychological laboratory" (Wolpe, 1981, p. 159). The main assumption of behavior therapy is that maladaptive behaviors are learned, so they can be unlearned. There are many principles of learning and many psychological disorders to which such methods and principles can be applied. In this section, we will list a few applications of learning theory that have become part of behavior therapy.

behavior therapy techniques of psychotherapy founded on principles of learning established in the psychological laboratory and aimed at changing one's behaviors

Systematic desensitization, applying classical conditioning to alleviate feelings of anxiety, particularly those associated with phobic disorders, is one of the first applications of learning theory to meet with success. It was introduced by Joseph Wolpe in the late 1950s (Wolpe, 1958, 1982), although others had used similar procedures earlier. Systematic desensitization is basically a matter of teaching a person first to relax totally and then to remain relaxed as he or she thinks about or is exposed to ever-increasing levels of stimuli that produce anxiety. If the person can remain calm and relaxed, that response can be conditioned to replace the anxious or fear response previously associated with a particular stimulus.

systematic desensitization classical conditioning procedures, used to alleviate anxiety, in which anxiety-producing stimuli are paired with a state of relaxation

A relatively new form of behavior therapy, *exposure and response prevention*, has shown promise as a treatment for obsessive-compulsive disorder (OCD), a disorder that is usually resistant to psychotherapy. In one clinic, patients are exposed for two hours, five days a week, for three weeks to whatever stimulus situation evokes their obsessional thinking or compulsions. They are asked to vividly imagine the consequences they fear *without* engaging in their usual compulsive or obsessional routine; the procedure is also repeated in homework assignments. This is followed by a maintenance program of phone calls or clinic visits. For example, a patient who is obsessed with dirt and germs is told

Behavior therapy techniques, such as systematic desensitization, are particularly useful in treating phobic disorders. A common disorder is agoraphobia, an intense, irrational fear of being in public places from which escape might be difficult.

to sit on the floor and imagine that she has become ill because of insufficient washing and cleaning. For the first two weeks she must not wash her hands (at all) and can only take a shower for ten minutes every other day. In the third week she can wash her hands for 30 seconds, five times a day. This program claims that 75 to 83 percent of the patients who complete the regimen show significant and lasting improvement (Foa, 1995).

aversion therapy a technique of behavior therapy in which an aversive stimulus, such as a shock, is paired with an undesired behavior

Aversion therapy is another example of learning applied to solving psychological problems. In **aversion therapy**, a stimulus that may be harmful but that produces a pleasant response is paired with an aversive, painful stimulus until the original stimulus is avoided. For example, every time you put a cigarette in your mouth, a painful shock is delivered to your lip. Every time you take a drink of alcohol, you get violently sick to your stomach from a nausea-producing drug. Every time a child molester is shown a picture of a young child, he gets an electric shock.

Techniques of aversion therapy do not sound like the sort of things anyone would agree to voluntarily. Many people do, however, volunteer for such treatments for two reasons: (1) aversion therapy is very effective at suppressing a specific behavior, at least for a while, and (2) it is seen as the lesser of two evils (shocks and nausea-producing drugs are not much fun, but people see the continuation of their inappropriate, often self-destructive behaviors as even more dangerous in the long run). Still, aversion therapy, in any form, is not commonly practiced, and when it is, it tends to suppress behaviors for only a relatively short time. During that time, other techniques may be used in an attempt to bring about a more lasting change in behavior. In other words, aversion therapy is seldom effective when used alone; it is usually used in conjunction with other therapy.

Contingency management and contingency contracting borrow from the learning principles of operant conditioning. The idea is to have a person appreciate the consequences of his or her behaviors. Appropriate behaviors lead to rewards and the opportunity to do valued things, whereas inappropriate behaviors do not lead to reinforcement and provide fewer opportunities.

In many cases, these procedures work very well. As operant conditioning would predict, their effectiveness is a function of the extent to which the therapist has control over the situation. If the therapist can manage the control of rewards and punishments, called **contingency management**, he or she stands a good chance of modifying the client's behavior. For example, in an institutional setting, if a patient (e.g., a severely disturbed person with schizophrenia) engages in the appropriate response (leaving her room to go to dinner), then the patient gets something she really wants (a chance to watch TV for an extra hour). In an outpatient setting, the therapist tries to arrange the situation so that the client learns to reinforce his or her own behaviors when they are appropriate.

contingency management bringing about changes in one's behaviors by controlling rewards and punishments

Contingency contracting amounts to establishing a contract with a client so that exhibiting certain behaviors (preparing dinner) results in certain rewards (watching TV). In many cases, contingency contracting involves establishing a *token economy*. What this means is that the person is first taught that some token—a checker, a poker chip, or just a check mark on a pad—can be saved. When enough tokens are accumulated, they are cashed in for something of value to the person. With contracting, the value of a token for a specific behavior is spelled out ahead of time. Because control over the environment of the learner is most complete in such circumstances, this technique is particularly effective in institutions and with young children.

contingency contracting establishing an agreement (contract) with one to reinforce appropriate behaviors; often involving token economies

Recognizing that not all learning can be explained in terms of classical or operant conditioning, it should be no surprise that some types of behavior therapy use learning principles other than those from simple conditioning. **Modeling**, a term introduced by Albert Bandura, involves the acquisition of an appropriate response through the imitation of a model. Modeling can be an effective means of learning. In a therapy situation, modeling amounts to having patients watch someone else perform an appropriate behavior, perhaps earning a reward for it (called *vicarious reinforcement*).

modeling the acquisition of new responses through the imitation of another who responds appropriately

Some phobias, particularly those in children, can be overcome through modeling. A child who is afraid of dogs, for example, may profit from watching another child (which would be more effective than using an adult) playing with a dog. Modeling is also a part of what is called *assertiveness training*, which involves helping individuals stand up for their rights and come to the realization that their feelings and opinions matter and should be expressed. Such training involves many processes, including direct instruction, group discussion, role-playing, and contingency management, but it often relies on modeling to help individuals learn appropriate ways to express how they feel and what they think in social situations.

BEFORE YOU GO ON

- What is the basic assumption of behavior therapy?

- What are systematic desensitization and exposure and response prevention?

- What are contingency management and contingency contracting?

- How is modeling used in therapy?

COGNITIVE TECHNIQUES

Psychotherapists who use cognitive techniques do not deny the importance of a person's behaviors; these therapies are often called *cognitive-behavioral*. Rather, they believe that what matters most are a client's beliefs, thoughts, perceptions, and attitudes about himself or herself and the environment (Weinland, 1996). The major principle is that to change how one feels and acts, therapy should first be directed at changing how one thinks. The goal of treatment is not only to produce a change in the way one thinks and behaves, but to teach the client how those changes were achieved. That is, the goal is not so much to provide a "cure" as it is to develop a strategy that can be applied to a wide range of contexts and experiences (Hollon, Shelton, & Loosen, 1991). As we've seen with other approaches to psychotherapy, there are several types of cognitive-behavioral therapy: One survey identified nearly two dozen types (Dobson, 1988). We'll examine just two: rational-emotive therapy and cognitive restructuring therapy.

Rational-Emotive Therapy

rational-emotive therapy (RET)
a form of cognitive therapy, associated with Ellis, aimed at changing a person's irrational beliefs or maladaptive cognitions

Rational-emotive therapy (RET) (now often *rational-emotive behavior therapy*) is associated with Albert Ellis (1970, 1991, 1995, 1997). Its basic premise is that psychological problems arise when people try to interpret what happens in the world (a cognitive activity) on the basis of irrational beliefs. "Rational-emotive therapy (RET) hypothesizes that people largely disturb themselves by thinking in a self-defeating, illogical, and unrealistic manner—especially by escalating their natural preferences and desires into absolutistic, dogmatic musts and commands on themselves, others, and their environmental conditions" (Ellis, 1987, p. 364).

When compared to person-centered techniques, RET is quite directive. Ellis takes exception with techniques of psychotherapy designed to help a person *feel* better without providing useful strategies by which the person can *get* better (Ellis, 1991). In rational-emotive therapy, the therapist takes an active role in interpreting the client's system of beliefs and encourages active change. Therapists often act as role models and make homework assignments that help clients bring their expectations and perceptions in line with reality. Some examples of irrational beliefs that people can form, and which lead to psychological problems are (Ellis, 1995):

- That one must always do tasks well because of a great desire to perform tasks well

- That one must always have the approval of others due to a strong need for approval

- That one must be loved by everyone for everything done

- That it is better to avoid problems than face them

- That one must always maintain perfect self control

Cognitive Restructuring Therapy

Similar to rational-emotive therapy is **cognitive restructuring therapy**, associated with Aaron Beck (1976, 1991, 1995). Although the goals are similar, cognitive restructuring therapy is less confrontational and direct than RET.

Beck's assumption is that considerable psychological distress stems from a few simple, but misguided, beliefs (cognitions). According to Beck, people with disorders (particularly those related to depression, for which cognitive restructuring was first designed) share certain characteristics. For example:

1. They tend to have very negative self-images. They do not value themselves or what they do.

2. They tend to take a very negative view of life experiences.

3. They overgeneralize. For example, having failed one test, a person comes to believe that there is no way he or she can do college work, withdraws from school and looks for a job, even though he or she believes that no one would offer a job to someone who is such a failure and a college dropout.

4. They actually seek out experiences that reinforce their negative expectations. The student in the preceding example may apply for a job as a stockbroker or a law clerk. Lacking even minimal experience, he or she will not be offered either job and, thus, will confirm his or her own worthlessness.

5. They tend to hold a rather dismal outlook for the future.

6. They tend to avoid seeing the bright side of any experience.

Sometimes people become very upset if they are not included or liked by everyone. Both Albert Ellis and Aaron Beck, as cognitive therapists, would argue that such is an irrational belief, and so long as it is held, the person will experience distress.

In cognitive restructuring therapy, the patient is given opportunities to test or demonstrate his or her beliefs. The patient and therapist make up a list of hypotheses based on patient assumptions and beliefs and then actually go out and test these hypotheses. Obviously, the therapist tries to exercise enough control over the situation so that the experi-ments do not confirm the patient's beliefs about himself or herself, but will lead instead to positive outcomes. Given the hypothesis "Nobody cares about me," the therapist need only find one person who does care to refute it. This approach, of leading a person to the self-discovery that negative attitudes directed toward oneself are often inappropriate, has proven very successful in the treatment of depression, although it has been extended to cover a wide range of psychological disorders (Beck, 1985, 1991; Beck & Freeman, 1990; Zinbarg et al., 1992).

cognitive restructuring therapy a form of cognitive therapy, associated with Beck, in which an individual is led to overcome negative self-images and pessimistic views of the future

BEFORE YOU GO ON

- What is the basic assumption of cognitive therapy?

- What is the basic logic behind rational-emotive therapy and cognitive restructuring therapy?

GROUP APPROACHES

Many patients profit from some type of *group therapy*. Group therapy is a label applied to a variety of situations in which a number of people are involved in a therapeutic setting at the same time. If nothing else, group therapy provides an economic advantage over individual psychotherapy: one therapist can interact with several people at once (Mackenzie, 1997).

In standard forms of group therapy, clients are brought together at the same time, under the guidance of a therapist, to share their feelings and experiences. Most groups are informal, and no particular form of psychotherapy is dominant. In other words, meeting with people in groups is something a psychotherapist with any sort of training or background might do from time to time.

Several possible benefits can be derived from group meetings, including an awareness that "I'm not the only one with problems." The sense of support that one can get from someone else with problems occasionally is even greater than that afforded by a therapist alone—a sort of "she really knows from experience the hell that I'm going through" logic. And there is truth in the notion that getting involved in helping someone else with a problem is, in itself, a therapeutic process. Yet another advantage of group therapy situations is that the person can learn new, more effective ways of "presenting" himself or herself to others (McRoberts, Burlingame, & Hoag, 1998).

family therapy a type of group therapy focusing on the roles, interdependence, and communication skills of family members

A group approach that has become popular is **family therapy**, which focuses on the roles, interdependence, and communication skills of family members. Family therapy is often begun after one member of a family enters psychotherapy. After discussing the person's problems for a while, other members of the family are invited to join in the therapy sessions. There is evidence that getting the family unit involved in therapy benefits patients with a wide range of disorders, from alcoholism and agoraphobia to depression and schizophrenia (Pinsof, Wynne, & Hambright, 1996; Feist, 1993; Goldfried et al., 1990).

Two related assumptions underlie a family therapy approach. One is that each family member is a part of a system (the family unit), and his or her feelings, thoughts, and behaviors necessarily impact on other family members (Minuchin & Fishman, 1981; Thomas, 1992). Bringing about a change (even a therapeutic one) in one member of the family system without involving the other members of the system will not last long. This is particularly true when the initial problem appears to be with a child or adolescent. We say "appears to be" because we can be confident that other family members have at least contributed to the troublesome symptoms of the child or adolescent. A therapist will have a difficult time bringing about significant and lasting change in a child whose parents refuse to become involved in therapy.

A second assumption often relevant in family therapy sessions is that difficulties arise from improper methods of family communication (Rivett, 1998; Satir, 1967). Quite often, individuals develop false beliefs about the feelings and needs of family members. The goal of therapy in such situations, then, is to meet with the family in a group setting to foster and encourage open expressions of feelings and desires. For example, it may be very helpful for an adolescent to learn that her parents are upset and anxious about work-related stress and financial affairs. The adolescent has assumed all along that her parents yelled at her and at each other because of something she was doing. And the parents didn't want to share their concerns over money with the adolescent for fear that it would upset her.

BEFORE YOU GO ON

- What is group therapy?

- What are some advantages of group therapy?

- What are two assumptions underlying family therapy?

EVALUATING PSYCHOTHERAPY

Evaluating psychotherapy has proven to be a difficult task. Is psychotherapy effective? Compared to what? Is one variety of psychotherapy better than another? These are obviously important questions, but the best we can do is offer partial answers. Yes, psychotherapy is certainly effective when compared to doing nothing. "By about 1980 a consensus of sorts was reached that psychotherapy, as a generic treatment process, was demonstrably more effective than no treatment" (VandenBos, 1986, p. 111; also see Gelso & Fassinger, 1990; Goldfried et al., 1990; Kingsbury, 1995; VandenBos, 1996).

More treatment often appears to be better than less treatment, with most improvement made early on (Howard et al., 1986). There are limits to this observation, however. In one study, time-limited therapy that actively involved the family in dealing with problems of children was as effective as therapy that used an unlimited number of sessions (Smyrnios & Kirby, 1993; also see Sechrest & Walsh, 1997). Whether short-term or long-term intervention will be best is often a function of known variables, such as the client's awareness of his or her problems, a willingness to change, and the extent to which the client lives in a supportive environment (Steenbarger, 1994).

Research also confirms the logical assertion that the sooner therapy begins, the better the prognosis (Kupfer, Frank, & Perel, 1989; Wyatt & Henter, 1997). There is also evidence that some therapists are more effective than others, regardless of what type of therapy is practiced (Garfield, 1997; Lafferty et al., 1989).

At this point, let's review just a few of the problems encountered when doing research on the effectiveness of psychotherapy. First, there is often little data on how people might have responded without treatment. In other words, we often do not have a baseline, or control group, for comparison. We know that sometimes there is a *spontaneous remission of symptoms*. Sometimes people "get better" without the formal intervention of a therapist. To say that people get better on their own is seldom literally true—there are many factors that can contribute to improve one's mental health, even if one is not "officially" in psychotherapy (Erwin, 1980). Perhaps the source of stress is removed; a nagging parent moves out of state, an aggravating boss gets transferred, or an interpersonal relationship begins that provides needed support.

Second, we all can't seem to agree on what we mean by *recovery*, or *cure*. These terms take on different meanings depending upon the goal of therapy. For some, it is the absence of observable symptoms for a specified period. For others, the goal of psychotherapy is something different: the self-report of "feeling better," personal growth, a relatively permanent change in behavior, insight into deep-seated conflicts, or a restructuring of cognitions.

These are commonly cited problems with designing studies to evaluate the outcome of psychotherapy. Even so, quality studies have been done. Most have focused on just one technique, and the results have generally been very positive (Barlow & Lehman, 1996; Clarkin, Pilkonis, & Magruder, 1996; Lipsey & Wilson, 1993; Marziali, 1984; Mueller et al., 1996; Scogin & McElreath, 1994).

One meta-analysis of 475 research articles showed positive results for psychotherapy and has become a commonly cited study of its effectiveness (Smith, Glass, & Miller, 1980). Another meta-analysis of 302 studies of psychotherapy outcomes came to the same conclusion: What psychotherapy provides is beneficial, and "the magnitude of the effects for a substantial portion of those treatments is in a range of practical significance by almost any reasonable criterion" (Lipsey & Wilson, 1993).

What about comparing psychotherapy methods? In general, there are very few differences; there is no evidence that any one type of therapy is universally better than any other (*Consumer Reports*, 1995; Stiles et al., 1986; Wampold, 1997). There *is* evidence that some types of therapy are better suited for some types of problems than for others, but even that evidence is sketchy. Which therapy is best suited for which disorder is one of the most active areas of research in psychotherapy (Davison, 1998; DeRubeis & Crits-Christoph, 1998; , 1988; Goldfried et al., 1990; Lipsey & Wilson, 1993).

Each variety of psychotherapy has its strengths and weaknesses. Psychoanalytic approaches can be time-consuming and expensive. Client-centered approaches require an introspective, nondependent client to be most useful. Group approaches may not be useful for clients who need personal attention. Behavioral methods work well with phobic disorders, and cognitive therapies appear to be well suited to patients with depression. A combination of behavioral and cognitive approaches seems particularly effective for the obsessive-compulsive disorders. No variety of psychotherapy is effective, by itself, for persons with bipolar disorder or schizophrenia. Many studies indicate that even when the primary treatment option is medical (say, an antidepressant drug), psychotherapy and medication together yield the best prognosis (Frank et al., 1990; Klerman, 1990). "Psychotherapy alone is not a good treatment for schizophrenia, but schizophrenic patients who take antipsychotic drugs can benefit from social skills training and related therapies" (Kingsbury, 1995, p. 8).

BEFORE YOU GO ON

- Is there any evidence that psychotherapy is effective?

Topic Review 13 B

1. Who may offer psychotherapy?

Many different mental health professionals can provide psychotherapy. These include clinical psychologists (Ph.D.s or Psy.D.s with graduate training in psychology and a one-year internship), psychiatrists (M.D.s with an internship and residency in a mental hospital), counseling psychologists (Ph.D.s in psychology specializing in less severe disorders and with an internship in a counseling setting), licensed counselors (perhaps with degrees in education), psychoanalysts (who specialize in Freudian therapy), clinical social workers (usually with a master's degree), and others, including pastoral counselors.

2. What are the major features of Freudian psychoanalysis?

Freudian psychoanalysis is aimed at uncovering repressed conflicts (often developed in childhood) so that they can be resolved. The process involves (1) free association, in which the patient is to say anything and everything that comes to mind, without editing; (2) resistance, in which a patient seems unable or unwilling to discuss some aspect of his or her life, suggesting that the resisted experiences may be anxiety-producing; (3) dream interpretation, in which one analyzes both the manifest and the latent content for insights into the nature of the patient's unconscious mind; and (4) transference, in which feelings once directed at a significant person in the patient's life become directed toward the analyst.

3. How is psychoanalysis different today from when it was practiced by Freud?

Although the principles of psychoanalysis have remained unchanged since Freud's day, some changes have evolved. There is now more effort to shorten the duration of analysis; there is less emphasis on childhood experiences and more concern with the here and now. Present-day analysis is also more directive than when it was practiced by Freud.

4. What are the basic ideas behind humanistic therapy techniques?

Although there are different humanistic approaches, they all share a focus on self-examination, personal growth, and development. These therapies focus on factors that foster psychological growth rather than uncovering deep-seated conflicts. A major premise is that the individual can take charge of himself or herself and grow and develop. Therapy focuses on that process.

5. What are the characteristics of client-centered therapy?

Client-centered or person-centered therapy, associated with Carl Rogers, is based on the belief that people can control their lives and solve their own problems if they can be helped to understand the true nature of their feelings. It promotes self-discovery and personal growth. The therapist reflects or mirrors the client's feelings, focuses on the here and now, and tries to be empathic, actively listening to and relating to the person's feelings. Throughout therapy, the therapist provides unconditional positive regard for the client.

6. What are the characteristics of Gestalt therapy?

Gestalt therapy, associated with Fritz Perls, has many of the same goals as Roger's person-centered approach, but is more directive and challenging, striving to integrate a person's thoughts, feelings, and behaviors.

7. What are the underlying assumptions of behavior therapy?

Behavior therapy is really a collection of several techniques that grew out of laboratory research on basic principles of learning. The main premise of behavior therapy is that maladaptive behaviors are learned, so they can be unlearned.

8. What are systematic desensitization and exposure and response prevention?

Systematic desensitization applies principles of classical conditioning to the treatment of anxiety. In systematic desensitization, a person is taught to relax totally and then remain relaxed as he or she thinks about or is exposed to anxiety-producing stimuli. The new relaxation response becomes classically conditioned to the stimulus, replacing the anxiety reaction. Exposure and response prevention is a treatment used for obsessive-compulsive disorder. Patients are exposed to the stimulus that evokes obsessive thinking and are then told to imagine the consequences of what they fear without engaging in their usual obsessive or compulsive routine. The procedure is repeated in homework assignments followed by a maintenance program of phone calls and clinic visits.

9. What is aversion therapy?

During aversion therapy, a stimulus is paired with an aversive, painful stimulus until the original stimulus is avoided. Although unpleasant, individuals still opt for aversion therapy because it is very effective in suppressing behavior and it is seen as better than the original behavior.

10. What are contingency management and contingency contracting?

Contingency management involves a health professional gaining control over the rewards and punishments that control a patient's behavior. Patients can be rewarded for productive behaviors and punished for unproductive behaviors. In contingency contracting, a contract is established with a patient specifying those behaviors that will be rewarded and those that will be punished. When enough rewards are accumulated, they may be traded for something the patient wants.

11. What is modeling, and how is it used as a therapy technique?

Modeling refers to the process of learning behavior by watching and imitating another person (a model). Modeling can be used to treat some disorders, like phobias. The client is shown a model interacting with a feared stimulus but not having the fear response. Through a process of observational learning, the patient finds that the feared stimulus is not dangerous.

12. What is the basic idea behind cognitive therapy techniques?

Cognitive therapists, while not denying the importance of a person's behavior, focus on an individual's thoughts, perceptions, and attitudes about himself or herself, and the environment. The major premise of cognitive therapy is that if a therapist wants to change how a patient feels, then the therapist has to change how that patient thinks, and the therapist must show the patient how those changes are achieved.

13. What is the basic logic behind rational-emotive therapy and cognitive restructuring therapy?

Cognitive therapies are designed to alter the way a person perceives and thinks about himself or herself and the environment. *Rational-emotive therapy (RET)* works on the premise that people with problems are operating on irrational assumptions about the world and themselves. RET is directive in its attempts to change people's cognitions. *Cognitive restructuring therapy* is somewhat less directive, but is based on the same sort of idea as RET. The underlying premise here is that people with psychological disorders have developed negative self-images and negative views (cognitions) about the future. The therapist provides opportunities for the patient to test those negative cognitions and discover that everything is not as bad as it may seem.

14. What is group therapy?

In group therapy clients are brought together at the same time under the guidance of a therapist. During group sessions members share their feelings and experiences. Group meetings are generally informal and no particular form of psychotherapy is dominant.

15. What are some advantages of group therapy?

There are several potential advantages to group therapy: (1) The basic problem may be an interpersonal one, and will be better understood and dealt with in an interpersonal situation, (2) There is value in realizing that one is not the only person in the world with a problem and that there are others who may have an even more difficult problem of the same nature, (3) There is therapeutic value in providing support for someone else, and (4) The dynamics of intragroup communication can be analyzed and changed in a group setting.

16. What are two assumptions underlying family therapy?

Family therapy is based on the assumptions that (1) family members can be seen as part of a system in which one member (and one member's problem) affects all of the others, and that (2) psychological problems often arise because of faulty communication, and that this is particularly critical within a family.

17. Is there any evidence that psychotherapy is effective?

Scientifically evaluating the appropriateness and effectiveness of psychotherapy has been very difficult. Nonetheless, in general, psychotherapy is effective. It is significantly better than leaving disorders untreated. There are data that suggest that some therapies may be better suited to some clients and to some disorders than they are to others. There is evidence that psychotherapy provides an advantage when offered with appropriate drug therapy. On the other hand, there is no evidence that, in general, any one type of therapy is better than any other.

Chapter 14

Social Psychology

Nearly 40 years ago, a New York City cocktail waitress named Kitty Genovese was brutally murdered in front of her apartment building as she returned from work about 3:30 in the morning. What made this particular murder noteworthy was that so many of Kitty Genovese's neighbors watched as she was bludgeoned and stabbed to death. Here is the account of the incident:

> For more than half an hour, 38 respectable law-abiding citizens in Queens watched a killer stalk and stab a woman in three separate attacks in Kew Gardens.

> Twice the sound of their voices and the sudden glow of their bedroom lights interrupted him and frightened him off. Each time he returned, sought her out, and stabbed her again. Not one person telephoned the police during the assault; one witness called after the woman was dead (New York Times, March 27, 1964).

Then there is the recent case of Vanessa Moretti. Vanessa and her father were driving to a beach in Italy. After they entered a tunnel, Vanessa's father began to feel ill so he pulled over. He was having a heart attack. His last words to his daughter were to get out of the tunnel and get help. Vanessa did what her father said. She got out of the car and walked the remaining length of the tunnel. Once outside, she tried to flag down a passing motorist for help. But, nobody would stop. Cars sped by so fast that they actually knocked Vanessa down. Finally, the exhausted Vanessa, now dirty and bleeding, got someone to stop. The police were called. Unfortunately, Vanessa's father did not survive.

**Topic 14A
Social
Cognitions:
Attitudes,
Attributions,
and
Attraction**

**Topic 14B
Social
Influence**

Topic 14A SOCIAL COGNITIONS: ATTITUDES, ATTRIBUTIONS, AND ATTRACTION

The stories of Kitty Genovese and Vanessa Moretti are strikingly similar and show that what happened to Kitty Genovese over 30 years ago was not a fluke, nor is it something that only happened in the past. The behavior of the "bystanders" in these two incidents raises some fundamental questions about what controls behavior. Were the bystanders simply uncaring, cold people who allowed these events to happen? Or, was it something about the social environment that had a chilling effect on their desire to help?

In this chapter, we will consider two major content areas in social psychology: (1) social cognition, or the perception and evaluation of oneself and others in social situations, and (2) social influence, or how others affect the reactions of the individual.

Key Questions to Answer

While reading this Topic, find the answers to the following key questions:

1. What is the definition of social psychology?

2. What is the basic premise of the cognitive approach to social psychology?

3. What is an attitude?

4. What are the three components of an attitude?

5. What is a possible fourth component of an attitude?

6. What are the three ways in which attitudes might be acquired?

7. What is cognitive dissonance theory?

8. What is the insufficient justification effect?

9. Under what conditions will disconfirmation of a belief increase the strength of that belief?

10. What is postdecisional dissonance, and how is it resolved?

11. What is self-perception theory?

12. What is persuasion, and what is the most widely accepted model of persuasion?

13. What are the three factors in the Yale Communication Model that influence persuasion?

14. What is the credibility of a communicator?

15. Other than credibility, what other source factors affect persuasion?

16. When should a one-sided or two-sided message be used?

17. What is discrepancy, and how does it relate to persuasion?

18. What are rational and emotional appeals?

19. What is the elaboration likelihood model?

20. What are attributions?

21. What errors are made in the attribution process?

22. What are the four approaches that account for interpersonal attraction?

23. What are four determinants of interpersonal attraction?

WHAT IS SOCIAL PSYCHOLOGY?

Social psychology is the field of psychology concerned with how others influence the thoughts, feelings, and behaviors of the individual. Social psychologists focus on the person or the individual in a group setting and not on the group *per se*, which is more likely to be the focus of sociologists. Because we are social organisms, we are familiar, each in our own way, with many of the concerns of social psychology.

To claim that we are familiar with the concerns of social psychology has certain implications. On the one hand, it means that social psychology is perceived as relevant because it deals with everyday situations that affect us all. On the other hand, it means that we are often willing to accept common sense and our personal experiences as the basis for our explanations about social behavior. Although common sense and personal experience may sometimes be valid, they are not acceptable for a scientific approach to understanding social behavior. Social psychology relies on experimentation and other scientific methods as sources of knowledge about social behavior.

Over the last 35 years, much of social psychology has taken on a cognitive flavor. That is, social psychologists are attempting to understand social behavior by examining the mental structures and processes reflected in such behavior. A basic premise of this approach, and of this Topic, is that we do not view our social environment solely on the basis of the stimulus information it presents us (Baldwin, 1992; Berscheid, 1994; Higgins & Bargh, 1987). Instead, the argument goes, we have developed cognitive structures or processes (for example, attitudes and schemas) that influence our interpretation of the world around us. "Discovering how people mentally organize and represent information about themselves and others has been a central task of social cognition research" (Berscheid, 1994, p. 84). Social cognition involves two related questions: What information about the social nature of the world do we have stored in memory? How does that information influence social judgments, choices, attractions, and behaviors (Sherman et al., 1989)?

ATTITUDES

Since the 1920s, a central concern in social psychology has been the nature of attitudes. An **attitude** is a relatively stable disposition to evaluate an object or event. An attitude has consequences for influencing one's beliefs, feelings, and behaviors toward that object or event (Olson & Zanna, 1993).

social psychology the field of psychology concerned with how others influence the thoughts, feelings, and behaviors of the individual

attitude a relatively stable evaluative disposition directed toward some object or event; it consists of feelings, behaviors, and beliefs

The concept of *evaluation* in this definition refers to a dimension of attitudes that includes such notions as being for or against, or positive or negative (Eagly & Chaiken, 1992). By *disposition* we mean a tendency, or a preparedness, to respond to the object of an attitude (actual responding isn't necessary). Note that, by definition, attitudes have *objects*. We do not have attitudes in general; we have attitudes about some object or event. We recognize that the word *attitude* is occasionally used differently in common speech. We may hear that someone has a "bad attitude" or "an attitude" in general, as in, "Boy, does he have an attitude!" In psychology, however, an attitude requires an object, that is, a specific object or event attached to the attitude.

Anything can be the object of an attitude, whether it be a person, an object, or an idea (Fazio, 1990; Petty & Cacioppo, 1986). You may have attitudes about this course, the car you drive, your father, the president, or the corner fast-food restaurant where you eat lunch. Some of our attitudes are more important than others, of course, but the fact that we have attitudes about so many things is precisely why the study of attitudes is so central in social psychology.

The Components of Attitudes

Although many definitions of an attitude have been proposed over the years, most of them suggest that attitudes comprise three components (Chaiken & Stangor, 1987). These components are *affect*, *behavior* and *cognition* (which make up the ABCs of attitudes). When we use the term "attitude" in everyday conversation, we are referring to the *affective component*, which consists of our feelings about the attitude object (Zanna & Rempel, 1988). For example, if you say that you like iced tea and don't like lemonade, you are expressing your feelings of affect about these beverages. It is this emotional expression that makes attitudes special and different from other cognitive schemas. The *behavioral component* consists of our response tendencies toward attitude objects. This component includes our behaviors and our intentions to act should the opportunity arise. So, based on your attitude, you would probably order iced tea with your lunch rather than lemonade. The *cognitive component* includes all of the information you have relating to an attitude object. The cognitive component represents the information storage and organization component of an attitude, making an attitude similar to other information-processing cognitive schemas. For example, you know that iced tea and lemonade are beverages and that lemonade has a sour flavor. We form a positive attitude toward a particular beverage because we know it is good for us (cognitive), because it is very convenient to buy (behavioral), or because we like the way it tastes (affective). By now, these three components of affect, behavior, and cognition, or ABCs, ought to be familiar.

Most of the time, the cognitive, affective, and behavioral components of attitudes are consistent. We think that classical music is relaxing and like to listen to it, so we buy classical music recordings. You believe that knowledge of psychology will be an asset in your career, you are enjoying your introductory psychology class, and you plan to take more psychology classes in the future. There are occasions, however, when behaviors are not consistent with beliefs and feelings (Ajzen & Fishbein, 1980). For example, we may have very strong, unfavorable beliefs and very negative feelings about someone, yet when we encounter that person at a social gathering, we smile, extend our hand, and say something pleasant. The social situation may "overpower" the cognitive and affective components of our attitudes. In other words, the components of an attitude may lack consistency, and it is the behavioral component that is most often inconsistent with the other two.

Because our actual behaviors may not reflect our true feelings or beliefs, some social psychologists (for example, Fazio, 1989) exclude the behavioral component from their definition, reserving the term *attitude* to refer only to the basic like or dislike for the attitudinal object. Others argue that *attitude* is a two-dimensional concept involving affect and cognition, but not behavior (Ajzen, 2001; Ajzen & Fishbein, 2000). Still others (Fishbein & Ajzen, 1975) add a fourth component: a **behavior intention**. Just as its name implies, a behavior intention is a specific intention to perform a given behavior. For example, you may have a positive attitude toward a particular candidate yet not vote because you do not form an intention to vote. A behavior intention is affected by three things (Ajzen, 1991): one's attitude toward a behavior (for example, your attitude toward voting), normative pressures (are your friends voting?), and the degree to which you perceive that the behavior will matter (will your vote count?). So, if you think that voting is important, all of your friends are going to vote, and you think that your vote will count, you will form an intention to vote. Such behavior intentions are better predictors of specific behaviors, like voting, than one's general political attitudes.

behavior intention a specific intention to perform a given behavior that relates to behavior better than general attitudes

Attitude Formation

As we go through life, we form many attitudes, some of which may stay with us our whole lives (e.g., religious attitudes), whereas others are held on a temporary basis (one's attitude toward a particular political candidate in a particular election). An interesting question concerns the origin of our attitudes. It is safe to say that we are not born with our attitudes in place. Instead, they are acquired through a process involving learning mechanisms such as observational learning and more basic conditioning processes.

People often imitate behaviors that they have seen reinforced in others (called vicarious reinforcement). To the extent we perceive others gaining reinforcers for having and expressing some attitude, we are likely to adopt that attitude ourselves. Advertising that relies on the testimonials of satisfied customers is appealing to this sort of *observational learning*. The consumer is shown that someone has used a certain product with success (received reinforcement), and the advertiser hopes that this will lead the observer to develop a favorable evaluation of the product. Obviously, the advertiser is going to show us only those people who are happy with their product or service. We seldom stop to think about how many people may have used the product or service and are unhappy with it.

Some attitudes are acquired through the associative process of classical conditioning. As shown in Figure 14.1, pleasant events (unconditioned stimuli) can be paired with an attitudinal object (conditioned stimulus). As a result of this association, the attitudinal object comes to elicit the same good feeling (a positive evaluation) originally produced by the unconditioned stimulus. The good feeling, originally an unconditioned response elicited by a pleasant event, now becomes a conditioned response elicited by the attitudinal object. Of course, negative attitudes can be acquired in the same way (for example, Cacioppo et al., 1992).

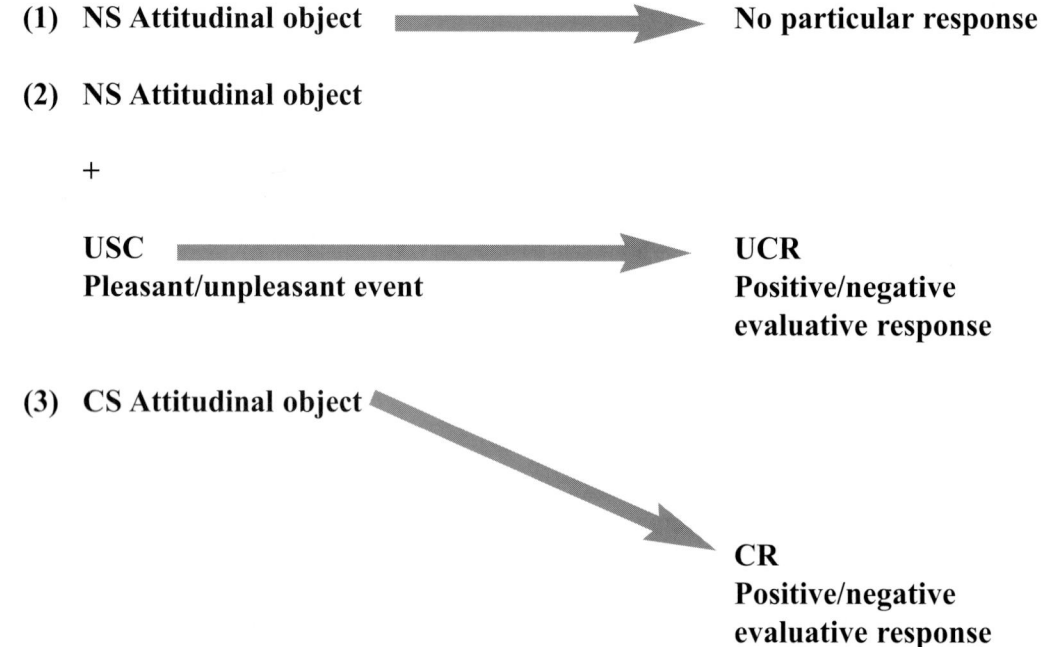

(1) NS Attitudinal object ⟶ **No particular response**

(2) NS Attitudinal object

+

USC ⟶ **UCR**
Pleasant/unpleasant event   **Positive/negative**
                                         evaluative response

(3) CS Attitudinal object

CR
Positive/negative
evaluative response

FIGURE 14.1

A schematic diagram of how attitudes may be formed through classical conditioning. At first, the attitudinal object is a neutral stimulus (NS), eliciting no particular response of interest. When it is paired with a stimulus (the unconditional stimulus, or UCS) that naturally produces an evaluative response (the unconditioned response, or UCR) the attitudinal object becomes a conditioned stimulus (CS) that elicits a learned, or conditioned, response (CR).

Some advertising uses conditioning techniques to change attitudes about a product by taking an originally neutral object (the product) and trying to create positive associations for it. For instance, a soft drink advertisement may depict attractive young people having a great time playing volleyball, dancing, or enjoying a concert while drinking a particular soft drink. The obvious intent is that we will associate the products with good times and having fun. That sports figures often wear brand name logos or trademarks on their uniforms also suggests that manufacturers want us to learn to associate their product with the skills of the athlete we are watching. Advertisements with sexual themes operate along the same lines.

Attitudes can also be formed as a result of the direct reinforcement of behaviors consistent with an attitudinal position, a matter of *operant conditioning*. Several studies have shown that verbal reinforcement (saying "good" or "that's right") when people agree with attitudinal statements leads to the development of attitudes consistent with the position expressed in those statements (Insko, 1965).

BEFORE YOU GO ON

- What is social psychology?
- What is an attitude, and what are its components?
- Describe how attitudes are formed.

Attitude Change and Persuasion

Once attitudes have been formed, can they be changed? Experience tells us that they can. Political polls regularly track changes in attitudes about politicians. Based on poll numbers, political strategists develop political advertisements designed to change your attitudes and behaviors about the candidates. What psychological mechanisms account for attitude change? In this section, we will explore social psychological models of attitude change, beginning with cognitive dissonance theory.

Cognitive Dissonance Theory

It seems reasonable that one's attitudes will affect one's behaviors and that attitude change will lead to behavior change. In 1957, Leon Festinger proposed just the reverse: that attitudes follow behavior. Festinger's theory involves a concept he called **cognitive dissonance**, which is a negative motivational state that arises when our attitudes, thoughts, and behaviors are out of balance or inconsistent. Cognitive dissonance often arises when we realize (a cognition) we have behaved in a manner inconsistent (dissonant) with other cognitions. Once dissonance is aroused, we are motivated to reduce or eliminate it. After all, like hunger, cognitive dissonance is a negative motivational state that we want to eliminate.

cognitive dissonance a negative motivational state that arises when our attitudes, thoughts, and behaviors are out of balance or inconsistent

An excellent example of how cognitive dissonance works is found in one of the original demonstrations of the phenomenon (Festinger & Carlsmith, 1959). Participants in the research were asked to perform an extremely boring task of rotating row after row of small wooden knobs. Following a lengthy knob-turning session, the experimenter explained that the research really had to do with the effects of motivation on such a task. Further, the participant was told that the person in the waiting area was to be the next participant in the project. This person was to be led to believe that the knob-turning task was interesting, fun, and educational. The experimenter explained that his assistant, who usually told these "lies" to the waiting participant, was absent. Would the participant do this "selling" job? The participant would be paid for his or her help. Participants invariably agreed and worked very hard to convince the next participant the project was fun and educational. Weeks later, at the end of the semester, all participants filled out a questionnaire that asked about their reactions to the knob-turning experiment.

The experimental manipulation was simple: some of the participants were paid $20 for trying to convince the waiting person (who was really not a participant, but was in on the experiment) that the obviously boring task was fun and interesting, whereas others were paid only $1. In all other respects, everyone was treated in the same way. Remember that this was the late 1950s, and for college students, $20 was a lot of money. The purpose of the experiment was to determine whether participants changed their attitudes toward the boring task.

At the end of the semester, which participants do you suppose expressed more positive attitudes about the project, the ones paid $20 or those paid $1? Doesn't it seem logical that those college students paid $20 would remember the task as being fun and enjoyable and indicate a willingness to participate in similar projects? Festinger and

Carlsmith predicted just the opposite. They reasoned that students paid only $1 would feel that their behavior had not been sufficiently justified. They had told a "lie" and had been given only a trivial amount of money for doing so. They would experience a great deal of tension or discomfort—cognitive dissonance would be created. The dollar that a participant was paid does not provide sufficient justification for the lie. In essence, one comes to the conclusion that "I lied for a lousy dollar." This is known as the *insufficient justification effect*. Because the participants could not undo the lie, they resolved the dissonance by changing their attitude about the project (to a more positive one) so that it fit better with their behavior—a sort of, "Well, I didn't really lie, because the experiment wasn't all that bad; in fact, it was kinda fun at that."

Participants paid $20, on the other hand, had plenty of justification for their actions. Sure, they lied, but they had good reason to do so and would experience little cognitive dissonance. They should not be expected to change their attitude about the experiment. "Yeah, I lied, but I got paid twenty bucks." The results of this experiment are presented in Figure 14.2. Seldom do we find differences in an experiment as clear-cut as this one.

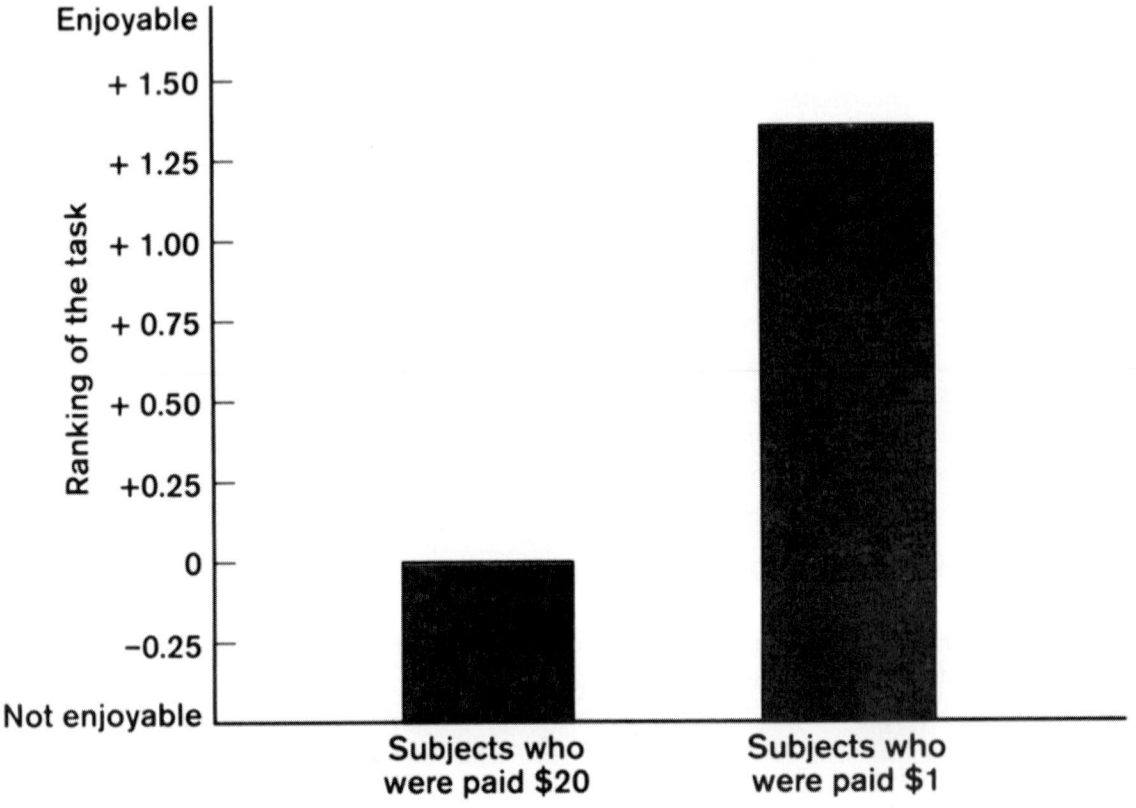

FIGURE 14.2

After being paid either $1 or $20 to "lie" about their participation in a boring task, subjects were later asked to rate that task in terms of enjoyment, interest, and educational value. As can be seen in the graph above, those paid $1 (those with cognitive dissonance) gave the task much higher ratings than did subjects paid $20 (from Festinger & Carlsmith, 1959).

The results of this experiment (and numerous others) suggest that one way to change people's attitudes is to get them to change their behaviors first. Additionally, there is a clear advantage in offering as little incentive as possible to bring about that change in behavior. Simply "buying one off" to change his or her behavior may get you compliance, but it will not produce the cognitive dissonance needed to bring about lasting attitude change.

You should be able to generate other examples of cognitive dissonance bringing about attitude change. Consider those students who have changed their attitude about a course, or a discipline, because they were required to take a class in it. For example, as a chemistry major, your (quite negative) attitudes about psychology might change because of the dissonance created when you are required to take a (very enjoyable and informative) course in introductory psychology.

Cognitive dissonance theory can help us understand behaviors that are seemingly incomprehensible. For example, why would members of a cult (for example, members of the People's Temple and Heaven's Gate) commit mass suicide? Strange behavior, but it does happen. We can interpret such behavior from a cognitive dissonance perspective. Festinger, Riecken, & Schachter (1982) found that members of a group that strongly adhere to a belief actually increase their strength in the belief after it is disconfirmed. Festinger and his colleagues joined a "doomsday" group that predicted the earth would end on a particular day. When the earth did not end, Festinger noticed that members increased their commitment to the belief and the group.

Festinger notes that there are several factors that contribute to this effect including that the person must hold the belief with great conviction and that there must be undeniable proof that the belief is false. However, the central psychological force driving this process is commitment. Commitment means that a person takes some significant, personally relevant behavioral steps related to the belief. For example, members of cult groups such as Jim Jones' former People's Temple, often gave up all of their worldly possessions to the cult and transferred power of attorney to the cult (so that Jim Jones was empowered to make all legal decisions for the member). Commitment is particularly strong when it is made public. A politician, for example, who publicly commits to a policy will find it harder to go back on that commitment than one expressed only in private. In the same way, members of doomsday groups and cults who make public commitments often find them inextricably bound to the group. Any break with the group is difficult and psychologically disturbing.

Dissonance is created when one's previous behavior (for example, a strong commitment to the group) is dissonant with the disconfirming evidence (the world is still here). One cannot undo all of the commitments made to the group—to admit that the belief was wrong would generate more dissonance. To reduce dissonance, the belief actually becomes stronger, and the believer rationalizes that the group's actions helped stave off the end of the earth. In the ultimate expression of this effect, individuals may be willing to go to their deaths (as in the People's Temple and the Branch Davidians) rather than face the prospect that they were wrong and all of the dissonance that would accrue.

There are many other situations that arouse dissonance. For example, situations that produce negative consequences are more likely to arouse dissonance than ones that produce positive consequences (Cooper & Scher, 1992). In such situations most of the negative affect is produced by feelings of personal responsibility for the negative event (Cooper & Fazio, 1984).

Dissonance is also aroused after you have made a choice between two mutually exclusive, equally attractive, but different alternatives. For example, imagine that you have to choose between two jobs. You can only have one of the jobs. Both are equally attractive, but they are different (one is near your favorite city, whereas the other is nearer to your family). After you make your decision, say you choose the job near the city, all of the positive cognitions associated with that job are consistent with your decision. However, all of the positive cognitions associated with the unchosen job are inconsistent with your decision. This inconsistency gives rise to **postdecisional dissonance**. How could you reduce the dissonance? Well, changing your decision won't help. That would just shift the source of the dissonance. What people tend to do is to think of negative things about the unchosen alternative. For example, one might begin to see being close to one's family as a drawback (for example, remaining dependent on the family, having to go to every family gathering).

postdecisional dissonance the cognitive dissonance experienced after making a decision between two mutually exclusive, equally attractive, different alternatives

Alternatives to Cognitive Dissonance Theory

Although cognitive dissonance theory has received strong support since it was first proposed, it is clear that the theory cannot account for all attitude change situations. For example, a person who smokes must surely know that it is unhealthy. Yet, the person continues to smoke. According to dissonance theory, this should create dissonance and put pressure on the person to change his or her behavior (i.e., stop smoking). But, as many smokers know, that often does not happen. Other approaches have been developed to account for situations that conflict with dissonance theory.

One alternative to classic dissonance reduction is rationalization. Here a person rationalizes away the negative aspects of continuing to smoke (as an example) in the face of evidence that it is harmful. A person may rationalize by saying that he or she now smokes only "light" cigarettes, or that even though smoking may hurt others it won't hurt me (called the illusion of unique invulnerability). Or, a person may find solace in the fact that her grandfather smoked three packs of filterless cigarettes per day for 80 years and then died in a scuba diving accident.

Another alternative approach to dissonance theory is *self-affirmation theory* which states that individuals may not always try to reduce dissonance if they can affirm their self-concept. Self-concept affirmation often takes the form of admitting a weakness (e.g., smoking), but at the same time affirming one's strengths in other areas. So a person who smokes may convince himself that he is a good parent or helpful in the community. In either case, the negative affect associated with dissonance is reduced.

self-perception theory an alternative to cognitive dissonance theory that says we keenly observe behavior, including our own, and look for an explanation for that behavior

Finally, **self-perception theory** (Bem, 1972) suggests that in dissonance arousing situations, we make careful observations of our behavior and then try to attribute a cause for that behavior. Self-perception theory suggests that there is no need to rely on dissonance, which is an internal motivational state. The theory suggests that thought processes replace the motivational aspects of cognitive dissonance. So, for example, the person paid $1 to lie may convince himself that he really did enjoy the task.

BEFORE YOU GO ON

- What is cognitive dissonance, and how does it relate to attitude change?

- Describe the conditions under which disconfirmation of a belief leads to an increase in the strength of that belief.

- When do we experience postdecisional dissonance?

- What are the alternatives to dissonance theory?

Persuasion

A wholly different approach to attitude change focuses on the process of **persuasion**, which is the application of rational and/or emotional arguments to convince others to change their attitudes or behavior (Horowitz & Bordens, 1995). The most widely accepted model of persuasion is the **Yale communication model** (Hovland, Janis, & Kelley, 1953). According to the Yale model (named after Yale University, where the research was done), the ability to persuade someone depends on three factors: the *source* of a message (who delivers the message), the characteristics of the *message* (what is said), and the nature of the *audience* (to whom the message is directed). According to the model these three factors affect internal processes such as attention to, comprehension of, and acceptance of a persuasive message. Change is measured in a person's attitudes, opinions (verbal expression), and overt behavior. In the sections that follow, we will explore how the source, message, and audience affect persuasion.

persuasion the application of rational and/or emotional arguments to change an individual's attitudes and behavior

Yale communication model the most widely accepted model of persuasion that considers the influence of the sources of a message, the structure of a message, and the audience for a message

The Source of Persuasive Communication

The most important characteristic of the source of a persuasive message is the communicator's **credibility**, or the believability, of the communicator. All other things being equal, a high credibility communicator will be more persuasive than a low credibility communicator (Hovland, Janis, & Kelley, 1953). There are two components comprising credibility: *expertise* and *trustworthiness*. Expertise refers to the qualifications, skills, and credentials of the communicator. For example, Secretary of State General Colin Powell (the former Chairman of the Joint Chiefs of Staff for the U.S. military) has a high level of expertise on military matters. You would be more impressed by a message coming from him about military matters than, say, a private pulled from the ranks or someone with no military experience. Trustworthiness refers to the motivations behind the communicator's attempt to persuade you. Trustworthiness goes to the question of "why is this person trying to convince me?" For example, you would probably trust an automotive review you read in *Consumer Reports* because they have no vested interest in convincing you to buy one car or another. On the other hand, you might have less trust of a review in a magazine that accepts large sums of money from a particular car maker. In this case, you might question the motives of the reviewer (honest review? or help sell cars made by the benefactor?). A communicator who argues against his or her own best interests (for example, a senator representing a tobacco-growing state arguing for strict control of cigarettes) is likely to be perceived as trustworthy.

credibility the believability of the communicator involving expertise and trustworthiness

To be effective, newscasters need to be judged to be credible, expert, and trustworthy.

Although credibility is the most important source characteristic in persuasion, there are others. For example, vocal pleasantness and facial expressiveness affect persuasiveness (Burgoon, Birk, & Pfau, 1990). Additionally, the attractiveness of the communicator (more persuasion with greater attractiveness), the similarity of the communicator to the target of the message, and the rate of speech (moderately fast delivery enhances persuasion) affect persuasion.

The Message and the Audience

How a message is put together can influence the amount of persuasion that occurs. One important message characteristic is the nature of the appeal made. In a *rational appeal,* one uses facts and figures to persuade an audience. For example, if we wanted people not to drink and drive, we could present facts and statistics concerning the number of alcohol-related traffic accidents and fatalities reported each year. Although rational appeals can be effective, emotional appeals can be even more effective. This is especially true of *fear appeals* which attempt to persuade through the arousal of the negative emotion of fear. A fear appeal attempting to persuade people not to drink and drive might depict graphic photographs of accident scenes involving drivers who were drunk.

Generally, fear appeals are effective. However, there are three conditions that are necessary for a fear appeal to be effective. First, the appeal must arouse a significant amount of fear. Second, the target of the appeal must believe that the dire consequences depicted in the appeal could happen to him or her. Finally, the appeal must include instructions about how to avoid the dire consequences depicted in the appeal (drink only at home; use a designated driver; take a taxi and retrieve your car tomorrow, etc.). This third condition is crucial. If it is not met, then the fear appeal will be ineffective, even if the other two conditions are met.

The audience to which an appeal is targeted also influences persuasion. For example, the opinions that members of the audience already hold play a part in persuasion. If a message is very different from audience members' preexisting opinions (known as high discrepancy) you get less persuasion than if the message is moderately different from the preexisting opinions (moderate discrepancy). This is because the content of the highly discrepant message is likely to be rejected by audience members. A moderately discrepant message will not be rejected as strongly as a highly discrepant message, allowing for persuasion to occur. Similarly, if there is too little discrepancy you will not get much persuasion. In this case, the persuasive message may be nothing more than a restatement of the audience member's opinion and little or no persuasion takes place.

It is important to note that audience and message characteristics often combine to affect persuasion. That is, whether a message is effective sometimes depends on the nature of the audience. For example, rational appeals tend to work best on well-educated audiences who are better able to make sense out of the facts and statistics presented. On the other hand, fear appeals work best with less educated audiences. In this case then, whether a fear appeal is maximally effective depends on the target audience.

The Elaboration Likelihood Model

The Yale model makes a key assumption about the persuasion process: that a person carefully attends to a message, carefully processes the content of the message, and changes attitudes when the content of the message is accepted. There are situations in which a person is persuaded even though he or she did not process information in a manner suggested by the Yale model. For example, after deciding a case in which the evidence was very unclear, resulting in a "not guilty" verdict, a juror indicated that he found the defendant not guilty because he "didn't like the way the prosecutor ran the show." Clearly, this juror, who was probably left hanging by the unclear evidence, turned to other factors (in this case, the behavior of the prosecutor) on which to base a decision. Because the Yale model has difficulty accounting for such examples of persuasion, another model has been proposed called the **elaboration likelihood model**. This model picks up where the Yale model left off, but it is not intended to replace it.

The elaboration likelihood model proposed by Petty and Cacioppo (1986) states that there are two routes to persuasion: the *central route* and the *peripheral route*. Central route processing is most likely to occur when an individual is motivated to process the content of a message and can understand the content of the message. In this case, the individual pays close attention to the nature and quality of the message, and creates a context for the message based on preexisting beliefs and ideas about the issue. These ideas are then used to expand and elaborate on the message. Who delivers the message and how it

elaboration likelihood model a model of persuasion stating that there are two routes to persuasion: the central route and the peripheral route

was delivered are not as important. For example, a juror who carefully listens to the evidence presented during a trial is likely to be persuaded by the strength of the message (evidence) presented. The individual undergoes a change in his or her underlying attitudes about the issue. Because of this persuasion, it is resistant to change. The juror will develop a firm belief in the defendant's guilt or innocence. Only new, stronger, persuasive arguments (perhaps by another juror during deliberation) will have a chance to change the juror's mind.

Peripheral route processing involves being persuaded by factors other than the content of the message. It is most likely to be used when the individual is not motivated, or is unable to understand the information contained in the message. Factors such as emotion, how a person looks, acts, and presents his or her arguments become the driving forces behind persuasion. The juror who found the defendant not guilty because he didn't like the prosecutor's actions was clearly using peripheral route processing. Emotional cues are powerful in the peripheral route processing (Petty & Cacioppo, 1986). For example, when using peripheral route processing, a strong fear appeal is likely to be effective even if the content of a message is weak (Gleicher & Petty, 1992). Finally, peripheral route processing often does produce attitude change. However, because the listener has not carefully processed the message, resulting attitudes tend to be unstable and easier to change than those based on central route processing (Kaswsin, Reddy, & Tulloch, 1990).

It is important to understand that most of us don't use central or peripheral route processing in the same way for every situation. We may use central route processing in one situation and peripheral route processing in another. Imagine, for example, a juror listening to evidence in a trial. That juror may be fascinated by the testimony of an expert on DNA evidence and as a consequence, pays close attention to what the witness says, using central route processing. However, the next witness who testifies about the angle of trajectory of a bullet may bore the same juror. In this case, our juror most likely won't pay close attention to the content of the message and will rely on peripheral route processing.

BEFORE YOU GO ON

- What is persuasion, and what is the most widely accepted model of persuasion?

- Describe what comprises credibility and how it affects persuasion.

- Describe what makes a fear appeal work.

- What is the relationship between discrepancy and persuasion?

- Describe the elaboration likelihood model.

ATTRIBUTION PROCESSES

Another facet of the cognitive orientation we find in social psychology is a focus on *attribution processes*. Social psychologists working with attributions are interested in understanding the cognitions we use when we try to explain the causes or sources of behavior (our own and the behavior of others) (Jones, 1990). We might ask, "Do we tend to attribute behaviors or events we observe in the world around us to internal or external sources, personal dispositions, or environmental factors?"

Internal and External Attributions

An **internal attribution** explains the source of a person's behavior in terms of some characteristic of the person, often a personality trait or disposition (for this reason they are sometimes called dispositional attributions). For example, if you have a friend who is chronically late, you might conclude that this is a personality characteristic. You would have made an internal attribution. An **external attribution** explains the source of a person's behavior in terms of the situation or context outside the individual, and are referred to as situational attributions. For example, if you have a friend who is hardly ever late, you will probably make an external attribution if he is late once or twice (an alarm clock failed to go off, heavy traffic, etc.).

We tend to rely on different types of information when making judgments about the sources of behavior. Imagine, for example, that your friend is late only when he is supposed to be at work. He is not late any other time. That information is useful because of its *distinctiveness* (lateness shows up only when he's dealing with work). As a result, you may take it as a signal of problems in the workplace. A second source of information is *consistency*, or how regular is the behavior pattern you observe. For example, if your friend is always late for work, this is a consistent pattern of behavior. Compare this with a person who is late occasionally. The final source of information is *consensus*, which is a question of what other people do in the same situation. If nobody else is consistently late for work, then consensus is low. If everyone is late for work, consensus is high. Compared to the other two types of information, consensus information tends to be underused.

Using information about distinctiveness, consensus, and consistency is important in determining the kinds of attributions we make about our own behaviors and about the behaviors of others (Kelley, 1967, 1973, 1992; Kelley & Michela, 1980). The manner in which the three sources of information mix determines the type of attribution you make. *High consensus* (everyone else is late for work), *high consistency* (my friend is always late), and *high distinctiveness* (my friend is only late for work) leads to an external attribution. That is, it must be something about the job situation causing lateness (perhaps a boss who doesn't care if people are late for work). On the other hand, *low consensus* (nobody else is late for work), *high consistency* (my friend is always late for work), and *low distinctiveness* (my friend is late for just about anything: golf games, dates, etc.) leads to an internal attribution. It must be something about your friend that causes his lateness.

One focus of research is how people make inferences about the behaviors of others. Current thinking is that there are two basic processes involved, the *trait inference process* and the *situational inference process* (Krull & Erickson, 1995). In some cases, we want to know about a particular person ("Just what kind of a guy is he, really?"). We might (1) note the person's behavior, (2) draw an inference about the presence of some trait the person has that led to that behavior, and (3) revise or modify that inference or attribution as we consider the situation more fully. In other cases, we want to know about a particular situation ("Just what kind of a party is this, really?"). In this case, we may reverse steps (2) and (3). First, we (1) note a person's behaviors, then we (2) infer that the situation has caused these behaviors, and then we (3) revise or modify our inferences on the basis of what we know or discover about the person we observed.

internal attribution an explanation of behavior in terms of something (a trait) within the person; a dispositional attribution

external attribution an explanation of behavior in terms of something outside the person; a situational attribution

We observe someone clearly behaving kindly toward an animal. Are we likely to attribute this behavior to "the way the person is" (an internal attribution) or to the situation as it exists at the moment (an external attribution)?

Another area of research deals with the errors we make in our social thinking. In general terms, we make attribution errors because preexisting cognitive biases influence our judgments of causality. An example of such a bias is the **fundamental attribution error**—the tendency to favor internal, or personal, attributions for behaviors rather than external, situational explanations (Jones, 1979; Ross, 1977). We see a man pick up a wallet that has been dropped on the pavement and race half a block to return it to its owner. We say to ourselves, "Now there's an honest man." (And we predict that he will act honestly in a variety of situations.) The truth is, however, that the fellow returned the wallet only because he knew that we saw him pick it up. If no one else was around, the wallet may not have been returned. The fundamental attribution error is the tendency to disregard, or discount, situational factors in favor of internal, dispositional factors when we make inferences about the causes of behaviors. There is evidence that biases such as the fundamental attribution error are more common in Western cultures. People from India, for example, make fewer dispositional attributions than Americans (Miller, 1984). Indians are more likely than Americans to explain behavior in terms of the situation or the environment than in terms of personality traits, abilities, or inabilities. That is, they are more likely to use a situational inference process than Americans.

There are other biases that lead us to make incorrect attributions about ourselves or others. One is called the **just world hypothesis**, in which people believe that we live in a world where good things happen only to good people and bad things happen only to bad people (Lerner, 1965, 1980). It's a sort of "everybody gets what they deserve" mentality. We see this bias (or fallacy) when we hear people claim that victims of rape often "ask

fundamental attribution error the tendency to overuse internal attributions when explaining behavior

just world hypothesis the belief that the world is just and that people get what they deserve

for it by the way they dress and act." In fact, even the victims of rape sometimes engage in self-blame in an attempt to grasp the random nature of the crime in which they were the victim (Janoff-Bulman, 1979; McCaul et al., 1990; Arata & Burkhart, 1998).

Another bias that affects our attributions is the **self-serving bias**. It occurs when we attribute successes or positive outcomes to personal, internal sources and failures or negative outcomes to situational, external sources (Harvey & Weary, 1984; Miller & Ross, 1975). We tend to think that we do well because we're able, talented, and work hard. Whereas when we do poorly it is the fault of someone or something else. "Boy, I did a great job of painting that room" versus "The room looks so shoddy because the paint was cheap and the brush was old" is an example. The same process is at work even in the social groups of which we feel a part. If someone in *our group* (be it an ethnic group, cultural group, social group, or gender group) succeeds, we're likely to attribute that success to internal, personal effort or an ability. If someone *outside our group* succeeds, we're likely to attribute that success to the situation (Finchilescu, 1994). Some cognitive theorists argue that depression can be explained as a failure to apply the self-serving bias. That is, some people may get into the habit of blaming themselves for failures and negative outcomes regardless of where the real blame resides or regardless of whether there even is any blame to attribute.

Yet another attribution error is the **actor-observer bias** (Jones & Nisbett, 1971; Monson & Snyder, 1977). This is a discrepancy between the way we explain our behavior (as actor) and the way we explain someone else's (as observer). Generally, we use external attributions when we talk about why we do things. When we explain someone else's behaviors, we are more likely to use internal attributions and refer to characteristics of the person. "I took that class because the instructor is excellent," versus "He took that class because he's so lazy." "I am dating Bill because he's so caring and considerate," versus "She's dating him only because she wants to be seen with an athlete." "I went there because the rates were lower than anyplace else," versus "He went there because he wanted to show off."

That we explain our own behaviors in ways that are different from the ways we explain the behaviors of others is not surprising. For one thing, we have more information about ourselves and our own past experiences than we do about anyone else. In fact, the more information we have about someone else, the less likely we are to use internal attributions to explain his or her behaviors. Also, in any situation, the actor gets a different view of what is happening than does the observer; that is, actors and observers attempt to attribute the causes of behavior on the basis of different information.

self-serving bias the tendency to attribute our successes to our own effort and abilities, and our failures to situational, external sources

actor-observer bias the overuse of internal attributions to explain the behaviors of others and external attributions to explain our own behaviors

BEFORE YOU GO ON

- What is an internal attribution and an external attribution?
- Describe the three sources of information used to make attributions.
- What mix of information leads to an internal or external attribution?
- Describe the various attribution errors.

INTERPERSONAL ATTRACTION

Interpersonal attraction is a favorable and powerful attitude toward another person. Interpersonal attraction reflects the extent to which a person has formed positive feelings and beliefs about another person and is prepared to act on those affects and cognitions.

interpersonal attraction a powerful, favorable attitude toward another person

Theories of Interpersonal Attraction

Social psychologists have put forth several theoretical models to explain the basis of interpersonal attraction. Let's briefly review four such theories.

The simplest theory is the *reinforcement-affect model* (Clore & Byrne, 1974; Lott & Lott, 1974) which states that we are attracted to (have positive attitudes toward) people that we associate with rewarding experiences. It also follows that we tend not to be attracted to those we associate with punishment. One implication of this point of view is that you're going to like your instructor more, and seek him or her out for other classes in the future, if you get (or earn) a high grade in his or her class than you will if you get a low grade.

Another popular theory of interpersonal attraction is *social exchange theory* (Kelley & Thibault, 1978; Thibault & Kelley, 1959). According to this theory, what matters most is a comparison of the costs and benefits of establishing or maintaining a relationship. For example, Leslie may judge that John is attractive but that entering into a relationship with him is not worth the grief she would get from friends and family, who believe John to be lazy and untrustworthy. On the other hand, if Leslie has recently gone through a series of failed relationships with other men who were not physically attractive, she might take a chance on John, judging (in her frustration) that he is "worth it." This theory takes into account a series of comparative judgments made in social situations. Being attracted to someone else is not just a matter of "Is this a good thing?" It's a matter of, "Is the reward I might get from this relationship worth the cost, and what other alternatives exist at the moment?"

There are many reasons why some persons are attracted to others. For example, we are attracted to those who provide rewards for us.

A third approach to interpersonal attraction is *equity theory*, which is more of an extension of social exchange theory than a departure from it (Greenberg & Cohen, 1982; Walster et al.,1978). Equity theory adds the appraisal of rewards and costs for both parties of a social relationship. That is, you may feel a relationship is worth the effort you have been putting into it, but if your partner in that relationship does not feel likewise, the relationship is in danger. What matters, then, is that both (or all) members of a relationship feel they are getting a fair deal (equity). Notice two things about this model: (1) Both members of a relationship do not have to share rewards equally. What matters is that the ratio of costs to rewards be equitable for both members. (2) If one person were to feel that he or she is getting more from a relationship than is deserved (on the basis of costs and compared to the other's rewards), the relationship would not be equitable and would be jeopardized. The best relationships are those in which all members receive an equal ratio of rewards to costs.

Another approach to understanding interpersonal relationships is one based on feelings or affect more than on cognitions. This model is referred to as *attachment theory* (Berscheid, 1994; Feeney & Noller, 1990; Hazan & Shaver, 1987). It suggests that interpersonal relationships can be classified into one of three types depending on the attitudes one has about such relationships (from Shaver, Hazan, & Bradshaw, 1988, p. 80):

Secure: "I find it relatively easy to get close to others and am comfortable depending on them and having them depend on me. I don't often worry about being abandoned or about someone getting too close to me."

Avoidant: "I am somewhat uncomfortable being close to others; I find it difficult to trust them completely, difficult to allow myself to depend on them. I get nervous when anyone gets too close, and partners often want me to be more intimate than I feel comfortable being."

Anxious/ambivalent: "I find that others are reluctant to get as close as I would like. I often worry that my partner doesn't really love me or won't stay with me. I want to merge completely with another person, and this desire sometimes scares people away."

One of the things that makes attachment theory appealing is the evidence that suggests that one's "style" of forming attachments with others is remarkably stable throughout the life span. It may be that the types of interpersonal relationships we form as adults are influenced by the types of attachments we developed as very young children.

Finally, we should remind you of a point we first discussed in the context of mate selection: few people enter into relationships having carefully considered all of the factors these models imply. That is, assessments of reinforcement, exchange, or equity value are seldom made at a conscious level; nor do we purposely seek out relationships that mirror those we had in childhood (Bargh, 1993).

Factors Affecting Interpersonal Attraction

Having reviewed four general models of interpersonal attraction, let's now look at some empirical evidence related to attraction. What determines who you will be attracted to?

What factors tend to provide the rewards, or the positive reward/cost ratios, that serve as the basis for strong relationships? We'll consider four common determinants of attraction.

Reciprocity, our first principle, is perhaps the most obvious: we tend to value and like people who like and value us (Backman & Secord, 1959; Curtis & Miller, 1986). We noted when discussing operant conditioning that the attention of others can be a powerful reinforcer. This is particularly true if the attention is positive, supportive, or affectionate. The value of someone else caring for us is particularly strong when that someone else initially seemed to have neutral or negative attitudes toward us (Aronson & Linder, 1965). In other words, we are most attracted to people who like us now, but who didn't originally.

Our second principle, *proximity*, suggests that physical closeness yields attraction. Sociologists, as well as your own experience, will tell you that people tend to establish friendships (and romances) with others with whom they have grown up, worked, or gone to school. Residents of apartments or dormitories, for example, tend to become friends with those other residents living closest to them (Festinger et al., 1950). Being around others gives us the opportunity to discover just who provides those interpersonal rewards we seek in friendship. Of course, with the advent of the Internet we have to redefine the definition of proximity. *Physical* closeness is becoming less and less important. One's ability to communicate with someone halfway around the world as if he or she were right next door brings people close together interpersonally and psychologically, if not physically.

Proximity leads to liking and attracting, which is one reason why children who go to the same school and live in the same neighborhood are likely to form friendships.

There may be a social-psychological phenomenon at work here called the **mere exposure phenomenon**. Research, pioneered by Robert Zajonc (1968), has shown with a variety of stimuli that liking tends to increase with repeated exposure. Examples of this phenomenon are abundant in everyday life. Have you ever bought a CD you had not heard previously, assuming you would like it because you have liked all the other CDs made by the performer? The first time you listen to your new CD, however, your reaction is lukewarm at best, and you are disappointed with your purchase. Not wanting to feel you've wasted your money, you play the CD a few more times. More often than not you soon realize you like this CD. The mere exposure effect has occurred. This also commonly happens in our formation of attitudes about other people. Familiarity is apt to breed attraction, not contempt. Although there is ample evidence that the mere exposure phenomenon is real, there remains considerable disagreement about why familiarity and repeated interactions breed attraction (Birnbaum & Mellers, 1979; Kunst-Wilson & Zajonc, 1980). However, there are limits. Too much exposure may lead to boredom and to devaluation (Bornstein, 1989; Bornstein, Kale, & Cornell, 1990).

Physical attractiveness is related to interpersonal attraction. The power of physical attractiveness in the context of dating has been demonstrated experimentally in a classic study directed by Elaine Walster (Walster et al., 1966). University of Minnesota freshmen completed several psychological tests as part of an orientation program. Students were then randomly matched for dates to an orientation dance, during which they took a break and evaluated their assigned partners. The researchers hoped to uncover intricate, complex, and subtle facts about interpersonal attraction, such as which personality traits might mesh in such a way as to produce attraction. As it turned out, none of these factors were important. The impact of physical attractiveness was so powerful that it wiped out all other effects. For both men and women, the more physically attractive their date, the more they liked that date and the more they wanted to date her or him again. Numerous studies of physical attractiveness followed this one. Some of these studies gave participants a chance to pick a date from a group of several potential partners (using descriptions or pictures). Not surprisingly, participants almost invariably selected the most attractive person to be their date (Reis et al., 1980).

We seldom have the luxury of asking for a date without the possibility of being turned down. When experiments added the possibility of rejection, an interesting effect emerged: people no longer chose the most attractive candidate, but selected partners whose level of physical attractiveness was more similar to their own. This behavior is called the **matching phenomenon** and occurs for physical attractiveness and social status (Schoen & Wooldredge, 1989). Even when we consider relationships between or among friends of the same sex, we find that such friends tend to be similar when rated for physical attractiveness (Cash & Derlega, 1978).

Our fourth determinant of interpersonal attraction is *similarity*. There is a large body of research on similarity and attraction, but the findings are consistent, and we can summarize them briefly. Much of this research has been done by Donn Byrne and his colleagues (Byrne, 1971; Smeaton et al., 1989). Simply put, the more similar another person is to you, the more you will tend to like that person and the more you are likely to believe that person likes you (Buss, 1985; Davis, 1985; Gonzales et al., 1983; Rubin,

mere exposure phenomenon the tendency to increase our liking of people and things as a result of recurring contact

matching phenomenon the tendency to select partners whose level of physical attractiveness matches our own

1973). We also tend to be repelled, or put off, by persons we believe to be dissimilar to us (Rosenbaum, 1986). Opposites may occasionally attract, but similarity is probably the glue that over the long haul holds together romances and friendships. It is this principle that makes it unusual, or difficult, for people to form significant interpersonal relationships with persons of other cultures or other ethnic groups (Stephan, 1985).

Why is similarity so important? Similarity enhances attraction because through a process of social comparison we can have our attitudes and beliefs verified by others. Such verification is immensely rewarding for people. Recall that reinforcement-affect theory tells us that we like things that are associated with reward. So, the rewards we derive from similar others verifying our attitudes serves to strengthen attraction to those individuals. Similarity also enhances attraction because we believe that we can predict how a similar person will act in social situations. This predictability is also rewarding, thus enhancing attraction. Finally, we may believe that individuals similar to ourselves will like us back. Once again, this is a source of interpersonal reward. Being liked by another person is, for most of us, very rewarding.

BEFORE YOU GO ON

- What is the definition of interpersonal attraction?

- Describe the theories of interpersonal attraction.

- What are the factors that influence interpersonal attraction?

- How does physical attraction affect interpersonal attraction?

- How does similarity affect interpersonal attraction?

The more similar another person is to you, the more you will tend to like that person. Our friends usually share our attitudes and enjoy doing the same things that we enjoy.

Topic Review 14A

1. **What is the definition of social psychology?**

   Social psychology is the field of psychology concerned with how others influence the thoughts, feelings, and behaviors of the individual. Social psychologists focus on the person or the individual in a group setting, and not on the group per se. Sociologists are more likely to focus on the behavior of larger groups.

2. **What is the basic premise of the cognitive approach to social psychology?**

   The cognitive approach to social psychology suggests that we don't simply respond to the information provided by social stimuli. Instead, we have a set of cognitive processes that help us make sense out of information from the social environment. Cognitive social psychologists try to discover how individuals organize and represent information about themselves and others.

3. **What is an attitude?**

   An attitude is a relatively stable evaluative disposition (positive or negative) directed toward some object or event.

4. **What are the three components of an attitude?**

   An attitude consists of feelings (affects), behaviors (action tendencies), and beliefs (cognitions). Although the affective and cognitive components of attitudes are often consistent with each other, they may be inconsistent with behavior because behavior is influenced by many situational variables.

5. **What is a possible fourth component of an attitude?**

   Fishbein and Ajzen (1975) suggest a model for attitudes that includes a fourth component: a behavior intention, which is a specific intention to perform a given behavior. Behavior intentions are formed based on three factors: one's attitude toward the target behavior, normative pressures, and the perceived consequences of behavior. Behavior intentions are better predictors of behavior than are general attitudes.

6. **What are the three ways in which attitudes might be acquired?**

   Attitudes may be acquired through classical conditioning: after positive or negative experiences are associated with an attitudinal object, the object by itself comes to produce a positive or negative evaluation. Attitudes may develop as a result of direct reinforcement (operant conditioning), or they may be formed when they are vicariously reinforced (observational learning).

7. **What is cognitive dissonance theory?**

   Cognitive dissonance theory is a theory of attitude change that proposes that attitude change occurs to reduce a negative motivational state called cognitive dissonance. Cognitive dissonance emerges whenever there is inconsistency between our cognitions (thoughts), attitudes, and behavior. Once dissonance is aroused, we are motivated to reduce or eliminate it.

8. **What is the insufficient justification effect?**

   The insufficient justification effect occurs when we behave in an inconsistent way and do not have sufficient reason for the behavior. For example, the participants paid only $1 to lie about an experiment changed their attitude toward the experiment more than participants paid $20 because the $1 was not sufficient to justify the lie. The inconsistency between the participant's attitude toward the experiment (boring) and their behavior (tell someone it was interesting) created cognitive dissonance which was resolved by changing the attitude toward the experiment.

9. **Under what conditions will disconfirmation of a belief increase the strength of that belief?**

   Festinger and his colleagues noted that under certain circumstances a disconfirmed belief is strengthened rather than abandoned. Festinger points out that five conditions must be met for this effect to occur: The belief must be held with deep conviction and relate to overt behavior, the believer must have taken steps toward commitment to the belief that cannot be easily undone, the belief must be specific and relate to real-world events, there must be undeniable evidence that the belief is false, and social support is needed after the belief has been disconfirmed.

10. What is postdecisional dissonance and how is it resolved?

Dissonance is aroused when you are forced to make a choice between two mutually exclusive, equally attractive, but different alternatives. It is resolved by developing negative cognitions concerning the unchosen alternative.

11. What is self-perception theory?

Self-perception theory was developed to account for dissonance-related attitude change. The theory proposes that dissonance is not needed for attitude change to occur. The theory says that we observe our behavior and then look for reasons why we might have behaved in the manner we did.

12. What is persuasion, and what is the most widely accepted model of persuasion?

Persuasion is the application of rational and/or emotional arguments to convince others to change their attitudes or behavior. The Yale communication model is the most widely accepted model of persuasion.

13. What are the three factors in the Yale communication model that influence persuasion?

The three factors outlined by the Yale communication model that affect persuasion are the source of a persuasive message (who delivers the message), the characteristics of the message, and the nature of the audience.

14. What is the credibility of a communicator?

A communicator's credibility refers to his or her believability. Credibility comprises two components: expertise (the qualifications of the source) and trustworthiness (the motivation of the source). All other things being equal, a communicator with high credibility is more persuasive than one with low credibility.

15. Other than credibility, what other source factors affect persuasion?

In addition to credibility, the attractiveness of the communicator, the similarity of the communicator to the audience, and the rate of speech of the communicator affect persuasion.

16. What is discrepancy and how does it relate to persuasion?

Discrepancy refers to the difference between the initial position of the audience and the content of a persuasive message. Too much or too little discrepancy leads to little or no attitude change. A moderate amount of discrepancy leads to the most persuasion.

17. What are rational and emotional appeals?

Rational appeals are persuasive messages that attempt to persuade by providing facts and figures. Emotional appeals try to persuade by arousing emotion, especially fear. Fear appeals are effective in producing attitude and behavior change when three conditions are met. First, the fear aroused must be quite high. Second, the target of the message must believe that the dire consequences depicted in the appeal could happen. Third, specific instructions must be given on how to avoid the dire consequences. The third factor is crucial. Without it, a fear appeal will not work, even if the first two conditions are met.

18. What is the elaboration likelihood model?

The elaboration likelihood model was proposed to account for situations in which persuasion occurs even in the absence of careful processing of a persuasive message. According to the model, messages can be processed along either a central route (involving careful processing of the content of the message) or a peripheral route (where the content of the message is not carefully considered. Rather, peripheral cues like the attractiveness of the communicator become important). A message will be processed along the central route if the audience can understand the message and is motivated to process it. Otherwise, the message will be processed along the peripheral route. Attitude change brought about by central processing is more enduring than change brought about by peripheral processing.

19. What are attributions?

Attributions are cognitions we use to explain the sources of the behaviors we see in our social worlds. Internal attributions identify the source of behavior as within the person and are also called dispositional attributions. External attributions find the source of behaviors to be outside the person and are also called situational attributions.

20. What errors are made in the attribution process?

The fundamental attribution error leads us to overuse internal, or personal, attributions when explaining behaviors. Those persons who hold to the just world hypothesis are likely to believe that good things happen only to good people and that bad things happen only to bad people, who in some way deserve their misfortune. With self-serving bias, we attribute our successes to our own efforts and actions and our failures to other, external factors. The actor-observer bias is the tendency to use external attributions to explain our own (as actor) behaviors, and internal attributions to explain the behaviors of others (as observer).

21. What are the four approaches that account for interpersonal attraction?

The reinforcement model claims that we are attracted to those persons we associate with rewards or reinforcers. The social exchange model adds cost to the equation, claiming that what matters in interpersonal relationships is the ratio of the benefits received to the costs invested in that relationship. The equity model suggests that both or all members of a relationship assess a benefit/cost ratio, and the best, most stable relationships are those in which the ratio is nearly the same (equitable) for both or all parties, no matter what the value of the benefits for any one member of the relationship. Attachment theory tells us that there are only a few relationship styles, and that each individual is consistent over his or her lifetime in the style used when relating to others.

22. What are four determinants of interpersonal attraction?

The principle of reciprocity states that we tend to like people who like us back. This is the most straightforward example of interpersonal attraction being based on a system of rewards. Proximity promotes attraction, in part, by means of the mere exposure effect: being near another person on a frequent basis gives us the opportunity to see what that other person has to offer. We also tend to be attracted to people we judge physically attractive. Finally, the principle of similarity suggests that we tend to be attracted to those we believe similar to ourselves.

Topic 14B SOCIAL INFLUENCE

So far, we have reviewed some of the ways in which our social nature has an impact on our cognitions—our perceptions and beliefs about ourselves and others. Now it is time to consider more direct influences of the social world on our everyday behaviors. We'll deal with the processes of conformity and obedience, and consider bystander apathy and intervention. We'll end by reviewing a few other situations in which social influence is a potent force in our lives.

Key Questions to Answer

While reading this Topic, find the answers to the following key questions:

1. What is conformity?

2. What were the methods and findings of Asch's conformity studies?

3. What were the different reasons given by Asch's participants for conforming?

4. What were the different reasons given by Asch's participants for not conforming?

5. What is the true partner effect?

6. What factors have been found to influence the rate of conformity?

7. How did Milgram study obedience?

8. What did Milgram find about factors that affect obedience?

9. What steps are involved in the decision to help in an emergency situation?

10. What effect does the presence of others have on a person's willingness to help in an emergency?

11. What explanations have been given for the bystander effect?

12. What is the relationship between empathy and altruism?

13. What are social loafing, social interference, and social facilitation?

14. What factors influence group decision-making?

15. What is group polarization?

16. What is groupthink, and what are its "symptoms"?

17. What does research suggest about the validity of groupthink?

CONFORMITY

One of the most direct forms of social influence occurs when we modify our behavior, under perceived pressure to do so, so that it is consistent with the behavior of others, a process referred to as **conformity**. Although we often think of conformity in a negative way, it is natural and often desirable. Conformity helps make social behaviors efficient and, at least to some degree, predictable.

conformity the changing of one's behavior, under perceived pressure, so that it is consistent with the behavior of others

When he began his research on conformity, Solomon Asch believed people are not that susceptible to social pressure when the situation in which they find themselves is clear-cut and unambiguous. Asch thought individuals would behave independently of group pressure when there was little doubt that his or her own judgments were accurate. He developed an interesting technique for testing his hypothesis (Asch, 1951, 1956).

A participant in Asch's experiment joined a group seated around a table. In his original study, the group consisted of seven people. Unknown to the participant, six of the people in the group were confederates of the experimenter; they were "in on" the experiment. The real participant was told that the study dealt with the ability to make perceptual judgments. The participant had to do nothing more than decide which of three lines was the same length as a standard line (Figure 14.3). The experimenter showed each set of lines to the group and collected responses, one by one, from each member of the group. There were 18 sets of lines to judge, and the real participant was always the last one to respond.

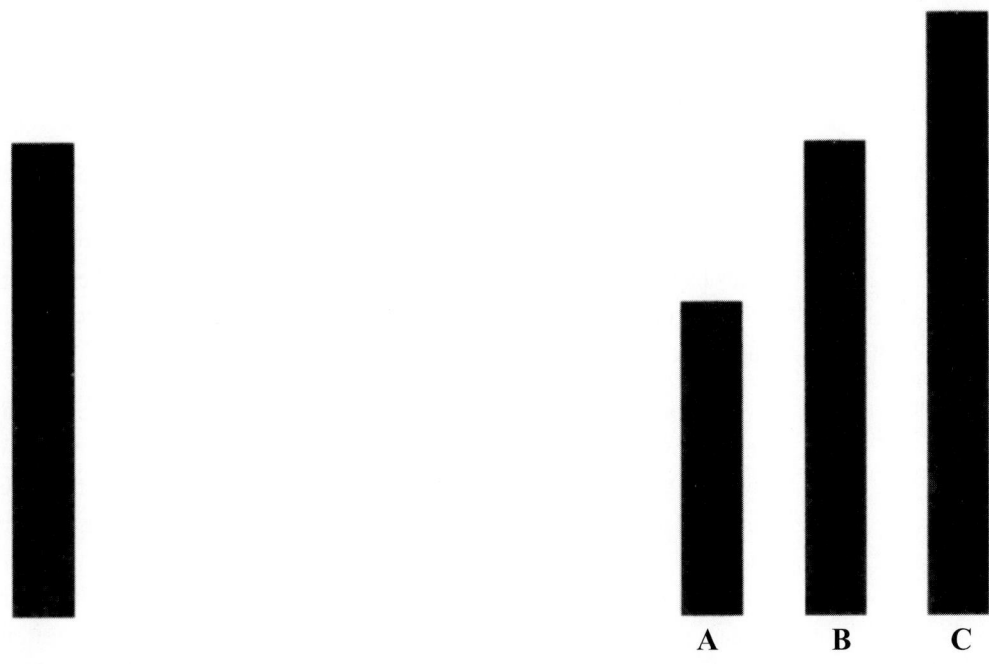

FIGURE 14.3

The type of stimuli used in Asch's conformity experiments. Subjects are to say which of the three lines on the right (A, B, or C) equals the line on the left. Associates of the experimenter will occasionally make incorrect choices, even though the correct choice is always as obvious as this one.

Each judgment involved unambiguous stimuli: the correct answer was obvious. On 12 of the 18 trials, however, the confederates gave a unanimous but *incorrect* answer. What would the "real" participants do? How would they resolve this conflict? Their eyes were telling them what the right answer was, but the group was saying something else.

The results of his initial study surprised Asch, because they did not confirm his hypothesis. When confederates gave "wrong" answers, conformity occurred 37 percent of the time. Participants responded with an incorrect answer that agreed with the majority on more than one-third of the trials. Moreover, three-quarters of Asch's participants conformed to the group pressure at least once.

Based on postexperimental interviews, Asch determined that participants conformed or remained independent for a variety of reasons. He categorized participants as yielding or independent. He found that some participants, although very few, yielded because they had come to accept the majority's judgments as correct. Most participants yielded because they did not have confidence in their own judgments. Another group of participants yielded because they did not want to appear to be defective in the eyes of the confederates. These individuals knew the majority was wrong, but went along anyway. Independent participants also fell into three categories. Some participants remained independent because they knew the majority was wrong and had confidence in their own judgments. Other participants remained independent because they felt a strong personal need to do so. These individuals might be called nonconformists or even anticonformists. The final group of independent participants remained independent because they wanted to perform well on the task.

In subsequent studies, Asch tried several variations of his original procedure. In one experiment, he varied the size of the unanimous, incorrect majority. As you might expect, the level of conformity increased as the size of the majority increased, leveling off at three or four people (Asch, 1956; Knowles, 1983). Participants gave incorrect judgments only 4 percent of the time when just one other incorrect judgment preceded their own. In another study, Asch found that participants gave an erroneous judgment only 10 percent of the time when there was but one dissenter among the six confederates who voiced an accurate judgment before the participants gave theirs. In other words, when the participants had any social support for what their eyes had told them, they tended to trust their own judgment. This is known as the **true partner effect**. If the true partner withdrew his support, conformity returned to its previous rate.

true partner effect the effect occurring when a person emerges to support the judgment of the minority in a conformity experiment leading to a reduction in conformity

Several factors have been found to influence the amount of conformity observed. If you believe that the majority facing you is highly competent, you are more likely to conform than if you believe the majority is less competent. The nature of the stimulus task used also affects levels of conformity. Remember that Asch used a simple line judgment task which had a clearly correct answer. As you increase the ambiguity of the stimulus, conformity increases. Research using the autokinetic effect, in which a stationary point of light is shown in a dark room and participants must estimate the amount that the light moves, shows a conformity rate of 70 percent (Sherif, 1936). When attitude items are used for which there is no clear "correct" answer, conformity rates approach 70 percent (Crutchfield, 1955).

There is also a small gender difference with women conforming more than men, especially when a male conducts the experiment and the experiment involves group pressure. Eagly (1987) has offered two explanations for the gender difference. First, gender may serve as a status variable in newly formed groups (such as those used in conformity experiments). Because the male gender role is traditionally seen as more powerful than the female gender role, females may conform more than males. Second, women are more sensitive than men to conformity pressures when opinions are stated publicly, as they typically are in conformity experiments (Eagly, Wood, & Fishbaugh, 1981).

Conformity involves yielding to the perceived pressure of a group. In most cases, it is assumed, group members are peers, or at least similar to the conformer. When one yields to the pressure of a perceived authority, the result is obedience. It is to this issue we turn next.

> ## BEFORE YOU GO ON
>
> - What is the definition of conformity?
> - Describe the experiment conducted by Asch on conformity and the results.
> - Describe the reasons why participants yielded or remained independent in Asch's experiment.
> - What is the true partner effect?
> - What factors affect conformity?

OBEDIENCE TO AUTHORITY

Adolph Eichmann, arguably the "architect" of the Holocaust, was captured by Israeli agents. He was brought to Israel where he was placed on trial for the crimes he committed against humanity. During his trial, Eichmann's principal defense was that he was a mid-level officer who was just "following orders." His contention was that his actions were taken at the behest of individuals who had the power to inflict punishment if he did not obey their orders.

Is "just following orders" a legitimate excuse? As we saw in the section on attributions, our predisposition is to attribute such behaviors internally. So, Eichmann becomes an inhuman monster and not a human being caught up in a highly unusual social situation. Which is it? Was Eichmann a monster, or was he a victim of circumstances?

This question preyed on the mind of social psychologist Stanley Milgram (1933-1984). Milgram was a student of Solomon Asch, so Milgram was interested in the conditions that lead to conformity. The participants in Asch's studies took the procedures seriously, but the consequences of either conforming or maintaining independence were rather trivial. At worst, participants might have experienced some discomfort as a result of voicing independent judgments. There were no external rewards or punishments for their behavior, and there was no one telling them how to respond. Milgram went beyond Asch's procedure. He wanted to see if an "ordinary" person placed in an "extraordinary" situation would obey an authority figure and inflict pain on an innocent victim. Milgram's research, conducted in the early 1960s, has become among the most famous and controversial in all of psychology. His experiments pressured participants to comply with the demand of an authority figure. The demand was both unreasonable and troubling (Milgram, 1963, 1965, 1974).

Obedience is not necessarily a bad thing. The smooth operation of any military endeavor requires a certain amount of obedience.

All of Milgram's studies involved the same basic procedure. Participants arrived at the laboratory to find that they would be participating with a second person (a confederate of the experimenter). The experimenter explained that the research dealt with the effects of punishment on learning and that one participant would serve as a "teacher," while the other would act as a "learner." The roles were assigned by a rigged drawing in which the actual participant was always assigned the role of teacher, while the confederate was always the learner. The participant watched as the learner was taken into a room and wired to electrodes to be used for delivering punishment in the form of electric shocks.

After the teacher received a sample shock of 45 volts, the teacher received his instructions. First, he was to read to the learner a list of four pairs of words. The teacher was then to read the first word of one of the pairs, and the learner was to supply the second word. The teacher sat in front of a rather imposing electric "shock generator" that had 30 switches. From left to right, the switches increased by increments of 15 volts, ranging from 15 volts to 450 volts. Labels were printed under the switches on the generator, ranging from "Slight" to "Moderate" to "Extreme Intensity" to "Danger: Severe Shock." The label at the 450-volt end read "XXX."

As the task proceeded, the learner periodically made errors according to a prearranged schedule. The teacher had been instructed to deliver an electric shock for every incorrect answer. With each error, the teacher was to move up the scale of shocks, giving the learner a more potent shock with each new mistake. (The learner, remember, was part of the act, and no one was actually receiving any shocks.)

Whenever the teacher hesitated or questioned whether he should continue, the experimenter was ready with a verbal prod, "Please continue," or "The experiment requires that you continue." If the participant protested, the experimenter became more assertive and offered an alternative prod, such as, "You have no choice; you must go on." Milgram was astonished by the results of his own study, and the results still amaze us. Twenty-six of Milgram's 40 participants—65 percent—obeyed the demands of the experimenter and went all the way to the highest shock and closed all of the switches. In fact, *no participant* stopped prior to the 300-volt level, the point at which the learner pounded on the wall in protest. One later variation of this study added vocal responses from the learner (voice feedback), who delivered an increasingly stronger series of demands to be let out of the experiment. The level of obedience in this study was still unbelievably high, as 25 of 40 participants—62.5 percent—continued to administer shocks to the 450-volt level. As shown in Figure 14.4, the level of obedience decreased as the distance between the "teacher" and "learner" decreased. Obedience dropped when the teacher and learner were in the same room (proximity). The lowest levels of obedience were observed when the "teacher" was required to force the "learner's" hand onto a shock plate (touch proximity).

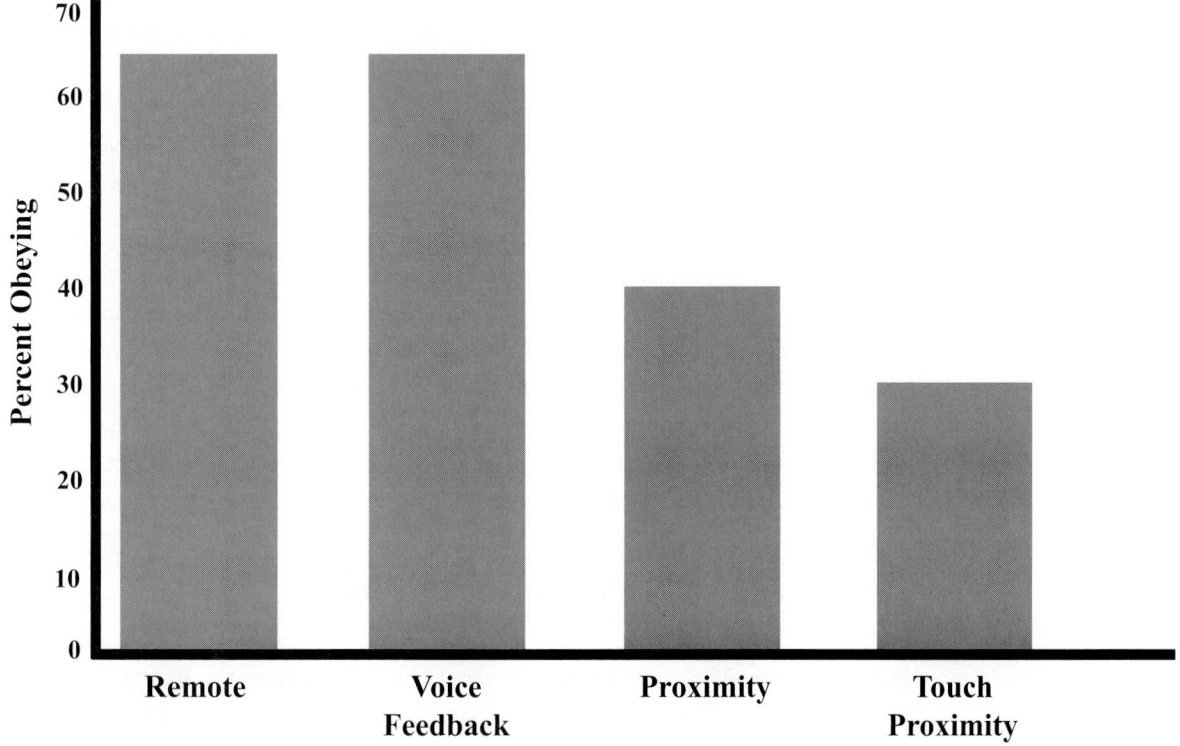

FIGURE 14.4

Results from Milgram's experiments on the distance between the teacher and the learner, and the level of shock administered.

The behavior of Milgram's participants indicated that they *were* concerned about the learner. All participants claimed that they experienced genuine and extreme stress in this situation. Some fidgeted, some trembled, many perspired profusely. Several giggled nervously. In short, the people caught up in this situation showed obvious signs of conflict and anxiety. Nonetheless, they continued to obey the orders of the experimenter even though they had good reason to believe they might be harming the learner.

Milgram's first study was performed with male participants ranging in age from 20 to 50. A later replication with adult women produced precisely the same results: 65 percent obeyed fully. Other variations of the procedure, however, uncovered several factors that could reduce the amount of obedience. Putting the learner and teacher in the same room, or having the experimenter deliver his orders over the telephone, reduced levels of obedience markedly. When the shocks were delivered by a team consisting of the participant and two confederates who refused to give the shocks, full-scale obedience dropped to only 10 percent. If the experimenter left the room and gave orders by telephone obedience also dropped. Obedience was also extremely low if there were conflicting authority figures; one urging the participant to continue delivering shocks and the other urging the participant to stop. When given the choice, participants obeyed the authority figure who said stop.

Attribution Errors and a Word of Caution

Upon first hearing about these distressing results, many people tend to think of Milgram's obedient participants as unfeeling, unusual, or even downright cruel and sadistic people (Safer, 1980). Nothing could be further from the truth. The participants were truly troubled by what was happening. If you thought Milgram's participants must be strange or different, perhaps you were a victim of what we identified in our last Topic as an *attribution error*. You were willing to attribute the participants' behavior to internal personality characteristics instead of recognizing the powerful situational forces at work.

Attributing negative personality characteristics to the "teachers" is particularly understandable in light of the unexpected nature of the results. In commenting on this research, many psychologists have suggested, in fact, that the most significant aspect of Milgram's findings is that they are so surprising. As part of his research, Milgram asked people, including a group of psychiatrists and a group of ministers, to predict what they would do under these circumstances, and asked them to predict how far others would go before refusing the authority. Respondents predicted very little obedience, expecting practically no one to proceed all the way to the final switch on the shock generator.

A Reminder About Ethics in Research

In reading about Milgram's research, it should have occurred to you that putting people in such a stressful situation could be considered ethically objectionable. Milgram himself was concerned with the welfare of his participants. He took great care to debrief them fully after each session. He informed them that they had not really administered any shocks and explained why deception had been used. It is, of course, standard practice in psychological experiments to conclude the session by disclosing the true purpose of the study and alleviating any anxiety that might have arisen.

Milgram reported that, after debriefing, the people in his studies were not upset at having been deceived. Their principal reaction was one of relief when they learned that no electric shock had been used. Milgram indicated that a follow-up study performed a year later with some of the same participants showed that no long-term adverse effects had been created by his procedure. Despite his precautions, Milgram was severely criticized for placing people in such an extremely stressful situation. One of the effects of his research was to establish in the scientific community a higher level of awareness of the need to protect the well-being of human research participants.

> ## BEFORE YOU GO ON
>
> - Describe the experiments conducted by Milgram on obedience, and what he found.
>
> - What happened when Milgram moved the teacher and learner closer together?
>
> - What factors did Milgram explore that could affect obedience, and what was found?
>
> - How could attribution errors affect how Milgram's participants are perceived?

BYSTANDER INTERVENTION

Remember the story of Kitty Genovese that opened this chapter? Here was a young woman brutally slain in full view of at least 38 witnesses, none of whom came to her aid. This tragic event stimulated public concern and sparked much commentary in the media. People wondered how all those witnesses could have shown such a lack of concern for another human being. *Apathy* and *alienation* were terms used to describe what had happened.

Bibb Latané and John Darley, two social psychologists who at the time were at universities in New York City, were not satisfied that terms such as *bystander apathy* or *alienation* adequately explained what happened in the Genovese case. They were not willing to attribute people's failure to help to internal, dispositional, or personality factors. They were convinced that situational factors make such events possible. Latané and Darley (1970) pointed out that there are logical reasons people should not be expected to offer help in an emergency. Emergencies tend to happen quickly and without warning. Except for medical technicians, firefighters, and a few other select categories of individuals, people are not prepared to deal with emergencies when they arise. In fact, one good predictor of who will intervene in an emergency turns out to be previous experience with similar emergency situations (Cramer et al., 1988; Huston et al., 1981).

A Cognitive Model of Bystander Intervention

Latané and Darley (1968) suggest that a series of cognitive events must occur before a bystander can intervene in an emergency (Figure 14.5). First, the bystander must *notice* what is going on. A person who is window shopping and fails to see someone collapse on the opposite side of the street cannot be expected to rush over and offer assistance. Second, if the bystander does notice something happen, he or she still must *label* the situation

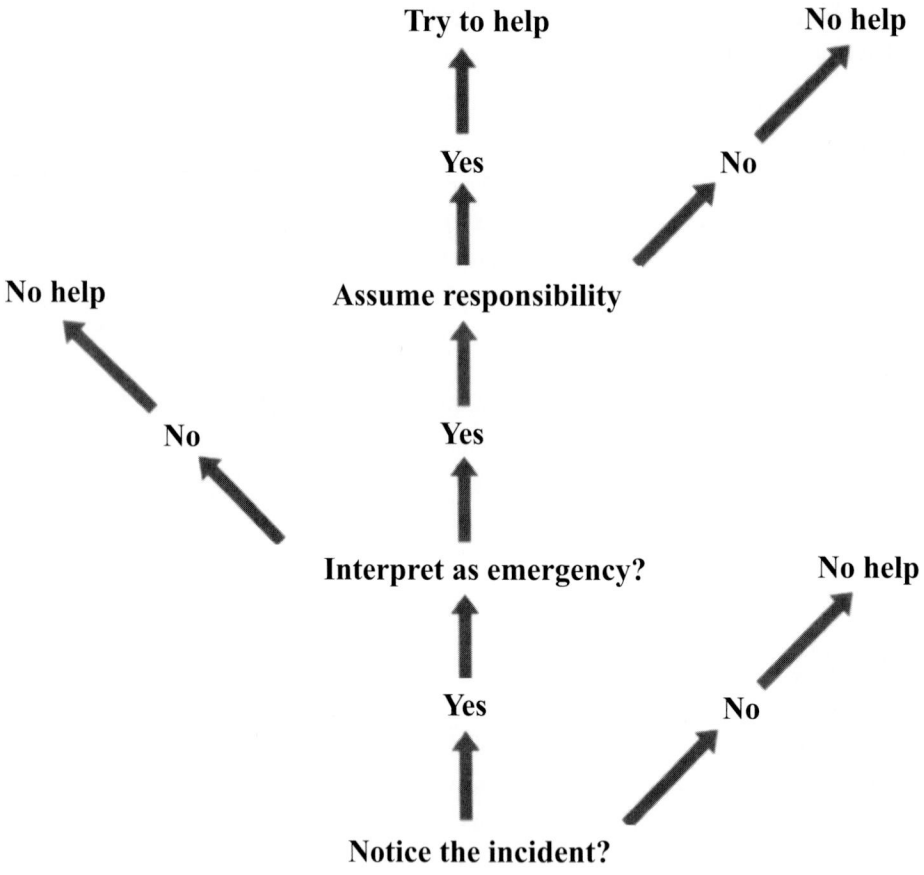

FIGURE 14.5

Some of the decisions and outcomes involved as a bystander considers intervening in an emergency situation (Latané & Darley, 1968)

as an emergency; perhaps the person who has collapsed is simply drunk or tired and not really having a stroke or a heart attack. The third step involves the decision that it is the bystander's (and not someone else's) *responsibility* to do something.

Even if the bystander has noticed something happening, has labeled the situation as one calling for action, and has assumed responsibility for helping, he or she still faces the decision of what form of assistance to offer. Should he or she try to give first aid? Should he or she try to find the nearest telephone, or simply start shouting for help? As a final step, the person must decide how to *implement* his or her decision to act. What is the best first aid under these circumstances? Just where can a phone be found? Thus, we can see that intervening on behalf of someone else in a social situation involves a series of cognitive choices.

A negative outcome at any of these steps will lead to a decision not to offer assistance. When one considers the cognitive events necessary for helping, it becomes apparent that the deck is stacked against the victim in an emergency. Ironically, it is the very presence of others that leads to this social-psychological phenomenon (Cunningham, 1984; Shotland, 1985). Perhaps we should be surprised that bystanders ever *do* offer help. There seem to be several psychological processes that account for what is called the **bystander effect** or *social inhibition of helping.* Let's review just three (Latané & Darley, 1970; Latané & Nida, 1981).

Audience Inhibition

Audience inhibition refers to our tendency to be hesitant to do things in front of others, especially strangers. We tend to be concerned about how others will evaluate us. In public, no one wants to do anything that might appear to be improper, incompetent, or silly. The bystander who intervenes risks embarrassment if he or she blunders, and that risk increases as the number of people present increases. People who are particularly sensitive to becoming embarrassed in public are most likely to be inhibited (Tice & Baumeister, 1985).

Pluralistic Ignorance

Emergencies tend to be ambiguous: is the man who has collapsed on the street ill or drunk? Is the commotion in a neighboring apartment an assault or a family quarrel that's just a little out of hand? When social reality is not clear, we often turn to others for clues. While someone is in the process of getting information from others, he or she will probably try to remain calm, cool, and collected, behaving as if there is no emergency. Everyone else, of course, is doing the very same thing, showing no outward sign of concern. The result is that each person is led by the others to think that the situation is really not an emergency after all, a phenomenon called **pluralistic ignorance** (Miller & McFarland, 1987). Pluralistic ignorance is the belief on the part of the individual that only she or he is confused and doesn't know what to do in an emergency, whereas everyone else is standing around doing nothing for a good reason. The group becomes paralyzed by a type of conformity—conformity to the inaction of others.

This process was demonstrated in a classic experiment by Latané and Darley (1968, 1970). Columbia University students reported to a campus building to participate in an interview. They were sent to a waiting room where they were to fill out some forms. While they did so, smoke began to billow through a vent in the wall. After six minutes (the point at which the procedure was terminated if the "emergency" had not been reported), there was enough smoke in the room to interfere with breathing and prevent seeing across the room.

When participants were alone in the waiting room, 75 percent of them came out to report the smoke. However, when two passive confederates were in the room with the participant, only 10 percent responded. Those people who reported the smoke did so quickly. Those from the groups who failed to do so generated all sorts of explanations for the smoke: steam, vapors from the air conditioner, smog introduced to simulate an urban environment, even "truth gas." In short, participants who remained unresponsive had been led by the inaction of others to conclude almost anything but the obvious—that something was very wrong.

bystander effect the phenomenon that a person is less likely to receive help when there are many bystanders as opposed to few or one

audience inhibition reluctance to intervene and offer assistance in front of others

pluralistic ignorance a condition in which the inaction of others leads each individual in a group to interpret a situation as a non-emergency, thus leading to general inactivity

Diffusion of Responsibility

In the Kitty Genovese murder, it was terribly clear that an emergency was in progress. There was little ambiguity about what was going on. Further, the 38 witnesses in the Genovese case were not in a face-to-face group that would allow social influence processes such as pluralistic ignorance to operate. Latané and Darley suggested that a third process is necessary to complete the explanation of bystander behavior.

A single bystander in an emergency situation must bear the full responsibility for offering assistance, but the witness who is part of a group shares that responsibility with other onlookers. The greater the number of other people present, the smaller is each individual's perceived obligation to intervene, a process referred to as **diffusion of responsibility**.

diffusion of responsibility the tendency to allow others to share in the obligation to intervene

Latané and Darley devised a clever demonstration of this phenomenon. College students arrived at a laboratory to take part in a group discussion on some of the personal problems they experienced as students attending an urban campus. To reduce embarrassment of talking about such matters in public, each group member was isolated in his or her own cubicle and could communicate with the others only through an intercom system. Actually, there were no other group members, only tape-recorded voices. Thus, there really was only one student in each group, and the perceived size of the group could be manipulated to see if diffusion of responsibility would occur.

The first person to "speak" mentioned that he was prone to seizures when under stress, such as when studying for an exam. The others, including the actual participant, then took turns talking about their problems. A second round of discussion began again with the seizure-prone student who, as he started talking, began to suffer one of his seizures. Clearly, something was wrong. As the "victim" began stammering, choking, and pleading for help, the typical participant became nervous—some trembled. The study had another feature in common with the Genovese episode: participants could not be sure if any other bystanders (members of the group) had taken any action. (In fact, remember, there were no others.)

As expected, the likelihood of helping decreased as the perceived size of the group increased. Eighty-five percent of those in two-person groups (just the participant and victim) left the cubicle to report the emergency. When the participant thought he or she was in a three-person group, 62 percent responded. Only 31 percent of the students who believed they were in a six-person group took any step to intervene. Additionally, help was given more slowly with more bystanders. So, a person is less likely to get help when there are many bystanders around and the help that is forthcoming takes longer to receive. The responsibility for reporting the seizure was divided (diffused) among those thought to be present.

Incidentally, diffusion of responsibility does come in forms less serious in their implications. Those of you with a few siblings can probably recall times at home when the telephone rang five or six times before anyone made a move to answer it, even though the entire family was home at the time. Some of you probably have been at parties where the doorbell went unanswered with everyone thinking that "someone else" would get it.

The Empathy-Altruism Connection

Traditionally, the focus of social psychologists interested in altruism has been the impact of the social environment on helping. However, other social psychologists point out that situational factors might interact with characteristics of the individual helper to affect helping. For example, true caring for a victim may motivate us to provide help (Batson 1987, 1990a,b). This caring is rooted in an emotional state called **empathy**, which is compassionate understanding of how the person in need feels. If someone needs our help, feelings of empathy would include sympathy, pity, and sorrow (Eisenberg & Miller, 1987). For example, if you read about the victims of an airplane crash and feel the anguish of those who suffered, you are feeling empathy. Batson suggests that empathy may lead to altruistic acts. According to this **empathy-altruism hypothesis**, empathy is one reason for helping those in need. However, it is not the only reason.

> **empathy** a compassionate understanding of how a person in need feels

You might be motivated to help a person in need to relieve your *personal distress* associated with not helping. This motive for helping is called **egoism**. For example, if you saw a motorist stranded on the side of the road and said to yourself, "I better do something or I'll feel terrible all day," your helping is designed to relieve your own distress and not the distress of the victim. So, empathy is focused on the distress and suffering of the *victim*, whereas egoism is focused on *your own* distress and suffering. This indicates that there are at least two paths to helping: empathy and egoism. Generally, research by Batson (1990a,b) and others (Dovidio, Allen, & Schroeder, 1990) supports the empathy-altruism hypothesis. Empathy is one important motivator for altruistic acts (Dovidio et al., 1990).

> **empathy-altruism hypothesis** a hypothesis stating that empathy is one reason for helping those in need

> **egoism** helping someone in need to avoid personal distress for not helping

The Bystander Effect: A Conclusion

The situational determinants of helping behavior continued to be a popular research topic for social psychologists throughout the 1970s. Many of these studies manipulated the size of the group witnessing the event that created the need for help in the first place. Latané and Nida (1981) reviewed nearly 50 studies involving almost 100 helping-not-helping situations. Although they involved a wide range of settings, procedures, and participants, the social inhibition of helping (the bystander effect) occurred in almost every instance. Latané and Nida combined the data from all of these studies in a meta-analysis. Their conclusion: A person is more likely to help when he or she is alone rather than in a group. The bystander effect is a remarkably consistent phenomenon, perhaps as predictable as any phenomenon in social psychology.

BEFORE YOU GO ON

- Describe the five steps a person goes through before giving help.
- What is the bystander effect?
- What explanations have been offered for the bystander effect?
- What are empathy and egoism?
- Describe the empathy-altruism hypothesis.

SOCIAL LOAFING AND FACILITATION

Latané, Williams, and Harkins (1979) have identified a process of social influence they call **social loafing**: the tendency to work less (to decrease individual effort) as the size of

> **social loafing** the tendency to decrease one's individual work effort as the size of the group in which one is working increases

Research on social loafing tells us that some people in some social situations may not work as hard as they would if they were working alone.

social facilitation improved performance due to the presence of others on a simple, well-learned task

social interference impaired performance due to the presence of others, especially on a complex task

the group in which one is working becomes larger. Their studies had participants shout or clap as loud as possible, either in groups or alone. If people were led to believe their performance could not be identified, they invested less effort in the task as group size increased. Other studies (Harkins & Petty, 1983; Karau & Williams, 1993; Weldon & Gargano, 1988; Williams & Karau, 1991) have used different, more cognitive tasks, such as evaluating poetry. The results tend to be consistent: when people can hide in the crowd, their effort (and hence their productivity) declines.

Although social loafing is a widespread phenomenon, it is not always predicted when one works in a group setting. Remember our earlier discussions of cultures that can be described in terms of the extent to which they exhibit collectivist or individualist characteristics? As you might predict, social loafing is significantly less likely in those (collectivist) cultures—such as in Japan, China, and other Asian countries—which place a high value on participation in group activities (Early, 1989; Gabrenya et al., 1985). In individualist cultures, such as in the United States and most Western countries, social loafing can be virtually eliminated if group members believe their effort is special and required for the group's success, or if group members believe that their performance can be identified and evaluated individually (Harkins, 1987; Harkins & Syzmanski, 1989; Williams et al., 1981, 1989). Indeed, there are situations in which social influence actually facilitates behavior.

Many years ago, psychologist Norman Triplett observed that bicycle riders competing against other cyclists outperformed those racing against a clock. He then performed what is considered the first laboratory experiment in social psychology (Triplett, 1898). Triplett had children wind a fishing reel as rapidly as they could. They engaged in this task either alone or with another child alongside doing the same thing. Just as he had noticed in his records of bicycle races, Triplett found that the children worked faster when another child was present. We now know that such an effect sometimes occurs not only with coactors (others engaged in the same task) but if a person performs before an audience. For example, joggers, both male and female, pick up the pace and run faster when going past a person sitting on a park bench (Worringham & Messick, 1983). When the presence of others improves an individual's performance on some task, it is called **social facilitation**.

Numerous studies of these phenomena were performed early in the twentieth century with a puzzling inconsistency in results. Sometimes social facilitation would occur, but on other occasions, the opposite would happen. Sometimes people performed more poorly in the presence of others than they did alone, an effect social psychologists called **social interference**. The inconsistency in these findings was so bewildering that most social psychologists eventually gave up investigating social facilitation.

In 1965, Robert Zajonc resurrected the topic of social facilitation by providing a plausible interpretation for the lack of consistency in social facilitation effects. In his examination of the research, Zajonc noticed that social facilitation occurred whenever the

Because of social facilitation, we tend to perform better when we are in the presence of others—at least when we are engaged in a simple or well-rehearsed task. Kayak teams, for example, paddle faster when racing against other teams than they do when they are racing against the clock.

behavior under study was simple, routine, or very well-learned (for example, bicycle riding or winding a fishing reel). Social interference, on the other hand, tended to occur whenever the behavior involved was complex or not well-learned. Zajonc's insight was that the presence of others creates increased arousal, which in turn energizes the dominant (most likely) response under the circumstances. When the dominant response is correct, as with a simple, well-practiced task, facilitation occurs. When the dominant response is incorrect, as with a complex task or one with which we have had little practice, the result is interference (Levine et al., 1993).

You may have experienced this effect yourself if you have ever tried to acquire a skill at a sport totally new to you. Whereas skilled athletes often perform better in front of audiences, the novice tends to do better when alone. (Even skilled athletes don't always perform better in front of audiences, sometimes "choking" in front of home crowds during important games [Baumeister, 1985].) You may have experienced—as a novice, that is— the frustration of making contact with a golf ball or tennis ball when there are others standing nearby, watching you.

In conclusion, we may safely assume that social interference and social loafing are more common phenomena than is social facilitation. Although there are occasions in which coworkers or an audience may enhance an individual's performance, the presence of others is more likely to inhibit it.

DECISION MAKING IN GROUPS

Many of the decisions we face in our daily lives are the sort that are made in group settings. Committees, boards, family groups, and group projects for a class are only a few examples. There is logic in the belief that group efforts to solve problems should be superior to the efforts of individuals. Having more people available should mean having more talent and knowledge available. It also seems logical that the cohesiveness of the group might contribute to a more productive effort (for some groups and some problems, this is exactly the case). But, we know better than to assume that just because a conclusion is logical it is necessarily true.

Decades of research show us that groups can, and often do, outperform individuals. Here is a partial list of what we know about group decision making:

- Groups outperform the average individual in the group mainly because groups recognize a correct answer to a problem faster, reject an incorrect answer, and have better memory systems than the average individual.

- Groups comprising high-quality members perform better than groups with low-quality members.

- As you increase the size of the group, you increase the resources available to the group. However, you also increase process loss (loss of productivity due to faulty group interaction). Additionally, in larger groups you get even less member participation than in smaller groups.

- When the problem a group must solve involves a great deal of interaction, interpersonal cohesiveness (how much members like each other) and task-based cohesiveness (mutual respect for skills and abilities) increase productivity. When a problem does not require much interaction, task-based cohesiveness increases productivity, but interpersonal cohesiveness does not.

Although it is generally true that groups outperform individuals, there are some liabilities attached to using groups to make decisions. In this section, we consider two aspects of group decision making that can lead, in some cases, to low-quality decisions.

Group Polarization

When he was an MIT graduate student in industrial management, James Stoner gave participants in his study a series of dilemmas to consider (Stoner, 1961). The result of each decision was to be a statement of how much risk the fictitious character in the dilemma should take. Much to his surprise, Stoner found that the decisions rendered by groups were much riskier than those individual group members made prior to the group decision. Stoner called this move away from conservative solutions a *risky shift*. For example, doctors, if asked individually, might claim that a patient's problem (whatever it might be) could be handled with medication and a change in diet. If these same doctors were to jointly discuss the patient's situation, they might conclude that a new and potentially dangerous (risky) surgical procedure was necessary.

Several hundred experimental studies later, we now know that this effect also occurs in the opposite direction, or a *cautious shift* (Levine & Moreland, 1990; Moscovici et al., 1985). In other words, the risky shift is simply a specific case of a more general **group polarization** effect—that group participation will make an individual's reactions more extreme, or polarized. Group discussion usually leads to an enhancement of the beliefs and attitudes of the group members that existed before the discussion began. One explanation for group polarization is that open discussion gives group members an opportunity to hear persuasive arguments they have not previously considered, leading to a strengthening of their original attitudes (Isenberg, 1986). Another possibility is that after comparing attitudinal positions with one another, some group members feel pressure to catch up with other group members who have more extreme attitudes (Hinsz & Davis, 1984).

group polarization the tendency for members of a group to give more extreme judgments following a discussion than they gave initially

BEFORE YOU GO ON

- What are social loafing, social facilitation, and social inhibition? When does each occur?

- Describe Zajonc's theory of social facilitation.

- What factors affect group decision making?

Groupthink

Irving Janis (1972, 1983a) has described a related phenomenon of influence he calls **groupthink**, an excessive concern for reaching a consensus in group decision making to the extent that critical evaluations are withheld. Janis maintains that this style of thinking emerges when group members are so interested in maintaining harmony in the group that differences of opinion or alternative courses of action are suppressed. Janis also maintained that groupthink is most likely to occur in cohesive groups.

groupthink an excessive concern for reaching a consensus in group decision making to the extent that critical evaluations of input are withheld

Janis (1972) saw some common threads running through bad group decisions that led to "historical fiascoes." He identified eight "symptoms" of groupthink:

1. *An illusion of invulnerability*: The group members believe that nothing can harm them, which leads to excessive optimism,

2. *Rationalization*: Rather than realistically evaluating information, group members collectively rationalize away damaging information,

3. *Unquestioned belief in the group's inherent morality*: The group sees itself on the side of what is right and just. This leads group members to ignore the moral implications and consequences of their actions,

4. *Stereotyped views of the enemy*: The "enemy" is characterized as too weak or stupid to put up any meaningful resistance to the group's planned course of action,

5. *Conformity pressures*: Direct pressure is placed on any member of the group who dissents from what the group wants to do,

6. *Self-censorship*: Because of the conformity pressure, individual members of the group who may want to say something keep silent because of the potential consequences,

7. *An illusion of unanimity*: Because of self-censorship, the group suffers the illusion that everyone agrees with the course of action planned by the group,

8. *Emergence of self-appointed mindguards*: Self-appointed mindguards emerge to protect the group from damaging outside information. These people intercept potentially damaging information and don't pass it along to the group.

By analyzing several key historical events such as responding to the bombing of Pearl Harbor, the Bay of Pigs invasion, and the Challenger explosion, in terms of groupthink, Janis found that such situations involved a cohesive decision-making group that was relatively isolated from outside judgments, a directive leader who supplied pressure to conform to his position, and an illusion of unanimity (see also, McCauley, 1989).

Generally, Janis' groupthink hypothesis has weathered the test of time. However, some research suggests that group cohesiveness may not be as crucial to the emergence of groupthink as Janis originally believed (Courtwright, 1978). Directive leadership and consensus seeking, which makes groups more concerned with morale and getting members to agree than with the quality of the decision are important precursors of groupthink (Flowers, 1977; Tetlock, Peterson, McGuire, Chang, & Feld, 1992). Finally, Gerald Whyte (1989) has proposed that group polarization, risk taking, and the potential for a fiasco occur when a group frames its decision in terms of potential failure. Whyte suggests that if a group frames possible outcomes in terms of potential failure the group is more likely to make a risky decision. Working in an environment that favors risky decisions enhances the likelihood of a disastrous group decision (Whyte, 1989).

BEFORE YOU GO ON

- What is group polarization?
- What is groupthink?
- What are the eight symptoms of groupthink?

Topic Review 14 B

1. What is conformity?

Conformity is a social influence process in which behavior is modified in response to perceived pressure from others so that the behavior is consistent with that of others. Conformity is often thought of in negative terms. However, conformity helps make social behavior efficient and predictable.

2. What were the methods and findings of Asch's conformity studies?

In Asch's studies, people made judgments about unambiguous perceptual stimuli: the length of lines. During some trials, confederates gave judgments that were clearly incorrect before the actual participant had a chance to respond. Although there were situations in which yielding to perceived group pressure could be lessened, many of Asch's participants followed suit and conformed.

3. What were the different reasons given by Asch's participants for conforming?

Based on post-experimental interviews, Asch categorized participants who conformed as "yielding" participants. Some, but very few, participants conformed because they accepted that the majority was correct in its judgments. A second group, making up the largest group of yielding participants, conformed because they had little confidence in their own judgments. The final group of yielding participants conformed because they didn't want to appear defective to others.

4. What were the different reasons given by Asch's participants for not conforming?

Asch's "independent" participants fell into one of three categories. First, some participants remained independent because they trusted their own senses and judgements. Others remained independent because they felt a great personal need to do so. Finally, other participants remained independent because they wanted to perform well on the task.

5. What is the true partner effect?

Asch found that if a member of the incorrect majority started to agree with the real participant in his experi-

ment, the conformity rate dropped drastically. If the true partner withdraws his support, the conformity rate went back to its original rate.

6. What factors have been found to influence the rate of conformity?

Several factors affect conformity rates. The size of the majority is one factor. Conformity increases as the size of the majority increases up to a point and then levels off. The more competent the majority is perceived to be, the greater the conformity. If the minority perceives him or herself to be competent, conformity decreases. Conformity increases if an ambiguous task is used. There is a small gender difference, with women conforming more than men when a male is the experimenter or if group pressure is involved. There are also cultural and sociopolitical climate relationships with conformity.

7. How did Milgram study obedience?

Participants in Milgram's experiments were led to believe they were administering more and more potent shocks to another person in a learning task. Whenever they hesitated to deliver shocks, an authority figure, the experimenter, prodded them to continue. All participants obeyed to some degree, and nearly two-thirds delivered what they thought was the most intense shock, even over the protests of the learner. Those who obeyed in Milgram's experiments were neither cruel nor inhumane. Rather, the experimenter created a powerful social situation that made it difficult to refuse the authority figure's orders.

8. What did Milgram find about factors that affect obedience?

Milgram found that a participant's gender did not relate to obedience rates. However, as Milgram moved the teacher and learner closer together (in the same room), obedience dropped. The lowest rate of obedience was observed when the teacher actually had to touch the learner to give him a shock. When a group administered the shocks and two group members refused to continue, obedience was reduced. Having the experimenter leave the room and deliver orders by telephone and adding an authority figure who tells the participant to stop the experiment also reduced obedience.

9. **What steps are involved in the decision to help in an emergency situation?**

Darley and Latané proposed that a person must pass through a series of cognitive events before he or she will help. First, a bystander must notice the emergency. Second, the bystander must label the situation. Third, the bystander must assume responsibility for helping. Fourth, the bystander must decide how to help. Finally, the bystander must implement the decision to help. A negative decision at any point will result in no help being offered.

10. **What effect does the presence of others have on a person's willingness to help in an emergency?**

The likelihood that someone will intervene on behalf of another in an emergency is lessened as a function of how many others (bystanders) are present at the time. The greater the number of bystanders present, the less likely a person in need will receive help. This is known as the bystander effect.

11. **What explanations have been given for the bystander effect?**

Several factors have been proposed to account for this phenomenon. Audience inhibition is the term used to describe the hesitancy to intervene in front of others, perhaps for fear of embarrassing oneself. Pluralistic ignorance occurs when others lead one to think (by their inactivity) that nothing is wrong in an ambiguous emergency situation. Diffusion of responsibility causes a member of a group to feel less obligated to intervene (less responsible) than if he or she were alone. Each of these processes tends to discourage helping and is more likely to operate as the number of persons present increases.

12. **What is the relationship between empathy and altruism?**

There are two forces that can motivate altruism: empathy and egoism. Empathy is an emotional state in which a person feels the suffering of a victim in need. Helping based on empathy is focused on relieving the suffering of the victim. Egosim motivates a person to help to avoid personal displeasure. The empathy-altruism hypothesis suggests that empathy is one important factor in motivating altruism.

13. **What are social loafing, social interference, and social facilitation?**

Social loafing occurs when one is less likely to invest full effort and energy in the task at hand as a member of a group than he or she would if working alone (at least in Western, individualist cultures). Data suggest that as group size increases, social loafing increases. It is also the case that the quality of one's performance tends to suffer when one works in a group, a phenomenon called social interference. On the other hand, when tasks are simple or well-rehearsed, performance may be enhanced, a process called social facilitation.

14. **What factors influence group decision making?**

Groups outperform the average individual because groups recognize a correct answer faster, reject an incorrect answer faster, and have better memory systems than the average person. Groups with high quality members perform better than groups with low quality members. Increasing group size increases resources available to the group, but also increases process loss. In larger groups member participation is less even than in smaller groups. Interpersonal cohesiveness and task-based cohesiveness enhance group performance when a problem requires a great deal of interaction. When a great deal of interaction is not required, only task-based cohesiveness increases productivity.

15. **What is group polarization?**

Although there are advantages to problem solving in a group setting, there are also liabilities. Group polarization (originally known as the risky shift) is the tendency for group discussion to solidify and enhance preexisting attitudes.

16. **What is groupthink, and what are its "symptoms"?**

Groupthink is an excessive concern for reaching a consensus at the expense of carefully considering alternative courses of action. Groupthink has been found to contribute to bad group decisions. Irving Janis identified eight symptoms of groupthink: An illusion of invulnerability, rationalization, an unquestioned belief in the group's morality, stereotyped views of the enemy, conformity pressures, self-censorship, an illusion of unanimity, and the emergence of self-appointed mindguards.

17. **What does research suggest about the validity of groupthink?**

Generally, the groupthink hypothesis has withstood the test of time. However, research shows that cohesiveness may not be as important as Janis originally thought. Directive leadership and consensus seeking are important factors in groupthink. Framing a problem in terms of potential failure may lead to excessive risk taking in groups, leading to bad decisions.

GLOSSARY

abnormal Referring to maladaptive cognitions, affects, and/or behaviors that are at odds with social expectations and result in distress and discomfort.

absolute threshold The physical intensity of a stimulus that one can detect 50 percent of the time.

accommodation The process in which the shape of the lens is changed by the ciliary muscles to focus an image on the retina.

acquired immune deficiency syndrome (AIDS) A deadly disease caused by a virus (HIV) that destroys the body's natural immune system; can be transmitted by an interchange of blood or semen.

aqueous humor Watery fluid found in the space between the cornea and the lens that nourishes the front of the eye.

acquisition The process in operant conditioning in which the rate of a reinforced response increases.

action potential The short-lived electrical burst caused by the sudden reversal of electric charges inside and outside a neuron in which the inside becomes positive (about +40 mV).

actor-observer bias The overuse of internal attributions to explain the behaviors of others and external attributions to explain our own behaviors.

adaptation A function in Piaget's theory involving a child adapting cognitive abilities to the demands of the environment.

adolescence The developmental period between childhood and adulthood, often begun at puberty and ending with full physical growth, generally between the ages of 12 and 20.

adrenal glands Endocrine glands that release adrenaline, or epinephrine, into the bloodstream to activate the body in times of stress or danger.

affects Mental processes that involve one's feelings, mood, or emotional state and that comprise part of the subject matter of psychology.

ageism Discrimination or prejudice against someone formed solely on the basis of age.

aggression Any behavior that is intended to inflict physical and/or psychological harm on another organism or the symbol of that organism.

aggressive script An internalized representation of an event that leads to increased aggression and a tendency to see the world as an aggressive, hostile place.

agoraphobia An exaggerated fear of venturing into the world alone.

algorithm A problem-solving strategy in which all possible solutions are generated and tested until an acceptable solution appears.

all-or-none principle The fact that a neuron will either produce a full impulse, or action potential, or will not fire at all.

Alzheimer's disease A form of dementia associated with personality changes, diagnosed at autopsy.

anorexia nervosa An eating disorder characterized by the reduction of body weight through self-starvation and/or increased activity.

anterograde amnesia The inability to form or retrieve new memories.

antianxiety drugs Chemicals that alleviate the symptoms of anxiety; also known as tranquilizers.

antidepressant drugs Chemicals that reduce the symptoms of depression.

antipsychotic drugs Chemicals, such as chlorpromazine, effective in reducing psychotic symptoms.

anxiety A general feeling of tension, apprehension, and dread that involves predictable physiological changes.

APA ethical guidelines A set of guidelines adopted by the American Psychological Association specifying ethical treatment of human and animal subjects used in psychological research.

applied behavior analysis An approach, based on operant conditioning, that attempts to find solutions to human environment problems in the real world.

aptitude tests Psychological tests of cognitive abilities used to predict future behaviors.

arbitrary symbolic reference The property of human language that there does not have to be any relationship between a word and its referent.

arousal One's level of activation or excitement.

assimilation In Piaget's theory, the process of adding, and "fitting in," new material or information to an existing schema.

association areas Those areas of the frontal, temporal, and parietal lobes in which mental processes (planning, thinking, problem solving, memory) occur and where incoming sensory information is integrated with outgoing motor responses.

attachment A strong emotional relationship between a child and parent or primary caregiver that develops over the first year of life.

attitude A relatively stable evaluative disposition directed toward some object or event; it consists of feelings, behaviors, and beliefs.

audience inhibition Reluctance to intervene and offer assistance in front of others.

autonomic nervous system (ANS) Neurons in the peripheral nervous system that activate smooth muscles and glands.

availability heuristic The assumption that whatever comes to mind readily must be more common or probable than what does not easily come to mind.

aversion therapy A technique of behavior therapy in which an aversive stimulus, such as a shock, is paired with an undesired behavior.

axon A long, tail-like extension of a neuron that carries impulses away from the cell body to other cells.

axon terminals The set of branching end points of an axon; where neurons begin to communicate with adjacent neurons.

babbling Speech phonemes produced in rhythmic, repetitive patterns.

basal ganglia A collection of structures in front of the limbic system involved in the control of large, slow movements; a source of much of the brain's dopamine.

baseline design An experimental design in which subjects are included in both the control and experimental groups; behavior observed while the subject is in the experimental phase of the experiment is compared to behavior observed in the control phase.

basilar membrane A structure within the cochlea that vibrates and thus stimulates the hair cells of the inner ear.

behavior The actions and responses of organisms that are the focus of psychological research and theory.

behavior genetics The study of how the interaction between genetic and environmental factors influences individual differences among specific individuals.

behavior intention A specific intention to perform a given behavior that relates to behavior better than general attitudes.

behavior therapy Techniques of psychotherapy founded on principles of learning established in the psychological laboratory and aimed at changing one's behaviors.

behavioral observation The assessment technique of drawing conclusions about one's personality based on observations of that person's behaviors.

behaviorism The school of psychology founded by Watson that emphasized the study of overt, observable behavior and not the mind.

bipolar disorder A mood disorder characterized by swings of mood between extreme depression and (shorter segments of) mania.

blind spot The small region of the retina containing no photoreceptors where the optic nerve leaves the eye.

brain stem The lowest part of the brain, just above the spinal cord, consisting of the medulla and the pons.

brightness constancy The perceptual constancy that allows one to perceive the apparent brightness of a familiar object as constant, despite changes in the actual amount or type of light under which it is viewed.

bulimia An eating disorder characterized by recurrent episodes of binge eating and then purging to remove the just-eaten food.

bystander effect The phenomenon that a person is less likely to receive help when there are many bystanders as opposed to few or one.

cell body The largest concentration of mass in a neuron; contains the cell's nucleus.

central nervous system (CNS) Neurons and supporting cells in the spinal cord and the brain.

cerebellum A spherical structure at the rear base of the brain that coordinates fine and rapid muscular movements.

cerebral cortex The large convoluted outer covering of the brain that is the seat of voluntary action and cognitive functioning.

chemical ions Electrically charged (+ or –) chemical particles present inside and outside the axon of a neuron.

chlamydia A common STD caused by a bacterial infection that can lead to PID and infertility in women if untreated.

chunk An imprecise concept referring to a meaningful unit of information represented in short-term memory.

ciliary muscles Small muscles attached to the lens that control its shape and focusing capability.

circular explanation An "explanation" that is not a true explanation, but rather does nothing more than give a new label for observed behavior.

classical conditioning Learning in which an originally neutral stimulus comes to elicit a new response after being paired with a stimulus that reflexively elicits that same response.

client-centered therapy The humanistic psychotherapy associated with Rogers, aimed at helping a person grow and self-actualize.

closure The Gestalt principle of organization claiming that we tend to perceive incomplete figures as whole.

clustering The process of recalling related items of information together.

cochlea The snail-like part of the inner ear where sound waves become neural impulses.

cognitions Mental events such as perceptions, beliefs, thoughts, and memories that comprise part of the subject matter of psychology.

cognitive development Age-related changes in a child's learning, memory, perception, attention, problem solving, and thinking.

cognitive dissonance A motivating discomfort or tension caused by a lack of balance or consonance among one's cognitions.

cognitive map A mental representation of the learning situation or physical environment.

cognitive restructuring therapy A form of cognitive therapy, associated with Beck, in which an individual is led to overcome negative self-images and pessimistic views of the future.

color constancy The perceptual constancy that allows one to perceive a familiar object as having a constant color, despite changes in the hue of the light illuminating the object.

common fate The Gestalt principle of organization claiming that we group together, within the same figure, elements of a scene that move together in the same direction and at the same speed.

communication function The function of the spinal cord involving transmission of information to and from the brain.

comorbidity The occurrence of two or more disorders within the same individual.

compromise memory The blending of conflicting information in memory so that an "averaged" version of information will be recalled.

compulsion Constantly intruding, repetitive, unwanted behavior.

concrete operations stage The third stage of development in Piaget's theory, from ages 7 to 12 years, when concepts can be manipulated, but not in an abstract fashion.

conditioned response In classical conditioning, the learned response (such as salivation in response to a tone) evoked by the CS after conditioning.

conditioned stimulus In classical conditioning, an originally neutral stimulus (such as a tone) that, when paired with a UCS, comes to evoke a new response.

cones Photosensitive cells of the retina that operate best at high levels of illumination and that are responsible for color vision.

conflict A stressor in which some goals can be satisfied only at the expense of others.

conformity The changing of one's behavior, under perceived pressure, so that it is consistent with the behavior of others.

confounding variable An extraneous variable that varies systematically with the independent variable in an experiment and clouds one's ability to clearly establish a causal relationship between the independent and dependent variables.

consciousness The awareness of the environment and of one's own mental processes.

conservation In Piaget's theory, an appreciation that changing the physical properties of an object does not necessarily change its essence.

construction memory framework (CMF) An emerging view of memory stating that we store patterns of features scattered over different parts of the brain with each feature representing a different aspect of what is experienced; retrieval involves successively reactivating features.

contingency contracting Establishing an agreement (contract) with one to reinforce appropriate behaviors, often involving token economies.

contingency management Bringing about changes in one's behaviors by controlling rewards and punishments.

continuity The Gestalt principle of organization claiming that a stimulus or a movement will be perceived as continuing in the same smooth direction as first established.

continuous reinforcement (CRF) schedule A reinforcement schedule in which every response is followed by a reinforcer.

contrast The extent to which a stimulus is in some physical way different from surrounding stimuli.

control group The group in the experiment that receives a zero level of the independent variable and provides a baseline of behavior to which performance of subjects in the experimental group is compared.

conventional morality The second level of moral reasoning in Kohlberg's theory in which a judgment is based on an accepted social convention, and social approval matters as much as or more than anything else.

convergence The tendency of the eyes to move toward each other as we focus on objects close up.

convergent thinking The reduction or focusing of many ideas or solutions into one, or a few.

conversion disorder A somatoform disorder involving a loss or altering of physical functioning with no underlying medical cause.

corpus callosum The network of nerve fibers that connects the two hemispheres of the cerebral cortex.

correlation coefficient A statistic that yields a number between −1 and +1 that shows the strength and nature of the relationship between variables: the sign of the coefficient shows the direction of the relationship between variables and the magnitude shows the strength of the relationship between variables.

correlational research A method of research in which variables are not manipulated; instead, two or more variables are measured and a relationship between or among them is investigated.

counterconditioning In systematic desensitization, when a new response (relaxation) is being acquired to "replace" an old one (fear).

credibility The believability of the communicator involving the expertise and trustworthiness of the communicator.

cross laterality The arrangement of nerve fibers crossing from the left side of the body to the right side of the brain, and from the right side of the body to the left side of the brain.

crowding The subjective feeling of discomfort caused by a sense of lack of space.

crystallized intelligence Abilities related to acquired knowledge, accumulated experiences, and general information.

dark adaptation The process by which our eyes become more sensitive to light as we spend time in the dark.

death instincts (thanatos) The inborn impulses, proposed by Freud, that compel one toward destruction; they include feelings of depression and aggression.

declarative memory A memory system that includes memory systems from which factual information and memories of events can be intentionally recalled.

defense mechanisms Unconsciously applied techniques that protect the self (ego) from feelings of anxiety.

delusions False beliefs; ideas firmly held regardless of evidence to the contrary.

dementia A condition characterized by the marked loss of intellectual abilities.

dendrites Extensions from a neuron's cell body that receive impulses.

denial A defense mechanism wherein one refuses to believe the realities of an anxiety-producing situation.

dependent variable The variable that provides the measure of a subject's behavior; its value depends upon what the subject does.

depressants Chemicals that reduce one's awareness of external stimuli, slow bodily functioning, and decrease levels of overt behavior, reduce one's awareness of external stimuli, slow bodily functioning, and decrease levels of overt behavior.

diagnosis The act of recognizing a disorder on the basis of a specified set of symptoms.

difference threshold The differences in a stimulus attribute that can be detected 50 percent of the time.

diffusion of responsibility The tendency to allow others to share in the obligation to intervene.

directionality problem A reason one should not infer a causal relationship between variables from correlational research; it is often logically difficult to specify the direction of causality between variables based on correlational data.

discrimination The process of differential reinforcement wherein one stimulus is reinforced while another stimulus is not.

discrimination learning The phenomenon in classical conditioning in which an organism learns to make a response to only one CS, but not to other CSs.

displacement A defense mechanism in which one's behaviors or motives (usually aggressive) are directed at a substitute rather than the real object of those behaviors or motives.

dissociative amnesia The inability to recall important personal information for no apparent reason.

dissociative disorders Disorders in which a person seeks to escape from some aspect of life or personality that is seen as a source of stress.

dissociative fugue Amnesic forgetfulness accompanied by a change in location.

dissociative identity disorder The existence within the same person of two or more distinct personalities or personality traits.

divergent thinking The creation of many ideas or possible solutions from one idea.

Down syndrome A condition of several symptoms, including mental retardation, caused by an extra (47th) chromosome.

drive A state of tension resulting from an unlearned need that arouses and directs an organism's behavior.

dualism A philosophical doctrine that states that humans possess both body and mind.

dysthymia A mild (but distressing) chronic form of depression.

eardrum The outermost membrane of the ear which is set in motion by the vibrations of a sound and transmits vibrations to the ossicles.

echoic memory The sensory memory system associated with the sense of hearing.

ego In Freud's theory, the aspect of personality that encompasses the sense of "self"; it is in contact with the real world and operates on the reality principle.

egoism Helping someone in need to avoid personal distress for not helping.

elaboration likelihood model A model of persuasion stating that there are two routes to persuasion: the central route and the peripheral route.

elaborative rehearsal A means of processing information into LTM that involves thinking about information, organizing it, and making it meaningful.

electroconvulsive shock therapy Treatment, usually for severe depression, in which an electric current passed across a patient's head causes a seizure.

embryonic stage The second prenatal developmental period from 2 to 8 weeks during which all the organ systems of the body are put into place.

emotion An experience that includes a subjective feeling, a cognitive interpretation, a physical reaction, and a behavioral expression.

empathic Able to understand and share the essence of another's feelings, or to view from another's perspective.

empathy A compassionate understanding of how a person in need feels.

empathy-altruism hypothesis A hypothesis stating that empathy is one reason for helping those in need.

empiricism A philosophical doctrine that states that the source of mental life is experience and observation.

encoding specificity principle The hypothesis that we can retrieve only what we have stored and that retrieval is enhanced to the extent that retrieval cues match encoding cues.

encoding The active process of representing or putting information into memory.

endocrine system A network of glands that secrete hormones directly into the bloodstream.

environmental psychology The field of applied psychology that studies how the general environment affects the behavior and mental processes of individuals and how individuals affect their environments.

episodic memory A subsystem of LTM, and a type of declarative memory in which personal experiences are stored.

equilibration In Piaget's theory, the idea that a child attempts to maintain a balance between cognitive abilities and demands of the environment. Once a child reaches a balance, the environment places more demands on the child, requiring cognitive change.

equity theory The view that workers are motivated to match their inputs and outcomes with those of fellow workers in similar positions.

etiology Referring to the source or cause of a disorder.

expectancy theory The view that workers make logical choices to do what they believe will result in their attaining outcomes of highest value.

experiment A series of operations used to investigate relationships between manipulated events and measured events, while other events are controlled or eliminated.

experimental group The group in an experiment that receives a nonzero level of the independent variable.

experimental research A method of research in which scientists manipulate one or more variable and then look for a relationship between manipulation and changes in behavior.

external attribution An explanation of behavior in terms of something outside the person; a situational attribution.

extinction The process in classical conditioning in which the strength of the CR decreases with repeated presentations of the CS alone (without the UCS).

extraneous variable A variable that is not controlled or eliminated from consideration in an experiment than can affect the outcome of the experiment.

factorial experiment An experiment that includes more than one independent variable.

family therapy A type of group therapy focusing on the roles, interdependence, and communication skills of family members.

fantasy A defense mechanism that involves the imagination or daydreaming as a reaction to stress and anxiety.

fetal stage The third stage of prenatal development, from week 8 until birth, during which the organs that developed in the embryonic stage develop further.

fetal alcohol syndrome (FAS) A cluster of symptoms (for example, low birth weight, poor muscle tone, and intellectual retardation) associated with a child born to a mother who was a heavy drinker of alcohol during pregnancy.

field experiment An experiment run in the real world and not in an artificial laboratory setting.

figure-ground relationship The Gestalt psychology principle that stimuli are selected and perceived as figures against a ground (background).

fixation In Freud's theory, an over-investment of psychic energy resulting from a failure to adequately deal with a crisis, leading to characteristics of a particular stage showing up in adult personality.

fixed interval (FI) schedule The partial reinforcement schedule calling for a reinforcer at the first response following a specified, or fixed, interval.

fixed ratio (FR) schedule The partial reinforcement schedule calls for delivering one reinforcer after a set number of responses (for example, one reinforcer after every five responses).

flashbulb memory A particularly clear and vivid (although not necessarily accurate) recollection from one's past.

fluid intelligence Abilities related to speed, adaptation, flexibility, and abstract reasoning.

formal operations stage The fourth stage in Piaget's theory, ages older than 12 years, when one can generate and test abstract hypotheses and manipulate symbolic concepts.

fovea The region at the center of the retina consisting solely of cones where acuity is best in daylight.

free association The procedure in psychoanalysis in which the patient is to express whatever comes to mind without editing responses.

frustration A stressor; the blocking or thwarting of goal-directed behavior.

frustration-aggression hypothesis The hypothesis that states that frustration gives rise to aggression and that aggression arises from frustration.

functional fixedness A type of mental set that interferes with problem solving involving the inability to discover a new use for an object because of prior experience with the object.

functionalism The school of psychology suggested by James that studied the adaptive functions of the mind and consciousness.

fundamental attribution error The tendency to overuse internal attributions when explaining behavior.

g-factor (g) General intelligence; a global measure of intellectual abilities.

gay The preferred term of reference for males with a homosexual orientation.

gender One's maleness or femaleness; socially ascribed characteristics of males and females, as opposed to their biological characteristics.

general adaptation syndrome (GAS) Selye's description of physiological reactions made to stressors, which include three stages: alarm, resistance, and exhaustion.

generalization The ability to apply research results beyond the restricted conditions of an experiment.

generalized anxiety disorder An anxiety disorder characterized by high levels of chronic anxiety with unrealistic, persistent worry.

generativity A concern in adulthood for one's family and for one's impact on future generations.

genital herpes (Herpes type II) the most common STD; a skin infection in the form of a rash or blisters in the genital area.

germinal stage The first stage prenatal development, lasting from conception to implantation into the uterine wall, around 2 weeks after conception.

gestalt Term meaning whole, totality, configuration; a gestalt is more than the sum of its parts.

gestalt psychology An approach to psychology that focuses on perception and how we select and organize information from the outside world.

gonorrhea A STD caused by a bacterial infection of moist tissues in the genital area.

group polarization The tendency for members of a group to give more extreme judgments following a discussion than they gave initially.

groupthink An excessive concern for reaching a consensus in group decision-making to the extent that critical evaluations of input are withheld.

habituation In classical conditioning, a simple form of learning in which an organism comes to ignore a stimulus of little or no consequence.

hair cells The receptor cells for hearing located in the cochlea and stimulated by the vibrating basilar membrane; they send neural impulses to the temporal lobe of the brain.

hallucinogens Chemicals that lead to the formation of hallucinations, usually visual.

health psychology The field of applied psychology that studies psychological factors affecting physical health and illness.

heterosexuality A sexual orientation involving being sexually attracted to and aroused by members of the opposite sex.

heuristic An informal, economical, yet reasonable method of testing problem solutions without the guarantee of success.

hindsight bias The belief that results from a psychological study are so obvious that no research was needed.

holophrastic speech The use of one word to communicate several meanings.

homeostasis A state of balance, or equilibrium, among internal, physiological conditions.

homosexuality A sexual orientation involving being sexually attracted to and aroused by members of one's own sex.

humanistic psychology An approach to psychology that proposed that the individual, or the self, should be the central concern of psychology.

hypnosis A state of consciousness characterized by (1) a marked increase in suggestibility, (2) a focusing of attention, (3) an exaggerated use of imagination, (4) an unwillingness or inability to act on one's own, and (5) an unquestioning acceptance of distortions of reality.

hypochrondriasis A somatoform disorder in which one is preoccupied with a fear of a serious disease.

hypothalamus A small structure near the limbic system in the center of the brain, associated with temperature regulation, feeding, drinking, and sex.

hypothesis A tentative explanation of some phenomenon that can be tested and then either supported or rejected.

iconic memory The sensory memory system associated with the sense of vision..

id In Freud's theory, the instinctive aspect of personality that seeks immediate gratification of impulses; it operates on the pleasure principle.

idealistic principle The force that governs the superego; opposed to the id, it seeks adherence to standards of ethics and morality.

identity crisis The effort to define and integrate one's sense of self and what one's attitudes, beliefs, and values should be.

illusion A perception that is at odds with (different from) what we consider physical reality.

imagery A memory strategy that involves forming mental images to improve memory.

incentives External stimuli an organism may be motivated to approach or avoid.

independent variable The variable in an experiment that is manipulated by the experimenter; its value is determined by the experimenter.

inductive technique Providing an age-appropriate explanation to a child for why a punished behavior is wrong .

industrial/organizational (I/O) psychologist One who uses scientific methods to study the affects, cognitions, and behaviors of persons in work settings.

inferiority complex The feeling that we are less able than others to solve life's problems and get along in the world.

information processing approach An approach to explaining cognitive development that proposes that cognitive development is represented by quantitative changes in basic information processing systems, such as attention and memory.

insanity A legal term related to whether one can understand the consequences of his or her actions and meaningfully participate in his or her defense.

insomnia The inability to fall asleep or stay asleep.

instinct An unlearned, complex pattern of behavior that occurs in the presence of certain stimuli.

integrative function The function of the spinal cord involving the control of the spinal reflexes.

intelligence One of the most difficult concepts in psychology to define. A theoretical definition is that intelligence is the capacity to understand one's world and one's resources to cope with it. Another definition is that intelligence is what intelligence tests measure.

interaction When the effect of one independent variable on the dependent variable differs over levels of a second independent variable.

interactionist theory of language development A theory of language development that acknowledges the roles of learning and biological mechanisms.

internal attribution An explanation of behavior in terms of something (a trait) within the person; a dispositional attribution.

interneurons Neurons within the spinal cord or brain.

interpersonal attraction A powerful, favorable attitude toward another person.

interview The assessment technique involving a conversational interchange between an interviewer and another in order to gain information about the latter's personality.

introspection The method used by structuralists to study the mind, which involves describing mental responses to conscious experience in great detail.

IQ (intelligence quotient) A measure of general intelligence that results from dividing one's mental age by one's chronological age and multiplying the result by 100.

iris The colored structure of the eye that reflexively opens or closes the pupil.

job analysis A complete and specific description of a job, including the qualities and behaviors required to do it well.

job satisfaction An attitude toward, or a collection of positive feelings about, one's job or job experiences.

just noticeable difference (j.n.d.) The minimal change that can be detected in a stimulus attribute, such as intensity.

just world hypothesis The belief that the world is just and that people get what they deserve.

kinesthetic sense The position sense that tells us the position of various parts of our bodies and what our muscles and joints are doing.

language A large collection of arbitrary symbols that have a shared significance for a language-using community and that follow certain combinatorial rules.

latent learning Hidden learning that is not demonstrated in performance until that performance is reinforced.

law of effect Thorndike's law stating that responses that lead to a "satisfying state of affairs" tend to be repeated; responses that do not lead to a satisfying state of affairs tend not to be repeated.

learning The demonstration of a relatively permanent change in behavior that occurs as the result of practice or experience.

learning theory of language development A theory of language development that postulates that language, like any other behavior is learned.

lens The structure behind the iris that changes shape to focus visual images in the eye.

lesbian The preferred term of reference for females with a homosexual orientation.

libido In Freud's theory, the energy that activates the sexual instincts.

life instincts (eros) Inborn impulses, proposed by Freud, that compel one toward survival; they include hunger, thirst, and sex.

limbic system A collection of structures near the middle of the brain involved in emotionality (amygdala and septum) and long-term memory storage (hippocampus).

lobotomy Psychosurgical technique in which the prefrontal lobes of the cerebral cortex are severed from lower brain centers.

loneliness A psychological state arising when our actual social relationships are discrepant from the relationships we would like to have.

long-term memory (LTM) A type of memory with virtually unlimited capacity and very long, if not limitless, duration.

maintenance rehearsal A process of rote repetition (reattending) to keep information in short-term memory.

major depression Feeling sad, low, helpless, with a loss of pleasure or interest in most normal activities.

mania A state of elevated mood, euphoria, or irritability with increased levels of activity.

matching phenomenon The tendency to select partners whose level of physical attractiveness matches our own.

meaningfulness The extent to which new information evokes associations with information already in LTM.

mechanism The philosophical doctrine suggesting that the human body is a piece of machinery subject to natural physical laws, which can be identified.

meditation Self-induced state of altered consciousness characterized by a focusing of attention and relaxation.

medulla The structure in the brain stem where cross laterality begins; it contains centers that monitor reflex functions, such as heart rate and respiration.

memory The cognitive capacity to encode, store, and retrieve information.

menarche A female's first menstrual period, a sure sign of the beginning of adolescence.

mental retardation A condition indicated by an IQ score below 70 that begins during development and is associated with an impairment in adaptive functioning.

mental set A predisposed (set) way to perceive or respond to something; an expectation.

mere exposure phenomenon The tendency to increase our liking of people and things as a result of recurring contact.

meta-analysis A statistical procedure used to combine the results of many studies to see more clearly if a relationship exists between independent and dependent variables.

Minnesota Multiphasic Personality Inventory (MMPI) A paper-and-pencil personality test designed to assess several dimensions of personality and to indicate the presence of a psychological disorder.

misinformation effect The biasing effect of postevent information on the recall of an event.

mnemonic device A strategy for improving retrieval that takes advantage of existing memories in order to make new material more meaningful.

modal model The model of memory stating that information is

processed through three distinct memory storage systems: sensory memory, short-term memory (STM), and long-term memory (LTM).

modeling The acquisition of new responses through the imitation of another who responds appropriately.

mood disorders Disorders where a disturbance of affect/mood is the defining symptom.

morpheme The smallest unit of meaning in a language.

motivation The process that arouses, directs, and maintains behavior.

motor areas Those areas at the rear of the frontal lobes that control voluntary muscular movement.

motor neurons Neurons that carry impulses away from the central nervous system to muscles and glands.

myelin A white fatty covering found on some axons that insulates and protects them and speeds impulses along.

narcolepsy Going to sleep, even during the day, without any intention to do so.

nativist theory of language development A theory of language development that postulates that there is a significant biological component to language development. One idea of this theory is that humans are born with a "language acquisition device."

need A lack or shortage of some biological essential resulting from deprivation.

need for affiliation The need to be with others and to form relationships.

need for intimacy The need to form and maintain close, affectionate relationships with others.

need for power The learned need to be in control of events or persons.

need to achieve (nAch) The learned need to meet or exceed some standard of excellence in one's behaviors.

negative correlation A correlation indicating that as the value of one variable increases, the value of the second decreases.

negative reinforcer A stimulus that increases the rate of a response when that stimulus is removed after the response is made; negative reinforcers are presented before a response is made.

negative symptoms of schizophrenia Emotional and social withdrawal, reduced energy and motivation, apathy and poor attention.

neo-Freudians Theorists (including Adler, Jung, and Horney) who supported the basics of psychoanalytic theory but differed from Freud.

neonate The newborn from birth through the first two weeks.

neural impulse A rapid and reversible change in the electrical charges inside and outside a neuron; it travels from dendrite to axon terminal of a neuron.

neural threshold The minimum amount of stimulation needed to fire a neuron.

neuron A nerve cell that transmits information from one part of the body to another via neural impulses.

neurotoxins Chemicals (poisons) that affect psychological processes through the nervous system.

neurotransmitters Chemical molecules released at the synapse that, in general, will either excite or inhibit a reaction in the cell on the other side of the synapse.

node A segment of exposed axon membrane between segments of myelin.

noise An intrusive, unwanted, or excessive experience of sound.

nondeclarative memory A long-term memory system (also known as procedural memory) that involves the acquisition, retention, and retrieval of performance skills.

norms In psychological testing, scores on a test taken by a large number of persons that can be used for making comparisons.

NREM (nonREM) sleep A period of sleep during which there are no rapid eye movements and is associated with fewer, more fragmented dreams.

object permanence The appreciation that an object no longer in view can still exist and reappear later.

obsessions Ideas or thoughts that constantly intrude into awareness.

obsessive-compulsive disorder An anxiety disorder characterized by a pattern of recurrent obsessions and compulsions.

operant conditioning A procedure that changes the rate of a response on the basis of the consequences that result from that response.

operational definition Defining a concept in terms of the procedures used to measure or create them.

optic chiasma The location in the brain where impulses from light in the left visual field cross to the right side of the brain, and impulses from light in the right visual field cross to the left side of the brain.

optic nerve The fiber consisting of many neurons that leaves the eye and carries impulses to the occipital lobe of the brain.

Opponent-process theory A theory of color vision suggesting that there are three pairs of visual mechanisms that respond to different wavelengths of light (blue-yellow, red-green, and black-white.

organization One of the functions in Piaget's theory involving a predisposition to integrate individual schemas into organized units.

orienting reflex The simple, unlearned response of orienting toward, or attending to, a new or unusual stimulus.

overlearning The practice, or rehearsal, of material over and above what is needed to learn it.

overregularization The over-application of an acquired language rule (e.g., for forming plurals) in a situation in which it is not appropriate.

panic disorder An anxiety disorder characterized by acute, recurrent, unpredictable attacks of anxiety.

partial reinforcement schedule A schedule in which responses are not reinforced every time they occur.

perception The cognitive process of selecting, organizing, and interpreting stimuli.

perceptual constancies Perceptual mechanisms that allow you to perceive various aspects of your world as constant.

performance criteria Specific behaviors or characteristics a person should have in order to do a job as well as possible.

peripheral nervous system (PNS) Neurons not found in the brain and spinal cord but in the periphery of the body.

personality The affects, behaviors, and cognitions that characterize a person in a variety of situations.

personality disorders Long-lasting patterns of perceiving, relating to, and thinking about the environment and oneself that are maladaptive and inflexible.

personal space The mobile "bubble" of space around you reserved for intimate relationships and into which others may enter only by invitation.

persuasion The application of rational and/or emotional arguments to change an individual's attitudes and behavior.

phenomenology The study of events as they are experienced by the individual, not as they actually occur.

pheromones Chemicals that produce an odor used as a method of communication between organisms.

phobic disorders Anxiety disorders characterized by persistent, excessive fear of some object, activity, or situation that leads to avoidance.

phoneme The smallest distinguishable unit of sound in the spoken form of a language.

phrenology A discredited science that sought to determine personal characteristics by the careful interpretation of bumps on the head.

pituitary gland The "master gland" of the endocrine system that influences many others; controls such processes as body growth rate, water retention, and the release of milk from the mammary glands.

placebo An inactive substance that produces an effect because a person believes it to be effective; something given to research participants that has no identifiable effect on performance.

pleasure principle The impulse of the id to seek immediate gratification to reduce tensions.

pluralistic ignorance A condition in which the inaction of others leads each individual in a group to interpret a situation as a non-emergency, thus leading to general inactivity.

pons A brain stem structure that forms a bridge that organizes fibers from the spinal cord to the brain and vice versa.

population density A quantitative measure of the number of persons (or animals) per unit of area.

positive disorganized symptoms of schizophrenia Disorders of thinking and speech, bizarre behaviors, and inappropriate affect.

positive psychotic symptoms of schizophrenia Hallucinations and delusions associated with schizophrenia.

positive reinforcer A stimulus that increases the rate of a response it follows; positive reinforcers are presented after a response has been made.

positive test strategy The heuristic of sticking with an acceptable decision or solution, even if better ones may exist.

positive correlation A correlation indicating that as the value of one variable increases (or decreases) the value of a second increases (or decreases) as well.

postconventional morality The highest level of moral reasoning in Kohlberg's theory in which moral reasoning reflects complex, internalized standards.

postdecisional dissonance The cognitive dissonance experienced after making a decision between two mutually exclusive, equally attractive, different alternatives.

posttraumatic stress disorder An anxiety disorder involving distressing symptoms that arise some time after the experience of a traumatic event.

pragmatics The study of how social contexts affect the meaning of linguistic events.

preconventional morality The first level of moral reasoning in Kohlberg's theory in which the prime interest of the child is simply with the punishment that comes from breaking a rule.

prenatal period The period of development from conception to birth.

preoperational stage The second stage of development in Piaget's theory, from ages 2 to 6 years, characterized by egocentrism and the beginning of symbol development.

primary mental abilities In Thurstone's model, the seven distinct abilities that constitute intelligence.

primary reinforcer A stimulus (usually biologically or physiologically based) that increases the rate of a response with no previous experience or learning required.

proactive interference The inhibition of retrieval of recently learned material caused by material learned previously.

problem A discrepancy between one's present state and one's goal state with no apparent way to get from one to the other.

productivity The property of human language that it is possible to produce an unlimited number of utterances with a limited number of speech sounds.

prognosis The prediction of the future course of a disease or disorder.

projection A defense mechanism that involves seeing one's own unacceptable, anxiety-producing characteristics in others.

projective technique A personality assessment technique requiring a person to respond to ambiguous stimuli in the hopes that the person will reveal aspects of his or her personality.

proximity The Gestalt principle of organization claiming that stimuli will be perceived as belonging together if they occur together in space or time.

psychoanalysis The form of psychotherapy associated with Freud, aimed at helping the patient gain insight into unconscious conflicts.

psychoanalytic psychology The school of psychology founded by Freud that emphasized innate strivings and the unconscious mind.

psychoanalytic approach The approach to personality associated with Freud and his followers that relies on instincts and the unconscious as explanatory concepts.

psychological test An objective, standardized measure of behavior.

psychology The science of human and animal behavior that also includes the study of mental processes that influence overt behavior.

psychophysics The study of the relationship between the physical attributes of stimuli and the psychological experiences they produce.

psychosurgery Surgical procedure designed to affect one's psychological or behavioral reactions.

puberty The stage of physical development at which one becomes capable of sexual reproduction.

punishment The administration of a punisher, which is a stimulus that decreases the rate, or probability, of a response that precedes it.

pupil The opening of the iris, which changes size in relation to the amount of light available and to emotional factors.

random assignment A technique used to equalize groups in an experiment before the experiment is run; each participant has an equal chance of being assigned to any group in the experiment.

rational-emotive therapy (RET) A form of cognitive therapy, associated with Ellis, aimed at changing a person's irrational beliefs or maladaptive cognitions.

rationalization A defense mechanism that excuses one's behaviors rather than facing the anxiety-producing reasons for them.

reality principle The force that governs the ego, arbitrating between the demands of the id and the realities of the world.

recall A direct measure of retrieval in which one is given the fewest possible cues to aid retrieval and must produce information to which he or she has been previously exposed.

receptor sites Places on a neuron where neurotransmitters can be received.

recognition A direct measure of retrieval in which an individual is required to identify material previously learned.

reconstructive memory An approach to memory suggesting that we retrieve features stored about an event and reconstruct a report of what was encoded and stored in memory.

regression A defense mechanism that involves returning to earlier, more primitive levels of behavior that were once effective.

reinforcement A process that increases the rate, or probability, of the response it follows.

reinforcer A stimulus that increases or maintains the rate, or probability, of a response it follows.

relearning The change in performance that occurs when one is required to learn material for a second time.

reliability In psychological testing, the extent to which a test measures whatever it measures consistently.

REM sleep A period of sleep during which the eyes move rapidly and is associated with vivid, story-like dreams.

representativeness heuristic The assumption that judgments made about a very typical member of some category will hold for all members of that category.

repressed memory Traumatic memories that pushed into an individual's unconscious that are very difficult to retrieve.

repression A defense mechanism referring to motivated forgetting of an anxiety-producing event or desire.

resistance In psychoanalysis, the inability or unwillingness to discuss freely some aspect of one's life.

resting potential The electrical tension resulting from the difference in electrical charge of a neuron where the inside is negatively charged and the outside is positively charged (about −70 mV).

reticular formation A network of nerve fibers extending from the base of the brain to the cerebrum that controls one's level of arousal.

retina Layers of cells at the back of the eye that contain the photosensitive rod and cone cells.

retinal disparity The phenomenon in which each retina receives a different (disparate) view of the same three-dimensional object.

retrieval The process of locating, removing, and using information stored in memory.

retroactive interference The inhibition of retrieval of previously learned material caused by material learned later.

retrograde amnesia The loss of the memory of events stored before the onset of the loss.

rods Photosensitive cells of the retina that are most active in low levels of illumination and do not respond differentially to various wavelengths of light.

Rorschach inkblot test A projective technique in which a person is asked to say what he or she sees in a series of inkblots.

s-factors Specific cognitive or intellectual skills; in Spearman's theory, part of intelligence in addition to "g".

salient detail A detail that captures our attention.

saltatory conduction The movement along myelinated axons in which the neural impulse "jumps" from node to node increasing the rate of neural transmission.

scanning An aspect of attention involving how efficiently and completely an individual looks at an object.

schema An organized mental representation of the world that are adaptive and formed by experience.

schizophrenia A family of serious disorders involving a distortion of reality, a retreat from others, disturbances in affect; often showing hallucinations and delusions.

science An organized body of knowledge gained through the application of scientific methods.

scientific method A method of acquiring knowledge involving observing a phenomenon, formulating hypotheses, further observing and experimenting, and refining and retesting hypotheses.

secondary drive A state of tension resulting from a learned, or acquired, need that motivates an organism's behavior.

secondary reinforcer A stimulus that increases the rate of a response because of an association with other reinforcers; also called conditioned, or learned, reinforcers.

selectivity An aspect of attention involving those aspects of a stimulus an individual picks out for attention.

self-perception theory An alternative to cognitive dissonance theory that says we keenly observe behavior, including our own, and then look for an explanation for that behavior.

self-serving bias The tendency to attribute our successes to our own effort and abilities, and our failures to situational, external sources.

semanticity The property of human language that gives language its meaning.

semantic memory A subsystem of LTM and a type of declarative memory in which vocabulary, facts, simple concepts, and rules are stored.

semantics The study of the meaning of words and sentences.

sensation The process of receiving information from the environment and changing it into nervous system activity.

sensorimotor stage The first stage of development in Piaget's theory, from birth to 2 years, when a child learns by sensing and doing.

sensory adaptation The process in which our sensory experience diminishes with continued exposure to a stimulus.

sensory areas Those areas of the cerebral cortex that ultimately receive neural impulses from sense receptors.

sensory memory A type of memory that stores large amounts of information for very brief periods (a few seconds or less).

sensory neurons Neurons that carry impulses from the sense receptors to the central nervous system.

sensory threshold The minimum intensity of a stimulus that will cause sense organs to operate.

sexual dysfunction Any one of a number of chronic difficulties or problems with sexual functioning.

sexually transmitted diseases (STDs) Contagious diseases that are usually transmitted through sexual contact.

shape constancy The perceptual constancy that allows one to perceive the shape of an object as constant despite different viewing angles and changes in the retinal image.

shaping A procedure of reinforcing successive approximations of a desired response until that desired response is made.

short-term memory (STM) A type of memory with limited capacity and limited duration; also called working memory.

signal detection theory The view that signal detection is decision-making; separating a signal from ground (background) noise.

similarity The Gestalt principle of organization claiming that stimuli will be perceived together if they share some common characteristics.

situationism An approach to explaining behavior which places greater emphasis on situational factors in determining behavior than stable personality traits.

size constancy The perceptual constancy that allows one to perceive the size of an object viewed at different distances as constant, despite changes in the size of the retinal image.

sleep apnea Patterns of sleep, usually short, during which breathing stops entirely.

social facilitation Improved performance due to the presence of others on a simple, well-learned task.

social intelligence In the cognitive theory of personality, all the skills, abilities, and knowledge that a person brings to all social situations.

social interference Impaired performance due to the presence of others, especially on a complex task.

social learning theory The theory that learning takes place through observation and imitation of models.

social loafing The tendency to decrease one's individual work effort as the size of the group in which one is working increases.

social phobias Significant, persistent fears of social or performance situations.

social psychology The field of psychology concerned with how others influence the thoughts, feelings, and behaviors of the individual.

socioeconomic status (SES) A measure that reflects one's income, education, and occupation.

somatic nervous system (SNS) Sensory and motor neurons outside the CNS that serve the sense receptors and the skeletal muscles.

somatoform disorders Disorders that involve some physical, bodily complaint.

specific phobia An intense irrational fear of some specific object or situation, such as a phobia of animals or enclosed spaces.

spinal cord A mass of interconnected neurons within the spinal column that transmits impulses to and from the brain and is involved in spinal reflex behaviors.

spinal reflexes Involuntary responses to a stimulus that involve sensory neurons, the spinal cord, and motor neurons.

split-brain procedure The surgical lesioning of the corpus callosum, which separates the functions of the left and right hemispheres of the cerebral cortex and is a treatment of last resort for epilepsy.

spontaneous recovery The phenomenon in classical conditioning in which a previously extinguished CR returns after a rest interval.

sport psychology The application of psychological principles to sport and physical activity at all levels of skill development.

state-dependent memory The hypothesis that retrieval can be enhanced by the extent to which one's state of mind at retrieval matches one's state of mind at encoding.

stimulants Chemicals that activate an organism, producing a heightened sense of arousal and an elevation of mood.

storage The process of holding encoded information in memory.

strategy In problem solving, a systematic plan for generating possible solutions that can be tested to see if they are correct.

stress A complex set of reactions to real or perceived threats to one's well-being that motivates adaptation.

stressors The sources or stimuli for stress, which include frustration, conflict, and life events.

structural-functional approach The approach Piaget took to explain cognitive development that says that structures (schemas) change with development, while functions remain fixed; cognitive development is a series of qualitative changes in intelligence.

structuralism The school of psychology founded by Wundt that studied the mind by attempting to break mental activity into its component parts.

subjective contours The perception of a contour (a line or plane) that is not there, but is suggested by other aspects of a scene.

sublimation A defense mechanism that involves taking sexual and aggressive energy, which may be inappropriate to express in their ray form, and channeling that energy into more socially acceptable pursuits.

subliminal perception The process of perceiving and responding to stimuli presented at levels of intensity that are below our absolute threshold—below our level of conscious processing.

superego In Freud's theory, the aspect of personality that refers to ethical or moral considerations; it operates on the idealistic principle.

sympathetic division (of the ANS) The division of the autonomic nervous system that takes over under conditions of emotional arousal and causes dilation of the pupils and increased respiration, blood pressure, and heart rate, among other reactions.

synapse Where one neuron communicates with other cells via neurotransmitters.

synaptic cleft The space between a neuron and the next cell at a synapse.

syntax The rules that govern how the morphemes of a language are to be combined in order to form meaningful utterances.

syphilis A STD caused by a bacterial infection; the disease may pass through four stages, ultimately resulting in death.

systematic desensitization Classical conditioning procedures, used to alleviate anxiety, in which anxiety-producing stimuli are paired with a state of relaxation.

taste buds Receptors for taste that are located on the tongue.

telegraphic speech Utterances characterized by the use of nouns, verbs, and adjectives, and few function words.

temperament theory A theory of the origins of personality, which suggests that one's temperamental qualities (such as activity level, sociability, and emotionality) are inborn and influence behavior.

territoriality The setting off and marking of a piece of territory (a location) as one's own.

thalamus A structure located just below the cerebral cortex, which is the last sensory relay station; projects sensory impulses to the appropriate areas of the cerebral cortex.

Thematic Apperception Test (TAT) A projective technique in which a person is asked to tell a series of short stories about a set of ambiguous pictures.

theory A set of assumptions concerning the causes for behavior, including statements of how the causes for behavior work; theories are rigorously evaluated and may be retained, modified, or rejected.

third-variable problem Reason one should not infer a causal relationship between variables from correlational research; a third, unmeasured variable could be the actual causal variable.

thyroid gland Endocrine gland that releases thyroxine, the hormone that regulates the pace of the body's functioning.

training A systematic and intentional process of altering the behaviors of employees to increase organizational effectiveness.

trait A distinguishable, relatively enduring way in which individuals can be described and in which they might differ.

transducer A mechanism that converts energy from one form to another—a basic process common to all of our senses.

transference In psychoanalysis, the situation in which the patient comes to feel about the analyst in the same way he or she once felt about some other important person.

tremors Involuntary trembling movements.

trichromatic theory A theory of color vision postulating the existing of three types of color photoreceptors in the eye (red, green, and blue).

true partner effect The effect occurring when a person emerges to support the judgment of the minority in a conformity experiment leading to a reduction in conformity.

Type A behavior pattern (TABP) A collection of behaviors (in which one is competitive achievement-oriented, impatient, easily aroused, and often hostile or angry) commonly associated with coronary heart disease.

unconditioned response (UCR) In classical conditioning, a response (e.g., salivation in response to food) reliably and reflexively evoked by a stimulus.

unconditioned stimulus (UCS) In classical conditioning, a stimulus (e.g., food powder) that reflexively and reliably evokes a response.

valenced state The idea that emotions can be classified as either positive or negative.

validity In psychological testing, the extent to which a test measures what it claims to be measuring.

variable interval (VI) schedule The partial reinforcement schedule calling for a reinforcer at the first response after a time interval whose length is randomly varied.

variable ratio (VR) schedule The partial reinforcement schedule that randomly changes the ratio of reinforcers to responses but maintains a given ratio as an average.

vesicles Small containers concentrated in a neuron's axon terminals that hold neurotransmitter molecules.

vestibular sense The position sense that conveys balance, where we are in relation to gravity, and acceleration or deceleration.

vicarious reinforcement (or punishment) Increasing the rate (with reinforcement) or decreasing the rate (with punishment) of responses due to observing the consequences of someone else's behaviors.

vitreous humor The thick fluid behind the lens of the eye that keeps the eyeball spherical.

vomeronasal organ (VNO) Organs located along the nasal septum believed to be involved in the detection of pheromones.

weapon focus The perceptual phenomenon in which an eyewitness's attention is drawn to a weapon that is present in a crime. The witness focuses attention on the weapon at the expense of other details.

Yale communication model The most widely accepted model of persuasion that considers the influence of the sources of a message, the structure of a message, and the audience for a message.

zygote The one-celled product of the union of sperm and ovum at conception.

REFERENCES

AARP. (1993). Census Bureau ups 65+ population estimates. *AARP Bulletin, 34,* 2.

AARP. (1995). Negative stereotypes still plague older workers on the job. *AARP Bulletin*, 36, April, p. 3.

Abel, E. L. (1981). Behavioral teratology. *Psychological Bulletin, 90,* 564-581.

Abel, E. L. (1984). *Fetal alcohol syndrome and fetal alcohol effects*, New York: Plenum.

Abravanel, E. & Sigafoos, A. D. (1984). Exploring the presence of imitation during early infancy. *Child Development, 55,* 381-392.

Ackerman, P. L. (1992). Predicting individual differences in complex skill acquisition: Dynamics of ability determinants. *Journal of Applied Psychology, 77,* 598-614.

Ackerman, P. L., & Kanfer, R. (1993). Integrating laboratory and field study for improving selection: Development of a battery for predicting air traffic controller success. *Journal of Applied Psychology, 78,* 413-432.

Adams, G. R. (1977). Physical attractiveness, personality, and social reactions to peer pressure. *Journal of Psychology,* 96, 287-296.

Adams, G. R., & Gullotta, T. (1983). *Adolescent life experiences.* Monterey, CA: Brooks/Cole.

Adams, J. L. (1974). Conceptual blockbusting. Stanford, CA: Stanford Alumni Association. Cited in A. L. Glass, K. J. Holyoak, & J. L. Santa (1979). *Cognition.* Reading, MA: Addison-Wesley.

Adams, J. S. (1965). Inequity in social exchange. In L. Berkowitz (Ed.), *Advances in experimental social psychology.* New York: Academic Press.

Adams, L. A., & Rickert, V. I. (1989). Reducing bedtime tantrums: Comparison between positive routines and graduated extinctions. *Pediatrics, 84,* 756-761.

Adams, R. M. (1992). The "hot hand" revisited: Successful basketball shooting as a function of intershot interval. *Perceptual and Motor Skills, 74,* 934.

Adams, R. M. (1995). Momentum in the performance of professional tournament pocket billiards players. *International Journal of Sport Psychology, 26,* 580-587.

Adelmann, P. K., & Zajonc, R. B. (1989). Facial efference and the experience of emotion. *Annual Review of Psychology, 40,* 249-280.

Adelson, B. (1984). When novices surpass experts: The difficulty of a task may interfere with expertise. *Journal of Experimental Psychology, 10,* 483-495.

Adler, L. L., & Gielen, U. P. (1994). *Cross-cultural topics in psychology.* Westport, CT: Praeger.

Adler, N., & Matthews, K. (1994). Health psychology: Why do some people get sick and some stay well? *Annual Review of Psychology, 45,* 229-259.

Adler, N. E., Boyce, T., Chesney, M. A., Cohen, S., Folkman, S., Kahn, R. L., & Syme, S. L. (1994). Socioeconomic status and health: The challenge of the gradient. *American Psychologist, 49,* 15-24.

Adler, N. E., & Stone, G. (1984). Psychology in the health system. In J. Ruffini (Ed.). *Advances in medical social science.* New York: Gordon & Breach.

Adler, R., & Cohen, N. (1993). Psychoneuroimmunology: Conditioning and stress. *Annual review of Psychology, 44,* 23-51.

Adler, T. (1989). Cocaine babies face behavior deficits. *APA Monitor, 20,* 14.

Adler, T. (1990). Does the "new" MMPI beat the "classic"? *APA Monitor, 21,* 18-19.

Agnew, H. W., Webb, W. W., & Williams, R. L. (1964). The effects of stage 4 sleep deprivation. *Electroencephalography and Clinical Neurophysiology, 17,* 68-70.

Aiello, R. R., & Aiello, T. D. (1974). The development of personal space: Proxemic behavior of children 6 through 16. *Human Ecology, 2,* 177-189.

Aiken, L. R. (1984). *Psychological testing and assessment* (4th ed.). Boston: Allyn & Bacon.

Ainsworth, M. D. S. (1979). Infant-mother attachment. *American Psychologist, 34,* 932-937.

Ainsworth, M. d. S. (1989). Attachments beyond infancy. *American Psychologist, 44,* 709-716.

Ajzen, I. (1991). The theory of planned behavior. *Organizational Behavior and Human Decision Processes, 50,* 179-211.

Ajzen I. (2001) Nature and operation of attitudes. *Annual review of psychology,* 52, 27-58.

Ajzen, I., & Fishbein, M. (1980). *Understanding attitudes*

and predicting social behavior. Englewood Cliffs, NJ: Prentice-Hall.

Ajzen I. & Fishbein, M. (2000). Attitudes and the attitude-behavior relation: Reasoned and automatic processes. IN W. Stroebe & M. Hewstone (Eds.) *European Review of Social Psychology.* Chicester, England: Wiley.

Akiskal, H. S., & Cassano, G. B. (Eds.). (1997). *Dysthymia and the spectrum of chronic depressions.* New York: Guilford Press.

Alba, J. W., & Hasher, L. (1983). Is memory schematic? *Psychological Bulletin, 93,* 201-231.

Albert, D. J., Petrovic, D. M., & Walsh, M. L. (1989). Competitive experience activates testosterone-dependent social aggression toward unfamiliar males. *Physiology and Behavior, 45,* 723-727.

Aldwin, C., & Stokals, D. (1988). The effects of environmental change on individuals and groups: Some neglected issues in stress research. *Journal of Environmental Psychology, 8,* 57-75.

Allen, J. L., Walker, L. D., Schroeder, D. A., & Johnson, D. E. (1987). Attributions and attribution-behavior relations: The effect of level of cognitive development. *Journal of Personality and Social Psychology, 52,* 1099-1109.

Allen, M. G. (1976). Twin studies of affective illness. *Archives of General Psychiatry, 33,* 1476-1478.

Allport, G. W. (1961). *Pattern and growth in personality.* New York: Holt, Rinehart & Winston.

Altman, I. (1975). *The environment and social behavior.* Monterey, CA: Brooks/Cole.

Amabile, T. M. (1985). Motivation and creativity. *Journal of Personality and Social Psychology,* 48, 393-399.

Amabile, T. M. (1988). A model of creativity and innovation in organizations. *Research in Organizational Behavior*, **10**, 123-167.

Amaro, H. (1995). Love, sex, and power: Considering women's realities in HIV prevention. *American Psychologist, 50,* 437-447.

Ambuel, B. (1995). Adolescents, unintended pregnancy, and abortion: The struggle for a compassionate social policy. *Current Directions in Psychological Science, 4,* 1-5.

American Academy of Sleep Medicine (2001). Sleep hygiene tips. Downloaded from the World Wide Web, January 31, 2001. http://www.asda.org/.

American Association of Retired Persons (1997). A Profile of Older Americans 1997. Downloaded from the World Wide Web, January 30, 2001. http://research.aarp.org/general/profile97.html#living.

American Automobile Association (1997). Road rage on the rise, AAA foundation reports. [On-line]. Available: http://webfirst.com/ aaa/text/roadrage.htm

American Cancer Society. (2000). *1998 Facts and figures: Tobacco use.* American Cancer Society.

American Diabetes Association (2001). The Dangerous Toll of Diabetes. Downloaded from the World Wide Web, January 30, 2001. http://www.diabetes.org/ada/facts.asp#youth.

American Heart Association. (2000). *Cigarette smoking and cardiovascular diseases.* American Heart Association.

American Sleep Apnea Association (2001). Information about sleep apnea: Sleep apnea defined. Downloaded from the World Wide Web, February 1, 2001. http://www.sleep-apnea.org/eninfo.html#defined.

American Psychiatric Association. (1987). *Diagnostic and statistical manual of mental disorders (3rd rev. ed.).* Washington, DC: American Psychiatric Association.

American Psychiatric Association. (1994). *Diagnostic and statistical manual of mental disorders (4th ed.).* Washington, DC: American Psychiatric Association.

American Psychiatric Association (1997). Practice guidelines for the treatment of patients with schizophrenia. *American Journal of Psychiatry*, **154**, Supplement, 1-63.

American Psychiatric Association. (2000). Diagnostic and statistical manual of mental disorders, Fourth Edition Text Revision (DSM-IV-TR). Washington: American Psychiatric Association.

American Psychological Association. (1992). Ethical principles of psychologists and code of conduct. *American Psychologist, 47,* 1597-1611.

Amoore, J. E. (1970). *Molecular basis of odor.* Springfield, IL: Thomas.

Anastasi, A. (1988). *Psychological testing* (6th ed.). New York: Macmillan.

Anderson, B. L. (1997). Psychological interventions for individuals with cancer. *Clinician's Research Digest; Supplemental Bulletin 16,* July, 1997.

Anderson, C. A. (1987). Temperature and aggression: Effects

on quarterly, yearly, and city rates of violent and nonviolent crime. *Journal of Personality and Social Psychology, 52,* 1161-1173.

Anderson, C. A. (1989). Temperature and aggression: Ubiquitous effects of heat on occurrence of human violence. *Psychological Bulletin, 106,* 74-96.

Anderson, C. A., & Anderson, D. C. (1984). Ambient temperature and violent crime: Tests of the linear and curvilinear hypotheses. *Journal of Personality and Social Psychology, 46,* 91-97.

Anderson, C. A., & Dill, K. E. (2000). Video games and aggressive thoughts, feelings, and behavior in the laboratory and in life. *Journal of Personality and Social Psychology,* 78, 772-790.

Anderson, C. A., & Morrow, M. (1995). Competitive aggression without interaction: Effects of competitive versus cooperative instructions on aggressive behavior in video games. *Personality and Social Psychology Bulletin,* 21, 1020-1030.

Anderson, J. R. (1976). *Language, memory, and thought.* Hillsdale, NJ: Erlbaum.

Anderson, J. R. (1980). *Cognitive psychology and its implications.* San Francisco: Freeman.

Anderson, J. R. (1983a). *The architecture of cognition.* Cambridge, MA: Harvard University Press.

Anderson, J. R. (1983b). A spreading activation theory of memory. *Journal of Verbal Learning and Verbal Behavior, 22,* 261-295.

Anderson, J. R. (1986). Knowledge compilation: The general learning mechanism. In R. Michalski, J. Carbonnell, & T. Mitchell (Eds.), *Machine learning II.* Palo Alto, CA: Tioga Press.

Anderson, J. R. (1987). Skill acquisition: Compilation of weak-method problem solutions. *Psychological Review, 94,* 192-210.

Anderson, R., & Nida, S. A. (1978). Effect of physical attractiveness on opposite- and same-sex evaluations. *Journal of Personality, 46,* 401-413.

Anderson, R. C., & Pichert, J. W. (1978). Recall of previously unrecallable information following a shift in perspective. *Journal of Verbal Learning and Verbal Behavior, 17,* 1-12.

Andreasen, N. C. (1982). Negative versus positive schizophrenia: Definition and validation. *Archives of General Psychiatry, 39,* 789-794.

Andreasen, N. C., Arndt, S., Alliger, R., Miller, D., & Flaum, M. (1995). Symptoms of schizophrenia: Methods, meanings, and mechanisms. *Archives of General Psychiatry, 52,* 341-351.

Andreasen, N. C., Ehrhardt, J. C., Swayze, V. W., Alliger, R. J, Yuh, W. T. C., Cohen, G., & Ziebell, S. (1990a). Magnetic resonance imaging of the brain in schizophrenia. *Archives of General Psychiatry, 47,* 35-44.

Andreasen, N. C., Flaum, M., Swayze, V. W., Tyrrell, G., & Arndt, S. (1990). Positive and negative symptoms in schizophrenia. *Archives of General Psychiatry, 47,* 615-621.

Andreasen, N. C., Olsen, S. A., Dennert, J. W., & Smith, M. R. (1982). Ventricular enlargement in schizophrenia: Definition and prevalence. *American Journal of Psychiatry, 139,* 292-296.

Andrews, R. J. (1963). Evolution of facial expression. *Science,* 142, 1034-1041.

Angoff, W. H. (1988). The nature-nurture debate, aptitudes, and group differences. *American Psychologist, 43,* 713-720.

Anisfeld, M. (1984). *Language development from birth to three.* Hillsdale, NJ: Erlbaum.

Anisman, H., & Zacharko, R. M. (1982). Depression: The predisposing influence of stress. *The Behavioral and Brain Sciences, 5,* 89-137.

Anshel, M. H. (1996). Effect of chronic aerobic exercise and progressive relaxation on motor performance and affect following acute stress. *Behavioral Medicine, 21,* 186-196.

Arata, C. M., & Burkhart, B. R. (1998) Coping appraisals and adjustment to nonstranger sexual assault. Violence Against Women, 4, 224-239.

Arendt, J., & Skene, D.J. (197). Efficacy of melatonin treatment in jet lag, shift work, and blindness. *Journal of Biological Rhythms,* 12, 604-617.

Arndt, S., Andreasen, N. C., Flaum, M., Miller, D., & Nopoulos, P. (1995). A longitudinal study of symptom dimensions in schizophrenia. *Archives of General Psychiatry,* 52, 352-360.

Arnett, J. (1995). The young and the restless: Adolescent reckless behavior. *Current Directions in Psychological Science, 4,* 67-71.

Arnot Ogden Medical Center (1998a). Frequently asked questions-viagra [On-line]. Available: http://external.aomc.org/HOD2/general/viagraFAQ.html

Arnot Ogden Medical Center (1998b). Synopsis of fatal outcome reports submitted to the FDA regarding viagra use [On-line]. Available: http://external.aomc.org/HOD2/general/viagraFORs.html

Aronson, E., & Linder, D. (1965). Gain and loss of esteem as determinants of interpersonal attractiveness. *Journal of Personality and Social Psychology, 1,* 156-171.

Aronson, E., Turner, J. A., & Carlsmith, J. M. (1963). Communicator credibility and communication discrepancy as a determinant of opinion change. *Journal of Abnormal and Social Psychology, 67,* 31-36.

Arvey, R. D., & Campion, J. E. (1982). The employee interview: A summary and review of recent research. *Personnel Psychology, 35,* 281-322.

Arvey, R. D., Miller, H. E., Gould, R., & Burch, P. (1987). Interview validity for selecting sales clerks. *Personnel Psychology, 40,* 1-12.

Asch, S. E. (1951). The effects of group pressure upon the modification and distortion of judgment. In H. Guetzkow (Ed.), *Groups, leadership, and men.* Pittsburgh: Carnegie Press.

Asch, S. E. (1956). Studies of independence and conformity: I. A minority of one against a unanimous majority. *Psychologal Monographs: General and Applied, 70 (Whole No. 416),* 1-7.

Aserinsky, E., & Kleitman, N. (1953). Regularly occurring periods of eye mobility and concomitant phenomena during sleep. *Science, 18,* 273-274.

Ashcraft, M. H. (1994). *Human Memory and Cognition* (2nd ed.). New York: HarperCollins.

Ashmore, R. D. (1990). Sex, gender, and the individual. In L. A. Pervin (Ed.), *Handbook of personality.* New York: Guilford.

Aslin, R. N., & Smith, L. B. (1988). Perceptual development. *Annual Review of Psychology, 39,* 435-473.

Aspinwall, L. G., & Taylor, S. E. (1992). Modeling cognitive adaptation: A longitudinal investigation of the impact of individual differences and coping on college adjustment and performance. *Journal of Personality and Social Psychology, 63,* 989-1003.

Atkinson, J. W., & Feather, N. T. (1966). *A theory of achievement motivation.* New York: Wiley.

Atkinson, J. W., & Litwin, G. H. (1960). Achievement motive and test anxiety conceived as motive to approach success and motive to avoid failure. *Journal of Abnormal and Social Psychology, 60,* 27-36.

Atkinson, R. C. (1975). Mnemotechnics in second-language learning. *American Psychologist, 30,* 821-828.

Atkinson, R. C., & Shiffrin, R. M. (1968). Human memory: A proposed system and its control processes. In K. W. Spence & J. T. Spence (Eds.), *The psychology of learning and motivation: Advances in research and theory.* New York: Academic Press.

Atwood, M. E., & Polson, P. G. (1976). A process model for water jug problems. *Cognitive Psychology, 8,* 191-216.

Auletta, K. (1984). Children of children. *Parade Magazine, 17,* 4-7.

Axelrod, S., & Apsche, J. (1983). *The effects of punishment on human behavior.* New York: Academic Press.

Azrin, N. H., & Holz, W. C. (1966). Punishment. In W. K. Honig (Ed.), Operant behavior: Areas of research and application. Englewood Cliffs, NJ: Prentice-Hall.

Azumi, K., & McMillan, C. J. (1976). Worker sentiment in the Japanese factory: Its organizational determinants. In L. Austin (Ed.), Japan: *The paradox of progress.* New Haven, CT: Yale University Press.

Babor, T. F., Berglas, S., Mendelson, J. H., Ellinboe, J., & Miller, K. (1983). Alcohol, effect and the disinhibition of behavior. *Psychopharmacology, 80,* 53-60.

Bachorowski, J., & Owren, M. J. (1995). Vocal expression of emotion: Acoustic properties of speech are associated with emotional intensity and context. *Psychological Science, 6,* 219-224.

Backman, C. W., & Secord, P. F. (1959). The effect of perceived liking on interpersonal attraction. *Human Relations, 12,* 379-384.

Badaway, A. A-B. (1998). Alcohol, aggression and serotonin: Metabolic aspects. *Alcohol and Alcoholism, 33,* 66-72.

Baddeley, A. (1990). *Human memory: Theory and practice.* Boston: Allyn & Bacon.

Baddeley, A. (1998). *Human Memory: Theory and Practice (Revised Edition).* Boston: Allyn & Bacon.

Baddeley, A. (1992). Working memory. *Science, 25,* 556-559.

Baddeley, A. D. (1982). Domains of recollection. *Psychological Review, 89,* 708-729.

Baer, L., Rauch, S. L., Ballantine, T., Martoza, R., Cosgrove, R., Cassem, E., et al. (1995). Cingulotomy for intractable obsessive-compulsive disorder. *Archives of General Psychiatry, 52,* 384-392.

Bagozzi, R. P., & Burnkrant, R. E. (1979). Attitude organization and the attitude-behavior relationship. *Journal of Personality and Social Psychology, 37,* 913-929.

Bahrick, H. P. (1984). Semantic memory content in perma-store. *Journal of Experimental Psychology: General, 13,* 1-29.

Bailey, D., Taylor, S. P. (1991). Effects of alcohol and aggressive disposition on human physical aggression. *Journal of Research in Personality, 25,* 334-342.

Bailey, J. M., & Pillard, R. C. (1991). A genetic study of male sexual orientation. *Archives of General Psychiatry, 48,* 1089-1096.

Baillargeon, R. (1993). The object concept revisited: New directions in the investigation of infants' physical knowledge. In C. E. Granrud (Ed.), *Visual perception and cognition in infancy.* Hillsdale, NJ: Lawrence Erlbaum Associates.

Baillargeon, R. (1995). How do infants learn about the physical world? Current Directions in Psychological *Science, 4,* 133-140.

Balay, J., & Shevrin, H. (1988). The subliminal psychodynamic activation method: A critical review. *American Psychologist, 43,* 161-174.

Baldwin, M. W. (1992). Relational schemas and the processing of social information. *Psychological Bulletin, 112,* 461-484.

Baley, S. (1985). The legalities of hiring in the 80s. *Personnel Journal, 64,* 112-115.

Ballenger, J. C. (1989). Toward an integrated model of panic disorder. *American Journal of Orthopsychiatry, 9,* 284-293.

Balleyguier, G., & Melhuish, E. C. (1996). The relationship between infant day care and socio-emotional development with French children. *European Journal of Psychology of Education*, 11, 193-199.

Baltes, M. M. (1995). Dependency in old age: Gains and losses. *Current Directions in Psychological Science, 4,* 14-19.

Baltes, P. B., & Baltes, M. M. (1990). Selective optimization with compensation. In P. B. Baltes & M. M. Baltes (Eds.), *Successful aging: Perspectives from the behavioral sciences.* New York: Cambridge University Press.

Bandura, A. (1965). Influence of models' reinforcement contingencies on the acquisition of imitative responses. *Journal of Personality and Social Psychology, 1,* 589-595.

Bandura, A. (1971). An analysis of modeling processes. In A. Bandura (Ed.), *Psychological modeling.* New York: Lieber-Atherton.

Bandura, A. (1974). Behavior theory and the models of man. *American Psychologist, 29,* 859-869.

Bandura, A. (1976). Modeling theory: Some traditions, trends and disputes. In W. S. Sahakian (Ed.), *Learning: Systems, models, and theories.* Skokie, IL: Rand McNally.

Bandura, A. (1977). *Social learning theory.* Englewood Cliffs, NJ: Prentice-Hall.

Bandura, A. (1978). The self-system in reciprocal determinism. *American Psychologist, 33,* 344-358.

Bandura, A. (1982). Self-efficacy mechanism in human agency. *American Psychologist, 37,* 122-147.

Bandura, A., Ross, D., & Ross, S. A. (1963). Imitation of film-mediated aggressive models. *Journal of Abnormal and Social Psychology, 66,* 3-11.

Bandura, A. (2001a). Social cognitive theory: An agentic perspective. *Annual Review of Psychology,* **52**, 1-26.

Bandura, A. (2001b). *On shaping one's future: The primacy of human agency.* Paper presented at the annual meeting of The American Psychological Society, Toronto, June 14, 2001.

Barber, T. F. X. (1972). Suggested (hypnotic) behavior: The trace paradigm vs. an alternative paradigm. In E. Fromm & R. E. Shorr (Eds.), *Hypnosis: Research developments and perspectives.* Chicago: Aldine-Atherton.

Barber, T. X., Spanos, N. P., & Chaves, J. F. (1974). *Hypnosis: Imagination and human potentialities.* New York: Pergamon Press.

Barefoot, J. C., Dahlstrom, W. D., & Williams, R. B. (1983). Hostility, CHD incidence, and total mortality: A 25-year follow-up study of 255 physicians. *Psychosomatic Medicine, 45,* 59-63.

Bargh, J. A. (1993). The four horsemen of automaticity: Awareness, intention, efficiency and control in social cognition. In R. S. Wyer & T. K. Srull (Eds.), *Handbook of social cognition.* Hillsdale, NJ: Erlbaum.

Barinaga, M. (1991). Is homosexuality biological? *Science, 253,* 956-957.

Barinaga, M. (1996). Developmental neurobiology: Guiding neurons to the cortex. *Science, 274,* 1100-1101.

Barinaga, M. (1995). "Obese" protein slims mice. *Science, 269,* 475-476.

Barker, R. (1968). *Ecological psychology.* Stanford, CA: Stanford University Press.

Barlow, D. H. & Lehman, C. L. (1996). Advances in the psychosocial treatment of anxiety disorders: Implications for National Health Care. *Archives of General Psychiatry, 53,* 727-735.

Barnette, R. C., Marshall, N. L., Raudenbush, S. W., & Brennan, R. T. (1993). Gender and the relationship between job experiences and psychological distress: A study of dual-earner couples. *Journal of Personality and Social Psychology, 64,* 794-806.

Baron, M., Freimer, N. F., Risch, N., Lerer, B., Alexander, J. R., et al. (1993). Diminished support for linkage between manic depressive illness and X-chromosome markers in three Israeli pedigrees. *Natural Genetics, 3,* 49-55.

Baron, R. A. (1977). *Human aggression.* New York: Plenum.

Baron, R. A., & Ransberger, V. M. (1978). Ambient temperature and the occurrence of collective violence: The "long hot summer" revisited. *Journal of Personality and Social Psychology, 36,* 351-360.

Barr, H. M., Streissguth, A. P., Darby, B. L., & Sampson, P. D. (1990). Prenatal exposure to alcohol, caffeine, tobacco, and aspirin: Effects on fine and gross motor performance in 4-year-old children. *Developmental Psychology, 26,* 339-348.

Barrett, G. V., & Depinet, R. L. (1991). A reconsideration of testing for competence rather than for intelligence. *American Psychologist, 46,* 1012-1024.

Barron, F., & Harrington, D. M. (1981). Creativity, intelligence, and personality. *Annual Review of Psychology, 32,* 439-476.

Barsalou, L. W. (1983). Ad hoc categories. *Memory and cognition, 11,* 211-227.

Barsalou, L. W. (1989). Intra-concept similarity and its implications for inter-concept similarity. In S. Vosniadou & A. Ortony (Eds.), *Similarity and analogical reasoning.* New York: Cambridge University Press.

Bartecchi, C. E., MacKenzie, T. D., & Schrier, R. W. (1995). The global tobacco epidemic. *Scientific American (May).*

Bartlett, F. C. (1932). Remembering. Cambridge: Cambridge University Press.

Bartoshuk, L. M., & Beauchamp, G. K. (1994). Chemical senses. *Annual Review of Psychology, 45,* 419-449.

Bartus, R. T., Dean, R. L., Beer, B., & Lippa, A. S. (1982). The cholinergic hypothesis of geriatric memory dysfunction. *Science, 217,* 408-417.

Basso, K. (1970). To give up words: Silence in Western Apache culture. Southwestern *Journal of Anthropology, 26,* 213-230.

Batson, C. D. (1987). Prosocial motivation: Is it ever truly altruism? In L. Berkowitz (Ed.). *Advances in experimental social psychology* (Vol. 20). New York: Academic Press.

Batson C. D. (1990a). How social an animal: The human capacity for caring. *American Psychologist, 45,* 336-346.

Batson C. D. (1990b). Good samaritans-or priests and Levites? *Personality and Social Psychology Bulletin, 16,* 758-768.

Baum, A., & Grunberg, N. E. (1991). Gender, stress, and health. *Health Psychology, 10,* 80-85.

Baumeister, A. A. (1987). Mental retardation: Some conceptions and dilemmas. *American Psychologist, 42,* 796-800.

Baumeister, R. F. (1985). The championship choke. *Psychology Today, 19,* 48-52.

Baumeister, R. F. (1987). How the self became a problem: A Psychological review of historical research. *Journal of Personality and Social Psychology, 52,* 163-176.

Baumeister, R. F., & Steinhilber, A. (1984). Paradoxical effects of supportive audiences on performance under pressure: The home field disadvantage in sports championships. *Journal of Personality and Social Psychology, 47,* 85-93.

Bausbaum, A. I., & Levine, J. D. (1991). Opiate analgesia: How central is a peripheral target? *New England Journal of Medicine, 325,* 1168-1169.

Bayley, N. & Schaefer, E. S. (1964). Correlations of maternal and child behaviors with the development of mental abilities: Data from the Berkeley Growth Study. *Monographs of the Society for Research in Child Development, 29,* 1-80.

Beauvais, F., Oetting, E. R., Wolf, W., & Edwards, R. W. (1989). American Indian youth and drugs: 1975-1987, a continuing problem. *American Journal of Public Health, 79,* 634-636.

Beck, A. T. (1967). *Depression: Clinical, experimental, and theoretical aspects.* New York: HarperCollins.

Beck, A. T. (1976). *Cognitive therapy and the emotional disorders.* New York: International University Press.

Beck, A. T. (1985). Theoretical perspectives in clinical anxiety. In A. H. Tuma & J. D. Master (Eds.), *Anxiety and the anxiety disorders.* Hillsdale, NJ: Erlbaum.

Beck, A. T. (1991). Cognitive therapy: A 30-year retrospective. *American Psychologist, 46,* 368-375.

Beck, A. T. (1995). *Cognitive therapy: Basics and beyond.* New York: Guilford.

Beck, A. T., & Emery, G. (1985). *Anxiety disorders and phobias: A cognitive perspective.* New York: Basic Books.

Beck, A. T., & Freeman, A. (1990). *Cognitive therapy of personality disorders.* New York: Guilford.

Beckman, L. J., & Houser, B. B. (1982). The consequences of childlessness on the social-psychologal well-being of older women. *Journal of Gerontology, 37,* 243-250.

Bee, H. (1992). *The developing child* (Sixth Edition). New York: Harper Collins.

Bee, H. (1995). *The developing child* (7th ed.). New York: HarperCollins.

Bee, H. (1996). *The journey of adulthood* (Third Edition). Upper Saddle River, NJ: Prentice Hall.

Beecroft, R. (1966). *Classical conditioning.* Goleta, CA: Psychonomic Press.

Beer, M., & Walton, A. E. (1987). Organization change and development. *Annual Review of Psychology, 38,* 339-367.

Begg, I., & Paivio, A. (1969). Concreteness and imagery in sentence meaning. *Journal of Verbal Learning and Verbal Behavior, 8,* 812-817.

Bekerian, D. A. (1993). In search of the typical eyewitness. *American Psychologist, 48,* 574-576.

Bell, I. R. (1994). Somatization disorder: Healthcare costs in the decade of the brain. *Biological psychiatry, 35,* 81-83.

Bell, P. A., Fisher, J. D., & Loomis, R. J. (1978). *Environmental psychology.* Philadelphia: Saunders.

Bellack, A. S. (1986). Schizophrenia: Behavior therapy's forgotten child. *Behavior Therapy, 17,* 199-214.

Bellack, A. S., & Mueser, K. T. (1986). A comprehensive treatment program for schizophrenia and chronic mental illness. *Community Mental Health Journal, 22,* 175-189.

Belsher, G., & Costello, C. G. (1988). Relapse after recovery from unipolar depression: A critical review. *Psychological Bulletin, 104,* 84-96.

Belsky, J. (1990). The "effects" of infant day care reconsidered. In N. Fox & G. G. Fein (Eds.), *Infant day care: The current debate.* Norwood, NJ: Ablex.

Belsky, J., Lang, M. E., & Rovine, M. (1985). Stability and change in marriage across the transition to parenthood: A second study. *Journal of Marriage and the Family, 47,* 855-865.

Belsky, J., Rovine, M., & Taylor, D. G. (1984). The Pennsylvania Infant and Family Development Project III: The origins of individual differences in infant-mother attachment-maternal and infant contributions. *Child Development, 55,* 718-728.

Belsky, J., & Rovine, M. (1988). Nonmaternal care in the first year of life and the security of infant-parent attachment. *Child Development, 59,* 157-167.

Beltramini, A. U., & Hertzig, M. E. (1983). Sleep and bedtime behavior in preschool-aged children. *Pediatrics, 71,* 153-158.

Bem, D. J. (1972). Self-perception theory. In L. Berkowitz (Ed.). *Advances in experimental social psychology* (Vol. 6). San Diego: Academic Press.

Bem, S. (1981). Gender schema theory: A cognitive account of sex typing. *Psychological Review, 88,* 354-364.

Ben-Porath, Y. S., & Butcher, J. N. (1989). The comparability of MMPI and MMPI-2 scales and profiles. *Psychological Assessment, 1,* 345-347.

Ben-Yehuda, N. (1980). The European witch craze. *American Journal of Sociology, 86,* 1-31.

Benbow, C. P. (1987). Possible biological correlates of precocious mathematical reasoning ability. *Trends in Neuroscience, 10,* 17-20.

Benbow, C. P. (1990). Gender differences: Searching for facts. *American Psychologist, 45,* 988.

Benedict, H. (1979). Early lexical development: Comprehension and production. *Journal of Child Language, 6,* 183-200.

Bennett, T. L. (1982). *Introduction to physiological psychology.* Monterey, CA: Brooks/Cole.

Bennett, W. (1980). The cigarette century. *Science, 80,* 36-43.

Benson, H. (1975). *The relaxation response.* New York: Morrow.

Berkowitz, L. (1978). What ever happened to the frustration-aggression hypothesis? *American Behavioral Scientist, 21,* 691-708.

Berkowitz, L. (1982). Aversive conditions as stimuli to aggression. *Advances in Experimental Social Psychology, 15,* 249-288.

Berkowitz, L. (1989). Frustration-aggression hypothesis: Examination and reformulation. *Psychological Bulletin, 106,* 59-73.

Berkowitz, L. (1990). On the formation and regulation of anger and aggression. *American Psychologist, 45,* 494-503.

Berkowitz, H. (1994). U. S. Firms Trip Over Their Tongues in Wooing the World. The *Journal Gazette, June 21,* Fort Wayne, IN.

Berlyne, D. E. (1960). *Conflict, arousal, and curiosity.* New York: McGraw-Hill.

Berlyne, D. E. (1971). *Aesthetics and psychobiology.* Englewood Cliffs, NJ: Prentice-Hall.

Bernstein, I. (1978). Learned taste aversion in children receiving chemotherapy. *Science, 200,* 1302-1303.

Bernstein, H. J., et al. (1998). Patient attitudes about ECT after treatment. *Psychiatric annals, 28,* 524-527.

Bernstein, R. (1981). The Y chromosome and primary sexual differentiation. *Journal of the American Medical Association, 245,* 1953-1956.

Berrettini, W. H., Golden, L. R., Gelernter, J., Gejman, P. V., Gershon, E. S., & Datera-Wadleigh, S. (1990). X-chromosome markers and manic-depressive illness. *Archives of General Psychiatry, 47,* 366-374.

Berry, J., Poortinga, Y., Segall, M., & Dasen P. (1992). *Cross-cultural psychology: Research and applications.* New York: Cambridge University Press.

Berscheid, E. (1994). Interpersonal relationships. *Annual Review of Psychology, 45,* 79-129.

Best, J. B. (1999). *Cognitive psychology* (Fifth edition). Belmont, CA: Wadsworth.

Bertenthal, B. I., & Campos, J. J. (1989). A systems approach to the organizing effects of self-produced locomotion during infancy. In C. Rovee-Collier & L. P. Lipsett (Eds.), *Advances in infancy research.* Norwood, NJ: Ablex.

Beutler, L. E., Crago, M., & Arizmendi, T. G. (1986). Therapist variables in psychotherapy process and outcome. In S. L. Garfield & A. E. Bergin (Eds.), *Handbook of psychotherapy and behavior change* (3rd ed.). New York: Wiley.

Beyer, S. (1990). Gender differences in the accuracy of self-evaluation and performance. *Journal of Personality and Social Psychology, 59,* 960-970.

Bhawuk, D. P. S., & Brislin, R. (1992). The measurement of intercultural sensitivity using the concepts of individualism and collectivism. *International Journal of Intercultural Relations, 16,* 413-436.

Billy, J. O. G., Tanfer, K., Grady, W. R., & Klepinger, D. H. (1993). The sexual behavior of men in the United States. *Family Planning Perspectives, 25,* 52-60.

Binder, J. L. (1993). Research findings on short-term psychodynamic therapy techniques. *Directions in Clinical Psychology, 3,* 10.3-10.13.

Birch, E. E., Gwiazda, J., & Held, R. (1983). The development of vergence does not account for the onset of stereopsis. *Perception, 12,* 331-336.

Birdwhistell, R. L. (1952). *Introduction to kinesics.* Louisville, KY: University of Louisville Press.

Birnbaum, M. H., & Mellers, B. A. (1979). Stimulus recognition may mediate exposure effects. *Journal of Personality and Social Psychology, 37,* 391-394.

Bjorklund, A., Dunnett, S. B., & Stenevi, U. (1980). Reinnervation of the denervated striatum by substantia nigra transplants: Functional consequences as revealed by pharmacological and sensorimotor testing. *Brain Research, 199,* 307-333.

Blair, P. S., & Fleming, P. J. (1996). Smoking and the sudden infant death syndrome: Results from 1993-5 case-control study for confidential inquiry into stillbirths and deaths in infancy. *British Medical Journal, 313,* 195-198.

Blanchard, D. C., & Blanchard, R. J. (1984). Affect and aggression: An animal model applied to human behavior. In R. J. Blanchard & D. C. Blanchard (Eds.). *Advances in the study of aggression* (Volume 1). New York: Academic Press.

Blanchard, D. C., & Blanchard, R. J. (1988).

Ethoexperimental approaches to the biology of emotion. *Annual Review of Psychology, 39,* 43-68.

Blaney, P. H. (1986). Affect and memory: A review. *Psychological Bulletin, 99,* 229-246.

Blashfield, R. K., & Breen, M. J. (1989). Face validity of the DSM-III-R personality disorders. *American Journal of Psychiatry, 146,* 1575-1579.

Blass, E. M., Ganchow, J. R., & Steiner, J. E. (1984). Classical conditioning in newborn human infants 2-48 hours of age. *Infant Behavior and Development, 7,* 223-235.

Bleier, R., Houston, L., & Byne, W. (1987). Can the corpus callosum predict gender, age, handedness, or cognitive differences? *Trends in Neuroscience, 9,* 391-394.

Bloch, D., & Simon, R. (Eds.). (1982). *The strength of family therapy: Selected papers of Nathan Ackerman.* New York: Brunner/Mazel.

Block, J. (1965). *The challenge of response sets.* Englewood Cliffs, NJ: Prentice-Hall.

Bloodworth, R. C. (1987). Major problems associated with marijuana abuse. *Psychiatric Medicine, 3,* 173-184.

Bloom, B. L. (1997). *Planned short-term psychotherapy,* Second Edition. Boston: Allyn & Bacon.

Bloom, F. E., Lazerson, A., & Hotstadter, L. (1985). *Brain, mind, and behavior.* San Francisco: Freeman.

Blum, J. E., Jarvik, L. F., & Clark, E. T. (1970). Rate of change on selective tests of intelligence: A twenty-year longitudinal study. *Journal of Gerontology, 25,* 171-176.

Bodick, N. C., Offen, W. W., Levey, A., et al. (1997). Effects of xanomelin, a selective muscarinic receptor agonist, on cognitive function and behavioral symptoms in Alzheimer disease. *Archives of neurology,* 54, 465-473.

Bolles, R. C. (1970). Species-specific defense reactions and avoidance learning. *Psychological Review, 7,* 32-48.

Bolles, R. C. (1972). Reinforcement, expectancy, and learning. *Psychological Review, 79,* 394-409.

Bolles, R. C. (1975). Learning, motivation, and cognition. In W. K. Estes (Ed.), *Handbook of learning and cognitive processes (Vol. 1).* Hillsdale, NJ: Erlbaum.

Bondareff, W., Mountjoy, C. Q., Wischik, C. M., Hauser, D. L., LaBree, L. D., & Roth, M. (1993). Evidence of subtypes of Alzheimer's disease and implications for etiology. *Archives of General Psychiatry, 50,* 350-356.

Bootzin, R. R., & Accella, J. R. (1984). *Abnormal psychology: Current perspectives* (4th ed.). New York: Random House.

Bootzin, R. R., & Rider, S. P. (1997). Behavioral techniques and biofeedback for insomnia. In M. R. Pressman & W. C. Orr (Eds.). *Understanding sleep: The evaluation and treatment of sleep disorders.* Washington, D. C.: American Psychological Association.

Boraod, J. C. (1992). Interhemispheric and introhemispheric control of emotion: A focus on unilateral brain damage. *Journal of Consulting and Clinical Psychology, 60,* 339-348.

Borbely, A. (1986). *Secrets of sleep.* New York: Basic Books.

Bordens, K. S., & Abbott, B. B. (1999). *Research design and methods: A process approach (Fourth Edition).* Mountain View, CA: Mayfield Publishing Company.

Bordens, K. S., & Abbott, B. B. (1991). *Research design and methods: A process approach.* Mountain View, CA: Mayfield.

Bornstein, R. F. (1989). Exposure and affect: Overview and meta-analysis of research 1968-1987. *Psychological Bulletin, 106,* 265-289.

Bornstein, R. F., Kale, A. R., & Cornell, K. R. (1990). Boredom as a limiting condition of the mere exposure effect. *Journal of Personality and Social Psychology, 58,* 791-800.

Bouchard, C., Tremblay, A., Després, J., et al. (1990). The response to long-term overfeeding in identical twins. *The New England Journal of Medicine, 322,* 1477-1482.

Bourne, L. E. (1992). Cognitive psychology: A brief overview. *Psychology Science Agenda, 5(5),* 5, 20.

Bourne, L. E., Dominowski, R. L., & Loftus, E. F. (1983). *Cognitive process.* Englewood Cliffs, NJ: Prentice-Hall.

Bousfield, W. A. (1953). The occurrence of clustering in the free recall of randomly arranged associates. *Journal of General Psychology, 49,* 229-240.

Bower, B. (1995). IQs evolutionary breakdown: Intelligence may have more facets than testers realize. *Science News, 147,* 220-222.

Bower, G. H. (1970). Imagery as a relational organizer in associative learning. *Journal of Verbal Learning and Verbal Behavior, 9,* 529-533.

Bower, G. H. (1972). Mental imagery and associative learning. In L. W. Gregg (Ed.), *Cognition in learning and memory.* New York: Wiley.

Bower, G. H. (1981). Mood and memory. *American Psychologist, 36,* 129-148.

Bower, G. H., & Clark, M. C. (1969). Narrative stories as mediators for serial learning. *Psychonomic Science, 14,* 181-182.

Bower, G. H., & Mayer, J. D. (1989). In search of mood-dependent retrieval. *Journal of Social Behavior and Personality, 4,* 133-168.

Bower, G. H., Monteiro, K. P., & Gilligan, S. G. (1978). Emotional mood as a context for learning and recall. *Journal of Verbal Learning and Verbal Behavior, 17,* 573-587.

Bower, G. H., & Springston, F. (1970). Pauses as recoding points in letter series. *Journal of Experimental Psychology, 83,* 421-430.

Bower, T. G. R., Broughton, J. M., & Moore, M. K. (1971). Infant responses to approaching objects: An indicator of response to distal variables. *Perception and Psychophysics, 9,* 193-196.

Bowers, J. S., & Schacter, D. L. (1990). Implicit memory and test awareness. *Journal of Experimental Psychology: Learning, Memory, and Cognition, 16,* 404-416.

Bowlby, J. (1982). *Attachment and loss: Vol. 1. Attachment* (2nd ed.). New York: Basic Books.

Bradbard, M. R., & Endsley, R. C. (1983). The effects of sex-typed labelling on preschool children's information seeking and retention. *Sex Roles, 9,* 247-260.

Bradley, D. R., & Dumais, S. T. (1975). Ambiguous cognitive contours. *Nature, 257,* 582-584.

Bradshaw, J. L., & Nettleton, N. C. (1983). *Human cerebral asymmetry.* Englewood Cliffs, NJ: Prentice-Hall.

Braine, M. D. S. (1976). Children's first word combinations. *Monographs for the Society for Research in Child Development, 4* (Serial No. 164).

Brandon, T. H. (1994). Negative affect as motivation to smoke. *Current Directions in Psychological Sciences, 3,* 33-37.

Bransford, J. D., & Johnson, M. K. (1972). Contextual prerequisites for understanding: Some investigations of comprehension and recall. *Journal of Verbal Learning and Verbal Behavior, 11,* 717-720.

Bratic, E. B. (1982). Healthy mothers, healthy babies coalition. *Prevention, 97,* 503-509.

Braun, P., Kochansky, G., Shapiro, R., Greenberg, S., Gudeman, J. E., Johnson, S., & Shore, M. (1981). Overview: Deinstitutionalization of psychiatric patients, a critical review of outcome studies. *American Journal of Psychiatry, 138,* 736-749.

Bray, D. W., Campbell, R. J., & Grant, D. L. (1974). *Formative years in business: A long-term AT&T study of managerial lives.* New York: Wiley.

Bregman, J., Dykens, E. Watson, M., & Leckman, J. (1987). Fragile X syndrome: Variability in phenotype expression. *Journal of the American Academy of Child and Adolescent Psychiatry, 26,* 463-471.

Brehm, J. W., & Self, E. A. (1989). The intensity of motivation. *Annual Review of Psychology, 40,* 109-131.

Breier, A., Schreiber, J. L., Dyer, J., & Pickar, D. (1991). National Institute of Mental Health longitudinal study of chronic schizophrenia: Prognosis and predictors of outcome. *Archives of General Psychiatry, 48,* 239-246.

Breland, K., & Breland, M. (1961). This misbehavior of organisms. *American Psychologist, 16,* 681-684.

Brett, J. F., Brief, A. P., Burke, M. J., George, J. M., & Webster, J. (1990). Negative affectivity and the reporting of stressful events. *Health Psychology, 9,* 57-68.

Brewer, J. B., Zhao, Z., Desmond, J. E., Glover, G. H., & Gabrieli, J. D. E. (1998). Making memories: Brain activity that predicts how well visual experience is remembered. *Science, 281,* 1185-1187.

Brewer, W. F., & Nakamura, G. V. (1984). The nature and function of schemas. In R. S. Wyler and T. K. Sroll (Eds.), *Handbook of social cognition.* Hillsdale, NJ: Erlbaum.

Briggs, G. G., Freeman, R. K, & Yaffe, S. J. (1986). *Drugs in pregnancy and lactation* (2nd ed.). Baltimore: Williams & Wilkins.

Brigham, J. C. (1991). *Social psychology* (2nd ed.). New York: HarperCollins.

Brinkerhoff, R. O. (1989). *Evaluating training programs in business and industry.* San Francisco: Jossey-Bass.

Brislin, R. W. (1990). *Applied cross-cultural psychology.* Newbury Park, CA: Sage.

Brislin, R. W. (1993). *Understanding culture's influence on behavior.* Fort Worth, TX: Harcourt Brace.

Brody, E. M. (1981). Women in the middle and family help to older people. *Gerontologist, 21,* 471-480.

Brody, E. M. (1985). Parent care as a normative family stress. *Gerontologist, 25,* 19-29.

Brown, J. (1958). Some tests of the decay theory of immediate memory. *Quarterly Journal of Experimental Psychology, 10,* 12-21.

Brown, J. (1976). An analysis of recognition and recall and of problems in their comparison. In J. Brown (Ed.), *Recall and recognition.* New York: Wiley.

Brown, J. D. (1991). Staying fit and staying well. *Journal of Personality and Social Psychology, 60,* 555-561.

Brown, J. I. (1973). *The Nelson-Denny reading test.* Boston: Houghton Mifflin.

Brown, K. W., & White, T. (1992). Syndromes of chronic schizophrenia and some clinical correlates. *British Journal of Psychiatry, 161,* 317-322.

Brown, N. A. (1985). Are offspring at risk from their father's exposure to toxins? *Nature, 316,* 110.

Brown, R. (1973). *A first language: The early stages.* Cambridge, MA: Harvard University Press.

Brown, R., Cazden, C. B., & Bellugi, U. (1969). The child's grammar from 1 to 3. *Symposia on child language (Vol. 2).* Minneapolis: University of Minnesota Press.

Brown, R., & Kulik, J. (1977). Flashbulb memories. *Cognition, 5,* 73-99.

Brown, R., & McNeill, D. (1966). The tip-of-the-tongue phenomenon. *Journal of Verbal Learning and Verbal Behavior, 5,* 325-337.

Brown, T. A., & Barlow, D. H. (1992). Comorbidity among anxiety disorders: Implications for treatment and DSM-IV. *Journal of Consulting and Clinical Psychology, 60,* 835-844.

Browne, M. A., & Mahoney, M. J. (1984). Sport psychology. *Annual Review of Psychology, 35,* 605-626.

Brownell, K. D. (1993). Whether obesity should be treated. *Health Psychology, 12,* 339-341.

Brownell, K. D., & Rodin, J. (1994). The dieting maelstrom: Is it possible and advisable to lose weight? *American Psychologist, 49,* 781-791.

Bruch, H. (1980). Preconditions for the development of anorexia nervosa. American *Journal of Psychoanalysis, 40,* 169-172.

Bruner, J. S. &Goodman, C. C. (1947). Value and need as organizing factors in perception. *Journal of Abnormal and Social Psychology, 42,* 33-44.

Bruner, J. S., Goodnow, J. J., & Austin, G. A. (1956). *A study of thinking.* New York: Wiley.

Bureau of Justice Statistics (1999). Sourcebook for criminal justice statistics, 1999 (Table 4.8, p. 347). Downloaded from the World Wide Web, January 30, 2001. http://www.albany.edu/sourcebook/1995/toc_4html.

Buck, R. (1980). Nonverbal behavior and the theory of emotion: The facial feedback hypothesis. *Journal of Personality and Social Psychology, 38,* 811-824.

Buck, R. (1985). Prime theory: An integrated view of motivation and emotion. *Psychological Review, 92,* 389-413.

Buckley, P. F., Buchanan, R. W., Schulz, S. C., & Tamminga, C. A. (1996). Catching up on schizophrenia. *Archives of General Psychiatry*, **53**, 456-462.

Buckout, R. (1975). Nearly 2000 witnesses can be wrong. Social *Action and the Law, 2, 7.*

Burger, J. M. (2000). *Personality* (Fifth Edition). Belmont, CA: Wadsworth.

Burgoon, J. K., Birk, T., & Pfau, M. (1990). Non-verbal behaviors, persuasion, and credibility. *Human Communication Research, 17,* 140-169.

Burisch, M. (1984). Approaches to personality inventory construction. *American Psychologist, 39,* 214-227.

Bushman, B. J., & Cooper, H. M. (1990). Effects of alcohol on human aggression: An integrative research review. *Psychological Bulletin, 107,* 341-354.

Bushnell, I. W. R., Sai, F., & Mullin, J. T. (1989). Neonatal recognition of the mother's face. *British Journal of Developmental Psychology, 7,* 3-15.

Buss, A. H. (1966). *Psychopathology.* New York: Wiley.

Buss, D. M. (1984). Evolutionary biology and personality psychology. *American Psychologist, 39,* 1135-1147.

Buss, D. M. (1985). Human mate selection. *American Scientist, 73,* 47-51.

Buss, D. M. (1989). Personality as traits. *American Psychologist, 44,* 1378-1388.

Buss, D. M., Abbott, M., Angleitner, A., Asherian, A.,

Biaggio, A., Blanco-Villasenor, A., et al. (1990). International preferences in mate selection: A study of 37 cultures. *Journal of Cross-Cultural Psychology, 21,* 5-47.

Buss, D. M., & Barnes, M. (1986). Preferences in human mate selection. *Journal of Personality and Social Psychology, 50,* 559-570.

Buss, D. M., & Plomin, R (1984). *Temperament: Early developing personality traits.* Hillsdale, NJ: Lawrence Erlbaum.

Butler, R., & Emr, M. (1982). SDAT research: Current trends. *Generations, 7,* 14-18.

Butler, R., & Lewis, M. (1981). *Aging and mental health.* St. Louis: Mosby.

Byrd, K. R. (1994). The narrative reconstruction of incest survivors. *American Psychologist, 49,* 439-440.

Byrne, D. (1971). *The attraction paradigm.* New York: Academic Press.

Cacioppo, J. T., Marshall-Goodell, B. S., Tassinary, L. G., & Petty, R. E. (1992). Rudimentary determinants of attitudes: Classical conditioning is more effective when prior knowledge about the attitude stimulus is low than high. *Journal of Experimental Social Psychology, 28,* 207-233.

Cacioppo, J. T., & Petty, R. E. (1989). Effects of message repetition on argument processing, recall, and persuasion. *Basic Applied Social Psychology, 10,* 3-12.

Calhoun, J. B. (1962). Population density and social pathology. *Scientific American, 206,* 139-148.

Calsyn, D. A., Saxon, A. J., Freeman, G., & Whittaker, S. (1992). Ineffectiveness of AIDS education and HIV antibody testing in reducing high-risk behaviors among injection drug users. *American Journal of Public Health, 82,* 573-575.

Campbell, J. P. (1988). Training design for performance improvement. In J. P. Campbell & R. J. Campbell (Eds.), *Productivity in organizations.* San Francisco: Jossey-Bass.

Campbell, J. P., McHenry, J. J., & Wise, L. L. (1990). Modeling job performance in a population of jobs. *Personnel Psychology, 43,* 313-333.

Campfield, L. A., Smith, F. J., Guisez, Y., Devos, R., & Burn, P. (1995). Recombinant mouse OB protein: Evidence for a peripheral signal linking adiposity and central neural networks. *Science, 269,* 546-549.

Campion, M. A., Palmer, D. K., & Campion, J. E. (1997). A review of structure in the selection interview. *Personnel Psychology,* 50, 655-702.

Campion, M. A., Palmer, D. K., & Campion, J. E. (1998). Structuring employment interviews to improve reliability, validity, and users' reactions. *Current Directions in Psychological Science,* 7, 77-82.

Campos, J. J. Heart rates: A sensitive tool for the study of emotional development. In L. Lipsett (Ed.), Developmental psychobiology: *The significance of infancy.* Hillsdale, NJ: Erlbaum.

Campos, J. J., Hiatt, S., Ramsey, D., Henderson, C., & Svejda, M. (1978). The emergence of fear on the visual cliff. In M. Lewis & L. A. Rosenbaum (Eds.), *The development of affect.* New York: Plenum.

Cannon, T. D., Mednick, S. A., & Parnas, J. (1990). Antecedents of predominantly negative- and predominantly positive-symptom schizophrenia in a high-risk population. *Archives of General Psychiatry, 47,* 622-632.

Cannon, W. B. (1932). *The wisdom of the body.* New York: Norton.

Cantor, N., & Kihlstrom, J. F. (1989). Social intelligence and cognitive assessments of personality. In R. S. Wyer & T. K. Srull (Eds.), *Advances in social cognition, volume II: Social intelligence and cognitive assessments of personality.* Hillsdale, NJ: Lawrence Erlbaum.

Cantor, N., & Langston, C. A. (1989). Ups and downs of life tasks in a life transition. In L. A. Pervin (Ed.). *Goal concepts in personality and social psychology.* Hillsdale, NJ: Lawrence Erlbaum Associates.

Caplan, N. (1989). *The boat people and achievement in America: A study of family life, hard work, and cultural values.* Ann Arbor: University of Michigan Press.

Carey, S. (1978). The child as word learner. In M. Halle, J. Bresnan, & G. A. Miller (Eds.), *Linguistic theory and psychological reality.* Cambridge, MA: MIT Press.

Carlson, N. R. (1991). *Physiology of behavior* (4th ed.). Boston: Allyn & Bacon.

Carlson, N. R. (1998). *Physiology of behavior* (6th ed.). Boston: Allyn & Bacon.

Carone, B. J., Harrow, M., & Westermeyer, J. F. (1991). Posthospital course and outcome in schizophrenia. *Archives of General Psychiatry, 48,* 247-253.

Carpenter, W. T., Jr., & Buchanan, R. W. (1994). Medical progress: Schizophrenia. *New England Journal of*

Medicine, 330, 681-690.

Carson, R. C. (1989). Personality. *Annual review of psychology, 40,* 227-248.

Carson, R. C., & Butcher, J. N. (1992). *Abnormal psychology and modern life* (9th ed.). New York: HarperCollins.

Carson, R. L. (1962). *Silent spring.* Boston: Houghton Mifflin.

Carson, T. P., & Carson, R. C. (1984). The affective disorders. In H. E. Adams & P. B. Sutker (Eds.), *Comprehensive handbook of psychpathology.* New York: Plenum.

Caruso, D. A. (1996). Maternal employment status, mother-infant interaction, and infant development in day care and non-day care groups. *Child and Youth Care Forum,* 25, 125-134.

Carver, C. S., & Gaines, J. G. (1987). Optimism, pessimism, and postpartum depression. *Cognitive Therapy and Research, 11,* 449-462.

Carver, C. S. & Scheier, M. F. (1999). Optimism. IN C. R. Snyder (Ed.), Coping: The psychology of what works. Pp. 182-204. New York: Oxford University Press.

Cash, T. F., & Derlega, V. J. (1978). The matching hypothesis: Physical attractiveness among same-sexed friends. *Personality and Social Psychology Bulletin, 4,* 240-243.

Cash, T. F., & Kilcullen, R. N. (1985). The eye of the beholder: Susceptibility to sexism and beautyism in the evaluation of managerial applicants. *Journal of Applied Social Psychology, 15,* 591-605.

Cattell, R. (1963). Theory of fluid and crystallized intelligence: A critical experiment. *Journal of Educational Psychology, 54,* 1-22.

Cattell, R. B. (1973). *Personality and mood by questionnaire.* San Francisco: Jossey-Bass.

Cattell, R. B. (1979). *The structure of personality in its environment.* New York: Springer.

Cavaliere, F. (1995). APA and CDC join forces to combat illness. *The APA Monitor, 26,* 1, 13.

Cavanaugh, J. C., & Park, D. C. (1993). Vitality for life: Psychological research for productive aging. *APS Observer, Special Issue: December.*

Ceci, S. J. (1994, May 5-7). *Childrens testimony: How reliable is it?* Invited address, Midwestern Psychological Association, Chicago, IL.

Ceci, S. J., & Bruck, M. (1996). *Jeopardy in the courtroom: A scientific analysis of childrens testimony.* Washington, D.C.: American Psychological Association.

Centers for Disease Control and Prevention (1996, August). Medical and lifestyle risk factors affecting fetal mortality. *Series 20 (31),* U. S. Department of Health and Human Services.

Centers for Disease Control (1999). Youth Risk Behavior Surveillance—United States, 1999. Downloaded from the World Wide Web, January 31, 2001. http://www.cdc.gov/mmwr/preview/mmwrhtml/ss4905a1.htm.

Centers for Disease Control (1993). Past month smokeless tobacco use among boys, grades 9-12—United States, 1993. Downloaded from the World Wide Web, January 31, 2001. http://www.cdc.gov/tobacco/research_data/spit/slt-boys.htm.

Centers for Disease Control (1999a). Youth Risk Behavior Surveillance—United States, 1999: State and Local Youth Risk Behavior Surveillance System Coordinators. Downloaded from the World Wide Web, January 30, 2001. http://www.cdc.gov/mmwr/preview/mmwrhtml/ss4095a1.htm.

Centers for Disease Control (1999c). Tobacco advertising and promotion fact sheet. Downloaded from the World Wide Web, January 30, 2001. http://www.cdc.gov/tobacco/sgr/sgr_2000/TobaccoAdvertising.pdf.

Centers for Disease Control (2000). Reducing children's use of tobacco: Fact sheets. Downloaded from the World Wide Web, January 30, 2001. http://www.cdc.gov/tobacco/youth.htm.

Cermak, L. S., & Craik, F. I. M. (Eds.). (1979). *Levels of processing in human memory.* Hillsdale, NJ: Erlbaum.

Cernoch, J. M., & Porter, R. H. (1985). Recognition of maternal axillary odors by infants. *Child Development, 56,* 1593-1598.

Chagnon, N. A. (1983). *Yanomamö: The fierce people* (3rd ed.). New York: Holt, Rinehart & Winston.

Chaiken, S., & Stangor, C. (1987). Attitudes and attitude change. *Annual Review of Psychology, 38,* 575-630.

Charney, D. S., Deutch, A. Y., Krystal, J. H., Southwick, S. M., & Davis, M. (1993). Psychobiological mechanisms of posttraumatic stress disorder. *Archives of General Psychiatry, 50,* 294-305.

Chase, M. H., & Morales, F. R. (1990). The atonia and myoclonia of active (REM) sleep. *Annual Review of Psychology, 41,* 557-584.

Chase, W. G., & Simon, H. A. (1973). The mind's eye in chess. In W. G. Chase (Ed.), *Visual information processing.* New York: Academic Press.

Chasnoff, I. J., Griffith, D. R., MacGregor, S., Dirkes, K., & Burns, K. (1989). Temporal patterns of cocaine use in pregnancy. *Journal of the American Medical Association, 261,* 1741-1744.

Cheesman, J., & Merikle, P. M. (1984). Priming with and without awareness. *Perception and Psychophysics, 36,* 387-395.

Cherney, I. D., & Ryalls, B. O. (1999). Gender-linked differences in the incidental memory of children and adults. *Journal of Experimental Child Psychology, 72,* 305-328.

Chi, M. T. H., & Glaser, R. (1985). Problem solving ability. In R. J. Sternberg (Ed.), *Advances in the psychology of human intelligence.* San Francisco: Freeman.

Chilman, C. S. (1980). Parent satisfactions, concerns, and goals for their children. *Family Relations, 29,* 339-346.

Chilman, C. S. (1983). Adolescent sexuality in a changing American society: *Social and psychological perspectives for the human services profession* (2nd ed.). New York: Wiley.

Chomsky, N. (1957). *Syntactic structures.* The Hague: Mouton.

Chomsky, N. (1965). *Aspects of a theory of syntax.* Cambridge, MA: Harvard University Press.

Chomsky, N. (1975). *Reflections on language.* New York: Pantheon Books.

Chomsky, N. (1986). *Knowledge of language: Its nature, origin, and use.* New York: Praeger.

Christiansen, K., & Knussmann, R. (1987). Androgen levels and components of aggressive behavior in men. *Hormones & Behavior, 21,* 170-180.

Chuang, H. T., Devins, G. M., Hunsley, J., & Gill, M. J. (1989). Psychosocial distress and well-being among gay and bisexual men with immunodeficiency virus infection. *American Journal of Psychiatry, 146,* 876-880.

Ciarrochi, J. V., Chan, A. Y. C., & Caputi, P. (2000). A critical evaluation of the emotional intelligence construct. Personality and individual differences. 28(3). 539-561.

CIBA-GEIGY. (1991). OCD: *When a habit isn't just a habit.* Pine Brook, NJ: CIBA-GEIGY Corporation.

Cinciripini, P. M., Cinciripini, L. G., Wallfisch, A., Haque, W., & Van Vunakis, H. (1996). Behavior therapy and the transdermal nicotine patch: Effects on cessation outcome, affect, and coping. *Journal of Consulting and Clinical Psychology, 64,* 314-323.

Clark, D. M., & Teasdale, J. D. (1985). Constraints on the effects of mood on memory. *Journal of Personality and Social Psychology,* 48, 1595-1608.

Clark, L. A., Watson, D., & Reynolds, S. (1995). Diagnosis and classification of psychopathology: Challenges to the current system and future directions. *Annual Review of Psychology, 46,* 121-153.

Clarkin, J. F., Pilkonis, P. A., & Magruder, K. M. (1996). Psychotherapy of depression: Implications for reform of the health care system. *Archives of General Psychiatry, 53,* 717-723.

Clarkson-Smith, L., & Hartley, A. A. (1989). Relationships between physical exercise and cognitive abilities in older adults. *Psychology and Aging, 4,* 183-189.

Clifford, B. R., & Lloyd-Bostock, S. (Eds.). (1983). *Evaluating witness evidence: Recent psychological research and new perspectives.* Norwood, NJ: Ablex.

Clifford, M. M., & Hatfield, E. (1973). The effect of physical attractiveness on teacher expectation. *Sociology of Education, 46,* 248-258.

Clinton, J. J. (1992). Acute pain management can be improved. *Journal of the American Medical Association, 267,* 2580.

Clore, G. L., & Byrne, D. (1974). A reinforcement-affect model of attraction. In T. L. Huston (Ed.), *Foundations of interpersonal attraction.* New York: Academic Press.

Coccaro, E. F., Kavoussi, R. J., & McNamee, B. (2000). Central neurotransmitter function in criminal aggression. In D. H. Fishbein, Ed. *The science, treatment, and prevention of antisocial behaviors.* (pp. 6-1-6-16). Kingston, NJ: Civic Research Institute.

Cohen, G. D. (1980). Fact sheet: Senile dementia (Alzheimer's disease). [No. ADM 80-929]. Washington, DC: Center for Studies of the Mental Health of the Aging.

Cohen, L. R., DeLoach, J., & Stauss, M. (1978). Infant visual perception. In J. Osofky (Ed.), *The handbook of infant development.* New York: Wiley.

Cohen, R. J., Montague, P., Nathanson, L. S., & Swerdlik, M. E. (1988). *Psychological testing: An introduction to tests and measurement.* Mountain View, CA: Mayfield Publishing Company.

Cohen, S. (1996). Psychological stress, immunity, and upper respiratory infections. *Current Directions in Psychological Science, 5,* 85-90.

Cohen, S., Doyle, W. J., Skoner, D. P., Fireman, P., Gwalyney, J., & Newsom, J. (1995). State and trait negative affect as predictors of objective and subjective symptoms of respiratory viral infections. *Journal of Personality and Social Psychology, 68,* 159-169.

Cohen, S., Evans, G. W., Krantz, D. S., Stokols, D., & Kelly, S. (1980). Aircraft noise and children: Longitudinal and cross-sectional evidence on the adaptation to noise and the effectiveness of noise abatement. *Journal of Personality and Social Psychology, 40,* 331-345.

Cohen, S., Evans, G. W., Stokols, D., & Krantz, D. S. (1986). *Behavior, health, and environmental stress.* New York: Plenum.

Cohen, S., & Lichtenstein, E. (1990). Perceived stress, quitting smoking, and smoking relapse. *Health Psychology, 9,* 466-478.

Cohen, S., Lichtenstein, E., Prochaska, J. O., Rossi, J. S., Gritz, E. R., Carr, C. R., et al. (1989). Debunking myths about self-quitting: Evidence from 10 prospective studies of persons who attempt to quit smoking by themselves. *American Psychologist, 44,* 1355-1365.

Cohen, S., & Williamson, G. M. (1991). Stress and infectious disease in humans. *Psychological Bulletin, 109,* 5-24.

Colby, A., & Kohlberg, L. (1984). Invariant sequence and internal consistency in moral judgment stages. In W. M. Kurtines & J. L. Gewitz (Eds.), *Morality, moral behavior, and moral development.* New York: Wiley.

Cole, K. N., Mills, P. E., Dale, P. S., & Jenkins. J. R. (1991). Effects of preschool integration for children with disabilities. *Exceptional Children,* **58,** 36-45.

Cole, J. O. (1988). Where are those new antidepressants we were promised? *Archives of General Psychiatry, 45,* 193-194.

Cole, R. E. (1979). *Work, mobility, and participation.* Berkeley: University of California Press.

Coleman, H. L. K., Wampold, B. E., & Casali, S. L. (1995). Ethnic minorities' ratings of ethnically similar and European-American counselors: A meta-analysis. *Journal of Counseling Psychology, 42,* 55-64.

Coles, R., & Stokes, G. (1985). *Sex and the American teenager.* New York: HarperCollins.

College Board. (1989). *College-bound seniors: 1989 SAT profile.* New York: College Entrance Examination Board.

Collins, A. M., & Loftus, E. F. (1975). A spreading activation theory of semantic processing. *Psychological Review, 82,* 407-428.

Collins, A. M., & Quillian, M. R. (1960). Retrieval time from semantic memory. *Journal of Verbal Learning and Verbal Behavior, 8,* 240-247.

Collins, W. A., & Gunnar, M. R. (1990). Social and personality development. *Annual Review of Psychology,* 41, 387-416.

Committee on an Aging society. (1986). *America's aging: Productive roles in an older society.* Washington, DC: National Academy Press.

Committee on Lesbian and Gay Concerns. (1991). Avoiding heterosexual bias in language. *American Psychologist,* 46, 973-974.

Compas, B. E., Hinden, B. R., & Gerhardt, C. A. (1995). Adolescent development: Pathways and processes of risk and resilience. *Annual Review of Psychology,* 46, 265-293.

Conger, J. J. (1991). *Adolescence and youth* (4th ed.). New York: HarperCollins.

Conger, J. J., & Peterson, A. C. (1984). *Adolescence and youth: Psychological development in a changing world.* New York: HarperCollins.

Conrad, R. (1963). Acoustic confusions and memory span for words. *Nature, 197,* 1029-1030.

Conrad, R. (1964). Acoustic confusions in immediate memory. *British Journal of Psychology, 55,* 75-84.

Consumer Reports. (1995, November). Mental health: Does therapy help?), 734-739.

Cooper, J., & Croyle, R. T. (1984). Attitudes and attitude change. *Annual Review of Psychology, 35,* 395-426.

Cooper, J., & Scher, S. J. (1992). Actions and attitudes: The role of responsibility and aversive consequences in persuasion. In T. Brock & S. Shavitt (Eds.), *The psychology of persuasion.* San Francisco: Freeman.

Cooper, J. R., Bloom, F. E., & Roth, R. E. (1996). *The biochemical basis of neuropharmacology* (Seventh Edition). New York: Oxford University Press.

Cooper, L., & Fazio, R. H. (1984). A new look at cognitive dissonance theory. In L. Berkowitz (Ed.), *Advances in experimental social psychology* (Vol. 17). San Diego: Academic Press.

Cooper, L. A., & Shepard, R. N. (1973). Chronometric studies of the rotation of mental images. In W. G. Chase (Ed.), *Visual information processing.* New York: Academic Press.

Cooper, M. K., Porter, J. A., Young, K. E., & Beachy, P. A. (1998). Teratogen-mediated inhibition of target tissue response to Shh signaling. *Science, 280,* 1603-1607.

Cordua, G. D., McGraw, K. O., & Drabman, R. S. (1979). Doctor or nurse: Children's perception of sex typed occupations. *Child Development, 50,* 590-593.

Coren, S. (1972). Subjective contours and apparent depth. *Psychological Review, 79,* 359-367.

Coren, S., & Girgus, J. S. (1978). *Seeing is deceiving: The psychology of visual illusions.* Hillsdale, NJ: Erlbaum.

Corkin, S. (1984). Lasting consequences of bilateral medial temporal lobectomy: Clinical course and experimental findings in H. M. *Seminars in Neurology, 4,* 249-259.

Cornblatt, B. A., & Erlenmeyer-Kimling, L. (1985). Global attention deviance as a marker of risk for schizophrenia: Specificity and predictive validity. *Journal of Abnormal Psychology, 94,* 470-486.

Costa, P. T., & McCrae, R. R. (1980). Still stable after all these years: Personality as a key to some issues in adulthood and old age. In P. B. Baltes & O. G. Brim, Jr. (Eds.), *Life-span development and behavior.* New York: Academic Press.

Costello, C. G. (1982). Fears and phobias in women: A community study. *Journal of Abnormal Psychology, 91,* 280-286.

Coté, T. R., Biggar, R. J., & Dannenberg, A. L. (1992). Risk of suicide among persons with AIDS: A national assessment. *Journal of the American Medical Association, 268,* 2066-2068.

Couce, M. E., Burguera B., Parisi J. E., Jensen M. D., & Lloyd R. V. (1997). Localization of leptin receptor in the human brain. *Neuroendocrinology,* 66, 145-50.

Coulter, W. A., & Morrow, H. W. (Eds.). (1978). *Adaptive behavior: Concepts and measurements.* New York: Grune & Stratton.

Council, J. R. (1993). Context effects in personality research. Current Directions in *Psychological Science, 2,* 3-34.

Courtwright, J. (1978). A laboratory investigation of groupthink. *Communication Monographs, 45,* 229-245.

Cowan, G., & Avants, S. K. (1988). Children's influence strategies: Structure, sex differences, and bilateral mother-child influences. *Child Development, 59,* 1303-1313.

Cowan, N. (1984). On short and long auditory stores. *Psychological Bulletin, 96,* 341-370.

Cowan, N. (1993). Activation, attention, and short-term memory. *Memory and Cognition, 21,* 162-167.

Cowan, N. (1994). Mechanisms of verbal short-term memory. Current Directions in *Psychological Science, 3,* 185-189.

Cowan, W. M. (1979). The development of the brain. In *The brain.* San Francisco: Freeman.

Cox, R. H. (1990). *Sport psychology: Concepts and applications.* Dubuque, IA: Brown.

Coyle, J. T., Price, D. L., & DeLong, M. H. (1983). Alzheimer's disease: A disorder of central cholinergic innervation. *Science, 219,* 1184-1189.

Coyne, J. C., & Downey, G. (1991). Social factors and psychopathology: Stress, social support, and coping processes. *Annual Review of Psychology, 42,* 401-425.

Coyne, J. C., Pepper, C. M., & Flynn, H. (1999). Significance of prior episodes of depression in two patient populations. *Journal of consulting and clinical psychology,* 67, 76-81.

Cozby, P. C. (1973). Self-disclosure: A literature review. *Psychological Bulletin, 79,* 73-91.

Craik, F. I. M. (1970). The fate of primary memory items in free recall. *Journal of Verbal Learning and Verbal Behavior, 9,* 143-148.

Craik, F. I. M., & Lockhart, R. S. (1972). Levels of processing: A framework for memory research. *Journal of Verbal Learning and Verbal Behavior, 11,* 671-684.

Craik, F. I. M., & Tulving, E. (1975). Depth of processing and the retention of words in episodic memory. *Journal of Experimental Psychology: General, 104,* 268-294.

Cramer, P. (2000). Defense mechanisms in psychology today:

Further processes for adaptation. *American psychologist.* 55, 637-646.

Cramer, R. E., McMaster, M. R., Bartell, P. A., & Dragna, M. (1988). Subject competence and minimization of the bystander effect. *Journal of Applied Social Psychology, 18,* 1133-1148.

Creekmore, C. R. (1984). Games athletes play. *Psychology Today, 19,* 40-44.

Creekmore, C. R. (1985). Cities won't drive you crazy. *Psychology Today, 19,* 46-53.

Crews, D. J., & Landers, D. M. (1987). A meta-analytic review of aerobic fitness and reactivity to psychosocial stressors. *Medicine and Science in Sport and Exercise 19,* 114-120.

Crockett, L. J., & Peterson, A. C. (1987). Pubertal status and psychosocial development: Findings from the Early Adolescence Study. In R. M. Lerner & T. T. Foch (Eds.), *Biological-psychosocial interactions in early adolescence: A life-span approach.* Hillsdale, NJ: Erlbaum.

Cromwell, R. L. (1993). Searching for the origins of schizophrenia. *Psychological Science, 4,* 276-279.

Cross-National Collaborative Group. (1992). The changing rate of major depression: Cross-national comparisons. *Journal of the American Medical Association, 268,* 3098-3105.

Crow, T. J. (1980). Molecular pathology of schizophrenia: More than one disease process? *The British Medical Journal, 280,* 66-68.

Crowder, R. G. (1993). Short-term memory: Where do we stand? *Memory and Cognition, 2,* 142-145.

Crutchfield, R. S. (1955). Conformity and character. *American Psychologist, 10,* 191-198.

Cruz, A. & Green, B. J. (2000). Thermal stimulation of taste. *Nature,* **403**, 889-892.

Cunningham, S. (1984). Genovese: 20 years later, few heed stranger's cries. *APA Monitor, 15,* 30.

Curtis, R. C., & Miller, K. (1986). Believing another likes or dislikes you: Behaviors making the beliefs come true. *Journal of Personality and Social Psychology, 51,* 284-290.

Cushner, K. (1990). Cross-cultural psychology and the formal classroom. In R. W. Brislin (Ed.), *Applied cross-cultural psychology.* Newbury Park, CA: Sage.

Cutler, W.B., Friedmann, E., & McCoy, N. L. (1998). Pheromonal influences on sociosexual behavior. *Archives of sexual behavior,* **27**, 1-13.

Cutler, W. B., Preti, g., Krieger, A., Huggins, G. R., Ramon Garcia, C., & Lawley, H. J. (1986). Human axillary secretions influence women's menstrual cycles: The role of donor extract from men. *Hormones and Behavior, 20,* 463-473.

Cutz, E., & Perrin, D. G. (1996). Maternal smoking and pulmonary neuroendicrine cells in sudden infant death syndrome. *Pediatrics,* 98, 668-672.

Dadler, H., & Gustavson, P. (1992). Competition by effective management of cultural diversity in the case of international construction projects. *International Studies of Management and Organizations, 22,* 81-93.

Dahlstrom, W. G. (1993). Tests: Small samples, large consequences. *American Psychologist, 48,* 393-399.

Damasio, A. R. (1997). Toward a neuropathology of emotion and mood. *Nature,* 386, 769-770.

Daniel, T. C. (1990). Measuring the quality of the natural environment: A psychophysical approach. *American Psychologist, 45,* 633-637.

Danmiller, J. L., & Stephens, B. R. (1988). A critical test of infant pattern preference models. *Child Development, 59,* 210-216.

Darley, J. M., & Fazio, R. H. (1980). Expectancy confirmation processes arising in the interaction sequence. *American Psychologist,* 35, 861-866.

Darley, J. M., & Schultz, T. R. (1990). Moral rules: Their content and acquisition. *Annual Review of Psychology, 41,* 525-556.

Darling, C. A., & Davidson, J. K. (1986). Coitally active university students: Sexual behaviors, concerns, and challenges. *Adolescence, 21,* 403-419.

Darwin, C. T., Turvey, M. T., & Crowder, R. G. (1972). An auditory analogue of the Sperling partial report procedure: Evidence for brief auditory storage. *Cognitive Psychology, 3,* 255-267.

Das, J. P. (1973). Cultural deprivation and cognitive competence. IN N. R. Ellis (Ed.), International review of research in mental retardation (Vol. 6), New York: Academic Press.

Dasen, P., & Heron, A. (1981). Cross-cultural tests of Piaget's theory. In H. C. Triandis & A. Heron (Eds.), *Handbook of cross-cultural psychology: Vol. 4. Developmental Psychology.* Boston: Allyn & Bacon.

Dasen, P. R., & de Ribaupierre, A. (1987). Neo-Piagetian theories: Cross-cultural and differential perspectives. I*nternational Journal of Psychology, 22,* 793-832.

Datan, N., Rodehever, D., & Hughes, F. (1987). Adult development and aging. *Annual Review of Psychology, 38,* 153-180.

Daubman, K. A., Heatherinton, L., & Ahn, Alicia (1992). Gender and the self-presentation of academic achievement. Sex Roles, 27, 187-204.

Davidson, G. C. (1998). Being bolder with the Boulder Model: The challenge of education and training in empirically supported treatments. *Journal of consulting and clinical psychology,* 66, 163-167.

Davison, G. C., & Neale, J. M. (1998). *Abnormal Psychology* (7th ed.). New York: John Wiley.

Davidoff, J. B. (1975). *Differences in visual perception: The individual eye.* New York: Academic Press.

Davidson, J. M., Smith, E. R., Rodgers, C. H., & Bloch, G. J. (1968). Relative thresholds of behavioral and somatic responses to estrogen. *Physiology and Behavior, 3,* 227-229.

Davidson, J. R. T., Hughs, D. C., George, L. K., & Blazer, D. G. (1994). The boundary of social phobia: Exploring the threshold. *Archives of General Psychiatry, 51,* 975-983.

Davis, K. (1985). Near and dear: Friendship and love compared. *Psychology Today, 19,* 22-30.

Davis, K. L., Mohs, R. C., Marin, D., et al. (1999). Cholinergic markers in elderly patients with early signs of Alzheimer disease. *Journal of the American Medical Association,* 281, 1401-1406.

Davis, L. E., & Cherns, A. B. (1975). *The quality of working life: Vol. I. Problems, prospects and the state of the art.* New York: Free Press.

Davies, M., Stankov, L., & Roberts, R. D. (1998). Emotional intelligence: In search of an elusive construct. *Journal of personality and social psychology,* 75(4), 989-1015.

de Cuevas, J. (1990, September/October). "No, she holded them loosely." *Harvard Magazine,* pp. 60-67.

DeAngelis, T. (1989). Behavior is included in report on smoking. *APA Monitor, 20,* 3-4.

DeAngelis, T. (1994). Ethnic-minority issues recognized in

DSM-IV. *Monitor, November,* p. 36.

deBoer, C. (1978). The polls: Attitudes toward work. *Public Opinion Quarterly, 42,* 414-423.

DeBono, K. G., & Harnish, R. J. (1988). Source expertise, source attractiveness, and the processing of persuasive information: A functional approach. *Journal of Personality and Social Psychology,* 55, 541-546.

DeCasper, A. J., & Fifer, W. P. (1980). Of human bonding: Newborns prefer their mother's voice. *Science, 208,* 1174-1176.

DeCasper, A. J., & Sigafoos, A. D. (1983). The intrauterine heartbeat: A potent reinforcer for newborns. *Infant Behavior and Development, 6,* 19-25.

Deffenbacher, J. L. (1988). Some recommendations and directions. *Counseling Psychology, 35,* 234-236.

DeGroot, A. D. (1965). *Thought and chance in chess.* The Hague: Mouton.

DeGroot, A. D. (1966). Perception and memory versus thought: Some old ideas and recent findings. In B. Kleinmuntz (Ed.), *Problem solving.* New York: Wiley.

DeJarlais, D. C., & Friedman, S. R. (1988). The psychology of preventing AIDS among intravenous drug users: A social learning conceptualization. *American Psychologist, 43,* 865-870.

Delaney-Black, V., Covington, C., Templin, T., Ager, J., Nordstrom-Klee, B., Martier, S., Leddick, L., Czerwinski, R. H., & Sokol, R. J. (2000). Teacher assessed behavior of children prenatally exposed to cocaine. *Pediatrics,* 106, 782-791.

Delgado, P. L., Price, L. H., Miller, H. L., Salomon, R. M., et al. (1994). Serotonin and the neurobiology of depression: Effects of tryptophan depletion in drug-free depressed patients. *Archives of general psychiatry,* 51, 865-874.

DeLongis, A., Folkman, S., & Lazarus, R. S. (1988). The impact of daily stress on health and mood: Psychological and social resources as mediators. *Journal of Personality and Social Psychology, 54,* 486-495.

Dembroski, T. M., & Costa, P. T., Jr. (1987). Coronary prone behavior: Components of the Type A pattern and hostility. *Journal of Personality, 55,* 211-235.

Dembroski, T. M., MacDougall, J. M., Williams, R. B., Haney, T. I., & Blumenthal, J. A. (1985). Components of Type A, hostility, and anger in relationship to angiographic findings. *Psychosomatic Medicine, 47,* 219-233.

Dement, W. C. (1974). *Some must watch while some must sleep.* San Francisco: Freeman.

De Radd, B. (1998). Five big, Big Five issues. *European psychologist,* 3(2), 113-124.

Deregowski, J. B. (1972). Pictorial perception and culture. *Scientific American, 83.*

Deregowski, J. B. (1973). Illusion and culture. In R. L. Gregory & G. H. Gombrich (Eds.), *Illusion in nature and art.* New York: Scribner's.

Derlega, V. J., Winstead, B. A., & Jones, W. H. (1991). *Personality: Contemporary theory and research.* Chicago: Nelson-Hall.

DeRubeis, R. J. & Crits-Christoph, P. (1998). Empirically supported individual and group psychotherapy treatments for adult mental disorders. *Journal of consulting and clinical psychology, 66,* 37-52.

Detterman, D. K., & Thompson, L. A. (1997). What is so special about special education? *American Psychologist,* **52,** 1082-1090.

Deutsch, J. A. (1973). The cholinergic synapse and the site of memory. In J. A. Deutsch (Ed.), *The physiological basis of memory.* New York: Academic Press.

deVilliers, J. G., & deVilliers, P. A. (1978). *Language acquisition.* Cambridge, MA: Harvard University Press.

Diamond, M., & Karlen, A. (1980). *Sexual decisions.* Boston: Litte, Brown.

Diamond, M. C., Lindner, B., Johnson, R., Bennett, E. L., & Rosenzweig, M. R. (1975). Differences in occipital cortical synapses from environmentally enriched, impoverished, and standard colony rats. *Journal of Neuroscience Research, 1,* 109-119.

Dibble, K. (1995). Hearing loss & music. *Journal of the audio engineering society,* **43(4),** 251-266

Digman, J. M. (1990). Personality structure: Emergence of the five-factor model. *Annual Review of Psychology, 41,* 417-440.

DiMatteo, M. R., & Friedman, H. S. (1988). *Social psychology and medicine.* Cambridge, MA: Oeleschlager, Gunn & Hain.

Dion, K. K. (1972). Physical attractiveness and evaluation of children's transgressions. *Journal of Personality and Social Psychology, 24,* 207-213.

Dion, K. K., Berscheid, E., & Walster (Hatfield), E. (1972). What is beautiful is good. *Journal of Personality and Social Psychology, 24,* 285-290.

Dirkes, M. A. (1978). The role of divergent production in the learning process. *American Psychologist, 33,* 815-820.

Dixon, N. F. (1971). *Subliminal perception: The nature of a controversy.* New York: McGraw-Hill.

Dixon, N. F. (1981). *Preconscious processing.* New York: Wiley.

Dobson, K. S. (1988). *Handbook of cognitive-behavioral therapies.* New York: Guilford.

Dodson, C., & Reisberg, D. (1991). Indirect testing of eyewitness memory: The (non) effect of misinformation. *Bulletin of the Psychonomic Society, 29,* 333-336.

Doll, R., & Peto, R. (1981). *The causes of cancer.* New York: Oxford University Press.

Dollard, J. Doob, L., Miller, N., Mowrer, O. H., & Sears, R. R. (1939). *Frustration and aggression.* New Haven, CT: Yale University Press.

Domjan, M. (1987). Animal learning comes of age. *American Psychologist, 42,* 556-564.

Donnenberg, G. R., & Hoffman, L. W. (1988). Gender differences in moral development. *Sex Roles, 18,* 701-717.

Doty, R. Y. (1986). Gender and endocrine-related influences on human olfactory perception. In H. Meiselman & R. S. Rivlin (Eds.), *Clinical measurement of taste and smell.* New York: Macmillan.

Douglass, H. M., Moffitt, T. E., Dar, R., McGee, R., & Silva, P. (1995). Obsessive-compulsive disorder in a birth cohort of 18-year-olds: Prevalence and predictors. *Journal of the American Academy of Child and Adolescent Psychiatry,* **34,** 1424-1431.

Dovidio, J. F., Allen, J. L., & Schroeder, D. A. (1990). Specificity of empathy-induced helping: Evidence for altruistic motivation. *Journal of Personality and Social Psychology, 59,* 249-260.

Doweiko, H. E. (1993). *Concepts of chemical dependency* (2nd ed.). Pacific Grove, CA: Brooks/Cole.

Drakeley, R. J., Herriot, P., & Jones, A. (1988). Biographical data, training success and turnover. *Journal of Occupational Psychology,* 61, 145-152.

Drews, C. D., & Murphy, C. C. (1996). The relationship between idiopathic mental retardation and maternal smoking during pregnancy. *Pediatrics*, 97, 547-553.

Duffy, E. (1962). *Activation and behavior.* New York: Wiley.

Duncan, J. (1985). Two techniques for investigating perception without awareness. *Perception and Pychophysics, 38,* 296-298.

Dunham, R. B. (1979). Job design and redesign. In S. Kerr (Ed.), *Organizational behavior.* Columbus, OH: Grid.

Dunker, K. (1945). On problem solving. *Psychological Monographs, 58 (Whole No. 27).*

Dunnette, M. D., & Borman, W. C. (197). *Personnel selection and classification systems. Annual Review of Psychology, 30,* 477-525.

Dupont, R. M., Jernigan, T. L., Heindel, W., Butters, N., Shafer, K., Wilson, T., Hesselin, J., & Gillin, C. (1995). Magnetic resonance imaging and mood disorders: Localization of white matter and other subcortical abnormalities. *Archives of General Psychiatry,* 52, 747-755.

Durand, V. M. & Barlow, D. H. (2000). *Abnormal psychology: An introduction.* Belmont, CA: Wadsworth.

Dweck, C. S. (1986). Motivational processes affecting learning. *American Psychologist, 41,* 1040-1048.

Dywan, J., & Bowers, K. (1983). The use of hypnosis to enhance recall. *Science, 222,* 184-185.

Eagly, A. H. (1987). *Sex differences in social behavior: A social-role interpretation.* Hillsdale, NJ: Lawrence Erlbaum Associates.

Eagly, A. H. (1995). The science and politics of comparing women and men. *American Psychologist, 50,* 145-158.

Eagly, A. H., & Chaiken, S. (1992). *The psychology of attitudes.* San Diego: Harcourt Brace Jovanovich.

Eagly, A. H., & Steffen, V. J. (1986). Gender and aggressive behavior: A meta-analytic review of the social psychological literature. *Psychological Bulletin, 100,* 309-330.

Eagly, A. H., Wood, W., & Fishbaugh, L. (1981). Sex differences in conformity: Surveillance by the group as a determinant of male conformity. *Journal of Personality and Social Psychology, 40,* 384-394.

Eaker, E. D., Packard, B., Wenger, N. K., et al. (1988). Coronary heart disease in women. *American Journal of Cardiology, 61,* 641-644.

Eaker, E. D., Pinsky, J., & Castelli, W. P. (1992). Myocardial infarction and coronary death among women: Psychosocial predictors from a 20-year follow-up on women in the Framingham study. *American Journal of Epidemiology, 135,* 854-864.

Early, P. C. (1986). Supervisors and shop stewards as sources of contextual information in goal-setting: A comparison of the U.S. with England. *Journal of Applied Psychology, 71,* 111-118.

Early, P. C. (1989). Social loafing and collectivism: A comparison of the United States and the People's Republic of China. *Administrative Science Quarterly, 34,* 555-581.

Eating Disorders Association (1999). Anorexia nervosa. Retrieved on June 19, 2001 from the World Wide Web: http://www.uq.net.au/eda/documents/anorexia.html

Eaton, W. O., & Enns, L. R. (1986). Sex differences in human motor activity level. *Psychological Bulletin, 100,* 19-28.

Eaton, W. W., Thara, R., Federman, B., Melton, B., & Liang, K. (1955). Structure and course of positive and negative symptoms in schizophrenia. *Archives of General Psychiatry, 52,* 127-134.

Eaton, W. W., Anthony, J. C., Gallo, J., Cai, G., et al. (1997). Natural history of diagnostic interview schedule/DSM-IV major depression: The Baltimore Epidemiological Catchment Area follow-up. *Archives of general psychiatry,* 54, 993-999.

Ebbinghaus, H. E. (1885/1964). *Memory: A contribution to experimental psychology.* New York: Dover.

Ebstein, R. P., Novick, O., Umansky, R., Priel, B., et al. (1996). Dopamine D4 Receptor (D4DR) Exon III polymorphism associated with the human personality trait of novelty seeking. *Nature Genetics, 12,* 78-80.

Eccles, J., Wigfield, A., Harold, R. D., & Blumenfeld, P. (1993). Age and gender differences in children's self- and task perceptions during elementary school. *Child Development, 64,* 830-847.

Edelman, G. (1992). *Bright air, brilliant fire: On the matter of mind.* New York: Basic Books.

Edmands, M. S. (1993). Caring for students with eating disorders on college and university campuses. *Advances in Medical psychotherapy, 6,* 59-75.

Edwards, C. P. (1977). The comparative study of the development of moral judgment and reasoning. In R. L. Munroe, R. Munroe, & B. B. Whiting (Eds.), *Handbook of cross-cultural human development.* New York: Garland.

Edwards, C. P. (1981). The development of moral reasoning in cross-cultural perspective. In R. H. Munroe, R. L. Munroe, & B. B. Whiting (Eds.), *Handbook of cross-cultural human development.* New York: Garland.

Edwards, L. K., & Edwards, A. L. (1991). A principal components analysis of the Minnesota Multiphasic Personality Inventory Factor Scales. *Journal of Personality and Social Psychology, 60,* 766-772.

Egeland, J. A., Gerhard, D. S., Pauls, D. L., Suddex, J. N., Kidd, K. K., Allen, C. R., Hostetter, A. M., & Housman, D. E. (1987). Bipolar affective disorders linked to DNA markers on chromosome 11. *Nature, 325,* 783-787.

Egeth, H. E. (1993). What do we not know about eyewitness identification? *American Psychologist, 48,* 577-580.

Eich, E. (1995). Searching for mood dependent memory. *Psychological Science, 6,* 67-75.

Eich, E., MacCauley, D., & Ryan, L. (1994). Mood dependent memory for events of the personal past. *Journal of Experimental Psychology: General, 123,* 201-215.

Eich, J. E., Weingartner, H., Stillman, R. C., & Gillan, J. C. (1975). State-dependent accessibility of retrieval cues in the retention of a categorized list. *Journal of Verbal Learning and Verbal Behavior,* 14, 408-417.

Eisenberg, N. & Lennon, R. (1983). Sex differences in empathy and related capacities. *Psychological Bulletin, 94,* 100-131.

Eisenberg, N., & Miller, P. A. (1987). The relation of empathy to prosocial and related behaviors. *Psychological Bulletin, 101,* 91-119.

Ekman, P. (1972). Universals and cultural differences in facial expression of emotion. In J. K. Cole (Ed.), *Nebraska symposium on motivation.* Lincoln: University of Nebraska Press.

Ekman, P. (1973). Cross-cultural studies in facial expression. In P. Ekman (Ed.), *Darwin and facial expressions: A century of research in review.* New York: Academic Press.

Ekman, P. (1992). Facial expression and emotion: New findings, new questions. *Psychological Science, 3,* 34-38.

Ekman, P. (1992a). An argument for basic emotions. *Journal of Cognition and Emotion, 6,* 169-200.

Ekman, P. (1993). Facial expression and emotion. *American Psychologist*, 48, 384-392.

Ekman, P., & Friesen, W. V. (1971). Constants across cultures in the face and emotion. *Journal of Personality and Social Psychology,* 17, 124-129.

Ekman, P., Friesen, W. V., O'Sullivan, M., Diacoyanni-Tarlatzis, I., Krause, R., et al. (1987). Universals and cultural differences in the judgment of facial expressions of emotion. *Journal of Personality and Social Psychology, 53,* 712-717.

Ekman, P., Levenson, R. W., & Friesen, W. V. (1983). Autonomic nervous system activity distinguishes among emotions. *Science, 221,* 1208-1210.

Elkis, H., Friedman, L., Wise, A., & Meltzer, H. Y. (1995). Meta-analysis of studies of ventricular enlargement and cortical sulcal prominence in mood disorders. *Archives of General Psychiatry, 52,* 735-746.

Ellis, A. (1970). *Reason and emotion in psychotherapy.* Secaucus, NJ: Stuart.

Ellis, A. (1973). *Humanistic psychotherapy: The rational-emotive approach.* New York: McGraw-Hill.

Ellis, A. (1987). The impossibility of achieving consistently good mental health. *American Psychologist, 42,* 364-375.

Ellis, A. (1991). How can psychological treatment aim to be briefer and better? The rational-emotive approach to brief therapy. In K. N. Anchor (Ed.), *Handbook of medical psychotherapy.* Toronto: Hogrefe & Huber.

Ellis, A. (1995). Rational emotive behavior therapy. In R. J. Corsini & D. Wedding (Eds.). *Current psychotherapies,* Fifth Edition. (pp. 162-196). Itasca, IL: Peacock.

Ellis, A. (1997). Using rational emotive behavior therapy techniques to cope with disability. *Professional psychology: Research and practice,* 28, 17-22.

Ellis, C. M., Lemmens, G., & Parkes, J. D. (1996). Melatonin and insomnia. *Journal of Sleep Research, 5,* 61-65.

Ellis, L., & Ames, M. A. (1987). Neurohormonal functioning and sexual orientation: A theory of homosexuality-heterosexuality. *Psychological Bulletin, 101,* 233-258.

Endler, N. S., Cox, B. J., Parker, J. D. A., & Bagby, R. M. (1992). Self-reports of depression and state-trait-anxiety: Evidence for differential assessment. *Journal of Personality and Social Psychology,* 63, 832-838.

Epstein, L. H., & Cluss, P. A. (1982). A behavioral medicine perspective on adherence to long-term medical regimes. *Journal of Consulting and Clinical Psychology, 50,*

950-971.

Epstein, S. (1979). The stability of behavior: On predicting most of the people much of the time. *Journal of Personality and Social Psychology, 37,* 1097-1126.

Epstein, S. (1994). Integration of the cognitive and the psychodynamic unconscious. *American Psychologist, 49,* 709-724.

Erdelyi, M. H. (1985). *Psychoanalysis: Freud's cognitive psychology.* New York: Freeman.

Erdelyi, M. H. (1992). Psychodynamics and the unconscious. *American Psychologist, 47,* 784-787.

Erdelyi, M. H., & Goldberg, B. (1979). Let's not sweep repression under the rug: Toward a cognitive psychology of repression. In J. F. Kihlstrom & F. J. Evans (Eds.), *Functional disorders of memory.* Hillsdale, NJ: Erlbaum.

Erez, M., & Early, P. C. (1987). Comparative analysis of goal-setting strategies across cultures. *Journal of Applied Psychology, 72,* 658-665.

Erez, M., & Early, P. C. (1993). *Culture, self-identity, and work.* New York: Oxford University Press.

Erez, M., & Zidon, I. (1984). Effect of goal acceptance on the relationship of goal difficulty to performance. *Journal of Applied Psychology, 69,* 69-78.

Ericsson, K. A., & Chase, W. G. (1982). Exceptional memory. *American Scientist*, 70, 607-615.

Erikson, E. H. (1963). *Childhood and society.* New York: Norton.

Erikson, E. H. (1965). *The challenge of youth.* Garden City, NY: Doubleday (Anchor Books).

Erikson, E. H. (1968). *Identity: Youth and crisis.* New York: Norton.

Erlenmeyer-Kimling, L. (1968). Studies on the offspring of two schizophrenic parents. In D. Rosenthal & S. S. Kety (Eds.), *The transmission of schizophrenia.* Elmsford, NY: Pergamon Press.

Erwin, E. (1980). Psychoanalytic therapy: The Eysenck argument. *American Psychologist, 35,* 435-443.

Erowid (2001). MDMA basics. Downloaded from the World Wide Web, February 1, 2001.http://www.erowid.org/chemicals/mdma/mdma_basics.shtml.

Etaugh, C. (1980). Effects of nonmaternal care on children. *American Psychologist, 35,* 309-316.

Evans, D. A., Funkenstein, H. H., Albert, M. S. et al. Prevalence of Alzheimer's disease in a community population of older persons: Higher than previously reported. *Journal of the American Medical Association*, 262, 2551-2556.

Evans, G. W., & Howard, R. B. (1973). Personal space. *Psychological Bulletin, 80,* 334-344.

Evans, G. W., Hygge, S., & Bullinger, M. (1995). Chronic noise and psychological stress. *Psychological Science, 6,* 333-338.

Evans, G. W. & Lepore, S. J. (1993). Nonauditory effects of noise on children. *Children's Environment, 10,* 31-51.

Evans, R. I., Rozelle, R. M., Maxwell, S. E., Raines, B. E., et al. (1981). Social modeling films to deter smoking in adolescents: Results of a three-year field investigation. *Journal of Applied Psychology, 66,* 399-414.

Eveleth, P., & Tanner, J. (1978). *Worldwide variations in human growth.* New York: Cambridge University Press.

Eysenck, H. J. (1952). The effects of psychotherapy.: An evaluation. *Journal of Consulting Psychology, 16,* 319-324.

Eysenck, H. J. (1960). *Behavior therapy and neurosis.* London: Pergamon.

Fackelman, K. A. (1992). Anatomy of Alzheimer's: Do immune proteins help destroy brain cells? *Science News, 142,* 394-396.

Fadiman, J., & Frager, R. (1994). *Personality and personal growth* (3rd ed.). New York: HarperCollins.

Fagan, J. F., & Singer, L. T. (1979). The role of single feature differences in infant recognition of faces. *Infant Behavior and Development, 2,* 39-45.

Fahn, S. (1992). Fetal-tissue transplants in Parkinson's disease. *New England Journal of Medicine, 327,* 1589-1590.

Fairburn, C. G., Jones, R. Peveler, R. C., Hope, R. A., & O'Conner, M. (1993). Psychotherapy and bulimia nervosa. *Archives of General Psychiatry, 50,* 419-428.

Fairburn, C. G., & Wilson, G. T. (Eds.). (1993). *Binge eating: Nature, assessment and treatment.* New York: Guilford.

Fairburn, C. G., Norman, P. A., Welch, S. L., O'Conner, M. E., Doll, H. A., & Peveler, R. C. (1995). A prospective study of outcome in bulimia nervosa and the long-term effects of three psychological treatments. *Archives of General Psychiatry, 52,* 304-312.

Falbo, T., & Peplau, L. A. (1980). Power strategies in intimate relationships. *Journal of Personality and Social Psychology,38,* 618-628.

Fantz, R. L. (1961). The origin of form perception. *Scientific American, 204,* 66-72.

Fantz, R. L. (1963). Pattern vision in newborn infants. *Science, 140,* 296-297.

Farlow, M. R. (2000). Therapeutic advances for Alzheimer's disease and other dementias. *The Medical Education Collaborative.* Golden, Colorado.

Farrell, M. P., & Rosenberg, S. D. (1981). *Men at midlife.* Boston: Auburn House.

Fast, J. (1970). *Body language.* New York: M. Evans.

Fazio, R. H. (1989). On the power and functionality of attitudes: The role of attitude accessibility. In A. R. Pratkanis, S. J. Breckler, & A. G. Greenwald (Eds.), *Attitude structure and function.* Hillsdale, NJ: Erlbaum.

Fazio, R. H. (1990). Multiple processes by which attitudes guide behavior. The MODE model as an integrative framework. *Advances in Experimental Psychology, 23,* 75-109.

Feeney, J. A., & Noller, P. (1990). Attachment style as a predictor of adult romantic relationships. *Journal of Personality and Social Psychology, 58,* 281-291.

Feighner, J. P. (1997). Are the new antidepressants Venlafaxine and Nefazodone really different? *The Harvard Mental Health Letter, 13(8),* p. 8.

Fein, G. G., Schwartz, P. M., Jacobson, S. W., & Jacobson, J. L. (1983). Environmental toxins and behavior development. *American Psychologist, 38,* 1188-1197.

Feingold, A. (1993). Cognitive gender differences: A developmental perspective. *Sex Roles, 29,* 91-112.

Feingold, A. (1994). Gender differences in personality: A meta-analysis. *Psychological Bulletin, 116,* 429-456.

Feingold, A. (1995). The additive effects of differences in central tendency and variability are important in comparisons between groups. *American Psychologist, 50,* 5-13.

Feist, S. C. (1993). Marriage and family therapy: Theories and applications. *Directions in Clinical Psychology, 3,* 4.3-4.24.

Feldman, S. S., & Elliott, G. R. (Eds.). (1990). *At the threshold: The developing adolescent.* Cambridge, MA: Harvard University Press.

Feng, A. S. & Ratnam, R. (2000). Neural basis of hearing in real-world situations. *Annual review of psychology,* **51,** 699-725.

Fenker, R. M., & Lambiotte, J. G. (1987). A performance enhancement program for a college football team: One incredible season. *The Sport Psychologist, 1,* 224-236.

Feshbach, S., Weiner, B., & Bohart, A. (1996). *Personality* (4th ed.). Lexington, MA: D. C. Heath & Co.

Festinger, L. (1957). *A theory of cognitive dissonance.* Stanford, CA: Stanford University Press.

Festinger, L., & Carlsmith, J. M. (1959). Cognitive consequences of forced compliance. *Journal of Abnormal and Social Psychology,* 58, 203-210.

Festinger, L., Riecken, H. W., & Schachter, S. (1993). When prophecy fails. In A. Pines & C. Maslach (Eds.), *Experiencing social psychology: readings and projects (Third Edition).* New York: McGraw Hill.

Festinger, L., Schachter, S., & Back, K. (1950). *Social processes in informal groups: A study of human factors in housing.* New York: HarperCollins.

Fielding, J. E., & Phenow, K. J. (1988). Health effects of involuntary smoking. *New England Journal of Medicine, 319,* 1452-1460.

Finchilescu, G. (1994). Intergroup attributions in minimal groups. *Journal of Social Psychology, 2,* 1-3.

Fink, M. (1997). What is the role of ECT in the treatment of mania? *The Harvard Mental Health Letter, June,* p. 8.

Finnegan, L. P. (1982). Outcome of children born to women dependent upon narcotics. In B. Stimmel (Ed.), *The effects of maternal alcohol and drug abuse on the newborn.* New York: Haworth.

Fiore, M. C., Novotny, T. E., Pierce, J. P., Hatzlandreu, E. J., Patel, K. M., & Davis, R. M. (1989). Trends in cigarette smoking in the United States: The changing influence of gender and race. *Journal of the American Medical Association, 261,* 49-55.

Fischhoff, B. (1990). Psychology and public policy: Tool or toolmaker? *American Psychologist, 45,* 647-653.

Fishbein, M., & Ajzen, I. (1975). *Belief, attitude, intention, and behavior: An introduction to theory and research.* Reading, MA: Addison-Wesley.

Fisher, A. C. (1977). Sport personality assessment: Facts, fallacies, and perspectives. *Motor Skills: Theory into*

Practice, 1, 87-97.

Fisher, J. D., & Fisher, W. A. (1992). Changing AIDS-risk behavior. *Psychological Bulletin, 111,* 455-474.

Fisher, S. & Greenberg, R. P. (1977). *The scientific credibility of Freud's theories and therapy.* New York: Basic Books.

Fishman, J. (1987). Type A on trial. *Psychology Today, 21,* 42-50.

Fitzgerald, L. (1993). Sexual harassment: Violence against women in the workplace. *American Psychologist, 48,* 1070-1076.

Flament, M. F., Rapoport, J. L., Berg, C. J., Sceery, W., Kilts, C., Mellstrom, B., & Linnoila, M. (1985). Clomipramine treatment of childhood obsessive-compulsive disorder: A double-blind study. *Archives of General Psychiatry, 42,* 977-983.

Flament, M. F., Whitaker, A., Rapoport, J. L., Davies, M., Berg, C. Z., Kalikow, K., Sceery, W., & Shaffer, D. (1988). Obsessive-compulsive disorder in adolescence: An epidemiologic study. *Journal of the American Academy of Child and Adolescent Psychiatry, 27,* 289-296.

Flavell, J. H. (1977). *Cognitive development.* Englewood Cliffs, NJ: Prentice Hall.

Flavell, J. H. (1982). On cognitive development. *Child Development, 53,* 1-10.

Fleishman, E. A., & Mumford, M. D. (1991). Evaluating classifications of job behavior: A construct of the ability requirement scales. *Personnel Psychology, 44,* 523-575.

Flexser, A. J., & Tulving, E. (1982). Priming and recognition failure. *Journal of Verbal Learning and Verbal Behavior, 21,* 237-248.

Flowers, M. (1977). A laboratory test of some implications of Janis groupthink hypothesis. *Journal of Personality and Social Psychology, 35,* 888-896.

Flynn, J. P., Vanegas, H., Foote, W., & Edwards, S. (1970). Neural mechanisms involved in a cat's attack on a rat. In R. E. Whalen, R. F. Thompson, M. Verzeano, & N. M. Weinberger (Eds.), *The neural control of behavior.* New York: Academic Press.

Foa, E. B. (1995). How do treatments for obsessive-compulsive disorder compare? *The Harvard Mental Health Letter, 12,* 8.

Foa, E. B., & Riggs, D. S. (1995). Posttraumatic stress disorder following assault: Theoretical considerations and empirical findings. *Current Directions in Psychological Science, 4,* 61-65.

Folkman, S. (1984). Personal control and stress and coping processes: A theoretical analysis. *Journal of Personality and Social Psychology, 46,* 839-852.

Folkman, S. & Moskowitz, J. T. (2000). Stress, positive emotion, and coping. *Current directions in psychological science, 9,* 115-118.

Folstein, S. E., & Rutter, M. L. (1977). Genetic influences and infantile autism. *Nature, 265,* 726-728.

Folstein, S. E., & Rutter, M. L. (1988). Autism: Familial aggregation and genetic implications. *Journal of Autism and Development Disorders, 18,* 3-30.

Fontenot, N. A. (1993). Effects of training in creativity and creative problem finding upon business people. *Journal of Social Psychology,* **133,** 11-22.

Food and Drug Administration (1995). FDA says tobacco and nicotine are drugs. Federal Register, 60. Downloaded from the World Wide Web, January 31, 2001. http://www.well-web.com/SMOKING/fdadrug.htm.

Ford, C. E., Wright, R. A., & Haythornwaite, J. (1985). Task performance and magnitude of goal valence. *Journal of Research in Personality, 19,* 253-260.

Ford, M. R., & Lowery, C. R. (1986). Gender differences in moral reasoning: A comparison of justice and care orientations. *Journal of Personality and Social Psychology, 4,* 777-783.

Foulkes, D. (1966). *The Psychology of Sleep.* New York: Charles Scribner.

Fowler, C. A., Wolford, G., Slade, R., & Tassinary, L. (1981). Lexical access with and without awareness. *Journal of Experimental Psychology: General, 110,* 341-362.

Fowler, R. D. (1992). Report to the Chief Executive Officer: A year of building for the future. *American Psychologist, 47,* 876-883.

Fowles, D. G. (1990). *A profile of older Americans: 1989.* Washington, DC: American Association of Retired Persons.

Fox, R., Aslin, R. N., Shea, S. L., & Dumais, S. T. (1980). Stereopsis in human infants. *Science, 207,* 323-324.

France, K. G. (1992). Behavior characteristics and security in sleep-disturbed infants treated with extinction. *Journal of Pediatric Psychology, 17,* 467-475.

France, K. G., & Hudson, S. M. (1993). Management of infant sleep disturbance: A review. *Clinical Psychology Review, 13,* 635-647.

Franco, P., Groswasser, J., Hassid, S., Lanquart, J. P., Scaillet, S., & Kahn, A. (1999). Prenatal exposure to cigarette smoking is associated with a decreased in arousal in infants. *Journal of Pediatrics, 135,* 34-38.

Frank, D. A., & McCarten, K. M. (1999). Level of in utero cocaine exposure and neonatal ultrasound findings. *Pediatrics,* 104, 1101-1105.

Frank, E., Kupfer, D. J., Perel, J. M., Cornes, C., Jarrett, D. B., et al. (1990). Three-year outcomes for maintenance therapies in recurrent depression. *Archives of General Psychiatry, 47,* 1093-1099.

Frankel, F. H. (1993). Adult reconstruction of childhood events in the multiple personality literature. *American Journal of Psychiatry, 150,* 954-958.

Frankenburg, W. K., & Dodds, J. B. (1967). The Denver Developmental Screening Test. *Journal of Pediatrics, 71,* 181-191.

Frazier, T. M., David, G. H., Goldstein, H., & Goldberg, I. D. (1961). Cigarette smoking and prematurity. *American Journal of Obstetrics and Gynecology, 81,* 988-996.

Frederickson, P. A. (1987). The relevance of sleep disorders medicine to psychiatric practice. *Psychiatric Annals, 17,* 91-100.

Free, M. L., & Oei, T. P. S. (1989). Biological and psychological processes in the treatment and maintenance of depression. *Clinical Psychology Review, 9,* 653-688.

Freed, C. R., Breeze, R. E., Rosenberg, N. L., et al. (1992). Survival of implanted fetal dopamine cells and neurologic improvement 12 to 46 months after transplantation for Parkinson's disease. *New England Journal of Medicine, 327,* 1549-1555.

Freedman, D. X. (1984). Psychiatric epidemiology counts. *Archives of General Psychiatry, 41,* 931-934.

Freedman, J. L. (1975). *Crowding and behavior.* New York: Viking Press.

Freud, A. (1958). *Adolescence: Psychoanalytic study of the child.* New York: Academic Press.

Freud, S. (1943). *A general introduction to psychoanalysis.* Garden City, NY: Garden City Publishing.

Freud, S. (1933). *New introductory lectures on psychoanaly-sis: Standard edition.* New York: Norton.

Freud, S. (1900). The interpretation of dreams. In J. Strachey (Ed.), *The complete psychological works of Sigmund Freud.* London: Hogarth Press.

Freud, S. (1900a). *The interpretation of dreams* (3rd ed) (A. A. Brill, Trans). Retrieved October 5, 2000, from the World Wide Web: http://www.yorku.ca/dept/psych/ classics/Freud/Dreams/ index.htm

Freud, S. (1900b/1952). *On dreams* (J. Starchey, Trans.). New York: W. W. Norton.

Freud, S. (1910). The origin and development of psychoanalysis. *American Journal of Psychology, 21,* 181-218. Retrieved October 5, 2000, from the World Wide Web: http://www. yorku.ca/dept/psych/classics/Freud/Origin/ index.htm

Fribourg, S. (1982). Cigarette smoking and sudden infant death syndrome. *Journal of Obstetrics and Gynecology, 142,* 934-941.

Fried, P. A. (1993). Prenatal exposure to tobacco and marijuana: Effects during pregnancy, infancy, and early childhood. *Clinical Obstetrics and Gynecology, 36,* 319-337.

Fried, P. A., & Watkinson, B. (2000). Visuoperceptual functioning differs in 9 to 12-year olds prenatally exposed to cigarettes and marijuana. *Neurotoxicology and Teratology,* 22, 11-20.

Friedman, H. S., & Booth-Kewley, S. (1987). The "disease-prone personality": A meta-analytic review of the construct. *American Psychologist, 42,* 539-555.

Friedman, H. S., Hawley, P. H., & Tucker, J. S. (1994). Personality, health and longevity. *Current Directions in Psychological Science,* 3, 37-41.

Friedman, H. S., Tucker, J. S., Schwartz, J. E., Tomlinson-Keasey, C., Martin, L. R., Wingard, D. L., & Cirqui, M. H. (1995). Psychosocial and behavioral predictors of longevity: The aging and death of the "Termites." *American Psychologist, 50,* 69-78.

Friedman, M., & Rosenman, R. (1959). Association of specific overt behavior patterns with blood and cardiovascular findings. *Journal of the American Medical Association, 169,* 1286.

Friedman, M. I., & Stricker, E. M. (1976). The physiological psychology of hunger: A physiological perspective. *Psychological Review,* 83, 409-431.

Friedman, S. (1972). Habituation and recovery of visual response in the alert human newborn. *Journal of Experimental Child Psychology, 13,* 339-349.

Frijda, N. H. (1988). The laws of emotion. *American Psychologist,* 43, 349-358.

Funder, D. C. (1996). *The Personality Puzzle.* New York: W. W. Norton.

Furstenberg, F. F., Brooks-Gunn, J., & Chase-Lansdale, L. (1989). Teenaged pregnancy and childbearing. *American Psychologist, 44,* 313-320.

Furumoto, L., & Scarborough, E. (1986). Placing women in the history of psychology: The first American women psychologists. *American Psychologist, 41,* 35-42.

Gabrena, W., Wang, Y., Latané, B. (1985). Social loafing on an optimizing task: Cross-cultural differences among Chinese and Americans. *Journal of Cross-cultural Psychology, 16,* 223-242.

Gabrieli, J. D. E. (1998). Cognitive neuroscience of memory. *Annual Review of Psychology, 48,* 87-115.

Gabrieli, J. D. E., Brewer, J. B., Desmond, J. E., & Glover, G. H. (1997). Separate neural bases of two fundamental memory processes in the human medial temporal lobe. *Science, 276,*264-266.

Gagné, R. M. (1984). Learning outcomes and their effects: Useful categories of human performance. *American Psychologist, 39,* 377-385.

Gagné , G. G. Jr., Furman M. J., Carpenter, L. L., & Price, L. H. (2000). Efficacy of continuation ECT and antidepressant drugs compared to long-term antidepressants alone in depressed patients. *American Journal of Psychiatry,* **157,** 1969-1965.

Galanter, E. (1962). Contemporary psychophysics. In R. Brown et al. (Eds.), *New directions in psychology.* New York: Holt, Rinehart & Winston.

Galbaud du Fort, G., Newman, S. C., & Bland, R. C. (1993). Psychiatric comorbidity and treatment seeking: Sources of selection bias in the study of clinical populations. *Journal of Nervous and Mental Disorders, 181,* 467-474.

Gallagher, J. J., & Ramey, C. T. (1987). *The malleability of children.* Baltimore: Paul H. Brooks.

Galton, F. (1879). *Hereditary genius: An inquiry into its laws and consequences.* Englewood Cliffs, NJ: Prentice-Hall.

Gans, J. E., & Blyth, D. A. (1990). American adolescents: How healthy are they? *AMA Profiles of Adolescent Health series.* Chicago: American Medical Association.

Garbarino, J. (1985). *Adolescent development: An ecological perspective.* Columbus, OH: Merrill.

Garcia, J., Ervin, F. R., & Koelling, R. A. (1966). Learning with prolonged delay of reinforcement. *Psychonomic Science, 5,* 121-122.

Garde, M. M., & Cowey, A. (2000) Deaf hearing: Unacknowledged detection of auditory stimuli in a patient with cerebral deafness. *Cortex, 36,* 71-80.

Gardner, H. (1983). *Frames of mind: The theory of multiple intelligences.* New York: Basic Books.

Gardner, H. (1993a). *Multiple intelligences: The theory in practice.* New York: Basic Books.

Gardner, H. (1993b). *Creating minds.* New York: Basic Books.

Gardner, H., & Hatch, T. (1989). Multiple intelligences go to school: Educational implications of the theory of multiple intelligences. *Educational Researcher, 18,* 6.

Gardner, M. (1993). The false memory syndrome. *Skeptical Inquirer,* 17, 370-375.

Garfield, S. L. (1981). Psychotherapy: A 40-year appraisal. *American Psychologist, 36,* 174-183.

Garfield, S. L. (1997). The therapist as a neglected variable in psychotherapy research. *Clinical Psychology: Science and Practice, 4(1),* 40-43.

Garfinkel, D., & Louden, M. et al. (1995). Melatonin: Is it the answer to a good night's sleep? *The Lancet, 50,* 541-545.

Garner, D. M., Olmsted, M. P., Davis, R., Rockert, W., Goldbloom, D., & Eagle, M. (1990). The association between bulimic symptoms and reported psychopathology. *International Journal of Eating Disorders, 9,* 1-15.

Garry, M., & Loftus, E. F. (1994). Repressed memories of childhood trauma: Could some of them be suggested? *USA Today, January, 22,* 82-84.

Gaugler, B. B., Rosenthal, D. B., Thornton, G. C., & Bentson, C. (1987). Meta-analysis of assessment center validity. *Journal of Applied Psychology, 72,* 493-511.

Gazzaniga, M. S. (1998). The split brain revisited. *Scientific American*, July, 50-55.

Gazzaniga, M. S., & Ledoux, J. E. (1978). *The integrated mind.* New York: Plenum.

Geary, D. C. (1995). Reflections of evolution and culture in children's cognition: Implications for mathematical development and instruction. *American Psychologist, 50,* 24-37.

Gefou-Madianou, D. (1992). *Alcohol, gender and culture.* New York: Routledge, Chapman Hall.

Geller, E. S. (1985). The behavior change approach to litter management. *Journal of Resource Management, 14,* 117-122.

Geller, E. S. (1986). Prevention of environmental problems. In B. A. Edelstein & L. Michelson (Eds.), *Handbook of prevention.* New York: Plenum.

Geller, E. S. (1989). Applied behavioral analysis and social marketing: An integration to preserve the environment. *Journal of Social Issues, 45,* 17-36.

Geller, E. S. (1992). It takes more than information to save energy. *American Psychologist, 47,* 814-815.

Geller, E. S., Berry, T. D., Ludwig, T. D., Evans, R. E., Gilmore, M. R., & Clarke, S. (1990). A conceptual framework for developing and evaluating behavior change interventions for injury control. *Health Education Research, 5,* 125-137.

Geller, E. S., Bruff, C. D., & Nimmer, J. G. (1985). "Flash for life": Community-based prompting for safety belt promotion. *Journal of Applied Behavioral Analysis, 18,* 309-314.

Geller, E. S., & Lehman, G. R. (1986). Motivating desirable waste management behavior: Applications of behavioral analysis. *Journal of Resource Management, 15,* 58-68.

Geller, E. S., & Nimmer, J. G. (1985). Social marketing and applied behavior analysis: An integration for quality of life intervention. Blacksburg: Virginia Polytechnic Institute and State University.

Geller, E. S., Rudd, J. R., Kalsher, M. J., Sreff, F. M., & Lehman, G. R. (1987). Employer-based programs to motivate safety belt use: A review of short-term and long-term effects. *Journal of Safety Research, 18,* 1-17.

Geller, E. S., Winett, R. A., & Everett, P. B. (1982). *Preserving the environment: New strategies for behavior change.* New York: Pergamon Press.

Gellhorn, E. (1964). Motion and emotion: The role of proprioception in the physiology and pathology of the emotions. *Psychological Review, 71,* 457-472.

Gelman, D., Doherty, S., Joseph, N., & Carroll, G. (1987, Spring). How infants learn to talk. *Newsweek*: On Health.

Gelman, R. (1978). Cognitive development. *Annual Review of Psychology, 29,* 297-332.

Gelso, C. J., & Fassinger, R. E. (1990). Counseling psychology: Theory and research on interventions. *Annual Review of Psychology,* 41, 355-386.

Gemberling, G. A., & Domjan, M. (1982). Selective associations in one-day-od rats: Taste toxicosis and texture-shock aversion learning. *Journal of Comparative and Physiological Psychology, 96,* 105-113.

Gendel, E. S., & Bonner, E. J. (1988). Sexual dysfunction. In H. H. Goldman (Ed.), *Review of general psychiatry* (2nd ed.), Norwalk, CT: Appleton and Lange.

George, L. (1992). Acupuncture: Drug free pain relief. *American Health, 11,* 45.

George, M. S., Ketter, T. A., Parekh, P. I., Horwitz, B., Herscovitch, P., & Post, R. M. (1995). Brain activity during transient sadness and happiness in healthy women. *American Journal of Psychiatry, 152,* 341-351.

Geracioti, T. D., & Liddle, R. A. (1988). Impaired cholecystokinin secretion in bulimia nervosa. *New England Journal of Medicine, 319,* 683-688.

Gerbert, B., & Maguire, B. (1989). Public acceptance of the Surgeon General's brochure on AIDS. *Public Health Report, 104,* 130-133.

Gerow, J. R., & Murphy, D. P. (1980). The validity of the Nelson-Denny Reading Test as a predictor of performance in introductory psychology. *Educational and Psychological Measurement, 40,* 553-556.

Gibson, E. J. (1987). Introductory essay: What does infant perception tell us about theories of perception? *Journal of Experimental Psychology: Perception and Performance, 13,* 515-523.

Gibson, E. J. (1988). Exploratory behavior in the development of perceiving, acting, and the acquiring of knowledge. *Annual Review of Psychology, 39,* 1-41.

Gibson, E. J., & Walk, R. D. (1960). The visual cliff. *Scientific American, 202,* 64-71.

Gilbert, L. A. (1994). Current perspectives on dual-career families. *Current Directions in Psychological Science, 3,* 101-104.

Gilbert, P. A., Harris, M. J., McAdams, L. A., & Jeste, D. (1995). Neuroleptic withdrawal in schizophrenic patients. *Archives of General Psychology, 52,* 173-188.

Gillam, B. (1980). Geometrical illusions. *Scientific American, 242,* 102-111.

Gilligan, C. (1982). *In a different voice.* Cambridge, MA: Harvard University Press.

Gilovich, T. Vallone, R., & Tversky, A. (1985). The hot hand in basketball: On the misperception of random sequences. *Cognitive Psychology, 17,* 295-314.

Gladue, B. A. (1994). The biopsychology of sexual orientation. *Current Directions in Psychological Science, 3,* 150-154.

Gladue, B. A., Green, R., & Hellman, R. E. (1984). Neuroendocrine response to estrogen and sexual orientation. *Science, 225,* 1496-1499.

Glaser, R. (1984). Education and thinking. *American Psychologist, 39,* 93-104.

Glasgow, R. E., & Lichtenstein, E. (1987). Long-term effects of behavioral smoking cessation interventions. *Behavior Therapy, 18,* 297-324.

Glass, A. L., Holyoak, K. J., & Santa, J. L. (1979). *Cognition.* Reading, MA: Addison-Wesley.

Glass, D. C., & Singer, J. E. (1972). *Urban stress.* Hillsdale, NJ: Erlbaum.

Glass, D. C., Singer, J. E., & Friedman, L. N. (1969). Psychic cost of adaptation to an environmental stressor. *Journal of Personality and Social Psychology, 12,* 200-210.

Gleaves, D. H. (1994). On "the reality of repressed memories." *American Psychologist, 49,* 440-441.

Gleicher, F. & Petty, R. E. (1992). Expectations of reassurance influence the nature of fear-stimulated attitude change. *Journal of Experimental Social Psychology, 28,* 86-100.

Glenn, N. D. (1990). Quantitative research on marital quality in the 1980s: A critical review. *Journal of Marriage and the Family, 52,* 818-831.

Glenn, N. D., & Weaver, C. N. (1981). The contribution of marital happiness to global happiness. *Journal of Marriage and the Family, 43,* 161-168.

Glickstein, M., & Yeo, C. (1990). The cerebellum and motor learning. *Journal of Cognitive Neuroscience, 2,* 69-80.

Gluck, M. A., & Myers, C. E. (1995). Representation and association in memory: A neurocomputational view of hippocampal function. *Current Directions in Psychological Science, 4,* 23-29.

Glucksberg, S., & Danks, J. H. (1968). Effects of discriminative labels and of nonsense labels upon the availability of novel function. *Journal of Verbal Learning and Verbal Behavior, 7,* 72-76.

Glucksberg, S. & Danks, J. H. (1975). *Experimental Psycholinguistics: An introduction.* New York: Lawrence Erlbaum Associates.

Golbus, M. S. (1980). Teratology for the obstetrician: Current status. *American Journal of Obstetrics and Gynecology, 55,* 269.

Gold, P. E. (1987). Sweet memories. *American Scientist, 75,* 151-155.

Gold, S. N., Hughes, D., & Hohnecker, L. (1994). Degrees of repression of sexual abuse memories. *American Psychologist, 49,* 441-442.

Goldberg, L. R. (1993). The structure of phenotypic personality traits. *American Psychologist, 48,* 26-34.

Goldfried, M. R., Greenberg, L. S., & Marmar, C. (1990). Individual psychotherapy: Process and outcome. *Annual Review of Psychology, 41,* 659-688.

Goldman-Rakic, P. S. (1995). More clues on "latent" schizophrenia point to developmental origins. *The American Journal of Psychiatry,* **152**, 1701-1703

Goldsmith, H. H., & Harman, C. (1994). Temperament and attachment; individuals and relationships. *Current Directions in Psychological Science, 3,* 53-57.

Goldstein, E.B. (1999). *Sensation and Perception,* Fifth Edition. Pacific Grove, CA: Brooks/Cole.

Goldstein, I. L. (1986). *Training in organizations.* Monterey, CA: Brooks/Cole.

Goldstein, I. L. (1989). *Training and development in organizations.* San Francisco: Jossey-Bass.

Goleman, D. (1995). *Emotional intelligence.* New York: Bantam.

Goleman, O. (1980). 1,528 little geniuses and how they grew. *Psychology Today, 14,* 28-53.

Gonzales, M. H., Davis, J. M., Loney, G. L., Lukens, C. K., & Junghans, C. M. (1983). Interactional approach to interpersonal attraction. *Journal of Personality and Social Psychology, 44,* 1192-1197.

Gooden, D., & Baddeley, A. D. (1975). Context-dependent memory in two natural environments: On and under water. *British Journal of Psychology, 66,* 325-331.

Goodman, G. S., & Reed, R. S. (1986). Age differences in eyewitness testimony. *Law and Human Behavior, 10,* 317-332.

Goodwin, D. W., Powell, B., Bremer, D., Hoine, H., & Stein, J. (1969). Alcohol and recall: State dependent effects in man. *Science, 163,* 1358-1360.

Gordon, C. T., State, R. C., Nelson, J. E., Hamburger, S. D., & Rapoport, J. L. (1993). A double-blind comparison of clomipramine, desipramine, and placebo in the treatment of autistic disorder. *Archives of General Psychiatry, 50,* 441-447.

Gorenstein, E. E. (1984). Debating mental illness. *American Psychologist, 39,* 50-56.

Gormezano, I. (1972). Investigations of defense and reward conditioning in the rabbit. In A. H. Black & W. F. Prokasy (Eds.), *Classical conditioning II: Current theory and research.* Englewood Cliffs, NJ: Prentice-Hall.

Gotlib, I. H. (1992). Interpersonal and cognitive aspects of depression. *Current Directions in Psychological Science, 1,* 149-156.

Gotlib, I. H. & Krasnoperova, E. (1998). Biased information processing as a vulnerability factor for depression. *Behavior therapy,* 29, 603-617.

Gottesman, I. I., & Bertelsen, A. (1989). Confirming unexpressed genotypes for schizophrenia. *Archives of General Psychiatry, 46,* 867-872.

Gottesman, I. I., & Shields, J. (1982). *Schizophrenia: The epigenetic puzzle.* Cambridge, UK: Cambridge University Press.

Gottlieb, B. H. (1981). *Social networks and social support.* Beverly Hills, CA: Sage.

Gottlieb, G. (1970). Conceptions of prenatal development. In L. R. Aronson, E. Robach, D. S. Lehrman, & J. S. Rosenblatt (Eds.), *Development and evolution of behavior.* San Francisco: Freeman.

Gottman, J. (1994). Why marriages fail. *Networker, 18,* 41-48.

Gough, H. G. (1985). A work orientation scale for the California Psychological Inventory. *Journal of Applied Psychology, 70,* 505-513.

Govoni, L. E., & Hayes, J. E. (1988). *Drugs and nursing implications* (6th ed.). Norwalk, CT: Appleton & Lange.

Gracely, R. H., Lynch, S., & Bennett, G. J. (1991). The central process responsible for A_LTM-medicated allodynia in some patients with RSD is sensitive to perfusion of the microenvironment of nociceptr terminals. Paper presented at the 21st Annual Meeting of the Society for Neuroscience. New Orleans.

Grady, C. L., McIntosh, A. R., Horowitz, B., Maisog, J. M., Ungerleider, L. G., Mentis, M. J., Pietrini, P., Schapiro, M. B., & Haxby, J. V. (1995). Age-related reductions in human recognition memory due to impaired encoding. *Science, 269,* 218-221.

Graf, P., & Mandler, G. (1984). Activation makes words more accessible, but not necessarily more retrievable. *Journal of Verbal Learning and Verbal Behavior, 23,* 553-568.

Graf, P., & Schachter, D. A. (1985). Implicit and explicit memory for new associations in normal and amnesic subjects. *Journal of Experimental Psychology: Learning, Memory, and Cognition, 11,* 501-518.

Graziano, A. M., & Raulin, M. L. (1993). *Research methods: A process of inquiry.* New York: HarperCollins.

Green, D. M., & Swets, J. A. (1966). *Signal detection theory and psychophysics.* New York: Wiley.

Greenberg, J., & Cohen, R. L. (1982). *Equity and justice in social behavior.* New York: Academic Press.

Greenberg, L. S., & Safran, J. D. (1987). *Emotion in psychotherapy.* New York: Guilford.

Greenberg, L. S., & Safran, J. D. (1989). Emotion in psychotherapy. *American Psychologist, 44,* 19-29.

Greeno, J. G. (1978). Natures of problem-solving abilities. In W. K. Estes (Ed.), *Handbook of learning and cognitive processes (Vol. 5).* Hillsdale, NJ: Erlbaum.

Greeno, J. G. (1989). A perspective on thinking. *American Psychologist, 44,* 134-141.

Greenough, W. T. (1984). Structural correlates of information storage in mammalian brain. *Trends in Neurosciences, 7,* 229-233.

Greenwald, A. G. (1992). New look 3: Unconsciousness reclaimed. *American Psychologist, 47,* 776-779.

Greenwald, A. G., Spangenberg, E. R., Pratkais, A. R., & Eskenazi, J. (1991). Double-blind tests of subliminal self-help audio tapes. *Psychological Science, 2,* 119-122.

Greer, S. (1964). Study of parental loss in neurotics and sociopaths. *Archives of General Psychiatry, 11,* 177-180.

Gregory, R. J. (1999). *Foundations of intellectual assessment.* Boston: Allyn and Bacon.

Gregory, R. L. (1977). *Eye and brain: The psychology of seeing* (3rd ed.). New York: New World Library.

Grice, G. R. (1948). The relation of secondary reinforcement to delayed reward in visual discrimination learning. *Journal of Experimental Psychology, 38,* 1-16.

Grinspoon, L. (1977). *Marijuana reconsidered* (2nd ed.). Cambridge, MA: Harvard University Press.

Grinspoon, L. (Ed.) (1995). Obsessive-compulsive disorder-Part I. *The Harvard Mental Health Letter*, **12**, 1-3.

Grinspoon, L. (1995). Schizophrenia update-Part I. *The Harvard Mental Health Letter, 11,* 1-4.

Grinspoon, L. (Ed.) (1996). Personality disorders: The anxious cluster—Part I. *The Harvard Mental Health Letter*, **12(8)**, 1-3.

Grinspoon, L. (Ed.) (1997). Mood disorders: An overview—Part I. *The Harvard Mental Health Letter*, **14(6)**, 1-4.

Grinspoon, L. (Ed.) (1997). Nicotine dependence—Part I. *The Harvard Mental Health Letter, 13(11),* 1-4.

Grinspoon, L. (Ed.) (1998). Mood disorders: An overview—Part II. *The Harvard Mental Health Letter*, **14(7)** 1-5

Grob, C., & Dobkin de Rois, M. (1992). Adolescent drug use in cross-cultural perspective. *Journal of Drug Issues, 22,* 121-138.

Gross, R. T., & Duke, P. M. (1980). The effect of early and late maturation on adolescent behavior. *The Pediatric Clinics of North America, 27,* 71-77.

Grossman, H. J. (Ed.). (1973). *Manual on terminology and classification in mental retardation.* Washington, DC: American Association on Mental Deficiency.

Groves, P. M., & Rebec, G. V. (1992). *Introduction to biological psychology* (4th ed.). Dubuque, IA: Brown.

Guilford, J. P. (1959a). *Personality.* New York: McGraw-Hill.

Guilford, J. P. (1959b). Traits of creativity. In H. H. Anderson (Ed.), *Creativity and its cultivation.* New York: HarperCollins.

Guilford, J. P. (1967). *The nature of human intelligence.* New York: McGraw-Hill.

Guilford, J. P. (1988). Some changes in the structure-of-intellect model. Educational and *Psychological Measurement, 48,* 1-4.

Guion, R. M., & Gibson, W. M. (1988). Personnel selection and placement. *Annual Review of Psychology, 39,* 349-374.

Gur, R. E., Resnick, S. M., Alavi, A., Gur, R. C., Caroff, S., Dann, R., et al. (1987). Regional brain function in schizophrenia. *Archives of General Psychiatry, 44,* 119-125.

Gurman, A. S., Kniskern, D. P., & Pinsof, W. M. (1986). Research on the process and outcome of marital and family therapy. In S. L. Garfield & A. E. Bergin (Eds.), *Handbook of psychotherapy and behavior change* (3rd ed.). New York: Wiley.

Gustafson, R. (1990). Wine and male physical aggression. *Journal of Drug Issues, 20,* 75-87.

Gutierrez, P. M. & Silk, K. R. (1998). Prescription privileges for psychologists: A review of the psychological literature. *Professional Psychology: Research and Practice, 29,* 213-222.

Guyton, A.C. (1972). *Organ physiology: Structure and function of the nervous system.* Philadelphia: W. B. Saunders.

Haaf, R. A., & Brown, C. J. (1976). Infants= response to face-like patterns: Developmental changes between 10 and 15 weeks of age. *Journal of Experimental Child Psychology, 22,* 155-160.

Haist, F., Shimamura, A. P., & Squire, L. R. (1992). On the relationship between recall and recognition memory. *Journal of Experimental Psychology: Learning, Memory and Cognition, 18,* 691-702.

Hake, D. F., & Foxx, R. M. (1978). Promoting gasoline conservation: The effects of reinforcement schedules, a leader, and self-recording. *Behavior Modification, 2,* 339-369.

Halaas, J. L., Gajiwala, K. S., Maffei, M., Cohen, S. L., Chait, B. T., et al. (1995). Weight-reducing effects of the plasma protein encoded by the obese gene. *Science, 269,* 543-546.

Halberstadt, A. G., & Saitta, M. B. (1987). Gender, nonverbal behavior, and perceived dominance: A test of the theory. *Journal of Personality and Social Psychology, 53,* 257-272.

Hall, C. S. (1954). *A primer of Freudian psychology.* New York: Mentor.

Hall, E. T. (1966). *The hidden dimension.* Garden City, NY: Doubleday.

Hall, G. S. (1904). *Adolescence.* Englewood Cliffs, NJ: Prentice-Hall.

Hall, J. A. (1978). Gender effects in decoding nonverbal cues.

Psychological Bulletin, 85, 845-857.

Hall, J. F. (1976). *Classical conditioning and instrumental conditioning: A contemporary approach.* Philadelphia: Lippincott.

Hall, W. G., & Oppenheim, R. W. (1987). Developmental psychology. *Annual Review of Psychology, 38,* 91-128.

Halpern, D. F. (1986). *Sex differences in cognitive abilities.* Hillsdale, NJ: Erlbaum.

Hamburg, D. A. (1992). *Today's children: Creating a future for a generation in crisis.* New York: New York Times Books.

Hamburg, D. A., & Takanishi, R. (1989). Preparing for life: The critical transition of adolescence. *American Psychologist, 44,* 825-827.

Hamer, D. H., Hu, S., Magnuson, V. L., Hu, N., & Pattatucci, A. M. L. (1993). A linkage between DNA markers on the X chromosome and male sexual orientation. *Science, 261,* 321-327.

Hammen, C., Burge, D. Burney, E., & Adrian, C. (1990). Longitudinal study of diagnoses in children of women with unipolar and bipolar affective disorder. *Archives of General Psychiatry, 47,* 1112-1117.

Hans, V. P. (1986). An analysis of public attitudes toward the insanity defense. Criminology, 4, 393-415.

Hansen, W. B., Hahn, G. L., & Wolkenstein, J. (1990). Perceived personal immunity: Beliefs about susceptibility to AIDS. *Journal of Sex Research, 27,* 622-628.

Harding, C. M. (1988). Course types in schizophrenia: An analysis of European and *American studies. Schizophrenia Bulletin, 14,* 633-642.

Hare, R. D. (1970). *Psychopathology: Theory and research.* New York: Wiley.

Hare, R. D. (1995). Psychopaths: New trends in research. *The Harvard Mental Health Letter,* 12, 4-5.

Hare, R. D., McPherson, L. M., & Forth, A. E. (1988). Male psychopaths and their criminal careers. *Journal of Consulting and Clinical Psychology, 56,* 710-714.

Harkins, S. (1987). Social loafing and social facilitation. *Journal of Experimental Social Psychology, 23,* 1-18.

Harkins, S. G., & Petty, R. E. (1982). Effects of task difficulty and task uniqueness on social loafing. *Journal of Personality and Social Psychology, 43,* 1214-1229.

Harkins, S. G., & Petty, R. E. (1983). Social context effects in persuasion: The effects of multiple sources and multiple targets. In P. B. Paulus (Ed.), *Basic group processes.* New York: Springer-Verlag.

Harkins, S. G., & Szymanski, K. (1989). Social loafing and group evaluation. *Journal of Personality and Social Psychology, 56,* 934-941.

Harlow, H. F. (1932). Social facilitation of feeding in the albino rat. *Journal of Genetic Psychology, 41,* 211-221.

Harlow, H. F. (1959). Love in infant monkeys. *Scientific American, 200,* 68-74.

Harlow, H. F., Harlow, M. K., & Suomi, S. J. (1971). From thought to therapy: Lessons from a private library. *American Scientist, 59,* 536-549.

Harris, B. (1979). What ever happened to Little Albert? *American Psychologist, 34,* 151-160.

Harris, D. V. (1973). *Involvement in sport: A somatopsychic rationale for physical activity.* Philadelphia: Lea & Febiger.

Harris, L., & Associates. (1975, 1981, 1983). *The myth and reality of aging in America.* Washington, DC: The National Council on Aging.

Harris, M. M. (1989). Reconsidering the employment interview: A review of recent literature and suggestions for future research. *Personnel Psychology, 42,* 691-726.

Harris, P. L. (1983). Infant cognition. In P. H. Mussen (Ed.), *Handbook of child psychology (Vol. 2).* New York: Wiley.

Harrow, M., Goldberg, J. F., Grossman, L. S., & Meltzer, H. Y. (1990). Outcome in manic disorders. *Archives of General Psychiatry, 47,* 665-671.

Hartman, S., Grigsby, D. W., Crino, M. D., & Chokar, J. (1986). The measurement of job satisfaction by action tendencies. *Educational and Psychological Measurement, 46,* 317-329.

Hartup, W. W. (1989). Social relationships and their developmental significance. *American Psychologist, 44,* 120-126.

Haruki, T., Shigehisa, T., Nedate, K., Wajima, M., & Ogawa, R. (1984). Effects of alien-reinforcement and its combined type of learning behavior and efficacy in relation to personality. *International Journal of Psychology, 19,* 527-545.

Harvey, J. H., & Weary, G. (1984). Current issues in attribution theory. *Annual Review of Psychology, 35,* 427-459.

Hastie, R., & Park, B. (1986). The relationship between memory and judgment depends on whether the judgment task is memory-based or on-line. *Psychological Review, 93,* 258-268.

Hastorf, A. H., & Cantril, H. (1954). They saw a game: A case study. *Journal of Abnormal and Social Psychology, 49,* 129-134.

Hatfield, E., & Sprecher, S. (1986). *Mirror, mirror...The importance of looks in everyday life.* Albany: State University of New York Press.

Havighurst, R. J. (1972). *Developmental tasks and education* (3rd ed.). New York: McKay.

Hayduk, L. A. (1983). Personal space: Where we now stand. *Psychological Bulletin, 94,* 293-335.

Hayes, C. D. (1987). *Risking the future (Vol. 1).* Washington, DC: National Academy Press.

Hayman, C. A. G., & Tulving, E. (1989). Contingent dissociation between recognition and fragment completion: The method of triangulation. *Journal of Experimental Psychology: Learning, Memory, and Cognition, 15,* 220-224.

Haynes, S. G., McMichael, A. J., & Tyroler, H. A. (1978). Survival after early and normal retirement. *Journal of Gerontology, 33,* 872-883.

Hayward, C., Killan, J. D., Hammer, L. D., Litt, I. F., Wilson, D. M., Simmonds, B., & Taylor, C. B. (1992). Pubertal stage and panic attack history in sixth- and seventh-grade girls. *American Journal of Psychiatry, 149,* 1239-1243.

Hazan, C. & Shaver, P. (1987). Romantic love conceptualized as an attachment process. *Journal of Personality and Social Psychology, 52,* 511-524.

Hebb, D. O. (1955). Drives and the C.N.S. (conceptual nervous system). *Psychological Review, 62,* 243-254.

Hecht, S. (1934). Vision: II. The nature of the photoreceptor process. In C. Murchison (Ed.), *Handbook of general experimental psychology.* Worcester, MA: Clark University Press.

Hedges, L. V., & Newell, A. (1995). Sex differences in mental test scores, variability, and numbers of high-scoring individuals. *Science, 269,* 41-45.

Heffernan, J. A., & Albee, G. W. (1985). Prevention perspectives. *American Psychologist, 40,* 202-204.

Hegarty, J. D., Baldessarini, R. J., Tohen, M., Waternaux, C.,

& Oepen, G. (1994). One hundred years of schizophrenia: A meta-analysis of the outcome literature. *The American Journal of Psychiatry,* **151**, 1409-1416.

Helweg-Larsen, M., & Collins, B. E. (1997). A social psychological perspective on the role of knowledge about AIDS in AIDS prevention. *Current Directions in Psychological Science, 6,* 23-26.

Heidbreder, E. (1946). The attainment of concepts. *Journal of General Psychology, 24,* 93-108.

Heinrichs, R. W. (1993). Schizophrenia and the brain: Conditions for a neuropsychology of madness. *American Psychologist, 48,* 221-233.

Hellige, J. B. (1990). Hemispheric asymmetry. *Annual Review of Psychology, 41,* 55-80.

Hobson, J. A. (1988). *The dreaming brain: How the brain creates both the sense and nonsense of dreams.* New York: Basic Books.

Hobson, J. A., & McCarley, R. W. (1977). The brain as a dream-state generator: An activation-synthesis hypothesis of the dream process. *American Journal of Psychiatry, 134,* 1335-1368.

Hellige, J. B. (Ed.). (1983). *Cerebral hemisphere asymmetry: Method, theory, and application.* New York: Praeger.

Helms, J. E. (1992). Why is there no study of cultural equivalence in standardized cognitive ability testing? *American Psychologist, 47,* 1083-1101.

Helzer, J. E., Robins, L. N., & McEnvoy, L. (1987). Posttraumatic stress disorder in the general population. *New England Journal of Medicine, 317,* 1630-1634.

Henley, T. B., Johnson, M. G., Jones, E. M., & Herzog, H. A. (1989). Definitions of psychology. *The Psychological Record, 39,* 143-152.

Hennessy, J., & Melhuish, E. C. (1991). Early day care and the development of school-age children. *Journal of Reproduction and Infant Psychology, 9,* 117-136.

Herek, G. M., & Glunt, E. K. (1988). An epidemic of stigma: Public reactions to AIDS. American Psychologist, 43, 886-891.

Herrnstein, R. J., & Murray, C. (1994). *The bell curve: Intelligence and class structure.* New York: Free Press.

Heshka, S., & Nelson, Y. (1972). Interpersonal speaking distance as a function of age, sex, and relationship. *Sociometry, 35,* 491-498.

Hetherington, E. M., & Parke, R. D. (1993). *Child psychology: A contemporary viewpoint.* New York: McGraw-Hill.

Hetherington, E. M., & Parke, R. D. (1999). *Child Psychology: A contemporary viewpoint (Fifth Edition).* Boston: McGraw Hill.

Higgins, E. T, & Bargh, J. A. (1987). Social cognition and social perception. *Annual Review of Psychology, 38,* 369-426.

Higley, J. D., Mehlman, P. T., Higley, S. B., Fernald, B. Vickers, J., Lindell, S. G. Taub, D. M., Soumi, S. J., & Linnoila, M. (1996). Excessive mortality in young free-ranging male nonhuman primates with low cerebrospinal fluid 5-hydroxyindoleacetic acid concentrations. *Archives of General Psychiatry, 53,* 537-543.

Hilgard, E. R. (1975). Hypnosis. *Annual Review of Psychology, 26,* 19-44.

Hilgard, E. R. (1978, January). Hypnosis and consciousness. *Human Nature,* pp. 42-49.

Hilgard, E. R. (1992). Divided consciousness and dissociation. *Consciousness and Cognition, 1,* 16-31.

Hilgard, E. R., & Hilgard, J. R. (1975). *Hypnosis in the relief of pain.* Los Altos, CA: W. Kaufman.

Hilgard, J. R. (1970). *Personality and hypnosis: A study of imaginative involvement.* Chicago: University of Chicago Press.

Hill, C. A. (1997). The distinctiveness of sexual motives in relation to sexual desire and desirable partner attributes. *Journal of Sex Research, 34,* 139-153.

Hill, C. A., & Preston, L. K. (1996). Individual differences in the experience of sexual motivation: Theory and measurement of dispositional sexual motives. *Journal of Sex Research, 33,* 27-45.

Hill, W. F. (1985). *Learning: A survey of psychological interpretations* (4th ed.). New York: HarperCollins.

Hines, P. J. (1997). Note bene: Unconscious odors. *Science, 278,* 1547-1551.

Hinrichs, J. R. (1976). Personnel training. In M. Dunnette (Ed.), *Handbook of industrial and organizational psychology.* Skokie, IL: Rand McNally.

Hinsz, V. B., & Davis, J. H. (1984). Persuasive arguments theory, group polarization, and choice shifts. *Personality and Social Psychology Bulletin, 10,* 260-268.

Hoaken, P. N. S., Giancola, P. R., & Pihl, R. O. (1998). Executive cognitive functions as mediators of alcohol-related aggression. *Alcohol and Alcoholism, 33,* 47-54.

Hobfoll, S. E. (1986). *Stress, social support, and women.* Washington, DC: Hemisphere.

Hobfoll, S. E. (1988). *The ecology of stress.* Washington, DC: Hemisphere.

Hobfoll, S. E. (1989). Conservation of resources: A new attempt at conceptualizing stress. *American Psychologist, 44,* 513-524.

Hobson, J. A. (1977). The reciprocal interaction model of sleep cycle control: Implications for PGO wave generation and dream amnesia. In R. R. Drucker-Colin & J. L. McGaugh (Eds.), *Neurobiology of sleep and memory.* New York: Academic Press.

Hobson, J. A. (1988). *The dreaming brain.* New York: Basic Books.

Hobson, J. A., & McCarley, R. W. (1977). The brain as a dream state generator: An activation-synthesis hypothesis of the dream process. *American Journal of Psychiatry, 134,* 1335-1348.

Hobson, J. A. (1994). *The chemistry of conscious states: How the brain changes its mind.* Boston: Little Brown.

Hofferth, S. L., & Hayes, C. D. (Eds.), (1987). *Risking the future: Adolescent sexuality, pregnancy, and childbearing.* Washington, DC: National Academy Press.

Hoffman, D. D. (1983). The interpretation of visual illusions. *Scientific American, 245,* 154-162.

Hoffmann, R. F. (1978). Developmental changes in human infant visual-evoked potentials to patterned stimuli recorded at different scalp locations. *Child Development, 49,* 110-118.

Hogan, J. (1989). Personality correlates of physical fitness. *Journal of Personality and Social Psychology, 56,* 284-288.

Hogan, R., & Nicholson, R. A. (1988). The meaning of personality test scores. *American Psychologist, 43,* 621-626.

Hogan, R., Hogan, J., & Roberts, B. W. (1996). Personality measurement and employment decisions: Questions and answers. *American Psychologist,* **51***,* 469-477.

Holden, C. (1980). A new visibility for gifted children. *Science, 210,* 879-882.

Hollander, E., DeCaria, C. M., Nitescu, A., Gully, R., Suckow, R. F., et al. (1992). Serotonergic function in obsessive-compulsive disorder. *Archives of General Psychiatry, 49,* 21-28.

Hollis, J. F., Connett, J. E., Stevens, V. J., & Greenlick, M. R. (1990). Stressful life events, Type A behavior, and the prediction of cardiovascular and total mortality over six years. *Journal of Behavioral Medicine, 13,* 263-281.

Hollon, S. D., Shelton, R. C., & Loosen, P. T. (1991). Cognitive therapy and pharmacotherapy for depression. *Journal of Consulting and Clinical Psychology, 59,* 88-99.

Holman, B. L., & Tumeh, S. S. (1990). Single-photon emission computed tomography (SPECT): Applications and potential. *Journal of the American Medical Association, 263,* 561-564.

Holmes, D. (1994). *Abnormal psychology* (2nd ed.). New York: HarperCollins.

Holmes, D. S. (1984). Meditation and somatic arousal reduction: A review of the experimental evidence. *American Psychologist, 39,* 1-10.

Holmes, D. S. (1985). To meditate or simply rest, that is the question: A response to the comments of Shapiro. *American Psychologist, 40,* 722-725.

Holmes, D. S. (1987). The influence of meditation versus rest on physiological arousal: A second examination. In M. West (Ed.), *The psychology of meditation.* Oxford: Oxford University Press.

Holmes, D. S. (2001). Abnormal psychology, Fourth edition. Needham Heights, MA: Allyn & Bacon.

Holmes, D.S. (2001). *Abnormal psychology*, Fourth Edition, (p. 239) Boston: Allyn & Bacon.

Holmes, T. S., & Holmes, T. H. (1970). Short-term intrusions into the life-style routine. *Journal of Psychosomatic Research, 14,* 121-132.

Holyoak, K. J., & Spellman, B. A. (1993). Thinking. *Annual Review of Psychology, 44,* 265-315.

Hood, R. D. (1990). Paternally mediated effects. In R. D. Hood (Ed.), *Developmental toxicology: Risk assessment and the future.* New York: Van Nostrand Reinhold.

Hoppock, R. (1935). Job satisfaction. New York: HarperCollins.

Hörmann, H. (1986). *Meaning and context.* New York: Plenum.

Horn, J., & Anderson, K. (1993). Who in America is trying to lose weight? *Annals of Internal Medicine, 119,* 672-676.

Horn, J. L. (1976). Human abilities: A review of research and theories in the early 1970s. *Annual Review of Psychology, 27,* 437-485.

Horn, J. L. (1982). The aging of human abilities. In J. Wolman, (Ed.), *Handbook of developmental psychology.* Englewood Cliffs, NJ: Prentice-Hall.

Horn, J. L. (1985). Remodeling old models of intelligence. In B. B. Wolman (Ed.), *Handbook of intelligence.* New York: Wiley.

Horn, J. L., & Cattell, R. B. (1966). Refinement and test of the theory of fluid and crystallized intelligence. *Journal of Educational Psychology, 57,* 253-276.

Horne, J. A. (1988). *Why we sleep: The function of sleep in humans and other mammals.* Oxford: Oxford University Press.

Horner, M. S. (1969). *Women's will to fail. Psychology Today, 3,* 36.

Horowitz, F. D., & O'Brien, M. (Eds.). (1985). *The gifted and talented: Developmental perspectives.* Washington, DC: American Psychological Association.

Horowitz, I. A., & Bordens, K. S. (1995). *Social psychology.* Mountain View, CA: Mayfield Publishing Company.

Hoshmand, T. L., & Polkinhorne, D. E. (1992). Redefining the science-practice relationship and professional training. *American Psychologist, 47,* 55-66.

Hostetler, A. J. (1987). Alzheimer's trials hinge on early diagnosis. *APA Monitor, 18,* 14-15.

Houston, B. K., & Vavak, C. R. (1991). Cynical hostility: Developmental factors, psycho-social correlates, and health behaviors. *Health Psychology, 10,* 9-17.

Houston, J. P. (1986). *Fundamentals of learning and memory* (3rd ed.). New York: Harcourt Brace Jovanovich.

Hovland, C. I., Janis, I. L., & Kelley, H. H. (1953). *Persuasion and communication.* New Haven, CT: Yale University Press.

Hovland, C. I., & Weiss, W. (1951). The influence of source credibility on communication effectiveness. *Public Opinion Quarterly, 15,* 635-650.

Howard, D. V. (1983). *Cognitive psychology.* New York: Macmillan.

Howard, K. I., Cornille, T. A., Lyons, J. S., Vessey, J. T., Lueger, R. J., & Saunders, S. M. (1996). Patterns of mental health service utilization. *Archives of General Psychiatry*, **53**, 696-703.

Howard, K. I., Kopata, S. M., Krause, M. S., & Orlinsky, D. E. (1986). The dose-effect relationship in psychotherapy. *American Psychologist, 41,* 159-164.

Howell, W. C., & Dipboye, R. L. (1982). *Essentials of industrial and organizational psychology.* Homewood, IL: Dorsey Press.

Howes, C. (1990). Can the age of entry into child care and the quality of child care predict adjustment in kindergarten? *Developmental Psychology, 26,* 292-303.

Hsia, J. (1988). Limits on affirmative action: Asian American access to higher education. *Educational Policy, 2,* 117-136.

Hsu, L. K. G. (1986). The treatment of anorexia nervosa. *American Journal of Psychiatry, 143,* 573-581.

Hubel, D. H. (1979). The brain. *Scientific American,* 241, 45-53.

Hubel, D. H., & Wiesel, T. N. (1979). Brain mechanisms of vision. *Scientific American, 241,* 150-162.

Huesmann, L. R. (1986). Psychological processes promoting the relationship between exposure to media violence and aggression. *Journal of Social Issues, 42,* 125-139.

Huesmann, L. R., & Malamuth, N. (1986). Media violence and antisocial behavior: An overview. *Journal of Social Issues, 42,* 1-6.

Hudson, W. (1960). Pictorial depth perception in subcultural groups in Africa. *Journal of Social Psychology, 52,* 183-208.

Hudspeth, A. J. (1997). How hearing happens. *Neuron,* **19**, 947-950.

Hughes, F. P., & Noppe, L. D. (1985). *Human development.* St. Paul, MN: West.

Hughes, J. Smith, T. W., Kosterlitz, H. W., Fothergill, L. A., Morgan, G. A., & Morris, H. R. (1975). Identification of two related peptides from the brain with potent opiate agonist activity. *Nature, 258,* 577-579.

Hughes, J. R., Gust, S. W., & Pechacek, T. F. (1987). Prevalence of tobacco dependence and withdrawal. *American Journal of Psychiatry, 144,* 205-208.

Hugick, L., & Leonard, J. (1991). Despite increasing hostility, one in four Americans still smokes. *Gallup Poll Monthly, 315,* 2-10.

Hui, C. H. (1990). Work attitudes, leadership styles, and managerial behaviors in different cultures. In R. W. Brislin (Ed.), *Applied cross-cultural psychology.* Newbury Park, CA: Sage.

Hulin, C. L., & Smith, P. C. (1964). Sex differences in job satisfaction. Journal of Applied Psychology, 48, 88-92.

Hull, C. L. (1943). *Principles of behavior.* Englewood Cliffs, NJ: Prentice-Hall.

Hunt, E. (1995). The role of intelligence in modern society. *American Scientist,* **83**, 356-368.

Hunt, M. (1987, August 30). Navigating the therapy maze. *The New York Times Magazine,* pp. 28-31, 37, 44, 46, 49.

Hunter, J. E. (1986). Cognitive ability, cognitive aptitudes, job knowledge, and job performance. *Journal of Vocational Behavior, 29,* 340-362.

Hunter, J. E., & Hunter, R. F. (1984). Validity and utility of alternative predictors of job performance. *Psychological Bulletin, 96,* 72-98.

Hunter, S., & Sundel, M. (Eds.). (1989). *Midlife myths.* Newbury Park, CA: Sage.

Huston, A. C. (1985). The development of sex-typing: Themes from recent research. *Developmental Review, 5,* 1-17.

Huston, T. L., Ruggiero, M., Conner, R., & Geis, G. (1981). Bystander intervention into crime: A study based on naturally occurring episodes. *Social Psychology Quarterly, 44,* 14-23.

Hyde, J. S. (1984). How large are gender differences in aggression? A developmental meta-analysis. *Developmental Psychology, 20,* 697-706.

Hyde, J. S. (1986). *Understanding human sexuality* (3rd ed.). New York: McGraw-Hill.

Hyde, J. S. (1994a). *Understanding human sexuality* (5th ed.). New York: McGraw-Hill.

Hyde, J. S. (1994b). Can meta-analysis make feminist transformations in psychology? *Psychology of Women Quarterly, 18,* 451-462.

Hyde, J. S., Fennema, E., & Lamon, S. J. (1990). Gender differences in mathematics performance: A meta-analysis. *Psychological Bulletin, 107,* 139-155.

Iacono, W. G., & Grove, W. M. (1993). Schizophrenia reviewed: Toward an integrative genetic model. *Psychological Science, 4,* 273-276.

Iaffaldano, M. T., & Muchinsky, P. M. (1985). Job satisfaction and job performance: A meta-analysis. *Psychological Bulletin, 97,* 251-273.

Ilgen, D. R., & Klein, H. J. (1989). Organizational behavior. *Annual Review of Psychology, 40,* 327-351.

Infante-Rivard, C., Fernandez, A., Gauthier, R., David, M., & Rivard, G. (1993). Fetal loss associated with caffeine intake before and during pregnancy. *Journal of the American Medical Association, 270,* 2940-2943.

Insko, C. A. (1965). Verbal reinforcement of attitude. *Journal of Personality and Social Psychology, 2,* 621-623.

Irvine, J., Garner, D. M., Craig, H. M., & Logan, A. G. (1991). Prevalence of Type A behavior in untreated hypertensive individuals. *Hypertension, 18,* 72-78.

Isabella, R. A., & Belsky, J. (1991). Interactional synchrony and the origins of inant-mother attachments: A replication study. *Child Development, 62,* 373-384.

Isenberg, D. J. (1986). Group polarization: A critical review and meta-analysis. *Journal of Personality and Social Psychology, 50,* 1141-1151.

Iso-Ahola, S. E., & Blanchard, W. J. (1986). Psychological momentum and competitive sport performance: A field study. *Perceptual and Motor Skills, 62,* 763-768.

Istvan, J. (1986). Stress, anxiety, and birth outcomes: A critical review of the evidence. *Psychological Bulletin, 100,* 331-348.

Ito, T. A., Miller, N., & Pollack, V. E. (1996). A meta-analysis on the moderating effects of inhibitory cues, triggering events, and self-focused attention. *Psychological Bulletin, 120,* 60-82.

Izard, C. E. (1972). *Patterns of emotion: A new analysis of anxiety and aggression.* New York: Academic Press.

Izard, C. E. (1977). *Human emotions.* New York: Plenum.

Izard, C. E. (1993). Four systems for emotional activation: Cognitive and metacognitive processes. *Psychological Review, 100,* 68-90.

Jackaway, R., & Teevan, R. (1976). Fear of failure and fear of success: Two dimensions of the same motive. *Sex Roles, 2,* 283-294.

Jacklin, C. N. (1989). Female and male: Issues of gender. *American Psychologist, 44,* 27-133.

Jacklin, C. N., & Maccoby, E. E. (1978). Social behavior at 33 months in same-sex and mixed-sex dyads. *Child Development, 49,* 557-569.

Jacobs, B. L. (1987). How hallucinogenic drugs work. *American Scientist, 75,* 386-392.

Jacobs, B. L., & Trulson, M. E. (1979). Mechanisms of action of LSD. *American Scientist, 67,* 396-404.

Jacobson, D. S. (1984). Neonatal correlates of prenatal exposure to smoking, caffeine, and alcohol. *Infant Behavior and Development, 7,* 253-265.

Jacobson, N. S. & Christensen, A. (1996). Studying the effectiveness of psychotherapy: How well can clinical trials do the job? *American Psychologist, 51,* 1031-1039.

Jacoby, L. L., & Dallas, M. (1981). On the relationship between autobiographical memory and perceptual learning. *Journal of Experimental Psychology: General, 3,* 306-340.

Jacoby, R., & Glauberman, N. (Eds.), *The bell curve debate.* New York: Time Books/Random House.

Jaffe, M. L. (1998). *Adolescence.* New York: John Wiley & Sons.

James, L. (1998a). Dr. Driving's world road rage survey: USA & Canada men/women contrasts [On-line]. Available: http:// www.aloha.net/~dyc/surveys/mf.html

James, L. (1998b). Dr. Driving's world road rage survey: USA & Canada age contrasts [On-line]. Available: http://www.aloha.net/~dyc/ survey/age.html

James, L. (1998c). *Principles of Driving Psychology* (Chapter 11). [On-line]. Available: http://www.aloha.net/~dyc/ch11.thml

James, L. (1998d). Congressional testimony by Dr. Leon James [On-line]. Available: http://www.aloha.net/~dyc/testimony.html#Heading5

James, W. (1890). *Principles of psychology.* New York: Holt, Rinehart & Winston.

James, W. (1892). *Psychology: Briefer course.* New York: Holt, Rinehart & Winston.

James, W. (1904). Does consciousness exist? *Journal of Philosophy, 1,* 477-491.

Janis, I. L. (1972). *Victims of groupthink.* Boston: Houghton Mifflin.

Janis, I. L. (1983a). *Groupthink: Psychological studies of policy decisions and fiascoes* (2nd ed.). Boston: Houghton Mifflin.

Janis, I. L. (1983b). The role of social support in adherence to stressful decisions. *American Psychologist, 38,* 143-160.

Janoff-Bulman, R. (1979). Characterological versus behavioral self-blame: Inquiries into depression and rape. *Journal of Personality and Social Psychology, 37,* 1798-1809.

Janssen, E., & Everaerd, W. (1993). Determinants of male sexual arousal. *Annual Review of Sex Research, 24,* 211-245.

Jaroff, L. (1993). Lies of the mind. *Time, November 29,* 52-59.

Jeffery, R. W. (1989). Risk behaviors and health: Contrasting individual and population perspectives. *American Psychologist, 44,* 1194-1202.

Jenkins, C. D. (1976). Recent evidence supporting psychological and social risk factors for coronary disease. *New England Journal of Medicine, 294,* 1033-1038.

Jenkins, J. G., & Dallenbach, K. M. (1924). Oblivescence during sleep and waking. *American Journal of Psychology, 35,* 605-612.

Jensen, A. R. (1969). How much can we boost IQ and scholastic achievement? *Harvard Educational Review, 39,* 1-123.

Jensen, A. R. (1980). *Bias in mental testing.* New York: Free Press.

Jensen, A. R. (1981). *Straight talk about mental tests.* London: Methuen.

Jessor, R. (1993). Successful adolescent development among youth in high-risk settings. *American Psychologist, 48,* 117-126.

Johnson, D. L. (1989). Schizophrenia as a brain disease. *American Psychologist, 44,* 553-555.

Johnson, E. H. (1978). Validation of concept-learning strategies. *Journal of Experimental Psychology, 107,* 237-265.

Johnson, J., Weissman, M. M., & Klerman, G. L. (1990). Panic disorder, comorbidity, and suicide attempts. *Archives of General Psychiatry, 47,* 805-808.

Johnson, M. K., & Hasher, L. (1987). Human learning and memory. *Annual Review of Psychology, 38,* 631-668.

Jones, E. E. (1979). The rocky road from acts to dispositions. *American Psychologist, 34,* 107-117.

Jones, E. E. (1990). *Interpersonal perception.* New York: Macmillan.

Jones, E. E., & Nisbett, R. E. (1971). *The actor and the observer: Divergent perceptions of behavior.* Morristown, NJ: General Learning Press.

Jones, K. L., Smith, D. W., Ulleland, C. N., & Streissgoth, A. P. (1973). Patterns of malformation in offspring of chronic alcoholic mothers. *Lancet, 3,* 1267-1271.

Jones, M. C. (1957). The careers of boys who were early or late maturing. *Child Development, 28,* 113-128.

Jones, M. C. (1924). A laboratory study of fear: The case of Peter. *Pedagogical Seminary, 31,* 308-315.

Jordan, B. K., Marmar, C. R., Fairbank, J. A., Schlenger, W. E., Kulka, R. A., Hough, R. L., & Weiss, D. S. (1992). Problems in families of male Vietnam veterans with post-traumatic stress disorder. *Journal of Consulting and Clinical Psychology, 60,* 916-926.

Jordan, J., Kaplan, A., Miller, J., Striver, I., & Surrey, J. (1991). *Women's growth in connection.* New York: Guilford.

Journal of the American Medical Association (1995). Editorial. The Brown and Williamson Documents: Where do we go from here? July 19, 274, 256-258.

Joyce, P. R., & Paykel, E. S. (1989). Predictors of drug response in depression. *Archives of General Psychiatry, 46,* 89-99.

Julien, R. M. (1985). *A primer of drug action* (4th ed.). San Francisco: Freeman.

Julien, R. M. (1988). *A primer of drug addiction* (5th ed.). New York: Freeman.

Julien, R. M. (1995). A primer of drug action, Seventh edition. New York: W. H. Freeman.

Kacmar, K. M., & Ferris, G. R. (1989). Theoretical and methodological considerations in the age-job satisfaction relationship. *Journal of Applied Psychology, 74,* 201-207.

Kagan, J. (1988). The meanings of personality predicates. *American Psychologist, 43,* 614-620.

Kagan, J., Resnick, J. S., & Snidman, N. (1988). Biological bases of childhood shyness. *Science, 240,* 167-171.

Kahn, D. A. (1995). New strategies in bipolar disorder: Part

II. Treatment. Journal of practical psychiatry and behavioral health, 3, 148-157.

Kahn, S., Zimmerman, G., Csikzentmihalyi, M., & Getzels, J. W. (1985). Relations between identity in young adulthood and intimacy at midlife. *Journal of Personality and Social Psychology, 49,* 1316-1322.

Kahneman, D., & Tversky, A. (1973). On the psychology of prediction. *Psychological Review, 80,* 237-251.

Kahneman, D., & Tversky, A. (1979). On the interpretation of intuitive probability: A reply to Jonathan Cohen. *Cognition, 7,* 409-411.

Kahneman, D., & Tversky, A. (1984). Choices, values, and frames. *American Psychologist, 39,* 341-350.

Kalat, J. W. (1984). *Biological psychology* (2nd ed.). Belmont, CA: Wadsworth.

Kales, A., Scharf, M. B., Kales, J. D., & Sodatos, C. R. (1979). Rebound insomnia: A potential hazard following withdrawal of certain benzodiazepines. *Journal of the American Medical Association, 241,* 1692-1695.

Kalish, R. A. (1976). Death and dying in a social context. In R. H. Binstock & E. Shanas (Eds.), *Handbook of aging and the social sciences.* New York: Van Nostrand Reinhold.

Kalish, R. A. (1982). *Late adulthood: Perspectives on human development.* Monterey, CA: Brooks/Cole.

Kalish, R. A. (1985). The social context of death and dying. In R. H. Binstock & E. Shanas (Eds.), *Handbook of aging and the social sciences (Second Edition).* New York: Van Nostrand-Reinhold.

Kamin, L. (1968). Attention-like processes in classical conditioning. In M. Jones (Ed.), *Miami symposium on the prediction of behavior: Aversive stimulation.* Miami: University of Miami Press.

Kamin, L. (1969). Predictability, surprise, attention, and conditioning. In R. Church & B. Campbell (Eds.), *Punishment and aversion behaviors.* Englewood Cliffs, NJ: Prentice-Hall.

Kamin, L. J. (1995). Behind the curve. *Scientific American, 272,* 99-103.

Kamiya, J., Barber, T. X., Miller, N. E., Shapiro, D., & Stoyva, J. (1977). *Biofeedback and self-control.* Chicago: Aldine.

Kandel, E. R., & Schwartz, J. H. (1982). Molecular biology of learning: Modulation of transmitter release. *Science,* 218, 433-443.

Kane, J. (1989). The current status of neuroleptics. *Journal of Clinical Psychiatry, 50,* 322-328.

Kanizsa, G. (1976). Subjective contours. *Scientific American, 234,* 48-52.

Kanner, A. D., Coyne, J. C., Schaefer, C., & Lazarus, R. S. (1981). Comparison of two modes of stress measurement: Daily hassles and uplifts versus major life events. *Journal of Behavioral Medicine, 4,* 1-39.

Kanner, L. (1943). Autistic disturbances of affective contact. *Nervous Child, 2,* 217-250.

Kaplan, G. M. (1991). The use of biofeedback in the treatment of chronic facial tics: A case study. *Medical Psychotherapy, 4,* 71-84.

Kaplan, H. S. (1974). *The new sex therapy: Active treatment of sexual dysfunction.* New York: Quadrangle.

Kaplan, H. S. (1975). *The illustrated manual of sex therapy.* New York: Quadrangle.

Kaplan, H. S., & Sadock, B. J. (1991). *Synopsis of psychiatry.* Baltimore: Williams & Wilkins.

Kaplan, R. M. (1984). The connection between clinical health promotion and health status. *American Psychologist, 39,* 755-765.

Kaplan, R. M., & Saccuzzo, D. P. (1989). *Psychological testing* (2nd ed.). Monterey, CA: Brooks/Cole.

Kaplan, R. M. & Saccuzzo, D. P. (2001). *Psychological testing: Principles, applications, and issue* (5th edition). Belmont, CA: Wadsworth.

Kaplan, S. (1987). Aesthetics, affect and cognition: Environmental preference from an evolutionary perspective. *Environment and Behavior, 19,* 3-32.

Karou, S. J., & Williams, K. D. (1993). Social loafing: A meta-analytic review and theoretical integration. *Journal of Personality and Social Psychology, 65,* 681-706.

Karoum, F., Karson, C. N., Bigelow, L. B., Lawson, W. B., & Wyatt, R. J. (1987). Preliminary evidence of reduced combined output of dopamine and its metabolites in chronic schizophrenia. *Archives of General Psychiatry, 44,* 604-607.

Kassin, S. M., Ellsworth, P. C., & Smith, V. L. (1989). The "general acceptance" of psychological research on eyewitness testimony: A survey of experts. *American Psychologist, 44,* 1089-1098.

Kassin, S. M., Reddy, M. E., & Tulloch, W. G. (1990). Juror interpretations of ambiguous evidence: The need for cognition, presentation order, and persuasion. *Law and Human Behavior, 14,* 43-56.

Kastenbaum, R., & Costa, P. (1977). Psychological perspectives on death. *Annual Review of Psychology, 28,* 225-249.

Katzell, R. A., & Guzzo, R. A. (1983). Psychological approaches to productivity improvement. *American Psychologist, 38,* 468-472.

Katzell, R. A., & Thompson, D. E. (1990). Work motivation: Theory and practice. *American Psychologist, 45,* 144-153.

Katzman, R. (1987). Alzheimer's disease. *New England Journal of Medicine, 314,* 964-973.

Kay, S. R. (1990). Significance of the positive-negative distinction in schizophrenia. *Schizophrenia Bulletin, 16,* 635-652.

Kay, S. R., & Singh, M. M. (1989). The positive-negtive distinction in drug-free schizophrenic patients. *Archives of General Psychiatry, 46,* 711-717.

Kazdin, A. E., Esveldt-Dawson, K., French, N. H., & Unis, A. S. (1987). Problem-solving skills training and relationship therapy in the treatment of antisocial child behavior. *Journal of Consulting and Clinical Psychology, 55,* 76-85.

Kazdin, A. E. & Mazurick, J. L. (1994). Dropping out of child psychotherapy: Distinguishing early and late dropouts over the course of treatment. Journal of consulting and clinical psychology, 62, 1069-1074.

Keating, D. P. (1980). Thinking processes in adolescents. In J. Adelson (Ed.), *Handbook of adolescent psychology.* New York: Wiley.

Keck, P. (2001). "Update on treatment advances in bipolar disorder." Presented at the Fourth Annual Symposium sponsored by NARSAD, the National Alliance for Research on Schizophrenia and Depression. January 20, Sarasota, FL.

Kee, D. W., & Bell, T. S. (1981). The development of organizational strategies in the storage and retrieval of categorical items in free recall learning. *Child Development, 52,* 1163-1171.

Keesey, R. E., & Powley, T. L. (1975). Hypothalamic regulation of body weight. *American Scientist, 63,* 558-565.

Keesey, R. E., & Powley, T. L. (1986). The regulation of body weight. *Annual Review of Psychology, 37,* 109-133.

Keith, P. M. (1983). A comparison of the resources of parents and childless men and women in very old age. *Family Relations, 32,* 403-409.

Kelley, H. H. (1967). Attribution theory in social psychology. In D. Levine (Ed.), *Nebraska symposium on motivation.* Lincoln: University of Nebraska Press.

Kelley, H. H. (1973). The process of causal attribution. *American Psychologist, 28,* 107-128.

Kelley, H. H. (1992). Common-sense psychology and scientific psychology. *Annual Review of Psychology, 43,* 1-24.

Kelley, H. H., & Michela, J. L. (1980). Attribution theory and research. *Annual Review of Psychology, 31,* 457-501.

Kelley, H. H., & Thibault, J. W. (1978). *Interpersonal relations: A theory of interdependence.* New York: Wiley.

Kelley, K. (1985). Sex, sex guilt, and authoritarianism: Differences in responses to explicit heterosexual and masturbatory slides. *The Journal of Sex Research, 21,* 68-85.

Kelly, G. A. (1964). Man's construction of his alternatives. In E. A. Southwell & M. Merbaum (Eds.), *Personality: Readings in theory and research.* Belmont, CA: Wadsworth.

Kelly, G. F. (1995). *Sexuality today: The human perspective.* Madison, WI: Brown & Benchmark.

Kelly, J. A., Kalichman, S. C., Kauth, M. R., Kilgore, H. G., Hood, H. V., et al. (1991). Situational factors associated with AIDS risk behavior lapses and coping strategies used by gay men who successfully avoid lapses. *American Journal of Public Health, 81,* 1335-1338.

Kelly, J. A., Murphy, D. A., Sikkema, K. J., & Kalichman, S. C. (1993). Psychological interventions to prevent HIV infection are urgently needed. *American Psychologist, 48,* 1023-1034.

Kelly, J. A., & St. Lawrence, J. S. (1988). *The AIDS health crisis.* New York: Plenum.

Kelly, J. A., St. Lawrence, J. S., Hood, H. V., & Brasfield, T. L. (1989). Behavior intervention to reduce AIDS risk activities. *Journal of Consulting and Clinical Psychology, 57,* 60-67.

Kempler, D., & Van Lanker, D. (1987). The right turn of phrase. *Psychology Today, 21,* 20-22.

Kendall, P. C., & Clarkin, J. F. (1992). Introduction to special section: Comorbidity and treatment implications. *Journal of Consulting and Clinical Psychology, 60,* 833-834.

Kendler, K. S., & Gruenberg, A. M. (1982). Genetic relationship between paranoid personality disorder and the "schizophrenic" spectrum disorders. *American Journal of Psychiatry, 139,* 1185-1186.

Kendler, K. S., Gruenberg, A. M., & Kinney, D. K. (1994). Independent diagnoses of adoptees and relatives as defined by the DSM-III-R in the Provincial and National Samples of the Danish Adoption Study of Schizophrenia. *Archives of General Psychiatry, 51,* 456-468.

Kendler, K. S., Neale, M. C., Kessler, R. C., Heath, A. C., & Eaves, L. J. (1993). A longitudinal twin study of 1-year prevalence of major depression in women. *Archives of General Psychiatry, 50,* 843-852.

Kendler, K. S., Walters, E. E., Truett, K. R., et al. (1994). Sources of individual differences in depressive symptoms: Analysis of two samples of twins and their families. American *Journal of Psychiatry, 51,* 1605-1614.

Kendrick, D. T., & Funder, D. C. (1988). Profiting from controversy: Lesson from the person-situation debate. *American Psychologist, 43,* 23-34.

Kendrick, D. T., & Funder, D. C. (1991). The person-situation debate: Do personality traits really exist? In V. J. Derlega et al. (Eds.), *Personality: Contemporary theory and research.* Chicago: Nelson-Hall.

Kentridge, R.W., & Heywood, C. A. (1999). The status of blindsight: Near-threshold vision, islands of cortex and the Riddoch phenomenon. *Journal of Consciousness Studies, 6,* 3-11.

Kentridge, R. W., & Heywood, C. A. (1997). Residual vision in multiple retinal locations within a scotoma: Implications for blindsight. *Journal of Cognitive Neuroscience, 9,* 191. Retrieved from the World Wide Web October 5, 2000, http://ehostvgw15.epnet.com/.

Kermis, M. D. (1984). *The psychology of human aging.* Boston: Allyn & Bacon.

Kershner, J. R., & Ledger, G. (1985). Effect of sex, intelligence, and style of thinking on creativity: A comparison of gifted and average IQ children. *Journal of Personality and Social Psychology, 48,* 1033-1040.

Kessler, R. C., McGonagle, K. A., Zhao, S., Nelson, C. P., et al. (1994). Lifetime and 12-month prevalence of DSM-III-R psychiatric disorders in the United States: Results from the National Comorbidity Survey. *Archives of General Psychiatry, 51,* 18-19.

Kessler, R. C., Sonnega, A., Bromet, E., Hughes, M., & Nelson, C. B. (1995). Popsttraumatic stress disorder in the National Comorbidity Survey. *Archives of General Psychiatry,* **52,** 1048-1060.

Kessler, R. C., Stang, P. E., Wittchen, H. U., & Ustun, T. B. (1998). Lifetime panic-depression comorbidity in the National Comorbidity Survey. Archives of general psychiatry, (55) 9, 801-808.

Kessler, S. (1980). The genetics of schizophrenia: A review. In S. J. Keith & L. R. Mosher (Eds.), *Special report: Schizophrenia.* Washington, DC: U.S. Government Printing Office.

Kett, J. F. (1977). *Rites of passage: Adolescence in America from 1790 to the present.* New York: Basic Books.

Kety, S. S., Wender, P. H., Jacobsen, B., Ingraham, L. J., Jansson, L., Faber, B., & Kinney, D. K. (1994). Mental illness in the biological and adoptive relatives of schizophrenic adoptees. *Archives of General Psychiatry, 51,* 442-455.

Key, M. R. (1975). *Male/female language.* Metuchen, NJ: Scarecrow Press.

Key, S. W., & Marble, M. (1996). NIH panel seeks to curb use. *Cancer Weekly Plus (August-September),* 19-21.

Kientzle, M. J. (1946). Properties of learning curves under varied distributions of practice. *Journal of Experimental Psychology, 36,* 187-211.

Kiester, E. (1984a). The playing fields of the mind. *Psychology Today, 18,* 18-24.

Kiester, E. (1984b). The uses of anger. *Psychology Today, 18,* 26.

Kiester, E., Jr. (1980). Images of the night: The physiological roots of dreaming. *Science 80, 1,* 36-43.

Kihlstrom, J. F. (1985). Hypnosis. *Annual Review of Psychology, 26,* 557-591.

Kihlstrom, J. F. (1987). The cognitive unconscious. *Science, 327,* 1445-1452.

Kimball, M. M. (1989). A new perspective on women's math achievement. *Psychological Bulletin, 105,* 198-214.

Kimble, G. A. (1981). Biological and cognitive constraints on learning. In L. Benjamin (Ed.), *The G. Stanley Hall Lecture Series (Vol. 1).* Washington, DC: American Psychological Association.

Kimble, G. A. (1989). Psychologist from the standpoint of a

generalist. *American Psychologist, 44,* 491-499.

Kimmel, D. C. (1988). Ageism, psychology, and public policy. *American Psychologist, 43,* 175-178.

Kimmel, H. D. (1974). Instrumental conditioning of autonomically-mediated responses in human beings. *American Psychologist, 29,* 325-335.

King, M., Murray, M. A., & Atkinson, T. (1982). Background, personality, job characteristics, and satisfaction with work in a national sample. *Human Relations, 35,* 119-133.

King, M. J., Zir, L. M., Kaltman, A. J., & Fox, A. C. (1973). Variant angina associated with angiographically demonstrated coronary artery system spasm and REM sleep. American *Journal of Medical Science, 265,* 419-422.

Kingsbury, S. J. (1995). Where does research on the effectiveness of psychotherapy stand today? *The Harvard Mental Health Letter, 12(3),* 8.

Kinsbourne, M. (1982). Hemispheric specialization and the growth of human understanding. *American Psychologist, 37,* 411-420.

Kinsey, A. C., Pomeroy, W. B., & Martin, C. E. (1948). *Sexual behavior in the human male.* Philadelphia: Saunders.

Kinsey, A. C., Pomeroy, W. B., Martin, C. E., & Gebhard, P. H. (1953). *Sexual behavior in the human female.* Philadelphia: Saunders.

Kirby, D. A., & Verrier, R. L. (1989). Differential effects of sleep stage on coronary hemodynamic function during stenosis. *Physiology and Behavior, 45,* 1017-1020.

Kirkpatrick, D. L. (1976). Evaluation of training. In R. L. Craig (Ed.), *Training and development handbook* (2nd ed.). New York: McGraw-Hill.

Kirscht, J. P. (1983). Preventive health behavior: A review of research and issues. *Health Psychology, 2,* 277-301.

Kitayama, S., Markus, H. R., Matsumoto, H., & Norasakkunkit, V. (1997). Individual and collective processes in the construction of the self: Self-enhancement in the United States and self-criticism in Japan. *Journal of personality and social psychology*, 72, 1245-1267.

Klayman, J., & Ha, Y-W. (1987). Confirmation, disconfirmation, and information in hypothesis testing. *Psychological Review, 94,* 211-228.

Klebanoff, M. A. (1999). Maternal Serum Paraxanthine, a Caffeine Metabolite, and the Risk of Spontaneous

Abortion. *New England Journal of Medicine*, 341, 1639-

Kleitman, N. (1963a). Patterns of dreaming. *Scientific American, 203,* 82-88.

Kleitman, N. (1963b). *Sleep and wakefulness.* Chicago: University of Chicago Press.

Klepinger, D. H., Billy, J. O. G., Tanfer, K., & Grady, W. R. (1993). Perceptions of AIDS risk and severity and their association with risk-related behavior among U.S. men. *Family Planning Perspectives, 25,* 74-82.

Klerman, G. L. (1990). Treatment of recurrent unipolar major depressive disorder. *Archives of General Psychiatry, 47,* 1158-1162.

Knapp, S., & VandeCreek, L. (1989). What psychologists need to know about AIDS. The *Journal of Training and Practice in Professional Psychology, 3,* 3-16.

Knittle, J. L. (1975). Early influences on development of adipose tissue. In G. A. Bray (Ed.), *Obesity in perspective.* Washington, DC: U.S. Government Printing Office.

Knowles, E. S. (1983). Social physics and the effects of others: Tests of the effects of audience size and distance on social judgments and behavior. *Journal of Personality and Social Psychology, 45,* 1263-1279.

Kobasa, S. C. (1979). Stressful life events, personality, and health: An inquiry into hardiness. *Journal of Personality and Social Psychology, 37,* 1-11.

Kobasa, S. C. (1982). The hardy personality: Toward a social psychology of stress and health. In G. S. Sanders & J. Suls (Eds.), *Social psychology of health and illness.* Hillsdale, NJ: Erlbaum.

Kobasa, S. C. (1987). Stress responses and personality. In R. C. Barnette, L. Beiner, & G. K. Baruch (Eds.), *Gender and stress.* New York: Free Press.

Kocel, K. M. (1977). Cognitive abilities: Handedness, familial sinistrality, and sex. *Annals of the New York Academy of Sciences, 299,* 233-243.

Kochanek, K. D., Maurer, J. D., & Rosenberg, H. M. (1994). Causes of death contributing to changes in life expectancy: United States, 1984C1989. *Vital and Health Statistics, 20,* 1-35.

Koestler, A. (1964). *The act of creation.* New York: Macmillan.

Kohlberg, L. (1963). Moral development and identification. In H. W. Stevenson (Ed.), *Child psychology.* Chicago:

University of Chicago Press.

Kohlberg, L. (1969). *Stages in the development of moral thought and action.* New York: Holt, Rinehart & Winston.

Kohlberg, L. (1981). *Philosophy of moral development.* New York: HarperCollins.

Kohlberg, L. (1985). *The psychology of moral development.* New York: HarperCollins.

Köhler, W. (1969). *The task of Gestalt psychology.* Princeton, NJ: Princeton University Press.

Kolata, G. (1987). What babies know, and noises parents make. *Science, 237,* 726.

Kolb, B. (1989). Brain development, plasticity, and behavior. *American Psychologist, 44,* 1203-1212.

Kolb, F. C., & Braun, J. (1995). Blindsight in normal observers *Nature, 377,* 336. Retrieved from the World Wide Web on October 5, 2000, http://ehostvgw15.epnet.com/

Korchin, S. J., & Scheldberg, D. (1981). The future of clinical assessment. *American Psychologist, 36,* 1147-1158.

Kornhuber, H. H. (1974). Cerebral cortex, cerebellum, and basal ganglia: An introduction to their motor function. In F. O. Schmitt & F. G. Worden (Eds.), *The neurosciences: Third study program.* Cambridge: MIT Press.

Koslow, D. R., & Salett, E. P. (1989). *Crossing cultures in mental health.* Washington, DC: SIETAR International.

Koss, M. P., & Butcher, J. N. (1986). Research on brief psychotherapy. In S. L. Garfield & A. E. Bergin (Eds.), *Handbook of psychotherapy and behavior change* (3rd ed.). New York: Wiley.

Kosslyn, S. M. (1987). Seeing and imagining in the cerebral hemispheres: A computational approach. *Psychological Review, 94,* 148-175.

Kraepelin, E. (1883). *Compendium der psychiatrie.* Leipzig: Abel.

Kramer, B. A. (1985). The use of ECT in California, 1977-1983. The *American Journal of Psychiatry, 142,* 1190-1192.

Krantz, D. S., & Glass, D. C. (1984). Personality, behavior patterns, and physical illness: Conceptual and methodological issues. In W. D. Gentry (Ed.), *Handbook of behavioral medicine.* New York: Guilford.

Krantz, D. S., Grunberg, N. E., & Braum, A. (1985). Health psychology. *Annual Review of Psychology, 36,* 349-383.

Kreutzer, J. S., Schneider, H. G., & Myatt, C. R. (1984). Alcohol, aggression, and assertiveness in men: Dosage and expectancy effects. *Journal of Studies on Alcohol, 45,* 275-278.

Kripke, D. F., & Gillin, J. C. (1985). Sleep disorders. In J. O. Cavenar (Ed.), *Psychiatry.* Philadelphia: Lippincott.

Krueger, J. M., & Obal, F. (1993). A neuronal group theory of sleep function. *Journal of Sleep Research, 2,* 63-69.

Krueger, W. C. F. (1929). The effect of overlearning on retention. *Journal of Experimental Psychology, 12,* 71-78.

Krull, D. S., & Erickson, D. J. (1995). Inferential hopscotch: How people draw social inferences from behavior. *Current Directions in Psychological Science, 4,* 35-38.

Krupat, E. (1985). *People in cities: The urban environment and its effects.* New York: Cambridge University Press.

Kübler-Ross, E. (1969). *On death and dying.* New York: Macmillan.

Kübler-Ross, E. (1981). *Living with death and dying.* New York: Macmillan.

Kunst-Wilson, W. R., & Zajonc, R. B. (1980). Affective discrimination that cannot be recognized. *Science, 207,* 557-558.

Kupfer, D. J, Frank, E., & Perel, J. M. (1989). The advantage of early treatment intervention in recurrent depression. *Archives of General Psychiatry, 46,* 771-775.

Labov, W. (1973). The boundaries of words and their meaning. In C. J. N. Bailey & R. W. Shuy (Eds.), *New ways of analyzing variations in English.* Washington, DC: Georgetown University Press.

Lafferty, P., Beuter, L. E., & Crago, M. (1989). Differences between more and less effective psychotherapists: A study of select therapist variables. *Journal of Consulting and Clinical Psychology, 57,* 76-80.

Laird, J. (1984). The real role of facial response in the experience of emotion: A reply to Tourangeau and Ellsworth, and others. *Journal of Personality and Social Psychology, 47,* 909-917.

Laird, J. M. A., & Bennett, G. J. (1991). Dorsal horn neurons in rats with an experimental peripheral mononeuropathy. Paper presented at the 21st Annual Meeting of the Society for Neuroscience, New Orleans.

Lakoff, R. (1975). *Language and women's place.* New York: HarperCollins.

Lam, D. A., & Miron, J. A. (1995). Seasonality of births in human populations. *Social Biology, 38,* 51-78.

Lamb, M. E. (1977). Father-infant and mother-infant interaction in the first year of life. *Child Development, 48,* 167-181.

Lamb, M. E. (1979). Paternal influences and the father's role: A personal perspective. *American Psychologist, 34,* 938-943.

Lamb, M. E., Hwang, C. P., Frodi, A. M., & Frodi, M. (1982). Security of mother and father infant attachment and its reaction to sociability with strangers in traditional and non-traditional Swedish families. *Infant Behavior and Development, 5,* 355-368.

Lamb, M. E., & Sternberg, K. J. (1990). Do we really know how day care affects children? *Journal of Applied Developmental Psychology, 11,* 499.

Landers, D. M. (1982). Arousal, attention, and skilled performance: Further considerations. *Quest, 33,* 271-283.

Landers, S. (1987). Panel urges teen contraception. *APA Monitor, 18,* 6.

Landesman, S., & Butterfield, E. C. (1987). Normalization and deinstitutionalization of mentally retarded individuals. *American Psychologist, 42,* 809-816.

Landesman, S., & Ramey, C. (1989). Developmental psychology and mental retardation: Integrating scientific principles with treatment practices. *American Psychologist, 44,* 409-415.

Landy, F. J. (1989). *Psychology of work behavior* (2nd ed.). Homewood, IL: Dorsey Press.

Landy, F. J., Shankster, L. J., & Köhler, S. S. (1994). Personnel selection and placement. *Annual Review of Psychology, 45,* 261-296.

Lanetto, R. (1980). *Children's conceptions of death.* New York: Springer.

Lang, P. J. (1985). The cognitive psychophysiology of emotion: Fear and anxiety. In A. H. Tuma & J. D. Maser (Eds.), *Anxiety and the anxiety disorders.* Hillsdale, NJ: Erlbaum.

Langer, S. K. (1951). *Philosophy in a new key.* New York: New American Library.

Laplace, A. C., Chermack, S. T., & Taylor, S. P. (1994). Effects of alcohol and drinking experience on human physical aggression. *Personality and Social Psychology Bulletin, 20,* 439-444.

Larner, A. J. (1995). The cortical neuritic dystrophy of Alzheimer's disease: Nature significance and possible pathogenesis. Dementia, 6, 218-224.

Larson, R., & Ham, M. (1993). Stress and "storm and stress" in early adolescence: The relationship of negative events with dysphoric affect. *Developmental Psychology, 29,* 130-140.

Larson, R., & Lampman-Petraitis, R. (1989). Daily emotional states as reported by children and adolescents. *Child Development, 60,* 1250-1260.

Lashley, K. S. (1950). In search of the engram. Symposia for the Society for *Experimental Biology, 4,* 454-482.

Lasky, R. E., & Kallio, K. D. (1978). Transformation rules in concept learning. *Memory and Cognition, 6,* 491-495.

Latane, B. (1981). The psychology of social impact. *American Psychologist, 36,* 343-356.

Latané, B., & Darley, J. M. (1968). Group inhibition of bystander intervention in emergencies. *Journal of Personality and Social Psychology, 10,* 215-221.

Latané, B., & Darley, J. M. (1970). *The unresponsive bystander: Why doesn't he help?* Englewood Cliffs, NJ: Prentice-Hall.

Latané, B., & Nida, S. (1981). Ten years of research on group size and helping. *Psychological Bulletin, 89,* 308-324.

Latané, B., Williams, K., & Harkins, S. (1979). Many hands make light work: The causes and consequences of social loafing. *Journal of Personality and Social Psychology, 37,* 822-832.

Latham, G. P. (1988). Human resource training and development. *Annual Review of Psychology, 39,* 545-582.

Lattal, K. A. (1992). B. F. Skinner and psychology: Introduction to the special issue. *American Psychologist, 47,* 1269-1272.

Lauer, J., & Lauer, R. (1985). Marriages made to last. *Psychology Today, 19,* 22-26.

Laumann, E. O., Michael, R., Michael, S., & Gagnon, J. (1994). *The social organization of sexuality.* Chicago: University of Chicago Press.

Laumann, E. O., Paik, A., & Rosen, R. C. (1999). Sexual dysfunction in the United States: Prevalence and predictors. *Journal of the American Medical Association, 281,* 537-544.

Lavond, D. g., Kim, J. J., & Thompson, R. F. (1993). Mammaliam brain substrates of aversive classical conditioning. *Annual Review of Psychology, 44,* 317-342.

Lawler, E. E. (1982). Strategies for improving the quality of work life. *American Psychologist, 37,* 486-493.

Lazarus, R. S. (1981). Little hassles can be hazardous to your health. *Psychology Today, 15,* 58-62.

Lazarus, R. S. (1991a). Cognition and motivation in emotion. *American Psychologist, 46,* 352-367.

Lazarus, R. S. (1991b). Progress on a cognitive-motivational-relational theory of emotion. *American Psychologist, 46,* 819-834.

Lazarus, R. S. (1991c). Emotion and adaptation. New York: Lazarus, R. S. (1993). From psychological stress to the emotions: A history of changing outlooks. *Annual Review of Psychology, 44,* 1-21.

Lazarus, R. S. (2000). Toward better research on stress and coping. American psychologist, 55, 665-673.

Lazarus, R. S., & Folkman, S. (1984). *Stress, appraisal, and coping.* New York: Springer.

Leahey, T. H., & Harris, R. J. (1989). *Human learning* (2nd ed.). Englewood Cliffs, NJ: Prentice-Hall.

Leary, M. (1983). *Understanding social anxiety: Social, personality, and clinical perspectives: Volume 153, Sage library of social research.* Beverly Hills, CA: Sage.

Leckman, J. F., Grice, D. E., Boardman, J., Zhang, H., Vitali, A., Bondi, C., Alsobrook, J., Peterson, B. S., Cohen, D. J., Pauls, D. L. (1997). Symptoms of obsessive-compulsive disorder. American journal of psychiatry, 154, 911-917.

LeDoux, J. E. (1995). Emotion: Clues from the brain. *Annual review of Psychology, 46,* 209-235.

Lee, I. M., Manson, J. E., Hennekens, C. H., & Paffenbarger, R. S. (1993). Body weight and mortality: A 27-year follow-up of middle-aged men. *Journal of the American Medical Association, 270,* 2823-2828.

Leger, D. W. (1992). *Biological foundations of behavior: An integrative approach.* New York: HarperCollins.

Lehrer, P. M., & Woolfolk, R. L. (1984). Are stress reduction techniques interchangeable, or do they have specific effects? A review of the comparative empirical literature. In L. Woolfolk & P. M. Lehrer (Eds.), *Principles and practice of stress management.* New York: Guilford.

Leigh, J. P., Markowitz, S. B., Fahs, M., Shin, C., &

Landrigan, P. J. (1997). Occupational injury and illness in the United States: Estimates of costs, morbidity, and mortality. *Archives of Internal Medicine, 157,* 1557-1568.

Lempers, J. D., Flavell, E. R., & Flavell, J. H. (1977). The development in very young children of tactile knowledge concerning visual perception. *Genetic Psychology Monographs, 95,* 3-53.

Lenneberg, E. H. (1967). *Biological foundations of language.* New York: Wiley.

Lenneberg, E. H., Rebelsky, F. G., & Nichols, I. A. (1965). The vocalizations of infants born to deaf and hearing parents. *Human Development, 8,* 23-27.

Lenzenweger, M. F., Dworkin, R. H., & Wethington, E. (1989). Models of positive and negative symptoms in schizophrenia: An empirical evaluation of latent structures. *Journal of Abnormal Psychology, 98,* 62-70.

Leon, G. R., & Roth, L. (1977). Obesity: Psychological causes, correlations and speculations. *Psychological Bulletin, 84,* 117-139.

Leonard, H. L., Swedo, S. E., Lenane, M. C., Rettew, D. C., Hamburger, S. D., et al. (1993). A 2- to 7-year follow-up study of 54 obsessive-compulsive children and adolescents. *Archives of General Psychiatry, 50,* 429-439.

Lerner, M. J. (1965). The effect of responsibility and choice on a partner's attractiveness following failure. *Journal of Personality, 33,* 178-187.

Lerner, M. J. (1980). *The belief in a just world.* New York: Plenum.

Lerner, R. M. (1978). Nature, nurture, and dynamic interactionism. *Human Development, 21,* 1-20.

Lerner, R. M. (1988). Early adolescent transitions: The lore and laws of adolescence. In M. D. Levine & E. R. McAnarney (Eds.). *Early adolescent transitions.* Lexington, MA: Lexington Books.

LeVay, S. (1991). A difference in hypothalamic structure between heterosexual and homosexual men. *Science, 253,* 1034-1037.

Leventhal, H., & Cleary, P. D. (1980). The smoking problem: A review of the research and theory in behavioral risk modification. *Psychological Bulletin, 88,* 370-405.

Levine, H. Z. (1983). Safety and health programs. *Personnel, 3,* 4-9.

Levine, J. D., Gordon, N. C., & Fields, H. L. (1979).

Naloxone dose dependently produces analgesia and hyper-algesia in post-operative pain. *Nature, 278,* 740-741.

Levine, J. M., & Moreland, R. L. (1990). Progress in small group research. *Annual Review of Psychology, 41,* 585-634.

Levine, J. M., Resnick, L. B., & Higgins, E. T. (1993). Social foundations of cognition. *Annual Review of Psychology, 44,* 585-612.

Levine, M., Toro, P. A., & Perkins, D. V. (1993). Social and community interventions. *Annual Review of Psychology, 44,* 525-558.

Levine, M. F., Taylor, J. C., & Davis, L. E. (1984). Defining quality of work life. *Human Relations, 37,* 81-104.

Levine, M. W., & Shefner, J. M. *Fundamentals of sensation and perception* (2nd ed.). Pacific Grove, CA: Brooks/Cole.

Levinson, D. J. (1978). *The seasons of a man's life.* New York: Ballantine Books.

Levinson, D. J. (1986). A conception of adult development. *American Psychologist, 41,* 3-13.

Levinson, D. J., Darrow, C. M., Klein, E. B., Levinson, M. H., & McKee, B. (1974). *The seasons of a man's life.* New York: Knopf.

Levinthal, C. F. (983). *Introduction to physiological psychology* (2nd ed.). Englewood Cliffs, NJ: Prentice-Hall.

Lewinsohn, P. M., Zeiss, A. M., & Duncan, E. M. (1989). Probability of relapse after recovery from an episode of depression. *Journal of Abnormal Psychology, 98,* 107-116.

Ley, B. W. (1985). Alcohol problems in special populations. In J. H. Mendelson & N. K. Mello (Eds.), *The diagnosis and treatment of alcoholism* (2nd ed.). New York: McGraw-Hill.

Ley, P. (1977). Psychological studies of doctor-patient communication. In S. Rachman (Ed.), *Contributions to medical psychology (Vol. 1).* Elmsford, NY: Pergamon Press.

Liben, L. S., & Signorella, M. L. (1993). Gender-schematic processing in children: The role of initial interpretations of stimuli. *Developmental Psychology, 29,* 141-149.

Libman, E., Creti, L., Amsel, R., Brender. W., & Fichten, C. S. (1997). What do older good and poor sleepers do during periods of nocturnal wakefulness? The sleep behaviors scale: 60+. *Psychology and Aging, 12,* 170-182.

Lidz, T. (1973). *The origin and treatment of schizophrenic disorders.* New York: Basic Books.

Liebert, D. T. (2000). Personal communication.

Lieberman, J., Jody, D., Geisler, S., Alvir, J., Loebel, A., et al. (1993). Time course and biological correlates of treatment response in first-episode schizophrenia. *Archives of General Psychiatry, 50,* 369-376.

Lieberman, M. A. (1983). The effects of social support on response to stress. In L. Goldbert & D. S. Breznitz (Eds.), *Handbook of stress management.* New York: Free Press.

Light, K. C. (1997). Stress in employed women: A woman's work is never don if she's a working mom. *Psychosomatic Medicine, 59,* 360-361.

Lightman, S. W., Pisarska, K., Berman, E. R., Pestone, M., et al. (1992). Discrepancy between self-reported and actual caloric intake in obese subjects. *New England Journal of Medicine, 327,* 1893-1898.

Lin, E., & Kleinman, A. (1988). Psychotherapy and clinical course of schizophrenia: A cross-cultural perspective. 555-567.

Lin, T. R., Dobbins, G. H., & Farh, J. L. (1992). A field study of race and similarity effects on interview ratings in conventional and situational interviews. *Journal of Applied Psychology, 77,* 363-371.

Lincoln, J. R., & Kalleberg, A. L. (1985). Work organization and workforce commitment: A study of plants and employees in the U.S. and Japan. *American Sociological Review, 50,* 738-760.

Lindley, A. A., Gray, R. H., Herman, A. A., & Becker, S. (2000). Maternal cigarette smoking during pregnancy and infant ponderal index at birth in the Swedish medical birth register, 1991-1992. *American Journal of Public Health, 90,* 420-423.

Lindsay, D. S., & Johnson, M. K. (1989). The reversed eye-witness suggestibility effect. *Bulletin of the Psychonomic Society, 27,* 111-113.

Lindsley, D. B., Bowden, J., & Magoun, H. W. (1949). Effect upon EEG of acute injury to the brain stem activating system. *Electroencephalography and Clinical Neurophysiology, 1,* 475-486.

Link, S. W. (1995). Rediscovering the past: Gustav Fechner and signal detection theory. *Psychological Science, 5,* 335-340.

Linn, M. C., & Peterson, A. C. (1985). Emergence and characterization of sex differences in spatial ability: A meta-analysis. *Child Development, 56,* 1479-1498.

Lipsey, M. W., & Wilson, D. B. (1993). The efficacy of psychological, educational, and behavioral treatment: Confirmation from meta-analysis. *American Psychologist, 48,* 1181-1209.

Litt, M. D. (1988). Self-efficacy and perceived control: Cognitive mediators of pain tolerance. *Journal of Personality and Social Psychology, 54,* 149-160.

Locke, E. A. (1968). Toward a theory of task motivation and incentives. *Organizational Behavior and Human Performance, 3,* 157-189.

Locke, E. A. (1976). The nature and causes of job satisfaction. In M. D. Dunnette (Ed.), *Handbook of industrial and organizational psychology.* Skokie, IL: Rand McNally.

Locke, E. A., & Latham, G. P. (1984). *Goal setting: A motivational technique that works.* Englewood Cliffs, NJ: Prentice-Hall.

Locke, E. A., Shaw, K. N., Saari, L. M., & Latham, G. (1981). Goal-setting and task performance: 1969-1980. *Psychological Bulletin, 90,* 124-152.

Lockhard, J. S., & Paulus, D. L. (Eds.). (1988). *Self-deception: An adaptive mechanism?* Englewood Cliffs, NJ: Prentice-Hall.

Lockyer, L., & Rutter, M. L. (1969). A five- to fifteen-year follow-up study of infantile psychosis. *British Journal of Psychiatry, 115,* 865-882.

Loftus, E. F. (1979a). *Eyewitness testimony.* Cambridge, MA: Harvard University Press.

Loftus, E. F. (1979b). The malleability of human memory. *American Scientist, 67,* 312-320.

Loftus, E. F. (1984). The eyewitness on trial. In B. D. Sales & A. Elwork (Eds.), *With liberty and justice for all.* Englewood Cliffs, NJ: Prentice-Hall.

Loftus, E. F. (1991). The glitter of everyday memory ... and the gold. *American Psychologist, 46,* 16-18.

Loftus, E. F. (1993a). The reality of repressed memories. *American Psychologist, 48,* 518-537.

Loftus, E. F. (1993b). Therapeutic memories of early childhood abuse: Fact or fiction. Paper presented at the Annual Meeting of the American Psychological Association, Toronto.

Loftus, E. F. (1994). The repressed memory controversy. *American Psychologist, 49,* 443-445.

Loftus, E. F. (1997). Researchers are showing how suggestion and imagination can create memories of events that did not actually occur. *Scientific American, (September),* 71-75.

Loftus, E. F., & Klinger, M. R. (1992). Is the unconscious smart or dumb? *American Psychologist, 47,* 761-765.

Loftus, E. F., & Loftus, G. R. (1980). On the permanence of stored information in the human brain. *American Psychologist, 35,* 409-420.

Loftus, E. F., Loftus, G. R., & Messo, J. (1987). Some facts about weapon focus. *Law and Human Behavior, 11,* 55-62.

Loftus, E. F., Miller, D. G., & Burns, H. J (1978). Semantic integration of verbal information into a visual memory. *Journal of Experimental Psychology: Human Learning and Memory, 4,* 19-31.

Loftus, E. F., Schooler, J. W., & Wagenaar, W. A. (1985). The fate of memory: Comment on McCloskey & Zaragoza. *Journal of Experimental Psychology: General, 114,* 375-380.

Loftus, E. F., & Zanni, G. (1975). Eyewitness testimony: The influence of wording on a question. *Bulletin of the Psychonomic Society, 5,* 86-88.

Londerville, S., & Main, M. (1981). Security of attachment and compliance in maternal training methods in the second year of life. *Developmental Psychology, 17,* 289-299.

Long, P. (1986). Medical mesmerism. *Psychology Today, 20(1),* 28-29.

Lonner, W. J. (1980). The search for psychological universals. In H. C. Triandis & W. W. Lambert (Eds.), *Handbook of cross-cultural psychology (Vol. I).* Boston: Allyn & Bacon.

Lord, C. G. (1980). Schemas and images as memory aids. *Journal of Personality and Social Psychology, 38,* 257-269.

Lorenz, K. (1969). *On aggression.* New York: Bantam Books.

Lott, A. J., & Lott, B. E. (1974). The role of reward in the formation of positive interpersonal attitudes. In T. L. Huston (Ed.), *Foundations of interpersonal attraction.* New York: Academic Press.

Lovaas, O. I. (1987). Behavioral treatment and normal educational and intellectual functioning in young autistic children. *Journal of Consulting and Clinical Psychology, 55,* 3-9.

Lovaas, O. I., & Smith, P. (1988). Intensive behavioral treatment for young autistic children. In B. Lahey & A. Kazdin (Eds.), *Advances in clinical child psychology (Vol. 2)*. New York: Plenum.

Lozoff, B. (1989). Nutrition and behavior. *American Psychologist, 44*, 231-236.

Lubin, B., Larsen, R. M., & Matarazzo, J. D. (1984). Patterns of psychological test usage in the United States: 1935-1982. *American Psychologist, 39*, 451-454.

Luborsky, I., Barber, J. P., & Beutler, L. (Eds.). (1993). Curative factors in dynamic psychotherapy. *Journal of Consulting and Clinical Psychology, 61*, 539-610.

Lucas, E. A., Foutz, A. S., Dement, W. C., & Mittler, M. M. (1979). Sleep cycle organization in narcoleptic and normal dogs. *Physiology and Behavior, 23*, 325-331.

Luecken, L. J., Suarez, E. C., Kuhn, C. M., et al., (1997). Stress in employed women: Impact of marital status and children at home on neurohormone output and home strain. *Psychosomatic Medicine, 59*, 352-359.

Lugaresi, E., R., Montagna, P., Baruzzi, A., Cortelli, P., Lugaresi, A., Tinuper, P., Zucconi, M., & Gambetti, P. (1986). Fatal familial insomnia and dyautonomia with selective degeneration of the thalamic nuclei. *New England Journal of Medicine, 315*, 997-1003.

Luh, C. W. (1922). The conditions of retention. *Psychological Monographs (Whole No. 142)*.

Lumer, E. D., Friston, K. J., & Rees, G. (1998). Neural correlates of perceptual rivalry in the human brain. *Science, 280,*1930-1934.

Lykken, D. T. (1957). A study of anxiety in sociopathic personality. *Journal of Abnormal and Social Psychology, 55*, 6-10.

Lykken, D. T. (1982). Fearlessness: Its carefree charm and deadly risk. *Psychology Today, 16*, 20-28.

Lykken, D. T., McGue, M., Tellegen, A., & Bouchard, T. J., Jr. (1992). Emergenesis: Genetic traits that may not run in families. *American Psychologist, 47*, 1565-1577.

Lynch, G., & Baudry, M. (1984). The biochemistry of memory: A new and specific hypothesis. *Science, 224*, 1057-1063.

Lyness, S. A. (1993). Predictors of differences between Type A and B individuals in heart rate and blood pressure reactivity. *Psychological Bulletin, 114*, 266-295.

Lynn, D. (1974). *The father: His role in child development.* Monterey, CA: Brooks/Cole.

Lynn, R. (1977). The intelligence of the Japanese. *Bulletin of the British Psychological Society, 30*, 69-72.

Lynn, R. (1982). IQ in Japan and the United States shows a greater disparity. *Nature, 297*, 222-223.

Lynn, R. (1987). The intelligence of the Mongoloids: A psychometric, evolutionary, and neurological theory. *Personality and Individual Differences, 8*, 813-844.

Lynn, R. (1991). Educational achievements of Asian Americans. *American Psychologist, 46*, 875-876.

Lynn, S. J., & Rhue, J. W. (1986). The fantasy-prone person: Hypnosis, imagination, and creativity. *Journal of Personality and Social Psychology, 51*, 404-408.

Lynn, S. J., Rhue, J. W., & Weekes, J. R. (1990). Hypnotic involuntariness: A social cognitive analysis. *Psychological Review, 97, 69-184.*

Lytton, H., & Romney, D. M. (1991). Parents' differential socialization of boys and girls: A meta-analysis. *Psychological Bulletin, 109*, 267-296.

Maccoby, E. E. (1988). Gender as a social category. *Developmental Psychology, 24*, 755-765.

Maccoby, E. E. (1990). Gender and relationships: A developmental account. *American Psychologist, 45*, 513-520.

Maccoby, E. E., & Jacklin, C. N. (1974). *The psychology of sex differences.* Stanford, CA: Stanford University Press.

Maccoby, E. E., & Jacklin, C. N. (1980) Sex differences in aggression: A rejoinder and reprise. *Child Development, 51*, 964-980.

Maccoby, E. E., & Jacklin, C. N. (1987). Gender segregation in childhood. In E. H. Reese (Ed.), *Advances in child development and behavior (Vol. 23)*. New York: Academic Press.

MacDonald, M. R., & Kuiper, N. A. (1983). Cognitive behavioral preparations for surgery: Some theoretical and methodological concerns. *Clinical Psychology Review, 3*, 27-39.

Mace, N. L., & Rabins, P. V. (1981). *The 36-hour day.* Baltimore: Johns Hopkins University Press.

Mackenzie, B. (1984). Explaining race differences in IQ: The logic, the methodology, and the evidence. *American Psychologist, 39*, 1214-1233.

MacKenzie, K. R. (1997). Time-managed group psychotherapy: Effective clinical applications. Washington, DC: American Psychiatric Press.

Mackintosh, N. J. (1975). A theory of attention: Variations in the associability of stimuli with reinforcement. *Psychological Review, 82,* 276-298.

Mackintosh, N. J. (1983). *Conditioning and associative learning.* New York: Oxford University Press.

Mackintosh, N. J. (1986). The biology of intelligence? *British Journal of Psychology, 77,* 1-18.

Mackowiak, P. A., Wasserman, S. S., & Levine, M. M. (1992). A critical appraisal of 98.6F, the upper limit of the normal body temperature, and other legacies of Carl Reinhold August Wunderlich. *Journal of the American Medical Association, 268,* 1578-1580.

MacMillan, J., & Kofoed, L. (1984). Sociobiology and antisocial personality: An alternative perspective. *Journal of Mental Disorders, 172,* 701-706.

Maddi, S. R., & Kobasa, S. C. (1984). *The hardy executive: Health and stress.* Homewood, IL: Dorsey Press.

Madigan, S., & O'Hara, R. (1992). Short-term memory at the turn of the century. Mary Whiton Calkin's memory research. *American Psychologist, 47,* 170-174.

Magee, W. J., Eaton, W. W., Wittchen, H., McGonagle, K. A., & Kessler, R. C. (1996). Agoraphobia, simple phobia, and social phobia in the National Comorbidity Survey. *Archives of General Psychiatry,* **53,** 159-168.

Magid, K. (1988). *High Risk: Children Without a Conscience.* New York: Bantam.

Magnusson, D. (1990). Personality development from an interactional perspective. In L. A. Pervin (Ed.), *Handbook of personality.* New York: Guilford.

Magnusson, D., & Edler, N. S. (Eds.). (1977). *Personality at the crossroads: An international perspective.* Hillsdale, NJ: Erlbaum.

Magsud, M. (1979). Resolution and moral dilemmas by Nigerian secondary school pupils. *Journal of Moral Education, 7,* 40-49.

Maguire, J. (1990). *Care and feeding of the brain.* New York: Doubleday.

Maharishi, Mahesh Yogi. (1963). *The science of living and art of being.* London: Unwin.

Mahowald, M. W., & Schenck, C. H. (1989). REM sleep behavior disorder. In M. H. Krygr, T. Roth, & W. C. Dement (Eds.), *Principles and practice of sleep medicine.* Philadelphia: Saunders.

Maier, N. R. F. (1931). Reasoning in humans: II. The solution of a problem and its appearance in consciousness. *Journal of Experimental Psychology, 105,* 181-194.

Malatesta, C. A., & Isard, C. E. (1984). The ontogenesis of human social signals: From biological imperative to symbol utilization. In N. A. Fox & R. J. Davidson (Eds.), *The psychobiology of affective development.* Hillsdale, NJ: Erlbaum.

Mandler, G. (1980). Recognizing: The judgment of previous occurrence. *Psychological Review, 87,* 252-271.

Mann, J. M., Tarantola, D. J. M., & Netter, T. W. (Eds.). (1992). *AIDS in the world.* Cambridge, MA: Harvard University Press.

Manning, M. L. (1983). Three myths concerning adolescence. *Adolescence, 18,* 823-829.

Marcia, J. E. (1980). Identity in adolescence. In J. H. Flavell & E. K. Markman (Eds.). *Handbook of adolescent psychology,* New York: John Wiley.

Marengo, J. T., & Harrow, M. (1987). Schizophrenic thought disorder at follow-up. *Archives of General Psychiatry, 44,* 651-659.

Markowitz, J. S., Weissman, M. M., Ouellete, R., Lish, J. D., & Klerman, G. L. (1989). Quality of life in panic disorder. *Archives of General Psychiatry, 46,* 984-992.

Marks, I. M. (1986). Epidemiology of anxiety. *Social Psychiatry, 21,* 167-171.

Marshall, J., Marquis, K. H., & Oskamp, S. (1971). Effects of kind of question and atmosphere of interrogation on accuracy and completeness of testimony. *Harvard Law Review,* 1620-1643.

Marschark, M., Richmond, C. L., Yuille, J. C., & Hunt, R. R. (1987). The role of imagery in memory: On shared and distinctive information. *Psychological Bulletin, 102,* 28-41.

Martin, B. J. (1986). Sleep deprivation and exercise. In K. B. Pandolf (Ed.), *Exercise and sport sciences review.* New York: Macmillan.

Martin, C. L. (1991). The role of cognition in understanding gender effects. In H. W. Reese (Ed.), *Advances in child development and behavior (Vol. 23).* New York: Academic Press.

Martin, G. B., & Clark, R. D. (1982). Distress crying in neonates: Species and peer specificity. *Developmental Psychology, 18,* 3-9.

Martin, R. J., White, B. D., & Hulsey, M. G. (1991). The regulation of body weight. *American Scientist, 79,* 528-541.

Martindale, C. (1981). *Cognition and consciousness.* Homewood, IL: Dorsey Press.

Marx, J. (1990). Alzheimer's pathology explored. *Science, 249,* 984-986.

Marziali, E. (1984). Prediction of outcome of brief psychotherapy from therapist interpretive interactions. *Archives of General Psychiatry, 41,* 301-304.

Maslow, A. H. (1943). A theory of human motivation. *Psychological Review, 50,* 370-396.

Maslow, A. H. (1954). *Motivation and personality.* New York: Harper.

Maslow, A. H. (1970). *Motivation and personality. (2nd ed.).* New York: HarperCollins.

Massaro, D. W. (1975). *Experimental psychology and information processing.* Skokie, IL: Rand McNally.

Masters, M. S., & Sanders, B. (1993). Is the gender difference in mental rotation disappearing? *Behavior Genetics, 23,* 337-341.

Masters, W., & Johnson, V. (1970). *Human sexual inadequacy.* Boston: Little, Brown.

Masters, W., & Johnson, V. (1979). *Homosexuality in perspective.* Boston: Little, Brown.

Masters, W., Johnson, V., & Kolodny, R. C. (1987). *Human sexuality* (3rd ed.). Glenview, IL: Scott, Foresman/Little, Brown.

Masters, W. H., Johnson, V. E., & Kolodny, R. C. (1992). *Human sexuality* (4th ed.). New York: HarperCollins.

Matarazzo, J. D. (1980). Behavioral health and behavioral medicine: Frontiers for a new health psychology. *American Psychologist, 35,* 807-817.

Matarazzo, J. D. (1990). Psychological assessment versus psychological testing: Validation from Binet to the school, clinic, and courtroom. *American Psychologist, 45,* 999-1017.

Mathews, A., & MacLeod, C. (1994). Cognitive approaches to emotion and emotional disorders. *Annual Review of Psychology, 45,* 25-50.

Matlin, M. W. (1983). *Perception.* Boston: Allyn & Bacon.

Matsumoto, D. (1987). The role of facial response in the experience of emotion: More methodological problems and a meta-analysis. *Journal of Personality and Social Psychology, 52,* 769-774.

Matthews, G. (1997). Intelligence, personality and information processing: An adaptive perspective. IN J. Kingma & W. Tomic, (Eds.), Advances in cognition and educational practice: Reflections on the concept of intelligence (Vol. 4), Greenwich, CT: Jai Press.

Matthews, K. A. (1982). Psychological perspectives on the Type A behavior pattern. *Psychological Bulletin, 91,* 293-323.

Matthews, K. A. (1988). Coronary heart disease and Type A behavior: Update on an alternative to the Booth-Kewley and Friedman (1987) quantitative review. *Psychological Bulletin, 104,* 373-380.

Matthews, K. A., Shumaker, S. A., Bowen, D. J., Langer, R. D., et al., (1997). Women's Health Initiative: Why now? What is it? What's new? *American Psychologist, 52,* 101-116.

Matthies, H. (1989). Neurobiological aspects of learning and memory. *Annual Review of Psychology, 40,* 381-404.

Mattson, S. N., Barron, S., & Riley, E. P. (1988). The behavioral effects of prenatal alcohol exposure. In K. Kuriyama, A. Takada, & H. Ishii (Eds.), *Biomedical and social aspects of alcohol and alcoholism.* Tokyo: Elsevier.

Maxhom, J. (February 12, 2000). Nicotine addiction. *British Medical Journal.* 391-392.

Maxman, J. S. (1991). *Psychotropic drugs: Fast facts.* New York: Norton.

Mayer, J. D., & Geher, G. (1996). Emotional intelligence and the identification of emotion. *Intelligence,* 22(2), 89-114.

Mayer, J. D., & Salovey, P. (1995). Emotional intelligence and the construction and regulation of feelings. Applied and preventative psychology, 4(3), 197-208.

Mayer, J. D. & Salovey P. (1997). What is emotional intelligence? IN P. Salovey, D. J. Sluyter, et. al. (Eds.), Emotional development and emotional intelligence: Educational implications. (pp. 3-34). New York: Basicbooks.

Mayer, R. E. (1983). *Thinking, problem solving, cognition.* San Francisco: Freeman.

Mayeux, R. & Sano, M. (1999). Treatment of Alzheimer's

disease. New England journal of medicine, 342, 1670-1679.

Mayo, E. (1933). *The human problems of an industrial civilization.* Cambridge, MA: Harvard University Press.

McAdams, D. P. (1989). *Intimacy.* New York: Doubleday.

McAdams, D. P. (1990). *The person: An introduction to personality psychology.* San Diego: Harcort, Brace, Jovanovich.

McAdoo, W. G., & DeMyer, M. K. (1978). Personality characteristics of parents. In M. Rutter & E. Schopler (Eds.), *Autism: A reappraisal of concepts and treatment.* New York: Plenum.

McAngus-Todd, N.P. &Cody, F. W. (2000). Vestibular responses to loud dance music: A physiological basis of the "rock and roll threshold?" *Journal of the acoustical society of America*, **107(1)**, 496-500.

McCann, I. L., & Holmes, D. S. (1984). Influence of aerobic exercise on depression. *Journal of Personality and Social Psychology, 46,* 1142-1147.

McCarthy, B. W., Ryan, M., & Johnson, F. (1975). *Sexual awareness.* San Francisco: Boyd & Fraser.

McCaul, K. D., Veltum, L. G., Boyechko, V., & Crawford, J. J. (1990). Understanding attributions of victim blame for rape: Sex, violence, and foreseeability. *Journal of Applied Social Psychology, 20,* 1-26.

McCauley, C. (1989). The nature of social influence in groupthink: Compliance and internalization. *Journal of Personality and Social Psychology, 57,* 250-260.

McClelland, D. C. (1958). Risk-taking in children with high and low need for achievement. In J. W. Atkinson (Ed.), *Motives in fantasy, action, and society.* New York: Van Nostrand Reinhold.

McClelland, D. C. (1973). Testing for competence rather than for "intelligence." *American Psychologist, 28,* 1-14.

McClelland, D. C. (1982). The need for power, sympathetic activation, and illness. *Motivation and Emotion, 6,* 31-41.

McClelland, D. C. (1985). *Human motivation.* Glenview, IL: Scott, Foresman.

McClelland, D. C. (1993). Intelligence is not the best predictor of job performance. *Current Directions in Psychological Science, 2,* 5-6.

McClelland, D. C., Atkinson, J. W., Clark, R. A., & Lowell, E. L. (1953). *The achievement motive.* Englewood Cliffs, NJ: Prentice-Hall.

McClelland, D. C., & Winter, D. G. (1969). *Motivating economic development.* New York: Free Press.

McClintock, M. K. (1971). Menstrual synchrony and suppression. *Nature, 229,* 244-245.

McClintock, M. K. (1979). Estrous synchrony and its mediation by airborne chemical communication. *Hormones and Behavior, 10,* 264.

McCloskey, M., & Egeth, H. (1983). Eyewitness identification: What can a psychologist tell a jury? *American Psychologist, 38,* 550-563.

McCloskey, M., Wible, C., & Cohen, N. J. (1988). Is there a special flashbulb-memory mechanism? *Journal of Experimental Psychology: General, 117,* 171-181.

McCloskey, M., & Zaragoza, M. (1985). Misleading postevent information and memory for events: Arguments and evidence against memory impairment hypotheses. *Journal of Experimental Psychology: General, 114,* 1-16.

McCormick, D. A., Clark, G. A., Lavond, D. G., & Thompson, R. F. (1982). Initial localization of the memory trace for a basic form of learning. *Proceedings, National Academy of Sciences, 79,* 2731-2735.

McCrae, R. (1984). Situational determinants of coping responses: Loss, threat, and challenge. *Journal of Personality and Social Psychology, 46,* 919-928.

McCrae, R. R., & Costa, P. T. (1984). Emerging lives, enduring dispositions: Personality in adulthood. Boston: Little, Brown.

McCrae, R. R., & Costa, P. T. (1986). Clinical assessment can benefit from recent advances in personality psychology. *American Psychologist, 41,* 1001-1002.

McCrae, R. R., & Costa, P. T. (1987). Validation of the five-factor model of personality across instruments and observers. Journal of *Personality and Social Psychology, 52,* 81-90.

McCrae, R. R., & Costa, P. T. (1994). The stability of personality: Observations and evaluations. *Current Directions in Psychological Science, 3,* 173-175.

McCrae, R. R., & Costa, P. T. (1997). Personality trait structure as a human universal. *American psychologist, 52(5),* 509-516.

McCrae, R. R., & John, O. P. (1992). An introduction to the five-factor model and its applications. *Journal of*

Personality, 60, 175-215.

McDougall, W. (1908). *An introduction to social psychology.* London: Methuen.

McEvoy, G. M., & Beatty, R. W. (1989). Assessment centers and subordinate appraisals of managers: A seven-year examination of predictive validity. *Personnel Psychology, 42,* 37-52.

McGaugh, J. L. (1983). Hormonal influences on memory. *Annual Review of Psychology, 34,* 297-323.

McGee, M. G. (1979). Human spatial abilities: Psychometric studies and environmental, genetic, hormonal, and neurological influences. *Psychological Bulletin, 86,* 889-918.

McGehee, D. S., Heath, M. J. S., Gelber, S., Devay, P., & Role, L. W. (1995). Nicotine enhancement of fast excitatory synaptic transmission in CNS by presynaptic receptors. *Science, 269,* 1692-1696.

McGeoch, J. A., & McDonald, W. T. (1931). Meaningful relation and retroactive inhibition. *American Journal of Psychology, 43,* 579-588.

McGinnis, J. M. (1985). Recent history of federal initiatives in prevention policy. *American Psychologist, 40,* 205-212.

McGinnis, J. M., & Foege, W. H. (1993). Actual causes of death in the United States. *Journal of the American Medical Association, 270,* 2207-2212.

McGlashen, T. H., & Fenton, W. S. (1992). The positive-negative distinction in schizophrenia: Review of natural history indicators. *Archives of General Psychiatry, 49,* 63-72.

McGlone, J. (1977). Sex differences in the cerebral organization of verbal functions in patients with unilateral lesions. *Brain, 100,* 775-793.

McGlone, J. (1978). Sex differences in functional brain asymmetry. *Cortex, 14,* 122-128.

McGlone, J. (1980). Sex differences in human brain asymmetry: A critical survey. The *Behavioral and Brain Sciences, 3,* 215-227.

McGrath, E., Keita, G. P., Strickland, B., & Russo, N. F. (Eds.). (1990). *Women and depression: Risk factors and treatment issues.* Washington, DC: American Psychological Association.

McGraw, K. O. (1987). *Developmental psychology.* San Diego: Harcourt Brace Jovanovich.

McGue, M., & Lykken, D. T. (1992). Genetic influence on

risk of divorce. Psychological *Science, 3,* 368-373.

McGuire, W. J. (1985). Attitudes and attitude change. In G. Lindzey & E. Aronson (Eds.), *Handbook of social psychology.* New York: Random House.

McKim, W. A. (1986). *Drugs and behavior.* Englewood Cliffs, NJ: Prentice-Hall.

McLeod, M. D., & Ellis, H. D. (1986). Modes of presentation in eyewitness testimony research. *Human Learning Journal of Practical Research and Applications, 5,* 39-44.

McLeod, J. D., & Kessler, R. C. (1990). Socioeconomic status and differences in vulnerability to undesirable life events. *Journal of Health and Social Behavior, 31,* 162-172.

McNally, R. J. & Shin, L. M. (1995). Association of intelligence with severity of posttraumatic stress disorder symptoms in Vietnam combat veterans. *American Journal of Psychiatry,* **152**, 936-938.

McNaughton, B. L., & Morris, R. G. M. (1987). Hippocampal synaptic enhancement and information storage within a distributed memory system. *Trends in Neuroscience, 10,* 408-415.

McNeil, D. (1970). *The acquisition of language: The study of developmental psycholinguistics.* New York: HarperCollins.

McRoberts, C., Burlingame, G. M., & Hoag, M. J. (1998). Comparative efficacy of individuals and group psychotherapy. Group dynamics, 2, 101-117.

Medin, D. L. (1989). Concepts and concept structure. *American Psychologist, 44,* 1469-1481.

Mednick, M. T. (1989). On the politics of psychological constructs: Stop the bandwagon, I want to get off. *American Psychologist, 44,* 1118-1123.

Mednick, M. T. S. (1979). The new psychology of women: A feminist analysis. In J. E. Gullahorn (Ed.), *Psychology and women: In transition.* New York: Wiley.

Mednick, S. A., Moffitt, T. E., & Stack, S. (1987). *The causes of crime: New biological approaches.* New York: Cambridge University Press.

Meer, J. (1986). The reason of age. *Psychology Today, 20,* 60-64.

Meichenbaum, D. (1977). *Cognitive-behavior modification: An integrative approach.* New York: Plenum.

Meichenbaum, D., & Turk, D. C. (1987). *Facilitating treat-*

ment adherence. New York: Plenum.

Mellman, T. A., Randolph, C. A., Brawman-Mintzer, O., Fores, L. P., & Milanes, F. J. (1992). Phenomenology and course of psychiatric disorders associated with combat-related post-traumatic stress disorder. *American Journal of Psychiatry, 149,* 1568-1574.

Meltzoff, A. N. (1995). Understanding the intentions of others: Re-enactment of intended acts by 18-month-old children. *Developmental Psychology, 31,* 838-850.

Meltzoff, A. N., & Moore, M. K. (1977). Imitation of facial and manual gestures by human neonates. *Science, 198,* 75-78.

Meltzoff, A. N., & Moore, M. K. (1983). Newborn infants imitate adult facial gestures. *Child Development, 54,* 702-709.

Meltzoff, A. N., & Moore, M. K. (1989). Imitation in newborn infants: Exploring the range of gestures imitated and the underlying mechanism. *Developmental Psychology, 25,* 954-962.

Melzack, R. (1973). *The puzzle of pain.* Baltimore: Penguin Books.

Melzack, R., & Wall, P. D. (1965). Pain mechanisms: A new theory. *Science, 150,* 971-979.

Mendelson, W. B. (1997). Efficacy of melatonin as a hypnotic agent. *Journal of Biological Rhythms, 12,* 651-657.

Meredith, N. (1986). Testing the talking cure. *Science 86,* 7(5), 30-37.

Mervis, J. (1986). NIMH data points the way to effective treatment. *APA Monitor, 17,* 1, 13.

Metcalf, J. (1990). Composite holographic associative recall model (CHARM) and blended memory in eyewitness testimony. *Journal of Experimental Psychology: General, 119,* 145-160.

Metcalfe, J., Funnell, M., & Gazzaniga, M. S. (1995). Right-hemisphere memory superiority: Studies of a split-brain patient. *Psychological Science, 6,* 157-164

Metcalfe, J., & Wiebe, D. (1987). Intuition and insight and noninsight problem solving. *Memory and Cognition, 15,* 238-246.

Michael, J. L. (1985). Behavior analysis: A radical perspective. In B. L. Hammonds (Ed.), *Psychology and learning.* Washington, DC: American Psychological Association.

Michael, R. T., Gagnon, J. H., Laumann, E. O., & Kolata, G. (1994). *Sex in America: A definitive study.* Boston: Little, Brown.

Middlemist, R. D., & Peterson, R. B. (1976). Test of equity theory by controlling for comparison of workers' efforts. *Organizational Behavior and Human Performance, 15,* 335-354.

Middlemist, R. D., Knowles, E. S., & Matter, C. F. (1976). Personal space invasions in the lavatory: Suggestive evidence for arousal. *Journal of Personality and Social Psychology, 33,* 541-546.

Milgram, S. (1963). Behavioral studies of obedience. *Journal of Abnormal and Social Psychology, 67,* 371-378.

Milgram, S. (1965). Some conditions of obedience and disobedience to authority. *Human Relations, 18,* 57-76.

Milgram, S. (1970). The experience of living in cities. *Science, 167,* 1461-1468.

Milgram, S. (1974). *Obedience to authority.* New York: HarperCollins.

Milgram, S. (1977). *The individual in a social world.* Reading, MA: Addison-Wesley.

Miller, D. T., & McFarland, C. (1987). Pluralistic ignorance: When similarity is interpreted as dissimilarity. *Journal of Personality and Social Psychology, 53,* 298-305.

Miller, D. T., & Ross, M. (1975). Self-serving biases in the attribution of causality: Fact or fiction? *Psychological Bulletin, 82,* 213-225.

Miller, J. G. (1984). Culture and the development of everyday social explanation. *Journal of Personality and Social Psychology, 46,* 961-978.

Miller, N. E. (1941). The frustration-aggression hypothesis. *Psychological Review, 48,* 337-342.

Miller, N. E. (1944). Experimental studies of conflict. In J. M. Hunt (Ed.), *Personality and the behavior disorders.* New York: Ronald Press.

Miller, N. E. (1978). Biofeedback and visceral learning. *Annual Review of Psychology, 29,* 373-404.

Miller, N. E. (1983). Behavioral medicine: Symbiosis between laboratory and clinic. *Annual Review of Psychology, 34,* 1-31.

Miller, R. C., & Berman, J. S. (1983). The efficacy of cognitive behavior therapies: A quantitative review of the research evidence. *Psychological Bulletin, 94,* 39-53.

Miller, R. R., & Spear, N. E. (Eds.). (1985). *Information processing in animals: Conditioned inhibition.* Hillsdale, NJ: Erlbaum.

Miller, T. Q., Smith, T. W., Turner, C. W., Guijarro, M. L., & Hallet, A. J. (1996). A meta-analytic review of research on hostility and physical health. *Psychological Bulletin,* 119, 322-348.

Miller, W. R. (1992). Client/treatment matching in addictive behaviors. *The Behavior Therapist, 15,* 7-8.

Millstein, S. G. (1989). Adolescent health: Challenges for behavioral scientists. *American Psychologist, 44,* 837-842.

Millstein, S. G., Peterson, A. C., & Nightingate, E. O. (Eds.). (1993). *Promoting the health of adolescents: New directions for the twenty-first century.* New York: Oxford University Press.

Milner, B. (1959). The memory deficit in bilateral hippocampal lesions. Psychiatric *Research Reports, 11,* 43-52.

Milner, B. (1965). Memory disturbances after bilateral hippocampal lesions. In B. Milner & S. Glickman (Eds.), *Cognitive processes and the brain.* New York: Van Nostrand Reinhold.

Milner, B., Corkin, S., & Teuber, H. L. (1968). Further analysis of the hippocampal amnesic syndrome: 14-year follow-up study of H. M. *Neuropsychologica, 6,* 215-234.

Minami, H., & Dallenbach, K. M. (1946). The effect of activity upon learning and retention in the cockroach. *American Journal of Psychology, 59,* 682-697.

Minuchin, S., & Fishman, H. C. (1981). *Family therapy techniques.* Cambridge, MA: Harvard University Press.

Mirin, S. M., Weiss, R. D., & Greenfield, S. F. (1991). Psychoactive substance abuse disorders. In A. J. Galenberg, E. L. Bassuk, & S. C. Schoonover (Eds.), *The practitioner's guide to psychoactive drugs.* New York: Plenum.

Mischel, W. (1968). *Personality and assessment.* New York: Wiley.

Mischel, W. (1973). Toward a cognitive social learning reconceptualization of personality. *Psychological Review, 80,* 252-283.

Mischel, W. (1979). On the interface of cognition and personality. *American Psychologist, 34,* 740-754.

Mischel, W. (1981). *Introduction to personality* (3rd ed.). New York: Holt, Rinehart & Winston.

Mischel, W., & Peake, P. K. (1982). Beyond déja vu in the search for cross-situational consistency. *Psychological Review, 89,* 730-755.

Mishkin, M., & Appenzeller, T. (1987). The anatomy of memory. *Scientific American, 256,* 80-89.

Mitler, M. M., Miller, J. C., Lipsitz, J. J., & Walsh, J. K. (1997). The sleep of long-haul truck drivers. *New England Journal of Medicine, 337,* 755-761.

Mobley, W. H. (1977). Intermediate linkages in the relationship between job satisfaction and employee turnover. *Journal of Applied Psychology, 62,* 237-240.

Moncher, M. S., Holden, G. W., & Trimble, J. E. (1990). Substance abuse among Native American youth. *Journal of Consulting and Clinical Psychology, 58,* 408-415.

Money, J. (1972). *Man woman/boy girl.* Baltimore: Johns Hopkins University Press.

Money, J. (1987). Sin, sickness, or status? Homosexual gender identity and psychoneuroendocrinology. *American Psychologist, 42,* 384-399.

Monson, T. C., & Snyder, M. (1977). Actors, observers, and the attribution process. *Journal of Experimental Social Psychology, 13,* 89-111.

Moon, C., & Fifer, W. P. (1990). Syllables as signals for 2-day old infants. *Infant Behavior and Development, 13,* 377-390.

Moore, K. (1992). *Facts at a glance.* Washington, DC: Childtrends.

Moore, K. L. (1982). *The developing human* (3rd ed.). Philadelphia: Saunders.

Moorecroft, W. H. (1987). An overview of sleep. In J. Gackenback (Ed.), *Sleep and dreams.* New York: Garland.

Moorecroft, W. H. (1989). *Sleep, dreaming, and sleep disorders.* Latham, MD: University Press of America.

Moran, J. S., Janes, H. R., Peterman, T. A., & Stone, K. M. (1990). Increase in condom sales following AIDS education and publicity, United States. *American Journal of Public Health, 80,* 607-608.

Morgan, C. T. (1961). *Introduction to psychology.* New York: McGraw Hill.

Morgan, W. P. (1980). The trait psychology controversy. *Research Quarterly for Exercise and Sport, 51,* 50-76.

Mori, D., & Pliner, P. L. (1987). "Eating lightly" and the

self-presentation of femininity. Journal of Social and Personality Psychology, 53, 693-702.

Morris, C. W. (1946). *Signs, language, and behavior.* Englewood Cliffs, NJ: Prentice-Hall.

Morris, L. A., & Halperin, J. (1979). Effects of written drug information on patient knowledge and compliance: A literature review. *American Journal of Public Health, 69,* 47-52.

Morrison, D. M. (1985). Adolescent contraceptive behavior: A review. *Psychological Bulletin, 98,* 538-568.

Moruzzi, G. (1975). The sleep-wake cycle. *Reviews of Psychology, 64,* 1-165.

Moruzzi, G., & Magoun, H. W. (1949). Brain stem reticular formation and activation of the EEG. *Electroencephalography and Clinical Neurophysiology, 1,* 455-473.

Moscovici, S., Lage, E., & Naffrechoux, M. (1969). Influences of a consistent minority on the response of a majority in a color perception task. *Sociometry, 32,* 365-380.

Moscovici, S., Mugny, G., & Van Avermaet, E. (1985). *Perspectives on minority influence.* New York: Cambridge University Press.

Mowday, R. T. (1983). Equity theory prediction of behavior in organizations. In R. M. Steers & L. W. Porter (Eds.), *Motivation and work behavior* (3rd ed.). New York: McGraw-Hill.

Mshelia, A. Y., & Lapidus, L. B. (1990). Depth picture perception in relation to cognitive style and training in non-Western children. *Journal of Cross-Cultural Psychology, 21,* 414-433.

Muchinsky, P. M. (1987). *Psychology applied to work* (2nd ed.). Homewood, IL: Dorsey Press.

Muchinsky, P. M., & Tuttle, M. L. (1979). Employee turnover: An empirical and methodological assessment. *Journal of Vocational Behavior, 14,* 43-77.

Mueller, T. I., Keller, M. B., Leon, A. C., Solomon, D. A., Shea, M. T., Coryell, W., & Endicott, J. (1996). Recovery after 5 years of unremitting major depressive disorder. *Archives of General Psychiatry, 53,* 794-799.

Mulac, A., Incontro, C. R., & James, M. R. (1985). Comparison of gender-linked language effect and sex role stereotypes. *Journal of Personality and Social Psychology, 49,* 1098-1109.

Mumford, M. D., Uhlman, C. E., & Kilcullen, R. N. (1992). The structure of life history: Implications for the construct validity of background data scales. *Human Performance, 5,* 109-137.

Munn, N. L. (1956). *Introduction to psychology.* Boston: Houghton Mifflin.

Murdoch, D. D., & Pihl, R. O. (1988). The influence of beverage type on aggression in males in the natural setting. *Aggressive Behavior, 14,* 325-335.

Murdock, B. B. (1974). *Human memory: Theory and data.* New York: Wiley.

Murray, D. J. (1983). *A history of Western psychology.* Englewood Cliffs, NJ: Prentice-Hall.

Murray, D. M., Johnson, C. A., Leupker, R. R., & Mittlemark, M. B. (1984). The prevention of cigarette smoking in children: A comparison of four strategies. *Journal of Applied Social Psychology, 14,* 274-288.

Murray, H. A. (1938). *Explorations in personality.* New York: Oxford University Press.

Murphy, S. L. (2000). Deaths: Final data for 1998. National vital statistics reports, 48(11), July 24, 2000.

Nakazima, S. (1962). A comparative study of the speech developments of Japanese and American English in children. *Studies in Phonology, 2,* 27-39.

NAMHC, [Basic Behavioral Science Task Force of the National Advisory Mental Health Council] (1996). Basic Behavioral Science Research for Mental Health: Sociocultural and environmental processes. *American Psychologist,* **51**, 722-731.

Namir, S., Wolcott, D. L., Fawzy, F. I., & Alumbaugh, M. J. (1987). Coping with AIDS: Psychological and health implications. *Journal of Applied Social Psychology, 17,* 309-328.

Nash, M. (1987). What, if anything, is regressed about hypnotic age regression? *Psychological Bulletin, 102,* 42-52.

National Academy of Sciences, National Research Council. (1989). *Diet and health: Implications for reducing chronic disease risk.* Washington, DC: National Academy Press.

National Association of Anorexia Nervosa and Associated Disorders (2001). Facts about eating disorders. Retrieved on June 19, 2001 from the World Wide Web: http://www.anad.org/ facts.htm

National Commission on Sleep Disorders Research

(NCSDR). (1993). *Wake up America: A national sleep alert.* Washington, DC: Department of Health and Human Services.

National Institute on Drug Abuse (1999a). Cocaine use and addiction. Downloaded from the World Wide Web, January 31, 2001. http://www.nida.nih.gov/ResearchReports/Cocaine/cocaine2.html#scope.

National Institute on Drug Abuse (1999a). Marijuana. Downloaded from the World Wide Web, February 1, 2001. http://www.nida.nih.gov/Infofax/marijuana.html.

National Institute on Drug Abuse (1999a). Ecstacy. Downloaded from the World Wide Web, February 1, 2001. http://www.nidanih.giv/Infofax/ecstacy.html.

National Institute of Mental Health (NIMH). (1981). *Depressive disorders: Causes and treatment (DHEW Publication No. ADM 81-108).* Washington, DC: U.S. Government Printing Office.

National Institute of Mental Health. (1984). The NIMH epidemiologic catchment area program. *Archives of General Psychiatry, 41,* 931-1011.

National Institute of Mental Health. (1989). *Information on lithium.* Rockville, MD: U.S. Department of Health and Human Services.

National Institute of Mental Health. (1990). *Bipolar disorder: Manic-depressive illness.* Washington, DC: U.S. Government Printing Office.

National Institute of Mental Health. (1991). *Information about D/Art and depression.* Rockville, MD: U.S. Department of Health and Human Services.

National Institute of Mental Health. (1993). The NIMH epidemiologic catchment area program. *Archives of General Psychiatry, 50.*

National Institute on Drug Abuse. (1987). *National household survey on drug abuse: Population estimates 1985.* Rockville, MD.

National Institutes of Health, Review Panel on Coronary Prone Behavior and Coronary Heart Disease. (1981). Coronary-prone behavior and coronary heart disease: A critical review. *Circulation, 63,* 1199-1215.

NDMDA [National Depressive and Manic-Depressive Association] (1996). *Depressive illness: The medical facts, the human challenge.* New York: The National Depressive and Manic Depressive Association.

Neisser, U. (1976). *Cognition and reality: Principles and implications of cognitive psychology.* San Francisco: W. H. Freeman.

Neisser, U. (1982). *Memory observed.* San Francisco: Freeman.

Neisser, U. (1991). A case of misplaced nostalgia. *American Psychologist, 46,* 34-36.

Nelson, K. (1993). The psychological and social origins of autobiographical memory. *Psychological Science, 4,* 7-14.

Nelson, K. (1986). *Event knowledge: Structure and function in development.* Hillsdale, NJ: Lawrence Erlbaum Associates.

Nemeth, C. (1986). Differential contributions of majority and minority influence. *Psychological Review, 93,* 23-32.

Neubauer, P. J. (1992). The impact of stress, hardiness, home and work environment on job satisfaction, illness, and absenteeism in critical care nurses. *Medical Psychotherapy, 5,* 109-122.

Neugarten, B. L., & Neugarten, D. A. (1986). Changing meanings of age in the aging society. In A. Piter & L. Bronte (Eds.), *Our aging society: Paradox and promise.* New York: Norton.

Neugarten, B. L., & Neugarten, D. A. (1989). Policy issues in an aging society. In M. Storandt & G. R. VandenBos (Eds.), *The adult years: Continuity and change.* Washington, DC: American Psychological Association.

Newby, R. W. (1987). Contextual areas in item recognition following verbal discrimination learning. *Journal of General Psychology, 114,* 281-287.

Newcomb, M. D., & Bentler, P. M. (1989). Substance abuse among children and teenagers. *American Psychologist, 44,* 242-248.

Newcomb, N., & Dubas, J. S. (1987). Individual differences in cognitive ability: Are they related to timing of puberty? In R. M. Lerner & T. T. Foch (Eds.), *Biological-psychosocial interactions in early adolescence: A life-span approach.* Hillsdale, NJ: Erlbaum.

Newell, A., Shaw, J. C., & Simon, H. A. (1962). The process of creative thinking. In H. E. Gruber, G. Terrell, & M. Wertheimer (Eds.), *Contemporary approaches to creative thinking.* New York: Atherton Press.

Newell, A., & Simon, H. A. (1972). *Human problem solving.*

Englewood Cliffs, NJ: Prentice-Hall.

Newman, B. M., & Newman, P. R. (1984). *Development through life: A psychosocial approach.* Homewood, IL: Dorsey Press.

Nickerson, R. S., & Adams, M. J. (1979). Long-term memory for a common object. *Cognitive Psychology, 11,* 287-307.

Nigg, J. T., & Goldsmith, H. H. (1994). Genetics of personality disorders: Perspectives from personality and psychopathology research. *Psychological Bulletin, 115,* 346-380.

NICHD Early Child Care Research Network (1997). The effects of infant child care on infant-mother attachment security: Results of the NICHD study of early child care. *Child Development, 68,* 860-879.

Nisan, M., & Kohlberg, L. (1982). Universality and variation in moral judgement: A longitudinal and cross-sectional study in Turkey. *Child Development, 53,* 865-876.

Nisbett, R. E. (1980). The trait construct in lay and professional psychology. In L. Festinger (Ed.). Retrospections on Social Psychology. New York: Oxford University Press.

Nisbett, R. E. (1972). Hunger, obesity, and the ventromedial hypothalamus. *Psychological Review, 79,* 433-453.

Norcross, J. C. (1986). *Handbook of eclectic psychotherapy.* New York: Brunner/Mazel.

Norman, G. R., Brooks, L. R., & Allen, S. W. (1989). Recall by expert medical practitioners and novices as a record of processing attention. *Journal of Experimental Psychology: Learning, Memory, and Cognition, 15,* 1166-1174.

Noyes, R., Reich, J., Christiansen, J., Suelzer, M., Pfohl, B., & Coryell, W. A. (1990). Outcome of panic disorder. *Archives of General Psychiatry, 47,* 809-818.

Oatley, K., & Jenkins, J. M. (1992). Human emotions: Function and dysfunction. *Annual Review of Psychology, 43,* 55-85.

Oden, G. C. (1987). Concept, knowledge, and thought. *Annual Review of Psychology, 38,* 203-227.

Oden, M. H. (1968). The fulfillment of promise: 40-year follow-up of the Terman gifted group. *Genetic Psychology Monographs, 77(1),* 3-93.

Oetting, E. R., & Beauvais, F. (1987). Peer cluster theory, socialization characteristics and adolescent drug use: A path analysis. *Journal of Counseling Psychology, 34,* 205-213.

Oetting, E. R., & Beauvais, F. (1990). Adolescent drug use: Findings of national and local surveys. *Journal of Consulting and Clinical Psychology, 58,* 385-394.

Offer, D., & Offer, J. (1975). *From teenage to young manhood: A psychological study.* New York: Basic Books.

Offermann, L. R., & Gowing, M. K. (1990). Organizations of the future: Changes and challenges. *American Psychologist, 45,* 95-108.

Offord, D. R., Boyle, M. H., Szatmari, P., Rae-Grant, N. I., Links, P. S., et al. (1987). Ontario child health study. *Archives of General Psychiatry, 44,* 832-836.

Ogata, S. N., Silk, K. R., Goodrich, S., Lohr, N. E., & Hill, E. M. (1990). Childhood sexual and physical abuse in patients with borderline personality. *American Journal of Psychiatry, 147,* 1008-1013.

Ogilvie, B. C., & Howe, M. A. (1984). Beating slumps at their game. *Psychology Today, 18,* 28-32.

Ohbuchi, K., & Kamgara, T. (1985). Attacker's intent and awareness of outcome, impression management and retaliation. *Journal of Experimental Social Psychology, 21,* 321-330.

Olfson, M., & Pincus, H. A. (1994). Outpatient psychotherapy in the United States, I: Volume, costs, and user characteristics. *American Journal of Psychiatry, 151,* 1281-1288.

Olio, K. A. (1994). Truth in memory. *American Psychologist, 49,* 442-443.

Oller, D. K. (1981. Infant vocalization. In R. E. Stark (Ed.), *Language behavior in infancy and early childhood.* New York: Elsevier.

Oller, D. K., & Eilers, R. E. (1988). The role of audition in infant babbling. *Child Development, 59,* 441-449.

Olson, J. M., & Zanna, M. P. (1993). Attitudes and attitude change. *Annual Review of Psychology, 44,* 117-154.

Olton, D. S. (1978). Characteristics of spatial memory. In S. H. Hule, H. F. Fowler, & W. K. Honig (Eds.), *Cognitive processes in animal behavior.* Hillsdale, NJ: Erlbaum.

Olton, D. S. (1979). Mazes, maps, and memory. *American Psychologist, 34,* 583-596.

Opalic, P. (1989). Existential and psychopathological evaluation of group psychotherapy of neurotic and psychotic patients. *International Journal of Group Psychotherapy, 39,* 389-422.

Orleans, C. T., & Slade, J. (Eds.) (1993). *Nicotine addiction: Principles and management.* New York: Oxford University Press.

Orlebeke, J. F., Knol, D. L., & Verhulst, F. C. (1999). Child behavior problems increased by maternal smoking during pregnancy. *Archives of Environmental Health*, 54, 15-19.

Orne, M. (1969). Demand characteristics and the concept of quasi-controls. In R. Rosenthal & R. Rosnow (Eds.), *Artifact in behavioral research.* New York: Academic Press.

Ornstein, P. A., Gordon, B. N., & Baker-Ward, L. E. (1992). Children's memory for salient events: Implications for testimony. In M. L. Howe, C. L. Brainerd, & V. F. Reyna (Eds,). *Development of long-term retention.* New York: Springer-Verlag.

Ornstein, P. A., Naus, M. J., & Liberty, C. (1975). Rehearsal and organizational processes in childhood memory. *Child Development, 46,* 818-830.

Ortony, A., Clore, G. L., & Collins, A. (1988). *The cognitive structure of emotions.* New York: Cambridge University Press.

Ortony, A., & Turner, T. J. (1990). What's basic about basic emotions? *Psychological Review, 97,* 315-331.

Ozer, D. J., & Reise, S. P. (1994). Personality assessment. *Annual Review of Psychology, 45,* 357-388.

Paivio, A. (1971). *Imagery and verbal processes.* New York: Holt, Rinehart & Winston.

Paivio, A. (1986). *Mental representations: A dual coding approach.* New York: Oxford University Press.

Palfai, T., & Jankiewicz, H. (1991). Drugs and human behavior. Dubuque, IA: Brown.

Paludi, M. A., & Gullo, D. F. (1986). The effect of sex labels on adults' knowledge of infant development. *Sex Roles, 16,* 19-30.

Pandey, J. (1990). The environment, culture, and behavior. In R. W. Brislin (Ed.), *Applied cross-cultural psychology.* Newbury Park CA: Sage.

Papilia, D. E., Camp, C. J., & Feldman, R. D. (1996). *Adult development and aging.* New York: McGraw-Hill.

Papolos, D. & Papolos, J. (1997). *Overcoming depression, Third edition.* New York: HarperCollins.

Putnam, F. W. (1989). *Diagnosis and treatment of multiple personality disorder.* New York: Guilford Press.

Parke, R. D. (1981). Fathers. Cambridge, MA: Harvard University Press.

Parke, R. D., & Tinsley, B. J. (1987). Family interaction in infancy. In J. D. Osofsky (Ed.), *Handbook of infant development* (2nd ed.). New York: Wiley.

Parker, E. S., Birnbaum, I. M., & Noble, E. P. (1976). Alcohol and memory: Storage and state dependency. *Journal of Verbal Learning and Verbal Behavior, 15,* 691-702.

Parson, A. (1993). Getting the point. *Harvard Health Letter, 18,* 6-9.

Pasewark, R. A. & Seidenzahl, D. (1979). Opinions concerning the insanity plea and criminality among mental patients. Bulletin of the American Academy of Psychiatry and Law, 7, 199-202.

Pate, J. E., Pumariega, A. J., Hester, C., & Garner, D. M. (1992). Cross-cultural patterns in eating disorders: A review. *Journal of the American Academy of Child and Adolescent Psychiatry, 31,* 802-809.

Paulus, D. L., & Bruce, M. N. (1992). The effect of acquaintancement on the validity of personality impressions: A longitudinal study. *Journal of Personality and Social Psychology, 63,* 816-824.

Pauly, I. B., & Goldstein, S. G. (1970, November). Prevalence of significant sexual problems in medical practice. *Medical Aspects of Human Sexuality,* pp. 48-63.

Paunonen, S. P., Jackson, D. N., Trzebinski, J., & Fosterling, F. (1992). Personality structures across cultures: A multimethod evaluation. *Journal of Personality and Social Psychology, 62,* 447-456.

Pavlov, I. (1927). *Conditioned reflexes.* New York: Oxford University Press.

Pavlov, I. (1928). *Lectures on conditioned reflexes: The higher nervous activity of animals (Vol. I) (H. Gantt, Trans.).* London: Lawrence and Wishart.

Pavlovich, M., & Greene, B. F. (1984). A self-instructional manual for installing low-cost/no-cost weatherization material: Experimental validation with scouts. *Journal of Applied Behavior Analysis, 17,* 105-109.

Pawlicki, R. E., & Heitkemper, T. (1985). Behavioral management of insomnia. *Journal of Psychosocial Nursing, 23,* 14-17.

Payne, J. W., Bettman, J. R., & Johnson, E. J. (1992).

Behavioral decision research: A constructive processing perspective. Annual *Review of Psychology, 43,* 87-131.

Peabody, D., & Goldberg, L. R. (1989). Some determinants of factor structures from personality trait descriptors. *Journal of Personality and Social Psychology, 57,* 552-567.

Pearce, J. M., & Hall, G. (1980). A model for Pavlovian conditioning: Variations in the effectiveness of conditioned but not of unconditioned stimuli. *Psychological Review, 87,* 532-552.

Pearson, J. C., Turner, L. H., & Todd-Mancillas, W. (1991). *Gender and communication* (2nd ed.). Dubuque, IA: Brown.

Pederson, D. R., Morgan, G., Sitko, C., Campbell, K., Ghesquire, K., & Acton, H. (1990). Maternal sensitivity and the security of infant-mother attachment: A Q-sort study. *Child Development, 61,* 1974-1983.

Peele, S., Brodsky, A., & Arnold, M. (1991). T*he truth about addition and recovery.* New York: Simon & Schuster.

Pelleymounter, M. A., Cullen, M. J., Baker, M. B., Hecht, R., Winters, D., Boone, T., & Collins, F. (1995). Effects of the obese gene product on body weight regulation in ob/ob mice. *Science, 269,* 540-543.

Penfield, W. (1975). *The mystery of the mind.* Princeton, NJ: Princeton University Press.

Penfield, W., & Rasmussen, T. (1950). *The cerebral cortex of man.* New York: Macmillan.

Peplau, L. A., & Perlman, D. (1982). Perspectives on loneliness. In L. A. Peplau & D. Perlman (Eds.), *Loneliness: A sourcebook of current theory, research and therapy.* New York: John Wiley.

Perls, F. S. (1967). Group vs. individual psychotherapy. ECT: A *Review of General Semantics, 34,* 306-312.

Perls, F. S. (1971). *Gestalt therapy verbatim.* New York: Bantam Books.

Perls, F. S., Hefferline, R. F., & Goodman, P. (1951). *Gestalt therapy.* New York: Julien Press.

Pervin, L. A., & John, O. P. (2001). *Personality: Theory and Research* (8th ed.). New York: John Wiley.

Peterson, A. C. (1988). Adolescent development. *Annual Review of Psychology, 39,* 583-607.

Peterson, A. C., & Ebata, A. T. (1987). Developmental transitions and adolescent problem behavior: Implications for prevention and intervention. In K. Hurrelmann (Ed.), *Social prevention and intervention.* New York: de Gruyter.

Peterson, L. R., & Peterson, M. J. (1959). Short-term retention of individual verbal items. *Journal of Experimental Psychology, 58,* 193-198.

Peto, R., Lopez, A. D., Boreham, J., Thun, M., & Heath, C., Jr. (1992). Mortality from tobacco in developing countries: Indirect estimation from national vital statistics. *Lancet, 339,* 1268-1278.

Petty, R. E., & Cacioppo, J. T. (1986). The elaboration likelihood model of persuasion. *Advances in Experimental Social Psychology, 19,* 123-205.

Petty, R. E. & Cacioppo, J. T. (1986). *Communication and persuasion.* New York: Springer-Verlag.

Petty, R. E., Harkins, S. G., Williams, K. D., & Latané, B. (1977). The effects of group size on cognitive effort and evaluation. *Personality and Social Psychology Bulletin, 3,* 579-582.

Petty, R. E., Ostrow, T. M., & Brock, T. C. (1981). *Cognitive responses in persuasive communications: A text in attitude change.* Hillsdale, NJ: Erlbaum.

Petty, R. E., Wells, G. L., & Brock, T. C. (1976). Distraction can enhance or reduce yielding to propaganda: Thought disruption versus effort justification. *Journal of Personality and Social Psychology, 34,* 874-884.

Phares, V., & Compas, B. E. (1993). Fathers and developmental psychopathology. Current Directions in *Psychological Science, 2,* 162-165.

Phillips, D., McCartney, K., & Scarr, S. (1987). Child-care quality and children's social development. *Developmental Psychology, 23,* 537-543.

Piaget, J. (1932/1948). *The moral judgment of the child.* New York: Free Press.

Piaget, J. (1952). *The origins of intelligence in children.* New York: W. W. Norton.

Piaget, J. (1954). *The construction of reality in the child.* New York: Basic Books.

Piaget, J. (1967). *Six psychological studies.* New York: Random House.

Pihl, R. O., Smith, M. & Farrell, B. (1984). Alcohol and aggression in men: A comparison of brewed and distilled beverages. *Journal of Alcohol Studies, 45,* 278-282.

Pihl, R. O., & Peterson, J. B.(1993). Alcohol, serotonin and aggression. *Alcohol Health and Research World, 17,* 113-

117.

Pihl, R. O., Peterson, J. B., & Lau, M. A. (1993). A biosocial model of the alcohol-aggression relationship. *Journal of Studies on Alcohol, 54,* 128-140.

Pihl, R. O., & Zacchia, C. (1986). Alcohol and aggression: A test of the affect-arousal hypothesis. *Aggressive Behavior, 12,* 367-375.

Pillemer, D. B., & White, S. H. (1989). Childhood events recalled by children and adults. In H. W. Reese (Ed.), *Advances in child development and behavior (Vol. 21).* New York: Academic Press.

Piner, K. E., & Kahle, L. R. (1984). Adapting to the stigmatizing label of mental illness: Foregone but not forgotten. *Journal of Personality and Social Psychology, 47,* 805-811.

Pinker, S. (1995). *The language instinct.* New York: Harper Perennial.

Pinsof, W. M., Wynne, L. C., & Hambright, A. B. (1996). The outcomes of couple and family therapy. Psychotherapy, 33, 321-331.

Plassman, B. L. (2000). Moderate to severe head injury increases later risk of Alzheimer's disease. Neurology, 55, 1158-1166.

Plawin, P., & Suied, M. (1988, December). Can't get no satisfaction. *Changing Times,* p. 106.

Plomin, R. (1990). *Nature and Nurture: An introduction to behavioral genetics.* Pacific Grove, CA: Brooks/Cole.

Plomin, R. (1988). The nature and nurture of cognitive abilities. In J. Sternberg (Ed.), *Advances in the psychology of human intelligence (Vol. 4).* Hillsdale, NJ: Erlbaum.

Plomin, R. (1989). Environment and genes: Determinants of behavior. *American Psychologist, 44,* 105-111.

Plomin, R., DeFries, J. C., & Fulker, D. W. (1988). *Nature and nurture during infancy and early childhood.* New York: Cambridge University Press.

Plutchik, R. (1980a). *Emotion: A psychoevolutionary synthesis.* New York: HarperCollins.

Plutchik, R. (1980b, February). A language for the emotions. *Psychology Today,* pp. 68-78.

Plutchik, R. (1994). *The psychology and biology of emotion.* New York: HarperCollins.

Pogue-Geile, M. F., & Zubin, J. (1988). Negative symptomatology and schizophrenia: A conceptual and empirical review. *International Journal of Mental Health, 16,* 3-45.

Pola, J., & Martin, L. (1977). Eye movements following autokinesis. *Bulletin of the Psychonomic Society, 10,* 397-398.

Pollack, H., Lantz, P. M., & Frohna, J. G. (2000). Maternal smoking and adverse birth outcomes among singletons and twins. *American Journal of Public Health,* 90, 395-400.

Pool, R. (1993). Evidence for homosexuality gene. *Science, 261,* 291-292.

Pope, H. G., & Hudson, J. I. (1986). Antidepressant therapy for bulimia: Current status. *Journal of Clinical Psychiatry, 47,* 339-345.

Pope, H. G., Hudson, J. I., Jonas, J. M., & Yurgelun-Todd, D. (1985). Antidepressant treatment of bulimia: A two-year follow-up study. *Journal of Clinical Psychopharmacology, 5,* 320-327.

Pope, H. G., Yurgelun-Todd, D. (1996). The residual cognitive effects of heavy marijuana use in college students. *Journal of the American Medical Association, 275,* 521-527.

Porter, L. W., & Steers, R. M. (1973). Organizational, work, and personal factors in employee turnover and absenteeism. *Psychological Bulletin, 80,* 151-176.

Posner, M. I. (1973). *Cognition: An introduction.* Glenview, IL: Scott, Foresman.

Posner, M. I., & Keele, S. W. (1968). On the genesis of abstract ideas. *Journal of Experimental Psychology, 77,* 353-363.

Posner, M. I., & Keele, S. W. (1970). Retention of abstract ideas. *Journal of Experimental Psychology, 83,* 304-308.

Post, R. B., & Leibowitz, H. W. (1985). A revised analysis of the role of efference in motion perception. *Perception, 14,* 631-643.

Powell, L. H., Shaker, L. A., Jones, B. A., Vaccarino, L. V., et al. (1993). Psychosocial predictors of mortality in 83 women with premature acute myocardial infarction. *Psychosomatic Medicine, 55,* 221-225.

Powell, R. A., & Boer, D. P. (1994). Did Freud mislead patients to confabulate memories of abuse? *Psychological Reports, 74,* 1283-1298.

Powers, S. I., Hauser, S. T., & Kilner, L. A. (1989). Adolescent mental health. *American Psychologist, 44,*

200-208.

Pressley, M., Levin, J. R., & Delaney, H. D. (1982). The mnemonic keyword method. *Review of Educational Research, 52,* 61-91.

Pribar, E. F., & Dinwiddie, S. H. (1992). Psychiatric correlates of incest in childhood. *American Journal of Psychiatry, 149,* 52-56.

Price-Williams, D. R., Gordon, W., & Ramirez, M. (1969). Skill and conservation. *Developmental Psychology, 1,* 769.

Prior, M., & Wherry, J. S. (1986). Autism, schizophrenia, and allied disorders. In H. C. Quay & J. S. Wherry (Eds.), *Psychopathological disorders of childhood* (3rd ed.). New York: Wiley.

Putnam, F. W., Guroff, J. J., Silberman, E. K., Barban, L., & Post, R. M. (1986). The clinical phenomenology of multiple personality disorder: Review of 100 recent cases. *Journal of Clinical Psychology, 47,* 285-293.

Pyle, R. L., Mitchell, J. E., & Eckert, E. D. (1981). Bulimia: Report of 34 cases. *Journal of Clinical Psychiatry, 42,* 60-64.

Pyle, R. L., Mitchell, J. E., Eckert, E. D., Hatsukami, D. K., Pomeroy, C., & Zimmerman, R. (1990). Maintenance treatment and 6-month outcome for bulimic patients who respond to initial treatment. *American Journal of Psychiatry, 147,* 871-875.

Pynes, J., & Bernardin, H. J. (1989). Predictive validity of an entry-level police officer assessment center. *Journal of Applied Psychology, 74,* 831-833.

Quadrel, M. J., Fishhoff, B., & Davis, W. (1993). Adolescent (in)vulnerability. *American Psychologist, 48,* 102-116.

Quay, H. C. (1965). Psychopathic personality as pathological sensation seeking. *American Journal of Psychiatry, 122,* 180-183.

Quina, K., Wingard, J. A., & Bates, H. G. (1987). Language style and gender stereotypes in person perception. *Psychology of Women Quarterly, 11,* 111-222.

Radford, A. (1990). *Syntactic theory and the acquisition of English syntax: The nature of early child grammars of English.* Oxford: Blackwell.

Rahe, R. H., & Arthur, R. J. (1978). Life changes and illness reports. In K. E. Gunderson & R. H. Rahe (Eds.), *Life stress and illness.* Springfield, IL: Thomas.

Raine, A., Venables, P. H., & Williams, M. (1990). Relationship between central and autonomic measures of arousal at age 15 years and criminality at age 24 years. *Archives of General Psychiatry, 46,* 1003-1007.

Rainville, P., Duncan, G. H., Price, D. D., Carrier, B., & Bushnell, M. C. (1997). Pain affect encoded in human anterior cingulate but not somatosensory cortex. *Science, 277,* 968-971.

Randall, T. (1993). Morphine receptor clone-improved analgesics, addiction therapy expected. *The Journal of the American Medical Association, 270,* 1165-1166.

Rapoport, J. L. (1991). Recent advances in obsessive-compulsive disorder. Psychiatric Clinics of North America, 15, 813-823.

Raskin, N. J. & Rogers, C. R. (1995). Person-centered therapy. In J. J. Corsini & D. Wedding (Eds.). Current psychotherapies, Fifth edition. (pp. 128-161). Itasca, IL: Peacock.

Rattner, A. (1988). Convicted but innocent: Wrongful conviction in the criminal justice system. *Law and Human Behavior, 12,* 283-294.

Ray, O. S., & Ksir, C. (1987). *Drugs, society, and human behavior.* St. Louis: Mosby.

Reason, J. T., & Lucas, D. (1984). Using cognitive diaries to investigate naturally-occurring memory blocks. In J. E. Harris, & P. E. Morris (Eds.), *Everyday memory: Actions and absent mindedness.* London: Academic Press.

Ree, M. J., & Earles, J. A. (1992). Intelligence is the best predictor of job performance. *Current Directions in Psychological Science, 1,* 86-89.

Ree, M. J., & Earles, J. A. (1993). g is to psychology what carbon is to chemistry: A reply to Sternberg and Wagner, McClelland, and Calfee. *Current Directions in Psychological Science, 2,* 11-12.

Reich, J. (1986). The epidemiology of anxiety. *The Journal of Nervous and Mental Disease, 174,* 129-136.

Reilly, R. R., & Chao, G. T. (1982). Validity and fairness of some alternative employee selection procedures. *Personnel Psychology, 35,* 1-62.

Reinisch, J. M., & Sanders, S. A. (1992). Effects of prenatal exposure to diethylstilbestrol (DES) on hemispheric laterality and spatial ability in human males. *Hormones and Behavior, 26,* 62-75.

Reinke, B. J., Ellicott, A. M., Harris, R. L., & Hancock, E.

(1985). Timing of psychological changes in women's lives. *Human Development, 28,* 259-280.

Reis, H. T., Nezlek, J., & Wheeler, L. (1980). Physical attractiveness in social interaction. *Journal of Personality and Social Psychology, 38,* 604-617.

Reis, S. M. (1989). Reflections on policy affecting the education of gifted and talented students: Past and future perspectives. *American Psychologist, 44,* 399-408.

Rescorla, R. A. (1968). Probability of shock in the presence and absence of CS in fear conditioning. *Journal of Comparative and Physiological Psychology, 66,* 1-5.

Rescorla, R. A. (1987). A Pavlovian analysis of goal-directed behavior. *American Psychologist, 42,* 119-129.

Rescorla, R. A. (1988). Pavlovian conditioning: It's not what you think it is. *American Psychologist, 43,* 151-160.

Rescorla, R. A., & Wagner, A. R. (1972). A theory of Pavlovian conditioning: Variations in the effectiveness of reinforcement and nonreinforcement. In A. H. Black & W. F. Prokasy (Eds.), *Classical conditioning II: Current research and theory.* Englewood Cliffs, NJ: Prentice-Hall.

Resnick, H. D., Kilpatrick, D. G., Dansky, B. S., Saunders, B. E., & Best, C. L. (1993). Prevalence of civilian trauma and posttraumatic stress disorder in a representative national sample of women. *Journal of Consulting and Clinical Psychology, 61,* 984-991.

Resnick, L. B. (1987). *Education and learning to think.* Washington, DC: National Academy Press.

Rest, J. R. (1983). Morality. In J. Flavell & E. Markman (Eds.), *Handbook of child development: Cognitive development.* New York: Wiley.

Reveley, M. A., Reveley, A. M., & Baldy, R. (1987). Left cerebral hemisphere hypodensity in discordant schizophrenic twins. *Archives of General Psychiatry, 44,* 624-632.

Revelle, W. (1987). Personality and motivation: Sources of inefficiency in cognitive performance. *Journal of Research in Personality, 21,* 436-452.

Revulsky, S. H. (1985). The general process approach to animal learning. In T. D. Johnston & A. T. Petrewicz (Eds.), *Issues in the ecological study of learning.* Hillsdale, NJ: Erlbaum.

Revulsky, S. H., & Garcia, J. (1970). Learned associations over long delays. In G. H. Bower & J. T. Spence (Eds.),

The psychology of learning and motivation (Vol. 4). New York: Academic Press.

Reynolds, A. G., & Flagg, P. W. (1983). *Cognitive psychology.* Boston: Little, Brown.

Reynolds, B. A., & Weiss, S. (1992). Generation of neurons and astrocytes from isolated cells of the adult mammalian nervous system. *Science, 225,* 1707-1710.

Rhodes, S. R. (1983). Age-related differences in work attitudes and behaviors: A review and conceptual analysis. *Psychological Bulletin, 93,* 328-367.

Rhyne, D. (1981). Bases of marital satisfaction among men and women. *Journal of Marriage and the Family, 43,* 941-954.

Rice, M. L. (1989). Children's language acquisition. *American Psychologist, 44,* 149-156.

Rice, P. L. (1999). Stress and health, Third edition. Pacific Grove, CA: Brooks/Cole.

Richardson, D. R., Vandenberg, R. J., & Humphries, S. A. (1986). Effect of power to harm on retaliative aggression among males and females. *Journal of Research in Personality, 20,* 402-419.

Richardson, J. D. (1991). Medical causes of male sexual dysfunction. *Medical Journal of Australia, 155,* 29-33.

Richardson-Klavehn, A., & Bjork, R. A. (1988). Measures of memory. *Annual Review of Psychology, 39,* 475-543.

Richmond, C. E., Bromley, L. M., & Woolf, C. J. (1993). Preoperative morphine pre-empts postoperative pain. *The Lancet, 342,* 73-75.

Rickels, K., Downing, R., Schweizer, E., & Hassman, H. (1993). Antidepressants for the treatment of generalized anxiety disorder. *Archives of General Psychiatry, 50,* 884-895.

Rickert, V. I., Vaughn, I., & Johnson, C. (1988). Reducing nocturnal awakenings and crying episodes in infants and young children: A comparison between scheduled awakenings and systematic ignoring. *Pediatrics, 81,* 203-212.

Riggio, R. E. (1990). *Introduction to industrial/organizational psychology.* Glenview, IL: Scott, Foresman.

Rinberg, D. & Davidowitz, H. (2000). Insect perception: Do cockroaches 'know' about fluid dynamics? *Nature,* **405,** 756-757.

Rist, M. C. (1990). Crack babies' in school. *Education Digest,*

55, 30-33.

Rivett, M. (1998). The family therapy journals in 1997: A thematic review. Journal of family therapy, 20, 423-430.

Robb-Nicholson, C. (1995). Posttraumatic stress. *Harvard Women's Health Watch, 11,* 2-3.

Roberts, G. W., Banspach, S. W., & Peacock, N. (1997). Behavioral scientists at the Centers for Disease Control and Prevention: Evolving and integrated roles. *American Psychologist, 52,* 143-146.

Robins, L. N., Helzer, J. E., Weissman, M. M., Orvaschel, H., Guenberg, E., Burke, J. D., & Regier, D. A. (1984). Lifetime prevalence of specific psychiatric disorders in three sites. *Archives of General Psychiatry, 41,* 949-958.

Roche, A. F., & Davila, G. H. (1972). Late adolescent growth in stature. *Pediatrics, 50,* 874-880.

Rock, I. (1986). The description and analysis of object and event perception. In K. R. Boff, L. Kaufman, & J. P. Thomas (Eds.), *Handbook of perception and human performance: Vol. 2. Cognitive processes and performance.* New York: Wiley.

Rodin, J. (1976). Crowding, perceived choice and response to controllable and uncontrollable outcomes. *Journal of Experimental Social Psychology, 12,* 564-578.

Rodin, J. (1981). Current status of the internal-external hypothesis of obesity: What went wrong? *American Psychologist, 36,* 361-372.

Rodin, J., & Salovey, P. (1989). Health psychology. *Annual Review of Psychology, 40,* 533-579.

Roediger, H. L. (1990). Implicit memory: Retention without remembering. *American Psychologist, 45,* 1043-1056.

Roehrs, T., & Roth, T. (1997). Hypnotics, alcohol and caffeine: Relation to insomnia. In M. R. Pressman & W. C. Orr (Eds.). *Understanding sleep: The evaluation and treatment of sleep disorders.* Washington, D. C.: American Psychological Association.

Rogers, C. R. (1959). A theory of therapy, personality, and interpersonal relationships as developed in the client-centered framework. In S. Koch (Ed.), *Psychology: A study of science.* New York: McGraw Hill.

Rollins, B. C., & Feldman, H. (1970). Marital satisfaction over the family life cycle. *Journal of Marriage and the Family, 32,* 20-27.

Rolls, B. J., Federoff, I. C., & Guthrie, J. F. (1991). Gender differences in eating behavior and body weight regulation. *Health Psychology, 10,* 133-142.

Rolls, E. T. (2000). Memory systems in the brain. In S. T. Fiske, D. L. Schacter, & C. Zahn-Waxler, (Eds.). *Annual review of psychology* (volume 52). (pp. 599-630). Palo Alto, CA: Annual Reviews.

Rook, K. S. (1987). Social support versus companionship: Effects of life stress, loneliness, and evaluation by others. *Journal of Personality and Social Psychology, 52,* 1132-1147.

Rorschach, H. (1921). *Psychodiagnostics.* Bern: Huber.

Rosch, E. (1973). Natural categories. *Cognitive Psychology, 4,* 328-350.

Rosch, E. (1975). Cognitive representations of semantic categories. *Journal of Experimental Psychology: General, 104,* 192-253.

Rosch, E. (1978). Principles of categorization. In E. Rosch & B. B. Lloyds (Eds.), *Cognition and categorization.* Hillsdale, NJ: Erlbaum.

Rose, A. S., & Blank, M. (1974). The potency of context in children's cognition: An illustration through conservation. *Child Development, 45,* 499-502.

Rosenbaum, M. E. (1986). The repulsion hypothesis: On the nondevelopment of relationships. *Journal of Personality and Social Psychology, 51,* 1156-1166.

Rosenman, R. H., Brand, R. J., Jenkins., C. D., Friedman, M., Straus,. R., & Wurm, M. (1975). Coronary heart disease in the Western Collaborative Group Study: Final follow-up experience of 8 1/2 years. *Journal of the American Medical Association, 233,* 872-877.

Rosenman, R. H., Friedman, M., Strauss, R., Wurm, M., Kositcheck, R., Hahn, W., & Werthessen, N. T. (1964). A predictive study of coronary heart disease. *Journal of the American Medical Association, 189,* 15-22.

Rosenthal, D. (1970). *Genetics of psychopathology.* New York: McGraw-Hill.

Rosenzweig, M. R. (1922). Psychological science around the world. *American Psychologist, 47,* 718-722.

Rosenzweig, M. R., Bennett, E. L., & Diamond, M. C. (1972). Brain changes in response to experiences. *Scientific American, 226,* 22-29.

Rosenzweig, M. R., Leiman, A. L., & Breedlove, S. M. (1996). *Biological psychology.* Sunderland, MA: Sinauer

Associates.

Rosnow, R. L., Skleder, A. A., & Rind, B. (1995). Reading other people: A hidden cognitive structure? *The General Psychologist, 31,* 1-10.

Ross, C. A. (1989). *Multiple personality disorder: Diagnosis, clinical features, and treatment.* New York: Wiley.

Ross, C. A. (1997). Dissociative identity disorder. New York: Wiley.

Ross, D., Read, J. D., & Toglia, M. P. (Eds.). (1993). *Eyewitness testimony: Current trends and developments.* New York: Cambridge University Press.

Ross, G., Kagan, J., Zelazo, P., & Kotelchuck, M. (1975). Separation protest in infants in home and laboratory. *Developmental Psychology, 11,* 256-257.

Ross, L. D. (1977). The intuitive psychologist and his short-comings: Distortions in the attributional process. In L. Berkowitz (Ed.), *Advances in experimental social psychology (Vol. 10).* New York: Academic Press.

Rossi, A. S. (1980). Aging and parenthood in the middle years. In P. B. Baltes & O. G. Brim, Jr. (Eds.), *Lifespan development and behavior (Vol. III).* New York: Academic Press.

Roth, E. M., & Shoben, E. J. (1983). The effect of context on the structure of categories. *Cognitive Psychology, 15,* 346-378.

Roth M., & Argyle, N. (1988). Anxiety, panic and phobic disorders: An overview. *Journal of Psychiatric Research, 22 (Suppl. 1),* 33-54.

Rothbaum, B. O., Foa, E. B., Murdock, T., Riggs, D., & Walsh, W. (1992). A prospective examination of post-traumatic stress disorder in rape victims. *Journal of Traumatic Stress, 5,* 455-475.

Rothenberg, S. A. (1997). Introduction to sleep disorders. In M. R. Pressman & W. C. Orr (Eds.), *Understanding sleep: The evaluation and treatment of sleep disorders.* Washington, D. C.: American Psychological Association.

Rothstein, H. R., Schmidt, F. L., Erwin, F. W., Owens, W. A., & Sparks, C. P. (1990). Biographical data in employment selection: Can validities be made generalizable? *Journal of Applied Psychology, 75,* 175-184.

Rotton, J., & Frey, J. (1985). Air pollution, weather, and violent crimes: Concomitant analysis of archival data. *Journal of Personality and Social Psychology, 49,* 1207-1220.

Rovee-Collier, C. K. (1984). The ontogeny of learning and memory in infancy. In R. Kail & N. E. Spear (Eds.), *Comparative perspectives on the development of memory.* Hillsdale, NJ: Lawrence Erlbaum Associates.

Rowe, D. C. (1981). Environmental and genetic influences on dimensions of perceived parenting: A twin study. *Developmental Psychology, 17,* 203-208.

Rowe, D. C. (1987). Resolving the person-situation debate. *American Psychologist, 42,* 218-227.

Rowe, J. W., & Kahn, R. L. (1987). Human aging: Usual and successful. *Science, 237,* 143-149.

Ruback, R. B., & Pandey, J. (1988). Crowding and perceived control in India. Unpublished manuscript, cited in J. Pandet (1990).

Rubin, D. C., & Kontis, T. C. (1983). A schema for common cents. Memory and *Cognition, 11,* 335-341.

Rubin, Z. (1973). *Liking and loving: An invitation to social psychology.* New York: Holt, Rinehart & Winston.

Rudd, M. D., Dahm, P. F., & Rajab, M. H. (1993). Diagnostic comorbidity in persons with suicidal ideation and behavior. American J*ournal of Psychiatry, 150,* 928-934.

Rushton, J. P. (1988). Race differences in behavior: A review and evolutionary analysis. *Personality and Individual Differences, 9,* 1009-1024.

Rushton, J. P., Fulker, D. W., Neale, M. C., Nias, D. K. B., & Eysenck, H. J. (1986). Altruism and aggression: The heritability of individual differences. *Journal of Personality and Social Psychology, 50,* 1192-1198.

Rutter, M., Graham, P., Chadwick, O., & Yule, W. (1976). Adolescent turmoil: Fact or fiction? *Journal of Child Psychology and Psychiatry, 17,* 35-56.

Rutter, M., & Schopler, E. (1987). Autism and pervasive developmental disorders: Concepts and diagnostic uses. *Journal of Autism and Developmental Disorders, 17,* 159-186.

Ryan, E. D., & Kovacic, C. R. (1966). Pain tolerance and athletic participation. *Journal of Personality and Social Psychology, 22,* 383-390.

Saal, F. E., & Knight, P. A. (1988). Industrial/organizational psychology. Monterey, CA: Brooks/Cole.

Saari, L. M., Johnson, T. R., McLaughlin, S. D., & Zimerle, D. M. (1988). A survey of management training and education practices in U.S. companies. Personnel Psychology,

41, 731-743.

Sachdev, P., Hay, P., & Cummings, S. (1992). Psychosurgical treatment of obsessive-compulsive disorder. *Archives of General Psychiatry, 49,* 582-583.

Sack, R.L., & Lewy, A.J. (1997). Melatonin as a chronobiotic: Treatment of circadian desynchrony in night workers and the blind. *Journal of Biological Rhythms,* 12, 595-603.

Sackeim, H. A. (1985). The case for ECT. *Psychology Today, 19,* 36-40.

Sackeim, H. A., Luber, B., Katzman, G. P., Moeller, J. R., Prudic, J., Devanand, D. P., & Nobler. (1996). The effects of electroconvulsive therapy on quantitative electroencephalograms: Relationship to clinical outcome. *Archives of General Psychiatry, 53,* 814-824.

Sadalla, E. K., & Oxley, D. (1984). The perception of room size. The rectangularity illusion. *Environment and Behavior, 16,* 394-405.

Saegert, S., & Winkel, G. H. (1990). Environmental psychology. Annual Review of Psychology, 41, 441-477.

Safer, M. (1980). Attributing evil to the subject, not the situation: Student reactions to Milgram's film on obedience. Personality and *Social Psychology Bulletin, 6,* 205-209.

Sakai, K. (1985). Neurons responsible for paradoxical sleep. In A. Wauquier (Ed.), *Sleep: Neurotransmitters and neuromodulators.* New York: Raven Press.

Salapatek, P. (1975). Pattern perception in early infancy. In L. B. Cohen & P. Salapatek (Eds.), *Infant perception: From sensation to cognition.* New York: Academic Press.

Salovey, P., & Mayer, J. D. (1994). Some final thoughts about personality and intelligence. IN R. J. Sternberg (Ed.) , Personality and intelligence. (pp. 303-318). New York: Cambridge University Press.

Salthouse, T. A. (1989). Age-related changes in basic cognitive processes. In M. Storandt & G. R. VandenBos (Eds.), *The adult years: Continuity and change.* Washington, DC: American Psychological Association.

Sameroff, A. J., & Cavanaugh, P. J. (1979). Learning in infancy: A developmental perspective. In J. D. Osofsky (Ed.), *Handbook of infant development.* New York: Wiley.

Samuelson, F. J. B. (1980). Watson's Little Albert, Cyril Burt's twins, and the need for a critical science. *American Psychologist, 35,* 619-625.

Sandler, J., Dare, C., & Holder, A. (1992). *The patient and the analyst: The basis of the psychoanalytic process* (2nd ed.). Madison, CT: International University Press.

Sands, L. P., Terry, H., & Meredith, W. (1989). Change and stability in adult intellectual functioning assessed by Wechsler item responses. *Psychology and Aging, 4,* 79-87.

Sanua, V. D. (1987). Standing against an established ideology: Infantile autism, a case in point. *Clinical Psychology, 4,* 96-110.

Satir, V. (1967). *Conjoint family therapy.* Palo Alto, CA: Science and Behavior Books.

Saunders, N. A., & Sullivan, C. E. (Eds.). (1994). *Sleep and breathing* (2nd ed.). New York: Marcel Dekker.

Sauser, W. J., & York, C. M. (1978). Sex differences in job satisfaction: A reexamination. *Personnel Psychology, 31,* 537-547.

Scarborough, E., & Furumoto, L. (1987). *Untold lives: The first generation of American women psychologists.* New York: Columbia University Press.

Scarr, S., & Eisenberg, M. (1993). Child care research: Issues, perspectives, and results. *Annual Review of Psychology, 44,* 613-644.

Scarr, S., & Kidd, K. K. (1983). Developmental behavior genetics. In P. H. Mussen (Ed.), *Handbook of child psychology, Vol. 2: Infancy and developmental psychobiology.* New York: Wiley.

Schacter, D. L. (1987). Implicit memory: History and current status. *Journal of Experimental Psychology: Learning, Memory, and Cognition, 13,* 501-518.

Schacter, D. L. (1992). Understanding implicit memory: A cognitive neuroscience approach. *American Psychologist, 47,* 559-569.

Schacter, D. L. (1996). *Searching for memory: The brain, mind and the past.* New York: Basic Books.

Schacter, D. L., Norman, K. A., & Koutstaal, W. (1998). The cognitive neuroscience of constructive memory. *Annual Review of Psychology, 48,* 289-318.

Schachter, S. (1971). Some extraordinary facts about obese humans and rats. *American Psychologist, 26,* 129-144.

Schachter, S., & Gross, L. P. (1968). Manipulated time and eating behavior. *Journal of Personality and Social Psychology, 1,* 98-106.

Schaffer, H. R., & Emerson, P. E. (1964). The development of social attachments in infancy. *Monographs for the society for research in child development, 29, Serial 94.*

Schaie, K. W. (1974). *Translations in gerontology-from lab to life: Intellectual functioning. American Psychologist, 29,* 802-807.

Schaie, K. W. (1983). The Seattle Longitudinal Study: A 21-year exploration of psychometric intelligence in adulthood. In K. W. Schaie (Ed.), *Longitudinal studies of adult psychological development.* New York: Guilford.

Schaie, K. W. (1993). The Seattle Longitudinal Studies of Adult Intelligence. *Current Directions in Psychological Science, 2,* 171-175.

Schaie, K. W., & Strother, C. R. (1968). A cross-sequential study of age changes in cognitive behavior. *Psychological Bulletin, 70,* 671-680.

Schaie, K. W., & Willis, S. L. (1986). *Adult development and aging* (2nd ed.). Boston: Little, Brown.

Scharf, B. (1978). Loudness. In E. C. Carterette & M. P. Friedman (Eds.), *Handbook of perception.* New York: Academic Press.

Scharli, H., & Harman, A. M.. (1999) Residual vision in a subject with damaged visual cortex. *Journal of Cognitive Neuroscience,* 11, 502. Retrieved from the World Wide Web October 5, 2000, http://ehostvgw15.epnet.com/

Scharli, H., Harman, A. M., &. Hogben, J. H. Blindsight in subjects with homonymous visual field defects. *Journal of Cognitive Neuroscience, 11,* 52. Retrieved from the World Wide Web on October 5, 2000, http://ehostvgw15.epnet.com/

Schau, C. G., Kahn, L., Diepold, J. H., & Cherry, F. (1980). The relationships of parental expectations and preschool children's verbal sex typing to their sex-typed toy play behavior. *Child Development, 51,* 266-270.

Scheerer, M. (1963). Problem solving. *Scientific American, 208,* 118-128.

Scheier, M. F., & Carver, C. S. (1992). Effects of optimism on psychological and physical well-being: Theoretical overview and empirical update. *Cognitive Therapy and Research, 16,* 206-228.

Scheier, M. F., & Carver, C. S. (1993). On the power of positive thinking: The benefits of being optimistic. *Current Directions in Psychological Science, 2,* 26-30.

Scheier, M. F., Matthews, K. A., Owens, J. F., Magovern, G. J., Lefebvre, R., Abbott, R. C., & Carver, C. S. (1989). Dispositional optimism and recovery from coronary artery bypass surgery: The beneficial effects of optimism on physical and psychological well-being. *Journal of Personality and Social Psychology, 57,* 1024-1040.

Schelling, T. C. (1992). Addictive drugs: The cigarette experience. *Science, 255,* 430-433.

Scher, S. J., & Cooper, J. (1989). Motivational basis of dissonance: The singular role of behavioral consequences. *Journal of Personality and Social Psychology, 56,* 899-906.

Scherer, K. R. (1986). Vocal affect expression: A review and model for future research. *Psychological Bulletin, 99,* 143-165.

Schiff, B. B., & Lamon, M. (1989). Inducing emotion by unilateral contraction of facial muscles: A new look at hemispheric specialization and the experience of emotion. *Neuropsychologia, 27,* 923-925.

Schiffman, H. R. (1990). *Sensation and perception: An integrated approach.* New York: Wiley.

Schmidt, F. L. (1992). What do data really mean? Research findings, meta-analysis, and cumulative knowledge in psychology. *American Psychologist, 47,* 1173-1181.

Schmidt, F. L., & Hunter, J. E. (1993). Tacit knowledge, practical intelligence, general mental ability, and job knowledge. *Current Directions in Psychological Science, 2,* 8-9.

Schmidt, F. L., Ones, D. S., & Hunter, J. E. (1992). Personnel selection. *Annual Review of Psychology, 43,* 627-670.

Schmitt, H. N., Schneider, J. R., & Cohen, S. A. (1990). Factors affecting validity of a regionally administered assessment center. *Personnel Psychology, 43,* 1-12.

Schmitt, N., & robertson, I. (1990). Personnel selection. *Annual Review of Psychology, 41,* 289-319.

Schmitt, R. C. (1966). Density, health, and social disorganization. *American Institute of Planners Journal, 32,* 38-40.

Schoen, R., & Wooldredge, J. (1989). Marriage choices in North Carolina, 1969-1971 and 1979-1981. *Journal of Marriage and the Family, 51,* 465-481.

Schooler, N. R., & Keith, S. J. (1993). The clinical research base for the treatment of schizophrenia. *Psychopharmacology Bulletin, 29,* 431-446.

Schou, M. (1997). Forty years of lithium treatment. *Archives of General Psychiatry, 54,* 9-13.

Schroeder, S. R., Schroeder, C. S., & Landesman, S. (1987).

Psychological services in educational settings to persons with mental retardation. *American Psychologist, 42,* 805-808.

Schuckit, M. A. (1989). *Drug and alcohol abuse: A clinical guide to diagnosis and treatment* (3rd ed.). New York: Plenum.

Schultz, *D. P., & Schultz, S. E. (1990).* Psychology and industry today. New York: Macmillan.

Schultz, R., & Alderman, D. (1974). Clinical research on the "stages of dying," *Omega, 5,* 137-144.

Schultz, R., & Decker, S. (1985). Long-term adjustment to physical disability: The role of social support, perceived control and self-blame. *Journal of Personality and Social Psychology, 48,* 1162-1172.

Schutte, N. S., Malouff, J. M., Hall, L. E., Haggerty, D. J., Cooper, J. T., Golden, C. J., & Dornheim, L. (1998). Development and validation of a measure of emotional intelligence. Personality and individual differences. 25(2), 167-177.

Schwartz, P. (1983). Length of day-care attendance and attachment behavior in eighteen-month-old infants. *Child Development, 54,* 1073-1078.

Scogin, F., & McElreath, L. (1994). Efficacy of psychosocial treatments for geriatric depression: A quantitative review. Journal of *Consulting and Clinical Psychology, 62,* 69-74.

Scott, K. G., & Carran, D. T. (1987). The epidemiology and prevention of mental retardation. *American Psychologist, 42,* 801-804.

Scott, M. D., & Pelliccioni, L., Jr. (1982). *Don't choke: How athletes become winners.* Englewood Cliffs, NJ: Prentice-Hall.

Sears, P. S., & Barbee, A. H. (1977). Career and life satisfaction among Terman's gifted women. In J. Stanley et al. (Eds.), *The gifted and the creative: Fifty year perspective.* Baltimore: Johns Hopkins University Press.

Sechrest, L. & Walsh, M. (1997). Dogma or data: Bragging rights. *American Psychologist, 52,* 536-540

Segall, M., Dasen, P., Berry, J., & Poortinga, Y. (1990). *Human behavior in global perspective.* Elmsford, NY: Pergamon.

Segall, M. H., Campbell, D. T., & Herskovits, M. J. (1966). *The influence of culture on visual perception.* Indianapolis: Bobbs-Merrill.

Segall, M. H., Lonner, W. J., & Berry, J. W. (1998). Cross-cultural psychology as a scholarly discipline: On the flowering of culture in behavioral research. *American psychologist,* 53, 1101-1110.

Seidenberg, M. S. (1997). Language acquisition and use: Learning and applying probabilistic constraints. *Science,* 275, 1599-1603.

Seligman, M. E. P. (1975). *Helplessness: On depression development and death.* San Francisco: Freeman.

Seligman, M. E. P. (1995). The effectiveness of psychotherapy: The Consumer Reports study. *American Psychologist, 50,* 965-974.

Seligman, M. E. P. (1996). Long-term psychotherapy is highly effective: The Consumer Reports study. *The Harvard Mental Health Letter, 13(1),* 5- 7.

Selkoe, D. J. (1990). Deciphering Alzheimer's disease: The amyloid precursor protein yields new clues. *Science, 248,* 1058.

Selye, H. (1974). *Stress without distress.* Philadelphia: Lippincott.

Selye, H. (1976). *The stress of life.* New York: McGraw-Hill.

Sennecker, P., & Hendrick, C. (1983). Androgyny and helping behavior. *Journal of Personality and Social Psychology, 45,* 916-925.

Serbin, L. A., Sprafkin, C., Elman, M., & Doyle, A. B. (1984). The early development of sex differentiated patterns of social influence. *Canadian Journal of Social Science, 14,* 350-363.

Serpell, R., & Deregowski, J. B. (1980). The skill of pictorial perception: An interpretation of cross-cultural evidence. *International Journal of Psychology, 15,* 145-180.

Shadish, W. R. (1984). Policy research: Lessons from the implementation of deinstitutionalization. *American Psychologist, 39,* 725-738.

Shadish, W. R., Montgomery, L. M., Wilson, P., Wilson, M. R., Bright, I., & Okwumabua, T. (1993). Effects of marital and family psychotherapies: A meta-analysis. *Journal of Consulting and Clinical Psychology, 61,* 992-1002.

Shadmehr, R., & Holcomb, H. H. (1997). Neural correlates of motor memory consolidation. *Science, 277,* 821-825.

Shaffer, D. R. (1996). *Developmental psychology: Childhood and adolescence (Fourth Edition.* Pacific Gorve, CA: Brooks/Cole.

Shaffer, D. (1999). *Developmental psychology: Childhood and adolescence* (5th ed.). Pacific Grove, CA: Brooks/Cole.

Shaffer, G. S., Saunders, V., & Owens, W. A. (1986). Additional evidence for the accuracy of biographical data: Long-term retest and observer ratings. *Personnel Psychology, 39,* 791-809.

Shaffer, M. (1982). *Life after stress.* New York: Knopf.

Shapiro, D. H., Jr. (1985). Clinical use of meditation as a self-regulation strategy: Comment on Holmes's conclusions and implications. *American Psychologist, 40,* 719-722.

Shaver, P., Hazan, C., & Bradshaw, D. (1988). Love as attachment: The integration of three behavioral systems. In R. J. Sternberg & M. L. Barnes (Eds.), *The psychology of love.* New Haven, CT: Yale University Press.

Shaywitz, B. A., Shaywitz, S. E., Pugh, K. R., Constable, R. T., Skudlarski, P., Fulbright, R. K., et al. (1995). Sex differences in the functional organization of the brain for language. *Nature, 373,* 607-609.

Shedler, J., & Block, J. (1990). Adolescent drug use and psychological health: A longitudinal study. *American Psychologist, 45,* 612-630.

Sheehan, P. W., Green, V., & Truesdale, P. (1992). Influence of rapport on hypnotically induced pseudomemory. *Journal of Abnormal Psychology, 101,* 690-700.

Sheehan, P. W., & Statham, D. (1989). Hypnosis, the timing of its introduction, and acceptance of misleading information. *Journal of Abnormal Psychology, 93,* 170-176.

Sheehan, P. W., Statham, D., Jamison, G. A., Ferguson, S. (1991). Ambiguity in suggestion and the occurrence of pseudomemory in the hypnotic interview. *Australian Journal of Clinical and Experimental Hypnosis, 19,* 1-18.

Sheer, D. E. (Ed.). (1961). *Electrical stimulation of the brain.* Austin: University of Texas Press.

Shekelle, B., Hulley, S. B., Neaton, J. D., Billings, J. H., Borhani, N. O., et al. (1985). The MRFIT behavior pattern study II: Type A behavior and the incidence of coronary heart disease. *American Journal of Epidemiology, 122,* 559-570.

Shekelle, R. B., Gale, M. E., & Norvis, M. (1985). Type A scores (Jenkins Activity Survey) and risk of recurrent coronary heart disease in the Aspirin Myocardial Infarction Study. *American Journal of Cardiology, 56,* 221-225.

Shelton, M., & Cook, M. (1993). Fetal alcohol syndrome: Facts and prevention. *Preventing School Failure, 37,* 44-47.

Sheridan, C. L., & Perkins, A. (1992). Cross-validation of an inventory of stressors for teenagers. *Medical Psychotherapy, 5,* 103-108.

Sheridan, C. L., & Smith, L. K. (1987). Toward a comprehensive scale of stress assessment: Norms, reliability, and validity. *International Journal of Psychometrics, 34,* 48-54.

Sheridan, K., Humfleet, G., Phair, J., & Lyons, J. (1990). The effects of AIDS education on the knowledge and attitudes of community leaders. *Journal of Community Psychology, 18,* 354-360.

Sherif, M. (1936). *The Psychology of Social Norms.* New York: Harper & Row.

Sherman, S. J., Judd, C. M., & Park, B. (1989). Social cognition. *Annual Review of Psychology, 40,* 281-326.

Sherman, R. T., & Thompson, R. A. (1990). Bulimia: A guide for family and friends. Lexington, MA: Lexington Books.

Shertzer, B. (1985). *Career planning* (3rd ed.). Boston: Houghton Mifflin.

Shiffman, L. B., Fischer, L. B., Zettler-Segal, M., & Benowitz, N. L. (1990). Nicotine exposure among nondependent smokers. *Archives of General Psychiatry, 47,* 333-340.

Shiffman, S. (1992). Relapse process and relapse prevention in addictive behaviors. The Behavior Therapist, 15, 99-111.

Shimamura, A. P. (1986). Priming effects in amnesia: Evidence for a dissociable memory function. *Quarterly Journal of Experimental Psychology, 38A,* 619-644.

Shipley, T. (1961). *Classics in psychology.* New York: Philosophical Library.

Shippee, G., & Gregory, W. L. (1982). Public commitment and energy conservation. *American Journal of Community Psychology, 10,* 81-93.

Shirley, M. C., Matt, D. A., & Burish, T. G. (1992). Comparison of frontalis, multiple muscle site, and reactive muscle site feedback in reducing arousal under stressful and nonstressful conditions. *Medical Psychotherapy, 5,* 133-148.

Shotland, R. L. (1985). When bystanders just stand by. *Psychology Today, 19,* 50-55.

Shulman, H. G. (1971). Similarity effects in short-term memory. *Psychological Bulletin, 75,* 399-415.

Shulman, H. G. (1972). Semantic confusion errors in short-term memory. *Journal of Verbal Learning and Verbal Behavior, 11,* 221-227.

Shweder, R. A., & Sullivan, M. A. (1993). Cultural psychology: Who needs it? *Annual Review of Psychology, 44,* 497-523.

Sibai, B. M., Caritis, S. N., Thom, E., Klebanoff, M., McNellis, D., et al. (1993). Prevention of preeclampsia with low-dose aspirin in healthy, nulliparous pregnant women. *New England Journal of Medicine, 329,* 1213-1218.

Siegler, R. S. (1983). Five generalizations about cognitive development. *American Psychologist, 38,* 263-277.

Siegler, R. S. (1989). Mechanisms of cognitive development. *Annual Review of Psychology, 40,* 353-379.

Signorella, M. L., Bigler, R. S., & Liben, L. S. (1997). A meta-analysis of children's memories for own-sex and other-sex information. *Journal of Applied Developmental Psychology,* 18, 429-445.

Silva, J. M., Hardy, C. J., & Crace, R. K. (1988). Analysis of momentum in intercollegiate tennis. *Journal of Sport and Exercise Psychology, 10,* 346-354.

Silver, E., Cirincione, C., & Steadman, H. J. (1994). Demythologizing inaccurate perceptions of the insanity defense. Law and human behavior, 18, 63-70.

Simkins-Bullock, J. A., & Wildman, B. G. (1991). An investigation into the relationships between gender and language. *Sex Roles, 24,* 149-160.

Simon, H. A. (1990). Invariants of human behavior. *Annual Review of Psychology, 41,* 1-19.

Simonton, D. K. (1997). Creative productivity: A predictive and explanatory model of career trajectories and landmarks. *Psychological Review,* **104,** 66-89.

Sims, E. A. H. (1990). Destiny rides again as twins overeat. New *England Journal of Medicine, 322,* 1522-1523.

Sinha, S., Anderson, J. P., Barbour, R., et al. (1999). Purification and cloning of amyloid precursor protein beta-secretase from human brain. Nature, 402, 537-540.

Sinton, C. M., Fitch, T. E., & Gershenfeld, H. K. (1999). The effects of leptin on REM sleep and slow wave delta in rats are reversed by food deprivation. *Journal of Sleep Research,* 8, 197-203.

Skinner, B. F. (1938). *The behavior of organisms: A behavioral analysis.* Englewood Cliffs, NJ: Prentice-Hall.

Skinner, B. F. (1956). A case history in the scientific method. *American Psychologist, 11,* 221-233.

Skinner, B. F. (1957). *Verbal behavior.* Englewood Cliffs, NJ: Prentice-Hall.

Skinner, B. F. (1983). Intellectual self-management in old age. *American Psychologist, 38,* 239-244.

Skinner, B. F. (1984). *A matter of consequence.* New York: Knopf.

Skinner, B. F. (1987). What ever happened to psychology as the science of behavior? *American Psychologist, 42,* 780-786.

Skinner, B. F. (1989). The origins of cognitive thought. *American Psychologist, 44,* 13-18.

Skinner, B. F. (1990). Can psychology be a science of mind? American Psychologist, 45, 1206-1210.

Skolnick, A. (1979). *The intimate environment* (2nd ed.). Boston: Little, Brown.

Slater, A., Morison, V., Town, C., & Rose, D. (1985). Movement perception and identity constancy in the newborn baby. *British Journal of Developmental Psychology, 3,* 211-220.

Slobin, D. I. (1979). *Psycholinguistics.* Glenview, IL: Scott, Foresman.

Slovic, P., & Fischoff, B. (1977). On the psychology of experimental surprise. *Journal of Experimental Psychology: Human Perception and Performance, 3,* 544-551.

Small, J. G., Klapper, M. H., Kellams, J. J., Miller, M. J., Milstein, V., Sharpley, P. H., & Small, I. F. (1988). Electroconvulsive treatment compared with lithium in the management of manic states. *Archives of General Psychiatry, 45,* 727-732.

Smalley, S. L. (1991). Genetic influences in autism. *Psychiatric Clinics of North America, 14,* 125-139.

Smeaton, G., Byrne, D., & Murnen, S. (1989). The repulsion hypothesis revisited: Similarity irrelevance or dissimilarity bias? *Journal of Personality and Social Psychology, 56,* 54-59.

Smetana, J. G., Killen, M., & Turiel, E. (1991). Children's reasoning about interpersonal and moral conflicts. *Child Development, 62,* 629-644.

Smith, A., & Stansfield, S. (1986). Aircraft noise exposure, noise sensitivity, and everyday errors. *Environment and Behavior, 18,* 214-226.

Smith, A. P. & Jones, D. M. (1992). Noise and performance. In D. M. Jones & A. P. Smith (Eds.), Handbook of human performance (Vol. 1). London: Academic Press.

Staples, S. L. (1996). Human response to environmental noise: Psychological research and public policy. *American Psychologist, 51,* 143-150.

Smith, C. P. (Ed.). (1992). *Motivation and personality: Handbook of thematic content analysis.* Cambridge: Cambridge University Press.

Smith, D. (1987). Conditions that facilitate the development of sport imagery training. *The Sport Psychologist, 1,* 237-247.

Smith, G. B., Schwebel, A. I., Dunn, R. L., & McIver, S. D. (1993). The role of psychologists in the treatment, management, and prevention of chronic mental illness. *American Psychologist, 48,* 966-971.

Smith, M. L., Glass, G. V., & Miller, T. I. (1980). *The benefits of psychotherapy.* Baltimore: Johns Hopkins University Press.

Smith, P. C. (1976). Behavior, results, and organizational effectiveness: The problem of criteria. In M. D. Dunnette (Ed.), *Handbook of industrial and organizational psychology.* Skokie, IL: Rand McNally.

Smith, S. (1979). Remembering in and out of context. *Journal of Experimental Psychology: Human Learning and Memory, 5,* 460-471.

Smith, T. W. (1992). Hostility and health: Current status of a psychosomatic hypothesis. *Health Psychology, 11,* 139-150.

Smither, R. D. (1994). *The psychology of work and human performance.* New York: HarperCollins.

Smyrnios, K. X., & Kirkby, R. J. (1993). Long-term comparison of brief versus unlimited psychodynamic treatments with children and their parents. *Journal of Consulting and Clinical Psychology, 61,* 1020-1027.

Snarey, J. (1987). A question of morality. *Psychology Today, 21,* 6-8.

Snarey, J. R., Reimer, J., & Kohlberg, L. (1985). Development of social-moral reasoning among kibbutz adolescents: A longitudinal cross-sectional study. *Developmental Psychology, 21,* 3-17.

Snow, M. E., Jacklin, C. N., & Maccoby, E. E. (1983). Sex-of-child differences in father-child interaction at one year of age. *Child Development, 54,* 227-232.

Snyder, S. H. (1984, November). Medicated minds. *Science 84,* pp. 141-142.

Snyderman, M., & Rothman, S. (1987). Survey of expert opinion on intelligence and aptitude testing. *American Psychologist, 42,* 137-144.

Sobal, J., & Stunkard, A. J. (1989). Socioeconomic status and obesity: A review of the literature. *Psychological Bulletin, 105,* 260-275.

Somers, V. K., Dyken, M. E., Mark, A. L., & Abboud, F. M. (1993). Sympathetic-nerve activity during sleep in normal subjects. *The New England Journal of Medicine, 328,* 303-307.

Sommer, R. (1969). *Personal space: The behavioral basis of designs.* Englewood Cliffs, NJ: Prentice-Hall.

Somerfield, M. R. & McCrae, R. R. (2000). Stress and coping research: Methodological challenges, theoretical advances, and clinical applications. American psychologist, 55, 620-625.

Sorensen, J. L., Wermuth, L. A., Gibson, D. R., Choi, K., et al. (1991). *Preventing AIDS in drug users and their sexual partners.* New York: Guilford.

Soyka, L. F., & Joffee, J. M. (1980). Male mediated drug effects on offspring. In R. H. Schwarz & S. J. Yaffe (Eds.), *Drug and chemical risks to the fetus and newborn.* New York: Alan R. Liss.

Spanos, N. P., & Barber, T. F. S. (1974). Toward convergence in hypnosis research. *American Psychologist, 29,* 500-511.

Spanos, N. P., Menary, E., Gabora, N. J., DuBreuil, S. C., & Dewhirst, B. (1991). Secondary identity enactments during past-life regression: A sociocognitive perspective. *Journal of Personality and Social Psychology, 61,* 308-320.

Spanos, N. P. (1994). Multiple identity enactments and multiple personality disorder: A socoiocognitive perspective. *Psychological Bulletin,* **116,** 143-165.

Spear, N. E., Miller, J. S., & Jagielo, J. A. (1990). Animal learning and memory. *Annual Review of Psychology, 41,*

169-211.

Spearman, C. (1904). "General intelligence" objectively determined and measured. *American Journal of Psychology, 15,* 201-293.

Spence, J. T. (1985). Gender identity and its implications for concepts of masculinity and femininity. In T. Sondregger (Ed.), *Nebraska symposium on motivation.* Lincoln: University of Nebraska Press.

Spencer, D. D., Robbins, R. J., Naftolin, F., et al. (1992). Unilateral transplantation of human fetal mesencephalic tissue into the caudate nucleus of patients with Parkinson's disease. *New England Journal of Medicine, 327,* 1541-1548.

Sperling, G. (1960). The information available in brief visual presentation. *Psychological Monographs, 74 (Whole No. 498).*

Sperling, G. (1963). A model for visual memory tasks. *Human Factors, 5,* 19-31.

Sperry, R. (1968). Hemispheric disconnection and unity in conscious awareness. *American Psychologist, 23,* 723-733.

Sperry, R. (1982). Some effects of disconnecting the cerebral hemispheres. *Science, 217,* 1223-1226.

Spitz, H. (1986). *The raising of intelligence: A selected history of attempts to raise retarded intelligence.* Hillsdale, NJ: Erlbaum.

Springer, J. P., & Deutsch, G. (1981). *Left brain, right brain.* San Francisco: Freeman.

Squire, L. R. (1986). Mechanisms of memory. *Science, 232,* 1612-1619.

Squire, L. R. (1987). *Memory and the brain.* New York: Oxford University Press.

Squire, L. R. (1992). Memory and the hippocampus: A synthesis from findings with rats, monkeys, and humans. *Psychological Review, 99,* 195-231.

Squire, L. R., Knowlton, B., & Mussen, G. (1993). The structure and organization of memory. *Annual Review of Psychology, 44,* 453-495.

Squire, L. R., & Slater, P. C. (1978). Bilateral and unilateral ECT: Effects on verbal and nonverbal memory. *American Journal of Psychiatry, 135,* 1316-1320.

Stall, R. D., Coates, T. J., & Huff, C. (1988). Behavioral risk reduction of HIV infection among gay and bisexual men: A review of results from the United States. *American Psychologist, 43,* 878-885.

Standing, L. (1973). Learning 10,000 pictures. *Quarterly Journal of Experimental Psychology, 25,* 207-222.

Standing, L., Canezio, J., & Haber, R. N. (1970). Perception and memory for pictures: Single-trial learning 2500 visual stimuli. *Psychonomic Science, 19,* 73-74.

Staw, B. M. (1984). Organized behavior: A review and reformation of the field's outcome variables. *Annual Review of Psychology, 35,* 627-666.

Steadman, H. J., Mulvey, E. P., Monahan, J., & Robbins, P. C. (1998). Violence by people discharged from acute psychiatric facilities and by others in the same area. Archives of general psychiatry, 55, 393-401.

Steblay, N. M., & Bothwell, R. K. (1994). Evidence for hypnotically refreshed testimony: The view from the laboratory. *Law and Human Behavior, 18,* 635-652.

Stechler, G., & Halton, A. (1982). Prenatal influences on human development. In B. B. Woolman (Ed.), *Handbook of developmental psychology.* Englewood Cliffs, NJ: Prentice-Hall.

Steele, C. M., & Aronson, J. (1995). Stereotype threat and the intellectual test performance of African-Americans. *Journal of Personality and Social Psychology, 69,* 797-811.

Steenbarger, B. N. (1994). Duration and outcome in psychotherapy: An integrative review. *Professional Psychology: Research and Practice, 25,* 111-119.

Stein, B. A. (1983). *Quality of work life in action: Managing for effectiveness.* New York: American Management Association.

Stein, J. A., Newcomb, M. D., & Bentler, P. M. (1990). The relative influence of vocational behavior and family involvement on self-esteem: Longitudinal analyses of young adult women and men. *Journal of Vocational Behavior, 36,* 320-328.

Stein, M. B., Walker, J. R., & Forde, D. R. (1996). Public-speaking fears in a community sample: Prevalence, impact on functioning, and diagnostic classification. *Archives of General Psychiatry,* **53**, 169-174.

Steiner, M., Steinberg, S., Stewart, D., Carter, D., Berger, C., Reid, R., Grover, D., & Steiner, D. (1995). Floxetine in the treatment of premenstrual dysphoria. *New England Journal of Medicine, 332,* 1529-1534.

Steinhausen, H. C., Göbel, D., Breinlinger, M., & Wolleben, B. (1986). A community survey of infantile autism. *Journal of the American Academy of Child Psychiatry, 25,* 186-189.

Stenchever, M. A., Williamson, R. A., Leonard, J., Karp, L. E., Ley, B., Shy, K., & Smith, D. (1981). Possible relationship between in utero diethylstilbestrol exposure and male infertility. *American Journal of Obstetrics and Gynecology, 140,* 186-193.

Stephan, W. (1985). Intergroup relations. In G. Lindsey & E. Aronson (Eds.), *Handbook of social psychology* (3rd ed.). New York: Random House.

Stern, D. (1977). *The first relationship.* Cambridge, MA: Harvard University Press.

Stern, L. (1985). *The structures and strategies of human memory.* Homewood, IL: Dorsey Press.

Stern, P. C. (1992). Psychological dimensions of global environmental change. *Annual Review of Psychology, 43,* 269-302.

Sternberg, R. J. (1979). The nature of mental abilities. *American Psychologist, 34,* 214-230.

Sternberg, R. J. (1981). Testing and cognitive psychology. *American Psychologist, 36,* 1181-1189.

Sternberg, R. J. (1985). *Beyond IQ.* New York: Cambridge University Press.

Sternberg, R. J. (1988). *The triarchic mind.* New York: Viking Press.

Sternberg, R. J. (1990). *Metaphors of mind: Conceptions of the nature of intelligence.* New York: Cambridge University Press.

Sternberg, R. J., & Kaufman, J. C. (1998). Human abilities. *Annual Review of Psychology, 48,* 479-502.

Sternberg, R. J., & Lubart. (1996). Investing in creativity. *American Psychologist,* **51**, 677-688.

Sternberg, R. J., & Wagner, R. K. (1993). The g-centric view of intelligence and job performance is wrong. *Current Directions in Psychological Science, 2,* 1-5.

Sternberg, R. J., & Wanger, R. K. (1993). The g-centric view of intelligence and job-performance is wrong. *Current Directions in Psychological Science,* **2**, 1-5.

Stevenson, H. W., Lee, S. Y., & Stigler, J. W. (1986). Mathematics achievement of Chinese, Japanese, and American children. *Science, 231,* 693-696.

Stiles, W. B., Shapiro, D. A., & Elliot, R. (1986). "Are all psychotherapies equivalent?" *American Psychologist, 41,* 165-180.

Stinnett, N., Walters, J., & Kaye, E. (1984). *Relationships in marriage and family* (2nd ed.). New York: Macmillan.

Stokols, D. (1972). On the distinction between density and crowding: Some implications for future research. *Psychological Review, 79,* 275-277.

Stokols, D. (1990). Instrumental and spiritual views of people-environment relations. *American Psychologist, 45,* 641-646.

Stokols, D. (1992). Establishing and maintaining healthy environments. *American Psychologist 47,* 6-22.

Stoner, J. A. F. (1961). A comparison of individual and group decisions involving risk. Unpublished master's thesis, Massachusetts Institute of Technology, Cambridge.

Storandt, M. (1983). Psychology's response to the graying of America. *American Psychologist, 38,* 323-326.

Streissguth, A. P., Aase, J. M., Clarren, S. K., Randels, S. P., La Due, R. A., & Smith, D. F. (1991). Fetal alcohol syndrome in adolescents and adults. *Journal of the American Medical Association, 265,* 1961-1967.

Strickland, B. R. (1992). Women and depression. *Psychological Science, 1,* 132-135.

Strupp, H. H. (1986). Psychotherapy: Research, practice, and public policy (How to avoid dead ends). *American Psychologist, 41,* 120-130.

Strupp, H. H. (1996). The tripartite model and the Consumer Reports study. *American Psychologist, 51,* 1017-1024.

Strupp, H. H., & Binder, J. L. (1984). Psychotherapy in a new key. New York: Guilford.

Stumpf, H. (1993). The factor structure of the Personality Research Form: A cross-national evaluation. *Journal of Personality, 61,* 27-48.

Stunkard, A. J. (1988). Some perspectives on human obesity: Its causes. *Bulletin of the New York Academy of Medicine, 64,* 902-923.

Stunkard, A. J., Harris, J. R., Pederson, N. L., & McClearn, G. E. (1900). The body-mass index of twins who have been reared apart. *New England Journal of Medicine, 322,* 1483-1487.

Stunkard, A. J., Storensen, T. I. A., Hanis, C., et al. (1986). An adoption study of human obesity. *New England Journal of Medicine, 314,* 193-198.

Sudesh, K., Swanson, M., & Trevathan, G. E. (1987). Persistence of sleep disturbances in preschool children. *Journal of Pediatrics, 110,* 642-646.

Sue, D. W., & Sue, D. (1990). *Counseling the culturally different: Theory and practice* (2nd ed.). New York: Wiley.

Sue, S. (1998). In search of cultural competence in psychotherapy and counseling. American psychologist, 53, 440-448.

Sue, S., & Okasaki, S. (1990). Asian-American educational achievements: A phenomenon in search of an explanation. *American Psychologist, 45,* 913-920.

Suinn, R. M. (1980). *Psychology in sports: Methods and applications.* Minneapolis: Burgess.

Suler, J. R. (1985). Meditation and somatic arousal: A comment on Holmes's review. *American Psychologist, 40,* 717.

Sulthana, P. (1987). The effect of frustration and inequity on the displacement of aggression. *Asian Journal of Psychology and Education, 19,* 26-33.

Surgeon General. (1988). The health consequences of smoking, Nicotine addiction. Rockville, MD: U.S. Department of Health and Human Services.

Surtman, R. J. (1985). Alzheimer's disease. *Scientific American, 247,* 62-74.

Sussman, E. (1996). Cocaine's role in drug-exposed babies' problems questioned. *Brown University Child and Adolescent Behavior Letter*, 12, 1-3.

Surwit, R. S., Feinglos, M. N., & Scovern, A. W. (1983). Diabetes and behavior. *American Psychologist, 38,* 255-262.

Suter, A. H. (1991). *Noise and its effects.* Washington, DC: Administrative Conference of the United States.

Suzuki, L. A. & Valencia, R. R. (1997). Race-ethnicity and measured intelligence: Educational implications. *American psychologist*, 52, 1103-1114.

Swaim, R. C., Oetting, E. R., Thurman, P. J., Beauvais, F., & Edwards, R. W. (1993). American Indian adolescent drug use and socialization characteristics: A cross-cultural comparison. *Journal of Cross-Cultural Psychology, 24,* 53-70.

Swedo, S. E., Rapoport, J. L., Leonard, H., Lenane, M., & Cheslow, D. (1989a). Obsessive-compulsive disorder in children and adolescents. *Archives of General Psychiatry,* 46, 335-341.

Swedo, S. E., Schapiro, M. B., Grady, C. L., Cheslow, D. L., et al. (1989b). Cerebral glucose metabolism in childhood-onset obsessive-compulsive disorder. *Archives of General Psychiatry, 46,* 518-523.

Switzer, R., & Taylor, R. B. (1983). Sociability versus privacy of residential choice: Impacts of personality and local social ties. *Basic and Applied Social Psychology, 4,* 123-136.

Szasz, T. S. (1960). *The myth of mental illness.* New York: HarperCollins.

Szasz, T. S. (1982). The psychiatric will: A new mechanism for protecting persons against "psychosis" and psychiatry. *American Psychologist 37,* 762-770.

Szymanski, S., Lieberman, J. A., Alvir, J. M., et al. (1995). Gender differences in onset of illness, treatment response, course, and biological indexes in first-episode schizophrenic patients. *The American Journal of Psychiatry,* **152,** 698-703.

Takahashi, Y. (1990). Is multiple personality disorder really rare in Japan? *Dissociation,* **3**, 57-59.

Takanishi, R. (1993). The opportunities of adolescence-research, intervention, and policy. *American Psychologist, 48,* 85-87.

Tandon, R., & Greden, J. F. (1989). Cholinergic hyperactivity and negative schizophrenic symptoms. *Archives of General Psychiatry, 46,* 745-753.

Tannenbaum, S. I., & Yukl, G. (1992). Training and development in work organizations. *Annual Review of Psychology, 43,* 399-441.

Tanner, J. M. (1973). Growing up. Scientific American, 179, 34-43.

Tanner, J. M. (1981). Growth and maturation during adolescence. *Nutrition Review, 39, 43-55.*

Tasto, D. L. (1969). Systematic desensitization, muscle relaxation, and visual imagery in the counterconditioning of a four-year-old phobic child. *Behavior Research and Therapy, 7,* 409-411.

Taub, A. (1998). Thumbs down on acupuncture. *Science,* 279, 159.

Taylor, R. (1994). Brave new nose: Sniffing out human sexual chemistry [On-line]. http://www.erox.com/SixthSense/StoryTwo.html

Taylor, W., Pearson, J., Mair, A., & Burns, W. (1965). *Study of noise and hearing in jute weaving. Journal of the Acoustical Society of America, 4,* 144-152.

Tedeschi, R. G., Park, C. L., & Calhoun, L. G. (Eds.) (1998). Posttraumatic growth. Mahwah, NJ: Erlbaum.

Tenopyr, M. L. (1981). The realities of employment testing. *American Psychologist, 36,* 1120-1127.

Teplin, L. A., Abram, K. M., & McClelland, G. M. (1994). Does psychiatric disorder predict violent crime among released jail detainees? A six-year longitudinal study. *American Psychologist, 49,* 335-342.

Terenius, L. (1982). Endorphins and modulation of pain. Advances in *Neurology, 33,* 59-64.

Termine, N., Hrynick, T., Kestenbaum, R., Gleitman, H., & Spelke, E. S. (1987). Perceptual completion of surfaces in infancy. *Journal of Experimental Psychology: Perception and Performance, 13,* 524-532.

Tesser, A., & Shaffer, D. R. (1990). Attitudes and attitude change. *Annual Review of Psychology, 41,* 479-523.

Tessier-Lavigne, M., & Goodman, C. S. (1996). The molecular biology of axon guidance. *Science, 274,* 1123-1133.

Tetlock, P. E., Peterson, R. S., McGuire, C., Shi-jie Chang, & Feld, P. (1992). Assessing political group dynamic: A test of the groupthink model. *Journal of Personality and Social Psychology, 63,* 4.3-425.

Thackwray-Emerson, D. (1989). The effect of self-motivation on headache reduction through biofeedback training. *Medical Psychotherapy, 2,* 125-130.

Thannickal, T., Moore, R.Y., Nienhuis, R. Ramanathan, L., Gulyani, S., Aldrich, M., Comford, M., & Siegel, J.M. (2000). Reduced number of hypocretin neurons in human narcolepsy. *Neuron, 27,* 469-474.

Thayer, W. P. (1983). Industrial/organizational psychology: Science and application. In C. J. Scheirer & A. M. Rogers (Eds.), *The G. Stanley Hall lecture series (Vol. 3).* Washington, DC: American Psychological Association.

Thibault, J. W., & Kelley, H. H. (1959). *The social psychology of groups.* New York: Wiley.

Thomas, A., & Chess, S. (1977). *Temperament and development.* New York: Brunner/Mazel.

Thomas, M. B. (1992). *An introduction to marital and family therapy.* New York: Macmillian.

Thompson, C. I. (1980). *Controls of eating.* Jamaica, NY: Spectrum.

Thompson, C. P. (1982). Memory for unique personal events: The roommate study. *Memory and Cognition, 10,* 324-332.

Thompson, J. W., & Blaine, J. D. (1987). Use of ECT in the United States in 1975 and 1980. *American Journal of Psychiatry, 144,* 557-562.

Thompson, R. (1969). Localization of the "visual memory system" in the white rat. *Journal of Comparative and Physiological Psychology, 2,* 1-17.

Thompson, R. (1981). Rapid forgetting of spatial habit in rats with hippocampal lesions. *Science, 212,* 941-947.

Thompson, R. (1986). The neurobiology of learning and memory. *Science, 233,* 941-947.

Thompson, R. (1990). Neural mechanisms of classical conditioning in mammals. *Philosophical Transactions of the Royal Society of London, 329,* 161-170.

Thorndike, A. L., Hagen, E. P., & Sattler, J. M. (1986). *The Stanford-Binet intelligence scale, Fourth edition: Technical manual.* Chicago: Riverside.

Thorndike, E. L. (1911). *Animal intelligence.* New York: Macmillan.

Thornton, G. C., III, & Cleveland, J. N. (1990). Developing managerial talent through simulation. *American Psychologist, 45,* 190-199.

Thurstone, L. L. (1938). Primary mental abilities. *Psychometric Monographs (No. 1).*

Tice, D. M., & Baumeister, R. F. (1985). Masculinity inhibits helping in emergencies: Personality does predict the bystander effect. *Journal of Personality and Social Psychology, 49,* 420-428.

Tice, D. M., & Baumeister, R. F. (1997). Longitudinal study of procrastination, performance, stress, and health: The costs and benefits of dawdling. *Psychological Science, 8,* 454-458.

Tilley, A. J., & Empson, J. A. C. (1978). REM sleep and memory consolidation. *Biological Psychology, 6,* 293-300.

Tobin-Richards, M., Boxer, A., & Peterson, A. C. (1984). The psychological impact of pubertal change: Sex differences in perceptions of self during early adolescence. In J. Brooks-Gunn & A. C. Peterson (Eds.), Girls at puberty: *Biological, psychological, and social perspectives.* New York: Plenum.

Tohen, M., Waternaux, C. M., & Tsuang, M. T. (1990). Outcome in mania. *Archives of General Psychiatry, 47,* 1106-1111.

Tolman, C. W. (1969). Social feeding in domestic chicks: Effects of food deprivation of non-feeding companions. *Psychonomic Science, 15,* 234.

Tolman, E. C. (1932). *Purposive behaviorism in animals and men.* Englewood Cliffs, NJ: Prentice-Hall.

Tolman, E. C., & Honzik, C. H. (1930). Introduction and removal of reward and maze performance in rats. *University of California Publication in Psychology, 4,* 257-275.

Tomkins, S. S. (1962). *Affect, imagery, consciousness: Vol. I. The positive affects.* New York: Springer.

Toro, P. A., Trickett, E. J., Wall, D. D., & Salem, D. A. (1991). Homelessness in the United States: An ecological perspective. *American Psychologist, 46,* 1208-1218.

Torrey, E. F. (1988). *Surviving schizophrenia: A family manual.* New York: HarperCollins.

Torrey, E. F., Taylor, E. H., Bracha, H. S., et al., (1994). Prenatal origin of schizophrenia in a subgroup of discordant monozygotic twins. *Schizophrenia Bulletin,* **20,** 423-432.

Torrey, T. W., & Feduccia, A. (1979). *Morphogenesis of the vertebrates.* New York: Wiley.

Travis, C. B. (1988). *Women and health psychology: Mental health issues.* Hillsdale, NJ: Erlbaum.

Treffert, D. A. (1988). The idiot savant: A review of the syndrome. *American Journal of Psychiatry, 145,* 563-572.

Triandis, H. C. (1990). Theoretical concepts that are applicable to the analysis of ethnocentrism. In R. W. Brislin (Ed.), *Applied cross-cultural psychology.* Newbury Park, CA: Sage.

Triandis, H. C. (1993). Collectivism and individualism as cultural syndromes. *Cross-Cultural Research, 27,* 155-180.

Triandis, H. C., Brislin, R., & Hui, C. H. (1988). Cross-cultural training across the individualism-collectivism divide. *International Journal of Intercultural Relations, 12,* 269-289.

Triplett, N. (1898). The dynamogenic factors in pacemaking and competition. *American Journal of Psychology, 9,* 507-533.

True, W. R., Rice, J., Eisen, S. A., Heath, A. C., Goldberg, J.,

Lyons, M. J., & Nowak, J. (1993). A twin study of genetic and environmental contributions to liability for posttraumatic stress symptoms. *Archives of General Psychiatry, 50,* 257-264.

Tucker, D. M. (1981). Lateral brain function, emotion, and conceptualization. *Psychological Bulletin, 89,* 19-46.

Tulsky, D., Zhu, J., & Ledbetter, M. (1997). WAIS-III and WMS-III technical manual. San Antonio, TX: Psychological Corporation.

Tulving, E. (1962). Subjective organization in free recall of "unrelated" words. *Psychological Review, 69,* 344-354.

Tulving, E. (1972). Episodic and semantic memory. In E. Tulving & W. Donaldson (Eds.), *Organization of memory.* New York: Academic Press.

Tulving, E. (1983). *Elements of episodic memory.* New York: Oxford University Press.

Tulving, E. (1985). How many memory systems are there? *American Psychologist, 40,* 385-398.

Tulving, E. (1986). What kind of a hypothesis is the distinction between episodic and semantic memory? *Journal of Experimental Psychology: Learning, Memory, and Cognition, 12,* 307-311.

Tulving, E., & Schacter, D. L. (1990). Priming and human memory systems. *Science, 247,* 301-306.

Tulving, E., & Thompson, D. M. (1973). Encoding specificity and retrieval processes in episodic memory. *Journal of Experimental Psychology: Learning, Memory, and Cognition, 8,* 336-342.

Tung, R. (1988). *The new expatriates: Managing human resources abroad.* New York: HarperCollins.

Turk, D. C. (1994). Perspectives on chronic pain: The role of psychological factors. *Current Directions in Psychological Science, 3,* 45-48.

Turnbull, C. (1961). Some observations regarding the experiences and behaviors of the Bambuti pygmies. *American Journal of Psychology, 74,* 304-308.

Turner, J. A., Deyo, R. A., Loesser, J. D., Von Korff, M., & Fordyce, W. E. (1994). The importance of placebo effects in pain treatment and research. *The Journal of the American Medical Association, 271,* 1609-1615.

Turner, J. S., & Helms, D. B. (1987). *Contemporary adulthood.* New York: Holt, Rinehart & Winston.

Tuttle, T. C. (1983). Organizational productivity: A challenge for psychologists. *American Psychologist, 38,* 479-486.

Tversky, A., & Kahneman, D. (1974). Judgment under uncertainty: Heuristics and biases. *Science, 125,* 1124-1131.

Tversky, A., & Tuchin, M. (1989). A reconciliation of the evidence on eyewitness testimony: Comments on McCloskey & Zaragoza. *Journal of Experimental Psychology: General, 118,*86-91.

Tyrer, P., & Shawcross, C. (1988). Monoamine oxidase inhibitors in anxiety disorders. *Journal of Psychiatric Research, 22 (Suppl. 1),* 87-98.

UNAIDS (2000). Study has dire AIDS warning. Joint United Nations Program on HIV/AIDS. Press Release. June 28, 2000.

U. S. Bureau of the Census. (1991). *Statistical Abstract of the United States* (111th ed.). Washington, DC: U.S. Government Printing Office.

U. S. Bureau of the Census. (1994). *Statistical Abstract of the United States* (114th ed.). Washington, DC: U. S. Government Printing Office.

U. S. Department of Health and Human Services. (2000). Healthy people 2000. Conference Edition, pp. 57-60.

U .S. General Accounting Office. (1992). *Elderly Americans: Health, housing, and nutritional gaps between the poor and the nonpoor.* Washington, DC: United States General Accounting Office.

Ulrich, R. E., Stachnick, T. J., & Stainton, N. R. (1963). Student acceptance of Generalized Personality Inventory. *Psychological Reports, 13,* 831-834.

Underwood, B. J. (1957). Interference and forgetting. *Psychological Review, 64,* 49-60.

Unger, R., & Crawford, M. (1992). *Women and gender: A feminist psychology.* New York: McGraw-Hill.

Valenstein, E. S. (1980). *The psychosurgery debate: Scientific, legal, and ethical perspectives.* San Francisco: Freeman.

Valenstein, E. S. (1986). *Great and desperate cures.* New York: Basic Books.

Vallerand, R. J., Colavecchio, P. G., & Pelletier, L. G. (1988). Psychological momentum and performance inferences: A preliminary test of the antecedents-consequences psychological momentum model. *Journal of Sport and Exercise Psychology, 10,* 92-108.

Valliant, G. E. (1983). *The natural history of alcoholism: Causes, patterns and paths to recovery.* Cambridge, MA: Harvard University Press.

Valliant, G. E., & Valliant, C. O. (1990). Natural history of male psychological health, XII: A 45-year study of predictors of successful aging at age 65. *American Journal of Psychiatry, 147,* 31-37.

Valtes, P. B., & Baltes, M. M. (1990). Selective optimization with compensation. In P. B. Baltes & M. M. Baltes (Eds.), *Successful aging: Perspectives from the behavioral sciences.* New York: Cambridge University Press.

Van Horn, J. D., & McManus, I. C. (1992). Ventricular enlargement in schizophrenia: A meta-analysis of studies of the ventricle/brain ratio (vbr). *British Journal of Psychiatry, 160,* 687-697.

van Ijzendoorn, M. H., & Kroonenberg, P. M. (1988). Cross-cultural patterns of attachment: A meta-analysis. *Child Development, 59,* 147-156.

Van Gundy, A. B. (1995). *Brain boosters for business advantage.* San Diego, CA: Pfeiffer.

VandenBos, G. R. (1986). Psychotherapy research: A special issue. *American Psychologist, 41,* 111-112.

VandenBos, G. R. (1996). Outcome assessment of psychotherapy. *American Psychologist, 51,* 1005-1006.

Vander Wall, S. B. (1982). An experimental analysis of cache recovery in the Clark's nutcracker. *Animal Behavior, 30,* 84-94.

VanderPlate, C., Aral, S. O., & Magder, L. (1988). The relationship among genital herpes simplex virus, stress, and social support, *Health Psychology, 7,* 159-168.

Varca, P. E. (1980). An analysis of home and away game performance of male college basketball teams. *Journal of Sport Psychology, 2,* 245-257.

Vargha-Khadem, F., Gadian, D. G., Watkins, K. E., Connelly, A., Ban Paesschen. W., & Mishkin, M. (1997). Differential effects of early hippocampal pathology on episodic and semantic memory. *Science, 277,* 376-380.

Vaughn, B. E., & Langlois, J. H. (1983). Physical attractiveness as a correlate of peer status and social competence in preschool children. *Developmental Psychology, 19,* 561-567.

Ventura, J., Nuechterlein, K. H., Lukoff, D., & Hardesty, J. P. (1989). A prospective study of stressful life events and schizophrenic relapse. *Journal of Abnormal Psychology, 98,* 407-411.

Verillo, R. T. (1975). Cutaneous sensation. In B. Scharf (Ed.), *Experimental sensory psychology.* Glenview, IL: Scott, Foresman.

Vernon, P. E. (1960). *The structure of human abilities* (rev. ed.). London: Methuen.

Vernon, P. E. (1979). *Intelligence: Heredity and environment.* San Francisco: Freeman.

Vertes, R. P. (1984). Brainstem control of the events of REM sleep. *Progress in Neurobiology, 22,* 241-288.

Viguera, A. C., Baldessarini, R. J., Hegarty, J. D., van Kammen, D. P., & Tohen, M. (1997). Clinical risk following abrupt and gradual withdrawal of maintenance neuroleptic treatment.

Vinacke, W. E. (1974). *The psychology of thinking* (2nd ed.). New York: McGraw-Hill.

Vitz, P. C. (1990). The use of stories in moral development. *American Psychologist, 45,* 709-720.

Voevodsky, J. (1974). Evaluations of a deceleration warning light for reducing rear-end automobile collisions. *Journal of Applied Psychology, 59,* 270-273.

Vokey, J. R., & Read, J. D. (1985). Subliminal messages: Between the devil and the media. *American Psychologist, 40,* 1231-1239.

Vorhees, C. F., & Mollnow, E. (1987). Behavioral tertatogenesis: Long-term influences on behavior from early exposure to environmental agents. In J. O. Osofsky (Ed.), Handbook of infant development (2nd ed.). New York: Wiley.

Vroom, V. (1964). *Work and motivation.* New York: Wiley.

Vurpillot, E. (1968). The development of scanning strategies and their relation to visual differentiation. *Journal of Experimental Child Psychology, 6,* 632-650.

Wadsworth, B. J. (1971). *Piaget's theory of cognitive development.* New York: David McKay Company, Inc.

Wagner, A. D., Schacter, D. L., Rotte, M., Koutstaal, A. M., Dale, A. M., Rosen, B. R., & Buckner, R. L. (1998). Building memories: Remembering and forgetting of verbal experiences as predicted by brain activity. *Science, 281,* 1188-1191.

Wagner, L. A., Kessler, R. C., Hughs, M., Anthony, J. C., & Nelson, C. B. (1995). Prevalence and correlates of drug use and dependence in the United States. *Archives of General Psychiatry, 52,* 219-229.

Wakefield, H., & Underwager, R. (1992). Recovered memories of alleged sexual abuse: Lawsuits against parents. *Behavioral Sciences and the Law, 10,* 483-507.

Walker, L. J. (1989). A longitudinal study of moral reasoning. *Child Development, 60,* 157-166.

Wallace, P. (1977). Individual discrimination of humans by odor. *Physiology and Behavior, 19,* 577-579.

Wallace, R. K., & Benson, H. (1972). The physiology of meditation. *Scientific American, 226,* 85-90.

Wallach, H. (1987). Perceiving a stable environment when one moves. Annual Review of Psychology, 38, 1-28.

Wallas, G. (1926). *The art of thought.* New York: Harcourt Brace Jovanovich.

Walsh, B. T., Hadigan, C. M., Devlin, M. J., Gladis, M., & Roose, S. P. (1991). Long-term outcome of antidepressant treatment for bulimia nervosa. *American Journal of Psychiatry, 148,* 1206-1212.

Walsh, B. T., Kissileff, H. R., Cassidy, S. M., & Dantzic, S. (1989). Eating behavior of women with bulimia. *Archives of General Psychiatry, 46,* 54-58.

Walster, E., Aronson, V., Abrahams, D., & Rottman, L. (1966). Importance of physical attractiveness in dating behavior. *Journal of Personality and Social Psychology, 4,* 508-516.

Walster, E., & Festinger, L. (1962). The effectiveness of "overheard" and persuasive communications. *Journal of Abnormal and Social Psychology, 65,* 395-402.

Walster, E., Walster, G. W., & Berschied, E. (1978). *Equity: Theory and research.* Boston: Allyn & Bacon.

Walters, G. C., & Grusec, J. E. (1977). *Punishment.* San Francisco: Freeman.

Walton, G. E., Bower, N. J. A., & Bower, T. G. R. (1992). Recognition of familiar faces by newborns. *Infant Behavior and Development, 15,* 265-269.

Walton, G. E., & Bower, T. G. R. (1993). Newborns form "prototypes" in less than 1 minute. *Psychological Science, 4,* 203-205.

Wamboldt, F. S., & Reiss, D. (1989). Defining a family heritage and a new relationship identity: Two central tasks in making of a marriage. *Family Process, 28,* 317-335.

Wampold, B. E., Mondin, G. W., Moody, M., Stich, F., Benson, K., & Ahn, H. (1997). A meta-analysis of outcome studies comparing bona fide psychotherapies: Empirically, "all must have prizes." Psychological bulletin, 122, 203-215.

Warner, L. A., Kessler, R. C., Hughes, M., Anthony, J. C., Nelson, C. B. (1995). Prevalence and correlates of drug use and dependence in the United States: Results from the National Comorbidity Survey. Archives of General Psychiatry, 52, 219-229.

Warrington, E. K., & Weiskrantz, L. (1968). New method of testing long-term retention with special reference to amnesic patients. Nature, 217, 972-974.

Warrington, E. K., & Weiskrantz, L. (1970). Amnesic syndrome: Consolidation or retrieval? Nature, 228, 629-630.

Washburn, M. F. (1908). The animal mind: A textbook of comparative psychology. New York: McMillan.

Waterman, A. S. (1985). Identity in the context of adolescent psychology. New Directions in Child Development, 30, 5-24.

Watkins, L. R. & Mayer, D. J. (1982). Organization of endrogenous opiate and nonopiate pain control systems. Science, 216, 219-229.

Watkins, M. J. (1990). Mediationism and the obfuscation of memory. American Psychologist, 45, 328-335.

Watson, C. J. (1981). An evaluation of some aspects of the Steers and Rhodes model of employee attendance. Journal of Applied Psychology, 66, 385-389.

Watson, J. B. (1919). Psychology from the standpoint of a behaviorist. Philadelphia: Lippincott.

Watson, J. B. (1925). Behaviorism. New York: Norton.

Watson, J. B. (1926). What is behaviorism? Harper's Monthly Magazine, 152, 723-729.

Watson, M. W., & Amgott-Kwan, T. (1984). Development of family-role concepts in school-age children. Developmental Psychology, 20, 953-959.

Waugh, N. C., & Norman, D. A. (1965). Primary memory. Psychological Review, 72, 89-104.

Weaver, C. N. (1980). Job satisfaction in the United States in the 1970s. Journal of Applied Psychology, 65, 364-367.

Webb, W. B. (1975). Sleep, the gentle tyrant. Englewood Cliffs, NJ: Prentice-Hall.

Webb, W. B. (1981). The return of consciousness. In L. T. Benjamin (Ed.), The G. Stanley Hall lecture series (Vol. I). Washington, DC: American Psychological Association.

Webb, W. B., & Cartwright, R. D. (1978). Sleep and dreams. Annual Review of Psychology, 29, 223-252.

Wechsler, D. (1958). The measurement and appraisal of adult intelligence (4th ed.). Baltimore: Williams & Wilkins.

Wechsler, D. (1975). Intelligence defined and undefined: A relativistic reappraisal. American Psychologist, 30, 135-139.

Wechsler, D. (1981). Manual for the Wechsler Adult Intelligence Scale-Revised. New York: The Psychological Corporation.

Weekley, J. A., & Gier, J. A. (1987). Reliability and validity of the situational interview for a sales position. Journal of Applied Psychology, 72, 484-487.

Weekes, J. R., Lynn, S. J., Green, J. P., & Brentar, J. T. (1992). Pseudomemory in hypnotized and task-motivated subjects. Journal of Abnormal Psychology, 101, 356-360.

Weil, A. T., Zinberg, N., & Nelson, J. M. (1968). Clinical and psychological effects of marijuana in man. Science, 162, 1234-1242.

Weinland, J. (1996). Cognitive behavior therapy: A primer. Journal of Psychological Practice, 2(1), 23-35.

Weisberg, R. W. (1986). Creativity: Genus and other myths. San Francisco: Freeman.

Weiskrantz, L., Warrington, E. K., Sanders, M. D., & Marshall, J. (1974). Visual capacity in the hemianopic field following a restricted occipital ablation. Brain, 97, 709-728.

Weisner, W. H., & Cronshaw, S. F. (1988). A meta-analytic investigation of the impact of interview format and degree of structure on the validity of the employment interview. Journal of Occupational Psychology, 61, 275-290.

Weiss, J. M. (1973). The natural history of antisocial attitudes: What happens to the psychopaths? Journal of Geriatric Psychology, 6, 236-242.

Weisberg, R. W. (1993). Creativity: Beyond the myth of genius. New York: Freeman.

Weissman, M. M. (1988). The epidemiology of anxiety disorders: Rates, risks and familial patterns. Journal of Psychiatric Research, 22 (Suppl. 1), 99-114.

Weissman, M. M., Bland, R. C., Canino, G. J., Faravelli, C. et. Al., (1997). The cross-national epidemiology of panic disorder. *Archives of General Psychiatry*, **54**, 305-309.

Weissman, M. M., & Klerman, G. L. (1992). The changing rate of major depression. *Journal of the American Medical Association, 268,* 3098.

Weissman, M. M., Klerman, G. L., Markowitz, J. S., & Ouellette, R. (1989). Suicidal ideation and suicide attempts in panic disorders and attacks. *The New England Journal of Medicine, 321,* 1209-1214.

Weissman, M. M. (1993). The epidemiology of personality disorders: A 1990 update. Journal of personality disorders: Supplement, Spring. 44-62.

Welch, W. W., Anderson, R. E., & Harris, L. J. (1982). The effects of schooling on mathematics achievement. *American Educational Research Journal, 19,* 145-153.

Weldon, E., & Gargano, G. M. (1988). Cognitive loading: The effects of accountability and shared responsibility on cognitive effort. *Personality and Social Psychology Bulletin, 14,* 159-171.

Wellman, H. M., & Gellman, S. A. (1992). Cognitive development: Fundamental theories of core domains. *Annual Review of Psychology, 43,* 337-375.

Wells, G. L. (1993). What do we know about eyewitness identification? *American Psychologist, 48,* 553-571.

Wells, G. W., Luus, C.A.E., & Windschitl, P. D. (1994). Maximizing the utility of eyewitness identification evidence. *Current Directions in Psychological Science, 3,* 194-197.

Wertheimer, M. (1961). Psychomotor coordination of auditory and visual space at birth. *Science, 134,* 1692.

Werker, J. F. (1989). Becoming a native listener. *American Scientist, 77,* 54-59.

Wessinger, C. M., & Fendrich, R. (1997) Islands of residual vision in hemianopic patients. *Journal of Cognitive Neuroscience, 9,* 203. Retrieved from the World Wide Web on October 5, 2000. http://ehostvgw15.epnet.com/

West, M. A. (1985). Meditation and somatic arousal reduction. *American Psychologist, 40,* 717-719.

Westen, D. (1998). The scientific legacy of Sigmund Freud: Toward a psychodynamically informed psychological science. *Psychological bulletin,* 124, 333-371.

Wheeler, R. J., & Frank, M. A. (1988). Identification of stress buffers. *Behavioral Medicine, 14,* 78-89.

Whetzel, D. L. & McDaniel, M. A. (1997). Employment interviews. IN D. L. Whetzel & G. R. Wheaton (Eds.) *Applied Measurement Methods in Industrial Psychology* (pp. 185-206). Palo Alto, CA: Consulting Psychologists Press.

Whitehurst, G. (1982). Language development. In B. Wolman (Ed.), *Handbook of developmental psychology.* Englewood Cliffs, NJ: Prentice-Hall.

Whiting, B., & Edwards, C. P. (1973). A cross-cultural analysis of sex differences in the behavior of children ages three through eleven. *Journal of Social Psychology, 91,* 177-188.

Whitman, F. L., Diamond, M., & Martin, J. (1993). Homosexual orientation in twins: A report on 61 pairs and three triplet sets. *Archives of Sexual Behavior, 22,* 187-206.

Whyte, G. (1989). Groupthink reconsidered. *Academy of Management Review, 14,* 40-56.

Whyte, L. L. (1960). *The unconscious before Freud.* New York: Basic Books.

Wickens, C. D. (1992). *Engineering psychology and human performance* (2nd ed.). New York: HarperCollins.

Wickens, D. D. (1973). Some characteristics of word encoding. *Memory and Cognition, 1,* 485-490.

Widner, H., Tetrud, J., Rehncrona, S., et al. (1992). Bilateral fetal mesencephalic grafting in two patients with Parkinsonism induced by 1-methyl-4-phenyl-1,2,3,6 tetrahydropridine (MPTP). *The New England Journal of Medicine, 327,* 1556-1563.

Wiggins, J. S., & Pincus, A. L. (1992). Personality: Structure and assessment. *Annual Review of Psychology, 43,* 473-504.

Wilcox, D., & Hager, R. (1980). Toward realistic expectations for orgasmic response in women. *Journal of Sex Research, 16,* 162-179.

Wilkes, J. (1986). Conversation with Ernest R. Hilgard: A study in hypnosis. *Psychology Today, 20(1),* 23-27.

Williams, J. E., & Best, D. L. (1990). *Measuring sex stereotypes: A multination study.* Newbury Park, CA: Sage.

Williams, K., Harkins, S., & Latané, B (1981). Identifiability as a deterrent to social loafing: Two cheering experiments. *Journal of Personality and Social Psychology, 40,* 303-311.

Williams, K., Nida, S. A., Baca, L. D., & Latané, B. (1989).

Social loafing and swimming: Effects of identifiability of individual and relay performance of intercollegiate swimmers. *Basic and Applied Social Psychology, 10,* 73-82.

Williams, K. D., & Karau, S. J. (1991). Social loafing and social compensation: The effects of expectations of co-worker performance. *Journal of Personality and Social Psychology, 61,* 570-581.

Williams, W. M., & Ceci, S. J. (1997). Are Americans becoming more or less alike: Trends in race, class, and ability differences in intelligence. *American Psychologist, 52,* 1226-1235.

Wilson, G. T. (1982). Adult disorders. In G. T. Wilson & C. M. Franks (Eds.), *Contemporary behavior therapy: Conceptual and empirical foundations.* New York: Guilford.

Wincze, J. P., & Carey, M. P. (1992). *Sexual dysfunctions: A guide for assessment and treatment.* New York: Guilford.

Winett, R. A. (1995). A framework for health promotion and disease prevention programs. *American Psychologist, 50,* 341-350.

Winett, R. A., Southard, D. R., & Walberg-Rankin, J. (1993). Nutrition promotion and dietary change: Framework to meet year 2000 goals. *Medicine, Exercise, Nutrition, and Health, 2,* 7-26.

Wing, L. (1989). *Diagnosis and treatment of autism.* New York: Plenum.

Wing, L., & Gould, J. (1979). Severe impairment of social interaction and associated abnormalities in children: Epidemiology and classification. *Journal of Autism and Developmental Disorders, 9,* 11-29.

Wingrove, J., Bond, A. J., Cleare, A. J., & Sherwood, R. (1999). Plasma tryptophan and trait aggression. *Journal of Psychopharmacology, 13,* 235-237.

Winner, E. (1996). *Gifted children: Myths and realities.* New York: Basic Books.

Winner, E. (2000). *Giftedness: Current theory and research.* Current directions in psychological science. 9(5), 153-155.

Winter, D. G. (1987). Leader appeal, leader performance, and the motive profiles of leaders and followers: A study of American presidents and elections. *Journal of Personality and Social Psychology, 52,* 196-202.

Winter, D. G. (1988). The power motive in women-and men. *Journal of Personality and Social Psychology, 54,* 510-519.

Winter, D. G., & Stewart, A. J. (1978). The power motive. In H. London & J. E. Exner (Eds.), *Dimensions of personality.* New York: Wiley.

Winters, K. C., Weintraub, S., & Neale, J. M. (1981). Validity of MMPI code types in identifying DSM-III schizophrenics. *Journal of Consulting and Clinical Psychology, 49,* 486-487.

Winton, W. M. (1987). Do introductory textbooks present the Yerkes-Dodson Law correctly? *American Psychologist, 42,* 202-203.

Wisensale, S. K. (1992). Toward the 21st century: Family change and public policy. *Family Relations, 41,* 417-422.

Witenberg, S. H., Blanchard, E. B., McCoy, G., Suls, J., & McGoldrick, M. D. (1983). Evaluation of compliance in home and center hemodialysis patients. *Health Psychology, 2,* 227-238.

Witmer, J. F., & Geller, E. S. (1976). Facilitating paper recycling: Effects of prompts, raffles, and contests. *Journal of Applied Behavior Analysis, 9,* 315-322.

Wittchen, H., Shanyang, Z., Kessler, R. C., & Eaton, W. (1994). DSM-III-R generalized anxiety disorder in the National Comorbidity Survey. *Archives of General Psychiatry, 51,* 355-364.

Wollen, K. A., Weber, A., & Lowry, D. H. (1972). Bizarreness versus interaction of mental images as determinants of learning. *Cognitive Psychology, 3,* 518-523.

Wolpe, J. (1958). *Psychotherapy by reciprocal inhibition.* Stanford, CA: Stanford University Press.

Wolpe, J. (1969). Basic principles and practices of behavior therapy of neuroses. *American Journal of Psychiatry, 125,* 1242-1247.

Wolpe, J. (1981). Behavior therapy versus psychoanalysis. *American Psychologist, 36,* 159-164.

Wolpe, J. (1982). *The practice of behavior therapy* (3rd ed.). New York: Pergamon Press.

Wong, M. Mei-ha., & Csilzenthmihalyi, M. (1991). Affiliation motivation and daily experience. *Journal of Personality and Social Psychology, 60,* 154-164.

Wood, C. (1986). The hostile heart. Psychology *Today, 20,* 10-12.

Woodruff, V. (1994). Studies say the kids are all right.

Working Woman, October, p. 12.

World Health Organization. (2000). Tobacco kills—Don't be duped, says WHO on World No Tobacco Day. Press Release WHO/38, May 30, 2000.

Worringham, C. J., & Messick, D. M. (1983). Social facilitation of running: An unobtrusive study. *Journal of Social Psychology, 121,* 23-29.

Worthen, J. B. (1997). Resiliency of bizarreness effects under varying conditions of verbal and imaginal elaboration and list composition. *Journal of Mental Imagery, 21,* 167-194.

Worthen, J. B. & Marshall, P. H. (1996). Intralist and extralist sources of distinctiveness and the bizarreness effect: The importance of contrast. *American Journal of Psychology, 109,* 239-263.

Wright, J. C., & Vlietstra, A. G. (1975). The development of selective attention: From perceptual exploration to logical search. In H. W. Reese (Ed.), *Advances in child development and behavior* (Volume 10). New York: Academic Press.

Wright, L. (1988). The Type A behavior pattern and coronary artery disease. *American Psychologist, 43,* 2-14.

Wright, P., Takei, N., Rifkin, L, & Murray, R. M. (1995). Maternal influenza, obstetric complications, and schizophrenia. *The American Journal of Psychiatry,* **152,** 1714-1720.

Wright, S.W., Lawrence L.M., & Wrenn K.D., et al. (1998). Randomized clinical trial of melatonin after night-shift work: Efficacy and neuropsychologic effects. *Annals of Emergency Medicine,* 32, 334-340.

Wundt, W. (1874). *Principles of physiological psychology.* Leipzig, Germany: Engelmann.

Wyatt, R. J. (1996). Neurodevelopmental abnormalities and schizophrenia. *Archives of General Psychiatry,* **53,** 11-15.

Wyatt, R. J. & Henter, I. D. (1997). Schizophrenia: The need for early treatment. *The Harvard Mental Health Letter, 14(1),* 4-6.

Wynchank, D., & Berk, M. (1998). Behavioral changes in dogs with acral lick dermatitis during a 2-month extension phase of treatment. Human psychopharmacology: Clinical and experimental, 13(6), 435-438.

Wysowski, D. K., & Baum, C. (1989). Antipsychotic drug use in the United States, 1976-1985. Archives of General Psychiatry, 46, 929-932.

Yalom, I. D. (1985). *The theory and practice of group psychotherapy.* New York: Basic Books.

Yaniv, I., & Meyer, D. E. (1987). Activation and metacognition of inaccessible stored information: Potential basis for incubation effects in problem solving. *Journal of Experimental Psychology: Learning, Memory, and Cognition, 13,* 187-205.

Yapko, M. (1993). The seduction of memory. *The Family Therapy Networker, 17,* 42-43.

Yates, A. (1989). Current perspectives on the eating disorders: I History, psychological and biological aspects. *Journal of the American Academy of Child and Adolescent Psychiatry, 28,* 813-828.

Yates, A. (1990). Current perspectives on eating disorders: II Treatment, outcome, and research directions. *Journal of the American Academy of Child and Adolescent Psychiatry, 29,* 1-9.

Yates, A. J. (1980). *Biofeedback and the modification of behavior.* New York: Plenum.

Yates, F. A. (1966). *The art of memory.* Chicago: University of Chicago Press.

Yen, S. H., Liu, W. K., Hall, F. L., Yan, S. D., Stern, D., & Dickson, D. W. (1995). Alzheimer neurofibrillary lesion: Molecular nature and potential roles of different components. Neurobiology of aging, 3, 381-387.

Yerkes, R. M. & Dodson, J. D. (1908). The relation of strength of stimulus to rapidity of habit-formation. *Journal of Comparative Neurology and Psychology, 18,* 459-482.

Youngstrom, N. (1991, May). Serious mental illness issues need leadership. *APA Monitor,* p. 27.

Yuille, J. C. (1993). We must study forensic eyewitnesses to know about them. *American Psychologist, 48,* 572-573.

Zadeh, L. (1965). Fuzzy sets. *Information and Control 8,* 338-353.

Zajonc, R. B. (1968). Attitudinal effects of mere exposure. *Journal of Personality and Social Psychology (Monograph Suppl.), 9,* 1-27.

Zajonc, R. B., & Markus, H. (1982). Affective and cognitive factors in preferences. *Journal of Consumer Research, 9,* 123-131.

Zanna, M. P., & Rempel, J. K. (1988). Attitudes: A new look at an old concept. In D. Bartal & A. W. Kruglanski (Eds.), *The social psychology of knowledge.* New York:

Cambridge University Press.

Zedeck, S. (1987). The science and practice of industrial and organizational psychology. College Park, MD: Society for Industrial and Organizational Psychology.

Zedeck, S., & Cascio, W. F. (1984). Psychological issues in personnel decisions. *Annual Review of Psychology, 35,* 461-518.

Zedeck, S., Tziner, A., & Middlestadt, S. E. (1983). Interviewer validity and reliability: An individual analysis approach. *Personnel Psychology, 36,* 230-237.

Zelnik, M., & Kantner, J. F. (1980). Sexual activity, contraceptive use, and pregnancy among metropolitan-area teenagers; 1971-1979. *Family Planning Perspectives, 12,* 230-237.

Zeman, A. (1998) The consciousness of sight. *British Medical Journal, 12/19/98,* 1696. Retrieved from the World Wide Web on October 5, 2000, *http://ehostvgw15.epnet.com/*

Zhdanova, I. V., & Wurtman, R. J. (1997). Efficacy of melatonin as a sleep-promoting agent. *Journal of Biological Rhythms, 12,* 644-651.

Zhdanova, I. V., Wurtman, R. J., Morabito, C., Piotrovska, V. R., & Lynch, H. J. (1996). Effects of low oral doses of melatonin, given 2-4 hours before habitual bedtime, on sleep in normal young humans. *Sleep, 19,* 423-431.

Zigler, E., & Hodapp, R. M. (1991). Behavioral functioning in individuals with mental retardation. *Annual Review of Psychology, 42,* 29-50.

Zilbergeld, B., & Evans, M. (1980). The inadequacy of Masters and Johnson. *Psychology Today, 14,* 28-43.

Zimmerman, M., & Coryell, W. (1989). DSM-III personality disorder diagnoses in a nonpatient sample. *Archives of General Psychiatry, 46,* 682-689.

Zinbarg, R. E., Barlow, D. H., Brown, T. A., & Hertz, R. M. (1992). Cognitive-behavioral approaches to the nature and treatment of anxiety disorders. *Annual Review of Psychology, 43,* 235-267.

Zohar, D. (1980). Safety climate in industrial organizations: Theoretical and applied implications. *Journal of Applied Psychology, 65,* 96-102.

Zuckerman, B., & Bresnahan, K. (1991). Developmental and behavioral consequences of prenatal drug and alcohol exposure. *The Pediatric Clinics of North America, 38,* 1387-1406.

Zuckerman, M. (1978). Sensation seeking and psychopathology. In R. D. Hare & D. Shalling (Eds.), *Psychopathic behavior.* New York: Wiley.

Zuckerman, M., Buchsbaum, M. S., & Murphy, D. L. (1980). Sensation seeking and its biological correlates. *Psychological Bulletin, 88,* 187-214.

Zuckerman, M., Eysenck, S., & Eysenck, H. J. (1978). Sensation seeking in England and America: Cross-cultural, age, and sex comparisons. *Journal of Consulting and Clinical Psychology, 46,* 139-149.

CREDITS

Photo Credits

Unless otherwise acknowledged, all photographs are the property of Alliance Press.

2 Corbis 5 Corbis 8 Corbis 9 Corbis 10 Corbis 12 Corbis 15 Corbis 24 Corbis 33 Corbis 71 Corbis 93 Corbis 143 Corbis 149 Corbis 151 Corbis 161 Corbis 169 Corbis 174 Corbis 187 Corbis 189 Corbis 195 Corbis 201 Corbis 215 Corbis 246 Corbis 301 Corbis 315 Corbis 316 Corbis 348 Corbis 358 Corbis 392 Corbis 394 Corbis 396 Corbis 398 Corbis 434 Corbis 449 Corbis 461 Corbis 465 Corbis 494 Corbis 500 Corbis 502 Corbis 522 Corbis 535 Corbis 541 Corbis 572 Corbis 592 Corbis 598 Corbis 610 Corbis 618 Corbis 619 Corbis

Text Credits

Figure 3.1 From "Contemporary Psychophysics" by Eugene Galanter from New Directions in Psychology. Copyright 1962 by Holt, Rinehart and Winston, Inc. Reprinted by permission of the author.

Figure 6.2 From "Short-term Retention of Individual Verbal Items" By Lloyd R. Peterson and Margaret J. Peterson from *Journal of Experimental Psychology* (September 1959), the American Psychological Association. Reprinted by permission of the authors.

Figure 6.4 From Long-Term Memory for a Common Object" by Ramond S. Nickerson and Marilyn Jager Adams in *Cognitive Psychology* 1979, 11. Copyright 1979 Academic Press. Reprinted by permission.

Figure 6.5 From "Narrative Stories as Mediators for Serial Learning" by Gordon H. Bower and Mical C. Clark from Psychonomic Science, Vol 14 (4), 1969. Copyright 1969 by Psychonomic Journals, Inc. Reprinted by permission.

Figure 6.6 From "Mnemotechnics in Second-Language Learning" by Richard C. Atkinson from *American Psychologist*, Volume 30, August 1975. Number 8. Published by the American Psychological Association. Reprinted by permission of the author.

Figure 6.8 From "Properties of Learning Curves under Varied Distribution of Practice" by Mary J. Kientzle from *Journal of Experimental Psychology* 36 (June 1946). Published by the American Psychological Association, Inc. Reprinted by permission of the author.

Figure 8.5 From "Human Mate Selection" by David M. Buss from *American Scientist* (January-February, 1985) . Reprinted by permission of American Scientist.

Figure 10.6 From Lazarus, 1993. Reproduced with permission from the *Annual Review of Psychology,* Volume 44, 1993 by Annual Reviews, Inc.

Subject Index